AMERICAN
PASSAGES

A LITERARY SURVEY

AMERICAN

PASSAGES

A LITERARY SURVEY

Instructor's Guide

W. W. NORTON

OREGON
PUBLIC
BROADCASTING

Annenberg/CPB

Copyright © 2004 by The Corporation for Public Broadcasting.

All rights reserved.
Printed in the United States of America.
First Edition.

Composition by PennSet, Inc.
Manufacturing by Maple-Vail.
Book design by Chris Welch.
Production manager: Diane O'Connor.

ISBN 0-393-97940-7 (pbk.)

W. W. Norton & Company, Inc., 500 Fifth Avenue, New York, N.Y. 10110
www.wwnorton.com

W. W. Norton & Company Ltd., Castle House, 75/76 Wells Street, London W1T 3QT

1 2 3 4 5 6 7 8 9 0

BRIEF CONTENTS

CONTENTS

WHAT IS AMERICAN LITERATURE?
An Overview

Unit 1

NATIVE VOICES
Resistance and Renewal in American Indian Literature

EXPLORING BORDERLANDS
Contact and Conflict in North America

UTOPIAN PROMISE

Puritan and Quaker Utopian Visions, 1620–1750

Unit 4

THE SPIRIT OF NATIONALISM
Declaring Independence, 1710–1850

MASCULINE HEROES
American Expansion, 1820–1900

Unit 6

AMERICAN GOTHIC
Ambiguity and Anxiety in the Nineteenth Century

Unit 7
SLAVERY AND FREEDOM
Race and Identity in Antebellum America

REGIONAL REALISM
Depicting the Local in American Literature, 1865–1900

Unit 9

SOCIAL REALISM

Class Consciousness in American Literature, 1875–1920

RHYTHMS IN POETRY
From the Beat of Blues to the Sounds of Everyday Speech

Unit 11

MODERNIST PORTRAITS
Experimentations in Style, World War I to World War II

Unit 12

MIGRANT STRUGGLE

The Bounty of the Land in Twentieth-Century American Literature, 1929–1995

SOUTHERN RENAISSANCE
Reinventing the South

Unit 14

BECOMING VISIBLE

Ethnic Writers and the Literary Mainstream, 1945–1969

Unit 15

POETRY OF LIBERATION
Protest Movements and American Counterculture

Unit 16

THE SEARCH FOR IDENTITY
American Prose Writers, 1970–Present

APPENDIX
Writing about Literature

PREFACE

A CONTEXTUAL APPROACH TO TEACHING AMERICAN LITERATURE

As an idea and as a classroom subject, American literature has been undergoing a transformation. As the nation has come to understand its own diversity, literary scholars and teachers have opened up the anthologies and the curriculum to include more works by American women and minority writers. This broadening of the canon has been accompanied by a shift in the way literature is being read and discussed. We are recovering the pleasure of reading imaginative literature within its own special historical moment, of understanding its response to the social forces and moral crises that helped to define that moment. These new options for reading can be both exhilarating and disconcerting for teachers and students. The aim of this *Instructor's Guide* and of the *American Passages* series is to support instructors as they experiment with these new strategies.

American Passages is organized in sixteen units, each of which covers one literary movement by exploring two or three authors in depth while linking their work to that of other writers associated with that movement. Featured authors reflect both traditional and newly recovered American voices. The *Instructor's Guide* provides instructional resources, including suggested thematic approaches, discussion questions, reading lists, and information for lecture and discussion to aid the instructor in offering a contextual approach. The goals of the *Instructor's Guide* are as follows:

1. **To encourage critical appreciation of American literature** within the structure, and in accordance with the traditional goals, of an American literature survey course:
   - to teach close reading skills and narrative strategies;
   - to introduce important American writers, styles, themes, and imaginative concerns;
   - to stimulate students to make connections among texts;
   - to illustrate how American literature has changed and evolved over time.
2. **To promote an understanding of American diversity and continuity** by presenting both canonical works and voices that have traditionally been unheard or discounted.
3. **To promote an understanding of American literature in broader contexts** by offering biographical, historical, and cultural contextual materials to support and enrich the readings.

Using Media to Explore Context

American Passages uses a combination of video, digital, and print media to aid the teaching of American literature in its cultural context.

Video Documentaries

For each unit there is a thirty-minute video documentary featuring two to four authors from the designated literary movement. To capture the artistic, political, historical, and literary settings for these authors, the documentaries draw upon an extensive archive of photographs, historical film clips, fine art, artifacts from popular culture, and other imaginative and historical resources. The videos include original interviews with literary scholars and historians, as well as readings and interviews featuring American authors, including, among others, Dorothy Allison, Sandra Cisneros, and Robert Stone. You will also find dramatized moments from the texts and montages to enhance student understanding of the author, the work, and the historical situation.

Online Archive and Slide Show Tool

The Online Archive is an extensive collection of materials illustrating the historical and cultural developments that influenced and were influenced by American literature. The Online Archive provides access to primary-source materials for student research and for classroom presentations. These materials include visual art, newspaper articles, sound files of traditional storytellers, government documents, diaries, musical recordings, maps, and photos of cultural artifacts. Occasionally, a unit contains questions about a work that is not included in the Online Archive or in *The Norton Anthology of American Literature* but is readily available from other Internet sources. You can find these works easily with the help of an online search engine such as Google.com.

The Online Archive is browseable for open-ended visits and easily searchable by students and instructors who have a specific writer or topic in mind. One advantage of the Online Archive is that its materials are situated within the site itself. Because the site is not dependent on URL links to other Web sites, it allows students to focus on content rather than on the acquisition of Web research skills; it provides materials that have been verified for accuracy and appropriateness; it invites inquiry into why specific materials have been included; and it ensures that the curriculum materials will be available whenever students and instructors want them.

All of the materials in the Online Archive are organized in a searchable database. Every item is cross-referenced by multiple fields, ensuring that users are presented with a wide and deep collection of materials upon each inquiry. Probing the database with a variety of approaches will yield different outcomes that can catalyze independent thought as users analyze and synthesize connections and relationships. Each artifact in the archive is accompanied by a caption and a brief description that helps make connections to the literature of its era.

The Online Archive includes a media composition feature (the Slide Show Tool) that allows students and instructors to compose audio and visual presentations using the materials in the archive. A "point and click" user interface allows Web site visitors to compose slide shows that integrate audio clips of authors, historical documents, fine art, musical selections, and other materials. The Slide Show Tool allows instructors to create class presentations with multimedia and to ask students to use the site for analysis and synthesis assignments. All materials are available for downloading onto personal CDs, e-mailing to others, or saving on individual computers for educational use.

COMPANION ANTHOLOGY AND STUDY GUIDES

The videos and digital media are complemented by *The Norton Anthology of American Literature*, available in both a six-volume edition and a one-volume shorter edition. Both versions contain a rich blend of canonical and newly recognized voices in American literature and draw on a wealth of traditions.

Also published by Norton, the *American Passages Study Guide* contains material (reproduced in the *Instructor's Guide*) that you may wish to assign, including the following:

- student overview and questions;
- video overviews and questions;
- author biographies and questions;
- contextual material and questions;
- personal and creative response projects and problem-based learning projects;
- glossary, selected bibliography, and further resources.

The *Study Guide* also contains resources not found in the *Instructor's Guide*:

- a guide to writing about literature;
- an overview of how to read literature across the disciplines of fine arts, history, material culture, architecture, religion, politics, music, psychology, cultural geography, folklore, and anthropology.

Instructor Overview

One of the most challenging aspects of teaching literature in its cultural context is seeing the forest for the trees. The Instructor Overview at the start of each unit is intended to provide a view of that forest. The overview offers information about key historical events as well as the artistic innovations and literary hallmarks of the movement. Preceding each overview is a series of Overview Questions to help you check for comprehension of this big picture and to be used as a framework for guiding the students through the unit. These questions are designed to tie in the five *American Passasges* Overview Questions (see pp. xxxiv–xxxv) to the specific content of each unit. A condensed version of this overview geared to students is available in the *Study Guide*, and you may find it helpful to have students read the overview and the questions before you begin the unit and before they watch the video documentary.

Tips on Using the Videos

Each of the sixteen videos is designed to introduce you and your students to the style, themes, and genres of one movement in American literature. Only a few of the ten authors covered in the unit curriculum materials can be featured in the video. When selecting authors to represent a particular literary moment, therefore, you may find it helpful to begin with one or more of the authors presented in the video.

The videos themselves have been designed to be "hooks": their goal is to intrigue the viewer rather than to deliver large amounts of information. Hence, you may have a richer class discussion if you have students read the Student Overview, the Video Overview, and the appropriate Author/Text Reviews before watching the video. The videos should lead the students back to the Overview Questions at the start of each unit; that is, they are designed to open up discussion rather than to be the final word. Once your students have watched the video, the Discussion Questions for the video will guide them from simple comprehension to more sophisticated analysis.

Author/Text Review

The Author/Text Review section provides biographical information about each author or a historical introduction to various anonymous texts, such as Native American Creation Stories, and commentary on what has made the author or texts important in the history of American literature. You may find it helpful to have students read these reviews before they read the works, to help focus their reading. Both the *Instructor's Guide* and the *Study Guide* provide information on 160 authors and texts.

Contexts

In each Context section, students can see how a literary work relates to an artistic, political, economic, or historical trend or event of the era. For example, for Unit 10, "Rhythms in Poetry," Context sections on the New Negro movement, radio, primitivism, and the cultural geography of Harlem invite students to consider questions that connect literature to culture: How does the poetry of Langston Hughes, for example, respond to the art deco style of Harlem Renaissance muralist Aaron Douglass? When you teach Unit 3, "Utopian Promise," the Context sections will help students understand how and why the writings of seventeenth-century Puritans and Quakers use the plain style and how that style reverberated through everyday life in the New England colonies.

Discussion Questions

In the *Study Guide*, as in the *Instructor's Guide*, there are questions on each video, author, and Context to help you prepare for class and to encourage group discussion. You may find it helpful to have students keep a journal about their reading or answer some of these questions before class or exams. The questions are arranged in three levels of sophistication and difficulty: Comprehension, Context, and Exploration.

Comprehension Questions are close-reading questions that help the students comprehend the work's basic subject and major themes. They also include questions that focus on the interpretation of specific parts of the text. Comprehension Questions are designed to be a point of entry: they're meant to ease students into the material, encourage attention, and help them to be more perceptive viewers and readers. Here is an example:

■ Why does Frederick Douglass refuse to narrate the details of his escape in his 1845 autobiography? What effect does this gap in information, and the reason Douglass provides for it, have on his *Narrative*?

Context Questions relate a specific literary work to a specific cultural-historical event, artifact, or person from the period. Some questions also compare works by one writer to works by other writers from the same unit. Others direct the reader to specific artifacts in the Online Archive. These artifacts are identified by their item number (e.g., [2356]). Context Questions usually provide background information before posing a specific problem. Here is an example:

■ Walt Whitman was the most photographed American writer who lived and died in the nineteenth century (there are 130 extant photographs of him). He frequently sent pictures of himself to friends and admirers and included portraits of himself in his editions of *Leaves of Grass*. Examine the Whitman portraits featured in the archive. How does Whitman present himself in the portraits? How does he manipulate clothing and expression to achieve different effects? How does his self-presentation change over time? Why do you think Whitman might have been so interested in circulating photographs of himself?

Exploration Questions encourage speculation about broader themes and issues. These questions are intertextual across the sixteen units. Here is an example:

■ In both "The Judge's History of the Settlement" and "The Slaughter of the Pigeons" James Fenimore Cooper describes the way "settlement" and "civilization" exploit and disrupt the natural abundance of the wilderness. While the Judge tends to view this process as "improvement," Natty condemns it as destructive and wasteful. What does Cooper's position seem to be here, with regard to the environmental impact of European American settlement? In what respects does he seem to side with the Judge's position, and in what respects does he seem to side with Natty? How does *The Pioneers* raise environmental issues that still concern us today? How do contemporary debates about North American environmental issues reflect or extend concerns raised in *The Pioneers*?

You may want to encourage students to review the Comprehension questions before attempting the more challenging Context and Exploration questions.

Personal and Creative Responses

You have undoubtedly noticed that each student has different ways of learning. You have probably also noticed that students play different roles in classroom discussion: some are facilitators, some are instigators, and some are listeners. You may also have noticed that some of your students tend to learn using visual cues while others prefer memorization. Some students may find it easier to understand things using logic while others prefer symbolism and metaphors. Perhaps you have students who could express themselves better if they were encouraged to be creative. If so, this section of the *Instructor's* and *Study Guides* will be useful. In it you will find suggestions for creative writing, journal exercises, and hands-on activities that allow your students to demonstrate what they know in a variety of different formats.

Problem-Based Learning Projects

Problem-based learning (PBL) works from the assumption that a good way to help students think across disciplinary boundaries is to give them hands-on experience as researchers. The PBL sections of the *Instructor's Guide* can help you encourage students to connect their readings and in-class explorations to personal experiences, public events, and life beyond the classroom. PBL features group participation. Sharing ideas and working on complex problems in small groups or pairs may help your students make more headway than they would on their own.

PBL takes time. A single problem may be the primary class activity for several weeks or even for the entire term. When the question at hand is broad and multifaceted, working it out can take many hours of prowling through archives and other resources and quite a bit of intensive discussion with others. PBL also requires perseverance and confidence, from both the student and the teacher. If you are interested in integrating PBL into your exploration of American writers and cultural history, be sure to consult a thorough guide to PBL. Following are a few suggestions to get you started.

First, PBL is not an add-on activity; it is a special way of organizing a classroom, a special form of student-centered learning. Instructors who try PBL must decide whether to try the strategy in a "pure" or a "hybrid" form, depending on the course content and the skill levels and interests of students. In its "pure" form, PBL consists of assigning a problem to a class, having students discuss it to decide what they might need to know in order to make headway with the problem, allowing students to divide the tasks among themselves, and coaching them as they go through the problem-solving process. This process takes the place of the traditional syllabus of assigned readings and paper topics. Here are some examples of PBL assignments that could work with ambitious students in a survey course:

- Choose a literary work that appeals to you—a poem, a short story, a play—from a historical period at least thirty years in the past. How would you present this work to a large contemporary American audience? Would you present it as a "timeless" work requiring no special knowledge of the year in which it was written? Or would you present it as a work very much *in* and *of* that year? Construct your answer by learning about that year. What was happening in public life? In the arts? In technology and politics and other literary circles? After you have created a summary of that year, evaluate the importance of what you have found with regard to understanding and appreciating the author and work you have selected.

■ Nearly every film is the product of many acts of selection, even educational films about literary history. Choose an *American Passages* video that caught your attention, and describe the strategy of the video as an introduction to an American historical period or literary movement. If you were rewriting or re-editing that film, what new or different material would you include? What would you decide to eliminate to make space for the new material and why? Propose and explain these changes; you will need to explore the Online Archive and to decide what is important, as well as what isn't, in telling the story of a bygone time.

■ What dramatic changes have taken place in the way that Americans have imagined and represented the North American wilderness? Where do you see shifts in style, mood, expectations, hopes, and fears? This is not a question limited to literary works; you will need to consider painting, photography, map-making, and other media through which Americans represent the natural world.

Depending upon the sophistication and motivation of the students, some problems may take several weeks. Notice that you have not assigned any readings to any student in particular: this means letting go of the idea that everyone is doing the same work. You may also have to change how you assess your students. Some practitioners of PBL suggest that you rely upon graded group work and self-assessment (see below); others suggest that you use a combination of graded group work and graded individual work. In either case, self-assessment is an important way to help students take responsibility for their learning.

Self-Assessment: Please rate yourself and your group members using the following chart:

	1 (low)	2	3	4	5 (high)
My commitment to this project was					
My analysis of the materials was					
Did I help my group members see connections?					
My writing for the project was					
Group Member #1 _____'s commitment to this project was					
Group Member #1 _____'s analysis of the materials was					
Did Group Member #1 _____ help you see connections?					

	1 (low)	2	3	4	5 (high)
Group Member #1 _____'s writing for the project was					
Group Member #2 _____'s commitment to this project was					

In a "pure" PBL classroom, the entire course would consist of three or four PBL problems such as the ones given above or those in the PBL section of the *Instructor's* and *Study Guides*. In a "hybrid" PBL classroom, PBL problems might be framed by assigned readings that provide some context for the problem or that introduce students to basic concepts. Another hybrid possibility is to assign specific novels and to have students solve problems about the novels.

Glossary (and Other Reference Sources)

As you and your students read the *Guides*, you will find words in **bold** such as **sentimentality**, **Creole**, and **Puritan**. These terms are defined in the Glossary at the end of each unit.

You may find that not every unfamiliar term is in the Glossary or that people and places you don't know are alluded to in the overviews and Contexts. For that reason, it's worth pointing your students toward some other general resources: two excellent starting places are *Benét's Reader's Encyclopedia of American Literature*, ed. George Perkins, Barbara Perkins, and Phillip Leininger (New York: Harper Collins, 1991), and James Hart's *Oxford Companion to American Literature*, with revisions and additions by Phillip W. Leininger, 6th ed. (New York: Oxford UP, 1995). These books provide biographical information on American authors, plot summaries of major works, and explanations of key references. Your students can find explanations of cultural references and identifications of historical figures and events at <www.britannica.com> or <www.encyclopedia.com>. If they are stumped by an extended metaphor or symbol, send them to *The Herder Dictionary of Symbols: Symbols from Art, Archaeology, Mythology, Literature, and Religion*, trans. Boris Matthews (Wilmette: Chiron Publications, 1993). If they encounter a word used in an unfamiliar way, they can determine what that word meant for people who lived before the twentieth century by looking in the *Oxford English Dictionary*. Similarly, they can discover the cultural significance of key concepts (such as the "sublime" or Prohibition) in the 11th edition of the *Encyclopaedia Britannica*. Most of these resources can be found in the reference room of a typical college or university library.

Selected Bibliography and Further Resources

The Selected Bibliography at the end of each unit lists the works that the writers of the *American Passages* guides found most useful when composing the unit materials. Further Resources is a list of other interesting materials, such as museum exhibits (virtual and actual), video recordings, sound recordings, and multimedia resources. These materials may enhance your students' learning and will provide rich contextual resources to help them understand the cultural milieu of the era they are studying.

TELLING THE STORY OF AMERICAN LITERATURE

One of the goals of this *Guide* is to help you teach your students to be literary historians—that is, to teach them to tell the story of how American literature has changed and evolved over time and to stimulate them to compare, contrast, and make connections between and among texts. When students make connections, they are telling a story: the story of how American literature came into being. Below are four organizing principles you might use to help your students narrate the story of American literature: one based on literary movements and historical change, one based on the Overview Questions, one based on Contexts, and one based on multiculturalism.

Literary Movements and Historical Change

American Passages is organized around sixteen literary movements or "units." A literary movement centers around a group of authors that share certain stylistic and thematic concerns. Each unit includes ten authors that are represented either in *The Norton Anthology* or in the Online Archive. Two to four of these authors are discussed in the video that accompanies the unit. The video calls attention to important historical and cultural influences on these authors, defines a genre that they share, and proposes some key thematic parallels.

Tracking literary movements can help your students see how American literature has changed and evolved over time. In general, people think about literary movements as reacting against earlier modes of writing and earlier movements. For example, just as modernism (Units 10–13) is often seen as a response to realism and the Gilded Age (Unit 9), so Romanticism is seen as a response to the Enlightenment (Unit 4). Most of the units focus on one era (see the chart below), but they will often include relevant authors from other eras to help draw out the connections and differences. (Note: The movements in parentheses are not limited to authors/works from the era in question, but they do cover some material from it.)

Century	Era	American Passages Literary Movements
Fifteenth–Seventeenth	Renaissance	(1: Native Voices) 2: Exploring Borderlands 3: Utopian Promise
Eighteenth	Enlightenment	(3: Utopian Promise) 4: Spirit of Nationalism (7: Slavery and Freedom)

Century	Era	American Passages Literary Movements
Nineteenth	Romanticist	4: Spirit of Nationalism 5: Masculine Heroes 6: American Gothic 7: Slavery and Freedom
Nineteenth	Realist	(1: Native Voices) 6: American Gothic 8: Regional Realism 9: Social Realism
Twentieth	Modernist	(1: Native Voices) 10: Rhythms in Poetry 11: Modernist Portraits 12: Migrant Struggle 13: Southern Renaissance
Twentieth	Postmodernist	1: Native Voices 2: Exploring Borderlands 12: Migrant Struggle 14: Becoming Visible 15: Poetry of Liberation 16: Search for Identity

Each of the units contains a timeline of historical events along with the dates of key literary texts by the authors discussed in the unit. These timelines are designed to help your students make connections between and among the movements, eras, and dates covered in each unit.

Overview Questions

The units are also connected by Overview Questions that will help start the thinking process for your students. While some of these questions will be more appropriate for some authors than for others, at least one of the Overview Questions should be provocative when asked about any particular author or group of authors. The Overview Questions are as follows:

1. **What is an American? How does literature create conceptions of the American experience and American identity?**
   This two-part question should trigger discussion about issues such as Who belongs to America? When and how does one become an American? How has the search for identity among American writers changed over time? It should also provoke discussion about the ways in which immigration, colonization, conquest, youth, race, class, and gender affect national identity.
2. **What is American literature? What are the distinctive voices and styles in American literature? How do social and political issues influence the American canon?**
   This multi-part question should instigate discussion about the aesthetics and reception of American literature. What is a masterpiece? When is some-

thing considered literature, and how is this category culturally and historically dependent? How has the canon of American literature changed and why? How have American writers used language to create art and meaning? What does literature do? This question should also invoke the issue of American exceptionalism: Is American literature different from the literature of other nations?

3. **How do place and time shape the authors' works and our understanding of them?**

   This question addresses America's location and the many ways in which place affects American literature's form and content. It should provoke discussion about how regionalism, geography, immigration, the frontier, and borders affect American literature, as well as the role of the vernacular in indicating place.

4. **What characteristics of a literary work have made it influential over time?**

   This question should spark discussion about the evolving impact of various pieces of American literature and about how American writers used language to create art and respond to and call for change. What is the individual's responsibility to uphold the community's traditions, and when are individuals compelled to resist them? What is the relationship between the individual and the community?

5. **How are American myths created, challenged, and re-imagined through this literature?**

   This question returns to the question "What is an American?" But it poses the question at a cultural rather than individual level. What are the myths that make up American culture? What is the American Dream? What are American myths, dreams, and nightmares? How have these changed over time?

Contexts

Another way that connections can be made across and between authors is through the five Contexts in each unit: three longer **Core Contexts** and two shorter **Extended Contexts**. The goal of the Contexts is not only to help your students read American literature in its cultural background but also to teach them close-reading skills and narrative strategies. Each Context features a brief narrative that introduces a key cultural metaphor or concept that had particular resonance for the writers in the unit and the average American of their era, questions that connect the Context to the authors in the unit, and a list of relevant items in the Online Archive. Some examples of Contexts include discussions of the concept of the Apocalypse (3: "Utopian Visions"), the sublime (4: "Spirit of Nationalism"), and baseball (14: "Becoming Visible"). The questions at the end of each Context will encourage your students to make connections across the Context, the writers in the unit, and the writers in other units.

The Core Contexts can be used in conjunction with an author or as stand-alone activities. You may find it helpful to skim the Context questions to see which authors are explicitly connected to that Context. While each Context is accompanied by a list of archive items, you may want to have your students search the Online Archive for other related materials. The Slide Show Tool on the Web site is ideal for creating assignments that draw connections between archive items from a Context and a text that a student has read. And you can create your own contexts and activities using the Slide Show Tool: these materials can then be e-mailed, viewed online, projected, or printed out on overhead transparencies.

Multiculturalism

In the past twenty years, the field of American literature has undergone a radical transformation. Just as the mainstream public has begun to understand America as more diverse, so scholars have moved to integrate more texts by women and ethnic minorities into the standard literary canon. These changes can be both exhilarating and disconcerting, as the breadth of American literature appears to be almost limitless. Each of the videos and units has been carefully balanced to pair canonical and noncanonical voices. Your students may find it helpful, however, to trace the development of American literature according to the rise of different ethnic and minority literatures. The following chart shows which ethnic and minority groups are represented in the videos and the units. As the chart indicates, we have set different multicultural literatures in dialogue with one another.

Group	Video Representation	*Instructor's Guide* and *Study Guide* Representation
African American literature	7: Slavery and Freedom 8: Regional Realism 10: Rhythms in Poetry 13: Southern Renaissance 14: Becoming Visible 15: Poetry of Liberation	4: Spirit of Nationalism 5: Masculine Heroes 7: Slavery and Freedom 8: Regional Realism 9: Social Realism 10: Rhythms in Poetry 11: Modernist Portraits 13: Southern Renaissance 14: Becoming Visible 15: Poetry of Liberation 16: Search for Identity
Native American literature	1: Native Voices 5: Masculine Heroes 14: Becoming Visible	1: Native Voices 2: Exploring Borderlands 3: Utopian Promise 4: Spirit of Nationalism 5: Masculine Heroes 7: Slavery and Freedom 8: Regional Realism 14: Becoming Visible 15: Poetry of Liberation 16: Search for Identity
Latino literature	2: Exploring Borderlands 10: Rhythms in Poetry	2: Exploring Borderlands 5: Masculine Heroes

GETTING STARTED

Defining Your Goals

Even if you have taught your American literature class a dozen times, it is worth asking yourself, What are my goals and what am I doing to accomplish these goals? The following chart provides examples of how to establish and meet class goals. This kind of preparatory exercise can help you identify the tasks that students find difficult.

Preparation for Activity	⇐ Activity That Teaches Skills	⇐Goal⇒	Assessment
Read the autobiographies of Benjamin Franklin *and* Frederick Douglass.	Have students read Booker T. Washington's *Up from Slavery*. Ask students to pay attention to the way Washington opens the story of his life.	**Understand conventions of autobiography**	To assess students' understanding of "as told to" auto-biographies, have students write an autobiography of a classmate and include authenticating documents at the beginning.
Have a brainstorming session about what kind of narrators students have seen in the literature they have read up to this point. What is going on at the end of the eighteenth century that allows for innovations in point of view?	Have students read Susanna Rowson's *Charlotte Temple* and discuss how she uses her authorial voice to forestall criticism, heighten dramatic tension, and manage readers' reactions to her tale.	**Understand conventions of narration in their cultural context**	*Quiz:* Ask students how Clappe's authorial voice compares to Rowson's when we get to Unit 5.

The Personal and Creative Responses section in each unit provides you with a variety of assessment tools ranging from journal exercises, to creative assignments, to multimedia presentations. You may find that varying the types of assessment tools you use produces welcome results.

Using Technology in the Classroom

How can using technology in the classroom help your teaching? If used appropriately, technology can help students become more engaged, enable them to see connections, and make your life easier. In the past few years, there has been an explosion of materials available on the Internet for teaching American studies. These materials include art, manuscripts, music, criticism, and language guides that are otherwise not available outside of archives, special-interest libraries, or large research institutions. Technology brings new resources to your students in an appealing and accessible format.

The *American Passages* videos are designed to be shown either as a series or as stand-alone episodes. You may want to show a video every class, every week, every other week, or once a term. If you are using the video as an overview for a more advanced course, you may want to use the Context and Exploration rather than the Comprehension questions. Researchers have shown that people are more likely to retain information if it relates to information that they already know, so you may want to precede the video with a short brainstorming session to ascertain what the students already know about the writers and/or movement the video covers. You may want to return to this brainstorming diagram after the video to map out how their perceptions have changed.

The *American Passages* Web site at <www.learner.org> includes an Online Archive of American cultural materials from the colonial period to the present that has been compiled specifically with the literary scholar in mind; this Online Archive is a rich resource for instructors and students alike. It is designed to support the curriculum in the *Instructor's* and *Study Guides*: you will find archival materials that relate to each of the 160 authors, as well as archival materials for all 80 of the Contexts. Items of general cultural significance have also been included. Each item contains an analytical description that links it to the *American Passages* curriculum materials. These items are not meant to duplicate the online holdings of other institutions such as the Library of Congress, the National Archives and Records Administration, and the Smithsonian, but rather are intended to exemplify the ways one might use resources from institutions such as these and others in conjunction with American literature.

The Web site Slide Show Tool is an excellent and easy way to project both passages and images. This software allows you to place text and image next to one another, providing for better illustrations of the relationship between text and artifact. You may find it helpful to have students pair their written assignments with slide shows that allow them to move back and forth among images, sounds, and texts. This user-friendly software allows you to save work for up to fourteen weeks. If you or your students wish to save a slide show for a longer period, you can download it in a "read only" format onto your own machine or you can simply revisit it at the Slide Show portion of the site.

For First-Time Teachers: The Student-Centered Classroom

How do the *American Passages* materials relate to other pedagogical theories, such as the student-centered classroom? The goal of the student-centered classroom is to get students to think, and hence to learn. In this classroom, the teacher becomes a facilitator, guiding the student toward better learning rather than disseminating wisdom. One way to get students more actively involved in the learning process is to ask them to do some of the preparation work and to give them time to show what they know.

If you are a first-time teacher, here are a couple of tips: if you have a quiet class or students who have trouble relating their views concisely, try having them freewrite on one of the discussion questions before starting the conversation. If you have one or two people who monopolize conversation and other means of engaging the rest of the class have failed, bring a small, soft ball to class and have students throw it to the person they want to respond to their comment. Make it a rule that you can't throw the ball back to the person who threw it at you. If you have students who say great things but never make connections to anything anyone else has said, have them do the freewriting exercise and then pass their paper to the person on their right (or left) and have that person respond. An alternative is to have the first person write a discussion question (something debatable, not a factoid). If you have problems with students asking "going-nowhere-factoid-questions," ask them to bring discussion questions that you can write on the board and use to talk about the difference between questions of fact and thought questions.

ACKNOWLEDGMENTS

American Passages is a multimedia series produced for Annenberg/CPB by Oregon Public Broadcasting in conjunction with W. W. Norton & Company.

Oregon Public Broadcasting (OPB)   An experienced producer of educational content with expertise in both traditional and new media approaches to formal education, community outreach, and television production, OPB has a long history of producing Web sites, teachers' guides, and other curriculum materials to accompany educational and PBS broadcast series. Working closely with national advisory boards, OPB's staff has produced curriculum materials in the humanities and sciences for a variety of grade levels and for teacher professional development. OPB is the third largest producer of documentary specials for PBS and has also produced programs for *NOVA, Frontline, American Experience*, and other series. In addition, OPB has undertaken co-productions with the BBC, NHK (Japan), ABC (Australia), and many other leading international producers.

W. W. Norton & Company   The companion texts, *The Norton Anthology of American Literature* and the *American Passages Instructor* and *Study Guides*, are produced and published by W. W. Norton & Company. A distinguished publisher in the areas of fiction, nonfiction, and poetry, W. W. Norton & Company has been independent since its founding in 1923, when William Warder Norton and Mary D. Herter Norton first published lectures delivered at the People's Institute, the adult education division of New York City's Cooper Union. The Nortons soon expanded their program beyond the Institute, publishing books by celebrated academics from America and abroad. By mid-century, the two major pillars of Norton's publishing program—trade books and college texts—were firmly established. In the 1950s, the Norton family transferred control of the company to its employees, and today—with a staff of 400 and a comparable number of trade, college, and professional titles published each year—W. W. Norton & Company stands as the largest and oldest publishing house owned wholly by its employees.

Annenberg/CPB   *American Passages* is funded by Annenberg/CPB, a partnership between the Annenberg Foundation and the Corporation for Public Broadcasting (CPB) that uses media and telecommunications to advance excellent teaching in American schools. Annenberg/CPB funds educational series and professional development workshops for teachers for the Annenberg/CPB Channel, which is distributed free by satellite and broadband to schools and other educational and community organizations.

The *American Passages* Advisors and Scholars

American Passages has been a team effort. Lead by Academic Director Laura Leibman, an Advisory Committee composed of specialists from across the field of American literature helped shape the program and the guides. These advisors are Randall Bass, Sacvan Bercovitch, Ann Green, Janice Gould, Terri Johanson, Mike McLeod, Bruce Michelson, Gary Nash, Sonia Saldívar-Hull, Greg Sarris, Pancho Savery, and Eric Sundquist.

Laura Leibman is associate professor of English and humanities at Reed College. She writes and teaches in the fields of technology and teaching, poetics, early American literature, and Native American literature and is working on a cultural edition of Experience Mayhew's *Indian Converts*.

Randall Bass is associate professor of English at Georgetown University. He is the director of the American Studies Crossroads Project and the editor of the electronic resources supporting the *Heath Anthology of American Literature*.

Sacvan Bercovitch is Powell M. Cabot Research Professor of American Literature at Harvard University. His publications include *Puritan Origins of the American Self*, *The American Jeremiad*, *The Office of* The Scarlet Letter, and *The Rites of Assent: Transformations in the Symbolic Construction of America*; he is General Editor of the multivolume *Cambridge History of American Literature*.

Janice M. Gould is an assistant professor and the Hallie Ford Chair in Creative Writing at Willamette University, where she teaches courses in imaginative writing and Native American literature. She has published three books of poetry—*Earthquake Weather*, *Beneath My Heart*, and *Alphabet*—and is the co-editor of *Speak to Me Words: Essays on Native American Poetry*.

Ann M. Green is professor of English at Jackson Community College. She teaches creative writing, film studies, and humanities. A specialist in collaborative learning, she writes and lectures about how to use virtual classroom software and bulletin board systems in computer-mediated classrooms.

Terri Johanson is the assistant commissioner for the Oregon Department of Community Colleges and Workforce Development. Her work focuses on how distributed learning modalities can be employed to create active learning environments. She is also co-director of the Oregon Technology Infusion Project (OTIP).

Michael McLeod is an independent producer and director. His recent projects include several programs for the PBS investigative series *Frontline*, documentary projects for PBS and *Discovery*, and the motion picture *A Place Apart*.

Bruce Michelson is professor of English and director of the Campus Honors Program at the University of Illinois at Urbana-Champaign. His most recent book is *Literary Wit*. He has also published books on Mark Twain and Richard Wilbur, as well as numerous articles on American writers. He is co-author of the Instructor's Guide for *The Norton Anthology of American Literature* and author of the *NAAL* Web site.

Gary B. Nash is professor of history at the University of California, Los Angeles. His publications include *Forbidden Love: The Secret History of Mixed-Race America, First City: Philadelphia and the Forging of Historical Memory, The Urban Crucible,* and *The Red, White, and Black: The Peoples of Early North America.*

Sonia Saldívar-Hull is professor of English at the University of Texas, San Antonio. She is the author of *Feminism on the Border: Chicana Gender Politics and Literature* and is the founding director of the Women's Studies Institute at the University of Texas, San Antonio.

Greg Sarris is professor of English at Loyola Marymount University. He is the author of numerous books, screenplays, and teleplays, including the award-winning HBO adaptation of his novel *Grand Avenue*. A specialist in Native American Studies, Sarris is the tribal chairman of the Coast Miwok and a member of the Pomo Indian tribe. Sarris served as special consultant for both the video and the print components of the *American Passages* project.

Pancho Savery is professor of English and humanities at Reed College. He is a poet and the co-editor of *Approaches to Teaching Ellison's* Invisible Man.

Eric J. Sundquist is Foundation Professor of Literature at the University of California, Los Angeles. He is the author of *To Wake the Nations: Race in the Making of American Literature, Faulkner: The House Divided,* and other books on American literature and culture.

The *Instructor* and *Study Guides* for *American Passages* were written under the guidance of this advisory committee by the following writers: Jolynn Parker (Units 2, 3, 4, 5, 7, 8, 9), David Pagano (Units 1, 6), Michael O'Conner (Units 12, 14), Kate Stephenson (Units 10, 15), Todd Chatman (Unit 13) , J. Susannah Shmurak (Unit 11), and Catherine M. Waitinas (Unit 16).

Jolynn Parker is finishing her doctorate at the University of Chicago. She has taught Early American literature at the University of Chicago and at Portland State University.

David Pagano received his Ph.D. in English from the University of California, Irvine. He is a lecturer in English at Old Dominion University, where he teaches American literature, film, and writing.

Michael O'Conner is an assistant professor of English and the academic webmaster at Millikin University in Decatur, Illinois. He teaches late-nineteenth and twentieth-century American literature, Web publishing, American science fiction, and business and professional writing.

Kate Stephenson received her Ph.D. in English from the University of Virginia, where she specialized in twentieth-century Anglo-American literature. She currently teaches at Trinity University in San Antonio, Texas.

Todd Chatman is a Ph.D. candidate in English at the University of Illinois, Urbana-Champaign, where he teaches American literature. His areas of specialization include late-twentieth-century American literature and critical theory.

J. Susannah Shmurak is a Ph.D. candidate in English at the University of Illinois at Urbana-Champaign. She specializes in late-nineteenth-century American literature and social history and has taught courses in both American and British literature.

Catherine M. Waitinas is a Ph.D. candidate in English at the University of Illinois at Urbana-Champaign, where she has taught American and British literature and business writing at the undergraduate and graduate levels. Her area of specialty is nineteenth-century American literature with a focus on Walt Whitman's democratic poetics.

These materials were edited by Laura Arnold, Eileen Connell, Julia Reidhead, and Marian Johnson, with assistance from Bruce Michelson, Katharine Ings, Nina Gielen, and Erin Dye. We would also like to thank W. W. Norton & Company production manager Diane O'Connor and Chris Welch, who supervised the design.

Julia A. Reidhead is Vice President and Director at W. W. Norton & Company, where she is senior English editor. Reidhead is in-house editor of *The Norton Anthology of American Literature*.

Eileen Connell is a field editor and English marketing associate at W. W. Norton & Company.

Marian Johnson is managing editor for college books at W. W. Norton & Company.

Katharine Ings is a freelance copyeditor and a professor of English at Manchester College.

Nina Gielen is a freelance project editor.

Erin Dye is an editorial assistant at W. W. Norton & Company.

American Passages would not be possible without the hard work of the research and production staff at Oregon Public Broadcasting. We would like to thank the following individuals: Project Manager Meighan Maloney; Unit Production Manager Catherine Stimac; Research Director Chris Lowe; Researchers and Assistant Editors Heather Chambers, Gina deLeo, Claire Dennerlein, Chris Moses, and Erin Forbes; Research Assistants Dane Bevan, Jyni Ekins, Sara Lawrence, Clint Sallee, Kristina Satter, Melinda Scharstein, and Beka Smith; Rights Coordinator Lisa Gewerth; Rights Assistants Laska Jimsen, Edgard Van Gansen, Lorrie Biggs, Andrea Rodriguez, and Renato Rodriquez; Image Coordinators Jon Baldivieso and Ronald Foss; Tuttle Intern Onye Ikwuakor.

AMERICAN
PASSAGES

A LITERARY SURVEY

```
┌─────────────────────────────────────────┐
│                                           │
├───────────────────────────────────────────┤
│                                           │
│         WHAT IS AMERICAN                   │
│                                           │
│      LITERATURE? AN OVERVIEW               │
│                                           │
├───────────────────────────────────────────┤
│                                           │
└─────────────────────────────────────────┘
```

WHAT IS AMERICAN LITERATURE? AN OVERVIEW

When the English preacher and writer Sidney Smith asked in 1820, "In the four quarters of the globe, who reads an American book?" little did he suspect that less than two hundred years later the answer in literate quarters would be "just about everyone." Indeed, just a few years after Smith posed his inflammatory question, the American writer Samuel Knapp would begin to assemble one of the first histories of American literature as part of a lecture series that he was giving. The course materials offered by *American Passages* continue in the tradition begun by Knapp in 1829.

One goal of this *Study Guide* is to help you learn to be a literary historian: that is, to introduce you to American literature as it has evolved over time and to stimulate you to make connections between and among texts. Like a literary historian, when you make these connections you are telling a story: the story of how American literature came into being. This Overview outlines four paths (there are many others) by which you can narrate the story of American literature: one based on literary movements and historical change, one based on the *American Passages* Overview Questions, one based on Contexts, and one based on multiculturalism.

TELLING THE STORY OF AMERICAN LITERATURE

Literary Movements and Historical Change

American Passages is organized around sixteen literary movements or "units." A literary movement centers around a group of authors that share certain stylistic and thematic concerns. Each unit includes ten authors that are represented either in *The Norton Anthology of American Literature* or in the Online Archive. Two to four of these authors are discussed in the video, which calls attention to important historical and cultural influences on these authors, defines a genre that they share, and proposes some key thematic parallels.

Tracking literary movements can help you see how American literature has changed and evolved over time. In general, people think about literary movements as reacting against earlier modes of writing and earlier movements. For example, just as **modernism** (Units 10–13) is often seen as a response to **realism** and the Gilded Age (Unit 9), so **Romanticism** is seen as a response to the **Enlightenment** (Unit 4). Most of the units focus on one era (see the chart below), but they will often include relevant authors from other eras to help draw out the connections and differences. (Note: The movements in parentheses are not limited to authors/works from the era in question, but they do cover some material from it.)

Century	Era	American Passages Literary Movements
Fifteenth–Seventeenth	Renaissance	(1: Native Voices) 2: Exploring Borderlands 3: Utopian Promise
Eighteenth	Enlightenment	(3: Utopian Promise) 4: Spirit of Nationalism (7: Slavery and Freedom)
Nineteenth	Romanticist	4: Spirit of Nationalism 5: Masculine Heroes 6: American Gothic 7: Slavery and Freedom
Nineteenth	Realist	(1: Native Voices) 6: American Gothic 8: Regional Realism 9: Social Realism
Twentieth	Modernist	(1: Native Voices) 10: Rhythms in Poetry 11: Modernist Portraits 12: Migrant Struggle 13: Southern Renaissance
Twentieth	Postmodernist	1: Native Voices 2: Exploring Borderlands 12: Migrant Struggle 14: Becoming Visible 15: Poetry of Liberation 16: Search for Identity

Each unit contains a timeline of historical events along with the dates of key literary texts by the movement's authors. These timelines are designed to help you make connections between and among the movements, eras, and authors covered in each unit.

Overview Questions

The Overview Questions at the start of each unit are tailored from the five *American Passages* Overview Questions that follow. They are meant to help you focus your viewing and reading and participate in discussion afterward.

1. **What is an American? How does literature create conceptions of the American experience and American identity?**
   This two-part question should trigger discussion about issues such as, Who belongs to America? When and how does one become an American? How has the search for identity among American writers changed over time? It can also encourage discussion about the ways in which immigration, colonization, conquest, youth, race, class, and gender affect national identity.

2. **What is American literature? What are the distinctive voices and styles in American literature? How do social and political issues influence the American canon?**
   This multi-part question should instigate discussion about the aesthetics and reception of American literature. What is a masterpiece? When is something considered literature, and how is this category culturally and historically dependent? How has the canon of American literature changed and why? How have American writers used language to create art and meaning? What does literature do? This question can also raise the issue of American exceptionalism: Is American literature different from the literature of other nations?

3. **How do place and time shape the authors' works and our understanding of them?**
   This question addresses America as a location and the many ways in which place impacts American literature's form and content. It can provoke discussion about how regionalism, geography, immigration, the frontier, and borders impact American literature, as well as the role of the vernacular in indicating place.

4. **What characteristics of a literary work have made it influential over time?**
   This question can be used to spark discussion about the evolving impact of various pieces of American literature and about how American writers used language both to create art and respond to and call for change. What is the individual's responsibility to uphold the community's traditions, and when are individuals compelled to resist them? What is the relationship between the individual and the community?

5. **How are American myths created, challenged, and re-imagined through this literature?**
   This question returns to "What is an American?" But it poses the question at a cultural rather than individual level. What are the myths that make up American culture? What is the American Dream? What are American myths, dreams, and nightmares? How have these changed over time?

Contexts

Another way that connections can be made across and between authors is through the five Contexts in each unit: three longer **Core Contexts** and two shorter **Extended Contexts**. The goal of the Contexts is both to help you read American literature in its cultural background and to teach you close-reading skills. Each Context consists of a brief narrative about an event, trend, or idea that had particular resonance for the writers in the unit as well as Americans of their era; questions that connect the Context to the authors in the unit; and a list of related texts and images in the Online Archive. Examples of Contexts include discussions of the concept of the Apocalypse (3: "Utopian Visions"), the sublime (4: "Spirit of Nationalism"), and baseball (14: "Becoming Visible").

The Contexts can be used in conjunction with an author or as stand-alone activities. The Slide Show Tool on the Web site is ideal for doing assignments that draw connections between archive items from a Context and a text you have read. And you can create your own contexts and activities using the Slide Show Tool: these materials can then be e-mailed, viewed online, projected, or printed out on overhead transparencies.

Multiculturalism

In the past twenty years, the field of American literature has undergone a radical transformation. Just as the mainstream public has begun to understand America as more diverse, so, too, have scholars moved to integrate more texts by women and ethnic minorities into the standard canon of literature taught and studied. These changes can be both exhilarating and disconcerting, as the breadth of American literature appears to be almost limitless. Each of the videos and units has been carefully balanced to pair canonical and noncanonical voices. You may find it helpful, however, to trace the development of American literature according to the rise of different ethnic and minority literatures. The following chart is designed to highlight which literatures are represented in the videos and the units. As the chart indicates, we have set different multicultural literatures in dialogue with one another.

Literature	Video Representation	*Study Guide* Representation
African American literature	7: Slavery and Freedom 8: Regional Realism 10: Rhythms in Poetry 13: Southern Renaissance 14: Becoming Visible 15: Poetry of Liberation	4: Spirit of Nationalism 5: Masculine Heroes 7: Slavery and Freedom 8: Regional Realism 9: Social Realism 10: Rhythms in Poetry 11: Modernist Portraits 13: Southern Renaissance 14: Becoming Visible 15: Poetry of Liberation 16: Search for Identity

Native American literature	1: Native Voices 5: Masculine Heroes 14: Becoming Visible	1: Native Voices 2: Exploring Borderlands 3: Utopian Promise 4: Spirit of Nationalism 5: Masculine Heroes 7: Slavery and Freedom 8: Regional Realism 14: Becoming Visible 15: Poetry of Liberation 16: Search for Identity
Latino literature	2: Exploring Borderlands 10: Rhythms in Poetry 12: Migrant Struggle 16: Search for Identity	2: Exploring Borderlands 5: Masculine Heroes 10: Rhythms in Poetry 12: Migrant Struggle 15: Poetry of Liberation 16: Search for Identity
Asian American literature	12: Migrant Struggle 16: Search for Identity	9: Social Realism 12: Migrant Struggle 16: Search for Identity
Jewish American literature	9: Social Realism 11: Modernist Portraits 14: Becoming Visible 15: Poetry of Liberation 16: Search for Identity	9: Social Realism 11: Modernist Portraits 14: Becoming Visible 15: Poetry of Liberation 16: Search for Identity
Women's literature	1: Native Voices 2: Exploring Borderlands 3: Utopian Promise 6: American Gothic 7: Slavery and Freedom 8: Regional Realism 9: Social Realism 11: Modernist Portraits 12: Migrant Struggle 13: Southern Renaissance 15: Poetry of Liberation 16: Search for Identity	1: Native Voices 2: Exploring Borderlands 3: Utopian Promise 4: Spirit of Nationalism 5: Masculine Heroes 6: American Gothic 7: Slavery and Freedom 8: Regional Realism 9: Social Realism 10: Rhythms in Poetry 11: Modernist Portraits 12: Migrant Struggle 13: Southern Renaissance 14: Becoming Visible 15: Poetry of Liberation 16: Search for Identity
Gay and lesbian literature	2: Exploring Borderlands 5: Masculine Heroes 10: Rhythms in Poetry 11: Modernist Portraits 15: Poetry of Liberation 16: Search for Identity	2: Exploring Borderlands 5: Masculine Heroes 10: Rhythms in Poetry 11: Modernist Portraits 12: Migrant Struggle 13: Southern Renaissance 14: Becoming Visible 15: Poetry of Liberation 16: Search for Identity

Literature cont'd	Video Representation	*Study Guide* Representation
Working-class literature	2: Exploring Borderlands 4: Spirit of Nationalism 5: Masculine Heroes 7: Slavery and Freedom 9: Social Realism 12: Migrant Struggle 16: Search for Identity	2: Exploring Borderlands 4: Spirit of Nationalism 5: Masculine Heroes 7: Slavery and Freedom 9: Social Realism 10: Rhythms in Poetry 12: Migrant Struggle 14: Becoming Visible 15: Poetry of Liberation 16: Search for Identity

LITERATURE IN ITS CULTURAL CONTEXT

When you study American literature in its cultural context, you enter a multi-disciplined and multi-voiced conversation where scholars and critics in different fields examine the same topic but ask very different questions about it. For example, how might a literary critic's understanding of nineteenth-century American culture compare to that of a historian of the same era? How can an art historian's understanding of popular visual metaphors enrich our readings of literature? The materials presented in this section of the *Study Guide* aim to help you enter that conversation. Below are some suggestions on how to begin.

Deep in the heart of the Vatican Museum is an exquisite marble statue from first- or second-century Rome. Over seven feet high, the statue depicts a scene from Virgil's *Aeneid* in which Laocoön and his sons are punished for warning the Trojans about the Trojan horse. Their bodies are entwined with large, devouring serpents, and Laocoön's face is turned upward in a dizzying portrait of anguish, his muscles rippling and bending beneath the snake's strong coils.

The emotion in the statue captured the heart and eye of critic Gotthold Ephraim Lessing, who used the work as the starting point for his seminal essay on the relationship between literature and art, "*Laocoön*: An Essay on the Limits of Painting and Poetry." For Lessing, one of the most common errors that students of culture can make is to assume that all aspects of culture develop in tandem with one another. As Lessing points out, each art has its own strengths. For example, literature works well with notions of time and story, and thus is more flexible than visual art in terms of imaginative freedom, whereas painting is a visual medium that can reach greater beauty, although it is static. For Lessing, the mixing of these two modes (temporal and spatial) carries great risk along with rewards. As you study literature in conjunction with any of the fine arts, you may find it helpful to ask whether you agree with Lessing that literature *is* primarily a temporal art. Consider too the particular strengths of the media discussed below. What do they offer that may not be available to writers? What modes do they use that complement our understanding of the literary arts?

Fine Arts

Albrecht Dürer created some of the most disturbing drawings known to humans: they are rife with images of death, the end of the world, and dark creatures that inhabit hell. Images such as *The Last Judgement* (below) can be found in the Online Archive. In *Knight, Death, and the Devil* (1513), a devout Christian knight is taunted by the Devil and Death, who gleefully shakes a quickly depleting hourglass, mocking the soldier with the passing of time. Perhaps the tension and anxiety in Dürer's print resonated with the American poet Randall Jarrell in his struggle with mental illness. In "The Knight, Death, and the Devil," Jarrell opens with a description of the scene:

> Cowhorn-crowned, shockheaded, cornshucked-bearded,
> Death is a scarecrow—his death's-head a teetotum . . .

[7995] Albrecht Dürer, *The Last Judgement* (1510), courtesy of the print collection of Connecticut College, New London.

Jarrell's description is filled with adjectives in much the same way that the print is crowded with detail. The poem is an instance of what critics call **ekphrasis**: the verbal description of a work of visual art, usually of a painting, photograph, or sculpture but sometimes of an urn, tapestry, or quilt. Ekphrasis attempts to bridge the gap between the verbal and the visual arts. Artists and writers have always influenced one another: sometimes directly as in the case of Dürer's drawing and Jarrell's poem, and other times indirectly.

The *Study Guide* will help you navigate through these webs of influence. For example, Unit 5 will introduce you to the Hudson River School, the great American landscape painters of the nineteenth century. In the Context focusing on these artists, you will learn of the interconnectedness of their visual motifs. In Unit 11, William Carlos Williams, whose poems "The Dance" and "Landscape with the Fall of Icarus" were inspired by two paintings by Breughel, will draw your attention to the use of ekphrasis. Williams's work is a significant example of how multiple traditions in art can influence a writer: in addition to his interest in European art, Williams imitated Chinese landscapes and poetic forms.

When you encounter works of fine art, such as paintings, photographs, or sculpture, in the Online Archive or the *Study Guide*, you may find two tools used by art historians helpful: **formal analysis** and **iconography**. Formal

[3694] Thomas Cole, *The Falls of Kaaterskill* (1826), courtesy of the Warner Collection of the Gulf States Paper Corporation, Tuscaloosa, Alabama.

analysis, like close readings of poems, seeks to describe the nature of the object without reference to the context in which it was created. A formal analysis addresses such questions as Where does the central interest in the work lie? How is the work composed and with what materials? How is lighting or shading used? What does the scene depict? What allusions (mythological, religious, artistic) are found in the work?

Once you have described the work of art using formal analysis, you may want to extend your reading by calling attention to the cultural climate in which the work was produced. This is called an iconographic reading. Here the Context sections of the *Study Guide* will be useful. You may notice, for example, a number of nineteenth-century paintings of ships in the Online Archive. One of the Contexts for Unit 6 argues that these ships can be read as symbols for nineteenth-century America, where it was common to refer to the nation as a "ship of state." The glowing light or wrecked hulls in the paintings reflect the artists' alternating optimism and pessimism about where the young country was headed.

Below are two possible readings of Thomas Cole's painting *The Falls of Kaaterskill* that employ the tools of formal analysis and iconography.

WRITER A: FORMAL ANALYSIS

In this painting by Hudson River School artist Thomas Cole, the falls that give the painting its name grab our attention. The shock of the white falls against the concentrated brightness of the rocks ensures that the waterfall will be the focus of the work. Even amidst this brightness, however, there is darkness and mystery in the painting, where the falls emerge out of a dark quarry and crash down onto broken tree limbs and staggered rocks. The descent is neither peaceful nor pastoral, unlike the presentation of nature in Cole's other works, such as the *Oxbow*. The enormity of the falls compared to the lone human figure that perches above them also adds to the sense of power the falls embody. Barely recognizable as human because it is so minute, the figure still pushes forward as if to embrace the cascade of the water in a painting that explores the tension between the individual and the power of nature.

WRITER B: ICONOGRAPHY

I agree with Writer A that this painting is all about the power of nature, but I would argue that it is about a particular kind of power: one that nineteenth-century thinkers called the "sublime." Cole's portrait of the falls is particularly indebted to the aesthetic ideas formulated by Edmund Burke in the eighteenth century. Burke was interested in categorizing aesthetic responses, and he distinguished the "sublime" from the "beautiful." While the beautiful is calm and harmonious, the sublime is majestic, wild, and even savage. While viewers are soothed by the beautiful, they are overwhelmed, awestruck, and sometimes terrified by the sublime. Often associated with huge, overpowering natural phenomena like mountains, waterfalls, or thunderstorms, the "delightful terror" inspired by sublime visions was supposed to both remind viewers of their own insignificance in the face of nature and divinity and inspire them with a sense of transcendence. Here the miniature figure is the object of our gaze even as he is obliterated by the grandeur of the water. During the nineteenth century, tourists often visited locales such as the Kaaterskill Falls in order to experience the "delightful terror" that they brought. This experience is also echoed in Ralph Waldo Emerson's essay "Nature," in which he writes of his desire to become a "transparent eyeball" that will be able to absorb the oversoul that surrounds him. The power that nature holds here is that of the divine: nature is one way we can experience higher realms.

How do these readings differ? Which do you find more compelling and why? What uses can you see for formal analysis or iconographic readings? When might you choose one of these strategies over the other?

History

As historian Ray Kierstead has pointed out, history is not just "one damn thing after another": rather, history is a way of telling stories about time or, some might say, making an argument about time. The Greek historian Herodotus is often called the father of history in the western world, as he was one of the first historians to notice patterns in world events. Herodotus saw that the course of empires followed a cyclical pattern of rise and fall: as one empire reaches its peak and self-destructs out of hubris (excessive pride), a new empire or new nations will be born to take its place. Thomas Cole's five-part series *The Course of Empire* (1833) mirrors this Herodotean notion of time as his scene moves from *savage*, to *pastoral*, to *consummation*, to *devastation*, to *desolation*. This vision of time has been tremendously influential in literature: whenever you read a work written in the **pastoral mode** (literature that looks back with nostalgia to an era of rural life, lost simplicity, and a time when nature and culture were one), ask yourself whether there is an implicit optimism or pessimism about what follows this lost rural ideal. For example, in Herman Melville's South Sea novel *Typee*, we find the narrator in a Tahitian village. He seeks to determine if he has entered a pastoral or savage setting: is he surrounded by savages, or is he plunged in a pastoral bliss? Implicit in both is a suggestion that there are earlier forms of civilization than the United States that the narrator has left behind. Any structural analysis of a work of literature (an analysis that pays attention to how a work is ordered) would do well to consider what notions of history are embedded within.

In addition to the structural significance of history, a dialogue between history and literature is crucial because much of the early literature of the United States can also be categorized as historical documents. It is helpful, therefore, to understand the genres of history. Like literature, history is comprised of different genres, or modes. Historian Elizabeth Boone defines the main traditional genres of history as **res gestae**, **geographical**, and **annals**. *Res gestae*, or "deeds done," organizes history through a list of accomplishments. This was a popular form of history for the ancient Greeks and Romans; for example, the autobiography of Julius Caesar chronicles his deeds, narrated in the third person. When Hernán Cortés and other explorers wrote accounts of their travels (often in the form of letters to the emperor), Caesar's autobiography served as their model. Geographical histories use travel through space to shape the narrative: Mary Rowlandson's captivity narrative is an example of a geographical history in that it follows her through a sequence of twenty geographic "removes" into Indian country and back. Annals, by contrast, use time as the organizing principle. Information is catalogued by year or month. Diaries and journals are a good example of this genre.

These three genres can also be found in the histories of the Aztecs and Mayans of Mesoamerica and in those of the native communities of the United States and Canada. For example, the migration legend, a popular indigenous form of history, is a geographical history, whereas trickster tales often tell the early history of the world through a series of deeds. Memoirists also mix genres; for example, the first section of William Bradford's *Of Plimouth Plantation* is a geographical history, whereas the second half is annals. Today the most common historical genres are intellectual history (the history of ideas), political history (the story of leaders), and diplomatic history (the history of foreign relations). To these categories we might add the newer categories of "social history" (a history of everyday life) and "gender history" (which focuses on the construction of gender roles).

Finally, history is a crucial tool for understanding literature because literature is written in—and arguably often reflects—a specific historical context. Readers of literary works can deepen their understanding by drawing on the tools of history, that is, the records people leave behind: political (or literary) documents, town records, census data, newspaper stories, captivity narratives, letters, journals, diaries, and the like. Even such objects as tools, graveyards, or trading goods can tell us important information about the nature of everyday life for a community, how it worshipped or what it thought of the relationship between life and death.

Material Culture

[6332] Archibald Gunn and Richard Felton Outcault, *New York Journal's Colored Comic Supplement* (1896), courtesy of the Library of Congress, Prints and Photographs Division [LC-USZC4-25531].

When you look at an object, it may call up associations from the past. For example, for the first-time viewer the clown figure in the image above may seem innocuous, yet at the end of the nineteenth century his popularity was so intense that it started a newspaper war fierce enough to spawn a whole new term for sensationalist, irresponsible journalism—"yellow journalism." Objects such as this comic supplement constitute "material culture," the objects of everyday life. In *Material Culture Studies in America*, Thomas Schlereth provides the following useful definition of material culture:

> Material culture can be considered to be the totality of artifacts in a culture, the vast universe of objects used by humankind to cope with the physical world, to facilitate social intercourse, to delight our fancy, and to create symbols of meaning. . . . Leland Ferguson argues that material culture includes all "the things that people leave behind . . . all of the things people make from the physical world—farm tools, ceramics, houses, furniture, toys, buttons, roads, cities." (2)

When we study material culture in conjunction with literature, we wed two notions of "culture" and explore how they relate. As critic John Storey notes, the first notion of culture is what is often called "high culture"—the "general process of intellectual, spiritual and aesthetic factors"; and the second is "lived culture"—the "particular way of life, whether of a people, a period or a group" (2). In a sense, material culture (as the objects of a lived culture) allows us to see how the prevailing intellectual ideas were played out in the daily lives of people in a particular era.

Thus, as Schlereth explains, through studying material culture we can learn about the "belief systems—the values, ideas, attitudes, and assumptions—of a particular community or society, usually across time" (3). In reading objects as embedded with meaning, we follow Schlereth's premise that "objects made or modified by humans, consciously or unconsciously, directly or indirectly, reflect the belief patterns of individuals who made, commissioned, purchased, or used them, and, by extension, the belief patterns of the larger society of which they are a part" (3). The study of material culture, then, can help us better understand the cultures that produced and consumed the literature we read today.

Thomas Schlereth suggests a number of useful models for studying material culture; his "Art History Paradigm" is particularly noteworthy in that it will help you approach works of "high art," such as paintings and sculptures, as well. The "Art History Paradigm" argues that the interpretive objective of examining the artifact is to "depict the historical development and intrinsic merit" of it. If you are interested in writing an "Art History Paradigm" reading of material culture, you might look at an object and ask yourself the following questions, taken from Sylvan Barnet's *Short Guide to Writing about Art*. These questions apply to *any* art object:

First, we need to know information about the artifact so we can place it in a historical context. You might ask yourself:

1. What is my first response to the work?
2. When and where was the work made?
3. Where would the work originally have been seen?
4. What purpose did the work serve?
5. In what condition has the work survived? (Barnet 21–22)

In addition, if the artifact is a drawing, painting, or advertisement, you might want to ask yourself questions such as these:

1. What is the subject matter? What (if anything) is happening?
2. If the picture is a portrait, how do the furnishings and the background and the angle of the head or the posture of the head and body (as well as the facial expression) contribute to our sense of the subject's character?
3. If the picture is a still life, does it suggest opulence or want?
4. In a landscape, what is the relation between human beings and nature? Are the figures at ease in nature, or are they dwarfed by it? Are they one with the horizon, or (because the viewpoint is low) do they stand out against the horizon and perhaps seem in touch with the heavens, or at least with open air? If there are woods, are these woods threatening, or are they an inviting place of refuge? If there is a clearing, is the clearing a vulnerable place or is it a place of refuge from ominous woods? Do the natural objects in the landscape somehow reflect the emotions of the figures? (Barnet 22–23; for more questions, see pp. 23–24)

Material culture is a rich and varied resource that ranges from kitchen utensils, to advertisements, to farming tools, to clothing. Unpacking the significance of objects that appear in the stories and poems you read may help you better understand characters and their motives.

Architecture

Most of the time we read the hidden meanings of buildings without even thinking twice. Consider the buildings below:

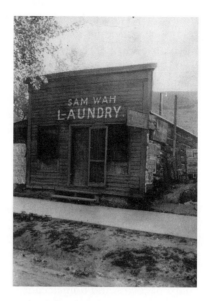

Above: **[9089]** Anonymous, Capitol Building at Washington, D.C. (1906), courtesy of Prints and Photographs Division, Library of Congress [LC-USZ62-121528].
Right: **[6889]** Anonymous, *Façade of the Sam Wah's Chinese Laundry* (c. 1890–1900), courtesy of the Denver Public Library.

Even if we had never seen either of these buildings before, it would not take us long to determine which was a government building and which was a small-town retail establishment. Our having seen thousands of buildings enables us to understand the purpose of a building from architectural clues.

When first seeing a work of architecture, it is helpful to unpack cultural assumptions. You might ask:

1. What is the purpose of this building? Is it public or private? What activities take place within it?
2. What features of the building reflect this purpose? Which of these features are necessary and which are merely conventional?
3. What buildings or building styles does this building allude to? What values are inherent in that allusion?
4. What parts of this building are principally decorative rather than functional? What does the ornament or lack of it say about the status of the owners or the people who work there?
5. What buildings surround this building? How do they affect the way the building is entered?
6. What types of people live or work in this building? How do they interact within the space? What do these findings say about the relative social status of the occupants? How does the building design restrict or encourage that status?
7. How are people supposed to enter and move through the building? What clues does the building give as to how this movement should take place?

These questions imply two basic assumptions about architecture: (1) architecture reflects and helps establish **social status** and social relations; and (2) architecture is often **processual**—that is, it guides the movement of people both between and among buildings and within them.

First, how does architecture embody notions of social status and social relations? Most twentieth-century American homes (domestic architecture) divide the space according to the age of the inhabitants: adults and children tend to have different bedrooms and "play" areas. Historically, this has not always been the case: in some societies, domestic space is divided based on social status and gender, rather than age. As you look at examples of American homes from before the twentieth century, you might look for clues as to how space was divided and what this arrangement says about the relationships among the inhabitants. Similarly, in fiction and nonfiction it is important to pay attention to what buildings tells us about characters and social relations. When in William Faulkner's "Barn Burning" the poor white father is told by a black servant in a nearby mansion that he must "Wipe yo foots, white man, fo you come in here," it is clear that he is being reminded through the encounter with the building and servant of his lower social status. The injunction to "wipe yo foots" is meant as an insult, just as the white man returns the insult when he refuses to wipe his feet, or when—as a result—he is told later that "you have ruined that rug. . . . It cost a hundred dollars. But you never had a hundred dollars. You never will." Floor plans, along with urban-planning documents and maps of towns and homesteads, can help provide a context for understanding the status of characters and relations between them.

A second concept to remember is that architecture is processual: the order of the rooms and the arrangement within the rooms encourage you to move through the building and to view the objects within the building in a particular order. While you can transgress this order—for example, in a museum you can skip an exhibit and go straight to the bathroom or cafeteria—when you do so, you are violating the normal order of the building. Though we don't think about it often, even domestic structures have a built-in order: a first-time visitor would be unlikely to visit the bedrooms of a house, unless invited to do so. The notion that architecture is processual is useful for thinking about architecture in conjunction with literature because characters often follow (or break!) these rules. Their comfort or discomfort with the rules can tell us much about their relationship to society. For example, that Gertrude Simmons Bonnin's (Zitkala Ša's) mother is uncomfortable cooking in a Western-style house and cooks instead in a tipi communicates important information about her relationship to Western culture.

The notion of architecture as processual applies both to an individual building and to a group of buildings. Plantation architecture is a good example of this. The stereotypical long tree-lined drive channeled visitors to the "big house." With its white pillars, the entryway resembled a Roman or Greek temple and emphasized the power of the patriarch who lived within. In contrast, the slave quarters were secondary, and their humble appearance emphasized the lower status of their residents. As you read a work of literature, pay attention to the description of the town, city, or homestead and how the buildings create a sense of social space.

Religion

While the Bill of Rights establishes the separation of church and state, the culture of America has always been profoundly religious. Though scholars, notably Perry Miller, have sought to create a cohesive story about American **religion**, America's religious traditions have been diverse since the earliest colonies: in addition to the indigenous religious traditions that had been evolving for millennia, Puritans, Quakers, Catholics, Jews, and Anglicans came to the Americas, bringing with them a wide range of theologies. For those interested in the religious history of the Americas, an essential resource is *Religions of the United States in Practice*, ed. Colleen McDannell. As this work and others like it show, the study of religion is itself interdisciplinary, drawing most commonly on the disciplines of literature and history, as well as theology. Although it necessarily oversimplifies three rich and varied traditions, the chart below can be a useful starting point for understanding some of the religious differences in early America. You might want to make a similar chart comparing Calvinism ("Puritanism") to the Quaker and Native American religious traditions during the first Great Awakening (1740s).

THE SECOND GREAT AWAKENING: EARLY NINETEENTH-CENTURY CALVINISM, UNITARIANISM, AND TRANSCENDENTALISM

Topic	Calvinism	Unitarianism	Transcendentalism
God	Supreme patriarch; Trinity	Supreme being; one person	Supreme mind ("Oversoul"); God animates everything
People	Innately sinful (Original Sin)	Innately good (*tabula rasa*)	Have part of the divine within
Who runs the world	God: all is predestined	Man: has free will to determine own fate	Supreme Mind: is present within all of us
Truth comes from	God, his texts	Within	Signs present everywhere in nature
Leaders of the movement in the 1820s (Second Great Awakening)	Timothy Dwight, Lyman Beecher	William Ellery Channing, early Emerson	Doesn't really begin until 1836; do see attacks on Locke (the Miracles debate) and essays on Carlyle in the 1820s
Main followers in the 1820s	Laboring classes	Wealthy Bostonians and land owners	Transcendental Club (begins 1836)

The chart on page 17 forces a question: What is religion, after all? The anthropologist Clifford Geertz in his essay "Religion as a Cultural System" suggests one important possibility. Geertz argues that religion is "a system of symbols which acts to establish powerful, pervasive, and long-lasting moods and motivations in men by formulating conceptions of a general order of existence and clothing these conceptions with such an aura of factuality that the moods and motivations seem uniquely realistic" (90). One of the most influential aspects of this definition is its ability to step outside of an understanding of religion as being about a creator: indeed, you might ask if Geertz's definition of religion is so broad as to apply, for example, to deeply held beliefs in the sciences. You will probably want to come up with your own definition of religion and to compare it with that of your classmates.

Most of the early American literary texts in *The Norton Anthology* deal with religion in one way or another. These include conversion narratives, sermons, creation stories, religious verse, and chants. How does one read a work of religious literature? Readers should remember that religious texts are often intended to be **performed** or to be **performative**. Many of the above genres were enacted—performed—in a specific context and for a specific audience. For example, when Samson Occom gave his "Sermon Preached at the Execution of Moses Paul," his intended audience was both Indians and white community members. It is crucial to consider who the intended audience is for a religious work. Many religious works are performative in that the words spoken are intended to bring about a particular deed. For example, saying the words "I do" performs the act of marriage—the words accomplish the act. An example of this performative power can be found both in Leslie Marmon Silko's novel *Ceremony* and in her autobiography *Storyteller* in the poem-myth "Long Time Ago." In this story, a witch has a performative power of language: as the witch tells the origin of the white people, the whites are created. The witch cannot take the words back "because it is already done." Other religious texts, such as conversion narratives, are thought to have this performative function. Preachers hoped that reading about or listening to a conversion would bring about more conversions. Whatever the traditions, as you read a religious text, it is important to consider its goal.

Politics

Where does literature begin and where do politics end? The definition of what constitutes literature has changed over time: types of texts that we might be likely to consider political, such as speeches, are found in *The Norton Anthology*. Political texts ask us to consider the social work of a piece of literature: tracts such as slave narratives or even sentimental novels such as *Uncle Tom's Cabin* had a great impact on American politics and political history. Understanding the political debates of an era can help us understand the popularity of a work in its own time. Similarly, political cartoons can provide us with insights into pervasive cultural metaphors, or **tropes**. For example, consider the following anti-slavery cartoon:

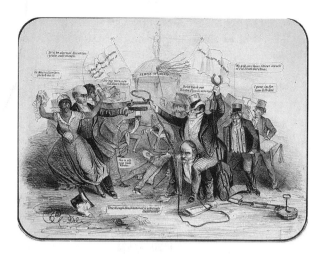

[6586] E. C. Dell, *Practical Illustration of the Fugitive Slave Law* (1851), courtesy of the Library of Congress.

Then, as now, cartoons were an effective way to garner support for or create distrust of individuals and groups within the United States. In this cartoon, the illustrator makes an analogy between protecting runaway slaves and protecting women from the animalistic passions of deviant men. This is a cultural metaphor that Harriet Jacobs and other slaves drew upon in their narratives, as did Harriet Beecher Stowe in *Uncle Tom's Cabin*.

In addition to providing important information about cultural tropes, political science offers a wealth of resources for better understanding the populations that are described and addressed in American literature. What segments of society comprised a reading public? Were they well educated? Was reading a leisure activity or a hard-won skill? Likewise, census data, immigration records, and political polls can tell us about whether the characters in a work of literature were representative of their era, or of the dreams and hopes—or nightmares—that a population faced.

Music

Some of the earliest American poems are songs: Sorrow Songs sung by the Aztecs as Hernán Cortés conquered Tenochtitlan; Sorrow Songs sung by slaves as they worked the soil of the New World and dreamed of a way out of bondage; or hymns sung by religious refugees as they embraced the hardships sent to them by their God. Poet Ezra Pound once said that there were three types of poems: those dominated by images, those dominated by the use of language and logic, and those dominated by the use of music and sound. Poetry is the literary genre perhaps most influenced by music, though fiction writers also use rhythms and melodies to set the tone of their work. Poetic forms are often borrowed from musical forms. Emily Dickinson's quatrains borrow from church hymns and popular songs, and Langston Hughes's verse borrows from the blues. This borrowing may occur both on a structural and on a rhythmic level. A poet may use the line length and stanza structure of a particular type of song or she may borrow just the beat from a musical mode. Recently, literary scholars have tended to view songs themselves as a form of literature, particularly for groups that did not traditionally record their verse in written form: for example, the Sorrow Songs of American slaves, the ballads of the cowboy, and the Nightway chant of the Navajo or the Ghost Dance songs of the Sioux.

Musical genres that have been particularly influential for American literature include hymns, blues, jazz, ballads, *corridos*, and chants. Hymns are one of the earliest musical influences on American poetry. One of the most popular early American books was the *Massachusetts Bay Psalm Book* by Reverend Richard Mather. Hymns and psalms from the Puritan colonies tend to be less ornate and less contrapuntal than church music from Catholic colonies of the same era. This difference is related to the general interest in a plain-style aesthetic held by the Puritans and Quakers. Psalms, or hymns, take their context from the Book of Psalms in the Bible but are written in rhyming quatrains of alternating iambic pentameter and tetrameter, the same form that a **ballad stanza** takes. The main difference between hymns and ballad stanzas is that hymns tend to be rhymed *abab*, while ballad stanzas are rhymed *abcb*. Ballad stanzas usually tell a story, whereas hymns are more meditative. Hymns are used differently in different communities: in a Wampanoag Indian praying town on Martha's Vineyard, many of the hymns were set to indigenous melodies; in the Spanish American colonies, Nahuatl (Aztec) speakers wrote hymns that combined the **jeremiad** tradition with Sorrow Songs lamenting the fall of their city; similarly, African American spirituals retain some of the rhythms and melodies brought over from Africa.

These African influences can also be found in **blues** and **jazz** and the poetic and narrative forms that they have inspired. People often think of the blues as a sort of melancholia, what people in the nineteenth century would have called the "hypos." The blues, however, have a rich range of associations and often rely upon humor and sexual innuendo to get their message across. According to scholar Steven Tracy, favorite subjects of blues songs and poems are relationships, love, poverty, politics, dreams, upward mobility, violence, death, sex, alcohol, skin color, and the harshness of the city versus the lost rural past. Traditional blues emerge out of the Sorrow Songs and take either a twelve- or eight-bar form. The meter of both of these forms is a swing; that is, the first beat is longer than the second, rather than the even meter of most Western music and verse: "GON-na," not "going to."

The lines of blues songs and poems are often given in a "call and response," a pattern that has its origins in African and slave oral traditions and that is also reflected in African American church oratory. The response line may comment on the call in a variety of ways; it may affirm, reject, undermine, emphasize, or increase the pathos of the call. The response may also mock the call: humor in the blues comes in many varieties and ranges from slapstick, to wry, to painful recognition. Blues poems borrow from the blues formally, metrically, and thematically.

Jazz and jazz poetry, like the blues, tend to use a swing meter, but unlike the blues rely on improvisation to create a new form, rather than adhering to the traditional song structures. Jazz is an example of what literary critic Henry Louis Gates Jr. has called "signifyin(g)": the rhetorical practice in Black

English vernacular of repeating with a "signal difference," or a comment on the initial version that calls attention to the change. John Coltrane's jazz rendition of "My Favorite Things" epitomizes the art of signifyin(g) and improvisation: in the original version of the song from *The Sound of Music*, Julie Andrews explains that the way to deal with scary events is to think of one's favorite things, such as "whiskers on kittens" and "sleigh bells." Out of context this seems innocuous enough, but given that the Von Trapp children must ultimately flee their home to escape the Nazis, such advice seems vapid at best. In Coltrane's version the beat is swung sideways and the melodic line is ripped apart and improvised upon and made anew: perhaps Coltrane references the original song to argue for a revolution through music, where platitudes (like those expressed in *The Sound of Music*) are replaced with radical rethinkings. Jazz poetry and fiction carry on this tradition of signification and revolution.

Another American musical form is the ballad. The ballad stanza lies behind many forms of popular American poetry, ranging from cowboy songs, to Civil War tunes, to borderlands *corridos*. Ballads in general, and *corridos* in particular, tell through song and verse the story of folk heroes who go against the status quo and subvert the social order. As oral historian Americo Paredes notes, *corridos* feature a hero who defends his rights, particularly with regard to territory; shows of bravado by the hero ("I am Joaquin!"); a lack of morality or repentance by the hero; and a family that will suffer after he is captured.

In *With a Pistol in His Hand*, Paredes explains that while ballads were popular throughout the United States during the nineteenth century, the **corrido** was the dominant form of balladry in the Texas border region between 1836 and 1930, in part because of the popularity of its subject: the racial conflict of the region and the ultimate triumph of the Chicano who sought to defend his civil rights. *Corridos* derive their power from the heraldic stories of Spain and Europe: a wronged man is made into an outlaw and is hunted down for his crime. The word *"corrido"* is derived from the Spanish *"correr"* ("to run"), signaling the rapid tempo and brisk narrative pace that usually characterize these songs. *Corridos* do not have refrains or choruses; rather, the lyrics move the listener through the narrative quickly and without digression. Like their English cousin the ballad, *corridos* consist of four-line stanzas in iambic tetrameter and trimeter.

The **chant** is another genre of American music useful for understanding American poetry. In his research on Native American verse patterns, anthropologist and linguist Dell Hymes has found that Native American verse tends to use repetition of numerical sets to build the underlying rhetorical and metrical form for song and verse. The most common pairs of numerical sets are 3 and 5 and 2 and 4. Often these numbers have deep associations within the communities that use them. For example, the Nightway chant relies on repetitions of 4 and a 4/4 beat to unify its message and emphasize the completeness and wholeness that the chant seeks to achieve. Look for numerical patterns in the other chants (such as the Ghost Dance songs) that appear in *The Norton Anthology* and the Online Archive and in the poetry of contemporary Native American poets.

Psychology

Although contemporary psychology has expanded beyond Freud, Freudian psychoanalysis has had an enduring influence on literary scholarship. The conversation among literary critics and scholars of psychoanalysis is rich and diverse, but at least two ideas are worth emphasizing here: the notions of the **cultural work of mourning** and the **cinematic gaze**.

One of the most important dialogues between psychology and literary analysis has been the application of Freud's theories about mourning to poetic elegies. Elegies are more than sad poems lamenting the loss of a beloved. As poet and literary critic Peter Sacks explains in *The English Elegy* (1985), **elegies** (and other artifacts of mourning such as mourners' rings and embroidery) attempt to take the reader, as well as the speaker, through the mourning process. The traditional structure of the elegy, Sacks argues, displays the speaker's transformation from an emotional state of melancholia (inconsolable identification between the ego and the dead) to one of consolable mourning. Using Freud and his analysis of the structure of mourning, Sacks suggests that the speaker in an elegy models the mourning process for the reader, ultimately warding off the reader's fears by laying claim to the power of art to reply to and ward off death. He notes that the poetic conventions that aid the movement from grief to consolation include the pastoral, myths, repetition and refrains, outbreaks of anger and cursing, the procession of mourners, and images of resurrection. In the movement out of grief, poetry and art come to replace the lost person and thereby console readers by reminding them of the ability of poetry to transcend mortality.

A second influence of psychoanalysis on literary analysis is the work of film critic Laura Mulvey, particularly her investigation of the cinematic gaze. Mulvey applies Freud's notion of **scopophilia** to the experience of watching films: in his *Three Essays on Sexuality*, Freud defines scopophilia as the pleasure associated with "taking other people as objects, subjecting them to a controlling and curious gaze." While watching a film may appear to be innocuous, Mulvey argues, "Among other things, the position of the spectators in the cinema is blatantly one of repression of their exhibitionism and projection of the repressed desire onto the performer" (9). In most films, this repressed desire belongs to an active male gaze and is projected onto a passive feminized body. When applied to literature, Mulvey's argument has significant implications: Who is the narrator of the story? How is this narration gendered? Who is the object of visual pleasure for the narrator? These questions can be profitably asked of Nathaniel Hawthorne's novel *The Blithedale Romance*, in which the story is channeled through the narrator, the bachelor Mr. Coverdale, who covets the two main female characters of the text and projects our desire as readers onto the women. This tension between the two desires (one of the women is chaste, the other is worldly) reflects what Mulvey identifies as the common splitting of the Western hero between integration into society via marriage and resistance to social demands and responsibilities.

Cultural Geography

In Margaret Fuller's autobiographical travel narrative *Summer on the Lakes* the author recounts passing time by watching what was considered by many to be the sublime spectacle of her generation: the cascading waters of Niagara Falls. As the water rushed over the precipice, Fuller recounts, "I felt nothing but a quiet satisfaction . . . everything looked as I thought it would." For readers of the nineteenth century, such a response was heretical: the falls were well known to invoke feelings of fear and trepidation in viewers. The experience, they believed, should be at once violent and beautiful, but surely not mere banal "satisfaction."

Margaret Fuller's response to Niagara, along with that of other writers and

[9026] George Barker, *Niagara Falls, N.Y., Close-Up View from Below* (1886), courtesy of the Library of Congress [LC-USZ62-97270].

tourists of her generation, brings into view the discipline of **cultural geography**, the intersection of the fields of cultural studies, geography, and urban planning. Cultural geography asks questions such as, What cultural forces influence our response to natural landscapes? What makes cityscapes culturally meaningful? What symbolism is embedded in the settings on which the national character is based, and how do these settings change with time? For surely, as Fuller's experience with Niagara Falls demonstrates, no two people experience a place in the same way, and those experiences are bound to change over time. As Niagara Falls came to represent a source of electrical power and mechanized miracles, its essence as a "natural wonder" changed for the American public.

Cultural geography and spatial analysis have had important ramifications for feminist literary studies as well. Feminist literary critics have explored how place and gender are mapped onto not only urban and rural space but also the body of characters themselves. As Margaret Higonnet suggests in *Reconfigured Spheres: Feminist Explorations of Literary Space (Theory and Applied Theory)*, "Feminist literary critics have begun to undertake new cartographies, to trace the ways writers inscribe gender onto the symbolic representations of space within texts, whether through images of physical confinement, of exile and exclusions, of property and territoriality, or of the body as the interface between individual and communal identities" (2). As you read the works in *The Norton Anthology of American Literature*, you might consider how the characters' bodies are themselves spaces mapped with cultural meanings.

Folklore

In the discipline of **folklore**, **myths** refer to stories that take place in a prehistoric time and involve supernatural, as well as sometimes human, beings. Myths may be stories of how the world was created (as in the Danbala story) or how Coyote stole the water from the waterfalls. Time may not function typically in myths and characters in myths may not be subject to ordinary rules. Myths often are about the creation of culture and the rules that govern the natural universe. In contrast, **legends** usually take place at the edges of historical record and involve heroes that are human yet have magical or extraordinary abilities. For example, the story of Troy is a legend for the ancient Greeks: it took place before the Dark Ages and involved both gods and heroes capable of superhuman feats. Other examples of legends include the migration legends told by American Indian communities about how they came to live on these lands.

Folklore also draws on contemporary events and contemporary notions of time and causality. Urban legends are one example of folklore, as are jokes. Jokes are an important cultural resource as they express the anxieties and boundaries of a community. In her work on resentment humor in Guatemala surrounding the controversial figure of Rigoberta Menchú, anthropologist Diane Nelson argues that jokes can also help restore jeopardized power relations and manipulate public opinion. Humor has a parallel purpose when it is part of religious or spiritual practice or part of myth, legend, or folklore. Trickster figures such as Coyote or Raven are good examples of the way in which sacred play can bring about what Paul Radin has called "the spirit of disorder, the enemy of boundaries" (185); such figures "add disorder and so make a whole, to render possible, within the fixed boundaries of what is permitted, an experience of what is not permitted." Humor is always worth keeping an eye out for in literature—it often represents more than comic relief.

Structuralism, or the investigation of underlying structures of thought and language, draws upon the conventions of folklore to explain the network of relations between units in a narrative. For structuralist theorist Mieke Bal, a tale is always composed of three levels: the **text**, the **fabula**, and the **story**. Bal defines these levels of the tale as follows: "a *narrative text* is a text in which an agent relates a narrative. A *story* is a fabula that is presented in a certain manner. A *fabula* is a series of logically and chronologically related events that are caused or experienced by actors" (5).

An example will help clarify Bal's distinctions: when we read Herman Melville's *Moby-Dick*, we hold a text in our hands in which an agent—Ishmael—narrates a narrative, namely the story of how the *Pequod* was lost at sea. The fabula of *Moby-Dick* is the sequence of events as they occurred (what we often call the "plot"), without all the narrative filler on whales and whaling. The story is the way in which the events are presented: When are events told out of sequence in order to heighten the tension? For example, although Ahab's monomaniacal obsession with Moby-Dick precedes the signing of Ishmael and Queequeg onto the *Pequod*, it is not revealed to them or to us until the ship has set sail. With its examinations of the layers within tales, structuralist theory is a crucial tool that literary scholars have used to better understand an author's rhetorical strategies.

Anthropology

Anthropology has had a significant influence on literary scholarship and vice versa. One of the conversations between anthropology and literature has come in the form of **dialogical anthropology**, as practiced by James Clifford and others. Dialogical anthropology argues that the interpretation of a text or event is necessarily an event in which both the creator and the interpreter of the text/event participate; thus, it is a dialogue.

Another conversation between anthropology and literary analysis has concerned kinship and social structure. **Kinship** consists of the ways in which social relations are passed along through families and community lines. For example, author and scholar Paula Gunn Allen has argued that Laguna Pueblo Indians originally were a matriarchal and matrifocal people; that is, unlike modern American culture, in which our names and identities are passed on through the paternal line, in Laguna culture, people belong to the mother's clan and women are at the center of the tribe's power systems. In Leslie Marmon Silko's novel *Ceremony*, Tayo's identity comes through his mother, his aunt, and his grandmother. In mainstream American fiction the story of the foundling, the child with unknown parents, is common, but Tayo has a family and does not search for or long for his white father as he attempts to heal. His father is not a part of his identity; rather, it is his mother's family that provides his identity. Importantly, the main male figure who helps Tayo heal is his maternal uncle Josiah, whereas his aunt's husband is almost completely absent. As you read texts from Native American cultures, you may find it helpful to trace identity through inheritance patterns. Creating family trees for texts not only may help you keep the characters straight but also can help you understand the influences among them.

Literary critics share with anthropologists and philosophers an interest in the subject of time. Anthropologists have argued that there are two basic notions of time: **chronological** and **nonlinear**, or **cyclical**. In the chronological notion of time familiar to most North Americans, time progresses in a linear fashion. Once an event has occurred, it is in the past and does not return or occur again in exactly the same fashion. Nonlinear time, which is less familiar to the majority of North Americans, is sometimes described as domelike, a concept of time in which events can be connected in a random fashion. Others describe nonlinear time as cyclical, with events repeating or reoccurring as instances of a prior experience.

These two modes of experiencing time—chronological and nonlinear—are not mutually exclusive: after all, even though the majority of North Americans believe that time progresses in a linear manner from past to present to future, they mark this linear time in a calendar fashion with recurring seasons, months, and dates. These different notions of time have had a great cultural impact, particularly on religious literature and Native American literature. Apocalyptic literature, for example, often predicts the end of linear time and the beginning of a timeless, pastoral state. Anthropologists and Native Americans have argued that American Indians traditionally have organized time in nonlinear and cyclical ways, a temporal organization that has influenced Native American written traditions, which sometimes lack a traditional chronological plot.

Implicit within any history, autobiography, or work of fiction is an underlying notion of time. As you read literary texts, consider the way time is constructed and presented in them.

GLOSSARY

annals   A mode of history that uses time as its organizing principle. Diaries and journals are good examples of this genre.

ballad stanza   A rhyming quatrain of alternating iambic pentameter and tetrameter lines. Variations of the ballad stanza are used in many forms of popular American poetry, from cowboy songs, to Civil War tunes, to borderlands *corridos*. Many hymns use a modified ballad stanza.

blues   A musical genre that developed out of Sorrow Songs and takes either a twelve- or eight-bar form. The meter of both of these forms is a swing; that is, the first beat is longer than the second.

chant   Native American music, often religious and performative in nature. Anthropologist and linguist Dell Hymes argues that Native American verse tends to repeat numerical units to build the underlying rhetorical and metrical form for song and verse. The most common pairs of numbers are 3/5 and 2/4. Often these numbers have deep associations within the communities that use them.

chronological time   The notion that time progresses in a linear fashion.

cinematic gaze   See **scopophilia**.

corridos   The dominant form of balladry in the Texas border region between 1836 and 1930. Popular subjects of *corridos* were the racial conflict of the region and the ultimate triumph of the Chicano seeking to defend his civil rights. The word *"corrido"* is derived from the Spanish *"correr"* ("to run"), signaling the rapid tempo and brisk narrative pace that usually characterize these songs.

cultural geography   The intersection among the fields of cultural studies, geography, and urban planning. Cultural geography asks questions such as, What cultural forces influence our response to natural landscapes? What makes cityscapes culturally meaningful? What symbolism is embedded in the settings on which our national character is based and how do these settings change with time?

cultural work of mourning   A Freudian term used to describe the psychological and cultural accomplishments of mourning for the dead. See **elegy**.

cyclical time   See **nonlinear time**.

dialogical anthropology   As practiced by James Clifford and others, the mode of anthropology that argues that the interpretation of a text or an event is necessarily a dialogical process, one in which both the creator and the interpreter of the text/event participate.

ekphrasis   The verbal description of a work of visual art, usually a painting, photograph, or sculpture. Ekphrasis attempts to bridge the gap between the verbal and the visual arts.

elegy   A poetic genre that attempts to take the reader, as well as the speaker, through the mourning process. The traditional structure of the elegy displays the speaker's transformation from an emotional state of melancholia to one of consolable mourning. The poetic conventions that aid this process include the pastoral, myths, repetition and refrains, outbreaks of anger and cursing, the procession of mourners, images of resurrection, and the movement from grief to consolation.

Enlightenment   An era in eighteenth-century American culture influenced by philosophers like Isaac Newton and John Locke, who argued that the universe is arranged in an orderly system, and that by the application of reason and intellect, human beings are capable of apprehending that system. This philosophy represented a radical shift from earlier notions that the world is ordered by a stern, inscrutable God whose plans are beyond human understanding and whose will can only be known through religious revelation.

fabula   According to narratologist Mieke Bal, "a series of logically and chronologically related events that are caused or experienced by actors." See **text** and **story**.

folklore   A genre that involves contemporary events and contemporary notions of time and causality. Urban legends are one example of folklore, as are jokes.

formal analysis   A tool of art historians. Like close readings of poems, formal analysis seeks to describe the nature of a work of art without attending to the context in which it was created. Questions that might be asked in formal analysis are, Where does the central interest in the work lie? How is the work composed? With what materials is it composed? How is lighting or shading used? What is the scene depicting? What allusions (mythological, religious, artistic) are found in the work?

geographical history   A historical mode that uses travel through space to shape a narrative: Mary Rowlandson's captivity narrative is an example of a geographical history in that it follows her through a sequence of twenty geographic "removes" into Indian country and back.

iconography   An analytical tool used by art historians. It calls attention to the cultural climate in which the work of art was produced.

jazz   A musical genre that, like the blues, tends to use a swing meter, but unlike the blues relies on improvisation to create a new form, rather than adhering to traditional song structures. Jazz is an example of what literary critic Henry Louis Gates Jr. has called "signifyin(g)"; that is, the rhetorical practice in Black English vernacular of repeating with a "signal difference," or a comment on the initial version that calls attention to the change.

kinship   The ways in which social relations are passed along through families and community lines. For example, author and scholar Paula Gunn Allen has argued that Laguna Pueblo Indians originally had a matriarchal and matrifocal kinship structure.

legends   Folklore term for stories that take place at the edges of the historical record and that involve heroes that are human yet possess magical or extraordinary abilities.

modernism   A movement in early-twentieth-century American culture that responded to technological innovation, increased urbanization, and the accompanying sense of a world changing too quickly to comprehend. Modernists tended to self-consciously oppose or reinvent traditional forms, which they believed to be out of step with the modern world.

myths   Stories that take place in a prehistoric time and involve both supernatural and human beings. Myths are often about the creation of the world and the rules that govern the natural universe.

nonlinear (or cyclical) time   Conception of time that holds that time does not progress in a linear fashion from past to present to future, and that moments repeat themselves either in a fixed pattern or in a random manner.

pastoral mode   Literature or art that looks back with nostalgia to an era of rural life, lost simplicity, and a time when nature and culture were one.

performative   Intended to bring about a particular deed. For example, saying "I do" performs the act of marriage—the words accomplish the act. An example of performative language can be found in Leslie Marmon Silko's novel *Ceremony* and in her autobiography *Storyteller* in the poem-myth "Long Time Ago." In this story a witch brings the white people into being by telling a story about them.

performed   Enacted in a specific context and for a specific audience.

postmodernism   A movement in late-twentieth-century American culture that rejected objectivity and stability in favor of more fluid understandings of reality. Postmodern philosophers argue that there are no absolutes and reject "essentializing" systems and ideas.

processual   According to architectural theory, the characteristic of buildings such that the order of the rooms and the arrangement within the rooms themselves control how one moves through the building and views the objects within it.

realism   A movement in late-nineteenth-century American culture in which writers and artists expressed a new commitment to the truthful, accurate representation of life as it was experienced by ordinary Americans. Realism was characterized by its uncompromising, literal representations of the particularities of the material world and the human condition. This passion for finding and presenting the truth led many American practitioners of realism to explore characters, places, and events that had never before seemed appropriate subject matter for literature.

religion   According to anthropologist Clifford Geertz, "A system of symbols which acts to establish powerful, pervasive, and long-lasting moods and motivations in men by formulating conceptions of a general order of existence and clothing these conceptions with such an aura of factuality that the moods and motivations seem uniquely realistic."

Renaissance   Literally "re-birth" (French); refers to the revival of the classical tradition in Europe during the fourteenth through sixteenth centuries. The Renaissance marked the end of the Middle Ages and the beginning of the Age of Exploration and modern science.

res gestae   Literally "deeds done" (Latin); the organization of history through a list of accomplishments. This was a popular form of history for the ancient Greeks and Romans, and these histories in turn served as the model for those of early explorers like Hernán Cortés.

Romanticism   A movement in early-nineteenth-century American culture that stressed creativity, sensation, subjectivity, emotion, and fulfillment. Romanticism saw nature as an inspiring force and emphasized the radically innovative individual, as opposed to the Enlightenment tendency to focus on the rationally ordered society.

scopophilia   According to Sigmund Freud, the pleasure associated with "taking other people as objects, subjecting them to a controlling and curious gaze." Scopophilia is a key term for psychoanalysis and film theory.

social status   The relative and culturally determined value attributed to persons within a society.

story   According to narratologist Mieke Bal, the level of a tale in which "a fabula . . . is presented in a certain manner." For example, although Ahab's obsession with the whale chronologically precedes the signing of Ishmael and Queequeg onto the *Pequod* in *Moby-Dick*, it is not revealed to them or to us until the ship has set sail. Here the fabula (the chronological tale) is presented in a more suspenseful manner. See **text** and **fabula**.

text   According to narratologist Mieke Bal, the level of a tale in which "an agent relates a narrative." For example, when we read *Moby-Dick*, we hold a text in our hands in which an agent—Ishmael—narrates a narrative, namely the story of how the *Pequod* was lost at sea. Also see **story** and **fabula**.

trope   A pervasive cultural metaphor.

SELECTED BIBLIOGRAPHY

Allen, Paula Gunn. *The Sacred Hoop: Recovering the Feminine in American Indian Traditions*. Boston: Beacon, 1986.

Austin, J. L. *How to Do Things with Words*. Boston: Harvard UP, 1962.

Bal, Mieke. *Narratology: Introduction to the Theory of Narrative*. Toronto: U of Toronto P, 1985.

Barnet, Sylvan. *A Short Guide to Writing about Art*. Boston: Little, Brown, 1981.

Boone, Elizabeth, and Walter Mignolo, eds. *Writing without Words: Alternative Literacies in Mesoamerica and the Andes*. Durham: Duke UP, 1994.

Clifford, James, and George E. Marcus, eds. *Writing Culture: The Poetics and Politics of Ethnography*. Berkeley: U of California P, 1986.

Dundes, Alan, ed. *Sacred Narrative: Readings in the Theory of Myth*. Berkeley: U of California P, 1984.

Freud, Sigmund. *A Case of Hysteria: Three Essays on Sexuality and Other Works*. Trans. James Strachey and Anna Freud. London: Hogarth, 1953.

Gates, Henry Louis Jr. *The Signifying Monkey: A Theory of African-American Literary Criticism*. New York: Oxford UP, 1988.

Geertz, Clifford. *Interpretation of Cultures*. New York: Basic Books, 1973.

Higonnet, Margaret, and Joan Templeton, eds. *Reconfigured Spheres: Feminist Explorations of Literary Space Theory and Applied Theory*. Amherst: U of Massachusetts P, 1994.

Hollander, John. *The Gazer's Spirit: Poems Speaking to Silent Works of Art*. Chicago: U of Chicago P, 1995.

Hymes, Dell. *"In Vain I Tried to Tell You": Essays in Native American Ethnopoetics*. Philadelphia: U of Pennsylvania P, 1981.

Kierstead, Ray. "Herodotus and the Invention of History." Humanities 110 Lecture. Reed College. 25 September 1998.

Lessing, Gotthold Ephraim. *Laocoön: An Essay upon the Limits of Painting and Poetry*. Trans. Ellen Frothingham. New York: Noonday, 1957.

McDannell, Colleen, ed. *Religions of the United States in Practice*. Vols. I & II. Princeton: Princeton UP, 2001.

Miller, Perry. *Errand into the Wilderness*. Cambridge: Belknap Press of Harvard UP, 1956.

Mulvey, Laura. "Afterthoughts on 'Visual Pleasure and Narrative Cinema' Inspired by King Vidor's *Duel in the Sun* (1946)." In Thornham, S., ed., *Feminist Film Theory: A Reader*. Edinburgh: Edinburgh UP, 1999.

———. "Visual Pleasure and Narrative Cinema." *Screen* 16.3 (Autumn 1975): 6–18.

Nelson, Diane M. "Maya Hackers and the Cyberspatialized Nation-State: Modernity, Ethnostalgia, and a Lizard Queen in Guatemala." *Cultural Anthropology* 11 (9): 287–308.

Paredes, Americo. *With a Pistol in His Hand*. Austin: U of Texas P, 1958.

Radin, Paul. *The Trickster: A Study in American Indian Mythology*. New York: Greenwood, 1956.

Sacks, Peter. *The English Elegy*. Baltimore: Johns Hopkins UP, 1985.

Schlereth, Thomas. *Material Culture Studies in America*. Nashville: American Association for State and Local History, 1982.

Storey, John. *Cultural Theory and Popular Culture*. Athens: U of Georgia P, 1993.

Tracy, Steven. *Langston Hughes and the Blues*. Urbana: U of Illinois P, 1988.

NATIVE VOICES

Resistance and Renewal in American Indian Literature

Authors and Works

Featured in the Video:
Luci Tapahonso, "They Are Silent and Quick," "A Breeze Swept Through" (poetry)

Simon J. Ortiz, "My Mother and My Sisters," "8:50 AM Ft. Lyons VAH" (poetry)

Leslie Marmon Silko, *Ceremony* (novel), *Storyteller* (short stories, poetry, photography)

Discussed in This Unit:
Louise Erdrich, "Fleur" (short story)

Chippewa songs (songs)

Black Elk and John G. Neihardt, *Black Elk Speaks* (autobiography)

Ghost Dance songs (songs)

Stories of the Beginning of the World (oral narrative)

Roger Williams, *A Key into the Language of America* (language primer)

Thomas Harriot, *A Brief and True Report of the New Found Land of Virginia* (ethnographic report)

Overview Questions

■ What is the relationship between Native American identity and American identity?

■ How does Native American literature reflect or help create a sense of what it means to be Native American in the United States?

■ What does this literature help reveal about the experience of having a multicultural identity?

■ How does the conception of American Indian identity depend upon the writer's identity?

■ What is Native American literature?

■ What makes Native American traditions from different regions distinctive?

■ How has Native American literature been influenced by politics on and off the reservation?

■ How are Native American oral traditions shaped by the landscapes in which they are composed?

■ What role does the land play in oral tradition?

■ How does the notion of time in American Indian narratives compare with notions of time in Western cultures?

■ How does the chronology of particular narratives reflect differing notions of time?

■ How do Yellow Woman stories and the Nightway or Enemyway chant influence Leslie Marmon Silko's *Ceremony* and *Storyteller*?

■ How do Navajo chantways influence the poetry of Luci Tapahonso?

■ How does the Ghost Dance influence the vision of Black Elk?

■ How does the Ghost Dance challenge nineteenth-century European American notions of Manifest Destiny?

■ How do Yellow Woman stories subvert the genre of captivity narratives?

■ How do the poems of Simon J. Ortiz challenge the notion of what it means to be an American hero?

Learning Objectives

After students have viewed the video, read the headnotes and literary selections in *The Norton Anthology of American Literature*, and explored related archival materials on the *American Passages* Web site, they should be able to

1. identify some of the genres, meanings, and purposes of American Indian oral narrative and song;

2. recognize the ways in which contemporary American Indian writers draw upon and transform the oral tradition in their written texts;

3. generalize about typical themes, concerns, and narrative forms in contemporary American Indian literature;
4. compare the migration legends and creation myths of the European explorers and the Iroquois and Pima Indians;
5. sketch out some differences between the values, beliefs, and assumptions of Native North Americans and Europeans at the time of first contact during the fifteenth and sixteenth centuries.

Instructor Overview

Native American traditions are rich and varied. There are over five hundred Native American languages, each one as different as English is from Arabic and as Arabic is from Swahili. Each Indian nation has its own myths, its own histories, its own personal stories. As Native American author N. Scott Momaday writes, "The voices are all around us, the three voices. You have the mythic and the historical and the personal and then they become a wheel, they revolve, they alternate. . . . Myth becomes history becomes memoir becomes myth." What unites these Native American cultures? What does it mean to study American Indian literature? To answer these questions is to begin to consider what it means to be American and Native American simultaneously.

The definition of Native American literature is closely tied to what people think constitutes the essence of Native American identity. Three views stand out in this highly contested debate: those of legal bloodlines, cultural traditions, and bicultural production. As literary critic Kenneth Lincoln notes, one "working definition of 'Indian,' though criteria vary from region to region, is minimally a quarter blood and tribal membership"; Native American literature, then, would be those works written by someone who legally is Native American, regardless of their content or style. A second perspective links Native American identity and literature with the preservation of cultural traditions. Literary critics who rely on this view focus on aspects of "traditional" Indian culture in contemporary American Indian literature, such as the continuance of oral traditions. A third trend in Native American studies defines American Indian identity and literature *not*

in terms of what they preserve (whether it be blood or culture), but rather as bicultural mixtures of Native and European American people and traditions. Some Native Americans have argued that since their indigenous cultures have always assimilated aspects of other cultures (including those of other American Indians), to be Indian is to be bicultural, or multicultural.

Many American Indians define themselves not primarily as "Native Americans" but as members of a specific tribe. It is important as you read the authors in this unit to remember that what you know about the Navajo and their religious traditions probably will not apply to the Chippewa, a people geographically, linguistically, and culturally separate from them. Some scholars have suggested, however, that Native American communities within a particular geographic region tend to be culturally more homologous because they are often from the same language family and because cultures are often shaped by the landscapes out of which they emerge. There are several key regions in Native American studies: the Plains, California, Midwest, Northeast, Northwest, South, and Southwest. The video focuses on the Southwest; however, in the unit you will find information about the other regions. You will also find a balance between information that is specific to the tribe of each author and information about qualities that are shared among American Indian peoples.

Oral traditions vary by region and tribe, and scholars have tended to examine the influence of the American Indian oral tradition upon contemporary American Indian written literature in two ways: (1) the content and (2) the style. When people explore how the content of the American Indian oral tradition has influenced contemporary literature, they usually turn to the stories and songs of American Indian peoples. These stories tend to focus on particular characters and to include standard events and elements. Some of the most common tale-types include gambler, trickster, creation, abduction, and migration legends. Contemporary authors can use these tale-types in their works; for example, Leslie Marmon Silko's *Ceremony* retells Yellow Woman stories—a Pueblo Abduction Cycle. In addition to looking at the content of the stories, scholars have looked at the style of contemporary American Indian literature to examine the influence of the oral tradition. Oral style has been characterized as empathetic, participatory, situational, and reliant on repetition. In the oral tradition, repetition is crucial both for ceremonial reasons and because it aids in the process of memorization and provides narrative cohesion. To repeat words is also to wield a certain power. Perhaps most importantly, the oral tradition is tied to the land: as author and critic Greg Sarris explains, "The landscape becomes the bible and each stone, each mountain, each set of trees or a river, or a section of the river becomes a text, because they become a way of remembering stories, and stories associated with that place."

The video, the archive, and the curriculum materials situate the writers featured in Unit 1 within several of the historical contexts and artistic movements that shaped their texts. Together, these materials articulate the diverse genres and cultural traditions that comprise and inform Native American literature.

Student Overview

Native American traditions are rich and varied. There are over five hundred Native American languages, each one as different as English is from Arabic and as Arabic is from Swahili. Each Indian nation has its own myths, its own histories, its own personal stories. As Native American author N. Scott Momaday writes, "The voices are all around us, the three voices. You have the mythic and the historical and the personal and then they become a wheel, they revolve, they alternate. . . . Myth becomes history becomes memoir becomes myth." What unites these Native American cultures? What does it mean to study American Indian literature? To answer these questions is to begin to consider what it means to be American and Native American simultaneously.

The definition of Native American literature is closely tied to what people think constitutes the essence of Native American identity. Three views stand out in this highly contested debate: those of legal bloodlines, cultural traditions, and bicultural production. As literary critic Kenneth Lincoln notes, one "working definition of 'Indian,' though criteria vary from region to region, is minimally a quarter blood and tribal membership"; Native American literature, then, would be those works

written by someone who legally is Native American, regardless of their content or style. A second perspective links Native American identity and literature with the preservation of cultural traditions. Literary critics who rely on this view focus on aspects of "traditional" Indian culture in contemporary American Indian literature, such as the continuance of oral traditions. A third trend in Native American studies defines American Indian identity and literature *not* in terms of what they preserve (whether it be blood or culture), but rather as bicultural mixtures of Native and European American people and traditions. Some Native Americans have argued that since their indigenous cultures have always assimilated aspects of other cultures (including those of other American Indians), to be Indian is to be bicultural, or multicultural.

Many American Indians define themselves not primarily as "Native Americans" but as members of a specific tribe. It is important as you read the authors in this unit to remember that what you know about the Navajo and their religious traditions probably will not apply to the Chippewa, a people geographically, linguistically, and culturally separate from them. Some scholars have suggested, however, that Native American communities within a particular geographic region tend to be culturally more homologous because they are often from the same language family and because cultures are often shaped by the landscapes out of which they emerge. There are several key regions in Native American studies: the Plains, California, Midwest, Northeast, Northwest, South, and Southwest. The video focuses on the Southwest; however, in the unit you will find information about the other regions. You will also find a balance between information that is specific to the tribe of each author and information about qualities that are shared among American Indian peoples.

Oral traditions vary by region and tribe, and scholars have tended to examine the influence of the American Indian oral tradition upon contemporary American Indian written literature in two ways: (1) the content and (2) the style. When people explore how the content of the American Indian oral tradition has influenced contemporary literature, they usually turn to the stories and songs of American Indian peoples. These stories tend to focus on particular characters and to include standard events and elements. Some of the most common tale-types include gambler, trickster, creation, abduction, and migration legends. Contemporary authors can use these tale-types in their works; for example, Leslie Marmon Silko's *Ceremony* retells Yellow Woman stories—a Pueblo abduction cycle. In addition to looking at the content of the stories, scholars have looked at the style of contemporary American Indian literature to examine the influence of the oral tradition. Oral style has been characterized as empathetic, participatory, situational, and reliant on repetition. In the oral tradition, repetition is crucial both for ceremonial reasons and because it aids in the process of memorization and provides narrative cohesion. To repeat words is also to wield a certain power. Perhaps most importantly, the oral tradition is tied to the land: as author and critic Greg Sarris explains, "The landscape becomes the bible and each stone, each mountain, each set of trees or a river, or a section of the river becomes a text, because they become a way of remembering stories, and stories associated with that place."

Video Overview

➤ **Authors covered:** Luci Tapahonso (Navajo), Simon J. Ortiz (Acoma Pueblo), Leslie Marmon Silko (Laguna Pueblo)

➤ **Who's interviewed:** Greg Sarris, author, professor of English (Loyola Marymount University) (Miwok chief/ Pomo); N. Scott Momaday, author (Kiowa); Simon J. Ortiz, author (Acoma Pueblo); Paula Gunn Allen, author, professor of English (University of California, Los Angeles) (Laguna Pueblo/Sioux); Joy Harjo, poet/musician, professor of English (University of California, Los Angeles) (Muscogee/Creek); Rex Lee Jim, author (Navajo)

➤ **Points covered:**

- American Indian oral traditions link people to the culture, myths, and land. Traditionally, the oral storyteller is a human individual who relates the mythological to others. Contemporary American Indian written literature draws on oral traditions even as it translates them into European forms. These stories are necessary for the culture to survive in the era after European contact. A kind of "cultural contact," this written literature deals with the interaction of Native and European cultures and identities. This video focuses on three Native American writers from the Southwest: Luci Tapahonso (Navajo), Simon J. Ortiz (Acoma Pueblo), and Leslie Marmon Silko (Laguna Pueblo).
- Luci Tapahonso's poems "They Are Silent and Quick" and "A Breeze Swept Through" draw on and are a product of Navajo language, tradition, and landscape.
- Simon J. Ortiz's writing reflects a renewed transmission of Acoma Pueblo cultural memory, as in "My Mother and My Sisters." It also conveys the often fractured and besieged state of being a Native American today, as in his poem "8:50 AM Ft. Lyons VAH." These poems reflect the bicultural world of contemporary Native Americans.
- Like "8:50 AM Ft. Lyons VAH," Leslie Marmon Silko's novel *Ceremony* deals with the post–World War II experience of Native Americans. The novel attempts to reintegrate the shattered experience of its protagonist, Tayo, with the old stories and worldviews. The Laguna ceremonies must be adapted to cope with the current world, or else the old ways will die. In *Storyteller*, Silko demonstrates the ways in which language does not merely reflect the world, but can directly affect it.
- Native American literature is particular to tribal people in its invocation of the concrete power of language to heal and guide, but it is also like all American literature in probing what it means to be American.

PREVIEW

Preview the video: Contemporary American Indian writers creatively employ and adapt native traditions even as they address contemporary American Indian life, and therefore American life in general. Luci Tapahonso, Simon J. Ortiz, and Leslie Marmon Silko are three writers who draw on their different southwestern native heritages to keep the old ideas and cultures alive in the form of new, relevant stories.

- **What to think about while watching:** What are some of the characteristics of Navajo and Pueblo oral traditions? In what sense do these writers draw on native oral traditions and beliefs? How do they speak to the experience of being American Indian? What does their written literature hope to do or achieve?
- **Tying the video to the unit content:** What are some

specific Navajo or Pueblo oral traditions or beliefs that you can see reflected in the written literature of these writers? What do these writers seem to be doing, or trying to say, by employing these traditions? How does Native American history, and the history of the contact between native peoples and Europeans, affect their contemporary writing? How are their texts a combination of Native American and European literary traditions?

DISCUSSION QUESTIONS FOR THE VIDEO

	What is an American? How does American literature create conceptions of the American experience and identity?	*What is American literature? What are its distinctive voices and styles? How do social and political issues influence the American canon?*	*How do place and time shape literature and our understanding of it?*
Compre-hension Questions	What are some differences between traditional Native American and European ways of seeing the world?	What are some elements of the "oral tradition"? What are some of the ways in which traditional Native American and European storytellers might differ? What social issues appear in Silko's *Ceremony*?	What part of the United States are Tapahonso, Ortiz, and Silko from? What tribe is each writer from? What part does World War II play in Silko's *Ceremony*?
Context Questions	How do elements of a specifically Native American worldview inform the work of the writers featured in the video?	How do the contemporary writers featured in the video draw on the oral tradition in their works?	How do the tribe, landscape, and environment with which each writer is familiar affect his or her work?
Exploration Questions	How much do you know about Native American history and culture? To what extent is it important for non–Native Americans to know these traditions? What do you gain by learning about them? What would you lose if you didn't know them?	What topics, styles, or ideas would you expect to see in a contemporary Native American written text? How do you imagine the text might differ from—and be similar to—literary works written by Americans with European, African, or Asian heritages? Would the absence of typically Native American concerns in a book by a Native American affect your judgment of that book?	Why do you think it might be important for these writers to incorporate the specifics of their own time and place into their texts? What would be lost if they did not incorporate such elements?

	Texts	Contexts
1490s		Columbus lands in the Bahamas, returns to Spain with first Indian slaves (1492)
1500s		Geographer Martin Waldseemüller names the "new" land "America" for Vespucci (1507)
1510s		Spanish Laws of Burgos forbid enslavement of Indians and advocate Christian conversion (1512)
1550s	Bernardino de Sahagún, *Florentine Codex* (c. 1558–85)	
1580s	Thomas Harriot, *A Brief and True Report of the New Found Land of Virginia* (1588)	Spanish begin settling New Mexico (1582)
1590s		First Spanish colony on the Rio Grande, establishing control over Pueblo Indians (1598)
1600s	Garcilaso de la Vega, *The Florida of the Inca* (1605)	
1620s		First Indian uprising in an English colony: Powhatan Confederacy attacks Jamestown (1622)
1630s		Pequot War (1637)
1640s	Roger Williams, *A Key into the Language of America* (1643)	
1670s		King Philip's War decimates native tribes in New England (1675–78)
1700s		Approximately fourteen hundred Indian slaves in the North American colonies (1708)
1750s		French and Indian War establishes English possession of Northeast (1755–63)
1760s	Samson Occom, *A Short Narrative of My Life* (1768)	Pontiac's War (1763–75)
1770s		Continental Congress establishes first treaty with Indian tribe, the Delaware (1778)
1780s		Northwest Ordinance approved by Confederation Congress (1787)

	Texts	Contexts
1790s		Congress enacts first law regulating trade and land sales with Indians (1790)
1810s		War of 1812, the last war in which Indians fight with a foreign colonial power against the United States (1812–14) First appropriation by Congress of a fund ($10,000) to "civilize" the Indians (1819)
1820s	Cherokee Memorials (1829–30)	Bureau of Indian Affairs established (1824) Cherokee Nation ratifies its new constitution (1827–28)
1830s	William Apess, "An Indian's Looking-Glass for the White Man" (1833)	Congress passes Indian Removal Act, legalizing removal of eastern Indians to west of the Mississippi (1830) Cherokees travel the Trail of Tears (1838–39)
1840s		Mexican War; Southwest is ceded to the United States (1846–48) Bureau of Indian Affairs shifts from War Department to the Department of the Interior (1849) California Gold Rush (1849)
1850s	John Rollin Ridge (Yellow Bird), *The Life and Adventures of Joaquin Murieta, the Celebrated California Bandit* (1854)	United States war against Plains Indians (1854)
1860s		Standing Bear court case establishes that Indians are "persons within the meaning of the law" (1868)
1870s	Cochise, "[I am alone]" (1872) Charlot, "[He has filled graves with our bones]" (1876) Lorenzo Asisara, "Punishment" (1877, 1890)	Congress appropriates first sum earmarked for federal administration of Indian education (1870) Congress passes a law putting an end to further treaties with Indian tribes (1871) General Custer and his Seventh Cavalry defeated by Sioux and Cheyenne in Battle of Little Big Horn (1876) Congress appropriates first funds for Indian police (1878) Carlisle Indian School founded (1879)
1880s		Geronimo and his band of Apaches captured, ending Indian fighting in Southwest (1886)

	Texts	Contexts
		Dawes Severalty (General Allotment) Act redistributes tribally held lands (1887)
		Paiute Wovoka inaugurates Ghost Dance religion (1889)
1890s	Franz Boas, *Chinook Texts* (1894) James Mooney, *The Ghost Dance Religion and the Sioux Outbreak of 1890* (1896)	Massacre of nearly 300 Indians at Wounded Knee ends Indian resistance to U.S. government (1890) Curtis Act dissolves tribal governments (1898)
1900s	Zitkala Ša (Gertrude Simmons Bonnin), "Impressions of an Indian Childhood," "The School Days of an Indian Girl," "An Indian Teacher among Indians" (1900)	
1910s	Frances Densmore, *Chippewa Songs* (1910) Selin Williams, "The Bungling Host" (1910) Charles Alexander Eastman, *From the Deep Woods to Civilization* (1916)	
1920s		Congress makes all Indians U.S. citizens and grants them the right to vote (1924)
1930s	Black Elk and John G. Neihardt, *Black Elk Speaks* (1932) Ella Cara Deloria, *Dakota Texts* (1932) Mourning Dove, *Coyote Stories* (1933) D'arcy McNickle, *The Surrounded* (1936)	Congress passes Wheeler-Howard (Indian Reorganization) Act, ending Dawes era (1934)
1940s		Founding of National Congress of American Indians (1944) Congress establishes Indian Claims Commission to judge all tribal claims (1946)
1950s	Paul Radin, *The Trickster* (1956)	Congress adopts House Concurrent Resolution 180, declaring its intent to terminate treaty relations with Indian tribes (1953)
1960s	Hugh Yellowman, "Coyote, Skunk, and the Prairie Dogs" (1966) N. Scott Momaday, *The Way to Rainy Mountain* (1969) Alexander Posey, *Poems of Alexander Lawrence Posey, Creek Indian Bard* (1969)	

	Texts	Contexts
1970s	Vine Deloria, *God Is Red* (1973) John Bierhorst, *Four Masterworks of American Indian Literature: Quetzalcoatl, The Ritual of Condolence, Cuceb, the Night Chant* (1974) Simon J. Ortiz, *Poems from the Veterans Hospital* (1977) Leslie Marmon Silko, *Ceremony* (1977)	American Indian Movement members occupy Wounded Knee and battle FBI agents (1973)
1980s	Joy Harjo, *She Had Some Horses* (1983) Louise Erdrich, "Fleur" (1986) Paula Gunn Allen, *The Sacred Hoop* (1986) Luci Tapahonso, *A Breeze Swept Through* (1989)	
1990s	Joy Harjo, *In Mad Love and War* (1990) Gerald Vizenor, *Landfill Meditations: Crossblood Stories* (1991) Simon J. Ortiz, *Woven Stone* (1992) Luci Tapahonso, *Saanii Dahataal: The Women Are Singing* (1993) Greg Sarris, *Mabel McKay: Weaving the Dream* (1994) Joy Harjo, *The Woman Who Fell from the Sky* (1994) Diane Glancy, *Firesticks* (1993)	Congress passes Native American Graves Protection and Repatriation Act, protecting Indian remains and sacred objects (1990)

AUTHOR/TEXT REVIEW

Luci Tapahonso (b. 1953)

A Navajo woman born in Shiprock, New Mexico, Luci Tapahonso grew up on a farm within the largest Indian reservation in the United States. For the Navajo, or Dine, as they call themselves, kinship and lineage define one's sense of self: Tapahonso's father was from the Bitter Water clan, her mother from the Salt Water clan. Tapahonso emphasizes the importance of her family to her craft: "When I write I can always hear their voices and I can hear the way that they would talk and just the beauty of how they structured stories and their expressions and their faces. So, my primary literary influence has been my family and my relatives."

Tapahonso's first language is Dine, the Navajo language, and Dine frequently appears in her poetry. Indeed, she often conceives, writes, and sings her poems entirely in Dine, translating them into English only for publication. This practice highlights the typical Native American conception of literature as **performative**, living, and inextricably linked to the specifics of culture, language, and place. For the Navajo, Tapahonso explains, language is powerful: "[The Navajo] say that when a child is born . . . the first breath they take is a holy thing, that it means that the power of the winds in the air that make up the universe are a part of you so that when you breathe you can actually feel your breath; that means that there's a sense of the holy imbued in you. So that each time you say something then . . . you can change things. . . . You can change the course of whatever it is that you're going to do." She goes on to explain that this belief in the efficacy of language makes all of the Dine careful speakers: "There's not really a way to say . . . you're sorry so . . . people have to be very careful about what they say and . . . you understand that words do have power and that you have the power to create or . . . the power to destroy. You have the power to heal, to comfort, to make people laugh." For the Dine, the poet or wordsmith has a special status. Tapahonso notes, "A person that speaks beautifully is thought to have . . . a really good upbringing . . . a lot of people [having] loved them, a lot of people [having] invested in them to make sure that they speak well. . . ."

Tapahonso received her B.A. and M.A. in 1980 and 1983, respectively, from the University of New Mexico, where she studied under Leslie Marmon Silko. She has taught as an assistant professor of English at the University of New Mexico and the University of Kansas, Lawrence, and currently teaches at the University of Arizona. Her books of poetry include *A Breeze Swept Through* (1989), *Saanii Dahataal: The Women are Singing* (1993) (in which "They Are Silent and Quick" appears), and *Blue Horses Rush In* (1997). In the preface to *Saanii Dahataal*, Tapahonso writes of two literary issues that appear as concerns for many other American Indian writers. First, she notes the centrality of storytelling to Indian life: "There is such a love of stories among Navajo people that it seems each time a group of more than two gather, the dialogue eventually evolves into sharing stories and memories, laughing, teasing. To be included in this way is a distinct way of showing affection and appreciation for each other." Tapahonso's words highlight the way in which stories are an essential aspect of maintaining Indian culture. Second, she de-emphasizes herself as a singular creative voice, as the "author" of her poems in the traditional Western sense. Rather, her writing is itself part of the web of an old culture—as is Tapahonso herself—and works toward the continual renewal of that culture. As Tapahonso explains, "Like many other relatives, [my paternal grandmother] had a profound understanding of the function of language. This writing, then, is not 'mine,' but a collection of many voices that range from centuries ago and continue into the future."

Tapahonso has served on the board of directors at the Phoenix Indian Center, has been a member of the New Mexico Arts Commission Literature Panel, and has been on the steering committees of the Returning the Gift Writers Festival, the Kansas Arts Commission Literature Panel, the Phoenix Arts Commission, and the Telluride Institute Writers Forum Advisory Board. She was also the commissioner of the Kansas Arts Commission.

TEACHING TIPS

■ The number 4 is important for Tapahonso's verse. As Tapahonso points out in her *American Passages* interview, many Navajo songs have four stanzas and ceremonies are structured in fours, as are many ordinary things. Play the excerpt from Tapahonso's interview in which she elaborates on the significance of the number 4, and then have your students read one of her poems that uses repetitions of 4. What meaning does the number bring to the poem?

■ Show your students the segment on the Navajo reservation from the documentary *Winds of Change: A Matter of Promises*, narrated by N. Scott Momaday. How do the Navajo strategies for adapting to cultural change compare to the strategies used by Tapahonso? This segment of the video, which introduces Navajo veterans and chantways, is also useful for setting up Ortiz's and Silko's work.

■ The traditional Navajo dwelling is called the hogan and is constructed out of earth and wooden poles according to instructions given by Talking God. Hogans are a good way to introduce students to some of the basic principles of Navajo oral tradition and chantways; as anthropologist Pierre Bourdieu reflects, the house is "a microcosm organized according to the same oppositions which govern all the universe." The entrances to hogans always face east. As Tapahonso explains, "In Navajo thinking everything begins in the East. So the beginning of day, the beginning of life . . . is seen as being situated in the East. The hogan given by Talking God is also the home of Dawn Woman, or Changing Woman, wife of the sun." Have students look at the image of the hogan in the archive. How is it different from a Western-style house? How does it reflect the values in the poem "A Breeze Swept Through"? Students may also enjoy "Starlore," Tapahonso's poem about a hogan, from *Blue Horses Rush In*.

[6850] Edward S. Curtis, *Head-and-Shoulders Portrait of Navajo Woman, Facing Front* (1904), courtesy of the Library of Congress [LC-USZ62-103498]. This woman's clothing is an example of bicultural production: while influenced by European dress, it also incorporates a Navajo blanket influenced by the designs of baskets and pottery. Sheep, who provide the wool for blankets as well as a source of food, are a crucial part of Navajo culture.

[8007] Luci Tapahonso, Reading: "They Are Silent and Quick" (2002), courtesy of Annenberg/CPB and *American Passages*. This poem shows (Dine) Navajo poet Luci Tapahonso moving between the English and Navajo languages. In the poem, Tapahonso discusses the importance of the oral tradition and storytelling.

[8963] Edward S. Curtis, *Navajo Hogan* (1905), courtesy of the Library of Congress [LC-USZ62-105863]. The hogan, a traditional Navajo dwelling, is constructed out of earth and wooden poles according to instructions from Talking God.

[9074] Luci Tapahonso, Reading: "A Breeze Swept Through" (2002), courtesy of Annenberg/CPB and *American Passages*. This poem shows (Dine) Navajo poet Luci Tapahonso moving between the English and Navajo languages. In the poem, Tapahonso retells the creation story of Dawn Woman.

[9080] Luci Tapahonso, Interview: "The Number Four and Its Significance" (2002), courtesy of Annenberg/CPB and *American Passages*. A recording from an interview with Tapahonso in which she discusses the number 4 and its significance in her poetry and for the Navajo; other interview excerpts can be found in archives [9076] through [9083].

QUESTIONS

Comprehension: The location of a poem or story—its setting—almost always conveys important information about its overall meaning. Where does "They Are Silent and Quick" seem to be set? Where are the narrator and her daughter, and where are the narrator's parents?

Comprehension: "A Breeze Swept Through" retells a Navajo creation story. Who or what is the "first born of Dawn Woman"?

Comprehension: What is the significance of the narrator's Navajo mother saying, "'There's nothing like that in Navajo stories'" in the third stanza of "They Are Silent and Quick"? How does this statement affect the narrator, her "aching," and her feelings about constituting one of three generations of women in her family? What do these emotions have to do with the setting of the poem?

Context: Why would Tapahonso compare dawn with birth in "A Breeze Swept Through"? What does her comparison suggest about the place of humans in the natural world?

Context: In *Language and Art in the Navajo Universe*, anthropologist Gary Witherspoon argues that for the Navajo, "the earth and its life-giving, life-sustaining, and life-producing qualities are associated with and derived from Changing Woman [Earth Mother]. It is not surprising, therefore, that women tend to dominate in social and economic affairs. Women are the heads of most domestic groups, the clans are matrilineal [i.e., they trace their descent through the maternal line], and the land and sheep traditionally were controlled by the women of residential groups." What role do women play in Tapahonso's poetry?

Exploration: The narrator of "They Are Silent and Quick" says, "There are no English words to describe this feeling." What do you think she means by this statement? At what point in her narrative does she switch from English? That is, where do the "breaks" occur in her English consciousness? You might compare these moments to when Gloria Anzaldúa (Unit 2), for example, switches to Spanish, or when writers like Jean Toomer (Unit 10) switch dialects.

Exploration: Navajo society is matrifocal; that is, in certain ways the community revolves around women (for example, families tend to reside with the mother's clan). In "A Breeze Swept Through," images of the female are vital to the force of the poem. Why is the poem gendered female? Would you describe the poem as empowering to women, especially Native American women? Why or why not?

Exploration: Compare the Navajo creation story in "A Breeze Swept Through" to the creation story in Genesis. How are humans characterized in each? How is the divine characterized? What are the relationships between the human and the divine in each story?

Simon J. Ortiz (b. 1941)

Simon J. Ortiz's world is one of mixtures and doublings, of multiple identities: he has an American name and an Acoma name, Hihdruutsi; he is from the Southwest but lives in Toronto, Canada. Born and raised in the Acoma Pueblo community in Albuquerque, New Mexico, Ortiz received his early education from the Bureau of Indian Affairs school on the Acoma reservation. He later attended the University of New Mexico. Ortiz currently teaches in the department of English at the University of Toronto.

[5887] Ansel Adams, *Looking across the Street toward Houses, "Acoma Pueblo"* (1933), courtesy of the National Archives and Records Administration, Still Pictures Branch.

Storytelling has always been a part of his life. As he explains, "I think that because storytelling is a process, that is a dynamic of culture. . . . [I]t was with that first utterance of sound that your parents or those who are closest to you in your family utter that first sound or that first word and you first conceive of it as sound that has meaning. It could be a murmur, it could be a song, it could be your name." His poetry explores the significance of individual origins and journeys, which he, like many American Indian writers, sees as forming a vital link in the continuity of life. Drawing on American Indian oral traditions, his poems emphasize orality, narrative, and the actual worldly effects of language. As Ortiz explains, storytelling is about more than just the style of the poetry: "The purpose of that story sharing or storytelling is . . . conversing, and the story listeners are conversing with us. We are sharing, or participating. And it's the storyteller participating by his telling, and the listener participating by his or her listening. So it's an exchange. It's a dialogue. It's an event."

Ortiz's poetry is also influenced by the sounds of the oral tradition and by the way that he conjures up concrete images and uses repetition. His poems, therefore, feel like they are being transmitted through the spoken word more than the written word. He has said that "Indians always tell a story. . . . The only way to continue is to tell a story and there is no other way. Your children will not survive unless you tell something about them—how they were born, how they came to this certain place, how they continued." Ortiz advocates a political literature, eschewing the idea that poetry should be above or beyond political concerns. While this is less obviously true of the poems featured in the video, it is more evident in such poems as "At the Salvation Army" (from *From Sand Creek*).

Perhaps most crucially, Ortiz's poetry grows out of his experience with the Pueblo landscape and the cultures that live with it. Like fellow Pueblo poet Leslie Marmon Silko, Ortiz expresses concern through his work that Western worldviews treat the land as a property to be used rather than as a life-force to be respected. Ortiz's books of poetry include *Going for Rain* (1976), *Poems from the Veterans Hospital* (1977) (in which "8:50 AM Ft. Lyons VAH" appears), *From Sand Creek* (1982), *Woven Stone* (1992) (in which "My Mother and My Sisters" appears), *After and Before the Lightning* (1994), and *Out There Somewhere* (2002).

[5876] Ansel Adams, *"Church, Acoma Pueblo" Corner View Showing Mostly Left Wall* (1933), courtesy of the National Archives and Records Administration. The Acoma Pueblo community of Albu-querque, New Mexico, was the childhood home of poet Simon J. Ortiz. Ortiz's poetry deals with political concerns and bears the marks of his oral heritage.

[5887] Ansel Adams, *Looking across the Street toward Houses, "Acoma Pueblo"* (1933), courtesy of the National Archives and Records Administration, Still Pictures Branch. Acoma Pueblo, the home of the Acoma Indians, is believed to be the oldest inhabited village in the United States. Atop a 367-foot mesa, this "Sky City" is well defended against enemies. Dwellings are built around a plaza that serves as the community's sacred center. The interconnectedness of the houses reflects the social bonds of the community.

[5891] Henry Kyllingstad, *Daisy Pino, an Acoma Girl, during On-the-Job Training at Brown's Cafe, Albuquerque, N. Mex.* (1951), courtesy of the National Archives and Records Administration. During the 1950s poor living conditions and high unemployment led many Native Americans to seek work off the reservation in cities. N. Scott Momaday, Sherman Alexie, and others write about the hardships and alienation experienced by "urban Indians."

[5971] Nancy Crampton, *Simon Ortiz Portrait* (n.d.), courtesy of Nancy Crampton. Simon J. Ortiz was born in the Acoma Pueblo community, to the Dyaamih clan. In Ortiz's native language there are no words for extended family members; everyone is either "father," "mother," "sister" or "brother."

[8304] Simon Ortiz, *Pottery in Acoma Pueblo Culture* (2002), courtesy of Annenberg/CPB and *American Passages*. Pueblo pottery is considered some of the most beautiful, and it has deep ties to storytelling traditions. In this excerpt from a poem by Simon Ortiz, we learn of the power of pottery in Acoma Pueblo culture.

■ Most students have heard little first-hand testimony from veterans about their experiences with war. Have your students interview veterans about their experiences, either veterans in their families or those at local VA hospitals. They may want to read them the poems that Ortiz has written and ask the veterans to comment on them.

■ Have your students write in their journals about some central family memory or legend as in "My Mother and My Sisters." What purpose does the dissemination and repetition of the story serve in their family? Is this story community-forming? Confidence-building? If the story is funny, as many such stories are, what purpose does the humor serve?

■ In his interview with *American Passages*, Simon J. Ortiz reflects that even though the Pueblo didn't have a written language before the arrival of the Spanish, they had "art forms and art objects, that communicated, that served as expressions of knowledge." Ask your students to focus on the image of the women creating pottery in "My Mother and My Sisters." What linguistic strategies does Ortiz use to let us know that what the women are doing is more important than just throwing and painting pottery?

QUESTIONS

Comprehension: What is "the building" in "8:50 AM Ft. Lyons VAH"? To which "three American wars" does the narrator probably refer?

Comprehension: The narrator of "My Mother and My Sisters" says that his mother paints "with movements whose origin has only to do with years of knowing." What does this description mean?

Comprehension: What is the relationship between the building and the geese in "8:50 AM Ft. Lyons VAH"? What does Ortiz seem to be saying by including them both in one brief poem?

Context: The VA Hospital in Albuquerque is located on over 500 acres on a high mesa and is designed in a village layout in Spanish-Pueblo architectural style. What is the significance of the architecture of the hospital in Ortiz's poem? What difference would it have made if the building were built in a style that imitated a pueblo or a kiva, the traditional site of Pueblo healing?

Context: "My Mother and My Sisters" includes two segments, the narrator's description of his mother and sister making pottery, and his mother telling the story of looking for pinons. What do these two segments have in common, or how do they illuminate each other? Consider the relationship between pottery-making and storytelling as art forms: how do they both involve the expression and transmission of cultural values and assumptions?

Context: Examine the jars from Acoma and Santo Domingo Pueblos featured in the "Singing Mothers" Web archive in this unit. Describe the shape of the jars. What potential uses might they have had? How has the potter used shape and geometry to create a sense of balance and rhythm? Compare the harmony-seeking principles in the pottery to those in Ortiz's poems.

Exploration: Poetry often invokes the five senses in order to make its message more vivid and immediate. There are two senses at work in "8:50 AM Ft. Lyons VAH": the Wisconsin horse's sighting of the geese and the sound the geese make. What is the relationship between sound and sight in the poem? What does the persona reflect on when he hears, and what does he reflect on when he sees? Which is more "healing"? Compare Ortiz's use of sensory impressions to that of other contemporary poets, such as Li-Young Lee and Sylvia Plath.

Exploration: Poetry is often addressed to an audience—a "you." The second, brief stanza of "My Mother and My Sisters" is written in the second person—that is, it is addressed to some "you." Who is this audience? What is the relationship between the reader and the narrator as a result of this pronoun? How does the second stanza affect your understanding of the poem? How does its inclusion support Ortiz's claim that poetry is a "dialogue" or "conversation"? You might contrast Ortiz's use of the pronoun "you" to that of other poets in such poems as "Daddy" by Sylvia Plath and "Black Art" by Amiri Baraka.

Leslie Marmon Silko (b. 1948)

Leslie Marmon Silko was born in Albuquerque, New Mexico, in the house where her father was also born. She grew up in Old Laguna, a town formed several centuries ago by Pueblo tribes. Her family is of mixed descent, with Plains Indian, Mexican, and European ancestors. She has both Laguna and white ancestors on her father's side and Plains tribe blood from her mother's side. Even the Laguna part of her heritage is multicultural: Hopi, Jemez, Zuni, Navajo, and Spanish peoples have influenced its culture and oral traditions. Like Louise Erdrich, Silko explores mixed identity in many of her works, particularly the situation of being "neither white nor fully traditional Indian." Silko received her B.A. from the University of New Mexico—graduating *magna cum laude* in 1969—and after three semesters of law school decided instead to become a teacher and a writer. She published *Laguna Woman*, a collection of poems, in 1974 and her first novel, *Ceremony*, in 1977. In many ways *Ceremony* was a Laguna answer to N. Scott Momaday's Pulitzer prize–winning *House Made of Dawn*. Like Momaday, Silko interweaves myth, history, and personal recollection, but in *Ceremony* the importance of the feminine landscape replaces the more male-centered story told by Momaday.

In *Ceremony*, Silko tells the story of Tayo, a mixed-blood Indian who fights in World War II and returns to Laguna physically intact but mentally fractured and deeply in shock from post-traumatic stress syndrome. As critic Greg Sarris puts it, the novel "is about a man who is displaced in World War II, taken away from his home, away from the stories, and about having to come home and reacquaint himself with, if you will, the landscape of who he is, his stories, what he knows from the landscape. And as he reacquaints himself with the landscape and the stories, he sees that his experience even in World War II was

[6113] Rudi Williams, *Korean War Army Veteran Ted Wood, an Abenaki Indian, in Full Dress Uniform* (1998), courtesy of DefenseLINK News, U.S. Department of Defense.

never disconnected. That in fact, from the one place we can see all places." This reconnection begins with the opening, in which we find Thought Woman, a mythic godlike figure, and Spider, creating a story. As the novel progresses, language heals both the characters and the readers; stories from the Pueblo oral tradition are interwoven with contemporary updates of traditional healing rituals and discussions of the development of the atomic bomb and uranium mining.

Among Silko's other works are *Storyteller* (1981), a collection of stories and poems; *Almanac of the Dead* (1991), a blistering, apocalyptic epic of North American minority, marginal, and underworld figures and their struggles for power; and *Gardens in the Dunes* (1999), which takes place around the turn of the twentieth century and explores the Ghost Dance and the cultural dismay of a young Laguna girl as she is taken in by a well-to-do white couple. Despite their often dark and disturbing qualities, all of Silko's works address the possibility of renewal or regeneration, particularly of American Indian cultures, values, and ways of life. This hope always rests in part with developing a nurturing and respectful relationship with the landscape of the Southwest. Place is never merely a "setting" in the Western sense; rather, it is inextricable from the life, values, and culture of a people—and their stories. The Laguna are a matrifocal community, and this worldview infuses Silko's work, which often retells female-centered myths around the figures of Yellow Woman and Thought/Spider Woman. Silko has said, "[Storytelling] is a way of interacting . . . a whole way of seeing yourself, the people around you, your life, the place of your life in the bigger context, not just in terms of nature and location but in terms of what has gone on before, what's happened to other people. It's a whole way of life."

TEACHING TIPS

■ In her book *The Sacred Hoop*, author and critic (and cousin of Silko) Paula Gunn Allen makes a rather bold statement about the position of women in American Indian cultures: she argues that "Traditional [American Indian] tribal lifestyles are more often **gynocratic** [governed by women] than not, and they are never patriarchal." Other scholars have refuted aspects of this statement (for example, people have argued that the Sioux and other Plains tribes were in fact patriarchal). However, it is clear that Allen's statement is important for understanding American Indian communities such as the Pueblos that were **matrilineal** (descended through the maternal line) and/or **matrifocal** (female-centered). Allen and others have argued that readers should pay attention to the way gender functions in texts by writers from gynocratic communities since gender is constructed differently in such communities than it is in mainstream American culture. As your students read *Ceremony*, you might want to ask them how gender is being constructed in this novel. How does Tayo compare to traditional European American male icons (e.g., John Wayne) or even to Black Elk? How do the female characters compare to female cultural icons in American culture?

■ Some readers have suggested that Tayo's encounter with Ts'eh in *Ceremony* resembles a Yellow Woman story. Told by the Pueblo peoples of the Southwest, **Yellow Woman stories** dramatize how humans interact with spirits in the world once it has been created. Although there is always variation, Yellow Woman stories often involve a young married woman who wanders beyond her village and has a sexual encounter with a spirit-man; sometimes she is killed, but usually she returns to her family and tribe having grown spiritually, and therefore has an empowering influence on the people in general. In her influential essay "Kochinnenako in Academe," Paula Gunn Allen points out that Yellow Woman stories are "female-centered, always told from the Yellow Woman's point of view," and that they generally highlight "her alienation from the people," but that her apparently transgressive acts "often have happy outcomes for Kochinnenako [Yellow Woman] and her people." This suggests, Allen argues, "that the behavior of women, at least at certain times or under certain circumstances, must be improper or nonconformist for the greater good of the whole." Like many Native American stories, these narratives have the communal function of both drawing socially important boundary lines and observing where they sometimes need to be transgressed. In particular, according to Allen, they emphasize "the central role that woman plays in the orderly life of the people." Leslie Marmon Silko frequently draws from the Yellow Woman tradition when she writes of empowered (especially sexually empowered) and empowering women like the spirit-being Ts'eh. Why do you think Silko includes Tayo and Ts'eh's encounter in her novel? What is the purpose of the Yellow Woman story? How does she update the story? What is the purpose of Silko's novel? What is the role of the oral tradition in general in *Ceremony*?

QUESTIONS

Comprehension: As the novel begins, what are some of the reasons Tayo is so miserable?

Comprehension: List as many "ceremonies" as you can from the novel. That is, if you think of *Ceremony* as a spiritual journey for Tayo, how many stages does it have? Who are his guides on the journey?

Comprehension: What exactly do the different ceremonies give to Tayo? How has he changed by the end of the novel?

Context: What is the role of Ts'eh in the novel? Can you compare her to other women characters in the novel? What about to Fleur and Pauline in the story by Louise Erdrich? Does it matter that the main character of *Ceremony* is a man? How would the novel be different if the main character were a woman?

Context: Compare Silko's portrait of Native American veterans to Ortiz's presentation of the issues surrounding veterans in "8:50 AM Ft. Lyons VAH."

Context: Do a close reading of Betonie's ceremony. How does Betonie's ceremony compare to the Navajo Nightway chant? What is the

Nation, is captured in this photograph. The traditional Native American reverence for the land is a cornerstone of the thinking of many contemporary writers as well as conservationists.

[6635] Skeet McAuley, *Fallout Shelter Directions* (1984), courtesy of *Sign Language, Contemporary Southwest Native America*, Aperture Foundation, Inc. Nuclear weapons were tested throughout the Southwest. Such weapons testing, for writers like Leslie Marmon Silko, does not accord with the respect that humans should show to the natural world if we are to retain our hopes for renewal and regeneration.

goal of each? What is the significance of innovations in the ceremony?

Exploration: How are time and space represented in the novel? How does Silko suggest characteristics of a "ceremonial" time and space, as opposed to the everyday European American senses of time and space? Indeed, it is worth keeping these questions in mind when reading all of the texts in this unit.

Exploration: In what sense is the novel a "ceremony" for the reader as well as for Tayo? How do you imagine Native American readers would respond differently to this book than would Americans of European heritage? What about readers of African or Asian heritages?

Exploration: Write your own modern Yellow Woman story using the theme of abduction and the traditional elements one would expect to find in Yellow Woman stories.

Stories of the Beginning of the World

Myths—deeply traditional stories that explain the origins of a phenomenon or cultural practice—serve as some of the foundational narratives for the stories told by a people. When authors re-create or adapt these myths for their own purposes, their audience must have a firm understanding of the myths in order to understand the stories that retell them. For instance, Herman Melville begins his novel *Moby-Dick* with the line "Call me Ishmael," which invokes the Bible. Similarly, the main characters in Native American literatures often refer back to classical tales from the oral tradition, such as coyote tales, cultural hero stories, migration legends, and **creation stories**. Each of these stories has a standard set of characters, events, and elements. Knowing these original stories can help you better understand the written literature that preceded them.

Like other Native American oral narratives such as **cultural hero** and **trickster** stories, creation stories have etiological features or tags; that is, they describe how some familiar characteristic of the world came to be. Often the particular landscape and environment of the tribe enters into such stories; sometimes the location of the tribe is identified as the center of the world. The ceremonies that accompany these creation myths often enact a ritual return to a combined sense of origin and center, where healing and renewal can be found.

[8113] Huron tribe, Pair of dolls (1830–50), courtesy of the Portland Art Museum, gift of Elizabeth Cole Butler [88.43.6-7].

Like the biblical account in Genesis, Creation stories tell about the beginning of the world and how the people first came to be. Predominant among the tribes of what is now Canada and the eastern United States were earth-diver stories, which tell of how the world was created by beings who gathered mud from beneath the waters created by a great flood. Common in the Southwest and elsewhere were **emergence stories**, which often describe how the people originated in the womb of the Earth Mother and were called to the surface by the Sun Father. Despite the many differences among various tribes' versions of these stories, they generally establish how the world was created, how people developed out of ambiguously formed beings (who often had both animal and human characteristics), what each tribe took to be the basic relationships among people and between people and nature, and the origins of important tribal customs and structures.

Trickster tales, one form of creation story, vary according to their community, but they also share certain basic qualities. Tricksters are more than deceivers or trick players who make us laugh with their scatological humor: by crossing society's boundaries they both break rules and show the importance of rules after the world has been created. They are also creators in their own right. Navajo story-teller Yellowman explains that he must tell about the trickster Coyote because, as he says, "If my children hear the stories, they will grow up to be good people; if they don't hear them, they will turn out to be bad. . . . Through the stories everything is made possible." As you read trickster tales, notice their unique characteristics. Consider the presence of traditional elements, such as animals (e.g., buffalo, coyote, spider, salmon), vegetables, minerals, landscape, weather, colors, directions, time, dances, and the supernatural.

TEACHING TIPS

■ It is important that students begin to have a sense of the traditions of their own region. Investigate what resources are available from Native American storytellers in your area. If possible, invite a local Native American storyteller to your class or play a recorded performance from an audio- or videocassette. Your reference librarian should be able to help you locate resources.

■ Students can learn about the performative nature of storytelling by telling stories themselves. Have students pick one of the legends, memorize it, and recite it *as an engaging story* to the class. You may want to have students work in groups so that they can coach one another or work on smaller segments.

QUESTIONS

Comprehension: What is a creation story? How does it differ from an emergence story?

Comprehension: What is a trickster? What does a trickster do?

Comprehension: What, according to the Pima and the Iroquois, existed at the beginning of time?

Comprehension: In the Iroquois creation story the monsters are concerned when Sky Woman sinks into the dark world. What does their reaction tell us about the nature of monsters and the lower world?

Comprehension: In the Pima emergence story, Juh-wert-a-Mah-kai had to rub his palm four times before the world was created. What else has to be done four times in the Pima stories? What does the number 4 come to mean by the end of the stories?

Context: Listen to the audio clip about Coyote [8008]. Compare him to the trickster figures found in the Winnebago, Sioux, Koasati, Coville, Clatsop Chinook, and Navajo stories. Which of the trickster figures does he most resemble? Which does he differ from the most?

Context: What are the themes and elements of some of the trickster tales? How do these compare to the gambler tales as described in the Extended Context "Sacred Play: Gambling in Native Cultures"?

Context: Examine the Iroquois cradle [8115] and the Huron dolls [8113]. Do these appear to have been created by the good or bad mind of the Iroquois creation story? How do you know?

Exploration: Is the Iroquois creation myth still an Iroquois text if it has been translated into English? Does such a translation so alter the meaning that it is no longer accurate to speak of it as Iroquoian, or should the fact of translation merely make readers more cautious, less eager to assume that they understand it? Is it better for non-Indians to have no access to such texts than to have texts that may be contaminated or inaccurate?

Exploration: The theme of rival twins is widespread in the Americas and in the Bible. What cultural anxieties or issues does this theme address? What might account for its popularity?

Louise Erdrich (b. 1954)

Born in Little Falls, Minnesota, Louise Erdrich is a member of the Turtle Mountain Chippewa tribe of North Dakota. The Chippewa are also called the Ojibwa, or, in their own Algonquian language, the Anishinabe, both of which terms appear in Erdrich's work. Erdrich's French-Chippewa mother and her German-American father were teachers for the Bureau of Indian Affairs in Wahpeton, Minnesota. Her maternal grandmother was tribal chairwoman on the Turtle Mountain Reservation. After attending Dartmouth College (where she studied under her future husband and collaborator, Michael Dorris), Erdrich received her M.A. from the Johns Hopkins University in 1979 and later edited the Boston Indian Council's newspaper, *The Circle*. Erdrich also held a variety of other jobs, such as lifeguard, waitress, prison poetry teacher, and construction flag signaler, which she has said greatly helped her writing. The winner of numerous prizes for her literature, she has published both fiction and poetry.

[7427] Linde, *Five Ojibwa Indians: Man, Woman, and Three Children in Canoe*—["*Typical Natives*"] (c. 1913), courtesy of the Library of Congress [LC-USZ62-101332].

In 1984 Erdrich published both her first volume of poetry, *Jacklight*, and her first novel, *Love Medicine*. The novel, a series of discrete stories spanning the years 1934 to 1984, is told by seven narrators and follows the relations among three Chippewa families: the Kashpaws, the Lamartine/Nanapushes, and the Morriseys. A number of Erdrich's later novels, including *The Beet Queen* (1986), *Tracks* (1988), *The Bingo Palace* (1994), and *Tales of Burning Love* (1996), focus on various members of these same families and their lives in and around a reservation in the fictional town of Argus, North Dakota. As do many writers of American Indian descent, Erdrich attributes her interest in literature in part to her cultural heritage. She has said, "People in [Indian] families make everything into a story. . . . People just sit and the stories start coming, one after another. I suppose that when you grow up constantly hearing the stories rise, break, and fall, it gets into you somehow." *Tracks* (Chapter 2 of which was published as "Fleur" in 1986) is typical of her novels in emphasizing how events are always understood and told by people with particular points of view, with their own assumptions, quirks, and belief systems. The story of the powerful Fleur Pillager is told by the fearful and confused Pauline Puyat, who later in the novel becomes Sister Leopolda and acts as an antagonist to Fleur. "Fleur" (subtitled "Pauline" in *Tracks*) explores both Fleur's power and Pauline's self-deception.

Many of Erdrich's novels are interwoven with characters or motifs from the Chippewa oral tradition. For the Chippewas the ultimate sources of existence were the **manitos**—extremely powerful beings who might be roughly characterized as spirits or gods that provided people with food (through hunting) and good health. In addition to Pau-Puk-Keewis, the Chippewa gambler, windigos, Nanabozho (the Chippewa cultural hero/trickster), and the underwater manito—all manitos from the Chippewa oral tradition—appear in Erdrich's work. Windigos are cannibals made of ice or people whose insides are ice. In other novels in the *Love Medicine* series, we learn that members of the Nanapush family (including Fleur) may have "gone windigo" during starving times long ago. Nanabozho was important to Chippewas as hunters, and he helped Chippewa culture. Critics have argued that Erdrich's character Gerry Morrisey is based both on this trickster/cultural hero (hence his supernatural ability to escape) and on Leonard Peltier—the Chippewa hero and activist. The underwater manito could both save people who fell through the ice and drown those who wandered—one of the worst ways that a Chippewa could die. Fleur encounters the underwater manito and survives, which tells us something about her power.

TEACHING TIPS

■ Have your students write a character sketch of Fleur. Does she change or surprise us, or is she constant? At what point do we know that Fleur is different from the other characters in the story? What linguistic and literary devices does Erdrich use to call attention to this difference?

■ It may be helpful to fill students in on some background about Fleur and the stories that people in her community tell about her, such as that during a starving time she went windigo or that she met with an underwater manito and survived. One ethnographer reports that the Chippewa of Parry Island say there are spirits everywhere, "or there were until the white man came, for today, the Indians say, most of them have moved away." Ask students to consider what it means that Fleur maintains this close relationship to the spirit realm even in the face of white settlement. What role does the supernatural play in the story?

[7178] Vera Palmer, Interview: "Erdrich and the Captivity Narrative" (2001), courtesy of Annenberg/CPB. Vera Palmer, a distinguished American Indian activist and scholar, earned her Ph.D. from Cornell University. In an *American Passages* interview she talks about Louise Erdrich's poem "Captivity."

[7427] Linde, *Five Ojibwa Indians: Man, Woman, and Three Children in Canoe*—["Typical Natives"] (c. 1913), courtesy of the Library of Congress [LC-USZ62-101332]. For the Chippewas the ultimate sources of existence were the manitos—powerful beings who might be roughly characterized as spirits or gods. The underwater manito could both save people who fell through the ice and drown those who wandered.

[7590] George Catlin, *Sha-Co-Pay (The Six)* [*Chief of the Plains Ojibwa*] (1842), courtesy of Tilt and Bogue, London. "The chief of that part of the Ojibbeway tribe who inhabit these northern regions, and whose name is Sha-co-pay (the Six), is a man of huge size; with dignity of manner, and pride and vanity, just about in proportion to his bulk."—George Catlin. This painting is one of 520 that resulted from an eight-year expedition during which Catlin visited over forty-five different tribes, participated in buffalo hunts, and observed ceremonies, games, dances and rituals.

QUESTIONS

Comprehension: Why is Fleur so threatening to the men? How do they respond to this threat?

Comprehension: By the end of the story, who does it seem did the actual locking up of the men in the meat locker?

Context: How are we meant to evaluate Fleur? How do the initial supernatural hints inform our feelings about her? What are we to make of her impossibly lucky poker playing? What is her relationship to her Chippewa heritage?

Context: How are we meant to evaluate the narrator, Pauline? What are we to make of her rejection of the Chippewa, her assertion that she "was made for better"? Why does she not help Fleur?

Exploration: What do you make of the fact that the story as originally published is "Fleur," but that its appearance in *Tracks* is subtitled "Pauline"? If possible, read the novel to answer this question; however, you might speculate about this apparent interchangeability based simply upon the events and narration of the story.

Exploration: Why does it matter that the main characters here are both women? You might think of the story as an exploration of the range of options that Chippewa women in 1913 had to exercise power. In that case, consider the varying forms of power that both women display and speculate on what you think Erdrich is saying about gender.

Chippewa Songs

Frances Densmore collected these Chippewa songs between 1907 and 1909. The songs reflect the culture of the Chippewa peoples who once lived along the shores of Lake Huron and Lake Superior, across Minnesota, and west to North Dakota. The Chippewa are Algonquian Indians; that is, they speak a language that is related to those others classified as part of the central Algonquian group. Chippewa and Ojibwa are the same word pronounced differently. They are composed of numerous tribes and bands, including the Turtle Mountain Band of which Louise Erdrich is a member. The Chippewa were the largest Great Lakes tribe and one of the most powerful tribes in North America. Because the Chippewa did not possess good farming lands, white settlement in their homelands was minimal, and hence they have been able to maintain much of their language and culture. Chippewa culture varies with geographic location: on the plains, for example, the Chippewa hunted buffalo. Most Ojibwa lived in the northern Great Lakes region and cultivated crops and supplemented their diet with hunting and gathering. They were skilled hunters, trappers, and fishers. The lakes and the spirits of the lake—the underwater manitos—became a central part of their cosmology.

Like other Algonquian peoples, the Chippewa lived in tipis. Theirs were dome-shaped and were made of birch bark that could be rolled up for easy transportation. Clothing was made out of buckskin and furs that were dyed. Today the Chippewa are renowned for their beautiful beadwork, particularly their beaded bandolier bags, named for the bandolier, an ammunition belt worn over the shoulder and across the chest. These decorative bags served many utilitarian purposes. The Ojibwa often passed the time and entertained each other with stories and songs such as the ones in *The Norton Anthology of American Literature*.

It is important to remember that while some songs are sacred and were both received and sung in a ceremonial context, others were not. As Frances Densmore, who collected a wide variety of songs among the Chippewa, explained in her 1915 article in *The Musical Quarterly*: "Among the Chippewa it was the custom for medicine men to build 'nests' in the trees, where they waited, fasting, until they secured a dream and its song. A man was very proud of a song received in this manner. . . . A medicine man always sang his principal dream song and related the dream before he began to treat a sick person." For Densmore, love songs were wholly removed from this more sacred and traditional context. She identified three levels of songs: "First, there still remain some of the old songs, sung by the old singers. . . . Second, there are old ceremonial and medicine songs belonging to men now dead, but which can be sung, and sung with reasonable correctness, by men who heard them given by their owners. . . . Third, there are comparatively modern songs, which represent a transitional culture. If differentiated from the really old songs, these are not devoid of interest, though it is scarcely worth while to collect a great many of them." Love songs were in this third, "modern" category.

[7428] Anonymous, *Rocky Boy (Stone Child), a Chippewa Chief, Three-Quarter Length, Standing, Dressed in Ornate Costume* (n.d.), courtesy of the National Archives and Records Administration, Still Pictures Branch.

TEACHING TIPS

■ Play your students some of the music from the Chippewa songs in the archive. What is the tone of the music? How does it compare to the tone of the Chippewa songs in *The Norton Anthology of American Literature*? Using Densmore's categories as a starting point, have students create their own categories for the types of music.

■ Early musicologist Frances Densmore has this to say about the thirty love songs she recorded: "Only one was inspired by happiness. All these songs were comparatively modern. Too frequently the words contained the information that the singer intended to drown disappointment in liquor. On moonlight nights one hears wailing songs of this kind issuing from the barred windows of the agency guardhouse. Let us hope that future students of Indian music will pass them by. Weird they are, and melodious they may be, but representative of true Indian character they assuredly are not." Ask students to refute Densmore's claim. Upon what assumptions is it based? What does she mean by "true Indian character"? Why does she think that these songs would be less worth collecting?

QUESTIONS

Comprehension: Musicologist Frances Densmore claims that the Chippewa love songs are "comparatively modern songs, which represent a transitional culture." Where do you see aspects of tra-

[7428] Anonymous, *Rocky Boy (Stone Child), A Chippewa Chief, Three-Quarter Length, Standing, Dressed in Ornate Costume* (n.d.), courtesy of the National Archives and Records Administration, Still Pictures Branch. Native American "Chief Songs" were sung by community members in praise of and to their chief. Fancy dress such as the outfit worn by Rocky Boy (Stone Child) reinforces authority and status in American Indian cultures. Rocky Boy was a famous chief, and the Rocky Boy Indian Reservation in Montana is named after him.

[9087] Cal Scott, *Music of Chippewa Songs* (2002), courtesy of Cal Scott Music. This is a sound recording of the music for the Chippewa songs featured in *The Norton Anthology of American Literature*.

[9106] Thomas Wyatt, "Whoso List to Hunt," from *The Poems of Sir Thomas Wiat* (1913), courtesy of University of London Press. English poet Thomas Wyatt here reflects on the relationship between hunting and loving, a relationship that is also posed in contemporary poems like "Jacklight" by Louise Erdrich.

ditional Chippewa culture in these songs? Where do you see European American influences?

Comprehension: What is the tone of each of the songs? How does the tone compare to love songs you hear on the radio?

Comprehension: Why are there several Chippewa songs about Sioux women? What do Sioux women represent?

Context: Compare the more whimsical Chippewa love songs to the more ceremonial Ghost Dance songs. What rhythmic or linguistic clues help the reader know that the Ghost Dance songs are more serious in nature?

Context: How are women represented in the songs? To what extent are these representations consonant with traditional Western stereotypes about women, and to what extent do they challenge those stereotypes?

Context: Compare the vision of love presented in the Chippewa love songs with that in Louise Erdrich's *Love Medicine* or *The Bingo Palace*. What does Lipsha mean by love?

Exploration: During the Renaissance, the Italian poet Petrarch refined a series of conceits that came to epitomize the way Western poets talked about the beloved. These include the idea of love as a battle or hunt, the power of the beloved's gaze being like a ray, the beauty of the beloved's person being like flowers or jewels, and the comparison of the beloved to a sun or star. Identify and examine Chippewa love conventions.

Exploration: Love is often depicted as a battle or hunt, in which the true test of passion comes in the pursuit. Compare the tension between the singer and the beloved in English poet Thomas Wyatt's "Whoso List to Hunt" and Chippewa poet Louise Erdrich's "Jacklight."

Black Elk (1863–1950) and John G. Neihardt (1881–1973)

Born into the Oglala Lakota, Black Elk was an important Sioux visionary and religious leader. As a young man he received a Great Vision in which the Six Grandfathers—powers of the West, the North, the East, the South, the Sky, and the Earth—appeared to him. This vision was powerful enough to remain an important part of his consciousness as he grew up, and he became a shamanic healer in his late teenage years. When, in 1886, Black Elk joined Buffalo Bill's Wild West Show, he became an Episcopalian, because all employees were required to be Christian. Though he later converted to Catholicism (in 1904), he passed on his vision to poet John G. Neihardt, and the record of this interaction became the 1932 book *Black Elk Speaks*. Much of the extant record of Native American narrative, poetry, and myth comes from transcriptions and translations often made by late-nineteenth- and early-twentieth-century, non–Native American anthropologists. John G. Neihardt, however, was not an anthropologist, and he did not speak Lakota; thus, his account of Black Elk's vision is not only filtered through several translators and transcribers but has been altered to fit Neihardt's own interpretation of Black Elk's world. These practices make *Black Elk Speaks* problematic if viewed as an authoritative American Indian text. In spite of these problems, the book has been—and continues to be—enormously influential.

John G. Neihardt, poet laureate of Nebraska, had a literary rather than a purely scientific motivation for speaking to Black Elk: he was gathering research material for the last volume of his epic poem, *A Cycle of the West*. In 1930 and 1931, he made several trips to Black Elk's cabin outside of Manderson, South Dakota, where they discussed poetry, spirituality, and Black Elk's life. *Black Elk Speaks* is also a product of the political upheavals of the 1930s. Even as *Black Elk Speaks* recounts the earlier period of

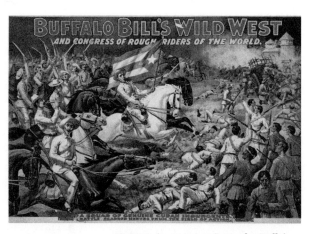

[2251] Anonymous, Poster for *Buffalo Bill's Wild West and Congress of Rough Riders of the World* (c. 1899), courtesy of the Library of Congress [LC-USZC4-2943].

renewal during the Ghost Dance Movement, the authors are speaking and writing during another important period of American Indian rejuvenation—the years leading up to the Indian Reorganization Act (IRA) or "Indian New Deal" of 1934. John Collier, the mastermind behind the IRA, suggests that the "Indian New Deal . . . held two purposes. One was the conservation of the biological Indian and of Indian culture, each with its special purposes. The other . . . was the conservation of the Indian's natural resources." As an acquaintance of Collier (and later an employee of the Bureau of Indian Affairs [BIA]), Neihardt was intimately acquainted with the movement leading up to the IRA. It is clear that the more bellicose aspects of Black Elk's story were excised by Neihardt in an effort not to offend white readers. The relationship between the two men was, however, reciprocal: while Neihardt found in Black Elk a fertile resource for understanding Native American culture, Black Elk saw in Neihardt someone who could disseminate a prophetic vision he had experienced some sixty years earlier.

During the 1960s and 1970s, *Black Elks Speaks* became an important text for Indian activists who wanted to access earlier visions of power. Vine Deloria went so far as to call it the Indian Bible. For literary scholars, however, the text raises questions about the limits of autobiography (how can an autobiography have been written by someone else?) and the oxymoron at the heart of the phrase "American Indian autobiography." As Arnold Krupat pointed out in 1981,

> Autobiography as a particular form of self-written life is a European invention of comparatively recent date. . . . [W]e may note that the autobiographical project, as we usually understand it, is marked by egocentric individualism, historicism, and writing. These are all present in European and Euro American culture after the revolutionary last quarter of the eighteenth century. But none has ever characterized the native cultures of the present-day United States.

Mixed-blood critic Hertha Wong has argued that precontact written texts—as well as the oral tradition—help explain one of the fundamental differences between American Indian and Western autobiogra-

[2251] Anonymous, Poster for *Buffalo Bill's Wild West and Congress of Rough Riders of the World* (c. 1899), courtesy of the Library of Congress [LC-USZC4-2943]. As a young man, Black Elk took part in Buffalo Bill's Wild West Show. This poster shows a band of Rough Riders battling Cuban insurgents. The famous charge at San Juan Hill had taken place the previous year.

[7418] Anonymous, Boy's moccasins, Lakota (n.d.), courtesy of the New York State Historical Association, Thaw Collection. Reservation-period (post-1880) beadwork on these dress moccasins shows how the American flag motif was incorporated into Native American design. This motif has been read as a sign of assimilation or as a way to capture the power of the enemy.

[8117] Mandan and Plains Indians, Moccasins (c. 1850–70), courtesy of the Portland Art Museum, gift of Elizabeth Cole Butler. Typical Plains clothing included buckskin aprons, leggings, and moccasins for men and buckskin dresses for women. Buffalo-skin robes were worn in cold weather. Decorated moccasins are common in portraits and photos of Plains Indians.

phies. Wong argues that the pictographic writings of the Sioux and other Plains tribes tended, like the oral tradition, to tell stories about the self which might be more accurately described as "communo-bio-oratory"(community-life-speaking) rather than "auto-bio-graphical" (self-life-writing), since they were about the person's life in the context of their human, spiritual, and natural communities and the writings were intended to be part of an oral recitation, rather than to stand on their own. *Black Elk Speaks* provides an opportunity to question our assumptions about the genres of biography and autobiography more generally.

TEACHING TIPS

■ Have your students pair up and interview one another about their lives. Then have them write an "autobiography" for their partner. Follow this up by having the interviewee write a short comment on his or her "autobiography." This activity illustrates the point that there is always a selection process in autobiography and also shows how the choice is lost when one is no longer the writer of the work.

■ In the oral tradition, repetition is crucial both for ceremonial reasons and because it aids in the process of memorization (which is how oral texts are preserved). In contrast, in written texts, we can turn back to earlier information if we need it; hence, repetition is less necessary. Ask students to pay attention in *Black Elk Speaks* both to what gets repeated and to how many times the reptition occurs. (In the Bible, the numbers 3, 4, and 7 are important. What numbers are important for Black Elk and why? What are their religious associations?) For many oral cultures, words have a great power to harm, heal, and create (think of the opening of the Bible, for example—originally an oral text). Thus, to repeat words is to wield a certain power. What kind of power does language have in *Black Elk Speaks*? In addition to its ceremonial uses, repetition is also a crucial way of providing narrative cohesion in oral narratives. Repeating aspects of a story enables items to be linked in the minds of the listeners: what events and ideas does Black Elk link in his text and with what effect?

QUESTIONS

Comprehension: Who is Black Elk? Why does he receive the vision?

Comprehension: What seems to be the purpose of the Grandfathers' council that Black Elk attends? What do the Grandfathers want to teach Black Elk?

Comprehension: What "four ascents" does Black Elk encounter?

Context: Consider the recurrence of the hoop in Black Elk's vision. For the Sioux, circles stand for the cyclical, interconnected nature of life itself. Given this, how does the appearance of the hoop affect the significance of *Black Elk Speaks*?

Context: Black Elk's revelation occurred when he was nine years old, in 1872—seventeen years before the Ghost Dance religion came to the Sioux nation. How does Black Elk's vision compare to the motifs present in the Ghost Dance songs and Wovoka's "Messiah letters"?

Context: What is the relationship between *Black Elk Speaks* and the policies of the Indian New Deal (e.g., does it affirm, respond to, complicate, or negate such goals)? Does Neihardt (or Black Elk) believe in the "continuity of the group"? What must be continued? What "certain kinds of changes" should be induced and which should be controlled? What "traditions" must be "conserved"?

Context: Examine the Lakota boy's moccasins decorated with American flags [7418] and compare them to the Plains moccasins [8117]. Is one of these more "traditional"? What are you assuming "traditional" means? How do you think Black Elk would have understood each of these artifacts?

Exploration: Consider the vision from *Black Elk Speaks* as literature. In what way is it like other literary texts with which you might be more familiar and that are more clearly fictional? Is this text "fictional" in any way? To what extent should we consider what we could call the text's multiple-authorship when interpreting it?

Exploration: Compare this vision with one or both of the most famous prophetic visions in the Western tradition, the biblical Books of Daniel and Revelation. How does Black Elk's vision compare to those granted to Daniel and John of Patmos? What are the most compelling clues in Black Elk's narrative that signify that he experienced a non-Western revelation (again, think especially of the hoop imagery)?

Ghost Dance Songs

One of the most tragic events in Native American history was the massacre of some two hundred Sioux men, women, and children at Wounded Knee, South Dakota, on the Pine Ridge Reservation, on December 15, 1890. The slaughter of the Sioux was provoked in part by the Seventh Cavalry's reaction to a multiday ceremony known as the Ghost Dance. A combination of traditional native religion and Christianity, the Ghost Dance religion had begun when a Paiute man, Wovoka, also called Jack Wilson, had a vision in 1889 shortly after a solar eclipse. After collapsing with severe scarlet fever, Wovoka found himself spiritually transported to a village where all the ancestors lived peacefully, surrounded by the old environment and engaging in the old activities. This precontact world would be soon restored to the indigenous people, God told Wovoka, so they should prepare themselves for its coming: they should live in peace, work, not lie or steal, and dance a Ghost Dance that would hasten the return of the old world: the buffalo would again be plentiful and the Europeans would be swept away.

[4219] Western Photograph Company, *Gathering Up the Dead at the Battlefield of Wounded Knee, South Dakota* (1891), courtesy of the Smithsonian Institution.

When Wovoka emerged from his fever, he began to spread this prophecy, which traveled widely among Plains Indians (as it had on a smaller scale in California in the early 1870s); before long 20,000 Sioux had begun to engage in the dance. Because this spiritual movement foretold the imminent destruction of the European invaders, it made U.S. officials extremely uneasy, and tensions reached the breaking point at Wounded Knee. By 1889, American Indians had already experienced several hundred years of physical and cultural violence, including the 1871 Congressional termination of treaties with native nations, which opened the door even wider for decimation of the land, destruction of the buffalo, and starvation of the people. The Ghost Dance offered a hope for a new world, in the form of the old world of the ancestors, but that hope largely vanished after the Wounded Knee massacre. The Ghost Dance songs accompanied the dance itself, which was a version of the communal dance form long present in North America. The songs generally involved apocalyptic visions experienced by the Ghost Dancers, but they also incorporated native customs and images, as well as aspects of the daily life of the tribe. In its *syncretism* (its combining of different spiritual traditions), the Ghost Dance thus illustrates the American Indian value of keeping rituals currently relevant to the life of the tribe.

Like most traditional Native American songs, the Ghost Dance songs were never meant to be written down, but were intended to be experienced in an oral, ritual setting as an accompaniment to physical movement. Here literature is meant to act on the community, to affect the world in which it is performed, rather than to be passively consumed by individual audience members. Records of the Ghost Dance movement and of Wounded Knee appear in *Black Elk Speaks* and in Charles Alexander Eastman's *From the Deep Woods to Civilization*, as well as in James Mooney's *The Ghost Dance Religion and the Sioux Outbreak of 1890*.

TEACHING TIPS

■ In his book *A Little Matter Called Genocide*, American Indian Movement (AIM) activist Ward Churchill places images of stacked bodies from Wounded Knee next to images of bodies from German concentration camps in World War II. These images have some shocking similarities and force the question: Was Wounded Knee a genocidal act? More importantly, what are the implications of calling it one? Ask your students to define the word "genocide" and then to debate when we should limit the use of the word.

■ Have your students read either Black Elk's or Eastman's description of the Ghost Dance movement before they read the Ghost Dance songs. Why were the whites in the area so scared? You may want to have your students read the sections surrounding the description so they know what led up to the incident.

■ Unlike the Chippewa songs included in this unit, the Ghost Dance songs were highly ritualistic and performative: they were intended to bring about the deeds they describe. If we take these songs seriously, this would be disastrous for many of their readers. What does it mean, then, to read these songs respectfully? Use this as a problem-solving activity for students. How can an audience respond to literature that may, at its heart, want to end that audience's very existence? How does the text change when read by those who identify with the author, those who are targeted by the author, and those who are not directly implicated by the text? (Amiri Baraka's "Black Art" poems pose issues related to these questions.)

QUESTIONS

Comprehension: What is the purpose of the Ghost Dance songs? How did they aim to accomplish this goal? In what context were they first performed?

Comprehension: According to the songs, what exactly is "approaching" or "coming"?

Context: Repetition is an important part of most Native American rituals. It can, for example, emphasize ideas and strengthen the bonds of the community. What is the effect of the repetition in these songs? Given that the "message" of the words could be conveyed without the repetition, how would the songs be different without it?

Context: Why do the songs evoke both imminent change in North American power structures and the details of traditional tribal ways of life (for example, the processing of meat)?

Exploration: Mixed-blood critic Hertha Wong has argued that the pictographic writings of the Sioux and other Plains tribes tended, like works in the oral tradition, to tell stories about the self which might be more accurately described as "communo-bio-oratory" (community-life-speaking) rather than "auto-bio-graphical" (self-life-writing). In other words, they were about the person's life in the context of his or her human, spiritual, and natural communities and the writings were intended to be part of an oral recitation, rather than stand on their own. How is Black Elk's narrative "communo-bio-oratory"? Is Black Elk's story community-centered? If so, how and who is his community? What is the role of the spoken word in his text?

Exploration: Compare these songs with both Black Elk's vision and the Book of Revelation. Keeping in mind that "apocalypse" is a transliteration of the Greek word for "revelation," consider how the Ghost Dance's vision of apocalypse compares to that in other works.

Non-Native Representations of Indians

Roger Williams (c. 1603–1683)

Although we do not have written texts by Algonquian Indians from the very early contact period, we can learn about their language and culture from the way it is presented by such Europeans as Roger

GHOST DANCE SONGS WEB ARCHIVE

[4219] Western Photograph Company, *Gathering up the Dead at the Battle Field of Wounded Knee, South Dakota* (1891), courtesy of the Smithsonian Institution. U.S. soldiers standing in front of a wagon full of dead Sioux. A blizzard delayed the burial of the dead. Eventually the Sioux were buried in a mass grave, with little effort made to identify the bodies.

[8102] Blackfeet tribe, Shirt (c. 1890), courtesy of the Portland Art Museum, gift of Elizabeth Cole Butler [86.126.32]. Shirts such as this one were worn by practitioners of the Ghost Dance religion. Clothing varied from tribe to tribe, but many believed that the shirts protected wearers from bullets and attack.

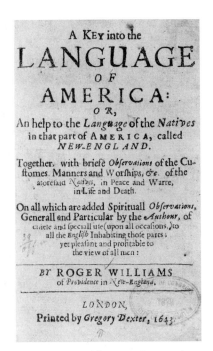

Roger Williams, *A Key into the Language of America* (1643), courtesy of the Rosenbach Museum & Library.

Williams, who lived among native communities. A Puritan whose unorthodox views alienated him from both the Massachusetts Bay and the Plymouth colonies, Williams has been reclaimed by some contemporary scholars as a democratic and pluralistic hero. Born in London, Williams studied at Cambridge, where he received his B.A. in 1627, but which he left in 1629, without having completed his M.A., to become a Puritan chaplain. He sailed to the New World on December 10, 1630; there tensions almost immediately arose between him and various members of the Puritan hierarchy (including, at different times, William Bradford, John Winthrop, and Cotton Mather—writers featured in Unit 3, "Utopian Promise").

The primary theological and political position that distinguished Williams was his assertion that church and state should be separate entities, with neither one having jurisdiction in the matters of the other. This was the first American articulation of the separation of church and state, appearing some 150 years before Thomas Jefferson's, and it did not sit at all well with the Puritan oligarchy (though it is worth noting that, unlike Jefferson's, Williams's concern was that the *church* not be corrupted by the *state*). In particular, Williams argued that the Massachusetts Bay Puritans should distance themselves from England (and therefore from English material support) by becoming Separatists, that their royal charter was invalid since Christians had no right to heathen lands, and that civil authorities should not meddle in spiritual affairs. When he was charged with subversion and spreading discord, he moved from Boston to Plymouth, where he established friendly trading relations with the Indians. Williams soon became pastor to Salem, where he continued preaching his subversive doctrines and in 1635 was indicted for heresy and divisiveness and sentenced to be banished. He escaped this fate only by fleeing to an Indian settlement, where he purchased land from the Narragansetts and founded Providence. This city became a haven for exiles and outcasts, from Anne Hutchinson to Baptists, Seekers, Antinomians, Quakers, and Jews.

Throughout his life Williams held important offices and fought for Native American rights, acting as negotiator for the Narragansetts during King Philip's War (which did not prevent them from being all but decimated by the end of that war). Although he produced various texts, his most famous is *A Key into the Language of America* (1643), which is in part a promotional tract for New World settlement in the tradition of Thomas Harriot's *A Brief and True Report of the New Found Land of Virginia*. *A Key into the Language of America*, however, is much more complicated ideologically: it is also an ethnographic study of Native American culture, a grammar of Native American languages, a defense of Native American cultures in the face of European allegations of immorality, and a lament for the "false religion" of the natives. Although Williams shared the common European assumption that only Christianity could save souls, this text does reveal his interest in analyzing American Indian language and culture on its own terms rather than by Western standards alone. Williams, like many Puritans, subscribed to the theory that Indians were ancestors of one of the "lost tribes" of Israel, applying a falsely Eurocentric view of native genealogy. Still, Williams remains one of the most powerful seventeenth-century European voices of sympathy and admiration for the American Indian.

TEACHING TIPS

■ Have your students write a natural history of, or promotional tract for, a place in which they have lived, using the standard structure of Renaissance travel literature. How does their work compare to Harriot's or Williams's?

■ Have your students write a first-contact narrative about meeting the Narragansetts or Wampanoags from a Puritan point of view. What is likely to have concerned them? What differences are they likely to have noticed? How is their text a **bicultural production**?

■ Ask your students to compare the Puritan creation stories (Genesis, for example) to those of the Native Americans in the East. What does each tell us about how they view humans? How they view the supernatural? How they view the relationship between the two?

QUESTIONS

Comprehension: What does Williams say about the religion of the natives?

Comprehension: According to Williams, why did he write *A Key into the Language of America*?

Context: What is the effect of Williams's constructing his book as "an implicit dialogue" that "respects the native language of it"? Keep in mind that there was a range of seventeenth-century opinion about how the Indians should be treated, with some advocating negotiation and partnership and others arguing for their elimination. Do you think Williams implies a value judgment when he describes the Narragansett language as "exceeding[ly] copious"?

Context: Compare Williams's attitude toward the Indians with Thomas Harriot's (below). What message about Native Americans does each try to convey to his Renaissance English readers?

Exploration: To what extent is Williams "ethnocentric"? That is, to what extent does he seem to assume that European culture and beliefs are true and correct and that, therefore, alternative cultures and beliefs must be inferior?

Exploration: Compare Williams's portrait of the Narragansetts to Mary Rowlandson's (Unit 3). What, besides circumstance, seems to account for his greater sympathy?

Exploration: Spanish American grammars of the New World from the sixteenth and seventeenth centuries tended to be organized in the same format as Latin grammars. Williams's grammar, on the other hand, is startlingly new in that it organizes its linguistic information by situation. What impact does this structure have upon the message Williams hopes to convey?

WILLIAMS WEB ARCHIVE

[1210] John Underhill, *The Figure of the Indians' Fort or Palizado in New England and the Manner of the Destroying It by Captayne Underhill and Captayne Mason* (1638), courtesy of the Library of Congress [LC-USZ62-32055]. In 1636, the English settlers engaged in a campaign to wipe out the Pequot tribe of New England. Captain John Underhill chronicled the Pequot War in his *News from America* (1638), providing this sketch of the Puritans, along with their Narragansett allies, encircling and destroying a Pequot village.

[1232] Roger Williams, *The Bloudy Tenent, of Persecution, for Cause of Conscience, Discussed, in a Conference Betweene Truth and Peace* (1644), courtesy of the Library of Congress. Roger Williams's *Bloudy Tenent of Persecution* was a plea to the Massachusetts legislature for freedom of conscience for himself and others in the Massachusetts Bay Colony.

[5219] Roger Williams, *A Key into the Language of America* (1643), courtesy of the Rosenbach Museum & Library. Williams held important offices and fought for Native American rights, including acting as negotiator for the Narragansetts during King Philip's War. In 1643 he published *A Key into the Language of America*. *A Key*, which deals with Narragansett language and culture, is an unusual and sympathetic mix of ethnography, grammar, and promotional tract.

[6942] Christopher Moses, Photo of Statue of Roger Williams, Providence, Rhode Island (2002), courtesy of Christopher Moses. A Puritan whose unorthodox views alienated him from both the Massachusetts Bay and the Plymouth colonies, Roger Williams has been reclaimed by some contemporary scholars as a democratic and pluralistic hero.

Thomas Harriot (1560–1621)

Born in England and educated at Oxford, Thomas Harriot was employed as a young man by the explorer Sir Walter Ralegh. In 1585 he accompanied Ralegh's New World expedition to Roanoke, where, as a naturalist, he collaborated with painter John White to study the landscape and its inhabitants. Although Harriot must have kept notebooks, none survives. The existing record of his observations is *A Brief and True Report of the New Found Land of Virginia* (1588), an optimistic account of native culture that seems to have been written at Ralegh's direction. Although this work lacks candor—Harriot avoids mentioning how the colonists fled a brutal storm by ship—it does acknowledge how the Indians were gradually devastated by disease and provides detailed descriptions of these native peoples in their soon-to-be-changing natural environment.

Harriot's account provides some of the only information we possess on the Roanoke people, who perished from disease soon after the Roanoke colony ceased to exist. South of the Potomac River the Virginian Algonquian peoples were united in the Powhatan Confederacy in the late 1500s. The leader of this confederacy, Powhatan, would eventually pledge his daughter to John Rolfe; and, if we are to believe John Smith, this same Indian princess, Pocahontas, saved Smith's life. Harriot's and John White's accounts provide us with important cultural information. Colonial accounts by travelers such as Harriot contribute to our limited understanding of the Native American communities whose own records have not survived.

TEACHING TIPS

■ Have your students write an ethnographic account of their own family, class, or school as if they were outside observers. You may want to have them do this in two stages: first, have them compose a description of behavior and practices without any analysis; second, have them switch papers with another student and analyze the "meanings" of the group. This short-circuits students' assumptions that they already know these meanings, and it can viscerally implant a sense of unease or even invasion on the part of the object of the ethnography.

■ Students often assume that Renaissance explorers used our own understandings of race and "otherness" when categorizing Native Americans, even though our notions of race today are much indebted to Enlightenment (i.e., eighteenth-century) thought. Show your students Konrad Kolble's map of the New World, which depicts four famous European explorers at its corners, and ask them to identify what makes these figures, literally and conceptually, different from the depictions of Native Americans? What does this map imply about what makes someone civilized or savage? How are these categories reflected in White's drawings and Harriot's descriptions?

[7429] John White, *The Manner of Attire and Painting Themselves, When They Goe to Their General Huntings or at Theire Solemne Feasts* (c. 1585), courtesy of The British Museum.

HARRIOT WEB ARCHIVE

[1368] Konrad Kolble, *Replica of a Map of the Americas with Portraits of Christopher Columbus, Amerigo Vespucci, Ferdinand Magellan and Francisco Pizarro Around Border* (1970), courtesy of the Library of Congress [LC-USZ62-89908]. In Konrad Kolble's facsimile of a map published in 1600 by Theodor de Bry, we see four of the most famous European explorers framing the New World, a testimony to its assumed possession by the Old.

Comprehension: What does Harriot emphasize about North America and its native inhabitants?

Comprehension: What precisely does Harriot object to in the religion of Native Americans?

Context: *A Brief and True Report of the New Found Land of Virginia* is largely an advertisement for European settlement in the New World. How do you see Harriot constructing his description of the New World in order to make it seem attractive to ambitious Europeans? How does his view of the New World compare to Williams's?

Context: To what extent is *A Brief and True Report* a conduct book for the English? Conduct books were manuals that sought to inculcate proper etiquette, behavior, and therefore values in their readers. In what ways does Harriot advise the English to behave in the New World?

Context: Compare Harriot's description of the Roanokes' dress with "The Manner of Their Attire and Painting Themselves" [7429]. Has White taken any liberties or filled in any gaps?

Exploration: Like Bernal Díaz del Castillo (Unit 2), Harriot emphasizes that he is giving a "true" report. How does Harriot establish the veracity of his report? Does he give any clues to what a false report might be? How do his attempts at establishing authority compare to those of Díaz del Castillo?

Exploration: How do Harriot's objections to native religion show his unspoken assumptions about what is spiritual and what is material?

[1900] John White, *The Manner of Their Fishing* (c. 1585), courtesy of the John Carter Brown Library, Brown University. One of John White's drawings not taken directly from real life: he shows a dip net and spear (daytime fishing techniques) and a fire in a canoe (used to attract fish at night). White combined disparate New World fishing methods and a mix of species in this and other paintings.

[7429] John White, *The Manner of Their Attire and Painting Themselves, When They Goe to Their General Huntings or at Theire Solemne Feasts* (c. 1585), courtesy of The British Museum. This is a portrait of an Algonquian Indian (either Secotan or Pomeiooc) from Virginia. Elite families and chiefs were elaborately decorated with paint, beads, and quills to signal their status and power. The pose, taken from sixteenth-century European portraits, emphasizes the importance of the subject and the occasion.

Suggested Author Pairings

LUCI TAPAHONSO AND LOUISE ERDRICH

Both Luci Tapahonso and Louise Erdrich emphasize the relationship of female power to Native American culture. Tapahonso's poems explore the relationship among generations of women, the image of birth as a renewal and a healing, and the power of such mythical female figures as Dawn Woman. She explores a worldview that itself emphasizes connection and change. You may want to contrast this female-centered space with the white town in "Fleur." At the beginning of "Fleur" Erdrich casts the male Chippewa as frightened by the spiritual connection Fleur has to nature, marked most clearly by her supposed multiple deaths and resurrections. Fleur (whose very name implies a link to nature) makes the men panic. Even Pauline, although a less sympathetic character than Fleur, manages to have a profound effect on her world and certainly can't be considered weak or yielding. You may also want to compare Tapahonso's verse style with the light-hearted Chippewa love songs, or compare their view of gender relations with that in Erdrich's work.

LESLIE MARMON SILKO AND SIMON J. ORTIZ

In their works Leslie Marmon Silko and Simon J. Ortiz engage with the intersection of modern warfare and native cultures. Tayo, the protagonist of Silko's *Ceremony*, takes a journey away from the European American contexts of World War II and alcoholism toward the native contexts of the Ts'eh, a mountain spirit. This journey is healing, a movement away from the corruption and destruction of the West and toward wholeness, harmony, and peace. Ortiz paints a powerful yet simple image of European American violence in "8:50 AM Ft. Lyons VAH": the straight line of the hospital wall blocks the view of the geese. That line stands not only for the hospital built to cope with the ravages of Western war, but also for the entirety of the West's antinatural worldview, where the living contours of the land and its creatures are cut and divided by the rigid measures of an arrogant technology. Both writers emphasize the power of the oral tradition and its constant adaptation to new contexts and experiences. Have your students compare the differences between the oral traditions of these closely related communities.

STORIES OF THE BEGINNING OF THE WORLD AND THE NARRATIVES OF ROGER WILLIAMS AND THOMAS HARRIOT

Stories of the Beginning of the World and the narratives of Roger Williams and Thomas Harriot provide two different views of the world and of native peoples. In the Stories of the Beginning of the World, we hear, through translators, of the cosmographies of the Iroquois and Pima peoples. These accounts contrast with Harriot's and Williams's views on how native cultures (specifically the Narragansett and Roanoke) are structured and what the communities value. It is worth calling students' attention to the differences in content and form of these accounts. In addition, you may want to discuss the different goals of the stories and Renaissance travel accounts. While the creation stories aim to integrate the listener into the community and its worldview, both Williams's and Harriot's works are in a sense advertisements for European settlement of the New World. While neither author's narrative is virulently racist and ethnocentric in the ways of many of their contemporaries' works (compare, say, the works of John Smith and William Bradford, two important Englishmen who have little or no sympathy for the Indians), they still aim to assimilate the "other" into the European cosmography.

BLACK ELK AND GHOST DANCE SONGS

Black Elk's narrative is usefully read alongside the Ghost Dance songs. It recounts the period of the Ghost Dance and the devastating experience of Wounded Knee, and it provides important contextual information on the goals of the Ghost Dance movement. Black Elk's vision might also be usefully compared to that of the Ghost Dance songs, as in many ways it signals the continuing renewal of Lakota culture, long after the Ghost Dance movement has ended. Students should pay attention to the use of repetition and significant numbers in both the vision and the songs. These texts illustrate the ways in which native spiritual traditions often appropriated and reinvented Christianity. Students should pay attention to the messianic nature of the Ghost Dance songs and their use of the Shaker (Christian) tradition, as well as to Black Elk's own continuing dedication to a Lakota brand of Catholicism. These texts provide a superb opportunity to discuss the problems inherent in translation. To what extent is the power of the vision in the songs lost in the movement into English and into a Western "literary" form?

CORE CONTEXTS

"God Is Red": The Clashes and Contacts of Native Religion and Christianity

Although Vine Deloria Jr. argues in his classic and polemical book *God Is Red: A Native View of Religion* that Christianity and Native religions are polar opposites, since the very first days of European-Indian contact, many Native Americans have adopted and adapted Christianity for their own purposes. As scholars have noted, native religions always sought out new forms of power that could be incorporated into their religious practices. Thus while white New England missionaries often assumed that they were converting natives into "red Puritans," practitioners of Native Christianity most often created an **emergent religion**: one that added new spiritual practices to an existing framework.

Although there are probably as many different forms of Native Christianity as there are Native Christians, a few basic generalizations provide an important starting point for understanding the forms taken by this melding of religions. For instance, Deloria argues that the fundamental difference between Christianity and native religion is an orientation to time in the former and an orientation to space in the latter. That is, Christianity is a time-based religion, predicated on the ideas that the universe has a definite beginning and a definite end and that human life is a sort of "dress rehearsal" for the last judgment and afterlife-placement. Native religion, Deloria claims, is space-based: it grows out of and accounts for the particular landscape of the tribe, has no conception of a primordial time when humans were pure but then fell into sin, and anticipates no future of a radically different order (as Christianity posits will come about at the Second Coming of Christ). For native religion, humans have always been and will always be the way they are, and the world will always be more or less as it is; even the afterlife is primarily a pleasant version of life in the tribe. Our job, writes Deloria, is to deal ethically and responsibly with each other

[2466] John Eliot, First page, *Genesis from the Holy Bible: Containing the Old Testament and the New* (1663), courtesy of the Annenberg Rare Book and Manuscript Library, University of Pennsylvania.

[4210] Anonymous, *John Collier and Hopi Men* (c. 1920), courtesy of CSULB, National Archives.

"GOD IS RED"
WEB ARCHIVE

[2059] N. C. Wyeth, *The Supplicant* (1919), courtesy of Reed College Library Special Collections, Portland, Oregon. Illustration from the N. C. Wyeth edition of *The Last of the Mohicans.* Here Cora pleads with the Delaware sachem Tamenund for the life of her sister, Alice. The theme of white women at the mercy of "savage" natives was made popular by early American captivity narratives.
[2466] John Eliot, First page, *Genesis from the Holy Bible: Containing the Old Testament and the New* (1663), courtesy of the Annenberg Rare Book and Manuscript Library, University of Pennsylvania. This translation of the first page of Genesis into Massachuset, an Algonquian language, was done with the help of John Sassamon (Massachuset), whose murder in 1675 for being an English informant began King Philip's War.
[2836] Bernard Picard, Illustration from *Cérémonies et Coutumes Religieuses des Peuples Idolâtres* (1723), courtesy of the Jay I. Kislak Foundation, Inc. European depictions of Native American ceremonies, such as this one from Picard's six-volume masterpiece on world religions, often tell us more about Europeans and their anxieties than about the actual experiences they record.

and with the web of all creation to which we are here and now connected—the land, the animals, the plants, the spirits of the ancestors—rather than to prepare for some future moment in which all will be transformed. Deloria's generalizations do not hold true for all native cultures: some tribes such as the Pomo of California do speak of a time in which the world was radically different. Even though Deloria's abstractions have been hotly debated by scholars, this healing vision of spiritual practice is reflected in the work of many contemporary Native American writers, especially and most elaborately in Silko's *Ceremony*, but also in the poetry of Ortiz and Tapahonso.

Native versions of Christianity often present a mixture of these two religious outlooks. For example, a popular story for missionaries was the idea that Native Americans were one of the lost tribes of Israelites. This story fit with the notion of Christianity as a time-based religion: from the missionaries' perspective, American Indians' history began with the arrival of the whites and moved forward with conversion and the eventual return of Christ. For early Native American Christian converts, however, the story was not so simple. Many, such as Guaman Poma of Peru and William Apess (Unit 4), argued that Native Americans were already Christians upon the arrival of the whites—in fact, they were much better Christians than the Europeans! This notion reflects the perspective that humans have always been and will always be the way they are and that the world will always be more or less as it is. Similarly, movements such as the Ghost Dance combine Christian apocalyptic thought with a basic faith in the interconnectedness of the land, the animals, the plants, the spirits of the ancestors. By appropriating elements of Christianity, Ghost Dance dancers and singers aimed to fight the enemy with its own weapons, in this case with religious firearms.

The history of Christianity and Native American communities has not always been uplifting. Since the earliest days of European settlement, Native Americans have been the object of strenuous conversion attempts that nevertheless failed to guarantee them equal treatment either before the law or in American religious life. Indeed, Native American converts were often viewed with suspicion both by their own communities and by European settlers: for example, Mary Rowlandson (Unit 3) has only unkind things to say about "Praying Indians" and indeed most praying Indians were forcibly interned and starved on an island in Boston Harbor during King Philip's War. Samson Occom (Unit 3), a Mohegan from Connecticut who was converted to Christianity at sixteen and later became a popular preacher in America and England, recalls similar mistreatment. In his *A Short Narrative of My Life* (1768), he sums up the years of discrimination and abuse he suffered: "I *must Say*, 'I believe [my mistreatment by white Christians] is because I am a poor Indian.' I Can't help that God has made me So; I did not make my self so.—"

Comprehension: According to Deloria, what is one basic difference between Native American religions and Christianity?

Comprehension: In what way does the Ghost Dance religion display the influence of Christianity?

Comprehension: What is an emergent religion?

Context: Find all the moments where the contemporary native writers in this unit blur the sacred and the secular. For example, is Tapahonso's "A Breeze Swept Through" a religious poem? Why or why not? In what sense might Ortiz's "8:50 AM Ft. Lyons VAH," despite its basically secular surface, be religious in a native sense?

Context: Using Ts'eh as an example, discuss the role gender plays in Pueblo religion.

Context: Reformer John Collier (1884–1968) created the American Indian Defense Association in 1923 to fight the assimilationist policies of the Dawes Severalty Act of 1887, and he was instrumental in salvaging religious rights for Indians. Consider the archive image of him and two Hopi men: what does their body language say about their relationship, and by extension the relationship in the early twentieth century between white and native cultures?

Exploration: You may never have seen a version of the Bible written in a nonmodern language, as in the archive image of the Bible translated into Massachuset, a native language. The Bible was originally written mostly in ancient Hebrew and Greek, so even the contemporary versions with which you might be more familiar are translations and therefore at some distance from the original. How do you think translation of sacred texts might affect their meaning? Does this "Indian Bible" seem less strange than, say, Chippewa songs in English?

Exploration: Compare Mary Rowlandson's vision of the Narragansetts and "Praying Indians" to Roger Williams's vision of the Narragansetts. What is the relationship between Puritanism and Narragansett religion in each text? What is the potential for conversion?

Exploration: Why do you think someone like Samson Occom would have converted to Christianity? How is it that a person can be brought up with one worldview and then later change it? Occom says that he was never really treated fairly by white Christians, but in what ways do you think he might have nevertheless benefited from being a Christian?

Exploration: Challenge Deloria's claims about Native American religions. For example, to what extent is myth an example of a "primordial time"?

Healing Arts: The Navajo Night Chant (Nightway)

Healing songs and chants are an important genre in Native American oral traditions. As a general rule, songs and chants seek to re-create a state rather than an event. Songs and chants are also rarely told in a

[3249] Joseph-Francois Lafitau, *An Iroquois Funeral as Observed by a French Missionary, Early 1700s* (1724), courtesy of the Library of Congress, Rare Books and Special Collections. Detail from *Moeurs des Sauvages Amériquians Comparées aux Moeurs des Premiers Temps* (Customs of the American Indians Compared with the Customs of Primitive Times [in Europe]). This drawing provides insight into Iroquois death rituals.

[4210] Anonymous, *John Collier and Hopi Men* (c. 1920), courtesy of CSULB, National Archives. Indian Commissioner John Collier helped fight the U.S. government's assimilationist policies and argued for the protection of American Indian cultures, religions, and languages. He is best known for the Indian Reorganization Act of 1934.

[6783] Edward S. Curtis, *Altar Peyote with Rattle (Osage)* (1930), courtesy of the Library of Congress [LC E77.C97]. The Osage Indians of Missouri were ardent practitioners of the Peyote Religion. Ceremonies include a prayer meeting in a house designed for the ritual and the singing of peyote songs. Taken from a cactus, peyote buttons have hallucinogenic properties. Peyote cults entered the United States from Mexico in the nineteenth century.

[7588] George Catlin, *Dog Feast*, from *The Manners, Customs, and Condition of the North American Indians* (1842), courtesy of Tilt and Bogue, London. In letter no. 28, Catlin remarks, "The dog-feast is given, I believe, by all tribes in North America; and by them all, I think, this faithful animal, as well as the horse, is sacrificed in several different ways, to appease offended Spirits or Deities" (*Letters and Notes on the Manners, Customs, and Condition of the North American Indians*).

[5951] Anonymous, *Rattle Shock Rite* (1980–2002), courtesy of the Museum of Northern Arizona Photo Archives.

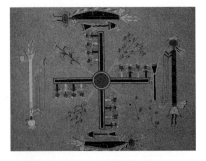

[5953] Anonymous, *Whirling logs* (n.d.), from J. C. Faris, *The Nightway: A History and a History of Documentation of a Navajo Ceremonial* (1990), courtesy of the Museum of Northern Arizona Photo Archives.

vacuum: the Night Chant, for example, is composed of a whole series of practices—including dances, the construction of sandpaintings, and the use of prayer sticks—that constitute a nine-day healing ceremony traditionally performed by the Navajo. Although the Night Chant is specific to the Navajo, it provides an important example of the interrelatedness of language, healing, and spirituality in native traditions. It is one of the great masterpieces of the oral tradition.

The Night Chant is a "way" insofar as it attempts not just to break into the natural course of an illness, but in facts sets the "patient" on the path or way toward reestablishing the natural harmony and balance that allow for health. For the Navajo, who migrated to the Southwest from the northern lands sometime between seven hundred and one thousand years ago, the Night Chant is one of many ceremonial chants meant to affect the world in some concrete manner. The Night Chant is a healing ceremony, a treatment for illness, especially paralysis, blindness, and deafness. In the words of anthropologist and ethnographer James C. Faris, Night Chant practices are those that "order, harmonize and re-establish and situate social relations." Hence the ceremony emphasizes humans' ability to control their world and their responsibility to use that control in the service of balance, respect, and healing. If the Holy People—the ancestors or the spirits—inflict suffering, it is because people have broken the rules; the Night Chant attempts to put the rules back together, to restore the conditions conducive to order, balance, and health.

The ceremony begins at sunset when the chanter, the medicine man who conducts the ceremony and the only one with the knowledge of proper Night Chant practice, enters the home of the patient, the one who is to be cured. After a ritual call for participation ("Come on the trail of song")—which emphasizes the role of not only the patient but all guests present to form a community of healing—the patient sits to the west of a fire. There follow elaborate chants, songs, and dances. The first four days are devoted to purification, after which the Holy People are called upon. On the sunrise of the ninth day, the patient is invited to look eastward and greet the dawn, representative of renewal. The chant is fundamentally narrative, although not necessarily continuous, and its specific details and enactments vary greatly among different medicine men and the particular needs of the patient. Faris emphasizes the flexibility and fluidity of the elements of the story. There is no central episode that must be retold in all cases for the ceremony to be effective; rather, specific episodes arise from local situations, and no single medicine man possesses the knowledge of every possible episode. But there is generally a basic storyline, which tells of a long-ago cultural hero of particular visionary power who gathers the details of how to properly conduct the ceremony from the Holy People. The Night Chant is therefore in part a perpetual retelling of itself; it is neither entertainment nor abstract teaching, but the ritual reenactment of its own origin. In this origin is the way toward order, which is the way toward healing. Through this retelling the singer aims to bring about **hózhó**, or holiness, harmony, beauty.

The sandpaintings reflect this goal of balance and harmony-seeking. Created for the ceremony and immediately wiped away, the sandpaintings elaborately echo some of the main patterns and images of the chant. As sacred artifacts, they are not intended to be recorded through film or painting. Because they are designed specifically to attract the attention of (and eventually embody) the Holy People, it would be a dangerous violation to allow them to exist after the proper time for spiritual contact had passed. Those included in the *American Passages* archive were painted by a priest based on sketches taken from the work of a medicine man who authorized them to be shown to the public. Reproductions such as these have usually been altered to diffuse their power. Surviving notes suggest that there are several in-accuracies in the Rattle Shock Rite image; for

[5742] Anonymous, *Navajo Shaman Drypainting a Remedy* (n.d.), courtesy of the American Museum of Natural History.

example, the owl feathers on the central figure should be spotted and decorations should be added to the belt of the central figure. Like the multiple levels of transmission that Black Elk's narrative went through (see above), the various mediations these images have undergone continue to define a communal center of identity and knowledge in opposition to the outsider—however sympathetic he or she may be.

QUESTIONS

Comprehension: Which tribe is the Night Chant associated with?

Comprehension: What is the Night Chant used for?

Comprehension: What acts does the Night Chant involve?

Context: In Silko's *Ceremony*, Betonie is a mixed-blood Navajo healer. In what sense can you see the Night Chant or something like it being used in this novel? How is what Tayo goes through like the ritual described above? To what extent does his ceremony take into consideration contemporary sources of illness? How does it seek to deal with these sources of pain?

Context: Examine one of the sandpaintings in the archive. How does it seek to achieve harmony and balance? How does it exemplify *hózhó*? Compare the strategies it uses for achieving harmony and balance to those in Tapahonso's poetry.

Context: Examine the Rattle Shock Rite image in the archive. Note that it is centered around four figures that represent gods of the North, South, East, and West. Why might these figures be important in *Ceremony*? Why do you think 4 might be such an essential number for many Native American beliefs (as opposed, say, to the 3 and 7 of Christianity)?

Context: Compare the text of the Night Chant to that of the Ghost Dance songs. What strategies does each use to achieve harmony and balance? How are these strategies related to the goal of each text?

Exploration: Why might a Navajo not want a non–Native American to know the details of the Night Chant? Does this seem reasonable to

"HEALING ARTS"
WEB ARCHIVE

[5741] Anonymous, *Two Navaho Shaman Dry Painting to Cure an Illness* (n.d.), courtesy of the American Museum of Natural History. Navajo sand paintings, or "dry" paintings, are meant to summon and embody the spirits of the holy people and therefore are wiped away immediately after the Night Chant ceremony.

[5742] Anonymous, *Navajo Shaman Drypainting a Remedy* (n.d.), courtesy of the American Museum of Natural History. The Navajo Night Chant is a nine-day healing ceremony that includes dances, sandpaintings, and prayer sticks. Sandpaintings reflect the Navajo value of *hózhó*, or holiness, harmony, beauty.

[5743] Anonymous, *Navajo Shaman Puts Finishing Touches on Remedy Painting* (n.d.), courtesy of the American Museum of Natural History. The Navajo use sandpaintings in an elaborate, nine-day ceremony designed to cure illness by restoring order, balance, and harmony. The paintings are wiped away as soon as the ritual is complete.

you? Are there things about your life you wouldn't want others to know, even though their knowledge would not affect your life? Navajos believe that knowing things about people *can* affect people. If knowledge could give people power over you, would you be less likely to give people access to personal information?

Exploration: Do you think the sandpainting images in the archive are aesthetically pleasing? How do you know "good" art when you see it? For example, to what extent is it reasonable to assume that realistic figures constitute good art?

Singing Mothers and Storytelling Grandfathers: The Art and Meaning of Pueblo Pottery

Pottery is an important Native American art form that dates back thousands of years. As Simon J. Ortiz notes, "[Pottery making] has more to do with a sense of touching than with seeing because fingers have to know the texture of clay and how the pottery is formed from lines of shale, strata and earth movements." Pueblo pottery is considered some of the most beautiful, and it has deep ties to storytelling traditions. Pueblo cultures, along with those of the Navajo and Apache, constitute the dominant native traditions in the American Southwest. Pottery dates back over fifteen hundred years to the Anasazi period, but in the past few decades there has been a tremendous revival in pottery-making among the Pueblo people, led in part by the Cochiti Pueblo potter Helen Cordero and her Storyteller dolls. Cordero's pottery challenged the appropriation of Native American art by white art collectors.

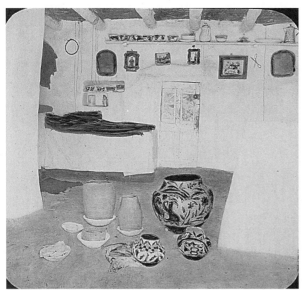

Native works of art and craft have a troubled history in mainstream American culture. Like so much of native culture, objects such as bowls and dolls were at least potentially sacred: if used in certain ritual contexts, they acted as embodied prayers to ancestors or gods. The kachinas in the archive are good examples of this: they are dolls, but they embody a ritual significance as well [8110, 8209]. As such, they were not to be handled and scrutinized by curious Europeans, even investigative anthropologists. Nevertheless, soon after the introduction of railroads into the Southwest, Indians (many of whom found themselves desperately poor after having their traditional ways of life disrupted) began producing pottery and other artifacts for European commercial consumption. This trade, which began in the 1880s, allowed a modest income for many Pueblo and other native peoples. In most cases, the objects differed in subtle but profoundly significant ways from the ones intended for tribal use, and so did not directly endanger the tribe's traditions: this practice continues to be a concern for some native writers who incorporate traditional material in their work.

Commercial production had the effect of making native-made objects into either mysterious oddities or "artworks" whose consumers had no sense of their sacred origin. Hence, for much of the twentieth century, many Indians felt invaded and exploited by the dissemination of their artifacts into white America.

As anthropologist Barbara Babcock and photographers Guy Monthan and Doris Monthan detail in their book *The Pueblo Storyteller*, in the late 1950s Helen Cordero began producing pottery that recaptured and transformed the traditional Pueblo ways of art. Cordero turned to the traditional construction of objects that possessed deep cultural significance: these are called fetishes (if used in ceremony), figurines, or effigies. Traditionally, clay for the Pueblo was a living substance with its own spirit, so that anything constructed from clay acquires, as Babcock writes, "a kind of personal and conscious existence as it [is] being made." All Pueblo ceremonies used clay objects, which are closely associated with the original creation of life in every known Pueblo creation story. Some of these objects were vessels and some were human figures—for example, those known as "kachina dolls." The dolls stand for kachinas, masked supernatural spirits who are said to enter into the bodies of Pueblo dancers during ceremonies and act as conduits between the world of humans and the world of spirits or gods.

Another such figure was the "Singing Mother" found among the Cochiti. These figures, which may not have been ceremonial but certainly partook of the Pueblo assumptions that made ceremonies possible, are the ones that Cordero's Storyteller dolls echo and revise. The figures of a mother singing to her child evoke fertility; as Babcock writes, they make "the connection between human reproduction and other, life-giving forms of generation." As such, childbirth and child raising are linked to the passing down of stories and songs across the generations, emphasizing the interlinking of all creation, including the inextricability of human culture and the natural world. Between 1900 and 1960, Pueblo artifacts made for trade were weak in quality and few in number. But Cordero first created a figure that evoked the Singing Mother on commission for a white folk art collector, and in the process managed to transform the old tradition into a living art form for the present. As always in native traditions, she emphasized the local and the specific: she changed the mother figure to a male, modeled on her grandfather whom she remembers as a powerful storyteller, and she added multiple children to the figures (there are as many as thirty on some pieces). None of her hundreds of figures are identical, nor are the many figures created by Pueblo potters inspired by her work. They are images of the passing down of tradition that are themselves the evolution of tradition. For potters like Cordero, the importance of the clay and its relationship to the stories of the oral tradition help keep the art traditions alive.

Indians (many of whom became desperately poor after having their traditional ways of life disrupted) began producing pottery and other artifacts for sale. **[8122]** Santo Domingo tribe, Jar (n.d.), courtesy of the Portland Art Museum, gift of Elizabeth Cole Butler [1481]. Native American pottery, traditionally sacred or utilitarian, began to be produced in its contemporary "decorative" form in the late nineteenth century. In the 1920s and 1930s, dealers, archaeologists, and tribal members formed the Indian Arts Fund to collect traditional Pueblo pottery and encourage its production.

Comprehension: What does the Singing Mother represent?

Comprehension: What is a kachina?

Comprehension: When and why did Helen Cordero begin producing her pottery?

Context: How can you see Native American artistic traditions being kept alive but transformed in the contemporary writers discussed in this unit? For example, how is *Ceremony* not only a reiteration of healing rituals but also a specific comment on the effects of World War II on Native Americans? What is Betonie's relationship to the Navajo community? How does this inform the way he uses ceremonies?

Exploration: It is a curious fact that there is very little evidence of Pueblo figurative ceramics from about 1500 to about 1875. This happens to correspond to the period of intense Spanish colonialism in the American Southwest. Why do you think we have this gap in the historical record?

Exploration: How is passing down traditions analogous to childbirth? In what ways are these acts similar, and in what ways different?

Exploration: Could those Pueblo who made pottery for white tourists be considered to be "selling out"? Would you have done the same thing? Does our contemporary culture show examples of once-sacred objects or ideas being used for profit?

EXTENDED CONTEXTS

Native Weavers and the Art of Basketry

> He breathed on her and gave her something that she could not see or hear or smell or touch, and it was preserved in a little basket, and by all of the arts of design and skilled handwork.
>
> —Kotai'aqan, *Columbia River Basketry*

Basketry, like pottery, is an art that is found in numerous Native American cultures but differs greatly from tribe to tribe. As Mary Dodge Schlick, the author of *Columbia River Basketry: Gift of the Ancestors, Gift of the Earth,* points out, for centuries baskets have been part of vast trade networks in which friends and acquaintances meet, gamble, and trade foodstuffs and goods: baskets are one way of carrying these valuables. Baskets also play important roles in spiritual and medicinal rituals, as attested to in Greg Sarris's work on Pomo basket weaver and healer Mabel McKay. McKay wove her baskets for collectors and for general consumption, and all were made under the guidance of a spirit who taught her healing songs and imbued her baskets with a spiritual power. Baskets like the Pomo feather baskets featured in the archive [6303, 8118, 8119] should be thought of as spiritual, as well as material, objects.

As archaeologist A. L. Kroeber and many others have noted, Pomo

[6303] Anonymous, Pomo feather gift basket (n.d.), courtesy of the Douglas F. Cooley Memorial Art Gallery, Reed College.

baskets are among the finest in the world. He writes, "To the Pomo, these served as gifts and treasures, and above all, they were destroyed in honor of the dead." The Pomo live in northern California and are known for the intricacy of their baskets, particularly their beaded baskets, feather baskets, and miniature baskets [6303]. Sometimes the baskets held medicines, but other times nothing at all; as Susan Billy, a Pomo basket weaver, explains, "People frequently ask me what these ceremonial baskets hold. They did not have to hold anything, because the basket itself was all that was needed. The basket contained the prayers and the wonderful, good energy that made it a ceremonial basket." Gift baskets were given to people of stature or people with whom one wanted to cement a relationship [8081, 8119]. Small gift baskets were sometimes worn.

Other Native American communities, including the Nez Perce of Oregon and Washington, also wore baskets. Baskets hats, such as the one in the archive [8118], play a part in the oral tradition of the Columbia River peoples. For example, in one Wishxam myth, Grandmother uses a basket hat to teach Little Raccoon about the consequences of misbehavior. In many Native American communities, baskets play an important role in women's culture. Knowledge of how to make a basket hat, among other skills, was a sign that a young woman had reached adulthood in Columbia River culture. Women still wear these hats at powwows and other ceremonies.

QUESTIONS

Comprehension: How is basketry like pottery in its significance for native cultures?

Comprehension: How are Pomo baskets potentially spiritual as well as material objects?

Context: In his book *The Gift*, Marcel Mauss argues that gifts must be reciprocated in honor and prestige, if not in kind. How might the Pomo gift baskets create a reciprocal relationship with the giver? How does this compare to other instances of giving, in, say, Leslie Marmon Silko's *Ceremony*?

Context: Look carefully at one of the baskets in the archive and take note of the strategies it uses to create order and harmony. Compare it to one of the coyote or trickster tales in *The Norton Anthology of American Literature*. How does Coyote undo society's order? Is balance reinstated by the end of the tale?

Exploration: If baskets such as the Pomo gift baskets have a "wonderful, good energy," do we have any right to keep them in museums? What do you think happens to this energy in museums? How should items with spiritual significance be displayed? (You may want to read the essay by Greg Sarris, "A Culture Under Glass: The Pomo Basket," in *Keeping Slug Woman Alive*.)

Exploration: What women's traditions exist in your family? How are they passed along from one generation to the next?

[6307] Anonymous, Water jar, pitched with horsehair lug handles (n.d.), courtesy of the Douglas F. Cooley Memorial Art Gallery, Reed College.

"NATIVE WEAVERS" WEB ARCHIVE

[6303] Anonymous, Pomo feather gift basket (n.d.), courtesy of the Douglas F. Cooley Memorial Art Gallery, Reed College. The series of quill stitches in this coiled Pomo basket indicates the weaver's desire to continue her work during a menstrual period, which would be bad luck if she did not substitute bird quills for plant materials.

[6307] Anonymous, Water jar, pitched with horsehair lug handles (n.d.), courtesy of the Douglas F. Cooley Memorial Art Gallery, Reed College. Basketry objects found on the North American continent have been dated to as far back as 9000 B.C.

[6310] Anonymous, Coiled basket tray, rattlesnake design (n.d.), courtesy of Reed College, Douglas F. Cooley Memorial Art Gallery. Like pottery, basketry is important for storing and transferring food and other supplies.

[7416] Anonymous, Tray, Apache, San Carlos, Arizona (n.d.), courtesy of the New York State Historical Association, Thaw Collection. Beginning in the late 1800s, many Native Americans used the American flag as a decorative motif in their arts and crafts. Notice the crossed flags in the design of this Apache basket.

[8081] Pomo tribe, Gift basket (c.1930), courtesy of the Portland Art Museum, Elizabeth Cole Butler Collection. The Pomo are a coastal native group in Sonoma County, California. The basket is made of willow, sedge root, clam shell beads, abalone shell, meadowlark feathers, quail feathers, mallard duck feathers, flicker feathers, and dogbane. Pomo baskets are known for their spiritual, ceremonial, and healing properties.

[8118] Plateau Indians, Basketry hat (c. 1900), courtesy of the Portland Art Museum, Elizabeth Cole Butler Collection. Nimíipuu (Nez Perce) women wore fez-shaped basket hats as part of their everyday clothing. This hat is made from vegetal fiber, wool yarn, and a leather fringe. The Nez Perce were one of the tribes encountered by Lewis and Clark during their search for the Northwest Passage.

[8202] Yokut, Basket (c. 1900), courtesy of the Portland Art Museum, gift of Elizabeth Cole Butler. Yokut Indian women (Central California) learned to weave at an early age. Baskets were indispensable to Yokut daily life. Yokut baskets are known for their ornate designs, including human figures and animals. This basket is made of sedge root, red bud, bracken fern root, grass, and quail feathers.

[6693] Anonymous, *Bone Game, Makah* (c. 1900), courtesy of Larry Johnson and the Washington State Historical Society.

Sacred Play: Gambling in Native Cultures

Gambling has long been a part of Native American cultures. Hand games, like gift exchange, are an important way to redistribute goods among community members. Gambling is not all fun and games, however. In the oral traditions of native peoples, gambler figures, like tricksters, tend to be threshold figures who can move between the world of the living and the world of the dead. Gambler myths, however, tend to have a more gothic edge than trickster tales. Gamblers often preside over the world of the dead, rather than merely visit it, and they are often associated with the end of the world. In contrast, the transgressive nature of the trickster is often a creative or generative force. Thus, gambler stories often are about an individual or community facing fear of annihilation. In Leslie Marmon Silko's *Ceremony*, for example, the tribes' Cultural Hero challenges the Gambler. The stakes are high: the Hero works on behalf of the community, but wages his life. These crucial encounters dramatize the people's belief about how the original world was altered to its current form.

As Kathryn Gabriel points out in *Gambler Way*, gambling can be seen as a way of tapping into cosmic forces. At times an attempt to gain insight into or even control the otherwise unpredictable future, the outcomes of games can suggest what the cosmic forces have in store. Dice and other gaming equipment are even sacrificed on Hopi and Zuni altars. As Gabriel says about gambling in these communities, "It is likely that the rites were performed to discover the probable outcome of human effort, representing a desire to secure the guidance of the natural powers that dominated humanity." Various native games, such as dice or hoop and pole, invoke and elaborate basic assumptions about the universe, from the nature of causality to the constant tension between opposing forces. Moreover, the communal nature of the games fosters identity within the group. Still, the games are competitive: winning was often seen as a blessing and an assurance of continued order and balance—hence the high stakes and profound meaning of native gambling (medicine men sometimes perform ceremonies to invoke the aid of spirits in winning). Many native myths involve gambling, where divine power helps the protagonist win games of chance over antagonistic opponents. Because these are sacred rites, tribal members are reluctant to discuss their details. The Navajo, for example, fear speaking about gambling away from sacred times and places, lest doing so bring down the wrath of the cosmic forces (much as they would be loath to casually discuss the Nightway). In cultures where there is no need for a straight-edge distinction between the sacred and the secular, practices like gambling both reveal and maintain profound cultural values and beliefs. Never trivial or merely parasitic to "real" or "productive" activity, gambling always conveys deep meaning in native culture.

These traditional associations of gambling are present in contemporary debates over bingo palaces and Indian casinos. Because Indian nations are sovereign states, gambling is legal on tribal ground. For many native communities, such as the Pequot of Connecticut, casino revenues have led to an economic and hence cultural renaissance. Libraries and museums as well as educational and language programs are now available where none existed before. Critics, however, argue that legalized gambling in any form is merely a way of taxing the poor and disenfranchised.

Indeed, Indian gambling has long had its detractors. European settlers professed shock when confronted with the intensity of native American gambling. In 1775, Captain Bernard Romans said of a Choctaw hoop and pole game that it was "plain proof of the evil consequences of a violent passion for gaming upon all kinds, classes, and orders of men." And indeed, from a Western point of view, the stakes of native gaming seemed high; traditionally, players would sometimes continue betting until losing everything they owned (even including the clothes on their backs), and Captain Romans notes that several Choctaw committed suicide after such losses. Gambling in most native cultures is not an idle pastime and certainly is not understood as vice or bad habit. First, it is a very pragmatic way of redistributing goods and food without the bloodshed of fighting or even war. But more profoundly, gambling is a form of what has been called "sacred play"; like many aspects of native life, it is inseparable from spirituality.

[1092] William J. Carpenter, *Life on the Plains* (1915), courtesy of the Library of Congress [LC-USZ62-99804].

TEACHING TIPS

■ Although Longfellow based his *Song of Hiawatha* on Iroquois history and mythology, chapter 16 on the gambler Pau-Puk-Keewis is based on the Chippewa oral tradition (as collected by Henry Schoolcraft in the first half of the nineteenth century). Kathryn Gabriel considers Pau-Puk-Keewis "the nearly perfect archetype of the destructive Native gambler"; she notes that he is "derived from *Pauppu-ke-nay*, the Ojibwa/Chippewa trickster grasshopper who has the ability to shape-shift." Ask your students to read the excerpt from *Hiawatha* in the archive and use it as a backdrop for discussing Native American Gambler figures and for understanding the characterization of Fleur in Erdrich's story.

■ Lawrence Johnson's 1999 documentary *Hand Game* is an excellent introduction to traditional Native American gambling practices. *Hand Game* looks at eight Indian communities including the Crow, Spokane, Flathead, and Blackfeet. It investigates the world of bone, grass, or stick game—the most widely played gambling game in North America. This video includes interesting interviews with gaming participants and could be usefully paired with stories about gambler figures.

"SACRED PLAY"
WEB ARCHIVE

[1092] William J. Carpenter, *Life on the Plains* (1915), courtesy of the Library of Congress [LC-USZ62-99804]. Navajo and cowboy playing cards. These cards show the type of interethnic male-male bonding seen in James Fenimore Cooper's novels. Interaction like this largely died out when white males started to bring their families to settle in the West.

[6651] Anonymous, *Men Playing a Game in Subterranean Lodge at Chino Village* (n.d.), courtesy of the John Carter Brown Library. In what looks not unlike a ritual or ceremonial formation, these men are engaged in game-playing in an underground lodge. In Native American cultures, gaming is a sacred activity that in some cases allows the players to tap into cosmic forces.

[6693] Anonymous, *Bone Game, Makah* (c. 1900), courtesy of Larry Johnson and the Washington State Historical Society. This game, called the "bone game" by the Makah tribe of the Pacific Northwest, is often referred to as the "hand game" or the "stick game." The activity is guessing which hand is holding a piece of bone, but the game is complex and involves drumming, singing, and trickery.

[8225] Henry Wadsworth Longfellow, "Pau-Puk-Keewis," from *The Song of Hiawatha* (1855), courtesy of Ticknor and Fields, Boston. The sixteenth chapter of Longfellow's famous *Song of Hiawatha* tells the story of the gambler Pau-Puk-Keewis. Although Longfellow based this work on Iroquois history and mythology, Pau-Puk-Keewis comes from the Chippewa oral tradition.

QUESTIONS

Comprehension: Why was gambling important to many Native American cultures?

Comprehension: What are the main attributes of a gambler figure? How does Silko's gambler fit within this paradigm?

Comprehension: Compare gambler and trickster figures.

Comprehension: What is the relationship between the gambler and the cultural hero?

Context: Why do the men in "Fleur" react so strongly to Fleur Pillager's uncanny winning of the game? How do gender politics and religion operate in the story to provoke the men's rancor?

Context: Read the Winnebago trickster tale. How does the Winnebago trickster compare to the gambler? What is the role of each in creating culture?

Context: Compare the depiction of gambling in Leslie Marmon Silko's *Ceremony* and Louise Erdrich's *The Bingo Palace*. What role does the oral tradition of the Pueblo and Chippewa, respectively, play in each?

Exploration: Imagine that you are an advertising executive who has been asked to design a campaign to gain acceptance for a new Indian gambling facility near your community. What rhetoric will you employ? What claims will you refute?

Exploration: Compare the role of gambling in Leslie Marmon Silko's *Ceremony* to the role of gambling in the high society novels of Edith Wharton and Henry James (Unit 9). To what extent is gambling in these novels also about characters' attempts to control the otherwise unpredictable future? How do their experiences differ?

ASSIGNMENTS

Personal and Creative Responses

1. *Journal:* First, freewrite in your journal on whatever you know about Native American literature and cultures. Then, write a narrative from the point of view of a person of your own age who has just encountered Native American culture for the first time. What do you imagine that person would be thinking? What would he or she find most memorable? What emotions would he or she be feeling? What would he or she say to or ask the Native Americans (assuming communication could occur)?

2. *Poet's Corner:* Use one of the poems by Tapahonso or Ortiz as a model for a poem about an experience of your own. What about this model is helpful to you in expressing yourself? What seems to interfere or be bothersome? If you have written poems in the past, "translate" one of them into this form so that it echoes elements of the oral tradition. How does changing the form of your poem affect what you understand to be its meaning?

3. *Doing History:* Stage a fictional dialogue between Wovoka, the

Paiute prophet of the Ghost Dance religion, and a thoughtful, middle-class white person in the midwestern United States, in which they try to explain themselves to each other. Imagine this exchange takes place in early 1890, after the Ghost Dance has begun to spread but before the catastrophe of Wounded Knee. Wovoka is preaching a peaceful yet clearly anti-white spirituality (read the Wovoka selection in *The Norton Anthology of American Literature* before you do this assignment). The white person, sympathetic to human suffering and not prejudiced against Native Americans, is both anxious about the subversive potential of the Ghost Dance and unavoidably implicated in the society that has nearly decimated native culture. What can these two people say to each other that might build a bridge between them?

4. *Multimedia:* As Paula Gunn Allen says in the video, virtually all objects and practices in traditional American Indian life are "messages": "content-laden information that you can read." Using the *American Passages* image database, construct a multimedia presentation in which you analyze the images of such items as pottery, baskets, sandpaintings, masks, and dances. What "argument" about their culture do they seem to be making? In what sense can these objects or practices be seen as *messages*, indicating the values or beliefs of the culture that produced them?

Problem-Based Learning Projects

1. You are a United States congressperson in 1924, speaking in favor of the act to grant citizenship to American Indians. Using texts and cultural artifacts from at least three different communities, prepare a presentation for Congress using images as well as testimony on why American Indians deserve to be full citizens.

2. You are a spokesperson for a museum that has been asked to return to a local tribe the five-hundred-year-old human bones and burial objects in its collection. What will the museum do with these objects if they aren't returned? How should the museum present information about Native American cultures if it doesn't use the burial objects? Help design a new exhibit for the museum.

3. You are part of a team charged with composing a new American history textbook for high school students. You have been asked to provide a brief sketch of the effects of European colonialism on Native American culture. How would you write such a sketch? Where would you want your reader to feel sympathy, anger, frustration, satisfaction? What is our current responsibility toward evaluating the actions of people in the past? Are the Europeans the bad guys? Are the Indians the good guys? Should our judgments be more complicated? Is there reason to believe any of us would have acted more ethically had we been alive four hundred years ago? Consider, as you write, that your audience will consist of readers from European as well as Indian backgrounds.

GLOSSARY

bicultural production   A text or object that retains the nature of the creator's original culture as well as influences from other cultures.

creation stories   American Indian narratives of how the world or the tribe began. The biblical book of Genesis also contains two creation stories, but Native American creation stories tend to emphasize the number 4, the humanlike nature of the original gods, a race of proto-humans, the essential connectedness of all creation, and the centrality of the tribe in question to the cosmic order.

cultural hero stories   Stories involving a hero who is human or has human characteristics and works on behalf of a community. These stories help dramatize the native people's belief about how the original world was altered to its current form.

emergence stories   Stories that describe how the people originated in the womb of the Earth Mother and were called to the surface by the Sun Father. Despite the many differences among various tribes' versions of these stories, they generally establish how the world was created; how people developed out of ambiguously formed beings (who often had both animal and human characteristics); what each tribe took to be the basic relationships among people and between people and nature; and the origins of important tribal customs and structures.

emergent religion   A religion in which new spiritual practices are added to an existing framework.

gynocratic   Governed by women, as opposed to patriarchal, meaning governed by men. American Indian communities such as the Pueblos were **matrilineal** (i.e., traced their descent through the maternal line) and/or **matrifocal** (female-centered).

hózhó   A Navajo term meaning holiness, harmony, or beauty. This term is used to describe Navajo art, song, and ritual that seeks balance and harmony.

manitos   Extremely powerful beings in the Chippewa cosmology who could be characterized as "spirits" or gods. Manitos provided people with food (through hunting) and good health. They include Pau-Puk-Keewis, the Chippewa gambler, windigos, Nanabozho (the Chippewa cultural hero/trickster), and the underwater manito.

oral tradition   The tradition of songs, stories, chants, and performances that comprised pre-Columbian Native American literature (actually "traditions," for each community had its own set of traditions). "Literature" is problematic here, however, insofar as these cultural events were never written down, frequently sacred, and always community-building. Many contemporary Native American writers employ themes and structures from the oral tradition in order to keep those traditions alive.

performative   One or more words that have immediate, concrete effects in the world. In the West, phrases such as "I now pronounce you husband and wife" or "Case dismissed" are examples of performative utterances. For many Indian cultures, much of the oral tradition was inherently performative—for example, it was used to cure or to invoke the spirits.

tale-types Groups of stories that tend to focus on particular characters and include standard events and elements. Some of the most common tale-types include gambler, trickster, creation, abduction, migration, and women's stories. Contemporary authors can use these tale-types in their works: for example, Leslie Marmon Silko's *Ceremony* retells Yellow Woman stories—a Pueblo Abduction Cycle.

trickster A common Native American legendary figure, usually male, but occasionally female or disguised in female form, and notorious for exaggerated biological drives and well-endowed physique. Partly divine, partly human, and partly animal, he is an often amoral and a comic troublemaker. Because stories about Trickster often represent him as transgressing cultural mores, they serve to explain and investigate the origins and values of those mores.

Yellow Woman stories Told by the Pueblo peoples of the Southwest, these stories dramatize how humans interact with spirits in the world once it has been created. Although there is always variation, Yellow Woman stories often involve a young married woman who wanders beyond her village and has a sexual encounter with a spirit-man; sometimes she is killed, but usually she returns to her family and tribe having grown spiritually, and therefore exerts an empowering influence on the people in general.

SELECTED BIBLIOGRAPHY

Allen, Paula Gunn. *The Sacred Hoop: Recovering the Feminine in American Indian Traditions*. Boston: Beacon Press, 1992.

Babcock, Barbara A., Guy Monthan, and Doris Monthan. *The Pueblo Storyteller: Development of a Figurative Ceramic Tradition*. Tucson: U of Arizona P, 1986.

Deloria, Vine Jr. *God Is Red: A Native View of Religion*. 2nd ed. Golden: Fulcrum Publishing, 1992.

Faris, James C. *The Nightway: A History and a History of Documentation of a Navajo Ceremonial*. Albuquerque: U of New Mexico P, 1990.

Gabriel, Kathryn. *Gambler Way: Indian Gaming in Mythology, History, and Archaeology in North America*. Boulder: Johnson Books, 1996.

Harjo, Joy, and Gloria Bird, eds. *Reinventing the Enemy's Language: Contemporary Native Women's Writings of North America*. New York: W. W. Norton and Company, 1997.

Hynes, Williams J., and William G. Doty, eds. *Mythical Trickster Figures: Contours, Contexts, and Criticisms*. Tuscaloosa: U of Alabama P, 1993.

Sarris, Greg. *Keeping Slug Woman Alive: A Holistic Approach to American Indian Texts*. Berkeley: U of California P, 1993.

———. *Mabel McKay: Weaving the Dream*. Berkeley: U of California P, 1994.

Schlick, Mary Dodds. *Columbia River Basketry: Gifts of the Ancestors, Gifts of the Earth*. Seattle: U of Washington P, 1994.

Schubnell, Matthias, ed. *Conversations with N. Scott Momaday*. Jackson: UP of Mississippi, 1997.

Swann, Brian, ed. *Smoothing the Ground: Essays on Native American Oral Literature*. Berkeley: U of California P, 1983.

Vecsey, Christopher. *Traditional Ojibwa Religion and Its Historical Changes*. Philadelphia: American Philosophical Society, 1983.

FURTHER RESOURCES

American Indian Music of the Southwest. Folkways Records, 1951.

Bates, Sara (curator), Jolene Rickard, and Paul Chaat Smith. *Indian Humor: American Indian Contemporary Arts*. San Francisco: American Indian Contemporary Arts, 1995.

Horse Capture, Joseph D., and George P. Horse Capture. *Beauty, Honor and Tradition: The Legacy of Plains Indian Shirts*. Minneapolis: U of Minnesota P, 2001.

Incident at Oglala: The Leonard Peltier Story. Directed by Michael Apted. Miramax Films, 1992.

Leslie Marmon Silko: A Film By Matteo Bellinelli. TSI Swiss Television, 2000.

Lovett, John R. Jr., and Donald L. DeWitt. *Guide to Native American Ledger Drawings and Pictographs in United States Museums, Libraries, and Archives*. Westport: Greenwood Press, 1998.

Moffitt, John F., and Santiago Sebastián. *O Brave New People: The European Invention of the American Indian*. Albuquerque: U of New Mexico P, 1996.

Monroe, Dan L., et al. (curators). *Gifts of the Spirit: Works by Nineteenth-Century and Contemporary Native American Artists*. Salem: Peabody Essex Museum, 1996.

Phillips, Ruth B. *Trading Identities: The Souvenir in Native North American Art from the Northeast, 1700–1900*. Seattle: U of Washington P, 1998.

Rushing, W. Jackson III, ed. *Native American Art in the Twentieth Century: Makers, Meanings, Histories*. New York: Routledge, 1999.

Winds of Change: A Matter of Promises. Narrated by N. Scott Momaday. Wisconsin Public Television. PBS Video, 1990.

Unit 2

EXPLORING BORDERLANDS

Contact and Conflict in North America

Authors and Works

Featured in the Video:

Bernal Díaz del Castillo, *The True History of the Conquest of New Spain* (history, exploration narrative)

Álvar Núñez Cabeza de Vaca, *The Relation of Álvar Núñez Cabeza de Vaca* (exploration narrative, captivity narrative, hagiography)

Americo Paredes, *George Washington Gomez* (novel), *With a Pistol in His Hand: A Border Ballad and Its Hero* (cultural criticism, music history)

Gloria Anzaldúa, *Borderlands/La Frontera: The New Mestiza* (memoir, poetry, cultural criticism, political theory)

Discussed in This Unit:

Christopher Columbus, letters

Bartolomé de las Casas, *The Very Brief Relation of the Devastation of the Indies* (history, protest literature)

Garcilaso de la Vega, *The Florida of the Inca* (history, folklore)

Samuel de Champlain, *The Voyages of Sieur de Champlain*, *The Voyages and Discoveries* (histories, exploration narratives)

John Smith, *The General History of Virginia, New England, and the Summer Isles* (history, captivity narrative, exploration narrative), *A Description of New England* (exploration narrative, promotional tract), *New England's Trials* (history, exploration narrative)

Adriaen Van der Donck, *A Description of New Netherland* (promotional tract)

Overview Questions

■ What is a *mestizo/a*? How has *mestizo/a* identity and consciousness altered and developed over the past four centuries?

■ What kinds of relationships did European explorers and colonizers have with the Native Americans they encountered in the New World? What stereotypes and conventions did they rely on to represent Indians in their narratives?

■ How did European colonizers use their narratives to mediate their relationships with authorities back in Europe?

■ How do writings that originated in South America, Mexico, the West Indies, and Canada fit into the American canon? Why have writings in Spanish, Dutch, and French been absent from the canon for so long? What responsibilities do we have as readers when we read these works in translation?

■ How do concepts of writing and literacy differ among cultures? How did these differences shape the colonial experience?

■ How does bilingualism affect *mestizo/a* narratives?

■ What characterizes a "borderland" or "contact zone"? What boundaries are challenged in a border region? How have conceptions of borderlands and contact zones changed over time?

■ What differentiates assimilation, acculturation, and transculturation? Which of these terms seems most appropriate for the colonial experiences described in the texts for this unit?

■ How did the Spanish, French, Dutch, and English approaches to colonizing the New World differ? How did those differences affect European–Native American relationships in different regions of the Americas? How did differences among native cultures in Mesoamerica, Florida, Virginia, the Middle Atlantic, and New France affect contact between Native Americans and colonizers?

■ How did the first European explorers envision the New World? How did their preconceptions affect their experiences in the Americas?

■ Why do early narratives of the New World so frequently invoke the language of wonder? What narrative strategies did explorers and colonizers use to describe their experience of wonder?

■ Most of the texts discussed in Unit 2 can be characterized as belonging to more than one genre. Why do texts that represent border and contact experiences so often combine different genres? What is the effect of this genre blurring?

■ How are early *mestizo* texts influenced by the oral tradition and pre-Conquest literary styles?

■ What kinds of images of America did the European writers featured in Unit 2 construct to promote colonization and settlement? What kinds of natural resources and environmental factors did they extol in their accounts of the New World?

■ How did European writers justify taking over Native American lands and resources?

■ How are Native American women characterized in colonizers' and *mestizos'* narratives? What archetypes and legends have developed about relationships between native women and European colonizers?

Learning Objectives

After students have viewed the video, read the headnotes and literary selections in *The Norton Anthology of American Literature*, and explored related archival materials on the *American Passages* Web site, they should be able to

1. explain the commercial, political, and religious structures and goals that underwrote European colonial ventures in the New World;
2. discuss the effects European colonization had on Native American populations in North and South America;
3. describe the differences among the Spanish, English, French, and Dutch models of colonization;
4. discuss the formation of *mestizo/a* identity and

its development in America since the sixteenth century;
5. identify primary differences among Native American cultures in Mesoamerica, Florida, Virginia, and New France and describe the hallmarks of their pre-Conquest literary traditions.

Instructor Overview

After the Spanish explorer Álvar Núñez Cabeza de Vaca was shipwrecked and stranded in the present-day southwestern United States, he spent years living among Native American groups while seeking out his own countrymen. When he finally encountered a group of Spaniards, he was surprised to realize that they did not seem to recognize him as European: "They were dumbfounded at the sight of me, strangely undressed and in company with Indians. They just stood staring for a long time, not thinking to hail me or come closer." At the same time, he found that his Indian companions refused to believe that he was of the same race as the "Christian slavers," or Spanish colonists, whom they associated with exploitation, cruelty, and enslavement. Somehow, in the process of living among the Indians and mixing their culture with his own European customs, Cabeza de Vaca had created a hybrid identity for himself that was neither wholly Indian nor wholly European. His unique experience was a product of the complex culture of the "contact zone," which scholar Mary Louise Pratt has characterized as an "interactive" and "improvisational" space where groups geographically and historically separated from one another come into contact and establish relationships. As Cabeza de Vaca's experience makes clear, contact and conquest were not one-way experiences in which Europeans simply imposed their will on passive Native Americans. Instead, contact is always characterized by intersecting practices and perspectives, even if power relations are often unequal. As diverse groups of Europeans explored, settled, and exploited the New World of North and South America in the fifteenth, sixteenth, and seventeenth centuries, they came into contact with diverse groups of Native Americans, creating contact zones from present-day Canada to the Caribbean. The dynamic, fluid cultures that arose out of the contact zones were marked by antagonism and violence as competing groups struggled for power. These contact zones could, however, also give rise to vibrant new traditions forged out of cooperation and innovation.

Unit 2, "Exploring Borderlands: Contact and Conflict in North America," examines the contact zones and colonial experiences of European explorers and the Native Americans they encountered. The unit also pays special attention to the way the contact zone between present-day Mexico and the southwestern United States evolved into a hybrid border region that continues to be influenced by the legacies of the different groups who first struggled there for dominance in the sixteenth century. After hundreds of years of war, intermarriage, trade, slavery, and religious struggles, a complex, syncretic culture has flourished in the space that marks the current U.S./Mexico border. As conquerors and conquered merged, a new *mestizo* identity (a blending of Indian, European, and African heritage) was created and continues to find expression in the work of contemporary Chicano and Chicana writers of the "borderland" region. Unit 2 explores a wide variety of contact and border experiences, including narratives by Christopher Columbus, Bartolomé de las Casas, Bernal Díaz del Castillo, Álvar Núñez Cabeza de Vaca, Garcilaso de la Vega, Samuel de Champlain, John Smith, Adriaen Van der Donck, Americo Paredes, and Gloria Anzaldúa. The unit provides contextual background and classroom materials designed to explore the multiple and diverse ways these writers represented encounters between cultures in contact zones and borderlands.

The video for Unit 2 focuses on four writers who challenge the geographical, cultural, political, and racial boundaries in the U.S./Mexico border region: Bernal Díaz del Castillo and Álvar Núñez Cabeza de Vaca wrote as Spanish foot soldiers who witnessed the brutal tactics of conquest and subjugation visited upon Native Americans. Writing centuries later, Americo Paredes and Gloria Anzaldúa protest the continued oppression and marginalization of people of *mestizo* ancestry in the United States. Their work also explores the dynamic, inclusive potential of the hybrid culture of the border region. All of these writers articulate the tensions inherent in power relations in border

regions, as well as the possibility for the formation of new identities in these interactive spaces.

In its coverage of these writers and their texts, the video introduces students to the complexity of the concept of the "border" and of cultural and racial boundaries more generally. How do the texts in Unit 2 represent the violence and exploitation that were part of the European exploration of the New World? What kinds of beliefs and expectations did European colonizers bring with them to the Americas? How did the sophisticated and varied cultures of native peoples impact the settlements Europeans created in America? How do European writers represent the experiences and cultures of indigenous peoples? How does gender complicate power relations in contact zones and borderlands? How has *mestizo* identity transformed over time? Unit 2 helps answer these questions by offering suggestions on how to connect these writers to their cultural contexts, to other units in the series, and to other key writers of the era. The curriculum materials help fill in the video's introduction to contact zones and borderlands by exploring the works of writers who articulated other, diverse experiences, such as Samuel de Champlain (who wrote as a French colonist in sixteenth- and seventeenth-century Canada), Adriaen Van der Donck (who described the Dutch colonial experience in New Netherland), and Garcilaso de la Vega (who drew on his mixed European and Incan heritage to write histories of Indian/Spanish interactions).

The video, the archive, and the curriculum materials situate Unit 2's writers within several of the historical contexts that shaped (and continue to shape) their texts: (1) the formation of the U.S./Mexican border and the impact of "borderlands" and boundaries on American culture; (2) Native American modes of writing and representing history, including contact histories; (3) traditional archetypes of Mexican and Mexican American femininity; (4) the discourse of "wonder" in contact narratives; and (5) metaphors of romance and eroticism that are common to conquest narratives.

The archive and curriculum materials suggest how the writers and texts featured in Unit 2 relate to those covered in other *American Passages* units: How does *mestizo/a* culture challenge dominant contemporary ideas about the origin of America and American identity? How did the history writing and *historias* of contact experiences shape subsequent American texts? How have concepts of Native American and Chicana femininity evolved over time? How have "borderlands" shaped American culture and politics? How do concepts of writing and literacy differ among cultures? How has transculturation shaped the American experience?

Student Overview

After the Spanish explorer Álvar Núñez Cabeza de Vaca was shipwrecked and stranded in the present-day southwestern United States, he spent years living among Native American groups while seeking out his own countrymen. When he finally encountered a group of Spaniards, he was surprised to realize that they did not seem to recognize him as European: "They were dumbfounded at the sight of me, strangely undressed and in company with Indians. They just stood staring for a long time, not thinking to hail me or come closer." At the same time, he found that his Indian companions refused to believe that he was of the same race as the "Christian slavers," or Spanish colonists, whom they associated with exploitation, cruelty, and enslavement. Somehow, in the process of living among the Indians and mixing their culture with his own European customs, Cabeza de Vaca had created a hybrid identity for himself that was neither wholly Indian nor wholly European. His unique experience was a product of the complex culture of the "contact zone," which scholar Mary Louise Pratt has characterized as an "interactive" and "improvisational" space where groups geographically and historically separated from one another come into contact and establish relationships. As Cabeza de Vaca's experience makes clear, contact and conquest were not one-way experiences in which Europeans simply imposed their will on passive Native Americans. Instead, contact is always characterized by intersecting practices and perspectives, even if power relations are often unequal. As diverse groups of Europeans explored, settled, and exploited the New World of North and South America in the fifteenth, sixteenth, and seventeenth centuries, they came into contact with diverse groups of Native Americans, creating contact zones from present-day Canada to the Caribbean. The dynamic, fluid cultures that arose out of the contact zones were marked by antagonism and violence as competing groups struggled for power. These contact zones could, however, also give rise to vibrant new traditions forged out of cooperation and innovation.

Unit 2, "Exploring Borderlands: Contact and Conflict in North America," examines the contact zones and colonial experiences of European explorers and the Native Americans they encountered. The unit also pays special attention to the way the contact zone between present-day Mexico and the southwestern United States evolved into a hybrid border region that continues to be influenced by the legacies of the different groups who first struggled there for dominance in the sixteenth century. After hundreds of years of war, intermarriage, trade, slavery, and religious struggles, a complex, syncretic culture has flourished in the space that marks the current U.S./Mexican border. As conquerors and conquered merged, a new **mestizo** identity (a blending of Indian, European, and African heritage) was created and continues to find expression in the work of contemporary Chicano and Chicana writers of the **borderland** region. Unit 2 explores the multiple and diverse ways that writers have represented encounters among cultures in contact zones and borderlands, from the fifteenth to the twenty-first century.

➤ **Authors covered:** Bernal Díaz del Castillo, Álvar Núñez Cabeza de Vaca, Americo Paredes, Gloria Anzaldúa

➤ **Who's interviewed:** Gloria Anzaldúa, author; Juan Bruce-Novoa, professor of Spanish and Portuguese (University of California, Irvine); Maria Herrera-Sobek, professor of Chicana studies (University of California, Santa Barbara); Sonia Saldívar-Hull, professor of English (University of Texas, San Antonio); Elliot Young, assistant professor of English (Lewis and Clark College)

➤ **Points covered:**

- The U.S./Mexico border region is an area with a long and complex history of challenging racial, political, cultural, and geographical boundaries. Contemporary Chicano/a literature and culture arise out of a literary history that begins with the narratives of Spanish exploration. Spaniards Bernal Díaz del Castillo and Álvar Núñez Cabeza de Vaca were eyewitnesses to the vibrant pre-Conquest indigenous cultures that existed in the area, as well as to the brutal realities of the sixteenth-century Spanish Conquest that devastated it. These writers helped begin a uniquely Latino and American literary tradition. After centuries of cultural and racial integration, twentieth-century critics and creative writers Americo Paredes and Gloria Anzaldúa have re-examined the history of the borderlands from the perspective of the *mestizo/a*.

- Bernal Díaz del Castillo served as a footsoldier in Hernán Cortés's campaign to conquer Mexico between 1519 and 1521. Many years later, he wrote about his unique perspective on the Conquest in his *True History of the Conquest of New Spain*. His narrative was one of the first accounts of Doña Marina, or La Malinche, the native woman who served as Cortés's translator, negotiator, and mistress. Doña Marina is a conflicted and contradictory figure within the tradition of Chicano/a literature: some see her as a traitor who sold out her own people to the Spanish, while others argue that she is better understood as an effective mediator between cultures.

- Cabeza de Vaca sailed to the New World in 1527 as part of a Spanish expedition to Florida. After being shipwrecked, he wandered for nine years among the Indians of the present-day U.S. Southwest before finding his way back to a Spanish settlement. In the process he became acculturated to Native American practices and learned Native American languages, thus becoming the first cultural *mestizo* in the region.

- Three hundred years after Cabeza de Vaca, Americo Paredes committed himself to studying and celebrating the legacy of *mestizo* culture in the border region. He collected and recorded the Chicano musical tradition of the *corridos*, subversive songs that narrate the struggles of Mexican heroes against Anglo oppression. His novel, *George Washington Gomez*, tells the story of a Chicano coming of age in the borderlands.

- Gloria Anzaldúa built on Paredes's legacy of Chicano activism to empower Chicana and *mestiza* women. Her 1987 book, *Borderlands/La Frontera*, gives voice to women of mixed identity and challenges traditional racial, cultural, linguistic, and gender boundaries. She has been part of the movement to recuperate and redefine Doña Marina as a heroine and inspiration to Chicanas.

PREVIEW

- **Preview the video:** Home to pre-Conquest indigenous peoples, European conquistadors, and *mestizos* of mixed racial and cultural background, the U.S./Mexico border region has long been a site of contact, conflict, and new beginnings. It is a place where geographical, cultural, political, and racial boundaries are challenged and restructured. Contemporary Chicano literature and culture arises out of a literary history that begins with the narratives of Spanish exploration. In the sixteenth century, Bernal Díaz del Castillo served as a footsoldier in the army of conquistadors that devastated the Aztec Empire in central Mexico. Much later, as an old man, he wrote about his experiences and offered insights into the Conquest from the perspective of a humble soldier. His narrative provides one of the earliest accounts of the controversial figure of Doña Marina, or La Malinche, the native woman who served as Cortés's mistress, interpreter, and negotiator. Doña Marina became a key symbol in the oral and literary traditions of later generations of Chicanos. Another Spanish soldier of the sixteenth century, Álvar Núñez Cabeza de Vaca, had a very different experience in the New World. Sailing to the Americas in 1527 as part of a Spanish expedition to Florida, he was shipwrecked off the coast of Texas. During his nine years in the border region, Cabeza de Vaca evolved into what some critics have called "the first cultural *mestizo*" and hence the first writer of Chicano literature. By learning the languages and becoming familiar with the culture of the many Native American tribes among which he moved, he constructed a mixed identity for himself. Centuries later, that mixed identity has become common in the border region. By the late twentieth century, people of mixed Spanish/Anglo/Indian/African blood who lived in this region began protesting the extent to which their culture had been marginalized by dominant Anglo society. Americo Paredes contributed to this movement by collecting and recording the musical border ballad tradition of the *corridos*, subversive songs about Chicano heroes who resist Anglo oppression. Building on Paredes's legacy, contemporary writer Gloria Anzaldúa explores the positive, inclusive possibilities that a mixed background offers to *mestizos* and *mestizas*. Protesting oppression based on race, class, and gender, she has given a voice to *mestiza* women inhabiting the borderlands and redefined the role of women as envisioned by Bernal Díaz del Castillo and other earlier writers.

- **What to think about while watching:** How has the southwestern border region changed over time? What political and social issues have shaped the literature of the borderlands? What is the relationship between the conquerors and conquered? How do these writers articulate an ideal of a mixed and inclusive identity? How does the Chicano notion of *"historia"* complicate traditional Anglo ideas about the distinction between history and fiction? What traditional stereotypes have been applied to *mestiza* women? How have women restructured and redefined the identities open to them in the borderlands?

- **Tying the video to the unit content:** Unit 2 expands on the issues discussed in the video to further explore the complex contact and conflict between different groups in different geographical border regions and contact zones. The curriculum materials offer background on Spanish, French, Dutch, and English writers and texts not featured in the video. The unit offers contextual background to expand on the video's introduction to the political issues, historical events, and literary styles that shaped the literature created in the borderlands.

	How do place and time shape literature and our understanding of it?	What is an American? How does American literature create conceptions of the American experience and identity?	How are American myths created, challenged, and re-imagined through these works of literature?
Comprehension Questions	What are borderlands? What boundaries besides geographical ones are challenged in border regions?	What is a *mestizo/mestiza*?	Who was Doña Marina, or La Malinche?
Context Questions	How does Cabeza de Vaca's almost anthropological account of his time among the natives resonate with Americo Paredes's sociological/anthropological approach to recording the traditional musical and folk traditions of Chicano culture?	How might Bernal Díaz's description of Tenochtitlán have inspired Chicano activists' ideas about Aztlán and its culture?	How do *corridos* celebrating the exploits of Gregorio Cortez invoke and rewrite the legacy of Hernán Cortés, the Spanish conquistador?
Exploration Questions	How have Native American, *mestizo*, and *mestiza* identities changed over the course of hundreds of years of contact and conflict between groups in the U.S./Mexico border region?	How has *mestizo* culture challenged dominant European American ideas about the origins of America? What does the term *Chicano* mean? Where does it come from? How does it differ from the terms Hispanic, Latino, or Spanish American? Which of these terms do you feel is most appropriate for the writers featured in the video and why?	What modes of protest do you think are most effective at enabling an oppressed group to challenge stereotypes and limitations imposed by the dominant culture?

	Texts	Contexts
1490s	Christopher Columbus, "Letter to Luis de Santangel Regarding the First Voyage" (1493)	Columbus sails from Spain for the New World, arrives in the Bahamas and claims the land for Spain (1492) Jews expelled from Spain by order of Ferdinand and Isabella (1492) Publication of the first Spanish grammar, *Gramática de la Lengua Castellana*, by Antonio Nebrija (1492) New World divided between Spain and Portugal by the Treaty of Tordesillas (1494) Bartolomé de las Casas sails with Columbus on his third voyage to America after receiving a law degree from the University of Salamanca (1498)
1500s		Martin Waldseemüller coins the name "America" on a map of the New World (1507)
1510s		Bartolomé de las Casas named "Protector to the Indians" after returning to Spain to petition the Crown for humane treatment of Native Americans (1516) Spanish-Aztec wars; Cortés conquers the Aztecs in Mexico (1519–21)
1520s	*Codex Boturini* (c. 1521–40?)	Explorer Giovanni da Verrazano is first European to enter New York Harbor (1524) Spanish explorers import first Africans as slaves to America, South Carolina (1526)
1530s	*Huejotzingo Codex* (1531)	La Virgen de Guadalupe appears to Juan Diego, an Incan Indian who had recently converted to Catholicism (1531)
1540s	Álvar Núñez Cabeza de Vaca, *The Relation of Álvar Núñez Cabeza de Vaca* (1542)	
1550s	Diego Muñoz de Camargo transcribes the *Lienzo de Tlaxcala* (c. 1550) Bartolomé de las Casas, *The Very Brief Relation of the Devastation of the Indies* (1552)	Bartolomé de las Casas debates with Juan Gines de Sepulveda; Casas argues that the Spanish conqests in the New World are unjust and inhumane (1550–51)
1560s	Bernal Díaz del Castillo begins his three-volume work *The True History of the Conquest of New Spain* (c. 1568, published in 1632)	

	Texts	Contexts
1570s	Fray Bernardino de Sahagún completes the *Florentine Codex* (1577)	
1580s	Thomas Harriot, *A Brief and True Report of the New Found Land of Virginia* (1588)	Sir Walter Raleigh and his English expedition reach "an island" and name it "Virginia" in honor of Queen Elizabeth (1584) John White named governor of colony at Roanoke Island, founded by Walter Raleigh (1587)
1590s	Theodor de Bry's *Grand Voyages* (six volumes) (1590–96)	
1600s	Garcilaso de la Vega, *The Florida of the Inca* (1605)	Samuel de Champlain makes his first voyage from France to Eastern Canada (1603) Jamestown colony established in Virginia (1607) Champlain founds Québec, to become the French capital in North America (1608)
1610s	Samuel de Champlain, *The Voyages of Sieur de Champlain* (1613)	
1620s	John Smith, *The General History of Virginia, New England, and the Summer Isles* (1624)	First Dutch settlers arrive in New Netherland (1624)
1640s	Adriaen Van der Donck, *A Description of New Netherland* (c. 1645) First publication of the story of the legend of La Virgen de Guadalupe (1648)	
1890s	*Lienzo de Tlaxcala* (1890)	Chicanos forced from their lands due to settlers arriving in Southwest to mine and develop land (1890–1900) Spanish-American War (1895–1902)
1940s	Americo Paredes, *George Washington Gomez: A Mexicotexan Novel* (1940; published in 1991)	The Fair Employment Practices Act helps eliminate discrimination in employment (1941) "Zoot Suit" riots take place in southern California (1943)
1980s	Gloria Anzaldúa, *Borderlands/La Frontera: The New Mestiza* (1987)	The Immigration Reform and Control Act (IRCA) creates a means through which some undocumented workers can become legal (1986) 70 percent of Hispanic female-headed households have children living in poverty (1987)

AUTHOR/TEXT REVIEW

Christopher Columbus (1451–1506)

In his 1828 biography of Christopher Columbus, American author Washington Irving styled Columbus as the archetypal American hero. Walt Whitman similarly lauded Columbus as an early mystic and religious seeker in his poem "Prayer of Columbus." Other authors and thinkers have not always agreed with these nineteenth-century hagiographies. In fact, Columbus has inspired controversy since he developed his bold plan to establish a new trade route to the eastern lands of India and Japan by sailing west from Europe. Although he failed in his attempt to reach Asia, he did land in the Bahamas and the Caribbean, where he laid the foundation for European colonization of that region. Since the fifteenth century, cultural commentators have argued over the nature of Columbus's accomplishment; his management of the Spanish colonies established in the Caribbean, his treatment of the native Indians who lived there, and especially his claim to the status of "discoverer" of America have provoked a variety of reactions ranging from adulation to censure. Columbus's reputation has long been troubled by the fact that his successes in navigation and exploration cannot be separated from the legacy of exploitation and violence that mark European involvement in the New World. Any account of his writings and his deeds must begin with the acknowledgment that Columbus's "discovery" of the Americas led to the destruction of as much as four-fifths of the native population of the region.

[7508] Vve. Turgis, *Depart de Christophe Colomb* (c. 1850–1900), courtesy of the Library of Congress [LC-USZC4-2029].

Columbus was born in Genoa, but left Italy as a young man to train as a sailor and navigator. Although many of his contemporaries dismissed his plan to sail westward as impracticable and misguided, Columbus eventually convinced King Ferdinand and Queen Isabella of Spain to finance an exploratory voyage in 1492 (the same year as the publication of the first Spanish grammar, a text which is often credited as essential to the colonization of the New World). Five months after setting sail from Granada, Columbus and his crew landed in the Bahamas and immediately claimed possession of the land for Spain by reading a proclamation that was certainly incomprehensible to the natives already living there. Columbus recorded his impressions of the voyage, the islands, and the natives in a logbook and in letters that he sent to his backers in Spain. Impressed with Columbus's inflated claims about the rich natural resources and wealth of the islands, Ferdinand and Isabella published his letters in Europe to assert their possession of this territory. Anxious to secure their control before other European powers could move into the region, the Spanish monarchs quickly sent Columbus on a second voyage of exploration and conquest in 1493.

Columbus returned to the island he had named Hispaniola to discover that all of the Spanish settlers he had left behind were dead, presumably because they had antagonized the native Taino Indians. The Tainos, who inhabited present-day Cuba, Jamaica, Haiti, the Dominican Republic, and Puerto Rico, are descendants of the

Arawaks and the early peoples of Mesoamerica. Although they had no calendar or writing system, the Tainos had a rich oral culture and were known for their ceremonial ball courts and their complex religious cosmology. Columbus attempted to enslave them and establish a new Spanish colony in Hispaniola, but the settlement soon devolved into rancor and violence after Columbus left to explore other islands in the region. He was forced to return to Spain in 1496 to settle the many political disagreements in which he had become embroiled. Upon his return to Europe, Columbus found his reputation tarnished by reports of his poor management of the colony and by his decision to enslave the Tainos. Nevertheless, he convinced the Spanish monarchs to fund a third voyage, begun in 1498. On this journey he reached the South American mainland, which he came to believe was the earthly paradise of Eden described in the Bible. This belief must have been severely tested when he returned to Hispaniola to find relations between the Indians and the Europeans in crisis and the settlers in open revolt against Columbus's inflexible management style. Refusing to recognize him as their leader, the colonists placed him under arrest and sent him back to Spain.

Although the Spanish court stripped him of all political authority, Columbus managed to obtain funding for a fourth and final voyage to the New World (1502–04), during which he explored Central America, was shipwrecked on Jamaica, and came to believe that God had spoken to him directly. Eventually rescued, he returned to Spain with his health ruined and his reputation damaged. He died in 1506, bitter about his colony's failure to provide him with the wealth and recognition he expected.

Unfortunately, the most important record of Columbus's explorations, his journal, has been lost. Contemporary scholars have access to only a transcribed version composed by Bartolomé de las Casas approximately forty years after Columbus's death. Columbus's letters, however, were translated and widely reprinted in his lifetime and thus provide more authoritative accounts of his experiences, as well as evidence of the way written travel accounts came to underwrite imperial pretensions to empire and conquest. Tellingly, many of Columbus's letters borrow from earlier travel narratives that described Asian and East Indian culture, thus interpolating the peoples and places he encountered into preexisting mythic categories. In many ways, Columbus's letters tell us more about the worldview and expectations of Renaissance Spaniards than about Native American peoples as they "actually were" in the fifteenth century.

TEACHING TIPS

■ Ask your students to imagine that they have been sent to cover Columbus's landing in Guanahani from the perspective of a present-day journalist. How would a journalist striving for objectivity recount Columbus's initial encounter with the Indians? What kind of evidence could this journalist gather about how the Europeans might have appeared to the Indians? You might point out the line

[1368] Konrad Kolble, *Replica of a Map of the Americas with Portraits of Christopher Columbus, Amerigo Vespucci, Ferdinand Magellan and Francisco Pizarro around Border* (1970), courtesy of the Library of Congress [LC-USZ62-89908]. Konrad Kolble's facsimile of a map published in 1600 by Theodor de Bry.

[2830] Simon Grynaeus and Johann Huttich, Detail from map in *Novus Orbis Regionum ac Insularum Veteribus Incognitarum* [Basle: Johann Hervagius, 1532] (1532), courtesy of the Jay I. Kislak Foundation, Inc. Map with detail of Native Americans practicing cannibalism. Scholars continue to debate whether indigenous peoples in the Americas practiced cannibalism, as the first explorers and colonizers claimed they did.

[2877] Mercator, *Orbis Terrae Compendios Descripto* (1587), courtesy of the Hargrett Rare Book and Manuscript Library/University of Georgia Libraries. Gerard Mercator was the most famous mapmaker after Ptolemy. His "Mercator Projection," while no longer considered good for global viewing, is still useful for navigation.

[6555] Thomas Nast, *A Belle Savage [Columbia Receiving Congratulations from All Parts of the World]* (1876), courtesy of the Library of Congress [LC-USZ62-105127]. This engraving, dating from the nation's first centennial, shows Columbia holding congratulatory papers from such foreign leaders as William Von Bismarck and Alexander II.

[7399] Cortés(?), *La Gran Ciudad de Temixtitan* (1524), courtesy of the Newberry Library, Chicago. This map of the Aztec city of Tenochtitlán is often attributed to Cortés. It is European in style, but the map-view contains information suggesting a native source.

[7508] Vve. Turgis, *Depart de Christophe Colomb* (c. 1850–1900), courtesy of the Library of Congress [LC-USZC4-2029]. This lithograph shows Columbus and his crew leaving the port of Palos, Spain, bound for the New World, with a large crowd gathered to see the spectacle.

from Columbus's "Letter to Luis de Santangel" in which he declares, "I have taken possession [of the island] for their highnesses, by proclamation made and with the royal standard unfurled, and no opposition was offered to me." Ask students to think about how the Arawaks might have perceived this act. Would they have understood Columbus's proclamation (read in Spanish)? Or the significance of the banner he "unfurled"? Why might they have decided against offering any opposition?

■ Ask your students to compare Columbus's descriptions of the islands' plants, natural features, and native inhabitants in the first and second letters featured in *The Norton Anthology of American Literature*. While the first letter is filled with the language of wonder and insists on the fertility and diversity of natural productions, the second letter is considerably less sanguine. Rather, Columbus seems preoccupied by the political strife created by the fractious colonists and by his resentment that his explorations have not generated great personal wealth. Ask students to consider what political project each letter was intended to serve. Why might Columbus insist that "Española is a marvel" in the first letter, and then portray it as an "exhausted," unhealthy place populated by "cruel savages" in his later account?

■ One of the cartographic innovations during the Renaissance was a more "objective" mapping style that used latitudinal and longitudinal lines. Some historians have argued that this mode of visually representing landscapes and landmass corresponds to more "scientific" narrative descriptions of the natural resources and characteristics of the New World. Have your students examine some of the early European maps featured in the archive and compare their visual styles to Columbus's narrative descriptions. What does his style of description have in common with the maps? Do your students agree with the idea that Columbus was attempting to create a kind of "verbal map" for the recipients of his letters?

QUESTIONS

Comprehension: In his "Letter to Luis de Santangel," Columbus declares that he has "taken possession" of the islands for "their highnesses" Ferdinand and Isabella of Spain. What procedures does Columbus follow in order to take possession? What kind of attitude toward the native inhabitants' rights underlies the ritual of possession that Columbus employed?

Comprehension: Why does Columbus open his "Letter to Ferdinand and Isabella Regarding the Fourth Voyage" with the statement that he cannot think of the Caribbean colonies without weeping? What has led to his disillusionment?

Context: Although Bartolomé de las Casas presented himself as a faithful and careful transcriber of Columbus's journals, scholars have been skeptical about the accuracy of his transcription of these documents. Given the attitudes about colonization that inflect Casas's *Very Brief Relation of the Devastation of the Indies*, what kind of bias might he have brought to the project of transcribing Columbus's experiences? How might his attitudes toward the Indians have differed from Columbus's?

Context: How do Columbus's descriptions of the natural resources he finds on the islands compare to John Smith's accounts of the plants and animals he found in New England? How do these explorers and colonizers deploy similar rhetoric in their accounts of the abundance and fertility of the New World? Do they value the same natural commodities? How do their visions of the economic possibilities of these two different regions compare?

Context: Columbus is clearly aware that the lands he "discovered" already have native Indian names. In his "Letter to Luis de Santangel," for example, he explains that the Arawak Indians call their island "Guanahani." Yet Columbus seems to have no reluctance about renaming the islands he visits, sometimes for religious reasons (San Salvador) and sometimes after Spanish royalty (Fernandina). Why does he feel justified in renaming the islands? What might he have hoped to accomplish in bestowing these Spanish names? How might his act of discovering and naming relate to the biblical account of Adam naming objects in Eden in the Book of Genesis?

Exploration: Columbus Day (the second Monday in October) has been celebrated as a national holiday since the early twentieth century. What are Americans supposed to be celebrating on that day? Should Americans continue to observe Columbus Day? Does the fact that the holiday was first instituted by Italian immigrant groups seeking to solidify their position in American society affect your assessment of its significance?

Exploration: How does the eighteenth- and nineteenth-century obsession with the figure of "Columbia" (discussed in Unit 4) relate to the actual experiences of the historical Columbus? Why might he have been an attractive figure to Americans immediately after the Revolutionary War? Why do you think they consistently allegorized and feminized their representations of Columbus?

[7511] Anonymous, *Landing of Columbus* (c. 1860–80), courtesy of the Library of Congress [LC-USZC4-4188]. This lithograph shows Columbus and members of his crew displaying objects to Native American men and women on shore.

[7512] George Schlegel, *Columbus Reception by the King Ferdinand and Queen Isabella of Spain after His First Return from America* (c. 1870), courtesy of the Library of Congress [LC-USZ62-96536]. This lithograph shows Columbus kneeling in front of the king and queen, who are surrounded by courtiers. Armed men and Indians look on.

[8344] Enrico Causici and Antonio Capellano, *Christopher Columbus* (1824), courtesy of the Architect of the Capitol. One of the sculptural reliefs in the Rotunda of the U.S. Capitol. The figure of Columbus looms large in U.S. cultural history, despite his exploitation of the native peoples he encountered on his voyages.

[8345] Randolph Rogers, *Columbus before the Council of Salamanca, 1487* (1860), courtesy of the Architect of the Capitol. Columbus at the Council of King Ferdinand presenting a chart from an unsuccessful voyage in order to gain support for his theory regarding a new route to India. On the sides are statuettes of Columbus's friend Juan Perez de Marchena and King Henry VII of England, a patron of navigation, both of whom agreed with Columbus's theory.

Bartolomé de las Casas (1474–1566)

Sometimes celebrated as the "conscience" of Spanish colonization, Bartolomé de las Casas was one of the first Europeans to recognize and protest the cruel treatment of Native Americans at the hands of their conquerors. By drawing on his considerable political, legal, and ecclesiastical connections, he became a powerful and eloquent —if ultimately unsuccessful—force in agitating for Indian rights.

While growing up and studying in the Spanish city of Seville, Casas closely followed news of the **conquistadors** and their exploits in the New World. His father and uncle joined Columbus's second expedition to the Indies in 1498, and his father returned with an Arawak Indian slave who must have provided the young Casas with details about the Caribbean world. In 1502, Casas joined Nicolas de

[2832] Bartolomé de las Casas (John Phillips, trans.), Illustration from *The Tears of the Indians* (1656), courtesy of the Robert Dechert Collection, Annenberg Rare Book and Manuscript Library, University of Pennsylvania.

Ovando's expedition to Hispaniola, where he participated in the brutal conquest of the Indians and received land and slave labor in return for his services under the ***encomienda***, or slave system. After over a decade of overseeing Indian slaves, Casas experienced a dramatic change of heart, perhaps precipitated by his decision to join the Dominican Order of Catholic priests. He became convinced that the Spanish *encomienda* was unjust and un-Christian, and he soon devoted himself to working toward its abolishment. While his commitment to Indian rights made him unpopular with many Spanish colonists and leaders, Casas never again wavered in his conviction that Native Americans deserved to be treated with respect and humanity. While he at one point advocated using African slaves to replace Indian labor, he later realized the hypocrisy of his proposal and renounced the idea, instead opting to oppose the enslavement of any peoples.

In 1515, Casas took his case to the Spanish court and was formally appointed "protector of the Indians." He also attained a commission to found an experimental colony on the coast of Venezuela based on principles of peace. The colony soon foundered, and Casas returned to Hispaniola, where he served as a friar in a monastery. By the 1530s he was again drawing on his political connections to legislate for protection of Native Americans, eventually persuading Pope Paul III to denounce the enslavement of Indians and convincing Charles V of Spain to make the practice illegal in Spanish colonies. Appointed bishop to the church of Chiapas, Mexico, in 1544, Casas encountered widespread, bitter, and violent resistance to his reform efforts. When Charles V retracted the ban on Indian slavery in the Americas in 1547, Casas returned to Spain. Until his death at the age of ninety-two, he continued his crusade by serving as attorney-at-large for the Indians in the Spanish courts and by publishing moving accounts of their tragic plight.

Casas's monumental *History of the Indies* and *The Very Brief Relation of the Devastation of the Indies* are among his most important writings. In these works, Casas offered a devastatingly vivid exposé of the brutality of the Spanish slave system. He also drew on his intimate knowledge of Indian culture to combat the popular argument that the native peoples were so docile, submissive, and mentally inferior as to be "natural slaves." The *Brief Relation* was widely translated and republished throughout Europe in Casas's lifetime, and its impassioned denunciation of the cruelty of the Spanish colonizers contributed to the perception (popular in Protestant countries) that the Spanish were especially violent and barbaric in their treatment of natives. Although he intended his work to spur reform, Casas's participation in the creation of the so-called **Black Legend** of Spanish colonial atrocities served mainly to make him extremely unpopular in Spain and may have fueled the equally problematic imperial pretensions of Protestant countries such as England and the Netherlands. Colonizers from these nations self-righteously justified their own repression and exploitation of Native Americans by arguing that their methods were more humane than those of the Spanish.

■ Have your class examine the painting from the 1531 *Huejotzingo Codex* featured in the archive. This codex served as evidence in a legal action brought by the Huejotzingo of Central Mexico to protest the heavy taxation they faced from their Spanish conquerors. This pictorial representation records the commodities and resources the Huejotzingo had already contributed to support Spanish expeditions: the eight small figures beneath the colored picture of the Madonna and child represent the slaves the tribe had sold in order to pay for the gold that went into making a banner for the Spanish expedition, while the rows of abstract shapes represent other commodities contributed to the campaign. After you have analyzed and interpreted the *Huejotzingo Codex* with your class, ask them to think about how the Spanish court might have responded to this document as a piece of legal evidence. Though it is an extremely sophisticated example of Native American record keeping and pictorial expression, it seems unlikely that Spanish judges would have appreciated its logic or understood its import without the explanation written in Spanish that accompanied it. Have students compare these paintings to the representation of slavery and the Conquest given in Casas's writings. What is the significance of his commitment to giving written expression to the injustices perpetrated against the Indians?

■ Students are sometimes startled by the graphic nature of Casas's accounts of Spanish atrocities. Gleefully drowning children, dismembering pregnant women, and torturing captives over smoldering fires, the Spanish conquerors in Casas's narrative engage in shocking brutality. Ask your students to consider why Casas might have chosen to represent so vividly the horror of the Spanish Conquest from the Indian point of view. How does his description reverse common European stereotypes about the "savagery" of American Indians? What kind of audience does he assume will read his work? Why might he think these accounts of violence will persuade them? Why does he consistently refer to the torture and murder of women and children? How effective is his strategy? You might have your students examine the graphic images of brutality that accompanied the English translation of Casas's work, entitled "Tears of the Indians," as they consider these questions.

QUESTIONS

Comprehension: What is the "Black Legend"?

Comprehension: What motivated the Spanish to act with such cruelty toward the Indians, according to Casas?

Comprehension: On what grounds does Casas attack Indian slavery? Why do you think he might have initially felt that replacing Indian slaves with African slaves was an acceptable alternative?

Context: Examine the frontispiece and illustration from the 1656 Protestant English translation of Casas's *Brief Relation* featured in the archive. How do the English publishers retitle Casas's *Brief*

[2831] Bartolomé de las Casas, Frontispiece to *The Tears of the Indians (las Casas): Being an Historical and True Account of the Cruel Massacres and Slaughters of above Twenty Millions of Innocent People; Committed by the Spaniards* (1656), courtesy of the Annenberg Rare Book and Manuscript Library, University of Pennsylvania. The English authorities used this 1656 translation to legitimize their conquest of Spanish Jamaica. Oliver Cromwell's nephew translated this volume.

[2832] Bartolomé de las Casas (John Phillips, trans.), Illustration from *The Tears of the Indians* (1656), courtesy of the Robert Dechert Collection, Annenberg Rare Book and Manuscript Library, University of Pennsylvania. This illustration details some of the atrocities committed by Spanish colonizers. Despite his intentions, Casas's work ultimately helped Protestant colonizers justify their own mistreatment of native peoples; they reasoned that their actions were not as reprehensible as those of the Spanish.

[7368] Anonymous, Sheet from the *Huejotzingo Codex* [1 of 8] (1531), courtesy of the Library of Congress, Manuscript Division. In 1531, the people of Huejotzingo asked conqueror Hernán Cortés to initiate a lawsuit against the high court of New Spain concerning the unjust use of indigenous labor and tribute. As part of this petition, eight pages of drawings were made on amatl (fig bark); these drawings are known today as the *Huejotzingo Codex*.

[7372] Anonymous, Sheet from the *Huejotzingo Codex* [6 of 8] (1531), courtesy of the Library of Congress, Manuscript Division. In 1531, the people of Huejotzingo asked conqueror Hernán Cortés to initiate a lawsuit against the high court of New Spain concerning the unjust use of indigenous labor and tribute. As part of this petition, eight pages of drawings were made on amatl (fig bark); these drawings are known today as the *Huejotzingo Codex*.

[7681] Anonymous, *Image of Bartolomé de las Casas* (1886), courtesy of *Narrative and Critical History of America*, Volume II (c. 1884–89), ed.

Justin Winsor, published by Boston and New York Houghton Mifflin and Company, The Riverside Press, Cambridge. Engraving of a young and determined-looking Casas writing at his desk, with a cross around his neck.
[9042] Laura Arnold, *The Great Chain of Being* (2003), courtesy of Laura Arnold. From the beginning of the Middle Ages through the early nineteenth century, "educated Europeans" conceived of the universe in terms of a hierarchical Great Chain of Being with God at its apex. In many ways, this hierarchy, still pervasive in Western theology and thought, stands in opposition to Native American and other belief systems that view the human and spirit worlds as co-existing on a horizontal plane.

Relation? What does the frontispiece's description of the contents of the book emphasize? What is the significance of the verse from Deuteronomy printed at the base of the page? How might the illustrations change or intensify a reader's reaction to Casas's narrative?

Context: According to a common European belief first coined by Aristotle and later adopted by Christian philosophers, the universe was structured according to immutable hierarchies. These hierarchies existed along the so-called **Great Chain of Being**, spanning from the dimensions of "non-being" (rocks and minerals) and extending through plants, animals, and man, all the way to God, as the representative of the highest form of "being." Within the category of "man," important hierarchies existed that separated more primitive peoples from more "cultured" or "advanced" societies. The following diagram shows the hierarchies of man as conceptualized in the Great Chain of Being:

Corporeal Man —— Man of Instinct —— Man of Feeling —— Thinking Man

How do you think Casas and his critics might have been influenced by the concept of the Great Chain of Being? Where do you think most Europeans felt Indians belonged on the chain? Where would Casas place them?

Context: In his *Brief Relation*, Casas challenges the popular notion that the Indians regarded European conquerors as divine gods: "[The Christians] committed other acts of force and violence and oppression which made the Indians realize that these men had not come from Heaven." How does Casas's insistence that the Indians do not revere or worship their conquerors compare to the opposite claims made by writers like Columbus, Cabeza de Vaca, and John Smith? What assumptions and justifications underwrite European accounts of Indians hailing them as powerful supernatural beings? How does this issue relate to European ideas about the "Great Chain of Being"?

Exploration: How do Casas's efforts to persuade readers of the evils of Indian enslavement compare to nineteenth-century abolitionists' efforts to convince Americans of the evils of African enslavement? How do Casas's narrative strategies compare to those adopted by writers like Frederick Douglass, Harriet Beecher Stowe, and Harriet Jacobs?

Exploration: In his tract "The Bloody Tenet of Persecution," Puritan Roger Williams (Unit 3) invokes many of the arguments employed by Casas in order to refute the claims of minister John Cotton that the Algonquians living in New England should not enjoy the same privileges as the British. What view of the Narragansett Indians is embedded in Roger Williams's *A Key into the Language of America*? What place does Williams give them in Puritan hierarchies? On what grounds does Williams make these claims?

Bernal Díaz del Castillo (1492–1584)

Bernal Díaz del Castillo was born in the Castile region of Spain in 1492, the same year that Christopher Columbus landed in the West Indies and declared himself "discoverer" of the New World. Coming of age in the exciting era of Spanish exploration and colonization, Díaz took advantage of an early opportunity to leave Europe for the Americas and joined an expedition bound for the colony of Darien (present-day Panama) in 1514. When he found the colony to be unstable and pervaded by political turmoil, he left for Cuba with a small contingent of other colonists. Although he based himself in Cuba, Díaz continued to join exploring parties in the region, eventually signing on with Hernán Cortés as a footsoldier in the Conquest of Mexico.

Because he saw the Conquest from the perspective of a common soldier rather than a nobleman or officer, Díaz formed different impressions of events than his superiors did. Much later in his life, he decided to write an account of those impressions, intending to offer a corrective to what he saw as the distortions and half-truths perpetuated by other historians. (Significantly, Díaz's work also serves as a corrective to Cortés's "great man" view of history in that it emphasizes the role of the ordinary footsoldier and lauds the role of natives such as La Malinche. Historians have argued that this is one of the first truly American histories in that it resonates with the democracy that would flourish later in the Americas.) Although Díaz claimed that he lacked eloquence and skill as a writer, his prose is vibrant and realistic and provides important insights into the clash between cultures that he witnessed. He offers convincing portraits of many of the central participants in the Conquest, including Cortés, Montezuma, and Doña Marina (La Malinche), and never shies away from representing the violent and destructive realities of war. His account of the beauty, wealth, and eventual devastation of the Aztec city of Tenochtitlán provides valuable evidence about traditional Aztec life and culture as well as insight into the experiences of soldiers on the ground during the siege of the city. Díaz's interest in and sympathetic portrayal of Doña Marina, the native woman who acted as translator, political negotiator, and mistress for Cortés, gives readers insight into the life of the woman who later took on mythical status as *"La Chingada"* ("the violated one").

Unlike some of the other conquistadors, Díaz did not gain wealth or fame as the result of his participation in the Conquest (at least according to his own account). The Crown endowed him with a modest *encomienda*, a grant that allowed the grantee to command Indians to labor for and pay tribute to him—in effect, a system of slavery. Díaz lived on his *encomienda* in Guatemala until his death at the age of ninety-two.

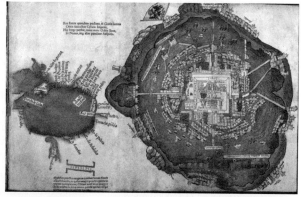

[7399] Cortés(?), *La Gran Ciudad de Temixtitan* (1524), courtesy of the Newberry Library, Chicago.

■ Díaz's narrative is infused with the language of wonder and invocations of the "Marvelous." He relies extensively on the narrative convention of claiming awestruck wordlessness: "I cannot attempt to describe [the wonders I saw]"; "I do not know how to describe this first glimpse of things never heard of, seen or dreamed before"; "with such wonderful sights to gaze on we did not know what to say." Ask your students to examine the text for moments when Díaz attempts to convey his sense of wonder. How successful is he? What narrative strategies besides the pose of wordlessness does he use? When does he describe the people and things he encounters as "other," and when does he draw parallels to their European counterparts? Be sure to point out that Díaz's invocation of wonder is used both to celebrate and to censure Aztec culture: he describes not only the beauty of Tenochtitlán (present-day Mexico City), but also the violent Aztec ritual of sacrifice and cannibalism in terms of wonder.

After you've discussed Díaz's participation in the discourse of wonder, ask your students to think about an object, place, or event that seemed radically new, striking, or awesome to them when they first saw it. Ask them to write their own account of their experience of "wonder." After they've finished writing, discuss their work as a class and talk about the difficulties they had finding words to convey their emotions and to describe accurately what they saw.

■ As the title *The True History of the Conquest of New Spain* indicates, Díaz claimed that his narrative was the simple, unvarnished truth. As he put it, "That which I have seen and the fighting I have gone through, with the help of God I will describe, quite simply, as a fair eyewitness without twisting events one way or another." As literary critic Stephen Greenblatt has pointed out, Díaz's pose of authenticity and accuracy should not be taken at face value. (The Spanish word **historia** means both "history" and "story," highlighting the extent to which any so-called "objective history" is always a subjective story inflected by personal biases and agendas.) Ask your class to think about how Díaz constructs the rhetorical device of his own neutrality in his *historia*. Then ask them to try to locate moments when the narrative is clearly not a dispassionate transcription of reality, but rather a personal and partisan account. You might look at Díaz's famous description of witnessing his countrymen being ritually sacrificed and cannibalized by the Aztecs on the altar of their god Huichilobos. How do Díaz's horror and personal fear affect his account of what he saw? How do his Christian beliefs color his narrative? How might an Aztec warrior's perspective on this scene be different? As contemporary readers, how might our knowledge of the destructiveness and brutality of European actions in the New World affect our understanding of this scene?

DÍAZ WEB ARCHIVE

[3699] Bernal Díaz del Castillo, *Historia Verdadera de la Conquista de la Nueva-España* (1632), courtesy of the Jay I. Kislak Foundation, Inc. Although Bernal Díaz del Castillo composed his *True History* in the late sixteenth century, it was not published until the seventeenth; the title page of the first edition is shown here.

[7368] Anonymous, Sheet from the *Huejotzingo Codex* [1 of 8] (1531), courtesy of the Library of Congress, Manuscript Division. In 1531, the people of Huejotzingo asked conqueror Hernán Cortés to initiate a lawsuit against the high court of New Spain concerning the unjust use of indigenous labor and tribute. As part of this petition, eight pages of drawings were made on amatl (fig bark); these drawings are known today as the *Huejotzingo Codex*.

[7399] Cortés(?), *La Gran Ciudad de Temixtitan* (1524), courtesy of the Newberry Library, Chicago. This map of the Aztec city of Tenochtitlán is often attributed to Cortés. It is European in style, but the map-view contains information suggesting a native source.

[7402] Anonymous, *Cortés, Montezuma and Doña Marina*, from the *Lienzo de Tlaxcala* Facsimile (1890), courtesy of the University of California, Berkeley, and the Bancroft Library. The *Lienzo de Tlaxcala* employs the res gestae strategy and provides an interesting counterpoint to the *Florentine Codex*. Here Cortés is depicted with Montezuma and Doña Marina.

QUESTIONS

Comprehension: What kinds of tensions and conflicts divide the Spanish camp? What distinctions does Díaz's narrative draw between different members of Cortés's army? How do class and rank affect individual Spaniards' feelings about the Conquest?

Comprehension: How does Díaz describe the city of Tenochtitlán? Compare his description to the map of Tenochtitlán featured in the archive. What aspects of the map match up with Díaz's description? How is the map different from Díaz's account? How does the bird's-eye perspective of the map compare to Díaz's narrative *historia*?

Context: The *Florentine Codex* (parts of which are featured in the archive) is a manuscript containing a hand-written version of the encyclopedic account of Aztec society assembled by Fray Bernardino de Sahagún. Beginning in the 1540s, Sahagún asked questions of groups of Nahuatl-speaking elders (presumably all male) from the heart of the former Aztec empire and had them record their responses. The book was illustrated by Aztec scribes in a style that reflected a mixture of pre-Conquest manuscript traditions and European illustration conventions. Compare the pictographic representations of the Conquest from Book 12 of the *Florentine Codex* to Díaz's account in the *True History*. In what points do these two histories agree? How do their different genres and styles (pictorial representations, narrative description) affect their perspective and representation of events?

Context: In their narratives, both Bartolomé de las Casas and Bernal Díaz describe the destruction and violence the Spanish visited on native cultures in the Americas, but their attitudes toward that violence seem quite different. How does Díaz's account compare to Casas's?

Exploration: Is it possible for a person claiming to be an eyewitness to write a "true history" of an event? What would constitute a "true history"?

Álvar Núñez Cabeza de Vaca (c. 1490–1558)

Often called the first culturally **Chicano** or *mestizo* writer, Álvar Núñez Cabeza de Vaca composed his *Relation* to narrate his extraordinary experience as a Spaniard who became integrated into Native American culture in the New World. Part hagiography, part captivity narrative, and part adventure story, the text recounts his ordeals from shipwreck to enslavement and details his rise to prominence as a trader and healer among various Native American groups. In the process, the *Relation* reveals the complex modes of acculturation through which Cabeza de Vaca forged a new, hybrid identity.

When Cabeza de Vaca set sail with Panfilo de Narváez in 1527 on an expedition to chart the Gulf Coast, he probably believed himself to be embarking on an auspicious career. He was a descendant of a noble family and had been chosen to serve as Emperor Charles V's representative and treasurer on an enterprise that seemed poised to

[7561] Fray Bernardino de Sahagún, *Florentine Codex*, Book 12, plate 45 (1500–99), courtesy of the School of American Research and the University of Utah Press. This plate shows Spanish soldiers leading Montezuma into the great palace. The *Florentine Codex* was illustrated by Aztec scribes in a style that reflected a mixture of pre-Conquest manuscript traditions and European illustration conventions.

[7575] Anonymous, *Florentine Codex*, Libro 12, plate 2 (1500–99), courtesy of the School of American Research and the University of Utah Press. This plate shows Spanish soldiers marching. Book 12 of the *Florentine Codex* depicts the deeds of Cortés and the Conquest of Mexico as it was described to Sahagún by Nahuatl-speaking elders and nobility.

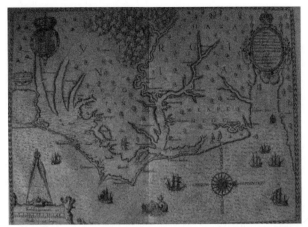

[7672] Anonymous, *New World Map*, from Thomas Hariot, *Admiranda Narratio Fida Tamen, de Commodis et Incolarum Ritibus Virginae* (1555), courtesy of the University of Pennsylvania, Jay I. Kislak Foundation, Inc.

garner him wealth and fame. But whatever hopes Cabeza de Vaca held for his future must have been shattered when Narváez, an incompetent leader, lost the ships under his command through a series of misadventures and left his crew marooned in Florida. After a plan to construct new ships ended in a disaster at sea, Cabeza de Vaca and the few other survivors from the expedition found themselves shipwrecked on the coast of present-day Texas and enslaved by the Han and Capoque clans of the Karankawa Indians. Cabeza de Vaca responded to his predicament (and freed himself from slavery) by learning the Native Americans' language and adapting himself to their culture, though he never relinquished his hope of eventually finding a Spanish outpost and being reunited with his countrymen. To this end, he began traveling north and west through North America, drawing on his skills as a trader and especially as a healer to ingratiate himself with the various tribes he encountered. Combining Christian rituals with traditional Native American customs, Cabeza de Vaca operated as a shaman, or spiritual healer, and acquired fame, respect, and power for his ability to heal and comfort the sick. The *Relation*'s account of his successful melding of different cultural and spiritual traditions reveals the importance of improvisation, adaptation, and flexibility to the process of acculturation.

Cabeza de Vaca and a small group of other survivors from the Narváez expedition reached present-day New Mexico in 1535. They gathered a large contingent of Native American followers and headed south to Mexico, hoping to find a Spanish settlement there. But when they eventually encountered a group of Spaniards, Cabeza de Vaca was appalled by their eagerness to enslave the natives and soon found himself in conflict with them. In his narrative, he ironically refers to these Spanish settlers by the same disparaging term the Indians used: "Christian slavers."

Cabeza de Vaca finally returned to Spain in 1537, where he continued to speak out against the conquistadors' mistreatment of Native American peoples. He wrote the *Relation* both to boost his own reputation and to offer his insights into Spanish colonial policy. In 1540 he received a grant from the emperor to lead an expedition to what is today Paraguay and help found the Rio de la Plata colony there. The other Spanish colonists in the region, however, were more interested in acquiring wealth than in upholding Cabeza de Vaca's enlightened policies toward the Indians. In 1545, they overthrew his government, arrested him, and sent him back to Spain in chains. Spanish authorities then exiled him to North Africa and forbade him ever to return to America.

■ At the conclusion of the excerpt from the *Relation* in *The Norton Anthology of American Literature*, Cabeza de Vaca explains that the Indians refused to believe that he and his group were of the same race as the "Christian slavers" they encountered in Mexico. Their "naked and barefoot" appearance as well as their gentleness and generosity seemed to separate them, in the Indians' minds, from other Spaniards. Ask your students to look at this segment of the narrative carefully, examining it for indications of Cabeza de Vaca's own racial and national identification. Does he see himself as "of the same people" as the Christian slavers? How has his identity as a European and as a conquistador altered over the course of his time among the Indians? To get at the issue of Cabeza de Vaca's hybrid identity, you might ask your students to chart his interesting use of pronouns in this concluding section of the *Relation*. When does he use "we" and "they"? Whom does he include when he refers to "we" and "us"?

■ In the section entitled "Our Life among the Avavares and Arbadaos," Cabeza de Vaca explains that exposure to the southwestern sun caused the members of the European group to "shed our skins twice a year like snakes." After pointing out the physical and mental transformation implied in this image of skin-shedding, ask your students to find other moments where Cabeza de Vaca symbolically indicates that he is undergoing a kind of metamorphosis. His accounts of acquiring a taste for native foods and his use of birth imagery might be good places to start this discussion.

QUESTIONS

Comprehension: How does Cabeza de Vaca survive among the various Native American groups he encounters? What skills does he draw on and develop? What strategies does he use to fit into native communities?

Comprehension: Why does Cabeza de Vaca come into conflict with Spaniards he encounters in Mexico? Why does he refer to his encounters with them as "confrontations" and "falling-outs"?

Context: How does Cabeza de Vaca's account of his experiences as a prisoner of the Malhados compare to John Smith's narrative of his imprisonment among the Chesapeake Bay Indians? What do the strategies they use to escape enslavement have in common? In what ways do their tactics for dealing with the natives differ? Who do you think was ultimately more successful?

Context: When Cabeza de Vaca traveled through what is now the southwestern United States and northern Mexico, there was of course no official border between the two areas. Nonetheless, do you think he might have had a sense of himself as inhabiting a kind of "borderland"? In what ways?

Context: When Spanish colonists arrived in the Americas, they sometimes encountered *berdaches*—Native American males who cross-dressed and performed female sex and social roles. While this form of transvestism was often widely accepted in native cul-

[2819] Álvar Núñez Cabeza de Vaca, Frontispiece to second edition of *La Relacion y Comentarios del Governador Alvar Nuñez Cabeza de Vaca, de lo Acaescido en las Dos Jornados que Hizo a las Indias* (1555), courtesy of the University of Pennsylvania, Jay I. Kislak Foundation, Inc. Sometimes considered the first captivity narrative, Cabeza de Vaca's account of his shipwreck and travels through Florida and northern Mexico is to some degree modeled after medieval romances.

[7672] Anonymous, *New World Map*, from Thomas Hariot, *Admiranda Narratio Fida Tamen, de Commodis et Incolarum Ritibus Virginae* (1555), courtesy of the University of Pennsylvania, Jay I. Kislak Foundation, Inc. European encounters with the New World presented a host of logistical problems for explorers; among them was the absence of cartographic data about the vast lands that were now being colonized. Early travelers contributed data that enabled the creation of maps like this one, which offer testimony to the various ways in which geographic space was conceived of during the era of early exploration.

[8766] Maria Herrera-Sobek, Interview: "De Vaca" (2002), courtesy of Annenberg/CPB. Maria Herrera-Sobek, professor of Chicana studies at the University of California, Santa Barbara, discusses de Vaca as a foundational figure for Chicanos.

tures, it frightened the Spanish. In his narrative, Cabeza de Vaca writes of the "soft" native men of Florida who dressed and worked as women. Why might the *berdache* have been so threatening to the Spanish? What notions of masculinity and femininity are implicit or explicit in the narratives about the conquest? How do the *berdaches* threaten (or reinforce) this gendered system?

Exploration: The captivity narrative has sometimes been called the first distinctly American genre, since it grew out of the cultural collision of colonists and America's native peoples. Literary critics and historians sometimes read the *Relation* as part of the captivity narrative genre (discussed in Unit 3). Do you think this is appropriate? What does Cabeza de Vaca's narrative have in common with Mary Rowlandson's account of her captivity among the Indians?

Exploration: Read Chicana poet Lorna Dee Cervantes's poem "Visions of Mexico While at a Writing Symposium in Port Townsend, Washington." How does her poem about her feelings of both closeness to and alienation from Mexican culture compare to Cabeza de Vaca's narrative? How does Cervantes's exploration of the meaning of the colonial experience and its relation to writing resonate with Cabeza de Vaca's struggles with this issue?

Garcilaso de la Vega (1539–1616)

One of the first American writers of mixed ethnic heritage, Garcilaso de la Vega signaled his *mestizo* identity by proudly appending the title "El Inca" to his name. He was descended from the Inca royal family through his mother, the princess Chimpu Ocllo, who was the granddaughter of one of the last Incan emperors. After the Spanish conquered the Incan dynasty in Peru, Chimpu Ocllo converted to Catholicism, assumed the name Isabel Suarez, and married Sebastian Garcilaso de la Vega, one of the Spanish conquistadors. Growing up as the child of this interracial marriage, Garcilaso de la Vega became fluent in both Spanish and the Inca language Quechua and acquired a detailed knowledge of Incan imperial history as well as the history of the Conquest.

After the death of his father in 1560, de la Vega journeyed to Spain to claim his inheritance. While he was never officially recognized as the son of a conquistador, he gained prestige by fighting in the wars of the Alpujarras. He eventually settled in Cordoba, where he studied Christianity and devoted himself to the pursuit of religion and literature. Most of his writings are historical narratives of the New World, including two volumes on Incan culture entitled *Commentarios Reales*, or *Royal Commentaries*, which draw on stories he learned from his mother and her

[7329] C. Colin, *Ferdinand Cortés and Hernando de Soto in the Camp of the Inca at Caxamalca. The Order of His Court and the Reverence with Which His Subjects Approached His Person, Astonished the Spaniards* (c. 1902), courtesy of the Library of Congress [LC-USZ62-104362].

relatives. Recuperating Indian traditions in the language of the colonizer, de la Vega's Incan histories are extraordinary testaments to the sophistication and civilization of pre-Conquest Peru. De la Vega's other work, *The Florida of the Inca* (1605), is a romanticized and fictionalized account of the de Soto expedition and of native life in Florida at the time of contact. De la Vega himself never went to Florida, so he compiled his account by synthesizing and drawing on other explorers' oral and written narratives. De la Vega's *mestizo* background provided him with a unique perspective on the history of Europeans in the New World, and, like his other writings, *The Florida of the Inca* reflects his commitment to mediating between two different cultures.

TEACHING TIPS

■ Ask your students how they would characterize the genre of de la Vega's account of Juan Ortiz. Is this conventional history? In what ways does it resemble a fable or fictional narrative? Remind your students that de la Vega was himself drawing on eyewitness oral accounts when he composed this work. Given this information, ask them to consider how the tale of Juan Ortiz resonates with the conventions of other narratives that derive from oral traditions (you might point them to the Native American tales featured in Unit 1).

■ It is sometimes difficult to ascertain whether de la Vega's sympathies lie with the conquistador figures or the Indians in his histories. Ask your students which characters in the Juan Ortiz narrative seem sympathetic. How do race and religion seem to impact de la Vega's characterization of the historical actors in this drama? In order to get your students to think deeply about this issue, you might ask them to rewrite Juan Ortiz's story from the perspective of one of the other characters, such as the cacique Hirrihigua, the eldest daughter, or Mucoco.

QUESTIONS

Comprehension: Why does the cacique Hirrihigua bear such enmity toward Juan Ortiz? What motivates his brutal treatment of his Spanish captive?

Comprehension: During the Renaissance the status of Native Americans was much debated: it was not uncommon to question whether they were fully human or even if they had souls. What criteria does Garcilaso de la Vega use to laud the Florida Indians? What do these criteria tell us about his perspective on what constitutes a fully human or even a "civilized" people? How does his definition of essential humanity compare to that of the conquistadors?

Comprehension: What is the role of Christianity and paganism in the narrative of Juan Ortiz? Which characters exemplify Christian qualities? How does de la Vega complicate traditional European ideas about Native American morality and religion?

DE LA VEGA WEB ARCHIVE

[2591] Theodor de Bry, *A Noblewoman of Pomeiock [Indian Woman and Young Girl]* (1590), courtesy of the John Carter Brown Library, Brown University. This engraving shows a native woman of the Virginia town of Pomeiock carrying a clay vessel, while a child holds a rattle and a doll. The woman resembles the female figures painted by Renaissance artists like Botticelli.

[2890] Robert W. Weir, *Embarkation of the Pilgrims* (1844), courtesy of the Architect of the Capitol. This painting shows Pilgrims praying on the deck of the *Speedwell* as it departs from Holland, on July 22, 1620, on its way to meet the *Mayflower* in England. The rainbow on the left symbolizes divine protection and hope.

[7329] C. Colin, *Ferdinand Cortés and Hernando de Soto in the Camp of the Inca at Caxamalca. The Order of His Court and the Reverence with Which His Subjects Approached His Person, Astonished the Spaniards* (c. 1902), courtesy of the Library of Congress [LC-USZ62-104362]. The Spanish conquistadors discovered a complex, highly developed society when they arrived in Peru. This image depicts an Incan court ritual that particularly impressed the Spanish. Garcilaso de la Vega's *Commentarios Reales* (Royal Commentaries) tells an Incan version of the conquest of Peru.

[8340] John Gadsby Chapman, *Baptism of Pocahontas* (1840), courtesy of the Architect of the Capitol. Pocahontas was the daughter of Powhatan, a powerful chief of the Algonquian Indians near colonial Virginia. Although her life has been much romanticized, it is known that she married Englishman John Rolfe in 1614. Before their marriage, Pocahontas converted to Christianity and was baptized and christened Rebecca.

[8359] William H. Powell, *Discovery of the Mississippi* (1855), courtesy of the Architect of the Capitol. At the center of this painting is Hernando de Soto, riding a white horse. In 1541 de Soto, a Spanish explorer, became the first European to see the Mississippi River. The painting shows Native Americans watching de Soto's approach, as a chief offers a peace pipe.

[8365] John Vanderlyn, *Landing of Columbus* (1847), courtesy of the Architect of the Capitol. Columbus is shown raising the royal flag in order to "claim" Guanahani, the West Indies island he renamed San Salvador, for Ferdinand and Isabella. As natives look on from behind a tree, crew members search for gold in the sand.

Context: How does Juan Ortiz's story compare to John Smith's account of his own salvation through the intervention of Pocahontas? Why do you think Pocahontas's story has received so much more attention and is so frequently retold? What is the effect of de la Vega's decision not to record Hirrihigua's daughter's name?

Context: Both Juan Ortiz and Cabeza de Vaca were stranded in North America as a result of the ill-fated Panfilo de Narváez expedition. How do Juan Ortiz's experiences compare to Cabeza de Vaca's?

Context: Garcilaso de la Vega praises the beauty of the native women in Florida, and even places them on the level of Cleopatra. What significance does the physical beauty of native peoples have in de la Vega's (or conquistadors') account? What is the rhetorical value of comparing the women to the Egyptian queen? Compare Garcilaso de la Vega's portrait of Native American women to those composed by other colonists, conquistadors, and engraver Theodor De Bry.

Context: De la Vega's narrative points to the often shaky distinction between "history" and "fiction" during the Renaissance. (In fact the Spanish word for history, *historia*, is also the word for story.) What parts of *The Florida of the Inca* seem to be the result of imagination rather than eyewitness testimony?

Exploration: While de la Vega's account of Juan Ortiz's relationship with Hirrihigua's daughter is one of the earliest descriptions of an interracial relationship between a European and a Native American, it certainly was not the last. Interracial relationships and romances between Native Americans and Europeans or European Americans fascinated nineteenth-century American writers as well. How does Juan Ortiz and Hirrihigua's daughter's story compare to later fictional interracial romances (such as Cooper's *The Last of the Mohicans*, Child's *Hobomok*, or Sedgwick's *Hope Leslie*)?

Exploration: Pan-Indianism usually refers to the nonviolent liberation philosophy of Native Americans and is based in part on the belief that Native Americans share a collective spiritual reality and certain essential cultural attributes that distinguish them from European Americans and other groups. In the preface to *Florida*, de la Vega makes an early move toward pan-Indianism when he claims that his Incan ancestry allows him to present a unique and more truthful perspective on the de Soto expedition and on the native peoples of Florida, although he had never set foot in Florida and presumably never spoke to a native Floridian. What evidence could you use to substantiate de la Vega's claim? What are the potential benefits and drawbacks of pan-Indianism as a rhetorical and political strategy?

Exploration: Eight paintings grace the Capitol rotunda in Washington, D.C., each of which depicts a key moment in the discovery and independence of the United States. One of these is William Powell's *Discovery of the Mississippi by Hernando de Soto,*

1541 A.D. There are three other images of discovery: *Landing of Columbus*, by John Vanderlyn, *Baptism of Pocahontas*, by John Chapman, and *Embarkation of the Pilgrims*, by Robert Weir. All were painted between 1840 and 1853. To what extent do these images still represent what we might consider the four key moments in the discovery of the United States? Would the de Soto expedition still play so large a role if these paintings were to be created today?

Samuel de Champlain (c. 1570–1635)

Often called the "Father of New France," Samuel de Champlain was a leader in exploring and claiming vast areas of North America for France. Born in the town of Brouage on the Atlantic coast of France, Champlain learned the arts of seafaring, navigation, and cartography early in his life. Because he was passionately interested in, as he put it, "obtain[ing] a knowledge of different countries, regions, and realms," Champlain accepted a post as commander of a Spanish trade ship that sailed to the West Indies and to New Spain in 1599. After returning to France, he was named "geographer royal" to the king and was sent to Canada as part of a 1603 expedition commissioned to confirm and further the North American discoveries made in the mid-1530s by Jacques Cartier. On this trip, Champlain and his party sailed up the St. Lawrence River to the site of present-day Montreal, where they helped establish the valuable fur trade with Native Americans that would become the central commercial enterprise of New France. In 1604, Champlain returned to Canada to explore the coastal areas that make up the present-day Maritime Provinces and New England. On another journey on the St. Lawrence in 1608, Champlain founded Quebec City, which eventually became the French capital in North America.

Champlain was soon appointed lieutenant general of the colony. Hoping to further French land claims and commercial interests, he sent delegates to explore as far west as the Great Lakes region. His scouts learned Native American customs and languages and established friendly relations with the Huron and Montagnais Indians in particular. The French eventually joined with these Indian allies to fight their traditional enemy, the Iroquois, in sustained conflict. Champlain recorded his experiences in New France in four books, which combine illustrations, maps, personal narrative, geographical and natural description, history, and ethnographic insights into Native American life. His combination of pictorial and verbal description lends his work an unusually vivid quality that literary critic Gordon Sayre has described as a "distinctive narrative storyboard effect."

In 1629, invading British troops unexpectedly captured Quebec and Champlain was taken to England as a prisoner. When a diplomatic treaty returned Canada to the French in 1632, Champlain was reinstalled as lieutenant general. He died three years later in Quebec on Christmas Day.

[2846] Samuel de Champlain, Illustration from *Les Voyages du Sieur de Champlain Capitaine Ordinaire pour Le Roy en la Nouvelle France en Années 1615 et 1618* (1619), courtesy of the Robert Dechert Collection, Annenberg Rare Book and Manuscript Library, University of Pennsylvania.

■ Ask your students to pay close attention to the incident in Chapter VIII of *The Voyages of Sieur de Champlain* in which French sailors and Indians have a violent skirmish over possession of some large iron kettles. In this passage, Champlain narrates the way cultural misunderstandings and the ill-considered actions of a few individuals can ignite destructive, large-scale confrontations. Have your students outline the progression of events and the actions that lead to the escalation of the fight. Who are the principal actors? What motivates them? What kinds of communication difficulties cause and exacerbate the situation? How do the French and Indian leaders ultimately diffuse the tension? Is the situation resolved satisfactorily for all parties? It might be useful to ask your students to compare Champlain's account of this encounter with some English and Spanish narratives of violent confrontations with Native Americans (William Bradford, John Smith, Christopher Columbus, or Bernal Díaz del Castillo, for example).

■ In *Cartography in Prehistoric, Ancient, and Medieval Europe and the Mediterranean*, J. Brian Harley and David Woodward argue that "maps are graphic representations that facilitate a spatial understanding of things, concepts, conditions, processes, or events in the human world." Have your students examine Champlain's "Map of New France," which is featured in the archive. How does this map help facilitate Champlain's view of New France and the Americas more generally? What key concepts and processes are represented in Champlain's map? You might call attention to details such as how he pictorially represents the landscape and the relative scale of the various pictures. How does Champlain depict Native Americans? Plants and animals? Natural resources? Europeans? How does the map differ from current maps? After you have discussed Champlain's map, ask your students to borrow his techniques to produce a map of their own city, their neighborhood, or an area they have visited recently. Discuss their maps as a class.

CHAMPLAIN WEB ARCHIVE

[1365] Anonymous, *The Battle of Ticonderoga* (1609), courtesy of the Library of Congress [LC-USZ62-108526]. This illustration depicts the French explorer Samuel de Champlain and his Native American allies fighting the Iroquois on the Ticonderoga Peninsula in 1609. As seen in the illustration, Champlain's mechanical firearms overpowered the Iroquois. **[2846]** Samuel de Champlain, Illustration from *Les Voyages du Sieur de Champlain Capitaine Ordinaire pour Le Roy en la Nouvelle France en Années 1615 et 1618* (1619), courtesy of the Robert Dechert Collection, Annenberg Rare Book and Manuscript Library, University of Pennsylvania. This engraving, made during one of Champlain's voyages, shows Huron funerary practices.

QUESTIONS

Comprehension: What kinds of misunderstandings and disagreements do Champlain and his party have with the Native Americans they encounter? How do they communicate? What kind of strategies do they use to diffuse tension?

Context: In Chapter VIII of *The Voyages of Sieur de Champlain*, Champlain describes the problems he has communicating with Native Americans. He finds that he cannot get answers to questions because "we did not understand their language, although they attempted to explain by signs." Later, he credits Etienne Brulé for his skill as both a cultural and a linguistic interpreter between the Indians and the French. John Smith, on the other hand, never mentions the language barrier that must have complicated his dealings with the Native Americans in Virginia, nor does he mention the presence of interpreters. Why might

Champlain and Smith have narrated their encounters with Native American languages so differently? How do their different accounts of linguistic communication shape their descriptions of their own positions within Native American communities?

Context: How does Champlain's concern with developing the fur trade compare to the Spanish explorers' interest in finding gold and setting up *encomiendas* in America? How might the differences in the production, trade, and value of these different commodities have led to substantive differences between the French and the Spanish settlements?

Context: How does Etienne Brulé survive the hostile Indians who torture him and are "prepared to put him to death"? Does Champlain's narrative of Brulé's "miraculous" escape describe divine intervention, or is he implying that Brulé simply benefited from a fortuitously timed thunderstorm? How does Champlain's narration of the role of prayer and religious icons in French interactions with natives compare to Columbus's or Díaz del Castillo's descriptions of Spanish religious practices during the Conquest?

Exploration: Both Champlain and William Bradford narrated their contact experiences with Native Americans on the coast of present-day Massachusetts. How do their accounts differ? What do they have in common? How do their descriptions of the coastal landscape and the area's natural resources compare?

Exploration: To what extent is the history of New France important for understanding American colonial history? Why do you think Champlain's voyages were not depicted in one of the four scenes of U.S. discovery in the Capitol Rotunda? (The four scenes are of Columbus, de Soto, Pocahontas, and the Pilgrims, and they date from the 1840s to 1850s.) Would Champlain's voyages be included today if the Rotunda paintings were replaced?

John Smith (1580–1631)

A consummate self-promoter, John Smith would be delighted with the privileged position that his adventures in Virginia have assumed within American mythology. The subject of a Disney animated film and popular legend, as well as scholarly inquiry, Smith and his writings have come to be regarded as representative of the colonial Virginia experience.

Despite his rather ordinary beginnings as the son of a yeoman farmer in England, Smith early hurled himself into a life of adventure. Upon his father's death in 1596, he journeyed to continental Europe and volunteered as a soldier in the Dutch fight for independence from Spain. After completing his tour of duty, he sailed on a privateer in the Mediterranean and then joined the Austrian army to fight against the Turks in Hungary and Romania. Wounded in battle, Smith was taken captive and held in slavery until he murdered his Turkish master and escaped. He made his way back to England in 1604.

Given Smith's history of daring exploits, it is perhaps not surpris-

[2869] Samuel de Champlain, *Carte Geographique de la Nouvelle Franse . . . Faict Len 1612* (1612), courtesy of the Osher Map Library, University of Southern Maine. Samuel de Champlain mapped the region from the St. Lawrence Valley through the Georgian Bay and Lake Ontario and along the Atlantic coast to Cape Cod between 1603 and 1616. This map, which uses Native American mapping techniques, shows Lake Ontario and Niagara Falls.

[3191] Samuel de Champlain, *Sketch of Wampanoag Wigwams at Plymouth* (1605), courtesy of the John Carter Brown Library, Brown University. The Wampanoag, meaning "Eastern people," probably numbered around 12,000 just before contact. They lived in small bands in beehive-shaped huts loosely clustered into villages, as shown in this sketch. English settlers in the Plymouth colony originally modeled their dwellings after these highly efficient native homes but soon abandoned them in favor of more "proper" British-style housing.

[1900] John White, *The Manner of Their Fishing* (c. 1585), courtesy of the John Carter Brown Library, Brown University.

ing that the Virginia Company, a group of investors interested in colonizing England's holdings in North America, selected him to serve on an expedition to form a settlement in Virginia. But while Smith's qualities of strength, boldness, self-sufficiency, and stubbornness may have made him a good soldier, they did not always suit him to the project of community-building at Jamestown. He quickly alienated most of the aristocratic members of the expedition and was nearly executed for insubordination. Still, his willingness to work hard, combined with his sheer ability to survive in the difficult climate and environment, made him valuable to the colony. After surviving a particularly virulent outbreak of illness that killed off many of the other members of the company, Smith successfully organized the remaining colonists into units to build shelters and fortifications. He also negotiated with Native Americans for food and other supplies. In recognition of his contributions, Smith was elected president of the Virginia colony's council in 1607.

Smith soon established himself as the most knowledgeable colonist at Jamestown on the geography of the region and the customs of the Native Americans who lived there. Although he understood that diplomatic relations with the native peoples were necessary to the survival of the colony, he never acknowledged the Native Americans he encountered as equals or as friends. He believed that his mission entailed making Virginia safe for colonial expansion at any cost, and he was perfectly willing to use deception and force to gain advantage over Powhatan and the Chesapeake Bay tribe. Even Smith's famous account of his rescue by the Indian princess Pocahontas does not offer a positive view of native culture. Instead, he portrays Pocahontas as alone among her tribe in her possession of "civilized" graces and insinuates that she welcomed European colonization.

Two years after becoming president of the Virginia colony's council, Smith was injured in an explosion and was forced to return to England. He made several subsequent brief voyages to the northern portions of the Virginia colony (an area for which he coined the name "New England"), but he never again returned to Jamestown or settled in North America. Although his offers to serve as an adviser in the new American colonies (including Plymouth) were consistently rebuffed, Smith devoted the rest of his life to writing about the New World and promoting exploration and colonization there. He wrote and compiled two works on Virginia (1608, 1612) and two works on New England (1616, 1620), eventually revising and combining them into *The General History of Virginia, New England, and the Summer Isles* (1624). All of Smith's writings are concerned both with encouraging colonial expansion and with fashioning his own image as the ideal colonist.

TEACHING TIPS

■ Your students will probably be anxious to discuss Smith's account of his rescue by Pocahontas since the story has assumed the status of a foundational American myth. (It is no accident a painting of Pocahontas being baptized hangs inside the Rotunda of the Capitol and that a sculpture of Pocahontas saving Smith hangs over the west door to the Rotunda today.) It is important to emphasize that Smith revised his story about his relationship with Pocahontas: in his initial narrative of the episode in his 1608 *True Relation* he does not mention her role in helping him escape captivity and avoid execution. It is only in the *General History*, written sixteen years after Smith's encounter with Powhatan, that he celebrates Pocahontas's intervention on his behalf. Some literary critics and historians have argued that Smith's inclusion of Pocahontas in the later narrative represents an effort to capitalize on her status as a celebrity in England. After she had converted to Christianity, married John Rolfe, traveled to England, and been presented at Court, Pocahontas was revered as an assimilated and fully Anglicized Native American—the ideal colonial subject. Thus, Smith's anxiousness to assert a significant relationship with her might be just one more example of his commitment to self-promotion. Ask students to think about what other reasons Smith might have had for revising his account in this way. What assumptions about Indian-European relations, gender, and politics underwrite this story? Why has the story achieved archetypal status? You might ask your class to generate a list of other examples of this trope of an attractive young woman intervening on behalf of her colonizer (for example, La Malinche, Sacajawea, and even contemporary news stories about women who defect from China, the Middle East, and other countries to be with American men). Why is this story continually repeated and celebrated? What kind of fantasy about American power does it represent?

■ Ask your class to analyze the role of literacy in Smith's relations with the Native Americans of Virginia. You might look, in particular, at his account of the native peoples' wonder at his "talking paper" when he demonstrates his ability to communicate with other colonists through writing. How do writing and literacy become emblems of European power for Smith? How might this status impact his relationship to his own text?

■ Ask your class to analyze the role of technology in colonization and in Smith's relations with the Native Americans of Virginia as presented in his narrative. For example, you might have students focus on Smith's description of his demonstration of a compass:

> Much they marveled at the playing of the fly and needle, which they could see so plainly and yet not touch it because of the glass that covered them. But when he demonstrated by that globe-like jewel the roundness of the earth and skies, the sphere of the sun, moon, and stars, and how the sun did chase the night round about the world continually, the greatness of the land and sea, the diversity of nations, variety of complexions, and how we were to them antipodes and many other such like matters, they all stood as amazed with admiration.

Here Smith indulges in a fantasy of the Indians' simultaneous bewilderment and understanding—they are awestruck by the unfamiliar instrument and do not understand the physical structure of glass, yet they seem to grasp Smith's complicated explanation of the cosmos. You might play up the unintentional humor of this moment. One wonders what exactly the Indians thought of Smith's operations with the compass, and what kind of response they were really expressing when Smith took them to be "amazed with admiration." Ask your students to think about why Smith is so invested in attributing the experience of wonder to the native peoples and why he problematizes that wonder with an assertion of transparency and communication.

QUESTIONS

Comprehension: What vision of colonial commerce does Smith offer in his description of New England's potential? How does Smith's model of colonial labor and trade differ from the model most Spanish colonizers adopted in Mexico and South America? For example, what kinds of commodities and economic potential does Columbus seem to value in his letters to the Spanish monarchs?

Comprehension: What problems does Smith have with the other English colonists in the Virginia Company? How does he represent his own leadership abilities? What role do class and nobility play in his leadership and in the colony in general?

Context: How does Smith mobilize the "discourse of wonder" in his narrative? At what point does he experience wonder himself? When does he displace the experience of wonder onto the natives he encounters?

Context: One of the models for heroic conduct that influenced Smith's self-fashioning was the figure of the knight or knight-errant, a traveling man of honor committed to helping people (often women) in trouble through his brave acts. One of the most popular and influential knight stories of Smith's day was Miguel Cervantes's story of Don Quixote, a middle-class man who becomes a knight-errant and works on the side of chivalry, the good, and endangered maidens. What knightlike traits does Smith possess? What does Smith gain rhetorically from placing himself in this tradition?

Context: Why does Smith interrupt his narrative in *The General History* with passages of translated classical verse? What general rhetorical purpose do classical allusions serve in the narrative?

Exploration: Like later colonial leaders William Bradford and John Winthrop (Unit 3), Smith hoped to secure the stable establishment of an English colony in America and his own authority within it. How do Smith's attempts to consolidate his own authority compare to Bradford's and Winthrop's? How do the conflicts and tensions between colonists in Jamestown compare to the conflicts and tensions within Plymouth and Massachusetts Bay?

Exploration: One of the models of the ideal conqueror for Spanish and British colonists alike was the Roman emperor Julius Caesar, who wrote his autobiographical commentaries *The Gallic War* in the third person and referred to himself as "he." What impact does Smith's choice of a third-person narrator have on *The General History*? Which other explorers use this strategy? How does Smith's narration compare to Henry Adams's self-conscious use of the third person in *The Education of Henry Adams* (Unit 9)? Why do you think Smith used first-person narration in his accounts of New England?

[7727] Anonymous, *How They Took Him Prisoner in the Ooze, 1607* (1629), courtesy of the Library of Congress [LC-USZ62-99524]. This image details the capture of a "heroic" John Smith by Native Americans. The caption reads: "Captain Smith bindeth a savage to his arme, fighteth with the King of Pamaunkee and all his company, and slew 3 of them."

Adriaen Van der Donck (1620–1655)

Adriaen Van der Donck began his professional life studying law at the University of Leyden in the Netherlands. Then, in 1641, he changed the course of his career by accepting a commission to travel to the Dutch commercial colony in America (present-day New York) to administer the estate of the wealthy patron Kiliaen Van Rennselaer. Van der Donck's assignment—to stifle the fur trade and instead promote agricultural settlement in Van Rennselaer's land in the Hudson Valley—soon brought him into conflict with the Dutch colonists, who were more interested in lucrative fur trapping and hunting than in farming. Uncomfortable with the climate of "great strife, uproar, quarreling . . . [and] mutual discord," as he put it, Van der Donck decided to leave Van Rennselaer's employment in 1646 and strike out on his own. After negotiating with the governor of New Netherland, William Kieft, he received a grant from the Dutch West India Company to purchase an estate just north of Manhattan. There, at the junction of the Hudson and Nepperhan Rivers, Van der Donck built one of the first saw mills in North America. His success and his status as an educated gentleman prompted settlers in the region to refer to him as "Jonk Herr" ("young gentleman," or "young nobleman"). Eventually, the name evolved into "Yonkers," now the name of a city north of Manhattan.

[2642] John Heaten, *Van Bergen Overmantel* (c. 1730–45), courtesy of the New York State Historical Association.

Van der Donck once again found himself at the center of political controversy when he clashed with the new governor of the colony, Pietr Stuyvesant, who arrived in New Netherland in 1647. Van der Donck wrote a lengthy formal complaint against the governor, entitled *Remonstrance of New Netherland*, and sailed back to the Netherlands to personally deliver it to government authorities in 1649. While residing in Europe, Van der Donck completed another work, the *Description of New Netherland*. This detailed account of the native inhabitants, plants, animals, and other natural resources of the colony was a **promotional tract**, meant to encourage immigration from the Netherlands and to defend Dutch imperial claims against rival European powers such as the French, Swedish, and English. Van der Donck returned to his adopted land in 1653 and died on his estate two years later.

■ Ask your students to pay attention to the way Van der Donck uses the discourse of the "sublime" (see Unit 4) to describe the landscape and natural productions of the Dutch colony. His descriptions of the beached whales, the power of the Great Falls on the Mohawk River, and the "grand and sublime" spectacle of bush burning all work to convey a sense of awesome natural power to the reader. Strikingly, Van der Donck's invocations of the sublime often end on a warning note: the beached whales die and infect the river; the waterfall leads to the destruction of an Indian family traveling by canoe; and the bush fires destroy gardens and homes. Ask students to think about what kind of relationship Van der Donck's narrative constructs between humans and the natural world. Why does he consistently offer ominous hints of danger? How might his narrative of the sublime complicate his book's efforts to serve as a promotional tract encouraging settlement?

■ Have your students compile a list of the anecdotes Van der Donck uses in the course of his description of New Netherland. (You might need to explain that an anecdote is a short account of a specific, often unusual or humorous, occurrence. It offers more personal, subjective insights than general descriptions of nature, geography, or communities.) After your students have charted Van der Donck's anecdotes, ask them to think about when and why he decides to rely on a specific story to supplement his narrative description. What kind of authority do anecdotes bring to his narrative? What issues and topics seem to demand the relation of specific stories? Do the anecdotes support or challenge Van der Donck's general claims about life in New Netherland?

QUESTIONS

Comprehension: In "Why This Country is Called New Netherland," Van der Donck is concerned with proving that the region was "first found or discovered by the Netherlanders." What evidence does he provide to refute other nations' potential claims to the Dutch colony?

Context: How does Van der Donck describe his own and other Dutch colonists' relationships with Native Americans in the region? When does he draw on Indian oral traditions to bolster his own historical account of New Netherland? When do the Dutch colonists rely on (and adopt) Indian knowledge and skills? How does Van der Donck's account of the relationship between colonists and natives compare to accounts by representatives of other European groups in North America, such as Samuel de Champlain or John Smith?

Context: How does Van der Donck's frequent discussion of "sublime" natural occurrences (such as waterfalls and bush fires) compare to the discourse of the "marvelous" as it appears in early contact narratives (such as those by Columbus, Smith, or Bernal Díaz del Castillo)?

Exploration: Compare Van der Donck's description of the falls to Thomas Cole's nineteenth-century masterpiece *The Falls of the Kaaterskill*. How does each create a sense of grandeur and awe? How do their visions of the sublime differ?

Exploration: How does Van der Donck's description of life in the New Netherland colony compare to the accounts of English colonists living in New England (such as William Bradford or John Winthrop) around the same time? How does Van der Donck's portrait of the Dutch relationship with Native Americans compare to Puritans' accounts of their interactions with native tribes?

Exploration: What is the role of timber in a European colonial or frontier settlement? How does Van der Donck's description of the abundance of lumber and of the settlers' and Indians' manner of dealing with the woods that are "always in our way" compare to James Fenimore Cooper's descriptions of the role of the woods in *The Pioneers*? How do these two writers characterize settlers' and natives' efforts to clear the land of woods and brush? How does each writer describe the effects of forest fires?

Exploration: Nineteenth-century writer Washington Irving (Unit 6) claimed in his fiction that the Dutch origins of New York could still be felt in the regional culture and geography. What, according to Van der Donck, are the essential attributes of New Netherland and of its Dutch colonizers? How does his portrait of New Netherland compare to Irving's nostalgic and mythic presentation of the area's Dutch ancestry in stories such as "Rip Van Winkle"?

[3694] Thomas Cole, *The Falls of the Kaaterskill* (1826), courtesy of the Warner Collection of the Gulf States Paper Corporation. Cole was one of the first American landscape artists and a founder of the Hudson River School of painting. Romantic depictions of wilderness became popular as the United States continued its westward expansion.

[9042] Laura Arnold, *The Great Chain of Being* (2003), courtesy of Laura Arnold. From the beginning of the Middle Ages through the early nineteenth century, "educated Europeans" conceived of the universe in terms of a hierarchical Great Chain of Being with God at its apex. In many ways, this hierarchy, still pervasive in Western theology and thought, stands in opposition to Native American and other belief systems that view the human and spirit worlds as co-existing on a horizontal plane.

Americo Paredes (1915–1999)

Born in the town of Brownsville on the border between south Texas and Mexico, Americo Paredes became an eloquent interpreter of the complicated, bicultural society that had grown out of the conflicts and tensions of this region. As the title of his second volume of poetry indicates, he found his identity *Between Two Worlds*. Paredes's pioneering work recording and elucidating Chicano folklore, as well as his commitment to furthering the field of Mexican American studies, left a lasting legacy that has inspired many writers and scholars interested in border cultures.

Paredes received his early education in Brownsville's public schools and at the local community college. He began writing poetry and fiction in the late 1930s. His novel *George Washington Gomez: A Mexicotexan Novel*, a bitter coming-of-age story of a Mexican American man who experiences discrimination in his childhood and copes by eventually renouncing his culture, was completed in 1940 but was not published until 1991. At the start of World War II, Paredes was sent overseas with the U.S. Army, where he served as a reporter for *The Stars and Stripes* and as an administrator for the International Red Cross.

After returning to Texas, Paredes entered college at the University

[6573] Anonymous, Cover art for Americo Paredes's *With a Pistol in His Hand* (1958), courtesy of the University of Texas Press.

of Texas at Austin. When he received his Ph.D. in folklore and Spanish in 1956, he became the first Mexican American student to earn a doctoral degree at that institution. Paredes wrote his dissertation on the story of the Mexican American folk hero Gregorio Cortez. In the late nineteenth century, Cortez avenged the unprovoked death of his brother at the hands of Anglo rangers (*rinches*) by killing a white sheriff. Cortez then successfully evaded the posses sent to capture him by drawing on his connections within the Chicano community and by skillfully navigating the southwestern landscape. When the *rinches* began punishing the Mexicans who helped Cortez, he surrendered himself to spare his people any further suffering. The story of Cortez, with its emphasis on heroic protest and resistance in the face of Anglo oppression, became legendary among Mexican Americans in the Texas border region and inspired many stories, drawings, and especially songs that celebrated Cortez's life and martyrdom. Paredes's dissertation, entitled *With a Pistol in His Hand: A Border Ballad and Its Hero*, explored the political and cultural importance of the Cortez story and of the ballads, or *corridos* (see Unit 5), which it inspired. This pioneering study of the development of folklore and the importance of conflict in border regions became enormously influential and has gone through over eight printings.

Paredes joined the faculty at the University of Texas in 1957. During his thirty-year teaching career, he was involved in the creation and administration of the Mexican American studies program and the Center for Intercultural Studies of Folklore and Ethnomusicology. His scholarship and creative work were instrumental in the movement to define and proclaim a unique "border identity" for people living in the land caught between the United States and Mexico, which has long been characterized by conflict and tension.

TEACHING TIPS

■ Read the Gregorio Cortez *corrido* aloud with your students. Ask them to think about what made Cortez such a heroic figure to Mexican Americans living in Texas. How does Cortez display his heroism? You might have them generate a list of qualities and characteristics that describe Cortez. After thoroughly discussing the *corrido*, ask your students to compare its plot, characterization of its hero, and themes to those of a contemporary song that they like.

■ Ask your students to think about the significance of the fact that Gregorio Cortez shares his name with the Spanish conquistador Hernán Cortés. Does Gregorio Cortez have more in common with Cortés or with the Aztecs he conquered? How might the creation of a specifically Mexican American Cortez challenge or build on the legacy of Cortés the conquistador?

■ Have students draw a map of the town in which George Washington Gomez lives, including the major landmarks and locales that Gomez visits. What distinguishes this as a border town? How is space divided in the town both symbolically and literally?

Comprehension: What is a *corrido*? Why do you think the story of Gregorio Cortez was such a popular subject for ballads?

Comprehension: What different names does the protagonist of *George Washington Gomez* go by? What is the significance of each name? When does he adopt different names in different situations?

Context: How does Gloria Anzaldúa's *Borderlands* both borrow from and challenge Paredes's definition of Mexican American *mestizo* identity? How does her description of the obstacles and prejudices that Chicana women face compare to Paredes's narrative of the obstacles and prejudices faced by a Chicano man like George Washington Gomez?

Context: Compare the vision of American masculinity as presented in *corridos* such as "The Ballad of Gregorio Cortez" with that presented in the narratives of Spanish and British colonial authors such as Cabeza de Vaca, Bernal Díaz del Castillo, and John Smith. What attributes do these men share? In what ways do the *corridos* present a new or different notion of American manhood?

Context: Gloria Anzaldúa calls the border "*una herida abierta,*" or, "an open wound." What is Paredes's implicit or explicit definition of the border? Do he and Anzaldúa agree on the experience of border life?

Exploration: Why do you think an "outlaw" figure like Gregorio Cortez became a folk hero in the border region? Can you think of similar rebel or outlaw contemporary figures who have acquired hero status? If so, in what contexts are they celebrated? Among what groups? When is rebellion against authority perceived as acceptable and even heroic?

Gloria Anzaldúa (b. 1942)

Gloria Anzaldúa's work is fundamentally concerned with articulating what she calls a "new *mestiza* consciousness," an identity characterized by hybridity, flexibility, and plurality and focused on the experiences of Chicanas (Mexican American women) and particularly *mestizas* (Chicana and Mexican women who have mixed Native American and Spanish heritage). Writing fiction, poetry, memoirs, and literary and cultural criticism (sometimes all within the same text), Anzaldúa has helped lend authority to women of color as well as lesbians, whom she identifies as empowered by the inclusiveness and expansiveness of *mestiza* identity.

Anzaldúa was born on a ranch in south Texas, near the border of Mexico. In her youth, she and her family labored as migrant agricultural workers. Although she felt stifled by the confines of a traditional Chicano home life in which gender roles tended to be rigid and rather limiting, Anzaldúa early found what she calls "an entry into a different way of being" through reading. Defying everyone's expectations, she went to college and earned a B.A. from Pan American University, an M.A. from the University of Texas at Austin,

[6575] Marcos Loya, *Americo Paredes with Guitar* (2001), courtesy of UCLA. This painting of Americo Paredes was done by Marcos Loya two years after Paredes's death. Loya is himself an accomplished Chicano guitarist.

[6581] Americo Paredes, Sheet music: *Gregorio Cortez* p.1 (n.d.), courtesy of the General Libraries, the University of Texas at Austin, © 2002. Cortez was a border hero who lives on in folk memory and whose story was told by Americo Paredes in *With a Pistol in His Hand*. The second page of the sheet music can be seen in the *American Passages* Archive [6583].

[7747] Danny Lyon, *Fifth and Mesa in the Second Ward. El Paso's "Barrio"* (1972), courtesy of the National Archives and Records Administration (NARA). Photograph by Danny Lyon for the Environmental Protection Agency's *Documerica* project. Lyon, one of the most creative documentary photographers of the late twentieth century, photographed the Rio Grande Valley and the Chicano barrio of South El Paso, Texas.

[9064] Anonymous, *El Corrido de Gregorio Cortez* (c. 1910), courtesy of Pedro Rocha and Lupe Martínez. Text of Cortez corrido. This *corrido* takes as its subject the murder of an Anglo-Texan sheriff by a Texas Mexican, Gregorio Cortez, and the ensuing chase, capture, and imprisonment of Cortez.

[5394] Dorothea Lange, *Mexican Mother in California* (1935), courtesy of the Library of Congress [LC-USF34-000825-ZC].

and did graduate work at the University of California at Santa Cruz. She has taught high-school English, been involved in education programs for the children of migrant workers, and taught creative writing and literature at a number of universities. A prolific writer, Anzaldúa has published stories, poems, critical theory, children's books, and a novel (*La Prieta*). Her work appears in both mainstream publications and alternative presses and journals. Anzaldúa's complex identity as a woman, a Chicana, a *mestiza*, and a lesbian is reflected in her pioneering contributions to gender studies, Chicano studies, queer theory, and creative writing. Her 1987 book, *Borderlands/La Frontera: The New Mestiza*, stands as a manifesto of her ideas about culture and identity construction.

Because she believes that language and identity are inextricably linked, Anzaldúa's writing often engages in daring narrative innovations intended to reflect the inclusiveness of the *mestiza* identity: by shifting between and combining different genres, points of view, and even languages, she attempts to represent the *mestiza*'s propensity to "shift out of habitual formations . . . [and] set patterns." In this way, her narrative literalizes her ideal of "border crossing." Her writing thus works against hegemonic structures that limit individual expression or impose stereotypes based on race, gender, nationality, or sexual orientation. Composed partially in untranslated Spanish and slipping between poetry and prose, Anzaldúa's texts consistently articulate her commitment to making writing a vehicle for personal freedom and political activism.

TEACHING TIPS

■ Students who do not read or speak Spanish may be frustrated by Anzaldúa's inclusion of words, phrases, and sentences in untranslated Spanish, and even students with a background in what Anzaldúa calls "Standard Spanish" may have difficulty understanding her use of regional Chicano dialects and Chicano slang known as *Caló*. Ask your students to pick a page of Anzaldúa's prose or poetry and look up the Spanish vocabulary both in a traditional Spanish dictionary and in a dictionary of Chicano Spanish such as *The Dictionary of Chicano Spanish/El diccionario del español chicano* by Roberto A. Galván and Richard V. Teschner. Ask your students to write a journal entry discussing why Anzaldúa challenges her readers in this way. What kind of audience is she hoping to reach? What kind of experience is she trying to provide for readers? What message does Anzaldúa send about the relative importance of English, Castillian Spanish, and *Caló*?

■ Ask your students to think about the significance of the title

Borderlands/La Frontera, the work from which the passages in *The Norton Anthology of American Literature* are drawn. Have your class discuss the importance of Anzaldúa's choice to incorporate both English and Spanish in the title and the significance of the slash, which itself functions as a kind of border within the title. How does the title reflect Anzaldúa's concern with articulating multiple perspectives and celebrating inclusivity? Anzaldúa has claimed that the capitalization of the word "Borderlands" throughout her text is a means of indicating that the border is less a physical place and more a state of mind or a cultural experience for *mestizas*. Ask your students to list and discuss the different kinds of psychological, cultural, sexual, racial, and spiritual borders that the text explores.

QUESTIONS

Comprehension: What is a Chicana? A *mestiza*? What does Anzaldúa mean when she calls for "a new *mestiza* consciousness"?

Context: Examine the "Visit Mexico" poster featured in the archive. What relationship does the poster seem to posit among Mexico, women, and food? Examine the portions of *Borderlands/La Frontera* in which Anzaldúa discusses cooking and the cultivation of corn. How does Anzaldúa restructure Chicanas' relationship to food and fertility? How do her comparison of *mestizas* to indigenous corn and her lyrical description of a woman making tortillas challenge the poster's image of a woman invitingly offering up a bounty of fruit?

Context: What traits and values characterize the "new *mestiza*" as Anzaldúa conceives of her? How does the new *mestiza* compare to the ideals of femininity expressed in the three traditional representations of women in Mexican culture, La Virgen de Guadalupe, La Malinche, and La Llorona? How might Anzaldúa's work help readers understand these traditional figures differently?

Context: Álvar Núñez Cabeza de Vaca has sometimes been called "the first *mestizo*" because he had a hybrid identity influenced by and oriented within both native and European cultures. How does de Vaca's narrative of the "first *mestizo*" experience compare to Anzaldúa's narrative of the "new *mestiza*"? How do these two writers articulate their intercultural and interlinguistic abilities? How do they benefit from their status as hybrid? When does their hybridity become problematic for them?

Context: Gloria Anzaldúa is not the first person to acknowledge the power of sexual deviance to shape people's experience of a "contact zone." Spanish exploration accounts and art representing the Conquest are rife with descriptions of the *berdaches*—Native American males who cross-dressed and performed female sex and social roles. What does Anzaldúa argue is the relationship between the "queer" and the borderlands? Compare Anzaldúa's notion to the role that transgendered figures play in Cabeza de Vaca's narrative.

Exploration: Do writers have a responsibility to make their work clear and easily understandable for readers? When might it be artistically or politically important for a writer to use languages or styles that might be unfamiliar to readers?

Exploration: Compare Anzaldúa's use of polyvocality in her poem "El sonavabitche" to Sarah Piatt's use of polyvocality in "The Palace-Burner" or "A Pique at Parting" (Unit 9). How does each poet use polyvocality to articulate her consciousness of her own status as a woman? How do they use polyvocality to register protest? Do you find one of the poems easier to understand? Why?

Exploration: In recent years queer writers and activists have sought to break down traditional ideas of normal and deviant and to argue for a more fluid notion of identity and sexuality. Compare Anzaldúa's use of the term *queer* and her construction of a queer identity to the notions of lesbianism developed by poets Audre Lorde and Adrienne Rich (Unit 15).

Suggested Author Pairings

CHRISTOPHER COLUMBUS AND JOHN SMITH

Both Columbus and Smith wrote not only in order to promote colonization of the New World but also to celebrate their own accomplishments and solidify their positions as leaders and even legends. While they had extremely different ideas about the kinds of labor and commodity extraction that should characterize their respective colonies, they had many personal qualities in common. Domineering and stubborn men, they were both controversial and sometimes decidedly unpopular figures within the colonies that they helped to found. At the close of their careers, both were frustrated by what they perceived as the lack of appreciation, respect, and financial compensation they had received from the monarchies and companies that had supported their expeditions. It might be useful to compare the defensive, frustrated tone of their later writings, and to explore the reasons why, despite their disappointments, neither ever completely gave up on the potential of the New World. Significantly, both have been presented in subsequent literature, art, and popular culture as archetypal American men who exemplify a particular kind of American heroism and masculinity.

BARTOLOMÉ DE LAS CASAS AND BERNAL DÍAZ DEL CASTILLO

Casas and Díaz both wrote narratives designed to serve as revisionist histories to other conquistadors' accounts of the Conquest of Mexico. Both narratives offer horrifying descriptions of the brutality and violence that characterized the Spanish Conquest, but to different ends. While Casas intended his descriptions to serve as protests and to incite reform, Díaz seems matter-of-fact about the necessity of violently quelling native opposition and condemns what he saw as the inherent savagery already existing within Aztec culture. Despite their different attitudes toward the Indians, both Casas and Díaz record important insights into pre-Conquest indigenous culture.

ÁLVAR NÚÑEZ CABEZA DE VACA AND GARCILASO DE LA VEGA

Cabeza de Vaca and de la Vega have been described as among the earliest *mestizo* writers. While Cabeza de Vaca was more a "cultural" *mestizo*, because he was not actually of mixed racial background, de la Vega was the child of an interracial marriage and was raised biculturally. Both writers lay claim to the authority of native views and knowledge, and both were interested in the role of the "white captive" who is at least partially acculturated into native society. They both left the Americas and spent their later years in Europe and, in Cabeza de Vaca's case, North Africa. Despite their physical distance from the New World, they wrote extensively about the effects of colonization and tried to serve as advocates for the native populations which were being exploited and destroyed.

SAMUEL DE CHAMPLAIN AND ADRIAEN VAN DER DONCK

Champlain and Van der Donck offer insight into the colonial practices of France and Holland during the age of exploration and colonization. Their accounts of the importance of fur and lumber provide an interesting counterpoint to the Spanish interest in gold, slaves, and spices. While Champlain was a well-respected governor and important leader in his colony, Van der Donck occupied a more tenuous position among his countrymen, a distinction that colors their narratives. You may want to guide students toward a discussion of why the Spanish American and British American colonies, rather than French or Dutch, have been seen as having a greater impact on the shape of American culture. Is such a view justified or does it merely reflect regional bias?

AMERICO PAREDES AND GLORIA ANZALDÚA

Paredes and Anzaldúa represent the twentieth-century Chicano/a and *mestizo/a* movements to celebrate the geographical and cultural heritage of the borderlands between the United States. and Mexico. Both express the plurality of their mixed identity by working in multiple genres—Paredes in musicology, fiction, and cultural criticism and Anzaldúa in poetry, memoir, political theory, and cultural criticism. Anzaldúa offers a feminist and queer reworking of the concerns that occupied Paredes and other early Chicano activists. Her work is dedicated to providing a voice to oppressed women of color in the border regions and to exploring the role of queers in Chicano/a culture and in the construction of America more broadly.

CORE CONTEXTS

Shared Spaces: Contact Zones and Borderlands

Gloria Anzaldúa has compared the U.S./Mexico border to an "open wound" that violently splits homes, bodies, and cultures. But while the physical demarcation of the border may be a space of divisiveness and pain, the regions on either side of the border—the "Borderlands," as Anzaldúa calls them—are vibrant, dynamic places of creation and innovation. Artistic, political, and cultural practices in the borderlands blend pre-Conquest, Indian, and European heritage to form new, syncretic traditions. (In perhaps the best-known example of this syncretism, the unique version of Catholicism found in the American Southwest and Mexico incorporates pre-Conquest Indian beliefs, figures, and symbols into European Catholic rituals and tenets.) Because the geographic placement of a national border is always arbitrary and artificial, the zones on either side of it contradict the notion that people and cultures can be kept separate or distinct from one another. Instead, borderlands are permeable places where traditions interconnect and cultures overlap. They are spaces marked by conflict, violence, and hatred, but they can also produce cooperation, innovation, and hybridity.

[5615] Anonymous, *Disturnell Map of Mexico* (c. 1850), courtesy of the Benson Latin American Collection, the University of Texas, Austin.

When European explorers first landed in the New World, they crossed previously intact boundaries, bringing cultures that had been separated geographically and historically into contact with one another for the first time. Scholar Mary Louise Pratt has coined the term **contact zone** to describe the space of this kind of meeting. As Pratt puts it, a contact zone is an area in which previously separated peoples "come into contact with each other and establish ongoing relations, usually involving conditions of coercion, radical inequality, and intractable conflict." Although unequal power relations characterized contact zones in the New World, with Europeans usually asserting dominance over native peoples, contact is never a one-way phenomenon. The interactive, improvisational nature of contact necessarily creates subjects who are impacted by relations with one another within a mutually constituted experience. The concept of **transculturation** usefully expresses the complicated power relations at work within the contact zone. A term coined by Cuban anthropologist Fernando Ortiz, transculturation refers to a process through which "members of subordinated or marginal groups select and invent from materials transmitted by a dominant culture." Transculturation emphasizes the agency involved in cultural change, as well as the loss that

[5761] N. Currier, *The Battle of Sacramento* (1847), courtesy of the Library of Congress [LC-USZC2-1966].

accompanies cultural acquisition. In these ways, "transculturation" differs from the older terms "assimilation" and "acculturation," which emphasize a more one-way transmission of culture from the colonizer to the colonized, from the dominant to the marginalized. The concept of transculturation makes clear that different groups living in contact zones do not share the *same* experience or necessarily see their relationship with one another in the same way. One need only examine the markedly different perspectives on the Conquest of Mexico offered by the Indian-authored codices and European-authored narratives to appreciate the profound disjunctions and misunderstandings that separated indigenous peoples and European colonizers. It is pre-cisely these disjunctions—the presence of multiple, diverse, and often hostile viewpoints—that give rise to the dynamism of contact zones.

Eventually, centuries of war, intermarriage, rape, slavery, and disease created a mixed culture in what had once been the contact zone of the New World. As conquerors and conquered merged, a new *mestizo* identity (a blending of Indian, European, and African heritage) was created in South America, Mexico, and what is today the southwestern United States.

By the nineteenth century, *mestizo* culture in northern Mexico was changed dramatically when European Americans began moving into the areas bordering and within Mexico, eventually annexing Texas for themselves. After the Mexican-American War, the United States and Mexico adopted the Treaty of Guadalupe Hidalgo (1848), which settled the location of the boundary between the nations at the Rio Bravo (or Rio Grande) River. The new boundary ran through the center of what had once been the Mexican province of Nuevo Santander, separating people who had long thought of one another as neighbors. Unhappy with what felt like an unnatural boundary, people in the region continued to cross the river to trade, travel, entertain one another, and practice their religion.

In the early twentieth century, the United States began to create and enforce stricter regulations in an attempt to control trade and movement over the border. In times of economic hardship, the United States deported Mexican and Mexican American workers, even deporting American citizens of Mexican descent during the Great Depression of the 1930s. (Ironically, the government performed a radical about-face and began encouraging Mexican workers to cross the border when the United States suffered from a labor shortage during World War II.) Despite rigid regulations, people on both sides of the border did and continue to collaborate on resisting and finding ways around the rules that order trade and social relations between Mexico and the United States. The borderlands have always been spaces of subversion, giving rise to patterns of illegal immigration and smuggling. These kinds of challenges to border regulations are recounted and celebrated in the *corridos*, or border ballads, that are sung in the region (see Unit 5).

As the stories recorded in the *corridos* testify, government regula-

[6587] Walter Barnes Studio, *A Young Paredes with His Guitar* (n.d.), courtesy of the University of Texas, Austin.

"SHARED SPACES"
WEB ARCHIVE

[5615] Anonymous, *Disturnell Map of Mexico* (c. 1850), courtesy of the Benson Latin American Collection, the University of Texas, Austin. Although the treaty of Guadalupe-Hidalgo officially ended the expansionist Mexican-American War in 1848, disputes continued between the Mexican and United States governments concerning, among other issues, the border of Texas.
[5761] N. Currier, *The Battle of Sacramento* (1847), courtesy of the Library of Congress [LC-USZC2-1966]. Americans charge against Mexicans during the battle near Rancho Sacramento, just north of Chihuahua, Mexico, on February 28, 1847. The heroism and forcefulness of the American soldiers contrast with the weakness of the Mexican forces and reflect American biases.
[6387] Jose Suarez, *Corrido: Venimos de Matamoros* [We Come from Matamoros] (1939), courtesy of the Library of Congress, American Memory. The alternate title for this Spanish-language *corrido*, which features vocals and guitar accompaniment, is "Bandit

Trouble on the Rio Grande Border 1915."

[6587] Walter Barnes Studio, *A Young Paredes with His Guitar* (n.d.), courtesy of the University of Texas, Austin. This photograph shows Americo Paredes strumming his guitar. Paredes devoted a good deal of his life to the study of Mexican border ballads, or *corridos*.

[6708] Judith F. Baca, *Pieces of Stardust* (1992), courtesy of the Social and Public Art Resource Center. Baca is an acclaimed muralist whose work is based on the belief that art can be a forum for social dialogue.

[6709] Judith F. Baca, *350,000 Mexican Americans Deported* segment from *The Great Wall of Los Angeles* (c. 1980), courtesy of the Social and Public Art Resource Center. Since 1976, muralist Baca has worked as the founder and artistic director of the Social and Public Art Resource Center in Los Angeles. She has headed a number of large-scale projects dealing with interracial relations.

[7584] Anonymous, *Florentine Codex*, Book 12, plate 40 (1500–99), courtesy of the School of American Research and the University of Utah Press. One of a series of plates showing Spanish soldiers marching from Itztapalapan to Tenochitlán. Assembled in the 1540s by Fray Bernardino de Sahagún, the *Florentine Codex* contains a mixture of Nahuatl (the language of the Aztec peoples) and pictographic illustrations describing Aztec society and culture.

[7746] Danny Lyon, *Young Men of the Second Ward, El Paso's Classic "Barrio" Near the Mexican Border* (n.d.), courtesy of the National Archives and Records Administration. Photograph by Danny Lyon for the Environmental Protection Agency's *Documerica* project. Lyon, one of the most creative documentary photographers of the late twentieth century, photographed the Rio Grande Valley and the Chicano barrio of South El Paso, Texas.

[7750] Danny Lyon, *Chicano Teenager in El Paso's Second Ward. A Classic "Barrio" Which Is Slowly Giving Way to Urban Renewal* (1972), courtesy of the National Archives and Records Administration. Another Lyon photo for the Environmental Protection Agency's

tions can never control the permeability of the borderlands. Music, food, language, fashion, and religious practices unite people on both sides of the border in everyday cultural experiences, and the borderlands continue to be spaces of dynamic transculturation and innovation. The *mestizo* identity formed within this space is always in flux, reflecting the complexity and diversity of border culture. Contemporary *mestizo* and *mestiza* writers like Gloria Anzaldúa strive to represent the breadth and hybridity of life in the borderlands, developing innovative narratives that reflect the decentered, many-sided quality of life in the region. In this way, *mestizo* identity challenges the artificial boundary imposed by the official border; in Anzaldúa's words, "the skin of the earth is seamless."

QUESTIONS

Comprehension: What is a "contact zone"?

Comprehension: What are "borderlands"?

Comprehension: What is transculturation? Why is it important for understanding the Chicano borderlands?

Comprehension: Historically, what kinds of conflict have been central to the culture of the U.S./Mexico border region?

Context: Listen to some of the *corridos* in the archive. What values do they espouse? How do they represent life in the borderlands?

Context: When Cabeza de Vaca traveled through what is today the American Southwest, there were no national borders, but he certainly experienced contact, and participated in intercultural trade, with a variety of Indian groups. How might Cabeza de Vaca's narrative be understood as a prehistory to the culture that would eventually develop in the borderlands? How does the absence of a clear national border make his experience different from that of later inhabitants of the borderlands?

Context: Do a close reading of the photo of the El Paso Barrio. What landmarks attest to the hybrid nature of the neighborhood? To what extent does the photo depict a scene of radical inequality and conflict, and to what extent is it celebratory of the neighborhood's culture?

Exploration: Why do Americans have such different attitudes toward the Canadian and Mexican borders? Is there a border culture around the Canadian border?

Exploration: What characteristics might some neighborhoods in cities that are not near the Mexican border share with the borderlands? Does a location have to be on an actual national border to be characterized by hybridity, conflict, and cultural and commercial trade?

Exploration: Should the seventeenth-century Massachusetts Puritan colonies be considered contact zones? Why or why not?

Writing without Words: A Native American View of Culture and the Conquest

While European writing systems rely primarily on phonetic alphabets, the written records of Native Americans used a combination of phonetic, pictographic, and ideographic transcription. For example, the Sioux recorded their exploits on buffalo hides, Algonquian and Iroquoian peoples used wampum, the ancient Incans used a complex knotting system called *quipu*, and Mayans often painted and carved their glyphs on their architecture. The Mesoamerican Aztec (or Nahua) peoples tended to preserve records in accordion-style books that were fashioned from animal skin or fig bark (*amatl*) and kept in vast libraries. After the Spanish Conquest these records were often painted on cloth. Today, these books are often referred to as *lienzos*, the Spanish word for linen, or as **codices**, a term that highlights the fact that they were written by hand, rather than printed. Originally the codices were written purely in indigenous scripts, but after the Conquest they were often combined with Nahuatl or Spanish written in the Roman alphabet. An elite class of scribes drawn primarily from Mesoamerican nobility created the codices. When the Spaniards entered the Aztec city of Tenochtitlán in 1519, they systematically burnt the libraries and destroyed the codices, at least in part out of fear of what they contained. The few surviving pre-Conquest records and the six hundred remaining codices, written just after the Conquest, continue to stun readers with their visual and verbal beauty and provide an important counternarrative to the stories told by the Spanish conquistadors.

Aztec histories are another primary resource for understanding indigenous culture and life in New Spain. Scholar Elizabeth Boone has identified three primary genres of Aztec histories: cartographic histories, *res gestae*, and annals. Cartographic histories such as the *Codex Boturini* organize Aztec histories around a geographic narrative. The *Codex Boturini* tells the story of the migration legend of the Aztec peoples as they left their homeland Atzlán ("land or place of wings" or "land of herons") in the present-day southwestern United States in 1 Tecpatl (1064 C.E.) and moved south to finally settle in Tenochtitlán in the Valley of Mexico (around 1325 C.E.). The opening sequence of the codex depicts an archetypal Aztec man and the goddess Chimalma (identified by the round shield attached by a line to her head) sitting on the far left in the Aztec homeland of Aztlán. From here we see the Aztecs leaving by boat in the year 1 Tecpatl (1 Flint) to travel to the cave of Curl Mountain (Colhuacan), where the god Huitzilopochtli was discovered. Footprints mark the direction the people traveled, and tonguelike scrolls ascend heavenward to mark the directions given by the god. This cartographic history differs from Western maps in several key ways: while Aztec maps tend to be

Documerica project. Lyon photographed the Rio Grande Valley and the Chicano barrio of South El Paso, Texas.

[7942] José Suarez and Joe K. Wells, *Corrido de las Elecciones de Brownsville* (1939), courtesy of the Library of Congress [AFC 1939/001 2610b1]. Audio file of a *corrido* composed by Benino Sandoval, based on the true story of Carlo Guillen, a notorious bandit.

[7974] Janjapp Dekker, *Sandra Cisneros with Virgen de Guadalupe Boots* (n.d.), courtesy of *El Andar Magazine*. Here, Cisneros wears boots with pictures of La Virgen de Guadalupe, a vision of the Virgin Mary that appeared to an Indian convert in the sixteenth century.

[9061] N. Currier, *Nuestra Señora de Guadalupe: Our Lady of Guadalupe* (1848), courtesy of the Library of Congress [LC-USZC2-2890]. This image shows a fairly Anglicized version of La Virgen de Guadalupe, buoyed by an angel.

[7801] Anonymous, *Codex Boturini* [sheet 1] (c. 1521–40?), from *Codex Boturini: An Inquiry into the Origin of the Antiquities of America*, by John Delafield, courtesy of the University of Oregon.

[7125] Anonymous, *Florentine Codex*, plate 50 (1500–99), courtesy of the School of American Research and the University of Utah Press.

relational, participatory, and situational, Western maps from the same period tend to be objective, distanced, and abstract.

A second important genre in Mesoamerican history is *res gestae*, or "deeds done." These histories focus on the accomplishments of either the Aztecs as a group or an individual great personage. Two important post-Conquest manuscripts that employ the *res gestae* strategy are Book Twelve of the *Florentine Codex* and the *Lienzo de Tlaxcala*. Assembled in the 1540s by Fray Bernardino de Sahagún, the *Florentine Codex* contains a mixture of Nahuatl (the language of the Aztec peoples) and pictographic illustrations describing Aztec society and culture. Book Twelve depicts the deeds of Cortés and the Conquest of Mexico as they were described to Sahagún by Nahuatl-speaking elders and nobility. The book was illustrated by Aztec scribes in a style that reflects a mixture of pre-Conquest manuscript traditions and European illustration convention. For example, speaking is represented by a small, curled speech-scroll moving between people, an icon used in pre-Conquest manuscripts. The *Lienzo de Tlaxcala* provides an interesting counternarrative to the *Florentine Codex*. Transcribed in the mid-sixteenth century by Diego Muñoz de Camargo, a first-generation *mestizo*, the *Lienzo de Tlaxcala* is based on wall paintings depicting the arrival of Cortés and the fall of Tenochtitlán recorded in the homes of Tlaxcalan royalty. These paintings served as a mnemonic device for poets who sang the story of the Conquest. Tlaxcala was a rival city-state of Tenochtitlán; consequently, the narrative lauds the role of the Tlaxcalans, as well as Doña Marina, in enabling the conquest of the Aztec capital.

A third genre in Mesoamerican histories is the annals, which organize their narratives around yearly events, such as payments of tribute, and which record the calendar year. Years appear in Aztec writings as icons with a double-bordered square. One of the most common recurrent year glyphs is 1 Tecpatl (1 Flint)—symbolized by a small double circle next to a long oval with a diagonal line (a flint knife). 1 Flint was a crucial year for the Aztecs as it was the year in which many great undertakings began, including the migration from Atzlán. Tribute records such as those found in the *Huejotzingo Codex* are helpful for understanding the material culture of the Aztecs as well as the transformation from Aztec empire to the *encomi-enda* system after the Conquest. To a certain extent, other codices emphasize a temporal progression as well. For example, pho-

[8015] Anonymous, *Lienzo de Tlaxcala* [title page] (1890) from *Homenjae a Cristobal Colon. Antiguedades Mexicanas; Publicadas por la Junta Colombina de Mexico en el Cuarto Centenario del Descubrimiento de America*, courtesy of the University of Oregon.

netic year glyphs in squares accompany the travels of the Aztecs throughout the *Codex Boturini*. These glyphs, along with Aztec calendars, reminded the Aztecs of the cyclical nature of time and the recurrence of cycles of conquest and destruction. Thus the Aztecs often recorded the Spanish Conquest not as the end of an era, but merely as a predictable catastrophe that echoed earlier troubles and would be followed by a period of renewal and power.

Meso-American writings are complemented by a rich and beautiful poetic tradition that was preserved primarily through oral transmission. Most Nahuatl (Aztec) poetry can be categorized as epic, dramatic, or lyric. Miniature epics such as "Foundation of Mexico in 1325" provide an intriguing view into life in the Aztec empire and are useful companions to the history recounted in the *Codex Boturini*. Lyric poems such as "I cry, I am sad . . ." provide examples of some of the broader aesthetic hallmarks of Aztec verse: most importantly, expressive metaphors, the use of parallel phrases in which the second half echoes the first half ("I cry, I am sad"), and the notion of *in Xóchitl, in Cuícatl* ("the flower, the song"). On the Aztec calendar, Xochiquetzal, the goddess of flower and song, is also the goddess of the arts and symbolized creation, nobility, and life. Through her, songs become a form of spiritual communication of which flowers are only one reminder. Dramatic poetry such as the "Hymn of the Dead" give us insights into the songs that might have accompanied the wall paintings in Tlaxcala or that were sung in Tenochtitlán after the fall. These songs provide a useful parallel to the Sorrow Songs sung by African American slaves in the eighteenth and nineteenth centuries (Unit 7). Like African American Sorrow Songs, these poems helped bind a community together and express the traumas of life under colonial rule.

In the twentieth century, Aztec culture and literature have played an important role in the formulation of Chicano nationalism and the style of Chicano poetry. In March 1969, Chicano nationalists drafted "El Plan Espiritual de Atzlán" (The Spiritual Plan of Atzlán). For Chicano nationalists, reclaiming an Aztec heritage is more than a way to acknowledge the long-standing claim of Mexican Americans to Atzlán, the southwestern United States. It is also a way to lay claim to a history of power, aesthetics, and one of the greatest cultures that has ever existed; hence many Chicano writers include references to Aztec history, literature, and culture in their own writings. In *Borderlands/La Frontera*, Gloria Anzaldúa claims her work is built upon *"Tlilli, Tlapalli*: The Path of the Red and Black Ink" created by the Aztecs. For Anzaldúa, the Aztecs represent an alternate aesthetic heritage upon which her work can be based. Along with Anzaldúa, Corky Gonzales, Pat Mora, Lorna de Cervantes (Unit 15), Francisco X. Alarcón, and Cordelia Candelaria are only a few of the Chicano/a writers who have placed themselves in this rich literary tradition.

QUESTIONS

Comprehension: What are the main genres of Mesoamerican history? What is an example of each?

Comprehension: What are some of the genres and hallmarks of Aztec poetry? How was this poetry originally used in Aztec culture?

Context: Use the genres of Aztec history to categorize Spanish writings about the Conquest. Do the works of Garcilaso de la Vega,

concerning the unjust use of indigenous labor and tribute. As part of this petition, eight pages of drawings were made on *amatl* (fig bark); these drawings are known today as the *Huejotzingo Codex*.

[7561] Fray Bernardino de Sahagún, *Florentine Codex*, Book 12, plate 45 (1500–99), courtesy of the School of American Research and the University of Utah Press. This plate shows Spanish soldiers leading Montezuma into the great palace.

[7586] Anonymous, *Florentine Codex*, Book 12, plate 68 (1500–99), courtesy of the School of American Research and the University of Utah Press. This plate is one of five which portray the massacre of participants in the Feast of Uizilopochtli. The *Florentine Codex* was illustrated by Aztec scribes in a style that reflected a mixture of pre-Conquest manuscript traditions and European illustration conventions. For example, speaking is represented by a small curled speech scroll moving between people, an icon used in pre-Conquest manuscripts.

[7801] Anonymous, *Codex Boturini* [sheet 1] (c. 1521–40?) from *Codex Boturini: An Inquiry into the Origin of the Antiquities of America*, by John Delafield, courtesy of the University of Oregon. Cartographic histories such as the *Codex Boturini* organize Aztec histories around a geographic narrative. The *Codex Boturini* tells the migration legend of the Aztec peoples as they left their homeland Atzlán ("land or place of wings" or "land of herons").

[8015] Anonymous, *Lienzo de Tlaxcala* [title page] (1890) from *Homenjae a Cristobal Colon. Antiguedades Mexicanas; Publicadas por la Junta Colombina de Mexico en el Cuarto Centenario del Descubrimiento de America*, courtesy of the University of Oregon. The *Lienzo de Tlaxcala* provides an interesting counternarrative to the *Florentine Codex*. Transcribed in the mid-sixteenth century by Diego Muñoz de Camargo, a first-generation *mestizo*, the *Lienzo de Tlaxcala* is based on wall paintings depicting the arrival of Cortés and the fall of Tenochtitlán recorded in the homes of Tlaxcalan royalty.

[9090] *I Cry, I Am Sad* (n.d.), courtesy of *La Literatura de los Aztecas*, by Angel M.

Columbus, Bartolomé de las Casas, Bernal Díaz del Castillo, and Cabeza de Vaca resemble cartographic histories, annals, or *res gestae*? What do these genres tell us about the focus of history in Spanish American culture? How is this focus similar to or different from Aztec historical values?

Context: Compare the excerpts from the *Florentine Codex* and the *Lienzo de Tlaxcala* found in the archive. Who or what is the focus of each work? Through what pictorial conventions do the works develop this emphasis?

Context: How do the pictorial texts featured in the archive compare to European texts in which writing is accompanied by illustrations? Might we consider Samuel de Champlain, who is noted for the "storyboard" quality of his illustrated narratives, to be using a form of pictorial writing? Why or why not?

Exploration: Compare "The Ruin of Mexico in Tlatelolco" to African American Sorrow Songs such as "I'll Fly Away" (Unit 7). How would you characterize the aesthetics of these two traditions? What sorrows does each group express? Where does their hope lie?

Exploration: Compare the view of the Conquest of Mexico presented in the *Lienzo de Tlaxcala*, the *Florentine Codex*, the "Hymn of the Dead," and "The Ruins of Mexico in Tlatelolco" with the Conquest of California by Anglos in the works of María Amparo Ruiz de Burton and John Rollin Ridge (Unit 5). What was the Conquest like for the conquered people in these texts? How are the modes of conquest similar and different?

Exploration: Compare the Nahuatl poetry in the archive with the poems of Lorna Dee Cervantes (Unit 15), Alberto Ríos (Unit 12), and Gloria Anzaldúa. What Aztec influences do you notice in either the style or the content of the contemporary poets?

Exploration: What do pictographic and ideographic writing systems gain from their ability to communicate visually as well as phonetically?

Exploration: How do the pictographic writings of Native Americans indigenous to Mexico and South America compare to the pictographic, autobiographical records composed by North American Indians (see the Core Context "Moving Pictures: Native American Self-Narration" in Unit 8)?

Model Women: La Virgen de Guadalupe, La Llorona, and La Malinche as Archetypes of Mexican Femininity

In Mexican culture, female identity has traditionally been structured around three principal archetypes: La Virgen de Guadalupe (a vision of the Virgin Mary that appeared to an Indian convert in the sixteenth century), La Llorona (a woman who, after being spurned by her lover, killed her children), and La Malinche (the Indian woman who served as Hernán Cortés's translator, negotiator, and mistress during the Conquest of Mexico). While these figures have usually represented a very limited spectrum of possibilities for women, Guadalupe, La Llorona, and La Malinche have also shown themselves to be flexible myths. They have been manipulated and restructured to meet the political and spiritual needs of different cultural moments in Mexican history.

Since her appearance in the sixteenth century, La Virgen de Guadalupe has been one of the most powerful symbols of Mexican national identity and pride. According to a legend first published in 1648, La Virgen de Guadalupe appeared several times in 1531 to Juan Diego, an Indian who had recently converted to Catholicism. She appeared on a hill outside Mexico City and spoke to him in his native language of Nahuatl, instructing him to lead his community in building a shrine to her on the hill. When the bishop of the Catholic Church in Mexico City demanded physical proof of Juan Diego's vision, the Virgen appeared to him again and told him to gather roses in his *tilma*, or peasant cloak, and to bring them to the bishop as evidence. When Juan Diego unwrapped his *tilma* to present the flowers to the bishop, he found the Virgen's image imprinted on the fabric. The *tilma* with La Virgen de Guadalupe's image hangs in the Basilica in Mexico City, where it is an object of pilgrimages and veneration. Today, the image of La Virgen—a young woman with dark hair, an olive complexion, humble downcast eyes, her hands clasped in prayer, and an angel at her feet—is reproduced on everything from T-shirts to candles to bumperstickers to tattoos.

In the colonial era, La Virgen de Guadalupe was celebrated as a long-suffering, loving mother and heralded as a symbol of obedience, forgiveness, and peace. The circumstances of her appearance were cited as evidence of Mexico City's favored status as an outpost of the Spanish empire. More recently, she has lost some of her passive, colonial attributes and evolved into an emblem of liberation, national pride, and Indian heritage. *Mestizo* activists have celebrated the Virgen's ties to Tonantzin, a pre-Conquest Aztec earth-mother deity. In their view, La Virgen de Guadalupe is best understood as an amalgamation of Christian and pre-Columbian religious imagery, since she appeared to Juan Diego on a hill that had originally served as the site of a shrine to Tonantzin, wears a cloak decorated with astral symbols sacred to the Aztecs, and has a dark complexion and some Native American facial features. Feminists including Gloria Anzaldúa and Sandra Cisneros have celebrated La Virgen de Guadalupe as a mystical, life-giving earth mother who symbolizes the power of womanhood and provides an alternative to more patriarchal spiritual figures.

Just as the image of La Virgen de Guadalupe has been manipulated and transformed to accommodate different political and cultural needs, the myth of the female phantom La Llorona has taken on many forms within Mexican culture. Translated as "The Weeping Woman," La Llorona began as an oral legend about a ghostly woman who can be heard wailing for her lost children. In some versions of the story, La Llorona is doomed to wander and weep to expiate her own guilt for murdering her children. The motivations for the mur-

Garibay and Cheyenne Jones, translator. This lyric Nahuatl poem shows some of the most pervasive aesthetic attributes of Aztec verse, including expressive metaphors and the use of parallel syntax.

[9091] *The Ruin of Mexico in Tlatelolco* (n.d.), courtesy of *La Literatura de los Aztecas*, by Angel M. Garibay and Cheyenne Jones, translator. Nahuatl poem. The Aztecs had a rich and beautiful poetic tradition that was preserved primarily through oral transmission.

[7124] Anonymous, *Florentine Codex*, plate 49 (1500–99), courtesy of the School of American Research and the University of Utah Press.

[9061] N. Currier, *Nuestra Señora de Guadalupe: Our Lady of Guadalupe* (1848), courtesy of the Library of Congress [LC-USZC2-2890].

ders range from depression or anger at being abandoned by their father (who is sometimes portrayed as an Anglo), to the need to conceal an illegitimate birth, to a selfish rejection of motherhood. In other versions, she is portrayed as a loving mother who loses her children in a tragic accident or to foul play. She is almost always represented as wandering near lakes and rivers, since in most versions of the myth her children died by drowning. At its most basic level, the story serves as a cautionary tale to keep young children away from dangerous bodies of water. At the same time, it constructs an archetype of failed motherhood and tragic femininity.

In some versions of the La Llorona story, the phantom woman appears in the streets of cities and towns and lures young men into following her, usually with tragic consequences. In these versions she represents a dangerous feminine sexuality, out to punish or destroy male pursuers just as she destroyed her children. Occasionally, La Llorona is conflated with the spirit of La Malinche, who is wailing because she is remorseful about having betrayed the native Mexican people by assisting Cortés. These versions of the myth reinforce stereotypes of women and women's sexuality as untrustworthy and traitorous.

The fact that La Llorona has been frequently conflated with La Malinche testifies to the symbolic importance of the Malinche legend. Identified as a slave, a princess, a *mestiza*, a cultural and linguistic translator, a mother, and a traitor, the figure of La Malinche functions as a powerful amalgamation of anxieties about race, gender, class, and nationality. According to Bernal Díaz del Castillo's account of La Malinche (whom he calls by her Spanish name, Doña Marina), she was born into a royal family but sold into slavery when her mother and stepfather decided her existence might threaten their son's position as sole heir to their throne. They gave La Malinche to a group of itinerant traders from Xicalango, who then sold her to a Tobascan chief, who in turn gave her as a gift to the conquistador Hernán Cortés. Since she had lived among so many different tribes, La Malinche had an extraordinary facility with native languages. Her rapid acquisition of Spanish made her an extremely valuable asset to Cortés, who called her *"mi lengua"* ("my tongue" or "my language") and used her to negotiate with the tribes he encountered on his march through Mexico. She also became his secretary, mistress, the mother of his child, and eventually the wife of one of his officers.

While European explorers' portraits of La Malinche are mostly positive, Mexican and Chicano writers have traditionally seen her as a traitor who sold out her own people to help Cortés destroy the Aztec Empire and conquer all of Mexico for Spain. Both she and Martín, the *mestizo* son she had by Cortés, are often viewed with contempt for embracing foreign domination and turning their backs on their native culture. In actuality, La Malinche's role was probably far less important to the fall of the Aztec Empire than Cortés's military skills, the Aztec chief Montezuma's weakness, the military contributions of rival indigenous tribes, and the spread of European diseases that decimated native populations. In any case, La Malinche had been repeatedly sold among tribes as a slave and thus probably did not perceive any particular group as "her people." Indeed, she may have felt that she was working with Cortés to conquer groups she herself identified as enemies for holding her in slavery.

Despite the facts of La Malinche's involvement with Cortés and the Conquest, she has functioned for centuries as a scapegoat for the destruction of Native American cultures in Mexico. Writer and critic Octavio Paz, for example, saw La Malinche as the central representative of a negative tradition of subjugation and cultural impoverishment that began with the Conquest. Assigning the pejorative name *"La Chingada"* ("the violated one"), Paz associated her with a history of shame, violation, and defamation. She is a symbolic reminder that indigenous people were "violated" by Spanish invaders, and that a woman enabled this violation (importantly, the word *"malinchista"* has come to mean "traitor" in Spanish). In this reading, La Malinche acquires the mythical status of a "Mexican Eve," who has brought about the "fall" of her people through her own selfishness or heedlessness.

Recently, feminist cultural critics have begun to resist such portraits of La Malinche, both because they are historically inaccurate and because they promote misogynistic attitudes toward women. Instead, they have attempted to rehabilitate the myth of La Malinche in order to celebrate her strength, flexibility, intelligence, and extraordinary skill at mediating between cultures. As a figure of mediation, she provides a model to *mestizas*, whose identity is built upon balancing a complex, multifaceted heritage. Chicana writer Cherríe Moraga has written a play about La Malinche, and she is a popular and recurrent figure in Chicana poetry.

QUESTIONS

Comprehension: Why do some critics understand La Virgen de Guadalupe as an amalgamation of Christian and indigenous pre-Columbian religious traditions? What characteristics mark her as a particularly Native American figure?

Comprehension: Why was La Malinche so valuable to Cortés? In what ways did she help him in his drive to conquer the Aztecs?

Context: How does Bernal Díaz del Castillo represent La Malinche in *The True History of the Conquest of New Spain*? How does his portrayal of her role in the Conquest compare to later representations of her "betrayal"?

Context: Examine the drawings of La Malinche with Cortés in the *Lienzo de Tlaxcala* featured in the archive. How does the *Lienzo* portray La Malinche's work as Cortés's *"lengua"* or "tongue"? What other roles does La Malinche seem to occupy in the drawings' representation of her position within Cortés's army?

Context: Compare the notions of womanhood present in Garcilaso de la Vega's *Florida of the Inca* to those at work in the narratives of Bernal Díaz del Castillo and Cabeza de Vaca. What role does

Boots (n.d.), courtesy of *El Andar* magazine. Here, Cisneros wears boots with pictures of La Virgen de Guadalupe, a vision of the Virgin Mary that appeared to an Indian convert in the sixteenth century.

[9061] N. Currier, *Nuestra Señora de Guadalupe: Our Lady of Guadalupe* (1848), courtesy of the Library of Congress [LC-USZC2-2890]. This image shows an Anglicized version of La Virgen de Guadalupe, buoyed by an angel.

each of these authors envision for women in the New World? What sorts of feminine behavior do they valorize?

Context: How does Gloria Anzaldúa's construction of a "new *mestiza* consciousness" challenge the traditional archetypes of Mexican femininity?

Exploration: The figures of La Virgen de Guadalupe, La Llorona, and La Malinche have historically structured the identities and opportunities available to Mexican and Chicana women. What kinds of archetypes shape the lives of women of other ethnicities in America?

Exploration: In Sandra Cisneros's novel *Woman Hollering Creek*, the creek of the title is named for La Llorona. Why do you think Cisneros makes this reference? How does *The House on Mango Street* (Unit 16) address the issue of cultural stereotypes about Mexican women? To what extent does it revise or accept these stereotypes?

Exploration: Compare the poetry of Lorna Dee Cervantes and Gloria Anzaldúa. How does each revise the myths and ideals that structure Chicana identity?

EXTENDED CONTEXTS

Working Wonders: The Experience of "*La Maravilla/The Marvelous*" in New World Encounters

Bernal Díaz del Castillo begins his *True History of the Conquest of New Spain* with an avowal that he will accurately and authentically describe the conquistadors' experiences in the Aztec Empire: "That which I have myself seen . . . with the help of God I will describe, quite simply, as a fair eyewitness, without twisting events one way or another." As Díaz del Castillo's narrative progresses, however, his promise of full disclosure is troubled at times by his inability to explain or articulate his responses to the radically unfamiliar sights. As he records his approach to the great Aztec city of Tenochtitlán, for example, his powers of description are immobilized by an intense experience of wonder at encountering a spectacle that no European had ever before seen. As he puts it, "We were astounded. . . . Indeed, some of our soldiers asked whether it was not all a dream. . . . It was all so wonderful that I do not know how to describe this first glimpse of things never heard of, seen, or dreamed of before." This experience of astonishment and an accompanying inability to find words to express the experience is characteristic of narratives that depict the first contact between Europeans and indigenous peoples in the New World. As scholar Stephen Greenblatt has claimed, "wonder" is "the central figure in the initial European response to the New World, the decisive emotional and intellectual experience in the presence of radical difference." Narratives that told of the wonder Europeans felt at encounters with the "marvelous" (a

[7511] Anonymous, *Landing of Columbus* (c. 1860–80), courtesy of the Library of Congress.

term the Spanish explorers frequently used to represent objects that were radically new or beyond description) could have aspects of horror, pleasure, desire, or fear, but the overwhelming impression was one of amazement and awe.

In narratives of New World exploration, the experience of wonder is triggered by unfamiliarity, and often by a sense of excess, or extreme beauty, or strangeness. The "marvelous" cannot be fit into existing categories of knowledge, leaving viewers almost paralyzed and unable to decide whether they should love, hate, repudiate, or embrace the sight at which they are marveling. When explorers protested that they could not find language to describe the marvelous sights of the New World, those protestations might reflect a sincere loss for words. Nonetheless, such claims could also serve as a useful rhetorical strategy. The discourse of wonder worked at times to represent extreme horror to readers and to dehumanize the natives. Díaz's gruesome description of the cannibalistic Aztec ritual he witnessed, for example, uses his horror to convey the barbarity of the native Mexicans. Moreover, expressions of wonder could serve as a means to aggrandize the explorers' own deeds and experiences. Columbus acted with calculation in promoting his own reputation and the importance of his expedition when he extravagantly claimed in his letters to Spain that the New World was "fertile to a limitless degree," that the islands he had seen were all "beyond comparison," and "most beautiful, of a thousand shapes . . . and filled with trees of a thousand kinds." His final comment, *Española es una maravilla* ("Hispaniola is a marvel"), testifies to the value of what he found and disarms skeptics who might try to detract from his accomplishments. Sometimes, the impulse to promote their discoveries in the New World led narrators to attempt to translate their experiences of wonder into terms of non-wonder—that is, to graft the familiar onto the unfamiliar in order to sell their audiences on the worth of what they found. When Columbus talks about the birds, animals, plants, and resources he found on the islands, he often compares them to their corresponding objects in Europe in order to make his experiences intelligible to his audience. When he writes of hearing nightingales singing on Hispaniola, for instance, he attempts to create a sense of comforting familiarity within the strangeness of the New World; in fact, nightingales are not native to the West Indies, and Columbus could not have heard any singing.

Some exploration narratives displace the experience of wonder onto the natives. Díaz's claims that the Indians viewed the in Spanish as *"Teules,"* or gods, conveys the difficulty the natives had in reconciling the Europeans with any existing conceptions they had of the earthly or the human. Similarly, Samuel de Champlain recounts that a group of hostile North American Indians freed explorer Etienne Brulé because the unfamiliar necklace he wore (and a fortuitous thunderstorm) convinced them he had divine powers. John Smith used his knowledge of writing and navigational technologies to inspire wonder in the Indians he encountered in Virginia. While it is difficult to know precisely what Native Americans felt when they

[2840] John Smith, Illustration from the *Generall Historie of Virginia, New-England, and the Summer Isles . . .* (1632), courtesy of the Robert Dechert Collection, Annenberg Rare Book and Manuscript Library, University of Pennsylvania.

"WORKING WONDERS"
WEB ARCHIVE

[1366] Theodor de Bry, *A Chief of Roanoke* (1590), courtesy of the Library of Congress [LC-USZ62-89909]. Full-length, front and back view of a Native American chief, with a river scene in the background.
[2518] Theodor de Bry, *The Town of Pomeiock* (1590), courtesy of the Library of Congress [LC-USZ62-54018]. Like many of de Bry's engravings, *The Town of Pomeiock* is based on a watercolor by John White, who accompanied Sir Walter Raleigh on his expedition to found a colony at Roanoke. The engraving shows a native town enclosed by a circular pole fence with two entrances.
[2840] John Smith, Illustration from the *Generall Historie of Virginia, New-England, and the Summer Isles . . .* (1632), courtesy of the Robert Dechert Collection, Annenberg Rare Book and Manuscript Library, University of Pennsylvania. This image shows a scene from Smith's captivity among the Native Americans of Virginia and his subse-

quent and legendary rescue by Pocahontas. This event was a central focus of his historical narrative. The full illustration of this panel is available in the *American Passages* Archive [2839].

[7399] Cortés(?), *La Gran Ciudad de Temixtitan* (1524), courtesy of the Newberry Library, Chicago. This map of the Aztec city of Tenochtitlán is often attributed to Cortés. It is European in style, but the map-view contains information suggesting a native source.

[7420] Theodor de Bry, *A Weroans, or Chieftain, of Virginia* (1590), courtesy of the Library of Congress [LC-USZ62-53338]. This engraving shows full-length, front and back portraits of a Native Virginian chief holding a bow and arrow. In the background is a hunting scene.

[7511] Anonymous, *Landing of Columbus* (c. 1860–80), courtesy of the Library of Congress. This lithograph shows Columbus and members of his crew displaying objects to Native American men and women on shore who seem overcome with curiosity and wonder.

first encountered Europeans, since almost all of the accounts of such moments were written by Europeans, it seems likely that they did experience a feeling of wonder when faced with the radical unfamiliarity of European culture. This sense of astonishment may have been one of the few things the Europeans and the Indians could recognize as something they had in common at the moment of contact.

QUESTIONS

Comprehension: What kinds of sights were considered "marvels" New World explorers?

Context: Examine the de Bry engravings of Native Americans in Virginia featured in the archive. How do the engravings portray people who were, for European viewers, radically unfamiliar? Do the pictures convey a sense of wonder or do they allow viewers to fit the people depicted into knowable categories? How does the artist make the Indians look more familiar to Europeans? How does he represent their "otherness"?

Context: Compare the descriptions of *"la maravilla"* (the marvelous) in Columbus and Bernal Díaz del Castillo's narratives. What are some of the rhetorical advantages of presenting America as marvelous? Whom are the writers trying to persuade and of what?

Exploration: The vision of the Americas as a place of wonder and marvel had important religious implications in that it helped solidify the notion that America was a type of New Jerusalem, an idea that was of particular importance to the New England Puritans (Unit 3). What role do religious associations of the New World play in the writings of the conquistadors? How do these compare to the religious associations at work in Puritan writings?

Exploration: What is the relationship between the experience of wonder and the experience of encountering the "sublime" (discussed in Unit 4)? To what extent has the view of the American landscape and peoples as "marvelous" been crucial to the construction of American identity over time?

[7402] Anonymous, *Cortés, Montezuma and Dona Marina*, from the *Lienzo de Tlaxcala* Facsimile (1890), courtesy of the University of California, Berkeley, and the Bancroft Library.

The Romance of Colonization

In his narrative of his third voyage to the Indies, Christopher Columbus arrived at the conclusion that the western hemisphere is not spherical, but "resembles the half of a round pear with a raised stalk . . . like a woman's nipple on a round ball." Columbus's conviction that he had found the "nipple" of the world in the West Indies is perhaps best understood as a particularly fantastic example of the convention of figuring European exploration in terms of an erotic encounter between masculine, European conquerors and the feminized land and peoples of the New World. The prevalence of gendered language in exploration narratives reveals an operative fantasy of the New World as a "virgin bride," beautiful, unspoiled, passive, and welcoming. By portraying themselves as "lovers" rather than conquerors, European explorers were able to rationalize their forceful—and often violent and brutal—conquest of American lands as an inevitable sexual consummation, desired by both parties involved. Conflating American land with its native inhabitants, this fantasy of conquest as romance relegates both land and Indians to the status of possessions, objects of value but without agency.

The complicated erotics beneath the rhetoric of colonization becomes most visible in the popular and recurring myth of the beautiful Indian maiden or princess who breaks with her own culture in order to affirm her loyalty to, and love for, a European man. One prototype of this myth is Garcilaso de la Vega's narrative of Juan Ortiz's relationship with the daughter of the Indian chief Hirrihuiga. In its celebration of a native woman's decision to disobey her father and rescue a European captive from execution at the hands of her tribe, de la Vega's narrative propounds a fantasy of Indian acceptance of white superiority and Indian willingness to give up traditional culture for European culture. Hirrihuiga's daughter's name is left unrecorded, thus highlighting her status as a generic and mythic ideal of native compliance.

John Smith's story of his rescue at the hands of Pocahontas is probably the most famous and most often retold example of the European tendency to figure conquest as romance. The fact that Pocahontas went on to marry a white man, bear his child, convert to Christianity, travel to England, and assimilate to Anglo culture makes her an ideal figure on which to build a fantasy of native assent to colonization. The story of her decision to fling her body between Smith and the Indian executioners' weapons has become a foundational national myth in the United States. Because it portrays traditional male Native American culture as cruel and barbaric—and glosses over the violence of European conquest by rendering Smith as passive and showing an Indian herself disrupting her tribe's ritual execution—the story symbolically justifies European destruction of Indian culture. The enduring cultural appeal of this national myth is attested to by the paintings and sculptures of Pocahontas that hang in the United States Capitol Building in Washington, D.C., and the success of contemporary representations of her life, such as Disney's 1995 animated film *Pocahontas*. Crucially, the idealization of romantic relationships between Indian women and their conquerors evades the historical reality that many Native American women were raped, tortured, and murdered by European invaders.

[5245] Salvador Brquez, *Dolores del Rios as Ramona* (1928), courtesy of the *Los Angeles Times*.

"THE ROMANCE OF COLONIZATION" WEB ARCHIVE

[1369] Theodor de Bry, *Florida Indians Planting Seeds of Beans or Maize* (1591), courtesy of the Library of Congress [LC-USZ62-3186]. This engraving shows Timucua men cultivating a field while Timucua women plant corn or beans.

[1371] Theodor de Bry, *Exercises of the Youths* (1591), courtesy of the Library of Congress [LC-USZ62-37992]. This engraving shows Native American men shooting arrows, running races, and throwing balls at a target on top of a tall pole.

[1900] John White, *The Manner of Their Fishing* (c. 1585), courtesy of the John Carter Brown Library, Brown University. One of John White's drawings not taken directly from real life: he shows a dip net and spear (daytime fishing techniques) and a fire in a canoe (used to attract fish at night). White combined disparate New World fishing methods and a mix of species in this and other paintings.

[2467] Anonymous, *Pocahontas* [reproduction of 1616 original] (c. 1900–1920), courtesy of the Library of Congress. Pocahontas, baptized as "Rebecca" before marrying John Rolfe, is shown in her English garb. The original of this painting was by William Sheppard, dated 1616, at Barton Rectory, Norfolk, England.

[2591] Theodor de Bry, *A Noblewoman of Pomeiock* [*Indian Woman and Young Girl*] (1590), courtesy of the John Carter Brown Library, Brown University. This engraving shows a native woman of the Virginia town of Pomeiock carrying a clay vessel, while a child holds a rattle and a doll. The woman resembles the female figures painted by Renaissance artists.

[3232] John Gadsby Chapman, *Baptism of Pocahontas, 1614* (c. 1837), courtesy of the Library of Congress. The Virginia Company instructed its governors to make conversion of the native population to Christianity a prime objective. Pocahontas, daughter of Powhatan, head of the Powhatan Confederacy, was the most famous early convert. She was baptized in 1614.

[5245] Salvador Brquez, *Dolores del Rios as Ramona* (1928), courtesy of the *Los Angeles Times*. Helen Hunt Jackson's *Ramona* failed to improve treatment of California Indians as she had hoped it would. Instead, the story's romantic depiction of California's Hispanic heritage became firmly entrenched in the mythology of the region.

[7125] Anonymous, *Florentine Codex*, Plate 50 (1500–99), courtesy of the School of American Research and the University of Utah Press. Here, the Spanish are shown looting Montezuma's treasure house. Assembled in the 1540s by Fray Bernardino de Sahagún, the *Florentine Codex* contains a mixture of Nahuatl (the language of the Aztec peoples) and pictographic illustrations describing Aztec society and culture.

[7402] Anonymous, *Cortés, Montezuma and Doña Marina*, from the *Lienzo de Tlaxcala* Facsimile (1890), courtesy of the University of California, Berkeley, and the Bancroft Library. The *Lienzo de Tlaxcala* employs the *res gestae* strategy and provides an interesting counterpoint to the *Florentine Codex*. Here Cortés is depicted with Montezuma and Doña Marina.

QUESTIONS

Comprehension: Why did European explorers and conquerors like to portray the New World as a "virgin bride"? What was at stake in their use of this image?

Context: Examine the sixteenth- and seventeenth-century illustrations of Native American youths featured in archive. How are the Indians portrayed? What kinds of physical characteristics do the artists idealize? How do these drawings participate in the mythologizing of New World inhabitants?

Context: How do the cultural myths that surround La Malinche in Mexico participate in, complicate, or challenge prevalent European and European American fantasies of the romance and erotics of colonization?

Exploration: The story of Pocahontas's rescue of John Smith still resonates in American culture; in 1995, Disney released a successful animated film based on this myth. Why is this story still so appealing to American audiences? How has it been reworked to reflect different values and beliefs in different periods of American culture?

ASSIGNMENTS

Personal and Creative Responses

1. *Artist's Workshop:* Draw your own pictographic representation of an event that has been important in your life, using the codices featured in the archive for inspiration. How will you organize the information you wish to present? How will you indicate the chronology of events? The principal characters?

2. *Journal:* Imagine that you are present in the West Indies, Virginia, or Canada when Europeans first land in the area and come into contact with the Native Americans who live there. Write your own account of the contact experience from the perspective of either a European colonizer or an Indian.

3. *Poet's Corner:* Drawing on Gloria Anzaldúa's *Borderlands/La Frontera* for inspiration, compose a personal narrative in which you switch between poetry and prose. How does the use of both genres affect your narrative? What difficulties did you encounter in trying to write both poetry and prose in the same text?

4. *Doing History:* Using a dictionary of Aztec pictographic and phonetic symbols or Donald Robertson's *Mexican Manuscript Painting of the Early Colonial Period*, interpret one of the pieces of pictorial writing in the archive. How does this form of storytelling differ from that of Western historiography?

5. *Multimedia:* Imagine that you have been asked to make a presentation on the role of women in borderlands and contact zones. What archetypes of femininity structure representations of women? How are women redefining their roles in borderlands?

Using the *American Passages* archive and slide-show software, create a multimedia presentation in which you explore the opportunities and limitations women have faced when cultures come into contact and conflict.

Problem-Based Learning Projects

1. Imagine that the parties in conflict during the Conquest of Mexico have decided to resolve their differences by hosting a diplomatic summit rather than using force against one another. Divide into groups representing the various parties involved (Cortés, Doña Marina, common footsoldiers like Bernal Díaz del Castillo, Montezuma, Aztec soldiers, and indigenous tribes who had been previously conquered by the Aztecs). Prepare for the summit by making a list of your concerns and demands; then meet as a group and begin the process of diplomacy. How will you resolve territorial disputes? How will you resolve conflicts over resources? Over religion? How will you form a government that will enable all groups to live peacefully in the region? Should some individuals or groups be expelled from the region? If so, whom? Groups may wish to form strategic alliances with one another to carry their points.

2. You have been asked to create a museum honoring the life and legacy of Álvar Núñez Cabeza de Vaca. Form a committee to draw up plans for the museum. Where will you locate it? What kinds of artifacts, images, and information will you feature within it? What points about Cabeza de Vaca's life will you highlight? Who will be your target audience?

3. The indigenous people who inhabited Mexico before the Spanish Conquest have decided to bring La Malinche to court to try her for what they see as her traitorous role in helping the Spanish conquistadors. Divide into groups and prepare her prosecution and defense.

[7429] John White, *The Manner of Attire and Painting Themselves, When They Goe to Their General Huntings or at Theire Solemne Feasts* (c. 1585), courtesy of The British Museum. Portrait of an Algonquian Indian (either Secotan or Pomeiock) from Virginia. Elite families and chiefs were elaborately decorated with paint, beads, and quills to signal their status and power. The body markings are painted for specific occasions, rather than permanently tattooed. The pose, taken from sixteenth-century European portraits, emphasizes the importance of the sitter and the occasion.

GLOSSARY

Black Legend   A widespread perception (especially popular in Protestant countries) that the Spanish colonizers were barbaric in their treatment of the natives. According to this myth, Spanish conquistadors were driven mainly by a lust for gold, and their claims that they were spreading Christianity in the New World were merely hypocritical justifications for their actions. Bartolomé de las Casas's *Brief Relation*, intended to spur reform in Spain, contributed to the spread of the so-called Black Legend in Northern Europe. Colonizers from other European nations often used the Black Legend to self-righteously justify their own repression and exploitation of Native Americans by arguing that their methods were more humane than those of the Spanish.

borderlands The regions on either side of a national border, characterized by their tendency to foster creation and innovation. Because the geographic placement of a national border is always arbitrary and artificial, the zones on either side of the border contradict the notion that people and cultures can be kept separate or distinct from one another. Instead, borderlands are permeable places where traditions interconnect and cultures overlap. They are spaces marked by conflict, violence, and hatred, but they can also produce cooperation, innovation, and hybridity.

Chicano/Chicana Men and women of Mexican American descent living in the United States. After the United States took possession of California, Texas, and other portions of the Southwest through the Treaty of Guadalupe-Hidalgo in 1848, Mexicans living in the region were deprived of their property and civil rights. In the late twentieth century, activists in the Chicano movement began to fight against this kind of discrimination. Part of their protest involved reclaiming and celebrating their unique history, language, and mixed Mexican and American heritage.

codex, codices Historical records preserved by the Mesoamerican Aztec (or Nahua) peoples in accordion-style books fashioned from animal skin or fig bark (*amatl*) and kept in vast libraries. After the Spanish Conquest these records were often painted on cloth. Today, these books are often referred to as *lienzos*, the Spanish word for linen, or as codices (codex in the singular), a term that highlights the fact that they were written by hand, rather than printed. Originally the codices were written purely in indigenous scripts, but after the Conquest these were often combined with Nahuatl or Spanish written in the Roman alphabet. An elite class of scribes drawn primarily from the Mesoamerican nobility created the codices. When the Spaniards entered the Aztec city of Tenochtitlán in 1519, they systematically burnt the libraries and destroyed the codices, at least in part out of fear of what they contained. The few surviving pre-Conquest records and the six hundred remaining codices written just after the Conquest continue to stun readers with their visual and verbal beauty and to provide an important counternarrative to the stories told by the Spanish conquistadors. Because we do not know who wrote, drew, and compiled the codices, they are usually named after the scholars and historians who have explicated them.

conquistadors Spanish explorers and soldiers who were sent to conquer indigenous populations, claim territory, and establish settlements in Mexico and South America in the sixteenth century. Many conquistadors journeyed to the New World in the hopes of acquiring vast fortunes by exploiting the resources there.

contact zone Term coined by scholar Mary Louise Pratt to describe the space of meeting between two cultures that had previously been separated geographically and historically. As Pratt puts it, a contact zone is an area in which previously separated peoples "come into contact with each other and establish ongoing relations, usually involving conditions of coercion, radical inequality, and intractable conflict." Although unequal power relations characterized contact zones in the New World, with Europeans usually asserting dominance over native peoples, contact is never a one-way phenomenon. The interactive, improvisational nature of contact necessarily creates subjects who are impacted by relations with one another within a mutually constituted experience.

encomienda   The system of forced tributary labor established by the Spanish in their colonies in Mexico and South America. Conquistadors like Bernal Díaz del Castillo were issued grants which gave them control over native populations who were expected to pay them in food, resources, and labor. While the grantee was supposedly obligated to protect, educate, and respect the freedom of the Indians in his *encomienda*, in reality the system quickly degenerated into the equivalent of slavery.

Great Chain of Being   According to a common European belief first coined by Aristotle and later adopted by Christian philosophers, the universe was structured according to immutable hierarchies. These hierarchies existed along the so-called "Great Chain of Being," spanning from the dimensions of "non-being" (rocks and minerals) and extending through plants, animals, and man all the way to God, as the representative of the highest form of "being." Within the category of "man," important hierarchies existed that separated more primitive peoples from more "cultured" or "advanced" societies. The following diagram shows the hierarchies of man as conceptualized in the Great Chain of Being:

Corporeal Man —— Man of Instinct —— Man of Feeling —— Thinking Man

European explorers and conquerors often deployed the Great Chain of Being to explain and make sense of the New World, as well as to justify their pretensions to superiority within it. They tended to structure promotional tracts around the Great Chain of Being, emphasizing the extent to which natural resources were "naturally" at the service of superior men. They also tended to characterize America's indigenous peoples as inhabiting a lower position on the scale of the "hierarchies of man" within the Great Chain of Being.

historia   In Spanish, the word *historia* means both "history" and "story," highlighting the extent to which any so-called "objective history" is always a subjective story inflected by personal biases and agendas.

lienzo   The Spanish word for "linen," often applied to Mesoamerican codices.

mestizo/mestiza   Men and women of mixed Indian, European, and African heritage. The *mestizo* identity has gained prominence in the American Southwest, where *mestizos* have proudly reclaimed their Native American heritage and identity that often went unacknowledged in the Chicano movement. *Mestizo* identity is characterized by plurality and inclusiveness.

promotional tract   A detailed account of the natural resources, plants, animals, and native inhabitants of a newly colonized area, intended to encourage immigration and solidify imperial claims. Such tracts were often structured by the notion of the Great Chain of Being.

transculturation A term coined by Cuban anthropologist Fernando Ortiz that refers to a process in which "members of subordinated or marginal groups select and invent from materials transmitted by a dominant culture." Transculturation emphasizes the agency involved in cultural change, as well as the loss that accompanies cultural acquisition. In these ways, "transculturation" differs from the older terms "assimilation" and "acculturation," which emphasize a more one-way transmission of culture from the colonizer to the colonized, from the dominant to the marginalized. For Ortiz, transculturation was a necessary concept for understanding Cuban and Spanish American culture more generally.

SELECTED BIBLIOGRAPHY

Bruce-Novoa, Juan. *RetroSpace: Collected Essays on Chicano Literature, Theory, and History.* Houston: Arte Publico Press, 1990.

Castillo, Ana, ed. *Goddess of the Americas/La Diosa de las Americas: Writings on La Virgen de Guadalupe.* New York: Riverhead Books, 1996.

Greenblatt, Stephen. *Marvelous Possessions: The Wonder of the New World.* Chicago: U of Chicago P, 1991.

Herrera-Sobek, Maria. *Reconstructing a Chicano/a Literary Heritage: Hispanic Colonial Literature of the Southwest.* Tucson: U of Arizona P, 1993.

Jara, Rene, and Nicholas Spadaccini, eds. *1492–1992: Re/Discovering Colonial Writing.* Minneapolis: U of Minnesota P, 1989.

Lockhart, James. *We People Here: Nahuatl Accounts of the Conquest of Mexico.* Berkeley: U of California P, 1993.

Pratt, Mary Louise. *Imperial Eyes: Travel Writing and Transculturation.* New York: Routledge, 1992.

Saldívar-Hull, Sonia. *Feminism on the Border: Chicana Gender Politics and Literature.* Berkeley: U of California P, 2000.

Sayre, Gordon M. *Les Sauvages Americains: Representations of Native Americans in French and English Colonial Literature.* Chapel Hill: U of North Carolina P, 1997.

Seed, Patricia. *Ceremonies of Possession in Europe's Conquest of the New World: 1492–1640.* Cambridge: Cambridge UP, 1995.

Swann, Brian, and Arnold Krupat, eds. *Recovering the Word: Essays on Native American Literature.* Berkeley: U of California P, 1987.

Tilton, Robert S. *Pocahontas: Evolution of an American Narrative.* Cambridge: Cambridge UP, 1994.

FURTHER RESOURCES

1492: An Ongoing Voyage [online exhibit]. Library of Congress <www.loc.gov/exhibits/1492/>.

The Ballad of Gregorio Cortez [videorecording]. Moctesuma Esparza Productions, Inc.; produced by Moctesuma Esparza and Michael Hausman; screenplay by Victor Villasenor; directed by Robert M. Young. Beverly Hills: Nelson Entertainment, 1988.

Boone, Elizabeth Hill, and Walter D. Mignolo, eds. *Writing Without Words: Alternative Literacies in Mesoamerica and the Andes.* Durham: Duke UP, 1994.

Cabeza de Vaca [videorecording]. Producciones Iguana in co-production with Instituto Mexicano de Cinematografia, Televisión Española, S.A.; screenplay by Guillermo Sheridan, Nicolás Echevarria; produced by Rafael Cruz, Jorge Sánchez, Julio Solórzano Foppa, Bertha Navarro; directed by Nicolás Echevarria. United States: New Horizons Home Video, 1993.

Conquistadors [videorecording]. Written and presented by Michael Wood; directed by David Wallace; produced by Rebecca Dobbs; executive produced by Leo Eaton, Laurence Rees. Coral Springs: PBS Home Video, 2001.

Doggett, Rachel, et al. *New World of Wonders: European Images of the Americas, 1492–1700.* Seattle: U of Washington P, 1992.

Gonzales, Manuel G. *Mexicanos: A History of Mexicans in the United States.* Bloomington: Indiana UP, 1999.

Harley, J. Brian, and David Woodward. *Cartography in Prehistoric, Ancient, and Medieval Europe and the Mediterranean.* Chicago: U of Chicago P, 1987.

Katzew, Ilona, et al. *New World Orders: Casta Painting and Colonial Latin America.* New York: Americas Society Art, 1996.

Pocahontas [videorecording]. Burbank: Walt Disney Home Video, 1995.

Robertson, Doñald. *Mexican Manuscript Painting of the Early Colonial Period: The Metropolitan Schools.* New Haven: Yale UP, 1959.

Authors and Works

Featured in the Video:

John Winthrop, "A Model of Christian Charity" (sermon) and *The Journal of John Winthrop* (journal)

Mary Rowlandson, *A Narrative of the Captivity and Restoration of Mrs. Mary Rowlandson* (captivity narrative)

William Penn, "Letter to the Lenni Lenapi Chiefs" (letter)

Discussed in This Unit:

William Bradford, *Of Plymouth Plantation* (history)

Thomas Morton, *New English Canaan* (satire)

Anne Bradstreet, poems

Edward Taylor, poems

Sarah Kemble Knight, *The Private Journal of a Journey from Boston to New York* (travel narrative)

John Woolman, *The Journal of John Woolman* (journal) and "Some Considerations on the Keeping of Negroes" (essay)

Samson Occom, *A Short Narrative of My Life* (autobiography) and "Sermon Preached at the Execution of Moses Paul, a Mohegan" (sermon)

Overview Questions

■ What different European and Native American groups inhabited the eastern shores of North America in the seventeenth and eighteenth centuries? What kinds of strategies did they adopt in order to forge community identities? What and whom did they exclude? What and whom did they embrace? How did their respective visions and ideals undermine, overlap, and compete with one another?

■ What qualities characterize the jeremiad form? How do jeremiads work to condemn a community's spiritual decline while at the same time reaffirming the community's identity and promise?

■ How did the Puritans use typology to understand and justify their experiences in the world?

■ How did the image of America as a "vast and unpeopled country" shape European immigrants' attitudes and ideals? How did they deal with the fact that millions of Native Americans already inhabited the land that they had come over to claim?

■ How did the Puritans' sense that they were living in the "end time" impact their culture? Why is apocalyptic imagery so prevalent in Puritan iconography and literature?

■ What is plain style? What values and beliefs influenced the development of this mode of expression?

■ Why has the jeremiad remained a central component of the rhetoric of American public life?

■ How do Puritan and Quaker texts work to form enduring myths about America's status as a chosen nation? About its inclusiveness and tolerance? About its role as a "City on a Hill" that should serve as an example to the rest of the world?

■ Are there texts, or passages in texts, in this unit that challenge the myths created by the dominant society?

■ Why are the Puritans, more than any other early immigrant group, considered such an important starting point for American national culture?

Learning Objectives

After students have viewed the video, read the headnotes and literary selections in *The Norton Anthology of American Literature*, and explored related archival materials on the *American Passages* Web site, they should be able to

1. discuss the variety of ways in which European settlers imagined Native Americans;

2. understand how myths about America's foundation were formulated, debated, and challenged by these seventeenth- and eighteenth-century writers;

3. explain the basic theological principles of the Quaker and Puritan faiths;

4. understand how the physical hardships of immigration and the challenges of living and traveling in unfamiliar landscapes shaped the culture of European immigrants in the New World.

Instructor Overview

Borrowing a phrase from the New England Calvinist minister Samuel Danforth, the historian Perry Miller described the Puritans who came to America to form the Massachusetts Bay Colony as having embarked upon an "errand into the wilderness." Here, the metaphor of the "errand" captures the immigrants' belief that they were on a sacred mission, ordained by God, to create a model community and thereby fulfill a divine covenant. While Miller was interested in the specific errand the Massachusetts Bay Colony Puritans envisioned for themselves, we might use his notion of the "errand" to consider the motivations behind the journeys of other groups who came to North America in the seventeenth and eighteenth centuries. What kind of errand did the Quakers in Pennsylvania believe they had embarked upon? The Pilgrims at Plymouth? The Anglicans, Catholics, and Sephardic Jews who also settled on the East Coast in the seventeenth century? Whatever they believed their errands to be, New World settlers were confronted with a variety of challenges—the physical difficulty of living in an unfamiliar land, friction with other immigrant groups, dissent within their own communities, conflicts with Native Americans—that complicated their attempts to create ideal communities. Unit 3, "The Promised Land," examines the Utopian visions and dystopic fears represented in the works of William Bradford, Thomas Morton, John Winthrop, Anne Bradstreet, Mary Rowlandson, Edward Taylor, William Penn, Sarah Kemble Knight, John Woolman, and Samson Occom. This unit provides contextual background and classroom materials that explore how these early texts contributed to American literary traditions and helped create enduring myths about America.

The video for Unit 3 focuses on three texts that together represent the diverse early American visions of "the promised land." John Winthrop's sermon "A Model of Christian Charity," Mary Rowlandson's narrative of her captivity among the Narragansett and Wampanoag Indians, and William Penn's "Letter to the Lenni Lenape Indians" all participate in a tradition of understanding personal and communal experience as the working of God's will. Thematically, stylistically, and generically, however, the texts are very distinct from one another, revealing important differences in the authors' religious convictions and positions within their communities.

Winthrop, a wealthy man and a leader within his Puritan congregation, delivered his lay sermon on board the ship *Arbella* before disembarking in Massachusetts. The sermon serves as an optimistic blueprint for the ideal Christian community, or "City upon a Hill," extolling the virtues of a clear social and spiritual hierarchy, interpreting the Puritan mission as the fulfillment of biblical prophecy, and exhorting fellow congregants to maintain their purity. A generation later, Rowlandson wrote from a different Puritan perspective, as a woman held captive by Native Americans whom she viewed as agents of the devil. Her narrative of her wanderings and sufferings is an example of a jeremiad, recounting the "trials and afflictions" that destroyed her earlier spiritual complacency and testifying to the sweetness of her repentance and eventual salvation. Penn, a Quaker and the wealthy proprietor of the Pennsylvania land charter, took an entirely different view of Native Americans in his letter to the Delaware Indians, written before he left England for the New World. His text is imbued with the tolerance and pacifism of Quaker belief, envisioning a utopian community in which Europeans and Native Americans would "live soberly & kindly together."

The video's coverage of Winthrop, Rowlandson, and Penn introduces students to these writers' influential utopian and dystopian visions of the promise of America. How do these texts serve to form enduring myths about America's status as a chosen nation? About its role as an example to the rest of the world? About its inclusiveness? How do these early visions of America's status overlap, undermine, or compete with one another? Unit 3 helps answer these questions by offering suggestions on how to connect these writers to their cultural contexts, to other units in the series, and to other key writers of the era. The curriculum materials help fill in the video's introduction to early articulations of "the promised land" by exploring writers who represent other, diverse traditions, such as Samson Occom (a Native American Calvinist minister), William Bradford (a Separatist Puritan), Thomas Morton (an Anglican protestor of Puritan doctrine), and many others.

The video, the archive, and the curriculum materials contextualize the writers of this era by examining several key stylistic characteristics and religious doctrines that shape their texts: (1) the role of typology—the Puritans' understanding of their lives as the fulfillment of biblical prophecy on both a communal and an individual level; (2) the importance of plain style—a mode of expression characterized by simplicity, accessibility, and the absence of ornament—in Puritan and Quaker speech, writing, clothing, architecture, furniture, and visual arts; (3) the diversity of Puritan and Quaker attitudes toward and ways of interacting with Native Americans; (4) the centrality of the Apocalypse, or the end of the world as it is prophesied in the Book of Revelation, to Puritan thought; and (5) the relevance of weaned affections—the idea that individuals must learn to wean themselves from earthly loves and focus only on spiritual matters—as a theological doctrine.

The archive and curriculum materials suggest how students might connect the readings in this unit to those in other units in the series. Students might ask, for example, Why are the Puritans considered such an important starting point for American culture and literature? Why do later writers such as Nathaniel Hawthorne and Louise Erdrich invoke the Puritans in their own work? How do Rowlandson's and Penn's perceptions of Native Americans compare to Christopher Columbus's, Thomas Harriot's, and John Smith's perceptions? How do the Native American perspectives offered in Unit 1 complicate Puritan and Quaker understandings of Indian culture? Why does Winthrop's metaphor of the "City on a Hill" resonate so deeply in American culture? How are the Utopian visions of the writers in Unit 3 adopted, reformulated, or undermined in the work of writers presented in later units?

Student Overview

Unit 3, "The Promised Land," explores the literatures and cultures produced by the different European and Native American groups who inhabited the eastern shores of North America in the seventeenth and eighteenth centuries. Many of the immigrant groups discussed in this unit—Puritans, Quakers, Anglicans, and others—arrived in the "New World" with optimistic plans for creating model societies that would fulfill God's will on earth. Most groups almost immediately encountered challenges that threatened those plans. The physical difficulties of living in an unfamiliar land, friction with other immigrant groups, dissent within their own communities, and conflicts with Native Americans complicated and undermined their attempts to build ideal communities. While groups such as the Puritans and the Quakers failed to turn their utopian dreams into realities, their visions, ideals, and even ideologies have left an indelible mark on conceptions of American national identity and continue to influence American literary traditions.

As the video demonstrates, John Winthrop's "A Model of Christian Charity," Mary Rowlandson's narrative of her captivity among the Narragansett Indians, and William Penn's "Letter to the Lenni Lenape Indians" all participate in a tradition of understanding personal and communal experience as the working of God's will. From Winthrop's vision of the Puritan congregation as "a City on a Hill" to Rowlandson's nightmarish account of personal and communal sin and redemption to Penn's idealistic commitment to peace and tolerance in his dealings with Native Americans, these texts demonstrate a shared belief in America's promise, even as they offer very different perspectives on how that promise should be realized. The study guide for Unit 3 also explores the diversity of early American visions of "the promised land" by examining the works of other writers from the period, such as William Bradford, Thomas Morton, Anne Bradstreet, Edward Taylor, Sarah Kemble Knight, John Woolman, and Samson Occom. The "Core Contexts" materials offer background on the religious doctrines, historical events, and stylistic developments that shaped the literature of this period.

A belief in America's potential to become an ideal society unites all of the writers discussed in Unit 3. Although the texts presented here offer radically different conceptions of an ideal society, they all participate in the formation of enduring myths that continue to shape our literary traditions and our national imagination: the ideas that America is a "chosen" nation, that America should be a beacon to the rest of the world, that America is a land of inclusiveness and tolerance, to name a few. For better and for worse, these early American texts helped create these ideas about America.

Video Overview

- **Authors covered:** John Winthrop, Mary Rowlandson, William Penn
- **Who's interviewed:** Gary Nash, award-winning author and professor of American history (UCLA); Michael J. Colacurcio, professor of American literary and intellectual history (UCLA); Priscilla Wald, professor of American literature (Duke); Emory Elliott, professor of English (UC, Riverside)
- **Points covered:**
  - Description of the diverse early settlers in America and their diverse utopian visions and expectations for the New World.
  - Introduction to the Puritans and their belief in their own status as God's "chosen people." John Winthrop's "Model of Christian Charity" explicates the nature of their "sacred errand" and outlines a blueprint for the model Puritan community.
  - Mary Rowlandson's narrative of her captivity among the Narragansett Indians offers a later, more dystopian vision of New England. Her text functions as a jeremiad, denouncing the sinfulness of her society, urging repentance, and providing a model for salvation. Louise Erdrich's 1984 poem "Captivity" offers a contemporary reinterpretation of Rowlandson's experience.
  - Introduction to the Quakers and their commitment to nonviolence, tolerance, and inclusiveness. Penn's "Letter to the Lenni Lenape Indians" shows a respect for Native Americans' culture and rights that is quite different from Puritan attitudes toward Native Americans. Theological differences between the Quakers and the Puritans led to hostility and persecution.
  - Internal doubts and external enemies plagued the Puritans, as evidenced by the witchcraft trials of the 1690s. Neither Quakers nor Puritans succeed in creating perfect communities, but they are the sources of lasting myths and guiding principles that have shaped America over the centuries.

PREVIEW
- **Preview the video:** In the seventeenth and eighteenth centuries, Puritans, Quakers, and other European immigrant groups arrived in the "New World" with optimistic plans to create utopian societies that would fulfill God's will on earth. John Winthrop's "A Model of Christian Charity," Mary Rowlandson's narrative of her captivity among the Narragansett Indians, and William Penn's "Letter to the Lenni Lenape Indians" all participate in a tradition of understanding personal and communal experience as the working of divine will. From Winthrop's vision of the Puritan congregation as "a City on a Hill" to Rowlandson's nightmarish account of personal and communal sin and redemption to Penn's idealistic commitment to peace and tolerance in his dealings with Native Americans, these texts demonstrate a shared belief in America's promise, even as they offer very different perspectives on how that promise should be realized. While groups like the Puritans and the Quakers failed to turn their utopian dreams into realities, their visions, ideals, and even ideologies have left an indelible mark on American conceptions of national identity and continue to shape American literary traditions.
- **What to think about while watching:** How did the Puritans and Quakers respond to the social and political pressures caused by their immigration to a "New World"? How did they react when they came into contact with other immigrant groups and with Native Americans? How do the writers and texts explored in the video formulate enduring myths about America? How have their values and beliefs shaped American culture and literature?
- **Tying the video to the unit content:** Unit 3 builds on the concepts outlined in the video to further explore the diversity of the utopian visions and dystopic fears that shaped the early American experience. The curriculum materials offer background on Puritan and Quaker writers and texts not featured in the video, as well as information about some of the other religious and cultural traditions that developed in America. The unit offers contextual background to flesh out the video's introduction to the historical events, theological beliefs, and stylistic characteristics that shaped Puritan and Quaker literature.

	What characteristics of a literary work make it influential over time?	**How are American myths created, challenged, and re-imagined through these works of literature?**	**What is American literature? What are the distinctive voices and styles in American literature? How do social and political issues influence the American canon?**
Comprehension Questions	What is new about Penn's "Letter to the Lenni Lenape"? How does he view Native Americans? How is his attitude toward Native Americans different from the Puritans' attitudes toward them?	What did John Winthrop mean when he proclaimed that New England would be "as a City on a Hill"? What benefits and responsibilities would such status incur for a community?	What are the characteristics of a jeremiad? How does Mary Rowlandson's text function as a jeremiad?
Context Questions	What is typology? What events and institutions did the Puritans choose to understand typologically? How did typology help them make sense of the world and their position within it?	How did internal doubts and external enemies problematize and challenge the Puritans' conception of their "sacred errand"? How did Native Americans and "witches" fit into the Puritans' sense of their mission?	Why do you think Louise Erdrich chose to reimagine Mary Rowlandson's experience in her poem "Captivity"? How does Erdrich's poem both draw from and challenge Rowlandson's narrative?
Exploratory Questions	Can you think of later, post-Puritan examples of jeremiads? Where can you see the influence of the jeremiad form in contemporary literature, culture, and politics? Why has the jeremiad remained a central component of the rhetoric of American public life?	How have Quaker beliefs and convictions influenced the development of American values?	Why do you think the Puritans, more than any other early immigrant group, have historically been considered the starting point for the United States's national culture? Why did leaders such as John F. Kennedy and Ronald Reagan choose to invoke John Winthrop's "City on a Hill" image in their late-twentieth-century speeches?

	Texts	Contexts
1620s	Mayflower Compact (1620)	Plymouth Colony (1620)
1630s	William Bradford, *Of Plymouth Plantation* (1630–50 [pub. 1868]) John Winthrop, *A Model of Christian Charity* (1630) Thomas Morton, *New English Canaan* (1637)	Thirty Years Wars of religion across Europe (1618–48) Antinomian Controversy (1635–37) Massachusetts Bay Colony (1630) Pequot War (1637)
1640s	Anne Bradstreet, poetry (1642–69)	English Civil War (1642–48) Revolution, Charles I executed (1649) Cromwell's Puritan Commonwealth (1649–61)

	Texts	Contexts
1650s	Anne Bradstreet, poetry (1642–69), *The Tenth Muse* (1650)	First Quakers to New England Halfway Covenant on problem of unconverted youth (1657–62) Boston authorities hang four Quakers (1659–60)
1660s		Charles II made king (1660) War with Dutch; English annex New Netherland (New York) (1664)
1670s	Edward Taylor, poetry (1674–98)	King Philip's War (1675)
1680s	William Penn, "Letter to the Lenni Lenape [Delaware] Indians" (1681) Mary Rowlandson, *Narrative of the Captivity and Restoration* (1682)	Pennyslvania founded (1681–82) Glorious Revolution removes Catholic James II; John Locke asserts principle of consent of governed (1688) War with France (1689–97)
1690s	Cotton Mather, *The Wonders of the Invisible World* (1693)	Salem witchcraft trials & executions (1692–93) Judge Samuel Sewall openly prays for forgiveness for Salem trials
1700s	Sarah Kemble Knight, *Journal* (written 1704–05, pub. 1825) Samuel Sewall, *The Selling of Joseph*, first American anti-slavery tract (1700)	War with France (1702–13) Eighteenth-century secularization of New England, growth of liberal philosophies, deism, scientific rationalism, imperial trade, and mercantilism
1730s	Jonathan Edwards, revivalist writings (1735–40s)	"Great Awakening," a revitalization of piety and enthusiastic religion that swept the British American colonies (1735–40s)
1740s		Peak years of British slave trade, involving New England shipping, southern colonies, Caribbean (1720–80) War with France (1744–48)
1750s	John Woolman, *Some Considerations on the Keeping of Negroes* (1745 [pub. 1754])	Emergence of organized religious anti-slavery in England (1750s) War with France (1754–63)
1760s	Samson Occom, *Narrative* (1768 [pub. 1982]) Briton Hammon, *Narrative*, first ex-slave narrative	French cede Canada and claims to Indian lands east of Mississippi River to British (1763)
1770s	John Woolman, "Journal" (1774)	American Revolution (1775–83) Declaration of Independence (1776)

[6324] Sarony and Major, *The Landing of the Pilgrims on Plymouth Rock, Dec. 11th, 1620* (1846), courtesy of the Library of Congress [LC-USZC4-4311].

William Bradford (1590–1657)

Born in 1590 in Yorkshire, England, William Bradford was orphaned at a young age and reared by his grandparents and uncles to be a farmer. Bradford broke with his family in early adolescence, affiliating himself with the **Separatist Puritans** and thereby making a religious commitment that would profoundly influence the course of his life. The Separatists dreamed of creating a purified religious community, free of the hierarchies and worldly rituals that they felt contaminated the Church of England. The sect was known as "Separatist" because, unlike most Puritan congregations, it rejected the Church of England entirely instead of attempting to reform it from within. Bradford and his fellow Separatists paid a high price for their controversial beliefs: religious persecution led them to flee England for safer harbors in Holland and eventually in America.

In 1620, Bradford and part of the congregation to which he belonged set sail for America on the *Mayflower*, bringing with them a patent granting them land in the territory of Virginia, where they hoped to set up their ideal church. Bad weather pushed them off course, and they landed well north of Virginia on the coast of what is now Plymouth, Massachusetts. There they began the difficult work of establishing a community in unfamiliar, and sometimes hostile, territory. Bradford was elected governor in 1621 and occupied that office, with only brief intermissions, until his death in 1657. In 1630 he began writing *Of Plymouth Plantation*, the history of his "Pilgrims'" religious and civil settlement in the New World.

Bradford's literary reputation depends, as scholar David Levin puts it, "as much on the quality of his historical intelligence as on the virtues of his style." Indeed, Bradford's text has long been celebrated for the "plain style" he endorses in its first paragraph. His simple yet artful prose, characterized by finely tuned sentences based upon the language and cadences of the Geneva Bible, is often regarded as a model of a specifically American style of writing. But, as Levin points out, Bradford's text is no less notable for its historiographic project, a complex balance of religious exhortation and unvarnished reportage. Clearly, *Of Plymouth Plantation* is meant to serve as an account of God's design in planting the Plymouth colony, interpreting events that might seem random or even commonplace to modern readers as evidence of God's hand at work on earth. Bradford's history extols the purity and strength of the first settlers in order to inspire subsequent generations to greater sanctity, combating what he perceived to be the spiritual decline of the community in the years following the initial settlement. While Bradford's desire to read God's will in the history of Plymouth colors his text—and frequently skews his understanding of non-Puritan people—his tendency toward exhortation is often balanced by an unflinching commitment to historical accuracy. He is surprisingly blunt in relating some of the troubles that plagued the Plymouth community, from rancorous differences between leaders to upsetting cases of sexual deviance among congregants. The result is a complicated, engaging document that has become an integral part of the mythology concerning the foundation of America.

■ Bradford wrote Book I of *Of Plymouth Plantation* in 1630 and Book II from about 1644 to 1650. The dates of composition are significant because they mark periods of crisis in the Plymouth settlement's sense of its own purpose and worth. In 1630, the **non-separating Puritans** led by John Winthrop arrived in nearby Massachusetts Bay. Not only did this group represent a competing strain of Puritanism, but it also was better funded than the Plymouth colony and in possession of a more legitimate charter to the New England territory (in fact, it would absorb the Plymouth group in 1691). In the late 1640s, Puritans led by Oliver Cromwell transformed the political and religious situation in England, making the American Puritans' project seem somewhat redundant and certainly less novel. Once you alert students to the historical contexts that inform the two parts of Bradford's text, you might ask them to consider how these events color Bradford's account. To some extent, his decision to recount the Plymouth group's voyage and landing seems to be a way of defending their primacy among New England settlers. How might his account of the hardships the group faced upon landing affirm their claim both to the land and to spiritual purity? You might also examine how Bradford's tone and outlook changed in the fourteen years that elapsed between the writing of Book I and Book II.

■ It is useful to point out that Bradford differs from most early American writers in portraying Native Americans as *immediately* hostile: in *Of Plymouth Plantation* the natives first run from the Puritans and then attack them with arrows before any other kind of contact can be established. Bradford's low estimation of the Indians is evident in his brutal, graphic account of the Plymouth group's genocidal war against the Pequots in Chapter XXVIII. For Bradford, the bloodiness and horror of the war seemed "a sweet sacrifice, and they [the Puritans] gave praise thereof to God, who had wrought so wonderfully for them, thus to enclose their enemies in their hands. . . ." You might ask students to analyze what assumptions lay behind Bradford's hatred of the Native Americans (he describes them as animals in Chapter IV) and how those assumptions were used to justify the colonization of Native American land.

■ Bradford's account of the Plymouth group's conflict with Thomas Morton and Morton's "consorts" at Merrymount is worth careful analysis and discussion, both because it provides insight into how the Puritans dealt with people who did not share their values and beliefs (both Native Americans and the English, in this case) and because it will serve as useful background when students read Morton's version of events in *New English Canaan*. You might ask students to consider whether Bradford is more outraged by what he perceives as Morton's "licentiousness" in matters of drink and sex or by Morton's decision to sell guns to Indians in exchange for fur pelts.

[6324] Sarony and Major, *The Landing of the Pilgrims on Plymouth Rock, Dec. 11th, 1620* (1846), courtesy of the Library of Congress [LC-USZC4-4311]. Although no evidence directly links the *Mayflower's* 1620 landing to Plymouth Rock, this location has come to represent the birthplace of English settlement in New England.

[6326] Jean Leon Gerome Ferris, *The First Thanksgiving 1621* (1932), courtesy of the Library of Congress [LC-USZ62-15915]. The Thanksgiving holiday has gained mythic status through representations of the event as a critical occasion of the Plymouth colony.

[6726] A. W. Anderson, *Plymouth Rock, in Front of Pilgrim Hall, 1834* (1909), courtesy of the Library of Congress [LC-USZ62-97130]. Although no evidence directly links the *Mayflower's* 1620 landing to Plymouth Rock, for many this location represents the birthplace of English settlement in New England.

[6940] Anonymous, Contemporary Model/Recreation of the *Mayflower* (2000–2001), courtesy of Plimoth Plantation, Inc. Thousands of tourists visit this model of the *Mayflower* each year, contributing to the Puritans' mythic status as the original American settlers.

■ In 1994, Sophie Cabot Black composed "Arguments," a series of poems in which she dramatizes the *Mayflower* landing from the perspective of Dorothy Bradford (William's wife), who died soon after the Separatist Puritans' arrival in the New World. Ask students to compare William Bradford's narrative of the *Mayflower* landing in *Of Plymouth Plantation* with Cabot Black's version of Dorothy Bradford's feelings about reaching America in "Landfall. 20th of November." How does Cabot Black revise William Bradford's narrative? Why did she choose Dorothy Bradford as the subject for her poems? See Sophie Cabot Black, *The Misunderstanding of Nature* (St. Paul, MN: Graywolf, 1994).

QUESTIONS

Comprehension: In Chapter IV, Bradford refers to America as a "vast and unpeopled" country, but his subsequent account of the Plymouth settlement attests to the fact that the land was far from uninhabited. What other kinds of people do the Plymouth settlers encounter on their voyage and in the New World? How does the presence of "strangers" work both to challenge and to solidify the Puritan community?

Comprehension: Why is Bradford so outraged by Thomas Morton? What is the nature of the conflict between Morton's Merrymount community and Bradford's Pilgrims? What kinds of values did each group espouse?

Context: What does Bradford mean when he refers to "plain style" in the introduction to *Of Plymouth Plantation*? What values and beliefs are reflected in his prose style? How does it compare to the prose styles of other writers discussed in this unit (Morton or Penn, for example)?

Exploration: Compare Bradford's account of the Puritans' "Arrival at Cape Cod" and "First Thanksgiving" with contemporary ideas about the landing at Plymouth Rock and the holiday. Why have these invented traditions and myths become so central to ideas about America's national beginnings? Why are the Puritans considered such an important starting point for America's national culture?

Thomas Morton (c. 1579–1647)

The historical record does not offer much detail about Thomas Morton's early life beyond the basic facts that he was born in England, received a traditional education, worked as an attorney, and had connections within the court of King Charles I. Those connections with wealthy court gentlemen probably enabled Morton's first visit to North America in 1622 and, as part of a trade venture, his settlement there in 1624. He established a fur-trading post at Mount Wollaston (modern-day Quincy), Massachusetts, and quickly began turning a steady profit dealing in beaver pelts. Morton called his community Mar-re-Mount, supposedly in reference to its position overlooking the sea; his Puritan neighbors saw through his pun and called it "Merrymount" in an indictment of what they viewed as the group's heedless indulgence in worldly pleasures. Indeed, the community at Mar-re-Mount did not share Puritan values and openly engaged in practices the Puritans condemned—drinking, dancing, and general "revelry." Tensions between Morton and the Puritans escalated, both because of the discrepancies between their respective moral systems and because of Morton's decision to trade rum and firearms with the local Native Americans, a practice the Plymouth group perceived as inimical to the safety of all European settlers in the region.

The situation came to a head with the famous Maypole incident in the spring of 1627, the conflict for which Morton is best known. When Morton invited local Native Americans—men, boys, and "lasses in beaver coats"—to dance around the eighty-foot maypole he had erected at Mar-re-Mount in a celebration of spring, the Puritans were so outraged by this open display of "profaneness" that they sent a military contingent out to arrest him. Morton was deported to England in 1628, where he stood trial and was acquitted. He returned to New England in 1629 as a free man only to have the Puritans seize his property, burn down his house, and banish him again. Back in England in 1630, Morton dedicated himself to creating difficulties for the Puritans, calling the legality of their colonial charter into question and condemning their religious practices. In 1643 he returned to New England, where he was imprisoned for slander until 1645 and died two years later in the northern part of the Massachusetts colony (present-day Maine).

Morton's only literary work is *New English Canaan* (1637), a satirical tract he drafted as part of his campaign against his Puritan enemies while in exile in England. Although part of the book is dedicated to chronicling Morton's skirmishes with the Puritans—and ruthlessly satirizing the Plymouth group—*New English Canaan* is not simply a history, nor is it wholly satirical. The book is also meant to serve as a promotional piece, celebrating the wealth and promise of the lands of New England and encouraging non-Puritans to settle there. Morton's florid, urbane writing style and witty irreverence make him unique among seventeenth-century New England writers.

[6740] Nicolaes Visscher, *Novi Belgii Novaeque Angliea Nec Non Partis Virginiae Tabula Multis in Locis Emendata* (1685), courtesy of the Library of Congress [97683561].

TEACHING TIPS

■ Ask students to read aloud a few sentences from the Morton selection. They will probably be struck by the difficulty of the prose and the proliferation of classical allusions. After reassuring them that Morton's style was intentionally highbrow and difficult (in many ways, the exact opposite of Bradford's prose), you might ask them to consider why Morton chose to write in this manner. Whom was he emulating? To what sort of audience was this text designed to appeal? Students who have some familiarity with English Renaissance writers will probably see the connection and understand that Morton was trying to establish himself as an educated, urbane Englishman who had more in common with people living in London than with the dour Puritans of colonial America.

[1210] John Underhill, *The Figure of the Indians' Fort or Palizado in New England and the Manner of Destroying It by Captayne Underhill and Captayne Mason* (1638), courtesy of the Library of Congress [LC-USZ62-32055]. In 1636, English settlers engaged in a genocidal campaign to wipe out the Pequot tribe. Captain John Underhill chronicled the Pequot War in his *News from America* (1638), providing this sketch of the Puritans, along with their Narragansett allies, encircling and destroying a Pequot village.

[3217] *The Bible and the Holy Scriptures Conteyned in the Olde and New Testament* (1560), courtesy of the Library of Congress. Title page from the Geneva Bible depicting the pursuit of the Hebrews by the Egyptians, as described in Exodus. Puritans who envisioned themselves as New Israelites used this Bible.

[6324] Sarony and Major, *The Landing of the Pilgrims on Plymouth Rock, Dec. 11th 1620* (1846), courtesy of the Library of Congress [LC-USZC4-4311]. Plymouth Rock has been used as a symbol of New England's settlement as the first event in American history—a myth not supported by the complex history of Native Americans and European exploration and settlement.

[6740] Nicolaes Visscher, *Novi Belgii Novaeque Angliae: Nec Non Partis Virginae Tabula Multis in Locis Emendata* (1685), courtesy of the Library of Congress [97683561]. This is a detail from the best-known map of New Netherland. The map details natural resources as well as geography. Beavers were a crucial, and profitable, trade item for places such Thomas Morton's Mar-re-Mount.

■ Compare Morton's account of the maypole incident with Bradford's. Ask students to generate a list of where the two stories agree on the facts and where they differ. What is at stake in these different accounts? Which is more persuasive? As your students draw their conclusions, ask them to consider the audiences Bradford and Morton were trying to reach.

QUESTIONS

Comprehension: What strategies does Morton use to satirize the Puritans in *New English Canaan*? How do the names he gives to the various characters in his tale undermine Puritan values and structures of authority? What is the significance of the title of his book?

Context: How does Morton's prose compare to Bradford's "plain style"? Bradford draws most of his metaphors and allusions from the Bible; what sources does Morton draw upon? What kind of identity is Morton trying to construct for himself through his literary style?

Exploration: Morton's portrait of Native Americans is quite different from the accounts offered by most other seventeenth-century American writers. What qualities does he ascribe to the Indians? How does his description of Native American culture compare to his description of Puritan culture? What reasons might Morton have had to portray the Indians so positively? Why do you think Morton's relationship to Native Americans was so threatening to the Puritans at Plymouth Plantation?

Exploration: What genre do you think *New English Canaan* falls into? Is it a history, a satire, a travel narrative, a promotional brochure, or some combination thereof?

Exploration: Read "The May-Pole of Merry Mount," Nathaniel Hawthorne's 1836 story about the conflict between Morton and the Puritans. How does Hawthorne portray the revelers? How does he portray the Puritans who confront them? With which group do his sympathies seem to lie? Why do you think Hawthorne chose this particular incident as the subject for his story?

John Winthrop (1588–1649)

Born into a wealthy landholding family in southern England in 1588, John Winthrop entered Trinity College, Cambridge, at the age of fourteen. At Trinity he considered studying to be a minister before ultimately deciding to become a lawyer. Although he did not choose to make the church his profession, Winthrop's faith and his commitment to Puritan ideals were nonetheless the dominant force in his life. While he and his fellow congregants shared many values and beliefs with the Separatist Puritans who had settled at Plymouth, they did not accept the doctrine of Separation. Rather than breaking entirely with the established Church of England, Winthrop and his group sought to reform it from within.

In 1629, uneasy about the English government's hostility toward

Puritanism and disgusted by what he perceived as the corruption of English society, Winthrop helped negotiate a charter forming the Massachusetts Bay Company and establishing the Puritans' right to found a colony in New England. The stockholders of the Company elected Winthrop governor, and, in 1630, he and nearly four hundred other Puritans set sail for the New World aboard the *Arbella*. In "A Model of Christian Charity," the lay sermon he delivered on the ship, Winthrop presented his vision of the ideal Christian community he hoped the Puritans would form when they arrived in Massachusetts. Premised on the belief that the Puritans were party to a **covenant**, or contract, with God, Winthrop's sermon uses this legal term to remind his followers of their spiritual and earthly duties as the "chosen people" of God. In "A Model of Christian Charity," he extols the virtues of a clear social and spiritual hierarchy, encourages the congregants to maintain an exemplary piety, and interprets the Puritan mission in typological terms (that is, as the fulfillment of biblical prophecy). Winthrop's famous proclamation that the new colony must be "as a City on a Hill"—truly a "model" society, unassailable in its virtue so that its enemies would have nothing to criticize and its admirers would have something to emulate—continues to resonate as an enduring myth of America.

[6751] Richard S. Greenough, *Statue of John Winthrop* (1876), courtesy of Architect of the Capitol.

Winthrop served as the governor of the Massachusetts Bay Colony for twelve of the nineteen years he lived there. His was a powerful voice in the shaping of Puritan social, religious, and political policies, and his *Journal* remains the most complete contemporary account of the first two decades of the Bay Colony's history. Composed during his busy career as a public servant, the *Journal* reflects Winthrop's often militant commitment to firmly establishing orthodoxy within his community. He chronicles both the external challenges the Puritans faced and the internal divisions—such as the religious controversies sparked by Roger Williams and Anne Hutchinson—that threatened to fracture the group's unity. Throughout, the *Journal* interprets events in Massachusetts as acts of providential significance, reading everyday occurrences as evidence of either God's favor or God's displeasure.

TEACHING TIPS

■ Review the Core Context on typology in this unit. Divide students into groups and ask them to locate typologizing moments in Winthrop's "Model of Christian Charity" or in his *Journal*. (The sermon is a particularly good source since Winthrop notes many parallels between the Puritans and the Old Testament Hebrews within it.) Ask students to consider the significance of the Puritans' insistence on understanding their own history as prefigured by the Bible. What kinds of pressures might this tendency to read biblical and divine significance into everyday affairs put on individuals and on communities? How might it work to comfort and reassure people?

■ The theological issues at stake in Winthrop's condemnation of Anne Hutchinson's Antinomianism are quite complicated, but even students bored by a discussion of the distinction between a covenant

[1363] Anonymous, *John Winthrop* (17th cent.), courtesy of American Antiquarian Society. John Winthrop was the first governor of Massachusetts Bay Colony. His somber-colored clothing marks him as a Puritan, while his ornate neck ruff indicates his wealth and social status.

[6751] Richard S. Greenough, *Statue of John Winthrop* (1876), courtesy of Architect of the Capitol. This statue was given, along with one of Samuel Adams, by the state of Massachusetts in 1876 to the National Statuary Hall Collection in the United States Capitol. The choice of Winthrop indicates his status both as a prominent American and as an allegorical representative of the nation's ideals.

[6942] Photo of a Statue of Roger Williams, Providence, Rhode Island (2002), courtesy of Christopher Moses. A Puritan whose unorthodox views alienated him from both the Massachusetts Bay and the Plymouth colonies, Roger Williams has been reclaimed by some contemporary scholars as a democratic and pluralist hero.

of works and a covenant of grace will be interested in the political and social implications of this controversy. Ask them to think about the role gender plays in Winthrop's attack on Hutchinson. Would her preaching be so threatening if she were not "a woman of a ready wit and bold spirit"?

■ In September 1638, Winthrop notes that Anne Hutchinson delivered a stillborn, misshapen child. In the sixteenth and seventeenth centuries, stillborn children and children with birth defects were called "monstrous births" and understood to represent either God's displeasure or the devil's influence over the mother. How does Winthrop describe Hutchinson's "monstrous birth" in his *Journal*? Why does her miscarriage seem so significant to him? Ask students to think about Winthrop's attitude toward motherhood, women's bodies, and childbirth. Keep in mind that Hutchinson served as a midwife within the Puritan community for many years prior to her banishment.

QUESTIONS

Comprehension: Winthrop's *Journal* chronicles a number of the problems and controversies that challenged the early settlers at Massachusetts Bay. What kinds of external and internal threats undermined the unity of the group? What happened to people who deviated from orthodox religious tenets? What rhetorical strategies does Winthrop adopt when characterizing people whose beliefs were different from his own?

Context: The "Model of Christian Charity" was composed before Winthrop and the Puritans disembarked in Massachusetts. How do the hopes and values the sermon espouses compare to the realities Winthrop later recorded in his *Journal*? Does Winthrop's sense of the community's mission and his own responsibility to further it change over time?

Exploration: Why has Winthrop's metaphor of the "City on a Hill" had so much influence on American culture? Do you see evidence of the endurance of this idea within contemporary public discourse?

Anne Bradstreet (c. 1612–1672)

Anne Bradstreet was born in England in 1612 to well-connected Puritan parents. Her father, Thomas Dudley, was unusual in his commitment to teaching his daughter literature, history, and philosophy, and Bradstreet benefited from an extensive classical education such as was usually reserved only for male children. Her sixty years of life were troubled by recurring sickness and ill health, beginning with an attack of smallpox when she was sixteen. Shortly after recovering, she married her father's assistant, Simon Bradstreet. She immigrated to America with her husband and parents in 1630 as part of the group that sailed with John Winthrop on the *Arbella*. Although she later admitted that her "heart rose" in protest against the "new world and new manners" she encountered when she landed in Massachusetts,

Bradstreet overcame her resentment and made a life for herself as a dutiful and respected Puritan daughter, wife, and mother.

Bradstreet and her family moved frequently, living in Boston, Newtown (modern Cambridge), and Ipswich before settling in North Andover. While her father and husband embarked on long and successful careers in public service—both would eventually occupy the position of governor—Bradstreet raised eight children and composed poetry. In 1650, her brother-in-law, John Woodbridge, brought a manuscript of her work with him on a trip to London and had it published without Bradstreet's knowledge. The volume, *The Tenth Muse, Lately Sprung Up In America*, was the first published collection of poetry written by a resident of America, and met with popular and critical success both in England and among the Puritan patriarchy. While Bradstreet did not publish again within her lifetime, a posthumous collection containing her corrections to the original volume and several new poems was printed six years after her death. The fact that she took the time to rework and correct the original volume suggests that she was planning for further publication and provides evidence that she took her vocation as a poet very seriously.

Bradstreet received acclaim in her own time for her long meditative poems on classical themes, but the poems that have interested modern readers are the more personal and intimate ones, reflecting her experiences with marriage, motherhood, childbirth, and housekeeping. This personal poetry is notable for the tensions it reveals between Bradstreet's affection for the things of this world—home, family, natural beauty—and her Puritan commitment to shunning earthly concerns in order to focus on the spiritual. Her evocations of the passion she felt for her husband and her children are poignantly balanced by her reminders to herself that such attachments should remain secondary to her love for Christ. Bradstreet's reflections on the issue of women's status within the Puritan community and on her own role as a female writer also create tensions within her poetry. Her self-conscious musings about her claims to literary authority and intellectual equality in "The Author to her Book" and "Prologue" provide rare insight into the pressures inherent in being both a woman and a writer in Puritan New England.

[1219] Anonymous, *The Mason Children: David, Joanna, Abigail* (1670), courtesy of Fine Arts Museums of San Francisco, gift of Mr. and Mrs. John D. Rockefeller 3rd, 1979.7.3.

TEACHING TIPS

■ When John Woodbridge, Bradstreet's brother-in-law, compiled her poetry for publication, he included a preface vouching for the book's authenticity and for his sister-in-law's character:

> . . . the worse effect of his [the reader's] reading will be unbelief, which will make him question whether it be a woman's work, and ask, is it possible? If any do, take this as an answer from him that dares to avow it; it is the work of a woman, honored, and esteemed where she lives, for her gracious demeanor, her eminent parts, her pious conversation, her courteous disposition, her exact diligence in her place, and discreet managing of her family occasions, and more than so, these

poems are the fruit but of some few hours, curtailed from her sleep and other refreshments.

Read this prefatory material aloud to your class and ask students why Woodbridge felt compelled to include it. What does this preface reveal about women's status in Puritan society? What does it tell us about the kinds of anxieties Bradstreet probably felt with regard to her poetry and its publication?

■ Have students read aloud "A Letter to Her Husband, Absent upon Public Employment." While students may initially respond to this as a conventional love poem, try to stress how unusual its secular tone is within the corpus of Puritan poetry. Even though some of the imagery has spiritual and biblical resonance, what emerges in this poem is Bradstreet's erotic attachment to her husband, not her understanding of her marriage as a metaphor for her union with Christ. Her reliance on pagan imagery (the sun god, the zodiac) is notable in this context.

QUESTIONS

Comprehension: Bradstreet's seventeenth-century language and syntax can be confusing. Pick one of her poems and write a line-by-line paraphrase of it in contemporary American English. What difficulties did you encounter in rewriting Bradstreet's images and ideas? What has the poem lost in translation?

Comprehension: Anne Bradstreet composed a number of "elegies," that is, poems that relate the experience of loss and the search for consolation. In an important sense, elegies are designed to defend the individual against death. Whose loss is mourned in "Before the Birth of One of Her Children," and how does Bradstreet console either the mourners or herself?

Context: What are some of the recurring themes and images in Bradstreet's poetry? How does she balance abstract, theological concerns with personal, material issues? What does Bradstreet's poetry tell us about motherhood and marriage in Puritan New England?

Context: In the poem "Here Follows Some Verses upon the Burning of Our House," how does Bradstreet struggle with her Puritan commitment to the doctrine of "weaned affections" (the idea that individuals must wean themselves from earthly, material concerns and focus only on spiritual matters)? How does she turn the experience of losing her possessions to spiritual use? Does she seem entirely resigned to casting away her "pelf" and "store"? In what terms does she describe the "house on high" that God has prepared for her?

Exploration: How sincere is Bradstreet's evaluation of her poetry as the "ill-formed offspring of my feeble brain"? Should we read this kind of self-abasement as a calculated rhetorical pose, a poetic convention, a defensive maneuver, or as evidence of extreme insecurity? Why does she make a point of avowing "Men have precedency" and "Men can do best"? Keep in mind that Bradstreet was writing in the immediate aftermath of the Antinomian controversy and the banishment of Anne Hutchinson. How might a consciousness of the dangers of female speech and female writing inform her work?

Exploration: Anne Bradstreet's poetry has often been compared to that by Sor Juana Inez de la Cruz, the first female poet to write in the Spanish American colony of New Spain (the area that is now Mexico and the southwestern United States). How does Bradstreet's "Prologue" compare to Sor Juana's "Prologue"? What justifications does each poet give for women composing poetry? How do their attitudes toward death compare?

Mary Rowlandson (c. 1636–1711)

Born around 1637 in Somerset, England, Mary White was the sixth of ten children. Her family immigrated to New England when she was very young, settling first in Salem and later in the frontier town of Lancaster, in the Massachusetts colony. In 1656, Mary married Joseph Rowlandson, the Harvard-educated Puritan minister of Lancaster, and for the next twenty years she occupied the role of a Puritan goodwife, tending to her home and raising children. Her life was radically disrupted on February 10, 1676, when a contingent of Narraganset Indians attacked and burned Lancaster, killing seventeen people and taking twenty-four others (including Rowlandson and three of her children) captive. This incident is the basis of Rowlandson's extraordinary account of her captivity among the Indians, a narrative which was widely read in her own time and which today is often regarded as one of the most significant early texts in the American canon. Rowlandson's tale shaped the conventions of the **captivity narrative**, a genre that influenced the development of both autobiographical writings and the novel in America.

The attack on Lancaster and on Rowlandson's home was part of a series of raids in the conflict that has become known as King Philip's War, named for the Indian leader Metacom (called "Philip" by the English). Although the war was immediately provoked by the Plymouth colony's decision to execute three members of the Wampanoag tribe, it should also be understood as the culmination of long-standing tensions between Native Americans and European settlers over land rights and colonial expansion. By the late seventeenth century, many Native Americans in the New England region were suffering the devastating effects of disease and starvation as European settlers encroached upon their homes and hunting grounds.

During her captivity, Rowlandson experienced the same physical hardships the Indians faced: she never had enough to eat and constantly relocated from one camp to another in a series of what she termed "removes." Her traumatic experience was made all the more harrowing by her Puritan conviction that all Native Americans were agents of Satan, sent to punish and torment her and her community. After eleven weeks and a journey of over 150 miles, Rowlandson was finally ransomed on May 2, 1676, for goods worth twenty pounds. Because Lancaster had been destroyed in the raid, she and her hus-

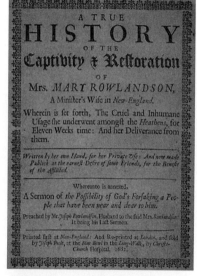

[2788] Mary Rowlandson, *A True History of the Captivity and Restoration of Mrs. Mary Rowlandson, A Minister's Wife in New England* (1682), courtesy of Annenberg Rare Book and Manuscript Library, University of Pennsylvania.

band spent the following year in Boston, then moved to Wethersfield, Connecticut, where Joseph Rowlandson became the town's minister. After he died in 1678, Mary Rowlandson married Captain Samuel Talcott and lived in Wethersfield with him until her death in 1711 at the age of seventy-three.

Rowlandson tells her readers that she composed her narrative out of gratitude for her deliverance from captivity and in the hopes of conveying the spiritual meaning of her experience to other members of the Puritan community. In many ways, her narrative conforms to the conventions of the **jeremiad**, a form usually associated with second-generation Puritan sermons but also relevant to many other kinds of Puritan writing. Drawing from the Old Testament books of Jeremiah and Isaiah, jeremiads work by lamenting the spiritual and moral decline of a community and interpreting recent misfortunes as God's just punishment for that decline. But at the same time that jeremiads bemoan their communities' fall from grace, they also read the misfortunes and punishments that result from that fall as paradoxical proofs of God's love and of the group's status as his "chosen people." According to jeremidic logic, God would not bother chastising or testing people he did not view as special or important to his divine plan. Rowlandson is careful to interpret her traumatic experience according to these orthodox spiritual ideals, understanding her captivity as God's punishment for her (and the entire Puritan community's) sinfulness and inadequacy and interpreting her deliverance as evidence of God's mercy.

But in spite of its standardized jeremidic rhetoric, Rowlandson's narrative is also marked by contradictions and tensions that sometimes seem to subvert accepted Puritan ideals. On occasion, the demands of life in the wilderness led Rowlandson to accommodate herself to Native American culture, which she viewed as "barbaric," in order to work actively for her own survival even as she cherished an ideal of waiting patiently and passively for God to lead her, and to express anger and resentment even as she preached the submissive acceptance of God's will. Thus, Rowlandson's *Narrative* provides important insight not only into orthodox Puritan ideals and values but also, however unintentionally, into the conflicted nature of her own Puritan identity.

TEACHING TIPS

■ When Rowlandson's *Narrative* was first published in 1682, it was printed with a "Preface" written by the influential Puritan minister Increase Mather, and with a sermon composed by her husband, Joseph Rowlandson. Some scholars have speculated that Joseph Rowlandson and Mather were also extensively involved in the production of the *Narrative* itself; the frequency and aptness of biblical quotations in the text might indicate the hand of an experienced cleric. After providing students with this background information, ask for their opinions on whether or not (or to what extent) Rowlandson was mediated and guided by Puritan authorities when composing this text. Ask them to offer specific textual evidence to back up their speculations.

You might point students toward the numerous biblical quotations and toward Rowlandson's explanations of how she accessed and derived comfort from these particular lines of scripture.

■ Rowlandson opens her *Narrative* with totalizing, dehumanizing descriptions of Native Americans as "hell-hounds," "ravenous beasts," and "barbarous creatures." As the text progresses, however, she seems to become more willing to see her captors as individuals, and even as people capable of humanity and charity. Ask students to analyze her portraits of individual Indians and to trace the evolution of her attitude toward Indians in general. Which Native Americans come in for the most criticism? Which does she view more positively? What might motivate her varying assessments? How might changes in Rowlandson's own status within the Wampanoag encampment influence her attitude toward individual Indians? You might point students toward her discussions of the various Native Americans who engage in economic transactions with her or give her food, her quite positive portrait of Metacom (or "Philip," as she calls him), and her bitter description of Weetamoo, a Wampanoag "squawsachem," or female leader.

■ Students may want to compare Rowlandson's description of Weetamoo to Benjamin Church's description of other Wampanoag squawsachems in his *Entertaining Passages Relating to Philip's War*. How does each text portray these Native American female leaders?

QUESTIONS

Comprehension: The subject of food receives a great deal of attention in Rowlandson's *Narrative*. How does Rowlandson's attitude toward food change over the course of her captivity? Why is she so concerned with recording the specifics of what she ate, how she acquired it, and how she prepared it? What kinds of conflicts arise over food? What do her descriptions of eating tell us about Native American culture and about Rowlandson's ability to acculturate?

Context: How does Rowlandson use typology within her *Narrative*? What kinds of biblical images does she rely on to make sense of her captivity? How does her use of typology compare with that of other writers in this unit (Winthrop or Taylor, for example)?

Context: In his preface to the first edition of Rowlandson's *Narrative*, published in 1682, Increase Mather describes her story as "a dispensation of publick note and of Universal concernment" and urges all Puritans to "view" and "ponder" the lessons it holds for them. Does Rowlandson always seem to understand her captivity in Mather's terms? How do the moments when Rowlandson narrates her experience as personal and individual complicate this imperative to function as a "public," representative lesson for the entire community?

Exploration: Many scholars view the captivity narrative as the first American genre and trace its influence in the development of other forms of American autobiographical and fictional writings. Why do you think the captivity narrative became so popular and influen-

ROWLANDSON WEB ARCHIVE

[2115] *Harper's Magazine, The Captivity of Mrs. Rowlandson* (1857), courtesy of the Library of Congress [LC-USZ62-113682]. This is an illustration from an 1857 *Harper's Magazine* feature on "The Adventures of the Early Settlers in New England." This woodcarving print depicts events chronicled in the *Narrative of the Captivity and Restoration of Mrs. Mary Rowlandson.*

[2788] Mary Rowlandson, *A True History of the Captivity and Restoration of Mrs. Mary Rowlandson, A Minister's Wife in New England* (1682), courtesy of Annenberg Rare Book and Manuscript Library, University of Pennsylvania. Subtitle: "Written by her own Hand, for her Private Use: And now made Publlick at the earnest Desire of some Friends, for the Benefit of the Afflicted."

[2916] Charles H. Lincoln, ed., *Map of Mrs. Rowlandson's Removes, Narratives of the Indian Wars* (1913), courtesy of Charles Scribner's Sons. This map shows Rowlandson's "removes" in terms of twentieth-century landmarks.

[4439] *Judea Capta* Coin (71 C.E.), courtesy of the American Numismatic Society. This Roman coin depicts the biblical image of *Judea capta* (Israel in bondage). Mary Rowlandson's *Narrative* typologizes her experience in terms of the *Judea capta* ideal, understanding her purifying ordeal in the wilderness as a parallel of God's punishment and ultimate redemption of the "New Israel."

[7178] Vera Palmer, Interview: "Erdrich and the Captivity Narrative" (2001), courtesy of Annenberg/CPB. Palmer, a distinguished American Indian activist and scholar (Ph.D. Cornell), discusses themes of the captivity narrative as they appear in the poetry of Louise Erdrich.

tial? What might make it seem particularly "American"? Can you think of any nineteenth- or twentieth-century novels or films that draw on the conventions of the captivity narrative?

Exploration: Compare Rowlandson's captivity narrative with Alvar Nuñez Cabeza de Vaca's *Relation* from Unit 2. How do these texts portray Native Americans differently? What do they have in common? What kind of audience does each author write for? How does each of these narratives differ from the Yellow Woman stories in Unit 1?

Edward Taylor (c. 1642–1729)

Edward Taylor was born in Leicestershire, England, in 1642 to Nonconformist parents of modest circumstances. In his mid-twenties, frustrated by the climate of intolerance toward Puritans, he fled England for Massachusetts. Entering Harvard with advanced standing, Taylor embarked on a course of study to prepare himself to become a minister. In 1671 he accepted a call to the ministry in the town of Westfield, a farming community on the fringes of the colony. He spent the rest of his life there, rarely leaving Westfield even for visits. Because the area was threatened by Indian attacks throughout the 1670s, Taylor's church building had to do double duty as a fort, delaying the formal organization of the congregation as a Puritan church until 1679. As the most educated man in Westfield, Taylor served the town by assuming the roles of physician and teacher as well as minister.

Taylor's education had left him with a lasting passion for books, and his library was a distinguished one, though many of the books were his own handwritten copies of volumes he could not afford to purchase in printed form. Much of Taylor's time was devoted to writing sermons for public presentation, but he also produced a large corpus of some of the most inventive poetry in colonial America. While he did not publish any of this poetry in his lifetime, viewing it instead as a personal aid to his spiritual meditations and as preparation for giving communion to his congregation, he did carefully collect and preserve his manuscripts. His collection was not published until the twentieth century, after it was discovered in the Yale University Library in 1937.

Taylor experimented with a variety of poetic forms, composing paraphrases of biblical psalms, elegies, love poems, a long poem called *God's Determinations* in the form of a debate about the nature of salvation, and his five-hundred-page *Metrical History of Christianity*. His best-known poems, a series of 217 verses called *Preparatory Meditations*, are lyric explorations of the Puritan soul and its relation to the sacrament. The poems' struggles with complicated theological issues are carefully contained within rigidly structured six-line stanzas of iambic pentameter. While the metaphors and metaphysical conceits in *Preparatory Meditations* are elaborate (they are sometimes compared to the work of the English poet John Donne), much of Taylor's other poetry is characterized by its plain-style aesthetic and its homely metaphors of farming and housekeeping. Taylor's work is not easily categorized because his poetic experiments are so varied, employing forms ranging from common meter to heroic couplets and imagery ranging from the traditionally typological to the metaphysical. Still, all of Taylor's work reflects his commitment to orthodox Puritan theology and his concern with ascertaining and sustaining a belief in his place among God's elect. His poems enact, in literary critic Sacvan Bercovitch's words, the "endless ritual celebration-exorcism of the Puritan self."

TEACHING TIPS

■ Taylor's use of puns and elaborate metaphors can make his work difficult for students to understand, especially when Taylor relies on archaic terms having to do with trades such as carpentry, weaving, smithing, printing, domestic economy, or horticulture. Have students use the *Oxford English Dictionary* to look up the complete history of unfamiliar terms (examples might include "nipper," "squitchen," "selvage," "knot," "stock," "fillet," "distaff," "huswifery," "quilt ball," "kenning," "rigalled," or "receipt"). Use their research to investigate both the cultural context of Taylor's imagery and his playful use of the different meanings of a single image.

■ Ask students to examine the different metrical forms and stanzaic patterns at work in Taylor's poetry. Why does he use heroic couplets in the "Preface" to *God's Determinations* (found in *The Norton Anthology of American Literature*) only to switch to other forms in the later sections of the poem? How does the predictable, relatively rigid ababcc verse form of the *Preparatory Meditations* relate to the complicated spiritual struggles explored within the poems? You can use students' formal analyses of the poems to investigate the relationship between the ritualistic and the sincere, the irrational and the rational, within Taylor's Puritan theology.

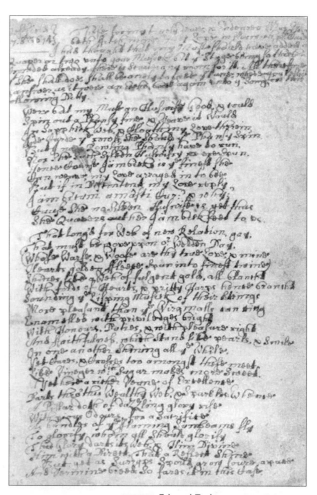

[6745] Edward Taylor, manuscript page of Taylor's *Poetical Writings* (year unknown), courtesy of Beinecke Rare Book and Manuscript Library, Yale University.

QUESTIONS

Comprehension: How does the main text of "Meditation 8" relate to the poem's prefatory biblical citation ("John 6.51. I am the Living Bread")? What is the extended metaphor at work in this poem? What is the significance of Taylor's focus on a basic domestic chore that is usually performed by women? Do you notice similar imagery in any of Taylor's other poems?

Context: Compare Taylor's "Prologue" to the *Preparatory Meditations* and "Meditation 22" with Bradstreet's "Prologue" and "The Author to Her Book." How do these Puritan poets deal with their anxiety about their own literary authority? Do they share similar concerns? How are they different? What conclusions do they arrive at?

Exploration: The only book of poetry known to have had a place in Taylor's personal library was Anne Bradstreet's *Tenth Muse*. Does his poetry seem influenced by her work? How is it different? How does his work fit or not fit within the tradition of "plain style"? Many critics have argued that Taylor's poetry is best understood within the tradition of the English metaphysical poets, such as John Donne and George Herbert. Metaphysical poetry is characterized by its ornate language and by its profusion of metaphors and paradoxes. Where do you see this style at work in Taylor's poetry? Does he seem more comfortable with one style than the other? Does he ever seem to meld the two?

William Penn (1644–1718)

William Penn was an unusual convert to Quakerism. Most Quakers came from relatively humble backgrounds and possessed little formal education, but Penn was Oxford-educated and a member of an elite and wealthy family. His father, an intimate of King Charles II, had served as an admiral in the Royal Navy and held substantial property in Ireland and England. Despite his conventional Anglican upbringing, Penn found himself drawn to the controversial religious ideas of non-conforming Protestants at an early age (he was expelled from Oxford for religious nonconformity). During a visit to Ireland, Penn encountered Quaker preaching, began to attend meetings regularly, and eventually converted to Quakerism in 1667.

Penn was attracted to Quakerism for many of the qualities that made it so controversial: the sect's belief that divine grace resided within all individuals in the form of an **"inner light,"** "spirit," or "Christ within" was powerfully egalitarian and radical in its implications, which Penn found appealing. Emphasizing the importance of unmediated, individual feeling in spiritual enlightenment, Quakers viewed scripture as secondary and rejected entirely the institution of professional clergy. Because they believed that all life was sacred, they refused to engage in violence or enlist in military service. Quakers' egalitarian spirituality also led to tolerance of people who did not share their beliefs and confidence in women's spiritual equality. Because these beliefs were threatening to the rigidly hierarchical social order of seventeenth-century England, Quakers were perceived as heretics and, as such, were persecuted.

After his conversion, Penn began preaching Quaker doctrine and lobbying extensively for religious tolerance; these activities resulted in his imprisonment on several occasions. Eventually, a combination of shrewd business acumen and a commitment to finding a safe haven for Quakers led Penn to make plans to found a colony in the New World. In 1681, he convinced Charles II to grant him a large piece of land west of the Delaware River and north of Maryland, to be called "Pennsylvania" in honor of Penn's father. As the sole proprietor, Penn had the power to sell plots of land, to make laws, and to establish a system of government. Because he believed in a limited monarchy and a system of checks and balances, Penn invested much of the power of the government in the settlers of Pennsylvania, creating a legislative assembly of freely elected representatives. Pennsylvanians enjoyed guaranteed civil rights and religious freedom from the start. Penn's commitment to civil liberties and cultural pluralism also moved him to make diplomatic relations with Native Americans a priority, a consideration that was unique to Pennsylvania among American colonies. Before setting up his government, Penn addressed a letter to the local Lenni Lenape Indians, acknowledging their right to the land and assuring them of his respect and his intention to always deal fairly with them. Thanks largely to the tone that Penn initially set, Native Americans and European settlers lived peacefully together in Pennsylvania for over half a century.

Despite its fine record of religious and racial tolerance, the colony did not always live up to Penn's utopian ideals or entrepreneurial vision. Legal entanglements, border conflicts with other colonies, debts, and political intrigue in both England and Pennsylvania caused problems. Penn was forced to move back and forth between England and the New World several times, trying to deal with personal debts and to settle conflicts within the colonial community. He left the colony forever in 1701. His final years were marred by a period of incarceration in debtors' prison, a debilitating stroke, and disappointment over the profligacy of his son. Although Penn was ultimately unable to transform his utopian vision into a political reality, his legacy lives on in the prolific collection of writings he produced (over 130 books, pamphlets, and letters) and in long-standing American ideals of tolerance, cultural pluralism, and the separation of church and state.

TEACHING TIPS

■ Students may assume that the seventeenth-century Quakers and Puritans were similar to one another since they shared some traits: both groups immigrated to escape persecution and dreamed of creating a utopian society that would purify the Christian religion and serve as a model to the rest of the world. It is crucial that students understand that, despite these similarities, the Quakers and Puritans were fundamentally different from one another and endorsed radically different values. The Puritans' insistence on rigid hierarchies, religious conformity, and a typological worldview were completely at odds with the Quakers' commitment to religious and racial tolerance, their pacifism, their support of women's spiritual equality, and their belief that written scripture was secondary to an individual's "inner light." The Puritans were so outraged by Quaker theology that they banished, tortured, and even executed Quakers who attempted to preach in

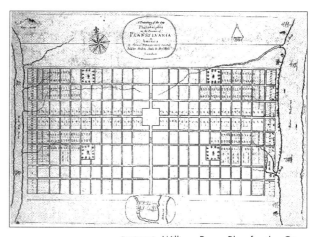

[1216] William Penn, Plan for the City of Philadelphia, in *A Letter from William Penn . . . to the Committee of the Free Society for Traders of That Province, Residing in London* (1683 [1881]).

PENN WEB ARCHIVE

[1211] John Sartain, *William Penn Portrait (The Armor Portrait) after 1666 Portrait, Penn Aged 22, Only One Taken from Life* (n.d.), courtesy of Pennsylvania State Museum. Penn at 22. The piece from which this portrait was copied was composed four years after his expulsion from Oxford as a result of his denunciation of the Anglican Church and sixteen years before his voyage to America.

[1214] Benjamin West, *William Penn's Treaty with the Indians* (1711), courtesy of the Philadelphia Academy of Fine Arts. The work portrays Penn's 1682 peace meeting with the Delaware tribe in Shackamaxon (present-day Kensington, Pennsylvania). Although there is no evidence that this meeting between Anglos and Indians actually took place, it has become part of American mythology—in large part because of West's painting.

[1216] William Penn, *Plan for the City of Philadelphia*, in *A Letter from William Penn . . . to the Committee of the Free Society of Traders of That Province, Residing in London* (1683 [1881]). Penn's plan reflects Quaker hopes for a colonial utopia of human reason informed by inner divine revelation. The right-angled plan treats the land like a Lockean blank slate and differs sharply from Native American settlement patterns.

Massachusetts. Ask your students to make a list of the differences between Quakers and Puritans. Have them consider how the values of each group have had a lasting effect on American values, politics, or national character.

■ In his "Letter to the Lenni Lenape Indians," Penn explains his belief that the Indians and the Quakers (and indeed all people) share the same God and are ruled by the same moral laws: "This great God has written his law in our hearts, by which we are taught and commanded to love and help and do good to one another, and not to do harm and mischief one unto another." This statement helps elucidate the Quakers' commitment to pacifism and their theological doctrine of the "inner light," or the manifestation of divine love that dwells inside and thus unites all humans. Ask your students to consider the implications of the idea that God "has written his law" in all people's hearts. Have them compare this notion to Puritan ideas about spiritual election. How might these different views of spirituality have affected the way Puritans and Quakers chose to deal with Native Americans?

QUESTIONS

Comprehension: In his "Letter to the Lenni Lenape," Penn acknowledges that Europeans before him have treated Native Americans with "unkindness and injustice." What specific problems do you think he is referring to? How does he propose to right these injustices? What is new about his approach? Why do you think he decided to acknowledge this history of European exploitation of Indians in his letter? What effect do you think it would have had on the Native Americans to whom the letter is addressed?

Context: Read the land deed documenting Penn's purchase of land from Machaloha, a member of the Delaware tribe, included in the archival material. What assumptions underwrite this legal document? Why do you think Penn decided to codify his purchase of Native American land in this way? How does the deed compare to the wampum belt included in the archival materials?

Context: Compare the migration legend of the Lenni Lenape (Delaware) Indians to the migrations stories told by Bradford in *Of Plymouth Plantation*. How does each speak of the place from which the came and the home they made upon arriving?

Exploration: What role did the Quaker tradition in Pennsylvania have in the development of America as a nation? Do you see any legacies of Quaker thought and practice within our culture today?

Sarah Kemble Knight (1666–1727)

Sarah Kemble was born in Boston in 1666, the daughter of Thomas Kemble, a successful merchant, and Elizabeth Trerice, who descended from an old and established Massachusetts family. In 1689, she married Richard Knight, a sea captain considerably older than herself. Even before her husband's death, Sarah Kemble Knight assumed many of the family's business responsibilities, running a shop in Boston, taking in lodgers, and working as a court scrivener copying legal documents. Her familiarity with legal issues—as well as her habitual independence—probably underwrote her decision in 1704 to journey to New Haven, Connecticut, to help settle the estate of her cousin Caleb Trowbridge on behalf of his widow. The overland trip from Boston to New Haven was long and difficult in the early eighteenth century; although the route was an established one used by postal riders, the road was rough and travelers found it necessary to hire local guides to conduct them from one town or rural inn to another. At the time, it was unusual for a woman to embark on such a journey alone.

Knight was a careful diarist, resolving to "enter my mind in my Journal" at the end of each day of travel. The resulting record is a unique and entertaining document, both because Knight's experience was so atypical and because her lively, often humorous narrative voice marks a break with the more somber tradition of Puritan journals and narratives. The *Private Journal* is in fact very secular in its content, tone, and style, containing little moral didacticism and almost no spiritual self-examination. Instead, Knight is witty, worldly, and sharply keyed in to the social distinctions and class hierarchies that structured colonial New England. All of Knight's experiences are filtered through her sense of her own middling social and economic position. She is ruthlessly sarcastic about the ignorance and poor taste displayed by the rustic "bumpkins" she encounters in the country, and extremely proud of "the wonderful civility" shown to her in the city by members of ranks of society higher than her own. She condones slavery and is appalled that some farmers allow their slaves to "sit at table and eat with them." Throughout the *Journal*, she refers to Native Americans in dehumanizing terms, comparing them to animals. Despite her off-putting prejudices, however, Knight manages to paint a vivid and engaging picture of a broad cross-section of early American society, describing both backwoods and urban life with humor and an ear for colloquial language.

Knight ended her journey in March 1705, returning safely to her home in Boston. In 1714 her daughter married John Livingston of New London, and Knight moved with them to Connecticut, where she continued her business and land dealings. When she died in 1727, she left her daughter a very large estate, attesting to her shrewdness and skill as a businessperson.

[7057] Annie Fisher, *Fisher's Tavern in Dedham*, courtesy of the Dedham Historical Society, Dedham, Massachusetts.

TEACHING TIPS

■ Early in her *Journal* Knight narrates a moment of fear and uncertainty brought on by feeling alone in the woods, acknowledging that she experienced some spiritual concern about her "call" to make such a journey:

Now returned my distressed apprehensions of the place where I was: the dolesome woods, my company next to none, going I knew not whither, and encompassed with terrifying darkness; the least of which was enough to startle a more masculine courage. Added to which the reflections, as in the afternoon of the day that my call was very questionable, which, till then I had not so prudently as I ought considered.

While this passage sounds akin to the kind of spiritual examination common in traditional Puritan autobiographical writings, Knight quickly undercuts its religious tone. Rather than recount an assurance of grace or gratitude for God's mercy, she instead reports her relief at catching a glimpse of the moon, which she proceeds to describe in neoclassical heroic couplets. You might ask students to focus on this passage in order to highlight the difference between the secularism of Knight's *Journal* and the profound religiosity of most of the other texts included in this unit. Ask them to consider the significance of Knight's homage to "Cynthia," the pagan goddess of the moon, in a moment of uncertainty and distress.

■ While Knight does not seem to have written her *Journal* for publication, she probably did circulate it in manuscript form for the amusement of her friends and relatives. Ask students to look for clues that might indicate the kind of audience Knight imagined reading her book. You might point out her lack of introspection, her sarcastic comments about social inferiors, and her inclusion of poetry and allusions to European literary texts. What kind of image was Knight trying to create for herself?

QUESTIONS

Comprehension: What kinds of prejudices color Knight's descriptions of the people she meets on her journey? What do her responses to people of different economic status and race reveal about the social hierarchy that structured colonial America?

Context: What role, if any, does spirituality play in Knight's worldview and her understanding of her journey? When does she bring up religion? How does her *Journal* compare to other journals and autobiographical narratives included in this unit (for example, those of Bradford, Rowlandson, and Woolman)?

Exploration: Literary critics disagree on the generic categorization of Knight's *Journal*. It has been read as participating in the traditions of the picaresque, mock-epic, and the captivity narrative, while it has also been cited as a foundational text in the development of American travel writing and the American comic tradition. How would you categorize the *Journal*? What kind of influence do you think it may have had on later American writing?

John Woolman (1720–1772)

John Woolman was born into a Quaker family in West Jersey (later New Jersey) in 1720. From an early age, he manifested a deep sensitivity toward spiritual matters that would become the basis for his lifelong commitment to Quaker precepts and devotion to what he called "the inward life." Woolman attended a local Quaker school, but, like many Quakers of the early eighteenth century, had no further formal education. Instead, he served an apprenticeship to a tailor and eventually established a business of his own: tailoring, dealing in retail goods, managing a farm, and writing legal documents. The success of his commercial ventures eventually gave Woolman cause for concern; he worried that the time and energy he devoted to his business was interfering with his faithfulness to the callings of God. True to his conscience, he deliberately scaled back his operations and found that "a humble man with the blessing of the Lord might live on a little."

At the age of twenty-three, Woolman felt called to the Quaker ministry, a vocation that involved speaking at meetings and traveling as an itinerant preacher. As a result of this spiritual commitment, he undertook many difficult missionary journeys, traveling to the southern colonies, into New York, through Native American lands in northern Pennsylvania, and to England. Woolman dedicated his ministry to fighting social injustice and spoke frequently against war, materialism, the exploitation of Indians, and the inhumane treatment of the poor. The cause that would become his passion and the focus of most of his energies, however, was the abolition of slavery. Convinced that slave holding was inconsistent with Christian principles, Woolman preached, wrote, and confronted individual slave holders in his quest to put an end to "this dark gloominess hanging over the land." In 1754 and 1762, he published the two parts of his treatise, *Some Considerations on the Keeping of Negroes*, a carefully argued, powerful plea for abolition. Woolman's convictions also moved him to renounce sugar and clothing colored with dyes since these commodities were produced by slave labor. While his activities did not lead to the abolition of slavery as an institution in his own time, Woolman did succeed in converting individuals and in persuading the organized Quaker church in Pennsylvania to officially adopt abolitionist resolutions. His writings and his example were also important in laying the groundwork for the abolitionist movement that would flourish in the nineteenth century.

Woolman died in 1772 after contracting smallpox while traveling through England on a preaching tour. He left behind a *Journal*, a kind of spiritual autobiography, which was published by the Society of Friends in 1774 and is the piece for which Woolman is best remembered. Written both as a personal exercise in self-examination and as a spiritual guide for others to consult, the *Journal* has remained popular for over two hundred years: it has never gone out of print since its first publication and has gone through over forty editions. Notable for its clear, plain writing style and its moving articulation of religious conviction, the *Journal* influenced such later American writers as John Green-

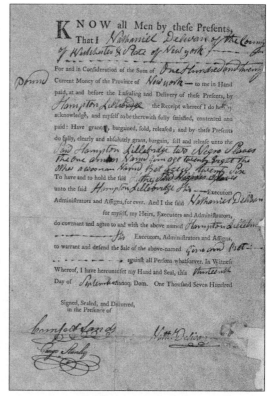

[6746] Nathaniel Delivan, *Bill of Sale for Slaves, New York* (1700), courtesy of the Library of Congress, Rare Books and Special Collections, Printed Ephemera Collection.

WOOLMAN WEB ARCHIVE

[1107] David H. Burr, *Map of New Jersey and Pennsylvania Exhibiting the Post Offices, Post Roads, Canals, Railroad* (1839), courtesy of the Library of Congress [LC-USZ62-96653]. This map provides a geographical context for Woolman's travels in Pennsylvania.
[1575] *To Be Sold, on Board the Ship Bance Island . . . Negroes, Just Arrived from Windward & Rice Coast* (c. 1780), courtesy of the Library of Congress [LC-USZ62-10293]. A newspaper advertisement for the sale of slaves at Ashley Ferry outside of Charleston, South Carolina. Plantation owners paid higher prices for slaves from the "Windward" or "Rice Coast," the rice-growing regions of West Africa that ranged from Senegal down to Sierra Leone and Liberia.

[2793] The Quaker Meeting, courtesy of George Fox University. Quaker churches like this one are "plain-style" buildings defined by their linear design, exposed structural supports, and open lighting. These unpretentious interiors have no altars or pulpits, creating unadorned spaces that allow congregants to concentrate on their individual relationships with God. Illustration from Sydney George Fisher, *The True William Penn* (Philadelphia: J. B. Lippincott, 1899).

[2909] Thomas Fairland, *George Fox* (1914), courtesy of the Library of Congress [LC-USZ62-49456]. Facsimile of portrait drawn on stone. George Fox (1624–1691) founded the Society of Friends, or Quakers, based on the principle of the direct guidance of the Holy Spirit. In the portrait Fox wears what would become known as a "Quaker hat."

[6746] Nathaniel Delivan, *Bill of Sale for Slaves, New York* (1700), courtesy of the Library of Congress, Rare Books and Special Collections, Printed Ephemera. Early opponents of slavery like John Woolman addressed the institution's existence in all of the British colonies. Hudson Valley wheat plantations used slaves, while merchants and ships from ports like Boston, New York, and Philadelphia brought slaves to those towns along with southern and Caribbean colonies.

leaf Whittier, Henry David Thoreau, and Theodore Dreiser. Woolman's commitment to social justice and his concern with issues that continue to haunt American culture—problems such as bigotry, violence, materialism, and poverty—have given his work a lasting relevance.

TEACHING TIPS

■ Woolman participates in a long tradition of Quaker journal-keeping begun by George Fox, the founder of the sect. Pious Quakers routinely composed spiritual autobiographies to be published after their deaths as examples and guides for those who read them. It seems clear, then, that Woolman carefully crafted and revised his *Journal* in anticipation of its eventual publication. Given this information, ask students to consider how Woolman's sense of audience and literary conventions might have influenced the composition and shaped the meaning of the *Journal*.

■ Woolman frequently explains his religious motivations in terms of "openings," or "drawings" sent to him by God. Ask students what they think he means by these terms. What rhetorical purpose do they serve? How do they work to justify Woolman's actions? Ask students to reflect on the potential problems this passive ideal of acting only when moved by God might pose for someone like Woolman. In explicating the tensions between activity and passivity in the *Journal*, you might point out Woolman's consistent use of the passive voice in his description of religious experiences.

QUESTIONS

Comprehension: What rhetorical strategies and appeals does Woolman use to argue against slavery in *Some Considerations on the Keeping of Negroes*? Which are most persuasive? Which do you think would have been most effective in persuading other eighteenth-century Americans to abolish slavery?

Context: Woolman's *Journal* has been celebrated as a particularly beautiful and effective example of "plain style." How does his use of this style compare to that of other plain stylists discussed in this unit (Bradford, Bradstreet, and Penn, for example)? What kinds of values and beliefs might Woolman's style reflect? Are they the same or different from the values held by Puritan plain stylists?

Exploration: How do Woolman's concerns prefigure later social movements in America (abolitionism, civil rights issues, the development of welfare programs, for example)? Can you trace his influence in any contemporary discussions of social justice issues? What might Woolman think of contemporary American society? How would he feel about the ongoing problems of racism, bigotry, poverty, violence, and materialism?

Samson Occom (1723–1792)

Samson Occom was born in 1723 in a Mohegan Indian community in Connecticut. At the age of sixteen he was "awakened and converted" to Christianity under the guidance of white itinerant ministers. Shortly thereafter, Occom began learning English and studying scripture under the tutelage of Eleazar Wheelock, a prominent missionary interested in training young Native American men to act as Christian ministers to their own people. In 1749, Occom left Wheelock to embark on such a mission. While teaching and preaching in Long Island, he met and married Mary Fowler, a Montauk Indian, with whom he had ten children. Occom was officially ordained as a minister in 1759.

Maintaining a close relationship with his mentor, Occom dedicated much of his early life to promoting Wheelock's missions and projects. In 1765, at Wheelock's behest, he embarked on an ambitious two-year speaking tour of England to raise money for a charity school for Indians in New England. The mission was a financial and public relations success, in large part because of Occom's popularity among the English. The novelty of a Christianized American Indian attracted a great deal of attention, and Occom's dedication to the project brought in large returns. While in England, he preached three hundred sermons and raised nearly twelve thousand pounds in contributions.

Upon his return to America, Occom was outraged to find his family living in poverty despite Wheelock's promise to provide for them during Occom's absence. His resentment toward Wheelock grew when he learned that the minister had decided to use the funds Occom had raised in England to turn the Indian school into Dartmouth College, an institution that quickly abandoned its focus on Native American students. Occom also complained that he was underpaid, for he had a large family to support and his wages never approached the salaries commanded by many white ministers. Finding himself in dire financial straits and feeling betrayed, Occom bitterly ended his long relationship with Wheelock. He devoted much of the rest of his life to preaching and raising funds for the resettlement of Christian Indians on lands belonging to the Oneida Indians in western New York. Though he eventually moved his family there and held the position of pastor within the settlement, the scheme was never entirely successful because of legal struggles and controversies over land claims. Occom died in New York in 1792.

[6747] John Warner Barber, *Sketch of Samson Occom's house* (1836), courtesy of the Connecticut Historical Society.

During his lifetime Occom wrote extensively and published two works, making him one of the few Native Americans of the period to leave a written record of his life and thought. While his best-known piece is probably the "Sermon at the Execution of Moses Paul," a transcription of the speech he delivered in 1772 before the execution of a fellow Christian Mohegan for the crime of murder, recent critical attention has also focused on Occom's brief autobiography. Occom wrote "A Short Narrative of My Life" in 1768 as a defense against the criticisms and personal attacks he withstood after his quarrel with Wheelock. In it, he seeks to prove the authenticity of both his spirituality and his Indian identity, as well as to expose the injustices he suf-

[1236] John Eliot, *The Holy Bible Containing the Old Testament and the New Translated into the Indian Language* (1663), courtesy of Annenberg Rare Book and Manuscript Library, University of Pennsylvania. Commonly known as the "Eliot Bible," this book was the first Bible published in New England and appeared over a hundred years before the first complete English edition of the Bible was published in the American colonies. It is written in Massachuset, the language of the Massachuset and Wampanoag Indians. John Eliot, the "Apostle to the Indians," composed his text to serve the cause of Native American conversion to Puritan Christianity.

[2850] Brass medal given to Christian Indians as a reward for service, courtesy of the National Museum of the American Indian, Smithsonian Institution, N38319/N38320. Photo by Carmelo Guadagno. Christianized Indians fought on both the Native and the British sides in King Philip's War, which led to confusion on the part of colonists as to who was a "good" and who was a "bad" Indian. Brass medals were awarded to those who served the British.

[6747] John Warner Barber, *Sketch of Samson Occom's house* (1836), courtesy of the Connecticut Historical Society. This illustration from Barber's *Historical Collections of Connecticut* is one of the few depictions of a private dwelling in the book. This house in Mohegan (present-day Montville, Connecticut) belonged to Occom. British-style housing, fenced yards, and individual property ownership were perceived by missionaries to be signs of a successful conversion to Christianity.

[6748] Anonymous, *Rev. Samson Occom, the Indian Preacher* (1802), courtesy of the Annenberg Rare Book and Manuscript Library, University of Pennsylvania. Between 1750 and 1766, Occom sat for at least three different portraits. This one emphasizes Occom's identity as a minister, rather than his Native American heritage. Others show him in Native American dress that resembles a Roman toga.

fered at the hands of whites. The document remained in the Dartmouth archives, unpublished, until 1982. It is one of the first autobiographical pieces in English by a Native American writer and thus offers a unique and important perspective on eighteenth-century American spiritual and social life.

TEACHING TIPS

■ You might provide students with some historical background on the Mohegan tribe so that they can situate Occom's experience within the broader context of Indian/white relations in the colonial period in New England. A member of the Algonquian language family, the Mohegans constituted the northernmost branch of the Pequot tribe. During the devastating Pequot War (chronicled from the English perspective in Bradford's *Of Plymouth Plantation*), the Mohegans sided with the English. This decision ensured a brief period of peace with European settlers following the war, but by the end of the seventeenth century, the tribe had been decimated by disease and by the colonists' continual encroachment on its lands. At the time of Occom's birth, the Mohegans numbered only about 350 and were confined to villages set aside for them in Connecticut.

■ Students may be unable to comprehend why seventeenth- and eighteenth-century Native Americans would have been interested in giving up their traditional beliefs in order to convert to Christianity. In fact, many Native Americans and African Americans embraced Christianity because it afforded them the same status as whites, as spiritual equals in the eyes of God. Of course, European colonists did not always respect this principle of spiritual equality. You might highlight the pointed contrasts Occom draws in his narrative between the Christian ideals espoused by whites and the actual treatment minority converts experienced at their hands.

QUESTIONS

Comprehension: When does Occom feel that he is being treated unfairly? What is his concept of justice? How does he deal with the prejudice and mistreatment he experiences? What rhetorical strategies does he use to present his complaints in his narrative?

Context: Compare Occom's description of Indian life and Indian identity with the perspectives on Indians offered by other writers in this unit (Bradford, Morton, Rowlandson, or Knight, for example). How does Occom's narrative of Native American life complicate or challenge the perspectives of the English writers? Does his account of Indian culture have anything in common with their accounts?

Exploration: In his life, Occom managed to inhabit what often seemed to be two very separate cultures: he wrote and preached in English and committed himself to the Christian theology taught by white people, yet never lost his commitment to his identity as an Indian. How does Occom's narrative provide evidence of the strategies he adopted in order to live in two separate cultures at the same time? What tensions does this hybrid or dual identity produce in the narrative? This problem of hybridity or duality is a major theme in many works by later American writers. You might compare Occom's piece to William Apess's "An Indian's Looking-Glass for the White Man," John Neihardt's *Black Elk Speaks*, or W. E. B. Du Bois's concept of double consciousness in *The Souls of Black Folk*.

Suggested Author Pairings

WILLIAM BRADFORD AND THOMAS MORTON

Both Bradford and Morton chronicle the challenges of life in and around the Plymouth colony, in a few cases treating the same events. To the extent that these accounts are fundamentally at odds with one another, they bring into relief the cultural values that their authors wished their respective communities to embody and foster. In *Of Plymouth Plantation*, Bradford sought not only to describe life and events in the Plymouth colony but also to locate within the colony's history a divine design that accorded with his Puritan beliefs. In contrast, Morton, a non-Puritan, devotes much of his *New English Canaan* to satirizing the Puritans in Plymouth and to promoting New England colonization more for its potential financial profits than for its spiritual possibilities. Even the differences in their rhetorical styles reveal their conflicting values and beliefs. When compared to Bradford's plain style, Morton's elevated language and classical allusions indicate a writer preoccupied with the kinds of worldly concerns and social hierarchies that the Plymouth colonists sought to eschew. The two writers also offer very different perspectives on Anglo relationships with Native Americans.

JOHN WINTHROP AND WILLIAM PENN

Both Winthrop and Penn were leaders when their respective colonies were founded, helping to shape systems of government and setting the tone for future American political formations and values. Of course, their views were very different from one another and thus form an illuminating contrast. Winthrop's "Model of Christian Charity" presents his vision of the ideal Christian community, encouraging Puritans to maintain an exemplary piety and interpreting the Puritan mission as that of a "chosen people" fulfilling biblical prophecy. Penn's "Letter to the Lenni Lenape Indians" (written, like Winthrop's "Model," prior to its author's actually arriving in America) reveals a different worldview, endorsing tolerance and religious and cultural pluralism in its respect for Native American culture and civil rights. The two documents, then, make plain the very different assumptions and values that underwrote Puritan and Quaker culture: a sense of exclusivity, shared orthodoxy, and "chosen-ness" on one hand, and tolerance and pluralism on the other. Both had an enduring effect on the development of American culture and American mythology.

ANNE BRADSTREET AND EDWARD TAYLOR

Bradstreet and Taylor, both poets and Puritans, are a natural pairing. Both deal eloquently with difficult Puritan theological issues, such as anxiety about election and the struggle to "wean" affections from worldly interests. In this vein, they are frequently celebrated for their poignant evocations of family life and domestic culture, manifested by their use of simple, homely metaphors. Although Bradstreet's work was published in her lifetime and Taylor's was not, they share concerns about the problem of literary authority and the writer's relationship to her or his audience: Taylor's "Prologue" and Bradstreet's "Prologue" and "The Author to Her Book" struggle with questions about the writer's agency and the compatibility of poetry and Puritan piety. While both were apparently uninterested in or unwilling to see their own work published (Bradstreet's poetry was published without her knowledge or consent), they both left carefully copied and preserved manuscripts at their deaths, suggesting that they took their vocations as poets very seriously. Bradstreet's work is obviously complicated by her position as a woman in a patriarchal society, creating tensions not present in Taylor's poems. Although both poets worked in the "plain style" on occasion, they both experimented with other poetic traditions. Bradstreet's poems tend more toward the classical, while Taylor's depend on biblical imagery and elaborate, extended poetic conceits.

MARY ROWLANDSON AND SARAH KEMBLE KNIGHT

Rowlandson's and Knight's narrative accounts of their respective journeys provide important insight into the role of women in early New England. Both texts chronicle journeys that were unusual undertakings for women—though obviously to totally different ends. Rowlandson's journey was an unwilling one, and she struggles to maintain the Puritan ideal of passive femininity even while actively working for her own survival. Knight, on the other hand, embarked on her travels voluntarily and clearly embraces her role as a businessperson, active in a traditionally masculine realm. While Rowlandson filters her every experience through scripture and searches constantly for signs of God's will, Knight barely mentions spiritual issues and concerns herself instead with witty social commentary. Perhaps their only point of overlap is their racism and intolerance of cultural practices different from their own. Written only twenty years apart, these two narratives reveal the diversity of the New England experience and the increasing secularization of Puritan culture.

JOHN WOOLMAN AND SAMSON OCCOM

Both Woolman's *Journal* and Occom's *Short Narrative* function as spiritual autobiographies, narrating their authors' conversion to and acceptance of Christianity. While Woolman's Quakerism was quite different from Occom's evangelical Christianity, both men experienced a profound conversion in early youth, and both found their calling as missionaries. Both wrote their pieces to persuade—Woolman's to serve as a guide for those seeking "inner light," and Occom's to plead for Indian rights and to salvage his reputation after his sincerity and commitment were attacked. Most importantly, Occom and Woolman share a concern with social justice and a desire to abolish racism, intolerance, and poverty. Though Occom's commitment to exposing and eradicating these social problems was the result of personal, first-hand experience while Woolman's was more a sympathetic response, both wrote movingly on these subjects. Many of the problems Woolman and Occom identified and worked to end continue to haunt American culture, giving their work enduring relevance.

CORE CONTEXTS

Apocalypse: The End of the World as They Knew It

John Winthrop reports in his *Journal* that in 1637 a Puritan woman was driven to despair by her inability to ascertain whether she was one of God's "elect," destined for heaven, or one of the damned: "having been in much trouble of mind about her spiritual estate, [she] at length grew into utter desperation, and could not endure to hear of any comfort, so as one day she took her little infant and threw it into a well, and then came into the house and said, now she was sure she should be damned for she had drowned her child." Although such a response to spiritual crisis was certainly extreme and anomalous, it was not uncommon for Puritans to experience intense anxiety about their spiritual condition. Puritan theology hinged on the concept of **election**, the idea that some individuals were predestined by God to be saved and taken to heaven while other individuals were doomed to hell. One's status as a member of the elect did not necessarily correlate with good works or moral behavior on earth, for God had extended a "covenant of grace" to his chosen people that did not have to be earned, only accepted with faith. Despite the apparent ease with which a believer could attain everlasting salvation, Puritans in practice agonized over the state of their souls, living in constant fear of damnation and scrutinizing their own feelings and behavior for indications of whether or not God had judged them worthy.

For the Puritans, anticipation of God's final judgment had relevance not just to the individual but to the community as a whole—and as a collective, they were far more confident about their spiritual status. Extending the notion of the covenant to the group, they operated under the conviction that they were the "chosen people of God," or the "New Israel," sent to New England to bring about the Kingdom of Christ on earth. Within the context of biblical history, they understood themselves to be living in the "end time" as it is prophesied in the Book of Revelation, with Christ's Second Coming near at hand. All around them, comets, eclipses, and other "wonders" pointed to the imminence of the Final Judgment. Puritan ministers performed complex analyses

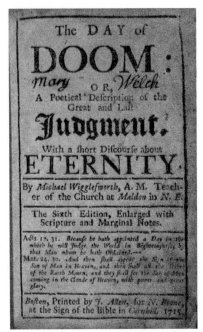

[4433] Michael Wigglesworth, *The Day of Doom. Or, A Short Description of the Great and Last Judgment. With a Short Discourse about Eternity. By Michael Wigglesworth. The Seventh Edition, Enlarged. With a Recommendatory Epistle (in Verse) By the Rev. Mr. John Mitchel* (1715), courtesy of the Tracy W. McGregor Library of American History, University of Virginia.

of scriptural predictions in order to pinpoint the exact day that New England would herald the **Apocalypse**, the time at which Christ would return and reign for a thousand years. According to the Puritans, this millennium would usher in the end of history: the earth would be destroyed, the elect would be ushered into heaven, and all others would be cast into hell.

The centrality of millennial apocalyptic beliefs to Puritan culture can be indexed by the extraordinary popularity of Michael Wigglesworth's poem "The Day of Doom." With its terrifying images of hellfire and damnation and its stern accounts of God's wrathfulness, the poem might seem grim and unappealing to modern readers. But Wigglesworth's lengthy verse description of the Apocalypse was a best-seller among seventeenth-century Puritans; scholars estimate that after its publication in 1662, one copy existed for every twenty-five New Englanders. Many Puritans were apparently moved to learn its 224 eight-line stanzas by heart. As the title indicates, the action takes place on Judgment Day, when a vengeful Christ divides humanity into two groups: the righteous sheep at his right hand and the sinful goats at his left. The goats' wickedness and religious heresy are exposed, and they are condemned to a burning lake in hell. The poem graphically describes the horrific punishments awaiting the non-elect:

> With iron bands they bind their hands,
>   and cursed feet together,
> And cast them all, both great and small,
>   into that lake forever.
> Where day and night, without respite,
>   they wail, and cry, and howl,
> For tort'ring pain, which they sustain
>   in body and in soul.

With its plain language and catchy rhyme scheme, "The Day of Doom" functioned for Puritans as a kind of "verse catechism," useful for teaching basic theological tenets. It frequently was employed to instruct children, who would thus grow up with a thorough understanding—however terrifying such knowledge might have been to them—of the coming Apocalypse.

In this cultural climate, death was approached with both fear and ecstatic expectancy, for it could bring either eternal torment or admittance to everlasting paradise. Only upon death could Puritans finally resolve the spiritual uncertainty that dominated their lives: death offered final and incontrovertible proof of their spiritual identity as either sheep or goats. The importance of death within Puritan culture is signaled by the attention they gave to funerary customs, including the carving of tombstones. Prior to the mid-1650s, Puritans usually left graves unmarked or indicated them only by simple wooden markers. Such non-decorative practices accorded with Puritans' rejection of all religious imagery as idolatrous "graven images" such as the Bible forbade. But by the 1660s, Puritans' preoccupation with death led them to erect elaborately carved gravestones decorated with symbolic images and engraved with language that both commemorated the deceased individual and expressed orthodox ways of understanding human mortality. Typical gravestone iconography ranged from traditional symbols of the transitory nature of earthly existence (skulls, skeletons, hourglasses, scythes) to emblems suggesting the possibility of resurrection and regeneration (wings, birds, flowers, trees, the sun). Eventually, gravestones also came to include representations of cherubs and human forms.

One of the most common images found on early Puritan gravestones is the winged death's-head, prominent on the pediment of the Joseph Tapping stone (Boston, 1678). At first glance, the image seems grim and despairing, a visual corollary to the Latin inscriptions on the lower right panel of the stone (*Vive Memor Loethi* and *Fugit Hora*, or "Live mindful of death" and "Time is fleeting"). Yet the wings attached to the death's-head suggest the possibility of resurrection and ascension to heaven, thus pictorially signifying the conceptual duality of Puritan attitudes toward death as both a fearful event and a potential means to eternal salvation. The architectural symbolism of columns and tablets on the Reverend Abraham Nott stone (Essex, Connecticut, 1756) similarly functions as a visual emblem of apocalyptic thinking, suggesting the rebuilding of the temple and the Second Coming of Christ as it is prophesied in Revelation. With their iconographic fusion of religious and aesthetic values, gravestones offer important evidence about the interrelationship of spiritual concerns and attitudes toward death in Puritan culture.

[4563] Anonymous, The Joseph Tapping Stone, King's Chapel, Boston, Massachusetts (1678), courtesy of Wesleyan University.

QUESTIONS

Comprehension: What kinds of images decorate the gravestones featured in the archive? Which images are most prominent? What do you think the images would have signified to Puritan viewers? How might the images have offered spiritual comfort to those mourning the dead?

Comprehension: Basing your opinion on the gravestones featured in the archive, how do you think Puritan gravestones changed over time? How might these differences reflect shifts in cultural values?

Comprehension: What is the concept of "election" in Puritan theology? Read Anne Bradstreet's spiritual reflections in her letter "To My Dear Children." How does she struggle with her faith and the question of her own election? What conclusions does she come to?

Context: In sermons delivered in the 1630s and 1640s, the Puritan minister John Cotton predicted that the Apocalypse would occur within the next fifteen years. Years later, at the end of the seventeenth century, his grandson Cotton Mather asserted that Puritans should expect the Apocalypse very soon. Using the timeline provided in this unit, examine the events that were occurring in New England in the 1630s, 1640s, and 1690s when these predictions were made. Why do you think Puritans living in this period would have felt that the end of the world was near at hand? What events and anxieties might have made these apocalyptic predictions seem realistic?

"APOCALYPSE" WEB ARCHIVE

[2121] Anonymous, *Goffe Rallying the men of Hadley* (1883), courtesy of the Library of Congress [LC-USZ62-75122]. Indian attacks on villages in western Massachusetts during King Philip's War challenged the viability of English settlement in New England and led many to question why they had fallen so far from God's favor and to wonder whether the Apocalypse was near.

[3370] Anonymous, The Rebekah Gerrish Stone (1743), courtesy of Wesleyan University Press. This stone depicts the conflict between time and death: a candle is flanked by a skeleton on the left, about to snuff out the fire, and a winged angel on the right, with an hourglass in hand, making a prohibitive gesture toward the skeleton. This dispute reflects the dual nature of time and Judgment found in Wigglesworth's "Day of Doom" and the more concrete dualism of the Apocalypse: some will be sent to hell and some to heaven.

[4427] John Stevens, The Mary Carr Stone (1721), courtesy of Wesleyan University Press. The Mary Carr Stone, in Old Common Burying-ground in Newport, Rhode Island, reads "Here lyeth the Body of Mary the Wife of John Carr, Dyed Sepr; ye 28th: 1721: in ye 21st: year of her age." The carving was made by the elder Stevens, a carver known for both the quality and the innovativeness of his work. The stone's imagery emphasizes rebirth. The sides and bottom feature intricate leaf patterns, pilasters, rosettes: flower and leaves were associated with the life of man (Job 14) and fecundity. At the top is a cherub with wings, and at the base is a pair of peacocks, symbols of immortality.

[4433] Michael Wigglesworth, The Day of Doom. Or, A Short Description of the Great and Last Judgment. With a Short Discourse about Eternity. By Michael Wigglesworth. The Seventh Edition, Enlarged. With a recommendatory epistle (in verse) by the Rev. Mr. John Mitchel (1715), courtesy of the Tracy W. McGregor Library of American History, University of Virginia. Originally published in 1662, this New England bestseller was often memorized by the pious: by 1715 it was already in its seventh edition. The poem tells of the coming of Christ on judgment day and the separating of the sheep (saved) from the goats (unsaved). A jeremiad, the text uses fire and brimstone to encourage sinful readers to repent.

Context: Compare Wigglesworth's "Day of Doom" with Taylor's "Meditation 42" and Bradstreet's "The Flesh and the Spirit." Compare the poets' visions of the afterlife. Do they have different views about God's wrathfulness? About his mercy? What do their descriptions of heaven have in common? How are they different?

Context: Examine the engraved images on the gravestones featured in the archive; then skim the poetry of Anne Bradstreet and Edward Taylor. Do you find any overlap in the imagery deployed? When you find similar imagery used (birds or flowers, for example), examine the context carefully. Do you think the stone carvers invested these symbols with the same meaning that Bradstreet or Taylor did? Why or why not?

Exploration: As you have read, apocalyptic thinking gained great cultural currency in New England in the seventeenth century. In our own time, anxiety about the Cold War and the dawning of the year 2000 created a great deal of interest in the Apocalypse. How does late-twentieth-century thinking about the Apocalypse compare to Puritan apocalyptic ideas? How do contemporary films and literature having to do with the Apocalypse compare to Puritan writings?

Exploration: Puritans often used Wigglesworth's "Day of Doom" to teach children basic religious and social principles. What effect do you think the poem would have on young children? How does the poem compare to Victorian and twentieth-century poetry created for children? How do you think American attitudes toward childhood have changed since the seventeenth century?

Exploration: Examine the Puritan gravestones in the archive; then think about other, later American graves you may have seen (Grant's tomb, Kennedy's eternal flame, battlefield grave markers, etc.). What kinds of cultural values and attitudes toward death do these later graves reflect? How are they different from Puritan values?

Souls in Need of Salvation, Satan's Agents, or Brothers in Peace?: English Settlers' Views of Native Americans

When English immigrants set sail for the "New World" in the early seventeenth century, many of them believed that they would be settling what William Bradford called "a vast and unpeopled country." When they arrived in America, however, they found not an empty wilderness but a developed region with a large population of Native Americans. Despite tendencies to view "the Indians" as a monolithic group, it is important to realize that Native American culture was extremely diverse; different tribes spoke different languages, created different political structures, and developed distinct cultural practices. Often, they fought among themselves over rights to land and game. Native American communities developed different strategies for dealing with the European settlers who began descending on their land in the seventeenth century: some opted to resist, some fled their traditional homelands, some sought accommodation, and some struck compromises. Cultural misunderstandings and intolerance plagued Indian-European relations, hampering negotiations and sometimes leading to violent confrontations.

Many Puritans who arrived in New England were convinced that the Indians they encountered represented remnants of the "Lost Tribes of Israel," a part of God's nation of chosen people that had gone astray and needed to be converted and saved. This belief was in fact one of the central premises of the Massachusetts Bay Colony charter: its colonial seal featured a picture of a Native American uttering the words "Come over and help us." Such imagery enabled the Puritan fantasy that Native Americans were voluntarily inviting them to North America, where they were anxiously awaiting the colonists' charity and spiritual instruction. In practice, Native Americans found that Puritan conversion practices could be extremely coercive and culturally insensitive. For Indians, accepting Christianity generally involved giving up their language, severing kinship ties with other Indians who had not been "saved," and abandoning their traditional homes to live in European-style "Praying Towns." Many Native Americans were understandably hostile toward Puritan missionaries, perceiving their work as a threat to Indian social bonds and cultural practices. Except for the persistence of a few zealous missionaries like John Eliot, Puritans' enthusiasm for proselytizing among the natives had waned by the late seventeenth century.

Puritan-Indian relations were further troubled by recurring disagreements over land use and land rights. Part of the problem stemmed from the groups' fundamentally different attitudes toward land ownership. To the New England Indians, "selling" land did not mean granting exclusive, perpetual ownership to the buyer; instead, it involved accepting a new neighbor and sharing resources. The Puritans, on the other hand, were committed to the notion of private property and expected Native Americans immediately and permanently to vacate their land upon its sale. Some Puritan settlers felt that they were entitled to Native American land because, in their view, the Indians were squandering the land's potential by failing to enclose it or to farm it in the English manner. The problems inevitably caused by these radically different concepts of land use and land ownership were compounded by the Puritans' increasing conviction that the Indians' claims were invalid anyway, because God intended to bestow New England upon the English. By 1676, the minister Increase Mather wrote confidently about the Puritans' property rights over "the Heathen People amongst whom we live, and whose Land the Lord God of our Fathers has given to us for a rightful possession."

As Mather's rhetoric makes clear, many Puritans saw Indians less as "the Lost Tribes" than as irredeemable "heathens." Shifting the biblical context through which they understood the Native Americans, Puritans likened them to the Canaanites or Amalekites, heathen peoples whom God sent as a scourge to test the nation of Israel and whose extermination was necessary for the fulfillment of his divine plan. This antagonistic perspective on the part of the Puritans enabled what critic Richard Slotkin calls "a new mythology of Puritan-Indian rela-

[2583] The First Seal of Massachusetts Bay Colony (1629), courtesy of the Massachusetts Secretary of the Commonwealth, Public Records Division.

[1210] John Underhill, *The Figure of the Indians' Fort or Palizado in New England and the Manner of the Destroying It by Captayne Underhill and Captayne Mason* (1638) courtesy of, the Library of Congress [LC-USZ62-32055].

"VIEWS OF NATIVE AMERICANS" WEB ARCHIVE

[1210] John Underhill, *The Figure of the Indians' Fort or Palizado in New England and the Manner of Destroying It by Captayne Underhill and Captayne Mason* (1638), courtesy of the Library of Congress [LC-USZ62-32055]. In 1636, the English settlers engaged in a campaign to wipe out the Pequot tribe. Captain John Underhill chronicled the Pequot War in his *News from America* (1638), providing this sketch of the Puritans, along with their Narragansett allies, encircling and destroying a Pequot village.

[2583] The First Seal of Massachusetts Bay Colony (1629), courtesy of the Massachusetts Bay Secretary of the Commonwealth, Public Records Division. The Massachusetts Bay Colony's official seal features a Native American uttering the words "Come

tionships in which war and exorcism replaced tutelage and conversion." As early as 1636, the English settlers engaged in a genocidal campaign to wipe out the Pequot tribe. In *Of Plymouth Plantation*, William Bradford described the carnage wrought by the Puritans as a "sweet sacrifice" and "gave the praise thereof to God, who had wrought so wonderfully." Captain John Underhill also chronicled the Pequot War in his *News from America* (1638), providing a sketch of the Puritans, along with their Narragansett allies, encircling and destroying a Pequot village. Puritan-Indian hostilities erupted again in 1676 with King Philip's War, one of the most devastating wars (in proportion to population) in American history. Former Puritan allies like the Narragansetts banded together with other Algonquian tribes to oppose the English. In her narrative of captivity among the Indians during King Philip's War, Mary Rowlandson frequently employs standard Puritan demonizing rhetoric, calling her captors "infidels," "hell-hounds," and "savages," and insisting that they are a "scourge" sent by God to chasten and test his chosen people. She reserves a special hatred for Native Americans who had experienced Christian conversion (the "Praying Indians"); in her view, they were nothing but hypocrites. Still, tensions and contradictions mark Rowlandson's narrative; she comes to see some Indians as individuals capable of humanity and charity, thus complicating her black-and-white worldview. English victories in both the Pequot War and King Philip's war, combined with the ravaging effects of European diseases like smallpox, resulted in the depletion of Native American populations in New England and enabled Puritans to seize most remaining Indian lands in the region by the early eighteenth century.

Unfortunately, we do not have extensive records of Indian/Puritan encounters during the seventeenth century composed from a Native American perspective. But some written accounts, pictographs, archaeological evidence, and transcriptions of oral traditions survive to give an indication of what Indians thought about the English settlers in New England. Some of the most interesting records remain from Natick, an Indian "Praying Town" east of Boston. Established in 1651 by missionary John Eliot, Natick consisted of English-style homesteads, three streets, a bridge across the Charles River, as well as a meetinghouse, which housed a school, and the governing body. The Indian residents of Natick were taught to read and write in their native language of Massachuset, using letters from the Roman alphabet. In 1988, anthropologists Kathleen Bragdon and Goddard Ives translated the town records from Natick into English and published an accompanying grammar for the Massachuset language under the title *Native Writings in Massachusett*. Our understanding of native lives and the Algonquian view of conquest has been further enhanced by Williams Simmons's ground-breaking collection of Algonquian oral tradition from southeastern New England, *The Spirit of New England Tribes, and*

Indian Converts (1727), and Experience Mayhew's biographies of four generations of Wampanoag men, women, and children from the island of Martha's Vineyard. These documents suggest that Indian converts often adapted Christianity to suit their needs and to face the trials of conquest, rather than merely being transformed into "Red Puritans."

In the colony of Pennsylvania, William Penn and the Quakers demonstrated that Indian-European relations did not have to be based on intolerance or violence toward native cultures. Initiating contact with the Delaware in his "Letter to the Lenni Lenape," Penn showed respect for Native American culture, pledged to treat Native Americans as equals, and acknowledged their land rights. The Pennsylvania seal provides a telling contrast to the seal of the Massachusetts Bay Colony, revealing important differences in the two colonies' attitudes toward and treatment of Native Americans. Rather than depicting the Indians as inferior beings in need of help, the Pennsylvania seal offers an image of harmony and equality: a Native American and a European share a pipe, while the motto proclaims "Let us look to the Most High who blessed our fathers with peace." Under Penn's leadership, the Quakers were scrupulously fair in their negotiations of land deals with Native Americans. The wampum belt featured in the archive, which functioned within Delaware culture as a kind of land deed, testifies to the Quakers' willingness to participate in and respect Indian cultural practices. As a result of their commitment to tolerance and mutual respect, the Quakers and Indians lived in peace in Pennsylvania for over half a century.

QUESTIONS

Comprehension: How did the Puritans' understanding of the Bible shape their attitudes toward Native Americans? How did Quaker theology shape their relationship with Native Americans? How did the theology of Native American Christians affect their attitudes towards whites?

Comprehension: How did Puritans justify seizing Native American land? Can you find examples of these justifications in any of the texts covered in this unit (Bradford, Rowlandson, Knight, Winthrop, or Occom, for example)?

Context: What does John Underhill's sketch of the Puritan attack on the Pequot community tell you about the Puritans' method of war or their feelings about that particular battle? How does the presence of Narragansett allies (the outer ring of figures in the sketch) complicate our understanding of the battle? How does the sketch compare with the written account of the Pequot War William Bradford gives in *Of Plymouth Plantation*?

Context: Samson Occom composed his "Short Narrative" almost a century after the conclusion of King Philip's War. How do white attitudes toward Native Americans seem to have changed by his time? How do they seem similar? How does his narrative challenge whites' ideas about Indians?

Exploration: How do later eighteenth-, nineteenth-, and twentieth-

over and help us." The "help" requested is the gift of the Gospel, as explained by John Winthrop in his "Reasons to be considered for iustifieing the undertakers of the intended Plantation in New England."

[2825] William Hubbard, *The Present State of New England. Being a Narrative of the Troubles with the Indians in New-England* (1677), courtesy of Special Collections, the University of Pennsylvania Library. Like Mary Rowlandson's captivity narrative, this history of King Philip's War views Native Americans as agents of Satan who have been sent to test the Puritans. It includes one of the early maps of New England.

[2850] Brass medal given Christian Indians as a reward for service, courtesy of the National Museum of the American Indian, Smithsonian Institution, N38319/N38320. Photo by Carmelo Guadagno. Christianized Indians fought on both the Native and the British sides in King Philip's War, which led to confusion on the part of colonists as to who was a "good" and who was a "bad" Indian. Brass medals were awarded to those who served the British.

[5054] Gleasons Pictorial, *In Honor of the Birthday of Governor John Winthrop, Born June 12th, 1587* (1854), courtesy of the Library of Congress [LC-USZ62-120506]. Woodprint engraving of head-and-shoulders portrait of Governor John Winthrop, flanked by statues of a Native American (left) and a pilgrim (right) and with a homestead below.

[5214] Iroquois Wampum belt, courtesy of the University of Pennsylvania Museum of Archaeology and Anthropology. Wampum, usually found in bead form and made from Quahog shells found along the southern New England coast, was an important item for exchange and political dealings among Indians; after European settlement, it came to resemble a type of currency.

[6326] Jean Leon Gerome Ferris, *The First Thanksgiving 1621* (1932), courtesy of the Library of Congress [LC-USZ62-15915]. The Thanksgiving holiday has gained mythic status through representations of the event as a critical occasion of the Plymouth colony.

century romanticized visions of Native Americans as "noble savages" relate to Puritan and Quaker ideas about Native Americans? Why do you think the "noble savage" concept became so popular later in American history?

Exploration: How do white Americans' attitudes toward Native Americans through the centuries compare to their attitudes toward other non-white groups?

Puritan Typology: Living the Bible

The Puritans developed **typology** as a mode both for reading scripture and for understanding the significance of historical and current events. In its strictest sense, typology refers to the practice of explicating signs in the Old Testament as foreshadowing events, personages, ceremonies, and objects in the New Testament. According to typological logic, Old Testament signs, or "types," prefigure their fulfillment or "antitype" in Christ. Applied more broadly, typology enabled Puritans to read biblical types as forecasting not just the events of the New Testament but also their own historical situation and experiences. In this way, individual Puritans could make sense of their own spiritual struggles and achievements by identifying themselves with biblical personages like Adam, Noah, or Job. But this broad understanding of typology was not restricted to individual typing; the Puritans also interpreted their group identity as the fulfillment of Old Testament prophecy, identifying their community as the "New Israel."

Tied to their typological understanding of their communal identity was the Puritans' belief that they had entered into a covenant with God. Like the Old Testament Hebrews, the Puritans felt themselves to be a "chosen nation," a people through whom God would fulfill his divine plan on earth. Their covenant, however, was not the same as the Old Testament covenant God had formed with the Israelites. The coming of Christ had changed the terms of the contract, enabling them to live under a "covenant of grace." According to this doctrine, God had freely extended salvation to the Puritans—salvation that did not have to be earned through good works, only accepted with faith. Right behavior would follow from acceptance of and faith in the covenant. On an individual level, Puritans agonized over the status of their covenant with God (that is, their election), but as a group they were more confident. Having entered into voluntary church covenants, and thus into a kind of national covenant with God, they were assured of the centrality of their role in the cosmic drama of God's plan. Like the Israelites of old, they had received a "special commission" from God and had come to the New World to fulfill their mission.

The typological implications of the Puritans' covenant theology are apparent in "A Model of Christian Charity," the sermon John Winthrop delivered on board the *Arbella* while traveling to New England. Proclaiming that "the God of Israel is among us" and has formed a "near bond of marriage between him and us, wherein he hath taken us to be his," Winthrop interprets the Puritans as the antitype of the Old

Testament Jews. His famous declaration that New England shall be "as a City upon a Hill" elevates the Puritan community to the status of an exemplary society with the potential to fulfill scriptural prophecies. The same typological worldview that characterizes Winthrop's speech also moved the Puritans to name some of the settlements they created in the New World after scriptural references—New Canaan and New Haven, for example.

As the Puritan community grew and changed, it became clear that typological interpretations were neither stable nor uniform. Different people could interpret events as having different kinds of typological significance, sometimes to ends that Puritan leaders considered unorthodox or subversive. During the divisive Antinomian Controversy (1637), for example, John Winthrop and Anne Hutchinson engaged in a kind of war of rival typological interpretations. During her trial, Hutchinson interpreted herself as the Old Testament figure of Daniel and the Puritan court as the lion's den: she claimed that God had told her that just as he "delivered Daniel out of the lion's den, I will also deliver thee." Seeing her own trial as the antitype of Daniel's encounter with the lions, she declared to the court that they would see "this scripture fulfilled this day." John Winthrop was outraged by this reading of events, sarcastically noting that if Hutchinson's typologizing were to be believed, "she must be delivered by miracle, and all we must be ruined." He went on to impose his own typological interpretation of Hutchinson's role in the fulfillment of biblical prophecy: "One would hardly have guessed her to have been an Antitype of Daniel, but rather of the Lions after they were let loose."

Despite these internal skirmishes over proper typologizing, Puritan leaders found that their typological interpretations of external threats, by uniting their congregants in a shared spiritual mission, could serve as an effective method for consolidating the community. For instance, Puritans justified their seizure of Native American lands and their wars against Native Americans by typologizing Indians as "Amalekites" or "Canaanites," heathen peoples whom God sent as a scourge to test the nation of Israel and whose extermination was necessary for the fulfillment of his divine plan. In this way, Puritans marshaled biblical typology to legitimate their destruction of Indian culture. Typologizing opposition and challenges as "tests," "scourges," or "punishments" sent by God allowed Puritans to read even their misfortunes as paradoxical proofs of God's love and of their status as his "chosen people." After all, they reasoned, God would not bother chastising or testing them if he did not view them as special. In her narrative of her captivity, Mary Rowlandson struggles to understand an experience that would otherwise have been inexplicably frightening and horrific as evidence of God's chastising hand, at first disciplining and ultimately delivering her. Rowlandson's story of holy affliction and deliverance touched a chord with the entire Puritan community. Ministers such as Increase Mather determined to read her individual experience as a communal lesson: God had not tested and punished Rowlandson alone; he had tested and punished the Puritan nation through her. In this way, Rowlandson herself functions as a type of the

[4439] *Judea Capta* coin (71 C.E.), courtesy of the American Numismatic Society.

[4781] Anonymous, Detail of the Eliakim Hayden Stone (1797), courtesy of Wesleyan University.

Old Testament *judea capta*, or Israel in bondage. Her purifying ordeal in the wilderness reflects God's punishment of the "New Israel" for its sins. Her redemption from captivity reflects New England's reinstatement in God's favor.

Of course, her narrative also offers evidence that typology provided Rowlandson with a more personal, individualized kind of comfort. She articulates her suffering through the words of Old Testament figures, drawing strength from understanding her own experience through theirs. Likening herself to Job, the good servant of God who is afflicted by a bewildering set of misfortunes in order to test the depth of his faith, Rowlandson seeks comfort in the notion that God's ways are beyond human understanding, but that his servants must remain patient and faithful. Like Rowlandson's narrative, the Eliakim Hayden gravestone (Essex, Connecticut, 1797) offers an example of typology applied to the individual life. The carved design of the stone shows Noah's ark, floating on the floodwaters, while a dove flies overhead with a cross in the background. Puritans understood the Old Testament story of Noah as a prefiguring, or type, of Christ, and the flood as a type of baptism. The cross and the dove carved on the stone, then, serve as antitypes representing Christ offering salvation for Adam's original sin. The epitaph clarifies the typological imagery: "As in Adame, all mankinde / Did guilt and death derive / So by the Righteousness of Christ / Shall all be made alive." Implicitly including Hayden's life within its typological reading—his soul is clearly one that has been "made alive" through Christ—the gravestone iconographically invokes biblical prophecy and folds the Puritan individual into its scriptural schema.

QUESTIONS

Comprehension: How does Rowlandson's *Narrative* understand her captivity as typologically significant both for herself as an individual and for her community as a whole? Does Rowlandson's need to understand her experience on two levels create tensions within the text? If so, how?

Comprehension: How would you interpret the Eliakim Hayden gravestone typologically? What do the images carved on the stone mean? What do you think the images that look like eyes at the top of the stone represent? How do the images relate to the rhymed aphorism in the epitaph?

Comprehension: How does John Winthrop use typological interpretations of current events to political ends? How do the typological interpretations in the "Model of Christian Charity" compare to his typological understanding of Anne Hutchinson seven years later? Do the motivations behind his typologizing change over time?

Context: Read Edward Taylor's "Meditation 8." How does Taylor join the Old Testament type of "manna" with the New Testament antitype of Christ as the bread of life? How does a typological reading change the significance of the homely metaphor of bread and bread baking in this poem?

Context: What kind of status did the Puritans' commitment to typology grant to the Bible? How might it work to blur the line between text and life? Why do you think the concept of typology never gained currency within Quaker theology?

Context: How does Mary Rowlandson typologize herself in her narrative? To which biblical personages does she choose to compare herself? Why?

Context: On September 2, 1772, Mohegan minister Samson Occom preached to a mixed audience of native peoples and whites about the execution of convicted murderer and drunkard Moses Paul, a Mohegan. For white ministers and their parishioners, American Indian drunkenness was only one of a long series of signs that confirmed their typological understanding of Native Americans as either helpless, "heathen," or satanic. Even Occom's supporters occasionally expressed fear that American Indians could never be incorporated into Christ's body politic. Occom uses as his inspiration a quotation from St. Paul's Epistle to the Romans, a letter that insists that Gentiles, not Israelites, are the true inheritors of Christ. How does Occom use typology to redefine the community to which he preaches?

Exploration: Why do you think the Puritans wished to interpret their relationship with God as a contract? What responsibilities, benefits, or anxieties do you think this contractual understanding of spirituality caused for the Puritans?

Exploration: What kinds of assumptions do people make when they embrace the idea that they are part of a "chosen nation"? Who is excluded from "chosen-ness"?

Exploration: Do you see the influence of typology in any later American writings? When do Americans seem most likely to turn to strategies like typology to make sense of the world and their place within it?

EXTENDED CONTEXTS

The Doctrine of Weaned Affections: In Search of Spiritual Milk

One of the most important theological doctrines for many Puritans is what has been called the "doctrine of **weaned affections.**" This doctrine holds that individuals must learn to wean themselves from earthly attachments and instead make spiritual matters their priority. Obviously, inappropriate earthly attachments included material possessions such as one's home, furniture, clothing, and valuables. But the doctrine of weaned affections could also proscribe things that we do not usually think of as incompatible with spirituality, such as a love of natural beauty, a dedication to secular learning, or even an intense devotion to one's spouse, children, or grandchildren. According to orthodox Puritan theology, anything tied to this world—even relation-

ships with family members—should be secondary to God. While the idea of weaned affections may have been emotionally practical given the seventeenth century's high mortality rates, it was still a difficult doctrine to live by. Mary Rowlandson's bitterness about being separated from her home, family, and domestic comforts attests to the power these attachments held for her, even though she insists that she welcomes and has been purified by God's testing of her spiritual commitment. Anne Bradstreet's vivid poetic evocations of her love for her family and her home also offer evidence of the tensions created by the doctrine of weaned affections. Her reflections on her relationships with nature, her husband, her children, her grandchildren, and even her house are poignantly balanced by her reminders to herself that her affections belong elsewhere.

Implicit in the language of "weaned affections" is the imagery of breast feeding, nursing, and weaning. In fact, Puritan ministers frequently employed breast and breastfeeding imagery in their sermons and poetry, appropriating this female bodily function as a metaphor for proper spiritual nourishment and dependence upon God. In the Puritans' symbolic understanding, the Bible was spiritual milk, and the minister was the breast at which his congregation suckled. Male ministers were comfortable figuring themselves as feminine "breasts" because the metaphor granted them a kind of spiritual, parental authority as vessels for God's word and providers of sustenance for their congregants. The Peter and Mary Tufts gravestone (Malden, Massachusetts, 1702) exemplifies the willingness of Puritan men to appropriate breast imagery to spiritual ends, featuring an obviously male, mustached figure with breasts.

Puritan children were taught from an early age about the importance of renouncing earthly nourishment and affection in favor of "spiritual milk." One of the first texts written and printed for an audience of children, John Cotton's *Spiritual Milk for Babes, Drawn Out of the Breasts of Both Testaments for their Souls Nourishment* (England, 1646; Boston, 1656), emphasized the doctrine of weaned affections. *Spiritual Milk* offered a formal catechism for children to memorize, imparting a sense of the corruption and depravity of the earthly human condition through a series of ritualized questions and answers:

Q: Are you then born a Sinner?
A: I was conceived in sin, and born in iniquity.
Q: What is your Birth-sin?
A: Adam's sin imputed to me, and a corrupt nature dwelling in me.
Q: What is your corrupt nature?
A: My corrupt nature is empty of Grace, bent unto sin, and only unto sin, and that continually.

Cotton's *Spiritual Milk* was often included in the *New England Primer*, a popular Puritan textbook designed to promote children's literacy and religious training. The *Primer* itself worked to instill in children a sense of the transitory nature of earthly existence and the necessity of focusing on spiritual concerns. Teaching the alphabet through moral aphorisms, the *Primer* preached "G: As runs the Glass / Man's life doth pass" and "Y: Youth forward slips / Death soonest nips." Puritans thus learned early that, since life on earth was fleeting, they should not become attached to things of this world and should instead reserve their most intense affections for the spiritual realm.

QUESTIONS

Comprehension: Why does the Tufts gravestone feature a man with breasts? What would this imagery have signified to Puritan viewers? How might it have served to comfort mourners?

Context: How does Anne Bradstreet deal with the doctrine of weaned affections in her poems "In Memory of My Dear Grandchild Elizabeth Bradstreet," "A Letter to Her Husband, Absent upon Public Employment," and "Here Follows Some Verses upon the Burning of Our House"? What tensions arise as a result of her love for her family and for her material possessions? To what spiritual use does she turn the experience of losing grandchildren and her home? Is she entirely resigned to the notion that "my hope and treasure lies above"?

Exploration: Although Cotton's catechism in *Spiritual Milk for Babes* may seem bleak and rather demoralizing for children, it was used as a teaching device through the nineteenth century. How do you think the worldview espoused in the catechism influenced American culture? Do you see evidence of Cotton's Puritan beliefs, or responses to them, at work in later American literature?

[4643] Anonymous, Detail of the left panel of the Peter and Mary Tufts Stone, Malden, Massachusetts (1702), courtesy of Wesleyan University. This detail from the Peter and Mary Tufts gravestone, erected in Malden, Massachusetts, around 1702, features a male figure with breasts. Puritan ministers frequently employed breast and breastfeeding imagery in their sermons and poetry, appropriating this female bodily function as a metaphor for proper spiritual nourishment and dependence upon God.

[6749] Anonymous, *New England Primer* (1807), courtesy of the Gettsyburg College Special Collections. The *New England Primer* (first published in Boston in 1690) was a popular Puritan textbook designed to promote children's literacy and religious training.

[7179] Emory Elliot, Interview: "Winthrop and the Puritan Motivations for Settlement" (2001), courtesy of Annenberg/CPB. Elliott, professor of English (University of California, Riverside), discusses John Winthrop and the rallying of the Puritans to work together.

Plain Style: Keeping It Simple

The term **plain style** refers to a mode of expression characterized by its clarity, accessibility, straightforward simplicity, and lack of ornamentation. In early America, the plain-style aesthetic had broad cultural relevance, shaping the language of prose and poetry, the design of furniture and buildings, and the style of painting and other visual arts. Rejecting ornamental flourishes and superfluous decoration as evidence of sinful vanity, plain stylists worked to glorify God in their productions rather than show off their own artistry or claim any renown for themselves. As the Puritan minister John Cotton put it, "God's altar needs not our polishings." By shunning extraneous embellishment, practitioners of the plain style hoped both to make their messages easily understandable and to avoid any distractions that might divert their audience's attention from God. The simplicity, humility, and directness of the plain-style aesthetic appealed to both Quakers and Puritans, for despite profound theological differences, both groups sought religious purity through the rejection of worldly interests.

Early Quaker and Puritan church architecture provide perhaps the clearest examples of the ideals of plain style, since these buildings are conspicuously free of the stained glass and carved and painted reli-

[4475] Old Ship Church, 88 Main Street, Hingham, Plymouth County, Massachusetts, interior (1681), courtesy of the Library of Congress [HABS, MASS,12-HING,5-].

gious decorations we tend to expect in houses of worship. Instead, Puritan and Quaker meetinghouses are consciously spare, defined by their linear design, exposure of structural supports, and open lighting. The unpretentious interiors have no carvings or altars (Quaker meetinghouses would not even have pulpits), creating unadorned spaces that allow congregants to concentrate on their individual relationships with God. These structures express the ideals of plain style and serve as examples of a distinctly American architecture.

Some seventeenth-century American paintings also reveal the influence of the plain-style aesthetic. The portraits of the Freake family painted by an unidentified Boston artist in the 1670s are characterized by a flatness of form and a precise linearity that render the human figures somewhat two-dimensional and deprive the subjects of sensuous, tactile qualities. While the portraits' depiction of the rich fabrics and expensive finery that mark the Freakes as a wealthy mercantile family is somewhat at odds with Puritan plain-style ideals, the flat, simple artistic style of the paintings shares in the plain-style aesthetic.

Plain-style ideals also shaped the development of literature among Puritan and Quaker writers. Though many Puritans used elaborate, highly ornate metaphorical language to convey their religious ideals, some developed a more simplified literary style (most famously William Bradford). Characterized by the absence of rhetorical flourishes and limited use of figurative language, texts composed in the plain-style tradition focus on making their meanings straightforward and accessible. When metaphors appear within plain-style texts, they usually derive from the Bible or refer to homely, everyday objects rather than classical allusions. But the restraint of plain-style writing does not signify a lack of artistry; rather, it can be elegant, powerful, and persuasive in its very simplicity.

"PLAIN STYLE" WEB ARCHIVE

QUESTIONS

Comprehension: Why would early congregants of the churches featured in the archive have found them architecturally suitable for Puritan or Quaker spiritual practices? What "plain-style" characteristics are visible in the construction of these churches? How does the plain style aesthetic embodied in this architecture complement Quaker and Puritan religious values and beliefs?

Context: Puritan poets Anne Bradstreet and Edward Taylor are sometimes identified as plain stylists and sometimes seen as part of other poetic traditions (such as classical, ornate, or metaphysical). When does their work seem to participate in the plain-style aesthetic? When does it seem to be doing something different? Do some topics or concepts lend themselves better to plain-style representation?

Exploration: Do you see the plain-style aesthetic as an influence on any later American art or literary movements? Do these later turns toward plainness and simplicity reflect the same values as the Puritan and Quaker use of plain style?

ASSIGNMENTS

Personal and Creative Responses

1. *Journal:* Try to imagine how one of Mary Rowlandson's Narragansett or Wampanoag captors would have experienced the events that she describes during her captivity. Remember that the Indians were provoked by the Plymouth colony's decision to execute members of the Wampanoag tribe, as well as by longstanding tensions with European settlers over land rights. By the late seventeenth century, many Native Americans in the New England region were suffering from disease and starvation as European settlers encroached upon their traditional homes and hunting grounds. Given this background information, write a short narrative of the conflict at Lancaster, the capture of Mrs. Rowlandson, and the subsequent journey into the wilderness from the point of view of a Native American.

2. *Poet's Corner:* Read Anne Bradstreet's "In Memory of My Dear Grandchild Elizabeth Bradstreet" and Edward Taylor's "Upon Wedlock, and Death of Children." Make a list of the images and metaphors the poets employ to characterize their familial relationships. How do Bradstreet and Taylor employ similar images to different ends? Draw upon Bradstreet's and Taylor's metaphors and images to write your own poem. Write about what these images signify to you personally; your poem need not be about family, religion, or God.

3. *Multimedia:* Imagine that you have embarked on a journey through colonial America. Explain the nature of your journey (you might be a traveling missionary, like John Woolman or Samson Occom; you could be a captive, like Mary Rowlandson; or you might be on a business trip, like Sarah Kemble Knight). Using the *American Passages* archive and slide-show software, create a multimedia photo album of the highlights of your journey. Include captions that explain and interpret your experience for a modern audience.

Problem-Based Learning Projects

1. You are a Puritan missionary. You believe that God has called you on a sacred mission to convert Native Americans and to "propagate the gospel and kingdom of Christ" among them. Write up notes for yourself and your assistants delineating the aspects of Puritan theology that you think are most important to convey to the Indians. Outline how you will present and teach these concepts to them. Finally, compose a memo justifying your conversion practices to the group that funds and oversees your work, the Society for the Propagation of the Gospel.

2. You are a Quaker missionary from Pennsylvania. You believe that God has called you on a sacred mission to convert the Puritans who live north of you in Massachusetts. Compose a journal entry to send

Massachusetts. Between 1671 and 1674, an unidentified artist known as the "Freake Painter" painted this portrait of Elizabeth and Mary Freake, the wife and daughter of Boston merchant and lawyer John Freake. The original 1671 painting depicted Elizabeth alone with her hands in her lap, holding a fan. Baby Mary was added in 1674, an addition that accentuates Elizabeth's virtues as a wife and mother.

[2793] The Quaker Meeting, courtesy of George Fox University. Quaker churches like this one are plain-style buildings defined by their linear design, exposure of structural supports, and open lighting. These unpretentious interiors have no altars or pulpits, creating unadorned spaces that allow congregants to concentrate on their individual relationship with God. Illustration from Sydney George Fisher, *The True William Penn*. (Philadelphia: J. B. Lippincott, 1899).

[4475] Old Ship Church, 88 Main Street, Hingham, Plymouth County, Massachusetts, Interior (1681), courtesy of the Library of Congress [HABS, MASS,12-HING,5-]. The Old Ship Church is named for the interior curve of the roof, which resembles a ship's hull. It is the oldest meetinghouse in continuous ecclesiastical use in the United States.

to your Quaker congregation at home, explaining your reasons for undertaking this mission and noting the concepts you wish to teach the Puritans. Explain what you think is wrong with Puritan theology and Puritan social practices, and outline what kinds of alternatives Quakerism offers.

3. You have been hired as the lawyer for Thomas Morton and the Marre-Mount community in the wake of the maypole incident. How will you defend them against the Puritan prosecution? Try to anticipate Puritan arguments as you compose your defense.

GLOSSARY

Apocalypse   The end of the world as it is prophesied in the Bible, especially in the Book of Revelation. Viewing their experiences through the lens of biblical history, the Puritans understood themselves to be living in the "end time," with Christ's Second Coming at hand. They believed that their purity as a nation would actually bring about the Apocalypse, at which time Christ would return and reign for a millennium. Then, the earth would be destroyed, the elect would be ushered into heaven, and all others would be cast into hell. Puritan ministers performed complex analyses of scriptural predictions in order to pinpoint the exact day the Apocalypse would occur.

captivity narrative   A uniquely American literary genre, the captivity narrative recounts the experience of a white European or, later, an American, during his or (more usually) her captivity and eventual release from hostile enemy captors (generally Native Americans). Enormously popular since their inception in the seventeenth century, captivity narratives influenced the development of both autobiographical writings and the novel in America.

covenant theology   The Puritans believed that they had formed a "covenant," or contract with God. Like the Old Testament Hebrews, they felt themselves to be a "chosen nation," the people through whom God would fulfill his divine plan on earth. Their covenant, however, was not the same as the Old Testament covenant God had formed with the Israelites. The coming of Christ had changed the terms of the contract, enabling them to live under a "covenant of grace." Right behavior would follow from their acceptance of and faith in the covenant. On an individual level, Puritans agonized over the status of their covenant with God, but as a group they were more confident. Having entered into voluntary church covenants, and thus into a kind of national covenant with God, they were assured of the centrality of their role in God's cosmic plan.

election   The Puritan belief that some individuals were predestined by God to be saved and taken to heaven while other individuals were doomed to hell. One's status as a member of the elect did not necessarily correlate with good works or moral behavior on earth, for God had extended a "covenant of grace" to his chosen people that did not have to be earned, only accepted with faith. Despite the apparent ease with which a believer could attain everlasting salvation, Puritans in practice agonized over the state of their souls, living in constant fear of damnation and scrutinizing their own feelings and behavior for indications of whether or not God had judged them worthy.

inner light   The Quaker concept of a manifestation of divine love that dwells within and thus unites all humans. Also called the "spirit," or the "Christ within," the inner light could be experienced without the mediation of a minister or the Bible and was thus powerfully egalitarian and radical in its implications. Quakers viewed the inner light as more important to spiritual development than the study of scripture.

jeremiad   A form usually associated with second generation Puritan sermons but which is also relevant to many other kinds of Puritan writing (Mary Rowlandson's *Narrative* is often cited as an example of a jeremiad). Drawing from the Old Testament books of Jeremiah and Isaiah, jeremiads lament the spiritual and moral decline of a community and interpret recent misfortunes as God's just punishment for that decline. But at the same time that jeremiads bemoan their communities' fall from grace, they also read the misfortunes and punishments that result from that fall as paradoxical proofs of God's love and of the group's status as his "chosen people." According to jeremidic logic, God would not bother chastising or testing people he did not view as special or important to his divine plan.

plain style   A mode of expression characterized by its clarity, accessibility, straightforwardness, simplicity, and lack of ornamentation. In early America, the plain-style aesthetic had broad cultural relevance, shaping the language of prose and poetry, the design of furniture and buildings, and the style of painting and other visual arts. Rejecting ornamental flourishes and superfluous decoration as sinful vanity, plain stylists worked to glorify God in their productions rather than to show off their own artistry or claim any renown for themselves. This aesthetic appealed to both Quakers and Puritans.

Puritans, Separatist and non-separating   All Puritans dreamed of creating a purified religious community, free from the hierarchies and worldly rituals they felt contaminated the established Church of England. While non-separating Puritans hoped that they could reform the church from within, the Separatists believed that they needed to break from the Church of England entirely. The Separatists represented a minority among Puritans, and they experienced even greater persecution in England than non-separating Puritans did. In America, the Plymouth colony led by William Bradford was Separatist while the Massachusetts Bay colony led by John Winthrop was non-separating.

typology   A Puritan method of both reading scripture and using it to understand the significance of historical and current events. In its strictest sense, typology refers to the practice of explicating signs in the Old Testament as foreshadowing events, personages, ceremonies, and objects in the New Testament. According to typological logic, Old

Testament signs, or "types," prefigure their fulfillment or "antitype" in Christ. Applied more broadly, typology enabled Puritans to read biblical types as forecasting not just the events of the New Testament but also their own historical situation and experiences. In this way, individual Puritans could make sense of their own spiritual struggles and achievements by identifying with biblical personages like Adam, Noah, or Job. But this broad understanding of typology was not restricted to individual typing; the Puritans also interpreted their group identity as the fulfillment of Old Testament prophecy, identifying their community as the "New Israel."

weaned affections This Puritan theological doctrine held that individuals must learn to wean themselves from earthly attachments and make spiritual matters their priority. Inappropriate earthly attachments included material possessions such as one's home, furniture, clothing, or valuables. The doctrine of weaned affections could also proscribe things that we do not usually think of as incompatible with spirituality, such as a love of natural beauty, or a dedication to secular learning, or even an intense devotion to one's spouse, children, or grandchildren. According to orthodox Puritan theology, anything tied to this world—even relationships with family members—should be secondary to God.

SELECTED BIBLIOGRAPHY

Bercovitch, Sacvan. *The Puritan Origins of the American Self*. New Haven: Yale UP, 1975.

———. *The American Jeremiad*. Madison: U of Wisconsin P, 1978.

Colacurcio, Michael. *Doctrine and Difference: Essays in the Literature of New England*. New York: Routledge, 1997.

Demos, John. *A Little Commonwealth: Family Life in Plymouth Colony*. New York: Oxford UP, 1970.

Levin, David. "William Bradford: The Value of Puritan Historiography." *Major Writers of Early American Literature*, ed. E. H. Emerson. Madison: U of Wisconsin P, 1972.

Miller, Perry. *Errand into the Wilderness*. Cambridge: Harvard UP, 1956.

Nash, Gary. *Philadelphia and the Forging of Historical Memory*. Philadelphia: U of Pennsylvania P, 2002.

Schweitzer, Ivy. *The Work of Self-Representation: Lyric Poetry in Colonial New England*. Chapel Hill: U of North Carolina P, 1991.

Slotkin, Richard, and James K. Folsom, eds. *So Dreadfull a Judgment: Puritan Responses to King Philip's War, 1676–1677*. Middletown, CT: Wesleyan UP, 1978.

Ulrich, Laurel Thatcher. *Good Wives: Images and Reality in the Lives of Women in Northern New England, 1650–1750*. New York: Knopf, 1980.

FURTHER RESOURCES

"Apocalypse: The Evolution of Apocalyptic Belief and How It Shaped the Western World" (A Frontline Special). PBS Video. P.O. Box 791. Alexandria, VA 22313-0791. 1-800-328-7271.

Delbanco, Andrew. *The Death of Satan: How Americans Have Lost the Sense of Evil*. New York: Farrar, Straus and Giroux, 1995.

Early American Psalmody: The Bay Psalm Book, Cambridge, 1640. Mission Music in California: Music of the Southwest. New York: Smithsonian Folkways [05108].

Hume, Ivor Noel. *A Guide to the Artifacts of Colonial America*. Philadelphia: U of Pennsylvania P, 1969.

Keller, Robert M. *The Dancing Master, 1651–1728 [computer file]: An Illustrated Compendium*. Annapolis, MD: Colonial Music Institute, 2000.

Ludwig, Allan I. *Graven Images: New England Stonecarving and Its Symbols, 1650–1815*. Hanover, NH: UP of New England, 1999.

Native Americans of the Northeast (Series). U of Massachusetts P. P.O. Box 429, Amherst, MA 01004 <info@umpress.umass.edu>. Customer Service: 413-545-2219. Fax: 1-800-488-1144.

Nicholls, David, ed. T*he Cambridge History of American Music*. Cambridge: Cambridge University Press, 1998. Opening chapters on Indian music, secular and sacred music to 1800, and African American music to 1900.

Plimouth Plantation. P.O. Box 1620, Plymouth, MA 02362. Phone: 508-746-1622. Fax: 508-746-4978.

The Plymouth Colony Archive Project at the University of Virginia. *Archives and Analysis of Plymouth Colony, 1620–1691*. Electronic Text Center, Alderman Library. Box 400148. University of Virginia. Charlottesville, VA 22904. Phone: 434-924-3230. Fax: 434-924-1431.

"Preserving America's Utopian Dream," Cultural Resource Management (online and in hard copy). Vol. 24, No. 9. National Park Service.

Religion and the Founding of the American Republic (Exhibit). The Library of Congress. 101 Independence Ave SE, Washington DC 20540. General Information: 202-707-5000. Exhibitions information: (202) 707-4604

The Religious Society of Friends <www.quaker.org>.

Simmons, William S. *Spirit of the New England Tribes: Indian History and Folklore, 1620–1984*. Hanover, NH: UP of New England, 1986.

St. George, Blaire. *Conversing by Signs: Poetics of Implication in Colonial New England Culture*. Chapel Hill: U of North Carolina P, 1998.

Authors and Works

Featured in the Video:

Benjamin Franklin, "The Way to Wealth," "Rules by Which a Great Empire May Be Reduced to a Small One," "Information to Those Who Would Remove to America," "Remarks Concerning the Savages of North America" (essays); *The Autobiography* (autobiography)

Ralph Waldo Emerson, from *Nature* (philosophy); "The American Scholar," "The Divinity School Address," "Last of the Anti-Slavery Lectures," "Thoreau" (lectures and addresses); "Self-Reliance," "The Poet," "Experience," "Fate" (essays)

Discussed in This Unit:

Jonathan Edwards, "Personal Narrative" (conversion narrative); "A Divine and Supernatural Light," "Sinners in the Hands of an Angry God" (sermons); "Letter to Rev. Dr. Benjamin Colman" (letter); from *Images or Shadows of Divine Things* (notebook entries, philosophy)

J. Hector St. John de Crèvecoeur, from *Letters from an American Farmer* (letters composed in voice of fictional persona)

Thomas Jefferson, Declaration of Independence (political document), from *Notes on the State of Virginia* (natural history, study of political and social structures)

Phillis Wheatley, "To the University of Cambridge, in New England," "On the Death of the Rev. Mr. George Whitefield," "To His Excellency General Washington" (poetry)

Royall Tyler, *The Contrast* (play)

Susanna Rowson, *Charlotte Temple: A Tale of Truth* (novel)

William Apess, "An Indian's Looking-Glass for the White Man" (essay)

Margaret Fuller, "The Great Lawsuit" (essay), "Autobiographical Romance" (short autobiography)

Overview Questions

■ To whom was the ethos of individualism available? How did this exclusivity change over time?

■ What literary strategies did American writers develop to distinguish themselves from British writers? How successful were they?

■ What virtues and values emerged as foundational to the American character? How did they change over time?

■ Why did fictional genres such as the novel and drama seem morally questionable to so many Americans? How did early national novels and plays attempt to make themselves seem wholesome and productive of national virtues?

■ How does "auto-American-biography" enable writers to construct themselves as ideal American citizens?

■ What different spiritual beliefs influenced eighteenth- and nineteenth-century American writing? How did Americans' spiritual beliefs change over time?

■ What is Transcendentalism? Who took part in the Transcendentalist movement and how did they influence later generations of writers and thinkers?

■ What relationship to nature did the Transcendentalists promote? How did they see the landscape as a resource for spiritual transformation?

■ Why and how did natural history come to be linked to national identity?

■ How did the aesthetic of the "sublime" shape American representations of and relations to nature?

■ What is neoclassicism? How did this aesthetic movement influence American art and literature?

■ What is Romantic Individualism?

■ What did early national writers and artists mean when they conceived of America as a "new Rome"?

■ What is the "self-made man"? Were opportunities for self-making open to all Americans equally? How did the limits of self-making change over time?

■ Why did Americans represent their nation through the allegorical figure of "Columbia"? What values and beliefs informed portraits of Columbia?

Learning Objectives

After students have viewed the video, read the headnotes and literary selections in *The Norton Anthology of American Literature*, and explored related archival materials on the *American Passages* Web site, they should be able to

1. explain the meaning of the term "individualism" and discuss the way ideals of individualism changed over the course of the eighteenth and nineteenth centuries;
2. discuss the importance of race and gender in negotiations of American political and cultural independence;
3. explain the relationship between eighteenth-century Enlightenment ideals and nineteenth-century Romanticism;
4. discuss transformations in American spiritual beliefs between the eighteenth and nineteenth centuries, from the Great Awakening to Deism to more Romantic conceptions of divinity.

Instructor Overview

In his answer to the difficult question "What is an American?" Farmer James, the narrator of J. Hector St. John de Crèvecoeur's *Letters from an American Farmer*, claims that Americans are characterized by their lack of distinction between rich and poor, by a "pleasing uniformity of decent competence," and by their respect for the "silken bands of mild government." As his letters continue, however, James's idyllic picture of American life becomes increasingly troubled. A horrifying encounter with a tortured African American slave in South Carolina, doubts about the morality and civilization of Americans living in backwoods settlements, and intense distress brought about by the violence of the Revolution leave the narrator uncertain about exactly what—

and who—is an American. The ambiguities and tensions surrounding this question characterized much of the literature of the eighteenth and nineteenth centuries. As the young nation struggled to define its values and beliefs, debates raged about what America should stand for and what it should be. Unit 4, "The Spirit of Nationalism: Declaring Independence, 1710–1850," examines the work of a wide variety of writers who participated in these debates, including Jonathan Edwards, Benjamin Franklin, J. Hector St. John de Crèvecoeur, Thomas Jefferson, Phillis Wheatley, Royall Tyler, Susanna Rowson, William Apess, Ralph Waldo Emerson, and Margaret Fuller. The unit provides contextual background and classroom materials designed to explore the role these texts have played in the formation of American values and in the creation of enduring myths about America.

The video for Unit 4 focuses on Benjamin Franklin and Ralph Waldo Emerson, two influential writers who articulated American ideals and celebrated the potential of the American individual. Franklin helped shape the foundational myth of the "American dream" by narrating his own rise from obscurity through hard work and virtue. His *Autobiography* served as a model that inspired many later Americans and helped define the autobiographical genre. Forty years later, Emerson built on Franklin's practical ideas of self-improvement and made them more personal and spiritual. He encouraged Americans to look inward, trust their intuition, and develop their own principles. His spiritual philosophy of the correspondence among nature, the individual soul, and God was influential both in his own time and for subsequent generations. Emerson's optimistic belief in the potential of all individuals had far-reaching implications and repercussions. Although Emerson was not especially active in social reform movements, he articulated ideas that inspired individuals to make America a more inclusive and equal society.

In its coverage of Franklin's and Emerson's development of American ideals, the video introduces students to the complexities and evolution of ideas about individualism and the national character. What makes an American? To whom is the ethos of individualism available? How did ideas about the rights and potential of the individual change over time? How were American ideals influenced by people's relationship to the natural world? How did changing spiritual beliefs shape national ideals? Unit 4 helps to answer these questions by situating Franklin and Emerson within their cultural contexts, as well as connecting them to other units in the series and to other key writers of the era. The curriculum materials fill in the video's introduction to the spirit of nationalism by exploring writers who represented other, diverse experiences, such as Phillis Wheatley (an African American slave who composed and published poetry), Susanna Rowson (an English-born novelist whose best-selling book portrayed the social consequences of the sexual double standard), and William Apess (a Pequot Indian who became a Methodist minister and champion of Native American rights).

The video, the archive, and the curriculum materials locate the writers featured in Unit 4 within several of the historical contexts and artistic movements that shaped their texts: (1) ideas about individualism, from the Enlightenment through the beginnings of Romantic Individualism; (2) the early national interest in classical Greece and Rome and the aesthetic of neoclassicism; (3) the symbolic connection between American natural history and the American nation; (4) the aesthetic of the sublime; and (5) the representation of America as the female allegorical figure Columbia.

The archive and curriculum materials suggest how the authors and texts featured in Unit 4 relate to those covered in other *American Passages* units: How have ideas of individualism changed over time? How have they influenced the genre of the autobiography and the slave narrative? How did later nineteenth- and twentieth-century American writers challenge and expand the definition of who should be considered an American? What is the place of nature and the wilderness in American philosophy and in American society?

Student Overview

In his answer to the difficult question "What is an American?" Farmer James, the narrator of J. Hector St. John de Crèvecoeur's *Letters from an American Farmer*, claims that Americans are characterized by their lack of distinction between rich and poor, by a "pleasing uniformity of decent competence," and by their respect for the "silken bands of mild government." As his letters continue, however, James's idyllic picture of American life becomes increasingly troubled. A horrifying encounter with a tortured African American slave in South Carolina, doubts about the morality and civilization of Americans living in backwoods settlements, and intense distress brought about by the violence of the Revolution leave the narrator uncertain about exactly what—and who—is American. The ambiguities and tensions surrounding this question characterized much of the literature of the eighteenth and nineteenth centuries. As the young nation struggled to define its values and beliefs, debates raged about what America should stand for and what it should be.

Unit 4, "The Spirit of Nationalism: Declaring Independence, 1710–1850," explores the struggle over who and what should be considered American. As the video makes clear, writers like Benjamin Franklin and Ralph Waldo Emerson provided foundational American ideals in their celebrations of individual potential. Franklin helped shape the myth of the "American dream" by narrating his own rise from obscurity through hard work and virtue. His *Autobiography* served as a model that inspired many later Americans and helped define the autobiographical genre. Forty years later, Emerson built on Franklin's practical ideas of self-improvement and made them more personal and spiritual. He encouraged Americans to look inward, trust their intuition, and develop their own principles. His spiritual philosophy of the correspondence among nature, the individual soul, and God was influential both in his own time and for subsequent generations. Franklin's and Emerson's belief in the potential of the individual inspired other writers and thinkers to push the boundaries of who and what are considered American.

➤ **Authors covered:** Benjamin Franklin, Ralph Waldo Emerson

➤ **Who's interviewed:** Michael J. Colacurcio, professor of American literary and intellectual history to 1900 (University of California, Los Angeles); Bruce Michelson, professor of English (University of Illinois, Urbana-Champaign); Carla Mulford, associate professor of English (Pennsylvania State University); Dana Nelson, professor of American literature (University of Kentucky); John Carlos Rowe, professor of English and comparative literature (University of California, Irvine); Rafia Zafar, director of African and Afro-American studies (Washington University, St. Louis)

➤ **Points covered:**

- In the wake of the political revolution that separated them from the Old World, Americans became determined to liberate themselves culturally as well. A new belief in the power and importance of the individual shaped what became a uniquely American philosophy and literary style.

- Benjamin Franklin helped shape the foundational myth of America and the "American dream." Relying on his own cleverness and hard work to rise from his station as a poor indentured apprentice and become a successful businessman, writer, philosopher, and politician, Franklin served as a model of the "self-made man." His witty, endearing representation of himself and his life in his *Autobiography* set a new standard for the autobiographical genre in America. In Franklin's time, prejudice and oppression limited the definition of who counted as an American, but Franklin's work inspired men and women of subsequent generations to strive to expand those boundaries.

- Forty years later, Ralph Waldo Emerson built on Franklin's practical ideals of self-improvement and virtue and made them more personal and spiritual. Emerson encouraged Americans to look inward and find power and inspiration within themselves. He turned to nature as a spiritual resource that could energize the nation politically and elevate it morally. His Transcendental ideas about the unity of nature, the individual soul, and God profoundly influenced his peers as well as subsequent generations of American writers and thinkers. His ideas about self-reliance, in particular, inspired such writers as Frederick Douglass, Booker T. Washington, and Anzia Yezierska. In a difficult historical period, Emerson was a prophet of hope and unbounded optimism. His ceaseless efforts on behalf of the individual generated important ideas about social reforms that would make America a more inclusive and equal society.

- Both Franklin and Emerson championed the rights and potential of the individual and called for independent thought. Through their own works, they gave new power to the genres of the autobiography and the moral essay. By writing about their experiences and offering their own lives as examples, they encouraged other Americans to examine themselves and trust in their own principles and beliefs.

PREVIEW

- **Preview the video:** In the wake of the Revolution that severed America's colonial ties to Great Britain, the new nation struggled to liberate itself culturally from the Old World values and aesthetics that structured life and art in Europe. Many Americans turned to the Enlightenment ideals of self-determination and individualism as the basis for the new culture they were in the process of forming. Benjamin Franklin, often called the "first American," helped shape the national ideal of the "self-made man" in his *Autobiography*, a book that traced his rise to prominence through hard work and virtue. Forty years later, Ralph Waldo Emerson also celebrated individualism, but in a more Romantic and spiritual context. Issuing a clarion call to Americans to break free of European traditions, Emerson encouraged individuals to use their intuition and intellect to cultivate spiritual power within themselves. He looked to nature both as a source of inspiration for the individual and as an expression of the correspondence among humans, God, and the material world. Although their understanding of individualism and their vision of national culture were profoundly different, both Franklin and Emerson committed themselves to championing independent thought and individual development.

- **Tying the video to the unit content:** Unit 4 expands on the video's introduction to Franklin's and Emerson's development of an American literature tied to an ethos of individualism. The curriculum materials offer background on a variety of other eighteenth- and nineteenth-century writers who modified or rejected English models and developed uniquely American literary styles and themes. Unit 4 examines genres not covered in the video—such as plays, novels, and poetry—and pays attention to the ways female, black, and Native American authors built on and transformed Franklin's and Emerson's ideas. The unit also offers contextual background to expand on the video's introduction to the political issues, historical events, and literary and aesthetic styles that shaped the development of a "spirit of nationalism."

	What is an American? How does literature create conceptions of the American experience and identity?	**What is American literature? What are its distinctive voices and styles? How do social and political issues influence the American canon?**	**What characteristics of a literary work have made it influential over time?**
Comprehension Questions	Who was excluded from the ideals of individualism and the "self-made man" that structured Franklin's beliefs?	What is Transcendentalism?	According to Emerson, what kind of relationship exists between individuals and nature? What is "nature" for Emerson?
Context Questions	How did Franklin construct his own life as a model for others to follow in his *Autobiography*? To what extent did Emerson share with Franklin a desire to serve as a model to his fellow Americans? How were Emerson's ideas about the importance of individual experience different from Franklin's?	When he embarked on his project to arrive at "moral perfection," what did Franklin stress as the most important virtues to cultivate? How do Franklin's "thirteen virtues" compare to the kinds of virtues Emerson seems to espouse?	How did Franklin organize his own time? How did Franklin's advocacy of schedules and efficiency influence the way Americans think about and structure industry and labor? How did Emerson challenge the assumptions behind Franklin's ideas about efficiency and industry?
Exploration Questions	How do Franklin's ideal of success and his notion of the "self-made man" conflict with or grow out of Puritan theology? How have Franklin's ideals influenced later American writers? How did later Americans challenge and transform the model of the "self-made man"?	How did Franklin's *Autobiography* influence later writers of autobiography? How did his book transform the autobiographical genre in America?	Emerson is often described as the writer with whom every other American writer has had to come to terms. What impact did Emerson's philosophy and transcendental ideals have on writers like Fuller, Thoreau, Whitman, or Dickinson? How did Emerson change ideas about individualism and about the artist's role in American society?

	Texts	Contexts
1730s	Benjamin Franklin, *Poor Richard's Almanac* (1733)	Clergyman Jonathan Edwards preaches "The Great Awakening," fueling religious revival in New England (1733)
1740s	Jonathan Edwards, "Sinners in the Hands of an Angry God" (1741)	King George's War between British and French colonies (1744–48)
1750s	Jonathan Edwards, *Freedom of the Will* (1754)	First American Masonic Hall inaugurated in Philadelphia (1755) Seven Years' War (French and Indian War) (1756–63)
1760s	Jonathan Edwards, "Personal Narrative" (1765)	First American medical school established at the College of Philadelphia (1765) British parliament enacts Stamp Act, prompting anti-tax protests in the colonies (1765) British parliament passes Townshend Acts requiring colonists to pay duties on tea and other imports (1767)
1770s	Benjamin Franklin, *Autobiography: Part One* (written 1771) Phillis Wheatley, *Poems on Various Subjects, Religious and Moral* (1773) Thomas Jefferson, Declaration of Independence (1776)	Boston Massacre (1770) Boston Tea Party (1773) First Continental Congress meets in Philadelphia (1774) American Revolution (1775–83) Declaration of Independence (1776) Thomas Paine writes pamphlet, *Common Sense*, in support of independence from England (1776)
1780s	J. Hector St. John de Crèvecoeur, *Letters from an American Farmer* (1782) Benjamin Franklin, *Autobiography: Part Two* (written 1784) Thomas Jefferson, *Notes on the State of Virginia* (1787) Royall Tyler, *The Contrast* (1787)	Shays's Rebellion, a revolt by debt-ridden Massachusetts farmers, suppressed by government forces (1786–87) United States Constitution ratified (1789) George Washington serves as first president of the United States (1789–97)
1790s	Susanna Rowson, *Charlotte Temple: A Tale of Truth* (1794)	Bill of Rights adopted (1791) Fugitive Slave Act passed, making it illegal to aid runaway slaves (1793)
1800s		Washington, D.C., replaces Philadelphia as the national capital (1800) Louisiana Purchase (1803) Lewis and Clark expedition (1804–06)

	Texts	Contexts
1810s		War of 1812 (1812–15)
		Spain cedes Florida to United States (1819)
1820s	William Apess, *A Son of the Forest* (1829)	Missouri Compromise (1820)
		Democratic Party formed (1828)
1830s	William Apess, "An Indian's Looking-Glass for the White Man" (1833), "Eulogy on King Philip" (1836)	Indian Removal Act (1830)
		Texas gains independence from Mexico (1836)
	Ralph Waldo Emerson, *Nature* (1836), "The American Scholar" (1837), "The Divinity School Address" (1838)	Samuel Morse develops the electric telegraph (1837)
		U.S. troops force the removal of Cherokee Indians westward from Georgia (1838)
1840s	Ralph Waldo Emerson, *Essays* (1841), *Essays: Second Series* (1844)	Migration over the Oregon Trail begins (1843)
	Margaret Fuller, "The Great Lawsuit: MAN *versus* MEN, WOMAN *versus* WOMEN" (1843), *Summer on the Lakes* (1844), *Woman in the Nineteenth Century* (1845)	U.S.-Mexican War; annexations include California (1846–48)
		California Gold Rush begins (1849)

AUTHOR/TEXT REVIEW

Jonathan Edwards (1703–1758)

Jonathan Edwards's writings articulate a complex synthesis of traditional Puritan piety, **Enlightenment** beliefs in the potential of the human will, and an almost mystical appreciation of natural beauty. Intrigued by his unique combination of scientific rationalism and ecstatic faith, scholars continue to debate whether Edwards should be understood as the last great Puritan or the first American Romantic. Born just after the turn of the century, Edwards is the quintessential transitional figure between seventeenth-century Puritan culture and eighteenth-century Enlightenment ideals. Descended from a long line of ministers, including the influential Solomon Stoddard, Edwards seemed destined for a life in the church. He showed remarkable promise as a child, entering Yale—at that time, a bastion of conservative religious training—when he was thirteen and graduating as valedictorian. While in college, Edwards complemented his traditional theological education by studying the Enlightenment philosophy of John Locke and Isaac Newton. He also developed a scientific interest in the natural world: his earliest known writings are scientific examinations of such natural phenomena as atoms, rainbows, and spiders. As a young man, Edwards adopted a regimen of intense study and meditation (he rose at four in the morning and would read for up to thirteen hours a day) that he would continue for the rest of his life.

After spending a short time in New York and then receiving his master's degree in theology at Yale, Edwards accepted a call to assist his grandfather, Solomon Stoddard, at his church in Northampton, Massachusetts. There he married Sarah Pierrepont, a woman renowned for her devotion to spiritual matters, and started what would become a family of eleven children. When Stoddard died in 1729, Edwards was made the sole pastor of the Northampton church. Throughout the following decades, Edwards had remarkable success in revitalizing religious commitment among his flock. The forceful language and vivid imagery of his sermons had a powerful effect on many of his parishioners, touching off an unprecedented wave of conversions within the church. This revival Edwards witnessed in Massachusetts found a corollary in the mass conversions effected by itinerant preachers like George Whitefield and Gilbert Tennent at the large camp meetings they held throughout the American southern and middle colonies.

The revitalization of spirituality and religious enthusiasm that swept through the American colonies from 1734 until around 1750 is referred to as the **Great Awakening**. Great Awakening preachers were united in their desire to promote what they called a "religion of the heart," through which converts would move beyond mere adherence to moral duties into an ecstatic experience of spiritual grace. Some of Edwards's parishioners were so moved by their conversions that they could not stop themselves from crying out or fainting. Converts at Tennent's and Whitefield's camp meetings had even more extreme physical reactions, including shouting, shaking, groveling on the

[6871] John Stevens, *The Mary Carr Stone* (1721), courtesy of Wesleyan University Press.

ground, and even falling unconscious. Although Edwards worried that the excessive enthusiasm and emotionalism that prevailed at camp meetings could be delusions rather than true conversions, he used some of the itinerant ministers' rhetorical strategies in his own sermons.

Despite his enormous successes in the 1730s and 1740s, Edwards was unable to sustain his popularity with his congregation. In his desire to purify the church, he attempted to abolish the practice of giving communion to anyone who had only been baptized; instead, he required a formal, public profession of conversion of all full church members. He also began to use the pulpit to chastise prominent church members for immorality. Although some of Edwards's followers continued to support his efforts, many felt that he had gone too far and turned bitterly against him. In 1750, the Northampton church voted to dismiss its pastor.

Although Edwards received many offers to serve as pastor at other churches both in America and abroad, he accepted a calling to Stockbridge, near Northampton, where he served as a missionary to the Housatonnuck Indians. His new position afforded him freedom to set his own schedule and allowed him to focus on his writings and philosophical inquiries. In 1754, he published *Freedom of the Will*, a work that was widely heralded as an important contribution to theological debates. In 1757, he received an offer from the College of New Jersey (known today as Princeton) to serve as its president. He was reluctant to accept, citing his own inadequacy and his fear that the new post would distract him from his writing. When the college offered him a reduced workload, Edwards agreed to take the position. Upon arriving, Edwards instituted and participated in what was at the time a controversial innoculation program against smallpox. He had a reaction to the vaccine, became ill, and died at the age of fifty-five.

TEACHING TIPS

■ Students have different responses to the vivid imagery Edwards employs in "Sinners in the Hands of an Angry God": some may find it surprising, others frightening, and still others are amused. Sometimes students will associate the "fire and brimstone" nature of the text with contemporary televangelism or TV talk shows and believe that Edwards was something of a religious huckster. You should stress to them that Edwards distrusted extreme enthusiasm and reportedly delivered his sermons in a sober monotone rather than ranting or shouting. Most of Edwards's sermons are characterized by a desire to make salvation emotionally and aesthetically appealing to his listeners, and the sternness and anger in "Sinners in the Hands of an Angry God" is somewhat anomalous for him. It is also important that students realize that Edwards actually managed to live in accordance with his strict beliefs: his devotion to his family, rigorous dedication to study, and lifelong focus on God testify to the conviction that underlies his rhetoric.

- Ask students to outline the structure and argument of one of Edwards's sermons ("A Divine and Supernatural Light" or "Sinners in the Hands of an Angry God" would work well). Have them pay attention to the way Edwards begins with a quotation from Scripture, elucidates the doctrine it contains, and elaborates on its applications in the lives of his listeners. Ask them to analyze the kinds of arguments and appeals Edwards relies upon to make his sermon meaningful and potent to his listeners. A careful analysis of Edwards's systematic, logically organized arguments should help students appreciate the way his intellect worked and the power his sermons had over his listeners.

QUESTIONS

Comprehension: What language does Edwards use to describe his experience of grace in his "Personal Narrative"? What kinds of difficulties does he seem to have articulating his experience? What imagery and metaphors does he employ?

Comprehension: What was the Great Awakening?

Context: Both Edwards and Emerson were profoundly affected by the beauty of the natural world and understood it to be an expression of God's glory. Compare Edwards's descriptions of his experiences in nature in the "Personal Narrative" with Emerson's descriptions in *Nature*. How are they similar? How are they different? How does Edwards use natural imagery in his sermons?

Exploration: During the Great Awakening preachers and clerics had a tremendous influence on American culture: they captivated audiences with their powerful messages and transformed people's beliefs and the way they lived their everyday lives. What charismatic figures seem to exert this kind of influence over American culture today?

Benjamin Franklin (1706–1790)

Benjamin Franklin's extraordinary energy and varied talents made him successful as a writer, humorist, statesman, diplomat, businessman, and scientist. The tale of his rise from humble beginnings through hard work and virtue has become a familiar lesson in the American dream. So exemplary is Franklin's story that his *Autobiography* is often considered, in literary critic Sacvan Bercovitch's term, an **auto-American-biography**. That is, it functions as a narrative that constructs a kind of ideal American citizen, even conflating Franklin's personal history with the founding of the nation.

Born the youngest son in a family of fifteen, Franklin rebelled at an early age against the narrow constraints of life in Puritan Boston. As a teenager, he rejected his family's pious Puritanism in favor of **Deism**, a persuasion that privileges reason over faith and rejects traditional religious tenets in favor of a general belief in a benevolent creator. He also rebelled against his lengthy apprenticeship in his brother's Boston print shop. After mastering the printing trade, Franklin violated his

EDWARDS WEB ARCHIVE

[3169] Jonathan Edwards, *Sinners in the Hands of an Angry God* (1741), courtesy of the New York Public Library. Edwards delivered this sermon on July 8, 1741, in Enfield, Connecticut. Edwards's preaching helped fan the flames of religious revival at the dawn of the first Great Awakening.

[4475] Anonymous, *Old Ship Church, 88 Main St., Hingham, Plymouth County, MA Interior* (1681), courtesy of the Library of Congress [HABS, MASS,12-HING,5-]. The Old Ship Church is the oldest meetinghouse in continuous ecclesiastical use in the United States. Puritan meetinghouses were square in shape, unadorned, and lacked altars, reflecting the plain-style aesthetic and a congregational emphasis.

[6871] John Stevens, *The Mary Carr Stone* (1721), courtesy of Wesleyan University Press. The Mary Carr stone rests in Old Common Burying-ground in Newport, Rhode Island. It reads, "Here lyeth the Body of Mary the Wife of John Carr, Dyed Sepr; ye 28th: 1721: in ye 21st: year of her age." The carving was made at the John Stevens Shop by the elder Stevens, a carver known for the quality and innovativeness of his work. Its imagery emphasizes rebirth. The sides and bottom show leaf patterns, pilasters, rosettes: flowers and leaves were associated with life (Job 14) and fecundity. At the top is a cherub with wings, and at the base is a pair of peacocks, symbols of immortality.

[8811] Emory Elliot, Interview: "Puritan Impact" (2001), courtesy of Annenberg/CPB. Elliott, professor of English at the University of California, Riverside, discusses the impact of Puritan thought and ideology on American culture.

[3143] Robert Feke, *Benjamin Franklin* (c. 1746), courtesy of Harvard University.

contract of indenture to his brother and ran away to Philadelphia, where he found another position as a printer's assistant. On his own in a new city, Franklin learned to look out for his own best interests, though he also was taken advantage of on occasion. Notably, he found himself stranded in England after gullibly accepting a spurious offer of assistance. Always one to turn adversity to his advantage, Franklin soon found work in England and acquired new printing skills.

Franklin returned to Philadelphia in 1726, convinced that virtue and hard work were the keys to success. Crucially, for Franklin, an *appearance* of virtue and industry was almost as important as actually possessing these qualities. He took pains to cultivate a reputation for hard work, carrying his own paper through the streets in a wheelbarrow and keeping his light burning late to ensure that others would notice his dedication to his business. Franklin prospered following this formula, and by 1732 he was operating his own print shop, publishing the *Pennsylvania Gazette*, and composing the best-selling *Poor Richard's Almanac*. As his wealth and stature increased, Franklin involved himself in a variety of benevolent social projects, including the formation of the first American lending library and the first American fire department. In the mid-1740s he began serious work on the scientific experiments that would win him international acclaim. Building on ideals of Enlightenment rationalism in his scientific inquiries, Franklin formulated the theory of electricity that still serves as the basis for our use of electric energy.

Franklin devoted the remaining years of his life primarily to politics, diplomacy, and writing. As a leading member of the Pennsylvania Assembly, he was sent to England in 1757 to articulate the colony's grievances against the Crown. Despite his best diplomatic efforts, he eventually resigned himself to the idea that American independence from British rule was necessary. In 1771, Franklin began composing his *Autobiography*, only to put the project on hold when the Revolution necessitated his return to America. He was selected as a Pennsylvania delegate to the Second Continental Congress and served on the committee that helped Thomas Jefferson draft the Declaration of Independence. Franklin then spent much of the war as America's minister to France, using his charm and charisma to ensure French support and eventually reach a peace accord with Great Britain. His last official public duty was his service at the Constitutional Convention of 1787.

TEACHING TIPS

■ Using Franklin's model, have students devise and follow their own "bold and arduous Project for arriving at moral Perfection" (being sure to point out the tongue-in-cheek nature of Franklin's pretensions to eradicating all of his faults). Ask your students to make a list of at least five qualities that they value—they need not choose Franklin's thirteen virtues—and to use a notebook to keep track of their adherence to them over the course of one week. At the end of the week, ask them to report on their experiences. Did their record keeping change their behavior during the week? What was most difficult about keeping this kind of record? Do they agree with Franklin that they were "by the endeavor made a better and happier man than I otherwise should have been, if I had not attempted it"?

■ Franklin composed his *Autobiography* during three different periods and died before it could be completed. The first part of the memoir (composed in 1771) is explicitly addressed to his son, William, while the second part (composed in 1784) was written ostensibly in response to the solicitous letters from Abel James and Benjamin Vaughan which Franklin includes at the beginning of Part Two. Critics have speculated that Franklin's strained relationship with his son—William remained a Loyalist during the Revolution—led Franklin to reject him as the designated audience for his memoir. Ask students to think about the shift in Franklin's intended audience between the first and second sections of the *Autobiography*. How does his relationship with his son inform the first part? (You might point out that the tradition of addressing a memoir or guidebook to one's son was something of a rhetorical convention in the seventeenth and eighteenth centuries. Puritan Thomas Sheperd also addressed his autobiography to his son a century earlier.) What kind of reader does Franklin seem to envision for the second part? Why does he include the letters from James and Vaughan? Franklin casually observes that the "Revolution occasioned the interruption" between his writing of the first and second part. How does the Revolution seem to have changed Franklin's narrative tone and/or purpose?

QUESTIONS

Comprehension: To what does Franklin attribute his success? What kind of advice does he offer to readers who want to model their life on his?

Comprehension: What is an "erratum"? Why does Franklin adopt this term?

Context: Benjamin Franklin and Jonathan Edwards were born within three years of each other, but, despite their similar ages, the two men had radically different perspectives and beliefs. Compare Franklin's *Autobiography* with Edwards's "Personal Narrative." How are these writers' views on morality, personal responsibility, human nature, and/or the limits of human knowledge similar? How are they different? How does Franklin both draw from and reject the Puritan tradition that was so important to Edwards?

Context: Examine the paintings and sculptures of Franklin featured in the archive. What different images of Franklin do these representations provide? If Franklin were choosing among them for an image for the cover of his *Autobiography*, which of the representations of himself do you think he would choose? Why?

Exploration: How did Franklin's *Autobiography* influence subsequent American autobiographies? How were his values translated and reinterpreted by writers like Frederick Douglass or Zitkala Ša?

J. Hector St. John de Crèvecoeur (1735–1813)

Although his writings evince a reverence for pastoral, quiet farm life, J. Hector St. John de Crèvecoeur led a restless existence marred by war, instability, and tragedy. Born in France to a privileged family, Crèvecoeur left for England as a young man and eventually traveled on to Canada. He worked as a surveyor in the French army during the French and Indian War and was wounded at the battle of Québec. In 1759, Crèvecoeur immigrated to rural New York, where he found employment as a surveyor, trader, and farmer. He married an American woman and became a naturalized citizen, adding the names "Hector" and "St. John" to his given name, perhaps in an attempt to seem more English. The outbreak of the American Revolution marred Crèvecoeur's idyllic farm life. Suspected of harboring Loyalist sympathies, he was persecuted and threatened by his neighbors. He tried to sail for France to escape harassment and to secure his children's inheritance, but both the English authorities and the Revolutionaries found him suspicious and made his departure difficult. After being imprisoned by the English, he was finally allowed to leave for France in 1780.

[1889] Paul Revere, *The Bloody Massacre Perpetrated in Kings Street Boston on March 5th 1770 by a Party of the 29th Regt.* (1770), courtesy of the Library of Congress [LC-USZC4-4600].

Once he had arrived safely in Europe, Crèvecoeur published a manuscript he had produced while in America. His book, *Letters from an American Farmer* (1782), was an account of rural life and travels through America told in the voice of a naïve, rustic narrator. These letters of "Farmer James" became popular in France and England and, trading on the book's success, Crèvecoeur became a minor celebrity. He was appointed a French consul to America and returned to New York in 1783. Tragically, he found his farm destroyed, his wife dead, and his children resettled in Boston. In 1790 he returned to France, where revolution and war once again tormented him. He lived obscurely in rural France until his death.

Although *Letters from an American Farmer* was initially read as a celebration of American culture and the American character, later generations of literary critics have puzzled over the exact nature of Crèvecoeur's attitude toward his adopted country. While his description of northern farm life is in some ways idyllic, later letters in the book engage the horrors of slaveholding in the South, the barbarity of the unsettled wilderness, and the terrors of revolution. A complex and ambivalent representation of American life, *Letters from an American Farmer* continues to challenge readers with its portrait of both the utopian and the dystopian possibilities of the nation.

TEACHING TIPS

■ Students tend to assume that the book's narrator, James, corresponds to Crèvecoeur himself and that *Letters from an American*

Farmer is an essentially autobiographical work. Be sure to make it clear to your class that James is an invented persona, and that Crèvecoeur sometimes uses the distance between himself and his narrator to produce ironic effects. You might focus on the horrific description of James's encounter with the tortured slave in Letter IX to make this point. How does the narrator react to the spectacle of the dying slave in the cage? Why doesn't he take any action to help the man? What are we to make of the line informing us that the narrator "mustered strength enough to walk away"? How does he interact with the owners of the slave when he eats dinner with them later that evening?

■ *Letters from an American Farmer* does not fall easily into a particular genre; it has been read as a travel narrative, an epistolary novel, an autobiography, a work of natural history, and a satire. To explore this question of genre and audience, ask students to imagine that they are Crèvecoeur's publisher and are responsible for marketing his book to eighteenth-century readers. Ask them to think about how they would describe and promote the book, and what readers they would hope to reach. Would the book be more interesting to Europeans or to Americans? How would they summarize the book for marketing purposes? Where would they shelve the book in a bookstore?

QUESTIONS

Comprehension: What kinds of problems does Crèvecoeur's narrator face in Letter XII, "Distresses of a Frontier Man"? How does this letter compare to the narrator's earlier descriptions of his life in America? What has caused the change in his tone?

Context: What answers does Crèvecoeur offer to the question he poses in the title of Letter III, "What Is an American"? What economic, social, religious, and racial qualities characterize an American in Crèvecoeur's view? How does his description of the American character compare to those offered by other authors in Unit 4 (Tyler, Franklin, or Emerson, for example)?

Context: How does Crèvecoeur describe Native Americans in *Letters from an American Farmer*? How do they fit into his ideas about who should be considered a true American? Why does his narrator contemplate living among the Indians in Letter XII? How does Crèvecoeur's description of Native American life compare to William Apess's account?

Exploration: For a text written before the nineteenth-century abolitionist movement, Letter IX contains an unusually graphic description of the shocking and terrifying abuses committed under the slave system. Why does Crèvecoeur include this description? What are readers supposed to make of his narrator's rather apathetic response to the horrible scene he encounters? How does Crèvecoeur's portrait of slavery compare to later, nineteenth-century accounts of slave abuse (texts by Frederick Douglass, Harriet Jacobs, or Harriet Beecher Stowe might make good comparisons)?

Thomas Jefferson (1743–1826)

President John F. Kennedy paid tribute to Thomas Jefferson's many accomplishments when he told a group of Nobel Prize winners that they were "the most extraordinary collection of talent, of human knowledge, that has ever been gathered together at the White House, with the possible exception of when Thomas Jefferson dined alone." Indeed, Jefferson's intellectual talents extended to a wide range of subjects and pursuits. He made important contributions to American culture as a writer, politician, farmer, horticulturist, inventor, book collector, art curator, architect, and scientist. His commitment to and eloquent articulation of ideals of liberty and justice (most famously in the Declaration of Independence) have made him a hero to many, while his ownership of slaves and sometimes disingenuous political rhetoric have disappointed others. As historian Joseph J. Ellis puts it, "The best and worst of American history are inextricably tangled together in Jefferson."

Jefferson was born into a prominent family in Albermarle County, Virginia. After his father's death in 1757 he was sent to the College of William and Mary, where he received an education in the classics as well as in eighteenth-century philosophy. Jefferson chose to pursue law as a career and studied with the influential legal scholar George Wythe. After setting up a successful law practice, he was elected to the Virginia legislature in 1769, thus embarking on his lengthy career in American politics. Jefferson soon became embroiled in the Revolutionary cause and published a fiery pamphlet on American rights. He also attended the Second Continental Congress as a strong advocate of independence. Jefferson was well known for his literary abilities, so he was a natural choice to serve on the committee selected to draft the Declaration of Independence. He accepted suggestions and editorial changes made by the committee and by the Congress (nervous congressional delegates removed his strong condemnation of slavery), but in essence the document is the product of Jefferson's pen.

After 1776, Jefferson returned to Virginia, where he was elected governor. While serving his term, he received a request for information about the land and culture of Virginia from François Marbois, a French diplomat. Jefferson composed the only full-length book of his career, *Notes on the State of Virginia*, in response. A comprehensive study of natural history, politics, and social customs, Jefferson's work attempts to make a scientific argument for America's potential as a land of freedom and prosperity. *Notes on the State of Virginia* contains insightful analysis of the natural world, intriguing political and social commentary, and some problematic racial stereotypes.

In 1784 Jefferson was appointed minister to France, and the years he spent abroad proved foundational to both his politics and his sense of aesthetics (he became enamored of French art and architecture). When he returned to the United States in 1789, he served as the first secretary of state under George Washington and later as vice president under John Adams. Jefferson's disagreements with Adams over the role of government in the new nation led to the formation of the first American political parties: Adams's Federalists and Jefferson's

[1196] Pendleton's Lithography, *Thomas Jefferson, Third President of the United States* (c. 1828), courtesy of the Library of Congress [LC-USZ62-117117].

Republicans. In what is sometimes termed the "Revolution of 1800," Jefferson defeated Adams and the Federalist Party to become the third president of the United States. He was the first president inaugurated in the new city of Washington, D.C., and during his term in office he oversaw the Louisiana Purchase and Lewis and Clark's expedition to the Pacific.

After the conclusion of his second term as president, Jefferson returned to Monticello, the elegant plantation he had built on his family lands in Virginia. In his final years, he helped found the University of Virginia and maintained an extensive correspondence with friends, acquaintances, and admirers in Europe and America. His productive retirement was troubled, however, by his enormous financial debts and his consciousness of the discrepancy between his professed political commitments and his position as a slaveowner. He died a few hours before John Adams on July 4, 1826, the fiftieth anniversary of the Declaration of Independence.

TEACHING TIPS

■ Students tend to view the Declaration of Independence as a kind of sacred document, forgetting that it was argued over and revised by the Second Continental Congress. Ask your class to examine the editorial changes to Jefferson's original draft indicated by the underlining and marginal notations featured in *The Norton Anthology of American Literature*. How did the Congress change Jefferson's original words? In what places did they tone down his language? Where did they make it stronger? In particular, you might focus on the removal of the passage condemning slavery (where Jefferson advances the unconvincing argument that the King set up the institution of slavery in America against the will of the white colonists) and the changes to Jefferson's indictment of "our British brethren."

■ Some background on Jefferson's vexed relationship with the question of slavery could enliven class discussion: Now that DNA tests have proven that he had children with his slave Sally Hemings, and that he held those children in slavery for most of his life, the discrepancy between Jefferson's belief that "all men are created equal" and the reality of his life as a plantation owner seems even more problematic. You should make it clear to students that Jefferson was by no means untroubled by the question of slavery—he sponsored unsuccessful political action to weaken or end slavery on several occasions and he devised elaborate architectural tricks at Monticello to disguise the slave labor that was foundational to its operations. But despite his discomfort with slavery, he never brought himself to free his slaves, nor did he free them after his death.

■ Ask one of your students to read aloud the speech that Jefferson attributes to the Native American chief Logan in Query VI of *Notes on the State of Virginia*. Jefferson (himself a notoriously poor speaker) once claimed that within the "whole orations of Demosthenes and Cicero and indeed in all of European oratory" one could not "produce a single passage superior to the speech of Logan." Ask students what

[1646] Anonymous, *The Providential Detection* (c. 1800), courtesy of Library Company of Philadelphia. Because Thomas Jefferson's beliefs were in accord with the religion and politics of the French Revolution, many Federalists believed him incapable of leadership as illustrated in this cartoon: the eye of God commanding the American Eagle to snatch away the Constitution of the United States.

[3679] Anonymous, *Daguerreotype photograph of Isaac Jefferson* (1847), courtesy of Special Collections, University of Virginia Library. Although he spoke out against the institution of slavery, Jefferson ran a large plantation through slave labor; recent DNA tests have provided conclusive evidence that Jefferson fathered children by his slave Sally Hemings.

[7781] Anonymous, *University of Virginia* (n.d.), courtesy of the National Park Service. Although Monticello is justly celebrated as an expression of Thomas Jefferson's aesthetic values, his true masterpiece is the design for the University of Virginia. Conceived of as an "academical village," the central campus of the university is composed of five neoclassical pavilions that housed five different branches of learning.

[9044] A. C. Brechin & Son, *Rotunda and Lawn, University of Virginia* (1911), courtesy of the Library of Congress [LC-USZ62-124456]. This early-twentieth-century shot shows the rotunda and lawn at the University of Virginia. Thomas Jefferson designed the university.

[9045] Anonymous, *University of Virginia, Pavilion VI* (after 1933), courtesy of the Library of Congress [HABS, VA,2-CHAR,1-O-]. This map shows the University of Virginia, Pavilion VI, East Lawn. A closeup can be seen at [9046].

[9047] Haines Photo Company, *Natural Bridge, VA* (1909), courtesy of the Library of Congress, Prints and Photographs Division [LC-USZ62-110212]. Sometimes dubbed one of the "Seven Wonders of the Natural World," Natural Bridge in Virginia has long attracted visitors. In his *Notes on the State of Virginia*, Thomas Jefferson called it "the most sublime of Nature's works."

kind of response they had when they listened to the speech. Why might Jefferson have chosen this as a model of oratory? What values does the speech uphold? What image of Native American culture does it provide? You might give students a summary of historian Hayden White's argument that the construction of the "Noble Savage" in America had more to do with debunking the idea of the superiority of hereditary aristocracies than with elevating "savages." Ask your students whether they think this theory illuminates Jefferson's discussion of Logan and whether it fits in with the rest of Jefferson's ideology.

QUESTIONS

Comprehension: What grievances against British rule are outlined in the Declaration of Independence?

Context: Examine the diagrams and photographs featured in the archive of the campus Jefferson designed for the University of Virginia. Why might Jefferson have chosen this design for his ideal "academical village," as he called it? What kind of educational space does the campus construct for its students? What values are reflected in its design? With these questions in mind, think about the design of your own campus or school. What do you think the architects of your campus had in mind when they planned it? How might their goals have been similar to or different from Jefferson's?

Context: Read the contextual material in "The Awful Truth: The Aesthetic of the Sublime" featured in this unit. Examine Jefferson's description of the Natural Bridge in Query V of *Notes on the State of Virginia* and then look at the image of the Natural Bridge featured in the archive. How does Jefferson describe the Natural Bridge? What effect does it have on him when he visits it? Why does he shift to the second person when he describes the Bridge's effects? Why does he view it as "the most sublime of Nature's works"? How does the Bridge compare to other natural or human-made wonders you may have visited (the Grand Canyon, the Rocky Mountains, the Empire State Building, the Hoover Dam, or Niagara Falls, for example)?

Exploration: The Puritans' Mayflower Compact, John Winthrop's "Model of Christian Charity," and the Declaration of Independence all function as early American articulations of shared values. How do these documents compare to one another? How did American values change over the course of 150 years? What does the Declaration, an eighteenth-century text, have in common with the Puritan documents?

Exploration: Sentences and phrases from the Declaration of Independence are often recycled in American political and cultural documents. Think of some instances when you may have heard the Declaration quoted. Which sections are quoted most often? Why? How do you think interpretations and uses of the language of the Declaration have changed since Jefferson's time?

Phillis Wheatley (c. 1753–1784)

One of the best known and most highly regarded pre-nineteenth-century American poets, Phillis Wheatley achieved poetic fame despite her status as an African American slave. Wheatley was kidnapped from West Africa (probably Senegal or Gambia) when she was six or seven years old, transported to America on a slave ship, and sold in Boston to the wealthy Wheatley family in 1761. Her mistress, Susannah Wheatley, soon recognized that her young slave was a remarkably intelligent, talented child and, apparently motivated by an unusual compassion and leniency, undertook the highly irregular project of providing her slave with an education. Phillis's domestic duties were curtailed and she quickly learned to read and write. Her exposure to Latin texts, and especially to English poets such as John Milton and Alexander Pope, provided her with models that profoundly influenced her subsequent work. The Wheatley family also instilled in Phillis a background in the Bible and in Christian tradition. Throughout her career, Phillis's evangelical Christianity was one of the most important forces in her thought and poetry.

In 1767, at the age of thirteen or fourteen, Phillis Wheatley published her first poem in *The Mercury*, a Newport, Rhode Island, newspaper. Three years later she composed an elegy on the death of the Reverend George Whitefield, the popular itinerant minister who had spread evangelical Christianity throughout the colonies. Published first in *The Massachusetts Spy* and eventually appearing in broadside and pamphlet form in New York, Philadelphia, Newport, and London, Wheatley's elegy for Whitefield brought her international recognition. Because her poetry was published as the work of "a Servant Girl . . . Belonging to Mr. J. Wheatley of Boston: And has been but 9 Years in this Country from Africa," Phillis's readers knew that she was an African American slave. By 1772, she had compiled a collection of twenty-eight poems that she hoped to publish as a book. Unfortunately, Wheatley's advertisements in the Boston newspapers seeking subscribers to help finance her proposed book yielded few patrons. With the help of Susannah Wheatley and the patronage of the Countess of Huntingdon, she then traveled to England, where her book, *Poems on Various Subjects, Religious and Moral*, was published by a British press in 1773. Though she was treated with great respect in London—important figures such as Benjamin Franklin, the Earl of Dartmouth, and the Lord Mayor of London hosted her during her stay—Phillis had to cut her trip short and return to Boston when she learned that Susannah Wheatley was gravely ill. Before her death in 1774 Susannah Wheatley granted Phillis her freedom.

[7388] Scipio Moorhead, *Phillis Wheatley, Negro Servant to Mr. John Wheatley of Boston* (1773), courtesy of the Library of Congress [LC-USZC4-5316].

Now independent of the Wheatley family, Phillis married John Peters, a free black man about whom little information is known. It is clear that the couple faced serious financial problems, forcing Phillis to work as a scullery maid in order to help support the family. Although she placed advertisements in an effort to fund a second volume of poetry and letters, she was never able to generate enough support to publish more of her work. She died in poverty.

Wheatley's poetry is characterized by a strict adherence to the con-

[1235] Ezekial Russell, *Poem by Phillis, A Negro Girl [of] Boston, on the Death of the Reverend George Whitefield* (1770), courtesy of the Library of Congress. Woodcut from the frontispiece of Wheatley's poem. An evangelical Christian, Phillis Wheatley drew heavily on religious themes for her work.

[1239] Phillis Wheatley, Frontispiece to *Poems on Various Subjects, Religious and Moral* (1773), courtesy of the Library of Congress. Wheatley was a respected poet in the late eighteenth century. Her work was resurrected by abolitionists just before the Civil War.

[1240] Phillis Wheatley, *To the Rev. Mr. Pitkin, on the Death of His Lady. [Signed] Phillis Wheatley, Boston, June 16th, 1772,* courtesy of the Library of Congress. Wheatley was greatly influenced by English poets such as John Milton and Alexander Pope. Her ability to master some of the conventions of their difficult styles was itself a form of protest against slavery.

[1241] Phillis Wheatley, *A Letter from Phillis Wheatley to Dear Obour. Dated Boston, March 21, 1774,* courtesy of the Library of Congress. Although Wheatley received great acclaim for her poetry, she was not able to find funding for her work after the death of her mistress, and she died in poverty.

[2734] David Bustill Bowser, *Rather Die Freemen than Live to Be Slaves—3rd United States Colored Troops* (c. 1865), courtesy of the Library of Congress [LC-USZ62-23098]. This regimental flag shows an African American soldier standing next to Columbia. Due to pressure on both the War Department and President Lincoln, black soldiers began serving in the Union Army beginning in 1863.

[6551] Kenyon Cox, *Columbia & Cuba—Magazine cover—Nude Study* (1898), courtesy of the Library of Congress, Prints and Photographs Division [LC-USZ62-68463]. An allegorical cover of an 1898 magazine, exemplifying the openness toward the human body of the late-nineteenth-century realists. The names of the women, "Columbia" and "Cuba," refer

ventions of neoclassical verse—that is, a reliance on carefully controlled iambic pentameter couplets and a focus on public, impersonal themes rather than personal self-expression. Some literary critics have understood the restraint and conventionality of her poetry as an indication that Wheatley lacked racial consciousness or was uninterested in protesting slavery. Recently, however, scholars have begun to find evidence that Wheatley actively addressed sociopolitical concerns and brought racial issues to the forefront in her work. Furthermore, since slaves were considered subhuman, Wheatley's ability to "master" the sophisticated style of neoclassicism itself functioned as a protest of slavery. Many of her poems contain pointed reminders to her audience that she is an African, and her celebrations of American ideals of liberty both implicitly and explicitly condemn African American slavery.

TEACHING TIPS

■ Ask students to read some passages from poems by Alexander Pope, the English poet who served as one of Wheatley's most important literary models (stanzas from *An Essay on Man* or *Imitations of Horace* would work well). Help them to analyze the construction of the heroic couplets Pope employed—that is, two sequential, rhymed lines in iambic pentameter—and ask them to pay attention to his ability to achieve rhythmic variety even while strictly adhering to this rigid metrical form. Have them then turn to Wheatley's poetry. Ask them to consider to what extent her work was influenced by Pope. How do the meter, rhythm, and thematic concerns of Wheatley's poetry both derive from and differ from Pope's model?

■ Wheatley made two revisions to her poem "To the University of Cambridge, in New England." Originally, the fourth line described Africa as "The sable land of error's darkest night," referring to what Wheatley perceived as the continent's paganism. The poem then went on to request the students at Harvard to "suppress the sable monster in its growth." In her revisions for the 1773 volume, Wheatley deleted the word "sable" from both lines, changing line 4 to "The land of errors, and Egyptian gloom," and altering line 28 to read "Suppress the deadly serpent in its egg." Provide students with a handout that delineates the revisions Wheatley made to her poem and ask them to think about the significance of her deletion of the word "sable." You might have them look up the etymology of the word in the Oxford English Dictionary in order to provide them with a clearer understanding of the connotations that "sable" would have held for eighteenth-century readers.

QUESTIONS

Comprehension: Examine the engraving of Phillis Wheatley that appeared in the 1773 edition of her *Poems* (reproduced in the archive). How does the portrait depict Wheatley? Why do you think her British publishers would have printed this picture of Wheatley, along with the caption describing her as the "negro servant of Mr. John Wheatley, of Boston," in the first edition of her book?

Context: In "To His Excellency General Washington," Wheatley refers to America as "Columbia"—a feminized personification of the "land Columbus found." While this designation of America as Columbia became commonplace in the years following the Revolution, Wheatley's use of the term marks its first-known appearance in print. Why might Wheatley have been interested in coining this description of America? How does she describe Columbia in her poem? What does the ideal of Columbia seem to signify for her? How does Wheatley's depiction of America as Columbia compare to other textual and visual representations of Columbia?

Context: In his efforts to support his arguments for the racial inferiority of black people in *Notes on the State of Virginia*, Thomas Jefferson famously dismissed the artistic merit of Wheatley's poetry: "Religion indeed has produced a Phyllis Whately [*sic*]; but it could not produce a poet. The compositions published under her name are below the dignity of criticism." Why do you think Jefferson felt compelled to denounce Wheatley in this way? What is at stake in his refusal to "dignify" her poetry with his criticism?

Exploration: Literary and cultural critic Henry Louis Gates Jr. has argued that Phillis Wheatley's poetry is enormously significant in that it "launched two traditions at once—the black American literary tradition *and* the black woman's literary tradition." How did Wheatley's poetry influence subsequent African American poets and writers, such as nineteenth-century writers of slave narratives or the poets of the Harlem Renaissance? How does her work deal with issues of gender? How do we reconcile Gates's claims for her status as a founder with the fact that Wheatley's work was largely forgotten after her death until abolitionists republished some of her poems in the mid-nineteenth century?

Royall Tyler (1757–1826)

Born into a wealthy Boston family, Royall Tyler would grow up to become the author of the first successful and widely performed American play. He entered Harvard at the age of fifteen and proved such a brilliant student that he earned baccalaureate degrees from both Harvard and Yale. After graduation, Tyler enlisted with the Boston Independent Company and fought intermittently in the American Revolution, eventually rising to the rank of major. When the focus of the war shifted to the South, Tyler's military duties abated and he turned his attention from the army to the law. He passed the Massachusetts bar in 1780 and soon established himself in a successful legal practice. He became engaged to Abigail Adams, the daughter of John Adams, but failed to impress the future president as a suitable match for his daughter. Adams apparently feared that Tyler's taste for

to the relationship of the nations during the Spanish-American War.

[7388] Scipio Moorhead, *Phillis Wheatley, Negro Servant to Mr. John Wheatley of Boston* (1773), courtesy of the Library of Congress [LC USZC4-5316]. Engraving of Wheatley seated at a desk, which appeared as an illustration in the 1773 edition of *Poems on Various Subjects, Religious and Moral.* By the age of fourteen, Wheatley had already published her first poem and was well on her way to publishing *Poems on Various Subjects, Religious and Moral,* which she traveled to Europe to promote.

[9019] Alexander Pope, *An Essay on Man* (1733), courtesy of *The Norton Anthology of English Literature,* Seventh Edition. The first stanza of Pope's *Essay on Man.* Phillis Wheatley emulated Pope's neoclassical style. Her mastery of this difficult meter was a form of protest against slavery.

[9020] Alexander Pope, *Imitations of Horace,* from *The Complete Poetical Works of Alexander Pope. With Life.* (c. 1886), courtesy of T. Y. Crowell & Co. The first two stanzas from Pope's "Imitations of Horace." Phillis Wheatley drew heavily on Pope's prosody, including his use of heroic couplets.

[9048] Deacon George Thomas, Figurehead of *America* (2002), courtesy of Claire Dennerlein and Paul Manson. Plaque on side of statue reads: "This figurehead is from the clipper ship 'America' built in 1874 at Quincy, Massachusetts, by Deacon George Thomas. In 1887 she was put on the Pacific coasting trade and was wrecked on San Juan Island in 1914." Seattle businessman and former mayor Robert Moran erected the figurehead at his resort in 1916 to commemorate the dying era of great shipbuilding in America.

literature and conversation indicated that the young man was "not devoted entirely to Study and to Business—to honour & virtue." Acquiescing to her father's wishes, Abigail Adams broke her engagement to Tyler and married her father's secretary instead.

In 1787, Tyler was recalled into military service, this time to help quell Shays's Rebellion, an insurrection of back-country farmers in Massachusetts who were resisting the government's economic policies, prosecution of debtors, and high taxes. After suppressing the rebellion Tyler was sent to New York City on official business. There

[4423] Anonymous, *The First Step* [*Godey's Lady's Book*] (1858), courtesy of Hope Greenberg, University of Vermont.

he attended the theater for the first time and developed what would become a consuming passion for plays. Inspired by the New York production of English playwright Richard Brinsley Sheridan's *The School for Scandal*, Tyler decided to write his own play, and, just over a month later, *The Contrast* was staged at the John Street Theater. Tyler's effort met with a warm response; the play received generally favorable reviews and was soon performed in other American cities. *The Contrast* is an important milestone in American literature because it was the first widely performed play that featured American characters and self-consciously promoted republican values and American patriotism. In early America, plays were often perceived as a morally questionable genre: Congress had banned theater during the Revolutionary War because it was "extravagant and dissipating," and in postwar society the stage continued to be dogged by its associations with dubious morality and hated British culture. Tyler met these criticisms head-on in his play, making his subject the "contrast" between virtuous, homespun American values (represented by the characters of Manly, Maria, and Jonathan) and foppish, insincere, European pretensions (represented by Dimple, Charlotte, and Jessamy).

Over the course of his long life, Tyler composed several more plays, as well as a number of essays and a novel. Literature was not a lucrative profession in the early nation, however, and he continued to support himself and his family by practicing law. He settled in Vermont in 1791, married in 1794, and rose to prominence as a professor of law at the University of Vermont and eventually as the chief justice of the state Supreme Court.

TEACHING TIPS

■ Have students read the review of *The Contrast* that appeared in *The New York Daily Advertiser* in 1787 (the text of the review is featured in the archive). The review, with its commentary on the acting and staging of the first New York production of Tyler's play, should help students recognize that eighteenth-century audiences experienced *The Contrast* as a performed spectacle rather than as a written text. Ask students to think about what the reviewer praised and what

he criticized. Why does he critique Maria and Manly's soliloquies? What values inform his claim that soliloquies "wound probability"?

■ Ask your students to assume parts and act out a scene from the play (the end of Act II, Scene 1 with Charlotte, Letitia, and Manly would work well, as would the concluding scene, Act V, Scene 2, which involves all of the main characters). Be sure that students have read through the play and the accompanying footnotes on their own before acting it out—the language and allusions can be obscure so you want to be certain that they understand the action and characters before performing the script. Ask students to think about which characters are the most enjoyable to play and which lines are the easiest to deliver. Is the play still funny? Why or why not? What are its most comedic aspects?

QUESTIONS

Comprehension: What is being "contrasted" in *The Contrast*? What values and characteristics mark some characters as more authentically "American" than others? What is "American-ness" being contrasted with in the play?

Comprehension: What does Maria's father Van Rough mean when he talks about "minding the main chance"? What does he seem to value in a son-in-law? How does his attitude toward marriage compare to Maria's and Manly's? Whose values win out in the conclusion of the play?

Context: The first reviewer of *The Contrast* declared that Tyler's characters "are drawn with spirit, particularly Charlotte's," but was disturbed by the "suddenness" of Maria's affections and by her "misplaced" song and soliloquy. What ideals of womanhood and femininity do Maria and Charlotte represent? Which of these women do you think best occupies the position of "heroine" in this play? Why do you think the reviewer found Charlotte such an appealing character? What are her faults? What are her virtues? How does she change over the course of the play? How do Charlotte and Maria relate to women portrayed in sentimental novels, such as the suffering Charlotte Temple or the evil Madame LaRue in Susanna Rowson's novel?

Context: Many literary critics have claimed that Colonel Manly is meant to be understood as a kind of George Washington figure. What characteristics relate him to George Washington? What kind of relationship to the military and to the Revolution does he have? What kind of relationship does he have with his sister? Why does Charlotte tease and make fun of Manly? What do you make of the fact that some of the humor of the play comes at Manly's expense? Why do you think Tyler named this character "Manly"?

Exploration: The character of the rustic, dialect-speaking Jonathan started a vogue in American literature for homespun "Yankee" types. Plays and novels from the early nineteenth century often feature naïve rural characters indebted to Tyler's portrait of the simple, sincere country bumpkin. Can you think of characters in nine-

TYLER WEB ARCHIVE

[3147] James Brown Marston, *The Old State House [Boston]* (1801), courtesy of the Massachusetts Historical Society. In this rare painting by the otherwise relatively unknown Marston, we see commerce at work in Boston's traditional center, only a few years after the seat of government had moved to the New State House on Beacon Hill. Royall Tyler hailed from the Boston of this era.

[4423] Anonymous, *The First Step [Godey's Lady's Book]* (1858), courtesy of Hope Greenberg, University of Vermont. These homespun Americans are similar to the characters in Royall Tyler's *The Contrast*, the first American comedy played in public by professional actors.

[5046] Gilbert Stuart, *George Washington* [Photograph of a painting] (1900), courtesy of the Library of Congress [LC-D416-29910]. The figure of Washington quickly became central to the new nation's understanding of itself. Colonel Manly in Royall Tyler's *The Contrast* may have been modeled after Washington.

[8565] Bruce Michelson, Interview: "Old World Ties" (2001), courtesy of Annenberg/CPB. Bruce Michelson, professor of English at the University of Illinois, Urbana-Champaign, discusses the relationship of the Old World to America, a theme that underlies Royall Tyler's *The Contrast*.

[9053] Candour, Review of *The Contrast*, from the *New York Daily Advertiser* (1787). This contemporary review of Royall Tyler's *The Contrast* was published in the *New York Daily Advertiser* in 1787.

teenth- and twentieth-century American literature, art, or film that bear a relationship to Jonathan? How have portraits of rural Americans changed over time?

Susanna Rowson (c. 1762–1824)

Susanna Rowson's colorful life story in some ways resembles one of the melodramatic plots of her popular novels and plays. Born in Portsmouth, England, Rowson was raised by her father and her aunt when her mother died shortly after childbirth. Her father, a lieutenant in the Royal Navy, received a commission in the American colonies and brought his daughter to live there in 1766. Rowson never forgot the physical discomfort of the harrowing ocean voyage that brought her to America (the ship was blown off course by a hurricane and then foundered in an ice storm off Boston Harbor). Settling in Nantasket, Massachusetts, the family enjoyed a comfortable life in the colonies until the Revolutionary War disrupted their situation. Because of her father's affiliation with English armed forces and his Loyalist sympathies, Rowson and her family became prisoners of war and were held under guard for three years until finally being sent back to England in a prisoner exchange. All of their property was confiscated by American officials.

Back in England, Rowson helped support her now destitute family by working as a governess and publishing novels and poetry. In 1786, she married William Rowson, a hardware merchant, actor, and trumpet player whose heavy drinking made it difficult for him to hold a job. When his hardware business failed, the couple decided to join a Scottish theater company and attempt to earn a living by acting. In 1793, believing they would find greater opportunities on the American stage, the Rowsons immigrated to the United States to appear with Thomas Wignell's theater company in Philadelphia. While William seemed to have difficulty holding down parts, Susanna played more than fifty-seven roles in two theatrical seasons and wrote several songs and plays for the company.

Rowson also contributed to the family's finances by arranging for the republication in 1794 of *Charlotte Temple: A Tale of Truth*, one of the novels she had originally published in England. (The novel first appeared in 1791 as *Charlotte: A Tale of Truth*.) The sentimental story of a naive English girl lured to America, seduced, made pregnant, and then abandoned there to die, *Charlotte Temple* struck a chord with American audiences and became the biggest best-seller in the nation's history until Harriet Beecher Stowe published *Uncle Tom's Cabin* over half a century later. As literary critics have noted, the book's power lies in its accessibility and appeal to a broad spectrum of readers; scholarship on inscriptions and marginalia found in extant eighteenth- and nineteenth-century copies of the book reveals that *Charlotte Temple* was owned by men as well as women and

[9059] William Waud, *Civilians Entering a Theater* (c. 1858–59), courtesy of the Library of Congress [LC-USZ62-15679].

by both wealthy and poor Americans. Although the tale is a rather formulaic example of a **seduction novel**—a popular genre characterized by its focus on a pathetic woman who has been seduced, abandoned, and left to die—*Charlotte Temple* touched its American readers profoundly. Many readers were so moved by Rowson's story and its purported status as a "tale of truth" that they refused to view it as a work of fiction. Thousands made pilgrimages to visit a gravestone in New York's Trinity Churchyard that was rumored to be Charlotte Temple's burial place.

Rowson did not own the American copyright to her enormously popular novel, so she made very little money off its best-seller status. In an effort to improve their financial situation, the Rowsons moved to Boston in 1796, where Susanna performed in the newly opened Federal Street Theater. In 1797 she retired from acting to start the Young Ladies' Academy of Boston, a prestigious school for girls. Dissatisfied with traditional textbooks used for girls' education, Rowson compiled her own spellers, geographies, and histories for her female pupils. Her school was unique in its progressive curriculum and commitment to providing young women with a serious and thorough education. The academy emphasized not only traditional female subjects such as music, drawing, and domestic economy but also subjects usually taught only to men, like mathematics and science.

Literary critics today disagree about the nature and extent of Rowson's feminist sympathies. While *Charlotte Temple* certainly evinces a tendency to view women as weak, helpless, and in need of male protection—its heroine is passive and dies after she is abandoned by the men in her life—the novel has also been read as subtly protesting women's tenuous position in society. Whatever the politics of her fiction, Rowson's own life was characterized by a resourcefulness that testifies to the possibilities for women's independent thought and action in eighteenth-century America.

TEACHING TIPS

■ In his book *Prodigals and Pilgrims*, cultural critic Jay Fliegelman argues that the cultural obsession with tales of female seduction in late-eighteenth-century America reflects the nation's anxiety about its own claims to virtue in its recent revolution against the "patriarchal authority" of England. Ask students what they think of this thesis and how it might apply to *Charlotte Temple*. You might explain that the figure of the seduced and abandoned woman became central to American fiction after the Revolution and that seduction stories usually ended formulaically with the tragic death of the long-suffering victim of seduction. Ask students to think about what this interest in female virtue and chastity might have signified in the new nation. How might a woman's "fall" from virtue be read as an allegory of the political and social conditions in the new nation?

■ Rowson frequently breaks into her narration of *Charlotte Temple* to address her readers directly, offering insights and defenses designed for the "sober matrons," "wise gentlemen," and "dear girls" she imag-

[3464] Harriet Beecher Stowe, *Uncle Tom's Cabin* book cover (1853), courtesy of the Institute for Advanced Technology in the Humanities, University of Virginia. *Uncle Tom's Cabin* outstripped Rowson's *Charlotte Temple* as the best-selling book of the nineteenth century. Both were sentimental novels, a genre that has traditionally been written by women.

[3472] Harriet Beecher Stowe, *Uncle Tom's Cabin*, cover (1892), courtesy of *Uncle Tom's Cabin* (Riverside Paper Series, No. 43), Boston: Houghton, Mifflin and Company, 1892. This cover of the classic *Uncle Tom's Cabin* shows a young African American boy holding a sign, which gives the title, subtitle, and author of the work.

[4060] Anonymous, *Led Astray* (1874), courtesy of the Library of Congress, Music Division. Illustration for sheet music, words by George Cooper, music by Violetta. Plots of seduction and abandonment and redemption of young women were a staple of sentimental fiction and were used as a quiet justification for women reformers.

[6749] Anonymous, *The New England Primer* (1807), courtesy of the Gettysburg College Special Collections. *The New England Primer* (first published in Boston in 1690) was a popular Puritan textbook designed to promote children's literacy and religious training. Dissatisfied with such traditional primers for her female students, Susanna Rowson developed her own textbooks.

[8934] Rafia Zafar, Interview: "Sentimental Novel" (2002), courtesy of Annenberg/CPB. Zafar, director of African and Afro-American studies at Washington University, St. Louis, discusses the conventions of the sentimental novel, with reference to Harriet Jacobs.

[9059] William Waud, *Civilians Entering a Theater* (c. 1858–59), courtesy of the Library of Congress [LC-USZ62-15679]. Susanna Rowson was a playwright and actress in Philadelphia and London and at the Federal Street Theater in Boston. She also wrote *Charlotte Temple*, which was the best-selling American novel until Harriet Beecher Stowe's *Uncle Tom's Cabin*.

ines make up her audience. Ask your students what effect these breaks in the narration have on their experience as readers of the novel. How does Rowson use her authorial voice to forestall criticism, heighten dramatic tension, and manage readers' reactions to her tale? You might have a student read Rowson's *Preface* aloud and then ask the class to analyze what kind of authorial voice she is presenting. What claims is she making for her story? What effect does she hope her novel will have? What tone does she adopt to address her readers?

QUESTIONS

Comprehension: How is Charlotte seduced away from her school? According to Rowson's narration, what decisions and personal qualities lead to Charlotte's downfall? What lessons does Rowson hope her readers will learn from her novel?

Context: Compare Charlotte Temple to Charlotte Manly in *The Contrast*. What ideals or stereotypes about womanhood do these characters exemplify? How do their relationships with "rakish" men turn out differently? What effect do you think the genre of each text has on its portrayal of these "fallen women" characters?

Context: In eighteenth-century America, many arbiters of taste condemned novel reading as a trivial or even dangerous occupation for young ladies to engage in. Thomas Jefferson, for instance, viewed novels as a "poison" that could "infect the mind" and warned that "a great obstacle to good education is the inordinate passion prevalent for novels, and the time lost in that reading which should be instructively employed." How does Rowson foresee and deflect this kind of criticism in *Charlotte Temple*? Do you think someone like Jefferson would have been convinced that Rowson's novel was in fact "wholesome" reading for young American women?

Exploration: *Charlotte Temple* was the first "best-seller" in American history; it had sold over 50,000 copies by 1812 and has gone through over two hundred editions in the course of its publishing history. The only other pre-twentieth-century American novel to circulate so widely was Harriet Beecher Stowe's enormously influential *Uncle Tom's Cabin* (1852). Why do you think these sentimental novels achieved such phenomenal popularity? What similarities of plot and narrative link *Charlotte Temple* and *Uncle Tom's Cabin*? To what kinds of people were these books designed to appeal?

William Apess (1798–1839)

William Apess composed the first published autobiography by a Native American. Born in Massachusetts, Apess was part of the Pequot tribe and claimed to count Metacomet, the Wampanoag leader known of the English as "King Philip," among his ancestors. Metacomet's courageous but unsuccessful resistance of the English settlers during King Philip's War (1675–78) probably made him an appealing historical figure to Apess, who devoted his own life to asserting and defending Indian rights.

Few details of Apess's life are known beyond those recorded in his 1829 autobiography, *A Son of the Forest*. Left by his parents to be raised by alcoholic and abusive grandparents, he was bound out as an indentured servant when he was very young. Apess lived with a series of white masters, but a combination of their unreasonable expectations and his own rebelliousness ensured that he never found a tenable situation as an apprentice or laborer. At the age of fifteen, Apess was converted to Methodism, an evangelical and radically egalitarian strain of the Protestant religion. Religious studies scholars have speculated that Methodism appealed to Native American communities not only because of its emphasis on equality, but also because its enthusiastic style and theology were more in keeping with Native American religions. Methodism was a controversial movement among European Americans, and Apess's involvement in ecstatic religious meetings did not sit well with his master. Encountering "persecution and affliction and sorrow" in his master's home, Apess ran away. He then enlisted in the army and served during an invasion of Canada in the War of 1812. In 1817, he returned to the Pequot community, where he soon began serving as a lay preacher. By 1829, the Methodist society had ordained him as a regular minister.

A Son of the Forest was published in 1830 in the midst of the national controversy over the Indian Removal Bill, the congressional act that legalized the federal government's decision to force Native Americans off their traditional homelands east of the Mississippi River. Apess's memoir implicitly challenges this injustice toward Native Americans by asserting Indians' humanity, worth, and potential, using his own life as an example. Conforming to some of the conventions of a spiritual conversion narrative, Apess's text situates his experiences within a Christian tradition and demonstrates his dedication to Christian values.

After the publication of *A Son of the Forest*, Apess became an increasingly outspoken critic of the wrongs white society perpetrated against Native Americans. In 1833 he published "An Indian's Looking-Glass for the White Man," an impassioned exposé of the disjunction between the rhetoric of white Christianity and the reality of whites' harsh treatment of Native Americans. In the mid-1830s, Apess also became involved in the Mashpee Indians' struggle for self-government and control over their own land and resources. (The Mashpee are one branch of Wampanoag Indians living in Massachusetts.) His efforts to publicize their case and to articulate their grievances helped them eventually win the right of self-governance from the Massachusetts State Legislature. Apess's final published work, the text of a lecture on King Philip that he delivered to a Boston audience in 1836, is a moving study of the history of white-Indian relations in early New England from the perspective of a Native American. Apparently exhausted by his efforts to fight for Indian rights, Apess stopped writing and publishing. Obituaries in New York newspapers report that he died of alcoholism.

[2121] Anonymous, *Goffe Rallying the Men of Hadley [in Defense of Indian Attack during King Philip's War, Hadley, Mass., 1675–76]* (1883), courtesy of the Library of Congress [LC-USZ62-75122].

APESS WEB ARCHIVE

[1236] John Eliot, *The Holy Bible Containing the Old Testament and the New. Translated into the Indian Language* (1663), courtesy of Annenberg Rare Book and Manuscript Library, University of Pennsylvania. Commonly known as "The Eliot Bible," this was the first Bible published in New England and appeared over one hundred years before the first complete English edition of the Bible was published in the American colonies. It is written in the language of the Massachuset and Wampanoag Indians. John Eliot, the "Apostle to the Indians," composed his text to serve the cause of Native American conversion to Puritan Christianity, putting his faith in Native American redemption through their direct exposure to God's word.

[2121] Anonymous, *Goffe Rallying the Men of Hadley* [in *Defense of Indian Attack During King Philip's War, Hadley, Mass., 1675–76*] (1883), courtesy of the Library of Congress [LC-USZ62-75122]. Villages in western Massachusetts were subject to attack by Indians during King Philip's War, an event that challenged the viability of English settlement in New England and led many to question why they had fallen so far from God's favor and to wonder at the potential coming of the Apocalypse.

[2469] John Foster, *Woodcut map of New England* (1677), courtesy of the American Antiquarian Society. This map is from William Hubbard's *The Present State of New-England, Being a Narrative of the Troubles with the Indians*, printed and published by Foster in Boston in 1677.

[8688] Arch C. Gerlach, editor, *Map of Early Indian Tribes, Culture Areas, and Linguistic Stocks*, from *The National Atlas of the United States, U.S. Dept. of the Interior, Geological Survey* (1970), courtesy of the General Libraries, the University of Texas at Austin. The Cherokee Nation originally lived in the southeastern part of what is now the United States, but after the unsuccessful petitions of the Cherokee Memorials, they were removed to present-day Oklahoma.

[9024] Samuel Occom, *A Sermon Preached at the Execution of Moses Paul, an Indian* (1772), courtesy of T. & S. Green. This was the first text written and published by a Native American in English. It went through ten editions in the ten years after it was published.

[9039] William Apess, *Eulogy on King Philip* (1837), courtesy of the Reed College Library. This eulogy defied the traditional white interpretation of King Philip and sought to highlight the wrongs perpetrated by the Pilgrims.

[9040] Anonymous, *Philip* [sic] *Alias Metacomet of the Pokanoket* (between 1850 and 1900), courtesy of the Library of Congress [LC-USZ62-96234]. This full-length portrait of Metacomet shows him holding a rifle, with other Indians and mountains in the background.

TEACHING TIPS

■ Review the history of King Philip's War with your students (the author biography of Mary Rowlandson and the context on "English Settlers' Views of Native Americans" in Unit 3 contain background on this topic). Ask them to consider why Apess might have been invested in claiming Metacomet as an ancestor. What qualities in Metacomet's history probably appealed to Apess? Why? How would Apess's perceptions of King Philip's War differ from white histories of the same event?

■ Ask students to pay attention to Apess's use of scripture in "An Indian's Looking-Glass." You might point out that he does not employ biblical quotations in the first half of his essay. Why does Apess use the Bible when he does? How does he use scripture to back up his arguments? What kinds of passages does he choose?

QUESTIONS

Comprehension: In "An Indian's Looking-Glass for the White Man" Apess claims that the Indians of New England are "the most mean, abject, miserable race of beings in the world." Why, according to Apess, has Native American society reached such a low point? What reasons does he give for the Indians' abjection?

Context: In the opening paragraphs of his "Eulogy on King Philip," Apess twice compares Metacomet to George Washington. Why do you think Apess would have been interested in likening his Native American ancestor to Washington? How does he compare the respective "American Revolutions" led by each man? What associations and sentiments might Apess have been trying to generate in his Boston audience?

Context: How does Apess's use of Christian values and biblical quotations in "An Indian's Looking-Glass" compare to Phillis Wheatley's use of Christian imagery and language in her poetry?

Exploration: Like Samson Occom, Apess trained as a minister and adopted white Christian values only to become frustrated by the disparity between Christian teachings and the harsh realities of white treatment of Native Americans. How does Apess's "An Indian's Looking-Glass" compare to Samson Occom's "A Short Narrative of My Life"? What experiences do they have in common? Do they use similar strategies to protest unfair treatment of Native Americans? How are their protests different? How do they characterize white prejudice?

Exploration: Apess was greatly influenced by the early Cherokee writers and the Cherokee struggle for their lands and for autonomy. Compare Apess's polemical works to the Cherokee Memorials. What rhetorical strategies do they share? What is the purpose of each work?

Ralph Waldo Emerson (1803–1882)

Ralph Waldo Emerson was the preeminent philosopher, writer, and thinker of his day, best known for articulating the **Transcendentalist** ideals of creative intuition, self-reliance, and the individual's unlimited potential. In contrast to the optimism that characterized his writings and philosophy, Emerson's own personal life was pervaded by tragedy. His father died in 1811, when Emerson was only eight years old, leaving his mother to struggle to support her five sons. After graduating from Harvard, Emerson suffered from serious eye strain and debilitating respiratory ailments. Later, he would live through the deaths of his beloved first wife, two of his brothers, and his eldest son.

Emerson also experienced career difficulties. He was unhappy in his first position as a schoolteacher, claiming that he was "hopeless" in the classroom. Leaving teaching to study theology, he was ordained in 1829, following nine generations of his ancestors into the ministry. As a Unitarian pastor, Emerson was part of a liberal New England religious movement which stressed the inherent goodness of humanity, the importance of reason and conscience over ritual, and the equality of all people before God. Eventually Emerson's role as a minister became a source of anxiety for him as he began to question church doctrine and to feel increasingly skeptical of revealed religion. In 1832 he resigned from the church and took a tour of Europe. There, he read widely and met with important intellectual and literary figures such as Coleridge, Wordsworth, Tennyson, Dickens, and Carlyle. Upon his return to the United States in 1834, Emerson used the legacy bequeathed to him by his deceased wife to embark on a new career as a writer and public lecturer. He settled in the quiet town of Concord, Massachusetts, where he lived with his second wife and received visits from a wide circle of friends and admirers.

Emerson's first book, *Nature* (1836), initially reached a relatively small audience, but the philosophy it articulated of the unity of souls, nature, and divinity functioned as a kind of manifesto for the group of intellectuals who came to be known as the Transcendental Club. Although the club was small and existed for only four years, it had an enormous impact on the development of American letters. It influenced such writers as Henry David Thoreau, Margaret Fuller, and Bronson Alcott, and it articulated ideas that inspired luminaries like Walt Whitman. As the leading figure in the Transcendentalist group, Emerson began to attract attention from a wider audience, especially after the publication of his *Essays* (1841) and *Essays: Second Series* (1844). "The American Scholar" and "The Divinity School Address," both lectures which were delivered at Harvard and subsequently published as pamphlets, brought him fame and some notoriety—"The Divinity School Address," in particular, was denounced for its outspoken criticisms of traditional religious educa-

[1029] Wilfred A. French, *The Old Manse* (n.d.), from F. B. Sanborn, *Emerson and His Friends in Concord* (1890), courtesy of Cornell University Library, *Making of America* Digital Collection.

[1029] Wilfred A. French, *The Old Manse* (n.d.), from F. B. Sanborn, *Emerson and His Friends in Concord* (1890), courtesy of Cornell University Library, *Making of America* Digital Collection. Ralph Waldo Emerson loaned his home at the Old Manse to Nathaniel Hawthorne for three years. This was one of his many efforts to encourage fellow authors.

[1030] Ralph Waldo Emerson, Letter, *Ralph Waldo Emerson to Walt Whitman* (1855), courtesy of the Library of Congress [LC-MSS-18630-5]. When this letter was written, Emerson was a well-known lecturer, and Whitman a young, aspiring poet. This is an example of Emerson's eagerness to support and encourage fellow writers.

[3662] Allen & Rowell Studio, *Ralph Waldo Emerson, Reading* (n.d.), courtesy of the National Portrait Gallery, Smithsonian Institution. Emerson was a prominent writer who articulated American ideals and celebrated the potential of the American individual. He supported the endeavors of such contemporaries as Hawthorne, Thoreau, and Whitman.

[3694] Thomas Cole, *The Falls of the Kaaterskill* (1826), courtesy of the Warner Collection of the Gulf States Paper Corporation. Cole was one of the first American landscape artists and a founder of the Hudson River School of painting. Romantic depictions of wilderness became popular as the United States continued its westward expansion.

[9037] Detroit Publishing Company, *Emerson House, Concord, Mass.* (1905), courtesy of the Library of Congress [LC-D4-11360 DLC]. Photo of Ralph Waldo Emerson's house in Concord, Massachusetts. Emerson moved here at the age of twenty-five and lived here for the rest of his life.

[9041] Christopher Cranch, *Transparent Eyeball* (n.d.), courtesy of Virginia Commonwealth University. Christopher Pearse Cranch was a contributor to such Transcendentalist publications as the *Dial* and the *Harbinger*, and he enjoyed drawing caricatures, such as this one, which satirizes Emerson's essay *Nature*.

tion, which Emerson found dogmatic. Despite the controversies provoked by some of his work, Emerson's impassioned calls for Americans to reject their deference to old, European traditions and to embrace experimentation were received with enthusiasm by a generation of writers, artists, and thinkers who strove to embody his ideals of American art.

Emerson continued writing to the end of his life, using his fame and influence to promote his own work as well as to support other writers. His endorsement of Whitman's *Leaves of Grass* (though he intended that endorsement to be private), his support for Thoreau's *Walden* project (Emerson allowed Thoreau to live on his land near Walden pond), and his loan of his home at the Old Manse to Hawthorne for three years were only the most famous of his many efforts to encourage fellow authors. Despite his activism on behalf of writers, Emerson was reluctant to become involved in any of the various social causes and reforms that enlisted his support. He eventually spoke and wrote on behalf of abolition, but his efforts came far too late to have much impact. He died in Concord, leaving a legacy of innovative thought and work that has had a lasting influence on the character of American letters.

TEACHING TIPS

■ Students sometimes find Emerson's work frustrating, overly abstract, and difficult to penetrate. You should reassure them that confusion is not an unusual response—one of the earliest reviews of *Nature* pronounced the book incomprehensible: "the effort of perusal is often painful, the thoughts excited are frequently bewildering, and the results to which they lead us, uncertain and obscure. The reader feels as in a disturbed dream." To help students overcome their confusion, you might read the "Introduction" to *Nature* with them, paying particular attention to Emerson's formulation of nature as the "Not Me." By dividing the universe into nature and the soul, Emerson was not claiming that these two essences have nothing to do with one another; rather, his point was that each particle of the universe is a microcosm of the whole. Be sure your students understand the concept of the microcosm. The key to Emerson's philosophy in *Nature* lies in his fundamental belief that everything in nature and in the soul is united in correspondence, that a universal divinity has traced its likeness on every object in nature, on every soul, and thus on every human production.

■ In order to help your students make connections and understand the important theological differences between various early American religious movements, provide them with copies of the chart below, or work on filling it out as a class on a chalkboard, overhead, or Power-Point slide:

Theological Principle	Puritans	Quakers	Deists	Transcendentalists
God is . . .				
Christ is . . .				
Man is . . .				
The Bible is . . .				
Man gets knowledge from . . .				
Man will be saved/will actualize his highest potential by . . .				

[9049] Ralph Waldo Emerson, *Divinity School Address* (1838), courtesy of rwe.org, The Works of Ralph Waldo Emerson. Emerson delivered this lecture to the senior class of the Divinity College of Cambridge. Emerson was himself a Unitarian minister for a period.
[9050] Ralph Waldo Emerson, *The American Scholar* (1837), courtesy of <rwe.org>, The Works of Ralph Waldo Emerson. Emerson addressed "The American Scholar" to the Phi Beta Kappa Society at Cambridge and stressed the importance of lived experience, especially for a scholar.
[9051] Ralph Waldo Emerson, *Nature*, Introduction and Chapter 1 (1836), courtesy of Project Gutenberg. The writing of *Nature* was interrupted by the death of Emerson's brother. Emerson's grief comes through in the essay with such thoughts as "nature is not always tricked in holiday attire, but the same scene which yesterday breathed perfume and glittered as for the frolic of the nymphs, is overspread with melancholy today."

■ Divide your class into groups and ask each group to put together a collection of their favorite aphorisms from Emerson's writings. Ask them why they chose certain statements and what they found particularly meaningful or illuminating about them. What kind of difficulties did they encounter in selecting aphorisms? Did members of the group disagree about which aphorisms to include? Is there a particular theme linking the collection of thoughts that they have put together? You might tell the class that literary critics have long debated how best to characterize Emerson's most basic "unit of thought." Ask them to weigh in on this question. How does Emerson organize texts? Does he develop his thoughts in sections, paragraphs, sentences, analogies? What kinds of insights do their collections of aphorisms provide into this question?

QUESTIONS

Comprehension: According to Emerson, what is "nature"?

Comprehension: Examine Christopher Cranch's caricature of the "Transparent Eyeball" featured in the archive. What passage from *Nature* is Cranch satirizing? What point do you think he is trying to make about Emerson's writing?

Comprehension: Emerson wrote, "A foolish consistency is the hobgoblin of little minds, adored by little statesmen and philosophers and divines. With consistency a great soul has simply nothing to do" ("Self-Reliance"). Why should great minds not overvalue consistency? Where in his own work does Emerson appear to be inconsistent?

Context: What kinds of cultural changes does Emerson call for in "The American Scholar"? How does his vision of American virtues and potential compare to Franklin's? To Jefferson's?

Context: Emerson opens Chapter 1 of *Nature* by pointing out that the stars afford humans insight into "the perpetual presence of the sublime." Review the explanation of the "sublime" featured in the context "The Awful Truth: The Aesthetic of the Sublime," and think about Emerson's relationship to this aesthetic movement. Why does Emerson open his book by invoking the idea of "sublimity"? What effect does he believe visions of sublime natural beauty have on viewers?

Exploration: By the end of his career, Emerson was undeniably a "public intellectual"—that is, his writings and lectures appealed to a general audience and not simply to professors or philosophers. Why do you think Emerson's work was appealing to a wide range of people? Can you think of current American thinkers and writers whom you would characterize as public intellectuals? What role do public intellectuals play in contemporary American society?

Exploration: What relationship does Transcendentalism have to traditional religious beliefs? Would you characterize Transcendentalism as a secular movement? Does it have anything in common with New England Puritanism? With Quaker doctrine? With Deism? (You can refer to the chart provided in Teaching Tips to work through these questions with students.)

[7129] Anonymous, *Margaret Fuller* (1840), courtesy of the Library of Congress [LC-USZ62-47039].

Margaret Fuller (1810–1850)

Margaret Fuller ranked among the most celebrated public intellectuals in her own day, an accomplishment that is especially remarkable given the social strictures and limitations women faced in the early nineteenth century. The foundation of her extraordinary career can be traced to the rigorous education she received from her father: under his tutelage she sometimes put in eighteen-hour days reading literary and philosophical texts in four languages. As her account of her early life in the "Autobiographical Romance" makes clear, Fuller developed into a prodigy but suffered emotionally in the absence of a normal childhood.

By her early twenties, Fuller had become integrally involved in the Transcendentalist movement, forming lasting intellectual and emotional relationships with men like Henry David Thoreau, Bronson Alcott, Theodore Parker, and, most importantly, Ralph Waldo Emerson. She was also involved in Brook Farm and can be found not too far below the surface of Nathaniel Hawthorne's character Zenobia in *The Blithedale Romance*. At Emerson's urging, she served as the editor of the Transcendentalist journal *The Dial* during its first two years of publication, overseeing submissions and sometimes writing the majority of its content herself. Because *The Dial* did not make money, Fuller supported herself during this time by leading "Conversations" for an elite group of educated Boston women. Fuller, frustrated that women were "not taught to think," designed her Conversations as discussion groups to encourage women to probe difficult questions and systematize their thinking in a supportive atmosphere. Fuller's charisma and her ability to draw out her students made the Conversations an enormous success.

The Conversations helped Fuller clarify her feminist ideas about the need to reform women's education and social status. In 1843, she articulated these ideas in a powerful essay for *The Dial* entitled "The Great Lawsuit: MAN *versus* MEN, WOMAN *versus* WOMEN." Arguing that women should be afforded the freedom "as a nature to grow, as an intellect to discern, as a soul to live freely," Fuller asserted that neither sex should be circumscribed by rigid boundaries or social expectations. She later expanded and revised the essay into the book-length study *Woman in the Nineteenth Century* (1845). The book was Fuller's most important and influential work, and, despite its unorthodox subject matter, it sold out its first edition.

In 1844, Fuller published her first travel account, *Summer on the Lakes*, a collection of essays about a trip to the Midwest. The book attracted the attention of Horace Greeley, who promptly hired Fuller as a paid columnist and literary critic for his newspaper, *The New York Daily Tribune*. Fuller spent two years living in New York, where she wrote nearly 250 reviews and essays for the newspaper. She produced astute critiques of literature and art, as well as reports on social issues such as poverty, prostitution, prison conditions, abolition, and the treatment of the insane. Fuller's growing interest in exposing contemporary social problems and suggesting practical, institutional reforms separated her from many members of the Transcendentalists, who tended to focus most of their energy on abstract theories or personal experience.

Fuller carried her interest in reform to Europe in 1846, when the *Tribune* sent her there as one of America's first foreign correspondents. Traveling through England, France, and Italy, Fuller met important writers, artists, philosophers and politicians of the day and sent her impressions back in her reports for the *Tribune*. She was deeply moved by Giuseppe Mazzini, the exiled Italian revolutionary who was working to unite his country under a republican government, and she traveled to Italy to report first-hand on the political instability in Rome. While in Italy, Fuller became romantically involved with Giovanni Ossoli, a Roman aristocrat much younger than herself. She gave birth to their son in 1848 while keeping their relationship secret from her friends and family. In the midst of this personal turmoil, Fuller managed to write regular reports of the Italian revolution for the *Tribune*, urging Americans to embrace the cause of Italian nationhood. She also became actively involved in the revolution, serving as a nurse during the siege of Rome. After the failure of the revolution, Fuller and Ossoli found their political and financial situation in Italy untenable and departed by ship for America with their infant son. Tragically, their ship foundered off the coast of Fire Island, New York. The entire family drowned.

The romantic story of Fuller's life and the accounts of her personal magnetism have tended to overshadow the importance of her written work. Generations of biographers, historians, and literary critics have frequently claimed that Fuller's dynamic personality and extraordinary experiences merit more interest than any of the texts she composed. Only recently have scholars begun to appreciate the stylistic sophistication and forward-thinking reformist agendas in her writing.

TEACHING TIPS

■ Ask students to consider why Fuller would have titled her essay "The Great Lawsuit." What kind of case is she pleading? Who are the principals involved in the "suit"? You might have the class read the first footnote to this essay in *The Norton Anthology of American Literature* to gain insight into what Fuller intended with the title. Ask your students whether they think they could stage this lawsuit as a mock court case. How might one try this case? Would it benefit from being performed? What would have to be changed or omitted from Fuller's original text?

■ Fuller was famous for her ability as a speaker and an interlocutor, a skill she marketed in the popular "Conversations" she ran for women in Boston. A student recalled her talent for facilitating discussion: "Whatever was said, Margaret knew how to seize the good meaning of it with hospitality, and to make the speaker feel glad, and not sorry, that she had spoken." Eventually the Conversations attracted so much attention that Fuller admitted men to the group. According to all in attendance, however, the inclusion of men disrupted the informal, hospitable atmosphere of the Conversations. As Emerson put it, the men apparently felt that they "must assert and dogmatize," and their more formal style of rhetorical debate silenced many of the female participants. After you provide students with this background information, ask them to think about Fuller's style of composition and argumentation in "The Great Lawsuit." How does she go about persuading readers to share her views? What kind of resolution does she seem to expect for her "lawsuit"? How does Fuller's model of argumentation differ from the masculine tradition that Emerson characterized as "asserting and dogmatizing"?

QUESTIONS

Comprehension: How does Fuller describe her relationship with her father in her "Autobiographical Romance"? How does she feel about the rigorous education she received?

Context: In Chapter 1 of *Summer on the Lakes* (included in the archive), Fuller describes her experience at Niagara Falls, a popular tourist destination in the nineteenth century. How does her initial emotional response to the Falls—"I felt nothing but a quiet satisfaction . . . everything looked as I thought it would"—relate to contemporary cultural ideals of the "sublime"? What kinds of expectations mediate her experience of the Falls? Why does she envy the "first discoverers of Niagara"? Does she ever come to feel the "sublimity" that she hoped to find in the scene? How?

Context: "The Great Lawsuit" echoes and builds on many of the ideas and values first articulated in Ralph Waldo Emerson's writings. How does Fuller's essay compare to some of Emerson's essays which also call for social and intellectual change among Americans ("The American Scholar" or "Self-Reliance," for example)? What ideals does Fuller have in common with Emerson? How is Emerson invoked in Fuller's writing style? How does Fuller extend Transcendentalist ideals in her discussion of the role of women in American society?

Exploration: How does Fuller's "Autobiographical Romance" relate to earlier traditions of American autobiography, such as Benjamin Franklin's or Frederick Douglass's narratives of their own lives? Does Fuller describe her development as a process of self-making in the same way that Franklin and Douglass do? How does her attitude toward literacy and education compare to Franklin's and Douglass's?

Exploration: George P. Landow, professor of English and art history at Brown University, argues that the sublime is "an aesthetic of power." For Landow, "the spectator of natural sublimity always experiences a situation of being overpowered by the size or energy of the sublime phenomenon, an endless desert, majestic mountain, raging ocean, or thundering waterfall: In the terms of descriptions of proper gender relations of the period, the enjoyer of the sublime, who is often described as being 'ravished' by the experience, takes an essentially feminine role. Under the influence of Edmund Burke who contrasted the bracing sublimity of masculine power to the relaxing effects of feminine beauty, sublimity became an explicitly gendered aesthetic category. Nonetheless, both men and women experienced it in the same way." Test Professor Landow's argument that men and women experience the sublime in the same way by comparing Fuller's experience of Niagara Falls in the first chapter of *Summer on the Lakes* with that of Nathaniel Hawthorne's male narrator in "My Visit to Niagara."

Suggested Author Pairings

JONATHAN EDWARDS AND BENJAMIN FRANKLIN

Born just three years apart at the beginning of the eighteenth century, Jonathan Edwards and Benjamin Franklin in some ways seem to inhabit different eras. Certainly Edwards's commitment to the Puritan beliefs of his ancestors and his passion for exploring his own spiritual nature is at odds with Franklin's secularism and practical drive for financial success and community standing. Nonetheless, both relied on and divergently engaged with their Puritan inheritance. For all his secularism, Franklin's commitment to virtue, thrift, and industriousness can be traced to Puritan values, while Edwards's brand of piety—though it is clearly based on strict Puritan models—is inflected with an almost Romantic interest in self-discovery. It might be useful to ask students to compare Edwards's "Personal Narrative" with Franklin's

Autobiography. While both men were interested in keeping track of their faults and cultivating their virtues, they take very different approaches to this project.

THOMAS JEFFERSON AND J. HECTOR ST. JOHN DE CRÈVECOEUR

Both Jefferson and Crèvecoeur grappled with the difficult question of what it meant to be an American at the end of the eighteenth century. Jefferson wrote a manifesto of American values in the Declaration of Independence, while Crèvecoeur laid out an answer to the broad question "What is an American?" in his *Letters from an American Farmer*. Crèvecoeur and Jefferson idealized agrarian life as the best expression of American values, though their cosmopolitanism and aristocratic tastes made both of them rather ironic spokesmen for agrarian simplicity. You might ask students to compare Jefferson's attempt to deal with the issue of slavery in his original draft of the Declaration with Crèvecoeur's narrator's problematic account of his meeting with a tortured slave in South Carolina.

ROYALL TYLER AND SUSANNA ROWSON

As writers of plays and novels, both Tyler and Rowson were targeted for participating in what were often considered trivial, immoral, and even dangerous genres. Ask students to think about how these two writers dealt with readers' and viewers' hostility toward their projects. Rowson frequently interrupts her narrative to address readers directly, while Tyler prefaces his play with a direct appeal to his viewers and includes a number of soliloquies in which characters address the audience. Both Tyler and Rowson take on the national obsession with female chastity—though their two Charlottes meet very different fates.

PHILLIS WHEATLEY AND WILLIAM APESS

As members of minority groups in the young nation, Wheatley and Apess offer poignant challenges to dominant views of who qualifies as an American. Wheatley's patriotic celebrations of American ideals in her poems are underlain with subtle critiques of the injustice of slavery and the difficulties of her own situation as an African American. Apess is much less subtle in his attacks on European American society—his "Indian's Looking-Glass for the White Man" is an openly angry protest against racial prejudice. Both Wheatley and Apess occupied difficult liminal positions in their respective societies. As a highly educated and cultivated woman, Wheatley lived a very different existence from other African American women and spent much of her early life among whites. As an ordained Methodist minister, Apess also found himself pulled between white culture and his own Native American community. Both Wheatley and Apess were profoundly religious and may have found Christianity appealing because of its potential to afford them equal status with European Americans as spiritual brethren in the eyes of God. They both draw attention in their work to the discrepancy between whites' professed beliefs about Christianity and the unfair treatment of racial minorities.

RALPH WALDO EMERSON AND MARGARET FULLER
Emerson and Fuller, good friends and lifelong supporters of one another's work, make an obvious pairing. They were both active in the Transcendentalist movement and frequently met to share ideas, discuss philosophy, and critique each other's work. But despite the fact that they shared important core beliefs about the power and potential of the individual, their writings have very different implications. In her eloquent case for the equality of the sexes, Fuller pushes Emerson's views in directions he never dared to go. Fuller's journalistic background and commitment to forwarding practical reforms also separate her from Emerson's more abstract and philosophical approach to the problems of American society.

CORE CONTEXTS

Every Man for Himself: American Individualism

Although the term "individualism" was not in general use until the 1820s, the foundational principles behind the concept were established by the mid-eighteenth century. Enlightenment philosophers like Newton and Locke argued that the universe is arranged in an orderly system, and that by the application of reason and intellect, human beings are capable of apprehending that system. This philosophy represented a radical shift from earlier notions that the world is ordered by a stern, inscrutable God whose plans are beyond human understanding and whose will can only be known through religious revelation. Enlightenment philosophy encouraged thinkers like Franklin and Jefferson to turn to Deism, a religion that privileges reason over faith and rejects traditional religious tenets in favor of a general belief in a benevolent creator. By privileging human understanding and the capacity of the individual, these new ideas reordered the way people thought about government, society, and rights.

The Declaration of Independence is emblematic of the eighteenth-century regard for the interests of the individual. Taking as unquestionably "self evident" the idea that "all men are created equal; that they are endowed by their Creator with inherent and inalienable rights; that among these are life, liberty, and the pursuit of happiness," the Declaration makes the rights and potential of the individual the cornerstone of American values. The fact that these lines from the Declaration are among the most quoted in all of American letters testifies to the power and resonance of this commitment to individual freedom in American culture. The Second Continental Congress affirmed the Declaration's privileging of the individual by making the signing of

[7259] Jean Leon Gerome Ferris, *Benjamin Franklin Reading Draft of Declaration of Independence, John Adams Seated, and Thomas Jefferson Standing and Holding Feather Pen and Paper, around Table* (1921), courtesy of the Library of Congress [LC-USZ62-96219].

[7065] Augustine de St. Aubin, *Benjamin Franklin, Ne a Boston, dans la Nouvelle Angleterre le 17. Janvier 1706* (n.d.), courtesy of the Edgar Fahs Smith Collection, Annenberg Rare Book & Manuscript Library, University of Pennsylvania.

[1495] John Neagle, *Pat Lyon at the Iron Forge* (1826), courtesy of Museum of Fine Arts, Boston. Reproduced with permission. © Museum of Fine Arts, Boston. Pat Lyon at the Forge, 1826–27; John Neagle, American (1796–1865). Oil on canvas; 93 3/4 x 68 in. (238.1 x 172.7 cm). Henry H. and Zoe Oliver Sherman Fund, 1975.806.

the document an important occasion. That is, by using the representatives' signatures as the means of validating this public document, they attested to the importance of individual identity and individual consent to government. John Hancock's famously large signature is thus a graphic emblem of the revolutionaries' commitment to individualism. Of course, the Declaration's assertion that "all men are created equal" conspicuously left out women and did not even seem to include "all men": when America achieved independence, many individuals found that their right to liberty was not considered self-evident. For African American slaves, Native Americans, and many others, the new nation's commitment to individual rights was mere rhetoric rather than reality.

But even though slavery and systemic inequality were an inescapable reality for many Americans, the nation nevertheless embraced the myth of the "self-made man" as representative of its national character. According to this myth, America's protection of individual freedom enabled anyone, no matter how humble his beginnings, to triumph through hard work and talent. One of the earliest and most influential expressions of this version of the "American dream" is Benjamin Franklin's narrative of his own rise from modest beginnings to a position of influence and wealth. So exemplary is Franklin's story that his *Autobiography* is often considered, in literary critic Sacvan Bercovitch's term, an "auto-American-biography." In other words, Franklin self-consciously uses the autobiographical form to foreground his narrative self-construction as an ideal American citizen. He repeatedly plays on the potential for self-making that print and authorship offer the individual, likening his own life to a book that can be edited, amended, and corrected for "errata." As he puts it in the opening lines of the *Autobiography*, "I should have no objection to a repetition of the same life from its beginning, only asking the advantage authors have in a second edition to correct some faults of the first." Franklin's conception of self thus hinges on the idea that the individual is the author of his own life, with full power to construct it as he wills. Franklin's presentation of himself as the ideal American individual was widely accepted. While he lived in France, he was celebrated as the embodiment of the virtue, naturalism, and simplicity that supposedly characterized the New World—an image he carefully maintained by shunning French fashion to dress plainly and wearing a primitive fur hat around Paris. So effective was Franklin's physical self-presentation that he became a kind of cult figure in France. Paintings, prints, busts, medallions, clocks, vases, plates, handkerchiefs, and even snuffboxes were manufactured emblazoned with Franklin's portrait. His American individualism had become a popular commodity.

By the nineteenth century, many Americans were more radical in their commitment to individualism. A growing concern over the people left out of the American dream fueled reform movements designed to extend individual rights to the historically disenfranchised and oppressed. Calls for the abolition of slavery, Native American rights, women's rights, prison reform, and help for the impoverished challenged American society to make good on its proclamation that all people are created equal. The industrialism that was transforming the American workplace became increasingly troubling to reformers, who felt that factories were stifling individual creativity and self-expression. As social critic Albert Brisbane put it in 1840, "Monotony, uniformity, intellectual inaction, and torpor reign . . . society is spiritually a desert." Ralph Waldo Emerson agreed, warning that "society everywhere is in conspiracy against the manhood of every one of its members . . . the virtue in most request is conformity."

Emerson's remedy for this stifling conformity was a radical call for self-reliance. His essay on this subject, "Self-Reliance," is a manifesto of what has come to be called **Romantic Individualism**. More radical and more mystical than Enlightenment ideas about individualism, Romantic Individualism asserts that every individual is endowed with not only reason but also an intuition that allows him to receive and interpret spiritual truths. Individuals thus have a responsibility to throw off the shackles of traditions and inherited conventions in order to live creatively according to their unique perception of truth. Emerson's intoxicating ideas about the power of the individual captivated many of his contemporaries, giving rise to the Transcendentalist movement (the group believed that only by *transcending* the limits of rationalism and received tradition could the individual fully realize his or her potential). Writers and thinkers like Margaret Fuller, Bronson Alcott, Theodore Parker, and Henry David Thoreau heeded Emerson's call and built on his ideas. Fuller pushed Romantic Individualism in the direction of women's rights, while Thoreau (Unit 12) embarked on a personal project to practice self-reliance by living alone in the woods at Walden Pond, free from the suffocating influences of modern commercial and industrial life.

QUESTIONS

Comprehension: According to the Declaration of Independence, what human rights are self-evident? What beliefs underlie Jefferson's use of the term "self-evident"?

Comprehension: How was Emerson's philosophy of individualism different from Enlightenment ideas about individualism?

Comprehension: What is Transcendentalism?

Context: How do texts by Phillis Wheatley and William Apess respond to and challenge traditional ideas of individualism? Are the same modes of autobiographical self-making that Franklin exploited available to them? Why or why not?

Context: Emerson claimed that, in stifling individualism, "society everywhere is in conspiracy against the manhood of every one of its members." What, for Emerson, does "manhood" have to do with individuality and nonconformity? How might you read Margaret Fuller's "The Great Lawsuit" essay as a response to this comment?

Context: Although Jefferson was clearly indebted to John Locke for much of the philosophy behind the Declaration of Independence, he did not borrow the Lockean ideal of "life, liberty, and property" but instead substituted "the pursuit of happiness" for "property." What do you think Jefferson meant by "the pursuit of happiness"? Why did he use this phrase?

Exploration: What rights are or should be guaranteed to an individual in American society? Is the government ever justified in curtailing those rights? Why or why not?

Exploration: Can you think of examples in contemporary American culture that testify to the persistence of the myth of the self-made man (or woman)? How do news programs, novels, television shows, and movies perpetuate the contemporary ideal of the self-made individual? What do current figures of the self-made American have in common with Franklin? In what ways are they different?

Exploration: Compare the Declaration of Independence with the Plymouth colonists' Mayflower Compact and Winthrop's "Model of Christian Charity." How does the Declaration's vision of the role of the individual within American society compare to these Puritan documents' assumptions about the place of the individual in America?

A New Rome: Neoclassicism in the New Nation

In Act III of Royall Tyler's *The Contrast*, the model American character, Colonel Manly, delivers an impassioned soliloquy: "When the Grecian states knew no other tools than the axe and the saw, the Grecians were a great, a free, and a happy people. . . . They exhibited to the world a noble spectacle—a number of independent states united by a similarity of language, sentiment, manners, common interest, and common consent." Manly's speech may sound strange to modern readers since his disquisition on ancient Greece seems to have little to do with the play's setting in eighteenth-century New York. Indeed, even the first reviewer of Tyler's play complained that the soliloquy seemed out of place: "A man can never be supposed in conversation with himself, to point out examples of imitation to his countrymen." Yet Tyler's seemingly unmotivated inclusion of comments on ancient Greece in his play was perfectly in keeping with the fascination with classical antiquity that characterized the early national period. In the late eighteenth and early nineteenth centuries, the United States, in search of foundational models to replace its former reliance on Great Britain, turned to examples from the ancient world, particularly the Roman republic, and, to a lesser extent, ancient Greece. Americans associated classical Greece and Rome with the virtuous, anti-aristocratic political and cultural ideals they hoped would prevail in the United States. Ancient Romans founded the first **republic**—a representational government in which power is held by the people and representatives are charged with the common welfare of all the people in the country— and Americans were anxious to emulate this model. Their growing interest in the art and culture of the ancient world was part of an aesthetic movement known as **neoclassicism**. The American neoclassical ideal did not entail a lavish imitation of ancient forms but rather demanded a modern interpretation and revitalization of old forms.

Neoclassicism may have found its most congenial home in the political climate of the new United States, but it did not originate there. The neoclassical aesthetic arose in Europe around the middle of the eighteenth century, an irony that many Americans, who wished to believe they were rejecting European examples, chose to ignore. In any case, classical models caught on quickly in the early republic. By the end of the eighteenth century, American newspapers and almanacs regularly quoted lines from Horace and Virgil. Correspondents to these periodicals often signed their pieces with Roman pseudonyms. (The authors of the Federalist Papers—Alexander Hamilton, John Jay, and James Madison—famously adopted the pen name "Publius" in honor of one of the founders and consuls of republican Rome.) George Washington was so fascinated by the self-sacrificing Roman patriot Cato that he had a play about him staged at Valley Forge to entertain and educate the American troops. After the Revolution, American army officers formed an honorary society named after the Roman hero Cincinnati. Even the names of some of the branches of government—"Senate" and "Congress," for example—hearkened back to the ancient Roman republic.

Neoclassical ideals also permeated American art and architecture. Artists eagerly adopted Roman models, creating statues of political and military leaders like George Washington wearing togas and crowned with laurel wreaths. Influenced by archaeological discoveries in Greece, Rome, and Egypt, furniture makers like Charles Honore Lannuier and Duncan Phyfe created pieces that incorporated classical motifs and design. But it was in architecture that the American neoclassical aesthetic achieved its best expression, a fact that was largely the result of Thomas Jefferson's commitment to infusing American buildings with classical principles of order and reason. Jefferson's passion for architecture was reinforced by his experiences in Paris, where he lived as the American minister to France from 1785 until 1789. Impressed both by the beautiful new houses built in Paris in the late eighteenth century and by ancient structures such as the Maison Carée (a Roman temple in Nîmes), Jefferson was anxious to reproduce and translate the French neoclassical aesthetic into American buildings.

When the Virginia legislature called upon him to find a designer for the Virginia State House, Jefferson decided to design the building himself. He created a neoclassical temple based on the model of the Maison Carée, thus symbolically infusing the site of the Virginia state government with ancient republican values of harmony and simplicity. Jefferson also modeled his own gracefully proportioned home, Monticello, on classical principles. A record of Jefferson's varied architectural ideas, Monticello was designed and redesigned many times in accord with its owner's ever-changing interests. In its final form, the house was built to resemble a single-story dwelling, even though it has two floors, and was divided into public and private areas arranged around a central parlor. Situated on an immense hill, Monticello commands an expansive view of the surrounding landscape, its central

[1639] Charles St. Memin, *George Washington* (1800), courtesy of the Library of Congress [LC-USZC4-4619].

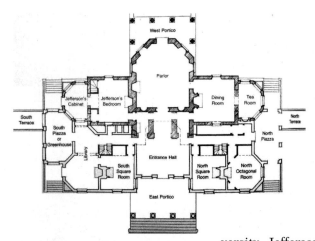

[1331] Thomas Jefferson, *Monticello Floor Plan* (n.d.), courtesy of the Thomas Jefferson Foundation.

"A NEW ROME"
WEB ARCHIVE

[1186] Christopher Pearse Cranch, *U.S. Capitol* (c. 1841), courtesy of the Architect of the Capitol. Washington, DC, was conceived of as a grand neoclassical city composed of orderly avenues and imposing government buildings. The White House and the Capitol were the first to be designed and constructed, though each took longer to complete than expected and neither is a true example of neoclassicism.
[1331] Thomas Jefferson, *Monticello Floor Plan* (n.d.), courtesy of the Thomas Jefferson Foundation. A record of Jefferson's varied architectural ideas, Monticello was designed and redesigned many times in accord with its owner's changing interests. In its final form, the house resembled a single-story dwelling, even though it has two floors, and was divided into public and private areas arranged around a central parlor.
[1639] Charles St. Memin, *George Washington* (1800), courtesy of the Library of Congress [LC-USZC4-4619]. Painting of Washington crowned by a laurel wreath, modeled after portraits of such classical Roman leaders as Julius Caesar.
[3700] John Plumbe, *Capitol's East End before Extension* (1846), courtesy of the

dome acting as a sort of symbolic eye asserting control and mastery over the countryside beneath it. Although Monticello is justly celebrated as an expression of Jefferson's aesthetic values, his true masterpiece is the design for the University of Virginia. Conceived of as an "academical village," the central campus of the university is composed of five neoclassical pavilions which housed five different branches of learning, along with a central domed "temple of learning" (based on the Pantheon in Rome) which housed the main library. Jefferson intended teachers and students to live together in this complex, working and residing in an integrated expression of the educational mission of the university. Jefferson also had an important hand in the design of Washington, D.C., the new federal city created as the site of the national government. Because the city was built from scratch on a rural landscape, Jefferson and the other planners were able to plan it as a carefully designed exercise in neoclassical order and harmony. Although bureaucratic disorganization, a lack of funding, and land use problems prevented the project from ever living up to its designers' visions, Washington, D.C., was conceived of as a grand neoclassical city made up of orderly avenues and imposing government buildings. The White House and the Capitol Building were the first to be designed and constructed, though each took longer to complete than expected and neither is a true example of neoclassicism. Noted neoclassical architect Benjamin Henry Latrobe, however, used his influence to add an American neoclassical touch to the Capitol once he was appointed Surveyor of Public Buildings in 1803. When he designed columns for the Senate wing and Senate rotunda, Latrobe Americanized the classical forms by substituting cornstalks and tobacco leaves for the traditional Corinthian acanthus decorations on the capitals of the columns. Latrobe's celebrated "corncob and tobacco capitals" exemplify the ideals behind American neoclassicism: they borrow from classical sources with originality and freedom, combining the stateliness of a traditional form with a tribute to American agriculture and natural productions. Although Latrobe certainly did not intend it, the agricultural decorations on the Senate building also serve to remind viewers that, just as Greece was a city-state whose economy was indebted to the institution of slavery, so was America's economy built on the slave labor that produced tobacco, cotton, rice, and sugar crops.

QUESTIONS

Comprehension: Why did so many Americans celebrate classical Greek and Roman traditions and aesthetics? What characteristics of ancient Greece and Rome made them appealing models to the young nation?

Comprehension: What is neoclassicism?

Comprehension: Examine the photographs and design plans for

Monticello and the University of Virginia featured in the archive. What do Jefferson's architectural projects have in common? What ideals inform the design of the campus? What kind of educational environment was Jefferson trying to construct at the university? How might the ideals that structure the buildings he designed be reflected in the Declaration of Independence, which is, in a sense, an "architectural plan" for the government of the new nation?

Context: Phillis Wheatley's poetry is often categorized as "neoclassical." What literary characteristics might make her work analogous to the neoclassical artifacts featured in the archive?

Context: The early American republic, like Greek democracy, was based on "equality," but for both communities equality could mean either (a) *isotes*: "proportionate equality or harmony," or (b) *isonomia*: "equal participation, the order of equality." For those who believed in *isotes*, one's rights and privileges were proportional to one's merits, rather than distributed in common shares to all members of society. Which of the writers in this unit believe in which kind of equality? What reasoning is behind their beliefs, and how do you know? Which of these values are reflected in neoclassical buildings such as Monticello and the University of Virginia? To what extent is our contemporary society based on either *isotes* or *isonomia*?

Context: Examine the original plans for Washington, D.C., featured in the archive. How does the design of the city uphold neoclassical ideals? Now examine the photographs and maps of present-day Washington, D.C. To what extent does the contemporary city live up to the plans of its designers? How does it diverge from them?

Exploration: Think about the designs and constructions for some contemporary American public buildings and/or monuments that you have seen (the Vietnam memorial, urban museums and skyscrapers, or government buildings, for example). What values do these examples of twentieth- and twenty-first-century public architecture reflect? How do these structures compare to eighteenth-century neoclassical structures?

Exploration: While the Puritans believed that they were constructing a "new Israel" or a "new Jerusalem" in America, many Revolutionary-era leaders believed they were constructing a "new Rome." How do these models differ from each other? What values are inherent in structuring a society as a rebuilding of Jerusalem? Of Rome? Can you think of any other historical periods or cities that have served as models for the American nation?

Mammoth Nation: Natural History and National Ideals

When Benjamin Franklin was abroad in England as a young man, he discovered that Europeans were fascinated by some of the natural "curiosities" he had brought over from the New World. Indeed, his "asbestos purse"—a clump of fibrous material that was impervious to fire—so interested a wealthy nobleman that it procured Franklin an

Library of Congress [LC-USZC4-3595]. Photograph of the U.S. Capitol Building, showing classical columns and frieze.

[6821] Robert King, *A Map of the City of Washington in the District of Columbia* (1818), courtesy of the Library of Congress. The city that L'Enfant had originally conceived of as "Washingtonople" had undergone many changes by the year that this map was drawn, including repairs made necessary by the War of 1812.

[7378] John Collier, *Monticello, Home of Thomas Jefferson. Charlottesville, VA* (1943), courtesy of the Library of Congress, Prints and Photographs Division [LC-USW36-756]. Monticello, which means "little mountain" in Italian, was a lifelong passion for Jefferson. The house is an excellent example of Roman neoclassicism, with its columned porticoes and classical central dome.

[7772] John Trumbull, *General George Washington Resigning His Commission* (c. 1823), courtesy of the U.S. Capitol Rotunda, Architect of the Capitol. On December 23, 1783, Washington resigned as commander-in-chief, and thereby established civilian, rather than military, leadership of the government.

[7781] Anonymous, *University of Virginia* (n.d.), courtesy of the National Park Service. Although Monticello is justly celebrated as an expression of Jefferson's aesthetic values, his true masterpiece is the University of Virginia.

[9025] E. Sachse & Company, *View of the University of Virginia, Charlottesville & Monticello, Taken from Lewis Mountain* (1856), courtesy of the Library of Congress [G3884.C4:2U5A35 1856.E2 Vault]. This panoramic view of the University of Virginia and its surroundings emphasizes Jefferson's classically influenced architectural style.

[9033] Peter Charles L'Enfant, *Plan of the City Intended for the Permanent Seat of the Government of the United States* (1791), courtesy of the Library of Congress [G3850 1791.L4 1887]. L'Enfant claimed that his plan for the capital city was "whol[l]y new"; it incorporated radiating avenues to connect significant focal points with open spaces and a grid of streets to be oriented north, south, east, and west.

invitation to the aristocrat's home and a substantial monetary reward. Similarly, Farmer James, the character who narrates Crèvecoeur's *Letters from an American Farmer*, is asked to give an account of American natural and agricultural history as well as American social customs in his correspondence with Mr. F. B., a European nobleman. It seemed that the national flora and fauna could afford a kind of cultural prestige, proving to Europeans, as well as to Americans themselves, the importance and worth of the very land upon which the new nation was situated. Eventually, many Americans came to tie their national pride to the landscape and wilderness, believing that a correlation existed between the strength and vigor of American nature and the strength and vigor of American society.

Thomas Jefferson illustrates the symbolic connection between American nature and the American nation in his "Query VI: Productions Mineral, Vegetable, and Animal" from *Notes on the State of Virginia*. Here he discusses American "natural productions" in order to refute the claims of French naturalist and writer Georges de Buffon, who had argued in his *Natural History of the Earth* that American plants, animals, and even people were inferior to European natural specimens. According to Buffon, "nature is less active, less energetic on one side of the globe than she is on the other," and American nature was weaker, smaller, less diverse, and more prone to degeneration than European nature. Outraged by this insult to America's worth and potential, Jefferson set out to prove, through long lists of statistics and scientific observation, that American natural productions were not simply equal to their European equivalents but actually superior to them. Jefferson includes detailed tables of all of the useful minerals, plants, and trees that exist in America and the relative weights of various animals and birds found in Europe and America. Not content to apply his hypothesis "to brute animals only," he goes on to dismiss Buffon's claim that the "savages" of North America were feeble and mentally inferior by arguing for the vigor and creativity of Indians. Although Jefferson intended to defend Native Americans from Buffon's slanders, his analysis participates in the Eurocentric assumption that Indians were "uncivilized." By categorizing Native Americans as "natural productions" on par with the animals and plants that he exhaustively lists and describes, Jefferson treats them as a homogeneous group waiting to be classified by white scientists. Later in the essay, Jefferson also addresses Buffon's claim that Europeans who relocate to America degenerate in their mental and artistic abilities, insisting that the American climate has "given hopeful proofs of genius."

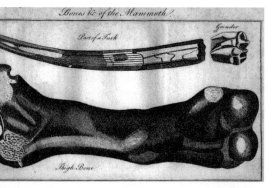

[7342] William Winterbotham, *Bones of the Mammoth* (1795), courtesy of Special Collections Research Center, University of Chicago Library.

But Jefferson finds his most compelling evidence for the superiority of the American environment in the existence of the "mammoth" or "mastodon," a giant quadruped six times the size of an elephant, whose bones had been found in some fossil pits. Insisting that the mammoth was not extinct and still roamed in the western territories (when he sent the Lewis and Clark expedition to the Pacific in 1804, Jefferson believed they would locate a live mammoth), Jefferson saw the existence of this enormous animal as proof of American superiority and uniqueness. Although the mastodon eventually proved to be an extinct, herbivorous creature, eighteenth-century Americans, in awe of the enormous teeth found on the fossilized mammoth jawbones, assumed that it had been a formidable carnivore. This investment in the fierceness and power of the mastodon testifies to the American desire to showcase an impressive, even frightening, natural specimen that would be superior in size and power to any creature found in Europe.

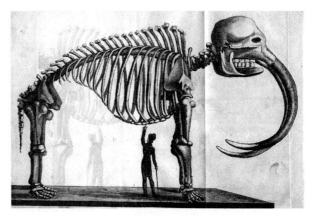

[7343] Thomas Ashe, *Skeleton of the Young Mammoth in the Museum at Philadelphia* (1806), courtesy of Special Collections Research Center, University of Chicago Library.

In 1801, Jefferson's hopes for further evidence of the mastodon were fulfilled when a pit of fossilized mammoth bones was discovered on a farm in upstate New York. His friend, the painter, inventor, naturalist, museum curator, and businessman Charles Willson Peale, immediately set out to exhume the bones and assemble a complete mastodon skeleton. Peale hired more than twenty-five men to help him with the labor of digging out the bones, transported the skeleton to Philadelphia, enlisted sculptor William Rush to create wooden models of missing bones, and finally assembled a complete skeleton. Considered a "wonder" and a "curiosity," the mastodon skeleton attracted a great deal of attention both in America and in Europe. Peale traveled with it, sold tickets to view it, and even auctioned off opportunities to eat dinner within the skeleton. He eventually brought it back to Philadelphia and made it the centerpiece of his museum of natural history there.

Peale's museum, housed for a time in Independence Hall, was itself an expression of the conjunction of national ideals and natural history. Intended to be a "world in miniature," Peale's collection of preserved natural specimens was carefully arranged to instruct spectators in the harmonious structure of nature. The museum did its best to reflect the diversity of the natural world: it housed 1824 birds, 250 quadrupeds, and 650 fish, all preserved through Peale's special taxidermy technique and all displayed against painted backdrops designed to evoke their natural environments. Tickets to the museum urged visitors to "explore the wondrous work!" presumably alluding both to the divine creation of the natural world represented in the museum and to Peale's labor in collecting and organizing the objects on display. Significantly, the walls of the museum were surmounted by a large collection of portraits of American politicians and leaders. (Peale had originally hoped to display mummified corpses of important men as specimens of the "highest order of nature," but when this proved impossible he settled for painted images.) The museum was meant to visually reinforce the idea that the world is organized by a "great chain of being," a universal hierarchy in which all existence is arranged from

[9029] T. W. Ingersoll, *U.S. Smithsonian Institute—Interior View* (1888), courtesy of the Library of Congress [LC-USZ62-95631]. Photograph of a dinosaur skeleton and various stuffed animals in the Museum of Natural History.

[9030] Thomas Jefferson, Query VI, from *Notes on the State of Virginia* (1785), courtesy of XRoads Virginia. This Query describes the animals and people native to North America and defends against the charge that North American natural resources were inferior to those of Europe.

[9031] Anonymous, *Captain Lewis & Clark Holding a Council with the Indians* (1810), courtesy of the Library of Congress [LC-USZ62-17372]. This etching shows Lewis and Clark standing over a council of Native Americans; it originally appeared in an 1810 book entitled *A Journal of the Voyages and Travels of a Corps of Discovery*.

[9042] Laura Arnold, "The Great Chain of Being" (2003), courtesy of Laura Arnold. From the beginning of the Middle Ages through the start of the nineteenth century, "educated" Europeans conceived of the universe in terms of a hierarchical Great Chain of Being, with God at its apex. The roots of this vertical hierarchy are still pervasive in Western theology and thought and stand in opposition to Native American and other belief systems that view the human and the spiritual as coexisting on a horizontal plane.

the lowest rung (minerals and plants) to the highest and most perfect (humans, and, ultimately, God). The paintings of American leaders ringing the tops of the galleries' walls visually asserted the dominance of human beings—and of the American political structure—over nature.

QUESTIONS

Comprehension: What was the nature of Jefferson's argument with Buffon?

Comprehension: Why were Americans so interested in mammoth bones in the late eighteenth century?

Context: How might eighteenth-century Americans' fascination with the mammoth bones relate to ideas of the sublime? Can fossilized bones be considered sublime objects?

Context: Read Jefferson's discussion of Native Americans in Query VI (the complete text is featured in the archive). What qualities and characteristics does he attribute to Native Americans? How does William Apess's account of Native American life complicate Jefferson's analysis?

Exploration: Dinosaurs and dinosaur bones continue to fascinate Americans. The assembled bones of a Tyrannosaurus Rex nicknamed "Sue" caused a sensation in the late 1990s, and contemporary films such as *Jurassic Park* and *Land Before Time* celebrate the power and size of prehistoric creatures. Does contemporary American interest in dinosaurs have anything in common with the eighteenth-century interest in the mammoth bones? Why are we as a nation so fascinated by dinosaurs?

Exploration: Compare Peale's museum to a contemporary science or history museum you have visited. How do twenty-first-century museums differ in their organization and mission from Peale's museum? What do they have in common?

Exploration: What values and assumptions underwrite contemporary discussions of the American wilderness and its place in national society? You might consider debates over the Alaskan Wildlife Refuge, Pacific Northwest old-growth forests, and the use of national parks and forests.

EXTENDED CONTEXTS

The Awful Truth: The Aesthetic of the Sublime

In Jefferson's famous description of the "Natural Bridge" rock formation in *Notes on the State of Virginia*, he declares that the bridge is a perfect example of a **sublime** view: "It is impossible for the emotions, arising from the sublime, to be felt beyond what they are here: so beautiful an arch, so elevated, so light, and springing, as it were, up to heaven, the rapture of the Spectator is really indescribable!" Despite his claim that the scene and the feelings it inspires are beyond description, Jefferson characteristically goes on to describe the Natural Bridge and his response to it in eloquent detail and in doing so provides a useful statement of the eighteenth-century aesthetic of the sublime in the process. While Jefferson clearly sees the scenery as thrillingly spectacular, he is also uncomfortably overwhelmed by it. He warns the reader that upon looking over the edge of the bridge "you involuntarily fall on your hands and feet, and creep to the parapet and peep over it. Looking down from this height . . . gave me a violent headache." Jefferson makes the effect of this "involuntary" and even "violent" physical response even more vivid for his reader by employing the second-person "you" and thus implicating the reader in these intense feelings. For Jefferson, the powerful effects the bridge has on its spectators are just as important to narrate as the conventional details of its size, measurements, and geological characteristics.

Jefferson's analysis of the Natural Bridge's sublimity is indebted to the aesthetic ideas formulated by Englishman Edmund Burke earlier in the eighteenth century. Burke was interested in categorizing aesthetic responses and distinguished the "sublime" from the "beautiful." While the beautiful is calm and harmonious, the sublime is majestic, wild, even savage. While viewers are soothed by the beautiful, they are overwhelmed, awe-struck, and sometimes terrified by the sublime. Often associated with huge, overpowering natural phenomena like mountains, waterfalls, or thunderstorms, the "delightful terror" inspired by sublime visions was supposed both to remind viewers of their own insignificance in the face of nature and divinity and to inspire them with a sense of transcendence. Thus Jefferson's seemingly paradoxical response of falling to a crouch, developing a headache, and then claiming that the "sensation becomes delightful in the extreme" is in fact a standard response to the sublime.

The idea of the sublime exerted an enormous influence over American art in the early nineteenth century. Hudson River School painters like Thomas Cole, Frederic Church, and Albert Bierstadt (featured in Unit 5) sought to capture the grandeur they found in the American wilderness as an expression of the greatness of the young nation. So ubiquitous was this aesthetic interest in the sublime that by mid-century, when Margaret Fuller visited Niagara Falls (a mecca for seekers of sublime views), she was disappointed to realize that her experience was inescapably mediated by other writers' and artists' descriptions of the scene's sublimity. She was left to lament, "When I arrived in sight of [the falls] I merely felt, 'ah, yes, here is the fall, just as I have seen it in pictures.' . . . I expected to be overwhelmed, to retire trembling from this giddy eminence, and gaze with unlimited wonder and awe upon the immense mass rolling on and on, but, somehow or other, I thought only of comparing the effect on my mind with what I had read and heard. . . . Happy were the first discoverers of Niagara, those who

[5932] Thomas Doughty, *In the Catskills* (1835), courtesy of Reynolda House, Museum of American Art.

[1181] Albert Bierstadt, *Valley of the Yosemite* (1864), courtesy of Museum of Fine Arts, Boston. Reproduced with permission. © Museum of Fine Arts, Boston. Valley of the Yosemite, 1864; Albert Bierstadt, American (born in Germany) (1830–1902). Oil on paperboard; 11 7/8 x 19 1/4 in. (30.2 x 48.9 cm). Gift of Martha C. Karolik for the M. and M. Karolik Collection of American Paintings, 1815–1865, 47.1236.

"THE AWFUL TRUTH"
WEB ARCHIVE

[1181] Albert Bierstadt, *Valley of the Yosemite* (1864), courtesy of Museum of Fine Arts, Boston. Reproduced with permission. © Museum of Fine Arts, Boston. Valley of the Yosemite, 1864; Albert Bierstadt, American (born in Germany) (1830–1902). Oil on paperboard; 11 7/8 x 19 1/4 in. (30.2 x 48.9 cm). Gift of Martha C. Karolik for the M. and M. Karolik Collection of American Paintings, 1815–1865, 47.1236. The romantic grandeur and luminism of Albert Bierstadt's western landscapes reflect Hudson River School influences. Realist writers like Bret Harte sought to imbue the same landscapes with the gritty realities of frontier life.
[3694] Thomas Cole, *The Falls of the Kaaterskill* (1826), courtesy of the Warner Collection of the Gulf States Paper Corporation. Cole was one of the first American landscape artists and a founder of the Hudson River School of

could come unawares upon this view and upon that, whose feelings were entirely their own." However overused the visual and linguistic vocabulary of the sublime had become by the mid-nineteenth century, it was nonetheless an important category through which Americans conceived of and organized their aesthetic experiences.

As European Americans moved west, they encountered more natural phenomena that fit within their view of the sublime. The Rocky Mountains, the Grand Canyon, and the geysers at Yellowstone, for example, were all described by early visitors in terms of their sublimity. Americans eventually came to ascribe sublime characteristics to humanmade objects as well: Whitman's description of the power of steam locomotives and Edward Weston's early-twentieth-century photographs of industrial architecture participate in the foundation of an aesthetic of the "technological sublime."

QUESTIONS

Comprehension: According to eighteenth-century aesthetic theory, what is the difference between the "beautiful" and the "sublime"? Give an example of each, either from literature or from your own experience.

Context: In eighteenth- and nineteenth-century America, the idea of the sublime was usually applied only to natural objects (and sometimes to encounters with Native Americans, who were perceived as "primitive" and more in touch with the natural world than whites). But sometimes the vocabulary of the sublime was used to describe other experiences. Do you think some individuals might have discussed their conversion experiences during the Great Awakening in terms of the sublime? How might listening to Jonathan Edwards's "Sinners in the Hands of an Angry God" compare to the experience of looking off the Natural Bridge or viewing Thomas Cole's painting *The Falls of the Kaaterskill*?

Exploration: Does a sense of the sublime still infuse contemporary American culture? Can you think of a late-twentieth-century novel, film, or painting that seems to participate in the aesthetic of the sublime?

Miss America: The Image of Columbia

In 1775, the African American poet Phillis Wheatley opened the poem she addressed to George Washington with the lines "Celestial choir! enthroned in realms of light, / Columbia's scenes of glorious toils I write." She goes on to describe the goddess Columbia as "divinely fair," with olive and laurel branches in her "golden hair." With these lines, Wheatley became the first writer to personify the new nation as the goddess "Columbia"—a feminized reference to Columbus, who was widely recognized as the "father" of America. Wheatley's use of the Columbia image is interesting both for its insistence on the goddess's Caucasian looks and for the profound influence it had on American culture. By the end of the Revolution, the figure of Columbia was everywhere. Popular songs and poems celebrated her; towns and cities were named for her (most notably the new seat of the federal government, the District of Columbia); and King's College in New York was renamed Columbia University. The adjective "Columbian" came to function as a kind of shorthand for patriotic allegiance to national ideals.

Although the image of Columbia was new when Wheatley developed it in 1775, iconographic representations of America as a woman had existed since the sixteenth century. The name "America," after all, is a feminization of explorer Amerigo Vespucci's Christian name. Sixteenth- and seventeenth-century drawings almost always represented the New World as a woman, and usually as a Native American. Pictured half-clothed in primitive garb, America in these representations is sometimes a savage cannibal woman and sometimes a regal Indian queen offering to share her natural bounty. British political cartoons produced during the Revolutionary War continued to portray America as a Native American woman, often picturing her as a rebellious Indian princess at war with her European mother, Britain.

As they fought to assert their independence, Americans apparently began to desire a new allegorical image to represent their nation. Scholar John Higham has suggested that Native American imagery may have become problematic because "white Americans were too close to real Indians in the eighteenth century to feel comfortable about identifying with any such personifications, no matter how idealized." In any case, Wheatley's Caucasian Roman goddess struck a chord. Her association with classical antiquity and the values of the Roman republic must have made her appealing to a nation that liked to conceive of itself as "a new Rome." Columbia was usually represented dressed in a white, toga-like gown, wearing a helmet, and carrying a liberty cap on a pole. She was often accompanied by the flag, the eagle, and documents like the Declaration of Independence and the Constitution. She appeared in paintings, statuary, and even on most of the coins produced by the United States Mint through the nineteenth century. Fearful that profiles of presidents or leaders would smack of imperialism and aristocracy, the young nation instead featured Columbia's profile on its money, accompanied by the word "Liberty."

Ironically, this celebration of the female figure as emblematic of American virtue and national character did not result in political gains for actual American women. Afforded only a symbolic and decorative position, they could not vote and were not considered citizens. In fact, the veneration of the feminized figure of Columbia in some ways displaces and obscures the important contributions that real women made to

painting. Romantic depictions of wilderness became popular as the United States continued its westward expansion.
[5932] Thomas Doughty, *In the Catskills* (1835), courtesy of Reynolda House, Museum of American Art. Landscape painting of river and boulders framed by trees in the foreground. An artist of the Hudson River School, Doughty painted the same American landscapes that writers such as Washington Irving described.
[9026] George Barker, *Niagara Falls, N.Y., Close-up View from Below* (1886), courtesy of the Library of Congress [LC-USZ62-97270]. Nineteenth-century photograph of the popular tourist attraction. Margaret Fuller and others commented on the sublimity of the Falls.
[9028] Thomas Moran, *The Tower of Tower Falls, Yellowstone* (1875), courtesy of the Library of Congress [LC-USZC4-3250]. It was in part by Moran's paintings that Congress was inspired to create Yellowstone National Park. Before color photography, painting captured an important dimension of the western landscape.

[5565] Kimmel and Foster, *The End of the Rebellion in the United States, 1865* (1866), courtesy of the Library of Congress [LC-USZ62-12764].

[3215] John Gast, *American Progress* (1872), courtesy of the Library of Congress [LC-USZC4-668]. Manifest Destiny is personified in the figure of America, who here leads a wave of civilization (settlers, railroads, and technology) across the continent. Symbols of the wilderness (Indians and animals) flee before her "progressive" influence.

[5565] Kimmel and Foster, *The End of the Rebellion in the United States, 1865* (1866), courtesy of the Library of Congress [LC-USZ62-12764]. The figure of Columbia, shown here in the turmoil of disunion surrounding the Civil War, was a prominent symbol of the classical republican virtues that framers of the new nation wished to emulate.

[6551] Kenyon Cox, *Columbia & Cuba—Magazine Cover—Nude Study* (1898), courtesy of the Library of Congress, Prints and Photographs Division [LC-USZ62-68463]. Cover of an 1898 magazine, exemplifying the openness toward the human body of the late-nineteenth-century realists. The names of the women, "Columbia" and "Cuba," refer to an imagined relationship between the nations during the Spanish-American War.

[6552] Washington Peale, *Three Days of May 1844, Columbia Mourns Her Citizens Slain* (1844), courtesy of the Library of Congress [LC-USZ62-46533]. This painting serves as a memorial to casualties of the "Bible Riots" that took place in May 1844 between Protestants and Irish Catholics in Kensington, Pennsylvania, a suburb of Philadelphia. The figure of Columbia places a wreath on a broken column and holds an American flag.

[6555] Thomas Nast, *A Belle Savage* [*Columbia Receiving Congratulations from All Parts of the World*] (1876), courtesy of the Library of Congress [LC-USZ62-105127]. This engraving dates from the nation's first centennial and shows Columbia holding congratulatory papers from such foreign leaders as William Von Bismarck and Alexander II.

[6556] Vincent Aderente, *Columbia Calls* (1916), courtesy of the Library of Congress [LC-USZC4-8315].

American society. The creation of the image of Columbia was probably not what Abigail Adams had in mind when she enjoined her husband, future president John Adams, to "remember the ladies."

QUESTIONS

Comprehension: Examine the representations of America as female featured in the archive. How did the depiction of America change over time? How is the Columbia in the eighteenth-century print by Edward Savage different from the Columbia featured on the World War I recruitment poster?

Context: How might the ideal of Columbia have influenced the depiction of female characters in eighteenth-century American texts? Consider Royall Tyler's *The Contrast* or Susanna Rowson's *Charlotte Temple*, for example.

Exploration: The U.S. Mint recently released a dollar coin emblazoned with an image of Sacajawea, the Native American woman who assisted the Lewis and Clark party on their journey to the Pacific. Purchase one of these coins at your local bank. How is Sacajawea portrayed on the coin? How does the representation of her compare to earlier representations of America as an Indian woman? How does she compare to images of Columbia? Why do you think the Mint decided to feature Sacajawea on this new coin? Your reason need not be the same as the Mint's "official" reason.

ASSIGNMENTS

Personal and Creative Responses

1. *Journal:* Think of an object or view you have seen or a phenomenon you have experienced that could be considered "sublime." Taking Margaret Fuller's description of Niagara Falls and Thomas Jefferson's account of the Natural Bridge as your model, write a description of your experience. How did the sight you viewed make you feel? What physical sensations did you experience? After you compose your account, think about the difficulties you encountered in translating your sublime experience into language. Does your written description effectively capture and explain your experience? If not, can you articulate what is missing from your account?

2. *Correspondence:* Imagine that you have been asked to compose a series of *Letters from an American Student*. Write a letter to your foreign correspondent in which you address the question "What is an American?" Be sure to include specific examples of values and behaviors that you see as representative of an American and an explanation of who qualifies as an American.

3. *Artist's Workshop:* Design or draw a figure that can function as a personification of contemporary America. How does your figure compare to eighteenth- and nineteenth-century images of

Columbia? What difficulties did you experience when trying to create a representative image?

4. *Multimedia:* In his lecture "The American Scholar," Ralph Waldo Emerson proclaimed, "the world is nothing, the man is all." Using Emerson's celebration of individualism as your inspiration, create a multimedia presentation that visually explores the importance of the individual within American culture. Include captions that explain and interpret the images you choose as exemplary of American individualism.

Problem-Based Learning Projects

1. You are a member of Jonathan Edwards's congregation at Northampton in 1750 when the church is debating about whether to dismiss Edwards from his position as pastor. Take a position on the debate and construct an argument to deliver to the congregation. What reasons will you give for your claim that Edwards should be removed or retained? What services has Edwards rendered to the church? What problems has he caused? What obligations and duties should pastors be responsible for performing? How has Edwards met or failed to meet his obligations? Would Edwards's time be better spent teaching the nearby Indians? Why or why not?

2. Both novels and plays were attacked in late-eighteenth-century America as frivolous, extravagant, and morally bankrupt. Cultural leaders like Thomas Jefferson proclaimed that novels were a "great obstacle to education" and insisted that Americans should spend their time in other pursuits. During the Revolutionary War, theater was seen as so dangerous that Congress declared it illegal. Imagine that you have been hired to produce a public relations campaign to promote either Susanna Rowson's novel *Charlotte Temple* or Royall Tyler's play *The Contrast*. How will you assure eighteenth-century Americans that the novel or play is worth their time and that it in fact produces good morals?

3. Imagine that Phillis Wheatley has asked you to be her literary agent. Given the racial prejudice that Wheatley faced in her attempts to publish her work, design a plan for marketing her poetry to an American publisher. What qualities of her work will you emphasize? What ethical questions are raised in making your choices? Be sure to anticipate the objections that you might hear from a white eighteenth-century publisher.

Propaganda poster calling for Americans to enlist to fight in World War I. The war encouraged disillusionment with, and distrust of, modernization and technology in both European and American writers.

[6908] Edward Savage, *Liberty* [*in the form of the Goddess of Youth; Giving Support to the Bald Eagle*] (1796), courtesy of the Library of Congress [LC-USZ62-15369]. This engraving shows Liberty, in the form of the goddess Hebe, making an offering to an eagle while she tramples on chains, a scepter, and other symbols of tyranny. At lower right is the city of Boston.

[9048] Deacon George Thomas, *Figurehead of "America"* (2002), courtesy of Claire Dennerlein and Paul Manson. Plaque on side of statue reads: "This figurehead is from the clipper ship 'America' built in 1874 at Quincy, Massachusetts, by Deacon George Thomas. In 1887 she was put on the Pacific coasting trade and was wrecked on San Juan Island in 1914." Seattle businessman and former mayor Robert Moran erected the figurehead at his resort in 1916 to commemorate the dying era of great ship-building in America.

GLOSSARY

auto-American-biography   A term coined by literary critic Sacvan Bercovitch for an autobiographical text in which the narrator self-consciously foregrounds his narrative construction of himself as an ideal American citizen. Benjamin Franklin's *Autobiography* is often understood as an auto-American-biography.

Deism　Eighteenth-century religious belief that privileges reason over faith and rejects traditional religious tenets in favor of a general belief in a benevolent creator. Deists do not believe in original sin and instead assume that human beings are basically good.

Enlightenment　Philosophy developed by thinkers such as Isaac Newton and John Locke, who argued that the universe is arranged in an orderly system, and that by the application of reason and intellect, human beings are capable of apprehending that system. Their philosophy represented a radical shift from earlier notions that the world is ordered by a stern, inscrutable God whose plans are beyond human understanding and whose will can only be known through religious revelation.

Great Awakening　The revitalization of spirituality and religious enthusiasm that swept through the American colonies from 1734 until around 1750. Ministers like Jonathan Edwards and the itinerant preachers George Whitefield and Gilbert Tennent promoted what they called a "religion of the heart," through which converts would move beyond mere adherence to moral duties into an ecstatic experience of spiritual grace. Great Awakening conversions were often characterized by physical reactions such as shouting, shaking, fainting, or even falling to the ground.

neoclassicism　Aesthetic movement characterized by interest in the art and culture of ancient Greece and Rome. In the late eighteenth and early nineteenth centuries, the United States, in search of foundational models to replace its former reliance on Great Britain, turned to examples from the ancient world, particularly the Roman republic, and, to a lesser extent, ancient Greece. Americans associated classical Greece and Rome with the virtuous, anti-aristocratic political and cultural ideals they hoped would prevail in the United States. The American neoclassical ideal did not entail a slavish imitation of ancient forms but rather demanded modern interpretations and revitalization of old forms.

republic　A government in which power is held by the people, government is representational, and representatives are charged with the common welfare of all the people in the country. Because the first republic was in ancient Rome, many eighteenth-century Americans were anxious to imitate Roman history and culture.

Romantic Individualism　The belief that individuals are endowed with not only reason but also an intuition that allows them to receive and interpret spiritual truths. Individuals thus have a responsibility to throw off the shackles of traditions and inherited conventions in order to live creatively according to their own unique perception of truth. Ralph Waldo Emerson's "Self-Reliance" is often considered to be a manifesto of Romantic Individualism.

seduction novel　A popular genre usually focusing on a pathetic, naïve female character who is seduced away from her protective family, made pregnant, and left to die by an unfaithful lover. Some literary critics have argued that the cultural obsession with tales of female seduction in late-eighteenth-century America reflects the nation's anxiety about its own claims to virtue in its recent revolution against the "patriarchal authority" of England. Susanna Rowson's *Charlotte Temple* is an example of a seduction novel.

sublime   An aesthetic ideal formulated by British philosopher Edmund Burke in the eighteenth century. Burke was interested in categorizing aesthetic responses and distinguished the "sublime" from the "beautiful." While the beautiful is calm and harmonious, the sublime is majestic, wild, even savage. While viewers are soothed by the beautiful, they are overwhelmed, awe-struck, and sometimes terrified by the sublime. Often associated with huge, overpowering natural phenomena like mountains, waterfalls, or thunderstorms, the "delightful terror" inspired by sublime visions was supposed both to remind viewers of their own insignificance in the face of nature and divinity and to inspire them with a sense of transcendence.

Transcendentalism   A nineteenth-century group of American writers and thinkers who believed that only by *transcending* the limits of rationalism and received tradition could the individual fully realize his or her potential. Ralph Waldo Emerson, Margaret Fuller, and Henry David Thoreau are among the most influential Transcendentalists.

SELECTED BIBLIOGRAPHY

Brawne, Michael. *The University of Virginia: The Lawn*. London: Phaidon Press, 1994.

Colacurcio, Michael J. *Doctrine and Difference: Essays in the Literature of New England*. New York: Routledge, 1997.

Davidson, Cathy N. *Revolution and the Word: The Rise of the Novel in America*. Oxford: Oxford UP, 1986.

Elkins, Stanley, and Eric McKitrick. *The Age of Federalism: The Early American Republic, 1788–1800*. Oxford: Oxford UP, 1993.

Ellis, Joseph J. *American Sphinx: The Character of Thomas Jefferson*. New York: Knopf, 1997.

Fliegelman, Jay. *Declaring Independence: Jefferson, Natural Language, and the Culture of Performance*. Stanford: Stanford UP, 1993.

Looby, Christopher. *Voicing America: Language, Literary Form, and the Origins of the United States*. Chicago: U of Chicago P, 1996.

Mulford, Carla. *Teaching the Literatures of Early America*. New York: Modern Language Association of America, 1999.

———, ed., with Angela Vietto and Amy E. Winans. *American Women Prose Writers to 1820*. Detroit: Gale Research, 1999.

Nelson, Dana. *The Word in Black and White: Reading "Race" in American Literature, 1638–1867*. New York: Oxford UP, 1992.

Rowe, John Carlos. *At Emerson's Tomb: The Politics of Classic American Literature*. New York: Columbia UP, 1997.

Zafar, Rafia. *We Wear the Mask: African Americans Write American Literature, 1760–1870*. New York: Columbia UP, 1997.

FURTHER RESOURCES

America Rock [videorecording]. Produced by Scholastic Rock, Inc. Burbank: ABC Video; distributed by Buena Vista Home Video, 1995.

Forbes, Jack D. *Africans and Native Americans: The Language of Race and the Evolution of Red-Black Peoples*. Urbana: U of Illinois P, 1993.

Franklin & His Friends: Portraying the Man of Science in Eighteenth-Century America [online exhibit, 1999]. National Portrait Gallery, Smithsonian Institution, 750 Ninth Street, NW, Suite 8300, Washington, DC, 20560-0973. Phone: (202) 275-1738; <www.npg.si.edu>.

George and Martha Washington: Portraits from the Presidential Years [online exhibit, 1999]. National Portrait Gallery, Smithsonian Institution, 750 Ninth Street, NW, Suite 8300, Washington, DC, 20560-0973. Phone: (202) 275-1738; <www.npg.si.edu>.

Higham, John. "Indian Princess and Roman Goddess: The First Female Symbols of America." *Proceedings of the American Antiquarian Society* 100 (1990): 45–79.

Jefferson's Blood [videorecording]. Produced and directed by Thomas Lennon; written by Shelby Steele and Thomas Lennon. Alexandria: PBS Video, 2000.

Marx, Leo. *The Machine in the Garden: Technology and the Pastoral Ideal in America*. New York: Oxford UP, 1964.

Novak, Barbara. *Nature and Culture: American Landscape Painting 1825–1875*. New York: Oxford UP, 1980.

On Time. An Exhibition at the National Museum of American History [virtual exhibit, 1999]. National Museum of American History, Smithsonian Institution, National Mall, 14th Street and Constitution Avenue, NW, Washington, D.C.

Rigal, Laura. *The American Manufactory: Art, Labor, and the World of Things in the Early Republic*. Princeton: Princeton UP, 1998.

Scott, Pamela. *Temple of Liberty: Building the Capitol for a New Nation* [exhibition catalog, Library of Congress exhibit]. New York: Oxford UP, 1995.

The Seneca Falls Convention [online exhibit]. National Portrait Gallery, Smithsonian Institution, 750 Ninth Street, NW, Suite 8300, Washington, DC, 20560-0973. Phone: (202) 275-1738; <www.npg.si.edu>.

Shields, John. *The American Aeneas: Classical Origins of the American Self*. Knoxville: U of Tennessee P, 2001.

Tool Chests: Symbol and Servant [virtual and actual exhibit, 1991]. Peter Liebold and Davus Shayt, curators. National Museum of American History, Smithsonian Institution, National Mall, 14th Street and Constitution Avenue, NW, Washington, DC.

MASCULINE HEROES

American Expansion, 1820–1900

Authors and Works

Featured in the Video:

James Fenimore Cooper, *The Pioneers* and *The Last of the Mohicans* (novels)

John Rollin Ridge (Yellow Bird), *The Life and Adventures of Joaquin Murieta* (novel)

Walt Whitman, *Leaves of Grass, Drum-Taps* (poetry), Preface to *Leaves of Grass* (literary criticism)

Discussed in This Unit:

Catharine Maria Sedgwick, "Cacoethes Scribendi" and "A Reminiscence of Federalism" (short stories), *Hope Leslie* (novel)

Cherokee Memorials, "Note on the Accompanying Memorials," "Memorial of the Cherokee Council," and "Memorial of the Cherokee Citizens" (political petitions)

Corridos (Mexican and Mexican American musical tradition)

Caroline Stansbury Kirkland, *A New Home—Who'll Follow?* (literary sketches)

Louise Amelia Smith Clappe, "California, in 1851 and 1852" (letters)

Maria Amparo Ruiz de Burton, *The Squatter and the Don* (novel)

Nat Love, *The Life and Adventures of Nat Love* (autobiography)

Overview Questions

■ How did racial tensions complicate and challenge the expansionist goals articulated in many American texts of the nineteenth century?

■ How did gender impact immigrants' experiences and opportunities in the American West?

■ How do texts by African American, Native American, and Latino writers expand and transform concepts of American citizenship, identity, and masculinity?

■ What are the distinguishing characteristics of the epic? How do writers in Unit 5 draw on and transform the tradition of the epic?

■ What characterizes the historical novel? What historical periods or events did nineteenth-century historical novelists see as appropriate subjects for their books? Why were historical novels so popular among nineteenth-century American readers?

■ What genres count as literature? How do letters, memoirs, and songs challenge the traditional borders of "the literary"?

■ What is a "frontier"? How have American ideas about the frontier changed over time?

■ What kinds of attitudes toward nature and the environment were prevalent in nineteenth-century American culture?

■ How did the concept of Manifest Destiny impact nineteenth-century American political policies and literary aesthetics?

■ What kinds of ideals and values do *corridos* advocate? How did *corridos* influence the development of Chicano literature?

■ What are the distinguishing characteristics of free verse? How did Whitman's development of free verse influence subsequent American poetry?

■ What ideals of masculinity helped shape the nineteenth-century figure of the American hero?

■ How were symbols and language usually associated with Anglo-American "patriotism" borrowed, appropriated, and transformed by African American, Native American, and Latino writers and artists?

■ How have American attitudes toward landscape and the environment changed over time?

■ How were the figures of the bandit and the outlaw represented in popular texts of the mid- to late nineteenth century? What kinds of myths came to surround these figures?

Learning Objectives

After students have viewed the video, read the head-notes and literary selections in *The Norton Anthology of American Literature*, and explored related archival materials on the *American Passages* Web site, they should be able to

1. understand the conflicts and tensions inherent in the American concept of the "frontier";
2. discuss the importance of gender in shaping the experiences and opportunities of immigrants and inhabitants of the American West;
3. discuss the importance of race and ethnicity in shaping the experiences and opportunities of immigrants and inhabitants of the American West;
4. understand nineteenth-century American debates about the relationship between humans and the natural environment and explain the impact of those debates on the development of American literature.

Instructor Overview

In 1893, Frederick Jackson Turner delivered a paper entitled "The Significance of the Frontier in American History" at the World's Columbian Exhibition in Chicago. Looking back over the course of American history, Turner concluded that the presence of unexplored land—"free land," as he termed it—gave a unique dynamism to American culture. For Turner, the frontier was "the meeting point between savagery and civilization." Ever since Turner made this famous pronouncement, Americans have been debating the definition and significance of the "frontier." As many scholars have pointed out, "frontier" is a term used by conquerors. It masks a reality of imperial invasion and colonialism under a veil of innocence and exceptionalism. That is, the idea of "free land" does not take into account the many other peoples who were displaced—sometimes violently—to make way for European-American expansion. As historian Patricia Nelson Limerick puts it, "the term 'frontier' blurs the fact of conquest."

To combat this problem, scholars have suggested other ways of thinking about the lands and histori-cal events we have traditionally associated with the "frontier." Along these lines, we might think of the frontier as a permeable zone where distinct cultures struggle and mix, or as a space of contact and contest among diverse groups. The Spanish word *la frontera*, which describes the borderlands between Mexico and the United States, is perhaps a more useful term than "frontier." Because the concept of a border does not contain a fantasy of "free land" or uninhabited space, it is a more realistic way to describe a place where cultures meet and where trade, violence, and cultural exchange shape a variety of individual experiences.

Whatever term we adopt, there are no simple ways to define or conceptualize nineteenth-century American expansion, a problem faced by all of the writers featured in Unit 5, "Masculine Heroes: American Expansion, 1820–1900." As they recorded and commented on the difficult issues that arose as European Americans moved west and north, the writers in Unit 5 also struggled with related issues of gender and race and their role in the formation of American identity. This unit explores representations of gender and American expansion in a wide variety of nineteenth-century works, including the musical *corridos* that developed in the southwestern borderlands and texts composed by James Fenimore Cooper, Catharine Maria Sedgwick, the Cherokee Memorialists, Caroline Stansbury Kirkland, John Rollin Ridge, Louise Amelia Smith Clappe, Walt Whitman, Maria Amparo Ruiz de Burton, and Nat Love. By focusing on these diverse authors, Unit 5 also traces the geographic movement of Anglo-American expansion, from the push into upstate New York and the "northwest territories" of Illinois and Ohio, to the colonization of California. Unit 5 provides contextual background and classroom materials designed to explore the way these writers both celebrated and challenged American ideals of masculinity and expansion. The video for Unit 5 focuses on three influential creators of masculine heroes: James Fenimore Cooper, John Rollin Ridge, and Walt Whitman. Cooper wrote the *Leather-Stocking Tales* about Natty Bumppo, a man who lives on the border between Native American and white culture and articulates tensions between "civilization" and "nature." John Rollin Ridge voiced his outrage at the atrocities committed by white Americans in California with his tale of the Mexican outlaw hero Joaquin Murieta. More sanguine about expansion, Walt Whitman used his innovative free-verse poetry to glorify the vastness of America's territories while adopting a tolerant, inclusive attitude toward all of its diverse inhabitants and to celebrate the poet as American hero. All of these writers created innovative literary styles and enduring themes that continue to influence American ideas about land, gender, and race.

In its coverage of these writers and texts, the video for Unit 5 introduces students to the complexities of the concept of the "frontier" and foregrounds the relationship between expansion and constructions of masculinity. How do these texts represent the violence and exploitation that were part of American expansion? How do they figure the expulsion of indigenous people from their traditional lands? How do they reconcile American ideals of democracy, equality, and freedom with the reality of conquest? How does race intersect with gender in the formation of American identity? What new literary forms emerge from the tensions of representing American expansion? Unit 5 helps answer these questions by offering suggestions on how to connect these writers to their cultural contexts, to other units in the series, and to other key writers of the era. The curriculum materials help fill in the video's introduction to territorial expansion and gender by exploring writers who articulated other, diverse experiences, such as the Cherokee Memorialists (who protested the federal government's decision to move them off their traditional homelands), Louise Clappe (a woman who lived in the predominantly male community of a Gold Rush camp), and Nat Love (an African American cowboy).

The video, the archive, and the curriculum materials situate these writers within several of the historical contexts and artistic movements that shaped their texts: (1) the transcontinental railroad and "Manifest Destiny"; (2) the California Gold Rush as a site of cultural exchange and conflict; (3) the social identity of the bachelor; (4) the use of American flag imagery in Native American Art; and (5) the aesthetic developed by the Hudson River School landscape painters.

The archive and the curriculum materials in Unit 5 suggest how these authors and texts relate to those covered in other *American Passages* units: How have American concepts of masculinity and heroism evolved over time? How have nineteenth-century ideas about landscape shaped contemporary aesthetics? How did Walt Whitman's development of free verse influence modern American poetry? How did the historical novel shape subsequent literary traditions? How have American ideas about the relationship between humans and their natural environment changed over time? How have notions of the "frontier" shaped American culture and politics?

Student Overview

In 1893, Frederick Jackson Turner delivered a paper entitled "The Significance of the Frontier in American History" at the World's Columbian Exhibition in Chicago. Looking back over the course of American history, Turner concluded that the presence of unexplored land—"free land," as he termed it—gave a unique dynamism to American culture. For Turner, the frontier was "the meeting point between savagery and civilization." Ever since Turner made this famous pronouncement, Americans have been debating the definition and significance of the "frontier." As many scholars have pointed out, "frontier" is a term used by conquerors. It masks a reality of imperial invasion and colonialism under a veil of innocence and exceptionalism. That is, the idea of "free land" does not take into account the many other peoples who were displaced—sometimes violently—to make way for European-American expansion. As historian Patricia Nelson Limerick puts it, "the term 'frontier' blurs the fact of conquest."

To combat this problem, scholars have suggested other ways of thinking about the lands and historical events we have traditionally associated with the "frontier." Along these lines, we might think of the frontier as a permeable zone where distinct cultures struggle and mix, or as a space of contact and contest among diverse groups. The Spanish word *la frontera*, which describes the borderlands between Mexico and the United States, is perhaps a more useful term than "frontier." Because the concept of a border does not contain a fantasy of "free land" or uninhabited space, it is a more realistic way to describe a place where cultures meet and where trade, violence, and cultural exchange shape a variety of individual experiences.

Whatever term we adopt, there are no simple ways to define or conceptualize nineteenth-century American expansion, a problem faced by all of the writers featured in Unit 5, "Masculine Heroes: American Expansion, 1820–1900." As they recorded and commented on the difficult issues that arose as European Americans moved west and north, the writers in Unit 5 also struggled with related issues of gender and race and their role in the formation of American identity. This unit explores representations of gender and American expansion in a wide variety of nineteenth-century works, including the musical *corridos* that developed in the southwestern border-lands and texts composed by James Fenimore Cooper, Catharine Maria Sedgwick, the Cherokee Memorialists, Caroline Stansbury Kirkland, John Rollin Ridge, Louise Amelia Smith Clappe, Walt Whitman, Maria Amparo Ruiz de Burton, and Nat Love. By focusing on these diverse authors, Unit 5 also traces the geographic movement of Anglo-American expansion, from the push into upstate New York and the "northwest territories" of Illinois and Ohio, to the colonization of California. Unit 5 explores the way these writers both celebrated and challenged American ideals of masculinity and expansion. The video for Unit 5 focuses on three influential creators of masculine heroes: James Fenimore Cooper, John Rollin Ridge, and Walt Whitman. Cooper wrote the *Leather-Stocking Tales* about Natty Bumppo, a man who lives on the border between Native American and white culture and articulates tensions between "civilization" and "nature." John Rollin Ridge voiced his outrage at the atrocities committed by white Americans in California with his tale of the Mexican outlaw hero Joaquin Murieta. More sanguine about expansion, Walt Whitman used his innovative free-verse poetry to glorify the vastness of America's territories while adopting a tolerant, inclusive attitude toward all of its diverse inhabitants and to celebrate the poet as American hero. All of these writers created innovative literary styles and enduring themes that continue to influence American ideas about land, gender, and race.

Video Overview

➤ **Authors covered:** James Fenimore Cooper, John Rollin Ridge (Yellow Bird), Walt Whitman

➤ **Who's interviewed:** Sherman Alexie, author and filmmaker; Blake Almendinger, professor of English (University of California, Los Angeles); Ramon Saldivar, professor of American literature (Stanford University); April Selley, associate professor of English (College of Saint Rose); Richard Slotkin, professor of American studies (Wesleyan University)

➤ **Points covered:**

• Introduction to nineteenth-century American ideas about expansion, immigration, and the movement west. Westward expansion created new identities and conflicts over who and what was American. Writers responded by creating masculine heroes who both challenged and celebrated the idea of the "frontier."

• James Fenimore Cooper invented the language for subsequent literature about American expansion with his *Leather-Stocking Tales*, which focus on the adventures of Natty Bumppo. A man living on the border between "wilderness" and "civilization" and between Native American and European culture, Natty challenges notions about American identity. Cooper's adoption of feminine imagery to describe the American landscape and his romantic yet ultimately dismissive view of Native Americans problematizes the role of gender and race in the construction of American identity.

• John Rollin Ridge, a Cherokee journalist, moved racial minorities from the sidelines of American literature into the spotlight with his creation of Joaquin Murieta, a Mexican outlaw who heroically fights the atrocities and injustices perpetrated by white American invaders in California. Ridge's own divided ethnicity (he had both European and Cherokee heritage) may have influenced his exploration of racial tensions in his novel.

• Walt Whitman was more celebratory of American expansion than either Cooper or Ridge, but also more inclusive and tolerant of diversity. Heeding Emerson's call for a national poet and a "true American voice," Whitman wanted his epic poetry collection *Leaves of*

Grass to express the plurality of voices that constitute America. His innovative style and development of free verse was foundational for modern American poetry.

• These authors constructed ideals of American masculinity and American expansion that are marked by tensions and contradictions. Celebrating Manifest Destiny and industrialization while also writing nostalgically about the people and cultures destroyed by American expansion, they created a complex portrait of the American frontier and the American hero that continues to shape popular culture in this country.

PREVIEW

• **Preview the video:** In the nineteenth century, the United States acquired vast new territories as a result of exploration, wars, treaties, and land purchases. As people of different racial, ethnic, and cultural backgrounds began moving into these territories, tensions developed over who and what should be considered "American." Writers responded by creating a literature centered on masculine heroes who both celebrate and question the ideals of American expansion. James Fenimore Cooper wrote the *Leather-Stocking Tales*, a series of five historical novels about the adventures of Natty Bumppo. A man who lives on the border between Native American and white culture, Natty articulates tensions between "civilization" and "nature." John Rollin Ridge voiced his outrage at the atrocities committed by white Americans in California with his tale of the Mexican outlaw hero Joaquin Murieta.

More sanguine about expansion, Walt Whitman glorified the vastness of America's territories while adopting a tolerant, inclusive attitude toward all of its diverse inhabitants. All of these writers created innovative literary styles and enduring themes that continue to influence American ideas about land and about masculinity.

• **What to think about while watching:** How do these authors both celebrate and challenge nineteenth-century American expansionist goals? What racial and ethnic groups inhabited the American West? How did racial tensions shape the American movement west? How do the writers and texts explored in the video create new American heroes and new ideals of masculinity? How have their efforts influenced American culture and literature?

• **Tying the video to the unit content:** Unit 5 expands on the issues outlined in the video to further explore the contradictions and tensions inherent in American ideas about the "frontier" and about borderlands. The curriculum materials offer background on Native American, Mexican, Mexican American, African American, and European-American writers and texts not featured in the video. Introducing literature by women into the discussion of the movement west, the curriculum materials build on the video's examination of the construction of masculinity and gender norms. Unit 5 offers contextual background to expand on the video's introduction to the political issues, historical events, and literary styles that shaped the literature of masculinity and western expansion in the United States.

	How do place and time shape the authors' works and our understanding of them?	What is an American? How does American literature create conceptions of the American experience and identity?	How are American myths created, challenged, and re-imagined through this literature?
Compre-hension Questions	Why did thousands of people go to California in the 1840s and 1850s?	What different groups inhabited the American West in the nine-teenth century?	What is "Manifest Destiny"? Who was excluded from the America that nineteenth-century propo-nents of Manifest Destiny envisioned?
Context Questions	What was the difference between Ridge's and Whitman's views of the railroad and the people who worked on it? What role did the railroad play in American expansion?	Why did Cooper use female body imagery to describe the American landscape? What role did women play in American expansion? How did this role conform to and devi-ate from nineteenth-century ideals of femininity and domesticity?	What is the relationship between Joaquin Murieta, the outlaw hero, and Natty Bumppo, the woods-man who lives on the border between Native American and white culture? How do these char-acters challenge the societies they live in? How are they implicated in the very systems they oppose?
Exploratory Questions	How did Cooper bring American history into his works? What events did he see as appropriate for his historical novels? How did his use of American history affect subsequent American literature?	How did Ridge critique U.S. policy in California in his novel The Life and Adventures of Joaquin Murieta? How did his creation of a bandit hero affect American mythology and the development of later American literary heroes?	How did Walt Whitman's ideals of inclusiveness shape American lit-erature and American poetry?

	Texts	Contexts
1820s	James Fenimore Cooper, *Precaution: A Novel* (1820), *The Spy: A Tale of the Neutral Ground* (1821), *The Pioneers, The Pilot: A Tale of the Sea* (1823), *The Last of the Mohicans* (1826), *The Red Rover* (1828) Catharine Maria Sedgwick, *A New-England Tale* (1822), *Redwood* (1824), *Hope Leslie* (1827)	Missouri Compromise (1820) Slave rebellion suppressed in Charleston, South Carolina (1822) Bureau of Indian Affairs established (1824) John Adams and Thomas Jefferson both die on July 4, the fiftieth anniversary of the Declaration of Independence (1826) Democratic Party formed (1828)
1830s	Catharine Maria Sedgwick, "Cacoethes Scribendi" (1830) Caroline Stansbury Kirkland, *A New Home—Who'll Follow?* (1839)	Indian Removal Act (1830) Anti-Slavery Society founded (1833) Texas gains its independence from Mexico (1836) U.S. troops force the removal of Cherokee Indians (1838)

	Texts	Contexts
1840s	Ralph Waldo Emerson, "The Poet" (1844)	Migration to Oregon over the Oregon Trail begins (1843) U.S.-Mexican War; annexations include California (1846–48) Seneca Falls convention on universal suffrage (1848) California Gold Rush begins (1849)
1850s	John Rollin Ridge, *The Life and Adventures of Joaquin Murieta, the Celebrated California Bandit* (1854) Louise Amelia Smith Clappe, "California in 1851, 1852. Residence in the Mines" (1854) Walt Whitman, *Leaves of Grass* (1855)	Compromise of 1850 strengthens Fugitive Slave Act while admitting California as a free state and abolishing slave trade in the District of Columbia (1850) Sioux Indians give up land in Iowa and Minnesota to U.S. government (1851)
1860s	Walt Whitman, *Drum-Taps* (1865)	Transcontinental telegraph service established between New York and San Francisco (1861) American Civil War (1861–65) Homestead Act (1862) Union Pacific and Central Pacific railroads meet at Promontory Point, Utah (1869)
1870s	Maria Amparo Ruiz de Burton, *Who Would Have Thought It?* (1872)	Battle of Little Bighorn ("Custer's Last Stand") (1876)
1880s	Walt Whitman, *Specimen Days* (1882) Maria Amparo Ruiz de Burton, *The Squatter and the Don* (1885)	President James Garfield assassinated (1881) Chinese Exclusion Act (1882)
1890s		Massacre at Wounded Knee, South Dakota (1890)
1900s	Nat Love, *The Life and Adventures of Nat Love* (1907)	Orville and Wilbur Wright achieve first powered flight, Kitty Hawk, North Carolina (1908) Ford Model T goes into production (1908)

AUTHOR/TEXT REVIEW

James Fenimore Cooper (1789–1851)

At the height of his fame in the early nineteenth century, James Fenimore Cooper was America's foremost novelist and one of the most successful writers in the world. Judgments on his stature as a novelist have been less generous since that time, but few would dispute the cultural significance of his innovative tales. Building on the example of the British novelist Sir Walter Scott, Cooper wrote the first American historical novels and in the process made subjects such as Native Americans, the western wilderness, and the democratic political system compelling and popular topics for fiction.

Cooper was raised in Cooperstown, the village his father founded in the forests of upstate New York. His third novel, *The Pioneers*, is closely based on his memories of growing up in this frontier community. Cooper was sent to Yale as an adolescent, but was quickly expelled for his poor academic performance and his habit of playing pranks. In need of a career, he enlisted in the merchant marines and the navy, experiences he would later draw on in his popular seafaring novels, including *The Pilot* and *The Red Rover*. Cooper inherited a substantial estate from his father in 1810, left the navy, and married Susan De Lancey, a woman from a wealthy New York family. Expecting to live as a privileged landowner, he was distressed when the following years brought financial setbacks, debt, and the loss of much of his inherited land.

In 1820, Cooper changed the course of his life when he wrote his first work of fiction, *Precaution*, a conventional novel of manners set in England. According to legend, Cooper wrote the book only because his wife challenged him to make good on his boast that he could write a better novel than the one she was reading. Despite his initial offhand attitude toward writing, Cooper took the American Revolution as the subject for his second book and composed the first important American historical novel, *The Spy* (1821). It met with enormous critical and financial success. In 1822 he moved his family to New York City to pursue his new career in earnest. Cooper founded the "Bread and Cheese" in the city, a social club for men committed to nurturing American culture. Through the club, Cooper associated with leading New York merchants, professionals, and artists, including many of the Hudson River School painters, whose depictions of nature are so frequently associated with Cooper's literary descriptions of the American wilderness. In 1823 Cooper published *The Pioneers*, the first of his five *Leather-Stocking* novels and the most autobiographical of his books. In it he introduced Natty Bumppo (known as the "Leather-Stocking"), who seized the American imagination as the independent backwoods hunter and friend to the Indians. Figured as a sort of personification of the American wilderness, Natty helped construct the mythology of the **frontier** and fuel American nostalgia for an idealized past before "civilization" intruded into the woods. Cooper followed *The Pioneers* with other successful novels, including *The Last of the Mohicans*, which chronicles Natty's adventures in upstate New York during the French and Indian War of 1754–63.

[1161] John Wesley Jarvis, *James Fenimore Cooper* (1822), courtesy of the New York State Historical Assocation.

At the peak of his success, Cooper took his family on a grand tour of Europe, where they were introduced to prominent political figures and artists. He continued writing and publishing novels from abroad, but many of these works were poorly received by the American press. Bitter at what he perceived as the American public's betrayal of him, Cooper announced in 1834 that he was going to give up novel writing and retire in seclusion to Cooperstown. From that point on he had a vexed relationship with his American audience, a problem exacerbated by his frequent involvement in petty lawsuits and his increasingly conservative harangues about the sociopolitical state of the country. Despite his threat to stop writing, Cooper actually wrote prolifically until his death, producing a total of thirty-two novels, along with several political tracts, works of history, and biographies.

TEACHING TIPS

■ Because it was set in England and featured only English characters, Cooper's first novel, *Precaution* (which he published anonymously), was assumed to be the work of a British citizen. Reviewers also concluded that the author was a woman because the novel centered on domestic scenes and social manners. Perhaps distressed by this misreading of his nationality and gender, Cooper focused many of his subsequent novels on American subjects and masculine heroes. After you give your students this background information, ask them to think about the strategies Cooper uses to identify his work as both "manly" and "American." What does Cooper see as appropriate behavior for a man and for an American? Which characters represent his ideals of American masculinity? How might his books respond to the notion, current in nineteenth-century America, that novel reading was a frivolous and feminine pursuit?

■ Although Cooper features prominent Native American characters and describes tribal customs in detail in his most famous novels, he was not personally familiar with Native American culture. In fact, even though many of his American readers took him to be an expert, Cooper's knowledge of Indian culture came largely from books, legends, and stereotypes. Ask your students to think about how Indians are portrayed in Cooper's novels, especially in *The Pioneers* and/or *The Last of the Mohicans*. You might have them pay special attention to the way he creates two separate versions of Native American character, celebrating "noble savages" like Uncas and Chingachgook while portraying other Native Americans as ferocious, barbarous, and inhumane. How does the Mohicans' doomed fate work to make them sympathetic and nonthreatening to Cooper's white audience? What kinds of prejudices do Cooper's negative depictions of the Mingo tribe appeal to? How are Cooper's stereotypes similar to or different from twentieth-century stereotypes depicted in Westerns, comic books, and other popular media?

[1161] John Wesley Jarvis, *James Fenimore Cooper* (1822), courtesy of the New York State Historical Association. Cooper is best known for his frontier novels of white-Indian relations. *The Pioneers* (1823), *The Last of the Mohicans* (1826), *The Prairie* (1827), *The Pathfinder* (1840), and *The Deerslayer* (1841) are known collectively as the *Leatherstocking Tales*.

[6974] Matthew Brady Studio, *James Fenimore Cooper* (c. 1850), courtesy of the National Archives and Records Administration. Brady photographed a number of famous Americans around 1850. This portrait of Cooper was taken shortly before the author's death in 1851.

[7314] Thomas Cole, Landscape Scene from *The Last of the Mohicans* (1827), courtesy of the New York State Historical Association. A founder of the Hudson River School, Cole painted several scenes from James Fenimore Cooper's novels. Cole was concerned that such industrial developments as the railroad would spoil the beauty of the Catskills.

[7734] Blake Allmendinger, Interview: "Male Bonding/Homo-Eroticism in Cooper's Novels" (2001), courtesy of Annenberg/CPB. Blake Allmendinger, professor of English at UCLA and author of *The Cowboy: Representations of Labor in American Work Culture* and *Ten Most Wanted: The New Western Literature*, discusses male bonding and homoeroticism in Cooper's novels.

[7735] Richard Slotkin, Interview: "Cooper's Critical American Hero, Relationship to Indians" (2001), courtesy of Annenberg/CPB. Richard Slotkin, professor of American Studies at Wesleyan University, discusses Cooper's hero and his relationship with Native Americans. Slotkin's trilogy on the myth of the frontier in America includes *Regeneration through Violence*, *The Fatal Environment*, and *Gunfighter Nation*.

[7530] F. O. C. Darley, *The Watch* [from the *Cooper Vignettes*] (1862), courtesy of Reed College. Cooper established a pattern in American literature of different races relating outside the bounds of society. In the example of Natty Bumppo and Chingachgook, white masculinity is developed through an ethnic "other" in the American wilderness.

Comprehension: Settings in works of fiction are often invented to symbolize or encapsulate the conflicts that will be developed in the story. How does Cooper describe the frontier community of Templeton in *The Pioneers*? How does the town function as a contact point between "civilization" and the wilderness? What kinds of hardships do the townspeople face? What is their vision of "progress"?

Comprehension: In 1863, German critic Gustav Freytag argued that the typical plot of a five-act play had a pyramidal shape. This pyramid consists of five stages: an introduction to the conflict, rising action (complication), climax, falling action, and a dénouement (unraveling). Although this pattern, known today as Freytag's pyramid, originally referred to drama, critics have applied the concept to fiction as well. How might we use Freytag's pyramid to analyze the plot development of *The Pioneers*? In what stage of the pyramid would the chapters "The Judge's History of the Settlement" and "The Slaughter of the Pigeons" fall? What is the nature of the conflict between Judge Temple and Natty Bumppo? How are their values opposed?

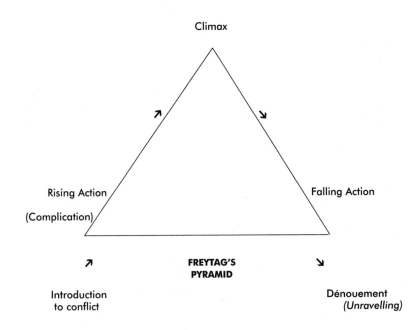

Context: Catharine Maria Sedgwick drew upon Cooper's development of the American historical novel when she wrote *Hope Leslie* in 1827. How does *Hope Leslie* compare to *The Pioneers*? Why do you think Sedgwick chose to write about the Puritans rather than the French and Indian War and post-Revolutionary period that Cooper chronicled? How does each book narrate the settlement of new territory by European-Americans? How are the novels' portraits of Native American characters similar? How are they different?

Context: Cooper was an enthusiastic admirer of the paintings of the Hudson River School artists. In a review of one of Thomas Cole's paintings, Cooper asserted that the picture was "the work of the highest genius this country has ever produced" and "one of the noblest works of art that has ever been wrought." Cole, in return, was an admirer of Cooper's prose and painted several scenes based on Cooper's descriptions of the landscape in *The Last of the Mohicans.* Why do you think Cooper and Cole were so interested in and enthusiastic about one another's work? How are their interests and subject matters similar? What do their attitudes toward land and landscape have in common?

Exploration: In both "The Judge's History of the Settlement" and "The Slaughter of the Pigeons," Cooper describes the way "settlement" and "civilization" exploit and disrupt the natural abundance of the wilderness. While the Judge tends to view this process as "improvement," Natty condemns it as destructive and wasteful. What is Cooper's position, on the environmental impact of European-American settlement? In what respects does he seem to side with the Judge's position, and in what respects does he seem to side with Natty? How does *The Pioneers* raise environmental issues that still concern us today? How do contemporary debates about issues such as logging old-growth forests, salmon fishing, and drilling for oil in the Alaskan National Wildlife Refuge grow out of some of the same controversies raised in *The Pioneers*?

Exploration: In 1895 Mark Twain published "Fenimore Cooper's Literary Offences," a hilarious indictment of Cooper's unrealistic dialogue and heavy-handed plots. What, in Twain's view, are Cooper's biggest "offences" against "literary art"? Why do you think Twain singled out Cooper? How did the development of both realism and regionalism (styles with which Twain is associated) represent a break with Cooper's style?

Exploration: Natty Bumppo has been described as the "first American hero" in U.S. national literature. What qualities make Natty heroic? How does he deal with the tensions between "wilderness" and "civilization" that structure life in and around Templeton? How does he deal with his existence on the border between Native American and Euro-American culture? How did Cooper's creation of Natty influence American literature? What subsequent literary heroes share some of Natty's qualities?

Exploration: In her article "'I Have Been, and Ever Shall Be, Your Friend': *Star Trek, The Deerslayer* and the American Romance," critic April Selley argues that the male-male bonding between Natty and his Native American sidekick Chingachgook laid the groundwork for later American heroes and their ethnic sidekicks (*Journal of Popular Culture* 20.1 [Summer 1986]: 89–104). These ethnic sidekicks, Selley argues, tend to be more effeminate, and thus enhance the masculinity of the European-American hero. Two famous examples of European-American heroes and ethnic sidekicks are the Lone Ranger and Tonto, and Captain Kirk and Spock. Do you agree with Selley's reading of Cooper's characters? Can you think of other examples that fit this model?

Catharine Maria Sedgwick (1789–1867)

Catharine Maria Sedgwick was one of the leading figures in early-nineteenth-century American literary culture. Although she is less well known today, she set a pattern for the development of both domestic novels and historical novels in this country. Male writers such as James Fenimore Cooper and William Cullen Bryant respected Sedgwick as a peer, while female authors such as Lydia Maria Child and Harriet Beecher Stowe regarded her as a literary role model. Born into a wealthy Massachusetts Federalist family, Sedgwick was the sixth of seven children. Her father, a prominent politician who occupied the position of Speaker of the U.S. House of Representatives during Washington's administration, took an interest in her education and provided her with a background in literature that would inspire her later development as a writer.

Sedgwick never married, choosing instead to devote herself to her writing and to caring for her parents and brothers. She spent time living in the homes of several of her brothers, and their unflagging support for her was a source of both private comfort and professional help and encouragement. Like many of her siblings, she renounced her parents' strict Calvinist faith for the tolerance and religious freedoms of the Unitarian Church, which she joined in 1821. Sedgwick's conversion was the impetus behind her first novel, *A New-England Tale*, which exposes the harshness of Calvinist theology. She hoped the novel would help convert readers who had not yet "escaped from the thraldom of orthodox despotism," as she put it. While her subsequent novels were more tempered in their critiques of orthodox religion, many of these later works were infused by Unitarian values.

Sedgwick's most celebrated novel is *Hope Leslie*, which takes the sixteenth-century Puritan colony in Massachusetts as its setting. Portraying Native American characters in a positive light, the novel advocates interracial friendships and recasts the Pequot War as an act of unfounded aggression against the Indians. While *Hope Leslie* considers the possibility of interracial marriage, it ultimately remains ambivalent about intimate relationships between Europeans and Indians. Sedgwick wrote several other novels and also produced many pieces of shorter fiction, which she published in collected editions and in magazines and literary journals.

Although she was sympathetic to causes such as abolitionism, Indian rights, and women's rights, Sedgwick never took an active role in these movements. Unlike many other nineteenth-century women writers, she was uncomfortable with overt political activism and tended to be conservative in her political commitments. In her posthumously published autobiography, she claimed that "an excessive love of approbation" made her reluctant to challenge social conventions. Although her legacy is perhaps less radical and her works less didacti-

[5519] A. B. Durand, *Catharine M. Sedgwick* (c. 1832), courtesy of the Library of Congress [LC-USZ62-113381].

cally political than those of the many female authors she inspired, Sedgwick was a pioneer among women writers and an important and insightful analyst of American society.

TEACHING TIPS

■ In an 1824 book review, a literary critic mistakenly attributed Sedgwick's second novel, *Redwood* (which she published anonymously), to James Fenimore Cooper. Sedgwick found the mistake amusing, commenting, "It is to be hoped that Mr. C's self-complacency will not be wounded by this mortifying news." Ask students to think about the assumptions about gender and authorship that underwrite Sedgwick's witty comment. Why might the reviewer have made the mistake he did? What does Sedgwick's work have in common with Cooper's?

■ Writing twenty-five years before Hawthorne's famous indictment of that "d—d mob of scribbling women," Sedgwick offered a satiric portrait of the phenomenon of female authorship in her short story "Cacoethes Scribendi." Ask students to consider the nature of Sedgwick's critique. How does the story question the quality of nineteenth-century women's writing? How does the title—which translates as "writer's itch"—mock women writers' pretensions and productivity? What was Sedgwick's own position within the culture of women writers that she satirizes? How might she have defended her own work from the criticisms she levels at other women writers in the story?

QUESTIONS

Comprehension: What separates the "opposed and contending parties" Sedgwick chronicles in her story "A Reminiscence of Federalism"? How do national party politics divide the small settlement of Carrington, Vermont? What is the narrator's attitude toward the characters' devotion to their political parties?

Comprehension: How does Sedgwick characterize the three women who compete for Everell Fletcher's affections in *Hope Leslie*? How does the novel deal with his relationship with Magawisca, the Pequot woman? What is Magawisca's fate?

Context: The "secluded and quiet village of H.," which is the setting for "Cacoethes Scribendi," is populated almost solely by women. How does the dominance of women affect the community? What is the women's relationship to the few men in the area? How does Sedgwick's description of this female village compare with other writers' accounts of western communities populated almost exclusively by men (works by Love, Clappe, or Ridge, for example)?

Context: How do the Native American characters in *Hope Leslie* articulate their attachment to their traditional lands? How do their attitudes toward their land and their culture compare with those expressed by the Cherokee memorialists?

Exploration: How does Sedgwick's portrait of the Pequot War in *Hope Leslie* undermine or challenge historical accounts of that event written by Puritans? How do Nelema and Magawisca's moving descriptions of the slaughter of the Pequots compare to John Underhill's account of the war? Or William Bradford's?

Exploration: Sedgwick's brother felt that his sister's first novel, *A New-England Tale*, had alienated some of its readers by its "unfavorable representation of the New England character." In response, Sedgwick determined to provide less hostile descriptions of Puritans and their descendants in her subsequent work. How does she portray the Puritan community in *Hope Leslie*? Which Puritans are sympathetic? How does she portray John Winthrop? How does her representation of Winthrop compare to his authorial persona in his *Journal*?

Cherokee Memorials

At the end of the eighteenth century, the Cherokee tribe was living in the mountain areas of northern Georgia and western North Carolina, on land guaranteed to them by the United States in the 1785 Treaty of Hopewell and the 1791 Holston Treaty. The Cherokee Nation had its own government, governing council, and by 1827 its own constitution, making it an independent sovereign nation. Increasingly, however, white settlers refused to respect Cherokee sovereignty and began encroaching on Cherokee land—especially when gold was discovered there in 1829. These illegal incursions by white settlers and prospectors were the basis for a series of ongoing disputes among the Cherokee Nation, the state of Georgia, and the federal government of the United States. In 1830 the United States Congress, with the support of President Andrew Jackson, attempted to legislate a permanent solution to the dispute by passing the **Indian Removal Act** by a narrow margin. The act stipulated that the government could forcibly relocate Native Americans living within their traditional lands in eastern states to areas west of the Mississippi designated as "Indian Territory." With this stroke, the federal government officially sanctioned the prevalent racist view that Native Americans had no valid claims to their homelands and should be moved westward to make way for white settlers and white culture.

During the debates over the Indian Removal Act, many Cherokee writers penned impassioned letters, pamphlets, and editorials to defend their tribe's right to its sovereignty and its land. Drawing on a long tradition of eloquence and a high rate of literacy and fluency in English among tribe members, the Cherokee produced articulate and compelling defenses of their position. In some cases they appealed to Congress and the courts directly with their letters and **memorials**— the nineteenth-century equivalent of petitions. The Cherokee Council, which was the official leadership body of the tribe, composed its own memorial to send to Congress, while also submitting twelve other memorials written by Cherokee citizens who, as the council put it, "wish to speak of their wishes and determination . . . themselves."

John Ridge (the father of John Rollin Ridge), who held the position of council clerk, probably authored the Council's official memorial with the help of the other council members. The document uses for-

[6823] F. W. Greenough, *Se-Quo-Yah* [*Sequoiah*] (c. 1836), courtesy of the Library of Congress, Prints and Photographs Division [LC-USZC4-4815].

mal, polished, legalistic language to articulate its claim that the forced removal of the Cherokee would be unnecessary, contrary to established agreements, and immoral. In its efforts to appeal to its white audience, the memorial stresses the Cherokees' commitment to "civilization" and their wish to "pursue agriculture and to educate their sons and daughters in the sciences," thus implying that the Cherokees' willingness to assimilate with white culture should strengthen their claim of sovereignty. At the same time, the memorial also insists on the Cherokees' separateness from the United States and on their historical claim to their land—a claim that long predates the arrival of Europeans in America. Perhaps most powerfully, the memorial skillfully employs American republican ideals of independence, natural rights, and self-government to point out the hypocrisy of nineteenth-century American policy and to support the Cherokees' claims. The citizens' memorials use many of the same rhetorical strategies, but are generally characterized by less formal language than the document composed by the council. The Cherokee memorials provided a model of rhetoric for subsequent Native American protest literature, such as William Apess's "An Indian's Looking-Glass for the White Man" (featured in Unit 4).

Tragically, for all their eloquence, the memorials were not effective. The state of Georgia, backed up by the federal government, continued to exert pressure upon the tribe to remove. Eventually, Ridge and some other leaders came to believe that resistance was futile and signed the Treaty of New Echota, agreeing to cede Cherokee lands to the state of Georgia. Most of the tribe, however, did not agree with the treaty and did not want to vacate their lands. In 1838, the United States government enforced the treaty by sending in federal troops and private contractors to compel the Cherokee to move west to what is now Oklahoma. One-third of the tribe died on the forced westward march, along what came to be known as the Trail of Tears.

TEACHING TIPS

■ Scholars have noted that the official memorial of the Cherokee Council employs pointed, though unstated, references to the language and logic of the Declaration of Independence. Most powerfully, by appealing to the ideals of independence and of natural human rights, the official memorial effectively points out the disjunction between American rhetoric of freedom and equality and the government's despotic treatment of the Cherokee. Ask students to consider the relationship between the Cherokee memorials and foundational American documents such as the Declaration of Independence. You might have students examine the Cherokee syllabary, and then discuss the way the Cherokee might be considered a culture in transition between oral and written expression. The Cherokee were the first tribe in the United States to develop a complete syllabary—that is, a written script that included characters for the vowel and consonant sounds of their language, thus enabling them to write in Cherokee.

■ In its opening paragraphs, the "Memorial of the Cherokee

[5595] Gales and Seaton's Register, Register of Debates, House of Representatives, 23rd Congress, 2nd Session, Pages 1007 through 1008, Cherokee Memorial (1835), courtesy of the Library of Congress. This is a record of Congress's reception of the Cherokee Council Memorial. Despite their petitions and appropriation of the republican ideals of natural rights and independence, the Cherokee people were forced off their lands in 1838.

[5916] John Ross to Abraham Lincoln, September 16, 1862 [Re: Relations between the U.S. and the Cherokee Nation] (1862), courtesy of the Library of Congress. During the early nineteenth century, Cherokee politics were highly factionalized. Author John Rollin Ridge's grandfather, Major Ridge, argued that it was useless to resist the U.S. government and hence supported removal. John Ross led the opposing faction, which urged complete resistance.

[6823] F. W. Greenough, Se-Quo-Yah [Sequoiah] (c. 1836), courtesy of the Library of Congress, Prints and Photographs Division [LC-USZC4-4815]. Half-length portrait of Sequoyah holding a tablet that shows the Cherokee alphabet. Sequoyah developed a Cherokee syllabary that enabled his people to write in their own language.

[8688] Arch C. Gerlach, editor, Map of Early Indian Tribes, Culture Areas, and Linguistic Stocks [from The National Atlas of the United States, U.S. Dept. of the Interior, Geological Survey] (1970), courtesy of the General Libraries, University of Texas at Austin. The Cherokee Nation originally lived in the southeastern part of what is now the United States, but after the unsuccessful petitions of the Cherokee memorials, the Cherokee people were removed to present-day Oklahoma.

Citizens" uses less formal language than the "Memorial of the Cherokee Council." It is sometimes characterized as reflecting traditional Cherokee oratorical practices in its rhetoric and language, while the Council's memorial is written in the conventional style of eighteenth-century government documents. Yet, by its closing, the Memorial of the Cherokee Citizens adopts more formal, legalistic language and sounds quite similar to the memorial of the Council. Ask students to consider the shift in tone and language in the Memorial of the Cherokee Citizens. Why might the memorialists have chosen to close their petition on a more formal note? What are the advantages and disadvantages of the two different styles at work in the memorial?

QUESTIONS

Comprehension: How are the "Memorial of the Cherokee Council" and the "Memorial of the Cherokee Citizens" different from one another? Why do you think the Cherokee chose to submit multiple memorials from different groups in the tribe rather than a single memorial?

Context: The Cherokee Council's memorial points out that, historically, the "phraseology, composition, etc." of treaties between the United States and the Cherokee were "always written by the Commissioners, on the part of the United States . . . as the Cherokees were unacquainted with letters." Given the council's awareness of this problem, what is the significance of the memorials' status as written texts? How does the Cherokees' "unlettered" history impact their written presentation of their situation?

Context: What kinds of attitudes toward land and land ownership do the Cherokee memorials endorse? How do their feelings about their relationship to their land compare to nineteenth-century white writers' attitudes toward land (in works by Cooper, Clappe, or Kirkland, for example)?

Exploration: How do the Cherokee memorials compare to early national documents proclaiming American sovereignty (such as the Declaration of Independence or the Constitution)? How do the Cherokee memorials exploit traditional American rhetoric of freedom and natural rights to their own ends?

Exploration: How does William Apess draw upon the rhetorical strategies and language developed by the Cherokee memorialists in his "Indian's Looking-Glass for the White Man"? How do Apess's reform goals compare to the memorialists' goal of retaining possession of their homeland?

Exploration: In *The Return of the Native: American Indian Political Resurgence,* sociologist and political scientist Stephen Cornell traces three basic stages in American Indian political resurgence. Cornell argues that while in the early contact period, Native American groups were able to maintain authority and status by playing European colonial powers off one another, in the years following the American Revolution, American Indian nations suffered a loss of land, social cohesion, and economic independence as

America expanded westward. This dislocation and disempowerment was in turn followed by militant activism in the 1960s and 1970s. Where do the Cherokee memorials fit into this continuum and what resistance strategies do they use? How do their resistance strategies compare to those of the Sioux during the Ghost Dance (Unit 1), or the Costanoans during the revolt against the Franciscan missionaries (Unit 7)?

Corridos

The *corrido*, a narrative ballad usually sung or spoken to music, was the most important literary genre of the southwestern **border** region, where it achieved its greatest popularity between the 1830s and the 1930s. Developed by Mexicans and Mexican Americans living in the former Mexican province of Nuevo Santander (currently Texas, New Mexico, Chihuahua, Coahuila, and Tamaulipas), corridos drew upon traditional Spanish ballad forms to articulate singers' experiences of cultural conflict in the borderlands. The word *corrido* is derived from the Spanish *correr* ("to run"), signaling the rapid tempo and brisk narrative pace that usually characterize these songs. *Corridos* do not have refrains or choruses; rather, the lyrics move the listener through the narrative quickly and without digression. Often composed within a short musical range of less than a single octave, *corridos* enable the performer to sing at high volume. Singers are often accompanied by guitar or the bajo sexto, a twelve-string guitar popular in Texas and New Mexico.

Corridos were usually composed to record political and social conflicts, current events, and extraordinary occurrences. While they were sometimes printed and distributed as broadsides, their primary mode of circulation was through oral performance. Some of the most famous of these broadsides were illustrated by Mexican artist José Guadalupe Posada on topics such as the Ku Klux Klan, the American "mosquito" (invaders), and episodes of violence in the Southwest. In this way, Latinos' borderland experiences—and political protests—were recorded in the memories and artistic expression of the people who learned the *corridos*. Many nineteenth-century *corridos* are still sung and recorded, and Mexicans and Mexican Americans continue to compose new *corridos*: popular musicians who use the *corrido* form include Los Tigres del Norte and the late singer Selena. Today, as then, *corridos* function as a kind of "musical newspaper" of the poor and oppressed; as musician and author Elijah Wald exposes in *Narcocorrido: A Journey into the Music of Drugs, Guns, and*

[7354] José Guadalupe Posada, *Verdaderos Versos de Macario Romero* [*The Truth about Macario Romero*] (1912), courtesy of the Library of Congress [LC-DIG-ppmsc-04557].

Guerrillas, contemporary *corridos* record the stories of drug traffickers, government corruption, bloody battles in Chiapas, and immigrant hardship in the United States.

Traditional *corridos* were a product of the dynamic culture within the border communities, where Mexicans, European Americans, and Native Americans vied for land rights, employment opportunities, and political authority. Expressing intercultural conflict from a Mexican point of view, the ballads often focus on an "outlaw" hero who defends his rights—as well as those of other Mexicans—against the unjust authority of Anglo *rinches* ("rangers") or other officials empowered by the American government after its annexation of Texas. The *rinches* were the Texas Rangers, who are sometimes celebrated outside of the corrido tradition as proponents of law and order in the Southwest. In reality, the Rangers were part of the European-American colonization movement and were partially responsible for the enormous number of lynchings of Mexicans and Chicanos in Texas and other areas of the Southwest.

Corridos serve as records of these and other injustices. Most *corrido* heroes are driven to crime only as a last resort or out of an honorable desire to avenge wrongs that have been perpetrated against them. For example, Gregorio Cortez kills two Texas sheriffs after they shoot his brother, and Rito Garcia shoots Anglo officers after they invade his home without a warrant. *Corridos* also celebrate figures who challenge political boundaries through their labor, such as *vaqueros* ("cowboys") and smugglers. "Kiansis," a corrido that asserts the *vaqueros'* superiority to Anglo cowboys, chronicles the Mexican cattlehands' drive into the American territory of Kansas. These songs provide an important counter story to western novelist Owen Wister's famous racist claim that only Anglos make good cowboys. Wister is the author of *The Virginian*, an early cowboy novel, and was a classmate of President Theodore Roosevelt (a popular target of early corridos' fury), who led the Rough Riders.

Some *corridos* close with their heroes' triumphant return to the Mexican community, while others narrate their capture, imprisonment, or execution. Whatever their fate, the men who are the subject of *corridos* are always celebrated as heroes because they defend their rights courageously and skillfully. Effectively translating political ideals of protest and resistance into a popular form, *corridos* functioned as powerful expressions of Mexican and Mexican American cultural pride. Today, they are recognized as one of the most important foundations for the rich Chicano literary tradition that developed in the twentieth century.

TEACHING TIPS

■ After your students read the featured *corridos* in their English translations (located in the archive), ask them to look at the Spanish lyrics as you play a recording of a *corrido* being performed. Even if they do not understand Spanish, they can focus on the rhythm and repetition of sounds in the original *corrido* through the lyrics. Ask

---

CORRIDOS WEB ARCHIVE

[5615] Anonymous, *Disturnell Map of Mexico* (c. 1850), courtesy of the Benson Latin American Collection, University of Texas at Austin. Although the treaty of Guadalupe-Hidalgo officially ended the Mexican-American War in 1848, disputes continued between the Mexican and U.S. governments concerning, among other issues, the border of Texas.

[5936] José Guadalupe Posada, *Corrido: Fusilamiento Bruno Martinez* (1920s), courtesy of Davidson Galleries. Political and social statements figured importantly in Posada's art. This Revolutionary-era print shows a *charro* bravely facing a group of onrushing *federales*. The title translates as *The Execution of Bruno Martinez*.

[6318] Lee Russell, *Backyards of Mexican Homes. Alamo, Texas* (1939), courtesy of the Library of Congress [LC USF34-032141-D]. *Corridos* grew out of the experience of the borderlands of the Southwest. As an oral history of a people, they document the everyday lives of the people who live in the lands that were once part of Mexico.

[6392] Mrs. Henry Krausse, *Corrido de los Rangers (Ballad of the Rangers)* (1939), courtesy of the Library of Congress. *Corridos* often expressed discontent with the oppression of Chicanos in the borderlands. This *corrido* tells of the 1912 feud between Texas Rangers and Brownsville officials.

them to think about how the music influences the effect of the ballad and what is lost in the English translation. Since this musical genre will be unfamiliar to many students, it might also be useful to play some political protest music that may be more familiar to them—sixties folk songs, for example. You can also ask students to compare the *corrido* in form and content to English-language ballads from the same region and era, for example, "The Dying Cowboy" and "The Dying Ranger." What rhetorical strategies does each use to develop sympathy (*pathos*) and to emphasize the moral character (*ethos*) of the protagonist?

■ Traditionally, *corridos* are composed by men, performed by men, and written about men. Ask students to consider how ideals of masculinity inform the *corridos* in the archive. What makes the male subject a hero? How does he deal with adversity, capture, or defeat? How is masculinity tied to ethnicity in these *corridos*? Ask your students to pay attention not only to the *corridos'* portraits of the courageous deeds of their heroes, but also to their descriptions of men who cry and men who complain.

QUESTIONS

Comprehension: What motivates the heroes of the *corridos* in the archive? What kinds of values do they espouse? How do they compare to their Anglo adversaries and rivals?

Context: Compare the *corrido* about Gregorio Cortez to John Ridge's novel, *Joaquin Murieta*. What do these title characters have in common? How do they interact with Anglo authority figures? How do their stories end? How does the *corrido* as a genre impact the portrait of Gregorio Cortez? How would Ridge's account of Murieta's life be different if it had been written as a *corrido*?

Exploration: While *corridos* were most popular between 1830 and 1930, they are still composed and sung today. Late-twentieth-century *corridos* include the "Recordado al Presidente," about the assassination of President John F. Kennedy in Texas, and the "Corrido de Cesar Chavez," about Chavez's organization of the United Farm Workers and their successful protest for better working conditions. How do the lyrics of these later *corridos* compare to the earlier *corridos*? What kinds of shifts in values do you see? How are the heroes of these later ballads different from heroes like Gregorio Cortez or Jacinto Trevino? How are they similar?

Exploration: Sandra Cisneros's *House on Mango Street* consists of a series of vignettes, each of which revolves around the young heroine, Esperanza. What analogies do you see between the structure of characterization used in the *corridos* and in Cisneros's novel?

[7354] José Guadalupe Posada, *Verdaderos Versos de Macario Romero* [*The Truth about Macario Romero*] (1912), courtesy of the Library of Congress [LC-DIG-ppmsc-04557]. Handbills printed with the lyrics to popular *corridos* were often sold to audiences for a small fee. This broadside features an illustration by José Guadalupe Posada.

[7505] Anonymous, *Music in Mexican Isurrecto Camp* (1911), courtesy of the Library of Congress [LC-USZ62-115488]. This photo emphasizes the close relationship between music and politics in the borderlands as musicians and armed men pose in a Revolutionary camp during the Mexican Civil War.

[9064] Anonymous, *El Corrido de Gregorio Cortez* (c. 1910), courtesy of Pedro Rocha and Lupe Martínez. This *corrido* takes as its subject the murder of an Anglo-Texan sheriff by a Texas Mexican, Gregorio Cortez, and the ensuing chase, capture, and imprisonment of Cortez. It formed the basis for Americo Paredes' novel, *With a Pistol in His Hand*.

Caroline Stansbury Kirkland (1801–1864)

Appearing well before either "regionalism" or "realism" had established themselves as literary movements, Caroline Kirkland's early writings anticipate these developments to such a degree that many critics now consider her to be among their founders. Born to a literary, middle-class family in New York, Caroline Stansbury received a good education at a series of distinguished schools and academies. In 1828, she married William Kirkland and moved to Geneva, New York, where the couple had four children and founded and ran a girls' school. In 1835, the Kirklands moved to Detroit, in the Michigan Territory, where William accepted a job as principal of the Detroit Female Seminary. He soon began purchasing large parcels of land in the Michigan backcountry and eventually moved his family to the frontier village of Pinckney, which he hoped would grow and thus increase the value of his land. The move into the backcountry inspired Kirkland to write her first work, a collection of realistic and often humorous sketches of frontier life called *A New Home—Who'll Follow?*, written under the pseudonym of "Mrs. Mary Clavers."

In 1843, after William lost the family's landholdings and capital to a swindling land agent, the family was forced to return to New York. There, Kirkland taught school and continued her writing career, publishing pieces in magazines and literary journals. In 1846, William died suddenly, leaving Kirkland to support herself and their children. Building on her literary connections, Kirkland took a job as the editor of the *Union Magazine of Literature and Art*, a position she held until 1851. Under her guidance, the magazine maintained a commitment to supporting both literary realism and women's writing. She also successfully compiled and sold several popular "gift books" (expensively printed books containing stories, essays, and poems, often given as gifts in the nineteenth century). Her literary celebrity enabled her to generate popular support for social reforms as well as for philanthropic work supporting the Union soldiers during the Civil War.

Today Kirkland is remembered chiefly for her innovative, realistic descriptions of western pioneer life in *A New Home*. Explicitly reacting against other writers' romanticized visions of the West, Kirkland was committed to providing her readers with an honest description of both the hardships and the joys of frontier life. Kirkland was also unique in offering a portrait of the West from something other than a masculinized point of view; rather than focusing on heroic tales of cowboys, outlaws, and dangerous adventures in the wilds of nature, Kirkland took as her subject the everyday experiences of hardworking women. Her witty, insightful commentary on problems of baking and ironing and getting along with one's neighbors is filtered through the persona of her narrator—an educated, middle-class woman who takes women's concerns seriously. Although her narrator in *A New Home* sometimes seems snobbish and overly invested in class distinctions by

[4340] Thomas Cole, *Home in the Woods* (1847), courtesy of Reynolda House, Museum of American Art.

today's standards, Kirkland's voice marks an important innovation in descriptions of the West.

TEACHING TIPS

■ Kirkland describes in detail many of the domestic commodities that circulate within her frontier community, both to complain about her ungrateful neighbors' habit of borrowing her possessions and to poke fun at pioneer women's pretensions in owning such luxuries as "silver tea-pots" and fancy dresses. Ask students to think about the role of commodities in Kirkland's narrative. How does she feel when she is accused of "introducing luxury" into the community when she displays her parlor carpet? How do commodities function to distinguish one "class" of women from another within the village? What kind of symbolic importance do the women in Pinckney attach to their furniture and household goods? How does gender structure the people of Pinckney's attitudes toward domestic objects, both decorative and useful? You might refer students to the contextual material on parlors featured in Unit 8.

■ Realism is usually thought of as a post–Civil War development in American literature, probably because male writers did not adopt it until the 1860s and 1870s. Kirkland's work provides clear evidence of an earlier incarnation of realism, yet she has never received the kind of critical attention afforded to the male writers who are seen as realism's "pioneers"—writers like Mark Twain and William Dean Howells. Ask students to think about the assumptions that inform our categorization and canonization of particular American writers. How does gender impact writers' reputations? How do we decide what constitutes a "school" or "movement" within American literature?

QUESTIONS

Comprehension: How do men and women experience frontier life differently, according to Kirkland's analysis in *A New Home*? What distinct problems and anxieties do women encounter in their new homes in the West?

Comprehension: Chapter 36 is titled "Classes of Emigrants." What characterizes the different "classes" that Kirkland describes? Which classes does she respect? Which does she condemn? How do issues of class structure Kirkland's portrait of life in the village of Pinckney?

Context: In many ways, Kirkland's sketches of frontier life read like letters home or journal entries. How does her project in *A New Home* compare to Louise Clappe's descriptive letters about life in the mines in California? How are the narrative personae that these writers develop similar? In what respects do they differ? What kind of audience does each writer assume?

Exploration: *A New Home—Who'll Follow?* sold well and received favorable notices from important reviewers such as William Cullen Bryant and Edgar Allan Poe. Yet Kirkland's book marks a distinct

KIRKLAND WEB ARCHIVE

[4340] Thomas Cole, *Home in the Woods* (1847), courtesy of Reynolda House, Museum of American Art. Painted just before the artist died in 1848, Thomas Cole's *Home in the Woods* depicts the pastoral bliss of a settler family amidst the destructive effect of human intrusion and settlement on wilderness.

[4423] Anonymous, *The First Step* [*Godey's Lady's Book*] (June 1858), courtesy of Hope Greenberg, University of Vermont. During the nineteenth century, a parlor was perceived as a necessary room in every home. Even Americans who lacked room for a formal parlor adorned their living spaces with decorative objects, such as the paintings and bureau-top items in this drawing.

[5806] J. F. Queen, *Home Sweet Home II* (1871), courtesy of the Library of Congress [LC-USZC4-2056]. Homesteading was often romanticized in American literature and decorative arts, as in this popular pastoral print of a woman feeding sheep.

[8703] Arch C. Gerlach, ed., *Map of Territorial Growth—1830* [from *The National Atlas of the United States*, U.S. Dept. of the Interior, Geological Survey] (1970), courtesy of the General Libraries, University of Texas at Austin. Spurred by the belief in Manifest Destiny and the search for a Northwest Passage, the United States acquired new land through wars, treaties, and purchase.

shift from previous popular descriptions of frontier life—it is neither romanticized nor sentimental nor filled with tales of masculine heroism and adventure. Why do you think Kirkland's work appealed to nineteenth-century readers? Do you think she appealed to the same kind of audience that read Cooper and Nat Love?

Louise Amelia Smith Clappe (1819–1906)

Born in New Jersey and educated at female academies in New England, Louise Clappe had an unusual background for a participant in and chronicler of the Gold Rush. She was raised by her father, a mathematics professor, after her mother's early death, and then by a guardian after she was orphaned in 1837. Her thorough education left her with a well-rounded knowledge of arts and literature.

In 1848, Louise Smith married Fayette Clapp, a young medical apprentice (Smith would later change the spelling of her married name to "Clappe"). Infected with "gold fever," he moved with his new wife to San Francisco in 1849 at the beginning of the Gold Rush. From San Francisco, the couple moved on to the mining camps springing up throughout northern California, where Fayette hoped to estab-

[7357] Sarony and Major, *View of San Francisco, Taken from the Western Hill at the Foot of Telegraph Hill, Looking Toward Ringon Point and Mission Valley* [detail] (c. 1851), courtesy of the Library of Congress [LC-USZC2-1716].

lish a profitable medical practice. In 1851 and 1852, the Clapps lived in Rich Bar and nearby Indian Bar, two boomtowns on the East Fork of the Feather River. The mining camps were makeshift and primitive, presenting their inhabitants with difficult living conditions, especially during the rainy winter. Clappe was one of relatively few women to live among the miners and prospectors—the first California census of 1850 indicates that the population of the state was over 90 percent male—but as Clappe's letters make clear, more women were immigrating to California along the Oregon Trail as the decade progressed.

While living in the mining camps, Clappe began writing descriptive letters about her experiences to her sister, Molly, who lived in Massachusetts. Drawing on traditions of literary letter writing begun by Caroline Kirkland and by Margaret Fuller in her *Summer on the Lakes, in 1843* (published in 1844), Clappe produced articulate epistles about her encounters. Witty, keenly observant, and often filled with literary references, Clappe's letters paint a vivid picture of the diversity and dynamism of the social world created by the Gold Rush. Clappe's perspective is surprisingly unconstrained by her status as a "proper lady"—she records everything she witnesses in the camps, from specialized mining techniques to incidents of mob justice to the prospectors' drunken gambling sprees. Her delight in the natural beauty of northern California also permeates her letters.

Left with an unsuccessful medical practice when the gold in the area was exhausted, Fayette Clapp moved his wife back to San Francisco in 1852. Soon after, the couple separated: while Fayette sailed to Hawaii and eventually returned to the Atlantic coast, Louise

Clappe remained in San Francisco and found work as a schoolteacher. In 1856, she formally filed for divorce and changed the spelling of her name from "Clapp" to "Clappe." In 1878, she retired from schoolteaching and moved back to New England, where she lived until her death.

Louise Clappe eventually published the letters she had written to her sister from the mining camps, using the title "California, in 1851 and 1852. Residence in the Mines." The letters appeared serially between 1854 and 1855 in the San Francisco magazine *The Pioneer*, where they became known as the "Shirley Letters" because Clappe signed them with the pseudonym "Shirley" or "Dame Shirley." If Clappe hoped to gain fame or fortune from her writings, she published a little too late, for public excitement over the Gold Rush had waned by 1854. Nonetheless, her letters have been important to historians for their unique perspective on life in the California mining camps, and her work is now recognized as an important literary accomplishment.

TEACHING TIPS

■ Clappe frequently employs literary allusions, referencing Shakespeare, Greek mythology, Romantic poets, and British writers such as Charles Dickens who were her contemporaries. Ask your students to consider the function of these self-conscious assertions of "literariness" in Clappe's letters. How do they affect the tone and voice of the letters? Why might Clappe have been interested in including these allusions in her work?

■ In Letter 12, Clappe tells her sister that she is committed to giving her a *"true* picture" of life in the mining camps. Ask your students to think about this "documentary" goal in Clappe's letters. Why does she feel bound to report everything that she observes, even the "disagreeable subjects"? In many ways, the letters read more like a diary than correspondence between two people—Clappe rarely asks about her sister or even specifically addresses her. Ask your students whether they believe Clappe envisioned another, wider audience for her writing, or whether she might have revised the letters before publishing them.

QUESTIONS

Comprehension: Based on Clappe's letters, what kind of role do you think women occupied within the mining camps (which were populated mainly by men)? What kinds of challenges would life in a mining town pose for women? What is Clappe's attitude toward the other women whom she encounters in Rich Bar? How do issues of class seem to color Clappe's descriptions of women?

Context: Compare Clappe's account of life in Rich Bar with Caroline Kirkland's narrative of life in the Michigan Territory. What do the two women have in common? How are their accounts of "settling" in new territory different? How do the different regional characteristics of the Midwest and California shape their narratives in different ways? How does each attempt to create a "true picture" of her life as a settler?

CLAPPE WEB ARCHIVE

[1303] Francis Samuel Marryat, *The Winter of 1849* (1855), courtesy of Bancroft Library, University of California, Berkeley. This illustration of residents trying to navigate San Francisco's flooded streets shows how rapidly growing cities and towns suffered from poor planning and local weather conditions.

[5228] Anonymous, *Montgomery Street, San Francisco, 1852* (n.d.), courtesy of the Library of Congress, Prints and Photographs Division [LC-USZ62-55762]. Rapid, primarily Euro-American immigration during the Gold Rush brought California to statehood in 1850, as a "free state" that forbade slavery. Yet demand for land and forced labor caused a genocidal-scale population decline among California Indians.

[5841] Currier and Ives, *Gold Mining in California* (c.1871), courtesy of the Library of Congress [LC-USZC2-1755]. This Currier and Ives lithograph presents a romantic and sanitized portrayal of life in the gold fields. In actuality, the mining process took an incredible toll on both miners and the surrounding environment.

[5599] Louise Amelia Smith Clappe, letter from *The Pioneer, Letters from the Mines* (1851), courtesy of the California History Room, California State Library. A well-educated woman from New Jersey, Louise Clappe wrote numerous letters to her sister about her experiences in the mining camps of California. In 1850 less than 10 percent of California's inhabitants were female.

[7357] Sarony and Major, *View of San Francisco, Taken from the Western Hill at the Foot of Telegraph Hill, Looking Toward Ringon Point and Mission Valley* [detail] (c. 1851), courtesy of the Library of Congress [LC-USZC2-1716]. Less than two years after the Gold Rush began, San Francisco had become a sprawling boom town that drew people from all over the world. This illustration shows both a busy city and a very active harbor crowded with ships.

Context: Examine the illustration entitled *The Winter of 1849* featured in the archive. How does the artist's depiction of life in a mining town compare to Clappe's account of her experiences?

Exploration: Scholars have noted that Bret Harte borrowed heavily from Clappe's letters in his stories "The Outcasts of Poker Flat" and "The Luck of Roaring Camp." Some scholars have also asserted that Mark Twain may have been inspired by an episode in Clappe's letters when he wrote "The Celebrated Jumping Frog of Calaveras County." What does Clappe have in common with these writers of literary regionalism? Why do you think they achieved greater fame and financial profit than she did?

[5513] Anonymous, *Walt Whitman* (1854), courtesy of the Library of Congress [LC-USZ62-79942].

Walt Whitman (1819–1892)

Walt Whitman's publication of *Leaves of Grass* in July 1855 represented nothing short of a radical shift in American poetry. Written in **free verse**—that is, having no regular meter or rhyme but instead relying on repetition and irregular stresses to achieve poetic effects—Whitman's poems flouted formal conventions in favor of an expansive, irregular, and often colloquial expression of poetic voice. Whitman unified his poems through the use of repetition of key opening words and ideas, parallelism between lines, and lists to bridge together the diversity he found around him. Critics have tended to see this mode of verse-making as more democratic, as it allows for both autonomy and unity in a startling new way. Whitman also flouted convention in his choice of subject matter: in his efforts to tell the epic story of American democracy in all its diversity, he excluded almost nothing from his focus and emphasized the body as much as the soul, the rude as much as the refined. Figuring himself and his poetry as the visionary representation of the American body politic, Whitman constructed an inclusive, all-embracing identity that could, as he characterized it, "contain multitudes." In the first edition of *Leaves of Grass* (which he printed himself), he did not include his name on the title page. Instead, he presented his readers with a picture of himself, dressed in casual working man's clothes, as the representative of the American collective self. Challenging tradition and shocking readers, Whitman's book was a revolutionary manifesto advocating a new style and a new purpose for American literature, as well as a new identity for the American poet.

No one could have predicted from Whitman's upbringing that he would emerge as a revolutionary poet. Born to a working-class family in New York, Walter Whitman received only six years of formal education before going to work at the age of eleven. He started out as an office boy and later became a printer's apprentice, a journalist, a teacher, and finally an editor. Over the course of his career, he edited or contributed to more than a dozen newspapers and magazines in the New York area, as well as working briefly in 1848 in New Orleans as an editor for the *New Orleans Crescent*. As a newspaperman, he was exposed to and participated in the important political debates of his time, usually affiliating himself with the radical Democrats.

By 1850 Whitman had largely withdrawn from his journalistic work in order to read literature and concentrate on his poetry. Given the ambition of the project—Whitman intended *Leaves of Grass* to be an American **epic**, that is, a narration of national identity on a grand, all-encompassing scale—it is perhaps unsurprising that he continued revising, rearranging, and expanding this collection for the rest of his life. Between 1855 and 1881 he published six different editions of *Leaves of Grass*. Many literary critics were shocked by Whitman's convention-defying style, reviewing the work as "reckless and indecent" and "a mass of stupid filth." Ralph Waldo Emerson, however, praised the book in a private letter to Whitman as "the most extraordinary piece of wit and wisdom that America has yet produced." Elated by this generous praise, Whitman immediately circulated Emerson's letter and supplemented it by anonymously writing and publishing several enthusiastic reviews of his own book.

In subsequent editions of *Leaves of Grass*, Whitman caused more controversy with his inclusion of a number of sexually explicit poems. The cluster titled *Enfans d'Adam* (Children of Adam) in the 1860 edition focuses on the "amative" love between man and woman, while *Calamus* celebrates the "adhesive" love that erotically links man and man. While many nineteenth-century critics do not seem to have grasped the homoerotic import of Whitman's "Calamus" poems, the sensuality and explicitness of all the "sex" poems made the collection extremely controversial.

With the onset of the Civil War, Whitman threw himself into nursing wounded soldiers in the hospital wards of Washington. His collection *Drum-Taps*, including his moving elegy on the death of Abraham Lincoln, records his struggle to come to terms with the violence and devastation of the war. Whitman remained in Washington after the war, serving as a clerk in the Bureau of Indian Affairs. Dismissed as a result of his controversial poetry, he found another government job in the Attorney General's office in 1865. Whitman suffered two severe blows in 1873 when he had a paralytic stroke and then lost his mother to heart disease. Devastated, he moved to Camden, New Jersey, to be near his brother. Although he was physically weakened, Whitman continued working on his poetry, meeting with influential artists and intellectuals of the time, and even making several journeys to the American West to see first-hand the expansive landscape he lovingly chronicled in his work. In 1881, he composed his final edition of *Leaves of Grass*, and in 1882, he published a prose companion to his poetry entitled *Specimen Days*.

TEACHING TIPS

■ Although students will probably pick up on the homoerotic imagery of many of Whitman's poems with little difficulty, it is worth reminding them that the male-male eroticism was not so clear to nineteenth-century readers, who were far more scandalized by his explicit descriptions of heterosexual sex. You might point out that the term "homosexual" did not exist in 1860, so Whitman's poems were

WHITMAN WEB ARCHIVE

[5130] Walt Whitman, *Leaves of Grass* (Brooklyn, 1855), courtesy of the Library of Congress. Frontispiece and title page to the first edition, first issue of Whitman's *Leaves of Grass*. Whitman became a new kind of American hero, writing exuberantly about the exploits of Americans and their beautiful land.
[5513] Anonymous, *Walt Whitman, Washington, D.C. 1863*, courtesy of the Library of Congress [LC-USZ62-98624]. Whitman spent much of the Civil War working in Washington hospitals, tending to the needs of wounded soldiers. His view of war and life would be forever changed by this experience.

[5758] Thomas Eakins, "Naked Series"—*Old Man, Seven Photographs* (c. 1880), courtesy of the Getty Museum. The model in these photographs looks strikingly like Walt Whitman. Debate continues as to whether or not the image is indeed of the poet "undisguised and naked."

[6242] Phillips & Taylor, *Walt Whitman, Half-Length Portrait, Seated, Facing Left, Wearing Hat and Sweater, Holding Butterfly* (1873), courtesy of the Library of Congress [LC-USZ62-77082]. Eve Sedgwick has noted that during the nineteenth century, before the term "homosexual" was invented, Whitman's writings, image, and name came to function as a code for men to communicate their homosexual identity and their homoerotic attractions to one another. Whitman was often photographed and liked to present himself in a variety of personae.

[6287] Frank Pearsall, *Walt Whitman, Half-Length Portrait, Seated, Facing Left, Left Hand under Chin* (1869), courtesy of the Library of Congress [LC-USZ62-89947]. Modernist poet Hart Crane considered himself an artist in Whitman's tradition of optimism and exuberance. Both tried to represent America and modernity.

[8267] Blake Allmendinger, Interview: "Whitman's Celebration of Expansion" (2001), courtesy of Annenberg/CPB. Blake Allmendinger, professor of English at UCLA and author of *The Cowboy: Representations of Labor in an American Work Culture* and *Ten Most Wanted: The New Western Literature*, discusses Whitman's celebration of expansion.

[8912] Allen Ginsberg, excerpt from "A Supermarket in California," a dramatic reading from *American Passages: A Literary Survey*, Episode 15: "Poetry of Liberation" (2002), courtesy of Annenberg/CPB. Walt Whitman had a tremendous influence on generations of free-verse poets, including Allen Ginsberg. This is a dramatic reading of an excerpt from Ginsberg's poem "A Supermarket in California," in which he addresses Whitman.

struggling to construct a new sexual identity and create a new language for erotic love between men. Ask your students to analyze stanzas VII and VIII of *Live Oak, with Moss* and/or the "Twenty-eight Bathers" section in *Song of Myself* in this context. Why does Whitman adopt a feminine persona in his narration of the "Twenty-eight Bathers"? How does Whitman struggle with his commitment to being a "public," national poet and his desire to record his private erotic feelings in *Live Oak, with Moss*? How does he describe his love for men, given that a vocabulary for homosexuality was unavailable to him?

■ Although the early editions of *Leaves of Grass* contain many eloquent celebrations of the vastness and grandeur of the American continent, Whitman had actually done very little traveling when he wrote them (his trip to New Orleans was his only significant travel experience until late in life). Ask students to think about why cities and landscapes Whitman could only imagine affected him so deeply. To what kinds of cultural myths and ideals was he responding? How might Whitman's lyrical descriptions of America's geographic expanse and demographic diversity have impacted his readers' ideas about the landscape and the nation?

■ When he wrote "The Poet" in 1844, Ralph Waldo Emerson proclaimed that "Poets are liberating gods . . . they are free, and they make free." He wished for the emergence of a poet "without impediment, who sees and handles that which others dream of, traverses the whole scale of experience, and is representative of man." Have students read Emerson's essay and stage a debate whether Whitman has indeed answered this passionate plea for a truly *American* poet.

QUESTIONS

Comprehension: Critics have called Whitman's 1855 Preface to *Leaves of Grass* a literary declaration of independence. What does Whitman call for in a national literature? Why does he feel America needs one? What kind of role does he envision for the new American poet?

Comprehension: In *Song of Myself*, Whitman attempts to reconcile and bring into harmony all the diverse people, ideas, and values that make up the American nation. Which groups of people does he choose to focus on particularly? How does he describe people of different races, social classes, genders, ages, and professions?

Context: Whitman was the most photographed American writer of the nineteenth century (there are 130 extant photographs of him). He frequently sent pictures of himself to friends and admirers and included portraits of himself in his editions of *Leaves of Grass*. Consider how Whitman presents himself in the portraits featured in the archive. How does he manipulate clothing and expression to achieve different effects? How does his self-presentation change over time? Why do you think Whitman might have been so interested in circulating photographs of himself?

Exploration: Why do you think Whitman's poetry was so controversial in the mid-nineteenth century? (Consider both his poems' for-

mal qualities and their subject matter as you answer this question.)
Do his poems still seem controversial? In what ways? Where do
you see Whitman's influence in later developments in American
poetry? (Do you see echoes of Whitman in Allen Ginsberg's *Howl*,
for example?)

Exploration: What is "epic" about *Song of Myself*? Can you think of
other American texts that might be described as epic? What do
these texts have in common? What defines an epic?

John Rollin Ridge (Yellow Bird) (1827–1867)

John Rollin Ridge was born in the Cherokee Nation (present-day
Georgia) into a prominent Native American family. Both his father and
his grandfather were Cherokee chiefs, landowners, and slave-owners.
During Ridge's youth, the tribe was troubled by white settlers' increasing encroachment on its lands and by mounting pressure from the
United States government to relocate to less desirable lands in Indian
Territory (present-day Oklahoma). A rift developed in the tribe
between those who were determined to defend their homeland against
white incursions and those who advocated compliance with white
demands. The Ridge family led the faction that wished to accommodate U.S. federal policy and was instrumental in signing the treaty that
led to the infamous Trail of Tears migration (1838–39). More than one-
third of the Cherokee who made the forced march to Oklahoma died
in the process, leaving many members of the tribe bitterly angry at
leaders like the Ridges, who were viewed as traitors for having advocated the disastrous treaty. In 1839 three members of the Ridge family
were assassinated, presumably for the role they had played in agreeing to the migration. John Ridge, just twelve years old at the time,
determined to avenge his father's death and to reassert his family's
leadership of the tribe.

[1190] Anonymous, *Joaquin, the Mountain Robber* (c. 1848), courtesy of the California State Library.

Despite his commitment to Cherokee politics, Ridge also identified
with his white mother's cultural heritage. He frequently wrote about
the need for Native Americans to assimilate to white culture and
become "civilized." He believed that Native Americans risked extinc-
tion unless they acculturated themselves to white values and customs.
Sent to school in New England for a time, he received a classical education and showed an early love for literature, writing his first poems
around the age of ten.

Ridge's life was radically disrupted in 1849 when he shot and killed
a man during a brawl. Rather than face prosecution for the crime, he
fled first to Missouri and then joined a Gold Rush party headed for
California. There he worked briefly as a miner, but found the labor
strenuous and unprofitable. He soon found work as a writer, journalist, and editor in the newspapers and literary journals springing up in
the boomtowns of northern California.

In 1854, Ridge published *The Life and Adventures of Joaquin
Murieta, the Celebrated California Bandit*, which is considered the first
novel written in California and the first novel published by a Native
American. His editor used Ridge's Cherokee name, "Yellow Bird," on

RIDGE WEB ARCHIVE

[1184] Anonymous, *John Rollin Ridge and Daughter Alice* (c. 1860), courtesy of Western History Collections, University of Oklahoma Libraries. John Rollin Ridge was born into an important Cherokee family in Georgia. His father was assassinated for signing the treaty that led to the Trail of Tears. Ridge later married a white woman and rejoined the Cherokee Nation in Oklahoma. Issues of assimilation and resistance resonate in his literary works as in his life.

[1190] Anonymous, *Joaquin, the Mountain Robber* (c. 1848), courtesy of the California State Library. The fact that no verifiable portrait of Murietta exists only enhances the legend of the California outlaw. Murietta's exploits were often exaggerated, and many acts committed by other bandits were erroneously attributed to him.

[4246] John Rollin Ridge, First page of *Joaquin Murieta* (c. 1854), courtesy of University of Oklahoma Press. This sensational novel tells the story of a Mexican American outlaw who seeks revenge on marauding Anglo American miners during the California Gold Rush. The work was originally attributed to "Yellow Bird," Ridge's Cherokee name.

[4249] John Rollin Ridge, Title page of *The Life and Adventures of Joaquin Murieta, The Celebrated California Bandit* (1955), courtesy of University of Oklahoma Press. This is considered both the first novel written in California and the first novel written by a Native American. Its publishers identified author John Rollin Ridge by his Cherokee name, "Yellow Bird."

[5832] Charles Christian Nahl, *Joaquin Murieta* (1859), courtesy of Bancroft Library, University of California at Berkeley. Charles Christian Nahl and John Rollin Ridge are two of the many artists inspired by the legend of Joaquin Murieta. Here Murieta is depicted as a Spanish American–style hero.

[6403] McKenney & Hall, *John Ridge, a Cherokee* (c. 1838), courtesy of the Library of Congress [LC-USZC4-3157]. Author John Rollin Ridge was born into a prominent Cherokee family. His father, John Ridge, was educated in New England and married a white woman.

the title page of the original edition, perhaps to highlight the novelty of the author's ethnicity. The work is a fictionalized account of the experiences of a legendary Mexican bandit who, though fundamentally a noble person, is driven to a life of crime by the persecution he suffers at the hands of Anglos. After having his profits stolen, his land seized, his brother unfairly executed, and his mistress raped before his eyes, Joaquin Murieta vows revenge and embarks on a crime spree, targeting the authorities of the Anglo establishment. While Ridge's story of Murieta is loosely based on a series of actual robberies and raids carried out by Mexican outlaws in California in the early 1850s, the tale is not modeled strictly on fact. Ridge's hero is a composite of several shadowy bandit figures about whom little historical information is known—though at least three of them do seem to have shared the first name "Joaquin." Despite its fictional status, Ridge's account of the adventures of Joaquin Murieta quickly came to be accepted as fact (by the 1880s, respected historians were citing details from his novel in the footnotes of their books on California history). As it gained currency, Ridge's story was also widely pirated and embellished by other novelists, playwrights, and screenwriters. Although Ridge's literary endeavors did not make very much money—he had received no profit from his novel by the time he died in California in 1867—he did create an enduring California legend and folk hero.

TEACHING TIPS

■ Some critics have claimed that the story of Joaquin Murieta appealed to Ridge because it shares some important similarities with his own life. Ask students to consider this theory. How does the disruption of Murieta's life by sudden violence compare to Ridge's early history? How does Murieta's obsession with revenge resonate with Ridge's own experiences? You might also ask students to consider the more general similarities between the Cherokees' forced migration from their traditional lands in Georgia to less desirable land in Oklahoma and the dispossession of Mexican miners and ranchers in California in the mid-nineteenth century.

■ Ridge concludes his novel by citing its "lesson" for his readers: "There is nothing so dangerous in its consequences as *injustice to individuals*—whether it arise from prejudice of color or from any other source . . . a wrong done to one man is a wrong to society and the world." Ask students to contemplate this moral and its applicability to the story of Joaquin Murieta. How does the novel justify this moral? How does Ridge use his narrative to generate sympathy for Murieta?

QUESTIONS

Comprehension: What drives Joaquin Murieta to a life of crime? What groups are the targets of his criminal activity? What groups and individuals does he spare? What kind of code does he live by?

Context: Compare Ridge's portrait of Joaquin Murieta to the *corridos'* descriptions of Latino bandits living on the border between Texas and Mexico. How do these texts participate in similar traditions? How do their descriptions of outlaws differ? How do these different kinds of texts (novels and ballads) use different strategies to shape their readers' attitudes toward the outlaws and border cultures that they portray?

Exploration: In 1967, Chicano activist Rodolfo "Corky" Gonzales published an epic poem which took the life of Joaquin Murieta as its subject. Compare Gonzales's *I Am Joaquin—Yo Soy Joaquin* with Ridge's earlier novelistic account. How does Gonzales's position as a late-twentieth-century activist and as a Chicano shape his portrait of Murieta?

Exploration: Although Ridge's narrative of Joaquin Murieta's life owes more to fiction than to fact, it was quickly accepted by many readers and even some professional historians as an accurate historical account. Why do you think the figure of Joaquin Murieta (or at least Ridge's description of him) was so appealing that people were anxious to believe in his reality? Why has the story of his life become such an important myth within California history? Can you think of other outlaw figures who occupy similarly important positions within the mythology of other regions of the United States?

The family favored assimilation and accommodation.
[8277] John Rollin Ridge, Excerpt from *The Life and Adventures of Joaquin Murieta, the Celebrated California Bandit.*

Maria Amparo Ruiz de Burton (c. 1832–1895)

Maria Amparo Ruiz was born into an aristocratic Latino family on the Baja peninsula in Mexico. Her grandfather, Don Jose Manuel Ruiz, owned a vast tract of land around Ensenada and served as the governor of Baja. The family's control of the area came to an end during the Mexican-American War (1845–48), when the American army occupied Baja and forced the surrender of its citizens. It was during this period that Maria Ruiz met Captain Henry S. Burton, an army officer from New England, and began a romantic relationship with him. At the close of the war, she took advantage of the terms of the Treaty of Guadelupe-Hidalgo to move to Alta California with her mother, where the two became American citizens. In 1849, Maria Ruiz married Henry Burton in Monterey, California. Embarking on a new life within a social circle made up of both native Latino Californio landholders and Anglos, she soon mastered the English language and gained a reputation for her beauty and her air of "true aristocracy," as one admirer put it. In 1853, the Burtons purchased the Jamul Ranch, a large parcel of land near San Diego, solidifying their position within California society.

In 1859, Henry Burton received military orders to return east and the family moved to the Atlantic coast. He was soon promoted, first to major and then to brigadier-general in the Union Army. Her husband's high-ranking position within the army enabled Ruiz de Burton to circulate in elite East Coast society and to see the inner workings of U.S. political and military life first-hand, experiences she would later draw upon in her novels. Henry Burton died of malarial fever in 1869, leaving Ruiz de Burton a thirty-seven-year-old widow with two children.

Ruiz de Burton returned to California after her husband's death,

RUIZ DE BURTON WEB ARCHIVE

undertaking a variety of land and business ventures in an attempt to secure her family's financial situation. She started a cement plant, a commercial-scale castor bean factory, and a water reservoir on her Jamul property, but turned little profit through these enterprises. Ruiz de Burton also found herself involved in a number of complicated legal battles over land titles, attempting both to safeguard her legal right to the Jamul Ranch and to claim her grandfather's Ensenada tract in Baja. When she died in Chicago, she was in the midst of raising political and financial support for her claim to the Mexican land.

Despite her financial and legal entanglements, Ruiz de Burton found time to begin a literary career in the 1870s, publishing two novels for an English-speaking audience. Both books critique the dominant Anglo society and express Ruiz de Burton's resentment over the discrimination and racism experienced by many Latinos residing within the United States. Her first novel, *Who Would Have Thought It?* (1872), which denounces what she viewed as the hypocritical sanctimoniousness of New England culture, was published anonymously, probably because its biting satire of Congregationalist religion, of abolitionism, and even of President Lincoln made it controversial. In 1885, Ruiz de Burton turned her attention to the situation in California in *The Squatter and the Don*, a fictional account of the land struggles experienced by many Californio families after U.S. annexation. The book is a historical novel about the relationship between Mercedes Alamar, the beautiful daughter of an aristocratic Californio family, and Clarence Darrell, an American who is affiliated with the Anglo squatters trying to claim the Alamar family's land. Chronicling the demise of the feudal Spanish rancho system in California, the novel questions whether the imposition of American monopoly capitalism (depicted in a scathing critique of the railroad industry) is an improvement over the old way of life. Because Ruiz de Burton writes from the perspective of the conquered Californio population, her work serves as an important corrective to Anglo writers' often celebratory, imperialist narratives of western expansion. Although Ruiz de Burton's work is not free from racist stereotypes—she portrays poor white squatters, Jews, African Americans, Indians, and the Chinese in racist terms—it does provide a unique perspective on crucial issues of race, class, gender, and power in nineteenth-century America.

TEACHING TIPS

■ *The Squatter and the Don* was originally published under the pseudonym "C. Loyal," shorthand for the term "Cuidado Leal" (Loyal Citizen), a conventional closing used in official government correspondence in nineteenth-century Mexico. Ask students to think about why Ruiz de Burton might have adopted this pen name. How does it resonate with her novel's critique of American political structures? Does this pseudonym suggest that she continued to see herself as a Mexican citizen even after her decision to become an American? Or was she reformulating the Mexican ideal of "loyal citizenship" within an American context?

■ Ruiz de Burton wrote and published both of her novels in English even though many of her central characters were Latino. Given this information, ask students to consider what kind of audience Ruiz de Burton envisioned for her novels. To whom was she addressing her critiques of American society? Why might she have chosen this audience? How did she work to make her stories—and her political points—appealing to English-speaking readers?

QUESTIONS

Comprehension: What is a "squatter"? What is a "Don"? Who is the novel's hero and what qualities does he embody?

Comprehension: What kinds of discrimination do the resident Californios face in *The Squatter and the Don*? How do the squatters jeopardize their claims to their ranches? What kinds of tactics do the Californios adopt in their efforts to maintain their land?

Context: How does Ruiz de Burton portray the railroad industry in *The Squatter and the Don*? How do the railroad monopolies impact the San Diego community in the novel? What does the railroad come to symbolize in the novel?

Exploration: Both Ruiz de Burton's *The Squatter and the Don* and Helen Hunt Jackson's *Ramona* are sentimental novels about ethnically diverse people living in the rapidly changing culture of nineteenth-century California. (See Unit 7 for an explanation and discussion of the sentimental novel.) How do these two texts share similar concerns? How are they different? How do their portraits of Native American characters compare? How does their treatment of interracial marriage compare?

Nat Love (1854–1921)

Born into slavery in Tennessee, Nat Love eventually found fame as "Deadwood Dick," the cowboy celebrated in western lore, dime novels, and his own autobiography, *The Life and Adventures of Nat Love* (1907). Because of Love's tendency toward hyperbole, his account of his life is sometimes understood as part of the western "tall tale" tradition. But his story also reflects the important reality of African American participation in the culture of the American West and functions as a crucial corrective to the stereotype of the "Old West" as the exclusive dominion of white men. In fact, at least five thousand African American men worked as cowboys, while countless others traveled through and settled in western lands in the nineteenth century.

Freed from slavery as a boy at the close of the Civil War, Love soon moved west to seek adventure and employment. He quickly found work as a ranch hand, cattle rustler, and "brand reader" (the skilled

and government communications outposts, guiding investment and commerce.
[5240] Helen Hunt Jackson, *Ramona* manuscript page (c. 1883), courtesy of Colorado College, Tutt Library Special Collections. Jackson wrote *Ramona* hoping that the novel would call attention to the mistreatment of California's Indians much as Harriet Beecher Stowe's *Uncle Tom's Cabin* had to the plight of slaves.
[5761] N. Currier, *The Battle of Sacramento* (1847), courtesy of the Library of Congress [LC-USZC2-1966]. Americans charge against Mexicans during the battle near Rancho Sacramento, just north of Chihuahua, Mexico, on February 28, 1847. The heroism of the American soldiers contrasts with the limpness of the Mexican forces and reflects American biases.
[6856] Oriana Day, *Mission San Gabriel Arcangel* [Oil on canvas, 20 x 30 in.] (late 19th century), courtesy of Fine Arts Museums of San Francisco; gift of Mrs. Eleanor Martin, 37556. As Ruiz de Burton makes clear, Mexican society was well established in California before the era of the Gold Rush. Missions often maintained large herds of cattle to provide their residents with a reliable source of meat.
[7264] William S. Smith, *The New Ship "Mechanic's Own," Built for the Mechanics' Mining Association by Messrs. Bishop & Simonson, Sailed from New York, Augt. 14th, 1849, for California* (1849), courtesy of the Library of Congress [LC-USZ62-114923]. Ships like the *Mechanic's Own* provided the crucial link between the United States and the western territories of California and Oregon. Writers such as Maria Amparo Ruiz de Burton, John Rollin Ridge, and Louise Amelia Smith Clappe wrote of the arrival of Euro-Americans in what had been Mexican American territory.
[7359] Fanny F. Palmer, *Westward the Course of Empire Takes Its Way* (1868), courtesy of the Library of Congress [LC-USZC2-3757]. Less than two years after the Gold Rush began, San Francisco had become a sprawling boom town that drew people from all over the world. This illustration shows both a busy city and a very active harbor crowded with ships.

[5307] Anonymous, *Deadwood Dick (Nat Love) in My Fighting Clothes* (c. 1870–90), courtesy of Duke University, Rare Book, Manuscript, and Special Collections Library.

hand who sorts cattle in mixed herds) in Texas, Arizona, and throughout the West. As Love's narrative demonstrates, the life of a nineteenth-century cowboy was a difficult one, demanding specialized knowledge and skills. Responsible for driving herds of cattle from the western ranches to the northern stockyards over hundreds of miles of arduous terrain, cowboys spent months at a time on the trail. Love was deservedly proud of his survival skills on the trail and his mastery of cattle-driving techniques. His talents at roping livestock and his skill on a horse earned him the moniker "Deadwood Dick"—a nickname he retained all his life—when he won a rodeo competition in Deadwood, South Dakota. Love's narrative indicates that he found a deep satisfaction in western life, celebrating the freedom of the open range and the "brotherhood of men" which bound cowboys to one another. Aside from his opening chapters, which critique the institution of slavery, Love does not often address issues of race except to express contempt for Native Americans and Mexicans. It seems clear that his solidarity with other cowboys and his pride in his individual accomplishments are more central to his narrative than a critical analysis of interracial relationships and tensions on the frontier. For Love, the frontier seemed to function as a place where he could be valued for his skills rather than his skin color.

By 1890, the Old West of open land and extensive cattle ranching that Love celebrates in his autobiography had changed dramatically. Railroads had made long cattle drives unnecessary, and the increasing settlement and fencing off of land had blocked the old cowboy trails. With his occupation outmoded by technology, Love responded by finding new employment and new challenges as a "Pullman Porter" on the Pullman rail line, a service job occupied almost exclusively by black men. Although the color line barred him from becoming a more highly paid manager or mechanic on the railroad, Love does not record dissatisfaction or resentment over his relegation to a service position. Rather, as his descriptions of his exciting adventures on the range give way to tame accounts of customer service and rail line procedure, Love insists on the gratification he finds in his role as a porter. For him, riding the railroad provided an opportunity to travel extensively, come in contact with a variety of people, and "justly appreciate the grandeur of our country."

TEACHING TIPS

■ During both his career as a cowboy and his stint as a railroad worker, Love records his feelings of awe for the natural beauty and vast expanses of the United States. Ask students to think about his relationship to the western landscape and to America as a nation. At the close of Chapter XX, after detailing the beauties of the land, Love exhorts his reader to "let your chest swell with pride that you are an American." He goes on to proclaim, "I have seen a large part of America, and am still seeing it . . . America, I love thee, Sweet land of Liberty, home of the brave and the free." How does the landscape contribute to Love's sense of pride in his country? How does Love's status as a former slave complicate his celebration of the "liberty" and "freedom" of the United States? You might ask students to look at images of Yosemite or the Grand Canyon as they think about this issue.

■ When Love is taken captive by the Native Americans he calls "Yellow Dog's Tribe," he attributes their generosity in sparing his life both to his own bravery and to the fact that he is black, since, as he puts it, the tribe "was composed largely of half breeds, and there was a large percentage of colored blood in the tribe." Despite this acknowledgment of shared racial heritage, Love conspicuously distances himself from the Native Americans who adopt him. Ask students to consider the racial politics of this scene. How does Love respond to his captivity? How does he portray his Native American/African American captors? What seems to be his role within the tribe's social hierarchy and how might it be influenced by race? How and why does he escape?

QUESTIONS

Comprehension: What kinds of labor does Love perform over the course of his life? How does he make his career choices? What motivates his transition from one job to another?

Context: Readers might expect Love to be somewhat bitter about the development of the railroad since it led to the demise of his cowboy lifestyle, yet he embraces his career as a Pullman Porter. What does Love find appealing about the railroad? Does his attitude reflect a typically American attitude toward technological change? What insights do his discussions of rail line procedure give us into the corporate structure and philosophy of the Pullman Company in the nineteenth century? What is Love's attitude toward the management of the railroad? How does his portrait of the railroad compare to Ruiz de Burton's?

Context: Examine the photographs of Nat Love featured in the archive, particularly the image of him in his cowboy gear and the image of him wearing his Pullman Porter uniform. In what kinds of conventions of portraiture do these photographs engage? How do Love's different "costumes" impact viewers' understanding of his identity in these pictures? Where are there points of overlap between these photographs of two very different stages in Love's life?

Context: In 1880, George M. Pullman, the president and founder of the Pullman Palace Car Company, began to transform the prairies south of Chicago into a model town for his railroad-car production workers. By creating the town Pullman hoped to improve the morale and health of his workers, while simultaneously increasing productivity and decreasing strikes and labor unrest. This model extended to the other workers for the Pullman Company, such as porters like Love. Compare Love's view of working for the Pullman Company to Pullman's philosophy.

Exploration: Why do you think pop cultural representations of the "Old West" usually portray both cowboys and pioneers as Anglo-

LOVE WEB ARCHIVE

[1012] Anonymous, *Devil's Gate on the Sweetwater* (1880), courtesy of the Denver Public Library. This classic view of Devil's Gate and the Sweetwater River in Natrona County, Wyoming, lay along the route of the Oregon Trail. This is the type of landscape that was ranched and tamed by men like Nat Love.

[1052] S. J. Morrow, *Deadwood in 1876: General View of the Dakota Hillside Above* (1876), courtesy of the National Archives and Records Administration (NARA), Still Pictures Branch. Rapidly growing settlements sprang up as merchants supplied goods and services to miners. Saloons and gambling halls added to the largely lawless conditions found in boomtowns such as Deadwood, South Dakota.

[5296] *Better Known in the Cattle Country as Deadwood Dick, by Himself* (1907), courtesy of Academic Affairs Library, University of North Carolina at Chapel Hill. Nat Love, who was also known as Deadwood Dick, wrote a 1907 autobiography that recounted his post-slavery experiences as both a cowboy and a railroad worker in the Old West.

[5306] Anonymous, *Nat Love (Deadwood Dick) in Pullman Porter Uniform* (c. 1890s), courtesy of Academic Affairs Library, University of North Carolina at Chapel Hill. This photograph of Love was taken shortly after he began his career as a railroad porter in 1890. The image of the wild, long-haired, gun-toting cowboy was replaced with that of the clean-cut, uniform-wearing company man.

[5307] Anonymous, *Deadwood Dick (Nat Love), In My Fighting Clothes* (c.1870–90), courtesy of Duke University, Rare Book, Manuscript, and Special Collections Library. This photo of Nat Love is from *The Life and Adventures of Nat Love Better Known in the Cattle Country as Deadwood Dick by Himself*. Love was one of thousands of ex-slaves who sought a new life in the West following the Civil War.

Americans? How does Nat Love's autobiography challenge traditional images of cowboy life? Does Love's narrative also participate in certain stereotypes?

Exploration: Compare Nat Love's depiction of African American–Native American relations to those in Briton Hammon's "Narrative" (Unit 7). How does each author respond to his captors? To what extent can each of the captivities be read on a spiritual or symbolic level? To what extent does race affect the nature of their captivities?

Suggested Author Pairings

JAMES FENIMORE COOPER, CATHARINE MARIA SEDGWICK, AND THE CHEROKEE MEMORIALISTS

Writing in the first half of the nineteenth century, these authors explored issues of Euro-American incursions into traditional Native American lands in the eastern United States. Cooper and Sedgwick both worked in the tradition of the historical novel. Though they focused on different time periods and geographic settings in their most famous works—Sedgwick set *Hope Leslie* in the Puritan community in seventeenth-century Massachusetts, while Cooper set his *Leather-Stocking* novels in the Great Lakes region in the eighteenth century—they both grappled with the questions of the evolving American character and the racial tensions that complicated Native American and Euro-American relations. Although Cooper and Sedgwick are sympathetic to many of their Native American characters, they still rely on stereotypical depictions and often present Native American culture as anachronistic and untenable in the modern world. The Cherokee memorials contrast interestingly with the works of Cooper and Sedgwick because the memorialists insist so forcefully on the living, vibrant, and evolving nature of Native American societies.

MARIA AMPARO RUIZ DE BURTON, LOUISE AMELIA SMITH CLAPPE, AND JOHN ROLLIN RIDGE

Burton, Clappe, and Ridge all write eloquently about the enormous economic and cultural changes shaping California at the end of the nineteenth century. Because they write from very different points of view—Ruiz de Burton as a Latina woman interested in the plight of displaced Latinos, Clappe as a white woman living in a Gold Rush boomtown, and Ridge as a Cherokee émigré to California who identifies with embattled Latinos—they supplement each other to create a rich picture of the diverse culture of California during the Gold Rush and railroad booms. Ridge's masculinist depiction of Joaquin Murieta as an outlaw hero makes an interesting contrast to Ruiz de Burton's explorations of powerful female characters and to Clappe's depiction of her own position as a woman in an environment dominated by male miners.

WALT WHITMAN AND THE *CORRIDOS*

Both Whitman's work and the *corridos* can be characterized as poetry that seeks to define a new kind of American hero. While the *corridos* adhere to formal conventions and metrical structure in a way that Whitman's poetry does not, they use their lyrics to question boundaries and celebrate resistance to rules and dominant conventions. These two poetic forms have had a lasting and ongoing influence on American verse and music—Whitman's development of free verse transformed American poetry, while the spirit of the *corridos* continues to live in contemporary Latino verse and song.

CAROLINE STANSBURY KIRKLAND AND NAT LOVE

Though they come from very different backgrounds and espoused extremely different values, Kirkland and Love both employed an autobiographical mode to narrate their impressions of life on what they considered the "frontier." Kirkland's interest in "domesticating" the West makes an effective contrast to Love's celebration of his time roaming the plains as a cowherd with no permanent home. (The extent to which Kirkland's model won out might be gauged by the fact that Love soon found the cowboy life untenable and took to the more domestic position of porter on the railroads.) Kirkland's female perspective is reflected in her chronicles of everyday experiences of hardworking women, an aspect of western life that usually went unreported. Love, on the other hand, is much more interested in constructing himself as a masculine hero and turns to "tall tales" and accounts of exciting adventures more often than realistic description to narrate his adventures in the West.

CORE CONTEXTS

America Unbridled: The Iron Horse and Manifest Destiny

The development of the railroad system transformed American culture, physically binding the country together and enabling people to travel long distances in short periods of time and in relative comfort. The railroad broke traditional geographic barriers that had restricted trade, commodity flow, and immigration, thus speeding the process of American expansion and producing unprecedented economic opportunities. In their early stages of development at the beginning of the nineteenth century, railroads were constructed mainly to link urban, metropolitan areas in the East. But with the ascension of the concept of **Manifest Destiny** over the course of the nineteenth century, Americans' desire for a transcontinental railroad intensified. A moral justification for expansion, Manifest Destiny refers to the popular belief that American control of the land that stretched from the Atlantic to the Pacific was inevitable and divinely sanctioned. Because of this culturally arrogant conviction of the

[7363] Union Pacific Railroad, *Map of the Union Pacific Rail Road and Its Connections* (1868), courtesy of the University of Michigan and the *Making of America* Project.

[1768] Anonymous, Poster circulated in Philadelphia in 1839 to discourage the coming of the railroad (1839), courtesy of the National Archives and Records Administration (NARA), Still Pictures Branch.

United States's "right" to western lands, American policy makers had few scruples about displacing Native Americans, Mexicans, and other groups who already inhabited the land from the Great Plains to California.

The transcontinental railroad seemed symbolic of America's destiny to stretch "from sea to shining sea," so public interest in and support for the railroads increased over the century. The nation's total mileage of track multiplied from 9,000 in 1850 to 30,000 in 1860. By 1870 there were 94,000 miles of railroad track in the United States, and by 1900 there were 199,000. While some of this construction filled out the urban eastern network, much of it went into the grand project of building the transcontinental lines that ran across the sparsely settled plains and through the rugged mountains and canyons of the West. Railways were also important to the development of National Parks. As Joshua Scott Johns points out in the online exhibit "All Aboard: The Role of the Railroads in Protecting, Promoting, and Selling Yellowstone and Yosemite National Parks," "From the earliest days of discovery to the crucial National Park Act of 1916, the process of park development was shaped by needs of the railroads—from acquiring investors to selling mass-market tourism, they modified their advertising strategies to win the patronage of new passengers with the promise of fulfilling their expectations of the West in 'America's playgrounds.'"

Although the railroads were the first "big business" enterprise in the United States and created enormous profits for the tycoons that ran them, the transcontinental project was largely fueled by government grants. Issuing both federal land and cash grants, the government subsidized the Union Pacific and the Central Pacific railroads' work of laying track from Omaha to Sacramento. The dubious financial practices of the men who ran the railroads—they controlled every aspect of the rail system from real estate to construction and thus found it easy to engage in profiteering—earned them the pejorative title "robber barons." Maria Amparo Ruiz de Burton offers a searing critique of the robber barons' monopolistic business practices in her novel *The Squatter and the Don*. Featuring the four men who headed the California railroad monopoly (known as the "Big Four") as characters in her book, she indicts their immoral business manipulations and unfair control over the economic resources of the state. In the novel, the Big Four, in collusion with Congress, ensure the failure of a proposed rail line, interfere with the prosperity of San Diego, and create financial hardships for honest working people. As Ruiz de Burton so vividly demonstrates in her portrait of the fate of San Diego, exclusion from the rail line could spell doom for a town.

While the railroad could have an enormously stimulating effect on local economies, promoting growth through easy immigration and the efficient transport of commodities, it could also lead to the failure of certain economies and the destruction of certain ways of life. By expediting the immigration of European American settlers, the railroad hastened Native Americans' expulsion from much of their traditional western land. The railroad famously led to the demise of the culture of the cowboys, making long-distance cattle herding obsolete because livestock could be transported more efficiently by rail car. Nat Love's career as a cowboy came to an end with the growth of the rail system, a setback he responded to by simply taking a job as a porter on the railroad. The expansion of the railroad also enabled the destruction of natural resources: the ease with which lumber could be shipped led to the demise of the white pine in the Great Lakes region. While buffalo herds were already endangered by wasteful European American hunting practices long before the completion of the transcontinental railroads, the trains sealed their doom by allowing passengers to shoot defenseless animals from inside the cars. As the train approached a herd, passengers opened the windows, pointed their rifles, and fired at random. The animals they killed were usually left to rot where they fell.

[7358] Anonymous, *Joining the Tracks for the First Transcontinental Railroad, Promontory, Utah Territory, 1869,* courtesy of the National Archives and Records Administration (NARA), Still Pictures Branch.

Nor was the railroad without physical dangers for its human passengers and employees. In its early years, travel by rail was a somewhat risky enterprise, as fires and derailments were common. But the dangers of riding in a train could not begin to compare to the hazards of laying track and building the rail line. The Union Pacific and Central Pacific exploited inexpensive labor, hiring primarily African Americans and Irish and Chinese immigrants to do the difficult work of constructing the transcontinental line. The Chinese workers (referred to as "coolies") who manned the Central Pacific crews, in particular, faced extremely dangerous working conditions as they graded and hauled the road through the rugged Sierra mountains. Many Chinese men died in the process of laying the transcontinental railroad. While the completion of the transcontinental line in May of 1869 was a much-celebrated national event—a golden spike was installed where the railroads met at Promontory, Utah—it is important to remember that this industrial feat came at the high price of many human lives.

Railroad companies also relied on exploitative labor practices to provide service to passengers within the cars. The porter positions on the Pullman Palace Car Company, for instance, were occupied almost exclusively by African American men who were not eligible for better-paying jobs as engineers or mechanics. Judging from his autobiography, Nat Love apparently found satisfaction in his career as a Pullman

Porter, but perhaps he did not feel comfortable recording any resentment or disappointment he might have felt. Eventually, labor dissatisfaction came to a head in the railroad industry. In 1893, railroad employees banded together to form the American Railway Union. A large-scale strike known as the Great Railroad Strike of 1877 crippled rail transit, and the Pullman employees went on strike in 1894. While none of these early attempts at labor organization resulted in significant reforms, they did lay the groundwork for later, more successful protests.

In the American imagination, railroads were symbols of optimism and democracy, creating economic opportunity and connecting the vast expanses of the country. And in important ways, the railroads really did function like this. People were able to travel through the country with new ease and speed and many Americans felt their country to be more unified as a result. In their development of efficient timetables, the railroads even created the Standard Time Zones that put citizens on the same schedules, a phenomenon that was originally known as "railroad time." Whatever its potential as an agent of democracy and unity, however, the railroad also enabled monopolies, natural destruction, and human exploitation.

QUESTIONS

Comprehension: What is the concept of Manifest Destiny?

Comprehension: What was the transcontinental railroad? How was it constructed? Why was it so important to nineteenth-century Americans?

Comprehension: Read the anti-railroad broadside featured in the archive. This piece of propaganda was part of a campaign to curtail railroad expansion in the urban areas of the East. What are the writer's objections to the railroad? What kinds of dangers does the railroad pose to the community?

Context: How does Walt Whitman describe the railroad in his poetry? Why might it have been an important symbol for him?

Context: Consider why Maria Amparo Ruiz de Burton featured the California railroad tycoons in her novel. Why did she use their real names? What risks did she take in doing so? What is the effect of the insertion of these "real people" into a piece of historical fiction?

Context: What was Nat Love's position on the Pullman line? Why do you think he included photographs of his experience working for the railroad in his autobiography? What do the photographs tell you about the nature of his work? What kind of satisfaction did he find in his job?

Exploration: Why do you think escaping slaves adopted the symbolic term "railroad" to describe their support system? What did the Underground Railroad have in common with a real railroad? Why might this symbol have appealed to abolitionists and runaways?

Exploration: Rail travel is no longer the primary mode most Americans use for long-distance travel. What kinds of transportation have replaced the railroad? Do they occupy a similar position in the popular imagination? Can you think of any industrial or technological developments of the twentieth century that have created the same kind of national excitement that the transcontinental railroad did in the nineteenth century?

Exploration: In "The Virgin and the Dynamo" (*The Education of Henry Adams*), Henry Adams claims that "his historical neck [was] broken by the sudden irruption of forces totally new" when he viewed the dynamo and steam engines at the Gallery of Machines at the Great Exposition of 1900. What was so revolutionary about turn-of-the-century technology that it would have this impact on Adams? What place did the railroads take in this technological revolution?

the Union Pacific Rail Road and Its Connections (1868), courtesy of the University of Michigan and the *Making of America* project. This map shows the route of the transcontinental railroad from the Atlantic to the Pacific; it was completed in 1869 after just seven years of construction. Union Pacific and Central Pacific Railroad companies worked from Sacramento, California, and Omaha, Nebraska, respectively, to meet at the midpoint of Promontory, Utah.

Competing Claims: The California Gold Rush

On January 24, 1848, gold was discovered in California at Sutter's Mill in the foothills of the Sierra Nevada Mountains. The find sparked a national and international craze as people from all over the world were seized by "gold fever" and headed to California to "strike it rich." Known as "Forty-niners" or "Argonauts" after the adventurers in Greek mythology who hunted the Golden Fleece, the immigrants contributed to an unprecedented population explosion in the American West. Over the course of a few months San Francisco was transformed from a village of 459 people to a city with more than 20,000 residents. The Gold Rush immigrants were overwhelmingly male, but beyond their sex they did not have much in common: the mines drew white Americans from the East Coast and the South, African Americans (both slaves and freemen), Europeans, South Americans, Australians, and Mexicans. In California, these diverse groups encountered the Hispanic and Native American populations that already inhabited the area. The many nations, colors, classes, and creeds represented in the gold fields made nineteenth-century California a place where access to resources, distributions of power, and notions of social order were debated and contested. Adding to the instability, few of the Gold Rush immigrants were interested in permanently settling in California; instead, they intended to amass a fortune quickly and then return home.

In reality, few people found the riches that the legends, stories, and promotional brochures promised. To the miners' disappointment, the streets of California were not paved in gold. Mining was dirty, frustrating, tiring work. Individual "placer" miners used picks to chip gold from rock deposits and pans and "sluice boxes" to sift gold from the dirt and gravel of riverbeds. Most miners lived in primitive, makeshift camps

[1303] Francis Samuel Marryat, *The Winter of 1849* (1855), courtesy of Bancroft Library, University of California, Berkeley.

[7407] Anonymous, *Portsmouth Square, San Francisco, California* (c. 1851), courtesy of the Library of Congress [LC-USZC4-7422].

[5841] Currier and Ives, *Gold Mining in California* (c. 1871), courtesy of the Library of Congress [LC-USZC2-1755].

"COMPETING CLAIMS"
WEB ARCHIVE

[1303] Francis Samuel Marryat, *The Winter of 1849* (1855), courtesy of Bancroft Library, University of California, Berkeley. This illustration of residents trying to navigate San Francisco's flooded streets shows how rapidly growing boom towns and cities on the West Coast suffered from poor planning and local weather conditions during periods of expansion.

[3721] Anonymous, *Panning at the Junction of the Eldorado and Bonanza Creeks, Klondike* (c. 1900), courtesy of the Denver Public Library. Although gold miners were primarily men, some women, like those pictured here, took part. Contrary to what most expected, mining was dirty, tiring work that led only a few to wealth.

[3725] Anonymous, *Hanging of Gilbert and Rosengrants at Leadville* (1881), courtesy of the Denver Public Library. Frontier justice was often swift and pub-

where diseases such as cholera and scurvy were rampant and mob violence was common. Many men found that their mining work produced only what Louise Clappe, in her descriptions of life in the mining camps, called "wages"—enough to live on from day to day but not enough to save. Commodities in the boomtowns were extremely expensive since high demand and scarce resources allowed merchants to charge steep "gold rush prices." Gambling halls, saloons, and brothels set up shop around the mining camps, selling alcohol and entertainment to the miners in their leisure time. A cycle of boom and bust ensured that many miners left California as poor as they had been when they arrived.

People who had the foresight to set up businesses outfitting the miners and supplying them with necessities made more stable fortunes. Companies in the East sold camp equipment, mining tools, and guidebooks to men planning to head to the gold fields. Merchants and entrepreneurs followed the miners to areas where strikes had been made and set up boarding houses, grocery stores, saloons, brothels, and other service businesses. Chinese immigrants, who often faced systematic discrimination and harassment in the mines, sometimes opened washhouses providing laundry services for miners. According to the Museum of the City of San Francisco, by 1876 there were 151,000 Chinese in the United States, of whom 116,000 were in the state of California. Their experiences did not go unrecorded: as literary critic Xiao-huang Yin recounts in *Chinese American Literature since the 1850s*, early Chinese immigrants recorded their experiences in numerous forms, ranging from newspaper stories, to autobiographical texts, to writings on the walls of Angel Island by detainees (Angel Island was a point of entry for many Asian American immigrants), to educational writings by students and scholars who came to America to complete their studies. These early testimonials provide an important counterpoint to other writings from the gold camps, writings that were often negative in their portrayals of Chinese immigrants. This alternative vision of life in early California becomes the setting for twentieth-century author Maxine Hong Kingston's novel *China Men* (1980).

The rags-to-riches stories of Mexican women making fortunes selling tortillas and white women turning enormous profits selling biscuits also speak to the extraordinary business opportunities in the mining camps. Many of these businesses were short-lived—boomtowns tended to disappear almost as quickly as they sprang up—but some entrepreneurs turned sizeable profits and were able to follow the miners to the next strike.

Sometimes, the cultural and racial diversity of the gold fields led to harmonious and mutually beneficial interaction: miners successfully shared tents, food, domestic labor, and economic partnerships with people of other ethnicities and language groups. But tension, conflict, and hostility could also characterize intercultural encounters in the mining camps. Because few mining towns had established police forces or stable systems of justice, miners could often get away with using violence and intimidation to harass their competition and force rival "placers" from their claims. Eventually, official United States policy formalized discrimination toward non-American miners with the passage of the Foreign Miners' Tax Laws of 1850 and 1852. Levying a steep licensing tax on all non-citizen miners, the Foreign Miners' Tax was aimed first at French- and Spanish-speaking miners and eventually at Chinese immigrants to the gold fields. The tax laws were controversial, drawing protests from both the affected miners and the merchants and entrepreneurs who made a living by supplying those miners. John Rollin Ridge's account of Joaquin Murieta chronicles the abuses and harassment suffered by Mexican miners—harassment that seemed particularly unjust since many Latinos had settled in the California territory long before Anglos arrived. Murieta is forced off his mining claim and his farm by unfair land laws and strong-arm tactics. After enduring a variety of other outrages, he is driven to a life of crime to avenge the injustices he and his fellow Mexicans have suffered. Ridge's novel thus mounts a subversive critique of official American policy toward the many non-Anglo miners who lived in California in the nineteenth century.

Eventually, gold became scarcer, European Americans solidified their dominance in California, and corporate, industrialized mining replaced the labor of the individual "placer" miners. New strikes in Nevada, Colorado, the Dakotas, and Montana briefly revived "gold fever" at various points later in the nineteenth century, but the peak of the dynamic, diverse, vibrant culture that characterized the California Gold Rush communities had passed by the mid-1850s.

QUESTIONS

Comprehension: What was a "placer" miner?

Comprehension: What different groups came to California during the Gold Rush? What did they have in common? What kinds of tensions and conflicts arose between groups?

Context: Compare Louise Clappe's descriptions of life in Rich Bar with the photograph of Deadwood, South Dakota, and the illustration of a California mining camp in the winter of 1849 featured in the archive. How does Clappe react to the makeshift quality of mining town buildings and the coarseness of mining town society?

Context: How does Louise Clappe's gender structure her narrative of her experiences in Rich Bar? What roles and opportunities are available to women in the camp community? How does she describe her interactions with other women?

Exploration: Many Americans' notions of the Gold Rush come from theme park reenactments and popular culture references. What references to the Gold Rush have you encountered in popular culture? How is the Gold Rush portrayed? Why do you think the Gold Rush occupies such an important place in the American national imagination?

lic. Here, residents of Leadville, Colorado, turn out in large numbers to watch the hanging of two men in 1881.

[5228] Anonymous, *Montgomery Street, San Francisco, 1852* (n.d.), courtesy of the Library of Congress, Prints and Photographs Division [LC-USZ62-55762]. Rapid, primarily white immigration during the Gold Rush brought California to statehood in 1850, as a "free state" that forbade slavery. Yet, demand for land and forced labor caused a genocidal-scale population decline among California Indians.

[5240] Helen Hunt Jackson, *Ramona* manuscript page (c. 1883), courtesy of Colorado College, Tutt Library Special Collections. Helen Hunt Jackson wrote *Ramona* hoping to call attention to the mistreatment of California's Indians, much as Harriet Beecher Stowe had to the plight of slaves with *Uncle Tom's Cabin*.

[5841] Currier and Ives, *Gold Mining in California* (c. 1871), courtesy of the Library of Congress [LC-USZC2-1755]. This Currier & Ives lithograph presents a romantic and sanitized portrayal of life in the gold fields. In actuality, the mining process exacted an incredible toll on both miners and the surrounding environment.

[7407] Anonymous, *Portsmouth Square, San Francisco, California* (c. 1851), courtesy of the Library of Congress [LC-USZC4-7422]. In July 1846, just two months after the start of the U.S.-Mexican War, John B. Montgomery, captain of the U.S.S. *Portsmouth*, raised the American flag in San Francisco for the first time. Days later the U.S. army took all of Upper California, though the war raged on for two more years. It was the first and by far the easiest victory for the United States.

[8597] State of California, *Chinese Immigration* (1877), courtesy of Vincent Voice Library, Michigan State University. The California Chinese Exclusion Act of 1877 was the result of growing anti-Chinese sentiment and a shaky labor market. Chinese workers came to the region in large numbers during the 1850s, drawn by the prospect of work from the Gold Rush and railroads. Many white laborers resented the Chinese taking jobs in an overcrowded market.

Exploration: Can you think of other moments in American history that have spurred the same kind of immigration, development, and/or excitement that the Gold Rush inspired (such as the late-twentieth-century "dot.com" boom, for example)? How do these periods of tremendous economic opportunities challenge the status quo? How do they enable new social formations?

Paradise of Bachelors: The Social World of Men in Nineteenth-Century America

Although both "bachelor" and "spinster" refer to unmarried individuals, the titles were far from equivalent in nineteenth-century American culture. While "old maids" were often perceived as socially undesirable, bachelors found social acceptance and even encouragement for their unmarried state. All-male social clubs flourished, with fraternities, professional clubs, service clubs, and "mystical orders" such as the Masons enjoying enormous growth in membership over the course of the nineteenth century. Often involving elaborate initiation ceremonies intended to create intimate bonds between members, these organizations took over some of the traditional functions of the family and provided sanctioned social outlets for men to interact with other men without the presence of women.

The work of westward expansion also created social formations in which men frequently lived without women and came to depend on other men for domestic comforts, economic assistance, and companionship. While Native American groups in the western United States continued to live in communities with roughly equal numbers of men and women, African American, Chinese, Latino, European, and Anglo-American immigrants for the most part lived and worked in communities with radically skewed sex ratios. The 1850 census in California, for example, revealed that more than 90 percent of the state's population was male. Certain professions, such as cattle herding and mining, attracted a high proportion of unmarried or unattached men because the labor was strenuous, time-consuming, and often necessitated living in primitive and makeshift camps—a lifestyle that was perceived as inappropriate or even dangerous for women. Nat Love's account of his life as a cowboy stresses the masculine values and codes of loyalty that bound cowboys together as a "brotherhood of men." Sharing physical hardships, economic concerns, and domestic chores, the cowboys in Love's narrative develop an intense camaraderie out of their interdependence.

Miners in the Gold Rush camps of California, too, found themselves surrounded by other single men hoping to "strike it rich." As historian Susan Lee Johnson observes, the scarcity of women led to "drastically altered divisions of labor in which men took on tasks that womenfolk

[1092] William J. Carpenter, *Life on the Plains* (1915), courtesy of the Library of Congress [LC-USZ62-99804].

would have performed back home." The most common type of household in the mining camps was a tent or cabin inhabited by two to five men who constituted an interdependent economic unit. They usually worked together at mining their claim, performed domestic chores for one another, and put their earnings in a common fund which was divided evenly among members of the household. Men who had never before cooked learned to prepare stew, bread, beans, and pies; and men who had never before done laundry learned to wash and mend clothes. Some men, disillusioned with the often futile search for gold, set up businesses performing chores normally associated with women, making a living by cooking food and doing laundry for the miners. These experiences with domesticity could exacerbate racial tensions—more than one miner commented negatively on the strange food and outlandish domestic practices of the different ethnic groups that he encountered in the camps—but the household intimacy inherent in camp life could also transcend racial difference. White men amicably shared tents, food, and economic responsibilities with Chinese, African American, and Latino miners. Critics have often been puzzled by the fact that Nat Love, who was African American, rarely mentions issues of race in his account of his life on the open range. But it seems clear that, in Love's experience at least, race was often secondary or irrelevant in the face of the economic and social interdependence that united the cowboys.

[3889] Thomas Eakins, *The Swimming Hole* (1884), courtesy of the Amon Carter Museum, Fort Worth, Texas.

Without the presence of women, the always unstable line dividing the **homosocial** from the **homosexual**—that is, dividing non-sexual male bonding activities from sexual contact between men—became even more blurred. As traditional notions of "normal" gender roles were challenged and unsettled, men could display both subtly and openly the erotic connections they felt for other men. When the miners at Angel Camp in southern California held dances, half of the men danced the part of women, wearing patches over the crotches of their pants to signal their "feminine" role. Men routinely shared beds in mining communities and on the range, and cowboys and miners settled into partnerships that other men recognized (and sometimes referred to) as "bachelor marriages."

It is difficult to find unambiguous references to homosexual relationships in nineteenth-century American writings, partly because there was no vocabulary to express such relationships at the time (the term "homosexual" did not exist until the late nineteenth century). Walt Whitman, who had several intimate relationships with men, struggled with this absence of language in his poetic efforts to describe and record his passionate same-sex relationships. In his *Calamus* poems and the "Twenty-eight Bathers" section of *Song of Myself*, for example, Whitman produced moving, evocative portraits of male homosexual love. But he often felt compelled to "shade and hide [his] thoughts," as he put it, because he was unable to speak as explicitly

[2061] Asher B. Durand, *Kindred Spirits* (1849), courtesy of the New York Public Library.

"PARADISE OF BACHELORS"
WEB ARCHIVE

[1092] William J. Carpenter, *Life on the Plains* (1915), courtesy of the Library of Congress [LC-USZ62-99804]. Navajo and cowboy playing cards. These cards show the type of interethnic male-male bonding that we see in James Fenimore Cooper's novels. This type of interaction largely died out when white males started to bring their families to settle in the West.

[2027] Anonymous, *Theodore Roosevelt, full-length portrait, standing alongside horse, facing left; wearing cowboy outfit* (1910), courtesy of the Library of Congress [LC-USZ62-91139]. With his infamous motto "Walk softly and carry a big stick," President Theodore Roosevelt is remembered as a trustbuster, one who worked to strengthen U.S. foreign policy, and one who was committed to the conservation of frontier land.

as he might have liked. Interestingly, Whitman's descriptions of heterosexual encounters caused more public outrage than his "Calamus" poems did, perhaps because his homoerotic imagery was new and innovative, and thus unfamiliar to much of his audience. Still, the implications of Whitman's poetry certainly reached some of his readers. Eve Sedgwick has noted that Whitman's writings, Whitman's image, and Whitman's name came to function as a kind of code for men to communicate their homosexual identity and their homoerotic attractions to one another: "Photographs of Whitman, gifts of Whitman's books, specimens of his handwriting, news of Whitman, admiring references to 'Whitman' which seem to have functioned as badges of homosexual recognition, were the currency of a new community that saw itself as created in Whitman's image." While certainly not all bachelors had homosexual experiences, the creation and legitimization of new social spheres made up of single men defined and enabled a variety of masculine identities and same-sex relationships.

QUESTIONS

Comprehension: How did all-male social clubs and communities both replicate and challenge more traditional family structures?

Comprehension: What kinds of domestic tasks did men perform on the range and in the mining camps? How did they usually divide up the labor?

Comprehension: Examine the photographs and illustrations of mining camps featured in the archive. What different ethnic groups do you see represented? How did these groups interact within mining communities?

Context: Walt Whitman had photographs taken of himself with several of his young male companions. Some of his friends were scandalized or upset by the pictures, calling them everything from "silly-idiotic" to "sickly." Other friends and acquaintances of Whitman admired the photos and requested copies. Whitman never distributed these pictures widely, instead keeping them to himself or sharing them only with a limited circle of friends. But in Section VII of *Live Oak, with Moss,* Whitman wrote that he hoped some future reader would "Publish my name and hang up my picture as that of the tenderest lover, The friend, the lover's portrait, of whom his friend, his lover, was fondest. . . ." What does Whitman mean in this poetic request to have his portrait hung? By what kind of portrait do you think he would like to be remembered? Why do you think he might have felt compelled to have his picture taken with his male companions? What do Whitman's friends' reactions to the photographs tell you about the social lives of nineteenth-century men?

Context: In her story "Cacoethes Scribendi" Catharine Maria Sedgwick (who herself remained unmarried all her life) describes a community populated almost solely by single women and widows. Does she have the same celebratory view of same-sex communities that writers like Whitman or Nat Love seemed to have? What kind of camaraderie binds the women together in her story? What divides them?

Context: Examine Louise Clappe's descriptions of life in the mining town of Rich Bar in her "Shirley Letters." How does Clappe's position as a woman in a mostly male community shape her letters? What is her sense of the male-male relationships that bind together the community? How does she describe the roles of other women in the town?

Context: Look at Thomas Eakins's painting *Swimming Hole* (1884), featured in the archive. Is this a homoerotic picture? How do you think nineteenth-century viewers would have responded to it?

Exploration: In his poetic celebrations of homoerotic love Whitman sometimes felt compelled to "shade and hide" his meanings. Can you think of other American writers who sometimes seem to hint at homosexual relationships but do not describe them explicitly? Hemingway, Dickinson, or Melville (especially in the "Counterpane" chapter of *Moby Dick*) might be appropriate figures to think about in this regard. What kinds of imagery and language do these writers rely on to convey their meanings?

Exploration: How did social reactions to unmarried men differ from social reactions to unmarried women in the nineteenth century? Did single women enjoy the same kinds of opportunities that single men did? How do you think cultural ideas about unmarried individuals (both men and women) have changed over time in America?

Exploration: How does Melville play on the construction of "the bachelor" in his short story "The Paradise of Bachelors and The Tartarus of Maids"? How do the opportunities available to bachelors compare to those open to single women in the story?

Exploration: Eve Sedgwick has argued that portraits and records of Whitman acted as a kind of code for men to convey homoerotic feelings to one another. Why do you think they chose Whitman to represent their identity? Can you think of any groups that use images or personalities in a similar way today? What kinds of material objects circulate as "code" today?

[2061] Asher B. Durand, *Kindred Spirits* (1849), courtesy of the New York Public Library. Durand's painting depicts Hudson River School founder Thomas Cole, left, and poet William Cullen Bryant in the Kaaterskill Clove. Both Cole and Bryant used the interaction between humans and nature as the primary theme for their work.

[3717] Charles D. Kirkland, *Cow Boy* (c. 1880), courtesy of the Denver Public Library, Western History Collection. As the nation's focus shifted to the West, the cowboy replaced the frontiersman of the eastern woodlands as the popular icon of American independence and self-sufficiency.

[3889] Thomas Eakins, *The Swimming Hole* (1884), courtesy of Amon Carter Museum, Fort Worth, Texas. The homosocial nature of nineteenth-century male relations is reflected in this painting, which shows a group of students swimming while their headmaster (Eakins) swims nearby.

[6242] Phillips and Taylor, *Walt Whitman, half-length portrait, seated, facing left, wearing hat and sweater, holding butterfly* (1873), courtesy of the Library of Congress [LC-USZ62-77082]. Eve Sedgwick has noted that even before the term "homosexual" was invented, Walt Whitman's writings, image, and name functioned as a code for men to communicate their homosexual identity to one another.

EXTENDED CONTEXTS

Star-Spangled Moccasins: The American Flag in Native American Culture

In a circa 1874 drawing, the Oglala warrior Sitting Bull depicted a Native American warrior proudly flying the stars and stripes of an American flag as he rides into battle. In many ways, this is a puzzling, even paradoxical, image. Why would the Oglala—who resisted U.S. encroachment on their lands—engage in a seemingly zealous show of American patriotism? Why would they embrace the flag of a country that they had historically perceived as hostile and oppressive? In fact,

[7414] William Henry Taylor, *Juanita, Wife of Navajo Chief Manuelito* (c. 1873), courtesy of Smithsonian Institution, National Anthropological Archives.

at the end of the nineteenth century, many Native Americans from many different tribes used flag imagery as a design element in their art, clothing, and crafts. While some of these objects were produced for sale or exchange with European Americans (the tourist trade was a growing component of many tribal economies), there is compelling evidence that many of these artifacts were used, worn, and treasured by Native Americans themselves. Not always literal or exact representations, Native American flag images often modify or abstract the pattern of the American flag, enlarging or shrinking the blue field, omitting stripes, or substituting other shapes for stars. But however the image is refashioned and transformed in Native American art, it is nonetheless recognizable as the American flag. These representations are a testament to the creativity and inventiveness of the Native American artisans who appropriated this symbol of European American power and dominance and adapted it to their own complex and diverse uses.

Many of the Great Plains tribes held the traditional belief that flags captured in battle were imbued with the power of the enemy, a belief probably reinforced by the fact that U.S. troops used the flag as a battle emblem when they attacked Native Americans. Upon capture, Native Americans believed that the flag transferred its power to its new owner, thus endowing him with the strength of his adversary. In this context, Sitting Bull's drawing of the Oglala warrior carrying the American flag into combat can be interpreted as a testament to the warrior's prowess and triumph in battle. Similarly, the Lakota tradition of decorating children's clothing with American flags can be understood as a method for ensuring their protection and safety through the flag's talismanic power. One of the few Lakota survivors of the massacre at Wounded Knee was a little girl who was found in the snow, wearing a bonnet beaded with American flag patterns.

Native Americans may also have adopted the flag on occasion as an expedient way to make their traditional practices seem less threatening to Reservation authorities. When U.S. authorities banned the Lakota summer Sun Dance ceremony because they saw it as pagan and subversive, the Lakota adapted parts of the ceremony into a sanctioned Fourth of July celebration. Because the traditional sacred colors of the Sun Dance are red and blue, the insertion of American flag imagery did not disrupt the spiritual significance of the ceremony. Native American art also frequently introduces traditional sacred symbols into the representation of the flag pattern itself. Substituting the usual five-pointed stars with four-armed Morning Stars and crosses, Native American artisans transformed the flag into a representation of their own religious and cultural traditions. The varied examples of flag imagery in Native American art point out the multivalence of this sym-

[7418] Anonymous, Boys' moccasins, Lakota (n.d.), courtesy of the New York State Historical Association, Thaw Collection.

bol. For some artists, the representation of the American flag may have been a means to signify assimilation with the dominant culture, while for others, redesigned images of the flag probably served as a means of proclaiming their cultural independence.

QUESTIONS

Comprehension: Look at the artifacts produced by Native American artisans featured in the archive. How do these representations of the American flag modify its usual design?

Context: Critics have noted that the Cherokee memorialists invoke some of the language and ideas of the American Declaration of Independence to argue their case to the U.S. Congress. How does their rhetorical strategy compare to the Native American artisans' use of the American flag in the items featured in the archive? Should these deployments of important American symbols be understood as simply "patriotic"?

Exploration: Think about moments when flags and flag imagery proliferate in American culture, such as on the Fourth of July, during a war, or in the wake of a tragedy like the attack on New York's World Trade Center on September 11, 2001. Why do Americans turn to the flag so often at these moments? Even though the display of the flag seems to be a symbol of national unity, how might the flag hold different meanings for different Americans at these times?

Picturing America: The Hudson River School Painters

In 1816 Governor Clinton of New York addressed the American Academy of Fine Arts, urging artists to create new movements and styles that would reflect the superiority of American morals and the grandeur of American scenery:

> For can there be a country in the world better calculated than ours to exercise and to exalt the imagination—to call into activity the creative powers of the mind, and to afford just views of the beautiful, the wonderful, and the sublime? Here Nature has conducted her operations on a magnificent scale: extensive and elevated mountains, . . . rivers of prodigious magnitude . . . , and boundless forests filled with wild beasts and savage men, and covered with the towering oak.

By the 1820s, artists had responded to his call. Thomas Cole caused a sensation in the New York art world with his large-scale paintings of the vast panoramas, rugged peaks, steep precipices, rushing waters, and dramatic light effects of the Hudson River Valley. Cole celebrated the primeval, unspoiled quality of the American wilderness, believing that it represented a perfect spiritual state and was a direct reflection of the divine work of the Creator. Cole's powerful landscapes and innovative ideas soon influenced other artists, including Asher Durand, Frederic Church, Albert Bierstadt, and Martin Johnson Heade. Originally known as simply "American" or "Native" painters, this group of artists is usually referred to as the **Hudson River School** today, in reference to their early focus on the landscape of the Hudson River Valley, which was the "frontier" of the late eighteenth century.

[7404] Asher B. Durand, *Progress (The Advance of Civilization)* (1853), courtesy of Gulf States Paper Corporation, Warner Collection.

The Hudson River School artists were interested in highlighting the awesome, monumental quality of the American wilderness by juxtaposing it against the minuteness of the human body: many of their paintings feature tiny human figures who are dwarfed by the vastness of the landscapes that surround them. But rather than conveying a sense of alienation or human insignificance, these pictures instead celebrate an ideal of harmony between people and nature. Fundamentally optimistic in their view of American expansion and the promise of democracy, the Hudson River School artists presented images of human industry coexisting in and even complementing the beauty of nature. In Asher Durand's *Progress* (1853), for example, a small city nestles within a stunning landscape, sending rail lines, telegraph poles, roads, and steamboats out into the wilderness. A group of Native Americans looks out over the scene in awestruck admiration and happiness. This romanticized vision of industrialization was part of the Hudson River School's aesthetic philosophy, which saw beauty in the contrast between primeval landscapes and pastoral scenes of towns and farms—an attitude in keeping with much of the prose and poetry of nineteenth-century America, from James Fenimore Cooper to Walt Whitman.

The Hudson River School was also noted for its commitment to an almost scientific attention to detail and clarity in the presentation of natural landscapes. Artists usually did their preliminary sketching out of doors, in the midst of the dramatic scenery that inspired them, then returned to their studios to paint the final canvas. While they were intent on faithfully reproducing the natural effects they observed, the Hudson River artists were not afraid to literally move mountains when it suited their sense of aesthetics. "Composing" landscapes by combining elements from different geographical locations, exaggerating heights and expanses, and playing with lighting, these artists created dramatic panoramas that they believed were faithful to the spirit, if not the reality, of the American landscape. After reading Cooper's *The Last of the Mohicans*, Cole even painted fictional scenes from the novel because it accorded so closely with his sense of America's identity and character. In their quest for new and spectacular effects, the Hudson River artists had journeyed far beyond the Hudson River by the mid-nineteenth century, traveling to Niagara

[1181] Albert Bierstadt, *Valley of the Yosemite* (1864), courtesy of the Museum of Fine Arts, Boston; gift of Martha C. Karolik for the M. and M. Karolik Collection of American Paintings, 1815–1865.

Falls, the Rocky Mountains, California, and even South America to record the expanse and grandeur of the continent.

QUESTIONS

Comprehension: How do the Hudson River artists usually depict human figures? What is the significance of the figures' size in relation to the vast landscapes?

Comprehension: How does Asher B. Durand portray Native Americans in his 1853 painting *Progress*? What assumptions underwrite his treatment of their response to "progress"? Why are they situated on a precipice overlooking the town?

Context: Read some of Cooper's descriptions of the view from the overlook he calls "Mt. Vision" in *The Pioneers*. How do these literary descriptions of the upstate New York landscape compare with the Hudson River School paintings? Why do you think Hudson River School paintings are frequently chosen as the cover illustrations for editions of Cooper's novels?

Context: How do Whitman's celebrations of the diversity—the "multitudes"—that make up the American body politic compare with the Hudson River School aesthetic? Which of Whitman's descriptions of American landscapes and cityscapes might fit within the ideals of the Hudson River School? What parts of America does Whitman celebrate that would probably fall outside of the scope of the Hudson River aesthetic?

Exploration: Many Hudson River School paintings present an idealized vision of harmony between humans and nature, between industrialization and the wilderness. Do you think Americans still subscribe to this optimistic view of the relationship between people and nature? How has the environmentalist movement complicated our understanding of "progress"?

Exploration: Art historians have pointed out that the Hudson River School painters developed a very "masculine" aesthetic. By picturing rugged, remote terrain, these artists interpolate the viewer as an active and intrepid explorer of the wilderness. How might the Hudson River artists compare to the figure of the explorer/hero in the literature of exploration?

ASSIGNMENTS

Personal and Creative Responses

1. *Journal:* Imagine that you live next door to Caroline Kirkland in the village of Pinckney, Michigan. Write a letter to a friend who is curious about your experience in Michigan. Include a description of how you feel about Kirkland and her family. Do you see her as an asset to the community? How do you feel about the descriptions of Pinckney that appear in the book she published?

ness became popular as the United States continued its westward expansion.
[5931] Worthington Whittredge, *The Old Hunting Grounds* (1864), courtesy of Reynolda House, Museum of American Art. The decaying Indian canoe among birch trees symbolizes the sentimental death of Native American culture found in James Fenimore Cooper's work and other frontier literature. After ten years of artistic training in Europe, Worthington Whittredge returned to America in 1859, impressed with the vast wilderness that still existed in his homeland.
[7404] Asher B. Durand, *Progress (The Advance of Civilization)* (1853), courtesy of Gulf States Paper Corporation, Warner Collection. The Native Americans in the lower left-hand corner of this painting observe the steady approach of American progress and settlement. Depictions of westward expansion such as this one helped publicize and legitimize what was seen as American progress, an ideology that began to be questioned only in the twentieth century.

2. *Journal:* Imagine that you are a miner in Rich Bar, California. Write a letter to a friend in which you detail your day-to-day life in the mining camp. You might also include a description of Louise Clappe. How do you and the rest of the miners in the community view her?

3. *Poet's Corner:* Using the translations of the *corridos* in the archive as models, write your own *corrido* about a contemporary person whom you view as a hero. Whom did you choose as the subject of your *corrido*? How did you use rhythm and repetition in your *corrido*? What problems did you encounter in fitting your subject into the *corrido* form?

4. *Poet's Corner:* Find a short poem that you like that uses conventional forms of meter and rhyme. Drawing inspiration from Whitman's poetry, translate the poem into free verse. How does the absence of rhyme and meter affect the poem? What problems did you encounter in translating the poem from one form to another?

5. *Artist's Workshop:* After looking at the Native American flag art in the archive, draw a design for a piece of clothing or other object on which you will put your own version of the American flag. Feel free to abstract or modify the patterns and designs of the flag. Explain the significance of the artifact you've designed and how your representation of the flag reflects your vision.

6. *Multimedia:* Referring to himself as the embodiment of America in "Song of Myself," Walt Whitman proclaimed, "I contain multitudes." What do you think he meant? What kinds of "multitudes" made up nineteenth-century American culture? Using the *American Passages* archive and slide-show software, create a multimedia presentation showing the diversity of American culture in the nineteenth century. Include captions that explain and interpret the images you choose.

Problem-Based Learning Projects

1. You are a lawyer hired by the Cherokee tribe to help them fight the Indian Removal Act, which they believe is unjust and should be overturned. You need to make your case convincing to the political authorities who can overturn the act. What courts or government agencies will you petition? How will you argue your position? What kind of evidence will you use? What kind of testimony will you solicit?

2. You are a Mexican or Chinese miner forced off your claim by the Foreign Miners' Tax, which you cannot afford to pay. Prepare a petition to the California legislature in which you argue for your right to continue mining even though you are not a citizen of the United States. Be sure to address the issue of how your presence—and the presence of other "foreign" immigrants—affects the economy, culture, and environment in California.

3. You have been asked to design an amusement park with a "frontier" theme. While your goal is to make the park fun, engaging, and accessible to children and families, you are also concerned that

your representation of the "frontier" be accurate. How will you interpret the idea of the frontier? What will you call your park? How will you portray the history of American expansion and westward migration? What activities and exhibits will you provide for visitors to the park?

GLOSSARY

border   Sometimes used as a replacement for the culturally insensitive term "frontier." Borders are places where cultures meet, and where trade, violence, and cultural exchange shape a variety of individual experiences.

corrido   A narrative ballad usually sung or spoken to music, the *corrido* was the most important literary genre of the southwestern border region, where it was popular between the 1830s and the 1930s. Developed by Mexicans and Mexican Americans, the *corridos* drew upon traditional Spanish ballad forms to articulate singers' experiences of cultural conflict in the borderlands. Characterized by a rapid tempo and brisk narrative pace, these ballads often focus on an "outlaw" hero who defends his rights—as well as those of other Mexicans—against the unjust authority of American officials.

epic   A long narrative poem celebrating the adventures and accomplishments of a hero. More generally, the term "epic" has come to be applied to any narration of national or cultural identity that has a broad, all-encompassing scope.

free verse   Poetry that does not adhere to conventional metrical patterns and has either irregular rhyme or no rhyme at all. Walt Whitman pioneered the use of free verse in American poetry, and his "Song of Myself" is a classic example.

frontier   Traditionally, the term Americans have used to describe the unexplored or contested land to the west of the eastern settlements on the Atlantic coast. Scholars have pointed out that the term "blurs the facts of conquest" and does not take into account the many other peoples who were displaced—sometimes violently—to make way for U.S. expansion.

homosocial/homosexual continuum   The relationship between non-sexual same-sex bonding activities and sexual contact between people of the same sex. While American culture has traditionally insisted that homosexuality is distinct from non-sexual same-sex relationships, scholars and theorists argue that the division between the two is always unstable.

Hudson River School   A group of landscape painters originally known as simply "American" or "Native" painters, the Hudson River School acquired its present name because of its early focus on the dramatic landscape of the Hudson River Valley in New York. While Thomas Cole is usually considered the "father" of the Hudson River tradition, other important painters including Asher Durand, Frederic Church, Albert Bierstadt, and Martin Johnson Heade contributed to the development of this movement. Highlighting the awesome, monumental quality of the American landscape, these artists were fundamentally optimistic about westward expansion and the promise of democracy. In their quest for new and spectacular effects, the Hudson River artists journeyed far beyond the Hudson River by the mid-nineteenth century, traveling to the Rocky Mountains, California, and even South America to record the expanse and grandeur of the continents.

Indian Removal Act of 1830   In 1830 the United States Congress, with the support of President Andrew Jackson, attempted to legislate a permanent solution to their land disputes with eastern Native American tribes by passing the Indian Removal Act. Passed by a narrow margin, the Act stipulated that the government could forcibly relocate Native Americans living within their traditional lands in eastern states to areas west of the Mississippi designated as "Indian Territory" (much of this land was in present-day Oklahoma). With this stroke, the federal government sanctioned the racist view that Native Americans had no valid claims to their homelands and should be moved westward to make way for white settlers and white culture. The Indian Removal Act enabled the tragic "Trail of Tears" migration, in which a third of the population of the Cherokee tribe died.

Manifest Destiny   The belief that American control of the land that stretched from the Atlantic to the Pacific was inevitable and divinely sanctioned. Because of this culturally arrogant conviction, American policy makers had few scruples about displacing Native Americans, Mexicans, and other groups inhabiting the land from the Great Plains to California.

memorial   A direct appeal to Congress, the courts, or another official federal body, a "memorial" was the nineteenth-century equivalent of a petition. The Cherokee tribe produced articulate and compelling memorials asking the United States Congress to allow them to stay in their traditional homelands east of the Mississippi. The Cherokee Council, which was the official leadership body of the tribe, composed its own memorial to send to Congress, while also submitting twelve other memorials written by Cherokee citizens. Despite their eloquence, the Cherokee memorials were not effective and the tribe was relocated in 1838.

SELECTED BIBLIOGRAPHY

Allmendinger, Blake. *The Cowboy: Representations of Labor in an American Work Culture*. New York: Oxford UP, 1992.

Chudacoff, Howard P. *The Age of the Bachelor: Creating an American Subculture*. Princeton: Princeton UP, 1999.

Herrera-Sobek, Maria. *Northward Bound: The Mexican Immigrant Experience in Ballad and Song*. Bloomington: Indiana UP, 1993.

Johnson, Susan Lee. *Roaring Camp: The Social World of the California Gold Rush*. New York: W. W. Norton and Company, 2000.

Leverenz, David. *Manhood and the American Renaissance*. Ithaca: Cornell UP, 1989.

Limerick, Patricia Nelson. "The Adventures of the Frontier in the Twentieth Century." In *The Frontier in American Culture*, ed. James R. Grossman. Berkeley: U of California P, 1994.

Matsumoto, Valerie J., and Blake Allmendinger, eds. *Over the Edge: Remapping the American West*. Berkeley: U of California P, 1999.

Nelson, Dana D. *National Manhood: Capitalist Citizenship and the Imagined Fraternity of White Men*. Durham: Duke UP, 1998.

Sedgwick, Eve Kosofsky. *Between Men: English Literature and Male Homosocial Desire*. New York: Columbia UP, 1985.

Slotkin, Richard. *Regeneration through Violence: The Mythology of the American Frontier, 1600–1860*. Middletown, CT: Wesleyan UP, 1973.

Yin, Xiao-huang. *Chinese American Literature since the 1850s*. Chicago: U of Illinois P, 2000.

FURTHER RESOURCES

The Ballad of Gregorio Cortez [videorecording]. Moctesuma Esparza Productions, Inc.; screenplay by Victor Villaseñor; produced by Moctesuma Esparza and Michael Hausman; directed by Robert M. Young. Santa Monica, CA: Metro Goldwyn Mayer Home Entertainment, 2000.

Carved in Silence [videorecording on Angel Island]. Produced and directed by Felicia Lowe; written by Felicia Lowe and Charlie Pearson. San Francisco, CA: Felicia Lowe Productions: distributed by Cross Current Media, 1987.

Corridos Sin Fronteras: A Traveling Exhibition and Educational Web Site Celebrating the Narrative Songs Known as Corridos. Smithsonian Institution Traveling Exhibition Service (SITES). Smithsonian Institution, PO Box 37012, QUAD Room 3146, MRC 706. Washington, DC 20013-7012. Phone (202) 357-3168; Fax (202) 357-4324.

Cowboy Songs, Ballads, and Cattle Calls from Texas [sound recording]. Cambridge: Rounder, 1999.

George Catlin and His Indian Gallery [virtual and actual exhibit]. Renwick Gallery. Smithsonian American Art Museum. 750 Ninth Street, NW, Suite 3100. Washington, DC 20001-4505. Phone (202) 275-1500.

Grossman, James R., ed. *The Frontier in American Culture: An Exhibition at the Newberry Library, August 26, 1994–January 7, 1995, Essays by Richard White, Patricia Nelson Limerick*. Berkeley: U of California P, 1994.

Herbst, Toby, and Joel Kopp. *The Flag in American Indian Art*. Seattle: U of Washington P, 1993.

Johns, Joshua Scott. *All Aboard: The Role of the Railroads in Protecting, Promoting, and Selling Yellowstone and Yosemite National Parks*. Aug. 1, 1996; <xraods.virginia.edu/~MA96/railroad/home.html>.

Minks, Louise. *The Hudson River School*. New York: Knickerbocker Press, 1998.

Paredes, Américo. *A Texas-Mexican Cancionero: Folksongs of the Lower Border*. Urbana: U of Illinois P, 1976.

Phillips, Sandra S., et al. *Crossing the Frontier: Photographs of the Developing West, 1849 to the Present*. San Francisco: San Francisco Museum of Modern Art, 1996.

Wald, Elijah. *Narcocorrido: A Journey into the Music of Drugs, Guns, and Guerrillas*. New York: Harper Collins, 2002.

AMERICAN GOTHIC

Ambiguity and Anxiety in the Nineteenth Century

Authors and Works

Featured in the Video:

Nathaniel Hawthorne, "Young Goodman Brown" and "Rappaccini's Daughter" (short stories)

Herman Melville, "Hawthorne and His Mosses" (essay) and *Moby-Dick* (novel)

Emily Dickinson, poems #258 [There's a certain Slant of light], #315 [He fumbles at your Soul], #465 [I heard a Fly buzz—when I died—], and #1129 [Tell all the Truth but tell it slant—]

Discussed in This Unit:

Charles Brockden Brown, *Wieland* (novel)

Washington Irving, "Rip Van Winkle" and "The Legend of Sleepy Hollow" (short stories)

William Gilmore Simms, "The Edge of the Swamp" (poem) and *The Forayers* (novel)

Edgar Allan Poe, "Ligeia" (short story)

Henry Ward Beecher, "The Strange Woman" (sermon)

Ambrose Bierce, "An Occurrence at Owl Creek Bridge" (short story)

Charlotte Perkins Gilman, "The Yellow Wall-paper" (short story)

Overview Questions

■ American gothic writing tends to question and analyze rather than offer helpful answers. How do these texts critique the common nineteenth-century assumption that America stands as the unique moral and social guiding light for the world (that it is, as John Winthrop said in 1630, "a City on a Hill")?

■ If the gothic explores what we might call the "dark side" of American life, what cultural fears and anxieties do we find expressed here? How does the form of this literature (especially narrative voice and point of view) help convey these anxieties?

■ Gothic writers addressed key nineteenth-century cultural trends such as westward expansion, technological and scientific progress, romantic individualism, the cult of true womanhood, and the debate over slavery and abolition. How can you see some of these trends reflected in the texts of this unit?

■ Who are the inheritors of the gothic mode today? Do they share similar concerns with these writers or are their concerns new to the twentieth and twenty-first centuries?

■ How do these writers explore and critique the ideas of self-reliance, free will, and the self-made man that you saw expressed by Franklin and Emerson in Unit 4?

Learning Objectives

After students have viewed the video, read the headnotes and literary selections in *The Norton Anthology of American Literature*, and explored related archival materials on the *American Passages* Web site, they should be able to

1. define what "gothic" means;
2. understand which American hopes, fears, and anxieties are explored and critiqued by writers in the gothic mode;
3. recognize the centrality of gothic literature to nineteenth- and twentieth-century American literature and culture;
4. evaluate the generally skeptical, pessimistic, or critical positions adopted by gothic writers;
5. discuss the role of gender and race in shaping the forms and themes of the American gothic tradition.

Instructor Overview

Americans saw many reasons to be optimistic in the second quarter of the nineteenth century. Philosophically, much of the nation had abandoned the bleak, deterministic theology of Calvin and had embraced either the Enlightenment faith in the power of human reason or a more gentle Protestant faith in a generous and forgiving God, or both. The election of Andrew Jackson in 1828 proved that a self-made man could rise from humble origins to the presidency. Requirements that voters own land were being relaxed or eliminated, so that democracy became a more achievable ideal. Spurred by a widespread belief in "Manifest Destiny," the young nation was expanding rapidly, growing well into the Midwest and eventually reaching the Pacific Ocean by the 1840s, gathering momentum and resources along the way. Industry became a powerful economic force, and cities began to bulge with immigrants eager for work. Reform and improvement (of daily life and labor by technology, and of social conditions by progressive activists) were spreading. And in the world of letters, writers like Ralph Waldo Emerson and Henry David Thoreau were arguing that Americans were in a perfect situation to cast off the fetters of European prejudice and habit and create a culture full of self-determined, empowered, and enlightened beings.

But if this picture represents one truth about nineteenth-century America, there are others as well. Almost 15 percent of the population was legally considered property (there were about 900,000 slaves in 1800 and about 3,200,000 by 1850). Only white, male property owners could vote. Women were largely confined to the home and certainly not expected to rise to positions of social authority. Native Americans were losing most of the power—and virtually all of the land—that they once held. How could all of these conditions exist, many asked, in the world's one modern nation created with the explicit purpose of establishing freedom and equality for all? In addition, rapid change was causing anxiety about the future: Where was America heading? How could it both grow exponentially and retain its unity and coherence? What if it lost its agricultural self-reliance and became beholden to the whims of European trade? Were the millions of immigrants good for the country, or did they bring dangerous and contagious influences? What were the human costs of city life and urban labor conditions? Was the Mexican War justified, or was it only a base attempt to grab more land and resources for European Americans?

It is this spirit of anxiety, fear, and even despair that writers in the gothic mode tap into. The three writers treated in the video, Nathaniel Hawthorne, Herman Melville, and Emily Dickinson, as well as the others represented in this unit, explore the "dark side" of nineteenth-century America. Charles Brockden Brown, Washington Irving, Edgar Allan Poe, Henry Ward Beecher, Charlotte Perkins Gilman, Ambrose Bierce, and William Gilmore Simms, among others, ask probing questions of their nation, challenging its tendency toward blind faith and unremitting optimism. Although these authors do at times write in styles that are not easily called "gothic," they illuminate their mutual concerns when they compose in the gothic mode. For the purposes of this unit, it will be useful to think of gothic literature as that which plunges its characters into mystery, torment, and fear in order to pose disturbing questions to our familiar and comfortable ideas of humanity, society, and the cosmos.

Sometimes these questions are asked in explicitly socio-political forms: for example, Gilman portrays a woman so oppressed by the patriarchal assumptions of her husband that she is driven insane; and Hawthorne rejects the promise that science will ameliorate the human condition when he tells the story of one researcher's obsessive and destructive botanical experiment on his daughter. But at least as often, these writers unveil their dark prophecies only by indirect glimpses—in the words of Dickinson, they "tell it slant." Sometimes by couching their insights in allegories, sometimes by focusing on the uncertainties and contradictions of the psyche, and often by combining allegory with psychological investigation, gothic writers often challenge America's optimism only by implication, forcing the reader to come to his or her own ethical conclusions. Thus, Melville's *Pequod* becomes not only a whaling vessel but also the American ship of state as a fractious and multicultural crew is led to a terrifying fate by a dangerous and potentially insane demagogue. Similarly, Hawthorne's Young Goodman Brown is both a tormented seventeenth-century Puritan and a representative of America's heritage of religious intolerance and self-righteousness. Charles Brockden Brown and Poe offer us characters who may be encountering the supernatural or may only be experiencing the projections of their own worst selves, their most base and uncontrollable prejudices and desires. In Dickinson's poems, a speaking subjectivity wonders how many of its sensations it can trust, and whether there is any comfort to be found beyond the visible world. It is best, then, not to look for direct political pamphleteering in these writers—no polemics against slavery or imperialism here. Rather, we see the cheery political *assumptions* of the nineteenth century challenged by the *staging* of characters and situations that seem impossible or out of place in an America of autonomy, optimism, and freedom. Finally, these writers urge us to ask: What is an American? What are our ideals, and to what extent does it seem within our power to realize them? What power, if any, rules us? How much are we in control of ourselves? How well do we even know ourselves? To what extent can we ever be sure of anything?

"American Gothic" contextualizes these questions in terms of five nineteenth-century cultural trends: (1) the image of the swamp; (2) interest in the occult; (3) the image of America as a "ship of state"; (4) abuse of reason and science; (5) the sentimentalization of death. Other *American Passages* units that bear comparison to this include Unit 3, "Utopian Promise," and Unit 4, "The Spirit of Nationalism," which lay out the forward-looking ideals established by the seventeenth and eighteenth centuries; Unit 7, "Slavery and Freedom," which explores the explicitly political literature of the most serious challenge to American ideals in the country's history; Unit 13, "Southern Renaissance," which shows how much of twentieth-century southern writing follows in the gothic tradition; and Unit 16, "The Search for Identity," which emphasizes literature that stages the fractures and contradictions of our own time.

Student Overview

"American Gothic" explores the "dark sides" of nineteenth-century American culture and identity. In a time of hope characterized by a widespread belief in America's **Manifest Destiny**, the rise of industry, increasing political freedom, and social reform movements, writers in the gothic mode speculate on the costs and dangers of the country's unbridled optimism. Sometimes explicitly and sometimes implicitly, they draw upon and explore the social anxieties of their time: the evils and threats of slavery, the cultural dominance of white men, the immigration of diverse and often mistrusted people, the possibility that Americans are fundamentally incapable of manifesting, in Abraham Lincoln's words, "the better angels of our nature"—indeed, the possibility that such angels are our own wishful delusions.

As you will see in the video, Nathaniel Hawthorne, Herman Melville, and Emily Dickinson, along with other writers of the **American Renaissance**, counter what they fear is America's smug, self-confident certainty not with conflicting certainties, but with potentially unanswerable questions. What is human nature? How much does selfish or uncontrollable desire, as opposed to altruistic or reasonable objectivity, motivate us? To what extent can America break from its European heritage of social caste and superstitious belief? What can Americans do about the massive contradictions involved in a country that was founded in the name of freedom and equality but sanctions the owning of black Americans, the dislocation of Native Americans, and the disenfranchisement of all but white male Americans?

In stories of obsessive or tormented characters who find their most basic assumptions about the world turned upside-down, these writers challenge their readers to question their own values and beliefs through exploring the ever-evolving character of American identity.

➢ **Authors covered:** Nathaniel Hawthorne, Herman Melville, Emily Dickinson

➢ **Who's interviewed:** Karen Halttunen, professor of history (University of California, Davis); Priscilla Wald, associate professor of English (Duke University); Emory Elliott, professor of English (University of California, Riverside); Nina Baym, general editor, *The Norton Anthology of American Literature*, and professor of English (University of Illinois, Urbana-Champaign); Robert Stone, author, poet, and professor of English (Yale University)

➢ **Points covered:**
- The gothic explores the dark or uncertain sides of human nature.
- Rapid social changes in the nineteenth century cause anxiety in America, nurturing a gothic sensibility in literature.
- Hawthorne's "Young Goodman Brown" and "Rappaccini's Daughter": "Goodman" as working through the painful inheritance of rigid Puritan faith; "Rappaccini" as expressing anxiety about both science and the oppression of women.
- Melville's "Hawthorne and His Mosses" and *Moby-Dick*: Melville's laudatory review of a book by Hawthorne shows their similar interest in the dark truths of humanity; Melville's adventurous life; the white whale as a symbol of ambiguity and uncertainty, and the ship as a microcosm of mid-nineteenth-century society; Ahab's hunt as a rage against God.
- Dickinson's poetry: Dickinson composes the terror of ordinary life; her Melville-like insistence that, because it is dangerous, the "truth" must be revealed only carefully and by glimpses; her use of the dash and popular verse; brief discussions of three poems.

PREVIEW

- **Preview the video:** Alongside the optimism of writers like Emerson, the nineteenth century produced a body of writing meant to question Americans' essential goodness. Nathaniel Hawthorne, Herman Melville, and Emily Dickinson wrote narratives and poems in which they asked difficult questions about God, truth, and humanity. They rarely provided hopeful answers.
- **What to think about while watching:** How do these writers expect their work to be received by the reader? How do they express the social and personal anxieties of their time? What assumptions or beliefs do they challenge? Why do they remain compelling today? What do they hope to achieve through their writing?
- **Tying the video to the unit content:** These writers are only three of the most important practitioners of the gothic mode in the nineteenth century. Many others also explored the disturbing or repressed aspects of American life, asking questions like: What are we afraid of? What is the worst we are capable of? What do we have a right to believe in? To what extent can our will and reason evade the lures of habit, prejudice, ignorance, and desire?

	What is an American? How does American literature create conceptions of the American experience and identity?	What is American literature? What are its distinctive voices and styles? How do social and political issues influence the American canon?	What characteristics of a literary work have made it influential over time?
Compre-hension Questions	How did America's Puritan heritage influence Hawthorne's "Young Goodman Brown"? Describe Rappaccini's scientific experiment with his daughter. In what sense is the *Pequod* a microcosm of American society?	How is gothic literature different from other kinds of writing that are contemporaneous with it? What were some nineteenth-century social conditions that contributed to the critical outlook of gothic literature? Why is the dash important in Dickinson's poems?	What happens to Young Goodman Brown in the forest? Describe Ahab's quest: what is he looking for, and why? What themes or topics does Dickinson tend to write about?
Context Questions	How did the Civil War and the tensions that precipitated it influence these three writers?	In what sense are these texts "pessimistic" compared to others of the nineteenth century?	Many of the gothic's concerns apply as well to the twenty-first century as to the nineteenth. What do these writers have to say about human nature and the human mind?
Exploration Questions	What do you think constitutes "an American"? Do these writers support or challenge your views about America?	All three of these writers are now considered "canonical," or essential for a complete understanding of American literary history, and many would call *Moby-Dick* the most important American novel ever. Melville's book was widely condemned during his lifetime, however, and only found broad appreciation by readers in the twentieth century. Why do you imagine so many people rejected it in the nineteenth century? How can a literary work be considered worthless at one time and great at another? Do you think *Moby-Dick* is a great novel? Why or why not?	Why wallow in the swampy regions of human nature? Are these works merely depressing, or do they have any positive or useful effects?

	Texts	Contexts
1790s	Charles Brockden Brown, *Wieland* (1798)	
1800s		United States purchases Louisiana Territory from France (1803) Foreign slave trade outlawed (1808)
1810s	Washington Irving, "Rip Van Winkle" (1819)	Second war against England (1812–14)
1820s	Washington Irving, "The Legend of Sleepy Hollow" (1820)	Second Great Awakening, a Christian revivalist movement, spreads across the country (1820s–30s) Monroe Doctrine warns European powers against future colonization in the Americas (1823) First U.S. railroad (1827) Andrew Jackson is president; the "Jacksonian impulse" urges westward expansion among whites (1829–37)
1830s	Nathaniel Hawthorne, "Young Goodman Brown" (1835) Edgar Allan Poe, "Ligeia" (1838)	Economic depression results in joblessness for one-third of labor force (1837)
1840s	Henry Ward Beecher, "The Strange Woman" (1843) Nathaniel Hawthorne, "Rappaccini's Daughter" (1844)	Samuel Morse invents telegraph (1844) United States annexes Texas (1845) Mexican War; Southwest is ceded to the United States (1846–48) California Gold Rush (1848–49)
1850s	Herman Melville, "Hawthorne and His Mosses" (1850), *Moby-Dick* (1851)	Fugitive Slave Act requires free states to return escaped slaves to slaveholders (1850) Dred Scott decision denies citizenship to African Americans (1857)
1860s	Emily Dickinson, 258 [There's a certain Slant of light] (1861), 315 [He fumbles at your Soul], 465 [I heard a Fly buzz—when I died—] (1862), 1129 [Tell all the Truth but tell it slant—] (1868)	Civil War (1861–65) First transcontinental railroad (1869)
1870s		Thomas Edison invents electric lightbulb (1879)
1890s	Ambrose Bierce, "An Occurrence at Owl Creek Bridge" (1890) Charlotte Perkins Gilman, "The Yellow Wall-paper" (1892)	Wounded Knee ends Native American armed resistance to U.S. government (1890)

AUTHOR/TEXT REVIEW

Charles Brockden Brown (1771–1810)

Born in Philadelphia to wealthy Quaker parents, Charles Brockden Brown was initially pressured by his family to study law. However, he had no real interest in the profession and would write in the evenings while studying law by day. After he finally admitted to his parents that he felt unable to appear before the bar, he began his writing career in earnest. Brown felt guilty for disappointing his family, but was rewarded with positive responses to his writing from Philadelphia literary circles.

Moving to New York in 1798 (and contracting and surviving yellow fever, an event which later found its way into his writing), Brown cultivated friends who were engaged in the fine arts and read widely. He was prolific in the following years, publishing the novels *Wieland* (1798), *Ormond* (1799), *Edgar Huntly* (1799), and the first part of *Arthur Mervyn* (1799). Supplementing these projects with work in journalism, Brown founded three different periodicals and became increasingly interested in politics and history.

Brown's **gothic** romances, which delve into the uncertainties and contradictions of human nature, were among the first important novels published in the United States. Fascinated by states of altered consciousness, such as sleepwalking and religious enthusiasm, he influenced the later psychic excavations of Edgar Allan Poe. He died of tuberculosis at the age of thirty-nine.

[7265] Anonymous, *Charles Brockden Brown* (c. 1925), courtesy of the Library of Congress [LC-USZ62-124378].

TEACHING TIP

■ Allow a free-ranging discussion of the metaphorical resonance of "hearing voices." You might begin by asking your students if any of them believe in ghosts and then expand the question to have them reflect on the idea of "ghosts" as one that stands for anything that haunts us (our past, our conscience, our conflicting values).

QUESTIONS

Comprehension: In Chapter IX of *Wieland*, we are privy to the complexities and subtleties of the thoughts of the narrator, Clara. How would you describe her state of mind?

Context: In what sense is Clara, as she says, "tormented by phantoms of [her] own creation"? How might Clara's words be applied to the interaction of spiritualism and gender described in the Core Context "The Spirit Is Willing: The Occult and Women in the Nineteenth Century"?

Exploration: How might the image of pausing at a closed door, debating whether or not to open it for fear of what might reveal itself, invite allegorical interpretations? Can you think of an experience in which a dilemma between knowledge and comfort presented itself? That is, are there ever times in real life when *not* knowing the truth seems preferable to knowing it?

BROWN WEB ARCHIVE

[7053] A. J. Dewey, *There's a Charm about the Old Love Still* (1901), courtesy of Duke University and the Library of Congress. Sheet-music illustration of a man and woman using a Ouija board. The nineteenth century witnessed a growing interest in spiritualism and the occult.

[7265] Anonymous, *Charles Brockden Brown* (1900–1950), courtesy of the Library of Congress [LC-USZ62-124378]. Portrait of Brown, whose novel *Wieland* is a precursor to the psychological novels of the Victorian era.

[8645] Emory Elliott, Interview: "The Gothic in Literature" (2001), courtesy of Annenberg/CPB. Emory Elliott, professor of English at University of California, Riverside, discusses the gothic in nineteenth-century American literature.

[9007] Charles Brockden Brown, *Wieland; or, The Transformation, an American Tale* (1799), courtesy of Project Gutenberg. *Wieland*, along with Brown's other novels *Edgar Huntly* and *Arthur Mervyn*, helped bring the gothic style to American literature.

IRVING WEB ARCHIVE

Washington Irving (1783–1859)

America's first international literary celebrity, as well as its first fully professional writer, was born in New York City, the eleventh child in a close-knit family. After writing satirical sketches and essays for his brother's newspapers for some years, Washington Irving captured the nation's attention with the fictitious *A History of New York*, supposedly written by a curious old gentleman named Diedrich Knickerbocker. In this work, which was accompanied by a publicity campaign involving newspaper reports on the putative whereabouts of the fictitious Knickerbocker, Irving made fun of the pretensions of bourgeois culture and democracy (including Thomas Jefferson), as well as American parochialism and history writing. In May 1815, Irving left the country for what would be a seventeen-year sojourn in Europe, where he worked first as an importer in Liverpool, then as an attaché to the American legation in Spain, and finally as secretary to the American legation in London. His diverse works range from *The Life and Voyages of Christopher Columbus* (1828) and *The Alhambra* (1832), both written during his stay in Spain, to *A Tour on the Prairies* (1835) and *The Adventures of Captain Bonneville, U.S.A.* (1837), studies of the American West written on his return from Europe, to a five-volume life of George Washington.

Irving's *Sketch Book* (1819–20), which included "Rip Van Winkle" and "The Legend of Sleepy Hollow," remains his most recognized and influential contribution to American literature (he is often credited with inaugurating the modern genre of the short story). He is sometimes read as a political reactionary, nostalgic for European aristocratic culture and disgusted with the American rabble. His work and life, however, complicate this view; for example, it is true that he seems to have preferred that art remain aloof from commercialism and beyond the world of utility, but he also was America's first commercially successful writer, who not only was very popular but depended for his living upon the mass consumption of his writing. Stories like those from *The Sketch Book* often display this tension, pitting an aesthetically oriented pre-Revolution America against a crass and utilitarian post-Revolution one—yet it is not always clear that the former is meant to be morally superior to the latter.

TEACHING TIP

■ You might begin exploring "Rip Van Winkle" through the "reader response" approach. Ask students which characters are sympathetic and why. Some students will see Rip's flexibility as admirable and his oppression by Dame Van Winkle as pitiable, while others will see Rip as a good-for-nothing. Explore how these different points of view change interpretations of the story: Is it good or bad to sleep through catastrophic historical change? To what extent should the masses actively be involved in the construction of society?

Comprehension: Describe Rip Van Winkle as husband and as citizen. As you articulate his relationship with his wife, consider whether you think Irving means us to feel more sympathy for Rip or for Dame Van Winkle.

Comprehension: How are we supposed to feel about Ichabod Crane? To what extent should we feel sympathy for him? On which of his characteristics or habits do you base your judgment?

Context: Note that Rip sleeps through the Revolutionary War; that is, he sleeps through America's transition from colony to nation. Why does it matter that Rip sleeps through these particular eighteen years? Describe his village before and after his fateful nap: which do you think Irving prefers? What is different and what is the same in the village before and after Rip's sleep?

Context: Like "Rip Van Winkle," "The Legend of Sleepy Hollow" suggests a distinction between Dutch colony and American nation (in the figures of Brom and Ichabod, respectively). What is Irving saying about the difference between the two communities?

Exploration: In 1820, Sydney Smith asked, "In the four corners of the globe, who reads an American book?" In *The Sketch Book of Geoffrey Crayon, Gent.* (1820), Irving responds by formulating America—and Americans—as a site of interest and inspiration. As you read "Rip Van Winkle," consider how Irving formulates national identity, particularly in relation to Europe. How do race, culture, and historical context figure into this formulation?

Nathaniel Hawthorne (1804–1864)

Hawthorne was born in Salem, Massachusetts, a descendant of the first Puritan colonists, including one of the judges of the Salem witchcraft trials, an ancestry that would haunt him throughout his life and provide a tormented inspiration for much of his writing. He graduated from Bowdoin College in Maine, where he had become friends with Henry Wadsworth Longfellow and Franklin Pierce, who later became president of the United States. Hawthorne had already begun writing at this point, acting as writer, editor, printer, and publisher of his own newspaper. In 1828 he published his first novel, *Fanshawe*, at his own expense. Soon thereafter, however, in a gesture of repudiation that he would later repeat with a collection of short stories, he tried to have all copies of the novel destroyed. In 1840 he joined the socialist-utopian commune of Brook Farm, but was unhappy with the drudgery of farm life and left after six months.

Hawthorne returned to Salem as Surveyor of the Custom House in 1846 and continued to write. His early endeavors were mostly short stories, which appeared anonymously in magazines and literary annuals. Only when he published these stories in collections, as in *Twice-Told Tales* (1837) and *Mosses from an Old Manse* (1846), did Hawthorne become a recognized literary force. In 1842 he married Sophia Peabody of Salem and began to focus on his new family, eventually moving them from Salem. His masterpiece, *The Scarlet Letter*,

[7242] John Plumbe, *Washington Irving* (1861), courtesy of the Library of Congress, Prints and Photographs [LC-USZ62-4238]. Portrait of Irving. Irving's work suggests nostalgia for European aristocratic culture over early-nineteenth-century American commercialism, but his position as America's first commercially successful writer complicates this view.

[7243] Currier & Ives, *Washington's Head-Quarters 1780: At Newburgh, on the Hudson* (1856), courtesy of the Library of Congress [LC-USZC2-3161]. Painting of stone farmhouse and bucolic surroundings along the Hudson River. General George Washington, his wife, officers, slaves, and servants occupied this modest house during the Revolutionary War. Washington Irving set many of his stories in this area.

[1549] T. H. Matteson, *The Trial of George Jacobs, August 5, 1692* (1855), courtesy of the Peabody Essex Museum, Salem, Massachusetts.

appeared in 1850 to international acclaim, with critics in Great Britain and the United States proclaiming Hawthorne America's finest romance writer. His philosophy of literature appears in that novel's introduction: "a neutral territory, somewhere between the real world and fairy-land, where the Actual and the Imaginary may meet, and each imbue itself with the nature of the other." His works explore the construction of reality through subjective perception, the past's inevitable and often malevolent hold on the present, and the agonizing ethical dilemmas encountered by individuals in society. Hawthorne frequently requires the reader to make a moral judgment, rather than passively receive a ready-made one. Hawthorne's other novels include *The House of the Seven Gables* (1851), *The Blithedale Romance* (1852), and *The Marble Faun* (1860).

TEACHING TIPS

■ To help your students contextualize "Young Goodman Brown," supply excerpts from Puritan writings—for example, one of Cotton Mather's trial descriptions in *Wonders of the Invisible World*—and ask them to determine exactly what in Puritanism Hawthorne seems to be criticizing (e.g., rigidity, right-and-wrong thinking, moral arbitrariness).

■ For "Rappaccini's Daughter," have the students discuss current ethical issues of science and "progress." Is Rappaccini a twisted and perverted emblem of the scientific method or does he stand for a general ethical failure of science?

■ Highlight the idea of "the beginning" in *The Scarlet Letter* both in terms of "The Custom-House" (i.e., how the frame narrative affects our understanding of Hester Prynne's story) and in terms of the novel as a foundation for American literary identity (i.e., how we might see it as establishing an American literary tradition).

QUESTIONS

Comprehension: What happens to Goodman Brown in the forest? Why does Hawthorne leave it up to the reader to decide whether the entire experience of Brown is a dream or real? To what extent does it matter that we decide one way or another?

Context: What does "Young Goodman Brown" seem to be saying about the ethics of American Puritanism? Hawthorne struggled with his own ancestors' roles in prosecuting the 1692 Salem witchcraft trials; what does the ironic revelation of "evil" hidden behind a façade of "good" suggest about Hawthorne's judgment of the Puritan worldview?

Context: Notice how the rational and objective pursuit of scientific truth blurs into the obsessive and personal pursuit of individual desire in "Rappaccini's Daughter" (this is true in different ways for all three of the male characters, Giovanni, Rappaccini, and Baglioni). Why might Hawthorne deliberately challenge the distinction between science and passion in this story?

Context: What are we to make of Rappaccini's final justification to Beatrice of his perverse experiment: "'Wouldst thou, then, have preferred the condition of a weak woman, exposed to all evil, and capable of none?'" Why does it matter that Beatrice is a woman? How would the story be different if Rappaccini had endowed a male child with the venomous powers of the poison plant? How can you relate this story to the nineteenth-century "cult of true womanhood" discussed in the Core Context "The Spirit Is Willing: The Occult and Women in the Nineteenth Century"?

Exploration: *The Scarlet Letter* has connections to both "Young Goodman Brown" and "Rappaccini's Daughter." Like the former, *The Scarlet Letter* deals with the wrenching implications of Puritan conceptions of sin; like the latter, it concerns the torments of gender inequality. Consider the representation of the human body in each of these texts to develop a theory that links these two themes. What, according to Hawthorne, is the relationship between the female body and sin?

William Gilmore Simms (1806–1870)

Born in Charleston, South Carolina, and remaining near his birthplace throughout his life, Simms was well-known as the author of romances such as *The Yemassee* (1835), *The Lily and the Totem* (1850), and *The Forayers* (1855). Some of the raw material for these works no doubt came from Simms's father, who was a soldier of fortune, wandering the South for years (leaving Simms in the care of a grandmother), eventually growing rich, and collecting stories and observations. Simms's novels represent the history of the American South and are influenced by Simms's knowledge of and affection for the region, including his respect for its landscape, institutions, and social structures. Perhaps his view of his homeland is best embodied in one of his protagonists (in *Voltmeier* [1869]), who at one point cries out, "I have the strength to endure, I *have* endured!" Capturing a vision of a defiant and exotic South, Simms's novels are frequently macabre, displaying characters living in harsh but strangely glamorous conditions.

Simms was politically active, helped develop the proslavery argument (he believed firmly that humans were part of the Great Chain of Being, with whites in a superior position to blacks), and submitted elaborate battle plans to the Confederacy during the Civil War. Like Charles Brockden Brown, he pursued literature rather than the law, with which he had flirted in his early adulthood. A prolific author, he wrote poetry, plays, histories of the South, novellas, biographies, magazine essays, medleys, and literary criticism. In an attempt to support his impoverished family late in life, he worked feverishly at various writing projects, eventually destroying his own health.

of the 1851 edition of *Twice-Told Tales*, a collection of Hawthorne's short stories that was originally published in 1837. **[7241]** Eric Muller, *Custom House, South Front and East Side* (1958), courtesy of the Library of Congress, Prints and Photographs Division, Historic American Buildings Survey [HABS, MASS, 5-SAL, 48-1]. This brick Custom House in Salem, Massachusetts, is an example of the Federal style of architecture. Much of Salem's wealth in the early nineteenth century was in the maritime trade.

[7245] *The International Magazine of Literature, Art and Science, William Gilmore Simms* (1852), courtesy of the *Making of America* Project, Cornell University Library.

SIMMS WEB ARCHIVE

[2742] Anonymous, *The Old Plantation* (c. 1790–1800), courtesy of © Colonial Williamsburg Foundation, Abby Aldrich Rockefeller Folk Art Museum, Colonial Williamsburg Foundation, Williamsburg, VA. Slaves dancing and playing music on a plantation, possibly in South Carolina. Writers such as William Gilmore Simms believed that slavery was justified by God.

[4308] Alfred Rudolph Waud, *Pictures of the South—Jefferson Davis's Mansion in Mississippi—Negro Quarters on Jefferson Davis's Plantation* (1866), courtesy of the Library of Congress, Prints and Photographs Division [LC-USZ62-116582]. These sketches show a plantation owned by Davis, president of the Confederate States of America. William Gilmore Simms believed that the discrepancy between the lives of slaves and those of their masters was part of the Great Chain of Being.

[4735] Anonymous, *Gloucester, Near Natchez, MS* (n.d.), courtesy of the Library of Congress, Prints and Photographs Division [LC-USZ62-58888]. A neoclassical plantation house designed as an expression of the good taste and prosperity of the owner.

[7245] *The International Magazine of Literature, Art and Science*, William Gilmore Simms (1852), courtesy of the *Making of America* Project, Cornell University Library. Simms, the antebellum South's most prolific author, was an astute observer of the cultural, social, and intellectual traditions of the region.

[9004] William Gilmore Simms, *The Life of Francis Marion* (1844), courtesy of Project Gutenberg. Simms was the most prolific southern writer of the antebellum period. This biography tells the story of Brigadier General Francis Marion, nicknamed the Swamp Fox, an American soldier in the Revolutionary War.

[9005] William Gilmore Simms, "The Edge of the Swamp" (c. 1853), courtesy of Coastal Carolina University. Simms's meditation on a swamp depicts it as a place of mystery and danger.

[9012] William Gilmore Simms, Introduction and Chapter I from *The Forayers; or, Raid of the Dog Days* (1855), courtesy of Belford, Clarke, Chicago, New York, 1885. The sixth in a series of eight novels set in the South during the Revolutionary War, *The Forayers* describes events leading up to the Battle of Eutaw Springs in the Orangeburg, South Carolina, area.

■ Have students sketch out images of various natural environments with an eye toward moving the emotions of their classmates in particular directions. How do their classmates respond to an open prairie, the ocean, a forest? Now have them sketch (or use the images of) a swamp, and evaluate their responses. Stress that the swamp is often "in-between": both threatening and concealing, both beyond civilization and a final sign of civilized resistance to tyranny.

QUESTIONS

Comprehension: Why is the swamp mysterious and dangerous in the poem "The Edge of the Swamp"? How does the swamp connect to the moral or message of the poem?

Comprehension: In what ways are the swamps in *The Forayers* symbolically different from the swamp in "The Edge of the Swamp"? In what ways are they similar?

Context: Consider this passage from *The Forayers* describing a path through a swamp: "The path grows sinuous and would be lost, but for certain marks upon the branches of the trees under which we are required to move. You would not see these marks. No one could see them, were they not shown, or decipher their mystic runes, were they not explored." How does this discussion of knowledge (of how a traveler might or might not be able to read the signs of passage through the swamp) relate to the many other examples of characters knowing, not knowing, or wrongly knowing that we have seen in this unit? Compare this swamp with the images in the Core Context "Swamps, Dismal and Otherwise." Which of the images does it most resemble? To what effect?

Edgar Allan Poe (1809–1849)

Born to the teenage actors Elizabeth Arnold and David Poe Jr. (in a time when acting was a highly disreputable career), Edgar Allan Poe was raised by a Richmond, Virginia, merchant named John Allan after both his parents died. Allan sent Poe to the University of Virginia, but Poe left after quarrelling with Allan in 1827. Allan had no patience for Poe's literary pretensions, and Poe found Allan cheap and cruel. Poe then sought out his father's relatives in Baltimore, where he published his first volume of poems, *Tamerlane and Other Poems*, and later secretly married his thirteen-year-old cousin, Virginia Clemm. He moved with his wife and her mother to Richmond, Philadelphia (where he wrote several of his most famous works, including "Ligeia," "The Fall of the House of Usher," and "The Tell-Tale Heart"), and then to New York City. Throughout these relocations, he worked editing magazines and newspapers, but found it difficult to hold onto any one job for very long. Poe's horror tales and detective stories (a genre he created) were written to capture the fancy of the popular reading public, but he earned his national reputation through a large number of critical essays and sketches. With the publication of "The Raven"

(1845), Poe secured his fame, but he was not succeeding as well in his personal life. His wife died in 1847, and Poe was increasingly ill and drinking uncontrollably. He died on a trip to Baltimore, four days after being found intoxicated near a polling booth on Election Day.

Poe was influenced by the fantastic romances of Charles Brockden Brown, Washington Irving, and Nathaniel Hawthorne. However, unlike most of his famous contemporaries, Poe rarely described American life in any direct way in his writings. Often set in exotic, vaguely medieval, or indeterminately distant locations, Poe's work seems more interested in altered states of consciousness than history or culture: his characters often swirl within madness, dreams, or intoxication, and may or may not encounter the supernatural. His literary reputation has been uneven, with some critics finding his extravagant prose and wild situations off-putting or absurd (and his poetry pedestrian and repetitive). Poe's defenders, however (including many nineteenth- and twentieth-century French intellectuals), see him as a brilliant allegorist of the convolutions of human consciousness. For example, there are many "doubles" in Poe: characters who mirror each other in profound but nonrealistic ways, suggesting not so much the subtleties of actual social relationships as the splits and fractures within a single psyche trying to relate to itself.

[7244] W. S. Hartshorn, *Edgar Allan Poe* (1848), courtesy of the Library of Congress [LC-USZ62-10610].

TEACHING TIPS

■ Poe works very well for spatial analysis and analyses of setting—that is, for considering the importance of the stories' spaces (e.g., houses, prisons) and the locations (e.g., "exotic" or medieval places and times). In preparation for class discussion, have students draw a picture of the setting of one of Poe's stories and ask them to annotate it with what each aspect of the setting symbolizes.

■ What is haunting Poe's houses? Ask students to contextualize Poe's use of the haunted house through comparing his use with Henry Ward Beecher's "haunted house" in "The Strange Woman."

■ Students are often quick to pick up on the "unnatural relations" between Usher and his sister in "The Fall of the House of Usher," but are unclear what to make of them. It can be helpful to point out that incest is a common theme in early national literature (Melville's *Pierre* is another famous example). Why would early national writers in general, and Poe in particular, be interested in incest as a theme?

QUESTIONS

Comprehension: Does "Ligeia" represent supernatural events? What difference does your answer make to our understanding of the story?

Comprehension: How does the setting of "Ligeia" affect your understanding of the story?

Context: In an essay about composing literature, Poe wrote the following: "the death, then, of a beautiful woman is, unquestionably,

POE WEB ARCHIVE

[3111] James William Carling, *The Raven* (c. 1882), courtesy of the Edgar Allan Poe Museum, Richmond, Virginia. This illustration, by James Carling for an 1882 edition of "The Raven," reflects the dark and foreboding tone of Poe's classic poem.

[7064] Cortlandt V. D. Hubbard, *Poe's Bedroom in Philadelphia* (1967), courtesy of the Library of Congress [HABS, PA,51-PHILA,663A-4]. This photograph shows Poe's bedroom on the second floor of the building now known as the "Edgar Allan Poe House." Poe wrote many of his most famous works during the six years he lived in Philadelphia.

[7244] W. S. Hartshorn, *Edgar Allan Poe* (1848), courtesy of the Library of Congress [LC-USZ62-10610]. Poe developed the detective story genre but was also known for his poetry, critical essays, and sketches.

[8643] Emory Elliott, Interview: "Mid-Nineteenth-Century America" (2001), courtesy of Annenberg/CPB. Emory Elliott, professor of English at the University of California, Riverside, discusses the climate of fear which characterized much of mid-nineteenth-century American life and culture.

the most poetical topic in the world—and equally is it beyond doubt that the lips best suited for such a topic are those of a bereaved lover." What do you think he meant by this? How does "Ligeia" fit into this philosophy of literature? Consider how the narrator describes Ligeia, how he feels and what he thinks about her: what does the story suggest about the proper roles or characteristics of men and women? How is Ligeia like and unlike the ideal woman as conceived by adherents of the cult of true womanhood?

Exploration: The narrator is unsure about many things in "Ligeia," including when and where he met Ligeia, her last name, and whether he is mad. In fact, it is possible to say that the story is *about* uncertainty: "Not the more could I define that sentiment, or analyze, or even steadily view it," says the narrator at one point. How does Poe explore the dilemma of **ambiguity** in "Ligeia"? What does he seem to be saying about the mind's attempt to establish certainty?

Henry Ward Beecher (1813–1887)

Born in Litchfield, Connecticut, Henry Ward Beecher was the son of the preacher Lyman Beecher and the brother of the novelist Harriet Beecher Stowe. He added to the discursive fame of his family by becoming a well-known preacher, orator, and lecturer. Beecher graduated from Amherst in 1834 and attended Lane Theological Seminary in Cincinnati. After two pastorates in Indiana, he moved in 1847 to the newly organized Congregational Plymouth Church in Brooklyn, New York.

Publicly vocal on contemporary issues, Beecher was a leader in the antislavery movement, a proponent of women's suffrage, and an advocate of the theory of evolution. He regularly attracted some twenty-five hundred auditors to his Sunday sermons, and he published an early pamphlet, *Seven Lectures to Young Men* (1844). In 1854, he raised money among his congregation for weapons to be used in the antislavery cause; these rifles came to be called "Beecher's Bibles." Beecher became editor of the *Independent* in 1861 and of the *Christian Union* in 1870. He visited England in 1863, spreading sympathy for the Union in a series of lectures.

[7240] James E. Cook, *Testimony in the Great Beecher-Tilton Scandal Case Illustrated* (1875), courtesy of the Library of Congress [LC-USZ62-121959].

In 1875, one of Beecher's parishioners (and a popular speaker in his own right), Theodore Tilton, brought a lawsuit against him for adultery with Tilton's wife—a charge first made by Victoria Woodhull in her newspaper *Woodhull & Claflin's Weekly*. After a long trial, this suit ended with the jury in disagreement; Beecher's friends claimed that he won. Despite being publicly embarrassed by the trial, Beecher remained influential for the rest of his life. His works include *The Life of Jesus, the Christ* (1871) and *Evolution and Religion* (1885).

■ Try applying the kind of gothic images Beecher uses to decry prostitution to another current social problem such as factory conditions in underdeveloped countries, child abuse, or the current "epidemic" of obesity in American children. Which of these problems lends itself to a gothic treatment that would likely persuade an audience of its injustice or intolerableness? Which aspects of each problem can be "gothicized," and which do not seem to work? Think in particular of how the gender and ages of the people involved affect your ability to perform this task.

QUESTIONS

Comprehension: According to Beecher, how exactly does the prostitute lure her young men? What exactly are the consequences for men who have a sexual encounter with the prostitute? In what sense are these elements "gothic"?

Context: Consider the gender politics of the sermon. How does Beecher draw on stereotypes and assumptions about women in general in order to make his point about prostitutes in particular? How does he invoke the cult of true womanhood?

Exploration: Why does "The Strange Woman" open with an attack on Chaucer, Shakespeare, and other famous writers? How is this section related to the main argument of the sermon? How would Melville (in "Hawthorne and His Mosses") disagree with Beecher about the aims and effects of literature?

Herman Melville (1819–1891)

Herman Melville's father was a New York City merchant who, when he died suddenly, left his family heavily in debt. Melville was only twelve at the time, but he was forced to leave school to go to work. After working in a variety of low-paying jobs (clerk, laborer, schoolteacher), in 1841 Melville joined a whaler sailing for the South Seas. Aboard a series of ships, he was away for three years. Ishmael, the narrator of Melville's 1851 *Moby-Dick*, surely speaks for the author as well when he says that "a whale-ship was my Yale College and my Harvard." In addition to learning the dangerous and difficult business of whaling itself, Melville also gained an unusually diverse cultural education. At one point, he and a crewmate jumped ship and lived for several weeks with a native tribe; upon his return to America, Melville transformed that experience into *Typee* (1846), a popular adventure tale that established him as a literary celebrity. A sequel, *Omoo*, soon followed, but Melville's appeal was dampened by his more philosophical works such as *Mardi* (1849), *Pierre* (1853), and even *Moby-Dick*. Some critics of these novels declared Melville unbalanced; the *New York Dispatch* charged him

[1540] William Huggins, *South Sea Whale Fishery* (1834), courtesy of The New Bedford Whaling Museum.

[1540] William Huggins, *South Sea Whale Fishery* (1834), courtesy of the New Bedford Whaling Museum. Colored aquatint of sperm whale and boats in rough seas. This popular scene was drawn on by American artists, such as author Herman Melville and painters Albert van Beest, R. Swain Gifford, and Benjamin Russell, as they played with the symbolism of America as "ship of state."

[2232] Rockwell Kent, *Whale beneath the Sea* (1930), courtesy of the Plattsburgh State Art Museum. This illustration dramatizes the smallness and vulnerability of the *Pequod* in relation to the whale and the vast ocean.

[2377] Rodney Dewey, *Herman Melville* (1861), courtesy of the Berkshire Athenaeum, Pittsfield, Massachusetts. Picture of Melville while he was living at Arrowhead, his home in the Berkshire Mountains in Massachusetts. All of his best-known works, including *Moby-Dick*, were written during the thirteen years that he lived at Arrowhead.

[2378] Anonymous, *Herman Melville* (c. 1885), courtesy of the Gansevoort-Lansing Collection, Manuscripts and Archives Division, The New York Public Library, Astor, Lenox and Tilden Foundations. Picture taken around the time of Melville's retirement from his job as a customs inspector for the New York Customs House, where he worked for over twenty years.

[2386] The International Magazine of Literature, Art and Science, *Herman Melville's Whale* (1851), courtesy of the *Making of America* Project, Cornell University Library. This review of *Moby-Dick* appeared in December 1851. *Moby-Dick's* unusual narrative structure and philosophical underpinnings were disliked by readers as well as critics.

[2387] *Putnam's Monthly Magazine of American Literature, Science and Art*, "Our Young Authors"—Melville (1853), courtesy of Cornell University, *Making of America* Digital Collection. This review of Melville's work is typical of the way in which it was received by his contemporaries. The author praises Melville's early adventure novel *Typee*, while disparaging the philosophical bent that characterizes many of his later novels.

later in his career with having "indulged himself in a trick of metaphysical and morbid meditations until he has perverted his fine mind from its healthy productive tendencies."

Melville had to struggle to regain the economic and critical popularity he had enjoyed with his ear-lier writing. After *Pierre*, he primarily wrote short stories for magazines like *Harper's*. Financial concerns burdened the family for years, but an inheritance late in life allowed Melville to work on his final narrative, *Billy Budd, Sailor*, the manuscript of which was found upon his death in 1891. Only after his death did Melville rise from the ranks of second-rate adventure novelists to his present status as one of America's most important writers. Many recent readers have praised his piercing social criticism; they point, for example, to his condemnation of racism in "Benito Cereno" (1855) and his critique of dehumanizing labor in "Bartleby, the Scrivener" (1853) and "The Paradise of Bachelors and the Tartarus of Maids" (1855). Many have also found compelling the self-reflective and multilayered nature of his narratives—narratives that continue to speak to the complexities of creating meaning in the American literary tradition.

TEACHING TIPS

■ Using illustrations of *Moby-Dick* from the nineteenth and twentieth centuries and selected passages from the novel, ask your students to write a character sketch of Ahab.

■ Divide your students into two (or more) groups and pose some current ethical issue of debate. Have one group respond as if it were Ahab, sharing his assumptions about the universe and people; have the other group speak as Ishmael, employing his beliefs and attitudes. What are the cores of their differing perspectives? How would they each respond to one of today's ethical questions?

QUESTIONS

Comprehension: Note the description of the *Pequod* in Chapter 16, "The Ship," in the archive. How does Ishmael characterize the ship and its crew? What does he mean when he says that the *Pequod* is "a cannibal of a craft"? How is this related to the idea of the "ship of state"?

Comprehension: How would you describe the relationship between Ishmael and Queequeg in Chapter 10, "A Bosom Friend," in the archive? Why should the two of them be "a cosy, loving pair"? How does Ishmael seem to feel about Queequeg's religious beliefs?

Comprehension: Why might Melville have chosen to tell the story of Ahab and the white whale from Ishmael's point of view? How do Ishmael's judgments and perspectives affect your understanding of Ahab's quest? And why begin the novel with the line "Call me Ishmael," as if the reader is not privy to the narrator's true name?

Context: Read carefully Ahab's diatribe against Moby-Dick in "The Quarter-Deck." He says that "all visible objects, man, are but as pasteboard masks," that the whale is like "the wall" that hems in a prisoner, and that "that inscrutable thing [in the whale] is chiefly what I hate." In the midst of a whale-hunt, why bring up pasteboard masks and prison walls? What does Ahab mean by "inscrutable"? What is the relationship between Ahab's speech and Ishmael's later assertion that Ahab identifies Moby-Dick with "all [Ahab's] intellectual and spiritual exasperations. The White Whale swam before him as the monomaniac incarnation of all those malicious agencies which some deep men feel eating in them"?

Context: In "The Whiteness of the Whale," Ishmael continues his assessment of Moby-Dick. He concludes that the whiteness presents "a dumb blankness, full of meaning." According to Ishmael, what is the significance of the whiteness of the whale?

Context: In what sense does *Moby-Dick* fit Melville's discussion of literature in "Hawthorne and His Mosses"?

Exploration: Melville wrote many texts that can be considered social critiques in a more clear-cut way than *Moby-Dick*. Read "Bartleby, the Scrivener," *Billy Budd, Sailor*, and *Benito Cereno*; then use the social critique in those texts to develop an interpretation of *Moby-Dick* as a social critique.

Emily Dickinson (1830–1886)

A lifelong resident of Amherst, Massachusetts, Emily Dickinson left her hometown for only one year, when she attended Mt. Holyoke Female Seminary. She was raised in an intellectual and socially prominent family and at the age of eighteen had received a better formal education than most of her American contemporaries, both male and female. Yet Dickinson led a largely sequestered existence, reading widely among works of classic and contemporary literature, devoting much of her time to writing poetry. She produced close to eighteen hundred poems, which are characterized by terse lines, "slant" rhymes, and keen observation. Because of the compressed and ambiguous nature of her work, where any given word can have multiple significations, Dickinson is sometimes called the first "modernist" poet. Most prominent in her style, which is quite unlike her contemporaries', is her use of the dash: she simultaneously separates and links words and ideas in complex ways, rather than allowing traditional punctuation to determine meaning absolutely. Dickinson's work often grapples profoundly with topics and ideas which would have been unacceptable to her community. Her poems are often skeptical and angry, challenging many of her contemporaries' assumptions about God, death, gender, nature, and the human body.

Except for a dozen poems, most of Dickinson's work was not published in her lifetime. She did, however, carefully collect her poems into handmade booklets, or "fascicles," of about twenty poems each. Her purpose in organizing her poetry this way remains unclear; she may have desired a private archive for retrieving poems she wished to revise, and it has been suggested that the fascicles are organized by theme. Scholars have long been fascinated by this and other mysteries

[2611] Walter Monteith Aikman, *The Tontine Coffee House, Wall & Walter Streets, about 1797* (n.d.), courtesy of the Library of Congress [LC-USZ62-98020]. The Tontine Coffee House was a place where the financial men of New York City met to discuss money matters. Melville depicted the potentially dehumanizing effects of life on Wall Street in works like "Bartleby, the Scrivener."

[9009] Herman Melville, Chapter 16 of *Moby-Dick*, "The Ship" (1851), courtesy of Project Gutenberg. In this chapter Ishmael describes how he decided to sign aboard the *Pequod*, following Queequeg's superstitious insistence that Ishmael choose the ship to which they would commit themselves. Rife with foreboding, this chapter also includes the first description of Ahab.

[9010] Herman Melville, Chapter 10 of *Moby-Dick*, "A Bosom Friend" (1851), courtesy of Project Gutenberg. In this chapter Ishmael cements his friendship with future shipmate Queequeg. "I'll try a pagan friend," Ishmael says, "since Christian kindness has proved but hollow courtesy."

[1617] Anonymous, *Emily Dickinson* (n.d.), courtesy of Amherst College Library.

of her intensely private life, including her sexuality. Dickinson never married, and the evidence suggests that she felt some variety of passionate affection for both men and women, especially for her sister-in-law, Susan, one of only a few people to whom she privately sent poems. A half-century after her death, the three volumes of *The Poems of Emily Dickinson* (1955) and two volumes of *The Letters of Emily Dickinson* (1958) appeared.

TEACHING TIPS

■ Have your students sing one of Dickinson's poems to the tune of a favorite ballad or hymn. For example, "I could not stop for death" works nicely with the tune of "Yellow Rose of Texas," "Amazing Grace," or even Lou Reed's "Sweet Jane." Why does Dickinson use these forms? How does she change or challenge them?

■ Focus on the "slant" (indirection and ambiguity) as the ruling trope of Dickinson's poetry.

QUESTIONS

Comprehension: Notice Dickinson's frequent use of dashes in place of more standard punctuation like commas and periods. Why did she rely so heavily on dashes? How do they affect your experience and understanding of the poems? How would the poems change with different punctuation?

Context: Unlike many of her contemporaries, Dickinson does not write poems with clear moral or ethical messages. Are her poems trying to "teach" us anything? What seems to be the purpose of these poems? Do they make you feel (and if so, feel how)? Do they make you think (and if so, think what)?

Context: Dickinson's most famous poem, #465, draws on the nineteenth century's fascination with deathbed scenes in literature. Unusually, however, this scene is described from the point of view of the deceased. What exactly does the poem's narrator experience, both sensuously and psychologically? How does the fly affect the narrator's experience of death?

Exploration: What might Dickinson mean when she writes "Tell all the Truth but tell it slant" (#1129)? Why is there a danger that Truth will blind us unless it "dazzle[s] gradually"? Why does the narrator refer to children in supporting this thesis?

Exploration: What, in poem #258, might "internal difference" mean? What are "the Meanings," and why are they contained in internal difference? Why does the natural experience of a certain winter light provoke reflection on internal difference?

Ambrose Bierce (1842–1914?)

Ambrose Bierce spent an unhappy childhood in Ohio and left home as a bitter and pessimistic young man. At the outbreak of the Civil War, Bierce joined the Union Army; he later brought his military experience vividly to life in some of his best stories. Bierce moved to San Francisco after the war and embarked on a career as a journalist. His "Prattler" column, originally printed in the *Argonaut* and then the *Wasp*, was picked up by William Randolph Hearst's *San Francisco Sunday Examiner* in 1886 and provided Bierce with an excellent outlet for his biting wit and his short stories. After divorcing his wife in 1891 and losing one son in a gunfight and the other to alcoholism, Bierce disappeared in Mexico in 1913, where legend says he was killed in the Mexican Revolution. His works include *Tales of Soldiers and Civilians* (1891; later retitled *In the Midst of Life*) and *The Devil's Dictionary* (1906).

[3320] J. H. E. Partington, *Ambrose Bierce* (1928), courtesy of the Library of Congress [LC-USZ62-20182].

TEACHING TIP

■ "An Occurrence at Owl Creek Bridge" is a textbook example of irony, with a surprising "twist ending." Have students practice this literary technique by writing brief narratives with unexpected, ironic endings. Briefly explore which ones work the best and what elements allow them to do so.

QUESTIONS

Comprehension: How does the ending of "An Occurrence at Owl Creek Bridge" change your sense of what happens earlier in the story?

Context: How might it matter that this story takes place in the South? How does this story relate to the Core Context "Swamps, Dismal and Otherwise" and the South's conflicting senses of identity?

Exploration: What does this story seem to be saying about perception and knowledge? We typically assume that perception precedes knowledge: I know the truth because I have seen it. To what extent does "An Occurrence at Owl Creek Bridge" argue that the opposite is sometimes true? You might compare it to the stories by Edgar Allan Poe and Nathaniel Hawthorne in this regard.

Charlotte Perkins Gilman (1860–1935)

Born in Hartford, Connecticut, Charlotte Perkins was raised by her mother. Her father abandoned the family shortly after her birth (her father was the nephew of siblings Harriet Beecher Stowe and Henry Ward Beecher). Gilman's mother moved her two children to her original home, Rhode Island, where she withheld physical expressions of love from them in an attempt to steel them against the future pain of broken relationships. Gilman worked as a governess, teacher, and greeting-card designer before reluctantly marrying Charles Stetson in 1884—she had become increasingly aware that women did not receive equal rights, and she was concerned that as a new wife and mother she would have difficulty beginning a writing career.

After the birth of her daughter, Gilman became depressed and was

GILMAN WEB ARCHIVE

advised to seek bed rest and to limit her intellectual endeavors. This "cure" so frustrated Gilman that she nearly went mad, recovering by thrusting her energies into the American Woman Suffrage Association. Soon after, she composed "The Yellow Wall-paper" (1892), which was based on her experience with depression. When her marriage broke up, Gilman sent her daughter to live with her ex-husband and his new wife, Gilman's former best friend. She married her first cousin, George Houghton Gilman, in 1900 and continued her writing career, producing books that advocated reform, including *Women and Economics* (1898), *Concerning Children* (1900), and *The Man-Made World* (1911), as well as the novels *Moving the Mountain* (1911), *Herland* (1915), and *With Her in Ourland* (1916). We can see that same reformist spirit in Gilman's most famous text, her critique of women's oppression under patriarchy, "The Yellow Wall-paper."

TEACHING TIPS

■ Have students debate about whether or not the narrator emerges "victorious" in "The Yellow Wall-paper." This question highlights different assumptions about the value of material and psychic freedom.

■ Emphasize the many ways in which John's treatment of the narrator in "The Yellow Wall-paper" is based on patriarchal assumptions about women—especially considering that postpartum depression is now recognized as a legitimate (and common) ailment. What are the signs of postpartum depression? How does knowledge of this condition help us understand the story?

QUESTIONS

Comprehension: Describe the narrator of "The Yellow Wall-paper" as precisely as you can. Why does she spend all of her time in the nursery? What is "wrong" with her? To what extent does she change over the course of the story?

Comprehension: Describe the wallpaper. Why is the narrator both fascinated and repulsed by it?

Comprehension: By the end of the story, the narrator seems to believe she has achieved a victory: " 'I've got out at last,' said I, 'in spite of you and Jane! And I've pulled off most of the paper, so you can't put me back!' " Do you agree that she has emerged victorious? If so, in what sense?

Context: How does the narrator's husband, John, treat her? She notes, "He says that with my imaginative power and habit of story-making, a nervous weakness like mine is sure to lead to all manner of excited fancies, and that I ought to use my will and good sense to check the tendency." Why does he emphasize her "imaginative power," and to what extent do you think Gilman wants us to agree with John's opinion? Think about this in terms of both nineteenth-century anxieties about the supposed promises of science and the ideals of the cult of true womanhood.

Exploration: Look at the advertisement for "Dr. Weiland's Celebrated Sugar Worm Lozenges" featured in the archive. In what sense can Gilman's story be seen as a response to the mid-nineteenth-century reverence for science?

Suggested Author Pairings

HERMAN MELVILLE AND WASHINGTON IRVING

In their texts treated in this unit, Herman Melville and Washington Irving arguably present veiled allegories of American experience. In *Moby-Dick*, the *Pequod* can stand as the mid-nineteenth-century ship of state, America's diverse and contentious community navigating treacherous waters and wary of the designs of its captain. Ahab might be the inverse of the messianic Andrew Jackson, the latter as confident of the divine sanction of westward expansion as the former is confident of the transcendental necessity of flouting God's cruelty. Aboard, too, are the African American Pip and the Native American Queequeg, members of two American groups who suffered during the Jacksonian expansion. Meanwhile, Irving constructs two conflicting worlds in his stories: the colonial Dutch community of easy aestheticism and the liberal-progressive United States of base commercialism. Rip Van Winkle has to construct a new identity when earthy colony becomes political country; and Ichabod Crane, the venial, craven representative of Yankee self-delusion, is punished for his blind hypocrisy.

EMILY DICKINSON, EDGAR ALLAN POE, AND CHARLES BROCKDEN BROWN

Dickinson, Poe, and Brown all ask us to explore a consciousness that doubts and questions its own reflections. All three employ death as the focal point of self-consciousness, the unknowable center around which our thoughts inevitably swirl (whether we are aware of it or not). Dickinson, in poem #315, emphasizes that our uncertainty about God is perennial, because only at or after death ("the Ethereal Blow") do we have any hope of sureness. She also ends her meditation on the subjective experience of winter light by suggesting that it withdraws "like the Distance / On the look of Death—." Neither Poe's nor Brown's narrators can be fully sure of the evidence of their senses: in each case, the narrative suggests that what the characters experience could be at least in part the projection of their own desires ("Ligeia") or fears (*Wieland*). And in each case, the threat of death looms large: the narrator of "Ligeia" cannot bear that death will have robbed him of his beloved, and Brown's Clara fears her own possible implication in the homicidal tendencies of her brother. (Hawthorne's "Young Goodman Brown" can also fit with this grouping.)

NATHANIEL HAWTHORNE, CHARLOTTE PERKINS GILMAN, AND HENRY WARD BEECHER

These authors, each in wildly different ways, reflect on how gender influences the supposedly objective progress of reason. For Hawthorne in "Rappaccini's Daughter," Giovanni's desire for Beatrice distracts him from the pursuit of scientific truth; and Rappaccini claims to perform his botanical experiment on pseudo-feminist grounds (so that Beatrice can now have some power in the world). Precisely what Hawthorne is saying about gender is debatable, although he seems to position the men as dangerously self-deluded and Beatrice as a social victim. Gilman's feminism is much more clear: her narrator is oppressed and psychically annihilated by the "objective" inhumanity of patriarchal psychiatric medicine. It is precisely her own creativity, thwarted as John forbids her from writing, that returns to assault her sanity in the form of the wallpaper. Henry Ward Beecher, equally unambiguous but far from feminist, depicts the seductive deviltry of the female body in his lecture. If they are to succeed in their social ambitions, suggestible young men must be careful to avoid the satanic snares of prostitutes. The female body here is the gothic threat, the dangerous and irrational force that threatens the American man.

AMBROSE BIERCE AND WILLIAM GILMORE SIMMS

These authors each depict the American South in gothic terms. For Simms, the South is the region of persevering self-reliance but, after the Civil War, also a shattered and beleaguered community that needs to rebuild its identity. When his characters journey through the swamps, they are both wandering in dangerously ill-defined territory and proving their mettle. In Bierce's "An Occurrence at Owl Creek Bridge," the southern Farquhar intends to burn a strategic bridge in order to thwart the Union forces. However, he is deceived twice: first by a mendacious Union scout, and second by his own imagination, as it conjures for him an elaborate scenario of heroism and bravery. Like so many other characters in the works treated in this unit, he cannot trust his own senses or awareness—even when he feels "preternaturally keen and alert." Unlike many of the other characters, though, his self-delusion provokes socio-historical questions: Was the South fooling itself in the face of the inevitable? Did slavery render the South ethically dead even as the region imagined it was heroically struggling to free itself from northern bondage? What, after all, is the identity of the South?

CORE CONTEXTS

Swamps, Dismal and Otherwise

According to David C. Miller in his book *Dark Eden*, the idea of the swamp underwent an important change in the mid-nineteenth century. The swamp, he says, had long been full of theological and folk-

[2767] H. L. Stevens, *In the Swamp* (1863), courtesy of the Library of Congress [LC-USZC4-2522].

loric implications: "It was the domain of sin, death, and decay; the stage for witchcraft; the habitat of weird and ferocious creatures." But the **Romanticism** of Emerson and Thoreau in the first part of the century had changed how nature was viewed. For many, nature was neither an impediment to be overcome by rational social progress nor a howling "wilderness" to be cultivated by Christian piety. Rather, nature became an object of human experience, a field of signs in which the apprehending consciousness could see analogies to his or her (usually "his") truest "nature." So the swamp, too, began to exhibit shifting associations as it became a screen on which the observer could project his or her own fears or desires. It was potentially threatening and consuming, but also potentially generative, creative, and thrilling. One could get lost and swallowed up in the swamp (could get, that is, "swamped"), or one could find a new source of energy and power. This shift was associated with sociocultural issues, as Miller observes: first, with "the erosion of patriarchal patterns of culture, motivated by an urge to control or suppress a 'female' nature as the source of heretical and potentially anarchic meaning"; second, with the South's power, conceived either as thrillingly resilient (as the South is assaulted by the North for its practices) or as cruelly inhuman (insofar as it practices slavery). The swamp, then, acts during this time as a figure for a variety of social and philosophical issues. And insofar as it tends to blend the threatening and the thrilling, it can be associated with gothic themes in general.

Swamps are part of the symbolism of slavery's suffocating evil in Harriet Beecher Stowe's *Uncle Tom's Cabin* and *Dred, A Tale of the Dismal Swamp*. Swamps can also be seen as symbolic of the problems of knowledge and repression in Herman Melville's *Pierre* and *The Confidence-Man*. According to Miller, however, swamps are most prominent as a symbol for, depending on the text, either the best or worst of southern society. They figure prominently in the work of southern writer William Gilmore Simms, for whom, in such novels as *The Forayers*, *The Scout*, and *Woodcraft*, the swamp stands for the conflicting connotations of the South. On the one hand, we have slavery and defeat, with their associations of stagnation, infirmity, self-pity, and lassitude. On the other hand, we have stalwart and fraternal community, with its associations of vigor, power, fecundity, and renewal. In the alternation between these two poles much of the gothic springs forth: When does comfort become stagnation? When does vigor become violence?

QUESTIONS

Comprehension: Which of the texts in Unit 6 contain swamps?
Context: Why was the swamp important in mid-nineteenth-century life and culture?

[1876] François Regis Gignoux, *View, Dismal Swamp, North Carolina* (1850), courtesy of Museum of Fine Arts, Boston. Copyright 2002 Museum of Fine Arts, Boston, François Regis Gignoux; American (born in France), 1816–1882. *View, Dismal Swamp, North Carolina*, 1850; Oil on canvas; 78.74 x 120.01 cm. (31 x 47 1/4 in.). Museum of Fine Arts, Boston. Bequest of Henry Herbert Edes, 1923, 23.184.

"SWAMP" WEB ARCHIVE

[1876] François Regis Gignoux, *View, Dismal Swamp, North Carolina* (1850), courtesy of Museum of Fine Arts, Boston. Copyright 2002 Musem of Fine Arts, Boston, François Regis Gignoux; American (born in France), 1816–1882. *View, Dismal Swamp, North Carolina*, 1850; Oil on canvas; 78.74 x 120.01 cm. (31 x 47 1/4 in.). Museum of Fine Arts, Boston. Bequest of Henry Herbert Edes, 1923, 23.184. Oil on canvas; southern swamp at sunset. As notions of nature changed in the mid-nineteenth century, the swamp began to be associated with the human potential to effect change on social problems.
[2719] Alfred Rudolph Waud, *Pictures of the South—Negro Quarters on Jefferson Davis's Plantation* (1866), courtesy of the Library of Congress, Prints and Photographs Division [LC-USZ62-116582]. Sketch of slave quarters and slaves on the plantation of Jefferson Davis, president of the Confederacy.

[2767] H. L. Stevens, *In the Swamp* (1863), courtesy of the Library of Congress [LC-USZC4-2522]. The swamp could be a refuge, especially for escaped slaves, displaced Native Americans, and exiled white communities such as the Acadians.

[3356] War Department, *Overseer Artayou Carrier whipped me. I was two months in bed sore from the whipping. My master come after I was whipped; He discharged the overseer. The very words of Poor Peter, Taken as he sat for his picture. Baton Rouge, Louisiana* (1863), courtesy of the Still Picture Branch, National Archive and Records Administration. For slaves, escape became increasingly difficult over the course of the nineteenth century because of the rigid laws enacted in response to abolitionist activity.

[5931] Worthington Whittredge, *The Old Hunting Grounds* (1864), courtesy of Reynolda House, Museum of American Art, Winston-Salem, North Carolina. The decaying Indian canoe among birch trees symbolizes the death of the Native American culture sentimentalized in Cooper's work and other frontier literature.

[8095] Alfred R. Waud, *Cyprus Swamp on the Opelousas Railroad, Louisiana* (1866), courtesy of the Library of Congress [LC-USZ62-108302]. The image of the swamp—dark, mysterious, and potentially dangerous—provides an apt allegory for many social and philosophical issues faced by the United States during the nineteenth century.

Context: What is the swamp's relation to society? What is its relation to more obviously threatening natural forces or objects such as storms, mountains, and volcanoes? Is the swamp a force or an object?

Context: Consider François Regis Gignoux's 1850 painting *View, Dismal Swamp, North Carolina* in relation to the opening pages of William Gilmore Simms's novels *The Scout* and *The Forayers*. How are these three swamps similar and different? What significance do Gignoux and Simms give them?

Context: To what extent does Ambrose Bierce's "An Occurrence at Owl Creek Bridge" draw on the symbolism of the swamp? In what ways does this story respond to the archive image of the runaway slave, "In the Swamp"?

Context: Analyze the significance of the swamp, or "tarn," in Edgar Allan Poe's "The Fall of the House of Usher."

Exploration: Have you ever seen a swamp? What was your reaction? What representations of swamps have you seen in the media or popular culture? What response did those images inspire?

Exploration: What comparisons can you make between Simms's swamps and other natural objects or phenomena in this unit: Melville's ocean or whale? Hawthorne's forest? Dickinson's winter light? Irving's Catskill Mountains? Gilman's botanical-motif wallpaper? What generalizations can you make about gothic literature's vision of nature?

The Spirit Is Willing: The Occult and Women in the Nineteenth Century

The nineteenth century saw an upsurge of interest in occult and supernatural phenomena, especially attempts to contact the spirits of dead loved ones. Enlightenment reason had by now taken its toll on the Calvinist faith of early America and its belief in **original sin**: far fewer people believed in a God who directly intervened in the affairs of the world, dispensing generous or harmful miracles as appropriate to convey his judgment. Indeed, the "invisible world," as Cotton Mather called the realm of divinity and spirits in 1693, had by the 1850s largely receded from the daily thoughts of many Americans. The Deist God was now prominent: this was the famous "clock-maker," who established the laws of the universe at the creation, but who never interfered with the mechanism after winding it up.

Our current notions of a clear distinction between science and religion did not exist much before the twentieth century. At least until the eighteenth century, science was called "natural philosophy" and was only one way of deepening one's understanding of self, nature, and divinity. Cotton Mather had also been a scientist, fascinated by God's creation as a way of reading the attitudes of the Creator, and Sir Isaac Newton wrote a lengthy treatise on the Book of Revelation. As Ann Braude argues in her book *Radical Spirits*, it should not be surprising, then, that many nineteenth-century Americans saw no less reason to believe in ghosts and mediums than they did to believe in what seemed like the equally improbable idea of the telegraph: both involved communication that crossed apparently insuperable barriers. **Spiritualism**, as the spirit-contacting movement was called, allowed Americans who were becoming more inclined to trust science than miracles to retain a belief in the afterlife based on what appeared to be repeatable, objective evidence and experiment.

It is not accidental that women were the main agents of nineteenth-century spiritualism. A science/religion that allowed direct contact with the invisible world without institutional hierarchy, it carved a place for women to provide religious leadership. In 1848, the Fox sisters, Margaret, Leah, and Catherine, reported hearing spirit rappings in their Arcadia, New York, home and went on to be the driving force in American spiritualism. They organized "performances" in which they demonstrated their abilities as mediums and drew condemnation from some male clergy. Women interfering with established religious structures had been an American anxiety at least since Anne Hutchinson in the seventeenth century—an anxiety especially apparent in the heavily gendered accusations of the Salem witch trials. Perhaps in response to the women who attempted to cross patriarchal boundaries, a social phenomenon sometimes called the **cult of true womanhood** developed and began to have widespread influence in nineteenth-century America. This ideology, or set of assumptions and beliefs, solidly relegated women to the home and explicitly rejected the possibility of women engaging in public leadership. Scholar Barbara Welter suggests that, through such vehicles as women's magazines and religious literature, the cult of true womanhood prescribed four cardinal virtues for women: piety, purity, submissiveness, and domesticity. Women, it was thought, had as their proper roles nurturer, comforter, and homemaker. In the public realm—whether political or religious—women, like children, were meant to be seen and not heard. "True" women in this sense were patriotic and God-fearing; anyone who opposed this ideology was seen as an enemy of God, civilization, and America itself. One of the most famous women to challenge this idea of womanhood was Victoria Woodhull, who combined a belief in spiritualism with crusades for women's suffrage and free love. She was also the first woman to address a joint session of Congress and ran for president in 1871 (an attempt that ended in failure when her past as a prostitute was exposed).

For all these reasons, we should not be surprised to see gothic writers reveal concerns about how gender relates to the spirit world. The narrator of Edgar Allan Poe's "Ligeia" imputes a witchlike, supernatural willpower to his beloved. He imagines that she is able to transcend the boundary between life and death and is therefore both exciting and threatening. Henry Ward Beecher, in his sermon "The Strange Woman," displays a similar fear as he warns against the almost supernatural power women's sexuality can wield over

[7053] A. J. Dewey, *There's a Charm about the Old Love Still* (1901), courtesy of the Library of Congress and Rare Book, Manuscript, and Special Collections Library, Duke University, Durham, NC.

[2498] Currier & Ives, *The Age of Brass; or, The Triumphs of Women's Rights* (1869), courtesy of the Library of Congress [LC-USZC2-1921].

[2245] Alexandre-Marie Colin, *The Three Witches from "Macbeth"* (1827), courtesy of the Sandor Korein. Paintings like this resonated with the mid-nineteenth-century American interest in the occult and the fear of what some saw as the supernatural power of women.

[2498] Currier & Ives, *The Age of Brass; or, The Triumphs of Women's Rights* (1869), courtesy of the Library of Congress [LC-USZC2-1921]. In this lithograph one woman scolds a cowed man, and another, in pantaloons, holds a sign reading "Vote for the Celebrated Man Tamer." Such cartoons played to predominantly male fears about the reversal of men's and women's public and private roles and were designed to reinforce the cult of true womanhood.

[2503] Unknown, *The Judiciary Committee of the House of Representatives Receiving a Deputation of Female Suffragists* (1871), courtesy of the Library of Congress, Prints and Photographs Division [LC-USZ62-2023]. Victoria Woodhull, backed by a group of women suffragists, is shown reading a speech to a skeptical judiciary committee. Her speech, about the legality of women's suffrage, was based on the Fourteenth and Fifteenth Constitutional amendments.

[7053] A. J. Dewey, *There's a Charm about the Old Love Still* (1901), courtesy of the Library of Congress and Rare Book, Manuscript, and Special Collections Library, Duke University, Durham, NC. This sheet music illustration shows a man and a woman using a Ouija board. The nineteenth century witnessed a growing interest in spiritualism and the occult.

[7248] N. Currier, *Mrs. Fish and the Misses Fox: The Original Mediums of the Mysterious Noises at Rochester, Western N.Y.* (1852), courtesy of the Library of Congress [LC-USZ62-2586]. The sisters, who claimed to communicate with the dead, are credited as the originators of modern spiritualism.

[9013] Henry Ward Beecher, *The Strange Woman* (1892), from *Addresses to Young Men*, published by H. Altemus,

impressionable young men. He comes close to suggesting that prostitutes, devil-like, are capable of mesmerizing and entrapping otherwise rational males. Arguably, Emily Dickinson exploits the association of the female with the mystical as she interrogates the assumptions of the largely patriarchal nineteenth-century worldview: although one must tell the truth "slant," Dickinson implies that she has access to it. Ironically, perhaps, given Beecher's social moralizing, spiritualism, whose proponents also critiqued marriage and advocated alternative medical treatments, became closely associated with the antebellum social reform ethos in general. The reform movements had always attracted many women who had a particular interest in creating a more equitable culture. Harriet Beecher Stowe, Henry's sister, was the most famous nineteenth-century literary woman to argue, through *Uncle Tom's Cabin* (1852), for social reform. It is useful to compare her reform ethos with the spiritualist one: for Stowe, it is the mystery of Christianity that shows the way to truth and justice.

QUESTIONS

Comprehension: Why was spiritualism threatening to some men? In the image "The Age of Brass, or the Triumph of Women's Rights," how are the women represented? What did the social empowerment of women have to do with spiritualism?

Context: What different emphases are provided by a reform movement that focuses on spirits, rather than one that focuses on traditional Christianity? What kind of reforms were Victoria Woodhull and the Fox sisters associated with? How can you relate women's reforms and spiritualism to Henry Ward Beecher's "The Strange Woman" or Edgar Allan Poe's "Ligeia"?

Context: Why would women have a particular interest in social reform movements?

Context: Why might spiritualism appeal to so many people (over one million Americans by 1855)? How might this popularity relate to the contemporaneous popularity of the gothic mode?

Exploration: Do you believe in spirits? Is it possible to reconcile such a belief with orthodox faiths?

Exploration: Is it fair to say that Dickinson presents herself as a latter-day mystic in her poems? How would this approach revise your reading of her work?

Exploration: What are the similarities and differences between Poe's character Ligeia and Beecher's "Strange Woman"?

Exploration: In what sense could you say all gothic literature is interested in social reform?

America on the Rocks: The Image of the "Ship of State"

Writers often create coherence in their writing by employing literary motifs—themes, characters, or verbal patterns that recur throughout the work. Sometimes writers draw these motifs out of their imagination, but other times they are popular symbols from a writer's era. One important cultural motif for nineteenth-century political discourse was the image of America as the **ship of state** and its history as a voyage. As David C. Miller observes, this is an ancient trope, reaching back at least to Sophocles, in whose *Antigone* Creon says to the chorus that "our Ship of State, which recent storms have threatened to destroy, has come safely to harbor at last, guided by the merciful wisdom of Heaven." And in the United States, the figure goes back at least to Roger Williams and John Winthrop, in the seventeenth century, who exploited its association with the Israelites' journey into the wilderness toward the promised land of Canaan. But in the years around *Moby-Dick*'s composition, as the nation seemed more and more headed toward sectional conflict over the issue of slavery, many voices warned that the ship of state was threatening to strike the rocks of civil war. For many Americans, America was not so much sailing into harbor as nearly foundering in treacherous socio-political seas. In 1850, Henry Wadsworth Longfellow wrote his poem "The Building of the Ship," which became popular with Unionists as it reminded Americans of the "blood and tears" that went into the creation

Philadelphia. In this sermon Beecher warns young men against the dangers of female sexuality, which he saw as a force possessing near-supernatural power over an unguarded man's will.

[7261] Currier & Ives, *A Squall off Cape Horn* (1840–90), courtesy of the Library of Congress [LC-USZC4-5632].

of the Union. Significantly, in the same year Daniel Webster defended the Compromise of 1850 in these terms: "The East, the North, and the stormy South combine to throw the whole sea into commotion, [. . .] I have a part to act, not for my own security or safety, for I am looking out for no fragment upon which to float away from the wreck, if wreck there must be, but for the good of the whole, and the preservation of all." The Compromise was meant to unite once and for all the North, the South, and the West, newly acquired in the Mexican War of 1848–49. Among other provisions, it allowed the admittance of California into the Union as a free state but required northern states to return escaped slaves to their former masters. However, it eased tensions between North and South only temporarily, and the Civil War came eleven years later. In fact, in 1851 Melville's own father-in-law, Lemuel Shaw, enforced the Fugitive Slave Act, putting the law officially into practice. One commentator responded to abolitionists who decried this law by figuring slavery as an implacable force: "Did you ever see a whale? Did you ever see a mighty whale struggling?"

It is possible to argue, then, as Alan Heimert did forty years ago, that Melville's epic consciously allegorizes America as the ship of state. He points out not only that the *Pequod* is manned by thirty isolates all "federated along one keel" (there were thirty states in the Union by 1850), but also that each of the three mates stands for one of the three major regions of the country: North, South, and West. Moreover, each one employs as harpooner the precise racial minority that the region he represents was built upon: a Pacific Indian serves Starbuck, the Yankee; a Native American throws for Stubb, whom Melville describes

[2603] *Harper's Weekly, The Africans of the Slave Bark "Wildfire"—The Slave Deck of the Bark "Wildfire," Brought into Key West on April 30, 1860—African Men Crowded onto the Lower Deck; African Women Crowded on an Upper Deck* (1860), courtesy of the Library of Congress [LC-USZ62-41678].

as "essentially Western"; and the African Daggoo carries Flask, who represents the South.

But even if the symbolism is not as tight as Heimert suggests (many readers might find this reading a little claustrophobic), there is no question that the spirit of the "ship of state" was in the air as Melville wrote. Other important literary texts of the time to evoke this image are Edgar Allan Poe's *The Narrative of Arthur Gordon Pym* and Henry David Thoreau's *Walden*. Of course, the other symbolically prominent vessel of the age was itself horribly literal: the slave ship. Its significance can be seen in images like *The Africans of the Slave Bark "Wildfire,"* which was the kind of visual rhetorical statement that abolitionists seized on to decry the cruelties of slavery. The two ships were symbolically inextricable, as the repeated but direct voyages of the one had much to do with the single but tumultuous journey of the other.

QUESTIONS

Comprehension: Why was there national tension in the 1850s?

Comprehension: In what sense might Melville's *Pequod* be allegorizing America?

Context: What aspects of a country are emphasized when it is thought of as the "ship of state"?

Context: How did the outcome of the Mexican War add to anxiety about the "voyage" of America?

Context: How do you imagine a typical northern white American of the mid-nineteenth century would react to the image of the slave bark *Wildfire*? A typical southern white American?

Exploration: Do you see any way to have avoided the Civil War? What advice would you have given Americans about the ship of state in 1850?

Exploration: In what ways is a country *not* like a ship? Why might employing the image of the ship of state actually be politically dangerous?

Exploration: Closely examine the details of the *Pequod* as described in Chapter XVI of *Moby-Dick*, "The Ship." What details support the idea that Melville intended this novel—at least in part—to represent America's voyage in the mid-nineteenth century?

EXTENDED CONTEXTS

Unnatural Reason/Weird Science

Alongside the enthusiasm for technological progress and the Industrial Revolution, the nineteenth century experienced widespread anxiety about the costs of technology and resulting urbanization and alienation. Herman Melville, in "The Paradise of Bachelors and the Tartarus of Maids," and Rebecca Harding Davis, in *Life in the Iron*

Mills, wrote of the dehumanizing potential of industrial labor. Melville, in "The Bell-Tower," and Hawthorne, in works like "Rappaccini's Daughter" and "The Birth-Mark," followed Mary Shelley's lead in *Frankenstein*, suggesting that scientific ambition can be easily associated with hubris—dangerously overweening pride that inevitably led to the destruction of the scientist. Moreover, industrial labor was seen by some as a challenge to republican individualism: the worker became a cog in the machine, no longer an autonomous producer. Many felt technology as a threat, a kind of monstrous "machine in the garden"—to borrow Leo Marx's term—one that invaded people's lives, producing potentially catastrophic side effects.

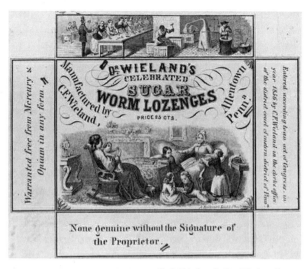

[3161] C. F. Wieland, *Dr. Wieland's Celebrated Sugar Worm Lozenges* (1856), courtesy of the Library of Congress [LC-USZ62-102488].

QUESTIONS

Comprehension: What sense do you get of the factory in view of the "Architectural Iron Works, 13th & 14th Sts., East River, New York"? Does this seem like an inviting place to work? Why or why not? Compare this image with the depiction of the factory in Herman Melville's "The Paradise of Bachelors and the Tartarus of Maids."

Context: How could you see "Molten Metal to Casts," in the archive, as an argument against industrial labor? How is this argument similar to and different from Harriet Beecher Stowe's abolitionist stance in *Uncle Tom's Cabin*?

Exploration: The archive images of "Dr. Wieland's Celebrated Sugar Worm Lozenges" and "Moorhead's Improved Graduated Magnetic Machine" implicitly promise that technology can improve daily life. Do you see these promises explored in any of the texts of Unit 6? In your own life? Do you trust these promises? Do these promises bear any resemblance to Rappaccini's experiment?

"Sleeping Beauty": Sentimentalizing Death in the Nineteenth Century

In the mid-nineteenth century, death was less often seen as the occasion for a final judgment of the sinning soul and more often as the passage to a comforting "home." As it had always been in America, death was still a family affair, much more a part of everyday life than in our own day; rather than in hospitals, people died at home, cared for by women relatives. With events like Unitarian Minister William Ellery Channing's repudiating the Calvinist theory of infant damnation in 1809, however, death—especially the death of children—became more an occasion for melancholy than an opportunity for pious reflections on depravity.

The **cult of sentiment** that continued from the eighteenth into the nineteenth century suggested that sympathy with another human was

shows iron workers transferring a crucible of molten metal to the casting area. Many states, and some private companies, printed their own notes prior to the nationalization of currency during the Civil War.

[7249] Anonymous, *Carter's Little Liver Pills* (c.1860), courtesy of the Library of Congress, Prints and Photographs Division, Samuel Rosenberg Collection [LC-USZ62-75898]. Trade card advertisement for liver pills, depicting a woman with a "wretched nervous headache" who is amazed that her husband could be chipper after a late night. The success of such nineteenth-century medications was due to the growing belief that science could improve the daily life of Americans.

[8650] Emory Elliott, Interview: "Hawthorne's Relation to the Puritan Past" (2001), courtesy of Annenberg/CPB. Emory Elliott, professor of English at the University of California, Riverside, reads an excerpt from Hawthorne's "Rappaccini's Daughter."

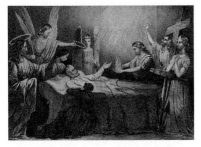

[2651] N. E. Talcott and J. H. Bufford, *Allegorical Representation of the Dying Christian* (1847), courtesy of the Library of Congress (LC-USZC4-3150].

"SLEEPING BEAUTY"
WEB ARCHIVE

[2651] N. E. Talcott and J. H. Bufford, *Allegorical Representation of the Dying Christian* (1847), courtesy of the Library of Congress [LC-USZC4-3150]. This lithograph shows a man on his deathbed making a peaceful transition to the afterlife. He is surrounded by Jesus Christ, angels, and women.

a paramount virtue. Especially associated with literature written by and for women—and the cult of true womanhood in general—the sentimental tradition taught that the homely virtues of empathy and pity were the route to moral edification for both sexes. This movement produced many tearful deathbed scenes in literature and art: the death of little Eva in *Uncle Tom's Cabin* is only one of many examples of angelically innocent children dying gracefully in order to rend the hearts of the onlookers and readers (in fact, childhood mortality was 30 to 50 percent in this era). On the other side of the Atlantic, Mary Shelley in *Frankenstein* and Charles Dickens in *The Old Curiosity Shop* employed this image as well. Through a sympathetic reaction to such a death, it was hoped that people would become more virtuous by tapping into their sentimentality, which would ease the demands of callous reason. Starting in the 1830s, "consolation literature"—roughly comparable to today's self-help books on dealing with grief—became popular, and life insurance companies took root. As Stanley B. Burns shows in *Sleeping Beauty: Memorial Photography in America*, by 1841 the brand-new technology of the daguerreotype was encouraging a vogue in post-mortem photography. In an age without public records, the dead could, in a way, be captured and held onto indefinitely.

Gothic literature responds to this era of sentimental death in a number of ways. Some writers, like Stowe, exploit the trend for sociopolitical purposes. In *Uncle Tom's Cabin*, the sentimental deaths of Eva and Uncle Tom are meant to edify the reader: as Stowe wrote in the novel's concluding chapter, "the man or woman who *feels* strongly, healthily and justly, on the great interests of humanity, is a constant benefactor to the human race." Writers like Poe and Brown inject death scenes with graphic physical descriptions to transfer the intense emotionality of sentiment into an aesthetic effect of horror. Dickinson, however, frequently writes about the moment of death—or its anticipation or aftermath—in decidedly unsentimental terms, as if to undercut the usual effect of the sentimental death.

QUESTIONS

Comprehension: What seems to be the message of the "Allegorical Representation of the Dying Christian"? How do you imagine it meant to make its viewers feel? How do Dickinson's "I heard a Fly buzz—when I died" or Melville's *Moby-Dick* (e.g., the death of Pip) challenge this allegory?

Exploration: Can you spot the use of sentimental death-scenes in literature or film today? How do they function in films like *Titanic*, *Steel Magnolias*, and *Terms of Endearment*? Why are films like these sometimes called—sometimes with affection, sometimes with disdain—"chick flicks"?

ASSIGNMENTS

Personal and Creative Responses

1. *Journal:* Write a letter to Goodman Brown, Rappaccini, Ahab, or Emily Dickinson in which you try to soothe their anxieties. What could you say to these tormented figures that might comfort them and ease their fears about people, society, or God? Do you think you could persuade them to adopt a more optimistic outlook? What points would you have to emphasize? Do you believe your own arguments?

2. *Poet's Corner:* First, try summarizing the "argument" of Dickinson's poem #1129 [Tell all the Truth but tell it slant—] in prose form. What problems do you encounter in doing so? Can you take into account *all* of the words and punctuation of the poem as you write your summary? If not, what do you have to leave out in order to make the argument coherent? Second, try writing a poem in the style of Dickinson that expresses one of your beliefs. Imitate her spare style, use dashes, and see how briefly and efficiently you can express your views. Are you able to translate the belief into a Dickinson-like poem? What problems do you encounter?

3. *Doing History:* Consider some gothic "texts" of our own day: you can find myriad examples in literature, film, television, and video games. Do you find in the current upsurge in gothic subject matter the spirit of Hawthorne, Melville, and Dickinson? Why or why not?

4. *Multimedia:* American gothic representation has always been interdisciplinary: as a mode that is meant to affect the emotions as well as the intellect, it can be seen in painting, photography, drama, film, television, and video games. Using the *American Passages* image database, construct a multimedia presentation in which you use visuals to develop a definition of "gothic." What elements or characteristics cause these images to cohere into an identifiable set of concerns, ideas, or assumptions?

5. *A Woman's View*: In 1999, Sena Jeter Naslund published *Ahab's Wife, or, The Star-Gazer*. In this novel Naslund imagines what life was like for Ahab's young wife. Write a response to one of the works you have read using the perspective of someone who is not given voice in the text. For example, you might rewrite the opening of *Moby-Dick* from Queequeg's perspective or a scene from *The Scarlet Letter* from Pearl's point of view.

Problem-Based Learning Projects

1. Because you have just studied the writers in this unit, you have been asked to help organize a new course being offered by the psychology department of your school, "Gothic Psychology." The idea is to introduce students to human psychology as represented by writers in the gothic tradition. Referring to the texts of this unit, outline the syllabus for the course.

[2654] James S. Baille, *The Mother's Grave* (1848), courtesy of the Library of Congress [LC-USZC4-1842]. Here a rosy-cheeked brother and sister dressed in mourning are joined by a dog at their mother's tombstone.

[2656] D. W. Kellogg, *Woman Mourning by Tomb* (c. 1842), courtesy of the Library of Congress, Prints and Photographs Division [LC-USZC4-1840]. Painting of crying woman leaning on tomb inscribed with the words "to the memory of Capt. John Williams, died April the 1, 1825."

[3111] James William Carling, *The Raven* (c. 1882), courtesy of the Edgar Allan Poe Museum, Richmond, Virginia. This illustration, created by James Carling for an 1882 edition of "The Raven," reflects the dark and foreboding tone of Poe's classic poem.

[8658] Priscilla Wald, "Dickinson Reading" (2001), courtesy of Annenberg/CPB. Wald, associate professor of English at Duke University, reads Emily Dickinson's "There's a certain Slant of light."

2. Congress is commissioning you to prepare a study about the effects on readers of violent, disturbing literature—e.g., gothic literature. You are told that among sociologists there are two schools of thought: one is that such literature acts to "purge" the violent tendencies of people, allowing them to vicariously "let off steam" in a safe environment; the other is that such literature only desensitizes people and therefore makes them more prone to violence. How would you evaluate this problem, and what recommendations would you make? What information would you need, and what resources would you have to consult? Who would you ask?

GLOSSARY

ambiguity Doubtfulness or uncertainness of interpretation. Much gothic literature is considered ambiguous insofar as it rarely presents a clear moral or message; it seems intended to be open to multiple meanings.

American Renaissance Standard if limiting description of the flowering of American art and thought in the mid-nineteenth century. The restricted "canonical" version is usually thought to include Emerson, Thoreau, Hawthorne, Melville, Poe, and Dickinson.

cult of sentiment Eighteenth- and nineteenth-century cultural phenomenon in which emotions and feelings, as opposed to reason and logic, were seen as the routes to moral and social improvement. Sentimentality emphasized the ability to empathize with another's sorrow or to experience profound beauty. It was associated especially with literature written by and for women.

cult of true womanhood Influential nineteenth-century ideal of femininity that stressed the importance of motherhood, homemaking, piety, and purity. While men were expected to work and act in the public realm of business and politics, women were to remain in the private, domestic sphere of the home.

gothic In the eighteenth century and following, generally used for "of the Middle Ages." Then, through negative association with the medieval—often seen as the "Dark Ages" following the intellectual and social flowering of Rome—the term "gothic" shifts to literature, art, or architecture which attempts to disturb or unsettle the orderly, "civilized" course of society. Gothic works probe the dark side of humanity or unveil socio-cultural anxiety.

Manifest Destiny Prevalent in America from its early days through the nineteenth century, the belief that divine providence mandated America to expand throughout the continent and to stand as a social model for the rest of the world.

original sin The Calvinist belief that, because of the fall of Adam and Eve, all humans are born inherently sinful. Only God's free grace can save us from hell.

Romanticism European American late-eighteenth-century and early-nineteenth-century intellectual movement that stressed human creativity, sensation, subjectivity, emotion, and fulfillment. Often associated with nature as an inspiring force, Romanticism emphasized the radically innovative individual, as opposed to the Enlightenment focus on the rationally ordered society. Gothicism is sometimes called "dark Romanticism."

ship of state   A metaphor for conceiving of society and government, in which the state is seen as a ship traversing treacherous waters (i.e., social conflict) and needs the steady guiding hand of a trustworthy captain (i.e., leadership) to steer it to safe harbor (i.e., peaceful consensus) before it founders (i.e., fails as a unified society). This metaphor represents part of the American tendency toward thinking via analogy (comparing how two apparently unlike things might clarify or explain each other) and typology (seeing cosmic or national history expressed or symbolized in everyday details).

spiritualism   A more comforting and optimistic idea of the afterlife than that offered by Calvinism: the belief that the human personality or soul continues to exist after death and can be contacted through the aid of a medium. Many in the mid-nineteenth century were hopeful that science would eventually prove the existence of spirits.

SELECTED BIBLIOGRAPHY

Baym, Nina. *American Women of Letters and the Nineteenth-Century Sciences: Styles of Affiliation.* New Brunswick: Rutgers UP, 2002.

Braude, Ann. *Radical Spirits: Spiritualism and Women's Rights in Nineteenth-Century America.* Bloomington: Indiana UP, 2001.

Burns, Stanley. *Sleeping Beauty: Memorial Photography in America.* Altadena: Twelvetrees Press, 1990.

Elliott, Emory, ed. *The Columbia History of the American Novel.* New York: Columbia UP, 1991.

Halttunen, Karen. *Murder Most Foul: The Killer and the American Gothic Imagination.* Cambridge: Harvard UP, 1998.

Heimert, Alan. "*Moby-Dick* and American Political Symbolism." *American Quarterly* 15.4 (Winter 1963): 498–534.

Leverenz, David. *Manhood and the American Renaissance.* Ithaca: Cornell UP, 1989.

Matthiessen, F. O. *American Renaissance: Art and Expression in the Age of Emerson and Whitman.* New York: Oxford UP, 1941.

Miller, David. *Dark Eden: The Swamp in Nineteenth-Century American Culture.* New York: Cambridge UP, 1989.

———, ed. *American Iconology: New Approaches to Nineteenth-Century Art and Literature.* New Haven: Yale UP, 1993.

Wald, Priscilla. *Constituting Americans: Cultural Anxiety and Narrative Form.* Durham: Duke UP, 1995.

Welter, Barbara. *Dimity Convictions: The American Woman in the Nineteenth Century.* Athens: Ohio UP, 1976.

FURTHER RESOURCES

American Decorative Arts: Gothic Revival Library (1859) (virtual and actual exhibit). The Metropolitan Museum of Art, 1000 Fifth Avenue at 82nd Street, New York, NY 10028-0198. General Information: (212) 535-7710. TTY: (212) 570-3828 or (212) 650-2551.

American Photographs: The First Century (exhibit). Smithsonian American Art Museum, Washington, DC 20560-0970. Phone: (202) 275-1500.

Dickinson Electronic Archives. Institute for Advanced Technology in the Humanities, University of Virginia.

Eisner, Will. *Moby-Dick* (comic book). Adapted from Herman Melville. NBM Publishing.

Godey's Lady's Book (online and in hard copy). UVM Electronic Text Archive.

Novak, Barbara. *Nature and Culture: American Landscape and Painting, 1825–1875.* New York: Oxford UP, 1995.

Poe Museum. 1914–16 East Main Street, Richmond, VA 23223. <info@poemuseum.org> Phone: (804) 648-5523 or (888)-21E-APOE.

Schultz, Elizabeth. *Unpainted to the Last: Moby-Dick and Twentieth-Century American Art.* Lawrence: UP of Kansas, 1995.

Stone, Robert. *Outerbridge Reach.* Boston: Houghton Mifflin, 1998.

Unit 7

SLAVERY AND FREEDOM

Race and Identity in Antebellum America

Authors and Works

Featured in the Video:

Frederick Douglass, *Narrative of the Life of Frederick Douglass* (autobiography/slave narrative), *My Bondage and My Freedom* (autobiography/slave narrative), "The Meaning of July Fourth for the Negro" (speech)

Harriet Jacobs, *Incidents in the Life of a Slave Girl* (autobiography/slave narrative)

Harriet Beecher Stowe, *Uncle Tom's Cabin* (sentimental novel)

Discussed in This Unit:

Sorrow Songs (African American musical tradition)

Briton Hammon, "Narrative of the Uncommon Sufferings and Surprizing Deliverance of Briton Hammon" (captivity narrative)

Lydia Maria Child, "Mrs. Child's Reply" (letter)

Abraham Lincoln, "A House Divided," "Gettysburg Address," "Second Inaugural Address" (speeches)

Lorenzo Asisara, "Punishment" (oral narrative, recorded by editor)

William and Ellen Craft, *Running a Thousand Miles for Freedom* (slave narrative)

Helen Hunt Jackson, *A Century of Dishonor* (history), *Ramona* (novel)

Overview Questions

■ How do racial divisions in nineteenth-century American culture exclude African Americans and Native Americans from American ideals of liberty and inclusion?

■ How do texts by African American and Native American writers expand and transform concepts of American identity and citizenship?

■ What are the distinguishing characteristics of

the genre of the slave narrative? How was the genre developed, adapted, and modified by the writers included in this unit? How does the slave narrative compare to the captivity narratives written in the seventeenth century (Mary Rowlandson's narrative, for example)?

■ How do ideals of domesticity, femininity, and sentimentality shape nineteenth-century American literature and reform movements?

■ How do the regional differences between the American North, South, and West (geographic, economic, and demographic) influence antebellum literature?

■ What is the relationship between oral expressions such as Sorrow Songs and printed literature? How did African American oral traditions influence American music and literature?

■ What is the relationship between slave narratives and captivity narratives? How did the genre of the slave narrative influence the development of autobiographical writing and the novel in America?

■ How does abolitionist rhetoric expand and transform the ideals set out in foundational national documents such as the Declaration of Independence?

■ How do black writers revise the myth of the "self-made man" to include African Americans?

■ How do both abolitionist and pro-slavery writers use biblical imagery and Christian ideals to support their positions?

Learning Objectives

After students have viewed the video, read the headnotes and literary selections in *The Norton Anthology of American Literature*, read this unit, and explored related archival materials on the *American Passages* Web site, they should be able to

1. understand how the antebellum debate about slavery transformed and expanded foundational ideas about American identity and citizenship;
2. see and discuss the different strategies slaves adopted to resist white authority and to develop their own distinct culture;
3. explain the importance of sentimentality and domesticity within the nineteenth-century literature of social reform;
4. understand the role of literature in both shaping and reflecting political reform movements.

Instructor Overview

When the founding fathers affirmed their commitment to the inalienable rights of "life, liberty, and the pursuit of happiness" in 1776, they opted not to struggle with the troubling question of how slavery fit into this ideal. But the contradiction inherent in the legally sanctioned enslavement of four million people in a country ostensibly founded on principles of freedom eventually became too discomfiting to ignore. By the mid-nineteenth century, the conflict over slavery had reached a crisis point, creating irresolvable tensions among the North, the South, and the West. In Abraham Lincoln's words, the nation had become as a "house divided against itself," embroiled in a domestic struggle that threatened to destroy the union. Many Americans concluded that the only solution lay in transforming American culture, and writers, both black and white, responded by creating a revolutionary literature committed to the overthrow of slavery. Autobiographies by former slaves, polemical speeches and editorials, and sentimental novels confronted their audiences with powerful narratives of the cruelty and destructiveness of slavery. These anti-slavery texts had overt designs upon their readers, using emotional rhetoric and didacticism to call the American populace to action in the interests of social reform. Anti-slavery literature also had the important effect of exposing the arbitrary nature of racial distinctions, thus challenging prejudices that had long been used to justify discrimination and inequality. Unit 7, "Slavery and Freedom," explores representations of race and identity in a wide variety of American texts, including the Sorrow Songs, which were developed communally within slave culture, and works composed by Briton Hammon, Lydia Maria Child, Frederick Douglass, Abraham Lincoln, Harriet Beecher Stowe, Harriet Jacobs, William Craft, Lorenzo Asisara, and Helen Hunt Jackson. The institution of slavery is often understood as a phenomenon limited to the antebellum period in the South. In fact, slavery existed in many other historical periods and geographical locations in America, including the northern colonies (mostly, though not exclusively, in the seventeenth and eighteenth centuries), and in California, where Anglos and Hispanic Californios enslaved Native Americans. Unit 7 includes materials about Native American enslavement in order to add another dimension to students' understanding of slavery. This unit provides contextual background and classroom materials designed to explore the way these writers both challenged traditional myths about America and helped to create new national ideals.

The video for Unit 7 focuses on three influential abolitionist texts. Frederick Douglass's *Narrative of the Life of Frederick Douglass*, Harriet Jacobs's autobiographical *Incidents in the Life of a Slave Girl*, and Harriet Beecher Stowe's *Uncle Tom's Cabin* all participate in the effort to convince readers slavery was unjust, but adopt very different rhetorical strategies to appeal to their audiences. Drawing on a variety of literary conventions, these texts expose the way race, gender, and social position inflect their writers' distinct approaches to the abolitionist cause.

Frederick Douglass's autobiography chronicles his early experiences of oppression, his rebellion, and his eventual heroic achievement of a fully liberated sense of self and identity. Emphasizing the importance of literacy and active resistance, he recasts the American myth of the "self-made man" to include African Americans. In *Incidents in the Life of a Slave Girl*, Harriet Jacobs modifies the conventions of the masculine slave narrative to chart her own life. Focusing on the specific plight of women held in slavery—and particularly on the sexual exploitation they often endured—her autobiography both appropriates and challenges the discourse of sentimentality. Situated squarely within the sentimental tradition, Harriet Beecher Stowe's *Uncle Tom's Cabin* unabashedly appeals to readers' emotions with affective scenes of pathos and tragedy. The novel sold hundreds of thousands of copies, bringing the abolitionist cause to the forefront of American consciousness.

In its coverage of these influential writers and texts, the video introduces students to the complexities of antebellum debates about slavery and race and foregrounds the relationship between literature and social reform. How do these texts critique an entrenched, racist ideology of white superiority? How do they recast American ideals of liberty and self-determination to include African Americans? What rhetorical strategies do they employ to effect social reform? How do they work within the constraints of literary and social conventions and yet still assert unique perspectives? Unit 7 helps answer these questions by offering suggestions on how to connect these writers to their nineteenth-century cultural contexts, to other units in the series, and to other key writers of the era. The curriculum materials help fill in the video's introduction to slavery and identity by exploring writers who articulated other, diverse experiences, such as Lorenzo Asisara (a Native American enslaved on a Franciscan Mission in California), Briton Hammon (an African American who endured both slavery in America and captivity among the Spanish), William Craft (a fugitive slave who escaped by disguising his wife as a white man), and many others.

The video, the archive, and the curriculum materials situate these writers within several of the historical contexts and stylistic conventions that shaped their texts: (1) the ideals of femininity and domesticity that shaped nineteenth-century women's lives; (2) the dynamic creole culture that African American slaves created out of the adversity of their situation; (3) slave strategies of rebellion and resistance; (4) the issue of "miscegenation"; and (5) the mythology of the plantation.

The archive and the curriculum materials suggest how these authors and texts relate to those covered in other *American Passages* units: How do antebellum African American autobiographies adapt and modify earlier literary traditions, such as the captivity narrative and the spiritual autobiography? How does the slave narrative provide a foundation for a rich tradition of African American writing, from W. E. B. Du Bois to Toni Morrison? How does abolitionist discourse revise enlightenment rhetoric from the revolutionary period? How does enslavement of Native Americans in nineteenth-century California resonate with sixteenth-, seventeenth-, and eighteenth-century discrimination against Indians? How and why has race remained a constant and controversial issue in American culture and literature?

Student Overview

Unit 7, "Slavery and Freedom: Race and Identity in Antebellum America," explores the problem that slavery posed to a country ostensibly founded on principles of freedom and equality. By the mid-nineteenth century, the nation had become, to quote Abraham Lincoln, like a "house divided against itself," embroiled in a domestic struggle over slavery that created irresolvable tensions among the North, the South, and the West. Many Americans concluded that the only solution lay in transforming American culture, and writers, both black and white, responded by creating a revolutionary literature committed to the overthrow of slavery. Autobiographies by former slaves, polemical speeches and editorials, and sentimental novels confronted their audiences with powerful narratives of the destructiveness and cruelty of slavery.

The video for Unit 7 focuses on three influential abolitionist texts. Frederick Douglass's *Narrative of the Life of Frederick Douglass*, Harriet Jacobs's autobiographical *Incidents in the Life of a Slave Girl*, and Harriet Beecher Stowe's *Uncle Tom's Cabin* all participate in the effort to convince readers that slavery is unjust, but adopt very different formal conventions and rhetorical strategies to appeal to their audiences. Douglass's autobiography chronicles his early experiences of oppression, his rebellion, and his eventual heroic achievement of a fully liberated sense of self and identity. In *Incidents in the Life of a Slave Girl*, Jacobs modifies the conventions of the masculine slave narrative to chart her own life. Focusing on the specific plight of women held in slavery, her autobiography both appropriates and challenges the discourse of sentimentality. Situated squarely within the sentimental tradition, Stowe's *Uncle Tom's Cabin* unabashedly appeals to its readers' emotions with affective scenes of pathos and tragedy.

All of the writers discussed in Unit 7 share an interest in the role of race in American culture as well as a commitment to promoting social reform. Focusing on such diverse issues as the enslavement of Native Americans in California and the implications of cross-dressing and racial passing, these texts help illuminate the ways abolitionist writers both challenged traditional myths about America and helped to create new ideals. By exploring problems of slavery and identity in antebellum texts, Unit 7 provides insight into the question of why race has remained a constant and controversial issue in American culture and literature.

Video Overview

➤ **Authors covered:** Frederick Douglass, Harriet Jacobs, Harriet Beecher Stowe

➤ **Who's interviewed:** Nina Baym, general editor, *The Norton Anthology of American Literature*, and professor of English (University of Illinois, Urbana-Champaign); Frederick Douglass IV, great-great grandson of Frederick Douglass; John Carlos Rowe, professor of English and comparative literature (University of California, Irvine); Richard Yarborough, associate professor of English and African American studies (University of California, Los Angeles); Rafia Zafar, director of African and African American studies (Washington University)

➤ **Points covered:**

- The video explains the development of a slave-based plantation economy in the American South and northern abolitionist opposition to slavery.
- Students will be introduced to the tradition of slave autobiographies and abolitionist fiction, literature which powerfully engaged readers' emotions in order to create social change. Abolitionist literature was instrumental in propelling the nation into the Civil War.
- Frederick Douglass's *Narrative of the Life of Frederick Douglass* (1845) generated a great deal of attention and sympathy for the abolitionist cause. Thematizing the importance of literacy and active resistance, his narrative recasts the American myth of the "self-made man" to include African Americans.
- With *Incidents in the Life of a Slave Girl*, Harriet Jacobs wrote the first female-authored slave narrative published in the United States. Focusing on the specific plight of enslaved African American women, her autobiography uses the discourse of sentimentality to appeal to a white female readership.
- Harriet Beecher Stowe's *Uncle Tom's Cabin* took the nation by storm in 1852. Unabashedly sentimental, the novel reflects Stowe's goal of making northerners actually feel the pain of enslaved African Americans. Although Stowe's use of racist stereotypes makes her story problematic for modern readers, *Uncle Tom's Cabin* was enormously important in generating support for the abolitionist cause in the nineteenth century.

- The writings of antebellum African Americans transformed the genre of autobiography in the United States and created the foundation for a rich tradition of African American literature.

PREVIEW

- **Preview the video:** In the early and mid-nineteenth century, America found itself increasingly divided over the volatile issue of slavery. The economy and cultural traditions of the southern states continued to depend on the institution of slave labor, while northern opposition to the destructive nature of the "peculiar institution" reached new heights. Determined to free the country from the blight of slavery, white and African American abolitionists wrote to generate public support for liberty and equality. Frederick Douglass and Harriet Jacobs published powerful autobiographical accounts of their experiences as slaves and their decisions to escape, helping to develop the genre of the slave narrative in the process. Harriet Beecher Stowe mobilized the literary tradition of sentimentality to further the abolitionist cause in her blockbuster novel, *Uncle Tom's Cabin*. A highly emotional —and sometimes racist—story of the tragedy of slavery and the power of Christian sacrifice, *Uncle Tom's Cabin* brought the issue of African American slavery to the forefront of American consciousness. All three of these writers profoundly influenced subsequent developments in American literature and offer important insight into how literature can both reflect and produce social change.
- **What to think about while watching:** What abuses of slavery do these writers bring to their readers' attention? What rhetorical strategies do they adopt to encourage their audience to support the abolitionist cause? How do race and gender influence their writing? How do the writers and texts explored in the video both transform traditional American myths and ideals as well as shape new

ones? How have their efforts influenced American culture and literature?

- **Tying the video to the unit content:** Unit 7 expands on the issues outlined in the video to explore further the evolution of American attitudes toward race and slavery in the nineteenth century. The curriculum materials offer background on abolitionist, African American, and Native American writers and texts not featured in the video. The unit offers contextual background to expand on the video's introduction to the political issues, historical events, and literary styles that shaped the literature of social protest and racial consciousness in the nineteenth century.

DISCUSSION QUESTIONS FOR THE VIDEO

	What is an American? How does American literature create conceptions of the American experience and identity?	*How are American myths created, challenged, and re-imagined through this literature?*	*What is American literature? What are the distinctive voices and styles in American literature? How do social and political issues influence the American canon?*
Comprehension Questions	How does Frederick Douglass learn to read? Why does literacy become so important to him?	What kinds of racial stereotypes does Stowe employ in developing the characters of *Uncle Tom's Cabin*?	What is "sentimentality"? To what kind of audience was sentimental rhetoric designed to appeal?
Context Questions	Why do you think Harriet Jacobs published under a pseudonym? What kinds of anxieties did she feel about making her story public? How did her narrative engage with nineteenth-century ideas about womanhood?	How do slave narratives recast the American ideal of the "self-made man" to fit African Americans? How does Frederick Douglass, for example, build on and transform the legacy of Benjamin Franklin?	What is the relationship between Jacobs's account of her slavery and escape and Douglass's account of his? How does she borrow and modify some of the conventions Douglass pioneered in his autobiography? Do you think they wrote for the same kind of audience? How are her concerns different from his?
Exploratory Questions	How do the writers featured in the video use formulas and conventions to tell their stories, yet still manage to speak in their own authentic voices?	How do you think abolitionist rhetoric might have influenced the civil rights movement in the 1960s? How do you think it influenced subsequent treatments of race in American literature?	How do slave narratives draw on the seventeenth-century tradition of captivity narratives? How did slave narratives influence the work of later African American authors (Charles W. Chesnutt, James Baldwin, Ralph Ellison, or Toni Morrison, for example)?

	Texts	Contexts
18th Century	Samuel Sewall, *The Selling of Joseph*, first American anti-slavery tract (1700) John Woolman, *On the Keeping of Negroes* (1754)	Peak years of British slave trade (1720–80) Growing religious criticism of slavery as sin, rise of free black and slave Christianity (1740s–90s)
1760s	Briton Hammon, "Narrative of the Uncommon Sufferings and Surprizing Deliverance of Briton Hammon" (1760)	Enlightenment political egalitarianism conflicts with emerging Enlightenment scientific racialism (post-1750)
1770s	Phillis Wheatley, *Poems* (1773)	American Revolution (1775–83) Declaration of Independence (1776) Spanish missions founded in Alta California (1769–1823)
1780s	Thomas Jefferson, *Notes on the State of Virginia* (1785) Olaudah Equiano, *Narrative of the Life* (1789)	Constitution accepts slavery, sets end of slave imports at 1808 (1789) Four of first five U.S. presidents are slave owners (1789–1825)
1790s		Haitian slave revolution leads to Louisiana Purchase (1791–1803) Invention of cotton gin (1793)
1800s		British slave trade abolished (1807) Slave imports to United States outlawed (1808)
1810s		Mexican independence wars (1810–20)
1820s	David Walker, *Appeal to the Colored Citizens of the World* (1829)	Missouri Compromise (1820) Denmark Vesey Conspiracy executions (South Carolina) (1822) Chumash Indian rebellion against California missions (1824) Andrew Jackson elected president (1828); "Jacksonian Democracy": white male equality, pro-slavery, anti-Indian wars and removals Mexico abolishes slavery (1829)
1830s		Influence of "Second Great Awakening" expands abolitionism (1830s) Nat Turner rebellion (Virginia) (1831) American Anti-Slavery Society formed (1833) British Empire abolishes slavery (1833–38) Mexican California missions secularized, rise of private peonage of native tenants (1833–36)

	Texts	Contexts
1840s	Frederick Douglass, *Narrative of the Life of Frederick Douglass* (1845)	New England textile industrialization tied to slave-grown southern cotton (1840s) Slave rebellion aboard *Amistad* (1841) U.S.–Mexican War; annexations include California (1846–48) California Indian population falls from c. 150,000 to c. 50,000 from disease, violence, and starvation (1848–70) California Gold Rush (1849–51)
1850s	Harriet Beecher Stowe, *Uncle Tom's Cabin* (1852) Frederick Douglass, "The Meaning of July Fourth for the Negro" (1852) Herman Melville, "Benito Cereno" (1855) Abraham Lincoln, "A House Divided Cannot Stand" (1858) Lydia Maria Child, "Mrs. Child's Answer" (1859)	Compromise of 1850: California a free state, other former Mexican territories open to slavery, Fugitive Slave Act Kansas-Nebraska Act, civil conflict in Kansas (1854–65) Dred Scott decision declares Negroes not national citizens (1857)
1860s	William Craft, *Running a Thousand Miles for Freedom: The Escape of William and Ellen Craft from Slavery* (1860) Harriet Jacobs, *Incidents in the Life of a Slave Girl* (1863) Abraham Lincoln, "Gettysburg Address" (1863) Abraham Lincoln, "Second Inaugural Address" (1865)	White population of California over 200,000, intensifying Indian peonage (1860) Civil War (1861–65) 13th Amendment to Constitution abolishes slavery (1865) "Congressional" or "Radical" Reconstruction; 14th and 15th Amendments expand civil rights, affirm black citizenship (1867–77) Formation of Ku Klux Klan (1867) First transcontinental railroad (1869)
1870s	Lorenzo Asisara, "Punishment" (oral testimony recorded 1877; published 1890)	Civil rights, anti-Klan laws (1870–72) End of Reconstruction (1877)
1880s	Helen Hunt Jackson, *Ramona* (1884)	White "Redemption" in South, spreading disenfranchisement, lynching, debt peonage of blacks (1880s) Dawes Act leads to wide Indian land losses (1887)

AUTHOR/TEXT REVIEW

SLAVE SONGS

UNITED STATES.

New York:
A. SIMPSON & CO.,
1867.

SORROW SONGS WEB ARCHIVE

[6753] William Francis Allen, Charles Pickard Ware, Lucy McKim Garrison, *Slave Songs of the United States* (1867). Title page of early collection of Sorrow Songs. Former abolitionists transcribed lyrics of the songs of ex-slaves to appeal for funding from northern whites to establish schools for freedpeople.

[7131] Anonymous, *Many Thousands Gone* (c. 1861–65), courtesy of Henry Edward Krehbiel, *Afro-American Folksongs: A Study in Racial and National Music* (4th ed., 1914), Fisk University. Sorrow Songs often referred to current events through religious language. The lyrics of "Many Thousand Gone" refer partly to the hundreds of thousands of slaves who escaped to the North, with some joining the Union

Sorrow Songs

Drawing on both African musical styles and western European sources, black slaves in the antebellum South created a rich musical tradition of **Sorrow Songs**, or spirituals. These songs fulfilled a variety of functions within slave culture: workers timed their labor to the tempo of their music, preserved and articulated communal values, and transcended the restrictions of slavery through meaningful self-expression. As Lawrence W. Levine points out, despite their name, Sorrow Songs do not express only sorrow or despair, but can be "pervaded by a sense of change, transcendence, ultimate justice, and personal worth." Characterized by their use of traditional West African rhythmic and harmonic patterns, the spirituals often employ a "call and response" pattern in which a leader sings or chants a few lines and the group repeats or offers variations on the lines in response. The songs thus draw upon many of the practices central to the African cultures the slaves had been forced to leave behind, emphasizing the primacy of the spoken word, celebrating verbal improvisation, and encouraging group participation. The spirituals included here were not rigidly codified or authored by a single person; instead, they are the result of communal authorship and a strong tradition of extemporaneous improvisations. Singers often mix lyrics from different songs together, graft lyrics onto new tunes, or create completely new stanzas in the course of performing a song. In some sense, then, the printed lyrics in this unit offer a false picture of the songs as "finished" or "frozen" when in fact they constantly change and evolve in performance.

The songs developed out of the slave tradition are mostly religious in nature, but their spiritual subjects often had concrete applications to the slaves' daily lives and their concerns in this world. The songs draw primarily on images of heaven and stories from the Old Testament, especially the story of Moses leading the enslaved Israelites out of Egypt to freedom. In "Go Down, Moses," for example, slave singers likened themselves to the Israelites and their oppressors to the Egyptian Pharoah. In this way, African Americans incorporated sacred prophecy into everyday life, articulating hope for both spiritual salvation and literal emancipation. Sorrow Songs could also function as a method of secret communication between slaves. Often incomprehensible to whites, the lyrics could protest slave conditions, mock masters and mistresses, call other slaves to secret meetings, and even aid runaways and revolts. The spiritual "Steal Away to Jesus," for instance, was used as a code song to assist people escaping along the Underground Railroad.

TEACHING TIPS

■ Use the sound files in the archive to play a recorded version of at least one of the songs included in this unit so students can have an aural experience of the music. If you have a strong voice or musical accompaniment, you might consider leading your class in a spiritual. Encourage students to improvise if they are moved to do so. The experience of participating in a performance should help students understand the important role of audience and communal authorship in the development of this musical tradition.

■ Students may be resistant to the idea that songs and oral traditions should be studied in a literature class. Engage them in the question of what constitutes literature and what appropriate objects of study in a literature class might be. How are these songs different from more "formal" poetry? (You might distribute a copy of a more traditional poem such as a sonnet so that the contrast will be clearer.) Does it matter that the songs are constantly changing? How does our understanding of the songs change when we study them in a literature classroom rather than in a music classroom?

QUESTIONS

Comprehension: Paraphrase one of the Sorrow Songs in your own words, eliminating repetition and ambiguity whenever possible. Compare your version to the original and think about what has been lost in your "translation." Why do you think repetition is central to many of the spirituals? What is the effect of repetition in the songs?

Context: In his *Narrative*, Frederick Douglass points out that slave songs reveal "at once the highest joy and the deepest sadness." What does he mean by this? Explain how a duality of expression and purpose inflects these songs.

Context: How do the spirituals challenge and protest the institution of slavery? What is subversive in these songs? Why do you think white masters and mistresses for the most part missed the rebellious implications of this music?

Exploration: How does the Sorrow Songs' use of Old Testament images—especially the image of the enslaved Israelites—compare to the New England Puritans' use of such images? Do the slave songs engage in a form of typologizing? Why or why not?

Exploration: Listen to a recording of one or more of the spirituals. How do you think these songs influenced the subsequent development of American musical culture? What is the relationship between these early African American songs and subsequent African American musical forms, such as jazz, blues, and hip-hop?

Briton Hammon (fl. 1760)

Briton Hammon's "Narrative of the Uncommon Sufferings and Surprizing Deliverance of Briton Hammon, A Negro Man," published in Boston in 1760, is generally recognized as the earliest published autobiography by an African American. Composed in the tradition of the popular Indian captivity genre, Hammon's narrative tells an exciting tale of travel, shipwreck, bondage among Native American and Spanish captors, and daring escapes. Unfortunately, no details of

army during the Civil War. Simultaneously, the song refers to the many who have died and gone to the afterlife.

[7132] Anonymous, *Steal Away to Jesus* (n.d.), courtesy of John Work, *Folk Songs of the American Negro* (1907), Fisk University. The lyrics to this song remind listeners that those who obey the Lord are assured of ultimate salvation, while unredeemed sinners, whether slaves or "masters," have cause to tremble. It might also refer to "stealing away" to forbidden worship meetings, or it could be an Underground Railroad code.

[7133] Anonymous, *Go Down, Moses* (n.d.), courtesy of Natalie Curtis-Burlin, *Negro Folk-Songs*, Hampton Series 6716, G. Schirmer (1918). Slaves used Old Testament texts to reject slave owners' claims that Christianity justified slavery. Singers adopted the voice of God commanding Moses to carry a message to Pharaoh (the slaveholder) to let "my people" (the slaves) go. The song is an example of the African tradition of *Nommo*, or the belief in the power of language.

[7134] Anonymous, *Didn't My Lord Deliver Daniel* (n.d.), courtesy of James Weldon Johnson, *The Book of American Negro Spirituals* (1925), Viking Press. These lyrics speak of African Americans' hope for delivery from both the enslavement of sin and human enslavement. Compiler James Weldon Johnson, a New Negro Renaissance intellectual and author, took pride in slave ancestors and their creations.

[6830] Peter Canot, *A View of the Entrance of the Harbour of the Havana, Taken from within the Wrecks* (1764), courtesy of the Library of Congress [LC-USZ62-105952].

Hammon's life are known beyond those recorded in the "Narrative." Although he does not discuss his race within the body of the text—only the title identifies him as a "Negro Man"—he does refer to himself as a "servant" and makes frequent mention of his "master." Thus, while it is unclear whether Hammon was held as a slave or worked as a servant, it is evident that he occupied a subordinate position within colonial society. In some ways, the "Narrative" reinforces traditional ideals of servitude as a benevolent institution: Hammon seems delighted when he is finally reunited with his "good old master" and happily returns to Boston with him. But Hammon's text also implicitly critiques slavery by figuring human captivity as a "barbarous" and "inhuman" practice that should be resisted.

Hammon's "Narrative" recounts the experiences of a person of marginal social status, someone whose life usually would have gone unrecorded. Sometimes viewed as a hybrid of an Indian captivity and **slave narrative**, Hammon's story is complicated by the fact that when he is finally redeemed from captivity, it is into a condition of servitude rather than of freedom. Ironically, he may actually have experienced greater freedom among the Native Americans and Spanish than he would have after returning to Boston with his master.

TEACHING TIPS

■ Critics have debated whether Hammon composed his "Narrative" entirely on his own or employed a white editor to write all or part of it. Some suggest that the religiously orthodox opening and closing of the text point to the hand of a white minister, while others argue that such formulaic qualities are merely traditional characteristics of the captivity genre and thus offer little insight into its authorship. Ask students what they think of this debate. How would it change our understanding of the text if we could establish whether Hammon wrote it on his own or dictated it to a white writer?

■ Hammon opens his "Narrative" with a modest disavowal of his own ability to properly "read" his experiences: "As my capacities and conditions of life are very low, it cannot be expected that I should make those remarks on the sufferings I have met with, or the kind providence of a good God for my preservation, as one in a higher station, but shall leave that to the reader as he goes along, and so I shall only relate matters of fact as they occur to my mind." Ask students to consider why Hammon begins his text this way. Why might this opening have been appealing to his audience? How sincere is Hammon's protestation of his own "low capacities"? Does he in fact restrict himself only to "matters of fact" in recounting his experiences?

QUESTIONS

Comprehension: How does Hammon view the Native Americans who capture him in Florida? How does he view the Spanish in Cuba? How does he feel about the Catholicism of his Spanish captors? How does captivity compare with servitude in his experience?

Comprehension: What role does Christianity play in Hammon's understanding of his experiences? When and how does he invoke God in the course of relating his story?

Context: What is the relationship between Hammon's "Narrative" and the narratives of slave escapes that became popular in the nineteenth century (such as those written by Douglass, Craft, or Jacobs, for example)? What historical factors might have caused the tone and subjects of slave narratives to change so dramatically?

Exploration: At several points in his text, Hammon describes his happiness at seeing the English flag, or "English Colours," and identifies himself as an "Englishman." What does being English seem to mean to Hammon? What insights does the "Narrative" provide us into the role of nationalism and national identity within the maritime world along the Atlantic coasts?

Exploration: How does Hammon's "Narrative" compare with the Indian captivity narratives written by Anglo-Americans in the seventeenth and eighteenth centuries (Mary Rowlandson's *Narrative*, for example)? How are Hammon's concerns different? In what ways are his experiences and reactions similar to those of white captives?

Lydia Maria Child (1802–1880)

Lydia Maria Child (born Lydia Francis) was raised outside of Boston in a community she described as made up of "hard-working people who had small opportunity for culture." Her parents ran a bakery while raising six children, leaving them little time for intellectual pursuits. Still, Child, encouraged by her Harvard-educated older brother, developed an early interest in books and learning. By 1820, she had completed her training as a teacher and begun working at a school in Maine. She soon moved back to Massachusetts, where she started a school for girls and kept house for her brother, who had become a Unitarian minister. When she joined the Unitarian Church herself, Child adopted a new name to signal her independence and new identity. Rebaptized as Lydia Maria, she preferred to be called Maria for the rest of her life.

Child embarked on her literary career after reading a piece in *The North American Review* in 1821 calling for American authors to take American colonial history and Native American life as subjects for their fiction. Taking up the challenge, Child wrote *Hobomok*, a tale of interracial marriage between a Puritan woman and an Indian man set in colonial Salem. Although *Hobomok* was published when Child was only twenty-two, the novel was an early illustration of the concern with social justice and commitment to ending racism that would dominate her subsequent work. While many critics pronounced the novel, with its moving portrait of racial intermarriage, "in very bad taste," it immediately catapulted Child to literary celebrity. Capitalizing on her success, she soon produced another historical novel and the first periodical for children published in the United States, *The Juvenile Miscellany*.

In 1828, Lydia Maria married David Child, a man who shared her commitment to radical social causes. Unfortunately, he was also

woman. As with the figure of the tragic mulatta, slavery is here feminized to invoke sympathy for the abolitionist cause. The *Illustrated London News* was founded in 1842 by Henry Ingram, a liberal who favored social reform.

[6830] Peter Canot, *A View of the Entrance of the Harbour of the Havana, Taken from within the Wrecks* (1764), courtesy of the Library of Congress [LC-USZ62-105952]. Havana, Cuba, was one of the ports visited by Briton Hammon as a sailor. Trade in sugar, slaves, and other commodities linked the Caribbean, Africa, North America, and Europe.

[6950] Briton Hammon, *Narrative of the Uncommon Sufferings and Surprizing Deliverance of Briton Hammon, A Negro Man . . .* [Frontispiece] (1760), courtesy of the Library of Congress, Rare Books and Special Collections Division. Front page of the earliest-known autobiographical narrative by an African American. Hammon's model helped establish a close relationship between the autobiographical genres of captivity narratives and slave narratives.

[6766] L. Schamer, *Lydia Maria Child* (1870), courtesy of the Library of Congress [LC-USZ62-5535].

CHILD WEB ARCHIVE

[1666] Anonymous, *The Harpers Ferry Insurrection—The US Marines Storming the Engine House—Insurgents Firing Through Holes in the Doors* (1859), courtesy of the Library of Congress [LC-USZ62-126970]. This illustration from *Frank Leslie's Illustrated Newspaper* depicts the end of John Brown's raid on the arsenal at Harpers Ferry.

[2773] Anonymous, *Attack on the Insurgents at the Bridge by the Railroad Men* (1859), courtesy of the Library of Congress [LC-USZ62-90728]. This illustration from *The Life, trial, and execution of Captain John Brown, known as "Old Brown of Ossawatomie"* depicts Brown's raid on the arsenal at Harpers Ferry, Virginia. Brown sought to overthrow slavery by armed slave revolt.

extremely impractical and prone to debt, leaving the couple dependent upon Child's literary efforts to support their household. While living with David, she successfully published housekeeping manuals, a history of the condition of women, and stories and articles for a variety of American journals. In 1833, Child changed the course of her career with the publication of *An Appeal in Favor of That Class of Americans Called Africans*, a sweeping indictment of slavery and racism addressed primarily to a female audience. The pamphlet was greeted with hostility and damaged Child's mainstream popularity, but it also pushed her to the forefront of the radical abolitionist movement in the North. Affiliated with **abolitionism**, the movement for women's rights, and advocacy of Native American rights, Child had marked herself as a radical and a reformer.

In 1841, Child informally separated from her husband and moved to New York City to edit *The National Anti-Slavery Standard*, an abolitionist newspaper, and to work as a correspondent for the Boston *Courier*. Composing weekly "Letters from New York," Child reported on a broad spectrum of urban life, including problems of poverty, crime, and racism. She eventually collected this groundbreaking journalistic work into the two-volume *Letters from New York* (1843, 1845).

In 1843, exhausted by divisions within the abolition movement, Child resigned as editor of the *Anti-Slavery Standard*. In 1850, ending nine years of independence, she reunited with her husband and moved to a village outside Boston where she cared for her ailing father and continued writing on behalf of the causes that had motivated her early career. While some of her work was very public, such as the stirring letters she wrote in defense of John Brown and his raid on Harpers Ferry, Child also worked behind the scenes, helping Harriet Jacobs edit her narrative, *Incidents in the Life of a Slave Girl*. All of Child's anti-slavery writing and editing work was crucial to the development of the abolitionist movement. Some 300,000 copies of the pamphlet collection of her abolitionist letters circulated in 1860, effectively galvanizing anti-slavery sentiment in the North.

Upon her death in Wayland, Massachusetts, Child left a legacy of pioneering literary achievement. In her nonfiction work, she gave voice to the perspectives and concerns of traditionally marginalized groups. In her fiction, she mixed sentimentality with calls for social reform, creating a powerful formula that would be imitated by writers like Harriet Beecher Stowe and Helen Hunt Jackson.

TEACHING TIPS

■ Child composed her "Reply" within the context of her defense of John Brown and his raid on Harpers Ferry. Since some students might be unfamiliar with this incident, you should provide them with the historical background. Brown was a white man who was committed to eradicating slavery by whatever means necessary—including violent resistance and aggression. On the night of October 16, 1859, Brown and a group of about twenty followers (including five black men) crossed from Maryland to Virginia in an attempt to take over the federal arsenal in Harpers Ferry. Their goal was to set up a base from which to organize, arm, and support slave insurrections throughout the South.

While Brown and his group managed to take the arsenal by surprise and seize several hostages, the Virginia militia quickly responded to defend the arsenal. By the morning of October 18, Brown's men had killed four people and wounded nine, while the Virginia militia had killed ten of Brown's group (including two of his sons) and captured seven (including Brown). Convicted of treason against the state and conspiracy to incite insurrection, Brown was hanged on December 2 at Charlestown, Virginia.

Although he failed to achieve his immediate purpose at Harpers Ferry, Brown succeeded in becoming a martyr for the abolitionist cause. Throughout the North, people responded with sympathy and admiration for Brown's action; Ralph Waldo Emerson even called him a "new saint." Southern commentators, on the other hand, declared him a "hoary-headed murderer." John Brown's raid, occurring as it did on the eve of the Civil War, became a touchstone for the conflicts that divided North and South.

After giving your students this background, you might ask them to stage a debate or mock trial of Brown (perhaps drawing some of their arguments from "Mrs. Child's Reply"). Ask some of the class to work as prosecutors, some as defenders, and some as the jury.

■ In *In Search of Our Mothers' Gardens*, African American writer Alice Walker argues that sometimes women's traditions are best represented by nonverbal artistry, such as quilts. For slave women who never wrote their narratives, quilts became a way to record their histories. These quilts were made from discarded scraps of material and clothing. Some quilts communicated messages in a straightforward way: for example, members of the Underground Railroad hung quilts with the color black on clotheslines to indicate a safe house. Other quilts were subtler. Like authors of slave narratives, African American quilters also used biblical references in their quilts. Ask students to examine the quilts featured in the archive. What stories are being told in them? How do the quilts draw on and transform biblical stories? How do these quilts compare to the written narratives of slavery included in this unit?

QUESTIONS

Comprehension: Consider the opening of Child's "Reply." What role do biblical quotations play in her argument against slavery? Why do you think this might have been an effective rhetorical strategy?

Context: Compare Child's abolitionist arguments in her "Reply" with the rhetorical strategies developed by some of the escaped slaves who composed narrative exposés of slavery (Douglass, Jacobs, or Craft, for example). Where does Child use strategies similar to those of the ex-slaves? How is her appeal to her readers different? How does her position as a non-slave and a white woman affect her appeal?

Exploration: "Mrs. Child's Reply" is part of a series of letters that

[3090] Harriet Powers, Pictorial quilt (c. 1895–98), courtesy of the Museum of Fine Arts, Boston. Many slave and freed women used quilts to record their histories. Some quilts communicated messages; for example, quilts using the color black are believed to have indicated a safe house on the Underground Railroad.

[3147] James Brown Marston, *The Old State House* [Boston] (1801), courtesy of the Massachusetts Historical Society. As the nineteenth century began, immigration, industrialization, and the advent of capitalism began to change American cities from barter economies to commercial ones (Gary Nash, *The Urban Crucible*). Boston became the stronghold for Unitarians, who were often associated with the new wealthy merchant class.

[3458] American Anti-Slavery Society of Philadelphia, *Declaration of the Anti-Slavery Convention, 1833* (1833), courtesy of the Library of Congress. At this convention, sixty abolitionist leaders declared their dedication to fighting slavery through nonviolent means. Abolitionists hoped to win sympathizers by using quotations from the Bible to emphasize the conflict between slavery and Christianity. The woodprint by R. S. Gilbert illustrates Psalm 91.13, "Thou shalt tread upon the lion and adder; the young lion and the dragon shalt thou trample under feet."

[6766] L. Schamer, *Lydia Maria Child* (1870), courtesy of the Library of Congress [LC-USZ62-5535]. Child was a prominent abolitionist and women's rights advocate. Her first novel, *Hobomok*, about "the noblest savage," was written in the sentimental literary tradition. Child edited Harriet Jacobs's *Incidents in the Life of a Slave Girl*.

[6949] Harriet Powers, Biblical quilt (c. 1886), courtesy of the Smithsonian Institution, National Museum of American History. Powers, a black woman from Athens, Georgia, made quilts depicting biblical scenes both before and after her emancipation. Both slaves and freed people used Christianity to interpret their hard circumstances and find hope.

Child exchanged with Governor Wise and Mrs. Mason of Virginia over the specific issue of John Brown's raid and the general question of the morality of slavery. Child's subsequent publication of the letters in pamphlet form was a great success. Why do you think Child decided to publish her argument in the form of letters between disputants rather than as a series of essays? Why do you think the collection of letters was popular with northern readers? How does Child's use of letters compare to later publications of letters, such as Amelia Clappe's "Shirley Letters"?

Abraham Lincoln (1809–1865)

Born to impoverished parents in backwoods Kentucky, Abraham Lincoln rose to become the sixteenth president of the United States. His remarkable story of success, his achievements in guiding the country through the Civil War, and his tragic death have afforded him iconic stature within the annals of American history and made him a hero to many. Lincoln had little formal schooling and was mostly self-educated, eventually training himself in the law. After setting up a successful legal practice in Illinois, he became interested in politics and was elected first to the state legislature and later to the U.S. Congress in 1846.

Lincoln's election to the presidency was the result of the complicated American political situation of the 1840s and 1850s, centered on the divisive issue of slavery. While Lincoln is often celebrated for his decision to free the slaves, he in fact came to his commitment to total emancipation only by degrees. Never an actual supporter of slavery, he was still somewhat ambivalent about its place within the country through much of his career: he fought to ban it from the western territories and new states but was reluctant to advocate abolition within the South itself. Lincoln's primary commitment was always to the preservation of the Union, and he was willing to reject abolitionist measures if they seemed to threaten that goal. Despite his attempts to seem flexible and moderate on the issue of slavery, however, his election to the presidency in 1860 polarized the nation. Seven southern states immediately seceded to form the Confederacy. Within a month of Lincoln's inauguration, the Civil War had begun. By 1863, Lincoln was ready to adopt a more radical position and signed the Emancipation Proclamation, finally committing the Union to the total abolition of slavery.

Lincoln's extraordinary skills as a writer and orator were crucial to his political successes and his ability to lead the country effectively through the war. In the early speeches of his career, he worked to connect with the "common man" in the audience, employing a clear, almost legalistic, logic and a satirical sense of humor. As he grew in confidence as a statesman, his speeches retained their clarity but became more powerful and resonant, often drawing upon biblical references and even the cadences of biblical prose. By turning to

[3228] Timothy O'Sullivan, *Incidents of the War. A Harvest of Death, Gettysburg, July, 1863,* courtesy of the Library of Congress [LC-B8184-7964-A DLC].

Christian rhetoric, Lincoln tried to unite the bitterly divided American populace and to garner popular support for a war that turned out to be longer and bloodier than anyone had anticipated. Since Lincoln's tragic assassination one month into his second term in office in 1865, his speeches have come to be revered as enduring expressions of formative American cultural ideals.

TEACHING TIPS

■ In order to appreciate the significance of Lincoln's "Gettysburg Address," students should have some background on the battle of Gettysburg. Fought in early July 1863, Gettysburg was the bloodiest battle of the Civil War, with a total of 51,000 casualties—more men died at Gettysburg than in any other battle on North American soil before or since. Gettysburg marked an important turning point in the Civil War; the Confederate Army never recovered from the heavy losses it suffered there. After giving students this background, ask them to think about how Lincoln grapples with the scope and nature of Gettysburg as a national tragedy in his address. You might have them consider how this speech compares with other presidential speeches following catastrophic events (such as Franklin Roosevelt's Pearl Harbor speech, or George W. Bush's responses to September 11, 2001).

■ Ask students to pay attention to the changes in Lincoln's rhetorical treatment of slavery between the "House Divided" speech (1858) and the "Second Inaugural" (1865). While the earlier speech is a rigorously logical, legalistic argument for keeping slavery out of the West, the "Second Inaugural" claims that slavery is an evil in the eyes of God and that the emancipation of the slaves was wrought by divine will. Ask students which speech they find more powerful or persuasive. Ask them to consider the different historical circumstances in which these two speeches were composed.

QUESTIONS

Comprehension: What kind of audience does Lincoln assume will be listening to his speeches? How do you think nineteenth-century audiences might have been different from audiences today?

Context: Why do you think Lincoln chose the verse from the New Testament "A house divided upon itself cannot stand" (Luke 11.17) as the basis for his speech? What significance would this image of a threatened home have for nineteenth-century Americans? How might it have resonated with American ideals of domesticity?

Context: Interestingly, Lincoln's now celebrated speech was not well received when he first delivered it on the battlefield at Gettysburg in November 1863. Apparently, it seemed too concise and simple to the audience, which preferred Edward Everett's lengthy two-hour sermon. Why do you think the speech was unsuccessful when Lincoln delivered it? Today the "Gettysburg Address" is often viewed as a model of eloquence. Why has it gained in popularity over time?

LINCOLN WEB ARCHIVE

[1708] Brady National Photographic Art Gallery, *Abraham Lincoln* (1864), courtesy of the Library of Congress, Prints and Photographs Division [LC-B816-1321]. This portrait photograph from January 1864, between the Gettysburg address and the second inaugural address, resembles most memorial images.

[1803] Abraham Lincoln, *Emancipation Proclamation* (1863), courtesy of the National Archives and Records Administration. This 1863 proclamation emancipated slaves held in areas in rebellion against the United States, but not those in Union-controlled areas.

[3228] Timothy O'Sullivan, *Incidents of the War. A Harvest of Death, Gettysburg, July, 1863*, courtesy of the Library of Congress [LC-B8184-7964-A DLC]. Dead Federal soldiers on the battlefield at Gettysburg, Pennsylvania. Graphic war photographs like this one inspired postwar literary realism.

[7163] Esther Bubley, *Inside the Lincoln Memorial* (1943), courtesy of the Library of Congress, Prints and Photographs Division [LC-USW3-040346-D]. After his assassination, Abraham Lincoln's image became iconic in the North and among African Americans, through ceremonies, popular songs and prints, statuary, and poetry such as Walt Whitman's "When Lilacs Last in the Dooryard Bloom'd."

Exploration: Today Lincoln is something of an American cultural icon—he is the subject of imposing monuments and his face even circulates on our money. What does Lincoln represent to contemporary Americans? Why is he viewed as such an important president? How does Lincoln's position within American cultural mythology compare to what you know about his biography and political choices? What kinds of myths are important to Lincoln's image?

Exploration: The Lincoln Memorial in Washington, D.C., is based upon one of the most famous architectural monuments in the world, the temple to Athena found on the Acropolis in Athens, Greece. Why would the architects of the Lincoln Memorial want to use the Parthenon as a model? What does this allusion signify about Lincoln and about America? What does it mean that inside we find Lincoln seated rather than the gold and ivory statue of Athena?

Exploration: Read "When Lilacs Last in the Dooryard Bloom'd," Walt Whitman's elegy for Lincoln. What does Whitman admire about Lincoln? Do Lincoln's speeches live up to this eulogy?

Harriet Beecher Stowe (1811–1896)

Harriet Beecher Stowe was born into a large New England religious family. Her father, Lyman Beecher, was a prominent Evangelical Calvinist minister, and her brother, Henry Ward Beecher, followed in their father's footsteps to become one of the best-known preachers in the country. Stowe's oldest sister, Catharine Beecher, ran a succession of girls' schools and gained national recognition for her theories of education, health, and domestic economy. When the family moved west to Cincinnati in 1832, the Beecher sisters founded a new religious school for young women. Because Ohio was a border state between North and South, Stowe met fugitive slaves and encountered fierce debates over slavery while she lived there, ultimately leading her to adopt the abolitionist cause.

In 1836, Harriet Beecher married Calvin Stowe, a widower and professor of biblical studies at a seminary in Cincinnati. She soon found herself overwhelmed by domestic concerns, raising seven children and managing a large household on a professor's small salary. To supplement the family's finances, Stowe published stories and sketches in magazines. In 1850, the Stowes moved back to New England when Calvin Stowe accepted a teaching job first in Maine and later in Massachusetts. Stowe's commitment to the abolitionist cause remained fierce, and, spurred by her outrage at the passage of the Fugitive Slave Act, she resolved to "write something that will make the whole nation feel what an accursed thing slavery is." *Uncle Tom's Cabin* appeared in 1851 in serial form in the weekly anti-slavery journal *The National Era*. It was published as a book the following year.

Although Stowe had set out to "make the whole nation feel" the horrors and injustice of slavery, she could not have anticipated the enormous and unprecedented impact her novel would have on the national psyche. *Uncle Tom's Cabin* sold over 350,000 copies in its first

[1328] A. S. Seer, *Uncle Tom's Cabin* (1879), courtesy of the Library of Congress [LC-USZ62-13513].

year of publication, and only the Bible sold more copies in the United States during the nineteenth century. The novel appealed to a wide audience by drawing upon mainstream religious and cultural beliefs: Stowe mobilized evangelical doctrine and the ideal of domesticity to argue that slavery was both un-Christian and destructive to family life. Above all, Stowe intended to convince the nation that slavery was a sin that harmed both slaves and the souls of slave owners. By treating human beings as property that could be bought and sold, slavery separated husbands and wives and parents and children, thus standing in opposition to both familial and Christian love. Using sentimental rhetoric and melodramatic situations, and writing in clear, accessible language, Stowe appealed to her culture's investment in the sacredness of home, family, and Christian salvation. The strategy was effective; when she visited the White House in 1862, President Lincoln is said to have remarked, "So you're the little woman who wrote the book that started this big war."

Whether or not *Uncle Tom's Cabin* was responsible for the Civil War, there is no denying that it brought slavery to the forefront of American consciousness. The novel has caused controversy since its publication, when southerners attempted to ban it and some northerners viewed it as inflammatory. In the twentieth century, the literary establishment has criticized *Uncle Tom's Cabin* for its unsophisticated sentimentality and emotionalism, its reliance on offensive racial stereotypes, its reinforcement of traditional gender roles, and its colonialist project of forming a separate state for free blacks in Africa. However out of touch the book is with contemporary values, Stowe's unparalleled ability to move readers—and effect social change—remains a testament to the power and importance of her first novel.

Uncle Tom's Cabin not only made Stowe famous, but also brought her enough wealth to free her from economic and domestic cares. She continued writing through the nineteenth century, producing many more novels and serving as an influential spokesperson on national affairs, literature, spirituality, and domestic practices.

TEACHING TIPS

■ For most of the twentieth century, *Uncle Tom's Cabin* was not considered an American literary classic. Because it is openly sentimental (that is, designed to appeal to the emotions) and lacks the formal complexity that is usually associated with literary merit, critics largely dismissed the novel as "propaganda" or "melodrama." But reassessment from feminist scholars like Jane Tompkins and Gillian Brown has changed the novel's place in the American canon. For this reason, *Uncle Tom's Cabin* is a great starting point for a discussion of literary values and the way the texts we read in college classes are selected and evaluated. Ask students to consider what constitutes a "classic" or a "masterpiece." What values underwrite these aesthetic judgments? How and why have our standards for the canon changed over time?

■ Many of Stowe's characters have taken on a life of their own in

[1328] A. S. Seer, *Uncle Tom's Cabin* (1879), courtesy of the Library of Congress [LC-USZ62-13513]. Situated squarely within the sentimental tradition, Harriet Beecher Stowe's *Uncle Tom's Cabin* unabashedly appeals to readers' emotions with scenes of pathos and tragedy. Though the novel seems melodramatic and even derogatory to modern readers, Stowe provided the sentimental appeal necessary to bring the abolitionist cause to the forefront of American consciousness in the mid-nineteenth century.

[2644] Edward Hicks, *Peaceable Kingdom* (c. 1834), courtesy of National Gallery of Art, 1980.62.15. Gift of Edgar William and Bernice Chrysler Garbisch. Hicks's Quaker biblical allegory alludes to William Penn's treaty with the Lenni Lenape Indians and influenced African American artist Robert Duncanson's painting of Little Eva and Uncle Tom, characters from *Uncle Tom's Cabin*. In these works, sentimentality obscured the tension between peace ideals and anti-slavery ideals.

[3457] Anonymous, *Harriet Beecher Stowe* (c. 1880), courtesy of the National Archives and Records Administration [208-N-25004]. Although *Uncle Tom's Cabin* dates from 1851, Stowe remained active for decades, composing both early New England regionalist literature and works dealing with how middle-class women's household work was changing in an industrializing society.

[5460] Courier Litho. Co., *Uncle Tom's Cabin—On the Levee* (1899), courtesy of the Library of Congress, Prints and Photographs Division, Theatrical Poster Collection. This poster for a theater production shows happy slaves dancing. Post–Civil War "Uncle Tom Shows" often were performed by whites in blackface. By presenting blacks as subservient in every way, such shows gave the term "Uncle Tom" its derogatory meaning.

[7221] Nina Baym, Interview: "The Publication Success of *Uncle Tom's Cabin*" (2001), courtesy of Annenberg/CPB. Baym, professor of English at the University of Illinois, is the general editor of *The Norton Anthology*

the American popular imagination. Ask students what springs to mind when they think of "Uncle Tom," "Simon Legree," "Little Eva," and "Poor Eliza." As a class, you can interrogate the racial and gender stereotypes conjured up by these familiar characters. Ask students to consider why these characters have found such a prominent place in American culture and how ideas about them have changed over time. You might show them the "Uncle Tom's Cabin ballet" scene in *The King and I* or some of the mass-produced trinkets and commodities emblazoned with "Uncle Tom's Cabin" images.

QUESTIONS

Comprehension: How does Stowe use racial and gender stereotypes in her characterization of Uncle Tom, Topsy, Little Eva, Eliza, George, and Simon Legree? Do any of these characters challenge common stereotypes? How?

Comprehension: Sometimes Stowe as the narrator of *Uncle Tom's Cabin* will address her audience directly as "you" and "dear reader." What is the effect of these direct appeals from the writer to the reader? Why do you think Stowe uses this technique?

Context: Compare Stowe's portraits of black women's sufferings in slavery (Eliza, Cassy, Emmeline) with Jacobs's account of her real-life experiences. How does Jacobs's narrative draw on some of the same sentimental conventions Stowe uses in her novel? How is Jacobs's story different?

Context: Stowe closes her novel by urging that all her readers involve themselves in the struggle against slavery: "There is one thing that every individual can do—they can see to it that *they feel right*. An atmosphere of sympathetic influence encircles every human being; and the man or woman who *feels* strongly . . . is a constant benefactor to the human race." What do you think Stowe means by "feeling right"? What kind of audience is she appealing to? Do you think her strategy is effective?

Exploration: *Uncle Tom's Cabin* achieves powerful results by allying a discourse of domesticity and sentimentality with a call for social reform. How does Stowe's formula influence later American literature? Can you think of other novels that adopt similar strategies?

Exploration: One of the most famous covers of an edition of *Uncle Tom's Cabin* reworks Edward Hicks's famous painting *A Peaceable Kingdom*. Examine both the original painting and the *Uncle Tom's Cabin* version. How does the painting for the cover of *Uncle Tom's Cabin* revise the original image? What aspects of *A Peaceable Kingdom* would have made it an appealing image to the creator of the *Uncle Tom's Cabin* cover?

Harriet Jacobs (c. 1813–1897)

Born into slavery in North Carolina, Harriet Ann Jacobs was raised both by her free black grandmother and by a white mistress who taught her to read. Upon her mistress's death, Jacobs was willed to

Mary Matilda Norcom and sent to live in her household. Mary's father, the prominent physician Dr. James Norcom, soon began making unwelcome sexual advances toward Jacobs, preying on her vulnerability as a slave. Rather than submit to her master, Jacobs chose to become involved with Samuel Sawyer, a white, slave-holding neighbor, with whom she had two children. In 1835, Dr. Norcom, angry at what he viewed as Jacobs's offenses against him, separated her from her children and sent her to work on a plantation in nearby Auburn. Jacobs soon escaped from the plantation but was unable to flee North Carolina. Instead, she was forced to hide in a cramped attic crawlspace in her grandmother's house for nearly seven years, keeping secret watch over her children. In 1842, Jacobs finally managed to escape to the North. Once there, she arranged for her children's escape as well.

In New York, Jacobs worked as a nursemaid in the home of the popular writer and editor Nathaniel Parker Willis. In 1849, she moved to Rochester to work in the Anti-Slavery Reading Room, where she got to know many prominent abolitionists (including Frederick Douglass) and familiarized herself with anti-slavery literature and feminism in the process. Jacobs eventually determined that she should publicize her own story of exploitation and escape in order to raise public awareness about the condition of women held in slavery. She initially approached Harriet Beecher Stowe, the celebrated author of *Uncle Tom's Cabin*, about writing her narrative, but ultimately Jacobs decided to compose her history herself. Adopting the pseudonym "Linda Brent" and disguising the names of the other characters in her story, she used her autobiographical narrative to reflect on the sexual harassment and psychological abuse that were so often the lot of the female slave. Because the book departed from the conventions of male-centered slave narratives and also challenged genteel notions of propriety by focusing on issues of sexuality, Jacobs found it difficult to find a publisher. Finally, a Boston firm agreed to publish the manuscript provided Jacobs could get Lydia Maria Child to write an introduction and act as editor. Child agreed to the project and, with the help of her introduction and minor editorial contributions, *Incidents in the Life of a Slave Girl* was published in 1861.

Jacobs's history is unique among slave narratives for its focus on the experiences of women, its treatment of sexual exploitation, its emphasis on family life and maternal values, and its self-conscious appeal to an audience of white, female readers. *Incidents* draws on the conventions of both seduction novels and domestic fiction—two popular eighteenth- and nineteenth-century sentimental literary forms. The book recounts Jacobs's efforts to maintain her virtue against her master's attempted seduction and celebrates family relationships and domestic ideals of femininity. Jacobs's deployment of sentimental discourse also works to problematize nineteenth-century notions of proper womanhood and exposes the extent to which such ideals were dependent upon economic and racial distinctions. As her story makes clear, the pressures and abuses enslaved black women faced could make it impossible for them to uphold bourgeois standards of virginity and motherhood. Relegated to the status of property, Jacobs faced

of *American Literature* and author of *American Women of Letters and the Nineteenth-Century Sciences: Styles of Affiliation*.

[6832] Sandy Point Plantation, Edenton, North Carolina (1933–40), courtesy of the Library of Congress, Historic American Buildings Survey [HABS, NC21-EDET.V,3-1].

an enormous struggle in her attempts to control her own sexuality, home life, and family relationships.

Jacobs was finally freed from slavery in 1853, when her New York employer's wife, Cornelia Willis, bought her from the Norcom family for three hundred dollars and then emancipated her. In her narrative, Jacobs notes both her gratitude to her employer and her discomfort with being purchased. Making use of her freedom, she remained active in the anti-slavery cause and did relief work among black refugees from the South during and after the Civil War. Jacobs died while living with her daughter in Washington, D.C.

TEACHING TIPS

■ *Incidents in the Life of a Slave Girl* did not receive a great deal of critical attention until the late twentieth century, mostly because modern scholars had doubts about its authenticity and the conditions of its authorship. For many years, the book was understood to be a novel written in the guise of a slave narrative or an embellished slave autobiography ghost-written by a white author. Critics often assumed that Lydia Maria Child had composed the narrative, even though she insists in her introduction that her editorial work was limited to "condensation and orderly arrangement." Through extensive research, Jean Fagan Yellin finally offered conclusive proof of Jacobs's authorship of *Incidents* and the authenticity of the events described in the text. Yellin's 1981 edition of Jacobs's work alerted scholars to its importance and transformed its position within the canon. Once you have provided students with this background information, ask them to consider why Jacobs's authorship was questioned for so long. Why would scholars have found it so difficult to believe that a black woman raised in slavery could have written this book? What qualities make the narrative seem fictional?

■ *Incidents in the Life of a Slave Girl* closes with Jacobs's reflections on the state of her domestic life after freedom: "Reader, my story ends with freedom; not, in the usual way, with marriage. . . . The dream of my life is not yet realized. I do not sit with my children in a home of my own. I still long for a hearthstone of my own, however humble. I wish it for my children's sake far more than for my own." Here, the narrative is clearly appealing to a readership of free, white women who would sympathize with this yearning for domestic stability, for "home and hearth." At the same time, this passage challenges the conventions of sentimental discourse by juxtaposing "freedom" and "marriage" in complex ways, both exposing domestic ideals as available only to the privileged and hinting that freedom is perhaps a preferable alternative to the patriarchal institution of marriage. You might use this passage to initiate a discussion of Jacobs's appropriations and revisions of the nineteenth-century ideology of domesticity and sentimentality.

Comprehension: What strategies does Jacobs adopt in her efforts to resist her master? How does she assert her rights over her own body and her children? How does she deal with the racism she encounters once she has escaped to the North?

Comprehension: How do Jacobs's relationships with family members and her children influence the decisions she makes?

Comprehension: Draw a diagram of the attic Jacobs hid in for seven years. How does your picture compare to Jacobs's description of the "loophole" in which she lived? What kinds of physical and emotional challenges would living in such enclosed quarters pose for an individual?

Context: How does *Incidents in the Life of a Slave Girl* compare to Frederick Douglass's narrative? What goals, values, and strategies do Jacobs and Douglass have in common? In what respects do they differ?

Context: How does Jacobs's text both appropriate and challenge conventions of domesticity and white ideals of femininity? What techniques does she adopt from sentimental novels such as *Uncle Tom's Cabin*? How does her text implicitly critique domestic ideals?

Exploration: Until the early 1980s, many scholars believed that Jacobs's narrative was a fictional rather than an autobiographical account (a theory that has subsequently been dismissed after conclusive evidence documenting Jacobs's life came to light). Why do you think critics read this text as a novel? How does it participate in novelistic conventions? How does our understanding of the text change once we know that it was really "written by herself," as the subtitle claims?

Frederick Douglass (1818–1895)

Frederick Douglass was one of the most influential African American thinkers of his day, in spite of his inauspicious beginnings. He was born into slavery on a plantation in Maryland, where he was called Frederick Augustus Washington Bailey. Douglass always suspected that his father was his mother's white owner, Captain Aaron Anthony. He spent his early childhood in privation on the plantation, then was sent to work as a house slave for the Auld family in Baltimore. There he came in contact with printed literature and quickly realized the relationship between literacy and personal freedom. With help from Mrs. Auld, Douglass learned how to read and write. In 1833, the Aulds sent him back to the plantation, where he soon acquired a reputation for resistance and insubordination. In an effort to make him more submissive, Douglass's owner sent him to Edward Covey, a "slave breaker" paid to discipline and train disobedient slaves. Instead of cowing Douglass, the experience with Covey only strengthened Douglass's resolve to acquire his freedom. Douglass was eventually sent back to Baltimore, where he learned the trade of ship caulking and achieved partial freedom by hiring himself out for work and paying a weekly fee to his owner. In 1838, Douglass escaped to the

[1055] W. M. Merrick, Map of the Washington and Alexandria Railroad (1865), courtesy of the National Archives and Records Administration. This period map of Washington, D.C., shows how the city looked at the end of the Civil War.

[6442] Keith White, *Harriet Jacobs* (1994), courtesy of the North Carolina Office of Archives and History. A rendering of the only known photograph of Harriet Jacobs. Jacobs's account of her sexual exploitation as a slave opened her up to attacks on her morality. This led her to publish under the pseudonym Linda Brent and may have led her to avoid being photographed.

[6832] Sandy Point Plantation, Edenton, North Carolina (1933–40), courtesy of the Library of Congress, Historic American Buildings Survey [HABS, NC21-EDET.V,3-1]. This nineteenth-century southern home is similar in style to the house of Harriet Jacobs's owner, Dr. James Norcom. Well-to-do slaveowning whites who were not part of the wealthiest planter class often built such houses.

[7223] Nina Baym, Interview: "Gender and Sexual Difference" (2001), courtesy of Annenberg/CPB. Baym, professor of English at the University of Illinois, is the general editor of *The Norton Anthology of American Literature* and author of *American Women of Letters and the Nineteenth-Century Sciences: Styles of Affiliation*.

DOUGLASS WEB ARCHIVE

North with financial and emotional support from Anna Murray, a free black woman he had met in Baltimore. The two married in New York and then moved to New Bedford, Massachusetts, where they adopted a new surname, "Douglass."

In 1839, Douglass bought his first copy of *The Liberator*, William Lloyd Garrison's radical abolitionist newspaper. He soon became involved in Garrison's abolitionist circle and emerged as an eloquent speaker for the cause of African American rights, addressing audiences all over the country with moving accounts of his experiences as a slave. In 1845, he published his *Narrative of the Life of Frederick Douglass* both to disseminate his story to a wide audience and to quell public doubts about the authenticity of his past as a slave. The book, an outstanding example of the **slave narrative** genre, was a bestseller both in the United States and abroad, catapulting Douglass to celebrity and making him an international leader in the anti-slavery fight.

Eventually, Douglass broke with Garrison because they disagreed about how best to achieve abolitionist goals. While Garrison disavowed the United States Constitution as a pro-slavery document and advocated only passive resistance, Douglass was becoming increasingly committed to working within electoral politics and to adopting active—and if necessary violent—strategies to ensure emancipation. Douglass moved to Rochester, New York, in 1847 to establish an abolitionist newspaper for the African American population, *The North Star* (later renamed *Frederick Douglass' Paper*). During the Civil War, he worked tirelessly for black rights and was instrumental in convincing Lincoln to enlist African Americans in the Union army. After the war, he held a variety of posts in the government and remained a prominent champion of not only African American rights but also all human rights, including women's suffrage. He revised his autobiography twice, publishing *My Bondage and My Freedom* in 1855 and *The Life and Times of Frederick Douglass* in 1881.

Douglass's original *Narrative* was a groundbreaking work of autobiography, setting the standard for many subsequent slave narratives in its eloquent articulation of a man's achievement of selfhood. Douglass powerfully appropriates the language and conventions of white middle-class American culture to condemn slavery and racism. Drawing on foundational republican ideals of human freedom and equality, he denounces the cruel contradictions and hypocrisies in American culture even as he affirms his hope for its future.

TEACHING TIPS

■ Douglass represents his violent physical encounter with Covey, the "slave breaker," as a crucial turning point in his journey toward independence and freedom—in his words, it is the moment "a slave was made a man." Ask students to analyze the importance of this passage. What are the implications of Douglass's physical assertion of strength and its resulting empowerment? You might ask them to consider how the episode compares to Tom's passive capitulation to

Simon Legree (another "slave breaker") in *Uncle Tom's Cabin*, to Lorenzo Asisara's account of his participation in an Indian revolt, and to Harriet Jacobs's account of the very different strategies she used to assert her independence.

■ As the *Narrative* makes clear, Douglass's achievement of literacy is a crucial step in his struggle for freedom. One of the texts he uses to learn to read is *The Columbian Orator*, a compendium of texts chosen for their evocation of American values. First published in 1797, *The Columbian Orator* was a mainstay of the American schoolroom through the nineteenth century. In it, Douglass would have encountered arguments for natural rights, human freedom, and even for emancipation (in this case, of Catholics). Ask students to consider the role of literacy in the *Narrative*. They might analyze Sophia Auld's dramatic shift in attitude toward teaching Douglass to read, Douglass's covert strategies for teaching himself, and his attempts to instruct other slaves in reading and writing. They might also look at the specific books Douglass mentions reading, such as *The Columbian Orator* and Cooper's *Last of the Mohicans*, to explore how these texts might have influenced Douglass's values and beliefs.

QUESTIONS

Comprehension: Why does Douglass refuse to narrate the details of his escape in his 1845 autobiography? What effect does this gap in information, and the reason Douglass provides for it, have on his narrative?

Context: Before Douglass's violent encounter with Covey, he is given a root by his friend, the slave Sandy Jenkins. Sandy claims that the root is a kind of talisman that will protect anyone who carries it. Although Douglass represents himself as skeptical of Sandy's superstitious belief in the root's power, he does at some level validate the effectiveness of the talisman in the course of his narrative. What is the significance of this invocation of African American folk magic at this point in the narrative?

Context: How does Douglass describe Sorrow Songs in his *Narrative*? How do they affect him personally? What does he believe they signify in slave culture? What does he mean when he says that though they seem "unmeaning jargon," they are "full of meaning" for the slaves?

Exploration: Douglass's autobiographical account of the process through which a "slave was made a man" has often been compared to Benjamin Franklin's narrative of his own self-making. What do these autobiographies have in common? How do these two writers' approach to literacy and writing compare? How does Douglass recast Franklin's ideals to fit the condition of an escaped slave?

Lorenzo Asisara (b. 1819)

While the institution of slavery is generally associated with African Americans and with the antebellum South, it was in fact present in

---

[3482] William Lloyd Garrison and Isaac Knapp, eds., *The Liberator* (May 21, 1831), courtesy of the Library of Congress, Rare Books and Special Collections Division. *The Liberator*, launched in 1831, called slavery a crime that should be ended immediately without compensation. Such radical abolitionism became identified with the paper's editor, William Lloyd Garrison.

[3538] Caleb Bingham, *The Columbian Orator . . . Calculated to Improve Youth and Others in the Ornamental and Useful Art of Eloquence* (1811), courtesy of the University of North Carolina at Chapel Hill Libraries. Frederick Douglass highlights Bingham's primer *The Columbian Orator* in describing his liberation through literacy. "Columbian" implies a distinctly American mode of rhetoric.

[3570] Anonymous, *Mrs. Auld Teaching Him to Read* (1892), courtesy of the University of North Carolina at Chapel Hill Libraries. This illustration from *The Life and Times of Frederick Douglass, Written by Himself*, depicts the northern wife of Douglass's owner introducing Douglass to reading.

[5150] J. Sartain, from a painting by M. C. Torrey, *William Lloyd Garrison* (n.d.), courtesy of the National Parks Service, Frederick Douglass National Historical Site. Garrison helped found the American Anti-Slavery Society, supported immediate emancipation and the Underground Railroad, and sponsored Frederick Douglass.

[6831] Frederick Douglass and Martin Delany, *The North Star* [banner] (1848), courtesy of the Library of Congress, Serial and Government Publications Division. *The North Star* was an abolitionist newspaper published by prominent black intellectuals Douglass and Delany in Rochester, New York. Its name symbolized a guiding light to freedom; escaping southern slaves used the North Star to find their way to the free states or to Canada.

[7220] Frederick Douglass IV, "Reading from the Narrative: Detesting My Enslavers Through the Power of Learning to Read" (2001), courtesy of Annenberg/CPB. Frederick Douglass IV is the great-great grandson of Frederick Douglass.

other regions and at other times in American history. Lorenzo Asisara's story is an example of the enslavement of Native Americans in the American Southwest. Asisara was born into the Costanoan Indian community in the Mission at Santa Cruz. The Costanos, or "coastal people," were Native Americans who traditionally resided along the Pacific coast from the San Francisco area south to Monterey. In his narrative "Punishment" (located in the archive), Asisara provides a rare eyewitness account of life within the Spanish Franciscan mission system from a Native American perspective. Transcribed from oral testimony Asisara gave in 1877 in an interview with field historian Thomas Savage, "Punishment" is an unusual narrative of mission discipline, the decline of the Franciscan order in California, and the decimation of the local Native American population.

[6856] *San Gabriel Mission* (1832), courtesy of the California Historical Society.

The Franciscan empire in California was the product of the Spanish colonial project in the New World. Catholic priests of the Franciscan order were sent to California to Christianize the local Native Americans, claiming their land and turning them into laborers for the missions in the process. Because Franciscan Christianization involved compelling the Indians to give up their lands, culture, native religious practices, and independence, it often could not be accomplished by voluntary conversion and instead necessitated the use of military force. Once the Native Americans were baptized at the missions they became unpaid laborers who were not free to leave—that is, they essentially became slaves. Between 1770 and 1834 over 90,000 California Indians (a third of the pre-contact population) were enslaved within the **Franciscan missions**. Rampant disease and high rates of mortality ravaged the mission Indian populations.

Understandably, many Indians resisted Spanish domination, and that resistance took a variety of forms. Some natives opted to sabotage the missions by laboring slowly and performing tasks poorly, while others resisted more actively by running away, assassinating priests, or even leading large-scale revolts. By the 1830s, the mission system had become untenable. The Mexican government passed a series of "secularization laws" designed to break up the Franciscan estates and distribute the property to surviving Native Americans. In practice, few Indians were granted land or resources from the missions because corrupt civil administrators plundered most of the wealth.

Lorenzo Asisara's narrative details the abuses of the priests at the Santa Cruz Mission, exposing their fraudulent financial dealings, sexual exploitation of mission Indians, and reliance on harsh physical punishments such as whipping and beating. "Punishment" also provides a unique first-hand account of a riot among young Indian men in defiance of Padre Ramon Olbes. Asisara's participation in this riot was not unprecedented within his family; in fact, his father, Venancio Llenco, also had a history of resisting Spanish domination, conspiring in the assassination of a priest in the Santa Cruz Mission in 1812.

Asisara was raised in the mission from birth, eventually serving as a sacristan, or assistant to the priests during church services. Once the mission was broken up, he married and found work as a shepherd and cattle herder. Widowed in 1845, he moved to Yerba Buena (San Francisco), where he was conscripted into the Mexican militia until Mexico surrendered California to the United States in 1846. Returning to Santa Cruz, Asisara joined his friend Jose Ricardo and moved onto a homestead that had been granted to the Indians upon the divestiture of the Santa Cruz Mission. In 1866, Asisara and Ricardo were driven off by whites anxious to claim possession of the land. Despite over fourteen years of service to the mission, Asisara received no lands or remuneration for his labor. He spent the rest of his life working as a ranch hand in Santa Cruz.

TEACHING TIPS

■ Students often believe that slavery in America was a phenomenon limited to the antebellum period in the South. In fact, African American slavery existed in the northern colonies in the seventeenth and eighteenth centuries, and many "indentured servants" throughout early America experienced slavery-like conditions. Asisara's narrative of the exploitation of Mission Indians in California should add another dimension to students' conceptions of the institution of slavery in America. Ask them to think about the similarities between the management of Franciscan missions and southern plantations. They might also consider why the stories of enslaved Mission Indians have historically received so little attention in American culture.

■ Have students read aloud Asisara's description of the riot that broke out when the Indians decided to defy Padre Olbes. How does the tension in the scene build? What touches off the riot? How does it escalate? Ask students to pay attention to Asisara's defense of the Indians' motivations in resisting Padre Olbes.

QUESTIONS

Comprehension: What kinds of abuses do Asisara and the other Mission Indians experience at the hands of the Franciscans? How do the Indians respond to these abuses? What sorts of strategies do they adopt to resist the Mission authorities and to improve their conditions?

Context: Compare Asisara's description of the riot in defiance of Padre Olbes with Frederick Douglass's account of his fight with Edward Covey. What similarities do you find between these two incidents of slave resistance? How are the incidents different? Does Asisara seem to acquire the same kind of self-confidence and sense of independence that Douglass does from his act of rebellion? Why or why not?

Exploration: Asisara's narrative implicitly critiques the piety and morality of the Catholic priests who enslaved California Indians under the pretext of converting them to Christianity. Can you think of other slave narratives that engage in similar critiques, calling the

ASISARA WEB ARCHIVE

[1279] Edward Vischer, *Indian Rancheria of José Antonio Venado, At San Luis Rey Mission, Near the Zanja. Caicha-Tribe, Quechumas* (1868), courtesy of the University of California, Berkeley, Bancroft Library. Made about a decade before the first recording of Asisara's testimony, this drawing illustrates the material circumstances of Native Americans on former California mission lands after secularization.

[1891] Rand McNally & Co., *New Enlarged Scale Railroad and County Map of California Showing Every Railroad Station and Office in the State* (1883), courtesy of the Library of Congress, Geography and Map Division [LC Railroad Maps, 189]. Building railroads required extensive mapping of natural geographical features. Later maps such as this one showed industrial transportation and government communications outposts.

[5228] Anonymous, *Montgomery Street, San Francisco, 1852* (n.d.), courtesy of the Library of Congress, Prints and Photographs Division [LC-USZ62-55762]. Rapid, mainly white immigration during the Gold Rush brought California to statehood in 1850, as a "free state" that forbade slavery. Yet demand for land and forced labor caused genocidal-scale population decline among California Indians.

[6856] Anonymous, *San Gabriel Mission* (1832), courtesy of the California Historical Society. Missions often maintained large herds of cattle as a reliable source of meat.

[7048] Lorenzo Asisara, "Punishment" [Narrative By Lorenzo Asisara, Translated And Edited By Edward D. Castillo] (1877). Asisara's narrative details abuses by the priests at the Santa Cruz Mission, exposing their fraudulent financial dealings, sexual exploitation of mission Indians, and reliance on harsh physical punishments.

religious pretensions of slaveholders into question? Why would this have been a popular and effective rhetorical strategy?

William and Ellen Craft (c. 1826–1897)

William and Ellen Craft's daring escape from slavery in 1848 made them famous throughout antebellum America, heroes in the eyes of abolitionists and criminals in the eyes of slavery supporters. The unusual circumstances of their flight to freedom were a major factor in their celebrity. Ellen, so light-skinned as to be nearly white, disguised herself in men's clothing and posed as a young white planter to effect her escape. Her husband, William, played the role of her slave. Together, they traveled from Georgia to Philadelphia by train and by boat, often staying in first-class accommodations and always directly under the noses of southern authorities. Americans everywhere were moved by their amazing story of boundary crossing, for the Crafts passed through not only the literal boundary that separated North from South, but also the social boundaries of race, class, and gender that divided the population of the United States.

At an early age, both William and Ellen witnessed the break-up of their families as a result of their enslavement. William's master sold his mother, father, brother, sister, and eventually William in order to pay off debts. Working for a variety of masters, William learned the craft of carpentry and labored in a cabinetmaker's shop. Ellen, born in 1826, was the daughter of Major James Smith, a wealthy white plantation owner, and Maria, his mulatto house slave. Major Smith's white wife, annoyed by the presence in her household of her husband's natural daughter by a slave, gave Ellen to her own daughter, Eliza, as a wedding present. At the age of eleven, Ellen was thus separated from her mother and sent to live in Macon, Georgia, as the slave of her white half-sister.

William and Ellen met in Macon in the early 1840s and married in 1846 in a slave ceremony that was not recognized as legal or binding in the southern states. Fearing the possibility of sale or separation, they decided not to have children while they were still enslaved. Instead, they formulated their bold escape plan, purchasing clothing for Ellen's disguise and asking their masters for a couple of days of vacation on the pretense of visiting friends and relatives. Since Ellen could not write (teaching slaves to read or write was a criminal offense in the South), she bound up her arm in a sling to discourage officials from asking her to sign documents. She also took the precaution of wearing a poultice on her face to disguise her femininity and to limit conversations with strangers. In this guise of a sickly white man accompanied by his slave, the couple took just four days to reach the North, where they were hidden by a Quaker family on a farm outside Philadelphia. A few weeks later, they moved on to the safer community of Boston.

In Boston, the Crafts were warmly received by abolitionists and by the free black community. They were invited to tour with noted abolitionist William Wells Brown, giving speeches and lectures on the

[6852] Anonymous, *Ellen Craft the Fugitive Slave* (1860), frontispiece of *Running a Thousand Miles for Freedom*, by William Craft.

nature and effects of slavery. Later, Brown would fictionalize their escape in *Clotel; or, The President's Daughter* (1853), one of the first novels by an African American. Eventually, William Craft established himself as a cabinetmaker, and Ellen found work as a seamstress. Their comfortable life in Boston came to an abrupt end, however, with the passage of the **Fugitive Slave Act of 1850**. Mandating that escaped slaves residing in the North had to be returned to their masters in the South, the law jeopardized William and Ellen's hard-earned freedom. When Ellen's former owner dispatched two slave-catchers to Boston to capture and return the fugitives, the city rallied to the Crafts' cause and drove the slave-catchers out of town. The incident left the Crafts feeling vulnerable, however, and they decided to immigrate to England where they could find safety and asylum.

In England, William and Ellen continued their work lecturing and speaking, profoundly influencing British attitudes toward slavery in the process. They also attended the Ockham school, an agricultural academy in Surrey, where they built on the education they had begun to acquire in Philadelphia and in Boston. While in England, the Crafts had four children and established themselves in business. Between 1862 and 1865, William planned and executed a series of journeys to Dahomey, Africa, to teach Christianity and agriculture to the Africans there, as well as to promote trade. The scheme was not entirely successful, leaving the Crafts deeply in debt.

Unemployed and in financial straits, the Crafts decided to return to the United States in 1869, after the conclusion of the Civil War. They purchased Hickory Hill, a plantation in Savannah, Georgia, hoping to run it as a cooperative managed by freed blacks. Reconstruction-era Georgia proved to be a hostile environment for their idealistic project; a band of angry whites burned down the plantation in 1870, entirely destroying the house, barn, and first-planted crop. Still committed to their vision, the Crafts refused to give up. In 1871, they took a lease on Woodville, a plantation outside of Savannah in a county where the majority of the population was black, and opened a school and cooperative farm there. Though they never again had to contend with the kind of overt violence they had encountered at Hickory Hill, they were dogged by perpetual hostility, discrimination, and debt for the remainder of their lives.

Today William and Ellen Craft are remembered primarily for their extraordinary escape from slavery and for William's gripping narrative of that escape. Published in 1860 in England, *Running a Thousand Miles for Freedom* was an immediate hit, going through two editions in two years. The narrative offers important testimony about the harshness of slavery, while also challenging common antebellum notions of race, class, and gender.

TEACHING TIPS

■ William is careful to insist that Ellen was reluctant to cross-dress: "My wife had no ambition whatever to assume this disguise, and would not have done so had it been possible to have obtained our lib-

CRAFT WEB ARCHIVE

[6828] Anonymous, *The Death of Clotel* (1853), courtesy of William Wells Brown, *Clotel; or, The President's Daughter: A Narrative of Slave Life in the United States* (1853). One of the first published novels by an African American, *Clotel* told the story of a slave daughter of Thomas Jefferson and contained Brown's own personal slave narrative, as well as a fictionalized version of William and Ellen Craft's story.

[6852] Anonymous, *Ellen Craft the Fugitive Slave* (1860), frontispiece of *Running a Thousand Miles for Freedom*, by William Craft. The light-skinned Ellen Craft escaped from slavery with her husband, William, by posing as a white man and her husband's master, symbolizing how slavery and resistance disrupted the "normal" social order.

[6876] Anonymous, *William Craft* (1879), courtesy of the Library of Congress, Rare Books and Special Collections Division. This illustration from William Still's *The Underground Railroad* shows a dignified Craft in respectable middle-class dress, contrasting with the appearance he needed to escape from slavery.

[6877] Anonymous, *Ellen Craft* (1879), courtesy of the Library of Congress, Rare Books and Special Collections Division. In this portrait published in William Still's *The Underground Railroad*, Craft is shown in conservative female dress and with her light skin.

[7846] William Craft, *Running a Thousand Miles for Freedom* (1860). Excerpts from Craft's slave narrative. William and Ellen Craft are remembered primarily for this gripping narrative of their extraordinary escape from slavery. Published in 1860 in England, *Running a Thousand Miles for Freedom* was an immediate bestseller, going through two editions in two years.

erty by more simple means." While he ironically refers to Ellen as "my master" throughout the narrative, he also highlights moments when she "breaks character" and behaves in a stereotypically feminine manner, acting "nervous and timid," "shrinking back" at crucial moments, and bursting into "violent sobs." Ask students to consider why William might have been invested in asserting his wife's normative femininity in this way. What kinds of tensions does her assumption of male clothing introduce into the narrative? What kinds of challenges does her "masculine" role pose for William as both her husband and the narrator of their story?

■ Although other abolitionists printed versions of the Crafts' story, William Craft did not publish his own narrative until 1860, twelve years after their escape. Many critics speculate that Craft waited so long because he wanted to write with complete independence—that is, without the aid of a white ghost-writer or editor—and needed to acquire literary skills in order to do so. Once you have provided students with this background information, ask them to think about the role of literacy in the narrative. Ellen's inability to write is figured as an important issue, and the Crafts' reading and writing lessons with the Quaker family in Philadelphia function as an important turning point in their quest for freedom. How are literacy and freedom bound together? What does literacy have to do with identity for the Crafts? How does the Crafts' attitude toward literacy compare to Frederick Douglass's?

QUESTIONS

Comprehension: What kinds of boundaries, both literal and symbolic, do the Crafts cross in the course of their escape? Which boundaries do they seem to have the most difficulty crossing?

Context: How does Ellen Craft's story compare with the "tragic mulatta" figure as she is characterized in *Uncle Tom's Cabin*? How does Ellen Craft's use of cross-dressing compare to Harriet Jacobs's use of cross-dressing in her escape? How does Craft's decision to "pass" for white complicate her narrative?

Exploration: Cross-dressing was a popular motif in early national literature (a famous example is the narrative of Deborah Sampson, who served as a soldier in the Revolutionary War). Can you think of other American texts that involve stories of cross-dressing or racial passing? How do these acts of disguise take on different meanings over time? How do they challenge our assumptions about race and gender?

Exploration: Feminist and queer theorist Marjorie Garber has argued that cross-dressing is usually a sign of "category crisis" in a text. That is, it points to the artificiality of other socially constructed categories such as race, class, or sexuality. What categories besides gender are "in crisis" in the Crafts' narrative?

Helen Hunt Jackson (1830–1885)

A committed activist for Native American rights, Helen Hunt Jackson provides an important context for understanding Indian slavery and exploitation in the California region. Born Helen Maria Fiske to strict, Calvinist parents and orphaned in her teens, Jackson was raised and educated in female boarding schools in Massachusetts and New York. In 1852 she married Edward Bissell Hunt of the politically and socially prominent Hunt family of New York. Edward was a career officer in the U.S. engineer corps, so the couple moved around a great deal as a result of his army postings. In 1854, the Hunts' first child died at the age of eleven months from a brain tumor. In 1863, after serving in the Civil War, Edward was killed while experimenting with a submarine explosive device. Two years later, the Hunts' only surviving child died of diphtheria. Devastated by these family tragedies, Jackson moved in 1866 to Newport, Rhode Island, to rest and recuperate. There she cultivated a literary circle of friends and found encouragement to produce her own creative work. Her first poems, about motherhood and the loss of her son, were favorably received and found a large audience. For Jackson, writing soon became both a passion and a profitable way to make a living. She was extremely prolific, producing hundreds of poems, essays, stories, book reviews, articles, and travel sketches for the leading periodicals of the day.

In 1873, poor health and respiratory problems prompted Jackson to move to Colorado Springs, where she believed the mountain air would cure her. She soon met and married William Sharpless Jackson, a Pennsylvania Quaker who had made his fortune as a banker in Colorado. Although her new husband was wealthy, Jackson continued to earn an independent living, publishing stories and travel sketches about life in the West.

In 1879, while she was visiting Boston, the course of her life and writing was forever changed when she attended a lecture given by Standing Bear, chief of the Ponca tribe, that detailed the abuses that his tribe had suffered at the hands of the U.S. government. Jackson was deeply moved by the Poncas' plight, declaring "I cannot think of anything else from morning to night." Although she had never identified herself with any of the prominent reform movements of the nineteenth century (such as abolitionism or women's suffrage), Jackson became committed to generating public support for Native American rights, devoting the remainder of her life to a crusade for justice for the Indians. In order to lend greater authority to her cause, she did exhaustive research in the Astor Library in New York, where she investigated documents related to United States Indian policy starting from the Revolutionary period. She gathered her findings together into a book, *A Century of Dishonor* (1881), narrating the history of cultural insensitivity, dishonest land dealings, and devastating violence that the American government had perpetrated upon various Indian tribes. Her work attracted the attention of President Chester Arthur, who appointed her a commissioner of Indian affairs among the Mission Indians of California.

Despite these successes, Jackson was frustrated by the slow pace of

[5244] Anonymous, *Ramona* (n.d.), courtesy of the San Diego Historical Society.

JACKSON WEB ARCHIVE

[5237] Anonymous, *Helen Hunt Jackson, Young Girl* (1845), courtesy of Colorado College, Tutt Library Special Collections. Born in 1830 to strict, Calvinist parents, Helen Hunt Jackson was orphaned in her teens and educated in female boarding schools in Massachusetts and New York. Jackson is most famous for her work on behalf of Native Americans, including her books *A Century of Dishonor* and *Ramona*.

[5238] Anonymous, *Helen Hunt Jackson* (c. 1875), courtesy of Colorado College, Tutt Library Special Collections. At the time of this portrait, Helen Hunt was a vocal advocate for Native American rights. In 1882 she was appointed as a special commissioner for Indian affairs, the first woman to hold such a position.

[5240] Helen Hunt Jackson, *Ramona* manuscript page (c. 1883), courtesy of Colorado College, Tutt Library Special Collections. Helen Hunt Jackson hoped that *Ramona* would call attention to the mistreatment of California's Indians in the same way that Harriet Beecher Stowe's *Uncle Tom's Cabin* had highlighted the plight of slaves.

[5244] Anonymous, *Ramona* (n.d.), courtesy of the San Diego Historical Society. Helen Hunt Jackson's novel *Ramona* explored prejudice, interracial marriage, and the injustices done to California Indians.

[7866] Helen Hunt Jackson, *Ramona: A Story* (1884), courtesy of the Reed College Library. *Ramona* is a sentimental novel about a virtuous half-Indian, half-white woman and her Indian husband, who are downtrodden by racism and unjust Indian policies. An immediate bestseller, *Ramona* has gone through over three hundred printings since its initial publication and has inspired many plays, films, and pageants.

reform and the sense that her activism was having little effect on government policy. In 1884, she adopted a new strategy to promote Indian reform, deciding to write a novel that would engage the sympathies of white Americans. The result, *Ramona*, is a sentimental novel about a virtuous half-Indian, half-white woman and her Indian husband, harassed and downtrodden by racial bigotry and unjust Indian policies. *Ramona* was an immediate bestseller; the novel has gone through over three hundred printings since its initial publication and has been the subject of many plays, films, and pageants. It is Jackson's most popular work, and the piece for which she is best remembered. She died of cancer one year after the publication of *Ramona*.

TEACHING TIPS

■ Jackson consciously modeled *Ramona* after *Uncle Tom's Cabin*; she hoped to "do one-hundredth part for the Indian as Mrs. Stowe did for the Negro" and later referred to herself as an "Indian Harriet Beecher Stowe." Ask students to think about the relationship between the two novels and the similarities of their goals for social reform. Ask them to consider why Jackson would have chosen Stowe as a model when her crusade for Indian rights seemed to be stalling. You might also ask students to research what social reforms were enacted around the time of *Ramona*'s publication. Ask them to consider why *Ramona* was not as effective a piece of social propaganda as *Uncle Tom's Cabin*.

■ *Ramona* depicts Spanish rule in California in romantic and nostalgic terms; it is mainly the encroaching white Americans who are characterized as greedy and cruel (perhaps to arouse the consciences of Jackson's white American readers). Ask students to think about Lorenzo Asisara's narrative of Indian life in the Spanish missions as they read *Ramona*. Ask them why Jackson would have ignored evidence that the Spanish system was often as unjust and exploitative as American policies were.

QUESTIONS

Comprehension: How does *Ramona* challenge stereotypes nineteenth-century Americans held about Native Americans? About Spanish settlers in California? How does the novel play into common stereotypes?

Context: Ramona is portrayed as the product of two cultures: European and Native American. How does she compare with the figure of the "tragic mulatta" (see the "Beyond the Pale" extended context later in this unit)? How does the resolution of Ramona's fate at the end of the novel undercut the message of Indian equality and the call for reform?

Exploration: Like Harriet Beecher Stowe, Helen Hunt Jackson claimed that her social reform novel was the result of something akin to divine inspiration; she insisted, "I did not write *Ramona*. It was written *through* me." What is at stake in this kind of denial of authorship? Why might it have served Stowe's and Jackson's purposes? How might their status as women writers and social activists have informed their claims to divine inspiration?

Suggested Author Pairings

LYDIA MARIA CHILD, HARRIET BEECHER STOWE, AND HELEN HUNT JACKSON

Women writers who worked within the nineteenth-century tradition of sentimentality and domesticity, Child, Stowe, and Jackson were enormously successful in reaching female audiences and convincing them to support various kinds of social reform. Their effectiveness stemmed from a willingness to make overt appeals to their readers' emotional investments in the sanctity of home and family. While Child was more radical than either Stowe or Jackson (she supported the very controversial causes of women's suffrage, penal reform, and interracial marriage), she shared with them a tendency to rely on racist stereotypes in constructing her sentimental plots. Jackson worked later in the century than Child and Stowe—her efforts were focused exclusively on helping oppressed Native Americans in California—but she employed the same literary conventions. In fact, she consciously modeled *Ramona* on *Uncle Tom's Cabin*, hoping to "do one-hundredth part for the Indian as Mrs. Stowe did for the Negro."

ABRAHAM LINCOLN AND SORROW SONGS

Lincoln's speeches and the Sorrow Songs developed by African Americans are the products of very different cultural formations and rhetorical traditions, yet both were intended for oral delivery. As spoken and sung texts, these works find their power in strategic repetition and in resonant imagery that is often drawn from the Bible. Lincoln's speeches and the Sorrow Songs make an interesting contrast because while the Sorrow Songs are the result of communal authorship and are constantly changing and evolving through improvisation, Lincoln's words are associated with his iconic persona and are unchanging (many of them, in fact, have actually been carved in stone).

BRITON HAMMON AND LORENZO ASISARA

Hammon's and Asisara's texts are both rather enigmatic since literary critics and historians know so little about the conditions and details of these men's lives. They are included in this module because their accounts touch so centrally on the issue of slavery, but neither manifests much self-consciousness about his own enslavement or the social institutions that oppress him. Both texts, too, are troubled by questions about their authorship and authenticity. Critics have debated whether Hammon composed his *Narrative* entirely on his own or whether he employed a white editor to write all or part of it. Asisara narrated his story to field historian Thomas Savage, who then wrote it up in its current form. Thus, readers have no direct access to Asisara's original words and must read his history through the mediation of his editor.

WILLIAM CRAFT, FREDERICK DOUGLASS, AND HARRIET JACOBS

Craft, Douglass, and Jacobs all wrote within the popular nineteenth-century genre of the slave narrative. Tracing their literal and emotional journeys from slavery to freedom, these writers explore issues of self-determination and the formation of identity. Authors of slave narratives were primarily concerned with gaining adherents to abolitionism by convincing white audiences of their intelligence and humanity—and, by extension, the intelligence and humanity of all African Americans held in slavery. Craft, Douglass, and Jacobs all detail the degradations and abuses they suffered while enslaved, although these sufferings encompass very different experiences for each writer. Craft deals more thoroughly with the details of his escape than do Douglass and Jacobs, who were perhaps more concerned that offering too many details might lead to their being recaptured. Craft's narrative is also different in that it covers the escape of himself and his wife—their story is that of a couple rather than an individual—and addresses issues of racial passing. Jacobs's narrative makes an effective contrast to the narratives of Craft and Douglass because she offers a woman's perspective and is fundamentally concerned with the particular plight of female slaves.

CORE CONTEXTS

The Radical in the Kitchen: Women, Domesticity, and Social Reform

The lives of most middle-class white women in nineteenth-century America were structured by an ideology known as the "Cult of Domesticity," or the **"Cult of True Womanhood."** This influential ideal of femininity stressed the importance of motherhood, homemaking, piety, and purity. While men were expected to work and act in the public realm of business and politics, women were to remain in the private, domestic sphere of the home. Charged with making the home a peaceful refuge of harmony and order—a haven from the stress of the competitive economic activity of the public domain—women were encouraged to eschew an interest in business or politics and devote themselves instead to the details of housekeeping and motherhood. Writers like Catharine Beecher, Harriet Beecher Stowe, and Lydia Maria Child published manuals offering exhaustive guidelines on the proper maintenance of the American home, instructing their readers in everything from the appropriate dimensions of furniture to the correct way to launder dish towels. Fastidious housekeeping was not sim-

[5476] Anonymous, Cover illustration for *Authentic Anecdotes of American Slavery* by Mrs. L. M. Child (1838), courtesy of the Library of Congress, African American Pamphlet Collection.

ply a display of cleanliness or good taste; rather, a well-managed home was believed to foster good morals and Christian behavior in the people who resided within it. In tending their houses, then, women were understood to be tending the nation's morals. Nineteenth-century proponents of the Cult of True Womanhood believed that women possessed an inherent, natural capacity for sympathy, piety, and purity that made them uniquely fit to manage the domestic sphere.

While this domestic ideology might seem restrictive or even degrading by today's standards, it can also be understood as a method through which women asserted power in antebellum America. Rather than seeing their role as peripheral or trivial, some nineteenth-century women viewed their homemaking and child-rearing as almost revolutionary cultural work—they believed it would bring about the foundation of a new, harmonious, Christian society. In this light, it is telling that Catharine Beecher and Harriet Beecher Stowe prefaced their manual, *The American Woman's Home* (1869), "To the Women of America, in whose hands rest the real destinies of the republic." As critic Jane Tompkins points out, domestic ideology had far-reaching implications in its efforts to "relocate the center of power in American life, placing it not in the government, nor in the courts of law, nor in the factories, nor in the marketplace, but in the kitchen. And that means that the new society will not be controlled by men, but by women." This "culture of the kitchen" was a powerful force in antebellum America, saturating popular magazines, advice books, religious journals, newspapers, and sentimental literature.

Domestic ideology, with its insistence on Christian morals and the redemptive power of love, was often aligned with social reform movements aimed at saving or rehabilitating the downtrodden and oppressed. Penal reform, poverty relief, women's suffrage, and especially abolitionism were popular outlets for middle-class women's sympathy and energy. Viewing the buying and selling of children and adults as an outrageous affront to the sanctity of family relationships, proponents of domesticity designated slavery a kind of national domestic problem for white American women to manage and settle. Domestic objects such as aprons and pinholders printed with pictures of suffering slaves functioned to remind women of the brutality of slavery as they performed their domestic work, and thus aligned that work with sympathy for slaves.

Gillian Brown has noted that slavery was particularly horrifying for proponents of domesticity because it "disregards the opposition between the family at home and the exterior workplace. The distinction between work and family is eradicated in the slave, for whom there is no separation between economic and private status." As Harriet Jacobs makes clear in *Incidents in the Life of a Slave Girl*, enslaved women could not live according to the ideology of "True Womanhood" because they could never be legally secure in marriage, motherhood, or home. Forced to labor for their white owners, they could not create private households of their own. Valued as chattel, they could be sold and separated from their children, husbands, and homes, as the advertisements from slave auctions featured in the

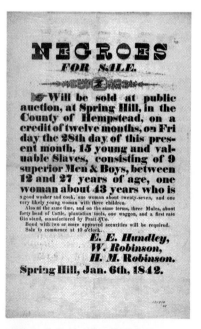

[6833] E. E. Hundley, W. Robinson, and H. M. Robinson, Slave Auction Broadside Advertisement, Arkansas (1842), courtesy of the Library of Congress, Rare Books and Special Collections Division [rbpe 00103300].

archive make vividly clear. Even the stereotypical figure of the African American "Mammy," an icon of nurturing motherhood and domesticity, could never really be part of the "Cult of Domesticity" because her work was forced rather than freely given and performed for her owners rather than for her family.

Harriet Beecher Stowe's *Uncle Tom's Cabin* is a clear example of **domestic fiction**: it uses the ideology of domesticity to mobilize a searing and powerful attack on slavery. By focusing on the slave system's destruction of families—both black and white—Stowe was able to portray slavery as a threat to the sanctity of the American home. Stowe's novel found its power in emotionally charged images of motherhood: an early and often cited episode portrays Eliza Harris, her child in her arms, desperately running across ice floes on the Ohio River to prevent her son from being sold away from her. Stowe's investment in the ideology of domesticity can be indexed by her reliance on descriptions of kitchens as a means to characterize the relative virtues of particular households in *Uncle Tom's Cabin*. In the St. Clair plantation, for example, the slave cook Dinah runs a disorganized and inefficient kitchen which "looked as if it had been arranged by a hurricane blowing through it." According to Stowe's logic, this badly managed kitchen is a direct reflection of the disorder and destructiveness caused by the slave system. Conversely, Rachel Halliday, the kindly Quaker woman who assists Eliza in her escape from slavery, keeps a perfectly ordered, welcoming kitchen in which every item of food seems imbued with a spirit of "motherliness and full-heartedness." Rachel's kitchen functions as the moral center of Stowe's book, its harmony and warmth a perfect manifestation of maternal love and Christian salvation.

If *Uncle Tom's Cabin* works by appealing to women's capacity to "feel" and sympathize, it also depends on depicting African Americans as possessing the same qualities of sentimentality and docility that were supposed to characterize the domestic woman. Thus, we learn that Uncle Tom has the "gentle, domestic heart" that "has been a peculiar characteristic of his unhappy race," and Stowe declares that African Americans "are not naturally daring and enterprising, but home-loving and affectionate." In her attempts to align the plight of black slaves with the concerns of middle-class white women, then, Stowe ends up perpetuating racist and sexist stereotypes. These problems certainly make the book less appealing to contemporary readers, but Stowe's sentimentality—however essentializing and racist—was a powerful political strategy in its own time. So successful was *Uncle Tom's Cabin* that Helen Hunt Jackson adopted the same formula over three decades later. Consciously modeling *Ramona* after Stowe's novel, Jackson hoped to unleash the same kind of moral outrage and social protest against the enslavement of Native Americans in California.

QUESTIONS

Comprehension: Examine the announcements of slave sales featured in the archive, paying attention to the way the people for sale are described and catalogued. What qualities do slaveholders seem to value in slaves? What aspects of the slaves' humanity are denied or ignored in the advertisements?

Comprehension: Look at *The American Woman's Home*'s diagram of a model kitchen featured in the archive. What qualities do Catharine Beecher and Harriet Beecher Stowe seem to value in a kitchen? Why do you think the kitchen was such an important room for proponents of the Cult of Domesticity?

Comprehension: Examine the nineteenth-century images of motherhood featured in the archive. How are mothers portrayed? What seems to make a good mother?

Context: How does Harriet Jacobs's *Incidents in the Life of a Slave Girl* participate in the tradition of domestic literature? To what extent does Jacobs idealize domesticity and traditional femininity? How does her narrative also work to critique these standards?

Context: Why do you think Abraham Lincoln chose the image of a "house divided" to characterize the problem of slavery in his speech of 1858? How would this metaphor have resonated with the domestic ideology of the period?

Context: In disguising herself as a man and escaping from slavery, Ellen Craft seems to transgress many of the ideals of "True Womanhood." How does William Craft's account of his wife in *Running a Thousand Miles for Freedom* work to reinscribe her within the confines of domestic ideology?

Context: During the nineteenth century, aprons and pincushions printed with pictures of suffering slaves were popular with middle-class white women. Why do you think these domestic items were popular? What kind of relationship do these artifacts signal between the position of the domestic housewife and the plight of the slave?

Exploration: The racist, stereotypical image of the African American "Mammy" has been a stock character in everything from novels and films to the packaging of pancake mix. Why has this image been so frequently reproduced? What kind of fantasy about African American women is at stake in this image?

Exploration: Many of the assumptions and values that underwrote the existence of the Cult of Domesticity in the nineteenth century are no longer prevalent today. How have our values as a culture shifted? How have attitudes toward women, and women's work, changed? Do you see any remnants of the Cult of Domesticity in contemporary culture?

Exploration: In the twentieth century, critics did not generally view the sentimental or domestic novels of the nineteenth century as "literary classics," yet they were extremely powerful and influential books in their own time. What makes a text a "classic"? Why were sentimental and domestic fiction excluded from the canon for so long? How do we determine what texts are studied in college classes?

Resistance, Rebellion, and Running Away:
Acts of Defiance in Slave Culture

Many white slaveholders liked to think of their slaves as "happy" or "contented," imagining that the slaves viewed the plantation as a family and the master as a benevolent father. But most slaves' lives were far from comfortable: even owners who had a reputation for kindness used the whip; southern slave codes enabled masters to work slaves up to sixteen hours a day; and families were routinely separated when individual slaves were sold. Whatever image they chose to present to their white masters, enslaved African Americans had many strategies for registering their discontent, protesting their situation, and resisting the discipline of slave life.

[5537] William Russell, Runaway Slave Advertisement (1847), courtesy of the Library of Congress, Rare Books and Special Collections Division, Printed Ephemera Collection.

Resistance could take subtle forms, such as performing assigned tasks slowly or poorly, breaking tools, or even singing songs that covertly mocked or criticized whites. Slaves could sabotage the efficiency of a plantation by stealing food that they would consume themselves, as well as commodities they could trade for money or other goods off the plantation. Resistance could take more violent forms, too. Some slaves set fire to houses, farm buildings, factories, and stores. Slaves who were pushed to their limits occasionally murdered their masters or overseers.

When a slave killed a white person, the incident tapped into slaveholders' biggest fear: that the slaves would rise up and violently overthrow the system that oppressed them. Whites lived in terror that they would experience something like the violent slave revolt that occurred at the end of the eighteenth century in Haiti, which resulted in the overthrow of white rule and the establishment of an independent black republic there. Such large-scale revolts never took place in the American South, probably because the white population was large and had an entrenched system of domination, controlling all the resources and weapons. Still, some courageous and daring slaves did try to organize rebellions, though they rarely saw their plans to fruition. In 1800, Gabriel Prosser, a slave on a plantation near Richmond, Virginia, enlisted as many as a thousand other slaves in a plot to seize key points in the city and execute white slave owners. The conspirators were betrayed before their insurrection got underway, resulting in the execution of twenty-five slaves and the deportation of ten others to the West Indies. Similarly, Denmark Vesey's plan to attack the white population of Charleston, seize ships in the harbor, and sail for Haiti was discovered before his operation could begin. Some historians believe that the uncovering of the Vesey plot, based primarily on rumors and the testimony of bullied and frightened slaves, really had more to do with white hysteria than with the existence of an actual conspiracy. Nonetheless, white authorities in Charleston executed thirty-five slaves as conspirators and deported thirty-four others.

At least two slave insurrections made it beyond the planning stage in the antebellum South. In 1811, a group of between three and five hundred slaves armed with farm implements marched on the city of New Orleans. They were quickly gunned down by militia and regular troops. The insurrection that attracted the most attention—and most frightened whites—was unquestionably Nat Turner's revolt in 1831 in rural Virginia. Turner, a slave foreman and religious exhorter, believed he had a messianic calling from God to unite slaves in a rebellion against white authority. His revolt began when he and a small group of others killed the white people in his plantation household, then continued on to neighboring farmhouses where they recruited other slaves to join in. These slave rebels killed at least fifty-five whites before the militia put down the rebellion. Understandably, this insurrection left a lasting impression on white communities throughout the South, who feared uprisings among their own slaves. Although largely unsuccessful in achieving their goals of revolution and emancipation, slave revolts and conspiracies had profound effects on southern culture. They forced whites to acknowledge that their slaves were neither "happy" nor "contented," but in fact had cause to rebel. And, as scholar Eugene Genovese comments, "they combated, in the most decisive way among both whites and blacks, the racist myth of black docility."

If full-scale revolts were infrequent occurrences, a far more common act of defiance among slaves was the decision to run away. Some individuals and small groups slipped into the woods for short periods to protest plantation conditions, while others fled long distances to effect a permanent escape within the free states. Both kinds of fugitivism worked to undermine the slave system and assert African American bravery and independence. Running away became an increasingly difficult proposition over the course of the nineteenth century, since, in response to abolitionist activity, the slave states developed rigid laws and institutions to catch, punish, and return fugitives. Advertisements publicized detailed descriptions of runaways and offered rewards for their apprehension. Ferocious dogs and professional slave catchers tracked and captured runaways, often inflicting brutal (and sometimes fatal) injuries in the process. The passage of the Fugitive Slave Act of 1850 made even the free territory of the northern states unsafe for escaped slaves; legally, they could be captured and returned to the South at any time without benefit of trial.

While many runaways braved these daunting impediments to successfully escape on their own, abolitionists and slaves also developed elaborate strategies like the famous **Underground Railroad** to aid fugitives. A system of concealed trails, hiding places, safe houses, and friendly supporters, the Underground Railroad helped spirit many escaped slaves to freedom, often in Canada. "Station masters" took enormous personal risks since providing aid to fugitive slaves was illegal. A few brave ex-slaves like Harriet Tubman even ventured back into slave states to assist runaways. Tubman made at least nineteen trips to the South to help organize escapes, reportedly using coded slave songs

[6585] Anonymous, *The Underground Railroad*, Charles T. Weber Painting (1893), courtesy of the Library of Congress, Prints and Photographs Division [LC-USZ62-28860].

to transmit messages to slaves planning on running. Once they reached safety, many fugitives worked tirelessly to free their family members still held in slavery. Escaped slaves like William and Ellen Craft, Frederick Douglass, and Harriet Jacobs wrote narratives about their experiences to raise awareness and inspire others.

Native Americans held in slavery in the missions and ranches of California adopted similar techniques of resistance to those used by enslaved African Americans in the South. Some of their strategies included sabotaging ranch and farm work, raiding livestock, resisting conversion to Christianity, and refusing to give up their native language. Many Native Americans fled the missions and ranches, escaping to communities of Indians living autonomously in inland California. And, as Lorenzo Asisara's narrative attests, Native Americans also engaged in riots and revolts, sometimes killing priests and other Spanish and American authorities when they felt they had no other recourse. The stories of these enslaved people reveal the inaccuracy of racist myths about the passivity or apathy of slaves, while also exposing the limits of white hegemony. Their resistance bears witness to their extraordinary personal courage, determination, and commitment to liberty.

QUESTIONS

Comprehension: What was the Underground Railroad? How did it work?

Comprehension: What kinds of strategies does Frederick Douglass use to resist the degradations of slavery? How do his strategies of resistance eventually enable his escape? What kinds of strategies does Harriet Jacobs use to resist her master's unwanted advances? How are her strategies of resistance different from Douglass's?

Comprehension: Examine the advertisements for runaways featured in the archive. What do they reveal about how slaves were treated? What do they reveal about white attitudes toward runaways and toward African Americans generally?

Context: How were Sorrow Songs encoded to enable slaves to pass covert messages and aid fugitives trying to escape? How do the lyrics subtly reveal subversive intentions?

Context: What kinds of strategies of resistance (if any) does Harriet Beecher Stowe advocate for abused slaves in *Uncle Tom's Cabin*? What are the implications of her idealization of nonviolence and an ethic of sacrifice? How do you think Frederick Douglass would have felt about the description of Tom's capitulation to Simon Legree?

Context: How does Lorenzo Asisara describe the riot he was involved in at the Franciscan mission? How does his attitude toward his own act of resistance compare to Frederick Douglass's? How might the presence of a white editor have influenced the way Asisara chose to narrate his story?

Exploration: How do you think the tradition of African American resistance that developed during slavery might have influenced civil rights activism in the 1960s (for example, Martin Luther King's strategy of nonviolence and civil disobedience, or the more militant strategies adopted by the Black Panthers and other groups)?

Exploration: Why has the exploitation and enslavement of Native Americans in California in the nineteenth century received so little attention?

Stirring Things Up: Slaves and the Creation of African American Culture

While it is important to understand the harshness and oppression that were inherent in slave life, it is equally important to appreciate the fact that African American slaves developed a vibrant life-affirming culture in the face of tremendous adversity. Because slaves came from many different regions of Africa—and thus brought with them a rich variety of cultural traditions—they were far from a homogeneous group. Bound together by shared labor, hardships, and joys in America, they formed what might be called a **creole** culture. "Creole" is a linguistic term for the phenomenon of two or more languages merging into one new language, but it can also usefully be applied to the phenomenon of two or more distinct cultures merging to form a new culture. Combining linguistic, musical, religious, and other cultural traditions from many regions of Africa with Native American, English, and other European traditions, slaves forged a dynamic culture that incorporated customs and practices from all of these places in innovative ways. The culture the slaves developed in turn influenced and transformed the cultural practices of their white masters. Slave culture was by no means homogeneous within the United States; it could vary as much as individual people do. Furthermore, slaves who lived in the low country of South Carolina might have little in common with urban slaves in New Orleans or slaves on a cotton plantation in Georgia. But everywhere, African American slaves dealt with adversity by forging communities that provided them with a sense of cohesion and pride.

Slaves transmitted jokes and wisdom through a sophisticated tradition of folk tales related to the West African legacy of "trickster tales." Often centering on the stories of animals who are not physically strong or intimidating (such as rabbits, monkeys, or spiders), trickster tales portray these supposedly "weaker" animals consistently outwitting the stronger animals who try to oppress or control them. Such stories have an obvious significance to a people oppressed by slavery. Slaves also drew on their African inheritance of trickster tales to create "John Tales," the stories of a slave trickster who outwitted whites.

Visitors to and memoirists of slave communities consistently celebrated the richness and beauty of the musical traditions the slaves created. Their famous spirituals, or Sorrow Songs, combined European Christian hymn traditions with sophisticated African rhythmic patterns and a "call and response" form in which a leader sings or chants a few lines and the group repeats or offers variations on the lines in response. The songs thus follow African traditions in allowing for

1877, African Americans faced increasing disenfranchisement, the spread of lynching, debt peonage, and scientific racism. But as this painting reflects, pro-abolitionist sentiment and a heroic view of slave resistance persisted.

[3090] Harriet Powers, Pictorial quilt (c. 1895–98), courtesy of the Museum of Fine Arts, Boston.

[2742] Anonymous, *The Old Plantation* (c. 1790–1800), courtesy of the Abby Aldrich Rockefeller Folk Art Center.

improvisation and communal authorship. Slaves used them to transmit communal ideals and values, take their minds off their labor, covertly protest their situation, subtly mock their white masters, and secretly pass messages and information to one another. African American slaves also made music with instruments such as drums, horns, and fiddles (sometimes crafted out of rustic objects) to play lively dance tunes at parties or "balls" held in the slave quarters. Because physical movement and dance are an important part of African musical traditions, slaves frequently incorporated expressive dances into their renditions of songs. Black musicians usually provided the music at white assemblies and parties in the antebellum South, so their musical and dance traditions also had a significant impact on white culture. The slaves' development of dance styles and songs has had an enormous impact on the character of music and dance in the United States (and indeed in much of the rest of the world) to the present day.

Some slaves gave up dancing when they "got religion" because white preachers insisted that such physical displays were sinful. But though they would forego dancing to maintain their piety, they created the "ring shout" as a replacement. Clapping and beating time, the slaves would sing religious songs and move around in a single file circle tapping their feet in the "shout step." Although the ring shout looked like dancing to many white observers, slaves insisted that it was not. They did not cross their feet when they performed it, and, by their definition, a dance involved crossing one's feet.

The evolution of the religious ring shout is indicative of the way slaves adapted themselves to Christianity: they absorbed what was useful and meaningful to them, combined it with African sources, and created something new. Most African slaves brought from their African religions a belief in a Creator, or Supreme God. They were thus able to graft their traditional beliefs onto the Christian figure of Jehovah. Many came to interpret Christ, the saints, and Old Testament figures within the context of the African religious system of minor, or lesser, gods. White masters usually taught their slaves about western religion in an effort to instill in them a Christian doctrine of obedience and humility, but most slaves rejected this version of the Bible in favor of a more empowering Christian spirituality. Turning to black slave preachers who celebrated the more redemptive possibilities of Christianity, slaves identified with the stories of Moses and the Israelites triumphing over those who had enslaved them. They also focused on the concept of heaven and eternal paradise as a reward for what they had endured in this world. Combined with their Christianity, many slaves maintained a traditional belief in magic and the supernatural. "Conjurers," charms, and spells were an integral part of life in many slave communities. Because white masters did not always approve of African American adaptations of Christianity, slaves often held secret meetings where they could practice their religion free from white interference. Even today, black and white Baptists in the South often attend different churches and have very different worship practices. Incorporating rituals of singing, shouting, and movement,

African American religion—like many of the other cultural practices the slaves developed—is an ecstatic, life-affirming experience.

Comprehension: What does the term "creole" mean? How can it be used to analyze the formation of cultural traditions?

Comprehension: What kinds of African religious traditions did slaves retain? How did they merge them with Christian traditions?

Comprehension: What is a "ring shout"?

Context: How does Harriet Beecher Stowe portray slave religion in *Uncle Tom's Cabin*? How accurate do you think her portrait of African American spirituality is? How do the slaves on Simon Legree's plantation exploit traditions of magic and superstition to resist Legree's cruelties?

Context: Examine the pictures of slave quarters featured in the archive. How do you think the physical environment of slave quarters might have fostered slave culture?

Context: Does Briton Hammon's text reflect "creolization"? Why or why not?

Exploration: Where do you see evidence of "creolization" in contemporary American culture?

Exploration: How do you think trickster tales influenced the development of African American literature and American literature generally? Can you think of texts that employ similar strategies to those of trickster tales?

and sand more common to the Caribbean region.

[7131] Anonymous, *Many Thousands Gone* (c. 1861–65), courtesy of Henry Edward Krehbiel, *Afro-American Folksongs: A Study in Racial and National Music* (4th ed., 1914), Fisk University. Sorrow Songs often referred to current events through religious language. The lyrics of this song refer partly to the slaves who crossed Union lines, often joining the Union army during the Civil War. The lyrics simultaneously look to the afterlife.

[7229] Orville Carrol, *Green Hill Plantation, Virginia, Kitchen, Exterior View* (1960), courtesy of the Library of Congress, Prints and Publications Division [HABS, VA,16-LONI.V,1B-2]. Large plantations resembled villages or small towns, with many outbuildings.

[7230] Orville Carrol, *Green Hill Plantation, Virginia, Kitchen, Interior View* (1960), courtesy of the Library of Congress, Prints and Publications Division [HABS, VA, 16-LONI.V, 1B-3]. The kitchen on a large plantation provided cooked food for those living in the main house. Slaves usually had their own fireplaces for cooking the separate rations provided them, typically corn and pork.

EXTENDED CONTEXTS

The Plantation: Cultivating a Myth

The ideal of gracious plantation life continues to dominate American images of the antebellum South: Hollywood movies and nostalgic novels have portrayed the Old South as a land of enormous wealth and leisure, filled with beautiful white-columned mansions, gallant gentlemen, and coquettish belles in hoop skirts. In reality, life on antebellum plantations was characterized by hard work. Time-consuming household chores and backbreaking labor in the fields structured the daily lives of the slaves, and even some of the white owners, who inhabited these estates. Few plantations lived up to the standards of size and wealth generally associated with plantation mythology; in fact, in 1860 there were only about 2,300 truly large-scale plantations in operation. The planter group (usually defined as those who owned at least twenty slaves) made up just 4 percent of the adult white male population of the South. Much more common were the small farms on which white landowners lived in modest cabins and owned few or no slaves.

Despite the fact that large plantations were far from representative

[6835] *Berry Hill Plantation* (main house) (after 1933), courtesy of the Library of Congress, Historic American Buildings Survey [HABS, VA, 42-BOSTS.V, 1-4].

[6834] *Green Hill Plantation and Quarters* (c. 1933–60), courtesy of the Library of Congress, Historic American Buildings Survey [HABS, VA, 16-LONI.V, 1-1].

**"THE PLANTATION"
WEB ARCHIVE**

[4327] Anonymous, *Slave Quarters on St. Georges Island, Florida* (n.d.), courtesy of the New York Historical Society. Slaves photographed in front of cabins on the Gulf Coast. Slave quarters throughout the U.S. were similar in size and shape, but these cabins were built of "tabby," an aggregate of shells, lime, and sand more common to the Caribbean region.

[4735] Anonymous, *Gloucester, Near Natchez, MS* (n.d.), courtesy of the Library of Congress, Prints and Photographs Division [LC-USZ62-58888]. Built in 1803, this neoclassical plantation house dates from the pioneering period of white settlement in Mississippi. The columns and hanging moss fit common images of plantations.

[5096] William F. Warnecke, *Margaret Mitchell* (1938), courtesy of the Library of Congress, Prints and Photographs Division [LC-USZ62-109613]. *Gone With the Wind*, Mitchell's best-selling 1936 novel of the Civil War South, won the Pulitzer Prize and became an immensely popular movie in 1939. Romanticizing wealthy slave owners and

of the general southern experience, the ideal of the plantation came to dominate southern culture, setting the tone of economic and social life and functioning as a standard to which many white men aspired. The architecture of the great plantations reinforced their status as icons of wealth, sophistication, and grandeur. Highly formalized in their layout, large plantations usually centered around the "big house," an imposing, often neoclassical structure designed as an expression of the good taste and prosperity of the owner. Wide terraces and long, tree-lined avenues controlled visitors' access to the plantation house, while extensive stretches of cultivated fields and fenced land demonstrated the planter's dominance over nature and society. Because few men even within the planter class could afford such splendor, landowners sometimes opted to dress up their modest homes with false fronts in order to emulate the plantation ideal. Many plain log cabins lay behind facades of Greek revival porches and neoclassical pediments.

Today, little remains of the landscape of antebellum plantation life besides the large mansions (many of which are still standing), but in the nineteenth century much of the work that sustained the plantation economy went on in smaller structures, or outbuildings, scattered over the estates. Detached kitchens, smokehouses, dairies, and water towers were important sites of domestic labor. Barns and mills were necessary in the production of the plantation's staple crop, whether it was tobacco, cotton, rice, or sugar. Slave quarters housed the workers whose forced labor was central to the entire system. While some planters tried to hide the reality of the enslaved labor that created their prosperity—Thomas Jefferson, for example, constructed underground passageways so that visitors to Monticello would not see slaves at work—others placed slave quarters in prominent locations to function as a display of their own wealth and power. The long avenue leading to the Hermitage, Henry McAlpin's Georgia plantation, was lined with more than seventy slave houses, apparently to impress visitors with a view of the inventory of his labor force. Usually small, simple, boxlike structures, slave quarters stood in stark contrast to the magnificent "big houses" they supported. Interestingly, some architectural historians have argued that slave houses may have held a different aesthetic significance for the slaves who lived in them than their masters may have envisioned. Rather than seeing their homes as inferior to and dependent upon the "big house," slaves may have seen in their small, square dwellings a likeness to traditional African architecture.

QUESTIONS

Comprehension: Examine the pictures of plantation "big houses," landscape plans, and slave quarters featured in the archive. How were the plantations laid out? What ideals are expressed in their landscape and architecture?

Context: How is plantation life described in *Uncle Tom's Cabin*? In

Jacobs's and Douglass's narratives? How do these texts critique the plantation system? What features of the plantation system are portrayed as the most destructive? Do any of these texts seem to perpetuate stereotypes associated with plantation life?

Exploration: Given that only a small fraction of the South's white population actually lived on large plantations, why do you think this image became so culturally dominant? Why do you think stereotypes of plantation life continue to loom large in the American imagination?

Exploration: Recently, expensive housing developments have begun using the term "plantation" to describe themselves. Thus, twenty-first-century homebuyers can purchase a house in "Oak Plantation" or "Main Street Plantation." What are the implications of this terminology? What associations do you think real estate developers are hoping the word "plantation" will have for potential purchasers?

Beyond the Pale: Interracial Relationships and "The Tragic Mulatta"

In nineteenth-century America, interracial romantic and sexual relationships were considered taboo within white culture. Viewed by many as leading to the "degeneration" of the white race, "racial mixing" was a locus of anxiety and alarm. Pseudoscientific theories backed up racist notions that conceived of black, white, and Native American people as essentially physically and psychologically different from one another, contending that those differences were traceable to people's blood. Antebellum Americans originally used the term "amalgamation" to describe interracial sex, but later coined the word **miscegenation**, with Latin roots, because it sounded more "scientific." Many states had laws on the books forbidding interracial sex, and social stigmas everywhere categorized interracial relationships as unacceptable. When Frederick Douglass (himself the child of a white man and a black woman) married his white assistant, Helen Pitts, after the death of his first wife, even some of his socially progressive black and white associates in the North were outraged. When Lincoln's political adversaries wanted to undermine his public approval, they accused him of endorsing miscegenation (which, in fact, he did not support).

Despite attempts to legislate against it, miscegenation has existed in America since the first settlements of European immigrants in the sixteenth century. Sexual relationships among Native Americans, blacks, and whites were far from anomalous. By the nineteenth century, sex between black slaves and their white masters and mistresses had become common enough that it was a source of intense anxiety in American culture. Some whites worried that black women

slavery while depicting blacks in racial stereotypes, it appealed to conventional white opinion.

[6834] *Green Hill Plantation and Quarters* (c. 1933–60), courtesy of the Library of Congress, Historic American Buildings Survey [HABS, VA,16-LONI.V,1-1]. Early-nineteenth-century plantation architecture in Campbell County, Virginia. This view of Green Hill provides an alternative to the romanticized image of the Old South.

[6835] *Berry Hill Plantation* [Main House] (after 1933), courtesy of the Library of Congress, Historic American Buildings Survey [HABS, VA, 42-BOSTS.V, 1-4]. Photograph of a Classic Revival mansion with octa-style Doric portico in Halifax County, Virginia, designed between 1835 and 1840. The richest planters used imposing architecture to demonstrate their wealth and sophistication.

[1851] Anonymous, *The Slave Sale* (c. 1855), courtesy of the Smithsonian Institute, National Museum of American History.

[6828] Anonymous, *The Death of Clotel*, in William Wells Brown, *Clotel; or, The President's Daughter: A Narrative of Slave Life in the United States* (1853).

were seducing white men, or that black men would rape white women. In reality, most interracial sex occurred because the powerless social position of enslaved black women left them vulnerable to rape by white men. In certain parts of the South, this kind of sexual exploitation was institutionalized; slave auctions of "fancy girls"—the term used to describe especially attractive young slave women—allowed white men to purchase concubines. The mixed-race children resulting from these sexual relationships, called "mulattos," legally followed the condition of their mothers and were thus considered slaves. While white masters occasionally freed or gave special treatment to the children they fathered by slave women, most simply worked and sold their own children like other slaves.

The plight of these mixed-race people was of particular interest to white abolitionists. They found a special poignancy in a person who was virtually white—a person with only one black great-grandparent could be held as a slave in the South—and was still treated as a slave and subject to all the cruelties of slavery. The figure of the practically white slave woman, or **tragic mulatta**, became a stock character in northern antebellum stories, novels, and plays, beginning with Lydia Maria Child's short story "The Quadroons" (1842). Beautiful, virtuous, and endowed with all the graces of white-middle-class "true womanhood," the tragic mulatta is usually portrayed as becoming involved with a white man whom she cannot marry because of her "single drop" of "black blood." Other popular sentimental plots explore the stories of mixed-race women who marry non-white men and then experience all the hardships and persecutions inflicted on their husband's race (Eliza Harris in *Uncle Tom's Cabin* and Ramona fit this paradigm). In any case, the fate of the mixed-race heroine in sentimental fiction usually involves tragedy. Although these stories stirred up abolitionist sentiment among white readers, they also had the effect of reinforcing racist assumptions. As many critics have pointed out, white readers may have found the tragic mulatta character sympathetic because she was so similar to themselves. In portraying only these mixed-race women as tragic, abolitionist authors implied that an enslaved white person was somehow more deserving of sympathy than an enslaved black person was. At the same time, the figure of the tragic mulatta also had radical, progressive potential: in mediating between racial categories, she exposed the arbitrary nature of racial distinctions. It is perhaps the radical, unsettling potential of the "tragic mulatta" figure that has given her currency in the work of later American novelists such as Nella Larsen (Unit 11) and Toni Morrison (Unit 16).

QUESTIONS

Comprehension: How were mixed-race people legally categorized in the antebellum South? Why do you think southern laws took the position they did with regard to mixed-race individuals? How did the laws protect the institution of slavery and ensure white hegemony?

Context: Ellen Craft exploited her nearly white looks to escape unde-
tected to the North. How does William Craft's characterization of
her in *Running a Thousand Miles for Freedom* engage with the tradition of the "tragic mulatta" figure? How does her story challenge
the assumptions behind the cultural construction of the tragic
mulatta?

Context: After their escape from slavery, the Crafts raised money by
selling portraits of Ellen in her white male planter disguise. How do
you think antebellum audiences would have reacted to the portrait
of Ellen Craft featured in the archive? Why do you think these portraits sold well in the North?

Context: In Helen Hunt Jackson's *Ramona*, the title character is the
child of a Native American and a European. How is her mixed-race
heritage handled in the novel? How does Jackson's treatment of a
Native American mixed-race woman compare to abolitionists' characterizations of African American mixed-race women?

Exploration: How do you think attitudes toward interracial relationships in the antebellum period affected subsequent portraits of
interracial relationships in American literature and film?

version of William and Ellen Craft's story.

[6852] Anonymous, *Ellen Craft the Fugitive Slave* (1860), frontispiece of *Running a Thousand Miles for Freedom* by William Craft. The light-skinned Ellen Craft escaped from slavery with her husband, William, by posing as a white man and her husband's master, symbolizing how slavery and resistance disrupted the "normal" social order.

[6877] Anonymous, *Ellen Craft* (1879), courtesy of the Library of Congress, Rare Books and Special Collections Division. In this portrait published in William Still's *The Underground Railroad*, Craft is shown in conservative female dress and with her light skin.

ASSIGNMENTS

Personal and Creative Responses

1. *Poet's Corner:* Listen to and read the lyrics of several slave spirituals. Using your knowledge of African American "call and response"
lyric patterns and techniques of improvisation, compose a new
verse or new lyrics to one of the songs. Your version need not be
about the African American slave experience, though it can be. How
does your improvisation change the meaning and effect of the
song?

2. *Journal:* Examine the advertisements for slave sales featured in the
archive. Pay attention to the descriptions of the specific people
offered for sale, especially their ages, occupations, relationships to
one another, and prices. Compose a short journal entry or narrative
about one of the people sold at these auctions, imagining their feelings about being separated from their families and purchased as
property.

3. *Journal:* Imagine that you are a participant in the riot Lorenzo
Asisara describes at the Santa Cruz Mission in defiance of Padre
Olbes. Compose an account of the riot, expanding on Asisara's narrative. What motivated you and your compatriots to revolt? What
did you hope to achieve through insurrection?

4. *Doing History:* Look at the watercolor painting *The Old Plantation*
(c. 1800) featured in the archive. This painting was found in South
Carolina without any records to clearly establish its artist, date of
composition, or even its subject. Based on your knowledge of
African American slave culture, what do you think is happening in

this painting? What was the artist trying to depict? Who do you think the artist might have been? Why did he or she paint this picture?

5. *Multimedia:* Imagine that you have been asked to speak at an abolitionist meeting in 1860 to raise public awareness about the devastating effects of slavery and to enlist others in the abolitionist movement. Even though it is 1860, you somehow have access to the *American Passages* archive and slide-show software, which is certain to dazzle your audience. Create a multimedia presentation that supports your argument for emancipation. Include captions that explain and interpret the images you choose within the context of your argument.

Problem-Based Learning Projects

1. You have been hired as a tour guide at a plantation house that has become a museum. The "big house" has been restored to its former grandeur and is now a popular tourist attraction, but the farm buildings, kitchens, and slave quarters no longer exist. You notice that many tourists focus on the beauty of the plantation house, but seem to have minimal awareness of the slave system that supported it. You are anxious to convince tourists that their romanticized notions of plantation culture are largely inaccurate. How will you structure your tour to inform them about the reality of life on a working plantation in antebellum America?

2. It is 1862 and you are a political consultant for President Lincoln. The president has decided to sign the Emancipation Proclamation, freeing all slaves held in bondage within the rebelling Confederate states. He has hired you to help him with public relations on the Emancipation Proclamation. Draft a plan for how the president and his staff should go about gaining public support and swaying public opinion in the North in favor of emancipation.

3. You are Harriet Jacobs's literary agent. Several publishers have already turned down the chance to publish *Incidents in the Life of a Slave Girl*, claiming that the book diverges too far from the traditional conventions of slave narratives, is too open about sensitive topics like sexual exploitation, and will not be interesting to the general public. You have a meeting scheduled with the Boston firm of Thayer and Eldridge (the eventual publishers of Jacobs's narrative). Prepare your sales pitch.

GLOSSARY

abolition   The movement to end slavery in the United States. While calls for abolition emerged from Quaker activists like John Woolman during the early eighteenth century and from proponents of natural rights during the American Revolution, abolitionism did not become an important political force in America until the early- to mid-nineteenth century.

creole   A linguistic term for the phenomenon of two or more languages merging into one new language; can also usefully be applied to the phenomenon of two or more cultures merging to form a new culture.

Cult of True Womanhood   This influential nineteenth-century ideal of femininity stressed the importance of motherhood, homemaking, piety, and purity. While men were expected to work and act in the public realm of business and politics, women were to remain in the private, domestic sphere of the home.

domestic fiction   Novels and stories that use traditional American ideals of domesticity to move readers to sympathy, and sometimes convince them of the importance of social reform. Domestic fiction usually involves sentimental plots and was written mostly by, for, and about women.

Franciscan mission   As part of the Spanish colonial project in the New World, Catholic priests of the Franciscan order were sent to California to Christianize the local Native Americans, claiming their land and turning them into laborers for the missions in the process. Because Franciscan Christianization involved compelling the Indians to give up their lands, culture, native belief practices, and independence, it often could not be accomplished by voluntary conversion and instead necessitated the use of military force. Once the Native Americans were baptized at the missions they became unpaid laborers who were not free to leave—that is, they essentially became slaves. Between 1770 and 1834 over 90,000 California Indians (a third of the pre-contact population) were enslaved within the Franciscan missions. Rampant disease and high rates of mortality ravaged the mission Indian populations.

Fugitive Slave Act of 1850   The passage of the Fugitive Slave Act of 1850 made even the free territory of the northern states unsafe for escaped slaves; legally, northerners were prevented from aiding or harboring escaped fugitives. Slaves could be captured and returned to the South at any time without benefit of trial. Because slave catchers enforcing the Act collected rewards for sending slaves to the South, they sometimes seized free blacks and sold them into slavery.

miscegenation   Pseudoscientific term for the mixing of races, derived from the Latin words *miscere* (to mix) and *genus* (species). Nineteenth-century ideas about miscegenation backed up racist notions that conceived of black, white, and Native American people as essentially physically and psychologically different from one another, contending that those differences were traceable to people's blood. Miscegenation was illegal in many states and culturally taboo throughout the United States in the nineteenth century. Even though many people did not want to acknowledge it, miscegenation was not uncommon in antebellum America.

slave narrative   A popular autobiographical genre in which escaped slaves recount their literal and emotional journeys from slavery to freedom, often emphasizing literacy and resistance to oppression. Authors of slave narratives were primarily concerned with gaining adherents to the abolitionist cause by convincing white readers of their intelligence and humanity—and, by extension, the intelligence and humanity of all African Americans held in slavery. They usually provide details of the degradations and abuses they suffered while enslaved, although these sufferings encompass very different experiences for each writer.

Sorrow Songs   Also called "spirituals," Sorrow Songs were developed within African American slave culture to ease the burden of labor, articulate communal values, and provide an outlet for meaningful self-expression. Drawing on both African musical styles and western European sources, Sorrow Songs are characterized by group authorship and improvisation.

tragic mulatta   The figure of the practically white slave woman, or "tragic mulatta," became a stock character in northern antebellum stories, novels, and plays, beginning with Lydia Maria Child's short story "The Quadroons" (1842). Beautiful, virtuous, and endowed with all the graces of white middle-class "true womanhood," the tragic mulatta is usually portrayed as becoming involved with a white man whom she cannot marry because of her "single drop" of "black blood." Her story usually ends in tragedy.

Underground Railroad   A system of concealed trails, hiding places, safe houses, and friendly supporters, the Underground Railroad was developed by abolitionists, ex-slaves, and slaves to spirit fugitives to freedom, often in Canada. "Station masters" took enormous personal risks since providing aid to fugitive slaves was illegal. A few brave ex-slaves like Harriet Tubman even ventured back into slave states to assist runaways. Tubman made at least nineteen trips to the South to help organize escapes, reportedly using coded slave songs to transmit messages to slaves planning on running.

SELECTED BIBLIOGRAPHY

Brown, Gillian. *Domestic Individualism: Imagining Self in Nineteenth-Century America*. Berkeley: U of California P, 1990.

Garber, Marjorie. *Vested Interests: Cross-Dressing and Cultural Anxiety*. New York: Routledge, 1992.

Genovese, Eugene. *Roll, Jordan, Roll: The World the Slaves Made*. New York: Vintage, 1976.

Levine, Lawrence W. *Black Culture and Black Consciousness: Afro-American Folk Thought from Slavery to Freedom*. Oxford: Oxford UP, 1979.

Sundquist, Eric J. *To Wake the Nations: Race in the Making of American Literature*. Cambridge, MA: Belknap Press of Harvard UP, 1993.

Tompkins, Jane. *Sensational Designs: The Cultural Work of American Fiction, 1790–1860*. Oxford: Oxford UP, 1985.

FURTHER RESOURCES

The African-American Mosaic: African-American Culture and History (Exhibit) and *Selected Civil War Photographs* (Exhibit). The Library of Congress. 101 Independence Ave, SE, Washington, DC, 20540. General Information (202) 707-5000. Exhibitions Information (202) 707-4604.

Amistad Research Center. Tilton Hall—Tulane University, 6823 St. Charles Avenue, New Orleans, LA 70118. Phone (504) 865-5535; fax (504) 865-5580.

Ayers, Edward L., and Anne S. Rubin. *Valley of the Shadow: Two Communities in the American Civil War*. Dual-Platform (Mac and Windows) CD with book and available Web site. New York: W. W. Norton & Company, 2000.

CivilWar@Smithsonian, <www.civilwar.si.edu>. National Portrait Gallery, Smithsonian Institution, 750 Ninth Street, NW, Suite 8300. Washington, DC, 20560-0973. Phone (202) 275-1738.

Collins, Lisa Gail. *The Art of History: African American Women Artists Engage the Past*. New Brunswick, NJ: Rutgers UP, 2002.

Davis, Natalie Zemon. *Slaves on Screen: Film and Historical Vision*. Cambridge, MA: Harvard UP, 2000.

The Frederick Douglass Museum and Cultural Center. 25 East Main Street, Suite 500, Rochester, NY, 14614-1874. Phone (716) 546-3960; fax (716) 546-7218.

Gerima, Haile. *Sankofa*. Mypheduh Films, Inc. PO Box 10035, Washington, DC, 20018-0035. Phone 1 (800) 524-3895 (outside the DC metro area); fax (202) 234-5735.

News from Native California. PO Box 9145, Berkeley, CA, 94610. Phone (510) 549-2802; fax (510) 549-1889. <news@heydaybooks.com>

The Ramona Pageant. 27400 Ramona Bowl Road, Hemet, CA, 92544. Phone (909) 658-3111, (800) 645-4465; fax (909) 658-2695.

Vlach, John Michael. *Back of the Big House: The Architecture of Plantation Slavery*. Chapel Hill: U of North Carolina P, 1993.

Wade in the Water, Volume I: African American Spirituals: The Concert Tradition. Smithsonian Folkways 40072.

REGIONAL REALISM

Depicting the Local in American Literature
1865–1900

Authors and Works

Featured in the Video:
Mark Twain (Samuel Clemens), *Adventures of Huckleberry Finn* (novel), "Fenimore Cooper's Literary Offenses" (satire, literary criticism)

Charles W. Chesnutt, "The Goophered Grapevine" and "The Wife of His Youth" (stories)

Kate Chopin, *The Awakening* (novel), "At the 'Cadian Ball" and "The Storm" (stories)

Discussed in This Unit:
Bret Harte, "The Outcasts of Poker Flat" (story)

Joel Chandler Harris, "The Wonderful Tar-Baby Story," "Mr. Rabbit Grossly Deceives Mr. Fox" (stories)

Sarah Orne Jewett, "The White Heron," "The Foreigner" (stories)

Mary E. Wilkins Freeman, "A New England Nun," "The Revolt of 'Mother'" (stories)

Charles Alexander Eastman (Ohiyesa), excerpts from *From the Deep Woods to Civilization* (autobiography)

Alexander Posey, letters of Fus Fixico (stories, political satire), poems

Zitkala-Ša (Gertrude Simmons Bonnin), "Impressions of an Indian Childhood," "The School Days of an Indian Girl," "An Indian Teacher among Indians" (autobiographical essays)

Overview Questions

■ How do regionalist writings reflect the distinct cultures and experiences of different ethnic groups?

■ How do realist texts represent gender? Are women authors' interpretations of realism different from male authors' interpretations? How?

■ What kinds of narrative conventions structure oral and visual autobiographies?

■ What regional and ethnic dialects were represented in late-nineteenth-century literature? Why were dialect stories so popular in late-nineteenth-century America?

■ What are the distinguishing characteristics of realism? What cultural values does realism reflect and promote?

■ What is regionalist writing? What historical events and cultural anxieties fueled regionalism's popularity in the late nineteenth century?

■ In the popular imagination of the late nineteenth century, what distinguished certain regions of the country from one another?

■ In what ways can regionalist texts be representative of the general "American" experience?

■ How did technology bind together the United States in the late nineteenth century?

■ What is dialect? How did different authors represent dialect?

■ How do narrators affect the tone of a fictional text? What kinds of narrators emerge in realist writing of the late nineteenth century?

■ What is a trickster figure? What cultural work do trickster figures perform?

■ How do regionalist texts participate in or challenge racial stereotypes?

■ How does class-consciousness inflect realist representations of American life? What classes of people are depicted in realist texts?

Learning Objectives

After students have viewed the video, read the headnotes and literary selections in *The Norton Anthology of American Literature*, and explored related archival materials on the *American Passages* Web site, they should be able to

1. understand the basic tenets of realism;
2. discuss the impact on American literature and culture of regionalist writers' emphasis on geographical settings and distinctive customs;
3. discuss the impact of race and gender on representations of regional cultures;
4. discuss the cultural values and assumptions that inform phonetic representations of racial and regional dialects in late-nineteenth-century American literature.

Instructor Overview

Midway through his adventures, Huck Finn comes to the "strange and unregular" conclusion that telling the truth might be the best way both to narrate his experiences and to accomplish his own ends. In a speech that is characteristically simultaneously humorous and profound, Mark Twain has Huck meditate on the nature of truth:

> I says to myself, I reckon a body that ups and tells the truth when he is in a tight place, is taking considerable many resks, though I ain't had no experience, and can't say for certain; but it looks so to me, anyway; and yet here's a case where I'm blest if it don't look to me like the truth is better, and actly *safer*, than a lie. I must lay it by in my mind, and think it over some time or other, it's so kind of strange and unregular.

Huck's radical decision to "up and tell the truth" despite the "resks" epitomizes the stylistic and thematic transformations shaping American literature during the second half of the nineteenth century. A new commitment to the accurate representation of American life as it was experienced by ordinary Americans infused literature with a new "realist" aesthetic. Realism was characterized by its uncompromising literal representations of daily life, and by its resistance to the emotional extravagance and fanciful settings that had characterized Romantic and sentimental fiction. This passion for finding and presenting the truth led many American practitioners of realism to explore characters, places, and events that had never before seemed appropriate subject matter for literature. American audiences, for their part, evinced a new willingness to read

about unrefined and even ugly subjects in the interest of gaining authentic accounts of the world around them.

Many writers expressed their realist aesthetic by emphasizing the particularities of geographic settings, evoking the distinctive customs, speech, and culture of specific regions of the United States in their work. This attention to the peculiarities of place flourished after the Civil War, as Americans began to conceive of themselves as part of a single, unified nation and as curiosity grew about regions of the country that had once seemed too far off and strange to matter. Regional realism may also have developed as an act of nostalgia and conservation in response to the rapid postwar industrialization and homogenization that was threatening older, traditional ways of life. By chronicling the specific details of regional culture, regional realism preserved a record of ways of life and habits of speech that were suddenly in danger of disappearing as a result of the newspapers, railroads, and mass-produced consumer goods that were standardizing American culture. Many regionalist writers became accomplished at transcribing the authentic rhythms and idioms of local dialect in their efforts to make their characters' dialogue mimic the way people really talked. Literalized, phonetic spellings forced readers to pronounce words as speakers of a regional dialect would pronounce them.

A commitment to capturing accurately the realities and peculiarities of regional culture distinguishes all of the authors featured in Unit 8, "Regional Realism: Depicting the Local in American Literature, 1865–1900." As they recorded and commented on the distinctive speech and customs that distinguished specific geographical areas, these writers also struggled with the role of class and gender in local life and in the construction of American identity. This unit explores the regional representations of a wide variety of late-nineteenth-century texts, including works composed by Mark Twain (Samuel Clemens), Bret Harte, Joel Chandler Harris, Sarah Orne Jewett, Kate Chopin, Mary E. Wilkins Freeman, Charles W. Chesnutt, Charles Alexander Eastman (Ohiyesa), Alexander Posey, and Zitkala-Ša (Gertrude Simmons Bonnin). The unit provides contextual background and classroom materials designed to explore the way these writers represented the distinguishing characteristics of American life in the South, in the West, in New

England, and on the Great Plains. The video for Unit 8 focuses on three influential practitioners of regional realism in the South: Mark Twain, Charles W. Chesnutt, and Kate Chopin. Twain used realism and regional dialect in his masterpiece, *Adventures of Huckleberry Finn*, to challenge readers to come to new conclusions about the role of race and class in America. His complex portrait of race relations in the 1840s continues to inspire controversy. Charles W. Chesnutt adopted the regional realist style to explore the contradictions of life on the "color line" between black and white society and to challenge racial stereotypes. Kate Chopin depicted the exotic culture of Creole and Cajun Louisiana, offering a controversial exploration of the constraints placed on women's individuality and sexuality in the process. All of these writers were committed to providing realistic representations of their local cultures and to constructing complicated, believable characters who faced complex moral dilemmas about the nature of their American identities.

In its coverage of these writers and texts, the video introduces students to the basic tenets of the aesthetic of regional realism and foregrounds the movement's relationship to the social and political challenges facing post–Civil War America. How do these texts both reflect and construct cultural values? How do regionalist writings portray the distinct cultures and experiences of different ethnic groups? How do they explore issues of gender? How do regional realist texts record the linguistic specificity of regional speech? Why were representations of dialect so popular in late-nineteenth-century America? In what ways did regional texts participate in the construction of a broader, more general "American" character? Unit 8 helps answer these questions by offering suggestions on how to connect these writers to their cultural contexts, to other units in the series, and to other key writers of the era. The curriculum materials expand the video's introduction to regional realism by exploring writers who represented different regions and different concerns about class and ethnicity, such as Bret Harte (who focused on the culture of the Old West in California), Joel Chandler Harris (a white writer who recorded the dialect and folktales of African American slave culture), and Zitkala-Ša (a Sioux woman who found herself caught between European American customs and traditional Indian culture).

The video, the archive, and the curriculum mate-rials situate these writers within several of the historical contexts and artistic movements that shaped their texts: (1) the development of "parlor culture" and ideals of domestic gentility; (2) Native American oral and visual autobiographical expressions; (3) the role of journalistic ideals in the development of the realist aesthetic; (4) the centrality of the "trickster" figure to expressions of ethnic identity; (5) the importance of developments in the study of anatomy and photography in visual expressions of realism.

The archive and the curriculum materials suggest how these authors and texts relate to those covered in other *American Passages* units: How have American ideas about realistic representation and the possibility of recording "truth" changed over time? How have realist ideals shaped contemporary aesthetics? How did the use of dialect impact later authors' dialogue and poetry? How have American ideas about the relationship between specific regions and the country as a whole changed over time?

Student Overview

In the second half of the nineteenth century, a new commitment to the truthful, accurate representation of American life as it was experienced by ordinary individuals infused literature with a new "realist" aesthetic. Realism was characterized by its uncompromising, literal representations of the particularities of the material world and the human condition. This passion for finding and presenting the truth led many American practitioners of realism to explore characters, places, and events that had never before seemed appropriate subject matter for literature. American audiences, for their part, evinced a new willingness to read about unrefined and even ugly or distasteful subjects in the interest of gaining authentic accounts of the world around them.

Many writers expressed their realist aesthetic by emphasizing the particularities of geographic settings, evoking the distinctive customs, speech, and culture of specific regions of the United States in their work. This attention to the peculiarities of place flourished after the Civil War, perhaps as a celebration of the new unification of a country long divided by political, racial, and religious differences. Regional realism may also have developed in response to the rapid postwar industrialization and homogenization that was destroying older, traditional ways of life. By chronicling the specific details of regional culture, regional realism preserved a record of ways of life and habits of speech that were suddenly in danger of disappearing as a result of the newspapers, railroads, and mass-produced consumer goods that were standardizing American culture. Many regionalist writers became accomplished at transcribing the authentic rhythms and idioms of local dialect in their efforts to make their characters' dialogue mimic the way people really talked. Literalized, phonetic spellings forced readers to pronounce words as speakers of a regional dialect would pronounce them.

A commitment to accurately capturing the realities and peculiarities of regional culture distinguishes all of the authors featured in Unit 8, "Regional Realism: Depicting the Local in American Literature, 1865–1900." As they recorded and commented on the distinctive speech and customs that distinguished specific geographical areas, these writers also struggled with the role of class and gender in local life and in the construction of American identity. As the video for Unit 8 makes clear, Mark Twain, Charles W. Chesnutt, and Kate Chopin adopted very different strategies in their efforts to provide realistic depictions of regional culture. Twain used realism and regional dialect in his masterpiece, *Adventures of Huckleberry Finn*, to challenge readers to come to new conclusions about the role of race and class in America. His complex evocation of racial tension continues to inspire controversy. Charles W. Chesnutt adopted the regional realist style to explore the contradictions of life on the "color line" between black and white society and to challenge racial stereotypes. Kate Chopin depicted the exotic culture of Creole and Cajun Louisiana, offering a controversial exploration of the constraints placed on women's individuality and sexuality in the process. Twain, Chesnutt, and Chopin, like all of the writers featured in Unit 8, were committed to providing realistic representations of their local cultures and to constructing complicated, believable characters who faced complex moral dilemmas about the nature of their American identities.

Video Overview

> **Authors covered:** Mark Twain (Samuel Clemens), Charles W. Chesnutt, Kate Chopin

> **Who's interviewed:** Jocelyn Chadwick, associate professor of education (Harvard University); Emory Elliott, professor of English (University of California, Riverside); Bruce Michelson, professor of English (University of Illinois, Urbana-Champaign); Nell Irvin Painter, professor of American history (Princeton University)

> **Points covered:**
- Introduction to the emergence of new, realistic sounding voices in American literature after the Civil War. Writers who represented regions, classes, and races that had not traditionally been given a voice in American literature demanded representation in the popular imagination and the right to satirize and criticize America in new ways. The American South was an important site for the formation of the literary movement, often called "regional realism."

- Samuel Clemens—better known as Mark Twain—transformed American literature with his skilled representation of regional dialect and his willingness to confront Americans with the difficult issues of racial and class inequality. Favoring the real over the fantastic or the romantic, Twain could make readers uncomfortable with his unsparing representations of the often unpleasant reality of the human condition. At the same time, his satiric portraits of American life often charm readers with their humor and comedy. His masterpiece, *Adventures of Huckleberry Finn,* continues to create controversy for its vivid evocation of racial tensions.

- Charles W. Chesnutt, a writer of mixed African American and white descent, created psychologically complex characters and representations of vernacular speech to challenge American stereotypes about race. His stories are often preoccupied with the problems faced by people of mixed blood who lived on what he called "the color line" between black and white society.

- Kate Chopin set her stories and novels within the distinctive culture of Louisiana Creole and Cajun society. Exploring the frustration of women bound by restrictive social conventions, her work is feminist in its implications. Chopin's frank depictions of both female sexual passion and discontent within marriage made her work extremely controversial in her own time.

- These southern practitioners of regional realism rejected idealistic romanticism in order to bear accurate witness to the reality of the world around them. In the process, they created complex characters faced with challenging moral dilemmas. Their work opened up new voices and new insights that democratized American literature and transformed national conceptions of what it means to be American.

PREVIEW

- **Preview the video:** American culture was changing rapidly in the post–Civil War era: new technologies such as the telegraph and the railroad bound the continent together, postwar racial tensions brought the issue of the "color line" to the forefront of American consciousness, and a new commitment to realistic representation transformed literary style. Writers responded to these cultural developments by producing texts that paid close attention to the specifics of people and place in particular regions of the country, evoking the distinctive culture of areas of America that had not been previously represented. The South was an important site for the development of this movement, often called "regional realism." Mark Twain used realism and regional dialect in his masterpiece, *Adventures of Huckleberry Finn*, to challenge readers to

come to new conclusions about the role of race and class in America. His complex evocation of racial tension continues to inspire controversy. Charles W. Chesnutt adopted the regional realist style to explore the contradictions of life on the "color line" between black and white society and to challenge racial stereotypes. Kate Chopin depicted the exotic culture of Creole and Cajun Louisiana, offering a controversial exploration of the constraints placed on women's individuality and sexuality in the process. All of these writers were committed to providing realistic representations of their local cultures and to constructing complicated, believable characters who faced complex moral dilemmas about the nature of their American identities.

- **What to think about while watching:** How do these authors challenge Americans to grapple with difficult issues regarding social class, region, and race? How do these writers react against romantic conventions to create a new aesthetic in American literature? Why is the realistic representation of dialect so important in late-nineteenth-century American literature? How do these depictions of regional life expand traditional ideas about American identity? How did the regional realist movement impact subsequent American fiction?

- **Tying the video to the unit content:** Unit 8 expands on the issues outlined in the video to further explore the scope and impact of regional realism on American literature and culture in areas outside of the South. The curriculum materials offer background on Native American, African American, and European American writers who represent the language, customs, and cultures of New England, California, and the midwestern plains. The unit offers contextual background to expand on the video's introduction to the political issues, historical events, and literary styles that shaped these realistic depictions of life in regional America.

	How do place and time shape the authors' works and our understanding of them?	What is an American? How does American literature create conceptions of the American experience and identity?	What characteristics of a literary work have made it influential over time?
Compre-hension Questions	What political and social problems faced the American South in the period after the Civil War known as Reconstruction?	What is the "plantation myth"? How do the featured southern regionalist writers challenge and transform ideas about life in the American South?	What is dialect? How did post–Civil War writers represent vernacular speech?
Context Questions	What role does the Mississippi River play in Mark Twain's depiction of Huck and Jim's journey southward in *Adventures of Huckleberry Finn*? What are the implications of the fact that they continue to drift further and further south over the course of their adventure? How do Twain's depictions of the culture of the border state of Missouri compare to Chopin's representations of life in the Deep South in Louisiana?	What is the difference between Chopin's portrait of mixed-race people in "Désirée's Baby" and Chesnutt's representations of mixed-race people in Cincinnati in "The Wife of His Youth"? What different attitudes and assumptions about race do these writers bring to their texts?	How does Twain's characterization of African Americans compare to Chesnutt's characterization of African Americans? How do both authors challenge and participate in racial stereotypes? How did their depictions of African American speech and culture influence later African American writers?
Exploration Questions	Why did the accurate representation of dialect play such an important role in regional realism? How did these writers' innovations in the creation of realistic-sounding dialogue affect later American literature?	What made Twain's *Adventures of Huckleberry Finn* and Chopin's *The Awakening* such controversial novels, both in their own time and in ours? How did their representations of southern culture unsettle assumptions and cause discomfort in their readers? How does their work continue to challenge readers?	Ernest Hemingway claimed that all subsequent American literature derived from *Huckleberry Finn*. What did Hemingway mean by this claim? Why did he see Twain's novel as so foundational to American identity and to American literary traditions?

	Texts	Contexts
1860s	Mark Twain (Samuel Clemens), *The Innocents Abroad* (1869) Bret Harte, "The Outcasts of Poker Flat," "Plain Language from Truthful James" (1869)	United States Secret Service established (1860) Transcontinental telegraph service established between New York and San Francisco (1861) Civil War (1861–65) Homestead Act (1862) Emancipation Act (1863) President Abraham Lincoln assassinated (1865) Ku Klux Klan formed (1866) First elevated railroad begins service in New York City (1867)
1870s	Bret Harte, *"The Luck of Roaring Camp" and Other Sketches* (1870) Mark Twain (Samuel Clemens), *The Adventures of Tom Sawyer* (1876) Sarah Orne Jewett, *Deephaven* (1877)	Fire destroys large portions of Chicago (1871) Yellowstone National Park established (1872) Battle of Little Bighorn (Custer's Last Stand) (1876) Alexander Graham Bell invents the telephone (1876) Edison patents the phonograph (1878)
1880s	Joel Chandler Harris, "The Wonderful Tar-Baby Story," "Mr. Rabbit Grossly Deceives Mr. Fox," *Uncle Remus: His Songs and Sayings* (1881) Sarah Orne Jewett, *The White Heron* (1886) Charles W. Chesnutt, "The Goophered Grapevine" (1887) Mark Twain (Samuel Clemens), *The Prince and the Pauper* (1882), *Life on the Mississippi* (1883), *Adventures of Huckleberry Finn* (1885), *A Connecticut Yankee in King Arthur's Court* (1889)	President James Garfield assassinated (1881) American Red Cross founded (1881) Chinese Exclusion Act (1882) American Federation of Labor launched (1886) Coca-Cola invented (1886)
1890s	Mary E. Wilkins Freeman, "The Revolt of 'Mother,' " "A New England Nun" (1891) Kate Chopin, "At the 'Cadian Ball" (1892), "Désirée's Baby," *At Fault* (1893), *Bayou Folk* (1894), *A Night in Acadie* (1897), *The Awakening* (1899) Sarah Orne Jewett, *The Country of the Pointed Firs* (1896) Mark Twain (Samuel Clemens), *Following the Equator* (1897) Charles W. Chesnutt, *The Conjure Woman*, "The Wife of His Youth" and Other Stories of the Color Line (1899)	Massacre at Wounded Knee, South Dakota (1890) Daughters of the American Revolution founded (1890) Pan-American Union formed (1890) National American Woman Suffrage Association founded (1890) Immigration Center established on Ellis Island (1892) World Columbian Exposition, Chicago (1893) Hawaii becomes a U.S. Protectorate (1893) Klondike Gold Rush (1896) Spanish-American War (1898)

	Texts	Contexts
1900s	Sarah Orne Jewett, "The Foreigner" (1900) Zitkala-Ša (Gertrude Simmons Bonnin), "Impressions of an Indian Childhood," "The School Days of an Indian Girl," "An Indian Teacher Among Indians" (1900) Charles Alexander Eastman (Ohiyesa), *Indian Boyhood* (1902) Alexander Posey, letters of Fus Fixico (1902–08), "Hotgun on the Death of Yadeka Harjo" (1908)	President William McKinley assassinated (1901) Orville and Wilbur Wright achieve first powered flight, Kitty Hawk, North Carolina (1903) International Workers of the World union founded (1905) First radio broadcast (1906) Ford Model T goes into production (1908)
1910s	Charles Alexander Eastman (Ohiyesa), *The Soul of an Indian* (1911), *The Indian Today* (1915), *From the Deep Woods to Civilization* (1916)	First movie studio opens in Hollywood (1911) World War I begins in Europe (1914) Panama Canal opens (1914) D. W. Griffith's *Birth of a Nation* (1915) United States enters World War I (1917) 18th Amendment to the Constitution (Prohibition) (1919)

AUTHOR/TEXT REVIEW

Mark Twain (Samuel Clemens) (1835–1910)

Samuel L. Clemens, better known by his pen name "Mark Twain," continues to enjoy a reputation, already attained by the end of his lifetime, as an icon of American literature. As such, he and his most enduringly popular novel, *Adventures of Huckleberry Finn*, have been subjects of high praise and, at times, subjects of probing questions about the cultural assumptions that shape definitions of "literature" and of "American-ness" at different historical moments. Indeed, Twain's fame stems in large part from his ability to raise questions about American identity and values in humorous ways through his writings, though they are often tinged with bitterness and despair.

Twain's life provided subjects and sources for many of his works. Born in Missouri, he grew up in the Mississippi river town of Hannibal, which, thinly disguised as St. Petersburg, became the boyhood home of his most famous characters, Tom Sawyer and Huck Finn. Clemens himself did not enjoy a long childhood. Following the death of his father, he left school at age twelve and worked for the next several years as a printer's apprentice to help support his mother and four siblings. During this time, he also began to try his hand at writing. In 1853 he embarked on a three-year period of travel as a journeyman printer, which took him through the Midwest and as far east as New York. This adventure was succeeded by an apprenticeship and subsequent job as a riverboat pilot, an exciting and lucrative experience that he would later recount in his 1883 memoir *Life on the Mississippi*. When the beginning of the Civil War ended Mississippi riverboat commerce in 1861, Twain enlisted for a brief period in the Confederate militia and then spent the next several years wandering through the West. He entered into a number of failed get-rich-quick schemes with his brother in the Nevada Territory (the subject of his 1872 memoir *Roughing It*) and published satirical sketches for western newspapers, first as an occasional contributor and then as a popular regular reporter and correspondent. In these pieces, he developed his skilled ear for **dialect,** establishing what would become his trademark humorous style of capturing the particularities of time, place, and personality by merely seeming to report what characters say in their own words, however unpopular or crude the sentiments. Following the convention of the age, these pieces appeared anonymously or under a pseudonym, for which Clemens chose "Mark Twain," the river pilot's term for a safe depth for passage.

Though Twain satirized genteel convention and corruption in print, he aspired to higher social status, vast riches, and greater fame for himself. He established his reputation in 1869 with the publication of *The Innocents Abroad*, a popular book about his experiences on the first large-scale American tourist excursion to Europe after the Civil War. Soon thereafter, in 1870, he married Olivia Langdon, the daughter of a wealthy coal merchant, and moved first to Buffalo and then into a fashionable mansion in Hartford, Connecticut, where his life began to assume the trappings of gentility. During the 1870s

[3777] Anonymous, *Mark Twain, Captain* (1895), courtesy of the Mark Twain House, Hartford, CT.

and 1880s, Twain began producing the novels for which he is best remembered today, including *The Adventures of Tom Sawyer* (1876), a simultaneously anti-sentimental and nostalgic tale of Missouri boyhood; *The Prince and the Pauper* (1882), a popular historical romance; *A Connecticut Yankee in King Arthur's Court* (1889), a social and political burlesque in the form of a parody of the historical novel; and, most notably, *Adventures of Huckleberry Finn* (1885). *Huckleberry Finn*, his greatest work, is remarkable above all for conjuring up a vivid sense of a time and place, for using humor and pathos to pose crucial questions about race relations and the legacy of slavery, and for experimenting with narration and dialect. Through the naïve perspective of Huck, a first-person boy narrator who speaks in slang and dialect, Twain exposes social inhibitions and injustices, the gaps between what the American people are supposed to be and what they are.

Twain's literary output dropped off in the remaining two decades of his life, during which time he lived abroad with his family for substantial periods. Those works that he did produce, such as *Following the Equator* (1897), a memoir of a trip around the world, reflect a new concern with global affairs, as well as an increasingly caustic and pessimistic tone. Nonetheless, during the final years of his life, he found himself celebrated everywhere, attaining fame at home and abroad as a kind of living literary institution and firmly securing a place for himself in the history of American letters.

TEACHING TIPS

■ Twain wrote the first sixteen chapters of *Huckleberry Finn* in the Centennial year 1876. He then found himself frustrated and uncertain about how to finish the story, abandoning it until 1883. Ask students to think about the relevance of the fact that this novel was begun on the anniversary of the Declaration of Independence. How does the book comment on the Declaration's ideals of "life, liberty, and the pursuit of happiness"? Ask your class to think about the breaking point at Chapter 16, given the information that Twain left his draft at that point for eight years. Why might he have found himself frustrated and uncertain about the trajectory of the story at that point? How did he resolve his problem? How does Huck and Jim's relationship change during the Grangerford and Shepherdson sequence?

■ Twain's repeated use of the word "nigger" throughout *Huckleberry Finn* has caused controversy since its publication and can make it a troubling book to teach. Parents and administrators angry about what they perceive as the book's racism have called for its removal from middle school and high school curricula. Ask your students to think about why Twain used this pejorative term—and it was considered pejorative both in his own time and in the historical period in which the novel is set—in a novel that many readers have understood to be an indictment of racism. What effect might Twain have been aiming for? Should we understand his use of the word as itself an example of racism? Is there a distinction to be made between Twain's

TWAIN WEB ARCHIVE

[3631] Edward Windsor Kemble, *Huckleberry Finn* (1884), courtesy of the Library of Congress [LC-USZ62-98767]. Shown with a shotgun and a rabbit, Huck Finn epitomizes the all-American traits of self-sufficiency and independence in this frontispiece illustration for the 1885 edition of *Adventures of Huckleberry Finn (Tom Sawyer's Comrade)*.

[3777] Anonymous, *Mark Twain, Captain* (1895), courtesy of the Mark Twain House, Hartford, CT. A riverboat pilot in his youth, Samuel L. Clemens chose the pseudonym "Mark Twain," a term meaning safe depth for passage. He used realism and regional dialect in his writing to challenge readers to come to new conclusions about the roles of race and class in America.

[4049] Anonymous, *Samuel L. Clemens about the time he wrote* Huckleberry Finn (c. 1885), courtesy of the Mark Twain House, Hartford, CT. During the 1870s and 1880s Twain began producing his best-known novels, including *The Adventures of Tom Sawyer* (1876), *The Prince and the Pauper* (1882), and *Adventures of Huckleberry Finn* (1885).

[4053] Anonymous, *Mark Twain in front of boyhood home, Hannibal, Missouri* (1902), courtesy of the Mark Twain House, Hartford, CT. Born in Missouri, Samuel L. Clemens grew up in the Mississippi river town of Hannibal, which, thinly disguised as St. Petersburg, became the boyhood home of Twain's most famous characters, Tom Sawyer and Huck Finn.

[5831] Anonymous, *Young Sam Clemens [Mark Twain]* (n.d.), courtesy of the Mark Twain House, Hartford, CT. This early photograph of Samuel L. Clemens reflects many of the ideals of realism, including the desire to document uncompromising, literal representations of the material world and the human condition.

[7838] Jocelyn Chadwick, Interview: "Controversy in the Reception of Twain's *Huckleberry Finn*" (2001), courtesy of Annenberg/CPB and *American Passages*. Jocelyn Chadwick, assistant professor of education at the Harvard Graduate School of Education, speaks on the controversial aspects of Mark Twain's *Huckleberry Finn*.

[7854] Bruce Michelson, Interview: "Stages of Controversy in *Huckleberry Finn*" (2001), courtesy of Annenberg/CPB and *American Passages*. Bruce Michelson, professor of English at the University of Illinois at Urbana-Champaign, speaks about the evolution of the controversy surrounding Mark Twain's *Huckleberry Finn*.

stand on slavery and his stand on racism? What is the impact of the presence of this word on our understanding of the novel today?

QUESTIONS

Comprehension: Why are Huck and Jim on the raft in *Huckleberry Finn*? What life experiences do these two characters have in common? How are they different from one another?

Context: According to Twain, what are James Fenimore Cooper's "literary offenses"? How does Twain's assessment reflect his own commitment to "realism" as an artistic ideal? Is his analysis a fair indictment of Cooper?

Context: How would you describe the narrative structure of *Huckleberry Finn*? Are some episodes in Huck and Jim's journey more important than other episodes? Does the novel have a climax? If so, what do you consider to be the climactic moment?

Context: Unlike Joel Chandler Harris, Charles W. Chesnutt, and Sarah Orne Jewett, Twain narrates the entire action of his novel through Huck's vernacular speech. Why do you think he does not employ an educated, urbane frame narrator like so many other authors who experimented with representing regional dialects? What roles do the frame narrators play in the stories by Harris, Chesnutt, and Jewett?

Exploration: In the past century and a half, many schools and libraries have banned *Huckleberry Finn* or have contemplated banning it. What makes this book so controversial? How might the reasons for Americans' discomfort with the novel have changed over time? How does *Huckleberry Finn* compare to other books that have been banned for one reason or another over the years (*The Catcher in the Rye*, *Lolita*, *Ulysses*, even *Harry Potter*)? For what reasons, if any, should a book be removed from a school's reading list or library?

Exploration: Critics disagree about Twain's portrait of Jim in *Huckleberry Finn*. How does the characterization of Jim participate in common nineteenth-century stereotypes of African Americans? How does Jim compare to some of the African American characters and writers discussed in Unit 7? Are there ways that Jim challenges racist stereotypes?

Bret Harte (1836–1902)

At the height of his career, in the 1860s and 1870s, Bret Harte was one of the most famous and most highly paid American writers. His popular accounts of life in Gold Rush–era California, including short stories such as "The Luck of Roaring Camp" and "The Outcasts of Poker Flat," seized the public imagination and made him an international celebrity. Harte's invention of prototypical "western" characters—the shady prospector, the cynical gambler, the tough cowboy, the prostitute with a heart of gold—created the mythology through which Americans learned to understand the culture of the "Old West."

Combining realistic descriptions of the specific regional characteristics of California life with sentimental plots, Harte hit on a formula that delighted nineteenth-century readers and continues to influence American narratives of the West.

Born in Albany, New York, Francis Bret Harte was tutored at home by his schoolteacher father, Henry Harte. When Henry died in 1845, the family relocated first to New York City and then to San Francisco when Harte's mother married Colonel Andrew Williams, an early mayor of Oakland, California. During his first six years in California, Harte drifted from job to job, working as a teacher, miner, and stagecoach guard for Wells Fargo. He ultimately found his calling as a printer's apprentice, journalist, and editorial assistant at the small newspapers *The Humboldt Times* and *The Northern Californian*. By 1865, Harte had graduated to positions with larger newspapers and magazines of San Francisco, eventually serving as the editor of the weekly *Californian,* where he commissioned pieces from the then-unknown writer Samuel Clemens. In 1868, Harte was hired as the first editor of the literary magazine *Overland Monthly*, a position that catapulted him to national fame when he used the magazine as the venue for his best stories and his popular poem "Plain Language from Truthful James," usually called "The Heathen Chinee."

Recognized as one of the most popular and marketable writers in America after his stint at the *Overland Monthly*, Harte received a deluge of offers of editorial positions and professional opportunities across the country. In 1871 he signed a one-year contract for $10,000 (a record-breaking salary for a writer at that time) with the *Atlantic Monthly* in Boston. Harte had promised the magazine a minimum of twelve stories and poems, but, distracted by his status as a celebrity, he grew careless about meeting his obligations. When the *Atlantic* refused to renew his contract at the end of the year, Harte found himself suddenly in need of a new source of income. To fill the gap, he began lecturing and writing plays, but his work never again achieved the success or acclaim he had come to expect. He eventually used his connections in the political world to attain diplomatic posts with the consulates in Germany and Scotland, jobs he held until he was relieved of his positions for "inattention to duty" in 1885. He lived out the rest of his life in London, where he became the permanent guest of the wealthy Van de Velde family. Harte remained a prolific writer until his death, publishing a volume of short stories almost yearly. While his fiction was favorably received in Europe, American critics generally dismissed his later work as repetitive, formulaic, and overly sentimental. Although Harte's reputation declined dramatically in the twentieth century, scholars have recently begun to reassess his important contributions to the development of regionalism and the genre of western fiction.

[3707] Louis Charles McClure, *The Gold Miner* (c. 1890), courtesy of Denver Public Library, Western History Collection.

TEACHING TIPS

■ Harte's literary reputation has suffered for what critics have historically understood as his sentimentality and romanticism. Recently,

[1147] Emanuel Gottlieb Leutze, *Westward the Course of Empire Takes Its Way* (1861), courtesy of the Smithsonian American Art Museum, Washington, DC. This painting's title became a popular motto for Manifest Destiny in America after 1850. Portraits of Captain William Clark and Daniel Boone flank a depiction of San Francisco Bay at the bottom of the image.

[1181] Albert Bierstadt, *Valley of the Yosemite* (1864), courtesy of the Museum of Fine Arts, Boston. Rerproduced with permission. © Museum of Fine Arts, Boston. Gift of Martha C. Karolik for the M. and M. Karolik Collection of American Paintings, 1825–1865, 47.1236. The romantic grandeur and luminism of Bierstadt's western landscapes reflect Hudson River School influences. Realist writers like Bret Harte sought to imbue the same landscapes with the gritty realities of frontier life.

[3707] Louis Charles McClure, *The Gold Miner* (c. 1890), courtesy of the Denver Public Library, Western History Collection. The discovery of gold and silver in the American West drew fortune seekers from all over the world. Miners often served as the vanguard of American expansion.

[5228] Anonymous, *Montgomery Street, San Francisco, 1852*, courtesy of the Library of Congress, Prints and Photographs Division [LC-USZ62-55762]. Rapid, mainly white immigration during the Gold Rush brought California to statehood in 1850 as a "free state" that forbade slavery. Yet demand for land and forced labor caused a genocidal-scale population decline among California Indians.

[5824] "Harte's *Poems*" (1871), courtesy of the Cornell University *Making of America* Digital Collection. This January 1871 review of Bret Harte's *Poems* reflects the way Harte's work helped shape notions of American manhood.

[5841] Currier and Ives, *Gold Mining in California* (c. 1871), courtesy of the Library of Congress [LC-USZC2-1755]. This lithograph presents a romantic and sanitized portrayal of life in the gold fields.

however, some literary scholars have claimed that Harte has been misunderstood and that his stories are much more cynical and ironic than has been appreciated. Ask students to think about whether they would characterize "The Outcasts of Poker Flat" as an example of sentimentality (you might refer back to Unit 7 for a discussion of sentimentality) or as participating in a more clearly realist tradition. How ironic is the tone of Harte's narration in this story? What is the relationship between irony and realism?

■ Have your students write articles for the Poker Flat newspaper in which they report on the fate of the "outcasts" from the perspective of a Poker Flat inhabitant.

QUESTIONS

Comprehension: Who are the central characters in "The Outcasts of Poker Flat"? How do they construct or participate in stereotypes about characters from the Old West? How do they challenge these stereotypes?

Context: Bret Harte was a mentor to Mark Twain, giving him some of his first writing assignments and, according to Twain, teaching him a great deal about his craft: "He trimmed and schooled me patiently until he changed me from an awkward utterer of coarse grotesqueness to a writer of paragraphs and chapters." Later, however, Twain attacked Harte's work as overly romantic, unbelievable, and repetitive. How is Harte's work similar to Twain's? What ideals and narrative strategies do they share? How are they different?

Exploration: Compare the plot and characters of "The Outcasts of Poker Flat" to the plot and characters of one or more Western movies (*Stagecoach*, *Butch Cassidy and the Sundance Kid*, *Unforgiven*, or *The Treasure of the Sierra Madre*, for example). How do subsequent American portraits of the Old West draw from Harte's depictions? What familiar ideas about the Old West seem to start in Harte's work?

Exploration: In the video for Unit 12 you will encounter two more key sentimental scenes in realist fiction: the breast-feeding of the dying man by Rose of Sharon in *The Grapes of Wrath* and the poisoning of Alejo by crop dusters. How do these compare to Mother Shipton's self-sacrifice in "The Outcasts of Poker Flat"? How do you see the relationship between sentimentality and realism?

Joel Chandler Harris (1848–1908)

Most famous for his creation of the black folk figure Uncle Remus, Joel Chandler Harris was also a journalist, humorist, and novelist. Born in rural Georgia to a single mother, Harris suffered poverty and social ostracism in his childhood. Many of his biographers suggest that his early insecurities led to lifelong shyness, which he compensated for by writing humorous stories and playing practical jokes. At thirteen, Harris was taken on as an apprentice typesetter at *The Countryman*, a weekly newspaper run by Joseph Addison Turner on his large plantation, called Turnwold. There, Harris received training in printing as well as what he later termed "a liberal education," enjoying the benefits of the extensive Turnwold library and receiving informal instruction from Turner. He also spent a great deal of time learning from the slaves on the Turnwold plantation, absorbing their stories, songs, and myths. Later, Harris drew on these experiences to compose his sketches and stories of African American life.

In 1864, Turnwold was attacked and destroyed by the advancing Union army, and by 1866, with his finances in ruins, Joseph Turner was forced to dismiss his young type-setter and close *The Countryman*. Harris found employment in Georgia cities, working as a typesetter, journalist, humorist, and editor for a variety of newspapers. In the late 1870s Harris began publishing a series of sketches written in African American **dialect** for the *Atlanta Constitution*, eventually using this forum to develop the character of Uncle Remus. A black slave who tells African American legends and folktales to a young white listener, Uncle Remus quickly achieved popularity with readers in the South as well as the North, where Harris's columns were syndicated in urban newspapers. Admirers praised the "accuracy" and "authenticity" of Harris's rendering of African American dialect and recounting of traditional African animal fables about trickster characters such as Brer Rabbit and Brer Fox. Building on the popularity of his newspaper columns, Harris published a book-length collection of Uncle Remus stories in 1880, titled *Uncle Remus: His Songs and Sayings*. The book sold out three printings in its initial months of publication, and, as late as 1904, Harris reported that it continued to sell four thousand copies yearly. Capitalizing on his success, Harris followed *Songs and Sayings* with several additional collections of Uncle Remus's animal fables. He also wrote local-color stories and novels focusing mainly on life among southern blacks and impoverished whites, but these works never attained the success and popularity of the Remus stories.

[1207] George Harper Houghton, *Family of slaves at the Gaines' house* (1861), courtesy of the Library of Congress [LC-USZC4-4575].

Harris also continued to work as a journalist until 1902, becoming a self-styled champion of reconciliation between the North and the South and between blacks and whites. In some respects, his ideas about race were enlightened for his time: Harris was a proponent of black education and argued that individuals should be judged according to their personal qualities rather than their race. At the same time, however, he perpetuated racial stereotypes in his writings. Literary critics have frequently pointed out the latent racism of the Uncle Remus tales, especially Harris's stereotyped portrait of Remus himself as a "contented darky" with nothing but happy memories of his life as a plantation slave. On the other hand, the **trickster** tales that Uncle Remus narrates—with their subversive focus on the triumph of seemingly weak

[2621] Robertson, Seibert & Shearman, *Oh Carry Me Back to Ole Virginny* (c. 1859), courtesy of the Library of Congress [LC-USZC4-2356].

characters over their aggressors—are characterized by poetic irony and a subtle critique of oppression and prejudice (a critique that Harris may never have fully appreciated). Whatever his intentions, Harris's work is undeniably important as a record of traditional African American folktales that might otherwise have been lost to history.

TEACHING TIPS

■ Students will probably have difficulty with Harris's rendering of Uncle Remus's dialect at first, but you should make it clear that such problems are to be expected and that the tales demand thorough and careful reading. It might be worthwhile to provide a gloss on a few of the more frequently used terms, such as "de" for "the," "gwyne" for "going," and "sezee" for "he says." You might ask them to compare a page of Harris's dialect to a page of Mark Twain's. When Twain writes in dialect, portraying the speech of Jim, what are the differences in strategy? Which works better for a modern reader? After students have become more comfortable reading Harris's and Twain's representation of African American speech, ask them to think about why these renditions of southern black dialect might have been so popular with white northern audiences in the late nineteenth century.

■ Harris always insisted that he did not invent the Uncle Remus tales but instead simply recorded the legends and stories he collected from African Americans. Although he obviously filtered and edited the tales, he would not publish any story that he could not authenticate as part of traditional black folklore. He even claimed that the central character of Uncle Remus "was not an invention of my own, but a human syndicate, three or four old darkies I had known. I just walloped them together into one person and called him Uncle Remus." After providing students with this background information, ask them to consider the implications of Harris's claims. How does his status as a recorder of folklore change our understanding of him as a writer? Should we read the Remus tales as faithful transcriptions of the stories as their black authors orally constructed them? To what extent might Harris have changed the stories in the act of recording them? Should we understand Uncle Remus as an "authentic" portrait of the African Americans Harris knew? Why might Harris have been invested in claiming this kind of accuracy and authenticity for his work?

QUESTIONS

Comprehension: Which animals are weak and which are strong in the Uncle Remus stories? How does Brer Rabbit succeed in reversing traditional power relations in his encounters with supposedly stronger animals? What qualities enable Brer Rabbit's success?

Comprehension: Examine the frame narratives surrounding the animal fables (in a story that describes the conditions of its own

Black English	Examples	Sentences to have students transcribe in Standard English
Predominantly active sentences with a reiteration of the subject	Brer Rabbit say he can't walk. Brer Fox say he tote 'im. Brer Rabbit say how? Brer Fox say in his arms.	Brer Rabbit come prancin' 'long twel he spy de Tar-Baby, en den he fotch up on his behime legs like he wuz 'stonished. De Tar-Baby, she sot dar, she did, en Brer Fox, he lay low.
Use of plural –s in addition to other plural markers	mens	Den one er de chilluns runned away fum de quarters one day, en died de nex' week.
Verb "to be": "is" and "are" exchanged or linking verb "to be" omitted altogether. Use of "ain't" for "isn't" or "aren't"	**Is** you deaf? W'at you doin' dar? Tar-Baby **ain't** sayin' nothin'.	"Youer stuck up, dat's w'at you is," says Brer Rabbit.
Tense indicated by context rather than verb endings ("ed" or "s" dropped)	Some say Jedge B'ar **come** 'long en loosed 'im.	Brer Rabbit say he can't walk. Brer Fox say he tote 'im. Brer Rabbit say how? Brer Fox say in his arms.
"th" is replaced by "t" or "d"	How you come on, **den**?	W'at you doin' dar, Settin' in de cornder Smokin' yo' seegyar?
"ng" is replaced by "n" at the end of words	I hear Miss Sally **callin'**.	Tu'n me loose, fo' I kick de natal stuffin' outen you.
Geneva Smitherman identifies different meanings for the term "nigger": 1. affection or endearment; 2. culturally Black, identifying with and sharing the values of Black people, as opposed to "African American," which has a more middle-class connotation; 3. expression of disapproval for a person's actions; 4. identifying Black folks—period	Now ef dey's an'thing a nigger lub, nex' ter 'possum, en chik'n, en watermillyums, it's scuppernon's.	I wouldn' spec' fer you ter b'lieve me 'less you know all 'bout de fac's. But ef you en young miss dere doan' min' list'n'in' ter a ole nigger run on a minute er two while you er restin', I kin 'splain to yer how it all happen.

Sources:
Mike Daley, "Black English and Rap Music," York University (May 14, 1998) <www.finearts.yorku.ca/mdaley/blackenglish.html>.
Geneva Smitherman, *Black Talk: Words and Phrases from the Hood to the Amen Corner* (Boston: Houghton Mifflin, 1994).

telling, the portion that sets up the "story within the story" is called the frame narrative). How is Uncle Remus portrayed? What is his relationship to the boy and the boy's family? How does Uncle Remus assert control over the stories and authority over the boy on occasion?

Context: Compare Harris's representation of Uncle Remus and his trickster stories to Charles Chesnutt's Uncle Julius in "The Goophered Grapevine." How are these portraits of African American storytellers different from one another? How do the trickster tales narrated by each of the "Uncles" compare? How do Chesnutt's accounts of Uncle Julius's history and motives complicate our understanding of "The Goophered Grapevine"?

Exploration: Stories about Brer Rabbit and his fellow animals have continued to entertain American readers—adults and children alike—through the twentieth century. Books featuring Uncle Remus have continued to sell well, and in 1946 Disney produced *Song of the South*, an animated feature film about the characters that populate the Uncle Remus stories (despite criticisms of the film's racial insensitivity, Disney re-released *Song of the South* as recently as 1986). Why do you think these stories and images have remained so popular? How might their significance to white and black audiences have changed over time?

Sarah Orne Jewett (1849–1909)

Sarah Orne Jewett's evocative sketches of village life in nineteenth-century Maine have earned her a place among the most important practitioners of American regional writing. Born in South Berwick, Maine, Jewett grew up steeped in the idioms and atmosphere of coastal New England. Her early experiences accompanying her father, a rural doctor, on house calls provided her with insight into the daily lives of the people who would eventually populate her fiction. Jewett's father encouraged her writing aspirations and instilled in her his taste for realistic description and restrained narration—qualities that characterized Jewett's best work.

As early as her teens, Jewett began writing and publishing fiction and poetry, placing one of her stories in the influential literary magazine the *Atlantic Monthly*. In 1877 she published *Deephaven*, her first book-length collection, and followed up on its success with several other collections of stories, four novels, and some children's literature. While Jewett's novels were well received, critics generally agree that her short fiction represents her most important literary accomplishment. In *The White Heron* (a collection of stories published in 1886) and especially in *The Country of the Pointed Firs* (1896), Jewett employed the flexible narrative structure of the "sketch" and the short story to create sensitive, realistic depictions of specific characters, customs, and places. The genre of the sketch—less formal than a novel and less dependent on traditional conventions of plotting and structure—enabled her to experiment with narrative form to compelling effect. Her masterpiece, *The Country of the Pointed Firs*, is a loosely

[9066] Joseph John Kirkbride, *Panorama of Mooseriver Village* (c. 1884–91), courtesy of the Library of Congress [LC-USZ62-61485].

linked collection of sketches unified by its narrator, a somewhat detached, cultured summer visitor to rural Maine.

Beginning in the late 1870s, Jewett found support and inspiration from an influential circle of New England women writers and artists. Her most important bond was with Annie Fields, the wife of prominent publisher James T. Fields. After her husband's death, Annie Fields began an intense, exclusive relationship with Jewett that endured until Jewett's death. In the nineteenth century, this kind of long-term union between two women who lived together was referred to as a **Boston marriage**. The two women regularly traveled together and spent much of every year living together in Fields's homes in Boston and on the New England shore. In recent years, literary critics and historians have become very interested in the nature of Jewett's and Fields's deep commitment to one another. While the question of whether or not their relationship was a sexual one has never been resolved, it is clear that the two women drew companionship and support from their mutual bond.

In 1901, Jewett received an honorary doctorate from Bowdoin College, her father's alma mater. The next year, she was seriously hurt in a carriage accident, sustaining injuries to her head and spine that left her unable to write. Eight years later she died in South Berwick, in the home in which she was born.

[5274] Arnold Genthe, *Sarah Orne Jewett* (n.d.), courtesy of the Library of Congress, Arnold Genthe Collection [LC-G4085-0430].

TEACHING TIPS

■ Sarah Orne Jewett had a deep interest in the occult, a theme that arises in "The Foreigner." Ask students to think about the role of the "other-worldly" in this story. Why does Jewett include the ending she does? How does it affect Mrs. Todd? How does it affect the narrator? How does the occult event serve to bind together women in the story? What is the relationship between Jewett's commitment to realistic depiction and her interest in the occult? Refer students to the contextual material featured in "The Spirit Is Willing: The Occult and Women in the Nineteenth Century" in Unit 6. Ask them to think about how this story relates to the experiences of the Fox sisters.

■ Jewett once told an editor who urged her to write a novel that she did not think she was capable of managing the narrative structure of a long work: "But I don't believe I could write a long story as you . . . advise me in this last letter. The story would have no plot. I could write you entertaining letters perhaps, from some desirable house where I was in most charming company, but I couldn't make a story about it." After you give students this background information, ask them how fair Jewett's self-deprecating analysis is to her ability to structure narrative. How do her stories challenge conventional plot structures? Do her plots move in a linear fashion? How does information come out? How are characters developed? How does she use the short story to experiment with narrative form?

QUESTIONS

Comprehension: In the story "The White Heron," how does Sylvia relate to her rural environment and to the animals—both wild and domestic—that she encounters within it? How is her relationship to wildlife different from the ornithologist's? Why does she ultimately decide not to tell him about the white heron?

Comprehension: "The Foreigner" tells the story of Mrs. Tolland, a foreign woman brought to Maine by her sea captain husband. When he dies at sea, she is left alone, living in the captain's house, in a community that continues to treat her as an outsider. What kinds of relationships do the characters in "The Foreigner" have to the objects in the Tollands' house? What objects are important to Mrs. Tolland? How does Mrs. Todd feel about the house? What attitude does Uncle Lorenzo take toward the house and its contents?

Context: "The Foreigner" contains numerous frames and distancing devices: the narrator recounts Mrs. Todd's story, while Mrs. Todd recounts both events that happened to her directly and events that she heard about from other people or through hearsay and gossip. What is the effect of this multiplicity of frames around the tale of Mrs. Tolland and her life and death? What links the various layers of the story together? Why do you think so many authors who wrote in the realist genre and experimented with dialect relied on frame narratives (Harris and Chesnutt, for example)?

Exploration: How do Jewett's depictions of New England characters and their values compare to other, earlier authors' interest in the same subject matter (Nathaniel Hawthorne, Catherine Maria Sedgwick, or Harriet Beecher Stowe, for example)?

Kate Chopin (1851–1904)

Writing at the end of the nineteenth century at the height of the popularity of "local color" fiction, Kate Chopin introduced American readers to a new fictional setting with her evocations of the diverse culture of Cajun and Creole Louisiana. But while much of Chopin's work falls into the category of **regionalism,** her stories and especially her novel, *The Awakening*, are also notable for their introduction of controversial subjects like women's sexuality, divorce, extramarital sex, and miscegenation.

Kate Chopin was born in St. Louis, Missouri, to a socially prominent, financially secure family. Her mother, Eliza Faris, descended from French Creole ancestors, and her father, Thomas O'Flaherty, was an Irish immigrant who had made his fortune as a merchant in St. Louis. Chopin learned to speak both French and English in her home and was sent to Catholic school. At the age of nineteen she married Oscar Chopin, a French Creole from a Louisiana planter family. After a glamorous European honeymoon, the couple settled in New Orleans, where Oscar went into business as a cotton broker and Kate became active in the city's social life. Her fluency in French and southern sympathies ensured that she fit easily into New Orleans society.

When the cotton brokerage business failed in 1879, the Chopins relocated to Natchitoches Parish in rural Louisiana, where they intended to operate one of Oscar's father's cotton plantations. But by 1883 Oscar Chopin had died of swamp fever, leaving Kate Chopin a thirty-two-year-old widow with six children to support and limited financial resources. After running the plantation on her own for a year, Chopin returned to St. Louis, where she moved into her mother's house and began writing poetry and short stories. Drawing on her experiences in New Orleans and Natchitoches, Chopin created realistic depictions of the distinctive customs of the region and captured the cadences and diction of Louisiana speech in her dialogue. By 1893, she had published her first novel, *At Fault*, and placed stories in such prestigious venues as the *Atlantic Monthly*, *Vogue*, and *Century*. In 1894 she published an extremely successful collection of short stories, *Bayou Folk*, and followed it up with another volume of stories about Louisiana entitled *A Night in Acadie*.

While her stories have been praised and frequently anthologized since their publication in the 1890s, critics today generally agree that Chopin's masterpiece is her 1899 novel, *The Awakening*. Taking up Chopin's recurring theme of the conflict between social constraints placed on women and their desire for independence, the novel tells the story of Edna Pontellier, a Creole woman who gradually awakens to her own dissatisfaction with her identity as a wife and mother. Focusing on her own needs and desires, Edna daringly flouts social conventions by moving out of her husband's house and entering into an adulterous affair. Due to its controversial subject matter and its sympathetic portrayal of its unconventional heroine, the novel provoked hostile reviews from critics who dismissed it as "trite and sordid" or even "perverse" and "vulgar." While Chopin did not completely abandon her writing career in the wake of *The Awakening*'s harsh reception, she was upset by the criticism and her literary output diminished. She died five years later of a cerebral hemorrhage. *The Awakening* sold poorly in its own day and was largely ignored until the mid-twentieth century, when it was recognized as a masterpiece of feminist and realist literature.

[2582] Thomas Anshutz, *A Rose* (1907), courtesy of the Metropolitan Museum of Art, Marguerite and Frank Cosgrove, Jr. Fund, 1993 (1993.324). Photograph © 1994 The Metropolitan Museum of Art.

TEACHING TIPS

■ Kate Chopin habitually wrote her stories and novels while sitting in the living room, surrounded by the noise of her busy household and subject to the demands of her six children. She wrote only one or two days a week and composed most of her stories in a single sitting without revision. She said of her own writing, "I am completely at the mercy of unconscious selection. To such an extent is this true, that what is called the polishing up process has always proved disastrous to my work, and I avoid it, preferring the integrity of crudities to artificialities." Ask students to consider what kinds of aesthetic values underwrite this description of a writer at work. Why was Chopin invested in presenting herself as someone who never revised? Why might she assume that readers would appreciate "crudities" over "artificialities"?

[2576] William Merritt Chase, *At the Seaside* (1892), courtesy of the Metropolitan Museum of Art. Kate Chopin evokes the symbolic landscape of the sea at the end of *The Awakening*. Chopin's protagonist finds considerable oppression in the forced camaraderie of female socialization, but a freeing independence in the solitary ocean.

[2582] Thomas Anshutz, *A Rose* (1907), courtesy of the Metropolitan Museum of Art, Marguerite and Frank A. Cosgrove, Jr. Fund, 1993 (1993.324). Photograph © 1994 The Metropolitan Museum of Art. Anshutz, a student of painter Thomas Eakins, was known for his unconventional subject matter, but here he uses his photographic clarity to make a fashionable portrait. The pose of the sitter reflects the sense that Anshutz has captured an informal, fleeting moment. It is this same attention to the emotional resonances of daily life that fills Chopin's *The Awakening*.

[4101] Anonymous, *Kate Chopin house* (c. 1883), courtesy of Northwestern University. Chopin wrote her stories and novels amidst the hustle and bustle of her living room, frequently interrupted by her six children.

[4106] Anonymous, *Kate Chopin with children* (c. 1878), courtesy of Northwestern University. Photograph of Chopin with four of her six children. Widowed at thirty-two, Chopin wrote poetry, stories, and novels to support her family.

[6094] Anonymous, *Frances Benjamin Johnston, full-length portrait, standing at edge of ocean in bathing suit, with left hand on boat, facing right* (1880), courtesy of the Library of Congress [LC-USZ62-120445]. Bathing was a popular fin de siècle pursuit, whether in the ocean or in mineral springs. Bathing costumes protected women's modesty.

[8521] Kate Chopin, "Désirée's Baby" (1893), courtesy of 4Literature.net. In this story Chopin addresses the question of miscegenation and the legacy of slavery in the South.

■ Chopin's original title for *The Awakening* was "The Solitary Soul." Ask students which title they prefer. Why might Chopin have changed the title? What different ideas does each title suggest about the novel's heroine and about her suicide?

Comprehension: How does Edna rebel against social conventions in *The Awakening*? How does her rebellion begin? Which of her actions seem most shocking to her community?

Context: Examine the nineteenth-century designs for bathing costumes and beach dresses featured in the archive. What kinds of attitudes toward women's bodies and women's athletic pursuits do these costumes reveal? How do these images affect your understanding of Edna's decision to swim naked into the Gulf at the end of *The Awakening*?

Context: As its subtitle indicates, the short story "The Storm" functions as a sequel to "At the 'Cadian Ball," offering a glimpse of the characters' lives several years after the action of the first story. How do the events of "The Storm" complicate the resolution of "At the 'Cadian Ball"? How are we meant to understand the final line, "So the storm passed and every one was happy"? Why do you think Chopin never submitted this story for publication?

Exploration: Literary critics disagree about how to interpret the meaning of Edna's suicide at the end of *The Awakening*. While some take the ending of the novel as an affirmation of Edna's strength and independence, others see it as psychologically out of character for Edna or as the pathetic act of a hopeless, defeated woman. How do you understand the ending of the novel? How does Chopin's representation of suicide resonate with descriptions of suicides or suicide attempts in later feminist American literature (by Dorothy Parker, Sylvia Plath, Anne Sexton, or Susanna Kaysen, for example)? You might refer to Anne Sexton's poem to Sylvia Plath, "Sylvia's Death," in particular.

Mary E. Wilkins Freeman (1852–1930)

In composing her well-received realist depictions of women's lives in New England villages, Mary E. Wilkins Freeman wrote about the people and places she had known all her life. Born in Randolph, Massachusetts, Freeman grew up in intimate familiarity with the economically depressed circumstances and strict Calvinist belief system that shaped the lives of the majority of her characters. At the age of fifteen, Freeman moved with her family to Brattleboro, Vermont, where her father opened a dry goods store in an effort to better their financial situation. After graduating from Brattleboro high school, Freeman spent one year at Mt. Holyoke Female Seminary but did not enjoy college life or living away from home. Returning to Vermont, she faced a series of misfortunes: her teaching career was unsuccessful, her sister died, her father's business failed, and her mother was forced to support the family by working as a housekeeper for the town's minister. Her family's poverty was difficult for Freeman to deal with; she found it particularly humiliating that she had to move into the servants' quarters at the home where her mother worked as a domestic.

In 1883, after both of her parents had died, Freeman moved back to Randolph to live with her childhood friend, Mary Wales. There she developed the writing career she had begun a few years earlier with the publication of some stories and poetry for children. She soon found a ready market for her realist representations of New England life, placing stories in the prestigious *Harper's New Monthly Magazine* and eventually publishing her own book-length collections of stories. Her work was well received by both critics and readers, who were charmed by her focus on a regional lifestyle that was rapidly becoming extinct. Freeman was a prolific writer: over the course of her career she published fifteen volumes of short stories (the work for which she is best known today), over fifty uncollected stories and essays, fourteen novels, three plays, three volumes of poetry, and eight children's books. With Wales's help, Freeman became a shrewd and successful businessperson. Her surviving letters reveal her deep concern with making a living as an author and with maximizing her fees and royalties.

While Freeman's successful career afforded her financial security and a great deal of autonomy, her best fiction focuses on the plight of women whose lives are bounded by poverty and the social constraints imposed on them by their strict religious beliefs and their position as women. Fascinated by the impact of traditional Puritan values of submissiveness, frugality, and self-denial on New England culture, Freeman often portrayed characters who create obstacles to their own happiness by their strict adherence to Calvinist morality. In other stories, however, she explored the rebellions and triumphs of seemingly meek women, depicting their strategies for gaining and maintaining control over their domestic situations with humor and sensitivity. She provided unflinching portraits of both the difficulties of "spinsterhood" and the often oppressive power dynamics that structured nineteenth-century marriage.

Freeman herself married late in life, wedding Dr. Charles Freeman when she was forty-nine. After an initial period of harmony, the marriage ended in separation when she had her husband institutionalized for alcoholism. In 1926 she was awarded the William Dean Howells Gold Medal for Fiction by the American Academy of Letters, and later that year she was inducted into the prestigious National Institute for Arts and Letters.

[1546] *Harper's Weekly*, Eight illustrations depicting a New England farmhouse, courtesy of the Library of Congress [LC-USZ62-102852].

[1546] *Harper's Weekly*, Eight illustrations depicting a New England farmhouse, courtesy of the Library of Congress [LC-USZ62-102852]. These illustrations show a variety of furnishings from a replica New England farmhouse exhibited at the Centennial Exposition of 1876. Spinning wheels, a desk, a clock, and kitchen implements are among the items shown.

[1895] Jerome Thompson, *Recreation* (1857), courtesy of the Fine Arts Museums of San Francisco, Museum Purchase, the M. H. de Young Memorial Museum, 47.13. By the second half of the nineteenth century, the outdoors was increasingly associated with relaxation, particularly for those who could afford leisure time and travel. Better roads and growing railroad systems made travel to suburban areas easier for residents of nearby cities.

[4423] Anonymous, *The First Step* [*Godey's Lady's Book*] (June 1858), courtesy of Hope Greenberg, University of Vermont. The parlor was perceived as a necessary room in even the most humble of homes. When there was no room for a formal parlor, Americans made an effort to adorn their living spaces with decorative objects, such as the paintings and bureau-top items in this drawing.

[8194] Bruce Michelson, Interview: "Women's Regionalist Writing" (2001), courtesy of Annenberg/CPB and *American Passages*. Bruce Michelson, professor of English at the University of Illinois at Urbana-Champaign, speaks about women's regionalist writing.

■ While "The Revolt of 'Mother' " is one of Freeman's most frequently anthologized stories, she herself was dissatisfied with what she viewed as its lack of realism. In an autobiographical essay she explained, "in the first place all fiction ought to be true, and 'The Revolt of "Mother" ' is not in the least true. . . . There never was in New England a woman like Mother. If there had been she most certainly would not have moved into that palatial barn. . . . New England women of that period coincided with their husbands in thinking that sources of wealth should be better housed than consumers." After you give students this background information, ask them to think about Freeman's literary values: Why does she insist that "all fiction ought to be true"? Given her conviction that the events in "The Revolt of 'Mother' " do not meet her realist standards, why did she plot the story around Mother's rebellion? You might ask students to outline what the plot would have looked like had Freeman characterized Mother as a more typical "New England woman of that period," and then have them share their outlines with the class.

■ Recently, scholars of lesbian studies have become interested in Freeman's work and career, examining her long and close relationship with her roommate, Mary Wales; her late and unsuccessful marriage; and her depictions of women who choose solitude or companionship with other women over relationships with men. While close female friendships had been socially acceptable in the late eighteenth and early nineteenth centuries, by the time Freeman wrote exclusive female relationships were undergoing redefinition. With the emergence of lesbian identity—and a new understanding of the sexual possibilities of same-sex relationships—close attachments between women were beginning to be portrayed as "unhealthy" or as a symptom of moral or biological degeneracy. Ask students to consider Freeman's portrayal of marriage and heterosexual romance in light of these issues. How does Freeman critique the power structure of heterosexual relationships? How radical is her position? What kinds of alternatives, if any, does she envision for characters involved in unsatisfying heterosexual unions?

QUESTIONS

Comprehension: In "A New England Nun," what kinds of pets does Louisa have? How do their lives symbolically suggest the limits of Louisa's own existence?

Context: Why are Mother and Nancy dissatisfied with their home in "The Revolt of 'Mother' "? What kinds of improvements do they wish for? How do their visions for their new home coincide with contemporary ideas about home decoration and parlor culture?

Context: In both "A New England Nun" and "The Revolt of 'Mother,' " Freeman narrates women's assertion of control over their own domestic situations. What kinds of strategies do Louisa and Mother employ to gain their ends? How empowering are their "revolts"? Should they be characterized as revolts? How do Freeman's depictions of women exercising domestic authority compare with Chopin's portrait of Edna Pontellier's drive for autonomy in *The Awakening*? Do Louisa or Mother experience anything like an "awakening"?

Exploration: Freeman was fascinated by the legacy of Puritanism in New England, explaining that her characters were "the descendants of the Massachusetts Bay Colonists, in whom can still be seen traces of will and conscience, so strong as to be almost exaggerations and deformities, which characterized their ancestors." How do Freeman's characters compare to the Puritans featured in Unit 3 (John Winthrop, Anne Bradsteet, or Mary Rowlandson, for example)? How do the scruples and morals that motivate Freeman's characters' actions resonate with Puritan values?

Charles W. Chesnutt (1858–1932)

Charles W. Chesnutt was a pioneer among African American fiction writers, addressing controversial issues of race in a realist style that commanded the attention and respect of the white literary establishment of the late nineteenth century. Born in Cleveland, Ohio, Chesnutt was the son of free parents who had moved north before the Civil War. During Reconstruction, the family returned to North Carolina and Chesnutt was raised among rural African Americans. His family's financial difficulties led him to take a job as a teacher while he was still a teenager. Building on his studious habits and intellectual curiosity, he eventually rose to the position of principal of the Fayetteville State Normal School for Negroes. In 1883, Chesnutt sought broader opportunities in the North, relocating to Cleveland and working as a clerk for a railway company while he studied law. He soon passed the state bar examination and founded his own successful practice as a court reporter.

Chesnutt first received national recognition as a writer in 1887, when his story "The Goophered Grapevine" appeared in the prestigious *Atlantic Monthly*. Narrated by an old black man named "Uncle Julius," written in African American dialect, and set in the rural South, the story seemed to have affinities with the regional folktales popularized by Joel Chandler Harris. But Chesnutt's Uncle Julius is a unique figure in nineteenth-century vernacular literature: he recounts plantation stories not out of sentimental nostalgia but in order to manipulate his white listeners to his own ends. The subversive humor and irony of Chesnutt's Uncle Julius stories subtly satirize nineteenth-century white people's condescending stereotypes of African Americans. Chesnutt soon negotiated a contract with Houghton Mifflin to publish a book-length collection of his stories, *The Conjure Woman*, which appeared in 1899. A second book, *"The Wife of His Youth" and Other Stories of the Color Line*, included stories which explore both urban and rural characters' experiences with race. Chesnutt followed this collection with a biography of Frederick Douglass and a series of novels that treat the plight of mixed-race people and social tensions in the South. Unfortunately, his novels never

[4112] Anonymous, *Two women hulling rice, Sapelo Island, Georgia* (c. 1900), courtesy of the Georgia Department of Archives and History.

[4112] Anonymous, *Two women hulling rice, Sapelo Island, Georgia* (c. 1900), courtesy of the Georgia Department of Archives and History. Technological advancements were slow to arrive in many parts of the country, particularly in the less industrialized South. Here, two African American women use a traditional mortar and pestle to remove the hulls from rice.

[4261] Anonymous, *Charles Chesnutt [portrait]* (1939), courtesy of Fisk University. Photograph of Charles W. Chesnutt, a pioneer African American author. Written in African American dialect, his "Uncle Julius" stories are similar to regional folktales popularized by white author Joel Chandler Harris. Chesnutt's work, however, intentionally and subtly satirized the condescending stereotypes of African Americans during the nineteenth century.

[4268] Anonymous, *Charles Chesnutt study* (1906), courtesy of Fisk University. Charles W. Chesnutt worked as a school principal, a stenographer, and, eventually, a lawyer. The expansion of the magazine industry gave Chesnutt his first opportunity to publish. His works depicted both average southern blacks and those of mixed blood who lived on the color line.

[4269] Anonymous, *Charles Chesnutt* (n.d.), courtesy of Fisk University Library's Special Collections. As a person of mixed race, Chesnutt felt removed from both white and black society. "I am too stuck up for colored folks," he wrote, "and, of course, not recognized by whites." From this distance, Chesnutt explored issues of race within the black community.

[4419] Anonymous, *African Americans in front of piano* (c. 1875–1900), courtesy of the New York Public Library. The values that informed parlor culture—the ability to devote the parlor space to formal display rather than stocking it with furnishings designed for private, daily use—were not limited to the wealthy or the urban in mid-nineteenth-century America.

achieved the popularity or acclaim of his short stories, and, by 1905, Chesnutt had difficulty publishing his work. As a new generation of African American writers produced the innovative literature associated with the Harlem Renaissance, Chesnutt found himself increasingly out of touch with both his black and his white audiences. Despite the decline at the end of his career, Chesnutt's contributions to African American letters were foundational and significant. In recognition of his efforts, the NAACP awarded him the Spingarn Medal in 1928 for his groundbreaking realist representations of the "life and struggle of Americans of Negro descent."

TEACHING TIPS

■ Unlike Joel Chandler Harris, Chesnutt insisted that his renditions of traditional African American folktales were not transcriptions but rather "the fruit of my own imagination." He frequently incorporated elements from his reading of classical Greek and Roman literature into his stories; for instance, in "The Goophered Grapevine," Henry is transformed into a kind of Bacchanalian vineyard figure. Ask students to think about the implications of Chesnutt's "imaginative" additions to traditional African American tales. Why might he have been interested in incorporating classical elements into these stories? Why did he want to be known as a creator of stories rather than as a transcriber of existing folktales? Why might Harris and Chesnutt have had such different approaches to their characterization of themselves as authors?

■ Because his Uncle Julius stories contain a frame narrative from the point of view of a rather condescending white man, many of Chesnutt's early readers probably assumed that the writer was white. In 1899, when he began to write full time, Chesnutt made his own racial identity more public. Ask students to think about the role of the white narrator in the Uncle Julius stories. Why might Chesnutt have adopted this narrative voice? Why might he have eventually felt compelled to publicize his own racial background as the stories became more popular? You might ask students to rewrite the frame narrative of Chesnutt's work so that it is clearly not a white narrator. What would need to be changed? What would get left as is? How does this change the nature of the story?

QUESTIONS

Comprehension: Why does Uncle Julius tell the white narrator the story of the "goophered" vineyard? What effect does the story have on the narrator? What do we learn about Julius's relationship to the land and its produce over the course of the tale?

Comprehension: What is the "Blue Vein Society" to which Ryder belongs in "The Wife of His Youth"? How do the Blue Veins participate in the construction of the social "color line" which Chesnutt found so fascinating? What values do the Blue Veins seem to promote among African Americans?

Context: Compare Uncle Julius to Joel Chandler Harris's Uncle Remus. What kinds of relationships do they have with their white auditors? What seems to motivate their storytelling sessions? How do the trickster tales related in Julius's and Remus's stories differ?

Context: Compare Chesnutt's representations of African American dialect to Alexander Posey's representations of the speech of Creek Indians. What characterizes each group's speech patterns? How do the speakers describe and relate to members of their own race? How do the speakers describe and relate to people of other races?

Exploration: Chesnutt was part of an early tradition of preserving traditional folktales and recording folk customs. His representations of African American beliefs about "conjuring" and "hoodoo"—spiritual practices that combined African, Caribbean, and Christian religious traditions—offer important insight into African American culture. How do Chesnutt's representations of "conjuring" relate to later African American writers' interest in these practices? How might Chesnutt have influenced Toni Morrison's interest in the supernatural?

Charles Alexander Eastman (Ohiyesa) (1858–1939)

A Santee Sioux, physician, government agent, and spokesperson for Indian rights, Charles Alexander Eastman was also the first well-known, widely read Native American author. A fully acculturated Indian, Eastman worked to create understanding between Native Americans and European Americans and sometimes found himself in the conflicted position of being caught between the two cultures. His writing resonates with his efforts both to make Indian traditions accessible to a white audience and to define his own identity as an Indian and as an American.

Eastman was separated from his parents at an early age when their tribe fled to Canada after the ill-fated Minnesota Dakota conflict. His father, Many Lightnings, was presumed dead so Eastman was given a traditional Sioux upbringing by his uncle and his grandmother. In 1869, however, Eastman found out that his father was not dead but had in fact changed his name to Jacob Eastman, adopted Euro-American customs, and converted to Christianity. Changing his son's name from Ohiyesa to Charles Alexander, Jacob Eastman took the boy from the Sioux community in Canada and raised him on a farm in South Dakota. With his father's encouragement, Eastman received a Euro-American education and eventually earned a degree from Dartmouth and an M.D. from Boston University.

In 1890 Eastman accepted what would be the first of many positions with the U.S. government, becoming an agency physician at the Sioux reservation in Pine Ridge, South Dakota. There he witnessed the aftermath of the tragic massacre at Wounded Knee, in which many

[1089] John S. (Jack) Coldwell, Jr., *U.S. allotting surveyor and his interpreter making an American citizen of Chief American Horse, Oglala Sioux* (c. 1907), courtesy of the Denver Public Library, Western History Department.

[1061] Anonymous, *Young-Man-Afraid-of-His-Horses (Tashun-Kakokipa), Oglala Sioux; standing in front of his lodge, Pine Ridge, South Dakota* (1891), courtesy of the National Archives and Records Administration (NARA), Still Picture Branch. Young-Man-Afraid-of-His-Horses initially resisted white encroachment into Lakota lands. In the late 1870s, realizing that the survival of his people was at stake, he became a friend to the whites and the president of the Pine Ridge Indian Council.

[1089] John S. (Jack) Coldwell, Jr., *U.S. allotting surveyor and his interpreter making an American citizen of Chief American Horse, Oglala Sioux* (c. 1907), courtesy of the Denver Public Library, Western History Department. According to the U.S. government and the Dawes Severalty Act of 1887, assimilation, or cultural conversion to European American ways of life, was the "ideal" goal for Native Americans. For some, compliance with U.S. policies meant the privileges of citizenship. But it was not until 1924 that the United States officially granted all Native Americans U.S. citizenship.

[1843] J. N. Choate, *Sioux boys as they were dressed on arrival at the Carlisle Indian School, Pennsylvania, 10/5/1879* (1879), courtesy of the National Archives and Records Administration (NARA), Still Pictures Branch. The mission of the Carlisle Indian School was to rid Indian children of their traditional ways and to "civilize" them for assimilation into white culture.

[4219] Western Photograph Company, *Gathering up the dead at the battlefield of Wounded Knee, South Dakota* (1891), courtesy of the Smithsonian Institution. U.S. soldiers standing in front of a wagon full of dead Sioux. A blizzard delayed the burial of the dead. Eventually the Sioux were buried in a mass grave, with little effort made to identify the bodies.

[7418] Anonymous, *Boy's moccasins, Lakotah* (n.d.), courtesy of the New York State Historical Association, Thaw Collection. Reservation period (post-1880) beadwork on these dress moccasins shows how the American flag

Sioux who had participated in the Ghost Dance religion were killed or injured in a raid by the U.S. Army. While at Pine Ridge, Eastman met and married Elaine Goodale, a reservation teacher and social worker. The couple soon relocated to St. Paul, Minnesota, where Eastman practiced medicine and eventually held other government jobs, at one point heading a federal project to give Anglicized surnames to Sioux Indians. In the early twentieth century, Eastman also helped establish the "scouting movement" in the United States, infusing the Boy Scouts and Girl Scouts with his interpretations of Native American culture.

With his wife's substantial editorial assistance, Eastman embarked on a successful literary career in 1900. His account of his traditional Sioux childhood, *Indian Boyhood*, was an enormous success and was reprinted at least ten times within his lifetime. He also published several collections of traditional Sioux lore and history, making traditional Native American animal tales accessible to a white audience. He advanced his interpretations of Indian spirituality and culture in *The Soul of the Indian* and *The Indian Today*. His moving autobiography, *From the Deep Woods to Civilization*, chronicles his experiences in the "white world" and among the Sioux at Pine Ridge. In 1921 Eastman separated from his wife, who, according to many scholars, had a significant role in the writing and editing of his work. He did not publish again in his lifetime. Although he continued to lecture and occasionally became involved in various Indian causes, Eastman spent most of the end of his life in seclusion in a remote cabin in Ontario.

TEACHING TIPS

■ In Chapters VI and VII of *From the Deep Woods to Civilization*, Eastman narrates the development of the **Ghost Dance** religion among the Sioux. Explain to your students that the Ghost Dance was a Native American response to Euro-American encroachments on their land and way of life. A powerful apocalyptic vision of the overthrow of white domination and a return to traditional Native American ways, the Ghost Dance sparked a pan-Indian, intertribal movement that frightened white authorities with its intensity. Started by the Paiute prophet Wovoka, who believed himself to be a Messianic figure, the Ghost Dance involved adopting traditional clothing and customs, singing and chanting traditional songs, and participating in a trance-inducing round dance designed to inspire dead Indian ancestors to return and reclaim their land. The movement ended tragically when white authorities killed 150 Sioux men, women, and children at Wounded Knee for their involvement in the Ghost Dance religion. After you give students this background information, ask them to evaluate Eastman's account of the Ghost Dance and the massacre at Wounded Knee. With whom are his sympathies? How does he portray the development of the Ghost Dance? How does he portray the massacre at Wounded Knee? What is his own relationship to the movement?

■ In the opening sentences of Chapter VI, Eastman explains his own, somewhat liminal position on the Pine Ridge Agency: "In

1890 a 'white doctor' who was also an Indian was something of a novelty." Ask students to analyze Eastman's characterization of his own identity. Why does he describe himself as a "white" doctor? Why does he put quotation marks around the word "white"? What problems are inherent in perceiving himself as simultaneously "white" and "also an Indian"?

QUESTIONS

Comprehension: What is Eastman's relationship to the other Sioux Indians at the Pine Ridge Agency? What kinds of distinctions does he perceive among the various Indians he encounters there? How do his education and upbringing set him apart? What kind of relationship does he have with non-Indian authorities at the Agency?

Comprehension: What was the Ghost Dance religion? How does Eastman represent it in his autobiography?

Context: Read Eastman's representation of the traditional Sioux tale "Turtle Story," featured in the archive. How does Smoky Day, the wise Indian narrator of the story, compare to Joel Chandler Harris's Uncle Remus? How does the tale itself compare to Uncle Remus's stories? What kinds of skills does the turtle rely on? How does he compare to the animal figures in the Remus stories?

Exploration: Eastman helped establish the Boy Scouts and Girl Scouts of America, establishing summer camps that he advertised as directed by a "real Indian" and publishing "Scout Books" on such topics as how to make tepees and canoes. He seemed invested in providing white children with "Indian" experiences in the outdoors. Why might Eastman have been interested in transmitting his interpretation of Native American culture in this way? How effective do you think the scouting movement has been in educating Euro-American children about Native American customs? Where do you see similar kinds of interest in (and commodification of) Indian culture at work in American society today?

Alexander Posey (1873–1908)

Alexander Posey recorded his insights into Creek Indian tribal politics and Native American customs in his poetry, journalism, and political satire. He lived through a crucial period in the history of the Creek Nation, when the tribe's land base and political autonomy were threatened by "progressive" reforms intended to force Indians to assimilate to Euro-American culture. The creation of the state of Oklahoma in the early twentieth century also significantly impacted the Creeks: fierce debates raged about whether to admit Oklahoma as a single state or whether to organize part of its territory into a separate Indian state. Posey registered these conflicts in his sharp and often satirical writing, in the process creating a unique record of both Native American politics and Native American literary developments. His interest in accurately representing the dialect and speech patterns of his Creek characters has made his work an important chronicle of his

motif was incorporated into Native American design.

[8507] Charles Eastman, "Turtle Story" (1909), courtesy of *Wigwam Evenings, Sioux Folk Tales*. This collection of Sioux tales by Eastman and his wife, Elaine Goodale Eastman, contains twenty-seven Sioux narratives, including creation stories and animal legends.

[5168] Russell Lee, *Street scene, Muskogee, Oklahoma* (1939), courtesy of the Library of Congress [LC-USF33-012332-M3 DLC].

own time and a source of inspiration for subsequent Native American writers.

Posey was born into a bicultural and bilingual family: his mother was a Creek Indian and his father was a white man who had been raised in the Creek community. He grew up learning to appreciate both Native American and Euro-American traditions and benefited from a traditional western education at the Bacone Indian University in Muskogee. It was at Bacone that Posey began composing poetry, most of which is heavily influenced by the British and American Romantic tradition. While some scholars see Posey's poetry as derivative and constrained by European traditions, others point out that the Romantic worldview that pervades his work in some ways coincides with traditional Indian beliefs. Like the Romantics, many Native American cultures are committed to a respect for nature, a belief in the interrelation of all things, and a refusal to impose a sharp division between the material and the spiritual.

After leaving Bacone in 1895, Posey was elected to the lower chamber of the Creek National Council and embarked on a long career of public service as an administrator to tribal schools. In 1902, he also began serving his community as a journalist, establishing the Eufaula *Indian Journal*, the first daily newspaper published by an Indian. As editor of the paper, Posey composed the works for which he is best known today: the Fus Fixico letters. Narrated by a Creek character named Fus Fixico (which translates as either "Warrior Bird" or "Heartless Bird"), the letters offer humorous political and cultural commentary written from the perspective and in the dialect of Indian speakers. Revolving around the conversations of four men—and usually centering on the monologues of Hotgun Harjo, a medicine man— the letters narrate Indian responses to political issues and lampoon the corruption that was rampant in Indian Territory. Posey's tendency to parody the names of Euro-American political figures with clever puns—"Rooster Feather" for President Roosevelt, "Itscocked" for Secretary of the Interior Ethan Allen Hitchcock—deflates the power of these public figures and critiques their pretensions to authority. The Fus Fixico letters do not always correspond to Posey's own convictions or political positions; instead, they offer a variety of perspectives on the difficult issues that faced the Creeks in his time. Tragically, Posey died before he was able to completely fulfill the promise of his innovative writing. He drowned at the age of thirty-five when his boat capsized on the North Canadian River.

POSEY WEB ARCHIVE

[1121] Harper's Weekly, *Scenes and Incidents of the Settlement of Oklahoma* [Land Rush pictures] (1889), courtesy of the Library of Congress [LC-USZ62-96521]. These illustrations from *Harper's Weekly*, May 18, 1889, are titled (from top to bottom): The arrival of the first train at Guthrie—The head of the line outside of the Guthrie land-office on the opening day—The Guthrie post-office.

[5168] Russell Lee, *Street scene, Muskogee, Oklahoma* (1939), courtesy of the Library of Congress [LC-USF33-012332-M3 DLC]. Alexander Posey

TEACHING TIPS

■ In a commencement address that he delivered at Bacone University, Posey celebrated the achievements of Sequoyah, the Cherokee who created a **syllabary** that enabled his tribe to record its language in written form. Later, Posey wrote one of his most famous poems, "Ode to Sequoyah," on the same subject. Have your students read "Ode to Sequoyah" out loud. Ask them to think about why Posey might have identified with Sequoyah. What is the role of writing in Indian culture, according to Posey? What is the relationship between Posey's representations of Indian dialect and Sequoyah's creation of a syllabary for the Cherokee language? You may want to define the ode, a subgenre of the lyric, for students. An ode (from the Greek *aeidein*, to sing, chant) is more than a poem that celebrates an occasion or individual; it is a poem that celebrates language and investigates its power to combat mortality and the ravages of time. Why is the form of the ode, then, an appropriate one for discussing Sequoyah? You may want to have students compare Posey's poem to classic odes such as John Keats's "Ode to a Grecian Urn" or Shelley's "Ode to the West Wind."

■ Although the Fus Fixico letters (found in the archive) were sometimes reprinted in Anglo newspapers like the *Kansas City Star* and Posey was frequently asked to contribute to larger, national newspapers, he generally confined his publication to the *Indian Journal*. Ask students to consider why Posey was not interested in syndicating his work to a larger audience. How might nineteenth-century white Americans have responded to the Fus Fixico letters? How might they have responded to Posey's representations of Indian dialect? Why might Posey have been invested in keeping his work specific to his local community?

QUESTIONS

Comprehension: How is the poem "Hotgun on the Death of Yadeka Harjo" different from Posey's other poetry? What is the role of dialect in this poem? How does the use of dialect affect the meter and rhyme scheme? How does the use of dialect impact the poem's status as an elegy (that is, a poem written as a memorial to someone who has died)?

Comprehension: What proper names appear in the Fus Fixico letters? Whose names are most frequently turned into puns?

Context: Both Posey and Joel Chandler Harris published their dialect stories in the form of newspaper columns. Why do you think dialect pieces were so popular with newspaper readers? What do the Fus Fixico letters have in common with Harris's Uncle Remus stories? How are they different? What kinds of audiences were Posey and Harris writing for?

Exploration: How might Posey's work have influenced subsequent Native American writers like N. Scott Momaday, Louise Erdrich, and Leslie Marmon Silko? Do you see a relationship between Posey's depiction of Indian language patterns and metaphors and these later writers' development of a Native American style?

Zitkala-Ša (Gertrude Simmons Bonnin) (1876–1938)

Writer, musician, educator, and Indian rights activist, Zitkala-Ša (or Red Bird) was born on the Sioux Pine Ridge Reservation in South

attended the Bacone Indian University in Muskogee. In his life as in his writing, Posey confronted the forms and traditions of European American culture while commenting on the difficult social and political issues facing the Creek Indians.

[5569] Anonymous, *Indian teams hauling 60 miles to market the 1100 bushels of wheat raised by the school* (c. 1900), courtesy of the National Archives and Records Administration [NWDNS-75-SE-39A]. Government attempts to "civilize" or assimilate Native Americans included the use of boarding schools and model colonies where Indians could learn farming or manufacturing techniques. This photo is from the Seger Colony in the Oklahoma Territory.

[6823] F. W. Greenough, *Se-Quo-Yah [Sequoyah]* (c. 1836), courtesy of the Library of Congress, Prints and Photographs Division [LC-USZC4-4815]. Half-length portrait of Sequoyah, dressed in a blue robe, holding a tablet that shows the Cherokee alphabet. Sequoyah developed a Cherokee syllabary that enabled his people to write in their own language.

[8508] Alexander Posey, "Ode to Sequoyah" (1910), courtesy of the Library of Congress [10022763]. Posey dedicated this ode to Sequoyah, the Cherokee who created a syllabary that enabled his tribe to record its language in written form. An ode (from the Greek *aeidein*, to sing, chant) is a poem that celebrates language and investigates its power to combat mortality and the ravages of time.

[9068] Alexander Posey, Letter 16 of the Fus Fixico letters (1903), courtesy of the Reed College Library. Posey offers humorous political and social commentary from a Native American perspective through the characters in his Fus Fixico Letters. In letter 16, Fus Fixico satirizes the policies of the Roosevelt Administration.

[9069] Alexander Posey, Letter 18 of the Fus Fixico letters (1903), courtesy of the Reed College Library. In letter 18, Fus Fixico comments on U.S. Indian policy and the propaganda that supported it. Fus Fixico uses humor to address governmental policies that essentially stripped Native Americans of their cultural heritage.

Dakota. After her white father abandoned the family, she was brought up by her Indian mother in traditional Sioux ways. At the age of eight, Zitkala-Ša's life was transformed when white missionaries came to Pine Ridge and convinced her to enroll in a boarding school in Wabash, Indiana. Part of a movement to "civilize" Indian children by removing them from their native culture and indoctrinating them in Euro-American ways, the school trained Indian pupils in manual labor, Christianity, and the English language. Zitkala-Ša found it a hostile environment and struggled to adapt.

After three years at school, Zitkala-Ša returned to Pine Ridge only to find herself estranged from her traditional culture and from her mother. While she was not completely comfortable with the Euro-American culture she encountered at school, she was also no longer at home with Sioux customs. She returned to school and eventually received scholarships to Earlham College in Indiana and to the New England Conservatory of Music to study violin. After completing her studies she became a music teacher at the Carlisle Indian School in Pennsylvania.

Frustrated by her position on the margins of both Indian and white culture and increasingly outraged by the injustices she saw visited on Native Americans, Zitkala-Ša resolved to express her feelings publicly in writing. Her reflective autobiographical essays on her experiences among the Sioux and in white culture appeared in the prestigious *Atlantic Monthly* in 1900. In these pieces, Zitkala-Ša explored what she called the "problem of her inner self," grappling with the question of her cultural identity and her relationship with her family. She also used the essays as occasions to expose the injustices perpetrated by whites on Native Americans and to critique the insensitivity of white strategies for "civilizing" Indians.

After the publication of the autobiographical essays, Zitkala-Ša composed an Indian opera called *Sun Dance* and compiled collections of traditional Sioux legends and stories that she translated into English. Her outspoken views eventually alienated authorities at the Carlisle School, so she left to work at Standing Rock Reservation. There she met and married Raymond Bonnin, another Sioux activist. Together they became involved in the Society of American Indians, founded the National Council of American Indians, and worked tirelessly on behalf of Native American causes. Zitkala-Ša died in Washington, D.C., and was buried in Arlington Cemetery.

[1801] J. N. Choate, *Group of Omaha boys in cadet uniforms, Carlisle Indian School, Pennsylvania* (1880), courtesy of the National Archives and Records Administration [NWDNS-75-IP-1-10].

TEACHING TIPS

■ In the preface to one of her collections of Sioux legends and traditional stories, Zitkala-Ša explained that her goal was to "transplant the native spirit of these tales—root and all—into the English language, since America in the last few centuries has acquired a second tongue." Ask students to consider the implications of "transplanting" stories from one language and culture into another. Why might Zitkala-Ša have chosen this plant metaphor to characterize her translation project? You might also ask them to analyze the role of language and translation in Zitkala-Ša's autobiographical writings. What kinds of problems does she encounter when she is forced to communicate in English at the missionary school? At one point, she describes the school authorities' English speech as creating a "bedlam within which I was securely tied." What kinds of emotional frustrations does her inability to understand or speak English create? How does her eventual success speaking English at a college oratorical contest resonate with these issues?

■ Have your students examine the images of the Indian boarding schools featured in the archive. They could also read Louise Erdrich's poem "Indian Boarding School: The Runaways." Ask your students to write poems or prose reflections on what the boarding school experience would have been like for the different people who lived and worked there (teachers, janitors, students, the people who lived in the town nearby).

QUESTIONS

Comprehension: How does Zitkala-Ša describe the education in traditional Sioux ways that she receives from her mother? What strategies does her mother use to teach her such skills as beadwork? What other values and skills does her mother teach her? How does the education she receives from her mother compare with the education she receives at the mission school? What kinds of discipline does she encounter at school?

Comprehension: As she rides the train on her first trip to school, Zitkala-Ša narrates her feelings about the telegraph poles that she sees out of the train windows: "I was quite breathless on seeing one familiar object. It was the telegraph pole which strode by at short paces. . . . Often I had stopped, on my way down the road, to hold my ear against the pole, and, hearing its low moaning, I used to wonder what the paleface had done to hurt it." Later, she characterizes her own fractured identity in similar terms: "Now a cold bare pole I seemed to be, planted in a strange earth." Why does the image of the telegraph pole recur in Zitkala-Ša's autobiographical essays? What is the significance of this symbol of technological progress and linguistic communication? How does it figure Zitkala-Ša's own concerns with language and with white culture? Why does Zitkala-Ša eventually come to see herself as a "cold bare pole"?

Context: Like fellow Sioux writer Charles Alexander Eastman, Zitkala-Ša found that her Euro-American education left her in a somewhat marginal social position: she did not feel wholly comfortable within white culture, but neither was she completely at home with traditional Sioux customs. How do Zitkala-Ša's efforts to solve the "problem of her inner self," as she puts it, compare to Eastman's attempts to construct a role for himself as a "white doctor" who is also an

ZITKALA-ŠA WEB ARCHIVE

[1056] William S. Soule, *Arapaho camp with buffalo meat drying near Fort Dodge, Kansas* (1870), courtesy of the National Archives and Records Administration (NARA) Still Picture Branch. Parlor culture was not limited to white, upper-class women; less privileged women struggled with the imposition of these values. In her essays, Zitkala-Ša poignantly narrates her Sioux mother's difficulty in making the transition from her traditional dwelling to a Euro-American style cottage.

[1801] J. N. Choate, *Group of Omaha boys in cadet uniforms, Carlisle Indian School, Pennsylvania* (1880), courtesy of the National Archives and Records Administration [NWDNS-75-IP-1-10]. Ten uniformed Omaha boys of various ages pose at the Carlisle Indian School in Carlisle, Pennsylvania. Many schools like Carlisle, which was one of the most famous and where Zitkala-Ša taught, opened in the nineteenth century with the purpose of immersing Native American children in "civilized" European American ways.

[5365] Frances Benjamin Johnston, *Carlisle Indian School* (1901), courtesy of the Library of Congress [LC-USZ62-119133]. Photograph of students at the Carlisle Indian School in Pennsylvania. Poet Marianne Moore taught at the school for four years.

[5810] Unknown, *Zitkala-Ša (Gertrude Bonnin), a Dakota Sioux Indian* (c. 1900), courtesy of the Library of Congress, Prints and Photographs Division [LC-USZ62-119349]. Portrait of Zitkala-Ša, a writer, musician, educator, and Indian rights activist. Much of Zitkala-Ša's work was driven by the injustices she witnessed against Native Americans and the feeling that she lived on the margins of both Indian and white culture.

[5819] Zitkala-Ša, *An Indian Teacher among Indians* (1900), courtesy of Cornell University, *Making of America Digital Collection.* Zitkala-Ša's essays on her experiences among the Sioux and in white culture appeared in the *Atlantic Monthly* in 1900.

[5820] Zitkala-Ša, *Impressions of an Indian Childhood* (1900), courtesy of Cornell University, *Making of America Digital Collection.* Frustrated by her position on the margins of both Indian and white culture and outraged by the injustices she saw visited on Native Americans, Zitkala-Ša resolved to express her feelings publicly in writing.

Indian? What strategies do the two writers adopt to deal with the conflicts they encounter upon returning to the Sioux agency? How are their attitudes toward their roles within traditional Sioux society different? How might gender have impacted their reactions to their status as "educated Indians"?

Exploration: In "The Indian Autobiography: Origins, Type, and Function," literary critic Arnold Krupat argues that American Indian autobiography is a textual equivalent to the frontier; it is "a ground on which two cultures meet." To what extent is this true of the form and content of Zitkala-Ša's writing? How does her work compare to earlier bicultural autobiographical accounts, like those of Mary Rowlandson, William Apess, or Frederick Douglass? How does she draw on and modify the tradition of literary self-making pioneered by these writers? How does her status as a woman and as a Native American impact her narration of her own life?

Suggested Author Pairings

JOEL CHANDLER HARRIS, CHARLES W. CHESNUTT, AND ALEXANDER POSEY

Authors of stories and sketches written in racialized dialect, Harris, Chesnutt, and Posey attempted to capture the rhythms and idioms of African American and Native American English speech. Harris and Chesnutt shared an interest in recording traditional African American folktales, but they created very different characters through which to narrate their stories. While Chesnutt's Uncle Julius on the surface resembles Harris's Uncle Remus—a stereotype of a contented slave anxious to serve and entertain white people—Uncle Julius is actually much more crafty and subversive, and much more skilled in looking out for his own best interest. Race is an important distinction between these authors. Critics sometimes argue that, as a white writer, Harris was not always sensitive to or aware of the cultural implications of the African American stories he recorded. Posey and Chesnutt, on the other hand, were of Native American and African American ancestry, respectively, though they sometimes found that their positions as writers and recorders of the culture distanced them from those communities.

MARK TWAIN AND BRET HARTE

Twain and Harte were humorists and journalists who got their start in the American West and ended up creating archetypal characters in American literature. While Harte's stories have shaped the genre of the Western, Twain created the naïve country boy narrator in *Huckleberry Finn*. Harte's work can be much more sentimental than Twain's, perhaps explaining why he fell out of popular favor as realism gained strength over the course of the century. Twain, on the other hand, remained a best-selling author, a celebrity, and an icon of American literature until his death and long after.

SARAH ORNE JEWETT, MARY E. WILKINS FREEMAN, AND KATE CHOPIN

Authors whose stories and novels participate in the regionalist tradition, Jewett, Freeman, and Chopin all focus on the position of women within the regional settings they so evocatively describe. Jewett and Freeman chronicle the impact of economic depression and lingering Puritan values on communities in rural New England, while Chopin records the French Catholic flavor of life in New Orleans and rural Louisiana. Chopin depicts Louisiana as in some ways less severe and repressed than Jewett and Freeman's New England, and her frank portrayal of women's sexual desire made her work more controversial than theirs. Still, she shares with Jewett and Freeman an interest in the effects of rigid social conventions on both downtrodden and rebellious women.

CHARLES ALEXANDER EASTMAN (OHIYESA) AND ZITKALA-ŠA (GERTRUDE SIMMONS BONNIN)

The fact that these authors are listed under both an Anglicized name and a traditional Native American name is significant, for they are characterized by the tensions created by their attempts to mediate between white and traditional Indian culture. Both Sioux Indians, they attended white boarding schools and colleges and found value in their Euro-American educations even though they were never completely at home in white culture. At the same time, they found that their acculturation into white ways separated them from other Native Americans. Eastman found himself in the awkward position of being a "'white doctor' who was also an Indian," while Zitkala-Ša felt out of place as "neither a wild Indian nor a tame one."

CORE CONTEXTS

The Best Seat in the House: Parlors and the Development of Gentility in Nineteenth-Century America

When Huckleberry Finn meets the rural Grangerford family in the course of his adventures on the Mississippi, he is awed by the grandeur of their house: "I hadn't seen no house out in the country before that was so nice and had so much style. . . . There warn't no bed in the parlor, not a sign of a bed." Huck's naïve description of the Grangerfords' "stylishness" is of course meant to be funny, but Mark Twain's satire of the family's genteel pretensions depends for its humor on his audience's knowledge of what might be called "parlor culture." By the mid-nineteenth century, middle-class Americans had come to believe that the appearance and physical layout of their homes could both express and construct an aura of domestic harmony, social success, and moral rectitude. In particular, the **parlor**—a formal space set aside for social ceremonies such as receiving guests or hosting tea par-

[4076] Anonymous, *Writing at the Quarry farm* [*Mark Twain*] (c. 1871–75), courtesy of the Mark Twain House, Hartford, CT.

ties—came to signify the refinement and comfort of respectable family living. Primarily designed for display rather than use, the parlor was generally the "best room" in the house and usually contained furnishings and knick-knacks that cost more than the objects in the house that were intended for everyday use. The fact that the Grangerfords do not have a bed in their parlor—that is, they can afford to devote the space to formal display rather than stock it with furnishings designed for private, daily use—marks them as genteel and cultured in Huck's eyes.

As Twain's satirical description of the Grangerfords' decorous parlor in backwoods Arkansas makes clear, the values that informed parlor culture were not limited to the wealthy or the urban in mid-nineteenth-century America. As industrialization and mass production made furniture and textiles affordable to even the lower middle classes, Americans everywhere began to create parlors to serve as visual assertions of their sophistication and good taste. Architectural plan books such as S. B. Reed's *House-Plans for Everybody* (1878) offered designs for inexpensive houses that, though small, included front parlors meant to signal respectability and refinement. Plans like the "Design for $600 Cottage" featured in the archive reveal that a parlor was perceived as necessary in even the most humble home. Even Americans whose dwellings were so small that there was no room for a formal parlor made an effort to adorn their living spaces with the decorative objects that were integral to parlor culture, such as the wreath, birdcage, and rocking chair visible in a nineteenth-century photograph of a primitive cabin on the Nebraska plains.

Intended to serve as a buffer zone between the outside world and the private domestic areas of the bedroom and kitchen, the parlor was a semi-public space that both protected people's privacy and publicized their accomplishments. Thick carpets muffled noises, while protective doilies and layers of lace curtains and heavy draperies shielded

the room and its furnishings from bright light and prying eyes. The large-scale, luxuriously upholstered furniture of the ideal "parlor suite" cradled the body even as it controlled posture. But while the parlor was shrouded and protected, it was at the same time designed to open itself to display. Curio cabinets, mantles, and shelves exhibited the photographs and knick-knacks that occupants felt expressed their individuality and good taste. Parlors often contained pianos, handmade artwork, and embroidery stands intended to show off the inhabitants' domestic accomplishments. The effect, though cluttered and oppressive by today's standards, was meant to be simultaneously comfortable and cultured, inviting and impressive.

While some social commentators complained that most parlors went unused—Americans often felt that their parlor furniture was "too good" to actually sit on—homeowners continued to perceive them as important rooms. The parlor could be used for evening parties at which guests would listen to piano performances, sing, or play specially developed "parlor games" such as charades, puzzles, or "Twenty Questions." At Christmastime, the decorated tree would stand in the parlor. Because they were not in constant use, parlors offered a secluded place for young couples to court one another. In Mary E. Wilkins Freeman's short story "The Revolt of 'Mother,'" Mother is particularly frustrated that her daughter, Nancy, is forced to host her fiancé in the family's kitchen because Father is unwilling to spend money on a parlor. Among wealthy city-dwellers, parlors were the location of choice for hosting "callers." The formal ritual of social calling, in which women paid brief visits or left specially designed "calling cards" at the homes of their female acquaintances, persisted into the early twentieth century and thus kept parlor culture alive. The ubiquity and conventionality of social calling is clear in Kate Chopin's novel, *The Awakening*. Edna Pontellier scandalizes her husband and her community when she stops receiving callers or making social visits and instead opts to structure her time according to her own desires.

As Chopin's novel illustrates, parlor culture could seem unappealing, suffocating, and overly regulated. It is significant that Edna's social revolt is enacted through her decision to spend her time in successively more unconventional domestic spaces: she first retreats to her painting studio, then to Mademoiselle Reisz's unfashionable and "dingy" apartment, and eventually takes the radical step of moving out of her husband's formal house and into a small home she calls the "pigeon house." While Edna's rejection of convention is to a certain extent enabled by her wealth, leisure, and social status, less privileged women struggled in their own ways with the imposition of the values of parlor culture. In her autobiographical essays, Zitkala-Ša poignantly narrates her Sioux mother's difficulty in making the transition from living in her traditional tipi to inhabiting a Euro-American style cottage. Never completely comfortable with the curtains and tablecloths in her cabin, Zitkala-Ša's mother continues to cook and perform most of her domestic chores in a nearby canvas tipi. As Zitkala-Ša explains it, "My mother had never gone to school, and though she meant always to give up her own customs for such of the white man's ways as pleased her, she made only compromises." Such "compromises" were, for many, more meaningful acts of self-expression than strict adherence to the norms of parlor culture.

QUESTIONS

Comprehension: What furnishings and objects characterized the ideal parlor? How did some Americans effect compromises with the requirements of parlor culture?

Comprehension: How did most Americans use their parlors? What kinds of domestic activities might have been considered improper in a parlor?

[5770] John C. Grabill, *Home of Mrs. American Horse* (1891), courtesy of the Library of Congress, American Memory, Grabill Collection [LOT 3076-2, no. 3638].

"BEST SEAT IN THE HOUSE" WEB ARCHIVE

[1056] William S. Soule, *Arapaho camp with buffalo meat drying near Fort Dodge, Kansas* (1870), courtesy of the National Archives and Records Administration (NARA) Still Picture Branch. Parlor culture was not limited to white, upper-class women; less privileged women also struggled with the imposition of these values. In her essays, Zitkala-Ša narrates her Sioux mother's difficulty in moving from her traditional dwelling to a European American–style cottage.

[1207] George Harper Houghton, *Family of slaves at the Gaines' house* (1861), courtesy of the Library of Congress [LC-USZC4-4575]. For many slaves, merely having a large enough home on the plantation where they worked proved problematic.

[3609] Anonymous, *Design for $600 Cottage* (1883), courtesy of Cornell University Library. Sketch and floor plan of modest four-room cottage with high, narrow windows and a chimney.

[4076] Unknown, *Writing at the Quarry farm [Mark Twain]* (c. 1871–75), courtesy of the Mark Twain House, Hartford, CT. Photograph of Mark Twain (Samuel Clemens) in a white suit, writing at a small round table in front of a modest fireplace at Quarry Farm. Though Clemens satirized the corruption and genteel conventions of high society, he aspired to higher social status himself.

[4423] Anonymous, *The First Step [Godey's Lady's Book]* (June 1858), courtesy of Hope Greenberg, University of Vermont. These homespun Americans might be the characters in Royall Tyler's *The Contrast*. The parlor was felt to be necessary in even the most humble homes. Even when there was no room for a formal parlor, Americans adorned their living spaces with decorative objects.

[5770] John C. Grabill, *Home of Mrs. American Horse* (1891), courtesy of the Library of Congress, American Memory, Grabill Collection [LOT 3076-2, no. 3638]. Uncovered tipi frame with Oglala women and children inside, most likely near the Pine Ridge Reservation, South Dakota. In contrast to typical Euro-American dwellings, canvas tipis were where Native American women performed most of their domestic chores.

[5799] Anonymous, *Ladies S.J.A. Glee Club 1897–1900 Breckenridge, Colo.* (c. 1897), courtesy of the Western History/Genealogy Department, Denver Public Library. Breckenridge, Colorado, was first settled in 1859 when gold was discovered in the Blue River. Glee clubs—or choral societies—were an important way of socializing in and domesticating the frontier town.

[8263] Anonymous, *One of the Many Parlors in a New York Apartment-Hotel* (1904), courtesy of *Cosmopolitan* [no. 38, Dec. 1904]. While most Americans, from the very rich to the humblest frontier family, had some parlor or leisure space in their homes, rooms such as this one in a Manhattan apartment exemplify the vast divide between the rich and the poor and the urban and the rural that existed in this country at the turn of the twentieth century.

Comprehension: Examine the architectural plans for Euro-American houses and the diagrams of traditional Native American tipis featured in the archive. What kinds of domestic values did these different spatial arrangements promote? Do they have any features in common?

Context: How is Mademoiselle Reisz's apartment described in *The Awakening*? Does she have a traditional parlor? How does her home compare with the Ratignolles' home? How do the two homes reflect their different inhabitants' attitudes toward social convention? How do Mademoiselle Reisz's and Madame Ratignolle's attitudes toward their shared hobby of piano playing differ?

Context: In Bret Harte's "The Outcasts of Poker Flat," the outcasts fix up and inhabit an abandoned cabin. How do they outfit the cabin's interior? How do they occupy themselves? Do the outcasts in some sense replicate parlor ideals in the abandoned cabin?

Context: Why does Mother move into the barn in Mary E. Wilkins Freeman's "The Revolt of 'Mother' "? What kind of reaction does her decision provoke in Father? Do her actions change the power dynamics within their marriage? If so, to what extent?

Exploration: Do contemporary American homes contain rooms similar to the nineteenth-century parlor? What kinds of rooms currently fulfill the roles that parlors used to fill?

Exploration: In contemporary American culture, consumers are inundated with decorating and homemaking advice: a "Home and Garden" channel on cable television dispenses round-the-clock insights on homemaking, while dozens of magazines suggest innumerable projects for improving one's domestic space. Why do you think these television shows and magazines are so popular? What kind of audience are they trying to reach? How do they promote particular cultural values by celebrating particular domestic arrangements and pursuits?

Exploration: How do contemporary films convey information about characters through their home decor?

Moving Pictures: Native American Self-Narration

In their coverage of Native American autobiographical texts, literary anthologies tend to focus on works by Indian authors who wrote their own stories in English (such as Zitkala-Ša or Charles Alexander Eastman) or on those who dictated their oral narratives to white translators and editors (such as Black Elk). But Native American autobiographical expressions are in fact part of a richer and more diverse tradition of representational practices that is often overlooked. Drawing on traditions of pictography, oral storytelling, performance, and dance, these acts of self-narration do not necessarily conform to Euro-American standards of autobiography: they are not written and they usually do not follow European conventions of chronological narration or closure. Instead, many Native American autobiographical texts rely on visual and oral expression, anecdotal orderings of significant events, and an emphasis on communal relationships rather than individual development. The collaborative mode of Native American self-expression could also extend to the performance of a text—friends and assistants could help storytellers, dancers, singers, and performers enact their autobiographical accounts. Given the nature of Native American ideas of self, narration, and representation, scholar Hertha Dawn Wong argues that "the word *autobiography* (or, self-life-writing) is inappropriate. . . . A more suitable term might be *communo-bio-oratory* (or, community-life-speaking), since its roots reflect the communal and often oral nature of early Native American autobiographical expressions." Thus, while non-written Native American texts can be difficult for non-Indians to understand, they are crucial records of Indian self-expression unmediated by the imposition of European cultural standards and expectations.

[9067] Anonymous, *Facsimile of an Indian Painting* (n.d.), courtesy of the Library of Congress [LC-USZ62-28805].

Of the more than five hundred languages that were spoken by indigenous peoples in North America prior to contact with Europeans, not one of them had a written alphabet. Instead, sophisticated forms of visual and oral notation and recording allowed authors to represent their stories to listeners, viewers, and participants. **Pictographic narratives** consisting of symbols, totems, and emblems conveyed expressions of personal and group identity as well as spiritual or military experiences. In Meso America in particular these systems were phonetic and quite complex. In some tribes this symbolic language was so highly evolved that individuals could "read" about one another by examining the pictures on robes, tipis, and shields without needing any accompanying oral explanation. An animal-skin tipi belonging to Kiowa chief Little Bluff, for example, was emblazoned with symbolic records of the Kiowas' military successes that would have been legible to any Plains Indian viewer. Images of American soldiers felled by braves' arrows and lances attest to the tribe's martial prowess, while vertical rows of tomahawks and decorated lances might have served as records of especially important exploits or as "coup" counts. A common Native American practice, **coup counting** was a historical record of an individual warrior's feats of bravery. Each time he touched an enemy in battle, either with his hand or with a special "coup stick," a Native American warrior acquired prestige and power—and the right to brag about his military successes. Rows of pictographic images could serve as a kind of account book or mnemonic device to enable a warrior to recite his triumphs. Clothing could serve a similar autobiographical function: painter and ethnographer George Catlin noted that Mandan chief Mah-to-toh-pa, or Four Bears, was famous for his pictographic buffalo skin robe. Drawing on the robe's visual "chart of his military life," Mah-to-toh-pa would point at the paintings on the back of the garment and dramatically re-enact the incidents depicted. As Wong has pointed out in her study of the robe, by combining the visual, oral, and performative, Mah-to-toh-pa constructed a vivid autobiographical narrative that did not rely on writing.

Native American naming practices could also serve as oral expressions of identity and personal development. Unlike European Americans, Indians could acquire multiple names over a lifetime, tak-

[5917] George Catlin, *Wi-Jun-Jon—The Pigeon's Egg Head Going to and Returning from Washington*, courtesy of the Library of Congress [LC-USZC2-3313].

[6823] F. W. Greenough, *Se-Quo-Yah* [*Sequoiah*] (c. 1836), courtesy of the Library of Congress, Prints and Photographs Division [LC-USZC4-4815].

ing one at birth, gaining others as a result of significant life events, and even keeping some secret. A new name would not necessarily replace earlier names but instead could exist in dynamic relation to them. Charles Alexander Eastman, for example, was assigned the name of "Hakadah," or "The Pitiful Last," because his mother died shortly after his birth. Later, when he performed admirably in a lacrosse game, he acquired the new name "Ohiyesa," or "The Winner." Eventually, he adopted the Anglicized name "Charles Alexander Eastman" at the request of his father, and then changed his title again when he received the degree of "Doctor." Kiowa warrior Ohettoint had several Indian names and was known variously as "High Forehead," "Charley Buffalo," "Padai," and "Twin." Such naming practices were understandably confusing to white authorities who wanted to compile accurate lists of tribal members. To help resolve this cultural misunderstanding, Eastman worked for several years to assign Anglicized surnames to Sioux individuals, hoping that more "American" names would help them register with the U.S. government and thus claim property rights guaranteed to them by law. Unfortunately, this kind of enforced assimilation left little room for the important autobiographical work performed by traditional Indian names.

As Native American cultures came into contact with Euro-Americans, their autobiographical practices changed significantly. Materials such as commercial paint, paper, and colored pencils acquired by trade, gift, or capture provided new media for recording pictographs. In response to these new materials and the shortage of old materials such as buffalo hides, Indians began to record pictographic tribal histories (sometimes called "Winter Counts") in partly used ledger books, army rosters, and daybooks acquired from whites. One unknown Cheyenne artist somehow acquired an envelope addressed in European script to "Commanding Officer, Company G, 2nd Cavalry" and used it as a canvas for his moving depiction of a courtship scene. In the pictograph, two lovers meet and then join each other in front of a tipi. Thus, the artist used the materials of the enemy's army to construct his own expression of romantic connection. White Bull, a Teton Dakota chief, created a hybrid pictographic autobiography in a business ledger, using traditional visual symbols as well as printed words to tell his life story. Commissioned by a white collector who paid White Bull fifty dollars for his work, the ledger graphically presents the author's genealogy and hunting and war record. White Bull portrays himself counting coup on an enemy warrior and interprets the image in script written in the Dakota language using the Dakota **syllabary**. By the nineteenth century, some tribes had developed scripts called syllabaries that included characters for their vowel and consonant sounds and thus enabled them to write in their own languages. First developed by Sequoyah for the Cherokee language, the syllabaries enabled the creation of hybrid Native American expressions. No longer visual or oral, texts written in syllabary adapted the Western technologies of writing to traditional Native American languages.

Comprehension: What is "counting coup"?

Comprehension: What is a syllabary? How did syllabaries transform Native American autobiographical expression?

Comprehension: Why might a Native American have had multiple names?

Context: After publishing their autobiographical pieces, both Zitkala-Ša and Charles Alexander Eastman put together collections of translations of the traditional folktales they had heard as children. Why do you think these two acculturated Sioux people might have felt compelled to translate their culture's stories into English and into print? What effect might this translation have on the stories?

Context: In his poetry and prose, Alexander Posey frequently celebrated the achievements of Sequoyah, the Cherokee who had invented the first syllabary for a Native American language. Why do you think Posey was so interested in the syllabary? What role did literacy play in his own work? How did Posey mediate between conventions of the English language and his desire to express authentic Native American speech patterns?

Exploration: What kinds of non-written expressions are important in American culture today? How do contemporary Americans engage in self-expression and self-narration through the use of non-written signs?

Exploration: How do Native American oral or pictorial autobiographical expressions compare to traditional Euro-American autobiography (Benjamin Franklin, or Henry Adams, for example)? How do they compare with early Native American autobiographical writings in English (Samson Occom or William Apess, for example)?

Exploration: To what extent are *Storyteller* by Leslie Marmon Silko and *The Way to Rainy Mountain* by N. Scott Momaday communo-bio-oratory (or, community-life-speaking) rather than autobiographical? How do these very experimental works relate to the works of Charles Eastman and Zitkala-Ša?

Black, White, and Yellow: Coloring the News in Late-Nineteenth-Century America

Americans in the late nineteenth century had unprecedented access to news, both of their immediate neighborhoods and of the world, as print technology, literacy, and appetites for information exploded. By 1900, there were twenty daily newspapers in circulation for every one that had existed in 1850. Industrialized printing presses enabled publishers to put out periodicals more cheaply than ever before—at one or two cents a copy, some newspapers sold in the 1890s were six times cheaper than they had been at the beginning of the century. Even high quality magazines and monthly periodicals could be purchased for just a few pennies. The changes in the cost and distribution of American newspapers meant, by the end of the century, that national

[8102] Shirt of the Blackfeet Tribe (c. 1890), courtesy of the Portland Art Museum, gift of Elizabeth Cole Butler [86.126.32]. Shirts such as this one were worn during the Ghost Dance Movement. Clothing varied from tribe to tribe, but many felt that the shirts would protect wearers from bullets and attack.

[8106] Anonymous, Girl's dress (c. 1890), courtesy of the Portland Art Museum, Portland, Oregon. This *hoestôtse*, or Cheyenne dress, incorporates beadwork as a means of expression. This style was developed by the Kiowa in the mid-1800s and copied by other Plains tribes.

[8112] Anonymous, Rawhide soled boots (c. 1900), courtesy of the Portland Art Museum, gift of Elizabeth Cole Butler. Fringes and beadwork on moccasins and clothing displayed the skill of the maker, as well as the status and social location of the wearer.

[9067] Anonymous, *Facsimile of an Indian Painting* (n.d.), courtesy of the Library of Congress [LC-USZ62-28805]. Paintings such as this one represent one of the ways that Native Americans recorded their perspectives on historical events even after contact and the introduction of written history by European Americans.

and international news reached even poor and rural Americans. Newspapers brought the nation together.

Many of the writers featured in this unit began their careers as printers' apprentices and journalists. Bret Harte and Mark Twain met when they were writing for newspapers in California; Alexander Posey founded and edited the first newspaper owned by a Native American; Joel Chandler Harris published his first Uncle Remus stories while working for the *Atlanta Constitution* and had them syndicated in newspapers throughout the North. Other important nineteenth-century writers got their start or in some cases published the majority of their work in magazines and monthly periodicals. Charles W. Chesnutt, Mary E. Wilkins Freeman, Sarah Orne Jewett, Kate Chopin, and Zitkala-Ša all published in the *Atlantic Monthly* and a variety of other literary journals. Undoubtedly, the close affiliation between journalists and fiction writers in the nineteenth century influenced the development of realism as a literary style. Borrowing ideals of truth, objectivity, and accuracy from journalistic techniques, these writers helped formulate the dominant aesthetic in American letters in this period.

William Dean Howells, a pre-eminent practitioner of literary realism and the editor of *Harper's Monthly* magazine, pronounced that realism "is nothing more and nothing less than the truthful treatment of material." For realists, this commitment to "truthfulness" often led them to explore characters, places, and events that had never before seemed appropriate subject matter for literature. Just as nineteenth-century newspapers democratized the news, realism democratized the scope of literature. The enfranchisement of "common" or "everyday" subject matter extended literary representation to ordinary people whom authors had previously ignored or romanticized. Perhaps influenced by their consumption of newspapers, American audiences evinced a new willingness to read about unrefined and even tragic or ugly subjects in the interest of gaining access to authentic accounts of the world around them. Journalistic coverage of the carnage and horror of the Civil War—an event that dramatically touched the lives of almost all Americans who lived through it—had exposed readers to realistic, if horrifying, depictions of actual events. As the stark photographs of the aftermath of Civil War battles featured in the archive make clear, these depictions could hardly fail to make a profound impression on readers and viewers. By the end of the century, journalism's aesthetic of truth and accuracy had found its way from the newspapers into the fiction of the country.

Unfortunately, the journalistic ideals that had such a powerful impact on American fiction did not always shape newspapers themselves. As the newspaper industry became big business—and as men like William Randolph Hearst and Joseph Pulitzer amassed enormous fortunes through their creation of publishing empires—journalistic integrity sometimes took a back seat to a desire to boost circulation and please readers. New techniques designed to sell papers rather than to provide accurate coverage of events started to shape the look and feel of American newspapers. Novelties like giant banner headlines, color inserts, provocative cartoons, and large engravings put a focus

[6551] Kenyon Cox, *Columbia & Cuba—Magazine Cover—Nude Study* (1898), courtesy of the Library of Congress, Prints and Photographs Division [LC-USZ62-68463].

on visual appeal rather than substance. The content of stories, too, privileged sensational impact over objectivity or thoroughness, focusing on scandal and human-interest stories to the exclusion of important events. The term **yellow journalism** was coined in the 1890s to characterize this new trend in news reporting. Named for R. F. Outcault's popular comic strip, which featured a yellow-robed character named the "yellow kid," the term refers to the circulation war that arose between Hearst's *New York Journal* and Pulitzer's *New York World*. The competition began when Hearst, determined to lure readers from Pulitzer's paper, hired Outcault away from the *World* to draw for the *Journal*. Pulitzer responded by commissioning a new cartoonist to draw a second "yellow kid" comic. Soon, the war between the two largest New York newspapers became a competition between two "yellow kids," and the term "yellow journalism" was coined to describe the sensationalist, irresponsible journalistic tactics the papers adopted in their attempts to outsell one another.

[6332] Archibald Gunn and Richard Felton Outcault, *New York Journal's Colored Comic Supplement* (1896), courtesy of the Library of Congress, Prints and Photographs Division [LC-USZC4-2553].

The Sioux writer Charles Alexander Eastman learned first-hand the potentially devastating impact yellow journalism could have on already tense situations. When the Ghost Dance movement was gaining momentum on the Pine Ridge Reservation, Eastman hoped to diffuse the anxiety the spiritual movement caused in white reservation authorities by assuring them of the non-threatening nature of the dancers' activities. Instead, rumors of a possible Indian attack—rumors started mainly by irresponsible journalists—increased the white authorities' fears. Eastman lamented, "of course, the press seized upon the opportunity to enlarge upon the strained situation and predict an 'Indian uprising.' The reporters were among us, and managed to secure much 'news' that no one else ever heard of." The reporters' specious news stories fueled an already fraught situation that eventually culminated in the tragic massacre of 150 Sioux men, women, and children at Wounded Knee in December 1890.

Yellow journalism also played a key role in the Spanish-American war, a conflict that has gone down in history as the first "media war." As the conflict between rebel Cubans and Spanish colonists escalated in Cuba in 1896, newspapers seized on the event as a chance to attract readers and increase their circulation. Dispatching the first "foreign war correspondents" to Cuba, the papers began printing inflammatory stories (often based on little or no evidence) about Spanish brutality and noble Cuban resistance. The papers commissioned some of the country's most popular artists to provide graphic illustrations of Spanish atrocities designed to whip the American public into a frenzy of outrage and war mongering. As *New York Journal* editor Hearst told artist Frederic

[4219] Western Photograph Company, *Gathering up the dead at the battlefield of Wounded Knee, South Dakota* (1891), courtesy of the Smithsonian Institution.

"BLACK, WHITE, AND YELLOW" WEB ARCHIVE

[1962] Timothy H. O'Sullivan, *Unfinished Confederate grave near the center of the battlefield of Gettysburg* [stereograph] (1863), courtesy of the Library of Congress, American Memory Collection [PR-065-793-22]. Photograph of dead Confederate soldiers in a shallow grave at Gettysburg. Journalistic coverage of the Civil War exposed readers to realistic depictions of actual events, paving the way for the aesthetic of truth and accuracy in American fiction.

[2818] Anonymous, *Refugees leaving the Old Homestead* (c. 1863), courtesy of the National Archives and Records Administration [NWDNS-LC-CC-306]. This photograph shows a family of Civil War refugees ready to leave the homestead. To escape the Rebels, Union families would gather as much of their belongings as would fit on a wagon and head north.

[3228] Timothy O'Sullivan, *Incidents of the War. A Harvest of Death, Gettysburg, July, 1863*, courtesy of the Library of Congress [LC-B8184-7964-A DLC]. Federal soldiers dead on the battlefield at Gettysburg, Pennsylvania. Graphic, bleak war photographs inspired postwar literary realism.

[4219] Western Photograph Company, *Gathering up the dead at the battlefield of Wounded Knee, South Dakota* (1891), courtesy of the Smithsonian Institution. U.S. soldiers standing in front of a wagon full of dead Sioux. A blizzard delayed the burial of the dead. Eventually the Sioux were buried in a mass grave, with little effort made to identify the bodies.

[5149] Kurz and Allison, *The Storming of Ft. Wagner* (1890), courtesy of the National Park Service, Frederick Douglass National Historic Site. This illustration shows soldiers of the 54th Massachusetts Regiment leading the Union charge against the Confederate stronghold of Fort Wagner, South Carolina. The 54th Massachussetts was the first black regiment recruited in the North during the Civil War.

[5808] Barthelmess, *Buffalo soldiers of the 25th Infantry, Ft. Keogh, Montana* (1890), courtesy of the Library of

Remington, "You furnish the pictures, I'll furnish the war." The newspapers' strategy worked: circulation increased dramatically and the American public demanded armed intervention. By 1898, President McKinley had become convinced that his political party would suffer if he did not engage in war with Spain, however unjustified. While it may not be fair to hold the newspapers responsible for the war, it is accurate to say that the press fueled pro-war sentiment and that the outcome of American involvement in nineteenth-century Cuba might have been very different without the sensational headlines and distorted reporting provided by the yellow journalists.

As newspapers began to shape the values and style of American culture in the late nineteenth century, artist William Harnett began to produce canvases that served as visual essays on the new role of newspapers in American life. Between 1875 and 1890, he painted over sixty still-life representations of newspapers. Never painting readers, Harnett instead offered tableaux of newspapers on tables surrounded by glasses, books, and other reading accoutrements. Often featuring matches, candles, pipes, and even smoldering embers next to the papers, he highlighted their potential to catch fire—that is, their tendency to inflame delicate situations. The papers in Harnett's paintings are not readable—he represented news copy as illegible marks—perhaps commenting on the fact that the content of the stories had become secondary to the circulation of the paper. Despite the blurred print, Harnett's representations consistently tricked his viewers: guards had to be posted at his exhibitions to restrain viewers from trying to touch the canvases. His paintings, then, are a visual corollary to the realist aesthetic that shaped American fiction, even as they subtly hint at the problems with the journalistic techniques that spurred the realist movement.

QUESTIONS

Comprehension: What does the term "yellow journalism" mean and how did it get its name?

Comprehension: What kinds of strategies did "yellow" newspapers use to boost their circulation and appeal to readers?

Comprehension: What are the ideals of "realism" as a literary style? How are they related to journalistic ideals?

Context: Both Joel Chandler Harris and Alexander Posey reached their broadest audiences by publishing their dialect stories in newspapers. Why do you think newspaper readers were so interested in stories written in ethnic or regional dialect?

Context: Examine the headlines, banners, and color supplements featured in the archive. How are these images different from traditional newspaper presentations? To what kinds of readers are these images trying to appeal?

Context: In *The Awakening*, Mr. Pontellier uses the public newspaper as a device for communicating with his wife and for avoiding scandal. How does he manipulate news of his family and domestic circumstances in the newspaper? Why does he feel it is necessary to offer public explanations of the family's domestic circumstances in the newspaper?

Exploration: Do you think "yellow journalism" is still a force in media coverage of the news in contemporary America? To what extent are the dual forces of realism and sentimentality still central to the art of journalism?

Exploration: How have twentieth- and twenty-first-century American military conflicts been shaped by media coverage? How do you think media coverage has shaped popular opinion either in favor of or in opposition to particular wars or military engagements?

Exploration: Today, many Americans get their news from sources other than printed newspapers. What other media have taken the place of newspapers in this country? How do these new media either lend themselves to or resist yellow journalism?

EXTENDED CONTEXTS

Monkeying Around: Trickster Figures and American Culture

Just like written literary traditions, oral storytelling traditions have genres and styles. The "trickster tale" is one of many genres of oral narrative tradition. The central figure in these tales is the "trickster," usually depicted as an animal. Characterized by paradox, duality, cleverness, shape-shifting, duplicity, and a knack for survival, trickster figures are appealing in their ability to assert their individuality and shatter boundaries and taboos. From traditional African American folktales about Brer Rabbit, Brer Tortoise, and the Signifying Monkey to Native American fables about Coyote, Raven, and Iktomi the Spider, trickster tales have served as powerful cultural expressions of ethnic identity. For many groups, these tales functioned as a means of representing and commenting on the mixing and meeting of cultures and the power relations such meetings entail, since the flexibility and polyvalent qualities of the trickster make him a useful figure for articulating resistance to dominant groups or oppressive colonizers. Trickster figures continue to be central to American culture. One need only turn on the television on Saturday morning to see their influence: the weekly celebrations of Bugs Bunny's exploits and his clever victories over the well-armed and supposedly more powerful Elmer Fudd are clear indications of the enduring appeal of the trickster tradition to new generations of Americans.

The trickster, by his very nature, is almost impossible to define. Because he is a master of dissolving boundaries, confounding certainties, and exploiting ambiguity, it is difficult to pin a clear description on him. As cultural critic Henry Louis Gates Jr. puts it in his influential study *The Signifying Monkey*:

> A partial list of [the trickster's] qualities might include individuality, satire, parody, irony, magic, indeterminacy, open-endedness, ambigu-

Congress [LC-USZC4-6161 DLC]. In 1866, Congress approved six new cavalry and infantry regiments comprised solely of African American enlisted troops. Called Buffalo Soldiers by the Native Americans, these units performed the same frontier duties as their white counterparts and later served with distinction in the Spanish-American War.

[6332] Archibald Gunn and Richard Felton Outcault, *New York Journal*'s colored comic supplement (1896), courtesy of the Library of Congress, Prints and Photographs Division [LC-USZC4-2553]. This color poster from the comic pages of William Randolph Hearst's *New York Journal* features a woman in dancing costume with a rope around the popular comic character "Yellow Kid," developed by artist Richard Felton Outcault.

[6551] Kenyon Cox, *Columbia & Cuba—Magazine Cover—Nude Study* (1898), courtesy of the Library of Congress, Prints and Photographs Division [LC-USZ62-68463]. An allegorical cover of an 1898 magazine, exemplifying the openness toward the human body of the late-nineteenth-century realists. The women's names, "Columbia" and "Cuba," refer to an imagined relationship between the nations during the Spanish American War.

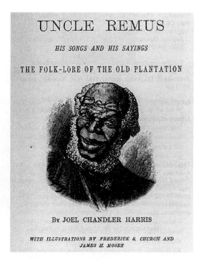

[1565] Joel Chandler Harris, *Uncle Remus* cover (c. 1880), courtesy of the University of Virginia.

ity, sexuality, chance, uncertainty, disruption and reconciliation, betrayal and loyalty, closure and disclosure, encasement and rupture. But it is a mistake to focus on one of these qualities as predominant. Esu [the trickster] possesses all of these characteristics, plus a plethora of others which, taken together, only begin to present an idea of the complexity of this classic figure of mediation and of the unity of opposed forces.

Perhaps one of the most useful evocations of the trickster's complex identity is the African carving of Esu which presents him as having two faces—one at the front of his head and one at the back—thus highlighting his duality and ambiguity.

Traditional African American folktales celebrate the way the trickster's duplicity allows him to escape unscathed from even the most seemingly hopeless situations. Brer Rabbit's ability to outwit the more powerful animals Brer Fox and Brer Bear makes him an appealing hero. While literary critics disagree about the extent to which Joel Chandler Harris understood the deep ironies of the African American stories he transcribed in his Uncle Remus tales, Harris was able to see the cultural usefulness of Brer Rabbit's trickster qualities to enslaved African Americans. In the introduction to one of his Uncle Remus collections, he explains, "It needs no scientific investigation to show why he [the black] selects as his hero the weakest and the most harmless of all animals, and brings him out victorious in contests with the bear, the wolf, and the fox." The manner in which these tales invert the roles of the powerful and the weak, so that the supposedly submissive figure cunningly outwits his powerful oppressor, offers a subversive moral that must have provided hope to oppressed slaves.

Native American trickster tales are similarly interested in the inversion of social norms and the breaking of boundaries; their tales of Coyote and other supernatural characters celebrate the trickster as simultaneously vulgar and sacred, wise and foolish, but always

surviving. In Charles Alexander Eastman's transcription of the traditional Sioux tale of the trickster turtle, Turtle's strategies exactly parallel Brer Rabbit's. Just as Brer Rabbit uses reverse psychology to convince Brer Fox to throw him into a briar patch—the environment in which he is most comfortable—so does Turtle convince his captors to confine him in water, a fluid medium which of course allows him to escape. The identity of the trickster continues to resonate in Native American culture today. Harry Fonseca's playful paintings about Coyote testify to the figure's enduring cultural importance. Fonseca's representations of Coyote show him skillfully mediating between the "old ways" and the new: in *Coyote in Front of Studio*, Coyote pairs a modern leather jacket and high-top sneakers with a traditional Plains Indian war bonnet and pipe bag. With two eyes on one side of his head, this Coyote embodies the duality and flexibility of contemporary

Indian culture, figuring both resistance and strategic accommodation to Euro-American culture.

QUESTIONS

Comprehension: What are some of the animals commonly chosen to represent trickster figures in African American and Native American traditional trickster tales? What qualities do these animals have in common?

Context: While *Adventures of Huckleberry Finn* does not contain any traditional animal trickster figures, many of Huck's adventures resonate with trickster traditions. How does Twain draw on traditional trickster schemes and qualities in his narrative of Jim and Huck's journey down the river? Which characters in the novel seem most trickster-like?

Exploration: How do characters such as the Joker in *Batman*, or the Road Runner or Bugs Bunny in *Looney Tunes* draw on trickster traditions? How are they similar to figures like Brer Rabbit or Iktomi? How are they different? What kinds of cultural values do they seem to espouse?

The Human Framed: Anatomy, Photography, and Realism in Nineteenth-Century America

Viewing Thomas Eakins's masterful depiction of medical surgery in his painting *The Gross Clinic*, an art critic writing for the *New York Herald* in 1876 was both impressed and repelled by its stark realism: "The painting is decidedly unpleasant and sickeningly real in all its gory details, though a startlingly life-like and strong work." Showing the famous surgeon Dr. Samuel David Gross in the midst of an operation, with blood on his hands and an open incision in the patient on the table before him, Eakins's controversial painting has come to be recognized as a masterpiece of uncompromising **realism**. Like much late-nineteenth-century American literature, American art after the Civil War became increasingly interested in providing viewers with accurate, unromanticized depictions of modern life and the human condition. As *The Gross Clinic* makes vividly, even brutally, clear, the realists' commitment to depicting physical truth prompted them to paint features and aspects of the human body that had previously seemed outside the boundaries of artistic representation.

Eakins was fascinated by the muscles and mechanisms of the human body. He became interested in anatomy in high school and went on to study the subject extensively at both the Pennsylvania Academy and the Jefferson Medical College, where he regularly dissected corpses. He eventually supplemented his income as an artist by teaching anatomy and dissection. While Eakins admitted that he felt a natural aversion to dissecting human bodies, he saw the task as necessary to his art. As he put it, "One dissects simply to increase his knowledge of how beautiful objects are put together to the end that one

[1565] Joel Chandler Harris, *Uncle Remus* cover (c. 1880), courtesy of the University of Virginia. Joel Chandler Harris's trickster tales that Uncle Remus narrates—with their subversive focus on the triumph of seemingly weak characters over their aggressors—are characterized by poetic irony and a subtle critique of oppression and prejudice.

[2616] James Brown, *Dancing for Eels* (1848), courtesy of the Library of Congress, Prints and Photographs Division [LC-USZC4-4542]. This lithograph with watercolor features a scene from a mid-nineteenth-century play intended to depict New York "as it is." A dancing black man in tattered clothes maintains the interest of observers of all types—the young, old, white, black, poor, and wealthy.

[5735] A. B. Frost, *Brer B'ar Tied Hard en Fas* (1892), courtesy of Houghton Mifflin. Illustration of Brer Rabbit tying Brer B'ar to a tree, taken from Joel Chandler Harris's *Uncle Remus and His Friends: Old Plantation Stories, Songs, and Ballads with Sketches of Negro Character*. As trickster tales, the African American fables published by Harris contain a subtle critique of oppression.

[8008] Greg Sarris, Interview: "Coyote" (2002), courtesy of Annenberg/CBP and *American Passages*. Greg Sarris, author, professor of English, and Pomo Indian, discusses the trickster Coyote.

[8507] Charles Eastman, "Turtle Story" (1909), courtesy of *Wigwam Evenings, Sioux Folk Tales*. This collection of Sioux tales by Eastman and his wife, Elaine Goodale Eastman, contains twenty-seven Sioux narratives, including creation stories and animal legends.

[1577] Thomas Eakins, *The Agnew Clinic* (1889), courtesy of the University of Pennsylvania Library, Schoenberg Center.

[3228] Timothy O'Sullivan, *Incidents of the War. A Harvest of Death, Gettysburg, July 1863*, courtesy of the Library of Congress [LC-B8184-7964-A DLC].

[3230] Anonymous, *Confederate and Union dead side by side in trenches at Fort Mahone* (1865), courtesy of the Library of Congress, Prints and Photographs Division [LC-B8171-3181].

might imitate them." Eakins put his extensive knowledge of the workings of the human body to use in all of his paintings, and especially in his series of representations of wrestlers, swimmers, boxers, and rowers in action.

Eakins and other realist painters found the new medium of photography enormously interesting, both because it enabled them to capture split-second moments of human movement and because it could allow them to try out various tableaux for their paintings. In 1885, photographer Eadweard Muybridge revolutionized both photography and the study of human and animal movement with his sequential pictures using stop-action shutters to capture details of motion too quick for the human eye. Originally hired by Leland Stanford, the governor of California, to settle a bet about the nature of a racehorse's gait, Muybridge developed a technique for photographing successive stages of the animal's motion, revealing that at top speed the horse had all four feet off the ground mid-stride. Muybridge continued his photographic investigations at the University of Pennsylvania, where he collaborated with Eakins, who was also interested in photographing motion. He soon published *Animal Locomotion*, an eleven-volume collection of over 100,000 photographs of humans and animals running, climbing, and jumping which he intended to function as a kind of dictionary of bodily movement.

The realists' passion for uncompromising analyses and representations of the human body did not always meet with public approval. Photographs and paintings that struck viewers as too "graphic"—like Eakins's *Gross Clinic*—came in for harsh criticism. Eakins eventually lost his position at the Pennsylvania Academy of Fine Arts because he insisted that his students, both male and female, view nude human models in order to better understand the human body. The realists' unconventional openness toward the body and all of its features may have flown in the face of traditional American beliefs about propriety and respectability, but it succeeded in transforming the face of American art and culture. These late-nineteenth-century photographers and painters created the technology that soon led to the development of the motion picture camera, and they pioneered an aesthetic of truth and realism that had a profound and lasting effect on American art.

Unfortunately, nineteenth-century Americans' interest in the scientific study of the human form could also lead in dangerous directions when it was used to justify racism and prejudice. The late part of the century saw a new vogue for "phrenology," the pseudo-scientific study of facial features based on the premise that external appearance is a reliable indicator of internal character. Phrenology, which had been popular in the eighteenth century, was resurrected in the last decades of the nineteenth century when immigration was changing the complexion and features of the American face. Proponents of "racial purity" worried that the hundreds of thousands of non-Northern

European immigrants who were arriving yearly (Italians, Greeks, Eastern European Jews, Chinese, and others) would contaminate or weaken the American body. Commentators like Joseph Simms devised racist charts and diagrams designed to "scientifically" classify racial facial characteristics on the basis of intelligence, sensitivity, creativity, and morality. Simms's book, *Physiognomy Illustrated; or, Nature's Revelations of Character: A Description of the Mental, Moral, and Volitive Dispositions of Mankind, as Manifested in the Human Form and Countenance*, predictably argued for the superiority of Caucasian facial features. Such distortions of the spirit and integrity of scientific inquiry were a tragic corollary to the nineteenth-century commitment to studying the human form.

QUESTIONS

Comprehension: What kinds of subjects did realist painters like Thomas Eakins favor? What did they want their paintings to accomplish? What kinds of values are reflected in their work?

Context: What is happening in the operating theater in Eakins's painting *The Agnew Clinic*? How does Eakins portray Dr. Agnew? What actions do his assistants perform? What parts of the patient are visible? Who do you think the woman is seated on the right? What is her role in the picture?

Context: Some Native American participants in the Ghost Dance religion came to believe that their spiritual practices would render their clothing impermeable to bullets. What kinds of views about the human body inform their beliefs? How does the Ghost Dancers' understanding of the relationship between the spirit and the body compare to European American realists' understanding of physicality?

Exploration: If Eakins and Muybridge were alive today, what kinds of modern technology do you think would most interest them? Why?

ASSIGNMENTS

Personal and Creative Responses

1. *Journal:* Write a journal entry or short narrative in which you imagine Jim's perspective on the final chapters of *Huckleberry Finn*, when Tom and Huck make a game out of Jim's captivity and escape on the Phelps farm. How might Jim narrate these events differently than Huck does in the novel?
2. *Poet's Corner:* Select a passage or poem written in dialect from one of the texts featured in this unit and translate it into "standard" English. What problems did you encounter in writing your translation? How does your translation change the meaning and effect of the passage?

gorical cover of an 1898 magazine, exemplifying the openness toward the human body of the late-nineteenth-century realists. The names of the women, "Columbia" and "Cuba," refer to an imagined relationship between the nations during the Spanish American War.

[8244] Eadweard Muybridge, *Animal Locomotion* (c. 1887), courtesy of the Library of Congress [LC-USZ62-103037]. Muybridge's innovative photographic techniques revolutionized the study of animal and human movement.

[8245] Eadweard Muybridge, *The Zoopraxiscope—A Couple Waltzing* (c. 1893), courtesy of the Library of Congress [LC-USZC4-7690]. Known as "the father of the motion picture," Muybridge invented the zoopraxiscope, which projected a moving image from still sequences, such as this couple dancing.

[8251] Pendelton's Lithography, *Dr. Spurzheim—Divisions of the Organs of Phrenology Marked Externally* (1834), courtesy of the Library of Congress [LC-USZC4-4556]. The pseudo-science of phrenology was revived in the late nineteenth century and was often used to provide a "factual" basis for racism.

[8252] Anonymous, *The Symbolical Head, Illustrating all the Phrenological Developments of the Human Head* (1842), courtesy of the Library of Congress [LC-USZ62-100747]. The late nineteenth century saw a renewed interest in phrenology, the study of facial features as indicators of qualities such as intelligence, creativity, and morality. Most late-nineteenth-century phrenological studies purported to prove that Caucasian features were superior.

3. *Journal:* Imagine you are a reporter stationed at the Sioux Pine Ridge reservation in the 1890s. Compose your own newspaper account of the Ghost Dance religion for publication in a newspaper geared to an audience of white settlers. How will you describe this spiritual movement? What aspects of the religion will you emphasize?

4. *Artist's Workshop:* Imagine you have won the lottery and are in the process of designing your dream house. Draw a floor plan for your ideal home. What rooms will you designate for specific activities? How large will you make the rooms? Will any of the rooms serve purposes similar to those served by the parlor in nineteenth-century homes?

5. *Multimedia:* Thomas Eakins believed that artists should represent the world as it is, not as they would like it to be. Using the *American Passages* archive and slide-show software, create a multimedia presentation in which you explore the influence of this realist ideal on some of the texts and contexts featured in this unit.

Problem-Based Learning Projects

1. Imagine you and your peers serve on the curriculum committee at your high school or college. A group of parents, students, and teachers has recently circulated a petition to remove *Huckleberry Finn* from the school's reading lists and library because of its racist language and offensive representations of African Americans. Other parents, students, and teachers have sent in letters insisting that the novel is a literary masterpiece and demanding that it continue to be taught at your school. Your committee is going to hold a community meeting to decide the issue. Take a side in the debate and prepare a presentation to articulate your point of view. How will you make your argument for or against *Huckleberry Finn*? What kind of evidence will you cite to support your claim for either the book's educational value or its inappropriateness? How will you construct your argument so it will address the concerns of parents and teachers as well as students?

2. The Native Americans at the Pine Ridge Reservation in South Dakota have decided to sue the government agents and missionaries who insist on taking young Indian children to mission schools and boarding schools at which they are forced to practice Euro-American customs. The Pine Ridge Indians have hired you as their legal team. How will you prepare your prosecution of the government and missionaries? What kinds of evidence will you use in the case? Whom will you call as witnesses?

GLOSSARY

Boston marriage   The nineteenth-century term used to describe two women who shared a household in a marriagelike arrangement.

Women involved in "Boston marriages" lived independently of men and drew emotional and material support from one another. It is not clear whether all or most "Boston marriages" involved sexual relationships—some probably did and others probably did not. In any case, couples like Sarah Orne Jewett and Annie Fields certainly found important companionship and support in their intense bond with one another.

coup counting   A common Native American practice of making a historical record of an individual warrior's feats of bravery. Each time he touched an enemy in battle, either with his hand or with a special "coup stick," a Native American warrior acquired prestige and power—and the right to brag about his military successes.

dialect   A unique, regional variant of a language in which pronunciation, grammar, and vocabulary diverge from standard conventions. Many regionalist writers became accomplished at transcribing the authentic rhythms and idioms of local dialect in their efforts to make their characters' dialogue mimic as closely as possible the way people really talked. Literalized, phonetic spellings forced readers to pronounce words as speakers of a regional dialect would pronounce them.

Ghost Dance   A Native American response to Euro-American encroachments on their land and way of life. A powerful apocalyptic vision of the overthrow of white domination and a return to traditional Native American ways, the Ghost Dance sparked a pan-Indian, intertribal movement that frightened white authorities with its intensity. Started by the Paiute prophet Wovoka, who believed himself to be a Messianic figure, the Ghost Dance involved adopting traditional clothing and customs, singing and chanting traditional songs, and participating in a trance-inducing round dance designed to inspire dead Indian ancestors to return and reclaim their land. The movement ended tragically when white authorities killed 150 Sioux men, women, and children at Wounded Knee for their involvement in the Ghost Dance religion.

parlor   In nineteenth-century homes, parlors were formal rooms set aside for social ceremonies such as receiving guests or hosting tea parties. Many Americans believed that parlors enabled them to enjoy the refinement and comfort of respectable family living. Designed for display, the parlor was generally the "best room" in the house and usually contained furnishings and knick-knacks that cost more than the objects in the house that were intended for everyday use.

pictographic narrative   Symbols, totems, and emblems which can convey expressions of personal and group identity as well as spiritual or military experiences. In some Native American tribes, this symbolic language was so highly evolved that individuals could "read" about one another by examining the pictures on robes, tipis, and shields without needing any accompanying oral explanation.

realism   A new commitment to the truthful, accurate representation of American life as it was experienced by ordinary Americans infused literature with a "realist" aesthetic in the last half of the nineteenth century. Realism was characterized by its uncompromising, literal representations of the particularities of the material world and the human condition. This passion for finding and presenting the truth led many American practitioners of realism to explore characters, places, and events that had never before seemed appropriate subject matter for literature.

regionalism   An expression of the realist aesthetic, regionalism emphasized the particularities of geographic settings, evoking the distinctive customs, speech, and culture of specific regions of the United States. This attention to the peculiarities of place flourished after the Civil War, perhaps as a celebration of the new unification of a country long divided by political, racial, and religious differences. Regional realism may also have developed in response to the rapid post war industrialization and homogenization that was destroying older, traditional ways of life. By chronicling the specific details of regional culture, regional realism preserved a record of ways of life and habits of speech that were suddenly in danger of disappearing as a result of the newspapers, railroads, and mass-produced consumer goods that were standardizing American culture and taste.

syllabary   First developed by Sequoyah for the Cherokee language, syllabaries were written scripts that included characters for the vowel and consonant sounds of individual Native American languages. Syllabaries enabled some Native Americans to write in their own languages.

trickster   Usually depicted as an animal, the "trickster" is a recurring figure in human cultures. Characterized by paradox, duality, cleverness, shape-shifting, duplicity, and a knack for survival, trickster figures seem to be universally appealing in their ability to assert their individuality and shatter boundaries and taboos. From traditional African American folktales about Brer Rabbit, Brer Tortoise, and the Signifying Monkey to Native American fables about Coyote, Raven, and Iktomi the Spider, trickster tales have served as powerful cultural expressions of ethnic identity.

yellow journalism   A term coined in the 1890s to describe the sensationalist, irresponsible journalistic tactics the papers adopted in their attempts to outsell one another. Such tactics included reporting false or embellished stories, reporting only one side of a controversy, and using visual novelties such as banner headlines and color inserts to attract readers.

SELECTED BIBLIOGRAPHY

Banta, Martha. *Imagining American Women: Ideas and Ideals in Cultural History*. New York: Columbia UP, 1987.

Gates, Henry Louis, Jr. *The Signifying Monkey: A Theory of African-American Literary Criticism*. New York: Oxford UP, 1988.

Grier, Katherine C. *Culture and Comfort: Parlor Making and Middle-Class Identity, 1850–1930*. Washington: Smithsonian Institution, 1988.

Krupat, Arnold, ed. *New Voices in Native American Literary Criticism.* Washington: Smithsonian Institution P, 1993.

Michelson, Bruce. *Literary Wit.* Amherst: U of Massachusetts P, 2000.

Painter, Nell Irvin. *Standing at Armageddon: The United States, 1877–1919.* New York: W. W. Norton & Company, 1989.

Sundquist, Eric J. *To Wake the Nations: Race in the Making of American Literature.* Cambridge: Belknap P of Harvard UP, 1993.

———, ed. *American Realism: New Essays.* Baltimore: Johns Hopkins UP, 1982.

Swann, Brian, ed. *Smoothing the Ground: Essays on Native American Oral Literature.* Berkeley: U of California P, 1983.

Wong, Hertha Dawn. *Sending My Heart Back Across the Years: Tradition and Innovation in Native American Autobiography.* New York: Oxford UP, 1992.

FURTHER RESOURCES

American Anthem: Masterworks from the American Folk Art Museum. Curated by Stacy C. Hollander and Brooke Davis Anderson. New York: American Folk Art Museum in association with Harry N. Abrams, 2001.

Carnes, Mark C. *Secret Ritual and Manhood in Victorian America.* New Haven: Yale UP, 1989.

Fried, Michael. *Realism, Writing, Disfiguration: On Thomas Eakins and Stephen Crane.* Chicago: U of Chicago P, 1987 .

Gilbert, James. *Perfect Cities: Chicago's Utopias of 1893.* Chicago: U of Chicago P, 1991.

Kaplan, Amy, and Donald Pease. *Cultures of United States Imperialism.* Durham: Duke UP, 1993.

Lucie-Smith, Edward. *American Realism.* New York: Abrams, 1994.

Mark Twain [videorecording]. Produced by Dayton Duncan & Ken Burns; written by Dayton Duncan & Geoffrey C. Ward; directed by Ken Burns; produced in association with WETA, Washington, DC. Burbank: Warner Home Video, 2001.

Nye, David. *American Technological Sublime.* Cambridge: MIT Press, 1994.

Thomas Eakins: An American Realist [actual and virtual exhibit]. Philadelphia Museum of Art. Benjamin Franklin Parkway and 26th Street, Philadelphia, PA, 19130. Main museum number: (215) 763-8100. *Thomas Eakins* [catalog], organized by Darrel Sewell with essays by Kathleen A. Foster [et al.]. Philadelphia, PA: Philadelphia Museum of Art in association with Yale UP, 2001.

Weinberg, H. Barbara. *American Impressionism and Realism: The Painting of Modern Life, 1885–1915* [exhibit]. New York: Metropolitan Museum of Art: Distributed by Harry N. Abrams, 1994.

Unit 9

SOCIAL REALISM

*Class Consciousness in American
Literature, 1875–1920*

Authors and Works

Featured in the Video:
Edith Wharton, "Souls Belated" (short story)
Anzia Yezierska, "The Lost 'Beautifulness'" (short story)

Discussed in This Unit:
Sarah Morgan Bryan Piatt, "The Palace-Burner," "A Pique at Parting," "Army of Occupation" (poetry)
Henry James, "Daisy Miller: A Study," "The Real Thing," "The Beast in the Jungle," "The Jolly Corner" (short stories); "The Art of Fiction" (literary criticism)
Booker T. Washington, excerpts from *Up from Slavery* (autobiography)
Abraham Cahan, "A Sweat-Shop Romance" (short story)
Sui Sin Far (Edith Maud Eaton), "Mrs. Spring Fragrance" (short story)
W. E. B. Du Bois, excerpts from *The Souls of Black Folk* (social and political criticism, music history)
Theodore Dreiser, "Old Rogaum and His Theresa" (short story)
Henry Adams, excerpts from *The Education of Henry Adams* (autobiography)

Overview Questions

■ What different ethnic groups inhabited America's urban areas around the turn of the century? How did their traditions and cultural values change American culture?

■ How do social realist texts represent gender? What kinds of issues inform social realist writing by women?

■ How did Booker T. Washington and Henry Adams transform the genre of the autobiography? How did their work change ideas about American identity?

■ How do social realist writings reflect the distinct cultures and political concerns of different ethnic groups?

■ What kinds of class structures divided American society at the turn of the century? Which classes of people are depicted in realist texts?

■ What political and social transformations in turn-of-the-century America led to the development of social realism? What kinds of political effects and reforms did social realist writers hope to produce?

■ How did industrialism change the demographics of urban and rural society in America?

■ How did immigrant culture shape life in lower-class cityscapes such as the Lower East Side of Manhattan?

■ How did social realist writers depict the contrasts between American and European customs and values? Why were so many social realists interested in this question?

■ How do realist writers describe the material conditions and physical surfaces of the world in which their fictional characters live? Why has their descriptive style sometimes been described as "documentary"?

■ What is "limited third-person narrative"?

■ How did the "gospel of wealth" build on and transform ideas about opportunity in America?

■ How did writers who represented immigrant experiences challenge and broaden the myth of the American Dream?

■ How did women activists and writers challenge ideas about the role of women in American society?

Learning Objectives

After students have viewed the video, read the headnotes and literary selections in *The Norton Anthology of American Literature*, and explored related archival materials on the *American Passages* Web site, they should be able to

1. explain the distinguishing characteristics of literary realism;
2. describe the social and economic conditions in turn-of-the-twentieth-century America that gave rise to social realism;
3. explain the difference between psychological and social realism;
4. discuss the political debates and reforms engendered by and reflected in social realist literature.

Instructor Overview

In 1884, Henry James announced that the "supreme virtue" of fiction, and the quality by which its success should be judged, resides in its ability to produce an "air of reality," or an "illusion of life." James, like many other American writers of the late nineteenth century, embraced an aesthetic of realism, which valued unsparing, accurate representations of the psychological and material realities of American life. Some realist writers, known as "social realists," were interested in exploring problems of economic inequality and in accurately capturing the experience of urban life that was transforming the nation at the end of the nineteenth century. Others, known as "psychological realists," were more concerned with delving beneath the surface of social life to probe the complex motivations and unconscious desires that shape their characters' perceptions. In their commitment to documenting the realities of everyday life in America, both social and psychological realists offered penetrating insight into the repression, instabilities, and inequalities that structured late-nineteenth-century American society.

Before the Civil War, America had been a nation made up primarily of farms and small towns. Most citizens worked in agriculture or in small, family-owned shops and businesses. By the 1870s, however, the growth of industrialism had transformed American lifestyles: more people lived in cities and worked in factories than ever before. Lured by economic opportunities, millions of immigrants from southern and Eastern Europe and China flooded urban centers like New York and San Francisco. Multiplying in size and serving as home to both wealthy socialites and impoverished immigrants, these cities reflected the astonishing diversity of the millions of people who lived and worked in them. While this confluence of people from radically different economic, social, and ethnic backgrounds created a rich and vibrant urban culture, it also led to social tensions and brought into relief the discrepancies between the very wealthy and the very poor. Socially conscious writers committed themselves to exploring and representing the impact of social class and ethnicity on American life, developing literary techniques designed to lend their texts an air of objective reality and psychological authenticity in the process. Some of these social realist authors wrote in order to protest the inequalities and exploitation that characterized American industrialization. Their work contributed to the growing Progressive political movements dedicated to eradicating social problems, including the oppression of women, prejudice against immigrants, discrimination against racial minorities, unsafe housing conditions, and exploitative labor practices. Other writers, such as Henry James and Edith Wharton, wrote about the experiences of the upper class.

All of the writers featured in Unit 9, "Social Realism: Class Consciousness in American Literature, 1875–1920," share an interest in realistically depicting American life at the close of the nineteenth century, though they focus on very different social classes and ethnic groups and deploy very different literary strategies. This unit surveys works composed by Sarah Morgan Bryan Piatt, Henry James, Booker T. Washington, Abraham Cahan, Edith Wharton, Sui Sin Far (Edith Maud Eaton), W. E. B. Du Bois, Theodore Dreiser, Henry Adams, and Anzia Yezierska. It provides contextual background and classroom materials designed to explore the way these writers represented the impact of social class and ethnicity on urban life around the turn of the twentieth century. The video for Unit 9 focuses on two writers who chronicled life at opposite ends of the social stratum in New York City: Edith Wharton created realistic, psychologically nuanced portraits of people enmeshed in urban high society, while Anzia Yezierska explored the tensions inherent in Jewish immigrant life on the Lower East Side of Manhattan. Although their depictions of New York and its inhabitants are radically different, both of these writers exposed the inconsistencies and inequalities of American urban life, with a special emphasis on the difficulties faced by women.

In its coverage of Wharton's and Yezierska's contrasting New York experiences, the video introduces students to the literary categories of social and psychological realism and foregrounds the relationship of these movements to the problems facing an increasingly industrialized and urbanized America. The video asks students to consider the connections between the literary aesthetic of realism and the historical circumstances of late-nineteenth-century America. How did social class emerge as a focus for American writers? What role did immigration play in the development of American urban culture? How did literary realists depict the tensions and conflicts inherent in an industrialized economy? What effect did social realist writers hope to have on the problems they exposed? How do issues of gender and ethnicity shape their accounts? How does the work of social realists relate to that of psychological realists? Unit 9 helps answer these questions by providing background and teaching suggestions intended to locate these writers within their cultural contexts and to connect them with other key writers of the era. The curriculum materials expand on the video's introduction to social and psychological realism by exploring writers who developed different literary techniques and chronicled the experiences of different groups, such as Sarah Morgan Bryan Piatt (a poet who experimented with realist techniques by using polyvocality and dialogue in her poems), W. E. B. Du Bois (an activist for African American rights), and Sui Sin Far (a Eurasian woman who depicted life among Chinese immigrants on the West Coast).

The video, the archive, and the curriculum materials situate these writers within several of the historical contexts that shaped their texts: (1) the explosion in immigration at the end of the nineteenth century; (2) the movement for woman suffrage; (3) ideas about capitalism and the "gospel of wealth" in newly industrialized America; (4) the creation of a vibrant immigrant community on the Lower East Side of Manhattan; and (5) African American activists' strategies for achieving racial equality through education.

The archive and the curriculum materials suggest how the authors and texts featured in Unit 9 relate to those covered in other *American Passages* units: How do concerns about social class continue to inform American literature? What is the relationship between social class and ethnicity? How have later American writers drawn from the example of social realists to produce fiction and poetry designed to register social protest? How did the movement toward creating psychologically complex characters influence subsequent American writing? Do Americans still believe literature has the power to effect social change? How have ideas about "realism" and "accuracy" in fiction changed over time?

Student Overview

In 1884, Henry James announced that the "supreme virtue" of fiction, and the quality by which its success should be judged, resides in its ability to produce an "air of reality," or an "illusion of life." James, like many other American writers of the late nineteenth century, embraced an aesthetic of **realism**, which valued unsparing, accurate representations of the psychological and material realities of American life. Some realist writers, known as "social realists," were interested in exploring problems of economic inequality and in accurately capturing the experience of urban life that was transforming the nation at the end of the nineteenth century. Others, known as "psychological realists," were more concerned with delving beneath the surface of social life to probe the complex motivations and unconscious desires that shape their characters' perceptions. In their commitment to documenting the realities of everyday life in America, both social and psychological realists offered penetrating insight into the repression, instabilities, and inequalities that structured late-nineteenth-century American society.

Before the Civil War, America had been a nation made up primarily of farms and small towns. Most citizens worked in agriculture or in small, family-owned shops and businesses. By the 1870s, however, the growth of industrialism had transformed American lifestyles: more people lived in cities and worked in factories than ever before. Lured by economic opportunities, millions of immigrants from southern and Eastern Europe and China flooded urban centers like New York and San Francisco. Multiplying in size and serving as home to both wealthy socialites and impoverished immigrants, these cities reflected the astonishing diversity of the millions of people who lived and worked in them. While this confluence of people from radically different economic, social, and ethnic backgrounds created a rich and vibrant urban culture, it also led to social tensions and brought into relief the discrepancies between the very wealthy and the very poor. Socially conscious writers committed themselves to exploring and representing the impact of social class and ethnicity on American life, developing literary techniques designed to lend their texts an air of objective reality and psychological authenticity in the process. Some of these social realist authors wrote in order to protest the inequalities and exploitation that characterized American industrialization. Their work contributed to the growing Progressive political movements dedicated to eradicating social problems, including the oppression of women, prejudice against immigrants, discrimination against racial minorities, unsafe housing conditions, and exploitative labor practices. Other writers, such as Henry James and Edith Wharton, wrote about the experiences of the upper class.

All of the writers featured in Unit 9, "Social Realism: Class Consciousness in American Literature, 1875–1920," share an interest in realistically depicting American life at the close of the nineteenth century, though they focus on very different social classes and ethnic groups and deploy very different literary strategies. As the video for Unit 9 makes clear, writers like Edith Wharton and Anzia Yezierska provided insight into the diversity of late-nineteenth-century New York City. While Wharton offered psychological, nuanced examinations of wealthy New Yorkers constrained by the rigid codes of their elite social class, Yezierska chronicled the experiences of Jewish immigrants living in poverty on the Lower East Side of Manhattan. Despite the differences in their subject matter, however, Wharton and Yezierska—along with all of the writers featured in Unit 9—shared a commitment to exposing the inconsistencies and inequalities of American urban life, and to exploring the impact of social class and ethnicity on the formation of American identity.

Video Overview

➢ **Authors covered:** Edith Wharton, Anzia Yezierska

➢ **Who's interviewed:** Judith Baskin, professor of religious studies and director of the Harold Schnitzer Family Program in Judaic Studies (University of Oregon); Bruce Michelson, professor of English (University of Illinois, Urbana-Champaign); Kathryn Oberdeck, associate professor of history (University of Illinois, Urbana-Champaign); Abby Werlock, author, former president and current member of the Edith Wharton Society

➢ **Points covered:**

• Introduction to the clash of cultures and social classes that resulted from the forces of urbanization, industrialization, and immigration in America at the turn of the century. Two very different sides of the "Gilded Age," as this period was called, were visible in New York. There, a few city blocks separated wealthy socialites from starving immigrants.

• Edith Wharton, a member of wealthy New York society, chronicled the world of her exclusive social set in detail. Her realist novels and stories depict the frustration of people trapped by social conventions, often focusing on the plight of society women who were treated as commodities or ornaments to be purchased and bartered by men. Her attention to the complex psychological and emotional motivations of her characters marks her work as part of the "psychological realist" movement.

• Anzia Yezierska wrote poignantly about her experiences as a Jewish immigrant in the Lower East Side of Manhattan. In her social realist fiction, she attempted

to explain immigrant culture to American-born readers and to broaden the boundaries of the American
dream to include immigrants, the impoverished, and
women. Yezierska's stories and novels often examine
the process of assimilation and acculturation, chronicling the tensions caused by immigrants' desire to be
part of both the Old World and the New.

• While Wharton concentrated on psychological realism
and Yezierska was more interested in social realism,
both of these women writers explored the inconsistencies and inequities of American society at the turn of
the century. In the process, they created complex characters who wrestled with the restraints of class and
convention. Wharton and Yezierska left a lasting literary legacy in their willingness to depict realistically
and to criticize American society.

PREVIEW

• **Preview the video:** In the decades between 1890 and
1920, America was transformed into an industrial,
urban, consumer society. This transformation created
unprecedented opportunities for the acquisition of
wealth, but also enabled the exploitation of large classes
of people. Immigrants arriving in waves from Eastern and
southern Europe had heard stories of a land where the
streets were paved with gold, but in many cases they
found only poverty and inequity in America. Writers
responded to the rapidly shifting class and social structure they saw around them by producing texts that realistically depicted both the problems and the promise of
industrial, urban America. In many cases, their goal was
to educate readers and to stimulate reform. Edith Wharton, a member of elite New York society, explored the
complexity of the social forms that governed her world in
carefully crafted novels and stories. Her psychologically
complex characters struggle with the conflict between
their desires and the authority of social convention. Anzia
Yezierska focused on a completely different social milieu,
chronicling the lives of poor Jewish immigrants on the
Lower East Side of New York. Her stories and novels work
to broaden the boundaries of the myth of the American
Dream and to make it available to women, immigrants,
and the poor. While Wharton and Yezierska moved in
very different social worlds and had very different concerns, they both were interested in the plight of women
who struggled against the constraints of class and convention.

• **What to think about while watching:** How do these
authors challenge readers to grapple with difficult issues
regarding social class, ethnic background, and gender?
How do these writers react against romantic conventions
and dedicate themselves to psychological and social realism? How does literary realism forward its goal of social
action and reform? How do social realists broaden and
transform the myth of the American Dream? How did
Wharton's and Yezierska's attention to class and gender
inform subsequent American fiction?

• **Tying the video to the unit content:** Unit 9 expands on
the issues featured in the video to explore the diversity of
social realist writing in America in the late nineteenth
century. The curriculum materials provide background on
African American, Asian American, Jewish American,
and European American writers who chronicle the experiences of different social classes and ethnicities, and who
advocate different ideas about social reform. The unit
offers contextual background to further develop the
video's introduction to the historical events, economic
and political issues, and literary styles that shaped social
realist literature.

	What is American literature? What are its distinctive voices and styles? How do social and political issues influence the American canon?	*What is an American? How does American literature create conceptions of the American experience and identity?*	*How are American myths created, challenged, and re-imagined through these works of literature?*
Compre-hension Questions	What is social realism? How did this literary movement depart from earlier nineteenth-century literary conventions?	What groups of immigrants came to America at the end of the nine-teenth century? Why did they leave their homes? How did they change the face of America?	What expectations and hopes did many immigrants have when they came to America? How was the reality of their experience different from what they imagined?
Context Questions	What kinds of social reform might Yezierska have been interested in promoting? How are her concerns different from Wharton's?	How do the characters Hannah Hayyeh and Lily Bart rebel against social and class conventions? How does their status as women affect their situations? How do their different social classes affect their situations?	How does Yezierska's work broaden and expand the possibili-ties of the American Dream?
Exploration Questions	How do you think the immigrant experience has changed since Yezierska wrote about it?	How has women's status in America changed since Wharton and Yezierska wrote about it?	Do you think American writers still view literature as an important instrument of social change? As an effective tool for reform?

	Texts	Contexts
1870s	Henry Adams, "The New York Gold Conspiracies" (1870) Sarah Morgan Bryan Piatt, "The Palace-Burner" (1874) Henry James, "Daisy Miller" (1878)	Battle of Little Bighorn ("Custer's Last Stand") (1876) Alexander Graham Bell invents the telephone (1876) Reconstruction ends as federal occupying troops leave the South (1877) Edison patents the phonograph (1878)
1880s	Henry Adams, *Democracy* (1880), *Esther* (1884), *History of the United States of America during the Administration of Thomas Jefferson and James Madison* (1889) Henry James, *The Portrait of a Lady* (1881), "The Art of Fiction" (1884)	American Red Cross founded (1881) Chinese Exclusion Act (1882)
1890s	Henry James, "The Real Thing" (1893), *The Turn of the Screw* (1898) Booker T. Washington, "Atlanta Exposition Address" (1895) Abraham Cahan, *Yekl: A Tale of the New York Ghetto* (1896), "A Sweat-Shop Romance" (1898) Edith Wharton, "Souls Belated" (1899)	Massacre at Wounded Knee, South Dakota (1890) National American Woman Suffrage Association founded (1890) U.S. Supreme Court upholds the legality of segregation and the institutions of Jim Crow in *Plessy v. Ferguson* (1896)
1900s	Theodore Dreiser, *Sister Carrie* (1900), "Old Rogaum and His Theresa" (1901) Booker T. Washington, *Up from Slavery* (1901) W. E. B. Du Bois, *The Souls of Black Folk* (1903), "The Talented Tenth" (1903) Henry James, "The Beast in the Jungle" (1903), "The Jolly Corner" (1909) Edith Wharton, *The House of Mirth* (1905)	Orville and Wilbur Wright achieve first powered flight, Kitty Hawk, North Carolina (1903) International Workers of the World union founded (1905) First radio broadcast from Plymouth, Massachusetts (1906) Ford Model T goes into production (1908)
1910s	Sui Sin Far, *Mrs. Spring Fragrance* (1912) Henry Adams, *Mont-Saint-Michel and Chartres* (1913), *The Education of Henry Adams* (1918) Abraham Cahan, *The Rise of David Levinsky* (1917) Anzia Yezierska, "The Fat of the Land" (1919)	World War I (1914–18) United States enters World War I (1917) Russian Revolution (1917)
1920s	Edith Wharton, *The Age of Innocence* (1920) Anzia Yezierska, *Hungry Hearts* (1920), "The Lost 'Beautifulness'" (1920) Theodore Dreiser, *An American Tragedy* (1925)	Wall Street Crash begins Great Depression (1929)

AUTHOR/TEXT REVIEW

Sarah Morgan Bryan Piatt (1836–1919)

A poet widely published in nineteenth-century America, Sarah Morgan Bryan Piatt saw hundreds of her verses appear in newspapers and magazines, and she published fifteen collected volumes of her work. The complexity and subtlety of some of her poetry tended to trouble critics, however, who accused her of being "wayward" and "enigmatic." Although she sometimes wrote within the genteel, sentimental tradition that dominated American women's poetry in the nineteenth century, Piatt—to her critics' dismay—also experimented with more challenging and allusive forms of expression. Piatt's subtle and often ironic aesthetic went largely unappreciated until contemporary feminist literary critics led a reassessment of her importance. Today Piatt's work is beginning to be recognized as a significant forerunner to the modernist poetry that emerged in the early twentieth century.

Sarah Piatt was raised in rural Kentucky and attended a women's college there. She received a liberal arts education, with a particular focus on the classics and on romantic poetry. Her interest in poetry was strengthened by her marriage in 1861 to John James Piatt, himself a poet. The couple eventually had seven children and John James, or J. J., took a variety of editorial and government jobs to support his large family. Over the course of his career, Piatt moved his family several times, living in Washington, D.C., Ohio, and Ireland. After growing up in the South, moving to the North, and living in Europe, Sarah Piatt developed a sophisticated awareness of cultural differences and the relativity of one's point of view, insights that permeate her poetry. With J. J. serving as editor and agent, Piatt published in many of the prestigious journals and magazines of the time and brought out a series of books. Despite her productivity, however, she and her husband both died in poverty.

[7634] Anonymous, *National Cemetery, Arlington, Virginia* (c. 1910–50), courtesy of the Library of Congress [LC-USZ62-91935].

Though Piatt's work sometimes deals with conventional sentimental themes such as children, romance, and death, she often uses her poetry to self-consciously deflate sentimental conventions. Her later work is characterized by a dramatic realism that relies on dialogue to elucidate her complex and subtle meaning. Many of Piatt's best poems do not rely on a single lyric voice but instead introduce multiple speakers (often children). This multitude of voices can be confusing to readers—an early reviewer complained that, by not making clear who is speaking and in what context, Piatt's poems leave "much to be supplied by intuition and imagination." But if engaging with Piatt's work can sometimes feel like trying to solve a difficult riddle, most readers will find the rich, complex results to be worth the effort.

[1927] William M. Smith, [Untitled] (1865), courtesy of the Library of Congress [LC-B8171-7861]. This picture shows African American soldiers who comprised the band of the 107th Colored Infantry: one of the many contradictions of the Civil War was that African American soldiers fought for the Confederacy to protect the institution of slavery, and others fought for the Union, where they were denied equal treatment before the law. Of the many writers whose work was affected by the Civil War, poet Sarah Morgan Bryan Piatt stands out for holding both the North and the South responsible for the war and its carnage. Though she lived in Union territory, her life and poetry were informed by the perspective of her southern childhood: her parents owned slaves, and she acknowledged her complicity in the forces that caused the devastation she described in her poems.

[7632] Keystone View Company, *Burial of Victims of the Maine in their Final Resting Place, Arlington Cemetery, VA, Dec. 28, 1899* (1899), courtesy of the Library of Congress, Prints and Photographs Division [LC-USZ62-92665]. Photograph of caskets, draped with the American flag and lined in rows, ready for burial at the Arlington Cemetery in Virginia. Four million people visit the cemetery annually to pay tribute to war heroes, to attend funeral services, and to view headstones that tell America's history.

[7634] Anonymous, *National Cemetery, Arlington, Virginia* (c. 1910–50), courtesy of the Library of Congress [LC-USZ62-91935]. Photograph of Arlington National Cemetery in Virginia, with the Memorial Amphitheater in the foreground. The amphitheater was dedicated in 1920 after a campaign for its construction by Judge Ivory G. Kimball, who wanted to have an assembling place for honoring defenders of America.

[9140] Robert Browning, "My Last Duchess" (1842), courtesy of Project Gutenberg. Browning's poem "My Last Duchess" is a quintessential example of the poetic genre of the dramatic monologue. The first-person speaker is a duke who hints at the murder of his wife, even as he arranges for a new marriage.

■ Many students will find "The Palace-Burner" difficult to penetrate because the context for the speaker's musings may not be readily apparent to them and because the poem includes the voices of both its primary speaker and her son. Be sure to explain that the speaker is reflecting on a picture she and her son are looking at in a newspaper. The two of them discuss the pictured woman, who was a radical and a "palace-burner" during the political struggles in France in the 1870s. Have your students read the poem out loud and then work through it slowly as a class. Who is speaking? Which questions are asked by the primary speaker's son? Which does she ask herself? Why does Piatt include these different voices in her poem without always clarifying who is speaking? In order to explain the "dramatic" quality of the poem, you might bring in one of Robert Browning's dramatic monologues ("My Last Duchess," "Porphyria's Lover," or "The Laboratory" would be good choices). Ask students to think about the effect of these dramatic monologues in which the voice of the speaker is not always that of the poet. What kind of challenges does the distance among the poet, the speaker, and the speaker's interlocutors pose for the reader? How do Piatt's dramatic poems compare to Browning's?

■ After reading and discussing "The Palace-Burner," ask your students to choose a picture that they find particularly moving in a magazine or newspaper and then write a poem or reflection in which they explain the effect the picture has on them. Have volunteers share their poems with the class and discuss the challenges they experienced in writing this kind of piece.

QUESTIONS

Comprehension: Who are the characters in "The Palace-Burner"? Who is speaking? What is the "picture in the newspaper" mentioned in the subtitle?

Context: How does the speaker in "A Pique at Parting" critique romantic conventions? How does her analysis of the power struggle between men and women compare to Lydia's experience in Edith Wharton's "Souls Belated"?

Context: Examine the picture of Arlington National Cemetery featured in the archive. How does it compare to Piatt's description of it in "Army of Occupation"? Why is Arlington such a powerful place for her?

Exploration: Why do you think Piatt was largely ignored by literary critics until recently? Why do you think feminist critics find her appealing now? How do Piatt's poems relate to the sentimental tradition within which many nineteenth-century women wrote? How do her poems anticipate the work of later American women poets, like Amy Lowell or H.D.? How do poems like Lowell's "The Captured Goddess" or H.D.'s "Helen" compare to Piatt's attempts to challenge traditional representations of women? How do later poets like Lowell and H.D. continue to wrestle with one of the problems that concerned Piatt—how to be a woman poet within a culture where women were perceived more as subjects for poetry than as writers of it?

Exploration: Why do you think Piatt is included in this unit on social realism? In what way might her poetry be understood as "realist"?

Henry James (1843–1916)

Known for his sophisticated style, precise language, extraordinary productivity, and innovative attention to the novel form, Henry James ranks among the greatest American writers. He was born in the mid-nineteenth century in New York City. His father, Henry James Sr., was a wealthy and eccentric philosopher who initiated his young son into what would become a lifelong habit of travel. The family, eventually consisting of five children, crossed the Atlantic Ocean repeatedly before 1860, and the James children were brought up and educated in Europe almost as much as they were in America.

When the family returned to America just before the Civil War, two of James's brothers enlisted in the Union Army, but Henry himself stayed out of the war because of an injury. After a brief period studying law at Harvard, he began publishing stories and reviews in the major American magazines of his day, and by 1869, had committed himself to a literary career. He traveled back and forth between Europe and America several times before finally deciding to settle in England, first in London and eventually at Lamb House, an eighteenth-century mansion located in a coastal town southeast of London. He became a naturalized British subject near the end of his life. James always maintained an active social life (he was famous for dining out almost every night of the week) and had a close relationship with his family, especially with his brother William, a pioneering American psychologist who was an important influence on James. But despite his familial and social ties, James spent much of his time alone at his writing desk. He never married, and he poured most of his emotional energy into his work.

Scholars traditionally have divided James's career into three phases: a lengthy apprenticeship (1864–81), the middle years (1882–95), and his major phase (1896–1916). James first achieved international fame with his story "Daisy Miller: A Study" (1878), which deals with the contrast between European and American manners by exploring a young girl's disregard for social codes. Although some readers considered the story shocking, it was widely reprinted. James's early phase culminated with *The Portrait of a Lady* (1881), a novel which many critics regard as one of his masterpieces. During what James referred to as his middle years, he produced several long political novels (none of which sold well), numerous short stories, some of his most influential literary criticism (including "The Art of Fiction"), and a disastrously unsuccessful play. James's major phase is characterized by his increasing complexity and subtlety as a writer and by the culmination of his development of a new

[1581] John Singer Sargent, *The Daughters of Edward Darley Boit* (1882), courtesy of Museum of Fine Arts, Boston. Reproduced with permission. © Museum of Fine Arts, Boston. *The Daughters of Edward Darley Boit*, 1882; John Singer Sargent, American (1856–1925). Oil on canvas; 87 3/8 x 87 5/8 in. (221.9 x 222.6 cm). Gift of Mary Louisa Boit, Julia Overing Boit, Jane Hubbard Boit, and Florence D. Boit in memory of their father, Edward Darley Boit [19.124].

modernist aesthetic for the novel form. It was also a period of intense productivity: he wrote thirty-seven stories, some of his most famous novellas (including the ghost story *The Turn of the Screw*), and several of his most important novels. Between 1906 and 1910 James embarked on the monumental project of revising his own work for publication in the twenty-four-volume New York edition of his *Collected Works*.

Throughout his career, James maintained an interest in contrasting European and American manners, and in exploring the ways psychologically complex characters deal with ambiguous social and intellectual problems. James has sometimes been criticized for the rarified quality of his work. For some readers, he seems to neglect "flesh and blood" problems in order to focus on the neurotic anxieties of over-privileged, self-absorbed characters. But for James, the value of fiction writing lay in providing "a personal, a direct impression of life," which to him was best achieved not by chronicling material conditions but rather by examining the subjective, psychological complexities of human beings. His interest in psychology led him to develop the use of **limited third-person narration**, which is often regarded as one of his major contributions to American fiction. By relying on narrators who are not omniscient but instead render descriptions and observations through the limitations of the central character, James opens his stories to ambiguity. Readers must do more work—and involve themselves more in the process of meaning-making—to understand the relationship of the stories to their narration.

TEACHING TIPS

■ Ask your students to write a short paraphrase of "what happens" in "The Jolly Corner" or "The Beast in the Jungle." When they are finished, discuss their summaries as a class. Because these stories are so complex—and focus so narrowly on their psychologically troubled main characters—students will have very different ideas about what should be considered the "action" of the story. You can use this project to make the point that "reality" is highly subjective in a James story. Readers will interpret the characters' psychological experiences differently, just as two characters in the same story will interpret the events differently.

■ With its ironic examination of the relationship between representations and reality, "The Real Thing" can serve as an excellent jumping-off point for a discussion of realism as an artistic movement. The story serves as a kind of fable about the artistic production of realistic representation. The reader, along with the artist in the story, comes to realize that it is precisely *because* the Monarchs represent British aristocratic values that they fail as models of the type. Artistic inspiration seems to depend on artificiality and pretense (figured by the lower-class models) and is hampered by the stifling presence of the "real thing." (To help your students understand the relationship between narrative and visual realism, you might have them examine some of the late-nineteenth-century realist paintings featured in the archive, such as John Singer Sargent's *The Daughters of Edward Darley Boit* or *Simplon Pass: The Tease*.) Ask your students to think about the implications of James's fable about the making of realistic art. What is the relationship between the artist and reality? What seems to be the goal of the "realist" art object? What is the relationship between the artist in the story and Henry James, the writer?

QUESTIONS

Comprehension: Why do Winterbourne's aunt, Mrs. Walker, and the rest of polite society in Europe shun Daisy Miller? What exactly do they find so shocking about her? How does she challenge conventional social codes?

Comprehension: According to James, what qualities characterize successful fiction? What kind of manifesto for fiction writing does he lay out in "The Art of Fiction"?

Context: Like Edith Wharton, Henry James frequently wrote about Americans traveling and living in Europe. What characteristics mark a typical "American" character for James? How does he see Americans as different from Europeans? How does his analysis of the contrast between Americans and Europeans compare to Wharton's?

Context: In "The Jolly Corner," Spencer Brydon is in the process of overseeing the conversion of one of his properties into "a tall mass of flats," while maintaining the other as an intact, but empty, mansion. What do these two types of housing structures represent to Brydon? Why does the realization that he has a "capacity for business and a sense for construction" create such harrowing anxieties for him? What is his relationship to the large family mansion on the "jolly corner"?

Context: James was once driven through the Lower East Side where he saw the crowded tenements and bustling commercial stalls of the Jewish section. He reported that he was disgusted by a sense of "a great swarming." How might knowledge of James's reaction to the tenements inform our understanding of "The Jolly Corner"? How do you think immigrants living in overcrowded tenements would react to Brydon's story of his frightening encounter with his empty mansion? For help in forming your response, see the material featured in the Lower East Side context in this unit.

Exploration: In 1879, James wrote the first critical-biographical book about Nathaniel Hawthorne's literary career. Why do you think James was so interested in Hawthorne? What values and interests do they share? How are they different from one another?

Booker T. Washington (1856–1915)

Born into slavery and poverty, Booker T. Washington grew up to become one of the most powerful African American public figures in the United States at the end of the nineteenth century. As a speaker, writer, and educator, Washington articulated ideas that had a tremendous influence on the state of race relations in America. In his autobiography, *Up from Slavery* (1901), he told the story of his life as the fulfillment of the mythic American Dream: he stresses that his success was achieved through hard work, perseverance, and virtue. Washington's skillful self-presentation and his remarkable abilities as a speaker, writer, and rhetorician played no small part in his rise to leadership and his consolidation of power within the African American community.

Washington was born on a plantation near Roanoke, Virginia. His childhood was spent in slavery, and he grew up, as he put it, in "the most miserable, desolate, and discouraging surroundings." Freed after the Civil War, he and his mother moved to West Virginia, where his stepfather had found work as a miner. Although he was eager to attend school, Washington was forced to help support his family by working in salt and coal mines and as a domestic servant. He eventually acquired a basic education by teaching himself the alphabet, studying with a local schoolteacher in the evenings, and convincing the wife of his white employer to give him lessons.

In 1872 Washington was admitted to the Hampton Institute, an industrial school established by the state of Virginia to educate freed blacks and Native Americans. Washington had to work as a janitor to support himself at Hampton, but he still managed to graduate with honors in three years. After college, Washington worked as a teacher until he was selected to serve as the principal of Tuskegee, a new school for black students in Alabama.

[1824] Palmer, *Instructor and Three Graduates with Diplomas and Geraniums* (1905), courtesy of the Wm. B. Becker Collection/ photographymuseum.com.

From 1881 until his death in 1915, Washington devoted much of his considerable energy and talent to establishing and maintaining Tuskegee as a prestigious black-run institution. Working with little money and few resources, he managed to transform the school from a small college of thirty students into a respected institution with an endowment of $2 million, a staff of two hundred, and a student body of four thousand. Convinced that African Americans would achieve social and economic advancement only through acquiring practical industrial and agricultural skills, Washington focused Tuskegee's curriculum on vocational subjects such as carpentry, masonry, farming, and domestic science. The school also stressed hygiene, manners, and religious instruction.

Building on Tuskegee's success, Washington concentrated on publicizing his educational and social philosophy on a broader level. In 1895 he captured national attention when he delivered a speech on race relations at the Atlanta Exposition. Later known as the "Atlanta Compromise," the speech emphasized the importance of attaining economic security through pragmatic, nonconfrontational means. Washington urged African Americans not to strain race relations by demanding civil rights, but instead to settle for peaceful coexistence and economic opportunity. As he put it, "in all things that are purely social we can be as separate as fingers, yet one as the hand in all things essential to mutual progress." While some African Americans resented Washington's willingness to sacrifice civil equality and political rights for menial jobs and toleration, many others saw Washington's plan in a positive light. In a climate in which African Americans were routinely oppressed, disenfranchised, and targeted for violence, it is perhaps understandable that Washington's promises of economic opportunity and peace would seem appealing. Organized opposition to Washington's "accommodationist" philosophy within the African American community would not arise until many years later (most notably under the leadership of W. E. B. Du Bois), and, following the Atlanta convention, Washington emerged as a powerful leader who commanded respect from both blacks and whites. The white press hailed him as the successor of Frederick Douglass and the undisputed leader of his race.

Washington consolidated his almost mythic position with the publication of *Up from Slavery*. Drawing on the literary models of Douglass's and Benjamin Franklin's autobiographies, he told his life story as an exemplary lesson in hard work, thrift, and virtue. With its deceptively simple and direct style, the book became a best-seller and was translated into more than ten languages.

Washington's willingness to compromise on African American civil equality—a philosophy that had ensured his popularity in his own time—has hurt his reputation with subsequent generations of American readers. Recent scholarship, however, has made the case that Washington's placating and accommodating stance was merely a public screen to gain favor with white authorities. According to this theory, Washington worked covertly to challenge racial injustice while maintaining a nonthreatening appearance. While critical debates continue on the nature of Washington's racial philosophy and political strategy, no one denies that he was an influential force in bringing African American concerns to public consciousness at the end of the nineteenth century.

TEACHING TIPS

■ In *Up from Slavery*, Washington reprints his Atlanta Exposition address, following it with excerpts from newspaper reviews praising the speech and a congratulatory letter from President Grover Cleveland. Ask students why they think Washington included all this supplementary material in his autobiography. What effect do the letters and newspaper reviews have on the reader's understanding of the speech? Ask students to imagine that they listened to the speech

[1824] Palmer, *Instructor and Three Graduates with Diplomas and Geraniums* (1905), courtesy of the Wm. B. Becker Collection/ photographymuseum.com. Former slave Booker T. Washington was deeply involved with the Tuskegee Institute throughout his lifetime. Washington advocated vocational training for African Americans as a means by which they could achieve economic advancement. His social philosophy was later criticized by such figures as W. E. B. Du Bois.

[3079] Richmond Barth, *Bust of Booker T. Washington* (c. 1920), courtesy of the National Archives and Records Administration [NWDNS-H-HN-BAR-38]. Washington was the most prominent African American at the turn of the twentieth century; he worked for most of his life to expand and support the Tuskegee Institute in Alabama; his best-known literary work is *Up from Slavery.*

[6937] R. V. Randolph, *Booker T. Washington* (1913), courtesy of the Library of Congress, Printed Ephemera Collection [Portfolio 189, Folder 2a]. This poetic tribute, published as a broadside, reads, in part, "Now 'Tuskegee and its People' know, / That fitness and efficiency win; / The Negro in Business will show, / The methods make a place for men"—an apt reference to Washington's vision that education in the mechanical arts would raise African Americans from their subjugated status.

[7852] Arthur Rothstein, *Tuskegee Institute, Alabama Students* (1942), courtesy of the Library of Congress [LC-USW3-000237-D]. Now designated a historic site by the National Park system, Tuskegee Institute was the lifelong project of Booker T. Washington and also the site of George Washington Carver's revolutionary agricultural experiments.

at the Atlanta Exposition and then have them write newspaper reviews or letters to Washington in which they articulate their responses to his philosophy.

■ The opening of *Up from Slavery* consciously engages with autobiographical conventions. Ask students to pay attention to the way Washington opens the story of his life. What is the effect of Washington's inability to say where and when he was born, or to give any details about his ancestry? How are we meant to understand the line "I suspect I must have been born somewhere and at sometime"? Is this humorous? Tragic? Both?

QUESTIONS

Comprehension: Washington closes Chapter 15 of *Up from Slavery* with some reflections on time management and organization. What kind of lessons and life tips does he impart to his readers? What values underlie his manner of structuring his work and leisure?

Context: Like Henry Adams, Washington uses his autobiography as an occasion to reflect on his own education and his educational philosophy more generally. How do Washington's ideas about education compare to Adams's? How might the two men's radically different backgrounds contribute to their different ideas on what constitutes a useful education?

Context: Examine the bust of Washington and the broadside poem celebrating his accomplishments featured in the archive. What vision of Washington as a man and as a leader do these pieces construct? How did Washington contribute to his own mythology in *Up from Slavery*?

Exploration: Many scholars have argued that Washington consciously modeled *Up from Slavery* on Benjamin Franklin's *Autobiography*. What do these two texts have in common? What structures and tropes does Washington borrow from Franklin? How does his life story complicate Franklin's construction of an exemplary American identity?

Abraham Cahan (1860–1951)

As a journalist and fiction writer, Abraham Cahan explored the social, cultural, and spiritual tensions of the Eastern European Jewish immigrant experience in New York. His sensitive treatment of the dual identities of Jewishness and Americanism, and of issues of accommodation and acculturation, made him an influential spokesperson for his community.

Born into an educated, Orthodox Jewish family in a small village near Vilna, Russia, Cahan trained to become a teacher. By the time he graduated from the Vilna Teachers' Institute in 1881, he had embraced the socialist cause and had become involved in radical intellectual circles. Because of these connections, he came under suspicion for anti-Czarist activities and was forced to flee Russia for the United States. Upon arrival in America, Cahan settled in New York's Lower East Side, at that time a neighborhood inhabited mainly by immigrants, including a large population of Eastern European Jews. He soon became a leading figure in the community, lecturing on socialism, organizing labor unions, teaching English to other immigrants, and writing stories and newspaper articles in Russian, English, and **Yiddish**.

Cahan's writing career was varied and long. He served as co-editor of the first Yiddish-language socialist weekly paper, the *Neie Tzeit*, and by 1890 edited the *Arbeiter Zeitung*, the newspaper of the United Hebrew Trades. In 1897 Cahan helped to found the influential and widely distributed Yiddish newspaper the *Jewish Daily Forward* and served as its editor for almost fifty years. In the *Forward*, Cahan pioneered the use of conversational, Americanized Yiddish that could be easily understood by his immigrant readers. He also introduced the popular **Bintl Briv** column. An early, Yiddish, "Dear Abby"–style advice column, the *Bintl Briv* (or "Bundle of Letters") printed questions from readers and offered authoritative advice on romantic, family, and social issues.

[3046] Lewis Hine, *Old Jewish Couple, Lower East Side* (1910), courtesy of the George Eastman House.

Cahan paralleled his career as a journalist with a distinguished career as a creative writer of short stories and novels, both in Yiddish and in English. In 1895, one of Cahan's Yiddish stories was translated and published in *Short Stories*, where it attracted the attention of the prominent literary critic and realist writer William Dean Howells. Impressed by the story, Howells encouraged Cahan to write a longer work focusing on the Jewish immigrant experience in New York. The result, *Yekl: A Tale of the New York Ghetto*, appeared in 1896 to great acclaim. In a front-page review of the novella for the *New York World*, Howells proclaimed Cahan "a new star of realism." After *Yekl* Cahan found himself an established part of the New York literary scene. In the decade that followed, he published a series of short stories and novels dealing primarily with the social realities of the Jewish immigrant experience. His career as a creative writer culminated with his masterpiece, *The Rise of David Levinsky* (1917). The story of a poor Jewish immigrant who rises to become a wealthy garment producer, the novel details the costs and conflicts of pursuing material success and assimilating into American capitalist society.

In 1946, Cahan suffered a stroke that slowed his writing career and led him to give up the day-to-day management of the *Daily Forward*. When he died, he was recognized as both an influential leader of the Jewish American community and the foremost chronicler of the Jewish immigrant experience. His ability to mediate between cultures and to articulate the struggles and successes of Jewish Americans left an enduring legacy that has shaped the work of a long line of important twentieth-century Jewish American writers.

[3046] Lewis Hine, *Old Jewish Couple, Lower East Side* (1910), courtesy of the George Eastman House. Upon arrival in the United States, Eastern European Jewish immigrants were faced with difficult questions: which aspects of their ethnic identity should they preserve, which reshape? Abraham Cahan addressed these and other topics in his *Bintl Briv* column.

[5023] Detroit Publishing Company, *Mulberry Street, New York City* (c. 1900), courtesy of the Library of Congress, Prints and Photographs Division [LC-USZC4-1584]. New York City received huge numbers of immigrants at the turn of the twentieth century. In the bustling streets of the Lower East Side, Old World met New in a population that ranged from Eastern European and Russian Jews to Irish Catholics.

[5124] T. De Thulstrup, *Home of the Poor* (1883), courtesy of the Library of Congress [LC-USZ62-75197]. This illustration shows an interior view of a crowded New York City tenement. The living conditions of the city's poor at the turn of the twentieth century eventually sparked a wave of social reform.

[7034] Anonymous, *Peddlers—New York's "Little Jerusalem"* (between 1908 and 1916), courtesy of the Library of Congress [LC-USZ62-95683]. New York's densely populated Lower East Side was home to innumerable vendors, as well as great poverty. Its largest ethnic community was Jews from Eastern Europe.

■ Cahan's *Bintl Briv* advice column was enormously popular with his immigrant readers. As he stated in his memoirs, "People often need the opportunity to be able to pour out their heavy-laden hearts. Among our immigrant masses this need was very marked. Hundreds of thousands of people, torn from their homes and their dear ones, were lonely souls who thirsted for expression, who wanted to hear an opinion, who wanted advice in solving their weighty problems." Have your students consider what kinds of problems the advice-seekers would probably have shared with the editor. How would their problems be specific to their position as Jewish immigrants? How would their concerns compare to those expressed in such contemporary advice columns as *Dear Abby*? Ask students to imagine that they are newly arrived immigrants in the United States. Have them compose their own *Bintl Briv* letters and/or answers. (A selection of *Bintl Briv* letters can be found in *Jewish American Literature: A Norton Anthology*.)

■ Ask your class to analyze the title of "A Sweat-Shop Romance." Why might Cahan have given the story this title? To what contradictory immigrant experiences does the title allude? What kinds of connotations do the words "sweat-shop" and "romance" have? Does a sweatshop seem a likely place for romance? As they try to define the term "sweat-shop," students could look at the pictures of Lower East Side dwellings and workplaces featured in the archive and read carefully Cahan's description of Lipman's "cockroach" shop.

QUESTIONS

Comprehension: Why does Beile refuse to obey Zlate's command to run an errand for her? Do you think her reasons have more to do with her reluctance to waste time and thus lose money or with her anger at being treated like a servant?

Comprehension: Lipman's factory is described as a "task shop." What is a task shop? How are the workers paid? What distinctions exist among the machine-operator, the baster, the finisher, and the presser?

Context: In both Anzia Yezierska's "The Lost 'Beautifulness'" and Cahan's "A Sweat-Shop Romance," the main characters are treated unfairly by fellow Jewish immigrants (the greedy landlord Mr. Rosenblatt in Yezierska's story, and the overbearing Zlate in Cahan's). What social and economic differences divide the Lower East Side Jewish community in these stories? How does wealth—and the adoption of American capitalist values—seem to affect the immigrants depicted in these stories?

Exploration: Cahan later expressed doubt about the romantic, happy ending of the story—in his memoirs he wondered, "How on earth did it pop into my head?" Do you think the story's romantic resolution troubles its status as a piece of realist writing?

Edith Wharton (1862–1937)

Edith Wharton was born into a wealthy, conservative New York family that traced its lineage back to the colonial settlement of the city. Although growing up within the upper echelon of New York society provided her with rich material for her fiction, the experience did not encourage Wharton to become a novelist. In the rather rigid social world in which she was raised, women were expected to become wives, not writers. Nonetheless, Wharton began experimenting with writing poetry and fiction at a young age. That she became a major figure of American letters is a testament to her extraordinary talent as a social observer and literary stylist.

Wharton debuted in New York society at the age of seventeen and married Bostonian Edward Wharton a few years later. Edward was thirteen years older than his wife and did not share her taste for art, literature, or intellectual pursuits. Given that the couple had little in common besides their privileged upbringing, it is perhaps not surprising that the marriage was not an emotionally satisfying one. Wharton soon found herself feeling stifled in her role as a society wife. When she eventually began suffering from depression and nervous complaints, her doctors encouraged her to write as a therapeutic release.

Wharton began her career by publishing a few poems and co-writing a popular guide to interior decoration. Still in print today, *The Decoration of Houses* is considered one of the most important American books about the art of interior design. By the 1890s, after the publication of a well-received collection of short stories, Wharton began to perceive authorship as her life's avocation. When her novel *The House of Mirth* became a best-seller in 1905, she found herself ranked among the most important American writers of the day. Her critical success proved inspiring; the productive years between 1905 and 1920 are traditionally understood as Wharton's major period.

Around 1910, Wharton moved permanently to France. After she divorced her husband in 1913, she devoted herself to travel, writing, and cultivating a wide circle of friends, including such artistic luminaries as Henry James, Jean Cocteau, and Sinclair Lewis. When World War I broke out in Europe, Wharton threw herself into charitable work in support of her adopted country.

Although she lived abroad, she continued to focus her fiction mainly on Americans. Much of her most-noted work, including the Pulitzer Prize–winning *The Age of Innocence* (1920), is set in the New York society she had known in the late nineteenth century. Themes that recur in almost all of Wharton's fiction include individuals' inability to successfully transcend repressive social conventions, the entrap-

[4621] Peter Powell, *Edith Wharton* (c. 1910), courtesy of the Yale Collection of American Literature, Beinecke Rare Book and Manuscript Library.

[2572] James Abbot McNeil Whistler, *Arrangement in Flesh Colour and Black: Portrait of Theodore Duret* (1883), courtesy of the Metropolitan Museum of Art, Wolfe Fund, Catharine Lorillard Wolfe Collection, 1919. (13.20) Photograph © 1984 The Metropolitan Museum of Art. French art critic and collector Theodore Duret is shown in full evening dress. This painting was ranked by many as the best portrait of Duret by any of the great realist artists of the period. Like novelists Henry James, Edith Wharton, and Kate Chopin, Whistler is interested in depicting the inner lives as well as the opulence of the upper classes. Ezra Pound's poem "To Whistler, American" lauds the artist.

[3636] Edward Harrison May, *Edith Jones* (1870), courtesy of the National Portrait Gallery, Smithsonian Institution. British painter Edward Harrison May painted portraits for affluent Americans and Europeans. Edith (Jones) Wharton was born into a prominent New York City family; much of her fiction paints the upper class in an ironic light.

[3643] Edward Harrison May, *Edith Jones at Age Nineteen* (1891), courtesy of the American Academy of Arts and Letters, New York City. Edith Jones made her debut in New York society at the age of seventeen and a few years later married the wealthy Edward Wharton of Boston. Her fiction details the confining traditions of upper-class life.

[4621] Peter Powell, *Edith Wharton* (c. 1910), courtesy of the Yale Collection of American Literature, Beinecke Rare Book and Manuscript Library. Photo of Wharton in a fur-collared coat. Wharton wrote a number of novels that depict upper-class society. She was particularly concerned about the status of women.

[4649] Anonymous, *Edith Wharton with a Dog on Her Lap, Henry James, Chauffeur Charles Cook, and Teddy Wharton, Holding Two Dogs* (c. 1904), courtesy of Lilly Library, Indiana University, Bloomington, IN. Wharton and James enjoyed a great friendship. Both were from prominent families, and both lived outside of the United States.

ment of women in marriage, the differences between American and European customs, and the rivalry between "old money" and the *nouveaux riches*. Wharton remained very productive into her old age—in the course of her career she published nineteen novels, eleven collections of short stories, and several nonfiction studies, memoirs, poems, and reviews—though critics generally agree that the quality of her work declined after 1920. However, her final unfinished novel, *The Buccaneers* (published posthumously in 1938), outshines everything else she wrote at the end of her career and suggests that her literary powers had not diminished with age. Wharton was consistently ranked among the most significant American writers of her generation, and she was the first woman to receive an honorary doctorate from Yale. She died of a stroke in France at the age of seventy-five.

TEACHING TIPS

■ When Lydia threatens to leave Gannett in "Souls Belated," he responds by asking her, "And where would you go if you left me?" Ask your students to brainstorm about the options Lydia would have if she left Gannett. (You might refer them to the Core Context "Making Amendments: The Woman Suffrage Movement" for insight into the limits women faced and the opportunities that were beginning to open to them at the end of the nineteenth century.) Be sure to point out that in Lydia's social class—much like Wharton's own—many professional occupations would be perceived as inappropriate for women. The exercise should help students realize why Lydia feels so trapped in her role as a companion to Gannett.

■ To make the context of the story clearer—and the characters' problems more compelling—you might explain to your students that divorce was neither as common nor as socially acceptable in Wharton's time as it is in twenty-first-century America. Along the same lines, it is important for students to understand that Lydia and Gannett are not being overly cautious in pretending to be married since sexual relationships outside of marriage were considered scandalous. Ask students to pay attention to Lydia's attitude toward the arrival of her divorce papers at the beginning of the story (she refers to them as "the *thing*," and the presence of the document seems to exacerbate her anxiety and frustration with her situation). You can compare Lydia's scruples about her divorce to Mrs. Linton/Cope's glee when the envelope containing her divorce arrives at the hotel. What conclusions are readers supposed to draw about these characters based on their reactions to their divorce documents? Why is the arrival of the legal document so important to these women?

QUESTIONS

Comprehension: Why is Lydia so reluctant to marry Gannett? Why does she insist that marriage would be "humiliating" and a "cheap compromise"?

Comprehension: What social codes structure the lives of the inhabitants of the Hotel Bellosguardo? Who are the social leaders?

Context: Like many of Wharton's stories and novels, "Souls Belated" presents marriage as a kind of imprisonment for women. Why does Lydia see marriage in this way? How does she attempt to escape this imprisonment? Why is she successful or unsuccessful? How do the restrictions and frustrations that Lydia faces compare to the restrictions faced by the impoverished Hannah Hayyeh in Anzia Yezierska's "The Lost 'Beautifulness'"?

Context: Based on your reading of Wharton's and James's stories of Americans living and traveling in Europe, what customs and values seem to separate Americans from Europeans?

Exploration: How does Lydia's attempt to rebel against marital conventions compare to Edna Pontellier's rebellion in Kate Chopin's *The Awakening*?

Sui Sin Far (Edith Maud Eaton) (1865–1914)

Writing around the turn of the twentieth century, Sui Sin Far, or Edith Maud Eaton, challenged entrenched social and political discrimination against Chinese immigrants and Chinese Americans by publishing eloquent stories and articles about Chinese culture in North America. Her goal was to encourage mutual understanding and respect between the Anglo and Asian communities. As she said, "I give my right hand to the Occidentals and my left to the Orientals, hoping that between them they will not utterly destroy the insignificant 'connecting link.'" With her cosmopolitan background and mixed ethnicity, Sui Sin Far was an excellent spokesperson for these multicultural ideals. Born in England in 1865, she was one of fourteen children raised by a white English father and a Chinese mother who had been educated in England. Because Sui Sin Far's father, Edward Eaton, was a struggling landscape painter, the family moved frequently and was always financially unstable. Eventually settling in Montreal, the Eatons raised their children to be creative, individualistic, and self-sufficient. Sui Sin Far started earning money to contribute to the family's finances while she was still a girl, selling crocheted lace and paintings on the street, publishing poetry, and eventually undertaking stenography and office work. Later, she supplemented her income by publishing articles and stories in magazines and newspapers.

Although she was educated in British and Canadian schools, spoke only English, and could easily "pass" as white, Sui Sin Far chose to embrace and emphasize her Chinese heritage. Soon after she began publishing, she adopted the name Sui Sin Far in place of her English name, Edith Maud Eaton. The Chinese name translates as "fragrant water flower" and signifies "dignity and indestructible love for family and homeland." Sui Sin Far began her writing career in Montreal but later moved on to a variety of urban centers with large Chinese immigrant communities. Over the course of her career, she lived in eastern and western Canada, Jamaica, California,

[6169] Anonymous, *Chinatown, New York City* (1909), courtesy of the Library of Congress [LC-USZ62-72475].

**SUI SIN FAR
WEB ARCHIVE**

[1111] Anonymous, *In the Heart of Chinatown, San Francisco, U.S.A.* (1892), courtesy of the Library of Congress, American Memory. Thousands of Chinese immigrants were hired to work on the transcontinental railroad and were often given the most dangerous jobs. While discrimination, biased immigration policies, and other hardships limited the rights of Chinese Americans well into the twentieth century, they nevertheless established vibrant communities which preserved many of their traditional ways, such as Chinatown in San Francisco. Cathy Song's poem "Chinatown" depicts her view of this neighborhood. Early examples of Chinese American literature include the poems from Angel Island and the works of Sui Sin Far.
[6164] Arnold Genthe, *Street of the Gamblers (By Day)* (1898), courtesy of the Library of Congress, Prints and Photographs Division [LC-USZC4-3890]. Photograph of pedestrians in

the Pacific Northwest, and Boston. In both her fiction and her journalism she worked to make the lives of Chinese immigrants understandable and sympathetic to a white audience, often highlighting the home life and domestic occupations of her Chinese women characters. Her presentation of Chinese characters who shared many of the same joys and concerns as European Americans was part of her ongoing effort to combat stereotypes of Chinese immigrants as "heathen," unclean, and untrustworthy. But even as Sui Sin Far dwelt on the similarities between Chinese and European Americans, she also used her stories and articles to document traditional Chinese customs and to provide her readers with insight into the unique culture that had developed in America's Chinatowns.

Sui Sin Far published nearly forty short stories and more than thirty articles about Chinese life in prominent national magazines. Near the end of her life she published two autobiographical accounts and collected some of her stories into a full-length book, *Mrs. Spring Fragrance*, which was well received by critics. When she died in Montreal, the Chinese community there erected a memorial to her inscribed with the characters "Yi bu wong hua," which translates as "The righteous one does not forget her country."

TEACHING TIPS

■ The original 1912 edition of *Mrs. Spring Fragrance* was published with an elaborate scarlet cover and "oriental" motifs inscribed on each page. Ask your students to consider the effects of this physical presentation, and why Sui Sin Far's book was bound this way. Why might the elaborate, ostentatiously Chinese-looking design have appealed to the white audience to whom the book was mar-keted? Ask your students to discuss how the experience of reading "Mrs. Spring Fragrance" might change if they read it in the original edition rather than in *The Norton Anthology of American Literature*.

■ Although Japan had been open to the West since 1853, "the Orient" remained a place of great mystery, reverence, and intrigue for modern Americans. Readers revelled in the exotic paraphernalia of Japanese daily life in works such as Matthew Calbraith Perry's *The Americans in Japan: An Abridgement of the Government Narrative of the U.S. Expedition to Japan*, and fascination with the Orient spilled over into U.S. architecture and literature, particularly in the poetry of Ezra Pound and William Carlos Williams (see the Core Context on "Orientalism" in Unit 10). Postcolonial theorist Edward Said has argued that for Westerners the Orient was "almost a European invention": the Orient becomes an "other" against which the West defines itself, rather than a place with its own reality. Have your students test whether Sui Sin Far's fiction breaks down or reinforces this "otherness" by having them diagram what constitutes Western and Chinese culture and identity in Sui Sin Far's work.

■ At one point in the story, Mrs. Spring Fragrance recites lines from "a beautiful American poem" by a "noble American named Tennyson." Of course, Tennyson, the poet laureate of Great Britain, was not an American. Ask your students to think about the function of this mention of Tennyson in the story (Mr. Spring Fragrance crucially misunderstands the meaning of the lines and becomes suspicious of his wife's affection and fidelity). Is the joke here on Mrs. Spring Fragrance for mistaking a British poem for an American one? Or is this a commentary on the state of American poetry and American literature generally? How does Mrs. Spring Fragrance's conflation of British and American culture compare to many Americans' inability to distinguish among various Asian cultures?

QUESTIONS

Comprehension: In what ways is Mrs. Spring Fragrance "Americanized"? What traditional Chinese values and customs does she retain?

Context: How does Sui Sin Far portray Mrs. Spring Fragrance's domestic activities and home life? How do her relationships with her neighbors and her husband compare to European American norms? How does Sui Sin Far's description of Mrs. Spring Fragrance's attachment to her home compare to Anzia Yezierska's portrait of Hanneh Hayyeh's joy in her kitchen?

Context: In "Mrs. Spring Fragrance," Sui Sin Far twice alludes to Mr. Spring Fragrance's brother, who has been detained in a "detention pen" at the Angel Island Immigration Center in San Francisco. Why does Sui Sin Far include these references to Mr. Spring Fragrance's brother, who is, after all, not an actor in the story? How does his immigration experience complicate the tone and resolution of the story?

Exploration: How might Sui Sin Far's work have influenced later Chinese American women writers, such as Amy Tan or Maxine Hong Kingston? Do these three authors deal with some of the same issues? How are Tan's and Kingston's concerns different from Sui Sin Far's?

Exploration: Could Sui Sin Far be considered a "regional realist," like the writers featured in Unit 8? Why or why not?

W. E. B. Du Bois (1868–1963)

With the publication of *The Souls of Black Folk* in 1903, W. E. B. Du Bois emerged as the intellectual leader of a new generation of African American activists who broke with the leadership and views of Booker T. Washington. Declaring that blacks should no longer accept second-class citizenship and should instead fight for suffrage, civil equality, and the right to education, Du Bois sent out what at the time was a revolutionary call for change in the racial status quo. In doing so, he became simultaneously one of the most influential and controversial black people in America.

San Francisco's Chinatown. Writing at the turn of the twentieth century, Sui Sin Far (Edith Maud Eaton) combatted stereotypes of Chinese immigrants as heathen, unclean, and untrustworthy and provided insight into the culture of America's Chinatowns.

[6169] Anonymous, *Chinatown, New York City* (1909), courtesy of the Library of Congress [LC-USZ62-72475]. Chinese immigrants brought their traditions and customs to America, where they established strong communities to provide familiar support in an otherwise unfamiliar world. Author Maxine Hong Kingston has written personal and deeply reflective portraits of Chinese immigrants' experiences.

[6171] Arnold Genthe, *Children Were the Pride, Joy, Beauty, and Chief Delight of the Quarter, Chinatown, San Francisco* (c. 1896–1906), courtesy of the Library of Congress, Prints and Photographs Division [LC-USZC4-5265]. Four children in traditional Chinese clothing on a sidewalk in San Francisco's Chinatown. Writing about the time this photograph was taken, Sui Sin Far (Edith Maud Eaton) sought to make the lives of Chinese immigrants understandable to white audiences.

[8183] Anonymous, *The Voyage, No. 8* (c. 1920), reprinted in *Island: Poetry and History of Chinese Immigrants on Angel Island, 1910–1940*, courtesy of the University of Washington Press. "How has anyone to know that my dwelling place would be a prison?" asks this poem, one of many written on the walls of the Angel Island Immigration Center by Chinese immigrants held there by U.S. authorities. Examples of these poems, which play a role in Maxine Hong Kingston's *China Men*, can be found in the archive, [8184] through [8191].

Born in Great Barrington, Massachusetts, Du Bois grew up far from the strife and racial divisions of the American South. Though he experienced discrimination as a child, it was not until he went south to attend Fisk University that he saw what he called "a world split into white and black halves, where the darker half was held back by race prejudice and legal bonds." Moved by the situation that he saw in the South, he decided to devote his life to fighting against racial prejudice and effecting legal and social change for blacks in America. After graduating from Fisk, Du Bois went on to receive an M.A. and Ph.D. from Harvard and to pursue advanced study in the emerging field of sociology at the University of Berlin.

When he returned to the United States in 1894, Du Bois found that in spite of his impressive academic record he could not get a permanent position at a major research university because of his race. Instead, he took a position teaching subjects outside his areas of interest at Wilberforce, a small all-black college in Ohio. In 1897 he left Wilberforce to take a temporary position at the University of Pennsylvania and later a permanent position at Atlanta University, where he conducted systematic, sociological studies of what was then termed "the Negro problem." But Du Bois's faith in the importance and efficacy of objective scientific inquiry was shaken by horrifying incidents of racial violence in the Reconstruction-era South. As he later put it, "one could not be a calm, cool, and detached scientist, while Negroes were being lynched, murdered, and starved." By the turn of the century, Du Bois had concluded that his scholarly studies were doing little to change the reality of everyday life for African Americans. Accordingly, he committed himself to more public political action.

One of Du Bois's first acts in his new role was to offer a strong critique of Booker T. Washington's position on African American rights. Espousing what often sounded like an acceptance of disenfranchisement, segregation, and second-class citizenship in exchange for low-level economic opportunities, Washington was popular with white audiences and had come to be regarded as the undisputed leader of the African American community. Although Du Bois had previously supported Washington's conciliatory philosophy, in *The Souls of Black Folk* he modified his position: "so far as Mr. Washington apologizes for injustice, North and South, does not rightly value the privilege and duty of voting, belittles the emasculating effects of caste distinctions and opposes the higher training and ambition of our brighter minds . . . we must unceasingly and firmly oppose [him]." Du Bois's shift from supporting to challenging Washington was typical of what would become a pattern in his career: he changed his mind or modified his views on so many different topics and issues that his ideology can be difficult to characterize.

In 1905 Du Bois joined with other critics of Washington to form the first all-black protest movement in American history, the Niagara Movement, which was dedicated to direct action to end racial discrimination. By 1910, the Niagara Movement was folded into a new organization, the National Association for the Advancement of

---

OPPOSE "BIRTH OF NATION."

Washington, D. C.—Officials of the N. A. C. P. say they will resist to the utmost any effort on the part of the managers here to show "The Birth of a Nation," which it is said is headed this way. With a failure to suppress the film in Boston, New York, Chicago, Atlantic City and Philadelphia, the lawyers in this city are dubious about the course that should be taken to keep the vile production out of Washington. No objection was raised to "The Nigger," which was played here to such large audiences that it had to make a return engagement. It was shown also at the Howard to overflowing audiences. "The Nigger'" had redeeming traits, but the second part of "The Birth of a Nation" is a libel upon a struggling race that was in no wise responsible for the sad conditions growing out of reconstruction days. It may be that the managers will listen to the appeal of the Colored people that they refuse to allow the film (or filth) to be shown in any of the local houses.

[5719] *Cleveland Advocate*, Article: Oppose "Birth of a Nation" (1915), courtesy of the Ohio Historical Society.

Colored People. Du Bois was recruited to serve as the NAACP's director of publicity and research and was for many years the only African American among the organization's leadership. In this position, Du Bois edited the association's official magazine, *Crisis*, and reached an enormous audience with his message of civil equality and educational opportunity.

Increasingly radical in his views and at odds with the leadership of the NAACP, Du Bois was forced to resign as editor of *Crisis* in 1934. He then began to focus his energies on working for broader, worldwide race reform and international understanding, leading a series of Pan-African conferences, working with the United Nations, and serving as chairman of the Peace Information Center. Du Bois eventually became convinced that communism offered the greatest hope for racial equality and world peace, a position that made him extremely controversial and alienated him from many more mainstream African American organizations. In 1961 he joined the Communist party and left the United States to live in Ghana, where he died at the age of ninety-five. Throughout his long career, Du Bois was an untiring champion of both African American and human rights in the United States and around the world.

TEACHING TIPS

■ Du Bois's articulation of "double-consciousness" and the "two-ness" of African Americans is one of the most famous passages in *The Souls of Black Folk*. You might begin your discussion of Du Bois by focusing on this passage, which appears early in Chapter 1, "Of Our Spiritual Strivings." Ask your students to think about Du Bois's claims that double-consciousness is both a gift (it enables a "second-sight" into American culture) and a curse (it denies African American individuals "true self-consciousness"). According to Du Bois, what kinds of stresses and tensions does double-consciousness create for African Americans? How can these tensions be resolved? Ask students to consider how Du Bois's formulation of double-consciousness impacted later twentieth-century artists interested in recording the experiences of racial minorities (Toni Morrison's and Ralph Ellison's work might lend themselves well to this discussion).

■ Divide your class into two groups and have them prepare a mock debate between Booker T. Washington and W. E. B. Du Bois. Ask them to imagine that the two leaders are meeting to formulate a platform of goals for the African American community at the turn of the twentieth century. What strategies would each leader advocate? How would they prioritize their goals? Ask each group to anticipate arguments and to be prepared to defend their strategies in the context of the historical circumstances of early-twentieth-century America.

[4801] Arthur Rothstein, *Sharecropper's Children* (1937), courtesy of the Library of Congress [LC-USF34-025464-D]. Photograph of three African American children on a porch. Landowners rarely kept sharecroppers' homes in good condition. Du Bois hoped that an educated "Talented Tenth" of African Americans would help lift such children out of poverty.

[5719] *Cleveland Advocate*, Article: *Oppose "Birth of a Nation"* (1915), courtesy of the Ohio Historical Society. Civil rights groups, including the National Association for the Advancement of Colored People, organized protests against D. W. Griffith's *The Birth of a Nation*. The film glorified the Ku Klux Klan and helped the organization gain new strength.

[7102] J. E. Purdy, *W. E. B. Du Bois* (1904), courtesy of the Library of Congress [LC-USZ62-28485]. Taken a year after the publication of *The Souls of Black Folk*, this portrait shows Du Bois as a refined and serious intellectual. In his lifetime Du Bois led the NAACP and championed the cause of African American advancement through education.

[7132] Anonymous, *Steal Away to Jesus* (n.d.), courtesy of John W. Work's *Folk Songs of the American Negro* (1907), Fisk University. These lyrics remind listeners that those who obey the divine Lord are assured ultimate salvation, while unredeemed sinners, whether slaves or masters, have cause to tremble. This song could also refer to "stealing away" to forbidden worship meetings, or it could be an Underground Railroad code.

Comprehension: What criticisms of Booker T. Washington does Du Bois offer in Chapter 3, "Of Mr. Booker T. Washington and Others"? On what points does he agree with Washington? On what issues does he disagree? How are his strategies for strengthening the African American community different from Washington's?

Comprehension: What does Du Bois mean when he talks about the "double-consciousness" and "two-ness" of African American identity?

Context: Du Bois repeatedly calls for African Americans to work toward attaining "self-conscious manhood" and complains that Booker T. Washington's policies are "emasculating" and in opposition to "true manhood." What is the role of masculinity and manhood in Du Bois's theories about racial struggle? How does his equation of racial strength and self-consciousness with masculinity compare to the depictions of minority women's struggles for strength and self-consciousness in works by writers such as Anzia Yezierska or Sui Sin Far?

Exploration: Like Du Bois, Frederick Douglass found himself "stirred" and "moved" by the haunting strains of the Sorrow Songs. How does Douglass's account of his relationship to the Sorrow Songs in Chapter 2 of his *Narrative* compare to Du Bois's discussion of the songs in Chapter 14, "The Sorrow Songs"?

Exploration: How do you think Du Bois's work and philosophy might have influenced later African American protest movements? You might think about Marcus Garvey, Martin Luther King and the Civil Rights movement in the 1960s, the Nation of Islam, and the Black Power movement.

Theodore Dreiser (1871–1945)

One of the foremost practitioners of American realism, Theodore Dreiser wrote novels and stories that explored such themes as the dangerous lure of urban environments, the conflict between Old World parents and their Americanized children, and the hollowness of the American drive for material success. Dreiser's own life provided him with many of the experiences and concerns that he later translated into his fiction. He was born into a large, impoverished family in Terre Haute, Indiana. His father, a German immigrant, tried to make his children conform to strict Old World values and dogmatic Catholicism, but Dreiser and most of his siblings rebelled. At fifteen Dreiser left home and took a series of odd jobs in Chicago. After spending a year in college through the help and support of a generous teacher, he became a journalist and wrote for newspapers in Chicago, St. Louis, and Pittsburgh.

By 1899 Dreiser was settled in New York, editing a magazine and selling his freelance writing. With the encouragement of his friends he decided to try his hand at a novel, to be based on the life of one of his sisters. The result, *Sister Carrie*, was published in 1900, but received neither critical attention nor praise. True to his interest in uncompromising realism, Dreiser had written a novel that portrayed characters who broke the bounds of respectability and engaged in illicit behavior without remorse or repercussions. Shocked by the book's controversial themes and worried about public opinion, the publisher refused to promote it and it sold poorly. Dreiser's disagreement with his publisher and his refusal to alter his novel marked the beginning of what would become a lasting commitment to resisting Victorian prudery and narrowness.

After his difficulties with *Sister Carrie*, Dreiser suffered a nervous breakdown and then opted to return to his career in journalism. He produced no new fiction for almost seven years. Then, in 1910, he lost his position as editor of a leading women's magazine and took his dismissal as an opportunity to return to fiction writing. The next fifteen years constituted a period of extraordinary productivity for Dreiser, leading to the publication of four novels, four works of travel narrative and autobiography, and numerous short stories and sketches. He published what many critics consider to be his masterpiece, *An American Tragedy*, in 1925. Based on an actual murder case in upstate New York, the book was hailed as a great American novel and generated substantial profits. With his reputation and finances secure, Dreiser's productivity dropped off; he completed no other novels until almost the end of his life.

[7110] H. C. White Co., *Making Link Sausages—Machines Stuff 10 Ft. per Second* (c. 1905), courtesy of the Library of Congress [LC-USZ62-50217].

Like many American intellectuals of the 1920s and 1930s, Dreiser was fascinated with socialism and the political experiment going on in the new Soviet Union. In 1927 he paid a lengthy visit to Moscow. Upon his return to the United States, he devoted himself to furthering proletarian causes and the Communist party. When he died in 1945 in California, his reputation as a writer and thinker was at a low point, but later critics have largely revived his standing as an innovative author who defied genteel and romantic traditions to offer realistic portraits of human nature and social conditions in America.

TEACHING TIPS

■ Ask your students to pay attention to Dreiser's use of regional dialects in "Old Rogaum and His Theresa." Which characters speak in dialect? How does Theresa's language separate her from her father? How does Connie Almerting talk? What conclusions are we supposed to draw from each character's different way of speaking? You might ask students to compare Dreiser's use of dialect to some of the "regional realist" writers featured in Unit 8.

■ As many critics have noted, the conclusion of "Old Rogaum and His Theresa," though not tragic, is not exactly a happy one. Readers are left with the uneasy feeling that the Rogaum family's disputes are not over. While both Theresa and her father are glad that she has safely returned to her home, the girl's desires still seem to be in conflict with her father's Old World ideas about proper conduct. After discussing the lack of resolution in the ending of the story, ask your students to write a sequel to "Old Rogaum and His Theresa" in which they speculate on how Theresa and her father will get along while she continues to live at home.

QUESTIONS

Comprehension: In "Old Rogaum and His Theresa," what attracts Theresa to the streets? Why is she reluctant to return to her home when her father calls her?

Context: What kind of neighborhood do the Rogaums live in? Does Dreiser give readers an idea about the different ethnic groups and socioeconomic classes that inhabit the neighborhood? How do you think the community compares to some of the New York neighborhoods whose pictures are featured in the archive?

Context: In "The Art of Fiction," Henry James claims that writers have a responsibility to represent "the strange irregular rhythm of life" rather than organized morality lessons, pat conclusions, or happy endings. How do you think James would have responded to "Old Rogaum and His Theresa"? Does it meet his criteria for good fiction? Why or why not?

Exploration: Much of the drama of "Old Rogaum and His Theresa" centers on the problem of female chastity. Theresa's exposure to the unscrupulous Connie Almerting and the elder Rogaums' encounter with the suicidal prostitute thematize the potential for young women to "go astray" in an urban setting like New York. Why does Dreiser focus on this issue? Does he seem to draw any conclusions? How does his portrait of young women's desires and temptations compare to earlier American treatments of the same subject (Susanna Rowson's *Charlotte Temple*, for example)?

Henry Adams (1838–1918)

From his early childhood on, Henry Adams was acutely aware of his heritage as part of the remarkable political dynasty of the Adams family. Both his great-grandfather and his grandfather had served as President of the United States, and his father, Charles Francis Adams, was a congressman and a diplomat. But while Henry Adams maintained a lively interest in politics and moved in powerful social circles in Washington, D.C., all his life, he found his true calling—and lasting fame—as a writer and a historian. Noted in his own time for his essays, biographies, novels, and histories, today Adams owes his reputation primarily to *The Education of Henry Adams*, his unique autobiographical study of the forces that shaped his own life and nineteenth-century America more generally.

Born in Boston, Adams grew up steeped in the traditions of his family and surrounded by some of the most influential politicians and thinkers of the day. He attended college at Harvard, traveled around Europe after his graduation, and then settled in Germany to study civil law and history. In 1860 he received the traditional family call to political service and took up a post as his father's private secretary in Washington, D.C. When President Lincoln named Adams's father, Charles Francis Adams, as his minister in Great Britain in 1861, Henry Adams relocated to London to serve as part of the diplomatic legation. He thus spent the entire Civil War period in England. He learned a great deal about international politics in the process but was constantly troubled by the feeling that he was missing out on participating in the most significant American event of his lifetime. Perhaps in an effort to involve himself in the political and cultural life of his own country, Adams took time away from his diplomatic work to write ambitious essays and reviews that were published in important American journals.

[7663] J. Alexander, *Cookie's Row, Villa No. 3* (1968), courtesy of the Library of Congress, Prints and Photographs Division [HABS, DC, GEO, 105-,DLC/PP-00:DC-2].

Returning to Washington in 1868, Adams devoted himself to a journalistic career, composing serious political pieces intended to expose corruption and encourage social and economic reform. Corruption and graft dominated American business and politics during President Grant's administration, however, and Adams was soon disillusioned by his failure to achieve real results. In 1870 he left Washington to serve as a professor of history at Harvard and as editor of the prestigious journal *The North American Review*. While at Harvard he introduced academic practices borrowed from German universities, such as the study of primary documentary sources and the use of seminar-style teaching.

Adams made a career change once again in the late 1870s, resigning his positions in Boston and returning to Washington to concentrate on historical research and writing. He published two historical biographies and the critically acclaimed nine-volume *History of the United States of America during the Administrations of Thomas Jefferson and James Madison*. This thorough study mixes diplomatic, social, and intellectual history in its examination of early-nineteenth-century America and is still regarded as a formative piece of historical analysis on the period. While he was at work on the *History* Adams also found time to experiment with novel writing, publishing two works of fiction, *Democracy* and *Esther*, in 1880 and 1884, respectively.

In 1885 Adams's life was shattered when his beloved wife, Marian, committed suicide. He never fully recovered, but in the tradition of his family, refused to give in to grief and pushed on with his research and writing. In the final decades of his life, Adams traveled again to Europe. While in France he was struck by the magnificence and harmonious beauty of the medieval cathedrals he visited, particularly at Chartres. The experience moved him to write *Mont-Saint-Michel and Chartres*, a study of medieval architecture and of the spiritual force that energized medieval culture. He developed a theory that medieval society had been unified by the spiritual power of the feminine force of the Virgin, while modern society had sacrificed this unity in its devotion to the chaotic forces of science and technology. His next book, *The Education of Henry Adams*, served as a corollary to *Mont-Saint-Michel and Chartres* in that it traced the disorder of the modern world by recounting what Adams thought of as his own "mis-education" and sense of uncertainty and failure. By figuring himself as a displaced eighteenth-century soul, unable to make proper use of his impulses toward harmony and civic virtue in the modern chaotic world, Adams eloquently articulated the plight and frustration of the modern American subject. Although both *Mont-Saint-Michel* and *The Education of Henry Adams* were originally printed privately and intended only for Adams's friends, they soon generated wide interest. *The Education of Henry Adams* was published and released to the public in 1918 and won the Pulitzer Prize in 1919, a year after its author's death.

TEACHING TIPS

■ Students often comment on the strangeness of Adams's use of the third person in a work in which he himself is the subject. Ask them to think about why Adams might have chosen this more detached way of writing his autobiography, and about what effect the third-person narration has on the reader's understanding of Adams as a character. You might ask students to write a journal entry about an incident from their own lives in the third person. Have them discuss the experience of writing about themselves in this way. What difficulties did they encounter? How did the use of the third person change their relationship to their own history?

■ Perhaps because Adams found his wife's suicide so devastating, he is completely silent about the event as he narrates his life. In fact, he never even mentions that he was married. Ask students what effect this absence has on the autobiography and how the knowledge of Adams's personal tragedy changes their understanding of him. You might have them examine the chapter entitled "Chaos," in which Adams vividly describes his reaction to his sister's tragic death. Might this episode be a displaced description of his reaction to his wife's suicide? How does this encounter with death affect Adams? What conclusions does he draw about life from this experience?

QUESTIONS

Comprehension: Adams sees the Virgin and the Dynamo as important symbols of their respected ages. What does the Virgin represent? What does the Dynamo represent? What conflict does Adams see between them?

Context: In 1870 Adams wrote an article entitled "The New York Gold Conspiracies," detailing the scandalous behavior of men like Jay Gould, who bankrupted the Erie Railroad through corporate mismanagement and became involved in a plot to corner the gold market. To Adams's surprise, the article was refused by the English periodicals *The Edinburgh Review* and *The Quarterly*. He was outraged by the power corrupt American businessmen, politicians, and corporations exerted over the free press, even in England: "One knew that the power of Erie was almost as great in England as in America, but one was hardly prepared to find it controlling the Quarterlies." How does the corporate culture created by the **robber barons** affect Adams? How does he respond to it in his memoir?

Context: What does Adams mean when he claims in his chapter "The Dynamo and the Virgin" that "The Woman had once been supreme" but that "an American Virgin would never dare command; an American Venus would never dare exist"? What kind of role did women occupy in America in the late nineteenth century, according to Adams? What kind of critique of sexual politics does he offer in this chapter? How does Adams's view of the limits of the American woman compare to Sarah Piatt's or Edith Wharton's views?

Exploration: How does Adams's autobiography compare to Benjamin Franklin's autobiography? What concerns do these two writers have in common? What values do they share? How do their attitudes toward spirituality and science compare? What makes the outcome of their lives, and their views of America's future, so different from one another?

Anzia Yezierska (c. 1880–1970)

In the course of a career that spanned more than fifty years, Anzia Yezierska recorded Eastern European women immigrants' struggles to find a place for themselves both within their traditional Jewish culture and within American society. Yezierska's goal as an author involved articulating Jewish women's experiences to a larger audience: she hoped her writing would "build a bridge of understanding between the American-born and myself."

Born in Plinsk, a Jewish shtetl outside Warsaw, Poland, Yezierska immigrated to New York with her large family when she was about fifteen years old. Settling in a tenement on the Lower East Side, the family attempted to live according to Old World values: Yezierska's father pursued Talmudic scholarship, his sons received an education, and his wife and daughters earned money to support the family. Like her mother and sisters Yezierska worked in sweatshops and as a domestic servant, but eventually she determined to rebel against her father's patriarchal values. In 1899 she left home to support herself and get an education.

In her pursuit of independence, Yezierska took a room on her own at the Clara de Hirsch Settlement House. A charitable institution created to help Jewish immigrant working women live on their own, the settlement house attempted to "Americanize" its tenants by replacing their traditional customs and values with those of European American culture. Thus, when the patrons of the Clara de

Hirsch house awarded Yezierska a scholarship to attend Columbia University, they stipulated that she had to study domestic science so she could learn the skills of a middle-class American housewife. Although Yezierska had little interest in domestic science, she used the opportunity to gain an education at Columbia.

After finishing her program, Yezierska briefly taught domestic science, then attended the American Academy of Dramatic Arts, where she studied acting and became involved in radical socialist circles. She also began writing stories about the experiences of Eastern European immigrants, focusing on the specific challenges faced by women. Although her stories were repeatedly rejected by prominent magazines and journals, Yezierska persisted. Around this time, she began using her given name of Anzia Yezierska rather than "Hattie Mayer," the name immigration authorities at Ellis Island had given her because it was easier for most European Americans to pronounce.

In 1910, Yezierska married attorney Jacob Gordon and annulled the marriage almost immediately. She then married businessman Arnold Levitas, with whom she had a daughter, Louise, in 1912. Yezierska soon found herself stifled by the demands of domestic life, and the couple had frequent disagreements. In 1915 she left her husband and moved to California to raise her daughter alone, but soon found this plan untenable. She returned to New York, gave custody of her daughter to her former husband, and decided to live on her own as a writer. She found support for her work in her friendship with John Dewey, a Columbia professor and a respected authority on education. Although Yezierska and Dewey were passionately devoted to one another and may have shared romantic feelings, their relationship apparently went unconsummated. His interest in and encouragement of her writing, however, proved inspirational for Yezierska.

Although she had successfully published two stories in 1915, Yezierska did not achieve real fame or critical recognition until 1919, when her story "The Fat of the Land" was awarded a prize as the best story of the year. This success enabled the publication of her first book-length collection, *Hungry Hearts*, in 1920. Yezierska's work attracted the attention of movie producer Samuel Goldwyn, who bought the rights to her stories and gave her a contract to write screenplays in Hollywood.

In California, her sudden rise to fame and fortune earned her the moniker "Sweatshop Cinderella." Although Yezierska's own semi-autobiographical work had contributed to this rags-to-riches image, she found herself uncomfortable with being touted as an example of the American Dream. Frustrated by the shallowness of Hollywood and by her own alienation from her roots, Yezierska returned to New York in the mid-1920s and continued publishing novels and stories about immigrant women struggling to establish their identities in America. Although she wrote and published well into her old age, Yezierska found little success as American readers became less inter-

[5088] Anonymous, *Anzia Yezierska after the Birth of Her Child* (c. 1912), courtesy of Melvin Henriksen.

ested in the immigrant experience. She died in poverty in a nursing home in California. Only recently has her critical reputation been rehabilitated by scholars interested in feminism and ethnic identity.

TEACHING TIPS

■ Yezierska was often praised for the authenticity of her representations of Yiddish-English immigrant speech. In order to appreciate her skill at reproducing dialect and "translating" the cadence and rhythm of Yiddish speech, ask your students to read some of the dialogue from "The Lost 'Beautifulness'" out loud. (The verbal exchanges when Hannah Hayyeh convinces the butcher and his customers to view her newly painted kitchen might work particularly well for this activity.) How does this speech sound different from "mainstream" American English speech? How are the vocabulary and sentence structure different? What effect does the use of dialect have on our understanding of the characters in the story? A footnote to the story in *The Norton Anthology of American Literature* explains that Yezierska probably intended readers to understand that the characters would actually be speaking Yiddish to one another and that she had translated their speech into English. Ask students to think about the implications of this assertion. If Yezierska was intent on translating Yiddish speech, why did she retain the unique idioms and rhythms of the language rather than render it in standard American English?

■ Many of Yezierska's works offer critiques of the hypocrisy or short-sightedness of charitable institutions and individuals. Her own experiences with charitable settlement houses and scholarships designed to enforce immigrant assimilation had convinced her that charity often leaves its recipients feeling imprisoned and disempowered. After giving students this background information, ask them to think about the figure of Mrs. Preston in "The Lost 'Beautifulness.'" Why does Hannah Hayyeh grow disenchanted with Mrs. Preston's patronage? You might point out Mrs. Preston's rather condescending contention that Hannah Hayyeh is an "artist of laundry" and her reluctance to change the status quo of class relations. (She insists, "We can't change the order of things overnight" and "We're doing our best.") Ask students how they think Yezierska intended readers to react to Mrs. Preston. Are we meant to think of her as a bad person? Or as someone who means well but is misguided? Is her character meant to offer a model or a lesson to readers who wish to offer charity to immigrants?

QUESTIONS

Comprehension: What motivates Hannah Hayyeh to paint her kitchen white? What sacrifices does she make in order to perform this improvement?

Comprehension: Why does Hannah Hayyeh refuse Mrs. Preston's

YEZIERSKA WEB ARCHIVE

[4716] Anonymous, *Anzia Yezierska at Typewriter* (n.d.), courtesy of the *New York Daily News*. After rising to prominence when Hollywood purchased the rights to *Hungry Hearts*, Anzia Yezierska refused to succumb to her image as a "Sweatshop Cinderella." Instead she returned to New York and continued writing about the experiences of immigrant women.

[5023] Detroit Publishing Company, *Mulberry Street, New York City* (c. 1900), courtesy of the Library of Congress, Prints and Photographs Division [LC-USZC4-1584]. New York City received huge numbers of immigrants at the turn of the twentieth century. In the bustling streets of the Lower East Side, Old World met New in a population that ranged from Eastern European and Russian Jews to Irish Catholics.

[5088] Anonymous, *Anzia Yezierska after the Birth of Her Child* (c. 1912), courtesy of Melvin Henriksen. Fiction writer Anzia Yezierska divorced twice and gave birth to one daughter. She developed a friendship with John Dewey, who was a lifelong proponent of educational reform and one of the most renowned philosophers of the twentieth century.

[5124] T. De Thulstrup, *Home of the Poor* (1883), courtesy of the Library of Congress [LC-USZ62-75197]. This illustration shows an interior view of a crowded New York City tenement. The living conditions of the city's poor at the turn of the twentieth century eventually sparked a wave of social reform.

[5126] Lewis Wickes Hines, *Rear View of Tenement, 134 1/2 Thompson St., New York City* (1912), courtesy of the Library of Congress, Prints and Photographs Division, National Child Labor Committee Collection [LC-USZ62-93116]. Photograph of the back of a tenement housing-complex in New York City. Like writer Theodore Dreiser, photographer Lewis Wickes Hines documented social conditions in America at the beginning of the twentieth century.

offer to give her money to cover the rent increase? How does the scene in which Hannah Hayyeh refuses Mrs. Preston's charity change their relationship?

Context: Examine the pictures of Lower East Side tenements featured in the archive. How do the pictures compare to Yezierska's description of Hannah Hayyeh's apartment? Given the tenement environment, why might Hannah Hayyeh's quest for "beautifulness" make such an impression on her neighbors and on Mrs. Preston?

Exploration: While she was studying at Columbia and the Academy of Dramatic Arts, Yezierska became interested in Ralph Waldo Emerson's philosophy of self-reliance. How do ideals of self-reliance inflect Yezierska's portrait of Hannah Hayyeh? In what ways might "The Lost 'Beautifulness'" critique Emerson's ideas about self-creation and personal responsibility? What were the limits of self-reliance for an impoverished immigrant woman at the turn of the twentieth century?

Suggested Author Pairings

HENRY JAMES, EDITH WHARTON, AND THEODORE DREISER

James, Wharton, and Dreiser are all considered masters of realist fiction. The short stories in *The Norton Anthology of American Literature* demonstrate the authors' ability to construct psychologically complex characters as they explore the tension between old and new customs and manners. While James and Wharton focus on wealthy, aristocratic, or *nouveaux riches* Americans at home or abroad, Dreiser attends to the immigrant and working-class experience in urban America. These authors also share an awareness of the social constraints that women faced in turn-of-the-century America, though they each had different perspectives on the nature and impact of those constraints.

BOOKER T. WASHINGTON AND W. E. B. DU BOIS

Washington and Du Bois make a natural pairing since they were associates and rivals. Washington's pragmatic, somewhat accommodationist approach to race relations makes a provocative contrast to the more uncompromising position Du Bois eventually adopted. Their opposed views on black education, in particular, make for revealing comparisons. Washington's and Du Bois's texts represent different stages in the struggle for African American rights, and reading them in tandem allows students to begin to gauge the evolution of the movement.

ABRAHAM CAHAN, ANZIA YEZIERSKA, AND SUI SIN FAR (EDITH MAUD EATON)

While Cahan and Yezierska chronicled the experiences of Eastern European Jewish immigrants in New York, Sui Sin Far explored the stories of Chinese immigrants living in Chinatowns along the West Coast. Despite the enormous cultural (and geographical) differences between these immigrant groups, they both had to deal with exploitation, prejudice, and the tensions caused by the process of "Americanization." Sui Sin Far and Yezierska both offer poignant—and at times ironic—examinations of immigrant women's relationship to bourgeois domesticity.

SARAH MORGAN BRYAN PIATT AND HENRY ADAMS

While Piatt's complex poems and Adams's elegant prose autobiography have little in common on the level of genre, these texts share a self-consciousness about—and willingness to experiment with—the formal possibilities of voice. Writing his autobiography in the third person, Adams almost seems to dissociate himself from this record of his own life in an effort to lend objectivity to its telling. Piatt adopts a different strategy, employing multiple voices and dialogue in her poetry rather than relying on a conventional single lyric voice. These writers' experiments with voice seem at some level intended to infuse their work with realism.

CORE CONTEXTS

The Gospel of Wealth: Robber Barons and the Rise of Monopoly Capitalism

John D. Rockefeller, the leader of the oil industry and the wealthiest man in the world in his day, once articulated his beliefs about money and power this way: "I believe the power to make money is a gift of God . . . to be developed and used to the best of our ability for the good of mankind. Having been endowed with the gift I possess, I believe it is my duty to make money and still more money, and to use the money I make for the good of my fellow man according to the dictates of my conscience." In justifying his incredible fortune in this way, Rockefeller expressed the ideology of "the gospel of wealth," a term coined by steel tycoon Andrew Carnegie. According to the gospel of wealth, unrestrained capitalism will reward the best and most virtuous people, who will then use their fortune to benefit all of society. The duty of the virtuous industrialist, then, is to seek as much profit as possible by whatever means necessary.

While not everyone agreed that big business unfettered by government regulations was a good idea, or that it benefited the right people, no one could deny that by the end of the nineteenth century a new class of financiers with unprecedented power and wealth had

[2855] Lewis W. Hine, *View of the Ewen Breaker of the Pennsylvania Coal Co.* (1911), courtesy of the National Archives and Records Administration.

"THE GOSPEL OF WEALTH" WEB ARCHIVE

[2855] Lewis W. Hine, *View of the Ewen Breaker of the Pennsylvania Coal Co.* (1911), courtesy of the National Archives and Records Administration. The thickness of the dust is visible in this photograph of children working for the Pennsylvania Coal Company. These children were often kicked or beaten by overseers.

[5749] John D. Rockefeller, *Address by J. D. Rockefeller, Jr.* (1920), courtesy of the Library of Congress. Rockefeller used his oil monopoly to become the richest man in the world during the first decade of the twentieth century. What he espoused as the "Gospel of Wealth" was criticized by others as the cruel and unfettered capitalism of "Robber Barons." Though Rockefeller donated huge sums to charity, many felt this inadequately redressed the damage done during his acquisition of wealth.

[7136] *Frank Leslie's Illustrated Newspaper, Boss Waving His Fist at Female Employee in a Sweatshop*

emerged in the United States. Industrialization had radically altered the character of the American economy by promoting the growth of giant corporations, **monopolies**, and **trusts** over the small businesses, shops, and farms that had formed the economic backbone of the prewar nation. These new corporations employed thousands of workers who were valued not for their artisanal skills but instead for their ability to perform menial tasks in factories and plants. Factory employment in the United States nearly doubled between 1850 and 1880. For many Americans, the growth of industrialism meant longer hours, unsatisfying working conditions, and a modest salary. But for a tiny minority, industrialism provided opportunities for extraordinary and unprecedented wealth.

In the economic climate of the late nineteenth century, some entrepreneurs were able to buy out or bankrupt all of their competitors to create monopolies. By 1900, a handful of men enjoyed virtually exclusive control over such important industries as steel, oil, banking, and railroads. Men like Carnegie, Rockefeller, J. P. Morgan, Jay Gould, and Leland Stanford developed innovative financial and management practices, centralizing control of their far-flung business interests through the use of trusts and holding companies. The men who ran the trusts made enormous profits and came to be regarded as aristocrats—to admirers, they were "princes of industry," while to critics, they were "robber barons." Many of these tycoons came from lowly or impoverished backgrounds and liked to remind people that they were examples of the fulfillment of the American Dream, in which a poor boy achieves success through hard work and virtue.

In accordance with the tenets of the gospel of wealth, many of these men gave tremendous sums of money to charity. They funded everything from churches to art museums to public swimming pools. Carnegie—who liked to call himself a "distributor of wealth"—by some calculations donated over 90 percent of his vast fortune to projects like the 2,811 libraries he founded in towns across the United States and all over the world. John D. Rockefeller gave lavishly to religious mission work, hospitals, schools, and countless other philanthropic organizations. Many of the industrialists endowed scholarship funds and universities, although ironically most of them did not have university degrees.

While the robber barons' philanthropic activities undoubtedly benefited countless people, some critics complained that their charitable works were motivated more by self-glorification and a desire for social acceptance than by a sincere desire to help the less fortunate. Other critics felt that no amount of charitable giving could outweigh the damage the robber barons caused with their unscrupulous business practices. They pointed out that these "captains of industry" were known for forcing their employees to labor in dangerous working conditions, paying poor wages, ruthlessly undermining fair competition, bribing politicians, and gouging consumers. Eventually, public outrage over monopolistic practices led to a call for the government to begin "trust-busting." In response, in 1890

Congress passed the Sherman Anti-Trust Act to punish corporations who engaged in "restraint of fair trade." In its first decade, the act was more symbolic than effective. More lasting reforms came through the efforts of labor unions that organized workers and staged protests demanding fair treatment.

QUESTIONS

Comprehension: What is a monopoly? What is a trust?

Comprehension: What is the "gospel of wealth"?

Context: Listen to the archive sound file of John D. Rockefeller's speech encouraging Americans to donate money to the war effort during World War I. What values and beliefs inform his lecture? How does he attempt to appeal to Americans?

Context: How does Henry Adams characterize industrialism in *The Education of Henry Adams*? Why is the Dynamo such an important symbol to him?

Context: Many of the authors featured in Unit 9 did not support unrestrained capitalism. W. E. B. Du Bois, Theodore Dreiser, Abraham Cahan, and Anzia Yezierska were all interested in socialist theories at some point in their careers. Why do you think socialism was so attractive to these social realists?

Exploration: What kinds of regulations has the government instituted to control large corporations since the days of the robber barons? Have "trustbusting" efforts succeeded? What effects has government regulation had on the U.S. economy?

Exploration: What responsibilities do wealthy people have to the rest of society?

Exploration: In *The Great Gatsby*, F. Scott Fitzgerald portrayed Jay Gatsby as an extremely wealthy but lonely and dissatisfied man. Do you think Fitzgerald might have modeled Gatsby after the robber barons? How is Gatsby influenced by the gospel of wealth?

Making Amendments: The Woman Suffrage Movement

When American women go to the polls to cast their ballots in local and federal elections, most of them do not realize that it took dedicated generations of women almost seventy-five years of activism to ensure their right to vote. Most of the women who first began working for suffrage in 1848 did not live to see the Nineteenth Amendment ratified in 1920. The struggle for female enfranchisement was long and difficult, and the "suffragettes," as suffrage activists were called, adopted many different strategies and tactics before reaching their goal.

The **woman suffrage** movement began at a convention in Seneca Falls, New York, when a group led by Elizabeth Cady Stanton adopted a resolution calling for the right to vote. At the time, the idea of woman suffrage was so radical that many delegates at the convention refused to sign Stanton's "Declaration of Sentiments,"

(1888), courtesy of the Library of Congress [LC-USZ62-79589]. The late nineteenth and early twentieth centuries saw some gain great wealth at the expense of multitudes, like this mistreated worker. Eventually, inhumane working conditions became a cause for social reformers.

[7255] Alfred R. Waud, *Bessemer Steel Manufacture* (1876), courtesy of the Library of Congress [LC-USZ62-1721]. One of six illustrations that appeared in *Harper's Weekly* showing the operations in a steel mill. Steel was big business at the end of the nineteenth century, and, in the days before the income tax, so-called "robber barons" amassed extravagant wealth.

[5605] L. Prang & Co., *Representative Women* (1870), courtesy of the Library of Congress [LC-USZ62-5535].

[2498] Currier & Ives, *The Age of Brass, or the Triumphs of Women's Rights* (1869), courtesy of the Library of Congress [LC-USZC2-1921].

with its call for the enfranchisement of women, even though they supported her other goals of ensuring higher education and property rights for women. However radical the goal of enfranchisement had once seemed, after the Civil War it emerged as one of the most important women's issues when activists realized that the right to vote was necessary both to effect social and political change and to symbolize women's full status as equal citizens. Because the woman suffrage movement had begun in the same reform milieu as abolitionism, many activists were tremendously disappointed when the Fourteenth and Fifteenth Amendments extended suffrage to African American men but not to black or white women. The issue was so volatile that in 1869 the women's rights movement split over whether or not to support the ratification of the Fifteenth Amendment, which guaranteed suffrage to black men.

One group of activists, led by Stanton and Susan B. Anthony, opposed the Fifteenth Amendment, but called for a Sixteenth Amendment that would give women the right to vote. Their organization, the National Woman Suffrage Association (NWSA), viewed suffrage as only one of many important feminist causes on their agenda, and they were unafraid to adopt radical policies and rhetoric to forward their goals. For example, in 1872 Susan B. Anthony went to the polls and tried to vote, hoping to get arrested and thus attract attention for the movement. She was indeed arrested, found guilty of "knowingly, wrongfully, and unlawfully voting," and issued a fine. In contrast, NWSA's rival association, the American Woman Suffrage Association (AWSA), led by Lucy Stone and Julia Ward Howe, was more moderate in its tone, promoted "partial suffrage" legislation, and worked to make feminist reforms appealing to mainstream Americans. AWSA supported the Fifteenth Amendment but vowed to continue working for woman suffrage.

Although they were no longer a united force, the suffrage organizations had made significant strides by the turn of the century. In the West, Wyoming, Utah, Colorado, and Idaho had all adopted woman suffrage by 1896. The suffrage movement also made gains through its alliance with the Women's Christian Temperance Union (WCTU). A more mainstream and conservative organization than either NWSA or AWSA, the WCTU encouraged its large membership to support suffrage as a way of protecting traditional family and domestic values. In particular, they hoped that women voters would be able to pass legislation mandating the prohibition of alcohol. The association of woman suffrage with the temperance movement was both a boon and a hindrance to the effort to achieve enfranchisement. On one hand, the Christian temperance platform attracted a broader base of support and made suffrage seem less radical to mainstream women. But on the other hand, the WCTU endorsement of suffrage fueled big business's fears that women voters would threaten their interests by tilting the nation toward reform. The

[2506] *Frank Leslie's Illustrated Newspaper, Woman Suffrage in Wyoming Territory. Scene at the Polls in Cheyenne* (1888), courtesy of the Library of Congress [LC-USZ62-2235].

brewing and liquor industry, especially, came to perceive woman suffrage as a significant threat and threw its considerable political clout behind stifling the movement.

In 1890, the NWSA and the AWSA finally put their differences behind them and joined forces to make a concerted push for enfranchisement. The new, unified movement, known as the National American Woman Suffrage Association (NAWSA), focused its efforts almost exclusively on winning the vote rather than on other feminist issues. Their strategy involved building support within individual states and winning suffrage referendums on a state-by-state basis. They hoped that when enough states had adopted suffrage amendments, the federal government would at last agree to approve an amendment to the Constitution. In pursuit of this strategy, NAWSA opted to disassociate the suffrage movement from its traditional affiliation with the cause of African American civil rights. Many suffrage activists either shared the racist sentiments so prevalent in turn-of-the-century America or believed that they had to comply with racist views in order to make their cause appealing to a wide constituency. In any case, whether motivated by racism or a misguided sense of expediency, by the late nineteenth century the suffrage movement excluded black women from meaningful participation and refused to take a strong position in support of black women's equal right to enfranchisement.

In their final push for the vote, the suffragists adopted other new—and sometimes radical—strategies. They borrowed newly developed advertising techniques, circulating catchy jingles with pro-suffrage lyrics and distributing stationery and buttons emblazoned with pro-suffrage designs. To attract public attention, they held open-air meetings and rallies in busy urban areas. Suffragists sponsored elaborate parades featuring decorated floats, horses, music, and hundreds of marchers wearing colorful banners. A more militant wing of the suffrage movement, led by Alice Paul, developed more radical tactics, including picketing the White House, getting arrested, and going on hunger strikes. Perhaps the suffrage activists' most successful strategy involved aggressive lobbying among politicians. By targeting and converting individual politicians—including President Woodrow Wilson—suffragists eventually convinced Congress to adopt the Nineteenth Amendment by a narrow margin. The fight for ratification demanded unabated effort and political maneuverings, but finally, on August 21, 1920, the Tennessee legislature completed the ratification process. Their victory came by a very slim margin and after years of struggle, but the suffragists had finally won for American women the right to vote.

The suffrage movement both contributed to and reflected the growing independence of American women by the turn of the century. Women were acquiring education, working in the business world, and achieving economic and social self-sufficiency in greater numbers than ever before. Some women began wearing trousers, smoking, and asserting their sexual freedom. These "**new women**," as such emancipated women were called, resisted the ideals of

speech, about the legality of women's suffrage, was based on the Fourteenth and Fifteenth Amendments to the Constitution.

[2506] *Frank Leslie's Illustrated Newspaper, Woman Suffrage in Wyoming Territory. Scene at the Polls in Cheyenne* (1888), courtesy of the Library of Congress [LC-USZ62-2235]. Woman suffrage was established in Wyoming in 1869. When Wyoming entered the union in 1890, it was the first state that allowed women the right to vote. Esther Morris is credited with convincing the territorial legislature to grant suffrage to women.

[5605] L. Prang & Co., *Representative Women* (1870), courtesy of the Library of Congress [LC-USZ62-5535]. Seven individual portraits of leaders in the woman suffrage movement: Lucretia Mott, Grace Greenwood, Elizabeth Cady Stanton, Anna E. Dickinson, Mary Ashton Rice Livermore, Lydia Maria Francis Child, and Susan B. Anthony.

[5005] Anonymous, *Immigrant Family Looking at Statue of Liberty from Ellis Island* (c. 1930), courtesy of the Library of Congress [LC-USZ62-50904].

domesticity and "true womanhood" that had dominated women's lives in the first part of the nineteenth century. Instead, they demanded new freedoms and transformed the position of women in the United States. Their legacy lives on in contemporary women's movements in support of such causes as economic equality and reproductive freedom.

QUESTIONS

Comprehension: Why did the suffrage movement split into two separate groups in 1869? How did the NWSA differ from the AWSA?

Comprehension: What was the relationship between the suffrage movement and the movement for African American rights? How did it change over time?

Comprehension: What was a "new woman"?

Context: Examine the anti-suffrage cartoon featured in the archive. How are women voters portrayed in this cartoon? What anxieties about woman suffrage underlie the humor of this cartoon?

Context: In Henry James's "Daisy Miller," Winterbourne describes Daisy Miller as an "American girl" of a "pronounced type." What characteristics does Winterbourne attribute to the "American girl"? Why is he so eager to label her as an example of a "type"? Does his vision of the "American girl" have anything in common with the concept of the "new woman"? Would Daisy see herself as a "new woman"?

Context: How do the debates and rifts within the woman suffrage movement compare to the debates and rifts that emerged within the movement for African American rights at the end of the nineteenth century? How do the strategies and philosophies employed by the NWSA, AWSA, and NAWSA compare to the strategies and philosophies developed by black leaders such as Booker T. Washington and W. E. B. Du Bois?

Exploration: What kinds of women's issues continue to be a focus for reform movements? What strategies do contemporary women's groups adopt to generate support for their causes?

Exploration: How have minority women writers like Toni Morrison and Gloria Anzaldúa broadened and revised nineteenth-century ideas about women's rights?

Coming to America: Immigrants at Ellis Island

Between 1892 and 1954, over twelve million immigrants first touched American soil at Ellis Island. A small island located just south of New York City and within view of the Statue of Liberty, Ellis Island was the site of the nation's largest immigrant reception center. On one day alone at the height of immigration, Ellis Island processed 11,750 individuals seeking entry into the United States. Despite its title of "reception center," Ellis Island was neither hospitable nor pleasant: immigrants lined up in an enormous hall and underwent intrusive inspections designed to weed out people with infectious diseases or political ideas that were considered dangerous or subversive. But despite the discomfort and bureaucracy, many newcomers were overjoyed to set foot on Ellis Island. In the shadow of the Statue of Liberty, they took to heart the promise chiseled into the base of the statue:

> Give me your tired, your poor,
> Your huddled masses yearning to breathe free,
> The wretched refuse of your teeming shore.
> Send these, the homeless, tempest-tossed to me,
> I lift my lamp beside the golden door!

Many immigrants arrived in America believing that marvelous opportunities awaited them behind the "golden door." In the last half of the nineteenth century, the vast majority of immigrants came from Eastern and southern Europe—Eastern European Jews made up an especially high percentage of immigrants. They left their homelands to escape persecution, oppression, famine, and poverty. These immigrants brought only the possessions they could carry with them and traveled in "steerage berths" in cramped compartments below the deck of the ship. Some immigrants who could not afford to pay for their passage were brought over as "contract labor." Under this system, businesses that wanted to hire cheap labor could pay the passage of immigrants willing to work for low wages in America. The cost of the workers' fares would then be deducted from their wages once they began working. Contract labor was effectively a form of indentured servitude, but the U.S. government did not make it illegal until 1885 and even then rarely prosecuted companies who engaged in this exploitative practice.

For many immigrants, America was not the Promised Land they had dreamed of. Low wages, long hours, and unhealthy and even dangerous working environments made earning an adequate living almost impossible. Overcrowded tenements and high rents made domestic arrangements difficult and caused problems within families and between neighbors. Many immigrants also had trouble assimilating to the customs and manners of America, or felt resentful about being forced to give up or modify their traditions. When Anzia Yezierska landed at Ellis Island, officials could not pronounce her name. They decided to rename her "Hattie Mayer," which they felt sounded more Anglicized. Yezierska resented this assault on her identity, and when she began to publish, she insisted on using her original, Eastern European name.

Immigrants also endured growing animosity and hostility from native-born Americans, who perceived these "foreigners" as threatening to the cultural and economic status quo. Immigrants' willing-

[5004] Underwood & Underwood, *Immigrants Just Arrived from Foreign Countries—Immigrant Building, Ellis Island. New York Harbor* (c. 1904), courtesy of the Library of Congress [LC-USZ62-15539].

[5092] Lewis Hine, *Young Russian Jewess at Ellis Island* (1905), courtesy of George Eastman House.

[5004] Underwood & Underwood, *Immigrants Just Arrived from Foreign Countries—Immigrant Building, Ellis Island. New York Harbor* (c. 1904), courtesy of the Library of Congress [LC-USZ62-15539]. People from Eastern and Southern Europe poured into the United States around the turn of the twentieth century. This reception center off New York City processed arriving immigrants and attempted to keep out people with infectious diseases or political ideologies perceived as threatening.

[5005] Anonymous, *Immigrant Family Looking at Statue of Liberty from Ellis Island* (c. 1930), courtesy of the Library of Congress [LC-USZ62-50904]. Many found the United States less idyllic than they had imagined it would be. The reception center at Ellis Island received more than 20 million of the 27 million immigrants who came to the United States between 1880 and 1930.

[5006] Anonymous, *Italian Immigrant Family at Ellis Island* (c. 1910), courtesy of the Library of Congress [LC-USZ62-67910]. Between 1880 and 1930, more people immigrated to America from Italy than from any other country. Many of these immigrants settled on New York's Lower East Side. Their lives were the basis for much of the literature of the social realists.

[5092] Lewis Hine, *Young Russian Jewess at Ellis Island* (1905), courtesy of George Eastman House. Millions of immigrants passed through Ellis Island at the turn of the twentieth century. Just off the coast of New York City, immigrants were greeted by the Statue of Liberty, but were also introduced to harsh and often callous immigration policies, which reflected the ambivalence with which the United States welcomed its newest residents.

[8183] Anonymous, *The Voyage, No. 8* (c. 1920), reprinted in *Island: Poetry and History of Chinese Immigrants on Angel Island, 1910–1940,* courtesy of the University of Washington Press. "How has anyone to know that my dwelling place would be a prison?" asks this poem, one of many written on the walls of the Angel Island detention center by

ness to work for low wages angered native-born Americans who resented competing with them for jobs, and the infusion of new religious and cultural practices caused some native-born people to fear that the "purity" of American culture was being assaulted. "Nativism," or the belief that native-born Americans were superior to and needed to be protected from immigrants, created deep divisions between immigrants and other Americans. Anti-Catholic and Anti-Semitic sentiments began to color public discourse. Nativists frequently scapegoated immigrants, blaming them for the spread of crime and disease.

Nativist hostility finally culminated in the passage of congressional bills restricting immigration. The Chinese, in particular, were the target of a specific law designed to forbid their entry into the United States: the Chinese Exclusion Act was adopted in 1882. As a result, the immigrant reception center on Angel Island off the coast of California was even less welcoming than Ellis Island. Many hopeful Chinese immigrants were denied entry and then held in detention centers for months. Poetry written in Chinese covers the walls of the detention centers, parsing out the aspirations, dreams, and despair of the inmates.

Given the difficulties faced by immigrants, it is perhaps not surprising that, according to some estimates, nearly a third of those who arrived in America in the late nineteenth and early twentieth centuries eventually returned to their homes in Europe or Asia. But millions of immigrants stayed, and their contributions to American society and culture enriched and transformed the nation.

QUESTIONS

Comprehension: How were Ellis Island and Angel Island different from one another?

Comprehension: What was "contract labor"?

Comprehension: What is "nativism"?

Context: In the story "Mrs. Spring Fragrance," Sui Sin Far mentions a peripheral character who is being detained at Angel Island. How does this character function in the story? Why does Sui Sin Far include this information about Angel Island in a story about Chinese immigrants who have been living in America for many years?

Context: What kinds of assimilation pressures do the Eastern European immigrant characters in Abraham Cahan's and Anzia Yezierska's stories encounter?

Context: Read the Emma Lazarus poem "The New Colossus" featured in the archive. How does this poem describe America and its relationship to immigrants? What comparison is Lazarus drawing between Ancient Greece and nineteenth-century America? What is the significance of personifying America as a woman?

Exploration: Should immigrants be expected to assimilate to American culture? If so, to what extent?

EXTENDED CONTEXTS

How the Other Half Lived: The Lower East Side

Touring the Lower East Side of Manhattan in the early years of the twentieth century, author Henry James was shocked by the "intensity of the material picture in the dense Yiddish quarter." An area populated almost entirely by impoverished immigrants, the Lower East Side must have astonished James, who had spent most of his life surrounded by wealth and privilege. The neighborhood was indeed "intense" and "dense"; in fact, by the turn of the century the area had a population density of 330,000 people per square mile. Photographs of the Lower East Side from the period show narrow streets, towering run-down tenements, crowds of adults and children, throngs of pushcarts and peddlers, and laundry hanging out of windows. It was a densely inhabited area that afforded little distinction between the sidewalk and the street, or between private homes and public spaces. Home to literally millions of immigrants, the Lower East Side could seem like a confusing, crowded maze because it contained countless mini-communities composed of different ethnic groups. Irish, German, Italian, Greek, Chinese, African, African American, and Arab families lived in different sections of the neighborhood. But by far the largest ethnic community consisted of Jews who had emigrated from Eastern Europe. While these groups all maintained separate and diverse traditions—and sometimes found that their differences created rivalries and hostility—they were united by their poverty, their status as outsiders, and their desire to find material success in America.

Most individuals living on the Lower East Side at the turn of the century lived in tenement apartments or slept in cheap lodging houses. Typical tenement flats consisted of two or three very small rooms in which a family of between four and eight would live with a boarder or two. Workspaces were no less congested—the "sweatshops" were crowded with underpaid laborers who worked between thirteen and eighteen hours a day, six and sometimes seven days a week. In these conditions, crime, disease, fires, and accidents were common occurrences. The appalling poverty of the Lower East Side became a popular topic for reformers and sensation-seeking journalists alike. Many books and articles offered titillating glimpses into this "vicious underworld" and hysterically warned that the Lower East Side was breeding a "criminal element" that would soon menace the rest of the city. Others proposed social and economic reforms to address the inequities that compelled immigrants to live and work in such squalid conditions. Most notably, Jacob A. Riis's newspaper articles, graphic photographs, and illustrated book-length exposé, *How the Other Half Lives: Studies Among the Tenements of New York* (1890), shocked Americans and led to some civic reforms designed to protect poor tenement-dwellers.

As crowded, exploitative, and oppressive as the Lower East Side may have been, however, it was not simply the pit of unmitigated

Chinese immigrants held there by U.S. authorities. Other examples of these poems can be found in the archive, [8184] through [8191].

[9092] Emma Lazarus, *The New Colossus* (1883), courtesy of the U.S. Department of State Web site. Lazarus's famous poem, which reads in part, "Give me your tired, your poor, / Your huddled masses yearning to breathe free," appears on the base of the Statue of Liberty in New York Harbor, an impressive sight that greeted immigrants as they began the difficult and sometimes degrading task of passing through the Ellis Island immigration facility.

[6352] Anonymous, *Hester Street, NY* (c. 1903), courtesy of the National Archives and Records Administration.

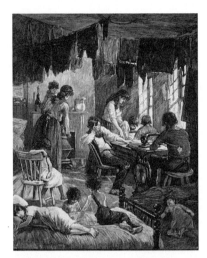

misery and evil that many nineteenth-century journalists portrayed. Rather, in spite of the rampant poverty and harsh working conditions, the neighborhood was a dynamic community infused with a vibrant and diverse cultural life. Ethnic restaurants and saloons offered an enticing variety of food and drink; halls hosted dances, weddings, union meetings, and scholarly lectures; theatres and music halls mounted plays and concerts; and synagogues, churches, temples, and schools served as important social centers. The inhabitants of the Lower East Side formed a thriving community in their crowded section of Manhattan, melding their old traditions with new ones to form a diverse culture that had a lasting impact on New York and on America.

QUESTIONS

Comprehension: What is a tenement? What is a sweatshop?

Context: How does Abraham Cahan describe the realities of labor in a sweatshop in his story "A Sweat-Shop Romance"? How does his description of life, work, and leisure among Jewish immigrants on the Lower East Side compare to the photographs and illustrations of Lower East Side life featured in the archive?

Exploration: How do contemporary journalists, writers, and filmmakers portray the slums and housing projects that still exist in many of America's urban areas? Do you think sensationalism still plays a role in depictions of urban poverty?

Elevating an Elite: W. E. B. Du Bois and the Talented Tenth

At the turn of the twentieth century, black people in the American South had yet to enjoy many of the rights and opportunities promised them by the Emancipation Proclamation, the Fifteenth Amendment, and the federal Civil Rights Act. Instead, many African Americans were denied the right to vote by expensive poll taxes, property requirements, or bogus "literacy tests." At the same time, "Jim Crow" laws enforced segregation in virtually all public spaces in the South, from railroad cars to schools. Violence against African Americans—including lynching—was on the rise.

Faced with this overwhelming, systematized oppression, African American leaders like Booker T. Washington and W. E. B. Du Bois concluded that education was their best strategy for achieving social advancement and civil rights. While they agreed on the need for education, however, they held extremely different ideas about what kind of curriculum would best suit their goal of asserting African American equality. Washington held that blacks should be trained only in practical, vocational skills such as farming, carpentry, mechanical trades, sewing, and cooking. The Tuskegee Institute, where Washington served as the director, dedicated itself to providing black students with these kinds of practical skills. Du Bois, on the other hand, insisted that broader educational opportunities should be available to at least some African Americans. His ideas centered on his theory of a **Talented Tenth**, an elite group of gifted and polished individuals who could benefit from a rigorous classical education and then lead their entire race forward.

In his 1903 essay "The Talented Tenth," Du Bois claimed that "The Negro race, like all races, is going to be saved by its exceptional men. The problem of education, then, among Negroes must first of all deal with the Talented Tenth; it is the problem of developing the Best of this race that they may guide the Mass away from the contamination and death of the Worst, in their own and other races." According to Du Bois, a small, uniquely endowed elite could alone make artistic and scholarly contributions to world development on behalf of the entire race. He perceived the relationship between this talented elite and the rest of the group as a symbiotic one: the larger group would support the talented elite, who would in turn raise the level of the entire group. The Talented Tenth would combat the degrading tendencies of what Du Bois called "The Submerged Tenth," a group he characterized as "criminals, prostitutes, and loafers." In Du Bois's scheme, the Talented Tenth would work not simply within the group but would also direct their efforts against the forces of racism.

While Du Bois intended his plan to benefit all African Americans, the theory of the Talented Tenth has obvious problematic implications. The elevation of an elite segment of African American society with special access to opportunities and resources would create sharp distinctions and classes within the community as a whole, and the belief that only a small group has the potential to make important contributions is profoundly anti-democratic. But despite the exclusivity of the notion of the Talented Tenth, Du Bois's ideas advocated broad educational opportunities for at least some African Americans and inspired many with hope.

QUESTIONS

Comprehension: According to Du Bois, what kinds of responsibilities do the Talented Tenth have to the rest of the group? In Du Bois's formulation, how would the Talented Tenth benefit the larger African American community?

Context: Early in his career, Du Bois was offered a position teaching at Tuskegee Institute, the vocational school that Booker T. Washington directed. Why do you think Du Bois decided not to accept the position? How are his ideas about black education at odds with Washington's mission for Tuskegee?

Exploration: In Charles W. Chesnutt's story "The Wife of His Youth," the main character is a member of an elite African American club that seems to consider itself akin to a "Talented Tenth." How does the story critique the elitism of this organization?

Exploration: What kinds of issues inform contemporary debates

ties. These harsh conditions challenged immigrants and contributed to a perception that immigrants were somehow "damaging" the country.

[5126] Lewis Wickes Hines, *Rear View of Tenement, 134 1/2 Thompson St., New York City* (1912), courtesy of the Library of Congress, Prints and Photographs Division, National Child Labor Committee Collection [LC-USZ62-93116]. Photograph of the back of a tenement housing complex in New York City. Like writer Theodore Dreiser, photographer Lewis Wickes Hines documented social conditions in America at the beginning of the twentieth century.

[6352] Anonymous, *Hester Street, NY* (c.1903), courtesy of the National Archives and Records Administration. Hester Street is one of many places on the Lower East Side of Manhattan that Anzia Yezierska described in her writing.

[7102] J. E. Purdy, *W. E. B. Du Bois* (1904), courtesy of the Library of Congress [LC-USZ62-28485].

about educational opportunities for minority groups? Why is affirmative action such a controversial policy in contemporary America?

ASSIGNMENTS

Personal and Creative Responses

1. *Journal:* Using the autobiographies of Booker T. Washington and Henry Adams for inspiration, compose a journal entry in which you describe your own education. What are the most valuable skills and life lessons you have learned? What circumstances or incidents have most shaped your development?

2. *Poet's Corner:* Examine Sarah Morgan Bryan Piatt's "The Palace-Burner," "A Pique at Parting," or "Her Word of Reproach." Pay attention to how Piatt uses dialogue and multiple voices to develop her ideas. Try rewriting one of these poems using a single lyric voice. How did your revision change the poem? What difficulties did you encounter in translating Piatt's many voices into a single voice?

3. *Multimedia:* Imagine that you have been asked to produce a documentary on turn-of-the-century New York. Using the *American Passages* archive and slide-show software, create a multimedia presentation in which you explore the different aspects of New York society at that time.

Problem-Based Learning Projects

1. Imagine that you and your peers sit on the town council of a small suburb of Pittsburgh in 1900. Andrew Carnegie, the wealthy Pittsburgh industrialist, has offered to donate funds to build and operate a library in your town. Some citizens of the town do not want to accept the gift because they believe that Carnegie's money is tainted by his unscrupulous business practices. Others believe that the benefits of a library outweigh any scruples they might have about accepting a robber baron's money. Deliberate as a council, come up with a plan of action, and prepare a statement of support for your plan.

2. You have been asked to create a museum dedicated to interpreting the immigrant experience in New York. Where will you house the museum? What kinds of information and activities will you provide?

3. It is 1905 and the state of Mississippi has allocated funds to charter a new school for African American students. Booker T. Washington and W. E. B. Du Bois are holding a meeting to discuss how the school should use its funds and what its educational mission should be. Imagine that you have been hired to help

Washington and Du Bois prepare for the meeting at which they will debate this issue. Divide into two groups and prepare your arguments.

GLOSSARY

Bintl Briv   A Yiddish, "Dear Abby"–style advice column introduced by Abraham Cahan in the Yiddish newspaper the *Jewish Daily Forward*. The *Bintl Briv* (or "Bundle of Letters") printed questions from readers and offered authoritative advice on romantic, family, and social issues. (A selection of *Bintl Briv* columns can be found in *Jewish American Literature: A Norton Anthology*.)

limited third-person narration   A mode of narration that relies on narrators who are not omniscient but instead render descriptions and observations through the limitations of the central character. Henry James's interest in psychology led him to develop the use of limited third-person narration, which is often regarded as one of his major contributions to American fiction. Readers must do more work —and involve themselves more in the process of meaning-making— to understand the relationship of the stories to their narration.

monopoly   Businesses that have exclusive control of a commodity or service and are thus able to manipulate the prices and availability of those commodities and services as well as to restrict potential competitors from entering the market.

"new woman"   A turn-of-the-century term for women who resisted the ideals of domesticity and "true womanhood" that had dominated women's lives in the first part of the nineteenth century. Such women challenged traditional social conventions by acquiring an education, working in the business world, asserting some degree of sexual freedom, and living independently of men. "New women" were also associated with such radical behaviors as wearing trousers and smoking.

realism   The literary commitment to the truthful, accurate representation of American life as it was experienced by ordinary Americans. A "realist" aesthetic infused literature in the last half of the nineteenth century. Realism was characterized by its uncompromising, literal representations of the particularities of the material world and the human condition. This passion for finding and presenting the truth led many American practitioners of realism to explore characters, places, and events that had previously seemed inappropriate subject matter for literature.

robber baron   A derisive term for the handful of enormously wealthy men who enjoyed virtually exclusive control over such important industries as steel, oil, banking, and railroads in the late nineteenth and early twentieth centuries. Robber barons were criticized for their ruthless and often unscrupulous business practices.

The Talented Tenth   An elite group of gifted and polished individuals who, according to W. E. B. du Bois's theory, could benefit from a rigorous classical education and then lead African Americans forward. Du Bois believed that the African American community should focus its resources on cultivating this group.

trust A combination of companies held in common by a board of trustees, which controls most or all of the stock of the constituent companies. This kind of organization allows large corporations to centralize their concerns and thus economize on expenses, regulate production, and discourage competition. For all practical purposes, the formation of steel, oil, bank, and railroad trusts made competition virtually impossible, since the monopolies enjoyed such tight control of their markets.

woman suffrage The movement for female enfranchisement. It took almost seventy-five years of activism before American women finally gained the right to vote in 1920.

Yiddish A language spoken mainly by European Jews. Based on German, Yiddish was also inflected by Hebrew, Slavic, and eventually American vocabularies. Abraham Cahan frequently wrote in Yiddish, and Anzia Yezierska incorporated Yiddish phrases and captured the cadence and rhythm of Yiddish speech in her characters' dialogue.

SELECTED BIBLIOGRAPHY

Andrews, William L., Frances Smith Foster, and Trudier Harris, eds. *The Concise Oxford Companion to African American Literature*. New York: Oxford UP, 2001.

Baskin, Judith R. *Women of the Word: Jewish Women and Jewish Writing*. Detroit: Wayne State UP, 1994.

Bederman, Gail. *Manliness and Civilization: A Cultural History of Gender and Race in the United States, 1880–1917*. Chicago: U of Chicago P, 1995.

DeMarco, Joseph P. *The Social Thought of W. E. B. Du Bois*. Lanham: UP of America, 1983.

Diner, Hasia R. *Lower East Side Memories: A Jewish Place in America*. Princeton: Princeton UP, 2000.

Graham, Sara Hunter. *Woman Suffrage and the New Democracy*. New Haven: Yale UP, 1996.

Kaplan, Amy. *The Social Construction of American Realism*. Chicago: U of Chicago P, 1988.

Maffi, Mario. *Gateway to the Promised Land: Ethnic Cultures on New York's Lower East Side*. New York: New York UP, 1995.

Oberdeck, Kathryn J. *The Evangelist and the Impresario: Religion, Entertainment, and Cultural Politics in America, 1884–1914*. Baltimore: Johns Hopkins UP, 1999.

Sundquist, Eric. *To Wake the Nations: Race in the Making of American Literature*. Cambridge: Belknap Press of Harvard UP, 1993.

Wheeler, Marjorie Spruhill, ed. *One Woman, One Vote: Rediscovering the Woman Suffrage Movement*. Troutdale: NewSage Press, 1995.

FURTHER RESOURCES

The Age of Innocence [videorecording]. Columbia Pictures; screenplay by Jay Cocks and Martin Scorsese; produced by Barbara De Fina; directed by Martin Scorsese. Burbank: Columbia TriStar Home Video, 1993.

Banta, Martha. *Imaging American Women: Idea and Ideals in Cultural History*. New York: Columbia UP, 1987.

Byron, Joseph. *New York Interiors at the Turn of the Century in 131 Photographs by Joseph Byron from the Byron Collection of the Museum of the City of New York*. Text by Clay Lancaster. New York: Dover Publications, 1976.

Chametzky, Jules, et al., eds. *Jewish American Literature: A Norton Anthology*. New York: W. W. Norton & Company, 2000.

LeGates, Richard T., and Frederic Stout, eds. *The City Reader*, 2nd ed. New York: Routledge, 2000.

Patton, Sharon F. *African-American Art*. New York: Oxford UP, 1998.

Rosten, Leo. *The New Joys of Yiddish*. Rev. by Lawrence Bush; illus. by R. O. Blechman. New York: Crown, 2001.

Sapoznik, Henry. *Klezmer!: Jewish Music from Old World to Our World* [book and sound recording]. New York: Schirmer Books, 1999.

Sears, Roebuck and Company. *The 1902 Edition of the Sears Roebuck Catalogue*. Intro. Cleveland Amory. New York: Bounty Books, 1969.

Yiddish Radio Project [broadcast]. Produced by Henry Sapoznik, Yair Reiner, and David Isay. Penguin Audiobooks; abridged edition (October 24, 2002).

Zurier, Rebecca. *Metropolitan Lives: The Ashcan Artists and Their New York*. Washington, DC: National Museum of American Art. New York: W. W. Norton and Company, 1995.

RHYTHMS IN POETRY

*From the Beat of Blues to the Sounds
of Everyday Speech*

Authors and Works

Featured in the Video:

T. S. Eliot, *The Waste Land* (poem)

Langston Hughes, "The Weary Blues," "The Negro Speaks of Rivers," "Montage of a Dream Deferred" (poems)

William Carlos Williams, "To a Poor Old Woman," "The Red Wheelbarrow," "This Is Just to Say" (poems)

Discussed in This Unit:

Ezra Pound, "In a Station of the Metro," *The Cantos* (poems)

Hilda Doolittle (H.D.), *The Walls Do Not Fall*, *Tribute to the Angels*, *The Flowering of the Rod* (long poems); *Pilate's Wife*, *Asphodel*, *Her* (prose pieces)

Jean Toomer, *Cane* (novel containing both prose and poetry)

Genevieve Taggard, "Everyday Alchemy," "With Child," "At Last the Women Are Moving" (poems)

Carl Sandburg, "Chicago," "Child of the Romans," "Cool Tombs" (poems)

Robert Frost, "Mowing," "Mending Wall," "After Apple-Picking," "Stopping by Woods," "Birches," "Out, Out—," "Design," "The Gift Outright" (poems)

Claude McKay, "If We Must Die," "The Lynching" (poems); *Home to Harlem* (novel)

Overview Questions

■ How did World War I affect the way that Americans imagined themselves? How is this change reflected in the writings of the era?

■ How do the authors in Unit 10 question or affirm individual identity? How do race and gender complicate what it means to be an American?

■ How do these writers use the vernacular? How does the idiom of Williams, for example, differ from that of Hughes?

■ How do these authors strive to broaden our concept of what it means to be American? How do they use different strategies to imagine and address marginalized peoples?

■ What qualities are common to all the writers in this unit?

■ How does the war affect the poetry of this period? How is this poetry also influenced by popular culture?

■ How do physical spaces influence this literature? How does the American city, specifically Harlem and Chicago, shape the production of American poetry of the 1920s and 1930s? What events changed the face of American cities in the 1920s and 1930s? How are those changes reflected in the poetry?

■ Does American literature have to be written within the borders of the United States? How do we categorize the literature of expatriate writers? Does poetry have to use an American idiom to be considered American?

■ How would you describe modernism, in contrast to other literary movements you have encountered or studied? What values and questions are reflected in the poetry of this movement?

■ How does the modernism of American poets writing in America differ from the modernism of those writing abroad? How do race and gender affect the way writers interpret modernism? What assumptions about literature have we inherited from the modernist poets? Can you see the modernist legacy in contemporary writers?

■ How do the African American authors in this unit re-imagine American identity? How do they challenge the way history has been told and recorded? What other myths about America are challenged by the poets in this unit?

■ How do the expatriate writers treat the question of American identity? Why does Greek mythology play a recurring role in American modernist verse?

Learning Objectives

After students have viewed the video, read the headnotes and literary selections in *The Norton Anthology of American Literature*, and explored related archival materials on the *American Passages* Web site, they should be able to

1. describe at least two different varieties of literary modernism and discuss how black and white modernist experiments may have influenced each other;
2. relate the historical and cultural developments and controversies of the time to poetry written between the world wars;
3. discuss how these authors imagine American identity;
4. analyze and compare basic poetic strategies such as the use of form, language, allusion, imagery, and rhythm in the poetry in this unit.

Instructor Overview

The opening decades of the twentieth century seemed to prove what Henry Adams and other historians had suspected: that technological change and social turmoil were propelling the West into unimaginable new territory, and that established ways of describing the human condition—including literary modes and strategies—were no longer appropriate. In 1903, modern aviation was little more than slapstick experiments with powered gliders on an empty beach; a dozen years later, in the middle of World War I, there were fleets of long-range lethal fighters in the air over battlefields where more soldiers would die than in any conflict in human history. Immediately after the armistice a pandemic of influenza killed millions more in their hometowns, and major American cities ran out of coffins.

In the United States, which had been spared the immense devastation inflicted in the European theaters of war, an economic boom brought heady hopes. Energized by new war-related technology, a pent-up demand for consumer goods, and an imperative to rebuild devastated landscapes in Belgium, France, and Italy, American heavy industry went to full throttle, offering high-paying jobs and setting off a migration of adventurous Americans, white and black, from small towns in the South to big cities in the East and Midwest. At the same time, disappointment, competition for work and for living space, and cross-cultural encounters brought new turmoil and violence.

In the summer of 1919, dubbed the Red Summer, race riots and lynchings erupted in many cities across America. Despite the optimism so evident in the music, fashion, and popular culture of the 1920s, racial tensions continued to fester, and starry-eyed investing and spending created an economic bubble, which burst in 1929. In that year, a series of bank failures overseas and a crash of stock markets all over the world brought on the Great Depression, which lasted nearly a decade and affected every industrialized country in the world. The bleak economic times brought about a renewed political and social awareness, as writers like Carl Sandburg, William Inge, John Steinbeck, and Genevieve Taggard brought special attention to the plight of millions. By the end of the 1930s, the threat of a new war loomed, and the vibrant 1920s seemed a distant memory.

Even before World War I, the artistic and literary communities of the West were haunted by a sense that new times required new ways of seeing and thinking. In Paris, the artistic practice of "cubism" appealed to many as a fresh way of representing the speed, diversity, and fragmentation of ordinary life. In the middle of the war, in a place called the Cabaret Voltaire in Zurich, experiments with "dadaism" challenged the arts and the individual mind to break free from the kind of logic that had carried European civilization into a storm of violence. During and after the war, American poets, from the aristocratic T. S. Eliot to the young African American Langston Hughes, looked to such experimental art for guidance in expressing the pace of modernity. The modernist poets strove to reinvent the fundamentals of poetry, to answer Ezra Pound's challenge to "make it new." Influenced by visual art, primitivism, orientalism, and jazz, writers searched for a distinctly American idiom. What should a modern American poetry sound like? What could white culture and African American culture learn from each other? How could American modernism become something unique and fundamentally different from British and European experiments?

The video for Unit 10 chronicles the different paths modernist poets took as they responded to the political, social, and economic changes shaping American life. As the video suggests, modernism was not a monolithic movement with one core idea and strategy. For modernist authors, the early twentieth century seemed to be a cultural and historical turning point. Their work is characterized by questions about objectivity and subjectivity, about conflicts between psychological or inward time and the relentless ticking of the mechanical and historical clock. They searched—often fruitlessly—for objective truth and a renewed sense of belonging in a secularized world, one without moral definition.

The prose and poetry they created offer very different strategies and aesthetic choices. T. S. Eliot, who spent most of his career abroad, ultimately turned to the high culture of the classical world and the European Renaissance. Committed to developing an American idiom, William Carlos Williams built poetry from everyday speech. Langston Hughes was also interested in creating music from the vernacular and the everyday, but he paid special attention to the dialects of African Americans. Determined to portray black experience with honesty and dignity, Hughes looked to jazz, folk tradition, and history as the foundations for his verse.

The video, archive, and curriculum in Unit 10 highlight early modernist intersections in America among art, politics, and culture. The key concepts covered include the Harlem Renaissance, orientalism, primitivism, the influence of radio, and the idea of the "New Negro." The materials also suggest ways that students might relate the authors and works to one another. Other units that provide complements to this one include Unit 7, "Slavery and Freedom," which offers background for the struggles and ideas explored by Harlem Renaissance writers; Unit 9, "Social Realism," which explores the rise of a modern political and social conscience in America; and Unit 11, "Modernist Portraits," and Unit 13, "Southern Renaissance," which present other varieties of modernist writing between the world wars. Finally, Unit 15, "Poetry of Liberation," and Unit 16, "Search for Identity," illustrate the

legacy of poets first interested in portraying the American vernacular and the black experience. These later authors also reflect an interest in formal experimentation, the mixing of literary genres, the introduction of shocking subject matter, an exploration of states of mind (as opposed to an emphasis on narrative), and a fascination with the everyday.

Student Overview

The opening decades of the twentieth century seemed to prove what Henry Adams and other historians had suspected: that technological change and social turmoil were propelling the West into unimaginable new territory, and that established ways of describing the human condition—including literary modes and strategies—were no longer appropriate. In 1903, modern aviation was little more than slapstick experiments with powered gliders on an empty beach; a dozen years later, in the middle of World War I, there were fleets of long-range lethal fighters in the air over battlefields where more soldiers would die than in any conflict in human history. Immediately after the armistice a pandemic of influenza killed millions more in their hometowns, and major American cities ran out of coffins.

In the United States, which had been spared the immense devastation inflicted in the European theaters of war, an economic boom brought heady hopes. Energized by new war-related technology, a pent-up demand for consumer goods, and an imperative to rebuild devastated landscapes in Belgium, France, and Italy, American heavy industry went to full throttle, offering high-paying jobs and setting off a migration of adventurous Americans, white and black, from small towns in the South to big cities in the East and Midwest. At the same time, disappointment, competition for work and for living space, and cross-cultural encounters brought new turmoil and violence.

In the summer of 1919, dubbed the Red Summer, race riots and lynchings erupted in many cities across America. Despite the optimism so evident in the music, fashion, and popular culture of the 1920s, racial tensions continued to fester, and starry-eyed investing and spending created an economic bubble, which burst in 1929. In that year, a series of bank failures overseas and a crash of stock markets all over the world brought on the Great Depression, which lasted nearly a decade and affected every industrialized country in the world. The bleak economic times brought about a renewed political and social awareness, as writers like Carl Sandburg, William Inge, John Steinbeck, and Genevieve Taggard brought special attention to the plight of millions. By the end of the 1930s, the threat of a new war loomed, and the vibrant 1920s seemed a distant memory.

Many of the writers of this period responded to the disruptions of modernity with an interest in "primitivism," a renewed taste for traditional art from Africa, Asia, the South Pacific, and the indigenous peoples of North America. With its aesthetic surprises and its aura of exoticism, such art seemed to promise fresh ways of perceiving, as well as escape from the excesses of civilization. Modernists expressed their sense of dislocation and alienation through fragmented form, and they looked to other cultures, particularly ancient civilizations and Asian traditions, as a respite from their urban, modern experience. Whatever their course, these poets recognized the dramatic changes introduced by modernity, from technology to urbanization, and they strove to write poetry that would respond to such change with fresh language. As they searched for this new poetic idiom, they raised questions central to their identity as Americans.

The video, archive, and curriculum in Unit 10 highlight early modernist intersections in American art, politics, and culture. The key concepts covered include the Harlem Renaissance, orientalism, primitivism, the influence of radio, and the idea of the "New Negro."

Video Overview

➢ **Authors covered:** T. S. Eliot, Langston Hughes, William Carlos Williams

➢ **Who's interviewed:** Lisa Steinman, chair of the English department (Reed College); Pancho Savery, professor of English (Reed College); Jacqueline Dirks, associate professor of history and humanities (Reed College); Rafia Zafar, director of African and Afro-American studies (Washington University); and Alice Walker, author and poet

➢ **Points covered:**

- Many American poets between the world wars favored common speech and strove to make their verse accessible to a large public. Others developed a style that could seem obscure.
- The historical, cultural, and economic events that shaped poetry of this period included the Great Migration, the Harlem Renaissance, World War I, and the Great Depression. In addition, rapidly advancing technology made possible department stores, skyscrapers, and public transportation; America was suddenly more urban than ever.
- When Ezra Pound urged poets to "make it new" in 1912, he helped to launch modern poetry, which left behind traditional forms and style in favor of free verse and vivid language. Pound wanted poets to con-

centrate on language and rhythm, to bring poetry "closer to the condition of music."

- Modernism was moving in two very different directions. While T. S. Eliot and Pound found inspiration and subjects in arcane traditions of classical and medieval Europe and Asia, William Carlos Williams and Langston Hughes looked to their own neighborhoods and personal experiences for inspiration, subjects, and styles. Hughes drew on African American culture, particularly the blues, jazz, and oral storytelling, to create poetry with distinctive rhythms and innovative use of the vernacular, a poetry meant to be heard. His poetry also reflects his social awareness and commitment to activism.
- In the 1920s, Harlem experienced a cultural and artistic flowering known as the Harlem Renaissance. While many African Americans took a great interest in the art and literature of the movement, white audiences were attracted to Harlem as well, to hear the music and experience the excitement of the popular culture.
- Alain Locke popularized the concept of the "New Negro," asserting that African Americans could achieve greater acceptance and social equality through art. He also believed that African Americans

could use art to define their identity and create a sense of racial pride and community.

- Williams and Pound were interested in the austere traditional poetry of China and Japan, in which ordinary objects can signify much beyond themselves.

PREVIEW

- **Preview the video:** The video offers historical background for Unit 10, focusing particularly on the effects of the Great Migration, urbanization, the rapid technological change of ordinary life, and racial prejudice. Centering on Hughes, Williams, and Eliot, the film shows how different strands of modernism developed and influenced one another. While Eliot wrote much of his poetry abroad, Williams and Hughes remained on American soil, both imaginatively and in the flesh. Eliot's work reflects an interest in and respect for Western European tradition, and he wrote obscure, incantatory poetry for an elite audience. Williams and Hughes, however, strove to make their poetry accessible to a much broader reading public, and their inspiration came primarily from everyday experience. They used the American idiom, and they challenged conventional concepts of both America and American poetry. In addition, Hughes's poetry is politically charged, and he incorporated elements of African American culture and history in his work. Despite their differences, all three influenced generations of poets to come.

- **What to think about while watching:** What different kinds of modernism are discussed in the video? How do the featured authors, Williams, Eliot, and Hughes, differ from one another in aesthetic philosophy? How do these differences appear in their poetry? How did black and white modernism influence each other? What qualities are common to all the poetry?

    What cultural, demographic, and technological forces were changing American life? The end of World War I and the threat of World War II affected all these poets at various times in their careers. The population distribution shifted dramatically in the early part of the century, and

technology was also rapidly changing the quality and pace of life. How did these changes influence art at the time?

- **Tying the video to the unit content:** Although the video focuses primarily on Williams, Eliot, and Hughes, it offers important historical background that brings the rest of the unit into focus. The portrayal of Harlem and the racial climate between the world wars connects the poetry of Cullen, McKay, and Brown, all of whom struggled with the problems of racial identity, equality, poetic tradition, and subject matter. Their political aims are shared in part by poets like Sandburg and Taggard, who are in tune with the struggles of working-class America. These poets all strive to represent lived experience honestly, and most of them rely on vernacular and dialect in their work. The effort to create an American identity was not limited to these poets. Indeed, Williams and Frost also did much to establish an American poetic identity by concentrating on American landscapes, language, and experience. Frost's wry, countrified New England narrative voice was often praised as a fundamental voice of America, and his determination to weave poetry out of everyday experience aligns him to some extent with Williams, who also looked to the ordinary for inspiration. Frost, however, was a lifelong believer in metaphor; Williams saw metaphor as a kind of dishonesty in art and strove for a poetry that could present ordinary experience unadorned and unmediated.

    Other authors in the unit, H.D., Pound, and Eliot, represent another strand of modernism that relied much more on the tradition of Western Europe. Their status as expatriates and their interest in classical traditions set them apart from the other authors in Unit 10. As the unit suggests, their work influenced these other writers, convincing them that their American rhythms were all the more important. In addition, Pound's role as mentor and founder of the imagist movement affected many of the writers who chose to stay in the United States. His concept of poetry as something new, as grounded in the particular and ordinary, was central to the work of all these poets.

	What is an American? How does American literature create conceptions of the American experience and identity?	**How do place and time shape literature and our understanding of it?**	**What characteristics of a work have made it influential over time?**
Comprehension Questions	What sources did the poets in this unit draw on for inspiration?	What kinds of historical and social events influenced art between the world wars? How did these forces shape poetry?	What is imagism? What are the features of this movement? How did it influence other poets besides Pound and Eliot?
Context Questions	What is the relationship between the two strands of modernism outlined in the video? How do they overlap?	How did patronage by wealthy whites affect the African American artists in this unit? How did the Great Migration, which brought together black Americans from all over the country, lead to changes in the racial climate? How did those changes affect the poetry of the time?	What are the aesthetic differences between the two strands of modernism covered in this unit? How have changing race and class politics affected the reception of these aesthetic innovations by subsequent generations of writers?
Exploration Questions	How does William Carlos Williams's "This Is Just to Say" compare to Li Young Lee's "Eating Together"? What poetic strategies do the poems share?	What comparison can you make between William Carlos Williams's "The Red Wheelbarrow" and other poems you have read this semester? What is distinctive about Williams's poem especially in terms of style and language?	How can you define American poetry? What other American literary figures might have been influenced by Williams, Eliot, and Hughes? What characteristics of their work do you see being continued in American poetry today?

	Texts	Contexts
1910s	Ezra Pound, "To Whistler, American" (1912), "In a Station of the Metro," "A Pact" (1913), *Cantos* (1917) Robert Frost, *A Boy's Will*, "Mowing" (1913), *North of Boston*, "After Apple-Picking" (1914), "Birches," "Out, Out—" (1916) William Carlos Williams, *The Tempers* (1913) H.D., "Oread" (1914), *Sea Garden*, "Mid-day" (1916), "Leda" (1919) Carl Sandburg, "Chicago" (1914), "Child of the Romans" (1916), "Cool Tombs" (1918) T. S. Eliot, "The Love Song of J. Alfred Prufrock" (1915) Claude McKay, *Harlem Shadows* (1918), "If We Must Die," "The Lynching" (1919) Genevieve Taggard, "Everyday Alchemy" (1919)	The Great Migration begins, prompting over 4,800,000 African Americans to move from southern to northern cities (1900–60) First movie studio opens in Hollywood (1911) Igor Stravinsky's ballet *The Rite of Spring* is performed (1913) World War I begins in Europe (1914) Panama Canal opens (1914) D. W. Griffith's film *Birth of a Nation* opens (1915) The United States enters World War I (1917) World War I ends (1918) Prohibition begins, spurring an increase in illegal sales of alcohol (1919–33) "The Red Summer": race riots and the number of lynchings increase (1919)
1920s	Ezra Pound, *Hugh Selwyn Mauberley: Life and Contacts* (1920) Claude McKay, "Tropics in New York," *Spring in New Hampshire* (1920), "Africa" (1921), *Home to Harlem* (1928), *Banjo* (1929) Langston Hughes, "Mexican Games," "The Negro Speaks of Rivers" (1921), *The Weary Blues*, "The Negro Artist and the Racial Mountain," "Brass Spittoons" (1926), "Mulatto" (1927) H.D., "At Baia" (1921), "Fragment 113" (1922), "Helen" (1924) Genevieve Taggard, "With Child" (1921), *For Eager Lovers* (1922), *May Days* (1926) Robert Frost, "Design" (1922), "Stopping by Woods on a Snowy Evening" (1923) T. S. Eliot, *The Waste Land* (1922), "The Hollow Men" (1925) William Carlos Williams, "The Red Wheelbarrow" (1923), *In the American Grain* (1925) Jean Toomer, *Cane* (1923)	Women gain the right to vote (1920) The Harlem Renaissance makes Harlem a spot for many artists and writers (1920–40) The Ku Klux Klan boasts a higher membership than ever (1921) *Shuffle Along*, the first all-black musical, opens (1921) First talking picture, *The Jazz Singer*, opens (1927) First experimental television broadcast in the United States (1928) The Stock Market collapses, beginning the Great Depression (1929)
1930s	T. S. Eliot, "Ash Wednesday" (1930), *Murder in the Cathedral* (1935) Genevieve Taggard, *The Life and Mind of Emily Dickinson* (1930), "At Last the Women Are Moving" (1935) Langston Hughes, "I Too" (1932) Jean Toomer, "The Blue Meridian" (1936) Robert Frost, "Two Tramps in Mud Time" (1936)	Nation of Islam founded (1930) Technicolor introduces full color film (1930) Maiden flight of first multipassenger commercial airliner (1933) The New Deal is introduced (1933) Artists' Union founded (1934) World War II begins in Europe (1939)

	Texts	Contexts
1940s	Langston Hughes, "Ballad of Booker T" (1941), "Democracy," "Note on Commercial Theater" (1949) Robert Frost, "The Gift Outright" (1942) T. S. Eliot, *Four Quartets* (1943), *The Cocktail Party* (1949) William Carlos Williams, "The Dance," "Burning of the Christmas Greens" (1944), *Paterson* (1946) H.D., *The Walls Do Not Fall* (1944), *Tribute to the Angels* (1945), *The Flowering of the Rod* (1946)	Attack on Pearl Harbor brings the United States into World War II (1941) Atlantic Charter issued by Roosevelt and Winston Churchill (1941) Conference among Roosevelt, Churchill, and Stalin in Yalta (1945) The United States drops atomic bombs on Hiroshima and Nagasaki; World War II ends (1945) United Nations established (1945) Central Intelligence Agency (CIA) established (1947) Pan Am begins round-the-world commercial flights (1947) North Atlantic Treaty Organization (NATO) established (1949)

AUTHOR/TEXT REVIEW

Robert Frost (1874–1963)

Although Robert Frost was born in San Francisco, where he spent his first eleven years, he is commonly associated with the rugged landscape and traditional values of rural New England. His father, William Frost, graduated with honors from Harvard and spent most of his life working as a journalist, but alcoholism led to an early death in 1885. In answer to William's wishes to be buried in Lawrence, Massachusetts, the family moved back east and settled in Lawrence. Robert quickly distinguished himself as both student and poet in high school, and he eventually married Elinor White, who with Frost was covaledictorian of their high school class. Frost attended Dartmouth for less than a year before dropping out to work odd jobs and write poems. Not finding the success he had hoped for, he decided in 1897 to return to college, this time attending Harvard as a special student. Although he didn't graduate from Harvard, he was influenced by many of the important thinkers in residence at the time, including George Santayana and William James. He left Harvard in 1899 and moved to a farm in Derry, New Hampshire. These early years of marriage were difficult financially for the Frosts, who had five children by 1905. Things began to look up when he accepted a position at Pinkerton Academy in 1906, where he spent five years teaching English, directing plays, and writing poetry.

In 1911, Frost sold his farm; he took his family to Scotland and London in the fall of 1912, a trip that proved invaluable to his writing career. Despite trouble getting his work published in America, Frost found a willing publisher in London, and *A Boy's Will* appeared in 1913. *North of Boston* followed in 1914. It was in London that Frost first met many of the leading young American poets, including Amy Lowell and Ezra Pound, who subsequently introduced Frost to Yeats, a poet he had long admired. The outbreak of World War I cut short Frost's time abroad and he returned to America in 1915. He had little trouble publishing his verse thereafter, and his growing reputation as a poet brought attractive offers at prestigious universities. He began teaching at Amherst in 1917. While he remained loyal to Amherst, Frost spent short periods at other institutions as poet in residence, and he lectured all over the United States. He eventually became an emissary to South America and later, during John F. Kennedy's presidency, to the Soviet Union. As the most famous poet of his time, Frost read at President Kennedy's inauguration.

Frost's poetry is widely recognized for its intense evocation of rural New England settings, its aphoristic lines, and its enigmatic voice—wise, clipped, and thematically evasive. Like other American modernists, Frost wrote in the American idiom, striving for colloquial language that evoked everyday speech. His poems usually have a narrative feel, and the characters are often engaged in manual labor, whether they are building a fence, picking apples, or chopping wood. Despite this penchant for the common and colloquial, Frost still believed very much in poetic form; he was famous for saying, in the

[5873] Dorothea Lange, *Napa Valley, CA. More Than Twenty-Five Years a Bindle-Stiff. Walks from the Mines to the Lumber Camps to the Farms* (1938), courtesy of the Library of Congress [LC-USF34-018799-E].

face of so much **free verse**, that writing without rhyme and meter was like playing tennis with the net down. For Frost much of the challenge and beauty in poetry comes from a tension between a dynamic, dangerous subject matter and the poise and restraint of literary form. Although Frost's poems often seem as simple and accessible as Sandburg's, his work reveals a darker underside, suggesting the complexity he sensed beneath the tranquil surfaces of New England country life. Frost's sagacious voice and gift for narrative lend his poems a popular appeal not shared by other modernists.

TEACHING TIP

■ While Frost's poems are wise and meditative, they almost always portray a narrator doing some sort of physical labor. Have the students write their own piece—either prose or poetry—in which they describe doing some sort of job. Then, ask them to reflect on the labor. How does this exercise help them understand the relationship between physical work and reflection? What is it about manual labor that seems to inspire Frost's writing? How does this connection to the land contribute to modern ideas about an American identity?

QUESTIONS

Comprehension: In "Mowing," Frost uses a form of whisper four times, but we never find out the secret. What is the effect of withholding the mystery from the reader? Does the narrator learn something we don't? What poetic form does Frost use? Why?

Comprehension: What does the wall symbolize in "Mending Wall"? Why does the neighbor repeat the cliché "Good fences make good neighbors," and how does the narrator interpret this? What season is it? Why do they have to repair the wall?

Comprehension: In "After Apple-Picking" why does the narrator refer repeatedly to sleep? How does the word change throughout the poem? What are the connotations of the word at the beginning of the work? Do they change at the end? What is the tone of this poem? Compare this poem to "Stopping by Woods on a Snowy Evening."

Comprehension: In both "Birches" and "Out, Out—" Frost portrays a young boy. How do the portraits differ? What is the tone of each poem? What does he seem to say about youth in each poem? How is death figured in each work? What is the relationship between the Shakespearean title "Out, Out—" and the rest of the poem?

Context: In comparison to that of the other poets in this unit, Frost's work seems strangely removed from the modern world, where world wars erupted and technology marched on rapidly. What kind of change does Frost write about? How does he reflect change in his poetry?

Exploration: What does Frost have to say about the relationship between the land and its inhabitants in "The Gift Outright"? How does he portray history and American identity? How do his ideas about history and the land compare to those of other writers in the unit?

Exploration: Compare Frost's use of traditional poetic forms to that of Claude McKay. What does each gain by using these forms?

Exploration: Compare Frost's depiction of apple picking to the depictions of fruit picking in the prose of Steinbeck, Carlos Bulosan, and Helena Maria Viramontes (all in Unit 12). What does fruit mean for each?

Exploration: A spider serves as the central symbol in both Frost's poem "Design" and Jonathan Edwards's sermon "Sinners in the Hands of an Angry God." What are the connotations of spiders? Why do spiders have particular resonance in a spiritual argument? How does the symbol function in each of these works?

Carl Sandburg (1878–1967)

Carl Sandburg was born in Galesburg, Illinois, to parents who had emigrated from Sweden. His father was a hard-working blacksmith, but the young Sandburg didn't exhibit his father's enthusiasm for manual labor and a steady home life. Sandburg left school after the eighth grade and then worked at a variety of odd jobs before volunteering in the Spanish American War in 1898. While serving in the war, he wrote columns about his experiences in the army for the Galesburg newspaper. After the war, Sandburg applied unsuccessfully to West Point. Eventually he attended Lombard College and worked at the local fire department to make ends meet. Although Sandburg became known around the institution for his writing, he didn't finish his degree, but instead spent the next decade traveling around the country, working odd jobs, including selling stereoscopic photographs. He also rode on the trains with hobos, an experience that explains his lifelong sympathy for the downtrodden. In 1904, he regained work at the Galesburg newspaper and also published his first collection of poems, *In Reckless Ecstasy*. Two years later he attended the fortieth anniversary of the Lincoln-Douglas debate in Galesburg, where he encountered the son of Abraham Lincoln. This experience intensified his interest in the president. In later life he wrote a magisterial four-volume biography of Lincoln as well as a book about his wife, Mary Todd. For the next few years, he worked a variety of jobs, until returning to Chicago, where he again landed work as a journalist. In 1914, he published several poems in the prestigious *Poetry* magazine, and he quickly became famous.

A public favorite, Sandburg began touring the country giving readings and lectures, and he wrote in a variety of genres, publishing children's books, articles, the aforementioned biographies and an autobiography, as well as his poetry. But his poetic colleagues, such as

[4848] Jack Delano, *Blue Island, Illinois. Switching a Train with Diesel Switch Engine on the Chicago and Rock Island Railroad* (1943), courtesy of the Library of Congress [LC-USW3-026606-E DLC].

Robert Frost and William Carlos Williams, considered Sandburg a poet with little craft. To an extent, they were right. Sandburg was more interested in subject matter than form or meter, and his poems often seem less polished. Despite what his contemporaries thought, Sandburg enjoyed wide public acclaim throughout his career. The governor of Illinois honored him by celebrating his seventy-fifth birthday as "Carl Sandburg Day," the king of Sweden recognized him, the U.S. Congress invited him to give an address, schools were named after him in his home state, and President Johnson bestowed on him the Medal of Freedom in 1964.

Deeply influenced by Walt Whitman, Sandburg shared his predecessor's devotion to American subject matter and common life. Sandburg strove to give poetic voice to a country whose poets seemed too willing to take a back seat to European tradition and to emulate Continental and other borrowed voices and forms. Based in Chicago, Sandburg was part of a school of poets who tried to wrest American poetry from the literary elite. Sandburg's poetry was ultimately more political than either Whitman's or William Carlos Williams's, and his sharp journalistic eye made a frequent appearance in his verse. A political socialist, Sandburg saw his poetry as rooted in the **vernacular** and the experiences of the working class.

TEACHING TIPS

■ Like Taggard and later Pound, Sandburg engaged with socialism. Have your students reread some of Taggard's poems about working-class people. How do Sandburg's poems reflect his political leanings? What themes and images associate him with socialism? How does his work differ from Taggard's social critiques?

■ Like many modernists, Sandburg uses the symbol of the modern city in his work. Have your students take turns reading "Chicago" aloud. Ask them to critique each other's performances, paying close attention to intonation, emphasis, and rhythm. How does reading the poem aloud help them to appreciate it on a deeper level? Are they now better able to answer more complicated questions like the following: How does Sandburg's portrayal of the city differ from that of other modernists? How does his portrayal of the city seem uniquely American?

QUESTIONS

Comprehension: In "Chicago," who is "they" in the section beginning in line 6? How does Sandburg portray Chicago? What is the effect of his use of personification? What is the tone of this poem?

Context: In "Child of the Romans," who are the people in the train? How do they compare to the shovelman? Where do our sympathies lie? What is the significance of the title? How does this poem compare to "Chicago"? What are some of the themes that appear in both poems?

Exploration: As mentioned earlier, the city was an important symbol in modernist poetry. Compare Sandburg's portrayal of the modern city in "Chicago" with Eliot's portrayal of London in *The Waste Land*.

Exploration: For many American poets, it was difficult to write in the shadow of the long and rich literary traditions of older, more established cultures, particularly those of Europe and the Orient. Thus, part of creating an American poetic identity meant making American history and culture legitimate or revered. With a much shorter history and tradition, American poets often felt they had to work harder to establish themselves and their poetry. In addition, the melting pot culture made it difficult to create a collective American identity. How does Sandburg portray history in "Cool Tombs"? What is he saying about Lincoln, Grant, and Pocahontas? How does his idea of history differ from Hughes's in "The Negro Speaks of Rivers"?

William Carlos Williams (1883–1963)

Born in Rutherford, New Jersey, William Carlos Williams was the son of an English immigrant and a mother born in Puerto Rico. After studying in Switzerland and Paris, Williams returned to America permanently, and came to regard with disdain the vogue of expatriate life followed by so many other writers of his generation. In 1902, Williams entered the University of Pennsylvania Medical School, and he later completed his residency in New York City. A practicing physician, Williams often wrote poetry in his office between visits with patients, and his verse bears the mark of a physician's precise, careful, and relentless seeing. Living and working near New York, Williams knew H.D. and other artists and writers associated with Greenwich Village, Harlem, and New England, and he maintained a life-long friendship with many of them, although they often disagreed heartily among themselves about the missions and direction of modern poetry. Ezra Pound helped Williams publish his first collection of poetry, *The Tempers*, in 1913. Williams would go on to publish many books of poetry, short stories, novels, essays, and an autobiography, but it is his poetry that has assured his fame.

Williams represents a strand of **modernism** that is markedly different from the work of expatriate poets T. S. Eliot and Pound. Unlike his contemporaries, Williams wanted to write poetry that used the American idiom and focused on the world available to him in northern New Jersey. When he wrote about art, he wrote from the perspective of an ordinary visitor in the gallery, not as an insider flaunting a special aesthetic education. He affirmed that poetry should sound like common American speech and should not take the form that Pound came to favor, a verse littered with esoteric allusions. The painters he favored were those a bit like himself, artists who celebrated the color and feel of ordinary life.

Williams's poetry is deceptively simple, and his verse can often achieve an austerity and surprise that link him to symbolism, imagism, and experimentation with haiku. Many of his poems, including the famous and brief "The Red Wheelbarrow" observation, depend on

[4996] Anonymous, *William Carlos Williams* (1963), courtesy of the Library of Congress [LC-USZ62-109601].

ingenious line breaks and visual organization for their poignancy. Williams's longest poem, *Paterson*, is an epic work that takes the industrial city of the title as its locale and chronicles the history of the people and place from its inception to the present. Williams draws on Joyce's circular structure in *Finnegans Wake* and echoes Eliot's use of the modern city in *The Waste Land*, but the specifically American diction and emphasis on the particular render it starkly original.

One of the most influential modern American poets, Williams received the Pulitzer Prize posthumously in 1963. His celebration of American colloquial speech and dedication to careful description are continued in the work of countless modern poets.

TEACHING TIPS

■ Students may assume that Williams is an "easy" poet, especially in comparison to Eliot and Pound, who composed more allusive poetry. The challenge with Williams will be to show students that these poems are more complicated than they appear. "The Red Wheelbarrow" and "This Is Just to Say" provide good starting points because they seem so straightforward. While in a sense they are, it is important to discuss with students how the form of "The Red Wheelbarrow" complements the subject. The line breaks and carefully crafted stanzas (three words, then one word) control not only the cadence of the poem, but the eye and ear of the reader. Williams forces us to stop and consider each image separately, as if we are looking at a series of photographs or Chinese ideograms. Only at the end of the poem can we see the entire image. Writing the poems out in paragraph form can help emphasize the inventiveness of Williams's economy and line breaks. The concentration on everyday images and colloquial speech in all his poetry is also clearly illustrated in these works. You might then broaden discussion by exploring how these poems compare with some of the imagist works of Ezra Pound, H.D., and Amy Lowell.

■ It is also helpful to point out to students how Williams's modernism differs from that of Eliot and Pound. Like the expatriate poets, Williams wanted to remake poetry, to wrest it from what he considered the stale and outmoded Victorian verse. Williams felt it was necessary, however, to write uniquely American poetry, verse grounded in his native idiom, landscape, and culture. He did not look to Europe for a sense of tradition, but rather set out to begin a new direction, though he certainly took much from poets like Walt Whitman. Unlike Frost, whose poetry Williams felt continued many of the stereotypes of America as rural, agricultural, innocent, and basically moral, he saw America in a less positive light. Like Eliot and Pound, he often showed the darker, more corrupt side of modern America. While Frost, Eliot, and Pound often make judgments and pronouncements about culture and society in their work, Williams resisted speaking more generally about human nature or the modern condition. He preferred to let the reader draw his or her own conclusions. His famous saying "No ideas but in things" speaks to this belief that the poet should deal with the concrete rather than the abstract. Like fellow poets H.D., Marianne Moore, and Ezra Pound, Williams probably saw Lawrence Binyon's exhibition of Chinese art at the British Museum, 1910–12, and he was certainly struck by Pound's use of Chinese poetics in "Cathay" (1915), about which he said that "the Chinese things" were "perhaps a few of the greatest poems ever written."

QUESTIONS

Comprehension: Williams is interested in representing the traditions of everyday life. For him, the ordinary often takes on extraordinary overtones. In "Burning the Christmas Greens" Williams describes the ritual of incinerating the holiday tree and greenery. Why does this ritual seem so important to the speaker? What connections does he make between the burning and the bystanders in the last few stanzas? Why are the onlookers suddenly "lost" in the penultimate stanza?

Context: In his architecture, Frank Lloyd Wright employed the technique of *tokonama*, or the use of a permanent element as a focus for contemplation and ceremony. To what extent does Williams use this strategy in his poetry? What in the poems is equivalent to the hearth that serves as the focus for Wright's architecture?

Exploration: "The Red Wheelbarrow" is one of Williams's most famous poems. What is the relationship between form and subject matter? Why do you think it has gained such an important place in American poetry? How does it differ from work by Eliot and Pound? What do you think each of those authors would say about this poem?

Ezra Pound (1885–1972)

Like T. S. Eliot, with whom he enjoyed a long friendship, Ezra Pound lived his early years in the United States but spent most of his life and career elsewhere. Born in Idaho, Pound spent his formative years on the East Coast. At sixteen, he attended the University of Pennsylvania and subsequently enrolled at Hamilton College. Eventually he returned to the University of Pennsylvania to study Romance languages and literature. After a year in Italy and Spain, Pound took a teaching job at Wabash College in Indiana, but soon left for a long sojourn in Europe.

While Ezra Pound's poetry remains important, his work as a mentor, editor, and theorist of literary modernism had a greater cultural impact. When Pound arrived in London, the literary scene seemed ripe for change. Cubism was shaking the art world; Stravinsky was composing radical music; T. E. Hulme was proclaiming the advent of literary voices that were powerful, new, and strange. In the years before the outbreak of World War I, Pound moved from one short-lived literary movement to another, sometimes as a leader, sometimes as an appropriator of ideas originated by others. Imagism and vorticism especially felt the impact of his presence, energy, and personality.

Intense, tightly focused, and borrowed from French experimentation at the close of the nineteenth century, imagism was supposed to spawn a new kind of European American poetry. In Pound's manifestos for the movement, imagism held to three principles: (1) "Direct treatment of the 'thing,' whether subjective or objective"; (2) "To use absolutely no word that does not contribute to the presentation"; (3) "As regarding rhythm: to compose in the sequence of the musical phrase, not in the sequence of the metronome." When imagism came under the influence of Amy Lowell, Pound nicknamed the movement "Amygism," resenting the fact that her tastes and hard work had eclipsed his own. With artist and writer Wyndham Lewis's help, Pound became the center of vorticism, which set out to produce poetry characterized by greater intensity and vigor than the imagist verse in Lowell's *Poetry* magazine. Both of these schools attracted their share of aspiring poets, but they remained smaller currents of modernism.

The important and abiding contribution of these hectic prewar years was the restlessness they witnessed, a deep dissatisfaction with any art that continued languidly in old forms, anything that did not "make it new." As the slaughter of millions along the Somme River, at Tannenberg, and at Verdun fostered a doubt that anything of the Belle Époque culture was worth saving, Pound and other radical experimenters seemed prophetic in their recognition that an unimaginable new era required literary voices and forms that had not been seen before.

With the publication of the manuscript of Eliot's poem *The Waste Land*, it has become clear just how significant Pound's influence was as an editor and arbiter of modernist taste. His editing of the poem was drastic and deft. Pound was also influential in the careers of the premier Irish modernist William Butler Yeats, the American imagist H.D., and many other modernists. Pound's most familiar poem is "In a Station of the Metro" (1916), his two-line haiku about people in the Paris subway. By his account, he worked for six months to achieve this poem, which began as more than thirty lines. Pound's most arcane and difficult works, *The Cantos*, are characterized by baffling shifts in time and perspective, abstruse allusions, and a cacophony of languages. He explained the nonlinear path of this modern epic as an attempt to emulate the Chinese ideogram, in which an image stands for a concept. At other times he suggested that the overall form was that of a fugue. Pound worked on *The Cantos* for most of his career, publishing the first in 1917. Although he never completed the project, he left a mass of stanzas which literary scholars have been decoding and annotating ever since.

Pound's later years were marked by unrest and conflict. In 1939, he visited the United States for the first time in twenty-nine years. Upon his return to Italy, he started speaking out against President Roosevelt on the radio, which continued as anti-Allied propaganda after World War II began. Eventually Pound's hatred of Jews and his enthusiasm for the Nazi agenda embarrassed even Mussolini. Indicted by the United States for treason against his country in 1943, Pound was arrested and imprisoned in Pisa when the Allied armies liberated Italy.

[7119] Shoshan, *Monkey Reaching for the Moon* (c. 1910), courtesy of the print collection of Connecticut College, New London.

POUND WEB ARCHIVE

[4006] Ernest Hemingway, *Letter, Ernest Hemingway to Archibald MacLeish discussing Ezra Pound's mental health and other literary matters, 10 August* (1943), courtesy of the Library of Congress, Archibald MacLeish Papers. The year this letter was written Pound was indicted for treason against the United States. He was brought to trial but was found mentally unstable and sent to a psychiatric hospital.

[4981] Alvin Langdon Coburn, *Portrait of Ezra Pound* (n.d.), courtesy of Yale University, Beinecke Rare Book and Manuscript Library, Yale Collection of American Literature, and New Directions Publishing Corp. An influential poet himself, Ezra Pound also supported other writers. He was deeply interested in Chinese and Japanese poetry, and his own work stressed economy and precision.

[4985] Olga Rudge, *Ezra Pound with Gargoyles at Provence* (1923), courtesy of Yale University, Beinecke Rare Book and Manuscript Library, Yale Collection of American Literature and New Directions Publishing Corp. Ezra Pound was born in Idaho but spent most of his life in Europe. Pound was charged with treason for broadcasting fascist propaganda to the United States during World War II, but the charges were dropped due to the efforts of a number of his fellow poets.

[4997] Janet Flanner-Solita Solano, *Group Portrait of American and European Artists and Performers in Paris* (1920), courtesy of the Library of Congress, Janet Flanner-Solita Solano Collection [LC-USZ62-113902]. Photograph of American and European artists in Paris, including Man Ray, Ezra Pound, and Martha Dennison. Many expatriate artists found inspiration in Paris's traditions and less restrictive culture.

[4998] *New York World-Telegram and Sun, Ezra Pound, Half-Length Portrait, Facing Front* (1943), courtesy of Yale University, Beinecke Rare Book and Manuscript Library, Yale Collection of American Literature and New Directions Publishing Corp. In part because of the generosity he had shown them, many of Ezra Pound's contemporaries were very loyal to him. While imprisoned in a psychiatric hospital after being charged with treason against the United States, Pound wrote his *Pisan Cantos* and was awarded the Bollingen–Library of Congress Award.

[7119] Shoshan, *Monkey Reaching for the Moon* (c. 1910), courtesy of the print collection of Connecticut College, New London. Japanese print showing a monkey hanging from a tree. Asian art became increasingly popular in the early twentieth century. Many modernist poets used Japanese and Chinese themes.

[8945] Lisa M. Steinman, Interview: "Rhythms in Poetry" (2003), courtesy of American Passages. Professor of English and humanities Lisa M. Steinman discusses Ezra Pound.

In 1945 he was put on trial in Washington, D.C., saved from execution by means of an insanity plea, and incarcerated in St. Elizabeth's, a psychiatric hospital. In 1958, after vocal support from many American poets, including Robert Frost, Pound was released and allowed to return to Venice, where he lived until his death.

TEACHING TIPS

■ It is helpful to note that Pound was an enthusiast about Chinese art and poetry. Have your students review the Core Context "Orientalism: Looking East."

■ Pound's later work is characterized by allusiveness, and it often proves obscure and difficult, particularly for first-time readers. Before asking your students to read "Hugh Selwyn Mauberley," ask them to research some of the allusions. Have groups report on different references, including perhaps the story of Odysseus, the Greek gods, Ariel's role in *The Tempest*, and Elizabeth Siddal/Pre-Raphaelite painting. Then ask them to discuss allusiveness in poetry—its strengths and its limitations.

QUESTIONS

Comprehension: In "A Pact," what is Pound saying about his relationship to Whitman? What does he mean when he says, "I make a pact with you"? What is the tone of this poem? If Pound was so intent on creating a new kind of poetry, why does he invoke Whitman here?

Context: In "Hugh Selwyn Mauberley," the narrator makes a timely reference to "kinema" (an early spelling of "cinema"), saying that "The 'age demanded' . . . a prose kinema" (lines 28–30). How might this poem be described as cinematic? How do you think the growing popularity of cinema in the 1920s and 1930s affected Pound's poetry?

Context: "Mauberley" also bears the burden of a war just fought. How does Pound portray World War I? What is his attitude toward it?

Exploration: Compare Williams's poems "Landscape with the Fall of Icarus" and "The Dance" with Pound's "To Whistler, American." What differences do you notice? What techniques do the poets use to capture the visual art? Why do you think Williams chooses a Flemish artist, while Pound chooses an American? How do the poets use visual art differently?

H.D. (Hilda Doolittle) (1886–1961)

Born in Bethlehem, Pennsylvania, Hilda Doolittle attended exclusive private schools in Philadelphia and was admitted to Bryn Mawr College. Her father was a professor of mathematics and astronomy at Lehigh University and the University of Pennsylvania. After attending Bryn Mawr for two years, H.D. stopped her formal schooling because of poor health.

Along the way, Hilda had fallen in love with young Ezra Pound. In 1911, when she traveled to England, Pound was waiting for her. Pound's friendship and encouragement enabled her to launch her own writing career. He helped her to publish her first poems in *Poetry*, and later in the anthology *Des Imagistes* (1914); he also gave her the pen-name H.D. by which she became widely known. Inspired by Pound's endorsement of *vers libre*, imagism, and vorticism, H.D. aimed to write tight, concise poems, resonant in the tradition of the haiku. Deeply interested in classical Greek literature, she brought Greek mythology and the words of classical poets into her own verse. Her poems are also characterized by their vivid descriptions of natural scenes and objects, which often stand for a feeling or mood. Her first collection of poetry, *Sea Garden* (1916), reflects the interests and techniques that were to remain central to her work.

Like many of the other poets in this unit, H.D. spent most of her adult life out of the United States. In 1913, she married fellow poet and imagist Richard Aldington, who shared her passion for Greek literature. The marriage soon ended, and H.D. was left as a single mother with little money. She soon forged a close relationship with a woman named Winifred Bryher, the daughter of a successful business-man. Bryher, who wrote historical novels herself, fell in love with H.D. and supported the poet financially for the rest of her life, allowing her the leisure to write and travel as she wished. H.D.'s companionship with Bryher probably inspired several prose pieces, namely *Pilate's Wife*, *Asphodel*, and *Her*, which dealt candidly with lesbianism, but they were not published until after her death. In 1933, with the encouragement of Bryher, H.D. left London to become a "pupil" (H.D.'s word) of Sigmund Freud. In 1939, she and Bryher returned to London, where they weathered the terrifying Blitz, the devastating German bombing campaign against London and other British cities. H.D. would write about this experience in her *The Walls Do Not Fall* (1944), *Tribute to the Angels* (1945), and *The Flowering of the Rod* (1946). These poems were later collected under one title, *Trilogy* (1973). After a long and prolific career, during which she published eight volumes of poetry, four novels, a memoir, and several critical works, H.D. died in Zurich.

[7105] *New York Times* Paris Bureau Collection, *London Has Its Biggest Raid of the War* (1941), courtesy of the National Archives and Records Administration.

TEACHING TIPS

■ Ask your students to review Pound's three tenets of imagism: (1) "Direct treatment of the 'thing,' whether subjective or objective"; (2) "To use absolutely no word that does not contribute to the presentation"; (3) "As regarding rhythm: to compose in the sequence of the musical phrase, not in the sequence of the metronome." Which of H.D.'s poems seem to adhere to Pound's ideas most closely?

■ *The Walls Do Not Fall* was written after living in London during the Blitz. Ask your students how the poem reflects the experience of war? What modernist or imagist techniques does H.D. employ? How does this longer poem compare to some of the earlier works in the unit? What strategies or ideas does she continue? What seems new?

H.D. WEB ARCHIVE

[7105] *New York Times* Paris Bureau Collection, *London Has Its Biggest Raid of the War* (1941), courtesy of the National Archives and Records Administration. Photograph of a London building destroyed by bombs. London experienced heavy fire bombing during World War II.
[7599] Euphronios, *Calyx-Krater* (c. 515 B.C.E.), courtesy of The Metropolitan Museum of Art, purchase, bequest of Joseph H. Durkee, gift of Darius Ogden Mills and gift of C. Ruxton Love, by exchange, 1972 (1972.11.10). Photograph ©1999 The Metropolitan Museum of Art. Greek bowl for mixing wine and water. Greek and Roman myths were central to the poetry of H.D., T. S. Eliot, and Robinson Jeffers.
[7981] Ando Hiroshige, *Inada/Buri/Warasa & Fugu* (1832), courtesy of the print collection of Connecticut College, New London. Woodcut of local fish by the Japanese painter and printmaker Ando Hiroshige. Imagist poets like H.D. and Pound were

attracted to the minimalist characteristics of such art.

[8005] Anonymous, *Hilda Doolittle, Bust Portrait, Facing Right* (1960), courtesy of the Library of Congress [LC-USZ62-122118]. H.D. was one of the founders of imagism, a school of poetry inspired in part by the minimalism of Oriental art, particularly the haiku form.

[9141] William B. Yeats, *Leda and the Swan* (1924), courtesy of Wikipedia <www.wikipedia.org/wiki/Leda_and_the _Swan>. Yeats's "Leda and the Swan" describes the rape of Leda, mother of Helen of Troy, by the Greek god Zeus, who came to her in the form of a swan. H.D. also treats this subject in "Leda."

[4995] Barry Hyams, *T. S. Eliot, Half-Length Portrait, Seated, Facing Slightly Right, Holding Eyeglasses* (1954), courtesy of the Library of Congress [LC-USZ62-109122].

QUESTIONS

Comprehension: In "At Baia," what is the relationship between the title and the subject matter? Why does H.D. locate this poem in an ancient Roman town? Why does the author use parentheses? What is the significance of the flower imagery?

Comprehension: In "Helen," how is Greece portrayed? How does this poem about Helen, whose face is said to have launched a thousand ships and begun the Trojan War, differ from other works about her? What is the tone of the poem? What is significant about the end?

Context: Pound was one of H.D.'s mentors and an influential friend throughout her career. How do H.D.'s early poems, particularly "Mid-day" and "Oread," follow the rules of imagism or vorticism as espoused by Pound?

Exploration: Compare H.D.'s "Leda" to Yeats's earlier poem, "Leda and the Swan." How do the poems differ? What is the tone of each? Does the reader sympathize with Leda? How does the diction differ?

T. S. Eliot (1888–1965)

Born in St. Louis, Thomas Stearns Eliot was one of seven children. Originally from New England, the Eliot family's lineage was bound to both religion and education. Eliot's grandfather, a graduate of Harvard Divinity School, moved to St. Louis in 1834, where he began a Unitarian Church and founded Washington University, which became one of the nation's elite educational institutions. Eliot's father was a successful business executive, but it was his mother, Charlotte Stearns, from whom he seems to have inherited his literary sensibility. She was a poet, and her biography of Eliot's grandfather, William Greenleaf Eliot, was published in 1904.

Although Eliot spent his formative early years in St. Louis, he maintained strong connections to New England, where the family summered following the aristocratic tradition of his ancestors. He graduated from Milton Academy, an elite private school in Massachusetts; and like many of his relatives, he then went to Harvard. Graduating in three years, Eliot stayed in Cambridge to study philosophy. While at Harvard, his most influential professors proved to be George Santayana and Irving Babbitt, who was vociferous in his dislike for lingering Romanticism and exhausted aesthetic traditions. As his poetry suggests, Eliot's formal education was intense and varied. He earned a master's degree from Harvard in 1910, the same year in which he wrote "The Love Song of J. Alfred Prufrock." He also studied at the Sorbonne in Paris and in Marburg, Germany, but when World War I exploded across northern Europe, he retreated to Oxford and London and never returned to America except as a visitor. Eliot read in an eclectic manner, to say the least, absorbing Dante, centuries of French poetry, and texts from Sanskrit. Eliot married his first wife, Vivien Haigh-Wood, on June 26, 1915, and it proved to be a turbulent marriage, ending in separation in 1932. Eliot's difficulties dealing with his wife's mental instability appear in subtle references in his poetry, most notably in Part II of *The Waste Land*.

In 1914, while in England, Eliot met Ezra Pound, who was to become one of the most influential figures in his life and career. It was Pound who first recognized Eliot's genius, proclaiming he "has actually trained himself and modernized himself on his own." Pound became Eliot's mentor and proponent, as he convinced editors to publish his work. Then as now, however, it was hard for anyone to make a decent living as a poet, so Eliot taught school for a while and eventually took a job as a clerk at Lloyd's Bank in London, where he worked while writing *The Waste Land* and other poems that made his reputation in the 1920s. The pressures of balancing a difficult marriage, Vivien's health problems, his father's death, and a developing writing career culminated in a mental breakdown in 1921. With most of *The Waste Land* completed, Eliot went to Lausanne, Switzerland, for rest and psychiatric treatment.

Pound helped Eliot edit *The Waste Land* extensively, reducing the poem by nearly half. Influenced by French poets like Laforgue, Mallarmé, and Rimbaud, and characterized by its fragmented form, esoteric allusions, spiritual searching, and apocalyptic imagery, *The Waste Land* stands as one of the most ambitious and innovative works of its time. In many ways the quintessential modernist text, this poem dispenses with linear sequence and narrative cohesion; complete with footnotes, it seemed to dare the reader to make sense of it. Although *The Waste Land* has become a centerpiece in survey courses of twentieth-century literature, in 1922 its voice and its themes seemed utterly new.

In the same year, Eliot started *Criterion*, a magazine that soon became an important voice on the literary scene. By the late 1920s, Eliot had established himself as a leading critic and arbiter of literary taste. His literary essays, including "Tradition and the Individual Talent" (1919), proved almost as influential as his poetry in shaping what came to be called "high modernism."

The Waste Land marks a turning point in Eliot's career because it seems to mark the end of a kind of spiritual despair. Eliot's poems in the years after, including "The Hollow Men" (1925) and "Ash Wednesday" (1930), suggest a transition that culminates in the spiritual solace that characterizes his elaborate meditations *Four Quartets*. Eliot did, in fact, become a dedicated member of the Church of England, and much of his later writing portrays this struggle for faith, including *Murder in the Cathedral*, *The Cocktail Party*, and various essays and books on religion. As well as writing poems and critical essays, Eliot also wrote plays, some of which were produced on Broadway and in London's West End. In 1948, Eliot was awarded the Nobel Prize for Literature.

TEACHING TIPS

■ Although written in free verse, "The Love Song of J. Alfred Prufrock" continues the long-standing poetic tradition of the dramatic monologue. Students will probably be most familiar with the dramatic monologues of English poet Robert Browning, such as "My Last

[4995] Barry Hyams, *T. S. Eliot, Half-Length Portrait, Seated, Facing Slightly Right, Holding Eyeglasses* (1954), courtesy of the Library of Congress [LC-USZ62-109122]. T. S. Eliot was born in St. Louis, Missouri, and studied at Harvard, but spent most of his adult life in Europe. Eliot was a student of Sanskrit and Buddhism, and his poetry was deeply influenced by orientalism as well as neoclassicism.

[6971] Underwood and Underwood, *Learning of German Retreat from Her District, French Woman Returns to Find Her Home a Heap of Ruins* (1917), courtesy of the Library of Congress [LC-USZ62-115012]. Photograph of woman looking at the ruins of her home in the Somme region. Many modernist writers were shaken by the unprecedented devastation of World War I.

[7105] *New York Times* Paris Bureau Collection, *London Has Its Biggest Raid of the War* (1941), courtesy of the National Archives and Records Administration. Photograph of a London building destroyed by bombs. London experienced heavy fire bombing during World War II.

[7658] Herbert Johnson, *Future Pastimes. Breaking the News to Her Papa—by Radio* (1922), courtesy of the Library of Congress. Cartoon depicting a young woman telling her father of her engagement over the radio. For some, the broadened communication made possible by the radio was inspiring. For others, like Ezra Pound, T. S. Eliot, and the father in this picture, the new technology was cause for alarm.

[8949] Lisa M. Steinman, Interview: "Rhythms in Poetry" (2003), courtesy of *American Passages*. Professor of English and humanities Lisa M. Steinman discusses *The Waste Land*.

[9140] Robert Browning, *My Last Duchess* (1842), courtesy of Project Gutenberg. Robert Browning's poem "My Last Duchess" is a quintessential example of the dramatic monologue. The first-person speaker is a duke who hints at the murder of his last wife, even as he arranges a new marriage. The dramatic monologue was a form later used by T. S. Eliot (see "The Love Song of J. Alfred Prufrock").

Duchess." Reading one of these famous poems can help students understand that the speaker is Prufrock, a fallible and possibly unreliable narrator and not the voice of Eliot himself. Try having your students stage the different parts of the monologue, using voices appropriate to the words. A similar strategy can be used for "Gerontion," which is also in the form of a dramatic monologue. Students often find the fragmented form, esoteric allusions, and disembodied speaker difficult and frustrating. Before discussing Eliot in class, have students write a line-by-line paraphrase of the poem and then a quick (three-to-four-sentence) plot synopsis. Begin class discussion by breaking into groups to compare the plot summaries and paraphrases. Each group should come up with a "master" version; then have the class discuss the poem as a whole.

■ Consider beginning your discussion of Eliot with "The Love Song of J. Alfred Prufrock." Encourage students to read the poem aloud and to listen to the sounds and rhythms. Instead of focusing on the footnotes, help them appreciate the lyric quality of Eliot's verse.

QUESTIONS

Comprehension: How would you describe the speaker in "The Love Song of J. Alfred Prufrock"? What are his fears? Is he a sympathetic character? Why does he ask so many questions? What is the significance of the title? How would you describe the tone of this poem?

Comprehension: Some readers have argued that Tiresias is the narrator of *The Waste Land*, a voice behind all the other voices. When he appears in "The Fire Sermon" in line 217, he says "I, Tiresias." Who is this figure in classical mythology? Why might Eliot choose to invoke him here? How does he relate to other themes in the poem?

Comprehension: In "Tradition and the Individual Talent" Eliot writes: "Poetry is not a turning loose of emotion but an escape from emotion; it is not the expression of personality, but an escape from personality." What does Eliot mean here? Does he follow his own dictum? What would he say of other poets in this unit?

Context: "Learning of German Retreat from Her District," in the archive, depicts some of the devastation inflicted upon the European landscape. In the video, critic Lisa Steinman argues that, like the war-torn buildings, *The Waste Land* "is, in fact, a kind of rubble of stuff that used to have meaning and used to go together and that doesn't seem to go together." What are the fragments from which *The Waste Land* is composed? From what cultures do these fragments originate? What sorts of images would you use to illustrate this text?

Context: Many readers have noted that *The Waste Land* is written in an apocalyptic mode; that is, it functions as a work of crisis literature that reveals truths about the past, present, and/or future in highly symbolic terms, and it is intended to provide hope and encouragement for people in the midst of severe trials and tribulations. What crises do the characters in *The Waste Land* face? Given this context, how do you read the ending of the poem? Is the final line triumphant or apocalyptic?

Context: How does Eliot's brand of modernism differ from Williams's? Do they share any ideas, beliefs, or techniques?

Exploration: What is the effect of the host of esoteric allusions in *The Waste Land*? Why do you think Eliot chooses the kinds of references he does? Why does he draw from so many different religions?

Exploration: In "Tradition and the Individual Talent," Eliot argues that "if the only form of tradition, of handing down, consisted in following the ways of the immediate generation before us in a blind or timid adherence to its successes, 'tradition' should positively be discouraged." What keeps Eliot's "The Love Song of J. Alfred Prufrock" from merely "blindly" or "timidly" adhering to the tradition of dramatic monologues? What is uniquely modern about Eliot's innovations?

Claude McKay (1889–1948)

Born in Jamaica, Claude McKay came to America to study agriculture at Tuskegee Institute, a historically black university founded by Booker T. Washington. After two years, he transferred to Kansas State College, but soon realized that his talents were better suited to writing than farming. In 1917, McKay arrived in Greenwich Village, where he sought out the company of artists and activists, both white and black. In fact, his ability to straddle both worlds easily became a source of envy and respect among his contemporaries. In those opening years of the Harlem Renaissance, McKay's poetry helped attract attention to the city and to the struggle for a new African American literary voice. While the earlier poetry that he had written in Jamaica used dialect, his writing in America relied on traditional poetic forms. His electrifying sonnet "If We Must Die" made him famous; it also worked as a call to arms for African Americans living through the **Red Summer** of 1919. In the poem, McKay urges African Americans to "face the murderous, cowardly pack" and to "nobly die" while "fighting back." These images of blacks rising up against their white oppressors gave voice to the frustration and rage of the African American people at a time when racism seemed to be spiraling out of control. Although McKay is often credited with helping to spark the Harlem Renaissance, he took great pains to distance himself, both physically and philosophically, from the movement in its heyday.

[3939] Underwood and Underwood, *Famous New York African American Soldiers Return Home* (1917), courtesy of the National Archives and Records Administration.

McKay left America for London in 1919, where he read Marx and Lenin and worked for a communist newspaper. Although he did return to America to oversee the publication of his first volumes of poetry, *Spring in New Hampshire* (1920) and *Harlem Shadows* (1922), McKay became disillusioned with African American leadership and the disappointing state of race relations in the United States. He felt that

[3939] Underwood and Underwood, *Famous New York African American Soldiers Return Home* (1917), courtesy of the National Archives and Records Administration. The 369th (former 15th New York City) regiment marches in Harlem, including Lieutenant James Reese Europe, a well-known musician. African American veterans advocated for civil rights. *Home to Harlem* (1928), by Harlem Renaissance writer Claude McKay, tells the story of an African American soldier's life after his return from the war.

[4766] Aaron Douglas, *The Judgement Day* (1927), courtesy of The Walter O. Evans Collection of African American Art. Aaron Douglas, American (1899–1979). Gouache on paper; 11 3/4" x 9". Douglas's painting incorporates images from jazz and African traditions and can be compared to "Harlem Shadows," by Claude McKay, and "The Weary Blues," by Langston Hughes.

[5289] Aaron Douglas, *Study for Aspects of Negro Life: The Negro Man in an African Setting* (1934), courtesy of The Art Institute of Chicago: Aaron Douglas, American, 1899–1979, Study for Aspects of Negro Life: the Negro in an African setting, before 1934, gouache on Whatman artist's board, 37.5 x 41 cm, Estate of Solomon Byron Smith; Margaret Fisher Fund, 1990.416. Sketch of Africans dancing and playing music. This became part of a Harlem mural sponsored by the Works Progress Administration chronicling African American history, from freedom in Africa to life in the contemporary United States. Africa and ancestry were themes of "The Negro Speaks of Rivers," by Langston Hughes, and "Africa," by Claude McKay.

[7390] Samuel Herman Gottscho, *New York City Views. Vendor in Greenwich Village Area* (1914), courtesy of the Library of Congress [LC-G622-T-81587]. Greenwich Village has long been home to both artists and activists. Jamaican-born poet Claude McKay lived there in 1917.

[7405] Carl Van Vechten, *Portrait of Josephine Baker* (1949), courtesy of the Library of Congress [LC-USZ62-93000]. Photograph of jazz musician Josephine

the leaders of the Harlem Renaissance, particularly Alain Locke and W. E. B. Du Bois, were discouraging artists from portraying black experience honestly. Refusing to enter the 1926 *Opportunity* prize contest, he wrote: "I must write what I feel what I know what I think what I have seen what is true and your Afro-American intelligentsia won't like it." McKay also felt that black editors, particularly of small magazines popular during the Harlem Renaissance, worried more about the reactions of white benefactors and audiences than they did about the integrity or political efficacy of the art. With sharp criticism for the leaders of the Harlem Renaissance, which he voiced throughout his career, McKay left America for Russia in 1922. While abroad, he wrote his bestseller *Home to Harlem* (1928) and *Banjo* (1929). His status as an exile, first as a Jamaican in America, and then as an American in Russia, colored his writing throughout his life. Poems like "Tropics in New York" represent this struggle with a double consciousness. McKay returned to America, but not until 1934, by which time the Harlem Renaissance had ended, its writers dispersed and the fire of the movement dimmed.

TEACHING TIPS

■ After reading Langston Hughes and some of the other poets in this unit who diverge from traditional forms, students will probably be struck by McKay's reliance on the sonnet. The sonnet form, however, has a long tradition of political engagement, one that goes back to the European Renaissance. In McKay's own lifetime, poets had skillfully reinvented the sonnet form to provide biting criticism of World War I, as seen in the work of British poet Wilfred Owen ("Dulce et Decorum Est"). The sonnet was particularly resonant for African American poets and was a popular form for men and women during the Harlem Renaissance. As critic Marcellus Blount argues, "For black poets, the sonnet has served as a zone of entrapment and liberation, mediation and self-possession . . . [black] poets have turned to the sonnet as an alternative space for performance, one that demonstrates the poet's craft while calling into question the marginality of black men and women in Euro-American discourse." What is the relationship between the highly structured form and McKay's subjects, for example, lynching ("The Lynching") and racial uprising ("If We Must Die")? Students should be encouraged to scan the poems, paying particular attention to where the meter or rhyme scheme intensifies or provides tension.

■ The violence in "The Lynching" and "If We Must Die," both written in 1919, becomes clearer and more significant when read about the historical context. The summer of 1919 was named the Red Summer because of the many racist uprisings around the country. Lynching reached a historical high that year, and blacks were appalled and frightened by the renewed vigor with which whites from Chicago to the Deep South were acting out their hatred and aggression.

Comprehension: In "Africa" who or what is the "harlot"? Why does McKay use this word?

Context: McKay uses several animal images in "If We Must Die." To whom does he refer each time? How do the images change? What do you associate with hogs? How are images of dogs associated with African American history, specifically slavery?

Exploration: How does McKay's language differ from that of other poets in this unit, particularly Harlem Renaissance writers? Why do you think he chooses to use this kind of diction? What kind of audience is he trying to reach? What kinds of political and social goals does his poetry seem to harbor?

Exploration: Compare McKay's use of the sonnet to that by African American poets Henrietta Cordelia Ray, Paul Laurence Dunbar, and Gwendolyn Brooks. How does each adapt the sonnet form? How does their use of the sonnet differ from that of some of the other famous modernist sonneteers such as E. E. Cummings, Edna St. Vincent Millay, and Robert Frost?

Baker in Paris. Paris was a major center for modernist artists, perhaps because it was less restrictive than American cities. Poet Claude McKay portrays the tensions of African American performers in "Harlem Dancer."

[9139] Wilfred Owen, *Dulce et Decorum Est* (1921), courtesy of Project Gutenberg. Wilfred Owen's poem "Dulce et Decorum Est" uses aspects of the sonnet form to critique his contemporaries' attitudes toward World War I. The sonnet form was also popular among writers of the Harlem Renaissance, most notably Claude McKay.

Genevieve Taggard (1894–1948)

Born in Waitsburg, Washington, Genevieve Taggard was raised in Hawaii, where her parents ran a school. Taggard attended the University of California at Berkeley on a scholarship. In 1920 she moved to New York City, where she worked for publisher B. W. Huebsch and, along with several other writers, including Maxwell Anderson, started a journal, the *Measure*. She also married writer Robert Wolf that year and they had a daughter, Marcia. In 1922, Taggard published her first collection of poetry, *For Eager Lovers*. Taggard spent most of the 1920s in Greenwich Village, where she socialized with other writers and artists. During this time she edited a poetry anthology called *May Days*, which collected work from the radical socialist journals *The Masses* and *The Liberator*. She also taught at Mount Holyoke, where she wrote a biography of Emily Dickinson, *The Life and Mind of Emily Dickinson*, which was published in 1930.

The 1930s marked a turning point in Taggard's career. The Great Depression sparked a renewal of social and political awareness among writers, and although Taggard had sympathized with socialism since her college years, only now did her poetry begin to show the imprint of her political leanings. As a contributing editor of the Marxist journal *The New Masses*, Taggard published poems, articles, and reviews. In her work she grapples with such timely issues as class prejudice, racism, feminism, and labor strikes. Unlike poets like Eliot and Pound, Taggard was very much concerned with the plight of the working class, and she used her poetry to raise social

[7106] *World-Telegram, Forgotten Women* (1933), courtesy of the Library of Congress [LC-USZ62-113263].

and political awareness. As her poetry suggests, Taggard remained an activist for most of her career. She participated in a host of organizations, including the Committee for the Protection of the Foreign Born, the United Committee to Aid Vermont Marble Workers, and the North American Committee to Aid Spanish Democracy. In addition, she was a member of the New York Teachers Union, the League of American Writers, and the U.S.-Soviet Friendship Committee.

In addition to her work as a social activist, Taggard was also deeply interested in radio and music. She saw radio as a means to make poetry and art accessible to the masses, and she often read her poems on the radio. Fascinated by the intersections between poetry and music, Taggard also wrote many poems that were later scored by such composers as William Shuman, Aaron Copland, Roy Harris, and Henry Leland Clarke.

After more than a decade of marriage, Taggard and Robert Wolf divorced in 1934. The next year she married journalist Kenneth Durant and moved to a farm in East Jamaica, Vermont, a landscape that provided inspiration for her poetry. She also joined the faculty of Sarah Lawrence College, where she taught until her retirement in 1947. Although Taggard died at the comparatively young age of fifty-three, she edited four books, wrote a biography, and published thirteen books of poetry.

TEACHING TIPS

■ Review the basic tenets of Marxism with your students, including concepts like the proletariat. Marx thought that the ideal society would be classless and that the workers would own the means of production: "From each according to his ability; to each according to his need." Taggard's poetry reflects her close ties to Marxism. What themes, images, or techniques does she use to articulate the relationship between her poetry and politics? What does she expect art to accomplish?

■ Many of Taggard's poems focus on the plight of working-class women. How does she portray the women in her poems? Which portraits are more sympathetic than others? Could Taggard be termed a feminist poet? Are there connections between Marxism and feminism that might be useful in understanding her work?

QUESTIONS

Comprehension: What is the meaning of the title "Everyday Alchemy"? What is Taggard saying about the relationship between the genders? How does her syntax help or hinder the message? Why does Taggard specify "poor" women? How should readers interpret the adjective "poor"?

Comprehension: In "With Child," who or what is the "it" in the last stanza? What is the tone of the poem?

Context: The turn of the twentieth century witnessed the first wave of feminism in America, culminating in women gaining the right to vote in 1920. Much of Taggard's poetry reflects this activism, though she concentrates on the working class. In "At Last the Women Are Moving," how are the women portrayed? What are they protesting? Why are the last two lines in italics?

Exploration: Unlike Eliot and Pound, Taggard wrote poetry for the masses, and her interest in radio broadcast enhanced her ability to reach a wide and diverse audience with her verse. How does her notion of poetry and audience differ from that of other writers in this unit? With whom does she seem to share a similar outlook?

Jean Toomer (1894–1967)

Born in Washington, D.C., Nathan Eugene Toomer was raised by his grandparents. He studied at several universities, including the University of Wisconsin, Massachusetts College of Agriculture, and New York University. After college, he held a variety of jobs, including ship fitter, car salesman, and physical education teacher. Enamored of the art scene in Greenwich Village, Toomer soon became part of the intellectual crowd, making friends with people like Waldo Frank, Sherwood Anderson, Hart Crane, Alfred Stieglitz, and the renowned benefactress Mabel Dodge. His short stories and poetry, which he published in *The Dial*, *Broom*, *The Liberator*, *Opportunity*, *Crisis*, and other magazines, received high praise from Allen Tate and Kenneth Burke; indeed, his work was well received in both the white and the black communities. His ability to straddle cultures became a mixed blessing for Toomer, as he struggled to secure a stable identity in a nation with a long habit of dividing itself along racial lines. Light-skinned enough to "pass," Toomer grappled with his complicated racial identity all his life. Toomer was not alone in this predicament; novelists James Weldon Johnson and Nella Larsen both explored the notion of passing in their fiction.

In 1923, Toomer's most famous work, *Cane*, won the approval of critics and his fellow artists, though the book never sold well. Sometimes referred to as a prose poem, *Cane* is not easily categorized; it includes verse and prose pieces. For young black writers, like Jessie Fauset and Charles S. Johnson, Toomer's unconventional work confirmed the belief that African American artists could form a movement and use art to fulfill political aims. At a time when the Harlem Renaissance was just beginning to take shape, Toomer's *Cane*, with its candid picture of rural and urban African American life, its picture of women, and its critique of modern industrialism, provided much-needed encouragement and promise; *Cane* endured as one of the most important works of the Harlem Renaissance.

[7104] Marion Post Wolcott, *Cut Sugarcane Being Carried to the Trucks for USSC* (1939), courtesy of the Library of Congress [LC-USF34-051089-E].

[3696] Dorothea Lange, *Plantation Overseer. Mississippi Delta, near Clarksdale, Mississippi* (1936), courtesy of the Library of Congress [LC-USF34-009596-C DLC]. White overseer and landowner with black workers. Sharecropping initially appealed to freedmen because it promised benefits they had previously been denied. However, most sharecroppers ended up working in conditions that weren't much better than slavery, while whites retained economic, social, and political power.

[4099] Anonymous, *Tenants* (c. 1880–1900), courtesy of Duke University, Rare Book, Manuscript, and Special Collections Library. Photograph of African American tenant farmers or sharecroppers in the field. Although sharecropping gave African American families more control over their labor, it was rarely lucrative.

[5510] J. C. Coovert, *White Cotton, Black Pickers and a Gin* (1915), courtesy of the Library of Congress [LC-USZ62-120480 DLC]. Cotton was an important but resource-taxing and labor-intensive southern crop. Although the Southern Agrarians romanticized agricultural life, work on cotton plantations was difficult and rarely lucrative for African Americans.

[7104] Marion Post Wolcott, *Cut Sugarcane Being Carried to the Trucks for USSC* (1939), courtesy of the Library of Congress [LC-USF34-051089-E]. Photograph of a worker for the United States Sugar Corporation in Clewiston, Florida. African Americans labored in harsh conditions for many southern agricultural companies.

Cane also proved to be Toomer's best work. He left New York for France, and although he received generous financial support from Mabel Dodge, he did not manage to publish anything that gained the acclaim of *Cane*. In 1924 he traveled to Fontainebleau to study with the Russian mystic George Gurdjieff, whose work he later taught in America. He experimented with communal living, and in 1932 he married a woman he met in one of these communities, Marjorie Latimer, a white woman from a prestigious New England family. She died in childbirth after only one year of marriage. In 1934, Toomer married another white woman, also named Marjorie. These marriages caught the attention of the media, and in his later years Toomer was often evasive about the question of his race. After the 1920s, Toomer virtually disappeared from the literary scene, but he did not stop writing. His unpublished plays, poems, and autobiographical sketches were collected in *The Wayward and the Seeking* (1980) after his death.

TEACHING TIPS

■ It's useful to talk about "passing" in relation to Jean Toomer. He was a pivotal figure in the Harlem Renaissance, despite his relatively early exit from New York, precisely because he was able to straddle both white and black cultures so easily. Toomer's choice later in life to live as white rather than black also raises interesting questions about his art. How does he represent the struggle with racial identity? What does it mean to have the ability to change one's racial identity?

■ Depending on their familiarity with postmodern literature, your students may not find it odd that Toomer mixes poetry and prose; however, during his own day this was a highly innovative strategy. Students should be encouraged to ask what the relationship is between the prose and verse sections, as well as to question why Toomer didn't just write *Cane* in one of these genres. What does Toomer say in verse that he couldn't say in prose, and vice versa?

QUESTIONS

Comprehension: What is the significance of the title *Cane*? What associations come to mind? In the second and last stanzas of "Georgia Dusk" Toomer uses "cane" as an adjective. What is he describing? Who is the "genius of the South"?

Context: Toomer's descriptions of Fern link her to the landscape of the South and raise a number of questions. What was happening in the South between 1900 and 1930? What does this tell us about her? How would you characterize the relationship between Fern and the landscape? Why is she described as "cream-colored"? Why does she have such a mysterious effect on men? Why does the narrator mention cities like New York, Chicago, and Washington? Why does the narrator ask so many questions? The narrator leaves our questions unanswered. What is the effect of this ambiguous ending?

Exploration: One of the most striking qualities of *Cane* is its use of multiple genres. In fact, one of the hallmarks of modernist literature is the authors' penchant for mixing genres, particularly prose and verse. Why does Toomer blend so many genres—poetry, short stories, sketches, and a play—in *Cane*? What effect does this shift among types of writing produce? How does his method compare to that of other writers in this unit?

Langston Hughes (1902–1967)

Langston Hughes stands as one of the most prolific writers in American history: he wrote poetry, two novels, two autobiographies, three volumes of short stories, several plays and musicals, over twenty years of newspaper columns, twelve children's books, and countless essays. Born in Joplin, Missouri, James Langston Hughes spent most of his childhood in the Midwest. Hughes moved to Harlem in 1921, where the famous Harlem Renaissance was taking shape under the leadership of intellectuals like Alain Locke and benefactors like Carl Van Vechten. It didn't take long for Hughes's literary talent to be recognized. Before the year's end, Jessie Fauset, perhaps the most prolific novelist of the Harlem Renaissance, published Hughes's first short story, "Mexican Games," in *The Brownie's Book*. Also, Hughes's widely anthologized poem dedicated to W. E. B. Du Bois, "The Negro Speaks of Rivers," appeared in *Crisis*. Despite his success, Hughes left the electrifying Harlem atmosphere for a two-year trip to Africa and Europe. His travels inspired in him a sense of awe for ancient and non-Western civilizations, an awe that reveals itself in the imagery of his later poetry.

Upon returning to America, Hughes worked as a busboy in a Washington, D.C., hotel until he was "discovered" once again, this time by poet Vachel Lindsay, and his poems were published in *Opportunity* and Alain Locke's *The New Negro*. Hughes's first collection of poetry, *The Weary Blues*, was published in 1926 with the help of his benefactor Van Vechten. In the same year, "The Negro Artist and the Racial Mountain," Hughes's groundbreaking essay on the obstacles facing black artists, appeared in response to George Schuyler's essay "Negro Art Hokum," which argued that there was no such thing as a quintessentially Negro art. Both essays were published in *The Nation*, and they sparked a dialogue that resonated throughout the Harlem community. Hughes's essay was important because it defended the possibility of an American art uniquely expressive of the black experience and because it challenged the elitism that often surfaced in the influential writings of Du Bois. For the last few years of the decade, patron Charlotte Mason, who also offered Zora Neale Hurston assistance, supported Hughes.

[4768] Aaron Douglas, *The Negro Speaks of Rivers* (1941), courtesy of The Walter O. Evans Collection of African American Art.

[3099] Anonymous, *Panorama of Joplin, MO* (c. 1910), courtesy of the Library of Congress. Langston Hughes was born in Joplin in 1902 and spent his childhood in Kansas, Illinois, and Ohio. He wrote his first poem in eighth grade and was named "class poet."

[3329] Anonymous, *Langston Hughes in Honolulu, Hawaii, August, 1933* (1933), courtesy of Yale University, Beinecke Rare Book and Manuscript Library, and the Langston Hughes estate. Hughes vacationing in Hawaii. By his early thirties, Hughes had traveled to France, where he experienced a society in which race mattered little, and to Africa, where he was first exposed to ancient, non-Western cultures.

[4554] Prentiss Taylor, *Scottsboro Limited* (1931), courtesy of the Library of Congress [LC-USZC4-4717]. Lithograph from *Scottsboro Limited*, a collection of four poems and a play by Langston Hughes protesting the incarceration, conviction, and death sentence of the Scottsboro boys, nine African American youths unjustly accused of raping two white women.

[4768] Aaron Douglas, *The Negro Speaks of Rivers* (1941), courtesy of The Walter O. Evans Collection of African American Art. Drawing of an African American man in a natural setting for Langston Hughes's poem "The Negro Speaks of Rivers." Aaron Douglas's art arose out of the Harlem Renaissance and New Negro Movement.

[5100] Gordon Parks, *Portrait of Langston Hughes* (1943), courtesy of the Library of Congress [LC-USW3-033841-C] and the Langston Hughes estate. Following the depression, Langston Hughes's vocal support of communism led to his being called on to testify before Congress in 1953. Hughes was drawn to communism's emphasis on racial equality.

[5183] Valerie Wilmer, *Langston Hughes in Front of Harlem Apartment* (1962), courtesy of Yale University, Beinecke Rare Book and Manuscript Library and the Langston Hughes Estate. Like William Carlos Williams and Carl Sandburg, Langston Hughes admired Walt Whitman and created literary per-

By the end of the decade, Hughes had become synonymous with the Harlem Renaissance.

When the Great Depression struck the United States, Hughes, like many of his contemporaries, including Genevieve Taggard, turned to social and political activism. He embraced communism with its emphasis on working-class issues and racial equality. After his visit to the Soviet Union in 1932, Hughes wrote radical essays and articles and reported on the Spanish Civil War for the *Baltimore Afro-American*. While he continued to publish poetry throughout his life, he also began writing plays and books for children. In 1953 his radical activities brought him before Senator McCarthy's committee, and the FBI considered him a security threat until 1959. During those six years, Hughes was unable to leave the United States.

Often called the poet laureate of Harlem, Hughes became famous for his innovative poetry, which appropriates the language, rhythm, and form of **jazz** and the blues. "The Weary Blues," for example, mimics the traditional form of twelve-bar blues. With its syncopated rhythm, southern dialect, and crooning diction, it is no surprise that much of Hughes's poetry has been set to music. While many intellectuals looked down on jazz and the blues as unrefined forms created by seedy characters, Hughes respected the artistry and originality of this new brand of African American music and recognized the unique contribution that it was making to American culture. Hughes wished to write about the black experience honestly. To Du Bois's dismay, he insisted on using dialect and portraying a range of characters, not just the educated upper class, and he wrote with compassion and dignity about working-class African Americans in poems like "Brass Spittoons" and "Elevator Boy." Hughes also wrote passionately about the American-ness of blacks at a time when political leaders like Marcus Garvey were encouraging scores of blacks to migrate back to Africa. Influenced by the work of Walt Whitman and Carl Sandburg, Hughes's poetry unites racial self-awareness with a larger American identity.

TEACHING TIPS

■ Hughes's poems are meant for the ear as much as the eye. Have your students close their books and begin your discussion of "The Weary Blues" by reading the poem aloud to them. Ask them how they imagine the speaker actually performing this song.

■ It is useful to point out that Hughes did not write the kind of poetry that Harlem Renaissance leaders like W. E. B. Du Bois and Alain Locke advocated. The intellectual leaders of the movement believed that art would bring about racial equality only if white audiences realized that black artists could produce polished works that were erudite and aesthetically sophisticated. The speakers in Hughes's poems, however, range from vagabonds to blues singers. You might begin a discussion of almost any Hughes poem by asking students to point out what is radical in the work and how the speaker differs from Alain Locke's concept of the "New Negro" and from the speakers of some of the elegant sonnets by Claude McKay.

QUESTIONS

Comprehension: In "The Negro Speaks of Rivers," Hughes offers a list of famous rivers. Where are these rivers? Why might he choose these specific rivers? What do they have in common?

Comprehension: In "I, Too" the speaker says, "I am the darker brother." What does he mean? Why does he eat in the kitchen? What does he mean when he says that he'll eat at the table "tomorrow"? What connection is the speaker making to America? What is the significance of the title?

Context: "Mulatto" was written at the height of the Harlem Renaissance. How does this poem conflict with the values and goals set forth by the leaders of this movement? Why might people like W. E. B. Du Bois and Alain Locke have objected to this poem?

Context: Hughes pays close attention to the structure of his poems, but he has a very different attitude toward poetic form than his contemporary Claude McKay. How does Hughes's verse differ from McKay's? Why do you think Hughes makes the choices he does? What is Hughes trying to convey about black experience and identity through his form?

Context: "Note on Commercial Theater" was written almost two decades after the Harlem Renaissance. What is Hughes objecting to in this poem? Are the same issues still relevant today?

Exploration: Hughes seems particularly concerned about American identity in his poetry. Why do you think he writes so often about America as opposed to Africa? How do poems like "I, Too" and "The Negro Speaks of Rivers" treat identity?

Exploration: Compare "I, Too" to the opening section of Walt Whitman's "Song of Myself." Why does Hughes allude to this poem? What does the allusion add to his work?

Suggested Author Pairings

LANGSTON HUGHES AND CARL SANDBURG

Both of these writers were preoccupied with creating a distinctly American voice, and both believed that art and politics were intimately connected. Whereas Hughes wrote about the plight of black Americans, Sandburg portrayed the working class. Unlike the expatriate writers in this unit, Hughes and Sandburg wrote in the American idiom and treasured the history not of the elite, but of the oppressed. Compare the way these two authors treat historical and social events. What values do they perceive as fundamentally American? How do they define American poetry? What are the political goals of these authors?

sonas that spoke to more than his own experience. In particular, Hughes was committed to portraying everyday African American life in his poetry.

[5196] Anonymous, *Langston Hughes at Age 3* (n.d.), courtesy of Yale University, Beinecke Rare Book and Manuscript Library, and the Langston Hughes estate. Langston Hughes was raised by his maternal grandmother, the widow of Lewis Sheridan Leary, who was killed at Harpers Ferry, and named for his great-uncle, John Mercer Langston (brother to his grandmother's second husband), who also played a part in the raid at Harpers Ferry.

[5198] Anonymous, *Langston Hughes at Age 22* (1924), courtesy of Yale University, Beinecke Rare Book and Manuscript Library, and the Langston Hughes estate. Poet Langston Hughes sought to portray the experiences of African Americans with honesty and challenged the elitism of W. E. B. Du Bois. Like Du Bois, however, he was an active social critic who fought for civil rights.

JEAN TOOMER AND CLAUDE MCKAY

Though both of these poets are regarded as central to the Harlem Renaissance, Toomer and McKay left Harlem early in the movement. Toomer often used dialect in his work, while McKay's poetry usually favors traditional European American poetic forms and diction. Yet both poets deal with radical subject matter in bold and original ways. The racial identity of both authors also provides rich fodder for discussion. Toomer, light enough to "pass," circulated among both black and white social groups in Harlem and lived his later life as a white man. McKay, born in Jamaica, struggled with forging his identity in America. What do these poets suggest about the varied and complicated notion of American identity? Must American poetry be written by native-born Americans? Must it be written in the United States?

H.D. AND WILLIAM CARLOS WILLIAMS

Both H.D. and William Carlos Williams wanted to pare down language to its essentials, and both believed that poetry should focus on the concrete rather than the abstract. Associated with imagism, H.D. was drawn to Greek literature and lived in Europe, while Williams grounded his poetry in American culture and history. These poets offer an interesting opportunity to explore not only varieties of imagism, but also what it means to be an American poet. How does the poetry of expatriate writers fit into the American tradition? Are poets like Williams, who write in the American idiom and who remained in the United States, more American than authors like H.D.?

ROBERT FROST AND T. S. ELIOT

Frost and Eliot, both giants of modern poetry, enjoyed incredible acclaim and success during their lifetimes. Hailed as the most famous living poet, Frost gave the inaugural address for President John F. Kennedy, and his lectures and readings around the country made him a virtual celebrity. Similarly, Eliot's role as poet, critic, and mentor cast a shadow of influence over the rest of the century. While both authors possess a wise voice, their poetry differs greatly. Associated with New England, Frost is a poet of the land, interested in the relationship between physical labor and reflection. His poetry is often narrative and usually meditative. He did not write in free verse, and his reflections are grounded in the American landscape, with its rugged beauty and pastoral associations. Frost's poetry is often concerned with moral and philosophical dilemmas as well as with ordinary experiences like mending fences and picking apples. Though his work can seem as dark as Eliot's at times, it also seems removed from modern society and historical events. In contrast, Eliot preferred to live and write in England. His expansive verse draws on many cultures, historical periods, religious traditions, and languages. His poetry, particularly *The Waste Land*, is difficult and allusive. In contrast to Frost's American landscapes, Eliot's poetry depicts society on the brink of radical, and perhaps destructive, change.

Both these poets sympathized with radical political philosophies, Taggard with socialism and Pound with fascism. These connections brought both authors under the scrutiny of the American government. While Taggard's poetry reflects her political ties, Pound's early work was written before his radical political leanings developed. How does Taggard's work reflect her commitment to socialism? How does gender influence her sympathies? How does Pound's poetry regard the common man or woman—as a potential reader and as a presence in modern culture? How might his attitude toward lowbrow and middle-class audiences foreshadow a move to the radical right?

CORE CONTEXTS

Harlem in the 1920s: The Cultural Heart of America

At its peak in the 1920s, Harlem was the cultural and artistic heart of America. Stretching north of Central Park from Park Avenue in the east to St. Nicholas Avenue in the west and all the way up to 155th Street, Harlem was a city within a city, where black businessmen like Phillip Payton owned huge apartment buildings and rented them to black families and where black families could buy from black merchants. Harlem pulsed with promise and expectation for black America. From 1913 through the end of World War II in 1945, hundreds of thousands of African Americans relocated from the South to the urban North. Known as the **Great Migration**, this dramatic resettlement changed the face of American cities as blacks arrived by the thousands in Chicago, Detroit, Cleveland, Philadelphia, and especially New York City. With renewed racism fueled by Jim Crow laws (legalized segregation in the South) and a nationwide resurgence of the Ku Klux Klan, African Americans looked to the urban North, where the world wars had created jobs and a hope of escape from rural poverty. As the most famous and vibrant cultural center of black American life, Harlem was transformed by this influx of people and talent. New arrivals like Langston Hughes and Zora Neale Hurston would become renowned artists. The move north was difficult, though. In Harlem, the South Side of Chicago, and other neighborhoods experiencing this sudden migration, housing conditions were often abysmal.

Artists and intellectuals also flocked to the cities. Some, like W. E. B. Du Bois, Alain Locke, and Marcus Garvey, were already famous, and some, like Langston Hughes, Aaron Douglas, and Zora Neale Hurston, hovered on the verge of fame. Harlem became such an important center of cultural vitality that it attracted many whites. The great photographer Alfred Stieglitz and bibliophile Arthur Schomburg were among the many nonblacks who mingled socially and intellectually with black artists and intellectuals, usually at parties hosted by people like Madam C. J. Walker, the first black woman millionaire,

[5479] Winold Reiss, *Drawing in Two Colors* (c. 1920), courtesy of the Library of Congress [LC-USZC4-5687].

[5496] Harry Olsen, *Jazzin' the Cotton Town Blues* (1920), courtesy of Duke University.

[3548] Anonymous, *Louis Armstrong Conducting Band, NBC Microphone in Foreground* (1937), courtesy of the Library of Congress [LC-USZ62-118977]. Louis Armstrong was one of the best-known jazz musicians of the 1930s. Jazz had an important influence in modernist writing and visual art.

[4553] James Allen, *Nella Larsen* (1928), courtesy of the Library of Congress. Portrait of Nella Larsen. The author of *Quicksand*, Larsen wrote novels and short stories that dealt with race, class, and gender. She was associated with the Harlem Renaissance.

[5289] Aaron Douglas, *Study for Aspects of Negro Life: The Negro Man in an African Setting* (1934), courtesy of The Art Institute of Chicago: Aaron Douglas, American, 1899–1979, Study for Aspects of Negro Life: the Negro in an African setting, before 1934, gouache on Whatman artist's board, 37.5 x 41 cm, Estate of Solomon Byron Smith; Margaret Fisher Fund, 1990.416. Sketch of Africans dancing and playing music. This became part of a Harlem mural sponsored by the Works Progress Administration chronicling African American history, from freedom in Africa to life in the contemporary United States. Africa and ancestry were themes of "The Negro Speaks of Rivers," by Langston Hughes, and "Africa," by Claude McKay.

[5479] Winold Reiss, *Drawing in Two Colors* (c. 1920), courtesy of the Library of Congress [LC-USZC4-5687]. Offset lithograph of African American man dancing; also titled *Interpretation of Harlem Jazz I*. Poets, novelists, and painters incorporated the imagery and rhythms of jazz in their art.

[5496] Harry Olsen, *Jazzin' the Cotton Town Blues* (1920), courtesy of Duke University. Sheet-music cover showing an African American band and couples dancing in formal attire. The New Negro Movement held that positive artistic representations of African Americans would lead to the acquisition of civil rights.

[7134] Anonymous, *Didn't My Lord Deliver Daniel* (n.d.), courtesy of *The Book of American Negro Spirituals*

and Carl Van Vechten, a white patron of the arts. By the mid-1920s, the Harlem Renaissance was in full swing.

Harlem became a hub of American popular culture, and thousands of people flooded to this small section of New York City to catch a glimpse of the nightlife, characterized by speakeasies, jazz clubs, and cabarets. As Langston Hughes wrote in 1926, "Harlem was in vogue." In these Harlem clubs, institutionalized racism took a peculiar form: although most of them, including the famous Cotton Club, featured black performers on stage, they banned blacks from the audience for fear of driving away white patrons. The injustice and irony of the situation was not lost on the artists of the period. In poems like "The Harlem Dancer," "He Was a Man," and "Visitors to the Black Belt," McKay, Brown, and Hughes criticize the veiled racism that made all things black—from jazz, dance, and variety shows—popular across America but unavailable to African American audiences.

On the other hand, African American artists gained respect and critical acclaim outside their own communities. The first all-black musical, *Shuffle Along*, opened at the 62nd Street Theater in midtown Manhattan in 1921, and African American performers like Josephine Baker and Paul Robeson became celebrities in Europe as well as in the United States. Jazz became a sensation in London, in Paris, even in Stalinist Russia, and many musicologists regard it as America's greatest musical contribution. From the black American experience in New Orleans, Chicago, and Harlem, jazz affirmed internationally the coming of age of African American culture.

Led by W. E. B. Du Bois, Alain Locke, Charles S. Johnson, and others, the Harlem Renaissance had specific political aims. These leaders believed that art could help African Americans achieve social, political, and economic equality in America. The movement placed great faith in the **Talented Tenth**, Du Bois's term for an educated class of African Americans empowered to improve the situation for all. If African Americans could prove themselves as writers and artists, Du Bois reasoned, then the rest of society would ultimately acknowledge their importance, and their right to equality under the law and in social arenas. Du Bois's ideas conflicted with those of Booker T. Washington, who championed economic independence through vocational education; and they also caused bitter controversy among Harlem Renaissance writers, especially Brown, Hurston, and Hughes, because their art did not always portray blacks in a positive light. But controversy became a source of vitality, and the Harlem Renaissance produced some of the most vibrant and powerful American art of the twentieth century.

QUESTIONS

Comprehension: What were some of the historical and social developments that contributed to the cultural prominence of Harlem?

Comprehension: How did the physical space of Harlem contribute to an artistic renaissance?

Context: Renaissance leaders like W. E. B. Du Bois and Alain Locke held distinct views about how black Americans could attain social equality in the United States. They believed that by demonstrating artistic ability and talent, African Americans could gain respect and acceptance for the race. They held that black artists should portray only positive attributes and dignified experiences of black Americans. However, many Harlem Renaissance authors and artists resisted that imperative. How do the authors in this unit reflect or challenge the values set forth by leaders of the Harlem Renaissance?

Context: Compare Aaron Douglas's *Study for Aspects of Negro Life*, in the archive, to Langston Hughes's poem "The Negro Speaks of Rivers." What is the relationship between Africa and the "New Negro" in each?

Exploration: Modernist poetry relies on the city as a symbol of modern culture and the human condition. How do Eliot's London, Sandburg's Chicago, and Hughes's Harlem all represent particular interpretations of the city and the modern condition?

Exploration: What do you think of Du Bois's concept of the Talented Tenth? What problems might this idea give rise to?

(1925), by James Weldon Johnson, Viking Press. Like many Sorrow Songs, these lyrics speak of the hope for delivery from sin and slavery. Compiler James Weldon Johnson, a major Harlem Renaissance intellectual and poet, self-consciously claimed slave ancestors and their creations as sources of cultural pride.

[7406] Staff photographer, *Duke Ellington, Half-Length Portrait, Seated at Piano, Facing Right* (1965), courtesy of the Library of Congress [LC-USZ62-123232]. Photograph of jazz musician Edward Kennedy "Duke" Ellington playing the piano. Black musicians such as Ellington were a major force in the development of jazz, arguably the first truly American art form. The rhythms and images of the jazz aesthetic deeply influenced the writers and visual artists of the Harlem Renaissance.

Orientalism: Looking East

Although Japan had been opened up to the West in 1853, for modern Americans the Orient remained a place of great mystery, reverence, and intrigue. American readers reveled in the exotic paraphernalia of Japanese daily life described in works such as Matthew Calbraith Perry's *The Americans in Japan: An Abridgement of the Government Narrative of the U.S. Expedition to Japan*, and fascination with the Orient spilled over into U.S. architecture. While many American architects were producing classical styles, Frank Lloyd Wright was inspired by Japanese architecture, from which he borrowed the concept of the *tokonama*. Defined as the use of a permanent element in the home as a focus for contemplation and ceremony, *tokonama* can be seen in Wright's use of the hearth as the vertical axis from which the horizontal floors radiate.

The modernist fascination with the art and aesthetics of ancient Japan and China is also reflected in the writings of modernist poets. Overall, American culture was primed for **orientalism**; between 1870 and 1882, the Chinese population in America rose dramatically, fueled by a fourfold increase in new immigrants, chiefly from Canton. Wealthy collectors took an interest in traditional East Asian art, which began appearing in newly constructed museums in Boston, New York, Chicago, and other major cities. Japan modernized rapidly and emerged as a formidable military power, defeating Russia decisively in

[7126] Eisen, *Asakusa Temple in Winter* (c. 1810), courtesy of the print collection of Connecticut College, New London.

[6662] Mary Cassatt, *The Fitting* (1891), courtesy of the Library of Congress.

[7128] Anonymous, *Frank Lloyd Wright Home & Studio* (c. 1933), courtesy of the Library of Congress [HABS, ILL, 16-OAKPA,5-2].

modern naval engagements that attracted the attention of the world. Moreover, the opulent, busy, literary and decorative styles of Victorian England and belle époque France were growing tiresome and predictable to young, independent thinkers, who hungered for aesthetic refreshment, for the austerity that the Japanese Zen tradition and the art of Imperial China seemed to embody.

Many modernist poets, artists, and architects, particularly Ezra Pound, T. S. Eliot, H.D., William Carlos Williams, Wallace Stevens, William Butler Yeats, Marianne Moore, Georgia O'Keefe, and Frank Lloyd Wright, expressed their own personal fascination with the Far East. Late-nineteenth-century and early-twentieth-century translations of Chinese poets like Qu Yuan, Tao Qian, Li Bo, Wang Wei, and Bo Juyi gained popularity in Western literary circles, helping to fuel this interest. For writers like Pound and Williams, the Orient did not represent a strange otherness, but rather an unexpected similarity in basic values. In 1913, Pound wrote that he felt "older and wiser" when looking at Japanese art, a sentiment shared by many of the modernist poets. When Wright set out to invent a "Prairie Style," an architectural vernacular expressive of the landscape and values of the American Midwest, he turned for inspiration to the temples and palaces of ancient Japan.

One of the leading thinkers and mentors of his time, Pound did much to shape modernism and its theoretical underpinnings. Pound's affinity for the Orient is conspicuous in his haiku-like poems, such as "In a Station of the Metro." He came to favor the poetry of China over that of Japan, and he spent much of his career studying and translating Chinese poetry. "The River Merchant's Wife: A Letter," one of his most anthologized poems, is a moving translation of a Chinese poem that depicts a lonely teenage wife longing for her husband with simplicity and emotion. Pound admired in Chinese poetry the impulse toward an economic, concrete verse, tendencies that became central to modernist poetry. Although his interest in China surfaces in a host of poems, *The Cantos* perhaps best illustrates his appropriation of techniques, themes, and allusions suggestive of Chinese poetry. The 1915 publication of *Cathay*, a collection of translated Chinese poems based partly on the writings of experts on the Orient, caught the interest of other modernist authors. Yeats experimented with the austerity and elegance of Japanese Noh drama, and the poetry of Wallace Stevens began to resonate with rhythms and images adapted from Chinese and Japanese poetry. Although Williams never discussed the place of the Orient in his own work, his early poetry also bears the mark of its influence.

Many characteristics that we associate with modernist poetry, including the use of ellipsis, allusion, and juxtaposition, have their roots in English translations of Chinese poetry. The Chinese ideogram, and the related concept that a concise visual experience can suggest philosophical and psychological meaning, became a central idea in imagism and early modernism.

QUESTIONS

Comprehension: What cultural forces combined to make the Orient popular in the West? What characteristics does Asian poetry, in English translation, share with early modernist poetry?

Comprehension: What role did Pound play in bringing the Orient into Western modernism?

Context: Reread William Carlos Williams's "Willow Poem" and "The Widow's Lament in Springtime." How do the content and style of these poems suggest oriental motifs and aesthetics?

Context: How do Pound's "In a Station of the Metro" and "The River-Merchant's Wife: A Letter" show the influence of Chinese and Japanese poetry? How do these poems differ from Williams's poetry discussed in the previous question?

Exploration: For American poetry, what are the advantages and complications of drawing inspiration from Chinese and Japanese literature and art?

Exploration: Pound challenged modern poets to "make it [poetry] new," but he also appropriates much from ancient Chinese poets. How do we reconcile his call for newness with his search into the past?

Primitivism: An Antidote for the Modern

Perhaps only a few times has a piece of music changed the course of history. On March 29, 1913, at the Théatre des Champs-Elysées in Paris, composer Igor Stravinsky conducted his ballet *The Rite of Spring*. The choreography seemed unnatural, the costumes outrageous, and the musical innovations ear-shattering; the ballet tells of pagan sacrifice, and many in the audience were repelled or elated by it. Riots erupted as the performance ended. The performance was a decisive historical moment, affirming that European and American modernism would need to reckon with **primitivism**, a fascination with art from cultures that nineteenth-century intellectuals and politicians had regarded with condescension and scorn.

Part of the continuing importance of the Harlem Renaissance was the complex way in which it engaged with the "primitive" art of the marginalized African cultures which African Americans recognized as a collective past but which the Middle Passage and three hundred years in North America had made distant. In looking to "primitive" cultures for inspiration, writers were trying to recover a lost fundamental identity, perhaps a purer form of language, and a more graceful and personal way of representing experience.

While many white Americans visiting Harlem or other black neigh-

[7170] Alfred Stieglitz, *Negro Art Exhibition, November, 1914* (1916), courtesy of the Library of Congress [LC-USZ62-100177].

[5289] Aaron Douglas, *Study for Aspects of Negro Life: The Negro Man in an African Setting* (1934), courtesy of The Art Institute of Chicago: Aaron Douglas, American, 1899–1979, Study for Aspects of Negro Life: the Negro in an African setting, before 1934, gouache on Whatman artist's board, 37.5 x 41 cm, Estate of Solomon Byron Smith; Margaret Fisher Fund, 1990.416.

borhoods expected African American artists to portray what were really little more than stereotypes, many black artists, like Claude McKay and Langston Hughes, sought deeper and richer connections with Africa; they experimented with primitivism, and their work shows a tension between their European intellectual heritage and their African lineage. This struggle to represent a split identity left many African American writers feeling conflicted. Many of the Harlem Renaissance poets explored the notion of the black American not only as a part of American history, but also as an indispensable foundation for the building of the country. Their poetry often suggested that the black person was more American than many of the country's white citizens.

This interest in African culture and tradition was not confined to Harlem. Indeed, Paris became known as the "Negro Colony" because so many African American artists moved there. As they mingled with other expatriates, they formed a network of learning and influence. Many of the artists studied formally at Parisian art schools, and their presence fostered an artistic exchange that changed modern art. The work of these black artists was recognized by French salons, publications, and exhibition spaces and contributed to modernist ferment on the Continent. Indeed, the connections between cubism and Africa are immediately recognizable in the angular lines, perspective, and subject matter of cubist paintings by Picasso and Braque.

Perhaps the best-known African American artist of the period was Aaron Douglas (1898–1979), who arrived in Harlem in 1924. An avid reader of African American journals like *Opportunity*, *Crisis*, and *Survey*, he was an active force on the art scene. Douglas soon adopted an abstract "African" style that borrowed much from African culture and cubism. His flat, stylized figures were immediately recognizable, and Douglas went on to illustrate the books of thirteen Harlem Renaissance writers, including Countee Cullen, Claude McKay, Langston Hughes, and James Weldon Johnson. Douglas's art, along with that of many of his contemporaries, was exhibited around the country by The Harmon Foundation, which was set up to expose white Americans to African American art. It remains one of the leading collections of African American visual art.

Many of the Harlem Renaissance writers and artists, including Douglas, Hughes, and Hurston, relied on white patrons for financial support. White Americans like Paul Kellogg, Albert C. Barnes, Carl Van Vechten, and Charlotte Osgood Mason were instrumental in making it possible for these artists to create and display their work. Although the patrons had good intentions, their patronage raised complicated questions. Some believed that black art was compromised by white patronage because the African American artists felt it necessary to please their benefactors. The patronage relationship also underscored the perception that most of these artists never broke the connection to the larger culture. Indeed, according to Harlem Renaissance expert Nathan Huggins, much of the art was ultimately created for white audiences. Some critics have also observed that the patrons were so interested in encouraging black art that they did so without due regard for skill and talent, and that the real genius of the Harlem Renaissance was overwhelmed by mediocre work. African American painter Romare Bearden (1911–1988), for example, complained that too much African American art was unoriginal and uninspired.

When Franklin Delano Roosevelt assumed office in 1933 and initiated a host of governmental programs to recharge the American economy, artists and writers were recruited and paid to produce murals and sculpture for public places, books about American places and history, and literary works for a broad and dispirited populace, eventually turning out over 100,000 paintings, 18,000 sculptures, and 2,500 murals for post offices, courthouses, schools, and other public buildings. The arts in the United States were saved from insolvency by massive federal support. Along with the opportunity, however, some artists felt a pressure to adapt the imagination to government service, to become, in a sense, public employees. Though the American artist never experienced the regimentation and thought-control which overwhelmed the arts in Nazi Germany, Fascist Italy, and the Soviet Union under Stalin, the freewheeling bohemianism down in Greenwich Village and up in Harlem gave way to production that was more predictable in intention and style.

The liberalism and populism of the Roosevelt administration and the **New Deal** intensified the interest in American folk culture, fostering a home-grown variation on the "primitive." As early as 1901, W. E. B. Du Bois had praised the power of Negro spirituals in *The Souls of Black Folk*. Decades later, African American authors like Zora Neale Hurston, who traveled to the black villages of Florida collecting folk tales, Langston Hughes, who wrote children's stories that drew on the folk tradition, and Jacob Lawrence, who painted ordinary African Americans in rural and urban settings and chronicled the Great Migration, contributed to a revival of interest in the culture of the common man and woman. Many poets, including Sterling Brown, experimented with writing exclusively in dialect—a move that not only recognized the importance of a black idiom, but also portrayed its vibrancy.

Ordinary American life colors the poetry of William Carlos Williams and Robert Frost. Frost revealed an enormous psychological and moral complexity behind the simple, austere surfaces of the New England back country; Williams found beauty in the most ordinary of urban places. Carl Sandburg, Vachel Lindsay, and Genevieve Taggard carried Whitman's legacy into the twentieth century, celebrating the sound of spontaneous vernacular voices and finding wonder in ordinary language and the pace of American speech.

Even so, an interest in the ancient, the primitive, and folk traditions could carry artists in very different directions. Modernist poets like H.D., T. S. Eliot, and Ezra Pound unearthed and alluded to arcane texts, near-forgotten medieval ballads, classical verse, and primordial myths that seem to transcend cultures.

"PRIMITIVISM" WEB ARCHIVE

[2944] Anonymous, *Aaron Douglas with Arthur Schomburg and the* Song of Towers *Mural* (1934), courtesy of Arthur Schomburg Photograph Collection, Photographs and Prints Division, Schomburg Center for Research in Black Culture, The New York Public Library, Astor, Lenox and Tilden Foundations. Douglas was commissioned to paint murals for the New York Public Library under the Works Progress Administration. This mural represents African American migration from the South to the urban North.

[4410] Anonymous, *Ernest Hemingway on Safari in Africa* (1933), courtesy of the National Archives and Records Administrations, JFK Library. Photograph of Hemingway with elephant carcass and gun. Hemingway traveled extensively and based his novels in various locales.

[4766] Aaron Douglas, *The Judgement Day* (1927), courtesy of The Walter O. Evans Collection of African American Art. Aaron Douglas, American (1899–1979). Gouache on paper; 11 3/4" x 9". Douglas's painting incorporates images from jazz and African traditions and can be compared to "Harlem Shadows," by Claude McKay, and "The Weary Blues," by Langston Hughes.

[5289] Aaron Douglas, *Study for Aspects of Negro Life: The Negro Man in an African Setting* (1934), courtesy of The Art Institute of Chicago: Aaron Douglas, American, 1899–1979, Study for Aspects of Negro Life: the Negro in an African setting, before 1934, gouache on Whatman artist's board, 37.5 x 41 cm, Estate of Solomon Byron Smith; Margaret Fisher Fund, 1990.416. Sketch of Africans dancing and playing music. This became part of a Harlem mural sponsored by the Works Progress Administration chronicling African American history, from freedom in Africa to life in the contemporary United States. Africa and ancestry were themes of "The Negro Speaks of Rivers," by Langston Hughes, and "Africa," by Claude McKay.

[7170] Alfred Stieglitz, *Negro Art Exhibition, November, 1914. Brancusi*

Sculpture, March 1914 (1916), courtesy of the Library of Congress [LC-USZ62-100177]. These photographs of two art exhibits illustrate the popularity of African American art and show how primitivism and African images influenced white artists such as Constantin Brancusi.

[7408] Carl Van Vechten, *Portrait of Bessie Smith Holding Feathers* (1936), courtesy of the Library of Congress [LC-USZ62-94955]. Writers and musicians of the Harlem Renaissance debated how best to depict African Americans, especially in terms of gender. Bessie Smith was a New Negro artist who embraced primitivism and the use of African images.

QUESTIONS

Comprehension: What were some of the manifestations and characteristics of primitivism in the literature of the 1920s and 1930s?

Context: H.D. draws on ancient mythology frequently in her poetry, often retelling the myths with a focus on female protagonists. Some of her favorite heroines are Helen of Troy, Leda (the mother of Helen), and Eurydice, the wife of Orpheus. Why do you think she chooses the particular stories and figures that she does? How does her use of mythology differ from that of Pound and of Eliot?

Context: Would you make a distinction between "primitive" and "folk" in American poetry? Which poems suggest such a difference?

Exploration: Imagine a debate between Sterling Brown and Robert Frost about the use of primitivism or folk traditions in American literature. What might be the key differences in their perspectives?

EXTENDED CONTEXTS

Broadcasting Modernization: Radio and the Battle over Poetry

With the creation of nationwide radio networks and the drop in the cost of home equipment, poetry, jazz, symphonic music, and fresh commentary on the news and the arts became available to a vastly expanded audience, including people who could not read. The immediacy of radio and the increased access to the arts that radio gave people of all classes revolutionized American culture.

For many American poets, including William Carlos Williams, Langston Hughes, and Robert Frost, this change was welcome. Their search for an American idiom and more accessible subject matter complemented this modern medium. For Sandburg and Taggard, the ability to reach a cross-section of the public increased the reach and influence of their words. The immediacy of radio created an intimacy between poet and audience, and the medium played a crucial role in turning the poet into a celebrity figure.

Other poets, including Ezra Pound and T. S. Eliot, regarded the popularization of art as a threat. They prided themselves on writing poetry that was allusive and difficult. For them, poetry was not meant to be mainstream. Broadcasting poetry seemed a degrading form of commercialization, a mass-consumer approach to art (although Eliot *did* present his work on the radio). To these artists, radio meant that art would become the territory of middlebrow taste.

[2360] Anonymous, *Listening to the Radio at Home* (1920), courtesy of the George H. Clark Radioana Collection, Archives Center, National Museum of American History, Smithsonian Institution.

Comprehension: How would you describe elitism in art? Where do you find it? Why did some modernists seek to be elite or obscure? Why did some poets resist the popularization of poetry through radio broadcast?

Context: Read Robert Frost's "The Road Not Taken" aloud. How does hearing the poem (as opposed to reading it) affect your interpretation and appreciation? What do you gain from hearing the poem read aloud? Are some possibilities lost in the process?

Context: Reread the poems of Carl Sandburg and T. S. Eliot. Which works do you think would work best on radio? What would be gained (or lost) by listening to these poems rather than reading them?

Context: We are often described as living in the "Information Age" in which access to all kinds of information, from instant news and sports to online texts of rare books, is instantly available to anyone with an Internet connection. Many American homes have multiple televisions. How have TV and the Internet affected the distribution and consumption of literature? Are there negative consequences of making art widely available to the public via radio, TV, and the Internet? How do these costs compare to the benefits? Do you think radio, TV, and the Internet have had a positive effect on the arts? How have these media affected the way the public appreciates or doesn't appreciate highbrow culture, specifically poetry?

The New Negro and the Reconstruction of African American Identity

The term "New Negro" came into use at the end of the nineteenth century, as a way of summarizing the various efforts of black Americans to put the culture of slavery behind them. By the 1920s, however, the term signified racial pride, economic independence, the struggle for social equality, and courageous expression in literature and the arts. When Alain Locke published his landmark anthology *The New Negro*, the term gained strong connections with the Harlem Renaissance. Small literary magazines abounded in Harlem during this period, and Locke's anthology had its origins in the March 1925 issue of *Survey Graphic*, a journal devoted to publishing young writers. The issue on Harlem was conceived by *Survey* editor Paul Kellogg, at a Civic Club dinner in November 1924, hosted by Charles S. Johnson, editor of *Opportunity*, a journal affiliated with the NAACP. Locke's collection of essays, poetry, and fiction quickly became landmark in the movement. Illustrated by Aaron Douglas, the book also included a bibliography of important artists, thinkers, and events of the Harlem Renaissance.

Leaders of the Harlem Renaissance believed that art should portray African Americans in a positive light, emphasizing literacy, artistic sophistication, and other qualities that could win respect among the dominant American majority. African American photographers, working in Harlem and across America, played an important role in con-

"BROADCASTING MODERNIZATION" WEB ARCHIVE

[2360] Anonymous, *Listening to the Radio at Home* (1920), courtesy of the George H. Clark Radioana Collection, Archives Center, National Museum of American History, Smithsonian Institution. Family seated around their radio in the early 1920s. Radio was the first affordable mass media entertainment to enter the homes of nearly all Americans. A powerful tool for rapid communication of news, radio helped advertise products and spread music like jazz and swing around the country.

[2363] Anonymous, *"Radiotron" Vacuum Tube Display* (1927), courtesy of the George H. Clark Radioana Collection, Archives Center, National Museum of American History, Smithsonian Institution. Department store display of vacuum tubes for radios. The advent of the radio allowed people from all walks of life to have access to poetry and classical music and set the stage for what was to become "pop culture."

[5177] Russell Lee, *Radio with Ornaments and Decorations* (1938), courtesy of the Library of Congress [LC-USF33-011602-M2 DLC]. Radio with photographs and knickknacks on top, in the home of a Farm Security Administration client near Caruthersville, Missouri. Radios made art and news accessible to a larger audience.

[5225] Russell Lee, *John Frost and Daughter Listening to Radio in Their Home* (1940), courtesy of the Library of Congress [LC-USF34-037961-D DLC]. Father and daughter inside a farm home in Tehama County, California, listen to the radio together. Radio was an important source of art, entertainment, and information for many families.

[5226] Marion Post Wolcott, *A More Well-to-Do Miner Listening to the Radio When He Returns Home in the Morning After Working on the Night Shift* (1938), courtesy of the Library of Congress [LC-USF34-050293-E]. Family seated around radio. Many poets, among them Genevieve Taggard, were excited about the advent of radio, especially because they were able to broadcast their poetry to a wide range of people.

[5594] Anonymous, *It Was Common Practice for Small Town and Country Dealers to Bring Radios Directly to Prospects and Customers Alike* (1925), courtesy of the George H. Clark Radioana Collection, Archives Center, National Museum of American History, Smithsonian Institution. Photograph of dealers delivering radios from vehicle. Increased geographical mobility and mass culture were intertwined. As travel became easier, small towns became less culturally isolated.

[6137] Doubleday, Page and Company, *Radio Broadcast* (1926), courtesy of the Library of Congress. Promotional material for radio broadcasting technology. Technological developments made art more accessible to larger audiences and contributed to a sense of breaking with the Victorian era.

veying that ideal. The photographs of James Van Der Zee emphasize values and concepts central to the New Negro and the aspirations of the race. With images of black war veterans, dignified parades, and "Striver's Row," he portrayed the pride, accomplishment, and patriotism associated with the New Negro.

Small circulation magazines, like *Survey*, *Opportunity*, *Fire*, and *Crisis*, helped to fuel the movement by providing forums for new poetry, fiction, and art. The annual prizes offered by *Opportunity* helped young writers like Langston Hughes and Zora Neale Hurston gain acceptance in New York literary circles. In turn, the editors of these magazines gained influence as discoverers of talent—and some of their choices sparked controversy, especially narratives and poems that portrayed African Americans talking in dialect, drinking in bars, or straying from the New Negro role model. There were also controversies when these publications engaged directly with racism, lynchings, miscegenation, and other unresolved dilemmas in black and white American life. The courage of these writers and their editors in representing life honestly and with dignity in works like "The Weary Blues" or *Cane* reflects the spirit of the New Negro and the Harlem Renaissance.

QUESTIONS

Comprehension: What does the "New Negro" signify, and how did the term become popular?

Comprehension: What social and cultural developments supported the flourishing of African American art?

Comprehension: Describe some of the debates that arose between leaders and artists of the Harlem Renaissance.

Context: How do the African American authors in this unit either fulfill or reject the concept of the New Negro? Does the poetry follow Alain Locke's aesthetic guidelines? What stereotypes does the art of this period embrace or deny?

Exploration: When Alain Locke published his article "The New Negro" in the 1925 publication of the same name, he ignited a wave of excitement and debate throughout the African American community. What was new about the concept of the New Negro? What political and social responsibilities did the New Negro artist have? What kinds of conflicts arose from these duties? Do you think that art can bring about political change? How do you think the concept of the New Negro has influenced African American identity today? Has it influenced current artists?

Exploration: Many of the authors in this unit interacted closely with powerful and wealthy white patrons. To some critics, these relationships lessened the integrity of the art. On the other hand, many argue that without the white support, much of the art of this period would not have been produced. What were some of the possible advantages and disadvantages of white patronage for these African American artists?

[4766] Aaron Douglas, *The Judgement Day* (1927), courtesy of The Walter O. Evans Collection of African American Art. Aaron Douglas, American (1899–1979). Gouache on paper; 11 3/4" x 9".

ASSIGNMENTS

Personal and Creative Responses

1. *Journal*: Try to imagine what it might have been like for a black person moving from a small town to Harlem in the 1920s. What would they have encountered? What would the atmosphere have been? What might they have done for fun on a weekend night? What kinds of frustrations might they have met with? What might have surprised or pleased them?

2. *Poet's Corner*: Reread William Carlos Williams's "This Is Just to Say." Choose a topic of your own and write a poem that imitates his style. Think about what kind of subject matter Williams writes about. What does his language sound like? What are the features of his verse? After you've written your poem, write a short paragraph analyzing what you wrote. What characteristics of Williams's work were you trying to capture?

[3012] Austin Hansen, *Count Basie and the Nicholas Brothers* (c. 1940s), courtesy of Joyce Hansen and the Schomburg Center for Research in Black Culture, New York Public Library.

3. *Poet's Corner*: Read Kenneth Koch's hilarious imitation of Williams's "This Is Just to Say": "Variations on a Theme by William Carlos Williams" (*Thank You, and Other Poems* [New York: Grove Press, 1962]). Ask your students to write their own parody of one of the modernist poems they have read.

4. *Doing History*: For the ancient Greeks, the Trojan War (c. 1200 B.C.E.) marked an important turning point in their collective identity. For the modernists, World War I functioned as an earth-shattering moment that signaled the end of the Victorian era and the beginning of the modern age. Reread some of H.D.'s poems that rely on classical mythology. Do some research on a myth that particularly interests you. How is H.D.'s telling of modern history enhanced by her use of past histories? What is added to her poetry when she uses histories steeped in myth rather than factual historical allusions?

5. *Multimedia*: Many of the artists in this unit looked to the visual arts and music for inspiration. Look at the paintings in the archive by Aaron Douglas and Jacob Lawrence, as well as items that reflect the primitivist and orientalist orientations of many modernist poets. In addition, listen to some jazz. How do the formal and aesthetic characteristics of these works relate to the poetry featured in this unit? What are specifically American images, sounds, or verses? What, if any, authentic national identity can be forged from these many sources?

[8083] Jacob Lawrence, *Rampart Street (aka Harlem Street)* (1941), courtesy of the Estate of Jacob Lawrence. Collection of the Portland Art Museum, Oregon. Gift of Jan de Graaff.

Problem-Based Learning Projects

1. You have been asked to illustrate a collection of poetry from the Harlem Renaissance using archival footage, photographs, artwork,

[3012] Austin Hansen, *Count Basie and the Nicholas Brothers* (c. 1940s), courtesy of Joyce Hansen and the Schomburg Center for Research in Black Culture, New York Public Library. Count Basie (pictured with Fayard and Harold Nicholas, internationally renowned tap dancers) was a leading figure in twentieth-century music, helping to define the style and nature of jazz and swing. Amiri Baraka and Michael Harper show jazz influences in their poetry.

[3939] Underwood and Underwood, *Famous New York African American Soldiers Return Home* (1917), courtesy of the National Archives and Records Administration. The 369th (former 15th New York City) regiment marches in Harlem, including Lieutenant James Reese Europe, a well-known musician. African American veterans advocated for civil rights. *Home to Harlem* (1928), by Harlem Renaissance writer Claude McKay, tells the story of an African American soldier's life after his return from the war.

[4012] Carl Van Vechten, *Portrait of James Baldwin* (1955), courtesy of the Library of Congress [LC-USZ62-42481]. James Baldwin is remembered as a civil rights activist and the author of plays, poetry, short stories, and novels, including *Go Tell It on the Mountain*.

[4565] Prentiss Taylor, *Zora Neale Hurston* (n.d.), courtesy of Yale University Collection of American Literature, Beinecke Rare Book and Manuscript Library. Used with the permission of the Estate of Zora Neale Hurston. Photograph of Hurston dancing on couch. Known for her flamboyance and charisma, Hurston was sometimes urged by other artists to represent African Americans in more "dignified" ways.

[4566] Anonymous, *Their Eyes Were Watching God* dustcover (1937), courtesy of Yale University, Beinecke Rare Book and Manuscript Library, Yale Collection of American Literature. Zora Neale Hurston's best-known book, *Their Eyes Were Watching God*, was criticized by some African American authors and

newspaper articles, and manifestos from the era. Which poems will you choose and why? How will you order them? How will you help bring these poems to life for your readers?

2. You are an art critic for the *New York Times*, and you've been asked to write a column on the influence of oriental art on modernist culture, drawing on poetry, paintings, architecture, and music. Which works will you choose? What historical events are key for understanding Asia's influence? What works of oriental art most influenced the modernists?

3. Using the video archive, prepare a slide show on primitivism during the modern era for schoolchildren in which you explain the relationship between the historical events and art of the time. As well as choosing the pictures, you should also write a script that you will deliver to your young audience.

4. You have been asked to do a poetry reading for National Public Radio. Make a list of the poems you would choose to read. Why have you chosen these particular works? Then, practice reading the poems aloud, paying particular attention to how you're reading. How do you know where to breathe, pause, or stop? What words do you emphasize? Analyze the other performance choices you make as you practice the broadcast.

GLOSSARY

free verse   Poetry that does not depend on traditional form and meter. Some of the features of free verse include enjambment, visual patterning, and varying line lengths. With the exception of Frost, McKay, and Cullen, most poets in this unit wrote in free verse.

Great Migration   The movement of thousands of African Americans from the South to the North. This mass relocation began at the turn of the twentieth century and continued through the 1920s, as black Americans left behind the racially divided South with its Jim Crow laws and enduring prejudices in the hopes that they would find equality and opportunity in the North. As the growing industrial section of the country, the North did offer more jobs, but dismal housing conditions, low wages, and racism made the North a disappointing destination for many blacks. Still, the steady increase in African Americans in the North, particularly in Harlem, made it possible for African Americans to build a sense of community and racial identity.

jazz   A style of music that developed in America in the early twentieth century in New Orleans and other southern cities. It is characterized by syncopated rhythms, improvisation, extremes in pitch and dynamics, call and response, and experimentation. Jazz draws on traditional African American music, and swing jazz, which was popular in the 1920s, and has often been described as following the patterns of speech. Indeed, the instruments in a jazz piece often seem to be "talking" back and forth to one another.

modernism   A literary movement that reached its peak in the

1920s, modernism developed in two rather different strands. American modernism, as practiced by Williams and Hughes, is characterized by an interest in portraying ordinary subject matter in concrete, vernacular language. Modernist poetry written in Europe, as characterized by Eliot, tends to be highly allusive. The poems are nonlinear and often refer to the modern condition, particularly the city, in a deeply critical manner. This strand of modernism tends to use a disembodied voice and a collage-like method.

New Deal   Federal programs developed by President Franklin D. Roosevelt's administration (1933–45) to restore economic stability and prosperity. The government created and funded thousands of jobs, many of them in public works and the arts.

orientalism   A term coined by literary and cultural critic Edward Said to denote a fascination with Asian culture. For Said, it is this fascination, and cultural appropriation, which is real—rather than any actual image of Asian cultures. Modernist poets like Pound and Williams implicitly critique modern society by turning to Asian culture, which they see as foreign and exotic. Viewed as an escape from or alternative to the increasingly mechanized and alienating modern world, the Orient is used as a symbol of a more tranquil life. Modernist poets were attracted by particular characteristics of Asian art, including the affinity with nature, appreciation of the ordinary, and commitment to clean, economic language. Like primitivism, orientalism can often seem patronizing and even racist because it tends to view all Asians and Asian culture stereotypically.

primitivism   An artistic style that privileges "simpler" times or cultures over a more "advanced" or modern way of life. Primitivism idealizes earlier times and it looks to rural living as an answer to the problems of modern civilization. Many twentieth-century poets idealized classical times by using mythology in their poetry. Other writers turned to Africa and images of the noble savage as an antidote to modern life.

Red Summer   Term coined by James Weldon Johnson to refer to the period between June 1919 and the end of that year, during which twenty-five race riots erupted around the country. In addition, more than seventy blacks were lynched in 1925, and the Ku Klux Klan experienced a frightening revival in the South and Midwest. After serving bravely in World War I, many black veterans were understandably bitter and resentful when they returned to the United States and lost the respect that they had experienced as members of the armed forces.

Talented Tenth   A term coined by W. E. B. Du Bois to refer to the upper echelons of the black race who would use their education and talent to improve the situation for African Americans. See the context on "the Talented Tenth" in Unit 9.

vernacular   Language that sounds colloquial or imitates the everyday speech patterns of a group of people. Poets like William Carlos Williams, Langston Hughes, and Robert Frost all write in the vernacular, but because they capture the conversational qualities of different groups of people, their verse sounds very different. In the modern period, many poets were interested in portraying characteris-

leaders because it did not emphasize racial oppression.

[4766] Aaron Douglas, *The Judgement Day* (1927), courtesy of The Walter O. Evans Collection of African American Art. Aaron Douglas, American (1899–1979). Gouache on paper; 11 3/4" x 9". Douglas's painting incorporates images from jazz and African traditions and can be compared to "Harlem Shadows," by Claude McKay, and "The Weary Blues," by Langston Hughes.

[5183] Valerie Wilmer, *Langston Hughes in Front of Harlem Apartment* (1962), courtesy of Yale University, Beinecke Rare Book and Manuscript Library and the Langston Hughes Estate. Like William Carlos Williams and Carl Sandburg, Langston Hughes admired Walt Whitman and created literary personas that spoke to more than his own experience. In particular, Hughes was committed to portraying everyday African American life in his poetry.

[8083] Jacob Lawrence, *Rampart Street (aka Harlem Street)* (1941), courtesy of the Estate of Jacob Lawrence, Collection of the Portland Art Museum, Oregon. Gift of Jan de Graaff. Jacob Lawrence, known for his visual dramatizations of African American life, often painted series on subjects like Harlem, events and figures in black history, and even Hiroshima. A number of critics have likened Lawrence's style to African American music, including jazz and boogie-woogie. Lawrence's paintings can be viewed in light of the poems of Langston Hughes and contrasted with the work of later African American artist Romare Bearden.

tically American speech and language. They felt that through language they could capture and create a uniquely American poetry and, perhaps also, a truly American identity.

SELECTED BIBLIOGRAPHY

Bell, Bernard W. *The Afro-American Novel and Its Tradition*. Boston: U of Massachusetts P, 1987.

Blount, Marcellus. "Caged Birds: Race and Gender in the Sonnet." *Engendering Men: The Question of Male Feminist Criticism*, ed. Joseph Boone and Michael Cadden. New York: Routledge, 1990. 225–238.

Douglas, Ann. *Terrible Honesty*. New York: Noonday Press, 1995.

Lewis, David Levering, ed. *The Portable Harlem Renaissance Reader*. New York: Penguin, 1994.

———. *When Harlem Was in Vogue*. New York: Penguin, 1979.

Levenson, Michael. *A Genealogy of Modernism*. Cambridge: Cambridge UP, 1984.

Locke, Alain, ed. *The New Negro*. New York: Simon and Schuster, 1997.

Moy, James S. *Marginal Sights: Staging the Chinese in America*. Iowa City: U of Iowa P, 1993.

Nicholls, Peter. *Modernisms: A Literary Guide*. Berkeley: U of California P, 1995.

North, Charles. " 'January morning,' or What Will You Not Be Experiencing?" *The Teachers & Writers Guide to Classic American Literature*, ed. Christopher Edgar and Gary Lenhart. Teachers & Writers, 2001.

Perkins, David. *A History of Modern Poetry*. Cambridge: Harvard UP, 1976.

Qian, Zhaoming. *Orientalism and Modernism: The Legacy of China in Pound and Williams*. Durham: Duke UP, 1995.

Sundquist, Eric J. *To Wake the Nations: Race in the Making of American Literature*. Cambridge: Harvard UP, 1993.

FURTHER RESOURCES

Against the Odds: The Artists of the Harlem Renaissance [videorecording]. Production of NJN; produced, written, and directed by Amber Edwards. [Alexandria, VA]: PBS Video [1994], 1993.

Alexander, Scott. *The Red Hot Jazz Archive* [electronic resource]. History of Jazz Before 1930. <www.redhotjazz.com/>.

Burns, Ken. *Empire of the Air: The Men Who Made Radio* [videorecording]. Produced by Florentine Films and WETA-TV. Alexandria, VA: PBS Video: Radio Pioneers Film Project, Inc., 1991.

Cahill, Holger, et al. *Masters of Popular Painting: Modern Primitives of Europe and America*. New York: Arno, 1966 [c. 1938].

Edwards, Justin D. *Exotic Journeys: Exploring the Erotics of U.S. Travel Literature, 1840–1930*. Hanover: UP of New England, 2001.

Ford, Edward R. *The Details of Modern Architecture*. Cambridge: MIT Press, 1990–96.

Locke, Alain. *The New Negro*. New York: Atheneum, 1968.

Museum of Modern Art (MOMA <www.moma.org>). 33rd Street at Queens Blvd., Long Island City, Queens. Phone: (212) 708-9400.

Patton, Sharon F. *African American Art*. Oxford: Oxford UP, 1998.

Said, Edward. *Orientalism*. New York: Pantheon Books, 1978.

Siskind, Aaron. *Harlem: Photographs 1932–1940*. Ed. Ann Banks. Washington, DC: National Museum of American Art, 1990.

Unit 11

MODERNIST PORTRAITS

Experimentations in Style,
World War I to World War II

Authors and Works

Featured in the Video:
Gertrude Stein, *Tender Buttons* (series of still lives)
F. Scott Fitzgerald, *Tender Is the Night*, *The Great Gatsby* (novels), "Babylon Revisited" (short story)
Ernest Hemingway, *A Farewell to Arms* (novel), "The Snows of Kilimanjaro" (short story)

Discussed in This Unit:
Susan Glaspell, *Trifles* (play)
Sherwood Anderson, *Winesburg, Ohio* (series of short stories)
Wallace Stevens, "The Snow Man," "The Emperor of Ice-Cream," "Disillusionment of Ten O'Clock," "Sunday Morning," "Gubbinal," "Thirteen Ways of Looking at a Blackbird" (poems)
Marianne Moore, "Poetry," "Nevertheless," "In Distrust of Merits" (poems)
Nella Larsen, *Quicksand* (novella)
John Dos Passos, *The Big Money* (novel)
Hart Crane, "Chaplinesque," *The Bridge* (poems)

Overview Questions

■ What issues shaped Americans' thinking during the modern era? How did American literature respond to the societal transformations of the post–World War I period?
■ How did political events, such as war and labor conflict, affect the works of the writers included in this unit?
■ What impact did World War I have on the way people thought about the modern world? What technological innovations influenced the way people perceived society and the individual's place within it?

■ How did the stylistic innovations of modernist prose affect the way later authors used language and narrative structure?
■ How were the myths of the "public enemy" shaped by historical and cultural changes during the modern era? How is this related to shifting notions of the American success story?
■ How did modernity transform the traditional notions of American self-reliance and independence? How did authors consider and rework modern social relations in their writing?

Learning Objectives

After students have viewed the video, read the headnotes and literary selections in *The Norton Anthology of American Literature*, and explored related archival materials on the *American Passages* Web site, they should be able to

1. recognize the different types of formal experimentation in the fiction of modernist writers such as Stein, Hemingway, Anderson, and Dos Passos, as well as in the poetry of Stevens, Moore, and Crane;
2. appreciate the diversity of modernist authors, especially the difference in subject matter treated by authors such as Glaspell, Fitzgerald, Larsen, Hemingway, and Stein;
3. understand the implications of the social and political transformations that reshaped American life during the modern era and the effect of these changes on the literature produced;
4. see connections between the art and literature of the modern era and be able to identify how popular culture informs both.

Instructor Overview

Between World War I and World War II, the lives of the majority of Americans underwent dramatic transformations. Though America did not officially participate in World War I until 1917, its entrance into the conflict marked a new level of U.S. involvement in European affairs and made a significant impression on those who served in the war, including a large number of writers. Following the war, and in part spurred by the increased production of a wartime economy, American consumer capitalism exploded, and the age of advertising and mass consumption reshaped the day-to-day lives of many Americans. The automobile, which debuted before the turn of the century, became an ever-increasing fact of daily life: in 1900 there were only eight thousand cars in America; by 1940 there were thirty-two million. Telephones and electrification, both innovations of the late nineteenth century, also became commonplace in American homes.

After the turn of the century, increasing numbers of Americans invested their money on Wall Street, which had become America's most prominent financial exchange in the second half of the nineteenth century. After World War I, the practice of investing by borrowing on "margin"—that is, investing money that investors themselves did not have—became more commonplace, enabling more people to invest—or gamble—in the market, often beyond their own means. Some became rich beyond their wildest dreams through Wall Street speculations in the 1920s; many more lost everything they had in the Wall Street crash of 1929. The ensuing Great Depression revealed that the booming capitalist economy of the 1920s was less stable than many had previously believed; in 1932 the federal government, led by President Franklin Delano Roosevelt, began formulating the New Deal, which initiated new ways to regulate business and the U.S. economy. In the meantime, nearly a quarter of the workforce was unemployed, and hunger and poverty remained widespread until the economy began to recover at the end of the decade, when World War II began in Europe.

Political changes likewise reshaped American life: after years of agitation for suffrage, women finally won the right to vote in 1919 (the Nineteenth Amendment was officially ratified in 1920). Also in 1919, Congress enacted the Eighteenth Amendment, ushering in the era of Prohibition by outlawing "the manufacture, sale, or transportation of intoxicating liquors." This law fueled a widespread illegal trade in alcohol; many historians believe that the increase in organized crime during Prohibition was a direct result of the new opportunities for illegal money-making provided by the Eighteenth Amendment. Prohibition, also known as the Volstead Act, was repealed in 1933, in part because politicians thought that reviving the liquor industry might provide jobs for the unemployed.

To a great extent the world of art and literature reflected the new pace and interests of American life, though many American practitioners of what would be labeled "modern" art lived in Europe, believing that the conventional values of American culture stifled their creativity. T. S. Eliot and Ezra Pound led the way for other authors who sought a cultural climate conducive to the production of great literature; from 1920 through 1929, more and more American authors took up residence in the culturally vibrant cities of Europe, especially Paris. Gertrude Stein, Ernest Hemingway, F. Scott Fitzgerald, and others formed a coterie in Paris and together strived to create a type of literature appropriate to what they considered a new "modern" world following World War I. Artists and writers alike developed new techniques and addressed new subjects in reaction to a now-outdated traditionalism.

Modernism also responded to a prevalent sense of loss and bewilderment prompted by the societal and technological changes of the early twentieth century. Disillusionment, confusion, and in some cases a sense of freedom characterized the "modern temper" of the first half of the twentieth century. It became increasingly evident that many traditional moral and social standards had shifted dramatically, particularly those governing the behavior of women, who began to assert new freedoms such as going out unchaperoned, wearing less constrictive clothing, and smoking in public. The pace of urbanization intensified, and more Americans lived in urban centers than in rural areas. This shift fundamentally changed the way people in communities interacted: whereas neighbors all knew each other in villages, residents were largely anonymous in cities, where the population tended to change rapidly. (This sense of the anonymity of the city appears in such works as *The Great Gatsby* and *Quicksand*, for example.) Further, immigration from Europe had accelerated markedly in the last decades of the nineteenth century, and cities appeared to be filled with foreigners. People thinking of themselves as native-born Americans pressed for reduced quotas of those immigrants whose cultures seemed most different from their own. Nativist sentiment helped push through stringent immigration acts in the first decades of the century, and immigrants faced discrimination and prejudice as they tried to adjust to American life (for more about immigration and literature see Unit 12). Ironically, those Americans who were truly native to the United States—American Indians—continued to face discrimination, and many lived on reservations where they had little access to paid work or adequate health care. Congress officially made all Native Americans citizens in 1924, but citizenship did not materially change the living conditions of most Native Americans; the Indian Reorganization Act of 1934 finally allowed Native Americans a greater measure of self-government.

This unit includes authors who represent diverse strands of modernism and who experimented with prose and poetry in a variety of ways. Gertrude Stein and Ernest Hemingway exemplify some of the ways prose writers tried to "make it new" following World War I: Hemingway's spare style and efforts to create "one true sentence" may be linked to the streamlining of other areas of American life during this period, while Stein's prose, which often defies reader comprehension, has ties to the fragmented images visible in cubist art. F. Scott Fitzgerald, whose prose style breaks conventions less radically than either Stein's or Hemingway's, chronicled many of the changes in the lifestyle of wealthy Americans during what he called the "Jazz Age." Sherwood Anderson and Susan Glaspell exemplify the continuation of regionalism—Anderson's *Winesburg, Ohio* examines the emotional and psychological lives of characters in a small midwestern town, and Glaspell's *Trifles* focuses on the trials faced by women in the isolated farm country of Iowa. The selection from John Dos Passos's *The Big Money* reveals another type of stylistic innovation: by incorporating snippets of popular culture materials in the text of his novel, Dos Passos calls our attention to the juxtaposition of national propaganda and the realities of labor strife that readers of a daily newspaper might otherwise miss. Nella Larsen's *Quicksand* provides an example of the fiction produced during the Harlem Renaissance; also experimenting with style and considering the possibilities for individuality in America and Europe, Larsen's novel questions the essence of African American identity in the larger context of the American arts. The poets Marianne Moore, Hart Crane, and Wallace Stevens share many of the same concerns as the prose writers, examining in their poetry the place of the individual in the complex and confusing modern world, while experimenting with form and style in their work.

Many of these writers spent significant periods of time abroad, especially in Paris, where they became involved with the Parisian artistic community, much of which centered around Stein's salon. The impact of European modernism was felt by all, however, whether or not they joined the expatriate community for any length of time. In their poetry and prose, these and other writers of the early twentieth century worked to create a literature appropriate to their time, breaking with tradition and reformulating the function of literature and art in the life of the individual and society at large.

In this unit, students will become familiar with many of the issues concerning prose modernism and its response to the modern world. The video focuses on Gertrude Stein, Ernest Hemingway, and F. Scott Fitzgerald and introduces students to some of the images and ideas linked to literary modernism, which may be further traced in the fiction of such authors as Nella Larsen and John Dos Passos, as well as in the poetry of Marianne Moore, Wallace Stevens, and Hart Crane. The work of Sherwood Anderson and Susan Glaspell provides a counterpoint to modern authors' focus on the city, revealing how ideas about modernity and the individual's place in the modern world also played out in rural settings. Together with the archive, this unit allows students to explore the formal characteristics of modernist prose, the diverse strains of American modernism, the relationships between modern literature and art, as well as a number of the sociopolitical contexts of this period in American history.

Several other units address different facets of modernism and have significant links to the works and ideas covered in this unit, including Unit 10, which examines the works of the leading expatriate modernist poets; Unit 12, which considers the social and political activism that informs the literature of immigration; Unit 13, which looks at the ways modernism played out in the writing of southern authors; and Unit 14, which shows the continuation of concerns about war and the conditions of everyday life in the work of writers after World War II.

Student Overview

The period between World War I and World War II was one of dramatic transformation for many Americans. The horror of World War I (1914–18), the most destructive conflict the world had yet seen, demonstrated to those who had blindly believed in technological progress that technology could also destroy. Postwar America and Europe underwent significant social change, resulting in a pervasive feeling of bewilderment and disillusion. The accelerated pace of urbanization during this period only heightened this sense of change, as did increasing immigration from eastern Europe and Asia. Americans found themselves living in a world that previous generations would not have recognized.

Also during this time, America's consumer economy took shape, as mass consumption and advertising became facts of American life. Many technological innovations became commonplace, and millions of Americans owned cars and telephones by the end of this period. American music changed as well; African American musicians created a new sound, introducing **jazz** to American audiences, and thereby changing popular music forever. The film industry burgeoned, and the 1927 film *The Jazz Singer* heralded the age of talking pictures. Political changes also transformed American life: following decades of struggle for suffrage, the Nineteenth Amendment gave women the right to vote in 1920. Congress also enacted the Eighteenth Amendment in 1919, which made it illegal to manufacture or sell alcohol: thus began **Prohibition**. The practice of "bootlegging" liquor fueled a thriving business in the trade of illegal alcohol, which helped to create a network of criminal organizations ruled by mob "bosses" such as Al Capone. These gangsters stirred the public imagination, and their lives of crime and extravagance were followed in the press and fictionalized by Hollywood in such films as *Public Enemy* (1931).

In this age of consumption and changing morals, greater numbers of Americans invested in Wall Street stocks, frequently by borrowing money on the "margin" to make their purchases—that is, investors used money that they themselves did not actually have. Though some became extremely wealthy through these investments, many Americans lost everything they owned in the crash of 1929. The Great Depression followed, lasting over a decade, until World War II (1939–45) helped to stimulate the economy once again.

Art and literature responded to many of these changes in American life, as artists and writers sought to make sense of societal transformations and provide a new form of art in tune with the modern world. Many American modernists actually chose to live in Europe rather than the United States, as they found the cultural climate of Europe more conducive to and tolerant of their experimental artistic endeavors. Gertrude Stein, Ernest Hemingway, F. Scott Fitzgerald, and others met one another in Paris while working to create a new type of art, one that discarded conventions of narrative structure and form. Painters and sculptors such as Pablo Picasso and Marcel Duchamp also rejected traditional artistic techniques and created abstract works that completely changed the way people thought about art. The innovations of these writers and artists profoundly altered the literature and art that would follow, as these "modernists" endeavored to create work that helped to define the modern world.

➤ **Authors covered:** Gertrude Stein, F. Scott Fitzgerald, Ernest Hemingway

➤ **Who's interviewed:** Emory Elliott, professor of English (the University of California, Riverside); Pancho Savery, professor of English (Reed College); Catharine Stimpson, Dean of the Graduate School of Arts and Science (New York University); Robert Stone, novelist, poet, and professor of English (Yale University); Linda Watts, Interdisciplinary Arts and Sciences director and professor of American studies (University of Washington, Bothell)

➤ **Points covered:**

- Following the devastation of World War I, many intellectuals and writers felt a sense of disillusionment with and alienation from modern, and especially modern American, culture.

- Numerous writers and artists sought refuge in Paris, which seemed more tolerant and appreciative of artistic pursuits. Paris became a center for writers seeking to create a new kind of literature.

- Societal standards and morals seemed to be changing, and the so-called "Lost Generation" tried to make sense of these societal changes in their writing, experimenting with form and style.

- Reacting against rigid Victorian value systems, people were increasingly attracted to Freud's ideas about the subconscious. Jazz allowed a freedom of expression not condoned by traditional moral codes.

- Gertrude Stein, a poet and prose writer interested in psychology and modern art, moved to Paris in the early twentieth century and soon became a central figure in the modern art movement there.

- Stein's home became an informal salon where numerous writers and artists congregated, and she promoted the work of other artists who later became influential figures, such as Hemingway and Picasso.

- Like other modernists, Stein chose to write character-driven, rather than plot-driven, fiction. Stein's "portraits" attempted to illuminate the inner workings of the human mind and investigate how language and consciousness interacted. She was less interested in representation than in words themselves and employed successive repetitions of words and phrases to force readers to look carefully at the words without thinking of them as representations of objects.

- Ernest Hemingway, another stylistic innovator, returned from service in World War I questioning much of what he had been taught about heroism and patriotism. He brought to his writing a journalist's eye for accuracy, stripping away rhetoric that had proved meaningless and creating a crisp and powerful prose style that would influence generations of writers to follow.

- Hemingway's characters search for meaning in exotic locations, such as Spain or the plains of Africa. "The Snows of Kilimanjaro," like much of Hemingway's writing, follows the thoughts of a dissatisfied man looking back on his life and questioning his place in the world.

- F. Scott Fitzgerald also moved to Paris following the war, having made a name for himself in the United States as a chronicler of what he termed the "Jazz Age" with his novel *This Side of Paradise.*

- Fitzgerald's novel *The Great Gatsby* examines the dark underside of the American dream. His work is haunted by loss, a sense that something is lacking in most modern American lives.

PREVIEW

- **Preview the video:** The video focuses on the three experimental prose writers of this period: Gertrude Stein, Ernest Hemingway, and F. Scott Fitzgerald. Responding to the disillusion following World War I and the excesses of the "roaring twenties," these expatriate writers looked for meaning in language and, in the process, profoundly influenced fiction writers who followed. Stein's sometimes incomprehensible prose portraits questioned the function of language and humans' ability to pin down meanings, while Hemingway's pared-down style offered readers what seemed a more accessible presentation of the world than fiction had previously provided. Fitzgerald's work examined the social mores of the "Jazz Age" and highlighted inconsistencies in the "American dream." Paris became a center where these and other authors congregated and helped to foster a flowering of modernist literature and art.

- **What to think about while watching:** What is new about these writers? How do they expand the definition of what it means to be American? How do they respond to the social and political tensions of the time? Ask students to think about why American authors found it easier to write about their subjects in Paris than in the United States. What aspects of these authors' work might have challenged conventions still in force in America?

- **Tying the video to the unit content:** This unit focuses on modernist writing between the world wars. In addition to the three prose writers addressed in the video, less-studied authors such as Sherwood Anderson, Nella Larsen, John Dos Passos, and Susan Glaspell provide further context for the prose that was produced in this period, while Wallace Stevens, Marianne Moore, and Hart Crane furnish examples of experimental poetry at the time. The archive material will allow more detailed consideration of the links between the experiments of writers and artists of the period and provide background information on World War I, mechanization, modern art, Paris, and the transatlantic nature of modernism.

DISCUSSION QUESTIONS FOR THE VIDEO

	What is an American? How does American literature create conceptions of the American experience and identity?	*How do place and time shape literature and our understanding of it?*	*How are American myths created, challenged, and re-imagined through these works of literature?*
Comprehension Questions	What brought the writers featured in the video to Europe?	What impact did World War I have on the thinking and writing of these authors?	What myths of American manhood did writers such as Hemingway believe in, and what shattered these myths?
Context Questions	What about the writing of Stein, Hemingway, and Fitzgerald struck readers as very "new"?	These writers lived much of their lives in Europe, especially Paris. Why did Europe seem more conducive to art than the United States?	In what way was the "Lost Generation" lost?
Exploration Questions	How are Stein, Hemingway, and Fitzgerald commenting on the behavior of Americans? What do they seem to be saying about the country of their birth?	Why do you think Hemingway's style appealed so strongly to his reading public? Why did he have such a pronounced influence on other writers?	What does Fitzgerald's portrayal of the American dream suggest about its viability in the modern world?

	Texts	Contexts
1910s	Gertrude Stein, *Tender Buttons* (1914) Wallace Stevens, "Sunday Morning" (1915) Susan Glaspell, *Trifles* (1916) Sherwood Anderson, *Winesburg, Ohio* (1919)	World War I (1914–18) Modernism in the arts begins around this time; artists and writers take new approaches to their work, often denying historical meanings and methods America officially enters World War I (1917) The 18th Amendment, also called the Volstead Act, is created, beginning Prohibition, which outlaws "the manufacture, sale or transportation of intoxicating liquors" (1919)
1920s	Marianne Moore, "Poetry" (1921) Hart Crane, "Chaplinesque" (1921), *The Bridge* (1926) F. Scott Fitzgerald, "Winter Dreams" (1922), *The Great Gatsby* (1925) Wallace Stevens, "The Emperor of Ice-Cream" (1923) Gertrude Stein, *The Making of Americans* (1925) Nella Larsen, *Quicksand* (1928) Ernest Hemingway, *A Farewell to Arms* (1929)	Women gain the right to vote (1920) Immigration controls are introduced, making it more difficult to enter the United States (1921) Congress officially makes Native Americans U.S. citizens (1924) The first talking film is created, *The Jazz Singer* (1927) Wall Street stock market crash spurs the Great Depression (1929)
1930s	F. Scott Fitzgerald, "Babylon Revisited" (1931), *Tender Is the Night* (1934) Wallace Stevens, "The Snow Man," "Disillusionment of Ten O'Clock," "Gubbinal," "Thirteen Ways of Looking at a Blackbird" (1931) John Dos Passos, *The Big Money* (1936) Ernest Hemingway, "The Snows of Kilimanjaro" (1936)	Franklin Delano Roosevelt is president; in 1933 he begins to implement the "New Deal" (1933–45) The 18th Amendment is repealed to provide jobs (1933) World War II (1939–45)
1940s	Marianne Moore, "Nevertheless" (1941), "In Distrust of Merits" (1944)	The Japanese attack Pearl Harbor, prompting the United States to enter World War II (1941)

AUTHOR/TEXT REVIEW

Gertrude Stein (1874–1946)

Gertrude Stein lived most of her life in Europe, yet considered herself an American, famously declaring that "America is my country and Paris is my hometown." In 1903, after dropping out of medical school, she joined her brother Leo in Paris and began to write. She and her brother began collecting modern art; paintings by Matisse, Picasso, and other avant-garde artists hung on the walls of her studio. In Paris she developed friendships with some of the foremost artists and writers of her time: Picasso, Hemingway, Matisse, and Fitzgerald, among many others. Her home at 27 Rue de Fleurus became a well-known gathering place for the artistic avant-garde as well as intellectuals and up-and-coming writers, who received advice and encouragement from Stein. In 1913 her brother Leo moved out and they divided their art collection. Her longtime companion and lover Alice B. Toklas lived with her from 1909 until Stein's death in 1946, and the two traveled together and hosted artists and expatriates at their house in Paris. Together they served France in both world wars, amassed an impressive collection of modern art, and created a gathering place for literati and artists seeking one another in a time of artistic experimentation.

[4004] Carl Van Vechten, *Portrait of Gertrude Stein* (1935), courtesy of the Library of Congress [LC-USZ62-103680].

Her first published book, *Three Lives* (1909), was composed of three stories written while examining a Cezanne painting and struck her as being "the first definite step away from the nineteenth century and into the twentieth century in literature." In the five hundred novels, stories, articles, plays, and poems Stein would write in her lifetime, she remained committed to experimentation with language and to breaking away from the traditions of the past. Her radical outlook on art and the central role she played in the modern art world made Stein a celebrity in America and Europe, and following World War I, she gave lectures at Oxford and Cambridge, as well as in numerous American cities on a lecture tour in the 1930s.

Stein is known for her radical experiments with language; in *The Making of Americans* (1925) she employs stream-of-consciousness and repetition to draw readers' attention to her language. *Tender Buttons* (1914) likewise challenges readers: Stein invents her own system of language here, and often meaning is not possible to determine. Stein wished to separate language from its use in representing the world of objects in the same way that abstract painters tried to separate painting from representation.

TEACHING TIPS

■ In *Really Reading Gertrude Stein*, poet Judy Grahn offers several suggestions that may help students appreciate what Stein was trying to do with her often confusing prose. Grahn suggests reading Stein's work aloud to help readers appreciate the sound of her writing and to involve them actively in the language Stein chooses. Grahn also cautions against being too serious in one's pursuit of meaning in Stein,

STEIN WEB ARCHIVE

[4003] Carl Van Vechten, *Portrait of Gertrude Stein, New York* (1934), courtesy of the Library of Congress [LC-USZ62-103678]. Stein became a celebrity in the United States and Europe because of her radical experiments with language and her importance to the world of modern art.

[4004] Carl Van Vechten, *Portrait of Gertrude Stein* (1935), courtesy of the Library of Congress [LC-USZ62-103680]. Photograph of Stein standing in front of American flag. Although Stein considered herself American, she lived in Paris, where she offered patronage to many promising expatriate American writers.

[4024] Henri Matisse, *Goldfish and Sculpture (Les Poissons)* (1911), courtesy of the Museum of Modern Art. Painting by modern artist Henri Matisse. Gertrude Stein and her brother Leo began collecting original works of modern art in the early 1900s, including paintings by Matisse and Picasso.

[7849] Linda Watts, Interview: "Gertrude Stein's Relationship to Feminism" (2002), courtesy of Annenberg/CPB. Watts, Interdisciplinary Arts and Sciences director and professor of American studies (University of Washington, Bothell), discusses Stein's feminist beliefs and commitment to women's rights. Although not aligned with the suffrage movement, Stein challenged restrictive gender norms.

[7850] Catharine Stimpson, Interview: "Gertrude Stein, Experimentalism, and Science" (2001), courtesy of Annenberg/CPB. Stimpson, dean of the Graduate School of Arts and Science (New York University), discusses the influence of Stein's scientific training on her literary work, particularly the expectations of trial and error in experiments.

and invites readers to skip around Stein's sometimes exceedingly lengthy meditations on people and objects. She reminds readers that there are ideas lurking behind the jumble of words and recommends paying attention to point of view in particular. It might be useful to tell students that getting a handle on Stein isn't supposed to be easy and that there isn't one right "answer."

■ To help students navigate the repetitious prose of *The Making of Americans*, preview the first few paragraphs in class before you ask students to read the selection in its entirety. A brief introduction to what Stein was trying to accomplish could be followed by a look at what she outlines as her project in the opening paragraphs. You might ask students to speculate about what "it" is in these paragraphs and about why so many people don't want to know "it" and why Stein does.

■ In a consideration of modernism, you might compare Stein's repetition in *The Making of Americans* to Ezra Pound's extremely spare poem "In a Station of the Metro" and ask students to think about how modernism can take such different forms. Ask them to speculate how these different techniques might achieve some similar ends (e.g., working in fragments, and thereby emphasizing the modern sense of perception as fragmentary).

■ *Tender Buttons* can be read as a series of still lifes, or portraits of objects. Traditionally, a still life is a painting of an inanimate object, such as flowers, food, or books. Still lifes allowed artists to demonstrate their skill in representing these objects realistically and by manipulating color, light, and texture. Like elegies, still lifes emphasize life's fleeting qualities and offer a stay against mortality by immortalizing these objects in paint. Using reproductions of modernist still lives by Cezanne, discuss with your students what innovations painters made in this genre in the first decades of the twentieth century. Was the goal to be as realistic as possible? If not, what was the goal of the modernist painter of still lifes? How may you apply these conclusions to the still lifes Stein presents in *Tender Buttons*?

QUESTIONS

Comprehension: Try to pinpoint some of the ways Stein uses the terms she has selected. What exactly does she mean by "repeating," in *The Making of Americans*, for example? What is it exactly that she repeatedly intends to "begin"?

Comprehension: What are the objects examined in *Tender Buttons*? Are there any hints about why they are described as they are? What is "A Piece of Coffee"? Why do you think "A Red Hat" begins, "A dark grey, a very dark grey, a quite dark grey is monstrous ordinarily"?

Context: Much of modern art and literature shows an interest in displaying the world as bewilderingly fractured and fragmented. Consider the fragmentation of Stein's writing in conjunction with a contemporary work of art by a cubist painter and with John Dos Passos's pastiche of headlines and newsreel materials. How do all these works represent the modern world and what comment might they be making on modern modes of living?

Exploration: You might make fruitful comparisons between Stein's *The Making of Americans* and Walt Whitman's *Song of Myself*, which seeks common attributes of humanity while also celebrating diversity. Find passages in both works that suggest to you common threads in the two writers' projects. Where do they diverge?

Susan Glaspell (1876–1948)

Born in Davenport, Iowa, Susan Glaspell grew up in a Midwest that was settled only decades before, but was developing rapidly as the post–Civil War economic boom transformed the United States. After graduating from high school, Glaspell worked as a reporter for the *Davenport Morning Republican* and then for Davenport's *Weekly Outlook*, where she edited the society pages. As a student at Drake University, Glaspell began writing for the college newspaper, and following her graduation became a statehouse reporter for the Des Moines *Daily News*, where she gained familiarity with the workings of American government. After two years as a journalist, she turned her attention to fiction, and her short stories appeared in magazines such as the *Ladies' Home Journal* and *Harper's*. For a short time in 1903, she studied English at the University of Chicago's graduate school. Her first novel, *The Glory of the Conquered*, was published in 1909.

[6016] Arthur Rothstein, *Douglas County Farmsteads, Nebraska* (1936), courtesy of the Library of Congress [LC-USF34-004276-D DLC].

Glaspell gave up journalism in 1901 and returned to Davenport, where she met the free-thinking George Cram Cook, a fellow member of the local progressive organization called the Monist Society. Though Cook was married when they met, he left his wife and married Glaspell, then thirty-six, and together they moved to the East Coast in 1913. Over the next ten years, they lived part of each year in New York's Greenwich Village and part in Provincetown, Massachusetts. Cook was a writer as well as a theatrical director, and the couple helped to found the Provincetown Players, a landmark organization in the development of American theater. The most famous of its members, Eugene O'Neill, authored plays such as *Long Day's Journey into Night* and *The Iceman Cometh*. Glaspell wrote nine plays for the Provincetown Players from 1916 to 1922, including her best-known one-act play *Trifles*. The commercial success of the Provincetown Players in some ways limited the company's ability to experiment, and in 1922 Glaspell and her husband left the group.

Glaspell continued to write through the 1930s and 1940s, publishing drama and fiction and remaining committed to writing experimental and overtly social work. Her play *Alison's Room*, which received the Pulitzer Prize for drama in 1930, follows the struggles of Alison Stanhope, a poet modeled upon Emily Dickinson, and considers the difficulties female artists face as a result of their gender. Much of Glaspell's work considers women's roles in society and the conflicts faced by American women who pursue individual fulfillment. *Trifles* examines the ways that expectations of women can confine them and offers a potential remedy for this problem in the communal efforts of women resisting the traditional roles to which men assign them. Glaspell's focus on the lives of women and their roles in American society challenged conventions of what could be shown on the American stage, and her stylistic innovations and promotion of new experiments in drama helped to shape American theater. After decades of critical neglect, Glaspell's significant contribution to the development of American drama has begun to be recognized.

TEACHING TIPS

■ Like many other female authors writing about women, Susan Glaspell did not receive much critical attention until the "rediscovery" of forgotten texts during the feminist movement of the 1960s and 1970s. *Trifles* is an especially effective play to help students consider what influences both our cultural values and the literary canon: the male characters' dismissal of women's realm of expertise parallels decisions made about what characterizes "great" literature. Students may have difficulty seeing what is at stake in the play's subtle storyline; the "clues" the women find in Minnie Wright's housekeeping may not be immediately obvious to students, as they are not to the men who ignore them. To be certain that they have understood the subtext of the dialogue and stage directions, you might ask students to explain what happens in several of the moments when the female characters discover something that the men cannot see.

■ Ask students to think about the dramatic form and their experience of reading a text that was not meant to be read but performed. You might ask them to consider the added dimensions of authorship in the case of drama: is the author of the script the sole author, or do the director, actors, and set and lighting designers complicate how we assign authorship? Ask them to think about how the dialogue and stage directions move the plot forward, and how the dramatic form shifts the way the story is presented. Glaspell adapted this play to the short-story form in "A Jury of Her Peers," which you might read in conjunction with the play to answer some of these questions.

QUESTIONS

Comprehension: What do Mrs. Peters and Mrs. Hale discover in Minnie Wright's house? How do you explain their decision not to tell the Sheriff and County Attorney about what they found? Why do you think the title of the play is *Trifles*?

Comprehension: According to Mrs. Peters and Mrs. Hale, what is the life of a farmer's wife like? How does the description of the life Minnie Wright must have led help to make sense of her behavior?

Context: At the time this play was produced, the suffrage movement in the United States had come close to reaching its goal: suffrage was granted to women in 1919. What does this play suggest about the way society viewed women and their fields of "expertise" (largely centered in the home)? Why do you think society evaluated women in this way?

Context: Examine the photograph of the "Women's club making a quilt" featured in the archive. What does the image suggest to you about the lives of these people? How does the image help you to understand what Mrs. Hale and Mrs. Peters say about the life of a farm woman?

Exploration: Consider other texts that deal with the challenges women face in their lives. What connections can you draw between *Trifles* and Harriet Jacobs's *Incidents in the Life of a Slave Girl* (1861), Louisa May Alcott's *Work* (1873), Charlotte Perkins Gilman's "The Yellow Wall-paper" (1892), Willa Cather's *O Pioneers!* (1913), and Maxine Hong Kingston's *The Woman Warrior* (1976)? What shapes the female characters' beliefs about themselves and their place in society? How do cultural traditions inform gender roles in these texts?

Sherwood Anderson (1876–1941)

Born in southern Ohio, Sherwood Anderson was the middle child of seven. His father, a harness maker, moved the family around a great deal during Anderson's childhood in search of work. In 1894 the family settled in Clyde, Ohio, which probably served as the model for Anderson's *Winesburg, Ohio*, though Anderson claimed he had no particular town in mind. After working in a variety of jobs and serving in the U.S. Army during the Spanish-American War, Anderson married into a successful business family and began managing businesses himself in 1906. Six years later he left both business and family and moved to Chicago, where he began his literary career. In Chicago he met many writers involved in what became known as the "Chicago Renaissance," including Theodore Dreiser, Edgar Lee Masters, and Carl Sandburg. In 1916 he published his first novel, *Windy McPherson's Son*, about a man who leaves a small town in Iowa to search for the meaning of life. In 1917 he published *Marching Men*, which follows a lawyer's efforts to reform the factory in his town. These works, like much of his other writing, examine individuals' search for meaning in small towns, removed from the developments of modern industry.

Anderson's best-known work is *Winesburg, Ohio* (1919), a collection of connected stories about residents of a small midwestern town. This work applied some of the experimental techniques of modernism (multiple perspectives and an interest in psychology in particular) to

[7201] Dorothea Lange, *Lobby of Only Hotel in Small Town* (1939), courtesy of the Library of Congress [LC-USF34-021148-E DLC].

[3062] Carl Mydans, *House on Laconia Street in a Suburb of Cincinnati, Ohio* (1935), courtesy of the Library of Congress [LC-USF34-000658-D]. Suburban scene of houses, street, and sidewalk. Anderson's most acclaimed work, *Winesburg, Ohio,* was likely based on his own childhood experiences in Ohio.

[5965] Carl Van Vechten, *Sherwood Anderson* (1933), courtesy of the Library of Congress [LC-USZ62-42477]. Photograph of Anderson seated in front of wall of books. Anderson, who frequently wrote about the Midwest, was often considered a regionalist.

[5966] Carl Van Vechten, *Portrait of Sherwood Anderson, Central Park* (1939), courtesy of the Library of Congress [LC-USZ62-117920]. Although Sherwood Anderson is often considered a midwestern regionalist, this photograph was taken in New York, an important center for many modernist writers and visual artists.

[7201] Dorothea Lange, *Lobby of Only Hotel in Small Town* (1939), courtesy of the Library of Congress [LC-USF34-021148-E DLC]. This photograph of a hotel lobby depicts one of the many intimate settings provided by small-town life. Such an environment contrasted sharply with the hustle and bustle of America's rapidly growing cities.

fiction and met with critical praise for its innovation and realism. Anderson's style of storytelling is simple, though the ideas his work contains are complex; following the lives of characters repressed by a society unsympathetic to individual desire, the stories reveal the inner workings of characters in conflict with societal expectations. Reviewing *Winesburg, Ohio*, a *Chicago Tribune* writer noted that "Mr. Anderson is frequently crude in his employment of English; he has not a nice sense of word values; but he has an intense vision of life; he is a cautious and interpretative observer; and he has recorded here a bit of life which should rank him with the most important contemporary writers in this country." H. L. Mencken called the book "some of the most remarkable writing done in America in our time."

None of Anderson's many subsequent publications proved as successful as *Winesburg, Ohio*. He published numerous novels and collections of stories and essays in the next two decades, including the novels *Poor White* (1920), *Many Marriages* (1923), and *Beyond Desire* (1932), as well as the short-story collections *The Triumph of the Egg* (1921) and *Horses and Men* (1923). The simplicity of his prose style and his choice of subject matter influenced many writers who followed him, most notably Hemingway and Faulkner, but these writers tended to belittle his contribution to literature and to their own work. Anderson died of peritonitis en route to South America on a goodwill trip.

TEACHING TIP

■ Students may find Anderson's spare tales confusing; their lack of narrative commentary and surprising plot developments might leave students wondering about "the point" of each story as well as the collection as a whole. You might start a class on these texts by addressing students' confusion, finding out what perplexed them about these characters' behavior, and asking them to speculate on what Anderson might be exploring in these plot twists. They will likely begin to notice that the three main characters have somehow been thwarted in the attainment of their desires and lash out in helpless protest against the restrictions in their lives.

QUESTIONS

Comprehension: What does Elizabeth Willard want for her son George? Why does she want "to cry out with joy" at the end of the story and why has "the expression of joy . . . become impossible"?

Comprehension: What troubles Elmer in "Queer"? Why is he so threatened by George Willard? What is he trying to escape at the end of the story?

Context: What links these stories together? What picture do they draw of the pressures of living in a small town?

Exploration: Sherwood Anderson's fiction may in part be considered "regionalist," writing that tends to look at areas of America removed from the more settled and populated areas of the

Northeast. What links do you see between *Winesburg, Ohio* and earlier stories we now label as "regionalist"? What connections can you make to the work of Sarah Orne Jewett and Mary Wilkins Freeman, for example, or to that of other writers in Unit 8? Where do Anderson's stories seem to diverge from the work of earlier regionalists?

Wallace Stevens (1879–1955)

Wallace Stevens grew up in Pennsylvania and attended Harvard University for three years, leaving in 1897 to pursue a career as a writer. At the age of twenty-one, he joined the editorial staff of *The New York Tribune*, but discovered that he did not enjoy journalism. A year later he enrolled at New York Law School and was admitted to the Bar in 1904. He became a member of the legal staff of the Hartford Accident and Indemnity Company in 1916 and remained with the company until he died in 1955. He prospered with the company and became vice president, all the time working on his writing. In 1914, he began publishing his poetry in the popular "little magazines" of the period. He joined the literary culture of New York City in the early part of his career and became friends with such figures as Marianne Moore and William Carlos Williams.

Harmonium (1923), his first published collection, sold fewer than one hundred copies but was reviewed favorably and established Stevens as a leading poet of his day. His second volume of poetry, *Ideas of Order*, did not appear until 1935, and in 1936 he followed it with *Owl's Clover*. *The Man with a Blue Guitar* was published in 1937, *Parts of a World* in 1942, *Transport to Summer* in 1947, and *The Auroras of Autumn* in 1950. His work is characterized by an interest in imagery and an attention to language, often revealing his belief that much of human meaning was created in the act of regarding the material world. In response to the modernist suspicion that humans could be sure of nothing, Stevens emphasized the importance of the activity of perception; though our perception is always extremely subjective, it is nonetheless meaningful. In "Thirteen Ways of Looking at a Blackbird," for example, the speaker takes pleasure in the different ways one may perceive a single object. In a world where religion had lost its force, Stevens believed that an appreciation of beauty—of nature, of music, of language—might help to reestablish human faith.

Three works in particular have received extensive critical attention: "Sunday Morning," in which a woman enjoys a Sunday at home rather than worshipping in church, and "The Comedian as the Letter C" and "Peter Quince at the Clavier," which consider the life of the mind and the life of the senses, locating meaning within appreciation of the world. Stevens's wit, insight, and careful diction earned him a place as one of the foremost poets of the twentieth century.

[6041] Paul Cezanne, *Bend in the Road* (1900), courtesy of the National Gallery of Art.

TEACHING TIPS

■ Though students may find Stevens's poetry difficult, some of the ways his poems engage the central concerns of modernism are quite

[6041] Paul Cezanne, *Bend in the Road* (1900), courtesy of the National Gallery of Art. Wallace Stevens argued that human faith could be found in the appreciation of beauty in nature, music, and art, rather than religion.

[8009] Gottscho-Schleisner, Inc., National Fire Group, Hartford, Connecticut, *Long View of First-Floor Office* (1942), courtesy of the Library of Congress [LC-G613-T-41579]. Poet Wallace Stevens earned his living at an office building like this: the Hartford Accident and Indemnity Company in Hartford, Connecticut, where he worked from 1916 until his death.

accessible. To help students better understand the issue of multiple perspectives, ask them to explain why the speaker of "Thirteen Ways of Looking at a Blackbird" feels it is important to look at the blackbird from so many different vantage points. You might include a creative response to help them further appreciate the idea of perspective by asking them to compose a similar poem of their own.

■ You might include Stevens in a consideration of other modern poets who use material objects to comment on the human condition in the modern world. The poetry of William Carlos Williams or Marianne Moore, for example, would help to elaborate on the modernist search for meaning in a world that challenges humans' ability to locate it.

QUESTIONS

Comprehension: Several of Stevens's poems question the possibility of finding meaning in one's life. What is meant by "the nothing that is" in "The Snow Man"? What is the significance of the statement "The only emperor is the emperor of ice-cream" in "The Emperor of Ice-Cream"? What do you think the speaker is disillusioned about in "Disillusionment of Ten O'Clock"?

Comprehension: What is "Sunday Morning" saying about organized religion and the individual's pursuit of pleasure? What is the significance of the question "What is divinity if it can come / Only in silent shadows and in dreams"?

Context: Consider what "Gubbinal" and "Thirteen Ways of Looking at a Blackbird" seem to be saying about the possibility for human objectivity. How might you interpret these poems as being especially modernist in their outlook on the primacy of individual perception? Do you see connections between this interest in multiple perspectives and the work of modern artists, such as Picasso, Duchamp, or Braque?

Exploration: Do you see similar concerns in Stevens's poetry as in T. S. Eliot's or Marianne Moore's? What issues seem to preoccupy these and other modernist poets? Do other writers (poets and fiction writers) from this time period or other time periods also seem concerned with these issues?

Marianne Moore (1887–1972)

Moore, like many other authors in this unit, was born in the Midwest but eventually settled in the East. She graduated from Bryn Mawr College in 1909, and, after traveling for two years with her mother abroad, taught at the Carlisle Indian School in Pennsylvania for four years. She continued to live with her family and in 1916 moved with her mother to Brooklyn, New York, to be with her brother, who was a minister there. In New York, Moore worked as a teacher and librarian, all the while producing poetry. Her first poems came out in "little magazines" such as *Poetry* and *Egoist*, and her connections with them introduced her to the artistic avant-garde. Unknown to Moore, in 1921 the poets H.D. and Winifred Bryher published her volume *Poems*. In 1924 Moore published another collection, *Observations*, which received the *Dial* magazine award for poetry. Moore became editor of the *Dial* in 1925 and remained there until the magazine ceased publication in 1929. Her work on the *Dial* introduced her to many key literary figures of the time, including Ezra Pound, Hart Crane, and James Joyce. Though she did not write much poetry while editing the *Dial*, her work for the magazine helped to sharpen her critical abilities, and her next book, *Selected Poems* (1935), is considered one of her most important. This volume contained some of her best-known poems, including "The Jerboa" and "Poetry." Moore was also an insightful critic and published many essays of literary criticism. In 1951 Moore's *Collected Poems* won the Pulitzer Prize, the Bollingen Prize, and the National Book Award, and she became something of a celebrity; the Brooklyn Dodgers, a baseball team Moore followed avidly, once asked her to throw out the ball that would open their season.

Moore's poetry is characterized by an attention to careful observation of the natural world in an attempt to find new connections between poetry and the world. She includes many references to scientific and historical texts that inform her thinking about the natural world; notably, she avoids literary allusions that would link her poetry to a literary tradition. Her verse structure and meter are subtle and complex, and readers must look carefully to understand her formal and linguistic choices. She came to favor a simpler style of diction in her later work, and her language is considerably more ornate in her earlier poems than in her later ones. In the face of World War II, many of Moore's poems became more social in theme, expressing her desire that humankind would work toward becoming more humane. In her poem "In Distrust of Merits," for example, she posits that the mutual distrust that promotes war may be overcome, suggesting that "contagion of trust can make trust." She asks readers to look inward to understand the causes of war and offers hope that if one can win internal battles, war may be averted in the future.

[4011] Carl Van Vechten, *Portrait of Marianne Moore* (1948), courtesy of the Library of Congress [LC-USZ62-42513].

TEACHING TIPS

■ Moore's poetry is a good place for students to start thinking about the different ways in which poems can be organized. For example, poems may be structured around a description, story, meditation, or argument. Choose a poem by Moore that has a more straightforward narrative, such as "A Grave" or "Baseball and Writing," and divide it into three to five parts that you feel correspond to the structural divisions of the poem. The more advanced students are, the more parts you can divide the poem into. Break students into groups and give each group one segment of the poem and ask them to determine where in the order of the poem the passage falls. Ask them to support their claim by hypothesizing about *why* they believe it is a particular section of the poem and what beginnings, middles, or ends usually look like. After having made their own claims, groups should talk with one another to compare passages and to determine the relationship between the various sections. This can be followed by a full class discussion of the poem and an analysis of one of Moore's more difficult structures, such as "Poetry" or "The Paper Nautilus."

■ The absence of specifically female experience in Moore's poetry is also worth noting and may become more apparent to students when contrasted to the work of Sylvia Plath or Anne Sexton, for example. Students might discuss why Moore felt that her identity as a woman and her identity as a poet were incompatible and then examine how her work takes on experiences that can be generalized to all of humankind, rather than focusing on the experience of women.

QUESTIONS

Comprehension: After reading "Poetry," consider what Moore says about why readers should care about poetry. What does she believe makes certain kinds of poetry important? What would she classify as "not poetry"?

Comprehension: What is "In Distrust of Merits" about? According to Moore, how does war happen? What does she mean in the last stanza of the poem when she says that "There never was a war that was / not inward"?

Context: How does Moore's poetic form communicate ideas differently than if, for instance, these poems were written as essays? What can "Nevertheless" or "In Distrust of Merits" achieve in poetic form that it could not attain as prose? How do the rhyme and rhythm of the poems influence your reading of them?

Context: In "Poetry," Moore describes how some poetry becomes too far removed from the things that are truly important and useful. Consider some of the other modernist poems you have read (by Eliot or Pound, for example); what do you believe Moore (or the speaker in this poem) would think about poems that rely heavily on literary allusions?

Exploration: Moore was a mentor to the poet Elizabeth Bishop, which Bishop acknowledges in her poem "Invitation to Miss Marianne Moore." Both poets are known for their animal poems, some of which are odes, poems that use the subject or occasion for the poem to investigate the potential power of the poet. Compare Bishop's "The Fish" to Moore's "To a Snail." What attracts the speaker of the poem to these animals? To what extent is the animal or the viewer of the animal like a poet? From what source does the power of the poet arise? What are the limitations of this power?

Nella Larsen (1891–1964)

Nella Larsen, like *Quicksand*'s Helga, was born to parents of different races: her father was West Indian and her mother was Danish. After her father died (when Larsen was two), her mother married a white man and raised Larsen in an all-white environment. Her adopted family was embarrassed by her dark skin, and Larsen always felt that she did not belong. From 1907 to 1908 she studied at a high school associated with Fisk University. She left Fisk and spent the next three years with relatives in Denmark, auditing classes at the University of Copenhagen. In 1912 she returned to the United States and pursued a nursing degree and career in New York. She married Elmer Samuel Imes, an African American physicist who worked at Fisk University. Larsen gave up nursing in 1922 and worked for the New York Public Library. She became involved with the artistic community in Harlem, and four years later, she decided to pursue a career as a writer.

Larsen completed two novels—*Quicksand* (1928) and *Passing* (1929), about a light-skinned black woman passing herself as white—which the prestigious publishing firm Alfred A. Knopf published. She was assisted by a white patron of Harlem Renaissance writers, Carl Van Vechten, himself the author of the controversial novel *Nigger Heaven*. While many believed that a celebration of the "primitive" aspects of African American culture benefited the advancement of the race, others thought that the depictions of blacks, and especially black women, in Van Vechten's and other authors' works contributed to a construction of racial identity that severely limited possibilities for African Americans.

Quicksand wrestles overtly with this problem of establishing an "authentic" racial identity: Helga prizes much about upper-class white culture, but also longs to understand and appreciate those things that distinguish African Americans. Throughout the novel, the mixed-race Helga finds herself torn in her loyalties and disconnected from both whites and blacks.

Larsen's novels were well received, and in 1930 she was awarded a Guggenheim fellowship in creative writing, the first African American woman to win one. She went to Spain to work, but she published little after receiving the award. One short story drew allegations of plagiarism, and Larsen probably stopped writing as a result of the controversy over her work. She returned to nursing and withdrew from the literary circles of which she had been a part. Her novels were largely forgotten until they were reissued in 1986, when her reputation as a significant Harlem Renaissance writer was revived.

[4553] James Allen, *Portrait of Nella Larsen* (1928), courtesy of the Library of Congress.

TEACHING TIPS

■ *Quicksand* would work well in conjunction with a unit on the Harlem Renaissance as well as one on modernism. You might teach this novel and the concerns it raises about black identity and sexuality together with Langston Hughes's "I, Too," or "Mulatto," or works by Zora Neale Hurston, Countee Cullen, or James Weldon Johnson's *Autobiography of an Ex-Colored Man*. *Quicksand* also shares many concerns with Harriet Jacobs's *Incidents in the Life of a Slave Girl*, and if you are reading *Uncle Tom's Cabin*, you might also consider how mixed-race women's sexuality is constructed (for more on the figure of the "tragic mulatta," see Unit 7). If you read *Quicksand* in the context of other Harlem Renaissance writers, you may want to spend some time giving students a sense of Harlem society in the 1920s. You could begin with a discussion of the "Great Migration" of African Americans

[4553] James Allen, *Portrait of Nella Larsen* (1928), courtesy of the Library of Congress. Author of *Quicksand*, Larsen wrote novels and short stories that explore the intersection of race, class, and gender. She composed during the Harlem Renaissance.

[7405] Carl Van Vechten, *Portrait of Josephine Baker* (1949), courtesy of the Library of Congress [LC-USZ62-93000]. Photograph of performer Josephine Baker in Paris. A major center for modernist artists, Paris was thought to be less restrictive than America.

[7406] *Duke Ellington, half-length portrait, seated at piano, facing right* (1965), courtesy of the Library of Congress [LC-USZ62-123232]. Photograph of jazz musician Duke Ellington playing the piano. Rhythms and images from jazz influenced writers and visual artists of the Harlem Renaissance.

[7408] Carl Van Vechten, *Portrait of Bessie Smith Holding Feathers* (1936), courtesy of the Library of Congress [LC-USZ62-94955]. Writers and musicians of the Harlem Renaissance debated how to best depict African Americans, especially in terms of gender. Some were influenced by primitivism, or an emphasis on earlier African images.

to the North and especially to northern cities as background for the coalescence of African American culture. The archive contains some photos you may want to assign or look at together in class; juxtaposing these with Larsen's descriptions of the activity and night life of Harlem could help locate Helga in a historical moment. For specific suggestions, see Unit 10.

■ *Quicksand* shares with other works in this unit a character's sense of alienation from America and search abroad for an environment more conducive to self-development. Like the selections by Fitzgerald and Hemingway, *Quicksand* concludes rather bleakly—Helga's attempted improvement of her life ends in ultimate failure, as do Dexter's, Charlie's, and Harry's. You might consider discussing with your class how Helga's difficulty adapting herself to American society differs from the problems the white authors explore.

■ You'll probably want to go over the varying positions different characters (Helga, Anne, Dr. Anderson, etc.) take on the "race problem," articulating the tenets of "uplift" and the concern that middle-class blacks were in danger of losing touch with their heritage. You may want to ask why certain characters find it intolerable to socialize with whites, even those sympathetic to the struggles facing African Americans. You might extend this discussion to consider contemporary viewpoints on African American identity and white America.

QUESTIONS

Comprehension: What does Helga find so objectionable about Naxos? What does she find appealing about social life in Harlem? Why do you think she tires of Harlem?

Comprehension: Helga wonders, "why couldn't she have two lives?" What are the two lives she wishes to lead and why do they seem to her so incompatible?

Comprehension: The furnishings of rooms and the clothing people wear receive a great deal of attention in this novel. What do furniture and clothing tell us about these characters? What is the impact of these descriptions on our understanding of the values and aspirations of Helga in particular?

Context: The novel begins with a poem by Langston Hughes about "Being neither white nor black." Why do you think Larsen presents Helga as being *neither* rather than being *both*?

Context: Bessie Smith's music is widely available. Compare her self-presentation in music and in the Van Vechten photo to that of Nella Larsen and her character. How does Smith's presentation of African American identity or culture complicate or contradict that presented in *Quicksand*?

Exploration: *Quicksand* follows Helga Crane's search for a place where she belongs. Consider how other works you've read also chronicle people's searches to find somewhere they feel at home. How are Helga's concerns similar to or different from those of the characters in Sherwood Anderson's *Winesburg, Ohio*, the speaker in

T. S. Eliot's "The Love Song of J. Alfred Prufrock," the narrator in Charlotte Perkins Gilman's "The Yellow Wall-paper," or other characters in works you've read? How do the issues raised in this novel contribute to your understanding of the work of other Harlem Renaissance writers such as Jean Toomer, Langston Hughes, Claude McKay, or Countee Cullen?

Exploration: Consider *Quicksand* in conjunction with Alice Walker's short story "Everyday Use." What does *Quicksand* have to say about the preservation of ethnic heritage, and how does Walker's story respond? These works were written over four decades apart; what seems to be different for the characters in Walker's story and what seems to have remained the same?

F. Scott Fitzgerald (1896–1940)

F. Scott Fitzgerald's best-known work, *The Great Gatsby*, has made him familiar to generations of students of American literature. Though the book sold poorly when it was first published, it has since become one of the most widely read American novels and justified Fitzgerald's reputation as one of the foremost chroniclers of the 1920s, which he famously labeled the "Jazz Age."

Fitzgerald was born in St. Paul, Minnesota, and educated primarily in East Coast schools. He attended Princeton University for three years, leaving without his degree to enlist in the U.S. Army during World War I, though peace was declared before he could see combat. While stationed in Alabama, he met and courted Zelda Sayre, who initially rejected him. He went to New York in 1919 to seek his fortune as a writer and to win over Zelda. His first novel, *This Side of Paradise*, became a best-seller and made Fitzgerald an overnight sensation; one week after its release he married Zelda. In addition to giving him fame and wealth, the book seemed to speak for the generation of which Fitzgerald was a part, and Fitzgerald's next books, two short-story collections called *Flappers and Philosophers* (1921) and *Tales of the Jazz Age* (1922), solidified his reputation as an insightful narrator of the social world of the 1920s.

Fitzgerald and Zelda lived well on the proceeds of these books and a second novel, *The Beautiful and Damned*, published in 1922. The couple had a daughter in 1921; in 1924 they moved to Europe to economize after several years of lavish living. In Europe they associated with other expatriate American writers, including Gertrude Stein, Ezra Pound, and Ernest Hemingway. While living in Paris, Fitzgerald composed *The Great Gatsby* (1925), the story of a self-made millionaire who pursues a corrupted version of the American dream, dealing in not-quite-legal businesses to make his fortune and win back the woman he loves.

Despite his success as a writer, Fitzgerald had difficulty getting out of debt, though he wrote prolifically and published short stories in

[4893] Anonymous, *(F. Scott) Fitzgeralds on a Street in Paris*, courtesy of Princeton University Library.

[4879] Anonymous, *F. Scott Fitzgerald* (1919), courtesy of Princeton University Library. Portrait of F. Scott Fitzgerald. Fitzgerald attended Princeton for three years before enlisting in the U.S. Army during World War I.

[4893] Anonymous, *(F. Scott) Fitzgeralds on a Street in Paris*, courtesy of Princeton University Library. Photograph of Fitzgerald with his wife, Zelda, and their daughter, Scottie, in an urban street scene. Fitzgerald was an expatriate American author who lived and wrote in Paris.

[4905] Anonymous, *F. Scott Fitzgerald with Friends in Freshman Dinks* (1913), courtesy of Princeton University Library. Photograph of Fitzgerald with two male classmates at Princeton, all wearing college jackets. Fitzgerald often wrote about educated and wealthy Americans.

[7822] Emory Elliot, Interview: "F. Scott Fitzgerald and the American Dream" (2001), courtesy of Annenberg/CPB. Elliot, professor of English at the University of California, Riverside, discusses Fitzgerald's mixed emotions concerning the American Dream. Some scholars argue that Fitzgerald's novel *The Great Gatsby* describes the corruption of this dream.

[7823] Catharine Stimpson, Interview: "F. Scott Fitzgerald's Alienation and Drinking" (2001), courtesy of Annenberg/CPB. Stimpson, dean of the Graduate School of Arts and Science, New York University, discusses heartbreak, drinking, and masculinity in the work and life of Fitzgerald and his contemporaries.

high-paying magazines such as the *Saturday Evening Post*. He abused alcohol, and in 1930 Zelda suffered a mental breakdown, which would lead to her spending much of the remainder of her life in mental institutions. After the stock market crash of 1929, Fitzgerald, like many other American expatriates, returned to the United States, where he wrote and published a fourth novel, *Tender Is the Night* (1934), which chronicles the decline of a young American psychiatrist, Dick Diver, whose marriage to a dependent patient interferes with his career. Though critics generally praised the novel, it sold poorly, and Fitzgerald tried screenwriting. He completed only one full screenplay, *Three Comrades* (1938), and was fired because of his drinking, which eventually ruined his health. He died of a heart attack when he was only forty-four.

TEACHING TIPS

■ The nuanced social interactions and high cultural styles that Fitzgerald describes in *The Great Gatsby* will probably seem somewhat alien to your students. In order to dramatize these scenes, you might show excerpts from the 1974 film version of the novel, starring Robert Redford and Mia Farrow, and ask students to compare their own visualizations of the scenes with the depictions in the movie. Have them focus on Fitzgerald's use of narrative point of view in one or more scenes, and ask them how it affects the presentation of these scenes in the film. Broaden the question to ask students about the significance of translating this novel—and other works, both popular and classic—into film versions.

■ Because *The Great Gatsby* is written in such a clear and evocative way, students may initially have trouble questioning the effects of Fitzgerald's use of language and other literary conventions such as point of view. Have students focus on certain descriptions—of setting, character, or even of mannerisms detailed in dialogue—and ask them to explain how the descriptions function to convey meaning in the novel. Additionally, ask students to imagine the story of *The Great Gatsby* retold from the point of view of a character other than Nick Carraway. How would such a change affect the structure of the narrative?

QUESTIONS

Comprehension: What about Judy Jones so fascinates Dexter in "Winter Dreams"? What in Judy's attitude attracts (or repels) Dexter? Why does the narrative describe her house repeatedly?

Comprehension: Though Dexter succeeds brilliantly in New York, we discover at the end of the story that his "dream was gone," that a part of himself has somehow been lost. What do you think Dexter has lost? Why does he come to recognize this after hearing about Judy seven years after he left Minnesota?

Comprehension: By calling his story "Babylon Revisited," Fitzgerald asks readers to compare the ancient city of Babylon—famed for its wealth and decadence, which eventually led to its downfall—to Paris in the 1920s. Why do you think Charlie's return to Paris to retrieve his daughter is a revisiting of Babylon?

Context: While wandering through early 1930s Paris, Charlie reflects on the way he lived there before the 1929 stock market crash. In retrospect, how does he view his conduct when he was wealthy and seemingly carefree? In light of what you've read about the 1920s and the stock market crash, what does this story appear to be saying about the lives many Americans lived after World War I?

Exploration: Consider other stories and poems that look back with longing or regret to a time past. Consider "Birches" by Robert Frost or "The Snows of Kilimanjaro" by Ernest Hemingway—why do you think these texts dwell on this sense of loss and remorse? Are there historical events or cultural developments that help to explain this shared preoccupation?

John Dos Passos (1896–1970)

John Dos Passos is one of the most overtly political authors in this unit. Involved in many radical political movements, Dos Passos saw the expansion of consumer capitalism in the first decades of the twentieth century as a dangerous threat to the health of the nation. The son of unmarried Portuguese American parents, Dos Passos grew up in Chicago. He attended prestigious East Coast schools, first the Choate School and then Harvard University. He graduated from Harvard in 1916 and joined the war effort before the United States entered World War I, becoming a member of a volunteer ambulance corps and later serving in the American medical corps.

Following the war he became a freelance journalist, while also working on fiction, poetry, essays, and plays. He wrote a novel drawing on his war experiences, *Three Soldiers* (1921), but his 1925 novel *Manhattan Transfer* established him as a serious fiction writer and displayed many techniques that writers who followed him would emulate. Political reform underwrote much of his fiction, and in 1926 he joined the board of *The New Masses*, a Communist magazine. Though not a party member, Dos Passos participated in Communist activities until 1934, when the Communists' disruption of a Socialist rally convinced him that the Communists were more concerned with achieving power than with the social reform about which he cared passionately.

From 1930 to 1936, Dos Passos published three bitingly satirical novels about contemporary American life, *The 42nd Parallel*, *1919*, and *The Big Money*, an excerpt of which is discussed in this unit. Together the novels form a trilogy called *U.S.A.*, and they attack all levels of American society, from the wealthiest businessman to the leaders of the labor movement. Dos Passos believed that American society had been thoroughly corrupted by the greed its thriving capitalist system promoted, and he saw little hope for real reform of such an entrenched system. His novels experimented with new techniques, especially drawing on those of the cinema, a relatively new cultural form (see the Context "Mass Culture Invasion: The Rise of Motion Pictures," Unit

[7200] Jack Delano, *Portrait of a Coal Miner* (1940), courtesy of the Library of Congress [LC-USF34-041334-D].

DOS PASSOS WEB ARCHIVE

[5940] Dorothea Lange, *Labor Strikes: NYC* (1934), courtesy of the National Archives and Records Administration [NLR-PHOCO-A-71134]. Labor demonstration on New York City street. John Dos Passos wrote explicitly political novels and argued that the greed encouraged by capitalism was destroying America.

[7200] Jack Delano, *Portrait of a Coal Miner* (1940), courtesy of the Library of Congress [LC-USF34-041334-D]. Photograph of a coal miner in work clothes. Authors such as John Dos Passos wrote about working-class people and labor rights.

[7423] Anonymous, *Harvard Hall, Harvard University, Cambridge, Mass.* (1935), courtesy of the Library of Congress [LC-USZ62-94158]. John Dos Passos attended prestigious schools on the East Coast, including Choate and Harvard University. Graduating from college in 1916, he joined the volunteer ambulance corps and served in World War I.

[7426] Herbert Photos, Inc., *Bartolomeo Vanzetti and Nicola Sacco, manacled together* (1927), courtesy of the Library of Congress [LC-USZ62-124547]. Sacco and Vanzetti, Italian immigrants and anarchists, surrounded by a crowd of onlookers and guards before entering a Dedham, Massachusetts, courthouse. In a series of incidents representative of the first American "red scare," these political radicals were accused of murder and received the death penalty, despite a lack of evidence.

13). His "Newsreel" sections mimic the weekly newsreels shown before films at local cinemas, blending together a patchwork of clips from newspapers, popular music, and speeches.

Dos Passos's politics shifted radically following World War II, as he saw the political left, with which he had identified himself, becoming more restrictive of individual liberty than the political right. His trilogy *District of Columbia* (1952) reexamined American society from this new perspective, attacking political fanaticism and bureaucracy.

TEACHING TIPS

■ Students will likely be bewildered by the opening sections of the selections "Newsreel" and "The Camera Eye." Encourage them to note what the headlines are about and to see trends in the snapshots. They should eventually see that many of the headlines are about labor struggles and many others are about money-making and business. This should lead them to realize that these issues are very much interrelated. The relationship between the wealthy and the struggling workers will arise again in the "Mary French" section, and Dos Passos will not make explicit what he is saying about these coexisting groups. Students should speculate on what Dos Passos implies about the parallel lives of the wealthy and poor that intersect in the character Mary French. Some background on capitalist expansion and the labor movement would be useful to help students understand what exactly is at stake in the work that Mary does and in the description in "The Camera Eye."

■ A look at modern art, especially political art, would work well with this selection. The collages of Picasso and Braque, for example, demonstrate visually the fragmentation associated with modernity that appears in the "Newsreel" pastiche. You might break students into groups to look at different images together and make connections to the Dos Passos excerpt. You might also ask them about the role of popular culture in the making of art and discuss why taking clips of songs and newspapers (which Picasso's collages, for instance, also do) and pasting them together should be considered art.

QUESTIONS

Comprehension: What are the different attitudes toward the labor movement espoused by different characters in *The Big Money*?

Comprehension: How do the three sections—"Newsreel," "The Camera Eye," and "Mary French"—work in conjunction with one another? What links between and among them do you see? How does the "Mary French" section develop the ideas briefly enumerated in the headlines of the "Newsreel"? What do the parallel lives of the labor activists and the New York elite say about one another? Why do you think Dos Passos draws them together in this section?

Context: Like Nella Larsen's *Quicksand*, this story examines an individual as well as a large social movement. What do these two narratives suggest about the way individuals must wrestle with their personal lives in the context of their involvement in larger social movements?

Context: Other works in this and other units use the form of the pastiche—the patching together of disparate elements, often with the intention of parodying the sources—that Dos Passos employs in the "Newsreel" section. Why do you think Dos Passos and authors such as T. S. Eliot and Gertrude Stein use this technique? What is the effect of jumbling together seemingly unrelated materials, and what does this technique achieve that could not be achieved any other way?

Exploration: Much modern art also patches together disparate elements to create a whole, as Dos Passos does in *The Big Money*. Take a look at some collage images. Picasso and Braque were especially fond of this technique and exhibited some of these works in the Armory Show of 1913. Do you see similarities between their work and Dos Passos's? What could their preference for such a technique be saying about modernity?

Ernest Hemingway (1899–1961)

Hemingway once stated that his goal as a writer was to create "one true sentence." The characteristic pared-down style he developed influenced a number of subsequent authors. Known for his emotionally recalcitrant characters, Hemingway created stories of men proving themselves in physically demanding conditions and trying to come to grips with a world that after the horror of World War I seemed largely out of their control.

Born and raised in a Chicago suburb, Hemingway was one of six children. His father was a doctor and his mother a schoolteacher. Following graduation from high school, Hemingway worked as a reporter for the *Kansas City Star*, but remained there only a few months. The eighteen-year-old Hemingway intended to join the army when the United States entered World War I in 1917, but a problem with his eye disqualified him. Instead, he became a volunteer ambulance driver in Italy and later served in the Italian infantry. He was wounded by shrapnel not long after and carried a fellow soldier to safety despite his own serious injury. This event profoundly influenced his future thinking about himself and his place in the world; brushes with death and the idea of wounds, both physical and psychological, would haunt his later fiction. As the first American wounded in Italy, Hemingway became known as a hero, which also became part of the persona he adopted in ensuing years. After only six months abroad, he returned to the United States, feeling that he had changed significantly while America had not. He became a correspondent for the *Toronto Star* and in 1920 married Hadley Richardson. The couple moved to Paris, where Hemingway met many significant literary figures, including

[3841] Anonymous, *Young Hemingway (far right) with His Family* (1906), courtesy of the John F. Kennedy Library.

[3841] Anonymous, *Young Hemingway (far right) with His Family* (1906), courtesy of the John F. Kennedy Library. Photograph of Ernest Hemingway as a child with his father, mother, brother, and sister. His family was wealthy and lived in a suburb of Chicago where residents generally espoused conservative politics. Hemingway's mother would dress him in girl's clothing well into his childhood.

[3850] Anonymous, *Hemingway in His World War I Ambulance Driver's Uniform* (1917), courtesy of the John F. Kennedy Library. Posed portrait of Hemingway in military dress. Hemingway incorporated into his works the brutality he witnessed during World War I.

[3854] Anonymous, *Hemingway Trying His Hand at Bullfighting in Pamplona, Spain* (1924), courtesy of the John F. Kennedy Library. Gelatin silver print of Hemingway in Spain. Bullfighting figures prominently in Hemingway's novel *The Sun Also Rises*.

[3860] Anonymous, *Hemingway on Safari in East Africa* (1934), courtesy of the National Archives and Records Administration, the John F. Kennedy Library. Hemingway posing with large antlers from animal carcass. Death and injury were important themes in Hemingway's writing, possibly due to the injuries he received and witnessed as an ambulance driver during World War I.

[4408] Anonymous, *Ernest Hemingway 1923 Passport Photograph* (1923), courtesy of the National Archives and Records Administration. Hemingway was one of many American authors who worked in Europe. The expatriate artists claimed that Europe offered freedom from restrictive American mores.

[5980] ABC Press Service, *Scene During the Siege of Teruel, Spain* (1938), courtesy of the Library of Congress [LC-USZ62-112445]. Photograph of fighting, casualties, and old building in Teruel, Spain. Teruel was the site of a Republican victory in the Spanish Civil War. Hemingway supported the Republicans, writing *The Fifth Column* to promote their cause.

Gertrude Stein and Ezra Pound. Stein especially encouraged his literary efforts. Sherwood Anderson and F. Scott Fitzgerald read his work, gave him advice, and helped secure the publication of *In Our Time*, a collection of his stories.

The novel that established his reputation as a literary figure, however, was *The Sun Also Rises*, published in 1926. Written in what would become known as the "Hemingway style," the novel's terse prose and dialogue would pave the way for a new style of fiction writing, stripped-down and spare in comparison to the novels that preceded it. *Men without Women*, another collection of short stories, was published in 1927. *A Farewell to Arms*, about an American officer's romance with a British nurse, appeared in 1929. Hemingway's interest in politics heightened in the 1930s; between 1936 and 1939 he served as a newspaper correspondent in Spain, covering the Spanish Civil War, the setting of his novel *For Whom the Bell Tolls* (1940). During World War II he again served as a correspondent, and following the war he settled in Cuba. His marriage to Hadley broke up in 1927; he married three more times.

While traveling in Africa in 1953, Hemingway survived a plane crash, which injured him badly. His health was never fully restored, and in the 1950s, despite winning the 1953 Pulitzer Prize for *The Old Man and the Sea* and the Nobel Prize for literature in 1954, Hemingway suffered from recurrent bouts of depression as well as paranoia. He committed suicide in 1961, at the age of sixty-two.

TEACHING TIP

■ "The Snows of Kilimanjaro" is a good text to use for considering how Hemingway defines masculinity. The places described in the story are largely places lacking women, places where men may prove themselves physically and mentally. Yet the story is ultimately about man's helplessness and powerlessness; as in other Hemingway works written following World War I (for example, *The Sun Also Rises*), masculinity is not particularly secure, and Hemingway's writing seeks to come to grips with this loss of power and control. Students may want to speculate about Harry's relationship with and attitude toward his wife and other women in his past.

QUESTIONS

Comprehension: Like Hemingway, the main character of "The Snows of Kilimanjaro" is a writer. What does the story suggest about the way writers think? What is the significance of the subjects Harry wants to address in his writing? How do you interpret the settings of the stories he wishes to write and the setting in which he is dying? What could the dream at the end of the story mean? What is the significance of his going to Kilimanjaro?

Comprehension: Hemingway was known for his stylistic innovations. In this story, he uses italics to construct a parallel narrative to the primary one. How do the italicized and un-italicized sections of the story work together? How are their styles different? What is revealed in the italicized sections that does not appear elsewhere?

Context: Harry is dying from gangrene that developed from a trivial and untreated scratch. What does this cause of death say about the masculine valor Harry prizes? Look at other post–World War I texts that deal with manhood and its relation to death, such as T. S. Eliot's "The Hollow Men" or E. E. Cummings's "next to of course god america i." What commentary do these works make on the amount of power and control men have over their lives?

Exploration: What modernist techniques does this story employ? What do you see in the narrative structure or style as specifically modernist? Consider this work in conjunction with T. S. Eliot's *The Waste Land* or "The Love Song of J. Alfred Prufrock" or the spare poetry of William Carlos Williams.

[5981] Arribas, *18, Julio* (1937), courtesy of the Library of Congress [LC-USZC4-3911]. Propaganda poster showing civilian with gun in front of ghost of soldier. On July 18, 1936, the Spanish Civil War began and Barrio, of the Republican Party, became prime minister.

[7824] Emory Elliot, Interview: "Hemingway's Masculinity" (2001), courtesy of Annenberg/CPB. Emory Elliot, professor of English at the University of California, Riverside, hypothesizes about why masculinity was such a significant issue in Ernest Hemingway's life and work.

Hart Crane (1899–1932)

Though Hart Crane only lived thirty-three years, the rich poetry he produced provides readers with an alternative view of modernity—his poems seek connectedness and optimism in a world many of his contemporaries saw as fragmented and hopeless. His life was not an easy one; his relationship with his parents was strained, he drank heavily, and he was homosexual at a time when homosexuality was not openly discussed, much less tolerated. Born in Ohio, Hart Crane moved to New York at the age of eighteen to pursue a career as a writer. Two years later, he returned to Ohio to try his hand at business in order to support himself while he worked at the craft of writing. Though he was not especially successful in business, in his four years in Cleveland Crane developed friendships with a variety of intellectuals and published several of the poems that established his literary reputation. "Chaplinesque" appeared in 1921 and "For the Marriage of Faustus and Helen" was published in 1922. In 1923 he returned to New York City to begin his writing career in earnest.

His first four years in New York were very productive: he finished his sequence *Voyages* and in 1926 published his first collection of poetry, entitled *White Buildings*. Ten of the fifteen poems that constitute his long work *The Bridge* were also completed during this period. Though he worked occasionally, he was supported primarily by friends and family, in particular a banker named Otto Kahn, who became something of a patron.

Crane thought of himself as a visionary in the tradition of the celebratory optimism of Walt Whitman. Crane was interested in the methods of modernism, but did not share completely the modernist pessimism about the state of the contemporary world. Rather than bemoan the loss of a time past, Crane's work sought affirmation and hope in the fabric of everyday life. In *The Bridge*, Crane employs the Brooklyn Bridge as a symbol to suggest the unifying potential of the

[7194] Samuel H. Gottscho, *New York City Views. Financial District, framed by Brooklyn Bridge*, courtesy of the Library of Congress [LC-G612-T01-21249].

[6027] Walker Evans, *Portrait of Poet Hart Crane* (1930), courtesy of the Library of Congress [LC-USZ62-122934]. Crane lived in New York City and socialized with important literary figures, including E. E. Cummings and Jean Toomer.

[6287] Frank Pearsall, *Walt Whitman, half-length portrait, seated, facing left, left hand under chin* (1869), courtesy of the Library of Congress [LC-USZ62-89947]. Modernist poet Hart Crane considered himself an artist in Whitman's tradition of optimism and exuberance. Both tried to represent the vastness of America in life and modernity.

[6548] A. E. Marey, *Going to See Chaplin* (1920), courtesy of the Gazette du Bon Ton. Line outside theater in Paris. Technology made movies available to mass audiences and facilitated popular culture, which often crossed national boundaries. Hart Crane's poem "Chaplinesque" referenced Charlie Chaplin, a popular comic actor.

[7194] Samuel H. Gottscho, *New York City Views. Financial District, framed by Brooklyn Bridge,* courtesy of the Library of Congress [LC-G612-T01-21249]. Hart Crane used the Brooklyn Bridge to represent modernization's unifying potential, while some authors perceived technology and urbanization to be fragmenting.

[7656] Anonymous, *Charlie Chaplin in The Vagabond* (1916), courtesy of the Library of Congress [LC-USZC4-6636]. In his poem "Chaplinesque," Hart Crane explored Chaplin's comic grace.

modern world: the bridge links far-flung reaches of the United States in a celebration of the possibilities of America and its people. Published in 1930, the poem did not receive favorable reviews from critics. It won an award from *Poetry* magazine, however, and Crane received a fellowship from the Guggenheim Foundation that year as well. Nonetheless, Crane was uncertain about his career in literature, and on his return from Mexico, where he had been working on another book, he jumped from the ship and drowned.

TEACHING TIPS

■ *The Bridge* could be fruitfully paired with Whitman's *Song of Myself* or "Crossing Brooklyn Ferry," as both poets aim to encompass and represent all aspects of America and American life. Ask students to find parallels in imagery, structure, and ideology between Crane's and Whitman's poems. Ask them to consider the difference between the symbol of the bridge as that which links times and places together as opposed to Whitman's use of himself as the connector of people from different times and places.

■ Because Crane uses visual references as touchstones for his poems, you might want to make your class's study of his work multimedia. The archive provides an image of the Brooklyn Bridge, which was constructed in the 1880s, when it was an engineering feat that surpassed all previous bridge construction and joined two of the most populous cities in the world. Consider presenting this information to extend your students' thinking about Crane's choice of the bridge as a symbol. Also ask them to consider the form of the Brooklyn Bridge, which, despite its modern construction, employs an almost medieval architectural vocabulary. You might also show a clip from a Charlie Chaplin film in conjunction with Crane's "Chaplinesque" and ask some of the same questions—what is it about this icon of silent film that appeals to Crane? How might Chaplin's body movements and the plots he involves himself in be attractive as a subject for poetry?

QUESTIONS

Comprehension: What does the speaker admire about Charlie Chaplin in "Chaplinesque"? What is the significance of the kitten in this poem? What do you think is meant by the assertion that the moon can "make / A grail of laughter of an empty ash can"?

Context: Look at photographs of the Brooklyn Bridge and read Crane's poem about it. Why does this bridge function as an effective symbol for Crane? What is the poem saying about contemporary American society? What is its attitude toward modernization?

Context: Crane's poetry relies heavily on metaphor, which he believed gave poetry its power to communicate with a reader. Choose a metaphor from one of Crane's poems and another from a poem by Marianne Moore. How do the two poets use these metaphors as vehicles for their ideas? What makes these metaphors effective? What similarities and differences do you see in the poets' approaches?

Exploration: Read Walt Whitman's "Crossing Brooklyn Ferry" and consider what it has in common with Crane's *The Bridge*. Do you see similarities in their outlook on modern life? Both employ symbols of modernity—the ferry, which brings commuters to work in Manhattan, and the Brooklyn Bridge, which joined Brooklyn to Manhattan three decades after Whitman first published his poem. Why do you think both poems are set in this space between two cities? What does each poem say about the possibilities for connection between people? About the relation of the present to the past?

Suggested Author Pairings

NELLA LARSEN, F. SCOTT FITZGERALD, SHERWOOD ANDERSON, AND SUSAN GLASPELL

All these authors comment on the status of American society, criticizing the ways individuals are restricted by their race, gender, class, or personal desires. Set in very different locations, these authors' works allow students to reflect on some of the different ways society may limit the individual. You might use Fitzgerald's *The Great Gatsby* to consider more fully the limitations of the American dream suggested by "Winter Dreams" and consider how gender complicates the limits on individual desires in *Trifles* and *Winesburg, Ohio. Quicksand* permits a discussion of the effects of both gender and race on the individual's pursuit of self-fulfillment. These texts may also be linked with texts from other units: you could pair some of Larsen's criticisms of race in America with those leveled by Harlem Renaissance poets such as Langston Hughes and Claude McKay. Glaspell's play connects well to several feminist authors in the nineteenth century; Fanny Fern's short essays and Charlotte Perkins Gilman's "The Yellow Wall-paper" might usefully extend your discussion of restrictions placed upon women. You might also select works that query how men are likewise limited by gender: Hemingway's *The Sun Also Rises*, John Cheever's "The Swimmer," and Raymond Carver's "Cathedral" would allow students to discuss how gender stereotypes may inhibit men as well as women. Anderson's stories would likewise complement this discussion, as *Winesburg, Ohio* examines the frustration of characters of both sexes.

GERTRUDE STEIN, JOHN DOS PASSOS, AND ERNEST HEMINGWAY

These authors' works highlight some of the stylistic innovations of modernism. Stein's idiosyncratic use of language, Dos Passos's inclusion of "newsreel" and "camera eye" materials, and Hemingway's nonlinear narrative all demonstrate some of the experiments being made by writers after World War I. These innovators in prose could also be taught with the most innovative of the modernist poets, Eliot, Pound, and perhaps Williams. Class discussion might focus on the different types of experimentation found in this prose and poetry, from choice of word to subject matter to form. These authors' works could also be paired fruitfully with some archive images of modern art. This juxtaposition would allow students to consider the breaks with tradition, the fragmentations of perspectives, and the celebrations of streamlined forms that were concurrently taking place in modern art.

HART CRANE AND JOHN DOS PASSOS

These writers employ popular culture in their work, and you might create a multimedia unit in which you pair a screening of a Charlie Chaplin film such as *The Kid* (1921) with a reading of "Chaplinesque." Dos Passos's work incorporates the newsreel, and again you might bring footage to class for students to watch. Ask students to think about the intersections of popular culture and art, and about how the newsreel material of *The Big Money* functions with respect to the rest of the novel. Several William Carlos Williams poems also reference popular culture, especially advertising, and you might also discuss some of the collage art of the cubists that incorporates remnants of newspapers and packaging.

WALLACE STEVENS, ERNEST HEMINGWAY, AND NELLA LARSEN

These authors all examine crises of faith and the difficulty of establishing meaning in the modern world. You might look at how the quest for meaning is treated differently in Stevens's poetry, Hemingway's short story, and Larsen's novel. "The Snows of Kilimanjaro" layers questions about meaning over concerns about authorship and artistic creativity, and *Quicksand* layers questions about personal identity and faith with those of race in America. This questioning of faith might also be traced through works in other units, especially in the modern poets Robert Frost and Langston Hughes.

SHERWOOD ANDERSON, MARIANNE MOORE, AND GERTRUDE STEIN

These writers employ something of a scientific approach to the world, observing people and objects carefully in their poetry and prose. Discussion might include a focus on individual psychology in the work of Stein and Anderson and the investigation of human nature in the works of Moore. Stein's portraits and descriptions focus less on the person or thing being described than on the variety of words one might use to describe them; the emphasis is on the language of communication rather than the information to be communicated. In contrast to Stein's treatment of the language of individual consciousness, Moore's poems seek universal truths and examine the vastly different effects of social forces on individuals.

CORE CONTEXTS

The War to End All Wars: The Impact of World War I

Considered by contemporary observers to be "the war to end all wars," World War I radically shifted the way people thought about the world and the relationships between different nations. Beginning as a localized conflict between Austria and Serbia, the war escalated through a series of complex treaties and agreements among thirty-two nations of Europe, all of which would eventually become involved in the war. Technological innovations had changed the face of warfare, which was now fought

[6972] National Photo Company, *Tank ploughing its way through a trench and starting toward the German line, during World War I, near Saint Michel, France* (c. 1918), courtesy of the Library of Congress [LC-USZ62-115011].

from a distance with bombs and poison gas. Opposing armies dug trenches on either side of contested areas of land, and soldiers found they could do little but wait for attack. The unimaginable horror of trench warfare—with the incredibly destructive bombs and deadly gas falling on soldiers waiting in wet and rat-infested holes—left a lasting impression on the soldiers lucky enough to return from the war. A new postwar condition emerged called "shell-shock"; many men returning home found themselves angry, depressed, confused, and haunted by nightmares of what they had seen on Europe's battlefields. Casualties reached staggeringly high numbers; it seemed that an entire generation of young men had died in the gruesome battles fought over mere yards of muddy ground. Ten million died in battle and twenty million more died of disease and hunger as a result of the war. Following the war, a severe flu epidemic spread around the globe as men returned home, and twenty million people died from complications associated with the flu.

In America, World War I had a lesser impact, though its effects were certainly felt. The American poet E. E. Cummings claimed that "World War I was the experience of my generation." Led by President Woodrow Wilson, the United States tried to maintain its isolation from the distant battles of European nations, believing America should not embroil itself in European squabbles. By 1917 the devastation that Europe had suffered along with the building pressure to protect U.S. economic interests in Europe swayed public opinion to support the war and "make the world safe for democracy." Despite patriotic propaganda, however, only 73,000 men volunteered to fill the million-man quota, and Congress called for a draft.

Support for America's late entrance into the European war was hardly unified: in response to the criticism leveled at the government by numerous socialists, intellectuals, pacifists, and isolationists, the Espionage Act of 1917 made it a criminal offense to speak out against the war. The hypocritical patriotism promoted by the government angered dissenters, who claimed that the war was yet another opportunity for big business to protect and expand itself at the expense of common soldiers who went to die on distant battlefields. Socialist

[6966] James Montgomery Flagg, *The Navy Needs You! Don't Read American History—Make It!* (1917), courtesy of the Library of Congress [2001700115].

[6971] Underwood and Underwood, *Learning of German retreat from her district, French woman returns to find her home a heap of ruins* (1917), courtesy of Library of Congress [LC-USZ62-115012].

"WAR TO END ALL WARS" WEB ARCHIVE

[6115] Charles Gustrine, *True Sons of Freedom* (1918), courtesy of the Library of Congress [LC-USZC4-2426]. Photograph of segregated African American regiment during World War I. African American soldiers often worked for civil rights both during and after their military service.
[6556] Vincent Aderente, *Columbia Calls* (1916), courtesy of the Library of Congress [LC-USZC4-8315]. Propaganda poster calling for Americans to enlist to fight in World War I.
[6963] American Lovers of Italy, *Ambulances in Italy, 1917* (1917), courtesy of the Library of Congress [LC-USZC4-7387]. Many modernist writers, including John Dos Passos and Ernest Hemingway, served as ambulance drivers or in other capacities during World War I.
[6965] Committee on Public Information, *Under Four Flags*, Third United States Official War Picture

agitator Charles Schenck distributed leaflets protesting the war and calling the draft "involuntary servitude" against which the Constitution was supposed to protect Americans. He called the draft "a monstrous deed against humanity in the interests of the financiers of Wall Street" (Zinn 356). The Espionage Act denied rights to free speech protected by the Constitution, but the Supreme Court nonetheless upheld the act, and objectors were jailed.

Historian Howard Zinn describes the war as a powerful unifying tool for a country split by class conflict and racial tensions; both before and after the war, the country seemed to many on the brink of revolution. (See Unit 12 for more on socialism and unions in the early twentieth century.) In contrast, many of the writers covered in this unit felt strongly about service to countries struggling to defend themselves, and some participated in the war even before the United States entered it: Hemingway, Stein, and Dos Passos all volunteered to drive ambulances in Europe, and Fitzgerald enlisted in the U.S. Army in 1917. Novelist Edith Wharton, then residing in France, also worked to help war refugees, for which she was awarded the Legion of Honor by the French government.

Fifty thousand American soldiers died in what became known as "The Great War" and those who returned home shared the disillusionment of their European counterparts. Many wrote about the war in the years following. It seemed proof positive that the frightening trends of modernization, advances in science and technology in particular, had terrifying and unimaginably destructive consequences. T. S. Eliot's *The Waste Land* depicts the world as a place devoid of life or meaning, a waste land not unlike the stretches of ground that separated opposing armies, over which they meaninglessly fought and refought, moving a few yards forward, only to be driven back, move forward, and be driven back again. Reporting in Europe generally neglected to mention the carnage on the battlefields, and the public was largely unaware of the extent of the destruction and the comparatively small gains made in return for the thousands of lives lost in each battle.

At the end of the war, the triumphant Allies—chief among them England, France, and the United States—demanded reparations from the defeated countries, especially Germany. Unable to make the reparation payments, Germany's economy collapsed. The harsh terms of the Treaty of Versailles in 1919 set the stage for Germany's aggressions leading up to what would become World War II.

Both during and after World War I, European and American writers expressed disillusionment with the lofty ideals that had led them into battle. In Britain a number of young writers such as Wilfred Owen and Sigfried Sassoon wrote poetry in response to what they had seen on the battlefields of France. E. E. Cummings—who, like Hemingway, Dos Passos, and Anderson, served as an ambulance driver in France— wrote "next to of course god america i," which questions the blind patriotism that young men like himself had been encouraged to feel. Their ideals shattered, young writers returning from war appeared to Gertrude Stein a "lost generation," a generation whose worldview had been radically altered by the most horrifying and destructive war anyone had yet experienced. The work these writers produced demonstrates their belief in the world as an uncertain and often illogical place, and their fiction and poetry often employ a similarly disorienting structure. By breaking with traditions of narrative and poetic form, these authors attempted to capture in the very fabric of their writing the confusion and dislocation fostered by modernity.

QUESTIONS

Comprehension: Why did World War I have such a pronounced impact on writers and thinkers? What made this war different from previous wars?

Comprehension: Examine the poster advertising war bonds located in the archive. How does this image appeal to its viewers? Why do you think this image was selected by the government? What does the text tell you about contemporary attitudes toward the war?

Comprehension: In Wallace Stevens's "Death of a Soldier," what is the speaker's attitude toward the death of this soldier? What does the poem seem to be saying about war in general? How does what you know about World War I help to explain this attitude?

Context: Read E. E. Cummings's "next to of course god america i." Pick out the different references to popular songs and sayings and consider what juxtaposing them in this way does to their meaning. What does the poem say about the popular rhetoric of patriotism? What is its attitude toward war?

Context: Though Hemingway's "The Snows of Kilimanjaro" is set in Africa, in Harry's flashback, readers get glimpses of his experiences in the war. How do the scenes of war figure in this story? How are they described and why do you think they are included in this story of a man dying in Africa? What comment do they make on war?

Context: Look at Robert Frost's poem "Fire and Ice" or T. S. Eliot's *The Waste Land*. Is there a way to read these poems as commenting on the war or its aftermath? What could Frost be saying about human nature and the effects of our actions or inactions? How does Eliot present the world he depicts? Why do you think the outlook of the poem is so bleak?

Exploration: Think of movies you've seen that depict wars. Consider different time periods: from *Birth of a Nation* (1915) to *All Quiet on the Western Front* (1930) to *Sergeant York* (1941) to *Paths of Glory* (1957) to *M*A*S*H* (1970) to *Platoon* (1986) to *Saving Private Ryan* (1998). How do these or other war movies you've seen portray war? Are conflicts shown as opportunities to demonstrate valor or pointless fights that ultimately achieve nothing (or a combination of both)? Which portrayals do you think are currently most accepted by society at large, and what do you think influences societal beliefs about war? How do you explain the shifting attitudes toward war represented in these films?

Exploration: Consider how World War I was presented to you in the history classes you've had. Did your class cover the protests against

(1918), courtesy of the Library of Congress [LC-USZC4-947]. Poster for U.S. World War I propaganda film. The U.S. government tried to sway public opinion in favor of fighting with the Allied powers.

[6966] James Montgomery Flagg, *The Navy Needs You! Don't Read American History — Make It!* (1917), courtesy of the Library of Congress [2001700115]. Recruitment poster showing businessman, sailor, and female figure with American flag. Reversing its previous policy of isolationism, the government solicited volunteers for World War I.

[6971] Underwood and Underwood, *Learning of German Retreat from Her District, French Woman Returns to Find Her Home a Heap of Ruins* (1917), courtesy of Library of Congress [LC-USZ62-115012]. Photograph of seated woman looking at the ruins of her home in the Somme region. Bombing damaged and destroyed many buildings in Europe. Images such as this illustrated the dangers of technology and modernization.

[6972] National Photo Company, *Tank Ploughing Its Way through a Trench and Starting toward the German Line, during World War I, near Saint Michel, France* (c. 1918), courtesy of the Library of Congress [LC-USZ62-115011]. Black-and-white photograph of a tank on a World War I battlefield. Devastation amplified by mechanized weapons and the horror of trench warfare created a sense of disillusionment in many modernist writers.

[6973] Central News Photo Service, *Another Sort of War Ruin—After Several Days in the Trenches* (1918), courtesy of the Library of Congress [LC-USZ62-115013]. Photograph of badly wounded soldier, assisted by comrade. Although many Americans approached World War I with optimism, their experiences with brutal trench warfare and mechanized weaponry were disillusioning.

[7669] William Allen Rogers, *Buy a Liberty Bond To-day!* (1918), courtesy of the Library of Congress [CAI-Rogers, no. 232]. War bonds were an important way to rally nationalism as well as raise money for war efforts. Here the artist uses a melting pot motif to enlist the aid of recent immigrants. Originally published in the *New York Herald*, May 1, 1918, p. 5.

[7803] Pancho Savery, Interview: "The Lost Generation Writing on World War I and Alienation" (2001), courtesy of Annenberg/CPB. Savery, of Reed College, discusses modernist writers' loss of innocence when faced with the brutal warfare of World War I and suggests that this disillusionment marks a break between the modern and Victorian eras.

[8246] George M. Cohan, *Over There!* [title page] (1917), courtesy of the Digital Scriptorium Rare Book, Manuscript, and Special Collections Library, Duke University. Title page for the sheet music to the song that rallied the nation to take action in World War I. Cohan also composed "You're a Grand Old Flag" and "Give My Regards to Broadway."

the war? If not, why do you suppose history books would leave out such things as the Espionage Act and the people who were imprisoned for violating it?

Exploration: Examine the images of World War I soldiers and battlefields included in the archive. How are these pictures presenting scenes of war? What do they seem to be asking the viewer to think and feel? Find other images of war you've seen in contemporary magazines and compare them to the World War I images. What has changed about the way war is presented visually to the public? What has remained the same? You might also look at some of the earliest photography of war: pictures of the Civil War. How was the camera being used to present war to newspaper readers?

Modernity and Technology: The Age of Machines

Americans' fascination with and dependence upon a variety of machines was well established by the closing years of the nineteenth century; in the early years of the twentieth century, this fascination only deepened as technological innovation became more and more widespread. Most major cities relied on some form of mechanized public transit to get residents from one side of growing metropolises to the other, and more Americans bought the automobiles Henry Ford turned out at astonishing rates. There were only eight thousand automobiles in America in 1900, and by 1920 there were more than eight million. By 1940 that number had risen to thirty-two million. Electricity became more common: in 1917, only 24 percent of homes in America were electrified, and in 1940, almost 90 percent were.

In his discussion of the machine age aesthetic, art historian Richard Guy Wilson contends that in America the machine became an integral part of the lives of a wider segment of society than was the case in Europe, infiltrating not only the workplace, but the home as well: refrigerators (up to seven million in 1934 from only sixty-five thousand in 1924), vacuum cleaners, and apartment building elevators became increasingly commonplace. The number of telephones jumped from one million in 1900 to twenty million in 1930, allowing Americans from far-flung parts of the country to communicate with one another. The radio, introduced in the 1920s, only enhanced the interconnectedness of Americans and their access to information and entertainment. (For more on the impact of the radio on American culture and poetry, see "Broadcasting Modernization: Radio and the Battle over Poetry" in Unit 10.)

[7033] Wilbur Wright, Orville Wright, Major John F. Curry, and Colonel Charles Lindbergh, who came to pay Orville a personal call at Wright Field (1927), courtesy of the Library of Congress [LC-DIG-ppprs-00765].

The development of the film industry likewise brought the "moving pictures" to an ever-widening audience, which increasingly looked to Hollywood for cues that would determine cultural values. With the advent of sound at the end of the 1920s, film became one of the major venues of American culture and Hollywood's influence expanded to become international in scope.

In 1903, brothers Wilbur and Orville Wright proved that man could fly; in Kitty Hawk, North Carolina, Orville had a successful flight of twelve seconds. In 1927 Charles Lindbergh completed the first transatlantic airplane flight, which took him more than thirty-three hours. After landing in Paris, he became an international hero and celebrity, one of the multiplying cultural links between the United States and Europe in an age of ever-faster international movement of people and ideas.

Literary critic Cecilia Tichi has argued that the machine age fundamentally changed the ways people viewed and thought about the world around them, as the human body itself came increasingly to be perceived as functioning like a machine. The efficiency expert Frederick Taylor developed a system to maximize profits by making factory workers as interchangeable as the parts in the machines they operated; as men and women came to be treated as interchangeable parts, their job security also lessened, for any worker could easily be replaced, a benefit for factory owners, but a significant disadvantage to the worker. These changes in the workplace certainly help to account for the rise in union membership coincident with the rise of **Taylorism**.

The power and possibility embodied by machines captured the imagination of everyday people, and especially fascinated artists and writers. The poet Hart Crane, for example, found the Brooklyn Bridge a compelling symbol of the possibility of the United States; his selecting a structure that represented the beginnings of American technological expertise and innovation suggests his belief in the potential of the machine-made world. Painters likewise turned to the machines of the early twentieth century for inspiration, finding the power and speed of machines appealing and adapting the streamlined look of ships and cars to their own work. Charles Sheeler, a painter and photographer working in the early twentieth century, likened the heavy machinery of industry to the massive architecture of European cathedrals, asserting that "Our factories are our substitutes for religious expression."

Architecture was also profoundly influenced by the possibilities opened up by machines, and city "skyscrapers" began to reach higher and higher. In 1909, the highest building in the world was the Metropolitan Life Tower, reaching 700 feet. In 1929, the Chrysler Building towered over it, its peak at an astounding 1046 feet. (It remained the tallest building in the world for only one year; the Empire State Building surpassed it in 1931.) The Chrysler Building, constructed for the Chrysler motorcar corporation, had a celebration of the machine built into its very fabric: architectural details used automotive motifs, and decorative elements were shaped like wheels and hood ornaments. The machine aesthetic influenced other areas of design as well,

[7024] Nathan Sherman, *Work with Care* (c. 1937), courtesy of the Library of Congress [LC-USZC2-1172 DLC].

[7032] Samuel H. Gottscho, *New York City Views. From foot 32 E.R., to Chrysler, Derrick boom* (1932), courtesy of the Library of Congress [LC-G612-T01-17832].

[4737] William France, *New York City, Northeast View from the Empire State Building* (1931), courtesy of the Library of Congress [LC-USZ62-118869]. New York City's skyline symbolized the economic and technological developments that encouraged taller buildings and urbanization.

[4766] Aaron Douglas, *The Judgement Day* (1927), courtesy of The Walter O. Evans Collection of African American Art. Aaron Douglas, American (1899–1979). Gouache on paper; 11 3/4 x 9 in. Douglas's painting incorporated images from jazz and African traditions, including music and dancing.

[4841] Ben Shahn, *Vacuum Cleaner Factory, Arthurdale, West Virginia* (1937), courtesy of the Library of Congress [LC-USF33-006352-M5]. Arthurdale was one of three New Deal subsistence farm projects in Preston County, West Virginia. Farming was intended to supplement other opportunities, such as in this vacuum factory or in the Mountain Craftsmen's Cooperative Association. Vacuum cleaners were a popular new item in the late 1920s and 1930s.

[4848] Jack Delano, *Blue Island, Illinois. Switching a Train with a Diesel Switch Engine on the Chicago and Rock Island Rail Road* (1943), courtesy of the Library of Congress [LC-USW3-026606-E DLC]. The Chicago and Rock Island Rail Road Company began operation in 1848. The 1930s saw the development of a lighter diesel engine capable of producing more horsepower that in turn brought great innovations to freight trains and streamlined "lightweight" passenger trains.

[6547] Anonymous, *Miss Katherine Stinson and Her Curtiss Aeroplane* (1910), courtesy of the Library of Congress [LC-USZ62-106324]. Curtiss biplane and early aviator Stinson (1891–1977), the fourth licensed woman pilot in the United States, was a talented stunt pilot who carried air mail, raised over two million dollars for the Red Cross, and trained pilots for the U.S. Air Force.

[6898] Anonymous, *Charles Lindbergh, Full-Length Portrait, Standing, Facing*

underpinning what came to be known as **art deco**, a streamlined style that drew on the vocabulary of machines, which designers applied to furniture, interior design, appliances, and jewelry. Music also experimented with the application of machine aesthetics to orchestral pieces, and works such as George Antheil's 1925 "Ballet Méchanique" were performed around the country.

The machine also demonstrated its tremendous power not only to create but to destroy in World War I, where distant machines lobbed powerful explosives at enemies too far away to see. Rather than facing individual enemies on the battlefield, combatants in World War I dug trenches and waited for shells and gas to drop on them, and the resulting casualties were gruesome and more numerous than in any previous war. No one had imagined that such horror was possible, and the dangers that modern mechanization imposed on humanity suddenly became apparent.

QUESTIONS

Comprehension: Why do critics call the early twentieth century the Machine Age? What made machines so significant at that moment in time?

Comprehension: What are some of the effects of the proliferation of machines after the turn of the century? How did they change the way people lived their day-to-day lives?

Comprehension: What values are promoted by the machine aesthetic? What do you see in the details of the Chrysler Building, for example, that demonstrates these values?

Context: How does the Brooklyn Bridge function as a symbol in Hart Crane's *The Bridge*? What attitudes does the poem express about the place of machinery in contemporary life?

Context: How do the images in the archive (the Aaron Douglas paintings, for example) respond to the machine aesthetic? How do they employ the vocabulary of machinery and to what effect?

Context: How are the lives of the characters of Fitzgerald's "Winter Dreams" affected by the machinery in it? What do the cars and boats that form part of the background say about Dexter and Judy Jones? (You might also consider this question in relation to Fitzgerald's novel *The Great Gatsby*.) What does this suggest to you about the role of machinery in the lives of the wealthy? Of the poor?

Exploration: Look at the advertisements included in the archive that juxtapose human bodies with machines. Why do you think this might be an attractive marketing strategy? Can you think of recent advertisements that ask consumers to think of their bodies in this way?

Exploration: How do different early-twentieth-century texts depict machines? Consider some of the novels, stories, and poems you've read from the first decades of the century—how does Fitzgerald portray the automobile in *The Great Gatsby*? What is the attitude expressed about machinery in Robert Frost's poem "Out, Out—"?

What is the function of the telephone in Dorothy Parker's story "The Telephone Call"? Do you see parallels in literature from other times or other nations? British novelist E. M. Forster's *Howards End*, for example? What do these connections suggest to you about the relationship of humans to machines?

Cultural Change, Cultural Exchange: The Jazz Age, the Depression, and Transatlantic Modernism

Popular history depicts the inter-war period as a time of raucous frivolity, speakeasies, flappers, and stock market millions. Indeed, unemployment during the 1920s in America was relatively low; some made sizable fortunes by speculating on Wall Street; and women wore shorter dresses and enjoyed a certain degree of freedom. But only an elite few enjoyed the easy lifestyle portrayed in overly nostalgic looks back at this decade; in America in the 1920s, one-tenth of a percent of the wealthiest families made as much money each year as 42 percent of the poorest families. Wealth was not enjoyed equally by everyone, and the twenties also witnessed growing numbers of labor strikes and a rise in what was called **nativism**, a preoccupation with protecting the interests of "native-born" Americans against those of increasing numbers of foreign immigrants. In 1924, the Immigration Act capped the number of immigrants permitted to enter the United States, particularly those from countries with cultures deemed unassimilable: while 34,000 British immigrants were allowed to enter, only 100 could come from any African nation or China.

At the same time in Europe, a spirit of experimentation and artistic freedom prevailed, and many artists moved abroad to find places to live that were more conducive to their work than the conservative and restrictive United States. These American expatriates contributed to the renovation of art and literature termed **modernism**. The label "modernist" applies to works of literature, art, and music produced during this time period that in a variety of ways reflect a "modern temper." Such work is characterized by a sense of loss, alienation, or confusion caused by changes in the social and physical world that served to dislocate individuals from traditional understandings of how the world functioned. Modernist works tend to break with conventions governing art: modernist writers often shied away from conventions of chronology, point of view, and coherence; modernist artists dismissed traditional conventions of representation, depicting fragmented and abstract images; composers rejected rules about melody and harmony. Much in modern society—moral values, gender roles, connection to one's work—seemed to have splintered apart, and modern art in some ways represented this sense of fragmentation. Marcel Duchamp's *Nude Descending a Staircase* provides a visual image of this fragmentation; John Dos Passos's pastiche of story and newspaper headlines textually represents a fragmented world.

Modernism was an international phenomenon. In the early twenti-

Front, Beside the Spirit of St. Louis (1927), courtesy of the Library of Congress [LC-USZ62-93443]. Lindbergh became an international celebrity after he completed the first transatlantic flight.

[7024] Nathan Sherman, *Work with Care* (c. 1937), courtesy of the Library of Congress [LC-USZC2-1172 DLC]. This woodprint was created as part of the Works Progress Administration (WPA) Federal Art Project. The WPA provided over nine million people with sustaining wages by employing them to build roads, beautify buildings, play concerts, and write histories, along with a wide range of other activities. President Roosevelt's plan was to provide multiple forms of relief to the unemployed.

[7032] Samuel H. Gottscho, *New York City Views. From Foot 32 E.R., to Chrysler, Derrick Boom* (1932), courtesy of the Library of Congress [LC-G612-T01-17832]. As technology developed, buildings grew taller and became known as "skyscrapers," making the modern cityscape profoundly different from the cityscapes of earlier ages.

[7033] Wilbur Wright, *Orville Wright, Major John F. Curry, and Colonel Charles Lindbergh, Who Came to Pay Orville a Personal Call at Wright Field* (1927), courtesy of the Library of Congress [LC-DIG-ppprs-00765]. These aviation and military leaders, photographed at Dayton, Ohio, helped mobilize developments in transportation, such as airplanes and automobiles, which facilitated cultural exchange between distant locations and contributed to a sense of rapid change.

[7194] Samuel H. Gottscho, *New York City Views. Financial District, Framed by Brooklyn Bridge,* courtesy of the Library of Congress [LC-G612-T01-21249]. Hart Crane used the Brooklyn Bridge to represent modernization's unifying potential, while some authors perceived technology and urbanization to be fragmenting.

[7479] Ford Motor Company, *Ford Automobile, Made between 1900 and 1920* (c. 1915), courtesy of the Library of Congress [LC-USZ62-118724]. The Ford Motor Company made automobiles available to more people, mass-producing and selling them for affordable prices.

[6548] A. E. Marey, *Going to See Chaplin* (1920), courtesy of the Gazette du Bon Ton.

[3547] Anonymous, *Louis Armstrong, Half-length Portrait, Facing Left, Playing Trumpet* (1937), courtesy of Library of Congress [LC-USZ62-118974].

eth century, travel and communication became increasingly easy, promoting the exchange of ideas among artists. Writers and artists in diverse countries answered the call to make a new kind of art for a new kind of world. They sought artistic inspiration from the cultural capitals of Europe; Fitzgerald, Hemingway, Stein, Anderson, Cummings, Joyce, and Picasso all lived and worked in Paris, which at the end of the nineteenth century had become a center for avant-garde art. Modernist artists of diverse nationalities worked in New York, Paris, and London, among a variety of other locations, and modernist thought traveled freely back and forth across the Atlantic and the borders of Europe through individuals and a vast array of publications. Paris was certainly a center for much of this thought, but modern art appeared in numerous other places, and modern architecture redefined cityscapes throughout the United States and Europe.

Nineteen thirteen was a watershed year for modernism: in New York, the Armory Show introduced abstract art to the American public, and in Paris music and dance took on new forms with the riot-provoking ballet *The Rite of Spring*, with its jarring music and erotic choreography. In her autobiography, arts patroness Mabel Dodge opined, "It seems as though everywhere, in that year of 1913, barriers went down and people reached each other who had never been in touch before; there were all sorts of new ways to communicate as well as new communications. The new spirit was abroad and swept us all together." In 1923, the sense that something important was happening in the world of letters that involved both Europe and America prompted Ford Madox Ford to start a magazine called *Transatlantic Review*, featuring the work of the multinational writers then residing, like Ford, in Paris.

European writers and artists also looked to other traditions for inspiration, especially in the cultures of Africa and Asia. Several historians have noted the significant influence of African American art and culture on the development of modernism. In part, modernists looked to the **primitive** as an antidote to the modern world and saw in African art and in people of African descent a link to a primordial past (for more on primitivism, see Unit 10). African American performers and writers found greater acceptance in Europe; Parisian audiences were fascinated by the new dance and music coming from performers Josephine Baker and Paul Robeson.

In 1929 the New York stock market crashed, wiping out the savings of millions of Americans and paralyzing industry; the economic collapse that ensued turned into a worldwide depression. Soon a quarter of the American work force was unemployed, and breadlines and soup kitchens attempted to meet the needs of the millions of Americans without sources of income or sustenance. Initially, economists and politicians predicted the depression would not last long, and those with money and power were unwilling to help the unemployed, whom they believed to be out of work as a result of their own shortcomings. It was not until President Franklin D. Roosevelt's New Deal that the federal government began to provide relief to the unemployed, largely through new work programs created by government spending. The depression did not end until the onset of World War II, when production accelerated once again and more work became available. Many Americans in Europe returned home during the depression, their sources of income destroyed by the crash. Nonetheless, the interaction of American and European artists had fundamentally changed the art and literature of the twentieth century.

[5935] Dorothea Lange, *Depression* (1935), courtesy of the National Archives and Records Administration.

QUESTIONS

Comprehension: What made modernism a transatlantic phenomenon? Which technological and social developments contributed to this cultural exchange?

Comprehension: What attracted American authors to Europe? What did they find there that they couldn't find in the United States?

Comprehension: How did political and economic changes in the United States affect the cultural climate of Europe? What impact did the stock market crash and the depression have on Americans living abroad?

Context: In addition to its setting in Africa, Hemingway's "The Snows of Kilimanjaro" references numerous other locations where Harry had spent time. What function does this catalog of different locales serve in the story? Why does Harry reminisce about them as he lies dying in Africa? Why is he concerned that he hasn't written about these places?

Context: How does Paris figure in "Babylon Revisited"? As Charlie looks back on the end of the 1920s after the Wall Street crash, what does he think of the life he lived in Paris? What does he believe contributed to the lifestyle he led then?

Context: What does *Quicksand*'s Helga Crane criticize about American culture? What does she find different in Denmark? What options are open to her there that are not available in the United States? What limitations do Danish cultural values impose on her? What does the novel suggest about the influence of location on individuals' lives?

Exploration: Transatlantic exchanges were not new in the twentieth century. Look at some of the writings of early visitors to the United States and consider what they hoped to find. What did Alexis De Tocqueville, Fanny Trollope, and Charles Dickens have to say about the young republic? What did nineteenth-century American authors such as Hawthorne and James find lacking in American culture that they sought in Europe?

Exploration: The things that contributed to transatlantic exchanges

"CULTURAL CHANGE/ CULTURAL EXCHANGE" WEB ARCHIVE

[3334] Anonymous, *The Trading Floor of the New York Stock Exchange just after the Crash of 1929* (1929), courtesy of the National Archives and Records Administration [1930-67B]. Photograph taken from above the Stock Exchange floor. The crash and ensuing depression brought many expatriate artists back to the United States.

[3547] Anonymous, *Louis Armstrong, Half-length Portrait, Facing Left, Playing Trumpet* (1937), courtesy of the Library of Congress [LC-USZ62-118974]. Innovations in music, prose, poetry, and painting mutually inspired each other. Writers tried to incorporate imagery and rhythms from jazz in their work. F. Scott Fitzgerald labeled the era the "Jazz Age."

[3548] Anonymous, *Louis Armstrong Conducting Band, NBC Microphone in Foreground* (1937), courtesy of the Library of Congress [LC-USZ62-118977]. Louis Armstrong was one of the best-known jazz musicians of the 1930s. Jazz was an important theme in modernist writing and visual art; its syncopated rhythms inspired both authors and painters.

[4022] Marcel Duchamp, *Nude Descending a Staircase (No. 2)* (1912), courtesy of the Philadelphia Museum of Art. Abstract painting exhibited at the Armory Show in New York in 1913. American audiences criticized and ridiculed the work, an example of cubism, a painting trend that incorporated fragmentation and geometrical shapes.

[5935] Dorothea Lange, *Depression* (1935), courtesy of the National Archives and Records Administration. Unemployed man leaning against vacant storefront. Many people lost their jobs and savings during the Great Depression. New Deal photographer Dorothea Lange captured many images of the hardships endured during this time.

[6520] Benson, Brown, Sterlin, and Lange, *Keep Jazzin' It Ras'* (1918), courtesy of the Brown University Library, Sheet Music Collection, The John Hay Library. Sheet music cover showing musicians and instruments. Jazz influenced poetry, prose, and painting, as artists tried to incorporate its images and rhythms.

[6540] Ethel M'Clellan Plummer, *Vanity Fair on the Avenue* (1914), courtesy of the Library of Congress [LC-USZC4-1408]. Four women in stylish attire. Popular culture and international cultural exchange, including high fashion, grew with technological advances.

[6548] A. E. Marey, *Going to see Chaplin* (1920), courtesy of the Gazette du Bon Ton. Individuals waiting to enter a theater in Paris. Technology made movies available to mass audiences and facilitated the production of popular culture, which often crossed national boundaries.

[6557] George Barbier, *La Belle Personne* (1925), courtesy of Chris Lowe. Painting of woman posed with fan, vase, and elegant curtain, table, and clothing. Definitions of female beauty and sexuality changed with modernization, diverging from restrictive Victorian standards.

between the world wars only intensified in the latter half of the twentieth century. How have jet airplanes, television, and the internet extended the cultural exchanges possible among distant nations? What are some examples of these exchanges and what impact do you think they have had on the development of art and literature? On national identity?

EXTENDED CONTEXTS

"An Explosion in a Shingle Factory": The Armory Show and the Advent of Modern Art

In 1913 the International Exhibition of Modern Art opened at the Sixty-Ninth Regiment Armory in New York City. Art historian Milton Brown calls it "the most important single exhibition ever held in America." Prior to what became known as the Armory Show, contemporary art and artists had received little attention from the American public, and this exhibition brought curious onlookers in numbers previously unimaginable. Displayed were works by avant-garde European artists such as Pablo Picasso, Henri Matisse, and Marcel Duchamp, all of whose abstract work had been shown in Europe beginning in 1905, with the *Fauviste* exhibition (where Gertrude Stein and her brother began collecting modern art). A similar exhibition in London in 1910 had prompted Virginia Woolf to tie a fundamental shift in the world to the display of those paintings, claiming that "in or about December, 1910, human character changed." **Cubism**, a style of painting that emphasized the underlying geometric forms of objects, shocked American viewers, many of whom thought that the artists were trying to conceal their own lack of artistic talent or were simply insane. Marcel Duchamp's *Nude Descending a Staircase* caused the greatest public furor, standing for all that was wrong in modern art in the eyes of its critics. It became a target of public ridicule, and parodies of the work appeared in newspapers and journals. As Brown puts it, "American critics were as unprepared for the European visitation as they were for an exhibition of art from Mars." An art critic for the *New York Times* thought the work resembled "an explosion in a shingle factory."

Nonetheless, the show radically changed art in America. Shown alongside these groundbreaking works from Europe, and compared to **dadaist** and **surrealist** works of the late 1910s and 1920s, the work of the American artists thinking of themselves as revolutionaries seemed to pale by comparison. The artists representing the Ashcan School— including George Bellows, John Sloan, George Luks, and William Glackens—who had broken with American academic art in choosing to paint scenes of everyday, and especially working-class, life, found themselves considerably less revolutionary than they had thought. While works such as Bellows's *Stag at Sharkey's* and Luks's *Hester Street* depicted subject matter generally not considered appropriate to art, their paintings did not move toward the level of abstraction favored by Picasso and Duchamp, for example.

Other arts were also undergoing significant change at this time. When the Ballet Russe performed the modern ballet *The Rite of Spring* in Paris in 1913, the dissonant music by Stravinsky and the daring and sometimes erotic ballet choreography shocked the opening night audience and nearly provoked a riot. Stravinsky's rejection of conventions governing rhythm and melody paralleled poets' rejection of conventions governing the meter of verse.

By 1915 some critics were announcing that a shift had occurred in the artistic climate of the United States and that America would soon itself become a capital of culture. After the war, however, American politics became increasingly conservative, with the Volstead Act, the Red Scare, and restrictions on immigration, and American artists again looked to Europe. But throughout the 1920s the spirit of experimentation persisted in different groups, notably the European surrealists, centered in New York, and by World War II artists in America were at the forefront of experimental art.

[6492] Anonymous, Armory Show Poster (1913), courtesy of the Smithsonian Institution, the Hirshhorn Museum and Sculpture Garden.

QUESTIONS

Comprehension: What was so new and shocking about the works exhibited in the Armory Show? How did these paintings differ from the art that had preceded them?

Context: What similarities can you see between the cubist paintings of the Armory Show and the literary techniques employed by writers like Stein and Dos Passos? Consider one of Picasso's cubist paintings and Stein's "Portrait of Picasso." How does Stein's use of language parallel the cubists' use of paint?

Exploration: Research other exhibitions and consider their impact on people's perception of the world. Virginia Woolf believed that modern art actually changed the way people saw things and thought; are there other exhibits of art (e.g., impressionist exhibits in France at the end of the nineteenth century, or an exhibit of Robert Mapplethorpe's photography in the late 1980s) that you believe have reshaped people's thinking? How did the many expositions of the nineteenth century (1851 in London, 1876 in Philadelphia, 1889 and 1900 in Paris, and the Columbian Exposition in Chicago in 1893, for example) change the way people understood the world they lived in? What is the role of the arts in shaping these beliefs and perceptions?

[4022] Marcel Duchamp, *Nude Descending a Staircase* (No. 2) (1912), courtesy of the Philadephia Museum of Art.

Experimentation and Modernity: Paris, 1900–1930

Paris became the unofficial center of literary and artistic culture not long after the turn of the century. Following World War I, a number of American authors and painters moved to Paris; some had served in the army and remained in Europe after the armistice, while others were lured from America by the vibrant cultural climate of the city and the extremely favorable monetary exchange rate. Artists and writers sought inspiration in the older culture of France, and many felt that Paris accorded them freedoms unavailable in the United States, which was still influenced in part by the Puritan work ethic and a repression of individual desire. Gertrude Stein commented on America's opposition to art: "Of course they came to Paris a great many of them to paint pictures and naturally they could not do that at home, or write they could not do that at home either, they could be dentists at home." Ezra Pound believed that American culture was essentially anti-culture and squashed the creativity of would-be writers.

Gertrude Stein made Paris her permanent home in 1903 and turned her apartment into an informal salon where literati and artists would congregate as Paris became a locus of expatriate artistic endeavor in the decades following. Hemingway, Fitzgerald, Picasso, Joyce, and many others called Paris home in the first decades of the twentieth century. The American Sylvia Beach founded a bookstore and publishing company and helped struggling authors get their work published, including James Joyce's controversial *Ulysses* in 1922.

Paris was a place of permissiveness, where eccentricity in dress and lifestyle was not only tolerated but also to a large degree encouraged. At the same time, Paris was steeped in tradition, both in its architecture and in its history as a center for cultural and intellectual life. It was in Paris that African American performers and authors who struggled with their careers in the United States found appreciative audiences. The nightlife of Paris did not suffer from the restrictiveness of Prohibition, and its cafés and bars offered authors a place to meet one another.

Literary critic Malcolm Bradbury views Paris as a critical location for the meeting of the international authors who would create modernism:

> Paris was the meeting place of two potent forces. One was the peaking of European Modernism, an artistic movement born of a transformation of consciousness in a volatile, troubled Europe. The other was a new stirring of American Modernity, a fundamental process of technological and social change. And what helped to bring about the meeting was the inward transformation of an American culture that was becoming morally and behaviourally far less culturally stable, far more experimental, and so responsive to *avant-garde* sentiment.

The blossoming of arts and letters that took place in Paris fundamentally changed the character of the literature of the United States, as American literature ceased to be simply a derivative of English literature, but itself became a force in the shaping of international arts and letters.

QUESTIONS

Comprehension: What about Paris attracted so many artists and writers? How did Paris influence modern art and literature?

Context: What role does Paris play in Fitzgerald's short story "Babylon Revisited"? How does Paris affect Charlie's fate? What do you think it is that Harry in "The Snows of Kilimanjaro" finds so appealing about Paris? Why does he want so much to have written about it?

Exploration: Why do you think Paris fostered the type of experimentation it did? What do you think contributes to the culture of a place?

[4930] Anonymous, *Hemingway in Paris*, courtesy of Princeton University Library, Department of Rare Books.

ASSIGNMENTS

Personal and Creative Responses

1. *Poet's Corner*: Choose a character from one of the prose works in this unit (e.g., "The Snows of Kilimanjaro," *Quicksand*, *Trifles*) and write a short poem from that character's point of view. You do not need to choose a main character. How, for example, do you believe Harry's wife ("The Snows of Kilimanjaro") would think? Or Minnie Wright, the absent focus of *Trifles*? How does the poetic form change the way you present information about the character?

2. *Journal:* Chronicle a moment in your life using the style of Gertrude Stein. Describe the same people and things from slightly different angles and experiment with departing from typical meanings of words. What happens to your thinking about your subject when you use this technique?

3. *Journal:* Imagine you are Nella Larsen and are considering your long-awaited third novella. What would this novella be about if you set it in present-day America? Where would you set it and what would happen?

4. *Doing History*: Look at the images of World War I and read the accounts by soldiers. Choose one image and write a narrative account of what you think is happening in it. What would an onlooker see, smell, and hear? What might a soldier feel and think? What's happened just before this picture was taken and what will happen next?

[7204] George Barbier, *La Redingote, ou le retour aux traditions* (1920), courtesy of the Gazette du Bon Ton.

5. *Multimedia*: You have been asked to design a virtual museum exhibit that shows the principles underlying modernism in literature, art, and music. Using the archive, create exhibition "rooms" where visitors may read texts, hear music, and see artwork to help them better understand how these different art forms interpreted the principles of modernism. Write short explanatory notes to go with each image, text, or sound clip.

Problem-Based Learning Projects

1. You belong to a group in which the members call themselves "modernists." It includes Gertrude Stein, Ernest Hemingway, Nella Larsen, and Susan Glaspell. Design a salon where you will hold

[4930] Anonymous, *Hemingway in Paris*, courtesy of Princeton University Library, Department of Rare Books. A photograph of Ernest Hemingway with motorcycle in Paris. Hemingway was one of many expatriate American writers who lived and worked in Paris, arguing that the atmosphere was less stifling than that of the United States.

[4997] Janet Flanner-Solita Solano, *Group Portrait of American and European Artists and Performers in Paris* (1920), courtesy of the Library of Congress [LC-USZ62-113902]. Photograph of American and European artists in Paris, including Man Ray, Ezra Pound, and Martha Dennison. Many expatriate artists found inspiration in Paris's traditions and less restrictive culture.

[6560] Zyg Brunner, *France Imagines New York* (n.d.), courtesy of Chris Lowe. Political cartoon by Zyg Brunner, an artist known for art deco influences, published in a French magazine. Paris was a center of modern art and cubism. New York was the site of the Armory Show exhibition.

[6561] Zyg Brunner, *America Imagines Paris* (n.d.), courtesy of Chris Lowe. Political cartoon by Zyg Brunner, an artist known for art deco influences, published in a French magazine. Paris was a major center of modern art and was perceived by Americans as permissive.

[7204] George Barbier, *La Redingote, ou le retour aux traditions* (1920), courtesy of the Gazette du Bon Ton. Many American artists who lived in Paris rather than the United States argued that Paris offered freedom from "Puritanical" American traditions.

your meetings. What works of art, music, and literature would you want around you? Whom would you invite to join you?

2. You are an editor of children's books at a large publishing house, and you have been asked to put together a book on modernism for three age groups: ages 7–10, 11–13, and 14–17. How will you present modernism to each of these groups? What works will you use to explain the ideas behind modernism to them? How will you alter your presentation for different age groups?

3. You are a member of the team responsible for designing an interdisciplinary exhibition about modernity and the 1920s and 1930s at a local museum. What art works, literary texts, film clips, music, photographs, and everyday objects would you include in this exhibition? What do you hope visitors to your exhibit will learn from your installation?

GLOSSARY

art deco A style in decorative arts and architecture that emphasizes streamlined, geometric forms and an affinity to the shapes and materials of industrial products. A response to the elaborate, organic forms of the prevalent art nouveau style at the turn of the twentieth century, art deco designs such as the Chrysler Building often celebrated the machine. Beginning about 1910 and lasting until the mid-1930s, the art deco style influenced the design of many significant buildings and interiors.

cubism A style of painting that developed in Paris in the first decade of the twentieth century and which emphasizes abstract forms rather than realistic representation in painting and sculpture. Reacting to the tradition of realistic art, cubists painted the underlying geometric forms that they believed were the basis of natural forms. Cubist art often incorporated multiple perspectives, which many viewers found disorienting. Some of the foremost practitioners of cubist art were Pablo Picasso, Georges Braque, and Fernand Leger.

dadaism A term used to describe a nihilist form of modern art. The word "dada" is a child's term for "hobbyhorse" in French and was picked at random from a dictionary by the original group of dada practitioners. Beginning in Zurich in 1916, with centers of activity in Berlin and Paris as well, dada was based on the principles of deliberate irrationality, anarchy, cynicism, and the rejection of the conventional laws of beauty and social organization. Dada is art designed to force viewers to question aesthetic conventions by shocking or confounding them. Unusual materials were often used; Marcel Duchamp, for example, displayed a urinal turned upside down and titled "Fountain." The dadaists disbanded in 1922, many of them becoming part of other modern art movements, particularly surrealism.

jazz Originated in cities such as New Orleans, St. Louis, and Chicago by African American musicians around the turn of the twentieth century, jazz developed in a variety of ways. Its roots are from

African American folk music, but as jazz developed, elements from other musical cultures—from contemporary Western classical music to musics of the Far East—were gradually assimilated, resulting in a broad range of sub-genres within the larger context known as "jazz." Jazz is characterized by solo and group improvisation, complex syncopation, and extended harmonies, as well as idiosyncratic interpretations of popular songs. Different styles of jazz have markedly different sounds, and the New Orleans jazz of Louis Armstrong sounds strikingly different from the urbane jazz of Duke Ellington in 1920s Harlem.

modernism   A term that refers rather broadly to literature and art produced under the influence of "modernity"; that is, in response to the conditions of the modern world, with its technological innovation, increased urbanization, and accompanying sense of a world changing too quickly to comprehend. Modernists tended to self-consciously oppose traditional forms, which they believed to be out of step with the modern world. Recently, critics have noted the variety of ways artists and writers labeled "modernist" approach their work, and the allusive poetry of T. S. Eliot, the spare prose of Ernest Hemingway, the political poetry of Langston Hughes, the radical linguistic experimentation of Gertrude Stein, and the regionalist work of Sherwood Anderson have all fallen into the category of modernism.

nativism   A term used to describe the sentiment of Americans who considered themselves "native," since their forebears had come to the United States generations earlier. Beginning in the late nineteenth century, millions of immigrants arrived in the United States each decade, and native-born Americans often found their different cultural attitudes difficult to tolerate. Increasing numbers of immigrants arrived from eastern European countries and Asia, whereas earlier waves of immigration had come primarily from northern and western European countries such as England, Ireland, and Germany. Immigration laws passed between 1917 and 1924 significantly restricted how many immigrants could come from each country, and they tended to allow many more immigrants from Germany and Ireland, for example, than from Asian or African nations.

primitivism   A term used to describe artistic and literary styles that borrow from cultures (usually non-European) considered less advanced than the artist's own. Primitivism in painting enjoyed a vogue in the early decades of the twentieth century, and artists such as Picasso incorporated style and symbol from African art, while literary figures looked to rural settings and "simple" folk for their stories and poems. These seemingly less complex societies and modes of life appeared to provide an answer to the confusion caused by the modern world.

Prohibition   The period in the United States between 1919 and 1933 when the Volstead Act or Eighteenth Amendment made it illegal to manufacture or sell alcohol. The law was not especially well enforced, and in the early years of the depression, many felt that Prohibition was not only an infringement on personal liberty but a detriment to the failing U.S. economy.

surrealism   An art and literary movement that aimed to tap the unconscious mind in the creation of art; founded by the French critic and poet André Breton in the mid-1920s. An outgrowth of dadaism, surrealism depicted scenes from dreams and employed Freudian symbolism. Some of the best-known surrealists are Salvador Dali and René Magritte. The surrealist movement in literature flourished mainly in France and often used automatic writing to establish a connection between the unconscious of the writer and that of the reader.

Taylorism   An approach to maximizing the efficiency of production developed by the industrial engineer Frederick Taylor in the first decade of the twentieth century. Taylor made careful analysis of the ways industries organized their human labor and machines and created systems to reduce the waste of time and energy. By simplifying the tasks of any individual laborer, Taylor's "scientific management" not only maximized the efficiency of production, but also made the laborer's job more repetitive and tedious. In a time when immigrants comprised a significant portion of the work force, such simple tasks allowed businesses to employ unskilled workers and pay them very little. This change in manual labor practice further alienated workers from meaningful work and created environments that made workers quite like the machines they operated.

SELECTED BIBLIOGRAPHY

Bradbury, Malcolm. *Dangerous Pilgrimages: Trans-Atlantic Mythologies and the Novel*. London: Secker & Warburg, 1995.

Brown, Milton W. *American Painting from the Armory Show to the Depression*. Princeton, NJ: Princeton UP, 1955.

Cooper, John M., Jr. *Pivotal Decades: The United States, 1900–1920*. New York: W. W. Norton and Company, 1992.

Dumenil, Lynn. *The Modern Temper: American Culture and Society in the 1920s*. New York: Hill and Wang, 1995.

Grahn, Judy. *Really Reading Gertrude Stein*. Santa Cruz: Crossing Press, 1990.

Orvell, Miles. *The Real Thing: Imitation and Authenticity in American Culture, 1880–1940*. Chapel Hill: U of North Carolina P, 1989.

Parrish, Michael E. *Anxious Decades: America in Prosperity and Depression, 1920–1941*. New York: W. W. Norton and Company, 1992.

Roberts, Mary Louise. *Civilization without Sexes: Reconstructing Gender in Postwar France, 1917–1927*. Chicago: U of Chicago P, 1994.

Ruth, David E. *Inventing the Public Enemy: The Gangster in American Culture, 1918–1934*. Chicago: U of Chicago P, 1996.

Tichi, Cecelia. *Shifting Gears: Technology, Literature, Culture in Modernist America*. Chapel Hill: U of North Carolina P, 1987.

Watts, Linda. *Gertrude Stein: A Study of the Short Fiction*. New York: Twayne, 1999.

Wilson, Richard Guy, Dianne H. Pilgrim, and Dickran Tashjian. *The Machine Age in America, 1918–1941*. New York: Brooklyn Museum in association with Harry Abrams, 1986.

Zinn, Howard. *People's History of the United States*. New York: HarperCollins, 1980. (See Chapters 14 and 15.)

FURTHER RESOURCES

"1913 Armory Show." (Online exhibit: <xroads.virginia.edu/~MUSEUM/Armory/armoryshow.html>.)

American Visions [interactive multimedia]: *20th Century Art from the Roy R. Neuberger Collection*. San Francisco, CA : Eden Interactive, 1994. To order: Eden Interactive, 224 Mississippi Street, San Francisco, CA, 94107.

Antheil, George. "Ballet Méchanique."

Association of American Painters and Sculptors. *The Armory Show: International Exhibition of Modern Art, 1913*. New York: Arno, 1972.

Chaplin, Charlie. *Modern Times*. 1936.

The Goldstein Museum of Design [Online exhibits: Costume, Decorative Arts, Graphic Design, Textile], Department of Design, Housing, and Apparel, College of Human Ecology, University of Minnesota, 244 McNeal Hall, 1985 Buford Avenue, St. Paul, MN, 55108. Phone: (612) 624-7434.

Inventing Entertainment: The Motion Pictures and Sound Recordings of the Edison Company (Online exhibit: American Memory Project. Library of Congress).

Kernfeld, Barry. *What to Listen for in Jazz* (book/CD). New Haven: Yale UP, 1995.

Prosperity and Thrift: The Coolidge Era and the Consumer Economy, 1921–1929 (Online exhibit: American Memory Project. Library of Congress. <lcweb2.loc.gov/ammem/coolhtml/>).

Winter, Robert. *Igor Stravinsky: The Rite of Spring*. Voyager CD-ROM. Phone: (888) 292-5584.

MIGRANT STRUGGLE

The Bounty of the Land in Twentieth-Century American Literature, 1929–1995

Authors and Works

Featured in the Video:
John Steinbeck, *The Grapes of Wrath* (novel)
Carlos Bulosan, *America Is in the Heart* (autobiography or creative nonfiction), "Be American" (short story)
Helena Maria Viramontes, *Under the Feet of Jesus* (novel)

Discussed in This Unit:
Henry David Thoreau, *Walden* (nonfiction), "Walking," "Resistance to Civil Government," "Life Without Principle" (essays)
Upton Sinclair, *The Jungle* (novel)
Robinson Jeffers, "Birds and Fishes," "Hurt Hawks," "November Surf" (poems)
Muriel Rukeyser, "Alloy," "The Conjugation of the Paramecium" (poems)
Tomas Rivera, . . . *y no se lo tragó la tierra/. . . And the Earth Did Not Devour Him* (novel)
Rudolfo Anaya, "The Christmas Play" (short story)
Albertos Ríos, "Advice to a First Cousin," "Refugio's Hair," "Day of the Refugios" (poems)

Overview Questions

■ How do the writers in this unit reflect the distinct cultures and experiences of different ethnic and socio-economic groups, including Sinclair's portrayal of European immigrants, Bulosan's depictions of Asian immigrants, and the **Latino/a** representations in the works of Viramontes, Rivera, and Ríos?

■ How do these works represent gender?

■ How do we have to expand our definitions of what is considered American after we read these works? Is citizenship the only thing that makes one an American? What other factors should one consider?

■ How do these works "give voice" to those who do not usually have a voice in our society?

■ What are the distinguishing characteristics of the many works depicting the migrant story? What cultural values are reflected and promoted in them?

■ What historical events and cultural anxieties in the United States helped to inspire these works? How have economic booms and busts affected the literature about the American landscape and its farmlands?

■ What role do politics and environmental conditions play in these works?

■ In what ways can the stories of migrants and working people represent the stereotypical "American" experience? In what ways are these stories similar to and different from the stories of earlier settlers of the United States, such as the Puritans or those who settled at Jamestown?

■ What negative effects of technology and industrialization are portrayed in these works? What positive effects?

■ How have the plots of these literary works helped to preserve and comment on important moments in U.S. history?

■ Is the theme of "social justice" present in every work? What distinguishes its various treatments?

■ How is the land or the environment used as a repeated symbol in these works?

■ Though most of the characters depicted in these works are considered outsiders or are **marginalized** by society, how can they also be considered universal? How do their struggles and dreams relate to all of us?

■ How do these works participate in or challenge racial stereotypes, especially concerning Filipinos and Latinos/as?

■ How is class consciousness present in migrant representations of American life? What classes of people are depicted in these texts? How do the different classes treat each other?

■ Do these works demonstrate that everyone can achieve the American Dream?

Learning Objectives

After students have viewed the video, read the headnotes and literary selections in *The Norton Anthology of American Literature*, and explored related archival materials on the *American Passages* Web site, they should be able to

1. understand the various expressions of migrant workers and the conditions they lived in and labored under;
2. discuss the impact on American literature and culture of these writers' emphasis on natural geographical settings and distinctive regional and ethnic customs;
3. discuss the importance of race, class, gender, culture, and socio-economic position in migrant workers' stories;
4. discuss the cultural values and assumptions that inform the differing migrant struggles examined in this unit;
5. understand the basic economic and environmental causes that led to a rise in the number of migrant and displaced workers in twentieth-century America;
6. understand eco-literature and the influence of the environment and the land on writers, literature, and society in relation to the rise of industrialization and technology.

Instructor Overview

The writers and works in Unit 12 explore the unfulfilled promises of the American Dream for segments of the population of the United States, especially immigrants and impoverished, dislocated workers. These "migrants" have the greatest confidence in the promises the United States has to offer; yet, ironically, these are the very people often denied access to its bounty. The coexistence of the migrants' disillusionment and their continued faith in the promise of America informs many of these works. Much of the literature of the migrant struggle explores human relationships with the environment and the land, especially in the West. Though modern economic systems tend to look at nature only as a commodity, writers from Thoreau to Viramontes resist or reject that view. Indeed, they are part of a tradition of writers and thinkers who, since the earliest days of the United States, have emphasized a strong bond between people and the land. In the later nineteenth and twentieth centuries, however, this bond gradually loosened, as technology and inexpensive labor allowed those who owned or controlled the land to work it less themselves and turn their energies toward increasing its productivity. Unfortunately, these changes had negative consequences. Poor land conservation practices and a long and severe drought eventually led to the environmental disaster known as the Dust Bowl during the 1930s.

The writers in this unit share an interest in the effects of economic and political systems on workers, writers, and activists. In their works, the losers tend to be ethnic immigrants and unskilled workers, those at the bottom of the hierarchy of business, industry, and American society itself. Many of these workers have been, and remain today, lower-class laborers of color; some are not U.S. citizens. Migrant workers labor at back-breaking picking and planting jobs few white middle-class Americans would want, and even today they are often denied basic employment benefits and rights.

In many ways, the cultural and literary contributions of those labeled "migrants" are just now becoming more broadly recognized. Though Carlos Bulosan gained national popularity during the 1940s as a spokesperson for Filipinos and other immigrants, the House Un-American Activities Committee blacklisted him in the 1950s for his socialist activities, and he died in relative obscurity. Other writers in this unit enjoyed more lasting acclaim. John Steinbeck's novel *The Grapes of Wrath*, for example, still resonates in the American consciousness with its story of a family of "Okies" looking for a better life on the West Coast. Steinbeck's reshaping of the American epic around the family and the worker, instead of around the solitary male hero, marked an important turning point in American literature.

As the writers in this unit show, the stories of the migrant struggle in American literature and American culture are as diverse as the people who live such struggles every day. Helena Maria Viramontes graphically reworks Steinbeck's story of migrant workers in *Under the Feet of Jesus*, this time through the eyes of a young Latina woman. Viramontes offers a totally different cultural perspective, but she also demonstrates that conditions have only slightly improved for migrants in the fifty years since Steinbeck's novel first appeared. Henry David Thoreau's ecological writing celebrates America, while his call for civil disobedience criticizes its faults. Robinson Jeffers's works convey both his love of the American landscape and his concern about the encroachment of civilization upon this landscape. This unit also explores works by leftist poet Muriel Rukeyser as well as those by Rudolfo Anaya, Tomas Rivera, and Alberto Ríos, who portray the lives of Latinos in the United States.

The literature of the migrant struggle often depicts characters with much stronger connections to the land than those who own it. From Thoreau to Steinbeck to Viramontes, these writers provide keen observations of the cultural changes occurring in the United States, with the rise of complex social structures made more and more possible by emerging technologies such as railroads, factories, and large corporate farms. These writers ask what is lost with this rise of technology and the lessening of direct connections to the land. Migrant workers often lose a sense of home as the agricultural industry envisions them as replaceable and disposable human harvesting-machines. Yet because these workers rely upon their burdensome work with the soil and its products to survive, they perceive the land as their only hope. They partake in the production of America's natural bounty but do not profit from their work. Not surprisingly, many of the texts discussed in this unit portray migrants as outsiders who see America's faults and virtues more clearly than do less marginalized members of American society.

The video, archive, and instructional materials accompanying this unit explore a wide and diverse range of writers who are linked more by theme than by time period. Most of the unit focuses on the period from the 1930s through the end of the twentieth century. The key issues covered are the migrant work force, immigration, the Great Depression, the Dust Bowl, WPA documentary photography and film, socialism, communism, the rise of unions, and the farm workers movement.

Student Overview

The writers and works in Unit 12 explore the unfulfilled promises of the American Dream for segments of the population of the United States, especially immigrants and impoverished, dislocated workers. These "migrants" have the greatest confidence in the promises the United States has to offer; yet, ironically, these are the very people often denied access to its bounty. The coexistence of the migrants' disillusionment and their continued faith in the promise of America informs many of these works. Much of the literature of the migrant struggle explores human relationships with the environment and the land, especially in the West. Though modern economic systems tend to look at nature only as a commodity, writers from Thoreau to Viramontes resist or reject that view. Indeed, they are part of a tradition of writers and thinkers who, since the earliest days of the United States, have emphasized a strong bond between people and the land. But in the nineteenth and twentieth centuries, this bond gradually loosened as technological and labor changes allowed those who owned or controlled the land to work it less themselves and turn their energies toward increasing its productivity. Unfortunately, these changes had negative consequences. Poor land conservation practices and a long and severe drought eventually led to the environmental disaster known as the Dust Bowl during the 1930s.

The writers in this unit share an interest in the effects of economic and political systems on workers, writers, and activists. In their works, the losers tend to be ethnic immigrants and unskilled workers, those at the bottom of the hierarchy of business, industry, and American society itself. Many of these workers have been, and remain today, lower-class laborers of color; some are not U.S. citizens. **Migrant workers** labor at back-breaking picking and planting jobs few white middle-class Americans would want, and even today they are often denied basic employment benefits and rights.

In many ways, the cultural and literary contributions of those labeled "migrants" are just now becoming more broadly recognized. Though Carlos Bulosan gained national popularity during the 1940s as a spokesperson for Filipinos and other immigrants, the House Un-American Activities Committee blacklisted him in the 1950s for his socialist activities, and he died in relative obscurity. Other writers in this unit enjoyed more lasting acclaim. John Steinbeck's novel *The Grapes of Wrath*, for example, still resonates in the American consciousness with its story of a family of "Okies" looking for a better life on the West Coast. Steinbeck's reshaping of the American epic around the family and the worker, instead of around the solitary male hero, marked an important turning point in American literature.

As the writers in this unit show, the stories of the migrant struggle in American literature and American culture are as diverse as the people who live such struggles every day. Helena Maria Viramontes graphically reworks Steinbeck's story of migrant workers in *Under the Feet of Jesus*, this time through the eyes of a young Latina woman. Viramontes offers a totally different cultural perspective, but she also demonstrates that conditions have only improved slightly for migrants in the fifty years since Steinbeck's novel first appeared. Henry David Thoreau's ecological writing celebrates America, while his call for civil disobedience criticizes its faults. Robinson Jeffers's works convey both his love of the American landscape and his concern about the encroachment of civilization on this landscape. This unit also explores works by leftist poet Muriel Rukeyser as well as those by Rudolfo Anaya, Tomas Rivera, and Alberto Ríos, who portray the lives of **Latinos** in the United States.

The literature of the migrant struggle often depicts characters with much stronger connections to the land than those who own it. From Thoreau to Steinbeck to Viramontes, these writers provide keen observations of the cultural changes occurring in the United States, with the rise of complex social structures made more and more possible by emerging technologies such as railroads, factories, and large corporate farms. These writers ask what is lost with this rise of technology and the lessening of direct connections to the land. Migrant workers often lose a sense of home as the agricultural industry envisions them as replaceable and disposable human harvesting-machines. Yet because these workers rely upon their burdensome work with the soil and its products to survive, they perceive the land as their only hope. They partake in the production of America's natural bounty but do not profit from their work. Not surprisingly, many of the texts discussed in this unit portray migrants as outsiders who see America's faults and virtues more clearly than do less marginalized members of American society.

Video Overview

- ➤ **Authors covered:** John Steinbeck, Carlos Bulosan, Helena Maria Viramontes
- ➤ **Who's interviewed:** Cherrie Moraga, Chicana/lesbian playwright and artist-in-residence (Stanford University); Louis Owens, professor of English (Choctaw/Cherokee) (University of California, Davis); Vicky Ruiz, professor of history and Chicano/Latino studies (University of California, Irvine); Sonia Saldivar-Hull, professor of English (University of Texas, San Antonio); Greg Sarris, professor of English (Loyola Marymount University) (Miwok Chief/Pomo); Helena Maria Viramontes, author
- ➤ **Points covered:**
  - American identity is a fluid concept that is defined in part by those who are pushed to the margins of American society.
  - The **Great Depression** and the **Dust Bowl** of the mid-1930s are foundational settings for many of these works.

- Eco-literature emphasizes people's relationships to the environment and often focuses on social justice.
- John Steinbeck published *The Grapes of Wrath* in 1939, generating attention and sympathy for the midwestern migrant workers who attempted to find employment in California during the Dust Bowl years. *The Grapes of Wrath* can be understood as a **jeremiad**: a literary work prophesying doom, or a lament or sermon recommending an immediate change in behavior or practices. Like many of the other works discussed in this unit, *The Grapes of Wrath* ends with an affirmation of humanity's basic goodness and a sense of hope for the future.
- Carlos Bulosan's *America Is in the Heart* explores the **American Dream's** promises and questions whether it is possible for all. Bulosan was one of many leftist artists and writers **blacklisted** during the anti-communism of the 1950s.

- The rise of farmworkers' unions in the 1960s and 1970s coincided with the civil rights movement.
- Helena Maria Viramontes is one of many important Latina writers that emerged in the 1980s and 1990s. Her novel *Under the Feet of Jesus* depicts strong and enduring female Mexican American characters.

PREVIEW

- **Preview the video:** In the nineteenth and twentieth centuries, waves of immigrants came to the United States from Europe and Asia seeking better lives for themselves and their families. Some came to escape hardship or oppression at home, or for freedom of religion, but many wished to pursue the American Dream. The idea that America's natural bounty was so large that it could accommodate all newcomers was appealing. After buying into the promises of this dream, however, many immigrants and migrants experienced a different reality. They discovered that only difficult low-paying jobs were available to them and that racism, prejudice, and hostility greeted them at nearly every turn. The writers discussed in the video offer glimpses of what it was, and is, like to be a marginalized person in the United States.
- **What to think about while watching:** What relationship have Americans had with the land? What does the American landscape mean to us? What power attaches to images such as "amber fields of grain," "purple mountain majesties," redwood forests, sweeping rivers, and unending cornfields. Is America's bounty meant to be available to everyone or only to a few? Who partakes in the advantages of the American way of life? Who doesn't? Who decides who participates?
- **Tying the video to the unit content:** Unit 12 materials incorporate a wide range of information that enhances and expands on the topics in the video and places these topics within a broader cultural and historical context. The materials also include information on additional writers associated with this unit in order to sample a wider range of migrant literature as well as eco-literature. For example, Robinson Jeffers displays a love of the American landscape while also admonishing those who destroy it in the name of capitalism. Muriel Rukeyser's verse explores the perils of labor and the promises of unionization. Rudolfo Anaya, Tomas Rivera, and Alberto Ríos all contribute to a larger picture of what it is like to be a marginalized ethnic worker in the United States while at the same time presenting the complex culture of Latino or Hispanic heritage. The unit also explores historical contexts relevant to this literature, including the Great Depression and Dust Bowl, the Works Progress Administration, documentary photography and films, socialism and communism, and the rise of trade unions, especially the farmworkers' unions.

	How do place and time shape literature and our understanding of it?	What is American literature? What are its distinctive voices and styles? How do social and political issues influence the American canon?	How are American myths created, challenged, and re-imagined through these works of literature?
Comprehension Questions	How is the West positively portrayed in early-twentieth-century American literature and culture? How does this change in the 1920s, 1930s, and 1940s?	What is eco-literature? What is *testimonio*?	What is a jeremiad, and how does Steinbeck use this form?
Context Questions	How have the geography and resources of the United States influenced American culture? How have Americans used and abused the land?	Why might Bulosan and his works have been "lost" for half a century? What forces worked against him, and what forces later advocated for him? Why did Steinbeck's *The Grapes of Wrath* receive social and political criticism when it was first published? How is *Under the Feet of Jesus* a feminist story? How does this affect its social message?	How does Steinbeck show that the American Dream can be dangerous? How is that reaffirmed by Viramontes? Does the promise of "home" play an important role in the works discussed in this unit? What about in the works of Viramontes and Rivera?
Exploration Questions	To what extent is the American Dream dependent on the bounty promised by the land? How do politics influence these works? Are American ideals considered, examined, and evaluated most during times of crisis?	Why is it so difficult for the impoverished and for minorities to make their stories heard? What is the role of literature in providing a voice for these struggles, and how does this form of expression relate to those used in politics or the media?	What is the American Dream? How has the American Dream changed over time? How do diverse cultures view the American Dream? How have significant historical events affected the dream? How will new opportunities and threats in the twenty-first century challenge the American Dream? What is your version of the American Dream? Who might be able to achieve your version of the dream, and who might not be able to achieve it?

	Texts	Contexts
1840s–70s	Henry David Thoreau, "A Week on the Concord and Merrimack Rivers" (1849), "Resistance to Civil Government" (1849), *Walden* (1854), "Life Without Principle" (1863)	Migration to Oregon over the Oregon Trail begins (1843) U.S.-Mexican War (1846–48) California Gold Rush begins (1849)
1900s	Upton Sinclair, *The Jungle* (1906)	International Workers of the World union founded (1905) Ford Model T goes into production (1908)
1910s	Upton Sinclair, *King Coal* (1917)	Russian Revolution (1917)
1920s	Robinson Jeffers, *Tamar and Other Poems* (1924), "Hurt Hawks" (1928), "November Surf" (1929) Upton Sinclair, *Oil!* (1927), *Boston* (1928)	Wall Street Crash begins Great Depression (1929)
1930s	John Steinbeck, *Cannery Row* (1935), *Tortilla Flat* (1935), *Dubious Battle* (1936), *Of Mice and Men* (1937), *The Long Valley* (1938), *Their Blood Is Strong* (1938), *The Grapes of Wrath* (1939) Muriel Rukeyser, "Alloy" (1938)	Dust Bowl (1931–39) President Roosevelt launches the New Deal (1933) Tydings-McDuffie Act (1934) Works Progress Administration (WPA) established (1935) House Un-American Activities Committee (HUAC) founded (1938)
1940s	Upton Sinclair, *World's End* (1940), *Between Two Worlds* (1941), *Dragon's Teeth* (1942) Carlos Bulosan, *Letter from America* (1942), *Chorus from America* (1942), *The Voice of Bataan* (1943), "Freedom from Want" (1943), "Four Freedoms" (1945), *America Is in the Heart* (1946) John Steinbeck, *The Pearl* (1945)	United States enters World War II (1939–45) after Japanese attack on Pearl Harbor (1941) Filipino Naturalization Act (1946) HUAC hearings on communism in the entertainment industry (1947)
1950s	John Steinbeck, *East of Eden* (1952)	Korean War (1950–53) Heyday of McCarthyism (1953–54) U.S. Supreme Court bans school segregation in *Brown v. Board of Education* (1954)
1960s	Carlos Bulosan, *The Sound of Falling Light* (1960) John Steinbeck, *The Winter of Our Discontent* (1961), *Travels with Charley* (1962) Robinson Jeffers, "Birds and Fishes" (1963) Muriel Rukeyser, "The Conjugation of the Paramecium" (1968)	Farm Workers Movement founded (1962) Rachel Carson publishes *Silent Spring* (1962) Cuban Missile Crisis (1962) Civil Rights Act (1964) Vietnam War (1964–75)

	Texts	Contexts
1970s	Tomas Rivera, . . . y no se lo tragó la tierra/. . . And the Earth Did Not Devour Him (1971), The Searchers (1973) Rudolfo Anaya, Bless Me, Ultima (1972), Heart of Aztlan (1976), Tortuga (1979) Muriel Rukeyser, The Collected Poems of Muriel Rukeyser (1978)	First "Earth Day" celebrated (1970) A Presidential Executive Order establishes the Environmental Protection Agency (EPA) as an independent agency of the Executive Branch (1970) Watergate scandal (1972) Moral Majority founded (1979) Iran hostage crisis (1979–81)
1980s	Alberto Ríos, Whispering to Fool the Wind (1982), The Iguana Killer (1984), Five Indiscretions (1985), "Advice to a First Cousin" (1985), "Seniors" (1985), The Dime Orchard Woman: Poems (1988) Helena Maria Viramontes, "The Moth" and Other Stories (1985) Tomas Rivera, The Harvest (1989)	Cold War ends (1989) Exxon Valdez runs aground in Alaska, spilling 11 million gallons of oil in one of the worst ecological disasters of the century (1989)
1990s	Rudolfo Anaya, Albuquerque (1992), Zia Summer (1995) Alberto Ríos, Teodora Luna's Two Kisses (1992), "Day of the Refugios" (1994), Pig Cookies and Other Stories (1995), Capirotada (1999), The Curtain of Trees: Stories (1999) Helena Maria Viramontes, Paris Rats in E.L.A. (1993), Under the Feet of Jesus (1995), Their Dogs Came with Them (1996) Carlos Bulosan, The Cry and the Dedication (first published, 1995)	Persian Gulf War (1990–91) Welfare Reform Act (1996)
2000s	Alberto Ríos, The Smallest Muscle in the Human Body (2002)	Terrorist attacks on the World Trade Center and the Pentagon (2001)

AUTHOR/TEXT REVIEW

Henry David Thoreau (1817–1862)

Best known as one of the first proponents of American Transcendentalism, Henry David Thoreau was also one of the first American naturalists and eco-literature writers. He was the third child of John Thoreau and Cynthia Dunbar and spent most of his life in and around Concord, Massachusetts. His father operated a pencil manufacturing

[5678] Currier & Ives, *Battle of Buena Vista. Fought Feby. 23rd, 1847. In Which the American Army Under Gen. Taylor Were Completely Victorious* (1847), courtesy of the Library of Congress, Prints and Photographs Division [LC-USZC4-2957].

business in the area. Thoreau attended Concord Academy and graduated from Harvard College in 1837. The next year he and his brother John opened an innovative school, which operated until 1841. Afterward, Thoreau worked as a tutor, handyman, carpenter, surveyor, essayist, and speaker. At the outbreak of the Mexican War, Thoreau protested slavery by refusing to pay his poll tax and was jailed for one night. His essay "Resistance to Civil Government" was written as a response to that event. During his life, he was an outspoken abolitionist and wrote a number of popular antislavery tracts. His books, *A Week on the Concord and Merrimack Rivers* (1849) and *Walden* (1854), and his journals, record observations of nature and meditations on humanity's place within it. Thoreau's most widely read book, *Walden*, documents two years he spent living in a small cabin beside Walden Pond just outside of Concord. This experiment in self-reliance gave Thoreau a way to practice his philosophy of living. (Recent scholars have noted that *Walden* conveniently neglects to acknowledge the extent of the domestic and practical help Thoreau's mother and sister provided.) Thoreau believed that people were too concerned with materialistic desires and that they should lead simpler and more purposeful lives. His rejection of the values of a rising consumer society complemented his reverence for nature and belief that humankind should live in harmony with it.

Considered by many of his fellow townspeople to be a loafer, Thoreau worked from time to time in his father's pencil factory, but the dust from the graphite aggravated the tuberculosis he would later die from. His legacy continues to inspire social and environmental activists. Thoreau's early biographies and published works attracted the attention of European socialists and Labor Party members, and his essays "Resistance to Civil Government" and "Life Without Principle" influenced Mahatma Gandhi's struggle for Indian independence and were also inspiring to Martin Luther King Jr. in his efforts to gain broader civil rights for African Americans. Edward Abbey, naturalist and author of *Desert Solitaire* and *The Monkey Wrench Gang*, is among the many environmental writers Thoreau inspired. Jon Krakauer's *Into the Wild*, the story of a young man who journeys alone into the Alaskan wilderness, pays homage to Thoreau's naturalist philosophy but shows what can happen if his ideas are taken too far.

■ After students have read selections from Thoreau's works, have them write about how Americans should properly "use" nature and lead their lives. Have them share their own beliefs regarding wilderness, technology, progress, success, and independent thinking. Offer them several Thoreau quotations with which to agree or disagree.

■ Have students cite recent instances of civil disobedience in the news. Discuss why individuals found it important to break the law and whether their action was justified. Debate the effectiveness of these instances of civil disobedience.

QUESTIONS

Comprehension: Why does Thoreau see the idea of "owned" property as immoral?

Comprehension: Take a look at the two introductions to *Walden* ("Economy" and "Where I Lived, and What I Lived For"). How does each of these chapters introduce what is to follow? What kind of readers does each ask us to be? Why wasn't "Economy" enough of an introduction? What does "Where I Lived . . ." add to our understanding of how to read *Walden*?

Context: Machine tools, steam engines, steamboats, railroads, textile machinery for factories, and the telegraph were all being developed and used more widely during Thoreau's lifetime. Thoreau's family owned a pencil factory, in which he worked from time to time. What changes in American society and culture were brought on by the Industrial Revolution? What were Thoreau's specific objections to those changes?

Exploration: Thoreau makes clear in his works how dependent industrialization is on cheap labor. He points to the role of slavery in developing the South's agricultural production and the abuse of Chinese and Irish immigrants in building the railroads as two examples. In "Life without Principle," he writes, "The ways by which you may get money almost without exception lead downward." Was Thoreau right in believing that for one person to succeed economically, he or she has to exploit others? Does that seem to be illustrated by the works discussed in this unit? What about bankers? Lawyers? Mechanics? Plumbers? Professors? Can you think of cases where one person's economic success does *not* depend upon the exploitation of others?

Upton Sinclair (1878–1968)

Upton Sinclair was born in Baltimore, Maryland, and is best known for his 1906 muckraking novel, *The Jungle*. He received a degree from the College of the City of New York and did graduate work at Columbia University. Early on, he supported himself as a journalist and a writer. His serials for boys' weekly magazines, the Cliff Faraday

[1031] Anonymous, *Emerson's Grave (1850–1920)*, courtesy of the Library of Congress [LC-D4-72358]. Emerson is buried on Author's Ridge in the Sleepy Hollow Cemetery of Concord, Massachusetts, alongside Nathaniel Hawthorne, Henry David Thoreau, and Louisa May Alcott. His epitaph, "The passive master lent his hand to the vast soul that o'er him planned," comes from his poem "The Problem."

[5678] Currier & Ives, *Battle of Buena Vista. Fought Feby. 23rd, 1847. In Which the American Army Under Gen. Taylor Were Completely Victorious* (1847), courtesy of the Library of Congress, Prints and Photographs Division [LC-USZC4-2957]. Painting of the Battle of Buena Vista, led by General Zachary Taylor. This popular scene of one of the major American victories of the war spoke to America's belief in Manifest Destiny. Thoreau was jailed for refusing to pay his poll tax, which would have helped finance the Mexican War.

[6964] Anonymous, *Thoreau's Cove, Lake Walden, Concord, Mass.* (n.d.), courtesy of the Library of Congress [LC-D4-34878DLC]. Photograph of woods and pond. Henry David Thoreau lived in a small cabin by Walden Pond for two years and wrote *A Week on the Concord and Merrimack Rivers* and *Walden*.

[7226] John Carlos Rowe, Interview: "Nature in the Slave Narrative Versus the Transcendentalism of Emerson and Thoreau" (2001), courtesy of *American Passages* and Annenberg/CPB. Professor of English and comparative studies John Carlos Rowe discusses the differences between the depiction of nature in Transcendentalist works and in slave narratives: in one genre, nature is a place for calm meditation; in the other, it is a place of terror.

[8581] John Carlos Rowe, Interview: "The Transcendental Critique of America" (2002), courtesy of *American Passages* and Annenberg/CPB. Professor John Carlos Rowe discusses the way in which the Transcendentalists criticized the American thirst for profit at the expense of nature and a high quality of life.

[7110] H. C. White Company, *Making Link Sausages—Machines Stuff 10 Ft. per Second* (c. 1905), courtesy of the Library of Congress [LC-USZ62-50217].

SINCLAIR WEB ARCHIVE

[1850] Lewis W. Hine, *The Children of John Meiskell* (1909), courtesy of the National Archives and Records Administration. Trained as both a teacher and a sociologist and photographer, Hine was hired by the National Child Labor Committee in 1908 to document child labor conditions in America. He traveled around the country photographing the horrible working conditions of children in mines, factories, textile mills, and canneries. The children in this picture, ages two to eleven, all worked thirteen-hour days in an oyster factory in Maryland. Their mother, Mrs. Meiskell, said, "This is worse than the days of slavery." Their plight might be compared to the depiction of child labor in Upton Sinclair's *The Jungle*, Stephen Crane's *Maggie, A Girl of the Streets*, and Rebecca Harding Davis's *Life in the Iron-Mills*.

[5637] Joseph C. Borden, Jr., *To the Arm and the Hammer, A Song for May Day* (1898), courtesy of the Library of

stories and the Mark Mallory stories, were particularly lucrative. Sinclair's later writing emphasized socialist causes. By 1904 he was a regular reader of the *Appeal to Reason*, a populist-socialist newspaper. Though his works were celebrated in Russia, he opposed the communist regime there after the 1917 revolution.

Sinclair wrote over a hundred books. In addition to *The Jungle*, important works include *King Coal* (1917); *Oil!* (1927), about the corruption of southern California society; *Boston* (1928), about the Sacco-Vanzetti trial; and the Lanny Budd series, which includes *World's End* (1940), *Between Two Worlds* (1941), and *Dragon's Teeth* (1942). The Lanny Budd series offers a Marxist interpretation of the years between the two world wars.

Sinclair is famous for his muckraking novels. Turn-of-the-twentieth-century writers and journalists who exposed scandals in politics and business through their writing were called "muckrakers." Muckrakers often had proletarian and socialist sympathies. Other writers associated with this movement include Jack London, David Graham Phillips, and Robert Herrick, along with Lincoln Steffens and Ida Tarbell.

Though Sinclair had to publish *The Jungle* himself after it was rejected by a number of publishers, it became his first popular literary success. The novel was inspired by journalistic investigations into the dirty and dangerous working conditions in the Chicago stockyards. Its protagonist, Jurgis Rudkus, a Lithuanian immigrant, endures the exploitation of the Brown and Durham meatpacking company as he witnesses the rest of his family being victimized and destroyed. Sinclair intended his novel to cause public outrage for the immigrants who were forced to work for substandard pay in the intolerable conditions of the stockyards. While the novel had little effect on working conditions, it did incite public concern about poor food quality and impurities in processed meats, which resulted in the passage of federal food inspection legislation.

TEACHING TIPS

■ Ask students to consider Sinclair's works as political commentaries and historic records. Suggest that they research a topic about which Sinclair wrote—the meatpacking industry or labor unions, for example; then have them share their assessment of the accuracy of Sinclair's representation.

■ The muckrakers used the media to alert the public to important issues and to initiate social change. Have students discuss how today's media is used to investigate social and economic problems. Have them list the topics covered in a week's worth of television "newsmagazine" shows. Ask them to compare and contrast the approaches and subjects of contemporary television investigative reports with those of the early-twentieth-century muckrakers.

QUESTIONS

Comprehension: What is Jurgis's original response to getting a job with the meatpacking company? What are we to make of that response?

Comprehension: Why did meatpacking companies almost always employ only immigrants?

Comprehension: How are European immigrants portrayed by Sinclair throughout *The Jungle*? How does this compare to his portrayal of nonimmigrants?

Context: Compare the living and working conditions of the Rudkus family with those portrayed by Bulosan in *America Is in the Heart*, by Rivera in *. . . y no se lo tragó la tierra/. . . And the Earth Did Not Devour Him*, and by Viramontes in *Under the Feet of Jesus*. What are the similarities and differences between the ethnic workers in all these works? What burdens do they share? How are their dreams similar or different?

Exploration: The Jungle is a novel in the tradition of literary naturalism. Compare it with earlier naturalistic works, such as Stephen Crane's *Maggie* or Theodore Dreiser's *Sister Carrie*. Note the differences in the way Sinclair incorporates socialist themes in his novel.

Exploration: To better understand popular opinion regarding European immigrants in the early twentieth century, investigate the Sacco-Vanzetti trial. Who was involved? What happened? Was the verdict right? In addition to Sinclair, which other important American writers wrote about the trial?

Congress [rbpe 0100230a]. Socialism was an important theme in Upton Sinclair's writing, although he opposed the communists that came into power after the Russian Revolution of 1917.

[6934] Drieser, *Breaker Boys* (c. 1900), courtesy of the Library of Congress [LC-D401-11590 DLC]. Investigative journalists and novelists such as Upton Sinclair, who sympathized with progressive and socialist causes, exposed corporations' abuses of power with photos of, and stories about, poor working conditions.

[7110] H. C. White Company, *Making Link Sausages—Machines Stuff 10 Ft. per Second* (c. 1905), courtesy of the Library of Congress [LC-USZ62-50217]. Photograph of Swift and Company's Chicago packing house. Mechanization and urbanization encouraged some writers' feelings of alienation from and nostalgia for the United States's agricultural past.

[7426] Herbert Photos, Inc., *Bartolomeo Vanzetti and Nicola Sacco, Manacled Together* (1927), courtesy of the Library of Congress [LC-USZ62-124547]. Sacco and Vanzetti surrounded by a crowd of onlookers and guards before entering a Dedham, Massachusetts, courthouse. Victims of the first Red Scare, these political radicals received the death penalty, despite a lack of evidence.

Robinson Jeffers (1887–1962)

Robinson Jeffers was born in Pittsburgh, Pennsylvania. His father was a minister and professor of Old Testament literature. When he was young, Jeffers traveled extensively in Europe, where he received his early education. In the United States, he attended Occidental College, the University of Southern California, and the University of Washington. An inheritance allowed Jeffers to devote himself to the writing of poetry. His first volume of verse was completed in 1912, and he published over twenty-five volumes of poetry during his life. In 1913, he moved to Carmel, California, and built a stone cottage and a large observation tower overlooking the Pacific Ocean. Much of his verse captures the images of his surroundings on the coast.

Published in 1924, *Tamar and Other Poems* demonstrates Jeffers's desire to break with the poetics of the past and write original, vigorous, and realistic verse. Here as in most of his works, Jeffers's major themes are lust and humankind's destructive self-obsessions. Jeffers integrates a broad knowledge of literature, religion, philosophy, languages, myth, and the sciences in his work. He represents a pantheistic universe that is revealed through constant and sometimes brutal

[7599] Euphronios, *Calyx-Krater* (c. 515 B.C.E.), courtesy of The Metropolitan Museum of Art.

[7341] Arthur Rothstein, *Strip Mining Operations with a Thirty-Two Cubic Yard Steam Shovel. Cherokee County, Kansas* (1936), courtesy of the Library of Congress, Prints & Photographs Division, FSA/OWI Collection [LC-USF34-004274-D DLC]. Heavy machinery at mining site. Meditative poets found inspiration in nature and were alarmed by increasing environmental destruction in the United States.

[7377] Lee Russell, *Grant County, Oregon. Malheur National Forest. Lumberjack Hitching Cable on Log Which Will Be Loaded Onto Trucks* (1942), courtesy of the Library of Congress [LC-USF34-073482-D DLC]. Picture of a Pacific Northwest lumberjack. Beat poet Gary Snyder went to Reed College in Oregon and worked as a logger before doing graduate work in anthropology. Snyder, like Robinson Jeffers, revered the rugged western landscape.

[7404] Asher B. Durand, *Progress (The Advance of Civilization)* (1853), courtesy of the Gulf States Paper Corporation, Warner Collection. The Native Americans in the lower left of this painting observe the steady approach of American progress and settlement. Depictions of westward expansion such as this one helped publicize and legitimize what was seen as American progress, an ideology that began to be questioned only in the twentieth century, by such writers as Robinson Jeffers.

[7599] Euphronios, *Calyx-Krater* (c. 515 B.C.E.), courtesy of The Metropolitan Museum of Art. Greek bowl intended for mixing wine and water. Greek and Roman myths were central to Robinson Jeffers's poetry.

change. Many of his images connote cycles of creation, growth, and destruction. Jeffers's representations of defaced and dehumanized landscapes have influenced modern environmentalists and writers of "eco-literature."

TEACHING TIPS

■ As *The Norton Anthology of American Literature* states, Jeffers "berated rather than celebrated American democracy, expressing his rage at the careless destruction of irrecoverable natural beauty." This stance aligns him with the modern environmental movement, but Jeffers's philosophy was controversial in his day. In "Hurt Hawks," he writes, "I'd sooner, except the penalties, kill a man than a hawk." Use this line as a basis for a class discussion on how far people should go to protect the environment. Remind them of some of the tactics of radical environmental groups, like Earth First, who have "spiked" trees to prevent them from being cut and harvested (a spiked tree has a steel rod placed in its trunk, making it dangerous for loggers to cut the tree with a chainsaw).

■ Have students research and discuss books that were influential in the environmental movement of the last fifty years. Guide them toward Rachel Carson's *Silent Spring*, Paul Ehrlich's *Population Bomb*, Aldo Leopold's *Sand County Almanac*, Daniel Quinn's *Ishmael*, and Joel Cohen's *How Many People Can the Earth Support?* Have them discuss the themes important in the environmental movement; then tie these themes back to Jeffers.

QUESTIONS

Comprehension: Reread the two sections of "Hurt Hawks." What is the difference between the hawks in each section? List some of the things the hawks might symbolize.

Comprehension: What kind of storm is referred to in line 11 of "November Surf"?

Context: How do the images of California in Jeffers's verse compare to the images of California in the works of other writers in this unit? How do Viramontes, Bulosan, and Steinbeck describe the land? What do these otherwise divergent images have in common?

Context: Animal symbolism is plentiful in many cultures. In the United States, dogs often represent loyalty, eagles freedom, and donkeys stubbornness. List the different animals catalogued in "Birds and Fishes." What might each type of animal represent for the poet or reader? Is the symbolic meaning particularly American?

Exploration: Read several Jeffers poems and summarize their representation of nature and humanity. Compare Jeffers's attitude to what you know about literary **modernism**. Based on this exercise, is Jeffers a modernist? What made the modernist writers lose faith in humanity and its institutions?

Exploration: Poems about animals can be understood as the poetic equivalent of still lives: places to show off the poet's powers of observation and empathy. Compare Jeffers's animal poems to those by Elizabeth Bishop ("The Fish" or "The Armadillo") and Marianne Moore ("The Jerboa," "To a Chameleon," or "Poetry").

John Steinbeck (1902–1968)

John Steinbeck's Pulitzer Prize–winning novel, *The Grapes of Wrath*, published in 1939, depicts the plight of the Joads, a family of Oklahoma sharecropper farmers who were driven off the land they worked by the Dust Bowl of the 1930s. The story of their journey to California to find work as agricultural laborers, a journey that they made along the often bleak Highway 66, helped secure Steinbeck's place in American literature.

Born in the Salinas Valley of California, Steinbeck attended Stanford University for a time and then spent a number of years traveling and studying on his own, while developing his craft as a writer. He lived in New York for a short while and attempted to earn money from his writing. He eventually returned to California. His first literary successes were his 1935 novel, *Tortilla Flat*, followed the next year by *In Dubious Battle*. *Tortilla Flat* was about people in a small town in northern California whose exploits mirrored those of the knights of King Arthur, while *In Dubious Battle* focused on a migrant fruit pickers' strike. In 1937, Steinbeck wrote *Of Mice and Men* about two drifters who dreamed of owning their own ranch. Steinbeck's 1938 story collection, *The Long Valley*, includes often-anthologized tales of a young boy, Jody, growing up in a West that is no longer a frontier. Steinbeck's other works include *Cannery Row* (1935), *The Pearl* (1945), *East of Eden* (1952), *The Winter of Our Discontent* (1961), and *Travels with Charley* (1962). He was most interested in the plight of disempowered outsiders, outcasts, and the underprivileged. He died in New York City in 1968, having won the Nobel Prize for literature five years earlier.

While doing research for *The Grapes of Wrath*, Steinbeck visited several of the camps the Farm Security Administration had built to house the homeless migrants who arrived in California from the Dust Bowl states. He spoke to the migrants there and listened to their stories. In fact, Steinbeck wrote a series of newspaper and journal articles about these workers and their plights, which were later gathered into a collection called *Their Blood Is Strong*, published in 1938. Steinbeck's ideas about social justice for the economic underclass of American society influenced both later American writers such as William Kennedy and popular songwriters such as Woody Guthrie, Bob Dylan, and Bruce Springsteen. His journalistic style has been imitated and admired by authors such as Dorothy Parker and Tom Wolfe.

TEACHING TIPS

■ Writer John Steinbeck and director John Ford had very different visions of *The Grapes of Wrath*. Ask students to watch the film after having read the book and compare the two versions of the story, espe-

[5872] Dorothea Lange, *Migrant Workers Near Manteca, Ca.* (1938), courtesy of the Library of Congress [LC-USF34-018767-C].

STEINBECK WEB ARCHIVE

[3343] Dorothea Lange, *People Living in Miserable Poverty, Elm Grove, Oklahoma County, Oklahoma* (1936), courtesy of the Library of Congress [LC-USF34-009695-E]. In *The Grapes of Wrath* Steinbeck depicts the life of Oklahoma farmers during the Dust Bowl. The Great Depression coincided with terrible droughts that killed crops and pushed families like the Joads west to California seeking better land and a better life.

[3347] Dorothea Lange, *Power Farming Displaces Tenants. Childress County, Texas Panhandle* (1938), courtesy of the Library of Congress [LC-USF34-TO1-018281-C DLC]. Alternately titled "Tractored Out." Mechanization made large farmers wealthy, but left small farmers, tenants, and sharecroppers without jobs. The increased use of machines instead of manual labor, coupled with drought and falling crop prices during the Great Depression, left many farmers homeless.

[5695] Anonymous, *Film Set during the Making of* The Grapes of Wrath, *with Part of Cast and Film Crew in Front of Small, Dilapidated House* (1939), courtesy of the Library of Congress [LC-USZ62-114292]. Photograph of set and actors for *The Grapes of Wrath,* one of John Steinbeck's most famous novels. The book centered on the Joads, a family of Oklahoma sharecroppers during the Dust Bowl who became migrant workers.

[5872] Dorothea Lange, *Migrant Workers Near Manteca, Ca.* (1938), courtesy of the Library of Congress [LC-USF34-018767-C]. Dorothea Lange's caption to this picture reads, "A former rehabilitation client harvesting milo maize. Now operating own farm under Tenant Purchase Act. A year and a half ahead on their payments. Average loan for purchase of farm and improvements in San Joaquin County is seven thousand four hundred and sixty-five dollars."

[5910] Anonymous, *Steinbeck Portrait* (n.d.), courtesy of the Center for Steinbeck Studies. Like many American authors, John Steinbeck, though never formally investigated, attracted the attention of the FBI in the 1940s due to his involvement with communist organizations.

[5911] Anonymous, *Younger Steinbeck Head Shot* (n.d.), courtesy of the Center for Steinbeck Studies. Steinbeck concluded his Nobel Prize acceptance speech with the following words: "Having taken God-like power, we must seek in ourselves for the responsibility and the wisdom we once prayed some deity might have. Man himself has become our greatest hazard and our only hope. So that today, Saint John the Apostle may well be paraphrased: In the end is the word, and the word is man, and the word is with man."

[8968] Louis Owens, Interview: "Steinbeck's Major Theme" (2002), courtesy of *American Passages* and Annenberg/CPB. Professor Louis Owens discusses Steinbeck's critique of America.

cially the altered ending. Ask why Ford may have wished to change the story in the way that he did. You might encourage them to research this topic, as there are many easily accessible works that discuss its significance.

■ Many of Steinbeck's fictional works focus on outsiders at odds with the local community. Throughout his career, Steinbeck was fascinated by the tales of King Arthur and the Knights of the Round Table. Discuss the themes and ethics underlying the Arthurian myths, focusing on Arthur's desire to unify a kingdom in conflict with itself. Examine some of the rules these tales propose for running society. Connect this discussion to *The Grapes of Wrath.*

QUESTIONS

Comprehension: Acts of charity and compassion occur from time to time in *The Grapes of Wrath.* Examine the scene near the end of Chapter 15 concerning the bread and the candy. Why did Steinbeck include such scenes in a novel that is often intent on showing American cruelty and social injustice?

Comprehension: Steinbeck's novel includes many images of the horrific condition of the land and juxtaposes them with images of the horrific social conditions brought on by industrialization and business. What is the purpose of such juxtaposed images?

Context: *The Grapes of Wrath* is sometimes referred to as a jeremiad: a lament of the spiritual and moral decline of a community and an interpretation of recent misfortunes as God's just punishment for that decline. (See Unit 3 for more discussion of this form in the American literary tradition.) Paradoxically, these misfortunes are seen as proof of God's love and of the group's status as a "chosen people." Do you think this novel fits well within that genre? Why or why not?

Context: Compare Chapter 11 of *The Grapes of Wrath* with the many Dust Bowl images in the *American Passages* archive. How do these photographs compare to Steinbeck's descriptions of the land?

Exploration: In his essay "Freedom from Want," Carlos Bulosan writes, "We are not really free unless we use what we produce. So long as the fruit of our labor is denied us, so long will want manifest itself in a world of slaves." Review the literary elements of slave narratives (focus on food and water, fear for the family, variations of hope and hopelessness, dehumanization, power and powerlessness, and the desire for education). Think about the ways that Steinbeck's novel about migrants compares and contrasts with the slave narratives of the nineteenth century. What qualities do they share? What are some differences?

Muriel Rukeyser (1913–1980)

Muriel Rukeyser was a political poet whose verse is noted for its intricate style and sophistication. She was born in New York City and attended Vassar College and Columbia University. Though from a wealthy family, Rukeyser was deeply concerned with the plight of laborers, the downtrodden, and the disadvantaged. She was shocked by the working conditions and meager wages of the lower classes and attracted to the solidarity she witnessed in the labor movement. Her political activism began in 1932 when she was covering the Scottsboro trials in Alabama for the *Student Review* and was briefly detained by the police because she was seen speaking with African American journalists. Later, she would lobby for the loyalists during the Spanish Civil War, speak out on behalf of Sacco and Vanzetti, protest the Vietnam War, and write against the persecution of Kurds in Iran. Her poems of social protest deal with the inequalities she witnessed in race, gender, and class, both in America and abroad. Rukeyser always considered herself a poet of the radical left, and her poems often connect an emotional reaction with a political or social event.

[7426] Herbert Photos, Inc., *Bartolomeo Vanzetti and Nicola Sacco, Manacled Together* (1927), courtesy of the Library of Congress [LC-USZ62-124547].

She published over twenty books of poetry, including *The Collected Poems of Muriel Rukeyser* (1978), seven books of prose, and five books of letters. In addition to writing poetry, Rukeyser translated works by Octavio Paz and Bertolt Brecht; wrote a biography of Wendell Willkie, an internationalist and strong opponent of American isolationism before World War II; and authored several children's books. Rukeyser never wrote in any particular poetical form, but instead preferred to experiment with language and structure. Her intricate and complex verse addresses a wide variety of subjects, including anthropology, war, the environment, biology, psychology, religion, and social issues such as women's rights, motherhood, lesbianism, and anti-Semitism.

TEACHING TIPS

■ Rukeyser often celebrates working people in her poems. Have students list ten categories of working people. For each category, have them come up with one or two powerful symbols that represent that category of worker or profession. Use the activity to discuss how symbols function in literary works.

■ Have students read "The Conjugation of the Paramecium," which on the surface appears to be a brief vignette about reproduction. Ask them to think about what the poem might mean. Remind students about Rukeyser's usual themes of social protest, the "uniting spirit" between common workers and laborers, and the emptiness of individual consumption.

QUESTIONS

Comprehension: In what ways does Rukeyser's "Alloy" condemn the steel-making industry?

Comprehension: Though the speaker of "Alloy" seems to be addressing "things," how is the poem really about people?

RUKEYSER WEB ARCHIVE

[4554] Prentiss Taylor, *Scottsboro Limited* (1931), courtesy of the Library of Congress [LC-USZC4-4717]. Lithograph from *Scottsboro Limited*, a collection of four poems and a play by Langston Hughes. This collection protested the incarceration, conviction, and death sentence of the Scottsboro boys, nine African American youths unjustly accused of raping two white women.

[6180] United Women's Contingent, *When Women Decide This War Should End, This War Will End: Join the United Women's Contingent on April 24* (1971), courtesy of the Library of Congress [LC-USZC4-6882]. Protest poster against the Vietnam War. The anti-war, civil rights, women's rights, and gay liberation movements were connected politically and artistically.

[7426] Herbert Photos, Inc., *Bartolomeo Vanzetti and Nicola Sacco, Manacled Together* (1927), courtesy of the Library of Congress [LC-USZ62-124547]. Sacco and Vanzetti surrounded by a crowd of onlookers and guards before entering a Dedham, Massachusetts, courthouse. Victims of the first Red

Scare, these political radicals received the death penalty, despite a lack of evidence.

[7650] Anonymous, *Ozzie Powell, Defendant in the Scottsboro Case, Full Length Portrait* (1936), courtesy of the Library of Congress [LC-USZ62-121575]. Photograph of Ozzie Powell, one of the nine defendants in the Scottsboro case, in Decatur, Alabama. Author Muriel Rukeyser's political activism began when she covered the Scottsboro trials and was questioned by police because she had been seen speaking with African American journalists. The Scottsboro case was characterized by extreme racial and social injustice.

Comprehension: Find the definition of "alloy" in the dictionary. Why might Rukeyser have used this word as the title of her poem?

Context: Steel production was a major industry in the United States in the late 1930s; however, relatively high labor costs and concerns about pollution and the environment gradually moved most steel production overseas. How does Rukeyser foreshadow the loss of this industry in "Alloy"?

Context: Who is "the gangster" referred to in the beginning of "Alloy" and what effect does that term have on the reader? Remember that gangsters loomed large in the public imagination in the 1920s and 1930s. Figures such as John Dillinger, Al Capone, and Bugsy Siegel dominated newspaper headlines for their involvement in drug dealing, prostitution, gambling, and loan sharking.

Exploration: Apprehension about the power of technology and industry continues as a major theme in late-twentieth-century science fiction movies. Analyze how such films as *Terminator* and *Minority Report* represent these fears. Pay particular attention to what the films' endings say about the place of technology in our lives.

Carlos Bulosan (1913–1956)

About 150,000 Filipinos immigrated to the United States between 1906 and 1946. Early on, many Filipinos came to America to seek an education and then return home. But starting in the 1920s, most came looking for work. Along the West Coast and in Hawaii and Alaska, they sought jobs as migrant workers, cannery workers, and domestic servants. They were subject to intense racism and discrimination, and Filipino men were beaten and driven out of town by mobs if they were seen with white women. It was within this atmosphere that Bulosan arrived in the United States.

[6061] Anonymous, *Filipino Man Processing Fruit* (c. 1930), courtesy of the James Earl Wood Collection of Photographs Relating to Filipinos in California, The Bancroft Library, University of California, Berkeley.

Carlos Bulosan is the first important literary voice for Filipinos in the United States. Bulosan's most famous novel, *America Is in the Heart*, was published in 1946. It depicts the terrible living and working conditions of Filipino immigrants struggling to survive in America. Bulosan came to the United States from the Philippines in the early 1930s. He washed dishes, worked in canneries, and picked fruits and vegetables up and down the West Coast, including the area in the Salinas Valley where many of John Steinbeck's novels take place. He eventually became a labor activist and tried to address racial and economic discrimination in the United States. After meeting labor organizer Chris Mensalves, he helped organize a union for fish cannery workers in California. During a long period of poor health, Bulosan read the works of many American writers, which helped improve his English and inspired him to become a writer. Bulosan gradually gained recognition and respect as a poet and social commentator. His work appeared in a number of prominent magazines and journals in the 1940s, including the *Saturday Evening Post*, *New Yorker*, *Harper's Bazaar*, and *Poetry*. Bulosan's works include poetry collections, *Letter from America* (1942),

Chorus from America (1942), and *The Voice of Bataan* (1943), as well as the novels *The Cry and the Dedication* (written in the 1950s and published posthumously in 1995) and *The Sound of Falling Light* (1960).

In the 1950s, at the height of the anti-communist movement, Bulosan's labor-organizing activities and early involvement with the communist party prompted Senator Joseph McCarthy and the House **Un-American Activities Committee** to blacklist him. Bulosan died in Seattle in poverty and relative obscurity in 1956. In the 1970s his works were "discovered" by the Asian American community, which recognized their historical and cultural importance. As one of the first writers to explore how Filipinos were forging an American identity, Bulosan influenced such Asian American writers as Jessica Hagedorn and Maxine Hong Kingston.

TEACHING TIPS

■ To give students a better contextual understanding of Bulosan's works, divide them into groups and have them prepare class presentations on (1) a brief history of the Philippines before 1895, (2) the interaction between the Philippines and the United States between 1895 and the 1950s, (3) the treatment of Filipino immigrants in the United States, especially in the mid-twentieth century, and (4) a recent history of the Philippines, focusing on the Marcos family.

■ Bulosan's writing depicts the economic and racial prejudice he encountered and observed in the United States. However, even after enduring open hostility, continuous threats, violence, and insufferable living and working conditions, he still fills his work with the hope of equality for all people. What other stories, films, or television programs can students recall where characters face constant adversity but never give up on their hopes and dreams? Examples might range from classical works, such as *The Odyssey*, to Jacobs's *Incidents in the Life of a Slave Girl*, to more recent works such as Hemingway's *The Old Man and the Sea*. They might also include works from popular culture, like *The Lord of the Rings*, *Star Wars*, or *Billy Elliot*. Discuss these examples in the context of Bulosan's works.

QUESTIONS

Comprehension: America Is in the Heart was criticized for its negative portrayal of the lives of Filipinos in the United States. Why would Bulosan show such a dark side to Filipino life in America, from constant drinking and gambling to stealing, prostitution, and murder? How do these portrayals help him make a point about the lives of these immigrants?

Comprehension: According to the narrator of "Be American," in what ways has Consorcio "become" an American?

Context: The status of Filipinos who immigrated to America was often indeterminate. Since the Philippines were a U.S. territory, immigrants were known as "nationals" and could enter the country freely until 1934, when the Tydings-McDuffie Act promised independence

BULOSAN WEB ARCHIVE

[1891] Rand McNally & Co., *New and Enlarged Scale Railroad and County Map of California Showing Every Railroad Station and Post Office in the State* (1883), courtesy of the Library of Congress, Geography and Map Division [LC Railroad maps, 189]. Building railroads, a major force in California's economic development, required extensive mapping of geographical features. Later maps like this one redefined territory through industrial transportation, political units, and government communications outposts, which guided investment and commerce.

[5385] Anonymous, *Carlos Bulosan* (n.d.), courtesy of *Filipinos: Forgotten Asian Americans*. Posed portrait of author Carlos Bulosan. Bulosan's semi-autobiographical work *America Is in the Heart* describes the lives of Filipino immigrants in America, particularly their difficult working and living conditions.

[5869] Dorothea Lange, *Filipino Migrant Workers* (1938), courtesy of the Library of Congress [LC-USF34-018671-D]. Large field with Filipino migrant laborers working in row. Filipinos migrated to the United States in three major waves. The first and second wave faced exploitative working conditions in agriculture, canneries, and other manual labor industries.

[6060] James Earl Wood, *Filipino Laborers, Wide Shot* (n.d.), courtesy of the University of California at Berkeley, Bancroft Library. Young Filipino working with boxes from cannery in field. Many Filipino immigrants found work at canneries, where conditions were often poor.

[6061] Anonymous, *Filipino Man Processing Fruit* (c. 1930), courtesy of the James Earl Wood Collection of Photographs Relating to Filipinos in California, The Bancroft Library, University of California, Berkeley. Photograph of a Filipino man preparing fruit to be sold. Despite the Philippines' status as a U.S. territory, Filipino immigrants faced discrimination and racism in twentieth-century America. Carlos Bulosan worked as a fruit picker when he first arrived in the United States.

[8976] Louis Owens, Interview: "Bulosan's View of American Capitalism" (2002), courtesy of *American Passages* and Annenberg/CPB. Professor Louis Owens discusses Carlos Bulosan's view of American capitalism.

to the Philippines in ten years. At the outbreak of World War II, Franklin Delano Roosevelt granted Filipino military enlistees U.S. citizenship, but it wasn't until 1946, when Truman signed the Filipino Naturalization Bill, that Filipinos became citizens. Keeping all this in mind, locate passages in Bulosan's work that demonstrate a sense of homelessness or a longing for identity and place.

Exploration: In *America Is in the Heart*, Bulosan recalls the creation of a culture of anti-colonial insurgency by Filipino peasants against those who had attempted to control the Philippines in the past (Spain and the United States). Why would this past make immigrant Filipinos especially good organizers of labor and **trade unions** to stand against the U.S. businesses and farms that exploited migrant workers?

Exploration: *America Is in the Heart*, an autobiography, includes stories and tales of incidents that did not actually happen to Bulosan but were culled from the lives of other Filipino Americans much like himself. How does Bulosan's use of the autobiographical genre compare with other famous American autobiographies, such as Franklin's *Autobiography*, Douglass's *Narrative*, Jacobs's *Incidents in the Life of a Slave Girl*, or Adams's *The Education of Henry Adams*? Consider stylistic as well as thematic similarities and differences.

[5979] Dorothea Lange, *Pinal County, Arizona. Mexican Boy Age 13, Coming in from Cotton Field at Noon* (1940), courtesy of the U.S. National Archives & Records Administration [CTL# NWDNS-83-G-41839].

Tomas Rivera (1935–1984)

Tomas Rivera was born in Crystal City, Texas. During his childhood, he accompanied his parents, who worked as farm laborers, on their journeys in the Midwest, from Missouri to Michigan to Minnesota. Rivera worked as a migrant farm laborer himself in the 1950s. He graduated from Southwest Texas State University with a degree in English and earned his Ph.D. in romance languages and literature from the University of Oklahoma. He was a professor of Spanish and held administrative positions at various universities, including the University of Texas at El Paso. Rivera's works include . . . *y no se lo tragó la tierra/* . . . *And the Earth Did Not Devour Him* (1971); *The Harvest* (1989), a short story collection; and *The Searchers* (1973), a volume of collected poetry. *This Migrant Earth* (1987) is an English translation by Rolando Hinojosa of . . . *y no se lo tragó la tierra/* . . . *And the Earth Did Not Devour Him*.

A number of Rivera's works explore the world of the migrant worker in America. Rivera did not view his writing as political but rather as a universal statement about the human condition. . . . *y no se lo tragó la tierra/* . . . *And the Earth Did Not Devour Him* is considered a milestone in the Mexican American literary canon. It is written in South Texas Spanish and does not follow a chronological storyline but presents a series of stream-of-consciousness vignettes and tales that are loosely united by an anonymous child-narrator reflecting on the lives of migrant workers in the late 1940s and early 1950s. Somewhat Faulknerian in style, it deftly portrays the economic and cultural conditions experienced by Mexican American migrant workers in the years following World War II.

■ Have your students brainstorm in small groups about migrant workers, keeping notes that they can use to present a report to the class. Collect the information from the groups and display it on a chalkboard or screen so that you can discuss it as a class. After they have read Rivera's novel, ask students to revisit their compiled information and make revisions. What changes in facts and opinions occur? Discuss those changes.

■ Have students compare different translations of the opening or closing paragraphs of *. . . y no se lo tragó la tierra/ . . . And the Earth Did Not Devour Him*. What differences do they find? Discuss the problems of reading translated works.

QUESTIONS

Comprehension: What is most shocking about the chapter "The Children Couldn't Wait"? What does this chapter say about the values and views of those who hire migrants? What broader social views are reflected in it?

Comprehension: The final chapter, "Under the House," seems to bind these discordant stories into a whole. Try to identify which italicized quotations go with which story. How does this chapter help unify the work?

Comprehension: . . . *y no se lo tragó la tierra/ . . . And the Earth Did Not Devour Him* demands that readers make connections among the twenty-seven episodes. Why is it important to the author that readers make these connections? Why might Rivera want readers to feel uncomfortable and somewhat lost until after they've experienced these bits and pieces of tales and conversations?

Context: Rivera's . . . *y no se lo tragó la tierra/ . . . And the Earth Did Not Devour Him* is very fragmented in style, somewhat in the nature of works by the U.S. and European modernists. What elements of literary **modernism** does Rivera's book embrace? How does it differ from other modernist works you have read?

Context: Have students imagine how Rivera's . . . *y no se lo tragó la tierra/ . . . And the Earth Did Not Devour Him* could be made into a film. What would such a film be like? What changes would need to be made in the plot or structure of the work to make it a viewable film? If possible, show the class the 1994 film by Severo Perez, *And the Earth Did Not Swallow Him*, based on the book.

Exploration: . . . *y no se lo tragó la tierra/ . . . And the Earth Did Not Devour Him* makes clear the extent of child labor that goes on among industries and farms that hire migrant workers. Research U.S. and international child labor laws. Which other works from this unit demonstrate child labor abuses?

[5864] Dorothea Lange, *Mexicans, Field Laborers, on Strike in Cotton Picking Season, Apply to Farm Security Administration for Relief. Bakersfield, California* (1938), courtesy of the Library of Congress [LC-USF34-018627]. The Farm Security Administration (1937–42) was formed under the Department of Agriculture. It provided low-cost loans and assistance to small farmers and sharecroppers, constructed camps for migrant workers, restored eroded soil, and put flood prevention practices into effect.

[5979] Dorothea Lange, *Pinal County, Arizona. Mexican Boy Age 13, Coming in from Cotton Field at Noon* (1940), courtesy of the U.S. National Archives & Records Administration [CTL# NWDNS-83-G-41839]. Dorothea Lange's full caption for this image reads, "Pinal County, Arizona. Mexican boy age 13, coming in from cotton field at noon. He picked 27 pounds of Pima cotton (earnings about $.45) during the morning. Note stamped work ticket in his hand."

[6138] Anonymous, *Mrs. Lionel Sanchez with Child during Migrant Hunger Strike* (1970), courtesy of the Denver Public Library, Western History Collection. This Hispanic American woman feeds her daughter from a bottle during a strike of Colorado migrant workers. Author Tomas Rivera worked as a migrant farm laborer in the 1950s; his novel *And The Earth Did Not Devour Him* is narrated by a child laborer.

[6364] Russell Lee, *Mexican Woman Cutting Spinach, La Pryor, Texas* (1939), courtesy of the Library of Congress [LC-USF33-012046-M3]. Agricultural worker in Texas. Author Tomas Rivera, who was born in Texas, experienced and wrote about migrant agricultural work.

Rudolfo Anaya (b. 1937)

Rudolfo Anaya was born in Pastura, New Mexico. His family moved to Albuquerque when he was fifteen. While working as a public school

teacher, he earned degrees from the University of New Mexico. Anaya's first novel, *Bless Me, Ultima* (1972), is the story of a boy growing up in a small New Mexico village during World War II. His second novel, *Heart of Aztlan* (1976), mixes mystical elements with an examination of social concerns for the twentieth-century Chicano worker. *Tortuga* (1979), his third novel, is another story about growing up as a **Hispanic** in America, this time from the perspective of a boy wearing a full body cast. Anaya has published many other books, including epic poems, short story collections, and nonfiction works. Two of his more recent works are *Albuquerque* (1992) and *Zia Summer* (1995).

Bless Me, Ultima focuses on the impact of World War II on a small community in New Mexico. The protagonist's participation in the war lessens his feeling of isolation from American society. As it did for other minority groups, World War II accelerated the process of assimilation and acculturation for Mexican Americans. The war prompted the movement of Mexican Americans into cities where industries were badly in need of labor. Many Mexican Americans joined the various branches of the armed forces. *Bless Me, Ultima* was one of the first novels to document this process.

Many of Anaya's works blend elements from Chicano and Anglo culture and explore how personal and public mythologies answer questions about an individual's place in the universe. Anaya is particularly influenced by the geography and culture of the area he grew up in, the Mexico–New Mexico border.

TEACHING TIPS

■ Have your students research *Bless Me, Ultima* (1972), the most frequently taught Latino juvenile book and one of the first Chicano books to enter the American literary canon. Ask them to explore why this novel is so popular with junior high and high school readers.

■ The antics in Anaya's "The Christmas Play" are reminiscent of the slapstick comedy of the Marx Brothers and the Three Stooges. If possible, show the class a Three Stooges episode and ask them to analyze it beyond the physical comedy. Many of the Three Stooges episodes have a background of the Stooges looking for work or food during the depression, which leads to their getting into trouble. Have the students discuss the film clip in that context. Another comparison to the comedy in this story is the traditional *actos* from the early days of the Teatro Campesino. Some of the *actos* of Luis Valdez contained comic figures that satirized the roles Chicanos were relegated to as irrelevant and stereotypical. Examining Anaya's story in this light might offer interesting insights into its meaning and purpose.

QUESTIONS

Comprehension: What is the overall tone of "The Christmas Play"? Why did the author choose this tone?
Comprehension: Why don't the boys care that they are messing up

Miss Violet's play? What is surprising about how Miss Violet treats the boys?

Comprehension: "The Christmas Play" begins and ends with images of a quiet tomb. Why is this important to the story?

Context: How do the tone and setting of "The Christmas Play" compare to the tones and settings of works by Helena Maria Viramontes and Tomas Rivera?

Exploration: Late-capitalist societies often value immediate access to goods, information, and institutional resources as basic features of everyday life. How does such an environment affect people's expectations of a "proper" education, and how does it compare with other environments' notions of education? While also considering how the process of becoming educated influences one's aesthetic preferences for art and literature, explore this question in relation to Anaya's story as well as the works of Harriet Jacobs, Frederick Douglass, and Mark Twain.

Alberto Ríos (b. 1952)

The son of a Mexican American father and a British mother, Alberto Ríos was born in Nogales, Arizona, on the Mexican border. Much of his work draws on the mixture of his parents' cultures and growing up in the American Southwest. He received his B.A. from the University of Arizona and earned an M.F.A. in creative writing in 1979. Ríos's collections of poetry include *Whispering to Fool the Wind* (1982), *Five Indiscretions* (1985), *The Dime Orchard Woman: Poems* (1988), *Teodora Luna's Two Kisses* (1992), and *The Smallest Muscle in the Human Body* (2002). He has also published three collections of stories, *The Iguana Killer* (1984), *Pig Cookies and Other Stories* (1995), and *The Curtain of Trees* (1999). In addition, he has written a memoir, *Capirotada* (1999), about growing up on the U.S.-Mexican border. Ríos has taught at Arizona State University since the early 1980s.

Ríos's storytelling draws on the oral traditions of his Latino heritage while celebrating its diversity and sense of community. His speakers and characters reveal the tensions of living in a racially charged area of the Southwest. **Magical realism**—a mixture of fantasy and realism—characterizes much of Ríos's work. Ríos thinks of teaching and writing as complementary activities. In one interview he explains, "When I sit down to write something, I'm not neglecting my teaching one bit. And when I speak aloud in front of a class, I'm not neglecting my writing one bit. They are two arms of the same body. They serve each other." Frequently taught and translated, Ríos's work has been adapted both for dance and as popular music.

TEACHING TIP

■ A skillful promoter of his own work and reputation, Ríos has an elaborate Web site hosted by Arizona State University. Review this Web site in class with your students or have them review it at home. What message about his own life and work does Ríos seem to be pro-

[5245] Salvador Brquez, *Dolores del Rios as Ramona* (1928), courtesy of the *Los Angeles Times.*

RÍOS WEB ARCHIVE

[2195] Robert Runyon, *Woman and Two Children, South Texas Border* (1920), courtesy of the Library of Congress. Photograph of woman and children at the Mexico-U.S. border. Folk music and literature from this region often highlight the conflicts between Anglos and Chicanos. See Americo Paredes's novel *George Washington Gomez.* Writer Alberto Ríos was born near the border, and much of his work deals with the interaction of Mexican and American cultures. His first book, *Whispering to Fool the Wind*, won the Walt Whitman Award.

[3551] Anonymous, *Latino. A Jitterbugging Yuma. Arizona 1942* (1942), courtesy of the Library of Congress. Latino youths dancing in Yuma, Arizona, near the hometown of writer Alberto Ríos. Ríos teaches English at Arizona State University. His memoir *Capirotada* recounts his childhood on the Mexico-U.S. border.

[5245] Salvador Brquez, *Dolores del Rios as Ramona* (1928), courtesy of the *Los Angeles Times*. Newspaper movie illustration. Helen Hunt Jackson's novel *Ramona* failed to improve treatment of California Indians as she had hoped it would. Instead, elements of the story's romantic depiction of California's Hispanic heritage became firmly entrenched in the mythology of the region.

[8754] Elliot Young, Interview: "Aztlán as the U.S. Southwest" (2002), courtesy of *American Passages* and Annenberg/CPB. Professor Elliot Young discusses Aztlán, the mythical city from which the Mexiques came before they arrived in central Mexico, and the role Aztlán plays in Chicano consciousness.

moting? Ask students to support their answers with specific evidence from the site.

QUESTIONS

Comprehension: In "Advice to a First Cousin," the speaker combines humor and superstition with wisdom. In the second part of the poem, who are the "scorpions" about which grandmother speaks? What is the moral? Why does this poem fit well into the oral tradition of storytelling?

Comprehension: "Refugio's Hair" tells how a woman's hair had to be cut off. What gives this poem its mythic quality? Instead of just telling a story, how does this poem incorporate religious or cultural icons?

Comprehension: What two cultures are represented in "Day of the Refugios"? Are they given equal time in the poem?

Context: Compare and contrast Ríos's poem "Seniors" with the ending of Viramontes's novel *Under the Feet of Jesus* or Anaya's story "The Christmas Play." What similar images and themes are displayed? How does the verse presentation differ from the prose presentations?

Exploration: In 1965, Congress amended the Immigration and Nationality Act, repealing the national-origin quotas and race-based policies that had all but prohibited the entrance of "less desirable" people who might not have had the "capacity to assimilate." This legislative change profoundly impacted U.S. demographics, allowing for an ethnic heterogeneity that went against the grain of "melting pot" cultural homogeneity. Research this topic, while also comparing the experiences of marginalized or oppressed groups as documented by authors writing before and after this date. Consider too a prominent theme in Ríos's work—that cultures can be woven together, preserving their best parts, without losing their unique traditions.

Helena Maria Viramontes (b. 1954)

Viramontes is a Chicana writer who was born in East Los Angeles, California. She attended Immaculate Heart College and the University of California, Irvine. She is co-founder of the Southern California Latino Writers and Film Makers group and teaches at Cornell University. Her first published book of short stories, *"The Moth" and Other Stories* (1985), focuses on everyday oppression in the lives of ordinary women, mostly Chicanas. In 1993 she published *Paris Rats in E.L.A.*, which she also rewrote as a screenplay. Her best-known work, the 1995 novel *Under the Feet of Jesus*, portrays the life of Estrella, a young migrant worker who must cope with the many difficult situations in which she and her family find themselves. Viramontes's most recent novel is *Their Dogs Came with Them* (1996), which explores the brutality of the Spanish Conquest of the Americas. Viramontes's powerful style is sweepingly realistic in scope and uses natural and religious symbolism.

Because Viramontes believes that writing can bring about social change, she tackles social issues in her work. In *Feminism on the Border*, Sonia Saldivar-Hull notes that many of Viramontes's works are not typical Latina "quest for origins" stories but rather seek to transform and rework concepts of the **Chicano** family. They tend to disrupt the notion of the monolithic Latino/a family as a refuge from racism and class exploitation and instead relocate "chicano families from secretive, barricaded sites of male rule to contested terrains where girls and women perform valued rituals that do not necessarily adhere to androcentric familial traditions." According to Saldivar-Hull, Viramontes's work permits both Chicanas and Chicanos to exist as unique subjects in a U.S. Latino/a America.

[6125] Anonymous, *Protest for Legislature to Improve Conditions [for Migrant Farm Workers]* (1969), courtesy of the Denver Public Library, Western History Collection.

TEACHING TIPS

■ Ask your students to imagine that producers have decided to make a film of *Under the Feet of Jesus* but want to extend the story beyond the novel's ending. Have them make a plot outline for a new section 6 and consider these questions: How would you carry on the story? Would you radically change the mood, tone, or theme of the story or keep it the same? How would Viramontes feel about this new ending?

■ Have students consider where their fresh produce comes from, other than shelves in the supermarket. Ask them to ponder on all the people who have touched the fruits and vegetables they eat.

QUESTIONS

Comprehension: Early in *Under the Feet of Jesus*, Estrella thinks, "It was always a question of work, and work depended on the harvest, the car running, their health, the condition of the road, how long the money held out, and the weather, which meant they could depend on nothing." How does this foreshadowing affect the novel?

Comprehension: Do you think Estrella was justified in the actions she took at the doctor's office? Was the nurse to blame? Why or why not?

Comprehension: Why does Viramontes use so many Spanish phrases and sentences in the novel? How does the presence of so much Spanish affect a reader's experience of the text?

Comprehension: What does the statue of Jesucristo represent or symbolize for Petra? What happens to the statue? What might this signify?

Context: Compare and contrast the racial, social, and economic conditions of the migrant workers in *Under the Feet of Jesus*, *America Is in the Heart*, and *The Grapes of Wrath*. Make a table or chart that clearly displays your findings. Create categories that are repeated in all these works.

Context: At the center of *Under the Feet of Jesus* are two women who must endure enormous suffering and hardship. How does having

VIRAMONTES
WEB ARCHIVE

[6125] Anonymous, *Protest for Legislature to Improve Conditions [for Migrant Farm Workers]* (1969), courtesy of the Denver Public Library, Western History Collection. Photograph of a migrant worker protest at the Capitol Building in Denver, Colorado. Hispanic and white men and women join together to urge improved living conditions for migrant workers. A priest holds a flag that says, "Huelga U.F.W.O.C. AFL-CIO Delano." Another man holds a sign that reads, "Denver Witnesses for Human Dignity."

[6708] Judith F. Baca, *Pieces of Stardust* (1992), courtesy of the Social and Public Art Resource Center, © Judith F. Baca, *Pieces of Stardust*, 1992. Judith Baca is an acclaimed muralist whose work is informed by the belief that art can be a forum for social dialogue, as well as a tool for social change. In this sense, her work shares much with the writings of Gloria Anzaldúa, Cherríe Moraga, and Helena Maria Viramontes and builds on the work of Mexican muralist Diego Rivera.

[7916] Helena Maria Viramontes, *Helena Maria Viramontes—Writer* (2002), courtesy of Annenberg/CPB. Frame of author Helena Maria Viramontes. Best known for her novel *Under the Feet of Jesus*, Viramontes deals with social justice in much of her work.

[8755] Helena Maria Viramontes, Interview: "Dominant Cultures in the United States" (2002), courtesy of *American Passages* and Annenberg/CPB. Helena Maria Viramontes discusses the message of the dominant U.S. cultures to the Chicano/a population.

[8981] Helena Maria Viramontes, Interview: "Looking for Hope" (2002), courtesy of *American Passages* and Annenberg/CPB. Helena Maria Viramontes discusses the importance of communication to the creation of hope.

women as protagonists make this work different from similar works with male protagonists?

Exploration: One definition of charity is benevolence or generosity toward others. Many claim that significant portions of our own social and governmental structures are based on this concept of charity. If this is the case, why is such a lack of charity by either socially dominant white characters or uncaring governmental organizations portrayed in the literary works associated with this unit? In what ways does this lack of charity seem to extend particularly to migrants, immigrants, and minorities?

Exploration: Compare Viramontes to the Chicana authors in Unit 2, particularly to Gloria Anzaldúa and her definition of the Borderlands as an open wound. How are these authors similar? How are they different? Do they concentrate on the same subjects and themes? How do the authors in Unit 2 provide a context for Viramontes's works?

Suggested Author Pairings

CARLOS BULOSAN AND HELENA MARIA VIRAMONTES

Both Bulosan and Viramontes focus on the importance of family and the connections among family members. How do these authors demonstrate the effects of class restrictions and racism on the family? How does each of them demonstrate the value of family in hard times? Do they have different approaches to their treatment of family issues? Which author seems more celebratory of family connections and relationships? Why might this be?

HENRY DAVID THOREAU AND JOHN STEINBECK

Both Thoreau and Steinbeck explore the social and moral disadvantages of increased mechanization and technology. Their harsh criticisms of "progress" and technology may seem counterintuitive to many Americans. After all, most of our institutions, and certainly the popular press, seem to praise these advances. Do these writers offer effective arguments against technology? How do their treatments of this subject overlap? How do they differ?

HELENA MARIA VIRAMONTES AND TOMAS RIVERA

Viramontes's *Under the Feet of Jesus* details the physical labor performed by migrant workers, while Rivera's *. . . y no se lo tragó la tierra/ . . . And the Earth Did Not Devour Him* more subtly alludes to such labor. Both works are coming-of-age stories as well as *testimonios*, narratives that bear witness to the migrant worker's plight. What effects do these themes have on the reader? How do Viramontes's and Rivera's representations of physical labor illuminate these themes?

In their writings, both Thoreau and Bulosan combine events from their own lives with events that happened to others. Discuss autobiography as a genre, and consider whether it is possible for any author to write an autobiography that is entirely without embellishment of some kind. Such a discussion could start with Benjamin Franklin's *Autobiography*, which begins with a letter of advice about growing up to a son who was in fact already grown when the *Autobiography* was written. Thoreau takes an experience that occurs over two years and condenses it to one in *Walden*; in addition, he downplays the extent to which his mother and sister made his "simple life" possible. Likewise, many of the events that Bulosan writes about in the first person in *America Is in the Heart* never really happened to him.

CORE CONTEXTS

The Great Depression and the Dust Bowl

The New York Stock Exchange collapse in October of 1929 marked the beginning of the Great Depression, which lasted until America entered World War II in the early 1940s. The longest and most severe economic depression in American history, the Great Depression caused untold economic hardship and great social upheaval throughout the United States and the world. From 1929 to 1932, stock prices fell dramatically in the United States, with many stocks losing over 80 percent of their value. Banks closed, unemployment skyrocketed, and factory and industrial production fell sharply. By 1932 nearly a third of the workforce in America was unable to find jobs. Many Americans lost their savings, their homes, and their livelihoods. Adding to the nation's difficulties, the ecological disaster of the Dust Bowl descended on the Midwest between 1935 and 1939. Constant drought and poor land management led to arid, lifeless growing conditions for struggling farmers and sharecroppers and ruined the little livelihood they had during the depression. Over 300,000 people were forced to leave the afflicted area and migrate to the West to look for employment. The advanced mechanization of industry, factory, and farm work also adversely affected some American workers during this period. Many work functions were taken over by machines, causing widespread worker displacement and relocation. The Great Depression, the Dust Bowl, and other factors caused a massive worker migration to alternate professions and alternate areas of the country. The Great Depression shaped the psyches of an entire generation; those who lived through the depression became acutely aware of the power of broad economic forces to impact individual lives.

[3343] Dorothea Lange, *People Living in Miserable Poverty, Elm Grove, Oklahoma County, Oklahoma* (1936), courtesy of the Library of Congress [LC-USF34-009695-E].

[5158] Ben Shahn, *Men Loafing in Crossville, Tennessee* (1937), courtesy of the Library of Congress [LC-USF33-OO6224-M4 DLC].

[2944] Anonymous, *Aaron Douglas with Arthur Schomburg and the Song of Towers Mural* (1934), courtesy of the Arthur Schomburg Photograph Collection, Photographs and Prints Division, Schomburg Center for Research in Black Culture, The New York Public Library, Astor, Lenox, and Tilden Foundations.

"THE GREAT DEPRESSION" WEB ARCHIVE

[2944] Anonymous, *Aaron Douglas with Arthur Schomburg and the Song of Towers Mural* (1934), courtesy of the Arthur Schomburg Photograph Collection, Photographs and Prints Division, Schomburg Center for Research in Black Culture, The New York Public Library, Astor, Lenox, and Tilden Foundations. Aaron Douglas was commissioned to paint murals for the New York Public Library under the Works Progress Administration. This mural represents the massive migration of African Americans from the South to the urban North during the early twentieth century.
[3334] Anonymous, *The Trading Floor of the New York Stock Exchange Just After the Crash of 1929* (1929), courtesy of the National Archives and Records Administration [1930-67B]. Photograph taken from above the stock exchange floor. The crash and ensuing depression brought many expatriate artists back to

The Great Depression helped Franklin Delano Roosevelt, a Democrat, unseat Herbert Hoover to win the presidency in 1932. Roosevelt quickly enacted major legislative initiatives to help Americans endure and recover from the economic downturn. Increased government regulations, extensive public-works projects, and other measures helped bolster public confidence that the economy would pull out of the depression. Roosevelt's "New Deal" included a broad range of legislation, such as the creation of the Federal Deposit Insurance Corporation (FDIC) to protect the savings of individuals, the Securities and Exchange Commission (SEC) to better regulate the stock market and other areas of investment, and the Federal Housing Administration (FHA) to better ensure the security of mortgages and home loans. The Roosevelt administration also created the Civilian Conservation Corps (CCC) to provide work relief and jobs to thousands of out-of-work men and the Tennessee Valley Authority (TVA) to assist with flood control and electricity generation. Nineteen thirty-three saw even more New Deal legislation, including an Agricultural Adjustment Act, a National Industrial Recovery Act, the Rural Electrification Administration, and a much-expanded public works effort, managed by the Public Works Administration. Under Roosevelt's guidance, the National Labor Relations Act and the Fair Labor Standards Act were passed. These two acts guaranteed the rights of workers to organize and bargain through unions and mandated maximum weekly work hours and minimum wages for many types of employees. The Social Security Act of 1935 helped guarantee unemployment insurance, created a retirement program for all American citizens, and instituted mechanisms to provide aid to dependent children. The unique combination of economic stagnation and disillusionment with big business and laissez-faire capitalism allowed Roosevelt to create and enact an impressive series of liberal reforms and social programs to assist a broad spectrum of the American public.

The effects of the depression were far-reaching on the arts in general and on literature in particular. The sense of loss, alienation, and fragmentation that developed after World War I increased. As the energy of the Roaring '20s dissipated, literature reflected new enervation and despair. For example, the lighthearted, optimistic tone of many of F. Scott Fitzgerald's earlier stories is absent from "Babylon Revisited" (1935). The depression also stifled the Harlem Renaissance. As economic resources to support African American writers, musicians, and artists dried up, African American writers and artists became increasingly disillusioned. Such works as Richard Wright's *Native Son* and Ralph Ellison's *Invisible Man* reflect this pessimistic outlook.

QUESTIONS

Comprehension: What were the major effects of the Great Depression on the country?
Comprehension: How did the Dust Bowl worsen conditions for many workers?

Comprehension: What was the Roosevelt administration's response to the Great Depression?

Context: Technology and mechanization helped reduce reliance on unskilled labor in many areas, and many people had to change professions or relocate. At the same time, as the literary works discussed in this unit show, migrant workers were often treated as easily replaceable pieces of equipment and forced to move from location to location. How do the authors in this unit allude to and implicitly or explicitly critique such treatment of humans? You might start with Bulosan's descriptions of Filipino migrants and compare them to the descriptions of Mexican Americans in Viramontes's and Rivera's works.

Exploration: Viktor Frankl's *Man's Search for Meaning* suggests that humor can be an important survival strategy. How does American literature develop humor as a strategy for dealing with oppression? Is there a tie between the works of Mark Twain or Flannery O'Connor and those of writers in this unit, such as Rudolfo Anaya or Tomas Rivera?

Documentary Photography and Film

In *Official Images: New Deal Photography*, Pete Daniel and Sally Stein ponder why so many photographs were taken and viewed during the depression era. They speculate, "Maybe people feeling deprived of material goods were attracted to those images that most closely resembled the look, surface, and solidity of things. Maybe, too, people feeling suddenly insecure about the future were comforted by photography's apparent matter-of-factness, even when the 'facts' were often distressing. Most likely, the appeal of photography contained contradictory impulses: to document and transform, to gain familiarity and distance" (viii). Whatever the reasons, the 1930s was one of the most photographically documented decades of all time.

As the country became more and more divided between those who favored social reform through government intervention and those who did not, documentary photography proved to be a powerful tool on the side of the reformers, revealing to a broad spectrum of the American public the horrific conditions brought on by both the depression and the Dust Bowl. Some of the documentary photographers' techniques found their way into literary works. For example, Steinbeck's use of documentary style in depicting people, places, and conditions during the depression contributed to the power of *The Grapes of Wrath*. And John Dos Passos used techniques he called "the camera eye" and the "newsreel" in *Manhattan Transfer* (1925) and in the USA Trilogy (*The 42nd Parallel* [1930]; *Nineteen Nineteen* [1932]; *The Big Money* [1936]). Like the documentary photographers, these authors sought to represent the suffering and despair of struggling American workers and families.

Early photographic pioneers such as Alfred Stieglitz, Edward Steichen, and Clarence White helped establish photography as an

the United States and diverted the focus of some away from wealth and luxury.

[3343] Dorothea Lange, *People Living in Miserable Poverty, Elm Grove, Oklahoma County, Oklahoma* (1936), courtesy of the Library of Congress [LC-USF34- 009695-E]. In *The Grapes of Wrath* Steinbeck depicts the life of Oklahoma farmers during the Dust Bowl, when terrible droughts killed crops and pushed families like the Joads west to California seeking better land and a better life.

[4792] Arthur Rothstein, *Farm Sale, Pettis County, Missouri* (1939), courtesy of the Library of Congress [LC-USF33-003448-M2]. Rothstein began his photography career while at Columbia University. After graduation, he became the first staff photographer for the Farm Security Administration. He is known mainly for his Dust Bowl images. By documenting the problems of the depression, he helped justify New Deal legislation. He went on to be a photographer for and director of *Look* magazine. As a child, author Tomas Rivera traveled throughout the Midwest with his parents, who were migrant farm laborers.

[4791] Arthur Rothstein, *Erosion on a Missouri Farm* (1936), courtesy of the Library of Congress [LC-USF34-001875-E]. Historian Donald Worster's book *Dust Bowl* opened people's eyes to the human causes of the Dust Bowl of the 1930s. Now ranked among the greatest manmade ecological disasters, the Dust Bowl worsened the effects of the Great Depression.

[5158] Ben Shahn, *Men Loafing in Crossville, Tennessee* (1937), courtesy of the Library of Congress [LC-USF33-006224-M4 DLC]. Unemployed men outside storefront in rural Tennessee during the Great Depression. Eventually, New Deal programs like the Civil Conservation Corps put many back to work on national projects such as road building and maintaining national parks.

[5935] Dorothea Lange, *Depression* (1935), courtesy of the National Archives and Records Administration. Unemployed man leaning against vacant storefront with "for lease" signs. Many lost their jobs and savings during the Great Depression. New Deal photographer Dorothea Lange captured images of the hardships during this time.

[3347] Dorothea Lange, *Power Farming Displaces Tenants. Childress County, Texas Panhandle* (1938), courtesy of the Library of Congress [LC-USF34-TO1-018281-C DLC].

emerging art form, but social documentary photography actually began with Jacob Riis's depictions of New York City slums in the 1880s, collected in his book *How the Other Half Lives*. Riis's groundbreaking work was followed by Lewis Hines's images of child labor abuses in factories, mills, and mines. The work of Riis and Hines inspired later photographers who worked for the Farm Security Administration (FSA). In 1935, the director of the FSA, Roy Stryker, hired a small corps of photographers to help inform the public of the brutal living and working conditions of displaced migrant workers. Among these photographers were Dorothea Lange, Ben Shahn, and Walker Evans. Lange and her sociologist husband studied poor farmworkers in southern California. Lange would later travel throughout the country documenting the stories of displaced workers through her images. Shahn, better known as a Works Progress Administration (WPA) painter, also photographed the harsh realities of American farming life, while Evans teamed up with writer James Agee to document southern sharecroppers' lives in *Let Us Now Praise Famous Men* (1941).

Documentary films also played an important role in depicting American life during the Great Depression and the Dust Bowl years. Partly to communicate to the public what the administration was doing to alleviate the suffering, the Roosevelt administration sponsored a number of documentary films directed by Pare Lorentz. Among these is *The Plow That Broke the Plains* (1936), the first film the United States government produced for commercial distribution. *The Plow That Broke the Plains* argues that a lack of ecological conservation and misuse of soil could have dire consequences. The film asserts that, by failing to practice land conservation and crop rotation, farmers themselves unwittingly created many of the conditions leading to the Dust Bowl. Many opponents of Roosevelt's New Deal legislation argued that this and other documentaries were designed to win approval for the broad range of social programs created by the government. Congress held a long and contentious debate about whether to fund the film, and some farmers protested the finished project. Today the film is hailed for its Whitmanesque free-verse script and its powerful and moving musical score. Lorentz's second

[5224] Dorothea Lange, *White Sharecropper Family, Formerly Mill Workers in the Gastonia Textile Mills. When the Mills Closed Down Seven Years Ago, They Came to This Farm Near Hartwell, Georgia* (1937), courtesy of the Library of Congress [LC-USF34-018147-C DLC].

Farm Security Administration film, *The River*, tells the story of the Mississippi River and its many tributaries. The film argues that, by controlling the river with dams, the country could avoid the disastrous seasonal flooding that stripped away valuable topsoil, put hundreds out of work, and destroyed homes and livestock.

Appreciated today primarily for their artistry and their sociological significance, the documentary photography and films of the Great

Depression provide an important historical record of the cultural and economic changes that were occurring in the country during that time.

QUESTIONS

Comprehension: What allowed the depression era to be so well documented?

Comprehension: What were the benefits of government-sponsored documentation of conditions in the country during the depression?

Context: How does the stark realism of these depression-era photographs relate to works by Bulosan, Steinbeck, and Viramontes?

Context: Compare the depression-era Dust Bowl photographs in the archive with pictures from contemporary newspaper articles about poverty (the Associated Press Web site is a good source for such images). Do the depression-era photographs have a distinctive style? Do the contemporary photographs seem more or less powerful to you than their depression-era counterparts? What accounts for these differences?

Exploration: A documentary is a work, such as a film or television program, that presents political, social, or historical subject matter in a factual and informative manner. Documentaries often include photographs, news footage, or interviews and are typically accompanied by narration. Think about photographs or documentaries that you have seen that help illustrate an era, a decade, a cause, or a movement. Search the archive, the Internet, or magazines, especially newsmagazines, for these definitive photographs, and put together a collection. You might focus on the 1950s, 1960s, or 1970s; the civil rights movement or Vietnam War protests; the women's liberation movement or the attacks on the World Trade Center and Pentagon. What about these collected photos helps convey a political or social message? How can the viewer judge whether that message is objective and accurate?

Unionism and the Farm Workers Movement

Industry, Perseverance and Frugality, make Fortune yield.
—Benjamin Franklin

Our movement is spreading like flames across a dry plain. We seek our basic, God-given rights as human beings. We shall do it without violence because it is our destiny. —Cesar Chavez

In some ways, social institutions like **trade unions** seem to stand in opposition to an American culture that praises hard-working individualism. The first European concepts of America envisioned this land as a new Eden, a place without toil or labor. The early Puritans and, later,

"DOCUMENTARY PHOTOGRAPHY AND FILM" WEB ARCHIVE

[3346] Marion Post Wolcott, *Rex Theatre for Colored People. Leland, Mississippi Delta* (1944), courtesy of the Library of Congress [LC-USF34-052508-D]. Photograph of front of all-black movie theater in the South. Blacks and whites attended separate theaters and other civic facilities in the South. In the North, African Americans were separated from white audiences for movies, plays, and music by more informal social codes of segregation.

[3347] Dorothea Lange, *Power Farming Displaces Tenants. Childress County, Texas Panhandle* (1938), courtesy of the Library of Congress [LC-USF34-TO1-018281-C DLC]. Alternately titled "Tractored Out." Mechanization made large farmers wealthy, but left small farmers, tenants, and sharecroppers without jobs. The rising use of machines instead of manual labor, coupled with drought and falling crop prices during the Great Depression, left many farmers homeless.

[4725] Arthur Rothstein, *Eroded Land, Alabama* (c. 1930s), courtesy of the National Archives and Records Administration [Photographs: FSA: Weather]. Farmer stands outside house, surveying eroded fields. Rothstein began his photography career while at Columbia University. After graduation, he became first staff photographer for the Farm Security Administration. He is mainly known for his Dust Bowl images. He went on to be a photographer for and director of *Look* magazine.

[4734] Marion Post Wolcott, *Picking Cotton Outside Clarksdale, Mississippi Delta, Mississippi* (1939), courtesy of the Library of Congress [LC-USF33-030629-M3]. Impoverished Mississippi farm worker harvesting cotton. Wolcott was a documentary photographer for the Farm Security Administration; her poignant photos strengthened support for many New Deal programs. The conflict between sharecroppers and landowners is depicted in William Faulkner's "Barn Burning."

[5224] Dorothea Lange, *White Sharecropper Family, Formerly Mill Workers in the Gastonia Textile Mills. When the Mills Closed Down Seven Years Ago, They Came to This Farm Near Hartwell, Georgia* (1937), courtesy of the Library of Congress [LC-USF34-018147-C DLC]. The less glamorous side of rural southern life; a white sharecropping family seated on the porch of their cabin. This family is an example of the poorer, "everyday people" that writers such as William Faulkner and Eudora Welty depicted.

[5864] Dorothea Lange, *Mexicans, Field Laborers, on Strike in Cotton Picking Season, Apply to Farm Security Administration for Relief. Bakersfield, California* (1938), courtesy of the Library of Congress [LC-USF34-018627].

the colonists and the citizens of the new Republic reshaped this naïve vision and wrote of the need for the American individual to work hard to tame and civilize a rugged and often hostile land. Benjamin Franklin's many pithy aphorisms about hard work remain engrained in the American consciousness, though the resonance of the agrarian ideal has faded. The capitalistic excesses of the Gilded Age and the rise of industrial robber barons, who benefited greatly at the expense of the common worker, helped to strip away people's confidence in their ability to prosper through hard work alone. Capitalism's excesses are represented in such literary works as Mark Twain and Charles Dudley Warner's *The Gilded Age* (1873), Twain's *A Connecticut Yankee in King Arthur's Court* (1889), William Dean Howell's *The Rise of Silas Lapham* (1885), Stephen Crane's *Maggie: A Girl of the Streets* (1893), Theodore Dreiser's *Sister Carrie* (1900), Frank Norris's *The Octopus* (1901), and Upton Sinclair's *The Jungle* (1906).

In the United States, the movement from an agrarian-based economy to an industrial one reflected a shift that had already occurred in much of Europe. Railroads, textiles, and the iron and steel industries all expanded in nineteenth-century America. The labor shortages and relatively good wages that resulted from this industrialization brought two major waves of immigrants from Europe. The first, arriving in the 1840s, included mostly Germans, English, Welsh, Scottish, and Irish. The second, in the 1880s, consisted mainly of people from Eastern Europe and the Balkans. This second wave of immigrants was treated more poorly than their predecessors had been. By and large, their assimilation into mainstream American culture was more difficult, as illustrated in literature by the treatment of the Rudkus family in Upton Sinclair's *The Jungle*. On the West Coast, Asian and Latino immigrants were arriving in great numbers and encountering racism as they sought work on the railroads and on large vegetable farms. Such writers as Carlos Bulosan, Amy Tan, Maxine Hong Kingston, and Tomas Rivera explore the stories of these immigrants. On both coasts, many immigrants found themselves working in industries that devalued their humanity by treating them as easily replaceable commodities.

Trade unions had begun to rise in Europe and the United States early in the nineteenth century. However, it was not until the formation of the American Federation of Labor (AFL) in 1886 that large organized union activities in America began. Union involvement and activity tended to increase during the early twentieth century, but also tended to fluctuate with the economic climate of the times. Originally, formally organized unions were made up almost exclusively of skilled workers. These unionized workers feared the influx of unskilled immigrants into the country and the workforce, and they sought to limit their influence. Early on, the AFL opposed unionization of these unskilled workers and in 1935 expelled a small group of unions that were trying to organize them. The expelled unions formed the Congress of Industrial Organizations (CIO), which later unionized the auto and steel industries. The AFL and CIO eventually merged in 1955.

Union activity in the United States often engendered violence and controversy. Influential industry leaders and large corporate farm owners went to great lengths to prevent or disrupt union activity through the jailing of leaders, the hiring of replacement workers, intimidation, and other legal and illegal means. They feared that unions would lead to higher wages and more benefits for workers, which would in turn make their products more costly and less competitive and thus cut into profits.

Compared to other types of union activity in the United States, the farm workers movement began modestly and relatively late. Led primarily by West Coast migrant workers who labored in fruit, vegetable, and flower fields, the movement attempted to address the harsh working conditions, low wages, substandard housing, and lack of benefits that existed for migrant workers. There had been attempts at addressing farm labor problems in the 1940s and 1950s. A small but active National Farm Labor Union attempted to expand in California in the 1940s and 1950s, but pressure from powerful corporate growers prevented more extensive union activities and membership. These growers relied upon 1951 legislation called Public Law 78, or the Bracero Program, to control Mexican agricultural workers who came to the United States seasonally. Despite union efforts, conditions in the field and wages remained poor. According to one history of the United Farm Workers:

> No ranches had portable field toilets. Workers' temporary housing was strictly segregated by race, and they paid two dollars or more per day for unheated metal shacks—often infested with mosquitoes—with no indoor plumbing or cooking facilities. Farm labor contractors played favorites with workers, selecting friends first, sometimes accepting bribes. Child labor was rampant, and many workers were injured or died in easily preventable accidents. The average life expectancy of a farm worker was 49 years. (UFW History)

In 1959, the AFL-CIO formed the Agricultural Workers Organizing Committee (AWOC), which consisted of Filipinos, Chicanos, Anglos, and African Americans. In 1962, Cesar Chavez started the National Farm Workers Association (NFWA). These organizations grew slowly, but in 1965 and 1966 a series of strikes finally led the two largest growers on the West Coast to recognize their employees as members of an organized labor union, especially when the two unions combined to create the United Farm Workers Organizing Committee (UFWOC).

As part of the farm workers movement, the **Chicano movement** was, and is, a force for socio-economic and cultural change in the Mexican American community. The movement generated a cultural renaissance in art, music, literature, and theatre. One of the most distinctive aspects of Chicano expression is El Teatro Campesino, or the Farm Workers' Theater. Founded in 1965 by Luis Valdez, El Teatro Campesino mounts productions that blend Spanish and English and often include music. Many artistic and political publications, including newspapers, magazines, and journals, arose out of the Chicano movement.

[6932] Student Mobilization Committee to End the War in S.E. Asia, *Pull Him Out Now: Join with the Hundreds and Thousands of Students, GI's, Women, Unionists, Puerto Ricans, Gay People . . .* (c. 1970), courtesy of the Library of Congress.

"UNIONISM/FARM WORKERS MOVEMENT" WEB ARCHIVE

[5864] Dorothea Lange, *Mexicans, Field Laborers, on Strike in Cotton Picking Season, Apply to Farm Security Administration for Relief. Bakersfield, California* (1938), courtesy of the Library of Congress [LC-USF34-018627]. The Farm Security Administration (1937–42) was formed under the Department of Agriculture. It provided low-cost loans and assistance to small farmers and sharecroppers, constructed camps for migrant workers, restored eroded soil, and put flood prevention practices into effect.

[5869] Dorothea Lange, *Filipino Migrant Workers* (1938), courtesy of the Library of Congress [LC-USF34-018671-D]. Large field with Filipino migrant laborers working in row. Filipinos migrated to the United States in three major waves. The first and second wave faced exploitative working conditions in agriculture, canneries, and other manual labor industries.

[6099] Cesar Chavez, *Migrant Workers Union Leader* (1972), courtesy of the National Archives and Records Administration [NWDNS-412-DA-1576]. Cesar Chavez speaking at a union event. Chavez organized the National Farm Workers Association in the 1960s to help migrant farm workers gain rights and better working conditions and pay. Lalo Guerrero composed his "Corrido de Cesar Chavez" after reading a newspaper account of Chavez's twenty-five day fast in 1968.

[6932] Student Mobilization Committee to End the War in S.E. Asia, *Pull Him Out Now: Join with the Hundreds and Thousands of Students, GI's, Women, Unionists, Puerto Ricans, Gay People . . .* (c. 1970), courtesy of the Library of Congress. Political poster protesting U.S. military involvement in Vietnam. The antiwar movement linked and encouraged a number of other movements, including the civil rights movement, the Chicano movement, and the farm workers movement. Many American poets protested the war, including Adrienne Rich, Robert Lowell, and Allen Ginsberg.

[8613] Vito Marcantonio, *Labor's Martyrs* (1937), courtesy of Special Collections, Michigan State University Libraries. Socialist publication describing the "great labor martyrs of the past 50 years." This pamphlet discusses the trial and public execution of "Chicago Anarchists" who organized the Haymarket bombing in 1887, as well as the trials of Sacco and Vanzetti in 1927 and the Scottsboro Boys in the 1930s. The pamphlet goes on to talk about the thriving state of the 1930s labor movement.

Union activity among farm workers continued to increase in the 1960s and 1970s. Aided by growing public awareness of discrimination against and abuses of minorities, fruit boycotts and other forms of public pressure, along with expanded union membership, eventually helped to provide relief from the worst problems faced by migrant farm workers. However, even today employers exploit migrant workers, and debates about immigration, housing, education, public services, citizenship issues, and discriminatory property ownership laws continue.

QUESTIONS

Comprehension: Why does the concept of "unionization" sometimes seem at odds with the American Dream?

Comprehension: Why didn't more widespread unionization of workers take place in the United States before the late 1800s?

Comprehension: What conditions led to the need for trade unions? Why were businesses and corporations opposed to the unions? What did they fear?

Comprehension: How did union activity lead to an artistic renaissance in some communities?

Context: Chapter 21 of *The Grapes of Wrath* offers a snapshot of some of the economic and cultural issues associated with the distrust of migrants and suggests that the sudden influx of workers into California was dangerous. Identify the particular perspectives or "voices" that Steinbeck presents in this chapter. Were these voices justified in their concerns or not?

Context: How does *America Is in the Heart* portray attempts to unionize Filipino and other minority migrant workers? What tactics do the local and state authorities and large farm owners use to try and squelch these efforts?

Exploration: Why did the migrant workers see unionization as the best way to improve working conditions and wages? Why didn't some of the original trade unions for skilled workers want to help unionize unskilled workers?

EXTENDED CONTEXTS

Socialism and Communism

Socialism can be understood as an economic theory or system of social organization whereby the means of producing and distributing goods are collectively owned or controlled. At its heart is the desire for a just and equitable distribution of wealth, property, and labor. Communism is an established system of government in which the state plans and controls the economy with the intent that goods should be shared equally among the people.

As industrialization gained momentum and technology improved, skilled workers and artisans became less important to the production of goods and were often replaced by factory wage earners with fewer technical skills. Unskilled workers soon dominated many industries, including shipping, transportation, and building. In the mid-to-late nineteenth century, most factories and jobs moved to the cities and unskilled workers followed. In an effort to receive better benefits, pay, and working conditions, these workers began to organize into trade unions. Many union leaders were inspired by socialist ideologies that promised just treatment for workers.

Though the ideals of socialism go back to classical times, contemporary socialism had its roots in the reaction to the industrial age and the treatment of workers as commodities. As the perception grew that capitalism and industrialism were causing widespread suffering, socialists called for fundamental changes to what they perceived as unfair economic and social systems. European socialist leaders championed different versions of socialist ideology. The utopian socialists, such as Comte Saint-Simon, Charles Fourier, and Robert Owen, envisioned a naturally occurring course of progress for humanity leading to shared wealth and resources for all. These thinkers influenced experiments with utopian societies in America, such as the Oneida Community and Brook Farm, the basis of Hawthorne's satire in *The Blithedale Romance*. Scientific socialists, such as Karl Marx and Friedrich Engels, argued that organized trade unions and radical political parties were needed to overthrow capitalist systems. Depictions of unions and leftist ideology appear in the works of Muriel Rukeyser, Carlos Bulosan, Upton Sinclair, and John Steinbeck, as well as in the writings of Ralph Waldo Ellison, Richard Wright, and Chaim Potok.

Some American laborers joined socialist movements, but the majority did not. There were three different socialist parties in the late nineteenth and early twentieth centuries: the Socialist Labor Party, formed in 1876; the Social Democratic Party, formed in 1898; and the Socialist Party, formed in 1901. Eugene V. Debs repeatedly ran for president on the Socialist Party ticket in the early twentieth century, but he never received more than 900,000 votes nationwide. Though socialist party membership dropped off during World War I, it grew somewhat during the Great Depression. After World War II, the Socialist Party in America split into conservative and progressive wings and lost much of its following, partly as a result of the anti-communist sentiment of the late 1940s and 1950s. Senator Joseph McCarthy and his followers fostered the perception that socialists and communists were closely associated.

Communism, in a broad sense, refers to radical political movements meant to overthrow capitalist systems of government. After the 1917 Russian Revolution brought the Bolsheviks to power, they

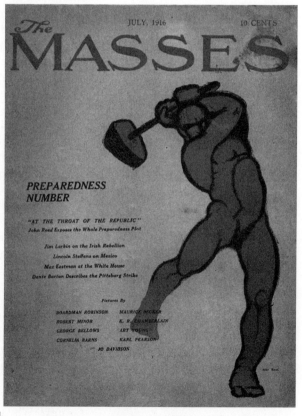

[7892] Robert Minor, Back cover of *The Masses*, July 1916 (1916), courtesy of Special Collections, Michigan State University Libraries.

[4775] Mabel Dwight, *In the Crowd* (1931), courtesy of the Library of Congress [LC-USZC4-6582].

renamed themselves the Communist Party. Eventually, under Lenin and then Stalin, the Soviet Union became the international leader of the communist movement. Many other countries became communist, including much of Eastern Europe, China, North Korea, Vietnam, and Cuba.

Although governments like that of the Soviet Union called for the overthrow of capitalistic systems, the United States did not perceive international communism as a serious threat until after World War II. A "cold war" began between the Soviet Union and the United States, with each vying for world domination. American fear of communism was enhanced by the emergence of Joseph McCarthy, a Wisconsin senator who spearheaded an anti-communist campaign from 1950 to 1954. During the same period, in the House of Representatives, the Un-American Activities Committee held numerous highly publicized hearings on suspected communists. The "Red Scare" campaign mounted by McCarthy and the Republican Party alleged that communists had infiltrated America and were intent on overthrowing the country. Arthur Miller's play *The Crucible* is perhaps the best-known literary response to this era. The anti-communist campaign and the public support it garnered allowed for unscrupulous congressional committee investigations, which Miller likened to the witch trials of centuries before, that sought to discredit or blacklist individuals with "known ties" to communists or socialists, even if those ties were well in the past. Many literary figures and people in the motion picture industry fell victim to these investigations.

The Cold War loomed large in the American consciousness throughout the late 1950s and the 1960s. Films and literature were the primary genres where these concerns surfaced. Movies like *Dr. Strangelove* and *Fail-Safe* expressed anxiety about atomic annihilation. Nuclear holocaust, Russian invasion, and the perceived rise of totalitarianism in American society were all themes in popular books and films like *Fahrenheit 451*, *Invasion of the Body Snatchers*, *It Came from Outer Space*, and *The Thing*. Similar themes appear in such popular works of fiction as Joseph Heller's *Catch-22*, Kurt Vonnegut's *Slaughterhouse-Five*, and Thomas Pynchon's *Gravity's Rainbow*. Each novel explores how coping with constant Cold War fears leads to alienation, absurdity, and paranoia.

QUESTIONS

Comprehension: How did American capitalism fail certain segments of the population? Why were people attracted to socialism and communism?

Comprehension: How did the fear of communism affect the United States in the 1950s? Was the government justified in the measures it took to root out communism?

Context: Why would a poet like Muriel Rukeyser, who was born into a wealthy family, support American communist and leftist organizations?

Context: In Chapter 26 of *The Grapes of Wrath*, Casey is called a "red son-of-a-bitch" just before he is killed. "Red" was a slang word for "communist." Does Casey seem to be a communist or socialist? What are his concerns? Why did Steinbeck portray Casey in this way?

Exploration: In the first decade of the twenty-first century, some people have compared the actions the U.S. government took in investigating possible communist "infiltrators and collaborators" in the 1950s to the post-9/11 suspension of civil rights for many people living in the United States. Are those comparisons fair? Do they help you understand why the government acted the way it did in the 1950s?

The Works Progress Administration (WPA)

During his acceptance speech at the 1932 Democratic National Convention, Franklin D. Roosevelt said, "I pledge you—I pledge myself to a new deal for the American people." One of the major components of the "new deal" was the **Works Progress Administration (WPA)**. The WPA provided over nine million people with work and sustaining wages by employing them to build roads, beautify buildings, play concerts, and write histories, along with a wide range of other activities. Created in 1935, the WPA was led by Roosevelt appointee Harry Hopkins. Whereas the previous president, Herbert Hoover, and his administration had refused to offer government assistance to individuals, Roosevelt's plan was to provide multiple forms of relief to the army of unemployed people created by the Great Depression.

The Civil Works Administration (CWA), the predecessor of the WPA, was created in the fall of 1933. In exchange for a weekly government check of fifteen dollars, previously unemployed workers repaired schools, built or beautified parks, constructed swimming pools and athletic fields, and taught people how to read. Writers and artists were also employed and paid for their services. About four million people found work under this program.

After the CWA expired, the WPA was formed and became the largest and farthest-reaching work-relief program of all those founded during the Roosevelt years. WPA workers participated in public service projects and programs, but the WPA is best remembered for its many artistic and literary projects. One division of the WPA, known as Federal Project Number One, included a Music Project, a Theater Project, an Arts Project, and a Writer's Project. The Federal Theater Project put on plays across the country, along with vaudeville shows, puppet circuses, and dance festivals. The Federal Music Project offered free concerts and music education across the country and created an Index of American Composers, cataloguing thousands of pieces of American music and gathering the biographies of U.S. composers. Artists such as Ben Shahn painted large murals inside and outside public buildings as part of the Arts Project. This project also included art education classes and seminars. As part of the Writer's Project, well-known authors like Richard Wright and John Steinbeck were paid to create

Vincent Voice Library, Michigan State University. Contains part of a speech made after the opening-night performance of *Thieves Paradise* on April 12, 1948. The speech talks about the presence of communism in Hollywood and "the menace of these traitors to the safety of America."

[8615] Anonymous, *The Story of the Sacco-Vanzetti Case* (1921), courtesy of Special Collections, Michigan State University Libraries. Written after the initial trial of Italian anarchists Nicola Sacco and Bartolomeo Vanzetti. Sacco and Vanzetti were originally arrested in 1920 on the charge of being "suspicious reds" but later charged with the murder of two men. They were found guilty and executed in 1927, though over one hundred people testified to their innocence. This pamphlet was partially designed to raise money for a new trial for them.

[7023] Nathan Sherman, *Work With Care* (1937), courtesy of the Library of Congress [LC-USZC2-1172].

regional histories of the areas they lived in. Other famous writers who were part of this project include Saul Bellow, John Cheever, Ralph Ellison, and Zora Neale Hurston, all of whom documented life histories and regional folklore. The Writer's Project also helped record many of the narratives of living African Americans who had been born into slavery.

QUESTIONS

Comprehension: Who do you think benefited the most from WPA projects? Who did not benefit?

Comprehension: How were the arts influenced by these government programs? What was created or saved that might have been lost had it not been for the WPA?

Context: In Chapter 34 of *America Is in the Heart*, Bulosan seems to both poke fun at and praise the WPA and some of its projects. How does he do so? What does this brief chapter tell us about Bulosan's general impression of the WPA?

Context: How do you think Henry David Thoreau, who wrote, "The government is best that governs least," would have reacted to the government programs of the 1930s? How do you think the American public would react to such initiatives today?

Exploration: Research President Johnson's efforts to enlarge government in the 1960s, especially the expansion of programs like Medicare, Medicaid, VISTA, and Head Start. In the 1980s and 1990s, these programs came under great scrutiny and were attacked as wasteful and counterproductive. Do you agree with this assessment? Why or why not?

"WPA" WEB ARCHIVE

ASSIGNMENTS

Personal and Creative Responses

1. *Poet's Corner:* Describe what "being an American" means to you. What makes Americans distinctive? Make a list of American characteristics. Now write a free-verse poem that explains why you do or do not see yourself as "American." Use Langston Hughes's "Theme for English B" as a model for your poem.

2. *Creative Writing:* Write a creative story about one day in the life of a person in a small midwestern town on the eastern edge of the state on a major east-west interstate highway. A highly contagious disease has broken out on the East Coast, and people are fleeing that part of the country and coming west in great numbers. No one knows who might be carrying the disease. How would you react to these travelers? What do the officials of your town and state do to protect residents from this disease? Include a scene of confrontation. Use Steinbeck's *The Grapes of Wrath* as a model.

3. *Journal:* Have you ever entered an environment in which you felt like an outsider? Perhaps you left home to go to college or moved to a new town or visited another country? Did you at times feel powerless, voiceless? Did you feel like you had little control over your own life? Describe the situation and what it felt like. How did you handle it? Now interview others using these questions, including students, relatives, or your parents. Write down your observations in a journal.

4. *Letter Writing:* Assume the role of Helena Maria Viramontes. Have Viramontes write a letter to John Steinbeck, explaining to Steinbeck what he left out or got wrong about migrant workers in *The Grapes of Wrath*. Then, write a reply from Steinbeck to Viramontes.

5. *Letter Writing:* Write a letter to a local, state, or national politician explaining a situation that you would like to see changed. Use an activist's voice, and list the reasons why the present situation is unfair and the changes you'd like to see take place. Justify the expenditure of money it would take to enact your changes.

6. *Presentation:* Tackle a project on any of the themes associated with this unit, such as migrant workers, labor unions, environmentalism, the Great Depression, or the Dust Bowl. Create a poster, put together a videotape, do a PowerPoint presentation, write and produce a radio play, make a map, or anything else that inspires you to explore your theme in more depth.

Problem-Based Learning Projects

1. Imagine that you have been asked to create a museum exhibit on the migrant struggle in the United States. Using the archive and literature in this unit, choose ten to fifteen items that you feel are representative of this topic. Then write a justification for the pieces that you will display. How did you decide on these items? What values seem most important in what you have chosen to display? How do your items reflect those values? What does it mean to be a migrant worker in the United States?

2. You are a high school teacher, and you've just finished teaching a unit on Hispanic and Latino/a writers. Imagine that you must now compose an essay exam for your students. Write three questions that you would like to have your students explore. What themes are important to the unit? What symbols or images have remained influential?

3. Imagine you are on the school board for your local district. A group of parents, students, and teachers has circulated a petition asking that more Hispanic literature that focuses on migrant issues be included in the curriculum. Other parents, students, and teachers have sent letters saying that the current curriculum is fine. The board is going to hold a community meeting to decide the issue. Take the position of wanting to include these works, and prepare a presentation to support your point of view. How will you make your

of photographers to document both the necessity for and the benefits of the program.

[7023] Nathan Sherman, *Work With Care* (1937), courtesy of the Library of Congress [LC-USZC2-1172]. This woodprint was created as part of the WPA Federal Art Project. The Works Progress Administration provided millions of people with work and sustaining wages by employing them to build roads, beautify buildings, play concerts, and write histories, along with a wide range of other activities. President Franklin D. Roosevelt's plan was to provide multiple forms of relief to the army of unemployed people created by the Great Depression.

argument? What kinds of evidence will you cite to demonstrate the educational value of these works? How will you construct your argument so that it addresses the concerns of those who think there is no reason to include these works in the curriculum?

4. You are a reporter for the *Chicago Tribune*, and you've been assigned to write an article on how U.S. employers take advantage of migrant workers. You want to begin the article with a history of employer–migrant worker relations in the United States. What would you include in your history? Where would you begin? Which groups would you focus on? What writers would you refer to and why?

GLOSSARY

American Dream   The belief that a better life is possible for anyone in the United States. Because of its near mythic status, the "American Dream" means different things to different people. One component of the American Dream is seen in the rags-to-riches tales of Benjamin Franklin and the nineteenth-century "Ragged Dick" stories. Another component is the notion of America as the "Gold Mountain," put forth by Chinese immigrants who came to the western United States in the 1850s, during the Gold Rush years, to make their fortunes. Sadly, few of them earned enough to pay for passage home and instead became miners, railroad builders, fishermen, service workers, and menial laborers.

blacklist   A list of persons or organizations that have incurred disapproval or suspicion and are to be denied employment or otherwise penalized. Suspicions of communism led to many Hollywood writers and producers/directors being blacklisted in the 1950s.

Chicano/Chicana   A Mexican American man or woman. Originally a derogatory term, it has been reclaimed as an acceptable, indeed proud, designation.

Chicano movement   A Mexican American movement to obtain civil rights and better wages and working conditions, improve educational opportunities, and increase appreciation for Chicano/a fine arts.

Dust Bowl   The area in the Midwest affected by a four-year drought (1935–39) that destroyed all cash crops and caused much of the topsoil to be stripped away by the wind in terrible dust storms.

eco-literature   Writing that explores our relationship to the environment and the land around us; nature writing. Eco-literature often combines stories of the land with tales of social injustice.

Great Depression   The period of great economic downturn in the United States and the world from 1929 to the early 1940s.

Hispanic   See Latino/Latina.

jeremiad   A literary work prophesying doom or a sermon strongly recommending an immediate change in behavior or practices.

Latino/Latina   A person of Latin American descent, often living in the United States. The *American Heritage Dictionary* notes that, although "Hispanic" and "Latino" are often used interchangeably, they are not identical. "Hispanic" is more global, referring to Spanish-speaking peoples around the world. But for some segments of the Spanish-speaking population, "Hispanic" can be offensive, bearing a stamp of Anglo labeling, whereas "Latino/Latina" is more a term of ethnic pride and distinct associations with a Latin American background.

magical realism   A primarily Latin American literary movement that arose in the 1960s. The Cuban writer Alejo Carpentier first applied the term to Latin American fiction in 1949. Works of magical realism combine realistic portrayals of ordinary events with elements of fantasy and myth, creating a fictional world both familiar and dreamlike. The best-known practitioner of magical realism is Colombian novelist Gabriel García Márquez, who has used the technique in such novels as *One Hundred Years of Solitude* (1967).

marginalize   To relegate or confine to a lower social standing or to proscribe as an outsider.

migrant workers   Workers who must travel to find employment. The term is often associated with agricultural workers on the West Coast and in the South.

modernism   A literary movement that reached its peak in the 1920s, modernism developed in two rather different strands. American modernism, as practiced by Williams and Hughes, is characterized by an interest in portraying ordinary subject matter by using concrete, vernacular language. Modernist poetry written in Europe, as characterized by Eliot, tends to be highly allusive. The poems are non-linear and often refer to the modern condition, particularly the city, in a deeply critical manner. This strand of modernism tends to use a disembodied voice and a collage-like method.

testimonio   A form of collective autobiographical witnessing that provides a voice to oppressed peoples. It generally plays an important role in developing and supporting international human rights, solidarity movements, and liberation struggles.

trade union   An association of laborers in a particular trade, mostly created to help lobby for higher wages, benefits, and improved working conditions.

Un-American Activities Committee   A committee of the U.S. House of Representatives, created in 1938 to investigate disloyalty and subversive organizations. It is associated today with the excesses of the Cold War and the unwarranted national fear of a communist takeover.

WPA   The Works Progress Administration, created in 1935 by the Roosevelt administration to provide millions of people with work and sustaining wages by employing them to build roads, beautify buildings, play concerts, and write histories, along with a wide range of other activities.

SELECTED BIBLIOGRAPHY

Britton, Sheilah. "Discovering the Alphabet of Life." *ASU Research Online*. <researchmag.asu.edu/articles/alphabet.html>.

Cheung, King-Kok, ed. *An Interethnic Companion to Asian American Literature*. Cambridge: Cambridge UP, 1997.

Craig, Albert M., et al. *The Heritage of World Civilization*. Combined Edition. Fifth Edition. Upper Saddle River: Prentice-Hall, 2000.

Craven, Wayne. *American Art: History and Culture*. New York: Brown and Benchmark, 1994.

Cross, Gary, and Rick Szostak. *Technology and American Society: A History*. Englewood Cliffs: Prentice-Hall, 1995.

Daniel, Pete, et al. *Official Images: New Deal Photography*. Washington DC and London: Smithsonian Institution Press, 1987.

Dictionary of Literary Biography. Vol. 122: *Chicano Writers*. Detroit: Gale, 1992.

Frankl, Viktor E. *Man's Search for Ultimate Meaning*. New York and London: Insight Books, 1997.

Hernández, Guillermo E. *Chicano Satire: A Study in Literary Culture*. Austin: U of Texas P, 1991.

Lim, Shirley Geok-lin, and Amy Ling, eds. *Reading the Literatures of Asian America*. Philadelphia: Temple UP, 1992.

Moraga, Cherríe, and Gloria Anzaldúa, eds. *"This bridge called my back": Writings by Radical Women of Color*. 2nd. Ed. New York: Kitchen Table, Women of Color Press, 1983.

Owens, Louis. *The Grapes of Wrath: Trouble in the Promised Land*. Boston: Twayne, 1989.

Reuben, Paul P. Chapter 7: "Early Twentieth Century—Robinson Jeffers." *Perspectives in American Literature—A Research and Reference Guide*. <www.csustan.edu/english/reuben/pal/chap7/jeffers.html>.

Rodgers, Daniel T. *The Work Ethic in Industrial America: 1850–1920*. Chicago: U of Chicago P, 1978.

Ruíz, Vicki. *Cannery Women, Cannery Lives: Mexican Women, Unionization, and the California Food Processing Industry, 1930–1950*. Albuquerque: U of New Mexico P, 1987.

Ryan, Bryan, ed. *Hispanic Writers: A Selection of Sketches from Contemporary Authors*. Detroit: Gale, 1991.

Saldívar-Hull, Sonia. *Feminism on the Border: Chicana Gender Politics and Literature*. Berkeley : U of California P, 2000.

Shindo, Charles J. "The Dust Bowl Myth." *Wilson Quarterly*, Autumn 2000.

"Viramontes, Helena Maria." *Contemporary Authors*. Vol. 159. Detroit: Gale, 1998.

Whitfield, Stephen J. *The Culture of the Cold War*. Baltimore: Johns Hopkins UP, 1991.

FURTHER RESOURCES

Art for the Millions: Essays from the 1930s by Artists and Administrators of the WPA Federal Art Project. Ed. and with an introduction by Francis V. O'Connor. Greenwich: New York Graphic Society, 1973.

"By the People, For the People: Posters from the WPA, 1933–1943." Teaching Resources, The Library of Congress. Also DeNoon, Christopher, *Posters of the WPA*. Los Angeles: Wheatley, 1987.

El Teatro Campesino: From the Fields to Hollywood (CD-ROM). El Teatro Campesino, P.O. Box 1240, San Juan Bautista, CA 95045. <info@elteatrocampesino.com>.

El Teatro Campesino Archives 1964–1988, California Ethnic and Multicultural Archives, Department of Special Collections, Donald C. Davidson Library, University of California, Santa Barbara, CA 93106. Phone: (805) 893-8563. Galería de la Raza/Studio 24, 2857 24th Street, San Francisco, CA 94110. Phone: (415) 826- 8009.

Ferris, Susan, writer/producer/director. "The Golden Cage: A Story of California Farmworkers." Documentary Film. 1990. 29 minutes.

From the Depression to the New Millennium. BeyondBooks.com <app.coxednet.org/bbdemo/ush12/2b.htm>.

The Grapes of Wrath. Film. Starring Henry Fonda, directed by John Ford. 1940.

Moss, Joyce, and George Wilson. *Literature and Its Times*. Detroit: Gale, 1997.

Netzley, Patricia D. *Social Protest Literature: An Encyclopedia of Works, Characters, Authors and Themes*. Santa Barbara: ABC-CLIO, 1999.

Perez, Severo, director. *And the Earth Did Not Swallow Him*. Film. Distributed by Facets Video, Kino on Video. 1994. 1 hour, 39 minutes.

Sayles, John, director. *Matewan*. Feature film about labor unions and a community dominated by a coal-mining company. 1987. Two hours, 12 minutes.

Unequal Sisters: A Multicultural Reader in U.S. Women's History. Ed. by Vicki L. Ruiz and Ellen Carol DuBois. New York: Routledge, 2000.

Unit 13

SOUTHERN RENAISSANCE

Reinventing the South

Authors and Works

Featured in the Video:
William Faulkner, *As I Lay Dying* and *Absalom, Absalom!* (novels)

Zora Neale Hurston, "How It Feels to Be Colored Me" (essay) and *Their Eyes Were Watching God* (novel)

Discussed in This Unit:
John Crowe Ransom, "Bells for John Whiteside's Daughter," "Here Lies a Lady," "Philomela," "Piazza Piece," and "Janet Waking" (poems)

Katherine Anne Porter, "Flowering Judas" (short story)

Thomas Wolfe, "The Lost Boy" (short story)

Robert Penn Warren, "Bearded Oaks," "Audubon," "American Portrait: Old Style," "Acquaintance with Time in Early Autumn," "Mortal Limit," and "After the Dinner Party" (poems)

Richard Wright, "The Man Who Was Almost a Man" (short story)

Eudora Welty, "Petrified Man" (short story)

Tennessee Williams, *A Streetcar Named Desire* (play)

Flannery O'Connor, "The Life You Save May Be Your Own" and "Good Country People" (short stories)

Overview Questions

■ How do Southern Renaissance writers portray American identity differently from writers from other regions? How do Southern Renaissance writers use race, class, and gender as part of identity? What roles do history, tradition, and heritage play in the work of these writers?

■ Many writers of the Southern Renaissance achieved popularity and/or critical acclaim during their lifetimes, but faded into obscurity for years before being "rescued" by later critics who recognized their achievements as among the greatest in American literature. What accounts for such a roller coaster of critical reception? What does the uneven critical reception of these writers tell us about American "literature" and what constitutes "greatness"? How do the different social and economic backgrounds of writers in the Southern Renaissance influence what and how they write?

■ What is "the South" for writers of the Southern Renaissance? How is "the South" both place and time, and how does it relate to "the North" and the United States more generally?

■ What stylistic and thematic interests do Southern Renaissance writers have in common? How do these writers attempt to connect the past and the future via style and theme?

■ How does the myth of the "Old South" appear to the writers of the Southern Renaissance? How do these writers portray the "New South"? In what ways do Southern Renaissance writers imagine or create a new "New South"?

Learning Objectives

After students have viewed the video, read the headnotes and literary selections in *The Norton Anthology of American Literature*, and explored related archival materials on the *American Passages* Web site, they should be able to

1. discuss and understand both why and how historical time (in the sense of past, present, and future) became such a dominant preoccupation for writers of the Southern Renaissance;

2. see and discuss the particular ways writers of the Southern Renaissance engaged various concepts around which southern society was organized, including gender, race, social and economic position, agrarian vs. urban ways of life, and tradition vs. innovation or "progress";

3. understand the thematic and stylistic innovations introduced and/or employed by writers of the Southern Renaissance and how these innovations relate to literary modernism and literary history more generally;

4. recognize the attempts of Southern Renaissance writers to *create* "the South" (or at least small pieces of it) as both a place and a constellation of values and experiences.

Instructor Overview

For many people in the United States, the first half of the twentieth century was a period of tremendous change in almost every facet of life. Breakthroughs in science—including Albert Einstein's theory of relativity, as well as the increasing influence of Charles Darwin's theories of evolution—challenged conventional views of both the world we live in and our place within it. In the social sciences, the increasingly popular ideas of Sigmund Freud became conceptual tools used by many to question the sexual and social restraints of a tradition-bound culture they saw as highly repressed. Meanwhile, technological advances began to create the vast array of consumer goods we take for granted today, including movies, automobiles, airplanes, radios, and myriad other items—all produced on a massive scale previously unknown in human history. The industry needed to produce all these goods helped accelerate yet another great shift in American life as people migrated in ever greater numbers from their traditional, rural homes—where agriculture was the main focus of life—to the ever-expanding urban, industrial centers, such as Charlotte, North Carolina, and Atlanta, Georgia. However, much of this migration was from the South to the booming cities of the North—notably Chicago and New York—a trend that began around the time of the Civil War and continued into the mid-twentieth century. The period marked the first time in American history

that fewer people lived in rural than urban areas, and as the focus of American life moved to the cities, the *consumption* of mass-produced goods became every bit as important as their production.

Historians sometimes refer to the massive social and cultural transformations of the early twentieth century as distinctively "modern." For many—and especially for many writers during the period—such great change and social upheaval raised questions: What kind of life is the best to live? Is the "modern" world headed in the right direction, or are we going the wrong way? For writers in the South, such questions often involved a desire to protect tradition and myth from being destroyed by the influx of new ways of thinking and living.

Such questions found expression in attempts by social reformers to legislate the kind of society they wished to inhabit. One prominent result of such efforts was the Eighteenth Amendment to the U.S. Constitution, which, from 1919 to 1933, banned the manufacture, sale, or transportation of intoxicants throughout the nation. According to historian Michael Parrish, "The prohibition battle divided the nation along sharp geographic, religious, and ethnic boundaries that defined much of America's political landscape" in the years following World War I. Specifically, the passage of the Eighteenth Amendment "symbolized the political and cultural victory of the small towns over the big cities; of evangelical and pietistic Protestants over Roman Catholics, Lutherans, and Jews; of old-stock Anglo-Saxons over newer immigrants; and finally, of rich over poor." Like the Eighteenth Amendment, the countless "Jim Crow" laws that divided the South into black and white were also attempts to legislate a certain kind of society—in this case, one based on the racial divisions that had segregated U.S. society since the introduction of slavery nearly three centuries earlier. The Ku Klux Klan, which had virtually disappeared in the first decade of the twentieth century, was reborn in 1915 and remained a formidable force in U.S. politics and race relations—particularly in the South—for the next ten years.

Unit 13, "Southern Renaissance," explores some of the ways writers who either lived in, wrote about, or were otherwise associated with the South between 1920 and 1950 responded to the many changes during the period. Not surprisingly, much of the writing in this unit features the struggle between those who embraced social change and those who were more skeptical or challenged social change outright. According to literary critic Richard H. King, "The writers and intellectuals of the South after the late 1920s were engaged in an attempt to come to terms not only with the inherited values of the southern tradition but also with a certain way of perceiving and dealing with the past, what Nietzsche called 'monumental' historical consciousness." In the work of John Crowe Ransom, Zora Neale Hurston, William Faulkner, Thomas Wolfe, Robert Penn Warren, Richard Wright, Katherine Anne Porter, Eudora Welty, Tennessee Williams, and Flannery O'Connor, the diverse wealth of voices in the early-twentieth-century South comes alive.

The video for Unit 13 explores some of the most influential texts from William Faulkner and Zora Neale Hurston, both of whom situate their writing firmly within the South even as they question southern myths and traditions. Both Faulkner and Hurston are concerned with questions of historical time: How does the past shape the present and future? To what extent are our lives predetermined by our skin color, economic situation, or what our ancestors have or have not done? In Faulkner's *Absalom, Absalom!*, for example, multiple narrators attempt to discover, understand, and cope with the legacy of Thomas Sutpen, a Virginian of low birth who created a grand plantation out of the Mississippi wilderness of the 1830s and 1840s. In contrast to the gothic and sometimes malevolent qualities of Faulkner's novel, in "How It Feels to Be Colored Me" Hurston takes a stand against letting her skin color or the legacy of slavery determine who she is or what her life will be. "I am not tragically colored," Hurston asserts, going on to ask, "How *can* any deny themselves the pleasure of my company? It's beyond me."

As the video explores the similarities and differences between these two influential writers, it introduces students to the complex relationship between writers and the place and time in and about which they write. How do Hurston and Faulkner depict "the South"? How do these texts engage the legacies of slavery as well as economic poverty? What innovative formal strategies did they use to bring their characters to life and to give their readers a rich sense of the South in the 1920s? What do Faulkner and Hurston seem to be saying about human possibility and about what America is or should be in the

early twentieth century? Unit 13 helps answer these and related questions by situating Faulkner and Hurston within their literary and historical contexts, and by guiding students to connections between these writers and others in their era, as well as to writers within other units.

Through an exploration of the historical and literary contexts with which the Southern Renaissance was most concerned, the video, the archive, and the curriculum materials work together to give students a broad understanding of "the South" within the larger fabric of U.S. history in the early twentieth century. Those contexts include (1) the goals, values, and influence of the literary group known as the "Southern Agrarians"; (2) the extensive and complicated history of racial segregation in the South as maintained by "Jim Crow" laws and etiquette; (3) the rise of the motion picture as popular entertainment and the ways in which mass culture began to reshape American life; (4) the ways in which the increasing ubiquity of automobiles and an improved national highway system increased geographic mobility and encouraged the breakdown of local isolation; and (5) the system of tenancy farming, or sharecropping, under which many of the South's poorest inhabitants—both black and white—labored in the early twentieth century.

The archive and curriculum materials also make connections with how writers of the Southern Renaissance relate to those covered in other *American Passages* units: How does the Southern Renaissance relate to the Harlem Renaissance and other regional literary movements? How do writers of the Southern Renaissance relate to literary modernism and the "Lost Generation" with which that movement is often associated? How did writers like Hurston and Wright break new ground for literature written by African Americans? How does the "southern gothic" tradition relate to earlier examples of the American gothic? How did southern writers benefit from the WPA, and what is their relationship to the farm workers' movement?

Student Overview

"Southern Renaissance" explores some of the ways writers who lived in, wrote about, or were otherwise associated with the South between 1920 and

1950 responded to the many changes during the period. Those changes included new developments in science, rapid industrialization, increasing urbanization, and large-scale immigration—primarily from the sagging South to the more robust North. Historians sometimes refer to these massive social and cultural transformations of the early twentieth century as distinctively "modern." For many of the writers covered in this unit, the change to "modern" times raised questions: What kind of life is the best to live? Is the "modern" world headed in the right direction, or are we going the wrong way?

As you will see in the video, writers such as William Faulkner and Zora Neale Hurston situate their writing firmly within the South even as they question southern myths and traditions. Both Faulkner and Hurston are concerned with how the past shapes the present and future. Like many of the other authors in this unit, Faulkner and Hurston raise many more questions: How much responsibility do we owe to the past? How should the history of racism in America be dealt with in the present? How does economic poverty shape human lives? What parts of southern tradition should we try to preserve,

and what should we abandon as we transition to the "modern" world?

Unit 13 will introduce you to the diverse wealth of voices in the early-twentieth-century South through the works of John Crowe Ransom, Zora Neale Hurston, William Faulkner, Thomas Wolfe, Robert Penn Warren, Richard Wright, Katherine Anne Porter, Eudora Welty, Tennessee Williams, and Flannery O'Connor. In addition, it explores some of the major historical and cultural contexts that shaped this writing, including (1) the goals, values, and influence of the literary group known as the "Southern Agrarians"; (2) the extensive and complicated history of racial segregation in the South as maintained by "Jim Crow" laws and etiquette; (3) the rise of the motion picture as popular entertainment and the ways in which mass culture began to reshape American life; (4) the ways in which the increasing ubiquity of automobiles and an improved national highway system increased geographic mobility and encouraged the breakdown of local isolation; and (5) the system of tenancy farming, or sharecropping, under which many of the South's poorest inhabitants—both black and white—labored in the early twentieth century.

Video Overview

➢ **Authors covered:** William Faulkner, Zora Neale Hurston

➢ **Who's interviewed:** Dorothy Allison, award-winning author; Don Doyle, professor of history (Vanderbilt University); Carla Kaplan, professor of literature, American studies, and gender studies (University of Southern California); Ramon Saldivar, professor of American literature (Stanford University); Alice Walker, award-winning author and poet; Rafia Zafar, director of African and Afro-American studies (Washington University, St. Louis)

➢ **Points covered:**
- After World War I, writers emerged in the segregated South to tell new stories. Continuing a tradition while challenging the past, writers such as William Faulkner and Zora Neale Hurston ushered in a renaissance of southern literature.
- Faulkner built upon the work of a group of writers known as the Southern Agrarians that emerged in the

late 1920s. The Southern Agrarians defended the South's rural way of life while the world was changing around them.
- Faulkner captured the complicated, often tangled layers of southern history in countless novels and short stories. Intricately weaving the importance of time and place into everything he wrote, Faulkner was also a modernist who rebelled against linear storytelling. *As I Lay Dying*, with its nearly ludicrous plot and modernist style, is a good example of this stylistic innovation, while *Absalom, Absalom!*—a soul-searching indictment of the South—shows how some poor nineteenth-century whites tried to elevate themselves through racism, as a reaction against their own oppression.
- While Faulkner explored myths about white southerners, Zora Neale Hurston turned to African American folk traditions to present a positive view of black southern life. Hurston was a flamboyant storyteller, an anthropologist, and a respected writer.

- In her essay "How It Feels to Be Colored Me" Hurston observes that race is created, not given. As a folklorist and author, she captured a vision of the South that was different from what was usually recorded. *Their Eyes Were Watching God* is a woman's coming-of-age story and a critique of African American folk society.

- Hurston's final work was the autobiographical *Dust Tracks on a Road*, from which her publishers removed all anti-white references prior to publication. In the 1950s she slipped into obscurity; she died in poverty in 1960 and was buried in an unmarked grave. Hurston's writing was "rediscovered" by Alice Walker in 1973. She's now seen as the most important African American woman who wrote before World War II.

- Writers like Faulkner and Hurston joined their voices with those of other writers from the South to revise southern myths. At the same time, they broke through regional barriers to speak to the American experience and to the universal human condition.

PREVIEW

- **Preview the video:** In the decades following World War I, the United States experienced massive social and cultural changes in response to economic, industrial, and technological upheavals. This was especially true in the South, which had never fully recovered—economically or socially—from the Civil War and the effects of Reconstruction. Within this environment, writers like William Faulkner and Zora Neale Hurston emerged to write about the South, both its mythical past and its often harsh contemporary realities—including deeply entrenched racism and the hardships of lives lived under crushing poverty. Joined by the likes of Flannery O'Connor and Tennessee Williams, these writers participated in a reinvigoration of southern literature which has come to be known as the "Southern Renaissance."

- **What to think about while watching:** What are the main social and cultural factors that influence these writers? How do these writers depict the South? Does "the South" seem to be the same place for both Faulkner and Hurston, or do they each see it differently? What assumptions or beliefs do these writers challenge? How and why do these writers convey the importance of time and place in their writing? What are the formal innovations these writers use to convey their characters' experiences? What does the history of the critical reception of these authors tell us about American literature and the literary canon?

- **Tying the video to the unit content:** Unit 13 builds upon the introductory nature of the video to provide students with a variety of ways to understand how writers in the South responded to certain changes in American life throughout the first half of the twentieth century. The curriculum materials offer additional background on both Hurston and Faulkner, as well as on some of their prominent contemporaries in the fields of fiction, poetry, and drama. The unit also explores in greater detail some of the important contexts of southern writing, including the history of racism as seen in Jim Crow laws; the sharecropping system on which much of the rural South depended at this time; and the Southern Agrarian movement, in which a group of southern writers sought to promote an alternative future for the South.

	What is American literature? What are its distinctive voices and styles? How do social and political issues influence the American canon?	*How do place and time shape literature and our understanding of it?*	*What characteristics of a literary work have made it influential over time?*
Compre-hension Questions	What were the main social and cultural issues Faulkner and Hurston addressed in their writing? How were their responses to these issues different or similar?	What are the differences and similarities between the settings and characters created by Faulkner and Hurston?	Traditionally, stories have been told in a "linear" fashion, meaning that the story starts at the beginning and proceeds chronologically from one action or event to the next in a more or less straight line. Faulkner rebelled against this linear model, jumbling the chronology of his stories and thereby challenging readers to reassemble the action of the story in a logical manner. Consider both the subject matter of Faulkner's writing and the historical period in which he wrote: Why might Faulkner have chosen to write nonlinear stories?
Context Questions	Both Faulkner and Hurston are known for their innovative use of dialect. How do the characters' dialects help us relate to their social and economic conditions?	After the Civil War, hundreds of thousands of southerners—most of them black—headed north in search of better lives. This move, known as the "Great Migration," continued well into the 1920s and 1930s. How did the "Great Migration" influence Hurston's writing?	In the video you learned that Faulkner's *Absalom, Absalom!* was published in the same year as Margaret Mitchell's *Gone With the Wind.* In what ways does Faulkner's novel contest the vision of the South in *Gone With the Wind?*
Exploration Questions	Faulkner received the Nobel Prize for literature in 1950, after which his books became increasingly popular. Hurston faded into obscurity at about this same time. What might account for the differences in the way these writers were received? Why do you think Hurston's work found a new audience in the 1970s? What historical events might have prepared that audience to be newly receptive to Hurston's work?	Like Faulkner and Hurston, many other writers are well known for their vivid evocations of the time and place about which they write. For example, F. Scott Fitzgerald (Unit 11) is famous for his depiction of elite New York City society in the 1920s, while Henry David Thoreau (Unit 12) is renowned for his descriptions of life in early-nineteenth-century New England. Compare the different strategies these writers use to evoke the periods and places about which they write. Why are these strategies effective for depicting each time and place?	Hurston was often criticized during her lifetime for her realistic—but not always flattering—portrayals of African Americans. What did such critics hope to achieve, and how does such criticism fit in the larger context of African American writing in the twentieth century?

	Texts	Contexts
1920s	Katherine Anne Porter, "Maria Concepcion" (1922), *Flowering Judas* (1930) William Faulkner, *The Marble Faun* (1924), *Soldier's Pay* (1926), *Mosquitos* (1927), *Sartoris* (1929), *The Sound and the Fury* (1929) John Crowe Ransom, *Here Lies a Lady* (1924)	Group of writers who would later come to be known as the Southern Agrarians publishes *The Fugitive* as an outlet for their poetry and criticism (1922–25) *State v. John Scopes* (the Scopes "Monkey" Trial), Dayton, Tennessee (1925) Wall Street crash begins the Great Depression (1929)
1930s	William Faulkner, *As I Lay Dying* (1930), *Sanctuary* (1931), *Light in August* (1932), *Absalom, Absalom!* (1936), "Barn Burning" (1938) Southern Agrarians publish *I'll Take My Stand*, by "Twelve Southerners" Zora Neale Hurston, "The Gilded Six-Bits" (1933), *Jonah's Gourd Vine* (1934), *Mules and Men* (1935), *Their Eyes Were Watching God* (1937) Margaret Mitchell, *Gone With the Wind* (1936) Katherine Anne Porter, *Noon Wine* (1937), "Pale Horse, Pale Rider" (1939) Richard Wright, *Uncle Tom's Children* (1938), "The Man Who Was Almost a Man" (1939)	"Scottsboro Boys" (nine African American youths) tried for the alleged rape of two white women, Victoria Price and Ruby Bates (1931–37) Faulkner in Hollywood on contract as a scriptwriter (1932–37) Eighteenth Amendment repealed; Prohibition ends (1933) World War II begins (1939)
1940s	William Faulkner, *The Hamlet* (1940), *Intruder in the Dust* (1948) Richard Wright, *Native Son* (1940), *Black Boy* (1945) Eudora Welty, "Petrified Man" (1941), *The Robber Bridegroom* (1942) Zora Neale Hurston, *Dust Tracks on a Road* (1942) Robert Penn Warren, "Bearded Oaks" (1942), *All the King's Men* (1946) Katherine Anne Porter, *The Leaning Tower* (1944) Tennessee Williams, *The Glass Menagerie* (1945), *A Streetcar Named Desire* (1947) *The Portable Faulkner*, ed. Malcolm Cowley (1946)	Japanese attack on Pearl Harbor brings United States into World War II (1941) United States drops atomic bombs on Hiroshima and Nagasaki; Japan surrenders, ending World War II. Cold War between United States and Soviet Union begins (1945) Jackie Robinson becomes first black major-league baseball player (1947)
1950s	Flannery O'Connor, "Good Country People" (1955) William Faulkner, *The Town* (1957), *The Mansion* (1959)	Senator Joseph McCarthy begins attacks on communism (1950) Korean War (1950–53) House Concurrent Resolution 108 dictates government's intention to "terminate" its treaty relations with the Native American tribes (1953) *Brown v. Board of Education* declares segregated schools unconstitutional (1954)

AUTHOR/TEXT REVIEW

John Crowe Ransom (1888–1974)

A leading force in southern letters from the 1920s on, John Crowe Ransom was born in Pulaski, Tennessee. Educated primarily at home in his early years by his parents, Ransom enrolled in Vanderbilt University as a young man of fifteen. Ransom's academic excellence earned him a Rhodes scholarship to Oxford University in England, after which he taught high school briefly in Connecticut before returning to Vanderbilt to begin his career as an English professor.

Ransom's first volume of poetry, *Poems about God*, was published in 1919. Around that same time, Ransom became the center of a small group of poets who called themselves the **Fugitives** after the name of the magazine they began publishing in 1922 as an outlet for their poetry. Ransom produced his best and best-known poetry in the 1920s, including "Bells for John Whiteside's Daughter," "Philomela," "Piazza Piece," "Equilibrists," and "Janet Waking." His poetry is known for its tendency to expose the ironies of existence, primarily through short lyrics about often somber or serious domestic scenes—such as the death of a child or a "lady young in beauty waiting until [her] true love comes"—into which Ransom introduces some unsettling twist.

Although Ransom is respected as an accomplished poet, he had always tended toward philosophical and theoretical pursuits and these came to dominate much of his literary output beginning in the late 1920s. Like many of his southern peers, Ransom was incensed by the "laughing stock" the national press made of the South in its coverage of the Scopes evolution trial of 1925. At the urging of Donald Davidson, Ransom joined with eleven other southern men (including several who were also members of the Fugitives) to produce *I'll Take My Stand*, a volume of essays that praised southern traditions and the agrarian ways of life that dominated the Old South. For the next several years, Ransom explored **Agrarianism** at greater depth, while at the same time he began to write critical essays that described and defended poetry which could represent reality fully and completely without retreating into untrustworthy realms of abstraction.

[3696] Dorothea Lange, *Plantation Overseer. Mississippi Delta, near Clarksdale, Mississippi* (1936), courtesy of the Library of Congress [LC-USF34-009596-C DLC].

Ransom's critical pursuits soon led to the publication in 1938 of *The World's Body*, a collection of essays which laid much of the groundwork for what came to be known as **New Criticism**, an influential critical movement that sought to focus the critic's attention on the work of literature itself—its language and formal qualities—rather than on the historical and biographical context of the work. In that same year, two of Ransom's former students—Cleanth Brooks and Robert Penn Warren—published *Understanding Poetry*, which expressed many of the critical principles Ransom was advocating, and which eventually became the standard text for teaching poetry in colleges and universities throughout the nation.

Ransom left Vanderbilt for a position at Ohio's Kenyon College in 1937. Two years later he founded the *Kenyon Review*, an influential literary journal that he edited until his retirement from Kenyon in 1959.

TEACHING TIPS

■ Although many of Ransom's poems focus on common domestic scenes, each uses unexpected words and turns of phrase to question the contradictions of everyday life. For example, in "Bells for John Whiteside's Daughter," a dead child's expression "Astonishes us all." At the end of the poem, the readers are "stopped" and "vexed" by the child's expression. Ask your students to think about the effect of these verbs in this context and to look for similar, unexpected language in Ransom's other poems.

■ Ransom is known for his frequent use of archaic language and references to classical texts and myths. Have your students identify some of these elements in Ransom's poems and discuss their contribution to the poems' overall effect.

QUESTIONS

Comprehension: What is "Janet Waking" about? Summarize the "events" the poem describes.

Context: As he contributed to the development of the New Criticism, Ransom argued that "criticism must become more scientific, or precise and systematic." Yet, in the 1920s, as a member of the Southern Agrarians, Ransom had denounced the increasing influence of modern science and the rationalization of human life. Why do you think Ransom eventually came to advocate a "scientific method" of literary criticism?

Exploration: As a writer of modern lyric poetry, Ransom argued that poetry could provide an alternative to science as a source of knowledge in the modern world. One of Ransom's contemporaries, T. S. Eliot, has been praised for writing poetry that challenges the authority of science and the value of its achievements. Yet Eliot (whom Ransom admired) depicted the world much differently in his poems than did Ransom. Compare Eliot's "The Hollow Men" with Ransom's "Philomela." If you consider each poem as an attempt to challenge the authority of science, what different strategies do these writers use to accomplish a similar goal?

Katherine Anne Porter (1890–1980)

"It is my firm belief," Katherine Anne Porter once said, "that all our lives we are preparing to be somebody or something, even if we do not do it consciously." Porter knew at a young age she wanted to be a writer, and she worked diligently and methodically toward that goal, achieving recognition as one of America's finest writers of short fiction by the time she reached the age of forty. Born Callie Russell Porter in a small log house in Indian Creek, Texas, Katherine Anne and her

three siblings were raised by their maternal grandmother after their mother died. The family lived in
poverty, and when Porter turned sixteen she married
a railroad clerk named John Henry Koontz—both to
leave home and to find the financial security she'd
never known. Porter did not take to domestic life,
however, and soon separated from her husband,
assumed the name Katherine Anne, and turned to a
life of travel and career changes. After a serious bout
with tuberculosis, Porter took her first job as a professional writer with the *Fort Worth Critic*, and from
there she went on to live and work in Denver, New
York City, Mexico, and Europe. Her first published
story, "Maria Concepcion," appeared in the prestigious *Century* magazine in 1922 and was soon followed by "The Martyr," which was about
the artist Diego Rivera. Porter's best-known story, "Flowering Judas,"
was published in 1930 in *Hound and Horn*; from then on, her reputation as a writer was secure.

Although her settings are often radically different (such as revolutionary Mexico and bohemian New York City), Porter's fiction is
characterized by a strong sense of locale, and much of her work
explores the tensions faced by women as they negotiate their place in
the modern world. Porter's careful attention to planning and revising
her work—sometimes over a period of several years—resulted in the
publication of only four story collections and one novel, each considered a literary event. Her books of short fiction are *Flowering Judas*
(1930), *Noon Wine* (1937), *Pale Horse, Pale Rider* (1939), and *The
Leaning Tower* (1944). Her novel *Ship of Fools* was begun in the early
1940s, but Porter developed and revised it for more than twenty years
before it was finally published in 1961. The novel was a commercial
success and was later made into a popular film. Porter's *Collected
Stories* was published in 1965, bringing her the National Book Award,
the Pulitzer Prize, and the Gold Medal for Fiction from the National
Institute of Arts and Letters.

TEACHING TIPS

■ "Flowering Judas" can be somewhat difficult for students to get
into at first because of the lack of explication for its foreign setting. In
preparation for reading the story, ask your students to look into the
history of Mexico in the early twentieth century, focusing on the abundance of revolutionary activity during the period. (The decade of
1910–20 was an especially turbulent time in Mexico, as different leaders in different regions of the country mounted military campaigns
against each other as well as the Mexican government. Many Mexicans
found themselves caught between military leaders at local and regional levels, and power shifted from one faction to another repeatedly
during the period.) After your students have read the story, ask them
to use their research to discuss what Porter means when she says that
Laura "wears the uniform of an idea, and has renounced vanities."

What does this suggest about Laura and the role she plays in the revolution?

■ In an interview in *The Paris Review*, Porter said that she had "no patience with this dreadful idea that whatever you have in you has to come out, that you can't suppress true talent. People can be destroyed; they can be bent, distorted, and completely crippled. To say that you can't destroy yourself is just as foolish as to say of a young man killed in war at twenty-one or twenty-two that that was his fate, that he wasn't going to have anything anyhow." Introduce your students to Porter's statements; then ask them to discuss them in small groups. Does Laura, the protagonist of "Flowering Judas," seem "bent" or "distorted" in any way? Does Porter's statement, above, give us a way of understanding these characters? What do Porter's thoughts suggest about authorship in general?

■ Good fictional characters commonly face a major problem or decision which develops from a misunderstanding, a value conflict with other characters, misinformation, or some other challenging situation. However, like many of the writers included in this unit, Porter often creates characters who seem challenged by some failing of their own—as a result of either some inner conflict or some past event that we as readers cannot directly access. Ask your students to analyze the characters in Porter's stories: What are these characters challenged by? Do these characters seem to be healthy human beings facing unusual obstacles, or do the characters themselves seem deficient in some way? For example, does Laura, the protagonist of "Flowering Judas," seem "bent" or "distorted" in any way? For purposes of comparison, invite your students to catalog the "deficiencies" of other protagonists, such as those created by Faulkner, O'Connor, or Williams. Why might southern authors create characters who seem to be, in some way, "damaged"?

QUESTIONS

Comprehension: What kinds of lives do the people in "Flowering Judas" lead? What clues does the story contain to help readers understand how its characters live?

Context: In her introduction to a 1940 edition of *Flowering Judas*, Porter wrote that she'd spent much of her life trying "to understand the logic of this majestic and terrible failure of the life of man in the Western World." Consider Porter's statement in light of World War I and World War II. How does "Flowering Judas" seem to reflect that "majestic and terrible failure"?

Context: The setting of "Flowering Judas" (revolutionary Mexico) might challenge students' concept of "southern" literature, yet thematically, the story is very much within the realm of the work of Porter's southern peers. For example, like similar characters in Faulkner's writing, Laura in "Flowering Judas" seems torn between repudiating her past and its traditions and accepting the revolutionary values of the world in which she finds herself. What does such a setting and theme suggest about the meaning of "southern literature" in this period and its dominant preoccupations?

Exploration: In a sense, Porter was as much a fiction as any of her characters; at a young age she changed her name, and throughout her life she lied about her birth date, marriages, education, and work habits. More importantly, she denied she'd been raised in poverty on a Texas dirt farm and claimed instead to be the descendant of a romantically degenerating "white-pillar" family of the Old South. Why do you think Porter lied about her background? How might her lies have changed the way her writing was received in the 1930s and 1940s? What does this suggest about American "literature" and the critical establishment? By way of comparison, you might also consider the fact that William Faulkner changed his name (he added the "u" to his last name) and lied about such things as being wounded in World War I. Why would these writers feel compelled to fictionalize their own lives?

Zora Neale Hurston (1891–1960)

Although she would later mislead people about her age and birthplace, Zora Neale Hurston was born in 1891 in Notasulga, Alabama, and later moved to the small, all-black town of Eatonville, Florida. Hurston would later write that she spent the first years of her life blissfully unaware of the racial oppression experienced by the vast majority of southern blacks in that era. "How It Feels to Be Colored Me," Hurston's famous essay recounting this experience, sets the unapologetic, joyful, and defiant tone of much of her writing. Speaking about herself and her African American peers who came of age after the Civil War and the immediate turmoil of **Reconstruction**, Hurston writes: "No one on earth ever had a greater chance for glory. The world to be won and nothing to be lost." Such exuberant optimism did not please many of her fellow writers in the 1920s and 1930s, and Hurston died in poverty and total anonymity. However, Hurston's prominent position in American literary history today suggests that perhaps she was more prescient than she could have known.

After spending the first thirteen years of her life in Eatonville, Hurston was sent to school in Jacksonville, Florida, where she was quickly initiated into the segregated, Jim Crow South. Determined to be undeterred by the experience, Hurston eventually made her way to Washington, D.C. There she attended Howard University before moving on to New York, where she earned a B.A. degree from Barnard College in 1928. At Barnard she worked with renowned anthropologist Franz Boas, and in 1927, under Boas's direction, Hurston traveled to Louisiana and southern Florida to study and collect African American folktales. That trip produced *Mules and Men*, published in 1935 and celebrated as the first collection of African American folklore compiled and published by an African American. "The Eatonville Anthology," an anthropologically based narrative, sketches vivid images of Hurston's hometown and reveals her skill as an anthropologist.

[4565] Prentiss Taylor, *Zora Neale Hurston*, courtesy of Yale Collection of American Literature, Beinecke Rare Book and Manuscript Library. Used with the permission of the Estate of Zora Neale Hurston.

[4565] Prentiss Taylor, *Zora Neale Hurston,* courtesy of Yale Collection of American Literature, Beinecke Rare Book and Manuscript Library. Used with the permission of the Estate of Zora Neale Hurston. Photograph of Hurston dancing on couch. Known for her flamboyance and charisma, Hurston was sometimes urged by other artists to represent African Americans in more "dignified" ways.

[4566] Anonymous, *Their Eyes Were Watching God* dustcover (1937), courtesy of Yale Collection of American Literature, Beinecke Rare Book and Manuscript Library. Zora Neale Hurston's best-known book, *Their Eyes Were Watching God,* was criticized by some African American authors and leaders because it did not emphasize and critique racial oppression.

[4811] Alan Lomax, *African American Child Singer for Singing Games* (1935), courtesy of the Library of Congress [LC-USZ62-130896 DLC]. Girl standing in rural scene. Zora Neale Hurston was raised in Eatonville, the first all-black township in Florida, about which she wrote "The Eatonville Anthology," an anthropological narrative. Hurston spent the first years of her life unaware of the racial oppression experienced by the vast majority of southern blacks in the era. "How It Feels to Be Colored Me," Hurston's famous essay recounting this experience, sets the unapologetic, joyful, and defiant tone of much of her writing.

[4819] Alan Lomax, *Zora Neale Hurston, Rochelle French, and Gabriel Brown, Eatonville, Florida* (1935), courtesy of the Library of Congress [LC-USZ61-1777 DLC]. Used with the permission of the Estate of Zora Neale Hurston. Hurston talking with residents of her all-black hometown, Eatonville. While attending Barnard, Hurston worked with renowned anthropologist Franz Boas, and in 1927, under Boas's direction, Hurston traveled to Louisiana and southern Florida to study and collect African American folktales.

[5342] Zora Neale Hurston, *Shove It Over* (1933), courtesy of the Library of Congress [AFS 3136A:1]. Used with the permission of the Estate of Zora Neale

Hurston's short story "The Gilded Six-Bits" conveys the author's exuberant and optimistic voice. That voice also characterizes her most famous work, *Their Eyes Were Watching God*, a novel that earned her the scorn and condemnation of other African American writers of her day, notably Langston Hughes and, later, Richard Wright. But while her critics urged her to write novels that would "uplift the race" by showing white readers the oppression and degradation experienced by African Americans, Hurston instead worked to promote a vision of "racial health—a sense of black people as complete, complex, *undiminished* human beings, a sense that is lacking in so much black writing and literature."

Hurston's writing won her great acclaim in the 1920s and 1930s, and her autobiography, *Dust Tracks on a Road* (1942), won an award from the *Saturday Review* for its contribution to positive race relations. Yet, despite her considerable success as a writer, Hurston virtually disappeared from the literary world from the late 1940s to the early 1970s. Thanks to an emerging black feminist movement and the special efforts of Alice Walker and Mary Helen Washington, Hurston was "rediscovered" in the mid-1970s. She is now widely regarded as the most important pre–World War II African American woman writer.

TEACHING TIPS

■ Hurston is often noted for her deft use of the South Florida African American vernacular and her masterful ability to integrate it smoothly with more standard English. Nevertheless, some students may initially be resistant to this; some might even be offended if they regard the vernacular as making Hurston's African American characters seem ignorant or comical. The audiobook version of *Their Eyes Were Watching God* can help students learn to read the dialect, while a few simple questions about Hurston's use of dialect should help your students appreciate the effect of this language. Why does Hurston have her characters talk this way? What does their language tell us about these characters? How is their use of vernacular related to the time and place about which Hurston is writing? Students should be encouraged to consult the table on Black English in Unit 8.

■ Although Hurston was trained as an anthropologist, her portrayals of southern life are not necessarily realistic. For example, in "The Gilded Six-Bits," Joe and Missie May are portrayed as childlike and simple. While this allows for a greater contrast between the couple's initial happiness and the estrangement that follows Missie May's infidelity, it hardly reflects the average life of African Americans in the rural South in 1933. The ease with which the couple's happiness is eventually restored is also not typical—infidelity was generally dealt with much more harshly in the rural South at this time. After pointing this out to your students, you might ask them to think about why Hurston chose to create characters like Missie May and Joe. What advantage is there for a writer in depicting the world as we wish it were, rather than as we actually find it? What are the disadvantages of this strategy? Such conversation should also help your students better understand the critical debates surrounding Hurston's work—both in her own time and today.

QUESTIONS

Comprehension: How would you characterize the tone of the short folktales that comprise "The Eatonville Anthology"?

Context: In 1933, the year Hurston wrote "The Gilded Six-Bits," the United States was being transformed by an increasingly mobile population. As automobiles became more affordable, the national highway system developed to allow people a greater freedom of movement than they'd ever experienced before. At the same time, chain department stores, national radio broadcasts, and a mature system of motion picture distribution meant that even remote, rural towns had begun to feel the effects of the new mass culture. In Hurston's story, Missie May and Joe seem to live a blissful and largely carefree existence, but their happiness is interrupted by the appearance of "Otis D. Slemmons, of spots and places." If Slemmons symbolizes many of the changes described above, what does Hurston seem to be saying about those changes?

Context: In "How It Feels to Be Colored Me," Hurston writes: "Someone is always at my elbow reminding me that I am the granddaughter of slaves. It fails to register depression with me. Slavery is sixty years in the past. The operation was successful and the patient is doing well, thank you." How does this perspective compare with the experience of other African Americans living in the segregated, Jim Crow South? Compare Hurston's sentiments here to those expressed by Richard Wright in "The Man Who Was Almost a Man."

Exploration: Both Zora Neale Hurston and Langston Hughes were closely associated with the literary movement known as the Harlem Renaissance (see Unit 10). However, unlike Harlem Renaissance writers who produced writing that focused on the experience of the growing population of urban, middle-class African Americans, Hurston and Hughes chose to write about African American folk cultures and to employ more vernacular in their writing. Read Hughes's "Mother to Son" and "The Weary Blues." How does Hughes's poetry complement the picture of African American life Hurston creates in "The Gilded Six-Bits"?

William Faulkner (1897–1962)

The man who would become one of twentieth-century American literature's best-known figures, William Cuthbert Falkner (he added the "u" to his last name later in life) was born in Albany, Mississippi. Four years later, the Falkners moved to nearby Oxford, which William would call home for the rest of his life. Faulkner's childhood was fairly

Hurston. This lining rhythm was collected from Charlie Jones on a railroad construction camp near Lakeland, Florida. Before mechanization, songs helped coordinate workers as they aligned railroad tracks using steel "lining bars."

[7305] R. H. Hoffman, *Anthropologist Franz Boas* (c. 1945), courtesy of the Library of Congress [LC-USZ62-93360 DLC]. One of the best-known anthropologists of the twentieth century, Franz Boas taught Zora Neale Hurston and Margaret Mead. His contributions to the field include historical particularism—the idea that anthropology should focus on the uniqueness and specificity of cultures rather than universal laws.

[6948] Jack E. Boucher, *South front and west side, Rowan Oak, Old Taylor Rd., Oxford, Lafayette County, MS* [*William Faulkner's old house*] (1975), courtesy of the Library of Congress [HABS, MISS, 36-OXFO, 9-4].

average for a young middle-class white boy of the period: he grew up surrounded by romantic and glorious tales of the **Old South**, many of them handed down from his grandfather, William Clark Falkner, a somewhat legendary figure who managed to become a colonel in the Civil War and went on to become a planter, lawyer, novelist, and builder of railroads before being shot dead by a former business partner in 1889. However, by the time Faulkner reached his late teens he began showing signs that his was not to be an average life. After dropping out of high school, he tried working in his grandfather's bank, but quickly gave that up and, in the face of his father's and the rest of his community's disapproval, decided to pursue a career as a poet. During this time, Faulkner was courting a local belle, Estelle Oldham, but when her family refused to approve of his unconventional behavior, Estelle married someone else, and Faulkner promptly left for Canada to join the RAF (Royal Air Force). (She later divorced her husband and married Faulkner in 1929.) Faulkner saw no action in World War I, and once it was over he returned to Oxford, where he briefly attended classes at the University of Mississippi. He continued to write poetry, publishing his first collection of poems, *The Marble Faun*, near the end of 1924 (the title consciously echoed that of Nathaniel Hawthorne's romantic novel about the conflict between American and Old World values). Despite this small success, Faulkner's writing life did not truly begin until he met another writer, Sherwood Anderson, who advised him to develop his prose and to concentrate on what he knew best—the Mississippi of his youth. It took three novels—*Soldier's Pay* (1926), *Mosquitos* (1927), and *Sartoris* (1929)—for Faulkner to develop his prose skills into their early greatness, but with the October 1929 publication of *The Sound and the Fury*, Faulkner's writing life had truly begun.

Like *Sartoris* and *The Sound and the Fury*, Faulkner's next novel, *As I Lay Dying* (1930), was set in Yoknapatawpha County, the fictional representation of the Oxford area that Faulkner would continue to develop in subsequent novels. Also like its predecessor, *As I Lay Dying* was written in a **stream of consciousness** style, using fifteen different narrators who deliver fifty-nine interior monologues from which readers must assemble the story, as if putting together a puzzle. The fragmented nature of Faulkner's narratives marks them as examples of literary modernism, a movement which sought to challenge artistic conventions and provide its audience with new ways of seeing the world. More recently, critics have explored the ways in which Faulkner's use of pastiche and multiple, often contradictory voices within a single work may have been a forerunner of what later came to be called postmodern fiction.

Although he continued to write throughout his life, critics generally agree that Faulkner produced his best work in the 1930s and early 1940s, including *Light in August* (1932) and *Absalom, Absalom!* (1936)—which many believe to be his masterpiece. Faulkner received the Nobel Prize in 1950.

■ Students will likely find *As I Lay Dying* confusing, difficult to relate to, and depressing. They are more likely to appreciate the novel if you preface their reading with a short introduction to Faulkner and to the modernist techniques he uses to tell his story. After students have read a few of the monologues, spend some class time letting them discuss the fragmentation and dislocation they feel; then use their comments to explore the epistemological and ontological questions the novel raises. How do Faulkner's characters know what they know? How do *we* know what we know? How do the Bundrens come to be who they are? How do *we* become who we are? Can we consider any of the novel's fifteen different narrators "reliable"? Working in groups, ask your students to write a character sketch of each of the novel's fifteen narrators. The sketch should describe the character and his or her context. After students have completed their sketches, ask each group to share their description and to tell the class whether their narrator is reliable and why.

■ Because Faulkner looms as such an imposing figure over the American literary canon, you may need to push your students to be critical of his authority. One way to do this is to ask your students to think about Faulkner's social position and compare it to that of the Bundren family in *As I Lay Dying*. To help your students understand the Bundrens a bit better, ask them to create a family/relationship tree that indicates with arrows how the characters are connected to one another and which gives the page number and chapter title in which we learn of the characters' personalities. Using their relationship trees as points of reference, ask your students to consider some of the following questions: What would someone of Faulkner's social standing typically think of people like the Bundrens? Is Faulkner making fun of the Bundrens, and if so, why? At what points do we want to laugh at the Bundrens? Why? At what points do we want to weep? Does the novel suggest any reasons for the Bundren's poverty? Why, for example, is Anse Bundren depicted as someone who never breaks a sweat?

QUESTIONS

Comprehension: Who are the Bundrens? What is their position in their community? What do their neighbors seem to think of them? How does their community's impression of the Bundrens affect our impression of them?

Comprehension: What drives Anse Bundren and his children to put themselves through all the trials required to bury Addie in Jefferson? Why don't the Bundrens just bury Addie at home? Do Anse and his children seem motivated by love and respect for their dead wife and mother, or are they driven by other forces?

Comprehension: In the opening scene of "Barn Burning," in which Mr. Harris has accused Abner Snopes of burning his barn, Harris suggests the judge question Sarty about the incident, but the judge hesitates and Harris eventually changes his mind. Why don't these

[3309] Letter, *Philip Avery Stone to John Sharp Williams requesting support for William Faulkner's appointment as postmaster at the University of Mississippi* (1922), courtesy of the Library of Congress [A86]. This position of postmaster was a way for Faulkner to earn an income and continue writing, as it paid a full salary, but did not require full-time work.

[5122] Anonymous, *Rowan Oak, Old Taylor Rd., Oxford, Lafayette County, MS*, courtesy of the Library of Congress [HABS, Miss, 36-OXFO, 9-]. William Faulkner's home in Mississippi. Highly formalized in their layout, large plantations usually centered on the "big house," an imposing, often neoclassical structure designed as an expression of the good taste and prosperity of the owner.

[6948] Jack E. Boucher, *South front and west side, Rowan Oak, Old Taylor Rd., Oxford, Lafayette County, MS* [*William Faulkner's old house*] (1975), courtesy of the Library of Congress [HABS, MISS, 36-OXFO, 9-4]. The myth of the "Old South" generally referred to the "plantation legend" of antebellum (and much postbellum) popular fiction that portrayed white southerners as genteel aristocrats and slavery as a benevolent, paternal institution from which blacks and whites benefited equally. Although Faulkner grew up in a neoclassical "big house," he challenged this myth in his fiction.

[7488] Anonymous, *William Faulkner Handed 1949 Nobel Prize of $30,000 for Literature* (1949), courtesy of AP/Wide World Photos. Some audiences eagerly anticipated Faulkner's acceptance of the Nobel Prize, as he rarely spoke publicly or dressed formally.

men want to ask Sarty to testify against his father? What does their reluctance to do so tell us about how they view the Snopes family?

Context: Compare Faulkner's depiction of a poor white southern family in "Barn Burning" to the Southern Agrarians' praise of the rural, soil-centered life. How does the Snopes family match up with the Agrarians' ideals?

Exploration: Faulkner's Yoknapatawpha County can sometimes seem like the land that time forgot. This is especially true in *As I Lay Dying*, in which much of the plot unfolds in rural areas which, while geographically not far from the somewhat modern community of Jefferson, seem separated from the modern world by a much wider gulf. While historians of the 1920s and 1930s emphasize the increasing pace of industrialization and technological change that was reshaping the world between the wars, the citizens of Yoknapatawpha County seem oblivious. Yet, in a more indirect sense, the effects of these global changes are inescapably woven into Faulkner's texts. Discuss the ways in which the larger changes in the "outside world" contribute to Faulkner's imaginary world.

Exploration: Because of the dark settings and disturbing themes of much of his writing, Faulkner is often regarded as a master of the **southern gothic**. How does Faulkner compare to other "gothic" writers, such as Edgar Allan Poe or Nathaniel Hawthorne? (See Unit 6.) In what ways are Hawthorne and Faulkner concerned with "the sins of the fathers"? How similar or different are their views of these "sins"?

Thomas Wolfe (1900–1938)

Known for his ability to produce lyrical torrents of largely autobiographical prose, Thomas Wolfe earned critical and commercial success with his first novel, *Look Homeward Angel* (1929), but struggled to live up to his own reputation for the rest of his short life.

Born Thomas Clayton Wolfe in Asheville, North Carolina, Wolfe was the youngest of eight children. He attended a private school in Asheville before going on to the University of North Carolina when he was just shy of his sixteenth birthday. It was at UNC that Wolfe began writing in earnest—first as a reporter for the school paper (of which he eventually became editor), and then as a budding playwright. After graduation, Wolfe went to Harvard to study playwriting at the 47 Workshop with George Pierce Baker. There, Wolfe produced two notable plays, *Mannerhouse* and *Welcome to Our City*, both of which featured a satirical style inspired by that of the most infamous critic of the South's cultural and intellectual sterility, H. L. Mencken. However, the sheer length of his plays (*Welcome to Our City* was nearly four hours from curtain to curtain) and his intensely personal narrative style were poorly suited

[7266] Marion Post Walcott, *Farmhouse and Barns near Asheville, North Carolina* (1939), courtesy of the Library of Congress [LC-USF34-052386-D DLC].

to drama, and Wolfe soon became frustrated by his lack of success as a playwright.

In August 1925, as he was returning to New York from Europe, Wolfe met and fell in love with Aline Bernstein. Almost twenty years Wolfe's senior and an accomplished scene designer in the New York theater, Bernstein encouraged Wolfe to pursue prose fiction instead of drama. With the publication of *Look Homeward, Angel* four years later, Wolfe's literary reputation finally seemed secure. A largely autobiographical story of a young Southerner coming of age, the novel was hailed by some as an American answer to James Joyce's *A Portrait of the Artist as a Young Man* and made such an impression that in 1947 even William Faulkner ranked Wolfe ahead of himself as the most important American writer of the 1920s and 1930s.

The success of *Look Homeward, Angel* allowed Wolfe to continue traveling and gathering material for his writing. Wolfe's experiences during these years—as well as his continued association with Bernstein—encouraged him to explore the Jewish themes with which some of his later writing was concerned. According to biographer Hugh Holman, "In 1936, leaving Berlin on a train, an incident with a Jew trying to escape Germany forced [Wolfe] to recognize the cruel nature of the Nazi state, and on returning home he wrote one of his most powerful short novels, *I Have a Thing To Tell You*, a strong indictment of Germany, which was serialized in the *New Republic*. Like many of his short novels, it was later incorporated in expanded form in one of his novels, in this case *You Can't Go Home Again*."

Yet, despite having plenty of new material, Wolfe struggled to produce a followup to *Look Homeward, Angel*, and eventually was forced to rely heavily on the talents of his editor at Scribner's, Maxwell Perkins (who also worked with F. Scott Fitzgerald and Ernest Hemingway), to help him pare down and shape the unwieldy manuscript that eventually became Wolfe's second novel, *Of Time and the River* (1935). The effort was a popular success, but critics charged that Wolfe's passionate but personal style was becoming tiresome and overindulgent; they also questioned whether Wolfe depended too heavily on Perkins to structure his work. In an effort to prove his ability as a writer, Wolfe changed publishers and worked furiously to produce a third novel. Mere months before his untimely death from tuberculosis, Wolfe delivered his final manuscript (thousands of pages) to his new editor, Edward Aswell at Harper's. After Wolfe's death, Aswell shaped the manuscript into two novels, *The Web and the Rock* (1939) and *You Can't Go Home Again* (1940). Both books continued the story of Wolfe's own life, but included a larger social vision that answered at least some of his critics' complaints.

TEACHING TIPS

■ As in *As I Lay Dying*, the narrative changes in the "The Lost Boy" can be confusing to students. Ask students to chart the narrative changes in the story by listing the different narrators, the page on which the narration changes, and the specific textual devices Wolfe uses to indicate the change. Use your students' charts to talk about the importance of the different narrators to the overall effect of the story.

■ Wolfe's career raises questions about what an "author" is or does. Can we call Wolfe the author of *Of Time and the River* if the book was largely "shaped" by his editor? What is authorship? To help students think about such questions, ask them to write a definition of authorship, then have them discuss their definitions. How important is it that the reader be able to define what an author is or does?

QUESTIONS

Comprehension: Why is Robert so concerned with "Time" in the first third of "The Lost Boy"? Notice how time seems to stop for Robert in certain places. How does his concern with the passage of time relate to the later sections of the story?

Context: Compare "The Lost Boy" to Richard Wright's "The Man Who Was Almost a Man." Like Wright, Wolfe was at least partially inspired by H. L. Mencken's sharp critiques of the South and its people. In what ways do both Wright and Wolfe seem concerned with "lost boys"? How are their lost boys similar? In what ways do they seem different?

Context: During Wolfe's life, new technologies of mass media—primarily radio and motion pictures—sparked the growth of a mass culture that brought many changes to the small southern communities Wolfe writes about. With this in mind, how might we read "The Lost Boy" as a story about Wolfe's life and literary career? In what ways was Wolfe himself "lost"? In what ways might we think of it as the story of "the South" more generally?

Exploration: Much of the fiction produced after World War II can be read as responding in some way to the horrific events of that conflict, including the Jewish Holocaust and the nuclear bombing of Hiroshima and Nagasaki. As you can see from Unit 15, "Poetry of Liberation," many writers in the second half of the twentieth century attempted to confront the question of what it means to be human after witnessing the extent of the cruelty humans can inflict on one another. Compare Thomas Wolfe to a few of the writers in Unit 15. In what ways are Wolfe's concerns similar to those of later writers? In what ways are they different?

Exploration: What is the role of critical taste in determining a work's value? Literary taste changed during the interval between the publication of Wolfe's first two books (1929–35). During that time, Marxist critics began demanding socially conscious fiction, while New Critics were looking for structurally unified works. Neither critical perspective was pleased by the lack of structure and the personal style that characterized Wolfe's books. How does the rise and fall of Wolfe's literary reputation compare with that of Zora Neale Hurston? What might the critical reception of these authors tell us about what makes "great" American literature?

Robert Penn Warren (1905–1989)

A prominent member of the Southern Agrarians as well as an accomplished poet and novelist, Robert Penn Warren was born in southern Kentucky and educated at Vanderbilt, the University of California, Yale, and Oxford. While at Vanderbilt he became one of the "Fugitive poets" and later contributed a somewhat reluctant defense of "separate but equal" racial segregation to *I'll Take My Stand*, the political manifesto of the Southern Agrarians, who were also associated with Vanderbilt. (Like many southerners, Warren later changed his mind about segregation.) He began teaching English at Louisiana State University in 1934 and there co-founded the *Southern Review*, which published provocative essays by the "New Critics," passionate advocates of "close reading," as well as fiction by emerging southern writers such as Eudora Welty. Warren's influence on the New Criticism was considerable; *Understanding Poetry*—which Warren co-authored with Cleanth Brooks while both were at Louisiana State—helped revolutionize the teaching of literature within the American university. That volume was followed in 1943 by *Understanding Fiction*. Warren left Louisiana State that same year.

[4730] Marion Post Walcott, *Political poster on sharecropper's house, Mississippi Delta, Mississippi* (1939), courtesy of the Library of Congress [LC-USF33-020570-M3].

Much of Warren's own prose and poetry grows out of his critical engagement with the history of the American South. That engagement was evident in his biography of abolitionist John Brown, which he undertook while at Yale and published in 1929. Warren's third and best-known novel, *All the King's Men*, which chronicles the rise and fall of a southern politician, received the Pulitzer Prize in 1946. Like Warren's second novel, *Heaven's Gate* (1943), *All the King's Men* was concerned with power and the way its pursuit and acquisition can destroy both the powerful and those around them. Warren returned to the theme in his fourth and perhaps second-best novel, *World Enough and Time*, published in 1950. Though he went on to write six more novels over the next thirty years, none would equal the power and eloquence of these earlier efforts.

The mid-fifties onward were fruitful years for Warren the poet. His long poem *Audubon* (1969), one of his most significant works, reveals a writer who celebrates the necessity that humans must face the darkness in their natures and forge ahead. Warren advocated a poetry "grounded in experience" and declared that the goal of the artist should be to stay within the limits of his/her gifts and, to the extent that those gifts allow, "to remain faithful to the complexities of the problems with which [he/she] is dealing." Warren's volumes of poetry include *Incarnations* (1968), *Now and Then* (1978), *Being Here* (1980), *Rumor Verified* (1981), and *Chief Joseph of the Nez Perce* (1983).

TEACHING TIPS

■ "Bearded Oaks," one of Warren's early poems, provides a good starting point for students. You might begin by trying to get students to think about the somewhat incongruous imagery within the poem: Where is the poem set? Who is the poem about? What doesn't seem to

[4730] Marion Post Walcott, *Political poster on sharecropper's house, Mississippi Delta, Mississippi* (1939), courtesy of the Library of Congress [LC-USF33-020570-M3]. Campaign poster for Joe Hidgon, chancery clerk. Living conditions for sharecroppers were generally poor as they rarely made large profits and often had enormous debts. African American sharecroppers were also barred from voting and often received no education.

[7284] Lewis Wickes Hine, *Starting Card in Motion, Picket Yarn Mill, High Point, North Carolina* (1937), courtesy of the National Archives and Records Administration [NWDNS-69-RP-230]. Young man working in factory. Southern Agrarian writers expressed mixed feelings about industrial development and extolled the region's rural, agricultural traditions.

[7611] Ralph Clynne, *Gloucester, Lower Woodville Rd., Natchez Vic., Adams County, MS* (1934), courtesy of the Library of Congress, Prints and Photographs Division [HABS, MISS, 1-NATCH. V, 1-1]. This photograph depicts the same plantation house shown in [4735] and [7654]. The house's dilapidated condition echoes the degradation of the myths of the South.

fit with this description of people "waiting" in the grass? Break your students into groups. Ask one group to describe the characters in the poem—who are they and what are they doing? Have the other group describe the poem's settings in their own words—what are the different settings, and how do they affect the meaning of the poem? Finally, have the groups work together to match the characters with the settings to arrive at a better idea of the meaning of the poem. Try to guide your students toward the poem's metaphysical concerns, its meditation on the inevitability of decay, and its fear that true human communication may not be possible. What does the allusion to an underwater setting suggest? What happens to organic matter under water? What is the significance of the "debate" that is "voiceless" here?

■ In poems such as "Audubon," Warren turned his lifelong interest in history into an exploration of the human condition. After they've read "Audubon," ask your students to re-create the poem in prose, paying attention to the dual nature of the poem. What history does the poem recount? What is the story of human nature it seems to be telling? Have your students write a short (one-page) prose story that attempts to capture these histories.

QUESTIONS

Comprehension: Much of Warren's poetry is grounded in particular places and relies for its effect on specific descriptions of landscape. Compare the setting of "Bearded Oaks" to that of "Mortal Limit." What settings and what kind of "mood" does each evoke? If we consider that both poems are concerned with the journey of life, how do their different settings help Warren create different variations on this similar theme?

Context: In "American Portrait: Old Style," the speaker tells us that his childhood friend, K, who was known as a good baseball pitcher in his youth, has grown old and thin. Review lines 105–09, in which K considers the passage of time. Compare K's actions to the position taken by the Southern Agrarians with regard to "modern progress" in the South. What might "the big brown insulator" symbolize? Also consider the speaker's conclusions in the final stanza of "American Portrait." How do the speaker's feelings about time and "progress" compare with K's, above? What might Warren's poem be saying about southern history and the passage of time more generally?

Exploration: In the late 1920s and 1930s, Robert Penn Warren expressed support for racial segregation, but he later changed his mind. Like Warren, other prominent writers of the early twentieth century expressed controversial views that later became very unpopular. For example, T. S. Eliot and Ezra Pound (Unit 10) were attracted to fascism and some of their writing has been called anti-Semitic. Yet, despite these unpopular views, writers like Warren, Eliot, and Pound are considered among America's best authors. As readers and critics, how should an author's political and social views affect our reception of his or her works?

Richard Wright (1908–1960)

Richard Wright grew up during some of the darkest days of racial seg-regation in the American South, and the horrors that he experienced and witnessed during that time became the material on which he built his reputation as one of the most important voices in American litera-ture in the first half of the twentieth century. The son of black share-croppers Nathan and Ella Wright, Richard was born in rural Mississippi. Wright's father abandoned his family when Richard was only five, and after that Wright moved around the South every few years before finally settling in Jackson, Mississippi, at the age of eleven. Forced by poverty to drop out of school, Wright went to work, first as a helper in an optical company and later as a porter in a cloth-ing store and a "hall-boy" in a hotel. As he details in "The Ethics of Living Jim Crow," each job taught Wright new lessons about the tenu-ousness of life for an African American in the segregated South.

Although his first story was published in an African American newspaper in Mississippi when Wright was in the eighth grade, Wright claimed to have awakened as a reader and writer during the mid-1920s, when he read H. L. Mencken's withering attacks on the South's social, racial, and intellectual failings. Yet it was to be more than ten years before Wright was able to find the voice that would gain him international fame, first with *Uncle Tom's Children* (a collection of short stories published in 1938), followed by *Native Son* in 1940, and finally the autobiographical *Black Boy* in 1945.

With *Native Son*, Wright said he was determined to create a book (and character) that was difficult to face. This determination sprang from the positive reception of *Uncle Tom's Children*, which did not have the effect on its readers for which Wright had hoped. "When the reviews of that book began to appear, I realized that I had made an awfully naïve mistake. I found that I had written a book which even bankers' daughters could read and weep over and feel good about. I swore to myself that if I ever wrote another book, no one would weep over it; that it would be so hard and deep that they would have to face it without the consolation of tears. It was this that made me get to work in dead earnest." Wright's effort paid off; he is now known for his unflinching, realistic, and purposely anti-romantic portraits of the racial prejudice, oppression, and hypocrisy he experienced and wit-nessed during much of his life.

[4013] Carl Van Vechten, *Portrait of Richard Wright* (1939), courtesy of the Library of Congress [LC-USZ62-42502 DLC].

TEACHING TIP

■ Richard Wright is probably best known for his aggressive por-trayal of African American characters like Dave, who are unhappy and unsatisfied with their lives but seemingly unable to do much to improve their situation. If you've read *Native Son*, it might be worth-while talking to your students about Bigger Thomas and the contro-versy surrounding that novel. This might be a good way to introduce them to "The Man Who Was Almost a Man," but it could also be part of a follow-up class in which you discuss Dave's possible destination and future. Where is he going on that train? What will he find there?

Does Wright suggest that it's inevitable that Dave will become Bigger Thomas, or does the story end more ambiguously than that? Use these questions to get your students thinking about the larger implications of the story; then ask them to consider contemporary parallels for Dave. Where might Dave be found today? Instead of plowing a field, what might Dave's job be? Have your students write for ten minutes in response to these questions; then ask them to share their responses with the class.

QUESTIONS

Comprehension: Dave thinks owning a gun will show those around him that he's a "man." What does being a man seem to mean to Dave? What are a few of the specific things Dave thinks a gun will change about his life?

Comprehension: Discuss the possible reasons Wright chose to have Dave kill the mule, Jenny. Why does Dave talk to Jenny like she can understand him? Why does he refer to her by name? Is Jenny more than a mule to Dave (at least for purposes of this story)? What kinds of things might a mule symbolize? How might such symbolism relate to Dave's situation in life or to the history of African Americans in the United States more generally?

Context: "The Man Who Was Almost a Man" is set in the midst of the Great Depression, a time of economic hardship for the vast majority of Americans. During this time (in what later came to be called the Great Migration), hundreds of thousands of southerners headed north in search of better lives, despite the fact that economic conditions were often no better there. At the end of Wright's story, Dave has hopped aboard the Illinois Central and is heading "away, away to somewhere, somewhere where he could be a man. . . ." The story does not tell us whether Dave is heading north or south. Do you think that "somewhere" exists? If so, what kind of future does this story suggest Dave is going to have?

Context: Like Zora Neale Hurston, Richard Wright saw himself as an outsider in the literary world, largely writing against the grain of what his critics thought he should be doing. But while Hurston wrote about African Americans who sometimes seem untouched, or at least "undiminished," by racism, poverty, and segregation, Wright created characters who are complete opposites of hers. For example, in "The Man Who Was Almost a Man," Dave's life seems greatly determined by his poverty and by his social position relative to the people around him—both black and white. If both writers hoped to improve the lives of African Americans through their work, what are some of the advantages and disadvantages of their different approaches to achieving this goal?

Context: In its coverage of the Scopes evolution trial in Dayton, Tennessee, in 1925, the national press, led by H. L. Mencken, ridiculed the South as backward, bigoted, and intellectually empty. But while Mencken's attacks on the South inspired Wright to begin writing about his own experiences of southern racial oppression, the Southern Agrarians responded very differently to Mencken's characterization of the South. Compare Wright's response to that of the Southern Agrarians. How do you account for the difference? What does this difference suggest about the Southern Agrarians? What does it suggest about Wright?

Exploration: In his 1949 essay "Everybody's Protest Novel," James Baldwin (Unit 14) attacked the way African Americans were portrayed in works ranging from *Uncle Tom's Cabin* by Harriet Beecher Stowe (Unit 7) to *Native Son* by Richard Wright. According to Baldwin, although the goal of these "protest novels" might have been to call attention to African American suffering as a way of improving the lives of blacks in America, the characters in these novels merely perpetuated stereotypes because they were flat, one-dimensional, and seemed trapped by their social conditions. After reading Stowe, Wright, and Baldwin, think about how the portrayal of African Americans changed in the century between Stowe and Baldwin. Do you agree or disagree with Baldwin's attack on his predecessors?

Eudora Welty (1909–2001)

Eudora Alice Welty was born in Jackson, Mississippi, where she lived nearly all of her life. A first-generation Mississippian, Welty grew up in comfortable circumstances and developed an early love of reading. After graduating from the local high school at age sixteen, Welty spent two years at Mississippi State College for Women before transferring to the University of Wisconsin, where she earned a B.A. in English in 1929. She declared her intention of becoming a writer, but decided to go into advertising after her father expressed concern that she would be unable to support herself and that writing was perhaps a waste of time. "He was not a lover of fiction," Welty once recalled, "because fiction is not true, and for that flaw it was forever inferior to fact." But Welty continued to write, and her job interviewing poor rural southerners and writing stories as a publicity agent for the Works Progress Administration (WPA) helped her develop her ability to capture dialogue and bring to life the variety of situations that would comprise her later fiction. In addition to her writing, the photographs Welty took to accompany her WPA stories have become an important part of her legacy as a southern storyteller. By 1936 Welty had begun publishing stories in several small but influential southern journals, and she quickly attracted the notice of established writers such as Robert Penn Warren and Katherine Anne Porter. Porter was especially encouraging; she eventually wrote the preface to Welty's first collection of stories, *A Curtain of Green*, published in 1941.

Welty's writing is rooted in the places she knew best—small southern towns peopled with seemingly ordinary characters who love to talk and whose conversation reveals their complex and often wryly amusing interior lives. Many of her best-known and most frequently anthologized stories—such as "Why I Live at the P.O." or "Petrified Man"—

[5169] Ben Shahn, *Two Women Walking along Street, Natchez, Mississippi* (1935), courtesy of the Library of Congress [LC-USF33-006093-M4 DLC].

[4672] Conrad A. Albrizio, *The New Deal* (1934), courtesy of National Archives and Records Administration (NARA), Franklin D. Roosevelt Library (NLR). A fresco of New York's Leonardo Da Vinci Art School. Showing working people, the mural was dedicated to President Roosevelt and commissioned by the WPA. Work was an important theme in depression-era art.

[5169] Ben Shahn, *Two Women Walking along Street, Natchez, Mississippi* (1935), courtesy of the Library of Congress [LC-USF33-006093-M4 DLC]. Eudora Welty was born into a family of means in Mississippi in 1909 and resided there for most of her life. Welty rooted much of her work in the daily life of small southern towns.

[5524] Dorothea Lange, *White Sharecropper Family, Formerly Mill Workers in the Gastonia Textile Mills. When the Mills Closed Down Seven Years Ago, They Came to This Farm Near Hartwell, Georgia* (1937), courtesy of the Library of Congress [LC-USF34-018147-CDLC]. The less glamorous side of rural southern life; a white share-cropping family seated on the porch of their cabin. This family is an example of the poorer, "everyday people" that writers such as William Faulkner and Eudora Welty focused on in their work.

feature characters who seem to thrive on the tension and unpredictability that arises from teasing, taunting, or bickering with each other, yet who generally seem to be friends despite their differences. By dramatizing the ordinary and everyday conversations of her characters, Welty often demonstrates that differences can bring people together, just as much as they can tear them apart.

Welty won numerous literary awards in her lifetime, including three O'Henry prizes, a Pulitzer, the American Book Award, the Modern Language Association Commonwealth Award, and the National Medal of Arts. Her story "Why I Live at the P.O." also inspired the developer of a popular email program to name his software after her. At the time of her death, Welty was considered by many to be the South's greatest living writer.

T E A C H I N G   T I P S

■ "Petrified Man" is narrated by an omniscient, third-person voice—a voice outside the story which refers to the characters as "he," "she," etc. How does this outside narrator depict Leota and Mrs. Fletcher? Since the story is primarily dialogue, it should be relatively easy for your students to pick out the narrator's descriptions of the characters. Have them list those descriptions, focusing on the adjectives applied to each character. Using these lists, ask your students to describe how the narrator seems to view these characters. How does this narrative voice affect our overall impression of the story?

■ In *The Eye of the Story*, a collection of her essays and reviews, Welty wrote that "a fiction writer's responsibility covers not only what he presents as the facts of a given story but what he chooses to stir up as their implications; in the end, these implications, too, become facts, in the larger, fictional sense. But it is not all right, not in good faith, for things *not* to mean what they say." Discuss Welty's comments with your students in the context of "Petrified Man." Using the chalkboard or an overhead projector, work with the class to produce two lists. One list should include the "facts" of the story; the other should include the "lies" of the story. What role do the "lies" serve for Leota? Does Mrs. Fletcher really believe them?

Q U E S T I O N S

Comprehension: What kind of relationship do Leota and Mrs. Fletcher seem to have? Describe these two characters. What kind of people are Leota and Mrs. Fletcher? Where does each of them live? How does each woman spend her day? How do they think of themselves? How do they seem to perceive each other? What specific clues does the text give us to help answer these questions?

Context: Like many other southern authors, Welty was greatly influenced by southern oral traditions. In "Losing Battles," for example, Welty attempted to write an entire narrative comprised solely of her characters' dialogue with one another. Think about the kinds of stories Leota tells, and compare those with, for example, the stories in

Zora Neale Hurston's *Eatonville Anthology*. What do the stories have in common? How do they differ? What does such a comparison suggest about southern oral traditions?

Exploration: Like many of the writers in Unit 8, (as well as many of the writers included under the category of the Southern Renaissance), Welty is often considered a **regional** writer because she writes almost exclusively about a particular geographic area, and that location seems to greatly determine her plots and characters. While this might be a useful way for literary scholars to group authors, it also risks reducing authors to a label that does not adequately describe their work. Consider the types of writing you've read that are grouped under the category of "regionalism." What are the pros and cons of such a label? What does such a label assume about literature? How might it be used by scholars to construct or manipulate the American literary canon? How does the South of Twain, Chopin, and Chesnutt differ from that of Welty and the Southern Agrarians?

Tennessee Williams (1911–1983)

"A morbid shyness once prevented me from having much direct communication with people," Tennessee Williams wrote, "and possibly that is why I began to write them plays and stories." Considered by many to be America's greatest playwright, Thomas Lanier Williams III was born in Columbus, Mississippi. Though some critics see Williams's work as overly obsessed with "perversion"—murder, rape, incest, and nymphomania—Williams's characters inhabit a world as emotionally unstable as their author's. Williams's mother, Edwina, was a southern belle who, despite enduring a lifetime of emotional and physical abuse from her husband, was a strong anchor for Williams and protected him from his father in his youth. Williams's father, CC, was a traveling salesman and an alcoholic with whom Williams was never close.

Williams was forever marked by the alienation and psychological pain of his childhood. After he flunked ROTC, his father forced him to drop out of the University of Missouri and got him a job in his shoe company's warehouse. Williams wrote furiously by night, but after three years the pressure of the factory work resulted in his first nervous breakdown, in 1935. Not long afterward, his beloved but reclusive sister, Rose, suffered a mental breakdown so devastating that their mother signed the papers to give her a prefrontal lobotomy. Williams changed his name to "Tennessee" while living in New Orleans, where he continued to write. During this period he also continued to explore his sexual attraction to men, which he'd discovered while finishing his undergraduate degree at the University of Iowa. Recognizing his homosexuality deepened a belief Williams had formed while watching his sister's slow decline—that the pressure to conform to the American mainstream could be a powerful and dangerous force. After producing several plays in local theaters, Williams enjoyed his first big success with *The Glass Menagerie* (1945) and followed it up with such power-

[7282] Dorothea Lange, *Antebellum Plantation House in Greene County, Georgia* (1937), courtesy of the Library of Congress [LC-USF34-017941-C DLC].

ful plays as the Pulitzer Prize–winning *A Streetcar Named Desire* and *Cat on a Hot Tin Roof* (1955). Other plays include *The Rose Tattoo* (1950), *Camino Real* (1953), and *The Night of the Iguana* (1961).

Although he continued writing throughout his life, by the early 1960s Williams had already produced his greatest work. The death of his longtime companion, Frank Merlo, in 1963, as well as Williams's continued abuse of alcohol and sleeping pills, forced Williams into a decline from which he never fully recovered. Williams wrote several more plays in the 1970s, including *Out Cry* (1971) and *Small Craft Warnings* (1972). He died after choking on the cap of a medicine bottle in a New York hotel room.

TEACHING TIPS

■ Have your students choose parts and stage an impromptu performance of the first scene in *A Streetcar Named Desire* to give them some idea of the difficulties involved with dramatic readings and to show them how performance can change their impression of a play. This will work best if your students have time to prepare, but it can also be done "cold." Students generally enjoy dramatic readings, and scene 1 sets out the major issues of the play, introduces all the main characters, and is a great way to begin a more general discussion of *Streetcar*.

■ Blanche and Stanley can be problematic characters, and student responses to *A Streetcar Named Desire* can sometimes be polarized by their reaction to either Stanley or Blanche. One way to deal with this is to ask students to focus on the characters independently. After you've polled them for initial reactions, divide your students into several groups. Ask half of the groups to describe Stanley and assess his pros and cons as a character; meanwhile, ask the other half of the groups to do the same with Blanche. You might provide your groups with some of the more common assessments of each character: Is Stanley a caged animal whose sexuality is so "natural" that his violence is somehow excusable or understandable? Or does he represent a patriarchal authority and social order that are threatened by the changing social mores of the 1950s? Is Blanche a representative of the Old South, of tradition and idealism, and as such a dying breed? Or is her struggle to come to terms with a reality that does not match her desires a more universal struggle that we all must face? Is the conflict between Stanley and Blanche one between the working class and a dying southern aristocracy? These are not, of course, the only ways to interpret Stanley and Blanche, nor are they mutually exclusive; however, they should provide a good basis for discussion and provoke your students to move beyond their "gut" reactions to these characters.

QUESTIONS

Comprehension: Who seems to be the protagonist in *A Streetcar Named Desire*? With whom do you sympathize?

Context: In light of Williams's homosexuality, it might be tempting to see the violence in Stanley Kowalski's interactions with Stella and Blanche as a critique of the strict heterosexual norms Williams had seen and experienced in his lifetime. However, the 1950s were a period of social repression in more ways than one, and *A Streetcar Named Desire* is a play that addresses multiple levels of 1950s culture. Besides sexuality, what other social norms might the play be attempting to address?

Context: Nearly thirty years before the debut of *A Streetcar Named Desire*, the American South was outraged by national press coverage of the Scopes evolution trial, which depicted the South as backward, hidebound, and repressed. The Southern Agrarian movement developed partially as a response to this experience and was an attempt by the writers involved to defend southern values and ways of life. How do you think the Southern Agrarians would have responded to *A Streetcar Named Desire*? How had the United States changed in the thirty years between the Scopes trial and the debut of Williams's play? Consider both the critical and the popular responses to the play.

Exploration: In describing the main character of his most successful play, *Death of a Salesman*, Arthur Miller said that in Willy Loman, "the past was as alive as what was happening at the moment, sometimes even crashing in to completely overwhelm his mind" (see Unit 14). Miller's description of Willy Loman could also describe Blanche DuBois in *A Streetcar Named Desire*, as she struggles to move beyond her past and the loss of Belle Reve. Why do you think two of the most important American plays of the twentieth century would be so concerned about the relation of the past to the present or the future? Consider this question in the larger context of the other southern writers in this unit: Which authors and works also seem centrally concerned with the way the past relates to the present, and why is this preoccupation so common to southern writers?

Flannery O'Connor (1925–1965)

Mary Flannery O'Connor was born in Savannah, Georgia, the daughter of devout Catholic parents of good social standing. She was educated at parochial schools in Savannah until 1938, when her father was diagnosed with lupus, a degenerative blood disease of which he died two years later. During her father's last years, the O'Connor family moved to Milledgeville, Georgia, where O'Connor would spend most of the rest of her life living with her mother. After finishing high school, O'Connor earned a degree in social science from a local college. In 1945, on the recommendation of one of her professors, she earned a fellowship to attend the Writer's Workshop of the State University of Iowa (now the University of Iowa), where she met John Crowe Ransom. During the next two years, O'Connor honed her skills as one of America's most distinguished writers of short stories. Her

first publication came with *Geranium* in 1946, followed by her first novel, *Wise Blood*, in 1952. *The Habit of Being* (1979) is a collection of O'Connor's letters.

Although she went on to publish a second novel, *The Violent Bear It Away* (1960), O'Connor is best known for her short stories, which are marked by their dark humor, masterful use of dialogue, and sometimes aggressive anti-sentimentalism. O'Connor's rural southern characters have been described as "repugnant, contemptible, and grotesque." But while deluded and deceitful characters like Tom T. Shiftlet in "The Life You Save May Be Your Own" or Hulga and Joy Hopewell in "Good Country People" are not necessarily likable, O'Connor deftly captures them in moments where they seem on the verge of realizing their deepest flaws. By showing the pain her characters feel as a result of their own shortcomings, O'Connor almost seems to suggest they deserve our pity as much as our scorn; yet she tends to leave them—and us—hanging just a moment before we can be sure.

O'Connor was diagnosed with lupus—the same disease that had killed her father—in December 1950. She continued to write for the next fourteen years and worked feverishly in the final weeks of her life to finish her second short-story collection, *Everything That Rises Must Converge*, before her death at the age of thirty-nine.

TEACHING TIPS

■ In *Mystery and Manners* O'Connor describes "Good Country People" as a story in which "a lady Ph.D. has her wooden leg stolen by a Bible salesman whom she has tried to seduce." Admitting that, "paraphrased this way, the situation is simply a low joke," O'Connor goes on to discuss the significance of the wooden leg as, among other things, a symbol of Hulga's wooden soul and emotional disability. "As the story goes on," O'Connor continues, "the wooden leg continues to accumulate meaning. The reader learns how the girl feels about it; and finally, by the time the Bible salesman comes along, the leg has accumulated so much meaning that it is, as the saying goes, loaded. And when the Bible salesman steals it, the reader realizes that he has taken away part of the girl's personality and has revealed her deeper affliction to her for the first time." Begin your discussion of the story by asking your students to think about O'Connor's simple paraphrase; then use that discussion to open up the multiple layers of meaning within the story.

■ The title of "The Life You Save May Be Your Own" comes from a warning to drivers that they should drive carefully. "Good Country People" begins with a description of Mrs. Freeman that characterizes her as very much like a car with three gears—neutral, forward, and reverse. Ask your students to think about O'Connor's apparent preoccupation with automobiles and travel. How might such references relate to the development of the federal highway system in the 1950s? What do these stories seem to be saying about an increasingly mobile population?

Comprehension: What is the significance of the names of O'Connor's characters such as Tom T. Shiftlet, Mrs. Hopewell, or Mrs. Freeman? Why might O'Connor name her characters in this way?

Comprehension: What is the role of the Freemans in "Good Country People"? Why does Mrs. Hopewell "keep" them? What does that mean?

Context: In the opening scene of "The Life You Save May Be Your Own," Tom T. Shiftlet says, "Lady, people don't care how they lie. Maybe the best I can tell you is, I'm a man; but listen lady . . . what is a man?" Why does Shiftlet ask such a question? Shiftlet also talks about the doctor who cuts out human hearts, denies he has any concern for money, and is unmistakably preoccupied with the car in the garage. What might these references symbolize? How do these aspects of Shiftlet's character relate to the changing South in the 1930s?

Exploration: In an essay entitled "Writing Short Stories" (from the collection *Mystery and Manners*), O'Connor wrote that "the great advantage of being a southern writer is that we don't have to go anywhere to look for manners; bad or good, we've got them in abundance. We in the South live in a society that is rich in contradiction, rich in irony, rich in contrast, and particularly rich in its speech." How does O'Connor make use of the richness of the South as she identifies it here? Do other southern writers seem to share O'Connor's assessment of the South, or do they portray it as something different?

Suggested Author Pairings

ZORA NEALE HURSTON, RICHARD WRIGHT, AND FLANNERY O'CONNOR

In the first half of the twentieth century, the increased mobility enabled by the spread of automobiles and good roads led to frequent collisions between the slow, trusting, tradition-bound way of life found in rural communities and the faster, more ruthless, and often more deceitful behavior found in the wider world. Such collisions form the basis of stories by Hurston, Wright, and O'Connor. In "The Gilded Six-Bits," the idyllic and childlike simplicity of Joe and Missie May's life together is nearly destroyed by the appearance of "Mister Otis D. Slemmons, of spots and places—Memphis, Chicago, Jacksonville, Philadelphia and so on." Something similar happens in O'Connor's "The Life You Save May Be Your Own," although O'Connor is much less clear about the ultimate consequences of Tom T. Shiftlet's arrival and eventual departure from the Carter's house. Did the older Lucynell Carter secretly want to be rid of her disabled daughter? (She was, after all, "ravenous for a son-in-law.") The ultimate effects of the wider world are nearly as ambiguous in Wright's "The Man Who Was Almost a Man." However, the fact that Dave first tries to get a gun through the Sears catalog marks the gun itself as something of an outsider, and it definitely destroys the life Dave has previously lived. As Dave hops the train "away to somewhere," we're left to wonder whether the end of his encounter with the wider world will be as unsuccessful as its beginning.

WILLIAM FAULKNER, FLANNERY O'CONNOR, AND TENNESSEE WILLIAMS

A great deal of writing by southern authors could be described as "gothic" in that many attempted in their writing to "unsettle" what they saw as prevailing trends in their society. However, these three writers each use gothic elements to special effect. Faulkner is generally considered a master of the southern gothic form and is often compared to Nathaniel Hawthorne for his dark and mysterious settings and for the way his writing explores the sin and guilt in the hearts of his characters and their world. While O'Connor's stories seem on the surface much less dark than Faulkner's, they are nearly always peopled with bizarre and even grotesque characters whose physical disabilities often symbolize their inner failings. With characters like Blanche DuBois and Stanley Kowalski, Williams's use of the gothic form falls somewhere between Faulkner and O'Connor, though toward the more deeply sinister end of the spectrum. But despite the different methods each author uses to explore the darker and more twisted sides of human nature and experience, each is concerned with how past mistakes develop into present imperfections and shape the possibilities for the future.

JOHN CROWE RANSOM, TENNESSEE WILLIAMS, AND KATHERINE ANNE PORTER

The struggle between myth and reality plays a prominent role in the work of these writers. In his contribution to the Southern Agrarian manifesto *I'll Take My Stand*, Ransom argued that myths, such as the romantic vision of the Old South, are necessary to hold a society together. Later, he argued for poetry as occupying the same role; by providing an alternative source of knowledge, poetry could challenge dominant beliefs and help society hold on to what it valued most. In *A Streetcar Named Desire*, Blanche struggles to accept that the reality of her life does not match any of the myths she was taught to believe about how life should be. And in Porter's "Flowering Judas," Laura seems to occupy a mythical space somewhere between revolutionary and southern belle, even as she must learn to accept the fact that her ideal of the revolutionary ("a revolutionist should be lean, animated by heroic faith, a vessel of abstract virtues") does not match the reality she finds in Braggioni. Many southern writers in this period address similar questions about the disillusionment produced by the conflict between their ideals and the reality in which they find themselves.

CORE CONTEXTS

Taking a Stand: The Southern Agrarians Respond to a Changing World

Many of the most prominent American writers of the early twentieth century responded to the social and cultural upheavals of the period by rebelling against them; however, that rebellion often took vastly different, even contradictory, forms. For example, one of the most influential literary rebellions of the period was that of the group of literary modernists who became known as the "Lost Generation," partially due to the fact that many of them were permanent or temporary expatriates. These writers left the United States because they found it lacking in the traditions and cultural richness they felt their creative lives required. Writing mostly from London and Paris in the 1910s and 1920s, modernists like Gertrude Stein, H. D., Ezra Pound, and T. S. Eliot experimented with new literary forms as they expressed despair and often cynicism about the course American culture seemed to be taking. As critic Lynn Dumenil has noted, "A theme that historians have called the **revolt against the village** pervaded the literature of the twenties. Both the young members of the Lost Generation and an older cadre of writers inveighed against the crudeness, materialism, and repression of their own society."

But while the Lost Generation often dominates literary histories of the era, theirs was not the only literary rebellion against changes in the "modern" world. At about the same time, a small group of critics and poets gathered in the South to challenge both the cynicism of the literary modernists and the more general "revolt against the village" in American culture. Because they praised the agrarian way of life in the South, this group became known as the Southern Agrarians.

Centered around Vanderbilt University in Nashville, Tennessee, these poets and critics—including John Crowe Ransom, Allen Tate, and Robert Penn Warren—first gained a degree of prominence for *The Fugitive*, the magazine they published from 1922 to 1925 as an outlet for their writing. According to critic J. A. Bryant, the group's goal as "the Fugitive poets" was simply to "demonstrate that a group of southerners could produce important work in the medium, devoid of sentimentality and carefully crafted, with special attention to the logical coherence of substance and trope."

The Fugitives' resistance to a great many prevailing social trends was catalyzed by the Scopes evolution trial, which took place in 1925 in Dayton, Tennessee. The trial (dramatized in the play *Inherit the Wind* by Jerome Lawrence and Robert E. Lee) pitted John Thomas Scopes, a young science teacher from Dayton who had dared to teach Darwin's theories of evolution in his science class, against the State of

[5224] Dorothea Lange, *White Sharecropper Family, Hartwell, Georgia* (1937), courtesy of the Library of Congress [LC-USF34-018147-C DLC].

[5158] Ben Shahn, *Men Loafing in Crossville, Tennessee* (1937), courtesy of the Library of Congress [LC-USF33-006224-M4 DLC].

Tennessee, which (with the support of the Ku Klux Klan) had recently passed a law forbidding the teaching of "any theory that denies the story of the Divine Creation of man as taught in the Bible." Much more than a battle over classroom policy, for many southerners the Scopes trial came to symbolize the clash between religious fundamentalism and modernism, between tradition and change, and between rural and urban ways of life. Although Scopes lost the case, many in the South—especially the writers who were to become the Southern Agrarians—were incensed at the media coverage of the trial, which portrayed the South as an ignorant backwater populated by "yokels" and "bigots."

In 1930, partially as a response to the Scopes trial, but also as an expression of their longstanding resentment against the North, the Southern Agrarians produced a manifesto called *I'll Take My Stand: The South and the Agrarian Tradition* by "Twelve Southerners." This collection of essays—whose title played on the defiance of the southern anthem "Dixie"—promoted traditional southern values and an agrarian way of life as an alternative to the course of the modern, industrial life they saw developing in the North. With essays by Ransom, Tate, and Warren, as well as contributions from Donald Davidson, John Gould Fletcher, Henry Blue Kline, Lyle Lanier, Andrew Lytle, H. C. Nixon, Frank Owsley, John Donald Wade, and Stark Young, the manifesto questioned the very definition of "progress" by asking: Progress toward what? According to the volume's introductory "Statement of Principles" (written by Ransom), those who advocated building a "New South" on the northern model "must come back to the support of the southern tradition." Industrial society, they claimed, was soulless and alienating, and besides, it caused more problems than it solved.

Citing "overproduction, unemployment, and a growing inequality in the distribution of wealth" as just a few of the "evils that follow in the wake of machines," the Agrarians condemned not only the means by which a new consumer culture was being built, but also consumption itself. "We have been deceived" by consumption, they wrote. "We have more time in which to consume, and many more products to be consumed. But the tempo of our labors communicates itself to our satisfactions, and these also have become brutal and hurried." What's more, they claimed, industrial society obscures "the God of nature" and makes it impossible for either religion or art to flourish. In short, the Agrarians expressed what critic Lynn Dumenil calls a dominant theme of the period—namely, despair at "the erosion of community and personal autonomy in the face of an increasingly nationalized and organized society."

"Opposed to the industrial society is the agrarian," they wrote, "which does not stand in particular need of definition." One of the reasons for the Agrarians' evasiveness about precisely what should replace the industrial model of progress was that they were a disparate

[3347] Dorothea Lange, *Power Farming Displaces Tenants. Childress County, Texas Panhandle* (1938), courtesy of the Library of Congress [LC-USF34-T01-018281-C DLC].

group who could not always agree on exactly what "the South" was or should be. Critics have noted that one of the things hidden in the Agrarians' lack of a specific plan for social reorganization is the underlying racism of the bulk of the essays in *I'll Take My Stand*. All twelve of the book's authors were white men, and their implicit advocacy of white supremacy is one of the reasons their attempt to establish a new cultural and literary movement has often been dismissed as simply a romantic and nostalgic attempt to return to a corrupt past. Critics remain divided about the value of the Agrarians' advocacy of an alternative in which land and other resources would be more equally distributed among the "plain (white) folk" around whom much of southern mythology revolved. Whatever their hopes might have been for leading the South in a new direction, the Agrarians' manifesto was never a big seller. Nevertheless, their work represents an important voice in the development of the South and southern literature.

QUESTIONS

Comprehension: What did the Agrarians want? What did they value?

Comprehension: What did the Agrarians dislike about "modern" life?

Comprehension: What was at stake in the Scopes evolution trial and how did the trial affect the South?

Context: How did the period of Reconstruction following the Civil War shape southern attitudes toward the North and the notion of "progress"?

Context: What did advocates for the "New South" hope to achieve? How do you see these aspirations reflected in the poetry of John Crowe Ransom and Robert Penn Warren?

Context: Why do you think some southerners felt threatened by the development of consumer culture? How does the *Birth of a Nation* advertisement from the archive [5703] relate to the Agrarians' fears about a consumer society?

Exploration: Consider *As I Lay Dying*. How does Faulkner relate to the Agrarians? Does his writing express nostalgia for the past or suggest that the South should move in a different direction?

Exploration: Some critics believe that if the white supremacist argument is removed from the Southern Agrarian agenda, what remains does not seem so different from other calls for reorganizing society in more just ways. For example, how does the Agrarians' agenda compare with the activities of U.S. labor movements during this period?

Exploration: Both the Agrarians and the writers of the "Lost Generation" (many of whom are covered in Unit 11) protested what they saw as the prevailing trends in American life. How were their protests similar? How did they differ? How do their concerns relate to modernism more generally?

Separate Is Not Equal: Enforcing the Codes of the Jim Crow South

Although the Civil War *officially* settled the status of African Americans as free individuals, many Americans—especially in the South—remained unconvinced even decades later. In the immediate chaos following the war, southern whites gradually assumed the responsibility of governing the former confederate states, taking as their greatest immediate concern the problem of controlling the four million former slaves. To this end, southern states quickly began enacting Black Codes which (like the antebellum Slave Codes that had preceded them) attempted to control the lives of African Americans in virtually every aspect. These repressive laws, as well as the southern states' refusal to ratify the Fourteenth Amendment (which provided equal protection to African Americans under the law), helped convince Congress that it needed to intervene in the process of rebuilding the South. However, the short period of Radical Reconstruction that followed (during which federal mandates enabled African Americans to vote and be elected as legislators and governors in the former confederate states) only further infuriated white southerners, making them more determined than ever to reestablish white supremacy in what they saw as their territory. Secret societies, such as the Knights of the White Camelia and the Knights of the Ku Klux Klan, flourished in the decade following the war. For members of these groups, depriving African Americans of political equality was a holy crusade, and they were willing to use any amount of force and intimidation (including whippings, beatings, arson, and murder) to ensure victory for their cause.

By 1876, the experiments of Reconstruction had largely ended and the southern states had returned to white control. Southern leaders moved quickly to establish elaborate election codes—usually involving poll taxes and literacy tests—to disenfranchise African Americans. By removing African Americans from the political sphere, southern whites were free to do as they pleased, and they vowed to keep the races completely separate. To that end, Tennessee passed the first law against intermarriage of the races in 1870, and it adopted the first "Jim Crow" law five years later. The rest of the South quickly followed suit.

Little more than updates to the post–Civil War Black Codes, "Jim Crow" laws got their name from one of the stock characters in the minstrel shows that were a mainstay of popular entertainment throughout the nineteenth century. Such shows popularized and reinforced the pervasive stereotypes of blacks as lazy, stupid, somehow less human, and inferior to whites. Thus, as the name suggests, Jim Crow was much more than a rigorous code of anti-black laws; it was also a way of life designed to reinforce the idea that whites were superior to blacks in all important ways. While the laws segregated schools, transportation, public buildings and almost every conceivable aspect of society, Jim Crow etiquette strictly regulated every possible interaction between blacks and whites, demanding, for example, that white

[2256] Russell Lee, *Negro Drinking at "Colored" Water Cooler in Streetcar Terminal, Oklahoma City, Oklahoma* (1939), courtesy of the Library of Congress [LC-USZ62-80126].

[3355] Jack Delano, *At the Bus Station in Durham, North Carolina* (1940), courtesy of the Library of Congress, Prints & Photographs Division, FSA/OWI Collection [LC-USF33-020522-MZ].

motorists be given the right-of-way at all intersections and that a black man should avoid even looking at a white woman if at all possible. In 1896, in the case of *Plessy v. Ferguson*, the Supreme Court ruled that the "separate but equal" ideology was entirely legal; it would be more than fifty years before that ideology was legally overturned.

African Americans who failed to abide by the rules of Jim Crow were dealt with severely. As Richard Wright recounts in "The Ethics of Living Jim Crow," when he dared throw rocks at a group of white boys who were taunting him, his mother beat him and "finished by telling me that I ought to be thankful to God as long as I lived that they didn't kill me." Wright's mother had good reason to give her son such a stern warning; if Jim Crow laws or etiquette were threatened or broken, violence was almost sure to follow. Vigilante white supremacist groups like the KKK needed very little encouragement to attack, and outbreaks of mob violence became a regular occurrence throughout the South.

The 3,446 lynchings of black men and women recorded between 1882 and 1969 are a stark measure of the degree to which vigilantism shaped race relations in the decades following Reconstruction. But even when the legal system was able to stop the summary justice of impassioned mobs, white supremacy often made it impossible for African Americans who were accused of crimes to get a fair trial. Such was the case with the so-called "Scottsboro Boys"—nine African American youths accused in 1931 of raping two white women one night after all of them had hopped aboard an Alabama train. Despite the lack of any physical evidence that the women had actually been harmed, eight of the nine defendants received death sentences (a mistrial was declared in the case of twelve-year-old defendant Roy Wright because the jury was split on whether to give him death or life in prison). Although the verdicts were affirmed by the Alabama Supreme Court, they were overturned by the United States Supreme Court, which said the defendants had not received competent counsel. In the multiple retrials that followed, Alabama courts continued to find the defendants guilty, despite growing evidence that the crimes had never, in fact, taken place. By 1936, the trials of the Scottsboro Boys had attracted so much attention that to some observers the case had become *The White People of Alabama v. The Rest of the World*. Although all of the defendants were eventually released, paroled, or had escaped from prison in Alabama, all had spent years in jail for a crime that most likely never happened. For many Americans, the case became a reminder of the deep prejudice that divided the South far into the twentieth century.

Thanks in part to prominent cases like those of the Scottsboro Boys, the ideology of Jim Crow was finally declared illegal by the land-

[9071] Anonymous, *Ku Klux Klan Parade, Washington, D.C., on Pennsylvania Avenue, N.W.* (1926), courtesy of the Library of Congress, Prints and Photographs Division [LC-USZ62-59666].

[2256] Russell Lee, *Negro Drinking at "Colored" Water Cooler in Streetcar Terminal, Oklahoma City, Oklahoma* (1939), courtesy of the Library of Congress [LC-USZ62-80126]. Jim Crow laws divided public facilities of many kinds throughout the South. Supposedly based on the "separate but equal" Supreme Court ruling, these divisions limited African Americans' access to many resources.

[3035] Anonymous, *Newspaper Headline: President Truman Wipes Out Segregation in Armed Forces* (1948), courtesy of the Library of Congress [microfilm 1057]. After Truman's executive order eliminated segregation in the military, many African American veterans of World War II became local leaders in civil rights struggles in the South.

[3355] Jack Delano, *At the Bus Station in Durham, North Carolina* (1940), courtesy of the Library of Congress, Prints & Photographs Division, FSA/OWI Collection [LC-USF33-020522-M2]. African American man in a segregated waiting room at bus station. Jim Crow laws severely divided the experiences of whites and African Americans in the South.

[3696] Dorothea Lange, *Plantation Overseer. Mississippi Delta, Near Clarksdale, Mississippi* (1936), courtesy of the Library of Congress [LC-USF34-009596-C DLC]. Sharecropping initially appealed to freedmen because it promised benefits they had previously been denied; however, the vast majority of sharecroppers worked in conditions that weren't much better than slavery.

[3933] Thomas Nast, *Andrew Johnson's Reconstruction and How It Works* (1866), courtesy of the Library of Congress [LC-USZC4-4591]. Cartoon depicting Andrew Johnson as Shakespeare's Iago betraying Othello, who represents African American Civil War veterans. Southerner Andrew Johnson, seventeenth President of the United States, took office after Lincoln's assassination. His notoriously racist politics thwarted processes of legal change and compensation to African Americans during Reconstruction.

mark 1954 Supreme Court decision *Brown v. Board of Education*, which legally ended segregation in U.S. public schools, beginning a trend toward greater equality in other aspects of race relations as well.

QUESTIONS

Comprehension: What was the role of the U.S. government in the Reconstruction of the South after the Civil War?

Comprehension: What is vigilantism?

Comprehension: How did white southerners justify Jim Crow laws and etiquette?

Context: Explain how the Jim Crow laws could be considered legal under the Fourteenth Amendment (which guaranteed African Americans equal protection under the law). What view of segregation does Zora Neale Hurston take in her depiction of Eatonville, Florida? How does this compare to the depiction of southern segregation in photos taken by white photographers from this era?

Context: How does the Jim Crow way of life affect Dave in Richard Wright's "The Man Who Was Almost a Man"?

Context: How was the Southern Agrarian literary movement related to the Jim Crow way of life?

Exploration: What does Zora Neale Hurston's essay "How It Feels to Be Colored Me" say about the white supremacy that was at the heart of the Jim Crow South? How does her vision of black-white relations compare to Harriet Jacobs's over fifty years earlier (Unit 7)?

Exploration: As the case of the Scottsboro Boys illustrates, African Americans in the Jim Crow South could end up in serious trouble just for being in the same place with whites at the wrong time. Do you think this is why Zora Neale Hurston's stories rarely include white characters? Consider the advantages and disadvantages of Hurston's approach to depicting race relations. How does Hurston's treatment of white characters compare to the work of other Harlem Renaissance writers such as Nella Larsen, Langston Hughes, Countee Cullen, and Jean Toomer?

Exploration: In her groundbreaking article "Visual Pleasure and Narrative Cinema," feminist theorist Laura Mulvey argues that film often employs a "male gaze": that is, films tend to be characterized by *scopophilia*—the pleasure involved in looking at other people's bodies as erotic objects. Although Mulvey is primarily concerned with the eroticization of women, people of color are also often objects of fetishization and domination in American literature; for, as the Scottsboro trials revealed, in the South sexual pleasure was always drawn upon racial lines during this era. For Mulvey visual pleasure is dependent upon an *objectification* of female characters and a narcissistic process of *identification* with an "ideal ego" seen on the screen. To what extent do the writers of the Southern Renaissance, particularly Faulkner, rely upon an objectification of either women or African Americans? Who is the "ideal ego" of these works? What does this imply about the authority and identity of the ideal reader?

Exploration: Some of the most influential writing in the decades leading up to the Civil War was published by former slaves and abolitionists. Writers like Frederick Douglass and Harriet Beecher Stowe saw the evils of slavery and worked tirelessly to end it (see Unit 7). However, as the history of Jim Crow laws shows, the work of abolishing slavery was only the beginning of a long process to confront the racism in American culture. That process was continued in the early twentieth century by prominent figures like Booker T. Washington and W. E. B. Du Bois (see Unit 9). Consider the context of the Jim Crow laws and the different ways these writers responded to their social conditions: How did racism change in America from the early nineteenth to the early twentieth century? How did the literary response to racism change in the same period?

Mass Culture Invasion: The Rise of Motion Pictures

In New York City, on April 23, 1896, Thomas Edison projected the first motion picture on a public screen in the United States. At the time, few foresaw the dramatic effects motion pictures would come to have on American culture in the coming decades. Beginning as a technological novelty, motion pictures soon became popular attractions in amusement parks, music halls, traveling fairs, wax museums, and vaudeville houses all over the country (and in other countries around the world). This upstart entertainment had a tough time competing, however, against the traditional stage arts that were considered to be of higher quality, and therefore appropriate for a higher economic and social class. It wasn't until the 1910s that film began to be taken seriously as many performance houses—formerly devoted exclusively to live drama—converted to present a mixed bill of motion pictures and live performance or abandoned live performance altogether in favor of film. With the rise of the star system during this same period (driven by the popularity of actors like Mary Pickford, Sarah Bernhardt, and Charlie Chaplin), motion pictures became an increasingly powerful force in American life. Although most of the major Hollywood motion picture studios would not be established until the mid-1920s, the motion picture was here to stay.

Along with broadcast radio and nationally circulated publications, motion pictures formed a large part of an ever-expanding "mass culture"—a culture consisting largely of standardized, mass-produced, and mass-distributed cultural products that included everything from movies to toothbrushes, and which meant that no matter where you traveled in the United States, you were likely to be able to find familiar products and entertainment. The rapid expansion of this mass culture formed a challenge to traditions of regional isolation and autonomy. In the South, the introduction of motion pictures into everyday life was fraught with controversy; therefore, the debates surrounding motion pictures often revealed a deeper and more pervasive anxiety about moral and social decay and offered, in some communities, a point around which conservative and "traditional" forces could rally. Many were quick to see that, while motion pictures offered new and

[4554] Prentiss Taylor, *Scottsboro Limited* (1931), courtesy of the Library of Congress [LC-USZC4-4717]. Lithograph from *Scottsboro Limited*, a collection including four poems and a play by Langston Hughes. The collection protested the incarceration, conviction, and death sentence of the Scottsboro boys, nine African American youths unjustly accused of raping two white women.

[7652] Anonymous, *Jim Crow Jubilee* (1847), courtesy of the Library of Congress [LC-USZ62-37348]. Jim Crow laws took their name from a character in minstrel shows. The shows and the character showcased racist stereotypes about African Americans, depicting them as lazy and less intelligent than whites.

[9071] Anonymous, Ku Klux Klan Parade, Washington, D.C., on Pennsylvania Avenue, N.W. (1926), courtesy of the Library of Congress, Prints and Photographs Division [LC-USZ62-59666]. This photograph of a huge KKK march on the National Mall in Washington, D.C., illustrates the mainstream acceptance of the group in the 1920s and 1930s. The Ku Klux Klan, organized under the guise of a civic organization, enforced Jim Crow laws and white supremacy with intimidation and violence. The group regained popular support after the release of *Birth of a Nation*.

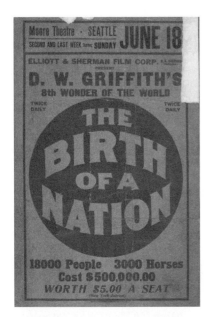

[5703] Riverside Printing Company, *Elliot & Sherman Film Corp. present D. W. Griffith's 8th Wonder of the World, "The Birth of a Nation"* (1915), courtesy of the Library of Congress [LC-USZC4-1971].

[3346] Marion Post Walcott, *Rex Theatre for Colored People, Leland, Mississippi Delta* (1944), courtesy of the Library of Congress [LC-USF32-052508-D].

unprecedented means by which to shape public opinion and teach the "right" values and behaviors, the medium was equally capable of teaching values a community didn't like. According to historian Gregory A. Waller, "The danger, of course, was that this powerful pedagogic tool would be (or had been) utterly prostituted in the name of profit and cheap amusement."

Many of these anxieties about the rise of mass culture—in the nation as a whole, but especially in the South—coalesced around D. W. Griffith's *The Birth of a Nation*, which premiered in 1915. According to Russell Merritt, whose documentary "The Making of *The Birth of a Nation*" explores both the film's technical achievements and its cultural reception, *The Birth of a Nation* was "a runaway success that paved the way for the feature movie as the most widely seen mass entertainment in history up to that time."

Griffith, who directed hundreds of short films, is often credited with defining the art of the motion picture. From a technical perspective, Griffith pioneered and/or popularized many stylistic and technical innovations, including closeups, establishing shots, medium shots, and backlighting. *The Birth of a Nation* also made use of the camera to achieve other novel effects, including composed shots, camera movement, split-screens, flashbacks, fades, irises, and dissolves. Audiences were also amazed by the realism and massive scale of Griffith's Civil War scenes, the detail and accuracy of his costuming, and the compelling combination of storytelling and editing that comprised the film.

While critics agree that *The Birth of a Nation* represented many technical and formal firsts for the motion picture, the response to the story it told was much more divided. The film was based on a dramatic adaptation of Thomas Dixon's novel *The Clansman* (1905), which "celebrated the Ku Klux Klan as savior of the South from vengeful and vindictive blacks." Released during the fiftieth anniversary of the close of the Civil War, the film seemed calculated to revive the spirits of southerners who had begun to doubt the righteousness of the "Lost Cause." The film's opening was promoted by klansmen dressed in full KKK regalia, and the Klan, which had all but disappeared in the first decade of the twentieth century, was revived and went on to become a major political force for the next ten years. Knowing his message would be controversial, Griffith prefaced the film with "A Plea for the Art of the Motion Picture," which addressed the potential that the film might be censored and asked that it be given "the liberty to show the dark side of wrong, that we may illuminate the bright side of virtue." Not unexpectedly, the National Association for the Advancement of Colored People and other civil rights groups protested the film vigorously and succeeded in persuading the U.S. Supreme Court to affirm "the right of state and local agencies to exercise prior restraint and censorship of motion pictures." This did little, however, to damage the success of *The Birth of a Nation*, which went on to become the most popular silent movie ever made. (Woodrow Wilson even showed it in the White House.) It was revived annually through the first half of the 1920s and remained the most profitable film for over two decades before passing that title to Disney's *Snow White and the Seven Dwarfs* in 1937.

The controversy surrounding *The Birth of a Nation* and the film's far-reaching influence provide vivid examples of the way the growth of motion pictures—and the mass culture of which they were a part—challenged the isolated autonomy of small communities throughout the country. However, by the 1930s, the new medium had gained enough acceptance that prominent southern writers such as William Faulkner had begun to interact with Hollywood. Faulkner went to Hollywood for the first time in 1932 to work as a scriptwriter, and he returned several times in succeeding years when he needed to supplement the meager income he was making as a writer. Meanwhile, Margaret Mitchell challenged Faulkner for the title of best-known southern writer when her romantic portrait of the Old South, *Gone With the Wind* (originally published in 1936, the same year as Faulkner's *Absalom, Absalom!*), was made into a popular film.

[5652] Ralph Barton, *Pearl White as a Dramatic Heroine* (1930), courtesy of the Library of Congress [LCPP003B-41012].

QUESTIONS

Comprehension: Why did traditionally isolated communities in the South object to the growing influence of motion pictures?

Comprehension: What reasons did those who attended live theater performances give for disliking motion pictures?

Context: Many communities strongly resisted Prohibition, which began in 1919. How might the cultural battle over Prohibition have been related to the controversies surrounding the spread of motion pictures?

Context: While many people in the South resisted the influences of film on their culture, Hollywood was highly influential in shaping the image of the South for the rest of the world. Films such as *The Birth of a Nation* and *Gone With the Wind* were wildly popular and often comprised everything non-southerners knew about the South. How do these Hollywood visions of the South compare to the South portrayed by southern writers such as the Southern Agrarians, Thomas Wolfe, or Flannery O'Connor?

Context: Motion pictures are never mentioned in Richard Wright's "The Man Who Was Almost a Man," yet the conflict at the center of that story—Dave's desire for a gun as a way to become a man—is related to the conflict surrounding motion pictures. Think about this connection and describe how it works.

Exploration: How did the growth of motion pictures relate to the growth of radio? (See Unit 10.) To what extent is film also a democratic medium?

Exploration: In its early years, the motion picture had to compete with live drama for its audience. In many respects, this competition was a battle between high and low culture. Are similar battles going

"MASS CULTURE INVASION" WEB ARCHIVE

[3346] Marion Post Walcott, *Rex Theatre for Colored People, Leland, Mississippi Delta* (1944), courtesy of the Library of Congress [LC-USF32-052508-D]. Photograph of all-black movie theater in the South. Blacks and whites attended separate theaters and other civic facilities in the South. In the North, African Americans were isolated from white audiences by more informal social codes of segregation.

[5652] Ralph Barton, *Pearl White as a Dramatic Heroine* (1930), courtesy of the Library of Congress [LCPP003B-41012]. Cartoon of woman in Roman clothing posing for movie director. The popularity of movies encouraged the growth of mass culture, leading some regionalists to worry about the erosion of southern traditions.

[5687] National Photo Company, *Margaret Gorman (Miss America 1921), and Stephen (?) Fegen Being Filmed for a Burlesque on the Burning of Rome by the Washington Producing Co.* (1922), courtesy of the Library of Congress [LC-USZ62-119624]. Films and beauty pageants played an important role in shaping the image of the "modern" American girl. Samuel Gompers, head of the American Federation of Labor, noted that Gorman "represents the type of womanhood America needs; strong, red-blooded, able to shoulder the responsibilities of home-making and motherhood. It is in her type that the hope of the country resides" (*New York Times*).

[5703] Riverside Printing Co., *Elliot & Sherman Film Corp Present D. W. Griffith's 8th Wonder of the World, "The Birth of a Nation"* (1915), courtesy of the Library of Congress [LC-USZC4-1971]. Advertising poster for *The Birth of a Nation*. The film was technologically innovative but racist. Glorifying the Ku Klux Klan, it was an adaptation of Thomas Dixon's novel *The Clansman*.

[5719] Cleveland Advocate, Article: *Oppose "Birth of a Nation"* (1915), courtesy of the Ohio Historical Society. Civil rights groups, including the NAACP, organized protests against *The Birth of a Nation*. The film glorified the Ku Klux Klan and helped the organization regain strength.

[7641] Anonymous, *NAACP Members Picketing outside the Republic Theatre, New York City, to Protest the Screening of the Movie "Birth of a Nation"* (1947), courtesy of the Library of Congress [LC-USZ62-84505]. Despite the protests of civil rights groups, *The Birth of a Nation* achieved massive popularity and even was shown in the White House.

on in our culture today? How does the divide between high and low culture relate to the battle for local control and the problems many communities had with the introduction of "mass" culture?

Exploration: The controversy surrounding *The Birth of a Nation* may not sound completely unfamiliar to you and may remind you of the controversy surrounding the use of derogatory language in *The Adventures of Huckleberry Finn* (Unit 8). Are there contemporary films that have caused similar controversies? How has the debate over the role of movies in our culture changed since 1915? How has it remained the same?

EXTENDED CONTEXTS

Hitting the Road: How Automobiles and Highways Transformed American Life

In 1900, Americans rarely moved or traveled beyond a radius of a few miles from where they were born. However, the introduction and rapid adoption of the automobile as America's primary means of transportation, combined with the development and construction of reliable roads on which those cars could travel, quickly transformed the traditional rootedness and stability of American life.

The first American automobile, the *Duryea*, was produced in 1893 and was little more than a horse-drawn buggy with an engine bolted on, with a top speed of approximately 15 miles per hour. By 1900, there were only about 8,000 cars in the United States. At that time, cars were handmade and cost well over $1,000 each, making them far too expensive for all but the wealthiest of Americans. However, in 1908, Henry Ford ushered in the era of the mass-produced automobile; by using a conveyor belt to move the car frame through each stage of its assembly, Ford was able to cut hundreds of dollars from the cost of building his Model-Ts, while at the same time cutting production time for each car from a day and a half to just 93 minutes. Ford's competitors quickly copied his production methods, and by 1920 millions of cars traveled American roads.

It took a while for American roads to catch up to American cars, though. In the early 1900s, the vast majority of roads in the United States were mere dirt tracks that quickly turned to treacherous and rut-filled swamps in the rain, then froze into rough and icy ridges in the winter. Only the most courageous or foolish travelers dared to venture far beyond major cities in their automobiles. As the number of cars rapidly multiplied, state and local governments experimented with an array of paving materials and road designs. During the Great Depression, the Works Progress Administration (WPA), whose purpose was to create jobs for millions of unemployed Americans, and the Civilian Conservation Corps (CCC) did much to improve America's roads. During the 1930s, WPA and CCC workers built 75,000 bridges and constructed or improved nearly 600,000 miles of public roads.

It was World War II, however, that finally convinced the U.S. government that it should do more to improve America's roads and enforce quality standards throughout the nation. As the commander of Allied forces in Europe, Dwight Eisenhower saw how Germany's *Autobahn* aided its war effort by allowing it to quickly and reliably move troops, supplies, and raw materials around the country. In 1944, Congress passed the Federal-Aid Highway Act, which established uniform design criteria for all U.S. highways. Twelve years later, the Federal-Aid Highway Act of 1956 established funding for nearly 45,000 miles of paved interstate highways—the largest peacetime construction project ever undertaken. About that effort Eisenhower would later write: "Its impact on the American economy—the jobs it would produce in manufacturing and construction, the rural areas it would open up—was beyond calculation."

Travel has always figured prominently in American literature, beginning with the Puritan trope of an errand into the wilderness and the narratives of Caveza de Vaca and other Spanish explorers to the New World. More recently, automobiles and the highway were important aspects of self-exploration and commentary in twentieth-century American literature. Writers like John Steinbeck, Jack Kerouac, and Zora Neale Hurston have invoked the highway as a rejection of the familiar and an embrace of the unknown. The advent of cars and other mechanized, high-speed travel has also come to represent the disconnectivity and rootlessness of society and has given voice to fears about changes brought about by technology and modernization. In contemporary Native American poetry, for example, cars are often used as metaphors for wreckage and social dislocation, illustrating one way that cars symbolize the impact of cultural exchange and the influence of technology and white culture upon migration stories and the cultures that produce them. For the writers of the Southern Renaissance, cars symbolized both progress and the possibilities of modernization as well as the threat of industrialization to more traditional practices and values.

Together, the mass-produced automobile and a reliable and uniform system of highways reshaped America. The ability of Americans to travel and move long distances broke down cultural barriers and meant that even remote rural areas could no longer remain isolated from the larger life of the nation, and the world.

QUESTIONS

Comprehension: Why was Henry Ford's assembly line production method such an important innovation? How did it change American industry as a whole?

Context: Increased mobility and the shambles of the southern economy after the Civil War opened up many opportunities to anyone willing to exploit them. Many northerners traveled or moved to the

[5170] Marion Post Walcott, *Saturday Afternoon, Clarksdale, Mississippi Delta, Mississippi* (1939), courtesy of the Library of Congress [LC-USF33-030640-M3 DLC].

[4835] Marion Post Walcott, *Negroes Brought in by Truck from Nearby Towns as Day Labor for Cotton Picking. Marcella Plantation, Mileston, Mississippi Delta, Mississippi* (1939), courtesy of the Library of Congress [LC-USF33-030601-M4 DLC].

"HITTING THE ROAD" WEB ARCHIVE

[4733] Dorothea Lange, *Mississippi Delta, on Mississippi Highway No. 1 between Greenville and Clarksdale. Negro Laborer's Family Being Moved from Arkansas to Mississippi by White Tenant* (1938), courtesy of the Library of Congress [LC-USF34-018952-E DLC]. The automobile is an important trope in American literature and culture: in this image the power relations between the workers and the tenant are reflected in their positions in the vehicle.

[4789] Arthur Rothstein, *Farm along Highway near Dickson, Tennessee* (1942), courtesy of the Library of Congress [LC-USF34-024597-D]. As highways reached rural locations, some worried that small-town and southern values and traditions would be eroded by access to travel and mass culture.

[4835] Marion Post Walcott, *Negroes Brought in by Truck from Nearby Towns as Day Labor for Cotton Picking. Marcella Plantation, Mileston, Mississippi Delta* (1939), courtesy of the Library of Congress [LC-USF33-030601-M4 DLC]. Cotton was an important but resource-taxing and labor-intensive crop in the South. Although the Southern Agrarians romanticized agricultural life, work on cotton plantations was difficult and rarely lucrative for African Americans.

[5170] Marion Post Walcott, *Saturday Afternoon, Clarksdale, Mississippi Delta* (1939), courtesy of the Library of Congress [LC-USF33-030640-M3 DLC]. A street scene in the Mississippi Delta. Older black men talking on sidewalk in downtown Clarksdale, Mississippi. Blanche Cutrer, the model for Blanche in *A Streetcar Named Desire*, was from Clarksdale.

[5594] Anonymous, *It Was Common Practice for Small Town and Country Dealers to Bring Radios Directly to Prospects and Customers Alike* (1925), courtesy of the George H. Clark Radioana Collection, Archives Center, National Museum of American History, Smithsonian Institution. Photograph of dealers delivering radios from vehicle. Growth in geographical mobility and mass culture were intertwined. As travel became easier, small towns became less culturally isolated.

[6422] Detroit Publishing Co., *Highway Construction Equipment, Probably Michigan State Highway Dept., Michigan* (1915), courtesy of the Library of Congress [LC-D418-629]. The mass development of automobiles and reliable roads altered travel, work, and residence patterns. Automobiles and roads became laden with cultural meanings, such as freedom and adventure.

South to exploit cheap labor and an abundance of raw materials and to capitalize on the relative naïveté of the largely rural population. How are these trends manifested in Zora Neale Hurston's "The Gilded Six-Bits" and Flannery O'Connor's "The Life You Save May Be Your Own"?

Exploration: How did the growing number of automobiles and the expanded and improved national highway system relate to the spread of mass culture in the early twentieth century?

Exploration: Trace the metaphors of transportation in the poetry of Joy Harjo (Unit 15) and Robert Penn Warren. What roles do cars, planes, trains, roads, and horses play in their verse?

Promises Unfulfilled: Sharecropping in the South

In the tumultuous South in the decades following the Civil War and Reconstruction, four million freedmen (former slaves) found themselves faced with choices many had scarcely imagined would ever be theirs: How should we make our way in the world? At the same time, while the war had ravaged the southern economy, that economy remained dependent on the production of cotton, which had traditionally been taken care of by slave labor in the plantation system. Therefore, southern farmers and plantation owners faced a dilemma of their own: What would replace slave labor in the southern economy?

Sharecropping was the system of tenant farming which gradually emerged as the answer to the dilemmas of both freedman and planter. In this system, freedmen and poor whites who were unable to afford land of their own contracted with landowners to work a particular piece of land in exchange for a share of the crops or revenue they produced in a given season. Typically, a small group of laborers—often a family but sometimes simply a group of workers who got along well together—would agree to cultivate a certain parcel of land in exchange for one-quarter to one-half the crop as wages, to be paid at the end of the season. The landowner would also generally provide the tenants with a small cabin to live in and food to eat.

Sharecropping initially appealed to freedmen because it promised benefits they had previously been denied, such as the right to work in families or groups of their choice, the freedom to work under their own supervision in their daily activities, and the potential that extra effort might eventually earn them enough profit that they could buy a small piece of land for themselves. However, the vast majority of sharecroppers ended up working in conditions that weren't much better than slavery. Landowners generally retained the right to dictate what their tenants planted and how they worked the land; some even kept their tenants under near-constant supervision. What's more, sharecropping rarely produced a profit for the tenants. In a good year, sharecroppers could earn enough to save a few dollars, but it was generally more likely that they would end up in debt at the end of the season. If a group of sharecroppers encountered a series of bad years—

due to poor weather, for example, or infestations of crop-destroying insects—they could quickly find themselves buried in more debt than they could ever hope to repay.

Despite its exploitative nature (and in part because of it), by the early 1900s sharecropping had become the norm throughout the South, allowing white landowners to continue to prosper while ensuring that those who could not afford land—both black and white—remained poor. During the Great Depression, government programs designed to aid southern agriculture only deepened the racial and class divides upon which sharecropping flourished. This was particularly true of the Agricultural Adjustment Act of 1933, which paid landowners to reduce their output and adopt production quotas in order to raise the profit they could make on what they did produce. When landowners agreed to take some of their acreage out of production, the tenants who had been working those acres found themselves homeless and jobless. Furthermore, government payments to landowners gave them the capital they needed to buy tractors and other farm equipment that further reduced their need for tenant labor. In 1934, the Southern Tenant Farmers Union (STFU) emerged to unite sharecroppers against these inhumane conditions, and for the next few years it made considerable gains. However, neither government aid nor the STFU could reverse falling cotton prices or the fact that mechanized farming methods were increasingly making sharecroppers obsolete. By the end of World War II, sharecropping had largely faded into history as farming became increasingly mechanized and former tenants were forced to migrate to cities, where industrial work was more plentiful.

[4833] Marion Post Walcott, *Tenant Family on Their Porch, Marcella Plantation, Mileston, Mississippi Delta, Mississippi* (1939), courtesy of the Library of Congress [LC-USF33-030534-M2].

[4806] Arthur Rothstein, *Evicted sharecroppers along Highway 60, New Madrid County, Missouri* (1939), courtesy of the Library of Congress [LC-USF33-002968-M1].

QUESTIONS

Comprehension: If sharecroppers were unable to make a satisfactory living by sharecropping, why did they continue doing it?

Context: As Abner Snopes looks upon his white landlord's plantation house in Faulkner's "Barn Burning," he tells his son, Sartie: "That's sweat. Nigger sweat. Maybe it ain't white enough yet to suit him. Maybe he wants to mix some white sweat with it." How does this illustrate the difference Snopes sees between himself and his fellow sharecroppers who are African American? How did white supremacy in the South draw on an argument of **paternalism** to maintain sharecropping as an exploitative system of agricultural production?

Exploration: The agrarian life associated with farming has always been an important but contested ideal in American life. Thomas Jefferson, for example, famously supported the ideal of the "gentleman farmer" (see Unit 4). Compare Jefferson's ideas about the agrarian life with the system of sharecropping as it developed in the South in the late nineteenth and early twentieth centuries. Why do you think Jefferson's ideal was never realized?

ASSIGNMENTS

Personal and Creative Responses

1. *Journal:* "The Man Who Was Almost a Man" by Richard Wright depicts the life of poor black southerners very differently from the way that life is depicted by Zora Neale Hurston in "The Gilded Six-Bits." Wright was, in fact, very critical of the way Hurston portrayed southern blacks; for him, Hurston's characters were too happy and lived too much in the moment with no thought for what might happen the next day. Wright worried that Hurston's white readers might get the idea that all African Americans in the South were as carefree and happy as those in Hurston's stories. Pretend you are Hurston and you have just heard Wright's critique of your work. Write a letter to Wright in which you explain and defend your creation of characters like Missie May and Joe.

2. *Doing History:* Study the images of sharecropping families in the archive and read accounts of what life was like for them. Choose one image and write an account of what a typical day might have been like for the family shown in that image. How early does their day begin? What kinds of things does each person have to do to keep the family going? What are the main concerns of the family members? What are their hopes for the future?

3. *Multimedia:* Study the images of southern life contained in the archive and create a short slide-show depicting the various facets of early-twentieth-century southern life. Write short captions for each image to help your audience understand the composition of southern communities in this period. What was the role of religion? Who had automobiles? What other forms of transportation did people use? How did men and women typically pass their time?

Problem-Based Learning Projects

1. Imagine you have been asked to help create a museum exhibit comparing the Old South to the New South. Working with one other student, search the archive and read the literature in this unit for images and descriptions of the various ideas of the South in the late nineteenth and early twentieth centuries. Choose ten to twelve items (images as well as short selections from written works) that depict the Old South and ten to twelve items that depict the New South; then write a "guide" to your collection that explains the role of each item in this exhibit.

2. The year is 1932. Imagine that you and several of your classmates live in Springcreek, a small southern town where the economy has been ravaged by the Great Depression and several years of poor cotton crops. You recently heard about a man who wants to build a rubber factory somewhere in your area. The factory will employ a hundred workers and attract many other businesses to the community in which it is built (including a movie theater and a department store). Some people in your town would love to have the factory in Springcreek. But because your town is so isolated, the rubber factory owner won't consider locating his business there unless he can be assured that the roads between Springcreek and the nearest city are good enough to ensure he'll be able to get needed supplies and ship his rubber goods to his customers. Lucky for you, the Works Progress Administration (WPA) has just offered to help build a highway between Springcreek and the city. There's just one problem: many Springcreek residents are opposed to the idea because they fear a highway, a factory, a movie theater, a department store, and other new businesses will threaten their traditional way of life. Working in a group, stage the town council meeting at which the residents of Springcreek debate the merits of allowing the rubber factory to be built in their town. Your meeting should include people who support the plan as well as people who oppose it, and both sides should have well-reasoned arguments to support their position. Appoint one person as mayor to listen to the debate and make a final decision on the matter.

3. One of the fundamental events that helped shape the Southern Renaissance was the Scopes "Monkey" trial, officially known as *The State of Tennessee v. John Thomas Scopes*. The trial pitted Scopes, a substitute science teacher in Dayton, Tennessee, against the Butler Act, Tennessee's statute that made it illegal to teach evolution in the state's public schools. Working with a group of your peers, research the background leading up to the trial, as well as the trial itself. Once you're familiar with the trial, work together to script a short, one-act play dramatizing the events of the trial, making sure there are enough roles for each of you so that you'll be able to "stage" a short re-enactment of the trial for your class. After your performance, invite your classmates to discuss how and why this trial was so important to the development of southern writing in the late 1920s and 1930s.

often owed more than they made. During the Great Depression, white and black sharecroppers and farmers, like this family, were displaced from their land and homes.

[4833] Marion Post Walcott, *Tenant Family on Their Porch, Marcella Plantation, Mileston, Mississippi Delta* (1939), courtesy of the Library of Congress [LC-USF33-030534-M2]. African American sharecropping family seated on their porch. Plantation owners were generally also the owners of sharecroppers' homes, which resembled, and sometimes were, old slave cabins. The plantation owners also controlled the rent and decided which crops should be planted. As payment, landlords usually received most of the profits.

GLOSSARY

Agrarianism The belief that society and daily life should be structured around the cultivation of the soil. According to literary critic and historian M. Thomas Inge, Agrarians believe that the direct contact with nature that comes from farming will bring humans closer to God and encourage the values of "honor, manliness, self-reliance, courage, moral integrity, and hospitality." Furthermore, Agrarians believe that urban life, capitalism, and technology destroy human dignity and independence while also encouraging vice and moral weakness. In the 1920s and 1930s a prominent group of southern writers—including John Crowe Ransom and Robert Penn Warren—loosely subscribed to the basic tenets of Agrarianism and therefore became known as the Southern Agrarians.

Fugitive Poets   Group of poets and critics centered at Vanderbilt University in the early 1920s. The group included John Crowe Ransom, Allen Tate, and Robert Penn Warren and first gained a degree of prominence for *The Fugitive*, the magazine they published from 1922 to 1925 as an outlet for their writing. According to critic J. A. Bryant, the group's goal was simply to "demonstrate that a group of southerners could produce important work in the medium, devoid of sentimentality and carefully crafted, with special attention to the logical coherence of substance and trope."

New Criticism   School of criticism which emerged primarily in the South and which argued that critics had for too long paid too much attention to the biographical and historical contexts of a work of literature. New Critics advocated a focus on "the thing itself"—the language and the structural and formal qualities of the poem, novel, play, or story with which the critic was concerned. The foundation of New Criticism was, and remains, the exercise of "close reading," which for poetry often means a word-by-word or line-by-line analysis of the poem, the goal of which is to discern the most coherent meaning within its language and form. Although the New Criticism had become the dominant critical practice by the mid-twentieth century, most contemporary critics merely use it as a starting point for various other critical approaches. Many southern writers are closely associated with New Criticism, including John Crowe Ransom, Robert Penn Warren, and Cleanth Brooks.

Old South   Refers to the romantic and sentimental myth of what the South once was. The myth of the Old South generally referred to the "plantation legend" of antebellum (and much postbellum) popular fiction which portrayed white southerners as genteel aristocrats and slavery as a benevolent, paternal institution from which blacks and whites benefited equally. The first few chapters of Margaret Mitchell's *Gone With the Wind* capture the myth of the Old South. Opposed to the myth of the Old South were ideas of the New South, including the view that southerners should try to "modernize" and reshape their region on the industrial model of the North.

paternalism   From the Latin *pater*, meaning to act like a father. In the context of the American South, paternalism generally refers to the attitude of many white southerners toward African Americans in the nineteenth century and continuing into the twentieth. According to the paternalist defense of slavery, African Americans were childlike and unable to take proper care of themselves; therefore, they needed white "masters" to take care of them and guide them through life. After the Civil War, the paternalist argument continued to be used as a pretext for the exploitative working conditions of sharecropping, as well as for the strict code of laws and etiquette known as Jim Crow.

Reconstruction   Period immediately following the Civil War during which the federal government attempted to force the former Confederate states to govern themselves according to the laws and customs of the rest of the United States. During this time (also known as the period of "Radical Reconstruction"), federal troops helped enforce universal male suffrage, and former leaders of the Confederate Army were barred from serving in public office. For the first time, African Americans were elected to serve as legislators and governors in southern states. Despite the fact that no state was ever controlled by a majority of African Americans, white southerners bitterly resented being forced to treat African Americans as equals, and by 1876 the period of Radical Reconstruction had effectively ended.

regionalism   Writing that emphasizes the importance of a regional setting and tradition to individuals' lives. While regional writing tends to focus on issues or experiences that are native to the place with which it is concerned, the best examples of regionalism have universal appeal as well.

revolt against the village   Theme in American literature in the 1920s and 1930s through which many writers (notably the members of the "Lost Generation"—see Unit 11) criticized their own society for its crudeness, materialism, and repression. Also refers more generally to early-twentieth-century changes in society—such as the rise of mass media and an increasingly mobile population—which appeared to threaten the cohesiveness and autonomy of the traditional community.

southern gothic   Style of writing marked by southern settings and characters which are somehow dark, mysterious, or grotesque, or which otherwise disturb or question the "normal" expectations of their readers. Writers associated with the southern gothic include William Faulkner, Flannery O'Connor, Tennessee Williams, and Carson McCullers. See also Unit 6.

stream of consciousness   Style of writing used by many modernists that attempts to portray the inner workings of a character's mind by cataloging or describing the character's thoughts and ideas in rapid succession and without any interpretation or explanation by an outside narrator. So-named by William James, who described human consciousness as a continuous stream of thoughts, impressions, emotions, and ideas. William Faulkner used this style in *As I Lay Dying*, which forces readers to assemble an overall narrative from the various thoughts, feelings, and observations of fifteen different characters. The stream-of-consciousness style challenged traditional narrative by abandoning the linear form in favor of the more confused and sometimes random jumps of the human mind.

SELECTED BIBLIOGRAPHY

Andrews, William (gen. ed.), Minrose C. Gwin, Trudier Harris, and Fred Hobson. *The Literature of the American South*. New York: W. W. Norton & Company, 1998.

Bryant, J. A., Jr. *Twentieth-Century Southern Literature*. Lexington: UP of Kentucky, 1997.

Doyle, Don. *Faulkner's County: The Historical Roots of Yoknapatawpha*. Chapel Hill: U of North Carolina P, 2001.

Dumenil, Lynn. *The Modern Temper: American Culture and Society in the 1920s*. New York: Hill and Wang, 1995.

Franklin, John Hope, and Alfred A. Moss, Jr. *From Slavery to Freedom: A History of African Americans*. 7th ed. New York: McGraw-Hill, 1997.

Heilbrun, Carolyn G. "On Katherine Anne Porter . . ." *American Short Story*, Vol. 2. Ed. Calvin Skaggs. New York: Dell, 1989. 296–300.

Hurston, Zora Neale. *I Love Myself When I Am Laughing . . . And Then Again When I Am Looking Mean and Impressive*. Ed. Alice Walker. Intro. Mary Helen Washington. Old Westbury, NY: The Feminist Press, 1979.

Kaplan, Carla. *The Erotics of Talk: Women's Writing and Feminist Paradigms*. New York: Oxford UP, 1996.

King, Richard H. *A Southern Renaissance: The Cultural Awakening of the American South, 1930–1955*. New York: Oxford UP, 1980.

Parrish, Michael E. *Anxious Decades: America in Prosperity and Depression, 1920–1941*. New York: W. W. Norton & Company, 1992.

Powell, William S. *Dictionary of North Carolina Biography*. Chapel Hill: U of North Carolina P, 1996.

Sundquist, Eric. *Faulkner: The House Divided*. Baltimore: Johns Hopkins UP, 1983.

Watt, Stephen, and Gary A. Richardson. *American Drama: Colonial to Contemporary*. New York: Harcourt Brace, 1995.

Woodward, C. Vann. *The Burden of Southern History*. 3rd ed. Baton Rouge: Louisiana State UP, 1993.

Wright, Richard. "How Bigger Was Born." *Native Son*. Perennial Classics ed. New York: Harper Collins, 1998. 433–62.

FURTHER RESOURCES

Arnett, Paul, and William Arnett, eds. *Souls Grown Deep: African American Vernacular Art of the South*. Vols. 1 & 2. Atlanta, GA: Tinwood Books [in association with the Schomburg Center for Research in Black Culture, the New York Public Library], 2000.

A Streetcar Named Desire [1951: videorecording]. Charles K. Feldman Group Productions. Burbank, CA: Warner Home Video, 1985. Starring: Vivien Leigh, Marlon Brando, Kim Hunter, Karl Malden. Producer, Charles K. Feldman; screenplay, Tennessee Williams; director, Elia Kazan; music, Alex North.

The Big Sleep [1945/46: videorecording]. Warner Bros.: a Howard Hawks production; Burbank, CA: Warner Home Video, 2000. Based on the novel by Raymond Chandler. Starring: Humphrey Bogart, Lauren Bacall, Martha Vickers, Dorothy Malone. Screenplay, William Faulkner, Leigh Brackett, Jules Furthman. Special features: the documentary *The Big Sleep Comparisons 1945/1946 Versions*; theatrical trailer. Side A: The 1946 theatrical release version. Side B: The 1945 pre-release version.

The Birth of a Nation [1915: videorecording]. Blackhawk Films. Film Preservation Associates; Chatsworth, CA: Image Entertainment [distributor], 1992. Starring: Lillian Gish, Mae Marsh, et al. Director: D. W. Griffith. Includes a 24-minute film, *The Making of The Birth of a Nation* . . . , by film historians Russell Merritt and David Shepard and a reproduction of the original program from the world's premiere of the film.

Center for the Study of the American South, University of North Carolina at Chapel Hill, 03A Manning Hall, Campus Box 3355, Chapel Hill, NC 27599. Phone: (919) 962-5665; Fax: (919) 962-4433; Email: csas@email.unc.edu. Includes *Southern Cultures* (a journal), Sounds of the South, and the Southern Oral History Project.

Conwill, Kinshasha, et al. *Testimony: Vernacular Art of the African American South*. New York: Harry N. Abrams in association with Exhibitions International and the Schomburg Center for Research in Black Culture, 2001.

Crossroads, Southern Routes: Music of the American South; Wade in the Water, Vol. 3: *African American Gospel: The Pioneering Composers; Been in the Storm So Long: Spirituals, Folk Tales and Children's Games; Black Banjo Songsters of North Carolina and Virginia*. Smithsonian Folkways Recordings. Smithsonian Folkways Mail Order: Smithsonian Folkways Recordings, Dept. 0607, Washington, DC, 20073-0607.

Delehanty, Randolph. *Art in the American South—Works from the Ogden Collection*. Baton Rouge: Louisiana State UP, 1996.

Edge, John T. *Southern Belly: The Ultimate Food Lover's Companion to the South*. Pen and ink illustrations by folk artist Blair Hobbs. Hill Street Press, 2000.

Inherit the Wind [1960: videorecording]. United Artists; Lomitas Productions, Inc.; produced and directed by Herman Shumlin; presented by Stanley Kramer. Farmington Hills, MI: CBS/FOX Video, 1985. Film dramatization of Scopes evolution trial.

Scottsboro: An American Tragedy [videorecording]. A Social Media Productions, Inc. production. Producers: Daniel Anker and Barak Goodman; writer and director: Barak Goodman; co-director: Daniel Anker. Alexandria, VA: PBS Home Video, 2001.

Their Eyes Were Watching God: Mules and Men, by Zora Neale Hurston, Ruby Dee (Reader). Harper Audio; ISBN: 0694524026; unabridged edition (November 2000). Abridged version: Caedmon Audio Cassette; ISBN: 1559945001 (November 1991).

Authors and Works

Featured in the Video:

Ralph Ellison, *Invisible Man* (novel), "Cadillac Flambé" (short story)

Philip Roth, *Portnoy's Complaint* (novel), "Defender of the Faith" (short story)

N. Scott Momaday, *The Way to Rainy Mountain*, *House Made of Dawn* (novels)

Discussed in This Unit:

Bernard Malamud, "The Magic Barrel" (short story)

Saul Bellow, "Looking for Mr. Green" (short story)

Arthur Miller, *Death of a Salesman* (play)

Gwendolyn Brooks, "The White Troops Had Their Orders But the Negroes Looked Like Men," "We Real Cool," "A Bronzeville Mother Loiters in Mississippi. Meanwhile a Mississippi Mother Burns Bacon," "The Last Quatrain of the Ballad of Emmett Till" (poems)

Grace Paley, "A Conversation with My Father" (short story)

James Baldwin, "Going to Meet the Man" (short story)

Paule Marshall, "Reena" (short story)

Overview Questions

■ How did this diverse array of minority and ethnic voices enrich an American literary tradition that once was defined almost exclusively by white men?

■ What relationship can we see between innovations in twentieth-century popular culture, especially jazz and rock and roll, and experimentation in literary style?

■ How do the writers in this unit greatly expand the conventional definitions of what it means to be an American?

■ Several of these writers experienced moral, political, or psychological crises during the course of their lives and in the process became disillusioned with radical agendas and mass movements. How do these crises show in their work, and what similarities do you see between their experience with political movements and that of authors from earlier periods in American literature?

■ What experimental styles and strategies become apparent in the literary works featured in this unit?

■ Much of the literature in this unit responds to an age in which the pressures of conformity and assimilation led to a climate of political protest. What resemblances and differences do you see between the moral issues that these writers address and those confronted by earlier American writers?

■ What relationship is conveyed between each writer and his or her own communities—both the ethnic or racial community in which he or she grew up, and the larger society encountered as an adult? How might the complexity of this relationship give each text and writer a special importance?

■ The suburbs expanded in the 1950s and after, rivaling cities and rural settings as places for Americans to live. How do some writers from this unit represent the suburban experience?

■ Almost all of the works included in this unit focus on the problems and challenges of forging identity. How do they achieve a measure of relevance for a broad range of American readers?

■ What modern American aspirations, myths, and fears are present in the work of these writers, and how does each writer address them?

■ What myths about American family life were reinforced in the popular culture of the 1950s and 1960s? How have those myths been challenged in literary works, and how have those myths endured or evolved today?

Learning Objectives

After students have viewed the video, read the head-notes and literary selections in *The Norton Anthology of American Literature*, and explored related archival materials on the *American Passages* Web site, they should be able to

1. see and discuss connections among Ralph Ellison's enthusiasm for jazz, his deep experience in classic American and European literature, and his own style and experiments as a writer;
2. hear and discuss the various ways in which these writers use American urban and ethnic dialects, speech patterns, and folkways in writing for a multiethnic audience;
3. understand how traditional American themes (growing up, breaking away from established values, finding love, pursuing dreams) are addressed and transformed by each of these authors;
4. understand how change in cultural and personal life is addressed in the work of several of these writers;
5. appreciate the dynamics of assimilation and acculturation;
6. define the "novel of identity" as a distinct literary genre and discuss how it relates to the broader tradition of the bildungsroman;
7. identify hallmarks of modern and contemporary Native American, African American, and Jewish American literature.

Instructor Overview

In the folk memory of the twenty-first century, the 1950s are recalled as a decade of bland conservatism and imaginative complacency in the United States. Television came of age in the 1950s, and it proclaimed that suburban ranch houses, station wagons, "Father Knows Best," and "The Man in the Gray Flannel Suit" were the icons and obsessions of postwar America. An investigation of newspapers, however, or a sampling of the literary and intellectual life of the 1950s will demonstrate that there was no shortage of vitality, independent thought, and moral uncertainty during this time in American history. As the severe housing shortage after World War II gave way to suburban sprawl and interstate highways, the dynamics of ordinary life were radically reinvented. Women who had worked in the defense industries and who remembered the scarcity and hardship of the 1930s and 1940s now faced the heady challenges of prosperity and conflicting social values. Propelled by the G.I. Bill, the vast expansion of the American college and university system brought higher education to millions of people from ordinary backgrounds—yet life after college did not always reflect the possibilities that had opened up to these bright and hopeful undergraduates. Women with college degrees, for instance, still faced an economic and social system that regarded them as aspiring housewives.

The G.I. Bill also changed the bloodlines of American thought. By the mid-1950s, the dominion of the New England Ivy League Brahmin with an Anglo-Saxon pedigree had ended, and the arts and intellectual life were energized by people with names and faces that Henry Adams and T. S. Eliot would have thought strange indeed. Many of the emerging authors, including Lionel Trilling, Ralph Ellison, Bernard Malamud, Gwendolyn Brooks, Delmore Schwartz, James Baldwin, Norman Mailer, Paule Marshall, Grace Paley, Philip Roth, and Saul Bellow, did not come from families that would have made the "Blue Book" of any prewar American social hierarchy.

Unit 14, "Becoming Visible," provides background and classroom materials on Baldwin, Bellow, Ellison, Arthur Miller, Roth, Paley, Malamud, Marshall, N. Scott Momaday, Richard Wright, and Brooks. The video for Unit 14 focuses on three of these authors and explores how writers from this period responded to the challenge of being American in a decade of Cold War, material comfort, moral anxiety, and deep concern about the place of independent thinkers and ethnic minorities within the United States. Ellison, Roth, and Momaday are known for their "novels of identity," works that relate a long adventure of growing up and achieving a self. Their heroes and journeys are sometimes emblematic of the aspirations and crises of people who had not previously figured so powerfully in the American imagination. Bellow, Malamud, and Miller also became famous as contributors to this expanded American mythology.

The video and curriculum materials for Unit 14 pay special attention to the mingling of American traditions in the works under discussion. *Invisible*

Man draws heavily on jazz, blues, and African American culture, as well as on the literary traditions of James Joyce, Mark Twain, Fyodor Dostoevsky, Franz Kafka, and Thomas Mann. In *Portnoy's Complaint*, Philip Roth echoes the Anglo-Saxon nostalgia of F. Scott Fitzgerald and Thomas Wolfe, as well as the exuberance of *yiddishkeit*, the folk culture of Eastern European Jews. N. Scott Momaday's *House Made of Dawn* is experimental in its use of collage, recalling moments in the works of William Faulkner, as well as the Kiowa oral tradition. Unit 14 also explores how these ethnic American writers won the attention of readers and critics beyond the reach of their own communities. What aspects of these works resonated for Americans living lives very different from the protagonists in these narratives? Unit 14 helps answer these questions by offering suggestions about how to connect these writers to other writers of the era, to their cultural context, and to other units in the series.

The video, the archive, and the curriculum materials situate writers of this generation with reference to several key issues of their day: (1) the rise of suburbs and the intensification of the conflict between individuality and conformity; (2) the migration to urban centers by ethnic minorities; (3) baseball as a symbol of national identity, and the consequent importance of desegregation in the sport; (4) anxiety over the threat of nuclear annihilation; (5) the plight of veterans returning to civilian life and seeking to be accepted as Americans, regardless of ethnicity; (6) the influence of jazz on American literature and style; and (7) the continuing impact of World War II on American social life.

The archive and curriculum materials suggest how students might connect the readings from this unit to those of other units in the series: How do the lives and work of Jewish American women differ from era to era? How does Ellison's protagonist compare with Dave Saunders in Wright's "The Man Who Was Almost a Man"? Similarly, students are encouraged to compare the rhetorical strategies used by Ellison and other African American writers of the 1950s and 1960s to those used by Frederick Douglass and Harriet Jacobs in Unit 7. Roth's emphasis on combat experience and ethnicity in imagining American manhood is compared to the construction of American masculinity discussed in Unit 5. Unit 14 is also designed to get students thinking about postmodernism and post–World War II American culture, topics that will be explored in Units 15 and 16. Why were the writers discussed in Unit 14 sometimes attacked by members of their own ethnic groups? How do the writers discussed in Units 15 and 16 respond to similar attacks and accusations?

Student Overview

In the folk memory of the twenty-first century, the 1950s are recalled as a decade of bland conservatism and imaginative complacency in the United States. Television came of age in the 1950s, and it proclaimed that suburban ranch houses, station wagons, "Father Knows Best," and "The Man in the Gray Flannel Suit" were the icons and obsessions of postwar America. An investigation of newspapers, however, or a sampling of the literary and intellectual life of the 1950s will demonstrate that there was no shortage of vitality, independent thought, and moral uncertainty during this time in American history. As the severe housing shortage after World War II gave way to suburban sprawl and interstate highways, the dynamics of ordinary life were radically reinvented. Women who had worked in the defense industries and who remembered the scarcity and hardship of the 1930s and 1940s now faced the heady challenges of prosperity and conflicting social values. Propelled by the G.I. Bill, the vast expansion of the American college and university system brought higher education to millions of people from ordinary backgrounds—yet life after college did not always reflect the possibilities that had opened up to these bright and hopeful undergraduates. Women with college degrees, for instance, still faced an economic and social system that regarded them as aspiring housewives.

The G.I. Bill also changed the bloodlines of American thought. By the mid 1950s, the dominion of the New England Ivy League Brahmin with an Anglo-Saxon pedigree had ended, and the arts and intellectual life were energized by people with names and faces that Henry Adams and T. S. Eliot would have thought strange indeed. Many of the emerging authors, including Lionel Trilling, Ralph Ellison, Bernard Malamud, Gwendolyn Brooks, Delmore Schwartz, James Baldwin, Norman Mailer, Paule Marshall, Grace Paley, Philip Roth, and Saul

Bellow, did not come from families that would have made the "Blue Book" of any prewar American social hierarchy.

Unit 14, "Becoming Visible," explores the expansion of American literary culture after World War II and the new voices entering America's cultural conversation. African Americans, Native Americans, American Jews, and citizens of many other ethnic backgrounds participated in the fight against Nazi Germany and the Japanese Empire; when the war was over, these people—as individuals and as groups—sought greater visibility and recognition within American society.

As the video explains, Ralph Ellison, N. Scott Momaday, and Philip Roth faced an artistic predicament shared by many other American minority writers. They experienced isolation from their own racial or ethnic literary communities, as well as from the larger culture, because of risks they took in their writing and their insistence on writing as individuals rather than as generic representatives of a larger group. Each of these three felt compelled to risk a great deal by saying things that would not, in Ralph Ellison's words in *Invisible Man*, "yes 'em to death."

This willingness to speak honestly, and in ways that might not please a wide audience, is shared by other writers discussed in Unit 14. Each affirmed the right to speak as an individual first and to give limited allegiance to coteries, hierarchies, and fashions. These writers thus join the ranks of Herman Melville, Margaret Fuller, Frederick Douglass, Emily Dickinson, Walt Whitman, and others who won widespread admiration only after a long and difficult conversation with the larger culture.

The video, the archive, and the curriculum materials for this unit connect the writers of this generation to the key issues of their day: (1) the rise of the suburbs after World War II, and the conflict between individuality and conformity that suburban life intensified; (2) the continuing migration to urban centers by ethnic minorities; (3) baseball as a symbol of American identity, and the impact of the desegregation of the sport in the early 1950s; (4) the arms race with the Soviet Union and the threat of nuclear annihilation; (5) the civil rights movement of the 1950s and 1960s and the special predicament of the minority veterans of the American armed forces; (6) the influence of jazz on American literature and fashion; and (7) the continuing impact of World War II on American ethnic communities.

On a thematic level, this unit explores ways in which American minority writers, including Ellison, Roth, and Momaday, achieved an important presence in the literary culture of the United States. How did our national literary traditions help these authors achieve recognition as American voices? What aspects of their work seemed to hit home for large numbers of readers during this era? Unit 14 helps answer these questions by offering suggestions on how to connect these writers to other writers of the era, to their cultural context, and to other units in the series.

Video Overview

➤ **Authors covered:** Ralph Ellison, Philip Roth, N. Scott Momaday

➤ **Who's interviewed:** Judith Baskin, professor of religious studies and director of the Harold Schnitzer Family Program in Judaic Studies (University of Oregon); John Callahan, Ralph Ellison's literary executor and Morgan S. Odell Professor of Humanities (Lewis and Clark College); Joy Harjo, poet/musician, professor of English (University of California, Los Angeles) (Muscogee/Creek); N. Scott Momaday, Pulitzer Prize–winning author; Greg Sarris, professor of English (Loyola Marymount University) (Miwok Chief/Pomo); Pancho Savery, professor of English (Reed College); Eric Sundquist, dean of the College of Arts and Sciences and professor of English (Northwestern University); Wendy Wasserstein, Tony Award, Dramatists Guild Award, and Pulitzer Prize–winning playwright

➤ **Points covered:**

• The decades after World War II were a conflicting time, characterized by prosperity and conformity for some and rebellion for others. Mass consumption, a movement to the suburbs from the inner cities, and a fear of communism helped to stifle dissent. During the 1950s and 1960s mainstream literary and popular culture embraced some ethnic writers who achieved both commercial success and literary acclaim.

• Writers Ralph Ellison, Philip Roth, and N. Scott Momaday grappled with issues of ethnicity and race and redefined what it meant to be American and part of the American literary canon. Each produced a **novel of identity** in which an existential hero goes on a journey of self-discovery. Widely appreciated for their universal appeal, these authors also tackled issues unique to their particular cultural and ethnic backgrounds.

• Ellison's *Invisible Man* sparked an ongoing debate about the obligations and consequences of a "black identity."

• Roth's *Portnoy's Complaint* explores the anxieties and aspirations of Jewish Americans as they attempt to adapt to life among the gentiles.

• N. Scott Momaday explores ethnic identity in *House Made of Dawn*. Influenced by the Native American oral tradition, Momaday's experimental style juxtaposes three kinds of voices: mythic, historical, and personal.

PREVIEW

• **Preview the video:** In the 1950s and 1960s, ethnic writers moved onto the bestseller lists and achieved recognition in literary circles. Ralph Ellison, Philip Roth, and N. Scott Momaday showed how Americans once at the margins were now closer to the country's cultural center. In doing so, all three writers expanded the boundaries of American literature and opened up the definition of what it is to be American. The video provides the backdrop for this era, as a post–World War II America began to enjoy a prosperity that led it toward conformity and mass consumption. However, the postwar economic boom and "white flight" to the suburbs increased the physical and class distance between the white middle class and ethnic minorities who remained in older neighborhoods closer to the city centers. Ellison, Roth, and Momaday helped to resist the imaginative segregation that accompanied these changes in the urban and suburban landscape. Ellison's adaptations from jazz and blues, Roth's ethnic comedic riffs, and Momaday's ingenious use of Native American narrative traditions all helped to make storytelling richer and expanded readers' awareness of where narrative art comes from and who is capable of creating it. The video also emphasizes the risk these authors took in their innovative approaches as representatives of their own communities, often facing fierce criticism and misunderstanding of their fiction and its intentions.

• **What to think about while watching:** How do Ellison, Roth, and Momaday expand the definition of what it means to be American? What traditions influenced each of these writers? How do they respond to the social and political tensions of the time, such as the pressure to conform and the need for overall recognition of civil rights for minorities? What American icons do the authors invoke and redefine in their works?

• **Tying the video to the unit content:** This unit focuses on "novels of identity" from the 1950s and 1960s, particularly those dealing with issues of ethnicity and race. In an era remembered now for conformity, but also for the cultural rebellions of the 1960s, these writers spoke both as individuals and as members of groups. In doing so, they exemplify a conflict between being American and being part of an ethnic community. Unit 14 provides background information that will help readers understand this literature.

The Context "With Justice for All: From World War II to the Civil Rights Movement" provides a surprising picture of how ethnic minorities who had served their country well in war were subjected to hatred and racism upon their return to civilian life. In one sense, these citizens were assimilated into the dominant culture through their service during the war but then were expected to return to disenfranchised minority status after the war was over. Alternatively, Japanese Americans were detained and confined without representation during the war because of widespread fear about their loyalties. Major works exploring such themes include Philip Roth's "Defender of the Faith," N. Scott Momaday's *House Made of Dawn*, and Ralph Ellison's *Invisible Man*. In the Context "Suburban Dreams: Levittown, New York" students learn how new suburban subdivisions intensified a pressure to assimilate and conform and eroded the sense of coherence and belonging that had been possible for many families when they lived in ethnic neighborhoods. Roth's *Portnoy's Complaint* and even Arthur Miller's *Death of a Salesman* explore the suburban setting, while Bellow's "Looking for Mr. Green" is set in the city. The Context "Living with the Atomic Bomb: Native Americans and the Postwar Uranium Boom and Nuclear Reactions" deals with Native Americans working in uranium mines and with the cultural paranoia of living with "the bomb" in the late 1950s and the 1960s. "Jazz Aesthetics" helps readers understand the influence of this music as it crossed over into other arts, such as writing and painting. Note the influences of jazz and the blues in Ellison's *Invisible Man* and "Cadillac Flambé," along with works by writers such as Gwendolyn Brooks, Langston Hughes, and James Baldwin. Finally, "Baseball: An American Pastime" discusses the influences of the "all-American" sport across the country, demonstrating how it reflected the ethnic and labor struggles that were occurring in the rest of American society. Note the use of baseball in the works of Ellison, Miller, Malamud, and Roth.

	What is American literature? What are the distinctive voices and styles in American literature? How do social and political issues influence the American canon?	**How are American myths created, challenged, and re-imagined through this literature?**	**What is an American? How does literature create conceptions of the American experience and American identity?**
Comprehension Questions	What changes in literary style are discussed in the video? Why did some Jewish American critics condemn Philip Roth's novels as anti-Semitic while Ellison was charged with not "being black enough"? Why is N. Scott Momaday's *The Way to Rainy Mountain* hard to classify?	How is the concept of "the American Dream" challenged in this unit? Why do so many people still think of the 1950s and 1960s as a wonderful, peaceful time, as envisioned in sitcoms like *Happy Days* or movies like *American Graffiti*? Who is excluded from these scenarios?	How do Roth, Ellison, and Momaday define America or Americans? Why does the Invisible Man leave the South? What is he looking for, and what does he find when he arrives in 1930s New York City? What does N. Scott Momaday mean when he describes his childhood as a "Pan-Indian experience"?
Context Questions	What traditions influenced each of these writers? How are these writers' ethnic traditions reflected in what and how they write?	Ellison, Roth, and Momaday explore the role of minority Americans in the armed forces, particularly in World War II. How does this war inform the construction of the American hero during the 1950s and 1960s?	How do the themes and styles of these writers reflect economic, cultural, and political changes in American culture in the 1940s, 1950s, and 1960s? Consider changes occurring with the civil rights movement, the Cold War, and the social rebellion sparked by the Vietnam War that extended to the needs of women, gay and lesbian Americans, and members of other minority groups.
Exploration Questions	Ellison's *Invisible Man* has been hailed as a classic novel of American literature. What makes a piece of literature a classic?	What American myths do you associate with the 1950s and 1960s? Some possibilities might be the idyllic imaginary world that television provided in programs like *Leave It to Beaver* or *My Three Sons*. Others might include the notions that "popularity leads to success in life," that "good always wins and evil always loses," or that "everyone has a fair chance at success if they just try hard." How do these myths relate to the authors and events covered in the video?	Ellison, Roth, and Momaday use ethnic stereotypes. When is using stereotypes useful and when is it not?

	Texts	Contexts
1940s	Saul Bellow, *The Dangling Man* (1944), *The Victim* (1947) Gwendolyn Brooks, *A Street in Bronzeville* (1945), "The White Troops Had Their Orders But the Negroes Looked Like Men" (1945), *Annie Allen* (1949) Arthur Miller, *All My Sons* (1947), *Death of a Salesman* (1949)	Executive Order 9066 signed by President Roosevelt, ordering all persons of Japanese ancestry out of the Pacific military zone to inland internment camps (1942; ends 1945) All-Girls Professional Baseball League (1943–54) Filipino Naturalization Act (1946) Jackie Robinson becomes the first African American to officially play Major League Baseball (1947)
1950s	Bernard Malamud, *The Natural* (1950), *The Assistant* (1957), "The Magic Barrel" (1958) Saul Bellow, "Looking for Mr. Green" (1952), *The Adventures of Augie March* (1953), *Henderson the Rain King* (1959) Ralph Ellison, *Invisible Man* (1952) James Baldwin, *Go Tell It on the Mountain* (1953), *The Amen Corner* (1955), *Notes of a Native Son* (1955), *Giovanni's Room* (1956) Gwendolyn Brooks, *Maud Martha* (1953), *Bronzeville Boys and Girls* (1956) Arthur Miller, *The Crucible* (1953), *A Memory of Two Mondays* (1955), *A View from the Bridge* (1955) Paule Marshall, *Brown Girl, Brownstones* (1959) Grace Paley, *Little Disturbances of Man* (1959) Philip Roth, *Goodbye Columbus* (1959), "Defender of the Faith" (1959)	Korean War (1950–53) Racial segregation in schools banned (1954) Rosa Parks arrested for refusing to give up her seat on a bus; sparks Montgomery bus boycott (1955) Supreme Court rules that bus segregation is illegal (1956) Voting Rights Bill passed by Congress (1957) President Eisenhower sends U.S. Army troops to Little Rock, Arkansas, to enforce desegregation in public schools (1957)
1960s	Gwendolyn Brooks, "We Real Cool" (1960), "A Bronzeville Mother Loiters in Mississippi. Meanwhile a Mississippi Mother Burns Bacon" (1960), *In the Mecca* (1968) Bernard Malamud, *The Tenant* (1960), *The Fixer* (1966) James Baldwin, *Nobody Knows My Name* (1961), *Another Country* (1962), *The Fire Next Time* (1963), "Going to Meet the Man" (1965) Paule Marshall, *Soul Clap Hands and Sing* (1961) Arthur Miller, *The Misfits* (1961), *After the Fall* (1964), *Incident at Vichy* (1965), *The Price* (1968) Philip Roth, *Letting Go* (1962), *When She Was Good* (1967), *Portnoy's Complaint* (1969) Saul Bellow, *Herzog* (1964) Ralph Ellison, *Shadow and Act* (1964) N. Scott Momaday, *The Journey to Tai-me* (1967), *House Made of Dawn* (1968), *The Way to Rainy Mountain* (1969)	Greensboro sit-in protests begin (1960) Civil rights march on Washington, D.C. (1963) President John F. Kennedy assassinated (1963) Civil Rights Act (1964) Vietnam War (1964–75) Malcolm X assassinated (1965) Voting Rights Act (1965) Black Panther Party for Self Defense founded by Huey Newton and Bobby Seale (1965) Martin Luther King Jr. assassinated (1968)

AUTHOR/TEXT REVIEW

Bernard Malamud (1914–1986)

In Saul Bellow's eulogy to Bernard Malamud, he writes that "a language is a spiritual mansion from which no one can evict us. Malamud in his novels and stories discovered a sort of communicative genius in the impoverished, harsh jargon of immigrant New York. He was a mythmaker, a fabulist, and a writer of exquisite parables. . . . The accent of hard-won and individual emotional truth is always heard in Malamud's words." Along with Bellow, Malamud is one of the most important contributors to the body of Jewish American writing coming out of the 1950s. Like Bellow, he captured the cadences of the speech and manners of the newly immigrated, working-class Jews and used reality and myth to "convey the most intimate details of existence."

Bernard Malamud was born in Brooklyn and graduated from Erasmus High School and the City College of New York. He received his M.A. from Columbia University in 1942 and taught at high schools in New York City as well as at Oregon State University and Bennington College. By 1950 his short stories had started to appear in *Partisan Review* and *Commentary*, and his first novel, *The Natural* (1950), a fable about an injured baseball hero gifted with miraculous powers, added the realm of the mythic to the already popular American pastime. His second novel, *The Assistant* (1957), tells the story of a young gentile hoodlum and an old Jewish grocer. *The Fixer* (1966), the story of a Jewish handyman unjustly imprisoned in Czarist Russia for the murder of a Christian boy, won the Pulitzer Prize.

[7855] Jack Delano, *Children Studying in a Hebrew School in Colchester, Connecticut* (1940), courtesy of the Library of Congress [LC-USF34-042452-D].

In the 1960s, Malamud tackled a subject central to Jewish experience and literature of the era: Jewish and African American relations. During the 1950s and 1960s, Jewish-black relations became increasingly strained as competition for inner-city housing became even greater than before. As anthropologist Karen Brodkin points out in *How Jews Became White Folks and What That Says about Race in America*, Jews had just begun to make the transition into being considered "white" during the 1950s and 1960s; one consequence of this transformation was that many Jews tried to distance themselves from other, less "white" ethnic groups, often in racist and unappealing ways. In *The Tenant* (1960), Malamud plays one minority's experience against another's. Interethnic tensions are also central to Jo Sinclair's path-breaking novel *The Changelings* (1955) and Saul Bellow's controversial *Mr. Sammler's Planet* (1970). These novels by Malamud and others provide an important counternarrative to the civil rights movement of the 1960s. Malamud's later works include *Dubin's Lives* (1979) and *God's Grace* (1982) as well as an important body of short fiction.

■ Before reading "The Magic Barrel," organize a student discussion on the problems of dating and finding a mate. Why is finding a date or a mate so difficult? What qualities do most students want in a date or a mate? What are the qualifications parents would set for the "perfect date" or mate? What mechanisms or customs did people use to find dates or mates in the past? What mechanisms do we use now? Do they work?

QUESTIONS

Comprehension: In what ways does Salzman in "The Magic Barrel" almost seem magical himself? Where does Malamud allude to Salzman's magical qualities? Why might Malamud want to include a sense of "magic" in this tale?

Comprehension: Why doesn't Malamud use a first-person narrator in "The Magic Barrel," as Roth does in "Defender of the Faith" and as Paley does in "A Conversation with My Father"? What are the advantages of an omniscient teller for this particular story?

Comprehension: Malamud was sometimes accused of sentimentalizing the ethnic experience in America. Is "The Magic Barrel" sentimental? What elements of the story complicate any answer to this question?

Context: Like Roth's "Defender of the Faith," Malamud's "The Magic Barrel" gives us a glimpse of a society in transition and of an individual quarreling with the traditional values that support his social identity. Compare the endings of the stories: what remains uncertain for both of the protagonists?

Exploration: Read aloud a sampling of the dialogue in "The Magic Barrel." What is your impression of its cadences, its sound? Are we listening to a conversation in American English? In translated Yiddish? Are we hearing voices in transition, as well as a tale of social values and personal identity? How can you tell?

Exploration: Several times, Malamud reminds readers of the long-standing suffering associated with being Jewish. Where does this suffering come from, historically and culturally, and why does it continue to exist? Why would this sense of cultural suffering be reinforced, especially after World War II?

Ralph Ellison (1914–1994)

Ralph Ellison grew up in Oklahoma City and attended college at the Tuskegee Institute, where he was a music major who admired both the classics of the European tradition and Kansas City **jazz**. After graduation he moved to New York City, where he met Richard Wright, who encouraged him to pursue his writing career. *Invisible Man* (1952), the result of seven years of writing, won the National Book Award and brought Ellison into the national spotlight. Critics disagreed about whether the book made a statement about African Americans, but

[7194] Samuel H. Gottscho, *New York City Views. Financial District, Framed by Brooklyn Bridge* (1934), courtesy of the Library of Congress [LC-G612-T01-21249]. River and New York City skyline. Bernard Malamud grew up and was educated in Brooklyn. Some of his work deals with Jewish and African American relations in the 1950s and 1960s.

[7855] Jack Delano, *Children Studying in a Hebrew School in Colchester, Connecticut* (1940), courtesy of the Library of Congress [LC-USF34-042452-D]. Novelist and short-story writer Bernard Malamud focused on the traits and language of recently immigrated and working-class Jews.

[8855] Eric Sundquist, Interview: "Becoming Visible" (2003), courtesy of *American Passages* and Annenberg/CPB. Professor Eric Sundquist discusses the means by which Jewish Americans became assimilated into American culture.

Ellison felt both sides had missed the point. He had never aimed to be a spokesperson and asked to be judged simply as a writer. After the enormous success of *Invisible Man*, Ellison began teaching, and from 1970 until his retirement he was the Albert Schweitzer Professor of the Humanities at New York University. His essays are collected in *Shadow and Act* (1964).

In the 1930s the communist party attracted much community attention as a force in the civil rights movement, and many African American intellectuals gravitated to it. Ellison found his way into the party because it seemed at the time to be the strongest and most promising force for change in African American life, a major presence in inner-city neighborhoods, with skilled organizers and an agenda that offered hope in the midst of a worldwide depression. Like Richard Wright and James Baldwin, however, Ellison broke with communism when he came to understand that the party, under the control of the Stalinist Soviet Union, was exploiting black Americans rather than genuinely championing their causes. This disappointment with the communist party is a central theme in Ellison's *Invisible Man*, contributing to the novel's pervading sense of alienation and dashed hopes. That mood is also palpable in his short story "Cadillac Flambé," in which a black man acts out of anger not only against the complacent racist remarks of a national politician, but also against his own susceptibility to consumerism, the dream that something purchased, something material, can bring fulfillment and peace.

By the early 1960s, *Invisible Man* was being praised at American universities as the greatest novel by an African American; later in that decade, however, as campus radicalism shook up literary and scholastic life in the United States, the book and its author were faulted for showing too much respect for traditions both literary and social. Ellison's wry humor and his public demeanor were liabilities at a time when artists tended to take themselves and racial politics very seriously. When the politics of the 1960s subsided, Ellison's reputation recovered.

ELLISON WEB ARCHIVE

[7140] Emory, *One of Our Main Purposes Is to Unify Brothers and Sisters in the North with Our Brothers and Sisters in the South* (c. 1970), courtesy of the Library of Congress [LC-USZC4-10248]. Political poster for the Black Panthers. In the 1960s and 1970s, the Black Panthers and black nationalist writers emphasized the need for solidarity among African Americans and people of African descent throughout the world.

TEACHING TIPS

■ Have a class discussion about the links between American capitalism, conspicuous consumption, the expansion of the suburbs, and the postwar era's movement toward **assimilation** and complacency. Also discuss the idea prevalent in the 1950s that, in a dangerous world where communists and enemies of the state lurk around every corner, you are either part of the problem or part of the solution. Discuss the complexities of what happens when you are "not allowed" to fit into or conform within the dominant society. Where are ethnic minorities left at such a time?

■ Ask your students to rewrite a paragraph or two of the Battle

Royal scene from *Invisible Man* using a different kind of narrator—
either third-person or omniscient. Read several of the paragraphs
aloud in class. How does narrative change affect the mood or tone of
the text? Why is perspective so crucial to the scene's power and meaning?

QUESTIONS

Comprehension: In "Cadillac Flambé," what seems to be the implied
threat when Lee Willie Minifee says he no longer wants a Cadillac,
a Ford, a Rambler, a Ninety-eight (Oldsmobile), a Chevy, or a
Chrysler?

Comprehension: Minifee states, "It is enough to make a citizen feel
alienated from his own times, from the abiding values and recent
developments within his own nation." How might this statement
relate to the African American veterans who had just returned from
serving in World War II?

Comprehension: What does the blindfold symbolize in Chapter 1 of
Invisible Man? How does the narrator's limited sight inform the way
we read the story?

Comprehension: Define surrealism for your students and situate it
historically. Ellison likes to place his characters in surreal circumstances: illuminated holes in the ground; lush lawns on which
expensive cars are burning; lurid evenings during which African
American boys beat each other for the amusement of a white audience. What does this surrealism accomplish? Is Ellison focusing on
something particular about contemporary life? What things can
make "real" life seem surreal?

Context: How does the use of the first-person narrator in *Invisible
Man* enhance the reader's understanding of what is happening to
the protagonist during the Battle Royal in Chapter 1?

Context: At the opening of both *Invisible Man* and "Cadillac Flambé,"
the main character portrays himself as essentially alone. If Ellison
means to speak for a large American minority group, what are the
advantages and risks of beginning with an isolated hero?

Context: In the video, John Callahan says that Ellison believed that
"every one of us is black" in a sense. How do "Cadillac Flambé" and
the excerpt from *Invisible Man* convey the sense that something
universal is being explored?

Exploration: Compare characteristics of the various works from the
1950s in this unit. Can you find specific instances of **existentialism**
(writing that embraces the view that the individual must create his
or her own meaning in an unknowable, chaotic, and seemingly
empty universe) in works by Ellison, Bellow, and others? Do these
works seem to differ substantially from works that fit into the categories of literary realism, **naturalism**, or modernism? How so?

Exploration: In *Shadow and Act*, Ellison writes, "I did not know my
true relationship to America . . . but I did know and accept how I
felt inside. And I also knew, thanks to the Renaissance Man, what I
expected of myself in the matter of personal discipline and creative

[7852] Arthur Rothstein, *Tuskegee
Institute, Alabama. Students* (1942),
courtesy of the Library of Congress [LC-
USW3-000237-D]. The Tuskegee
Institute was the lifelong project of
Booker T. Washington and also the site
of George Washington Carver's revolutionary agricultural experiments.
Tuskegee was the model for the college
in Ralph Ellison's *Invisible Man*. Note the
neoclassical architecture.

[7865] Charles Keck, *Statue of Booker
T. Washington* (1922), courtesy of the
Library of Congress [LC-USZ62-
103181]. "I am standing puzzled,
unable to decide whether the veil is
really being lifted, or lowered more
firmly in place; whether I am witnessing
a revelation or a more efficient blinding."—Ralph Ellison, *Invisible Man*. The
narrator's comment reflects the debate
over how African Americans should
be educated. Born into slavery but
freed after the Civil War, Booker T.
Washington devoted his life to the
advancement of African Americans.
Although he was respected by both
blacks and whites, Washington came
under criticism for his willingness to
trade social equality for economic
opportunity.

[8613] Vito Marcantonio, *Labor's
Martyrs* (1937), courtesy of Special
Collections, Michigan State University
Libraries. This socialist publication
describing the "great labor martyrs of
the past 50 years" discusses the trial and
public execution of the "Chicago
Anarchists" who organized the
Haymarket bombing in 1887 as well as
the trials of Sacco and Vanzetti in 1927
and the Scottsboro Boys in the 1930s. It
also talks about the thriving state of the
1930s labor movement. Labor activism
is depicted in Ralph Ellison's *Invisible
Man* and Carlos Bulosan's *America Is in
the Heart*.

[8849] John Callahan, Interview:
"Becoming Visible" (2003), courtesy of
American Passages and Annenberg/
CPB. John Callahan discusses Ralph
Ellison's conception of African influence
on all Americans.

quality. . . . I rejected all negative definitions imposed on me by others." How does this quotation ring true not only with Ellison's writing but also with that of other key figures in this unit, such as Momaday and Roth?

[3048] Anonymous, *Free Classes in English! Learn to Speak, Read, & Write the Language of your Children . . . Special Classes for Educated Foreign Born. N.Y.C.* (1936), courtesy of the Library of Congress [LC-USZC2-946].

BELLOW WEB ARCHIVE

[3046] Lewis Hine, *Old Jewish Couple, Lower East Side* (1910), courtesy of George Eastman House. Upon arrival in the United States, Eastern European Jewish immigrants found themselves faced with difficult questions: which aspects of their ethnic identity should they preserve and which should they reshape? Writers like Abraham Cahan and Anzia Yezierska asked these ques-

Saul Bellow (b. 1915)

Saul Bellow remains one of the most important post–World War II Jewish American writers. Like Roth, Malamud, and Paley, he offers a Jewish perspective on themes of alienation and "otherness" during an age of postwar fragmentation, materialism, and **conformity**. Like Anzia Yezierska and Abraham Cahan a generation before him, he translates the Yiddish American experience into English.

Born to parents who emigrated from St. Petersburg, Russia, in 1913, Bellow, the fourth and youngest child, grew up in the Jewish ghetto of Montreal and learned to speak both Yiddish and English. In 1924 he moved with his family to Chicago, the city that would influence much of his early fiction. He attended the University of Chicago and then transferred to Northwestern University, from which he graduated in 1937 with a degree in anthropology and sociology. He then moved to New York. His plan was to begin graduate work at New York University, but he married instead and eventually moved back to Chicago in 1962. Chicago became the setting for many of his novels of the 1970s and 1980s. In 1993 he accepted a position in the English department at Boston University. Early in his career, Bellow cultivated a friendship with fellow writer Ralph Ellison—an often-forgotten point in the controversy surrounding his much debated stance on Jewish–African American relations and the attacks he endured for the supposed racism of such novels as *Mr. Sammler's Planet* (1970).

Bellow wrote his first book, *Dangling Man* (1944), while serving in the Merchant Marine during World War II and followed it with *The Victim* in 1947. In 1976 his novel *Humboldt's Gift* won the Pulitzer Prize. His analysis of American cultural anxiety and his belief in the possibility of greatness in spite of human frailty and failure are at the core of much of his work. Bellow's prolific output includes the frequently anthologized novella *Seize the Day* (1956), *The Adventures of Augie March* (1953), *Henderson the Rain King* (1959), *Herzog* (1964), *The Dean's December* (1982), and *Ravelstein* (2000). He has also written plays and short stories.

TEACHING TIPS

■ "Looking for Mr. Green" is set during the depression. You may find it helpful to review some of the materials in Unit 12 to help students understand the lingering legacies of the Roosevelt administration's methods of assisting the poor and destitute. You might remind them that during the Great Depression over a third of the U.S. population needed and received government relief just to survive. Also review the state of race relations in the 1950s to understand some reasons why distrust of "the man" (the white man in a position of power or authority) would be so prevalent at this time. Have students put together a slide show using depression-era photographs that might help to illustrate issues presented in "Mr. Green."

■ Have your students build a "character trait" description of the narrator, George Grebe, describing their ideas about his personality and character. Where would he go for fun? What would he do? With whom would he hang out? What would his politics be? What kinds of movies would he like?

QUESTIONS

Comprehension: In "Looking for Mr. Green," why might Bellow name an elusive black man "Mr. Green"? How does that name contribute to the atmosphere or themes of the story?

Comprehension: What are the obvious differences between George Grebe's attitude towards African Americans and the attitude of the Italian grocer? What purpose do these differences serve in the story? What does the author's attitude seem to be regarding racism and stereotyping?

Comprehension: What are readers to make of the ending of "Looking for Mr. Green"? Does Grebe feel a true or a false sense of elation? Does Grebe seem more cynical or idealistic to you?

Context: Bellow was born in poverty in an ethnic neighborhood in a French Canadian city. He graduated from Northwestern University, a prestigious American school. What transformations, expansions, and compromises might be required in making a journey from poverty to an exclusive American institution of higher education? Are the effects of such a journey evident in "Looking for Mr. Green," particularly in the personality of Grebe?

Context: Many of the literary works of the mid-twentieth century focus on protagonists who create illusions of a better world in order to cope with the harsh and unpleasant reality they find themselves in. Can you think of stories where this happens? Do you think this is happening in "Looking for Mr. Green"?

Exploration: Bellow often gives his protagonists unusual names, and assertion of ethnicity is not always the obvious objective. For example, a grebe (*Podicipedidae*) is a small, stocky bird that spends most of its time in the water and is ungainly on land. Why call a protagonist "Grebe"? How does the name affect our response to Grebe? Bellow's naming his character after a bird may remind us of a famous parallel: Washington Irving's Ichabod Crane from "The Legend of Sleepy Hollow." If "Grebe" recalls "Crane," who also goes into a strange place as a confused, over-educated, inquisitive outsider, what thematic parallels should we consider between "Looking for Mr. Green" and "The Legend of Sleepy Hollow"?

Exploration: One of Bellow's favorite themes is that a liberal arts education, the kind acquired with great effort and expense at institutions like Columbia, Amherst, Chicago, Georgetown, and other elite universities, teaches no skills for surviving in the "real" world. How are such American campuses designed to be places apart? When

tions in the early twentieth century, from the perspective of the Lower East Side; later writers like Saul Bellow and Philip Roth reflected on the transformation of Jewish identity in the United States.

[3048] Anonymous, *Free Classes in English! Learn to Speak, Read, & Write the Language of your Children . . . Special Classes for Educated Foreign Born. N.Y.C.* (1936), courtesy of the Library of Congress [LC-USZC2-946]. Sign in Hebrew and English advertising free English-language and naturalization classes aimed at European Jewish immigrants. The classes were offered through the Works Progress Administration's Adult Education Program in New York City. Most Jewish immigrants in New York and other major cities lived in tight-knit communities where Hebrew or Yiddish was spoken.

[6248] Anonymous, *Ginsberg with Classmates, the Columbia Campus Quadrangle* (1948), courtesy of the Department of Special Collections, Stanford University Libraries. Allen Ginsberg had a precarious relationship with Columbia University: as a sophomore, he was expelled for sketching obscene drawings and phrases on his dorm window, which he said he did to demonstrate its dustiness. And although he eventually graduated, Ginsberg's final years at the school were complicated after he allowed an addict friend to store stolen items in his apartment: in order to avoid prosecution, Ginsberg pled insanity and spent eight months at the Columbia Psychiatric Institute.

[9072] U.S. Department of the Interior, *Map of Chicago, 1970* [from *The National Atlas of the United States of America*, U.S. Geological Survey] (1970), courtesy of the General Libraries, The University of Texas at Austin. At the age of nine, Saul Bellow moved from the Jewish ghetto of Montreal to Chicago, where he would reside for much of his adult life. Bellow's "human understanding and subtle analysis of contemporary culture," in the words of his Nobel Prize citation, reflect in part his witnessing Chicago's transformation from a stockyard and rail town to a booming metropolis of business and industry.

you consider the relationship between the landscape of a great campus and the landscape of a major city, what questions can you form about the relationship between education and life?

[8611] Wives of the Hollywood Ten, *For Justice and Peace* (1950), courtesy of Special Collections, Michigan State University Libraries.

MILLER WEB ARCHIVE

[3024] Gottscho-Schleisner, Inc., *Levittown House of Mrs. Dorothy Aiskelly, Residence at 44 Sparrow Lane* (1958), courtesy of the Library of Congress [LC-G613-72794]. The postwar generation saw the development of so-called "Levittowns," homogeneous suburbs that were first conceptualized by William Levitt in response to the postwar housing crunch. These communities were typically middle-class and white. Jewish Americans flocked to the suburbs during this era. Philip Roth satirizes Jewish suburban life in *Goodbye, Columbus*, and Arthur Miller dramatizes the plight of the suburban Willy Loman in *Death of a Salesman*.

Arthur Miller (b. 1915)

Arthur Miller was born in Manhattan to a German Jewish family. His father, a successful clothing manufacturer, lost the business in the 1929 stock market crash, and the family was forced to move to Brooklyn. After working two years to earn tuition, Miller enrolled at the University of Michigan to study journalism and began writing plays as well. Following graduation he worked for the Federal Theater Project, writing for radio, and eventually married Mary Slattery. His first Broadway success, *All My Sons*, was produced in 1947 and won the Drama Critics' Circle Award. *Death of a Salesman* (1949) won the Pulitzer Prize. He also has won Tony Awards, an Obie, and the John F. Kennedy Lifetime Achievement Award and has earned honorary degrees from Harvard and Oxford Universities.

Miller's inspiration for *The Crucible* (1953) came from the McCarthy hearings in Washington, during which those suspected of communist sympathies were subpoenaed to appear before the House Un-American Activities Committee and "confess" as well as name other "suspected" subversives. Miller himself was a victim of **McCarthyism** and in 1957 was convicted of contempt for refusing to identify writers with supposed communist allegiances, a conviction which the Supreme Court overturned on appeal a year later. *The Crucible*, a rather transparent allegory of the communist witch hunts of that era, received unfavorable reviews. Nevertheless, this morally complex play has remained one of Miller's most powerful and popular creations.

Miller is perhaps best known for *Death of a Salesman*, a tragic homage to the average American middle-class, mid-century man, personified by salesman Willy Loman. Alienated from work, community, and family, Loman hungers for prosperity and personal glory but is trapped by his circumstances.

TEACHING TIPS

■ Have your students brainstorm about the many versions of the American Dream. Categorize these versions as a class. Discuss which versions are mostly based on illusion and which are more realistic and possible. Explore for whom they might be possible and who could probably not realize these dreams.

■ In *Death of a Salesman*, Willy says, "The man who makes an appearance in the business world, the man who creates personal interest, is the man who gets ahead. Be liked and you will never want." Discuss with students the differences between character and personality. You might have students explore how Americans once idolized mainly people who had good "character." Then discuss how that has seemed to change to an appreciation for public figures with interesting personalities, or those who are "well liked." After this discussion, apply the conversation to *Death of a Salesman*.

■ Have students consider Willy's definition of masculinity and its dependence on a triad of sexual appeal, work, and sports. This is one of the places where you could discuss what is considered Jewish about the text. When Willy wants his sons not to be bookish but instead to be sports heroes and be "liked," he engages in a classic juxtaposition of Jewish and American conceptions of manhood.

■ Have students view selected segments of *Death of a Salesman* on film. Use these segments as a springboard for discussing Miller's critique of mid-twentieth-century life in America. Note that this play is set entirely in the house and in this sense depends upon classical (Greek) dramatic conventions, in which everything happens around the ancestral house, and we are just told about other events/places. What kind of house is the Loman house? How does it symbolize the action that will take place?

QUESTIONS

Comprehension: Why does Willy Loman continue to idolize his son Biff throughout most of the play?

Comprehension: Does Willy Loman learn anything by the end of the play? Or does he continue to see the world as one of limitless promises?

Comprehension: Examine the role of Linda Loman. Is she typical of a housewife of this era? What do we make of her when reading the play today?

Comprehension: What do Charley and Bernard seem to represent in the story? Are they living a different version of the American Dream? What is their version?

Context: One of the risks of literary naturalism is caricature and condescension. How do the mixed modes of *Death of a Salesman*—its dream-sequences and interludes of surrealism—help it resist these pitfalls?

Context: How important to the play is the design and style of its set? What audience might Miller have had in mind when he wrote the play? Is *Death of a Salesman* a "period piece" about a particular era or a play that can be reimagined as relevant to our own time? How do we account for its perennial popularity in high school and college English courses?

Exploration: Ellison and Bellow fill their stories with the music, food, and popular tastes of Harlem and Chicago. Why are there so few such details in Miller's portrait of the Loman household?

Exploration: Does *Death of a Salesman* attempt to refute the American Dream, as some critics have noted? Is the play devoid of hope? What myths are challenged in this play, and how are they transformed?

[6240] Anonymous, *Look Behind the Mask! Communism Is Death* (n.d.), courtesy of the Library of Congress [LC-USZ62-80757]. Propaganda poster depicting Stalin and a skull. U.S. anti-communism peaked during the 1950s Red Scare. Many political, union, and popular-culture figures were accused of being communists. Writers responded to the Red Scare with such works as Arthur Miller's *The Crucible*.

[6404] Joseph Glanvill, Frontispiece, *Saducismus Triumphatus: Or Full and Plain Evidence Concerning Witches and Apparitions* (1681), courtesy of the Annenberg Rare Book & Manuscript Library, University of Pennsylvania. Fear of witchcraft was widespread in Puritan New England, as evidenced by the Salem witch trials. Nathaniel Hawthorne dramatized this fear in such works as "Young Goodman Brown." In the twentieth century, Arthur Miller made a powerful connection between McCarthyism and America's history of the witch hunt in *The Crucible*.

[8567] Carla Mulford, Interview: "Becoming Visible" (2003), courtesy of *American Passages* and Annenberg/CPB. Professor Carla Mulford discusses the origins of the American Dream.

[8611] Wives of the Hollywood Ten, *For Justice and Peace* (1950), courtesy of Special Collections, Michigan State University Libraries. When members of the movie industry were questioned by the House Un-American Activities Committee in 1947, ten Hollywood producers, directors, and screenwriters refused to testify about their possible communist ties. They were briefly put in jail and then blacklisted from Hollywood studios. The "Committee for the Hollywood Ten" was formed to fight on their behalf.

[8612] Anonymous, *Facts on the Blacklists in Radio and Television* (1950), courtesy of Special Collections, Michigan State University Libraries. By 1950, the number of movie industry people blacklisted had grown to over two hundred. Blacklists were issued by "independent" sources like the Catholic Church and religious/moral citizen watchgroups. These lists usually devastated the careers of those targeted.

Gwendolyn Brooks (1917–2000)

Born in Topeka, Kansas, Gwendolyn Elizabeth Brooks grew up in Chicago. As a child she attended both all-white and all-black schools, as well as the integrated Englewood High School. This background helped create for her a rich perspective on race and identity issues in the city that had such an impact on her work. By the time she was thirteen, her first poem, "Even-tide" (1930), was published, and by 1934 she had worked for and was a weekly contributor to the *Chicago Defender*, in which over one hundred of her poems appeared. Brooks won her first major award, the Midwest Writers Conference Poetry Award, in 1943, and in 1945 her first book, *A Street in Bronzeville*, was published. With her second book, *Annie Allen* (1949), she became the first African American to win the Pulitzer Prize for poetry. Other books soon followed, such as *Maud Martha* (1953), *Bronzeville Boys and Girls* (1956), and *In the Mecca* (1968).

A pivotal moment in Brooks's life occurred in 1967 when she attended the Second Black Writers' Conference at Fisk University, where she encountered young black poets writing "as blacks, about blacks, to blacks." She began conducting poetry workshops for gang members and inner-city black youth and became associated with more militant political groups. Stylistically, she combined the sermonizing style of black preachers, street talk, and some of the more standard forms of verse, and her later work echoes the rhythms of jazz and the combinations of African chants. Brooks's work also addresses issues of abortion, violence, abandonment by men, and the struggles of raising children in poverty. Her penetrating insights into and commentary on African American life, ethnicity, and identity are vividly and powerfully articulated in her poetry and prose.

[7851] Jack Delano, *Chicago, Illinois. A Poetry Study Circle at the South Side Community Art Center* (1944), courtesy of the Library of Congress [LC-USW3-000701-D].

BROOKS WEB ARCHIVE

[3010] Austin Hansen, *Woman and Baby Evicted from Their Harlem Apartment, 1950s* (c. 1950s), courtesy of Joyce Hansen and the Schomburg Center for Research in Black Culture, New York Public Library. This photo's echoes of the traditional iconography of the Madonna and Child comment ironically on life in inner-city New York. Gwendolyn Brooks's work addresses the struggles of raising children in poverty.

[3013] Austin Hansen, *The Apollo Theater in Harlem* (c. 1940s), courtesy of Joyce Hansen and the Schomburg Center. Printed on back of photo: "Exterior view of the Apollo Theatre, with marquee advertising appearances by Jimmie Lunceford and his band and other acts, 1940s." Beginning in the 1930s, the Apollo Theater, in the heart of Harlem, played a crucial role in the development of black music. Famous performers like Ella Fitzgerald and Sarah Vaughan got their first break at the Apollo's Amateur Night. The experience of watching such performers inspired Langston Hughes's "The Weary Blues"

TEACHING TIPS

■ Brooks's work changed during the Black Arts movement of the 1960s. Have a group of students research the Black Arts movement (or read the materials on it in Unit 15) as well as the concept of Black Power and present their findings to the class. In an era in which black men were disempowered, disenfranchised, and often incarcerated, images of black men as strong and influential were particularly empowering. Ask students to consider both the "Black Is Beautiful" cultural program and the self-presentation of leaders such as Malcolm X and Martin Luther King Jr. What strategies do these images share with Brooks's presentation of black male subjectivity?

■ Have students create a poetry family tree for one of Brooks's poems that puts an attribute of the poem on each branch and traces it back to an earlier or contemporary poet. They should define each attribute on their trees and list the influencing poet's name and birth/death dates.

QUESTIONS

Comprehension: Reread "The White Troops Had Their Orders But the Negroes Looked Like Men." What is the "formula" in the first line? To what might a "box for dark men and a box for other" allude?

Comprehension: "A Bronzeville Mother Loiters in Mississippi. Meanwhile a Mississippi Mother Burns Bacon" is a long and unusual title for a long poem. In the poem, details from ordinary life, northern and southern, are interspersed with meditations on the perils of growing up black in America. What holds the poem together? What is the effect of the changes in pace and focus? Why do the lines grow briefer at the very end? You might compare the mixture of the ordinary and meditative here with Romare Bearden's use of magazine and newspaper images in canonical settings.

Comprehension: What is the controlling tone of "We Real Cool"?

Context: What do Brooks's poems suggest about the special challenges of being an African American poet in a time when many other genres and media compete for attention? What do her poems suggest about the challenges of being a poet who deals with social and moral problems? How does poetry, in Brooks's hands, become an effective means for observing and teaching?

Exploration: Brooks's poetry shows the influences of many writers: Walt Whitman, Langston Hughes, Marianne Moore, Claude McKay, Elizabeth Bishop, William Carlos Williams, and the Beats, to name a few. Which of her poems particularly recall the work of one or more of these forebears? Within those poems, what stylistic experiments or other strategies make the work uniquely her own?

Grace Paley (b. 1922)

Of her early writing, Paley notes, "I didn't yet realize that you have to have two ears. One ear is that literary ear," and the other is "the ear of the language of home . . . the language of your street and your people." Such an intuitive ear helped define her as one of the twentieth century's most noted American writers and "urban chroniclers."

Grace Paley was born to Russian Jewish immigrants in New York City and grew up listening to the stories of her family, sometimes told in English, sometimes in Russian or Yiddish. She attended Hunter College and the Merchants and Bankers Business and Secretarial School, although she never received a degree from either. She attributes her political activism to her parents, both of whom were political exiles in Europe and later were active members of a variety of progressive movements. A self-described "combative pacifist and cooperative anarchist," Paley has continued to play an active role in peace, feminist, and anti–nuclear war movements throughout her

and Gwendolyn Brooks's "Queen of the Blues."

[7138] Anonymous, *Leroi Jones (Amiri Baraka) Leads the Black Arts Parade Down 125th Toward the Black Arts Theater Repertory/School on 130th Street, New York City* (1965), courtesy of *The Liberator*. Inspired by civil rights activism and black nationalism, Baraka (Jones) and other African American artists opened the Black Arts Theater in Harlem in 1965.

[7851] Jack Delano, *Chicago, Illinois. A Poetry Study Circle at the South Side Community Art Center* (1944), courtesy of the Library of Congress [LC-USW3-000701-D]. Gwendolyn Brooks's engagement with poetry began as early in her life as her strong association with Chicago's black community. In her early work, Brooks followed in the modernist tradition of Pound and Eliot and in the Harlem Renaissance tradition of poets such as Langston Hughes and Countee Cullen. Following the 1967 Second Black Writers Conference, Brooks began writing specifically for black audiences under the auspices of African American publishers.

[7863] Committee for the Defense of Soviet Political Prisoners, *The Left and the Soviet Union: Is a Broad-Based Left Wing Defense of Soviet Political Prisoners Possible?* (n.d.), courtesy of the Library of Congress.

[3043] John A. Gentry, LCpl, *Vietnam . . . Private First Class Joseph Big Medicine Jr., a Cheyenne Indian, Writes a Letter to His Family in the United States* (1969), courtesy of the National Archives and Records Administration. Soldier from Company G, 2nd Battalion, 1st Marine Regiment, on clear, search, and destroy mission near An Hoa. U.S. military involvement in Vietnam encouraged antiwar protests and distrust of the government. Writer Grace Paley described herself as a "combative pacifist and cooperative anarchist" and was deeply involved in the antiwar movement.

[3296] Dick DeMarsico, *Protesting A-Bomb Tests* (1962), courtesy of the Library of Congress [LC-USZ62-126854]. Demonstrators protesting U.S. tests of atomic weapons. The use of nuclear weapons in World War II prompted a variety of responses from U.S. citizens, including fear, protest, and feelings of alienation.

[6180] United Women's Contingent, *When Women Decide This War Should End, This War Will End: Join the United Women's Contingent on April 24* (1971), courtesy of the Library of Congress [LC-USZC4-6882]. Protest poster against the Vietnam War. The antiwar, civil rights, women's rights, and gay liberation movements were connected politically and artistically. In 1961, writer and activist Grace Paley founded the Greenwich Village Peace Center, which was integral to draft resistance during the Vietnam War.

[7360] Frank Moffit, SPC 5, *Vietnam . . . A Sky Trooper from the 1st Cavalry Division (Airmobile) Keeps Track of the Time He Has Left on His "Short Time" Helmet* (1968), courtesy of the National Archives and Records Administration. Soldier, part of Operation Pershing, near Bong Son. By 1968, many Americans were ambivalent about U.S. involvement in Vietnam. Most of the soldiers drafted after 1965 were troubled by their role in what they saw as a morally ambiguous conflict. A variety of American poets protested the war, including Allen Ginsberg, Denise Levertov, Robert Bly, Robert Lowell, Adrienne Rich, James Wright, and Galway Kinnell.

life. Paley balanced married life, motherhood, and teaching creative writing at such institutions as Sarah Lawrence, Syracuse, and Dartmouth.

Although she began her career as a poet, Paley is best known for her short stories. Her first collection, *Little Disturbances of Man* (1959), while highly praised by novelist Philip Roth, was not an immediate success. It did help her to establish a steady readership that grew over time and positioned her as a contemporary local-color writer. Her second collection, *Enormous Changes at the Last Minute* (1974), was published fifteen years later. Paley's other collections include *Later the Same Day* (1985), *The Collected Stories* (1994), and her most recent, a collection of essays, *Just as I Thought* (1999). Her insight into the complexities of post–World War II Jewish American urban life is vibrant and telling, her characters opinionated, stubborn, angry, and outspoken. Critic John Leonard notes that her writing combines "a Magical Socialism" with "Groucho Marxism." Through her stories, Paley has been able to capture the cadences and complexities of everyday life and give voice to the causes of those who are both American and part of an ethnic community.

TEACHING TIPS

■ Invite a speaker to discuss what it was like to be young in the late 1960s and early 1970s. You could also have your students interview their parents and grandparents about what it was like to be alive during this era. (It would be useful to have more than one generation commenting on what those years were like.) Alternatively, have students volunteer their impressions of hippies, "free love," campus antiwar protests, the drug culture, etc. Then discuss "A Conversation with My Father" in the context of your students' comments.

■ Have students discuss how place or a sense of place affects a person's identity. Ask how they might be different if they had grown up in a different location or environment. Then discuss Paley's story in terms of place and identity.

QUESTIONS

Comprehension: In "A Conversation with My Father," how do the narrator and her father have different concepts of the truth and of what fiction is supposed to do?

Comprehension: "A Conversation with My Father" seems to call into question Paley's own career as a conscientious creator of and experimenter in self-consciously "literary" trends. The narrator's father asks for a simple, readable story: why does the narrator listen to the complaints of an eighty-six-year-old man?

Comprehension: Does the father teach the writer an important lesson about fiction? About life or the relationship of art to life? What does he mean by those last words: "Tragedy! You too. When will you look it in the face?"

Context: Compare the dialogue in "A Conversation with My Father" to the dialogue in "The Magic Barrel." Do you hear differences in the voices? Consider carefully the voice of the writer herself: in becoming a New York artist, has she lost or forgotten something of who she once was?

Exploration: Use Grace Paley's work as a springboard for an exploration of **metafiction**. Read another piece of metafiction, such as Pynchon's "Entropy." Think about whether such works as *The Way to Rainy Mountain* or *Invisible Man* qualify as metafiction.

James Baldwin (1924–1987)

The eldest of nine children, James Baldwin was born in Harlem. An excellent student who read and wrote from an early age, he developed his writing with the encouragement of his high school teacher, poet Countee Cullen. Influenced by his stepfather, a factory worker and Pentecostal preacher, Baldwin originally planned on becoming a minister himself; he composed and delivered his own sermons in a storefront church at the age of fourteen and developed a style that would influence much of his later work. After graduating from high school, he moved to Greenwich Village and began to write full time. His book reviews and essays in *The New Leader*, *The Nation*, and *Partisan Review*, along with the aid of author Richard Wright, helped earn him a fellowship, but his career did not blossom until he moved to France in 1948, where he wrote essays critiquing America's failed promises. Baldwin returned to the United States in 1957, chiefly to join in the struggle for African American civil rights. Not surprisingly, he emerged as one of the movement's most vocal participants, composing powerful commentaries in a style that incorporated the rhythms of gospel and the themes of preaching. His first novels, *Go Tell It on the Mountain* (1953) and *The Amen Corner* (1955), explore both his painful relationship with his stepfather and his search for his racial heritage. *Notes of a Native Son* (1955), *The Fire Next Time* (1963), and "Going to Meet the Man" (1965) helped establish him as a leading black voice of the 1950s and 1960s.

In most of his works, Baldwin intertwines issues of race and sexuality. *Giovanni's Room* (1956), for instance, explores a homosexual relationship between a white American expatriate and a young Italian man. Similarly, *Another Country* (1962) ruminates about what it means to be black and homosexual in a white society. Baldwin explained his diverse thematic interests this way: "I have not written about being a Negro at such length because I expect that to be my only subject, but because it was the gate I had to unlock before I could hope to write about anything else." Although Baldwin's move to France was in response to discrimination and bigotry in the United States, he never considered himself an expatriate. Rather, he referred to himself as a "commuter" with active and vocal interest in racial issues in his homeland. He became one of the most prolific spokespersons for black America, and *Notes of a Native Son* remains to this day a key text of the civil rights movement.

[2256] Russell Lee, *Negro Drinking at "Colored" Water Cooler in Streetcar Terminal, Oklahoma City, Oklahoma* (1939), courtesy of the Library of Congress [LC-USZ62-80126]. Jim Crow laws in the South insulated whites and oppressed and demoralized African Americans. Many black writers, from W. E. B. Du Bois to James Baldwin, examined the negative economic, physical, and psychological effects of segregation in their work and challenged other black and white Americans to do the same.

[3355] Jack Delano, *At the Bus Station in Durham, North Carolina* (1940), courtesy of the Library of Congress, Prints and Photographs Division, FSA/OWI Collection [LC-USF33-020522-M2]. African American man in a segregated waiting room at bus station. Jim Crow laws severely divided the experiences of whites and African Americans in the South.

[4012] Carl Van Vechten, *Portrait of James Baldwin* (1955), courtesy of the Library of Congress [LC-USZ62-42481]. Photographer Van Vechten was an important patron of Harlem Renaissance writers and artists. The Harlem Renaissance laid an important foundation for writers like Ralph Ellison, James Baldwin, Gwendolyn Brooks, Alice Walker, and Toni Morrison. James Baldwin is remembered as a civil rights activist and author of plays, poetry, and novels, including *Go Tell It on the Mountain*.

[5085] Esther Bubley, *A Rest Stop for Greyhound Bus Passengers on the Way from Louisville, Kentucky, to Nashville, Tennessee, with Separate Accommodations for Colored Passengers* (1943), courtesy of the Library of Congress [LC-USZ62-62919]. "If one race be inferior to the other socially, the Constitution of the United States cannot put them upon the same plane," wrote Justice Brown of the United States Supreme Court in the 1896 case *Plessy v. Ferguson*, which upheld the legality of segregation in the United States. Not until 1954, in *Brown v. Board of Education*, did the Court find the "separate but equal" doctrine unconstitutional.

TEACHING TIPS

■ Before they read "Going to Meet the Man," have students research the post–Civil War lynchings that took place in the United States, even up until the mid-twentieth century. They may be surprised to find that nearly two thousand lynchings of African Americans by whites took place in the twentieth century. You may wish to use the story of Emmett Till and his 1955 lynching as a focus of the research. Till was a fourteen-year-old African American from Chicago who was visiting relatives in Mississippi. After an incident where he apparently "whistled" at a white woman in a store, he was found shot and battered almost beyond recognition. An all-white jury acquitted the men accused of the crime. This miscarriage of justice led to demonstrations by African Americans throughout the South and helped to spark the civil rights movement.

■ Show students portions of the 1915 D. W. Griffith film *Birth of a Nation*, which is still used today as a recruitment tool for the Ku Klux Klan and is still taught in film classes for its groundbreaking cinematography. Discuss its racist message and have students research why this film was one of the biggest blockbusters of its time. Make sure to preview the film ahead of time (it is three hours long) to select applicable scenes and to prepare students for its content. Finally, ask them to make connections between the film and Baldwin's story.

QUESTIONS

Comprehension: Baldwin's story is full of sound, with juxtapositions of moaning, singing, and screaming, along with passages pointing out silence. Describe how sound is used in "Going to Meet the Man" to intensify the action and memories and to provide an understanding of Jesse's mental state.

Comprehension: Sexuality, violence, guilt, and hatred are intertwined in this story. What connections do you see among them in Jesse's mind? Why does the story end in the way it does and what is ironic about that ending?

Comprehension: What is ironic about Jesse's relationship with his young friend, Otis? Do you think Jesse's life could have been different if he had more liberal parents, even growing up in the South?

Context: Was publishing "Going to Meet the Man" in the midst of the civil rights struggle of the 1960s an act of special significance? What aspects of the story help you construct your answer?

Context: Do you believe that Baldwin excuses Jesse and his actions in any way because of the culture Jesse was brought up in? Why or why not?

Exploration: More than thirty years after the first publication of "Going to Meet the Man," American writers and film directors are often faulted for imagining the psychological life of someone of the other gender or from a different race or culture. How does Baldwin succeed or fail in his representation of Jesse, a white deputy sheriff in a small southern town?

Exploration: Compare the racism in "Going to Meet the Man" with the racism encountered in a novel (or movie) like Harper Lee's *To Kill a Mockingbird*. What are the differences and similarities?

Exploration: In *Gender Trouble* (1990), feminist theorist Judith Butler argues that gender is not constant but rather is fluid and changes with a given context. In this sense, one "performs" one's gender. Test Butler's theory using Baldwin's characters. Does Jesse's gender depend on the circumstances in which he finds himself?

Paule Marshall (b. 1929)

Born Valenza Pauline Burke to parents who had emigrated from Barbados to New York, Paule Marshall explores the contrasts between her West Indian heritage—a heritage of slavery and colonial exploitation—and her Brooklyn background and confronts the issues of identity and assimilation that face Caribbean American families. Maintaining one's identity and voice while dealing with these issues remains a common theme in her work.

Marshall graduated from Brooklyn College in 1953 and worked for a popular African American magazine, *Our World*. Her first novel, *Brown Girl, Brownstones*, was published in 1959. *Praisesong for the Widow* (1983) established her as a major writer and won her the Columbus Foundation American Book Award. Other works include *Soul Clap Hands and Sing* (1961), *Reena and Other Short Stories* (1983), *Daughters* (1991), and *The Fisher King* (2000).

While Marshall claims that she is indebted to the "literary giants," both black and white, she notes that "they were preceded in my life by another set of giants . . . the group of women around the table long ago—this is why the best of my work must be attributed to them; it stands as testimony to the rich language and culture they so freely passed on to me in the wordshop of the kitchen." Indeed, her early novels focus on the power of the **oral tradition** and the idea of women as oral translators of their culture who are able to define themselves and their world based on their ability to articulate their feelings. In Marshall's works, conversation becomes a means of empowerment, and addressing the spiritual over the material offers important affirmation. Marshall's focus on the Afro-diasporic culture as well as black women protagonists as voices of the immigrant community has opened new avenues of discussion and expanded the concept of what it means to be American.

TEACHING TIPS

■ Before teaching Marshall, have students record an oral history. Instruct them to inconspicuously write down the topics, threads, and themes of a family conversation they overhear, or perhaps a conversation in a dorm or a lunchroom between friends. In addition, have them record the conversation at the same time that they are transcribing it and then compare what they have written to what was recorded. Have them then examine and analyze the dynamics of conversation in con-

[6715] Romare Bearden, *The Return of Ulysses* (1976), courtesy of the Romare Bearden Foundation/Licensed by VAGA, New York, NY.

[4327] Anonymous, *Slave Quarters on St. Georges Island, Florida* (n.d.), courtesy of the collection of The New-York Historical Society. Slaves photographed in front of cabins near the Gulf of Mexico. Slave quarters throughout the South were similar in size and shape, but these cabins were built of "tabby," an aggregate of shells, lime, and sand more common to the Caribbean region. Contemporary writer Paule Marshall's work explores connections between her West Indian heritage and her Brooklyn upbringing.

[6715] Romare Bearden, *The Return of Ulysses* (1976), courtesy of the Romare Bearden Foundation/Licensed by VAGA, New York, NY. Romare Bearden's paintings and collages distinguish him as one of the great artists in the twentieth-century African American aesthetic tradition. Derek Walcott's long poem *Omeros* is a Caribbean retelling of the Odysseus (Ulysses) myth, and Caribbean American author Paule Marshall's writing emphasizes the need for black Americans to reclaim their African heritage.

[7194] Samuel H. Gottscho, *New York City Views. Financial District, Framed by Brooklyn Bridge* (n.d.), courtesy of the Library of Congress [LC-G612-T01-21249]. River and New York City skyline. Hart Crane used the figure of the Brooklyn Bridge to represent modernization's unifying potential; some authors saw technology and urbanization as fragmenting.

[7641] Anonymous, *NAACP Members Picketing Outside the Republic Theatre, New York City, to Protest the Screening of the Movie* Birth of a Nation (1947), courtesy of the Library of Congress [LC-USZ62-84505]. Despite the protests of civil rights groups, D. W. Griffith's *Birth of a Nation* achieved massive popularity.

trast to more formal types of communicating. Try to have them pluck out any serious themes or topics amidst all the casual conversation and remarks. Discuss how they write down colloquial or accented English when it is present.

■ To prepare for Marshall, have groups of students research both the history and the culture of Barbados in particular and Caribbean culture in general. Have them present their findings in class. Then, after they've read "Reena," have them discuss their research in relation to the story's use of characterization and setting.

QUESTIONS

Comprehension: What kinds of pressures contributed to the divorce between Reena and her husband?

Comprehension: Of the stories discussed in Unit 14, "Reena," in which a writer hears about an old friend's life, covers the broadest landscape and the longest expanse of time. Does "Reena" hold together as a short story? How does the narrator create coherence in her account of Reena's adventures?

Comprehension: In what ways is "Reena" a universal story about women in America, rather than an exploration of the lives of urban African American women?

Context: "Reena" ends with a long overview of the modern African American experience, a sequence of paragraphs from Reena herself that read at times like an opinion piece in a newspaper. Comment on how effective you find this overview as the ending to a short story.

Context: Reena and the narrator, who is also African American, speak to each other in dialect only infrequently, and only when they are being ironic. Otherwise, their exchanges are in an English more standard than that used by Malamud's or Paley's characters. Why might Marshall have these intimate friends talk to each other in this way?

Exploration: Compare Marshall's style of writing in "Reena" with the styles of other African American writers, such as Hughes, Hurston, Wright, Brooks, Morrison, and Walker. What is so comfortable and familiar about the way Marshall composes her art?

Philip Roth (b. 1933)

Philip Roth was born in Newark, New Jersey. His father was a struggling businessman for most of Roth's young life, and financial setbacks were not unusual for the family. Roth attended the Newark branch of Rutgers University for several years, then transferred to Bucknell University, from which he graduated in 1954. After earning an M.A. in English literature from the University of Chicago, he went on to teach there, as well as at the University of Iowa and Princeton University, among other schools. In 1959 he published *Goodbye, Columbus*, a collection of five stories and a novella that won the

National Book Award for Fiction. Roth continued teaching during the 1960s and published two somewhat disappointing novels, *Letting Go* (1962) and *When She Was Good* (1967), both of which took him some distance from the topic of Jewish Americans and assimilation, which he had explored so effectively in *Goodbye, Columbus*.

In 1969, Roth re-emerged as an exciting writer with the publication of *Portnoy's Complaint*, an over-the-top exploration of Alexander Portnoy, a neurotic Jewish American male who struggles both to satisfy and be satisfied by the cultural, economic, and sexual demands of American society. After the success of *Portnoy's Complaint*, which challenged the generic boundaries of the **bildungsroman**, Roth composed novels of increasingly fantastical showmanship, among them *Our Gang* (1970) and *The Breast* (1971). In the late 1970s, he began publishing work that has brought him steady attention, respect, and awards. One of his most recent novels, *The Human Stain* (2000), takes up the subject famously found in the novels of Nella Larsen and James Weldon Johnson—that of a light-skinned African American who passes for white.

Roth has been a wanderer—in his upbringing, his various homes, and the subjects he has chosen for his fiction: suburban life, an American Jewish boyhood, the United States Army, baseball, love and marriage, the art and predicament of being an author. He can be funny and poignant about divided loyalties, about growing up and growing away from old neighborhoods and traditions, about friendship, duty, sex, and the mutual exploitation that can characterize a life in which art, business, and show business commingle.

[4764] Anonymous, *Current Photo of Philip Roth* (n.d.), courtesy of Nancy Crampton and Houghton Mifflin Publishing.

TEACHING TIPS

■ Mark Twain once said, "The Jew has made a marvelous fight in this world, in all the ages; and has done it with his hands tied behind him." What role has humor played in this fight? Students might be most familiar with Jewish humor from *Seinfeld*. Or perhaps they have seen some Woody Allen movies. It might be worthwhile to show clips of either. Then have the class brainstorm about Jewish stereotypes and list elements of this humor and what makes it distinctive from and similar to other types of humor.

■ Have your students discuss the manner in which Jews are sometimes portrayed in canonical literature, especially by non-Jewish writers. Common controversial literary renditions of Jewish characters might include Shakespeare's Shylock in *The Merchant of Venice*, Dickens's Fagin in *Oliver Twist*, Fitzgerald's Meyer Wolfsheim in *The Great Gatsby*, and Hemingway's Robert Cohn in *The Sun Also Rises*. Then have your students compare these portrayals to Roth's characterizations. What similarities and differences do they see? How might Roth be playing off these other characterizations?

ROTH WEB ARCHIVE

[3024] Gottscho-Schleisner, Inc., *Levittown House of Mrs. Dorothy Aiskelly, Residence at 44 Sparrow Lane* (1958), courtesy of the Library of Congress [LC-G613-72794]. The postwar generation saw the development of so-called "Levittowns," homogeneous suburbs that were first conceptualized by William Levitt in response to the postwar housing crunch. These communities were typically middle-class and white. Jews, only recently being considered "white," also flocked to the suburbs during this era. Philip Roth satirizes Jewish suburban life in *Goodbye, Columbus*, and Arthur Miller dramatizes the plight of the suburban Willy Loman in *Death of a Salesman*.

[3048] Anonymous, *Free Classes in English! Learn to Speak, Read, & Write the Language of your Children . . . Special Classes for Educated Foreign Born. N.Y.C.* (1936), courtesy of the

Library of Congress [LC-USZC2-946]. Sign in Hebrew and English advertising free English-language and naturalization classes aimed at European Jewish immigrants. The classes were offered through the Works Progress Administration's Adult Education Program in New York City. Most Jewish immigrants in New York and other major cities lived in tight-knit communities where Hebrew or Yiddish was spoken.

[4743] Anonymous, *Roth National Book Award* (1960), courtesy of the Associated Press (AP), Wide World Photos Office. The narrator of "Defender of the Faith," published in Roth's award-winning *Goodbye, Columbus*, makes poignant reference to the contradictions of military service and Jewish assimilation in the wake of World War II.

[4764] Anonymous, *Current Photo of Philip Roth* (n.d.), courtesy of Nancy Crampton and Houghton Mifflin Publishing. Philip Roth's works vary from somber and unresolved questionings of Jewish American life, like his early story "Defender of the Faith" and his later *American Pastoral*, to more fantastical works like his 1971 novel *The Breast*.

[8854] Eric Sundquist, Interview: "Becoming Visible" (2003), courtesy of *American Passages* and Annenberg/CPB. Professor Eric Sundquist discusses Philip Roth's *Portnoy's Complaint*.

QUESTIONS

Comprehension: "Defender of the Faith" is a story about rules and loyalties—to country, to personal heritage, to friends and pseudo-friends. Is the story a situation comedy; that is, is it a story with a stock setting, stereotypical characters, a recurring motif, running jokes, and catchphrases? How would you describe its tone?

Comprehension: In "Defender of the Faith," what experiences and ethics separate Grossbart and Marx? What brings them together? Does Grossbart get what he deserves? Which side of Marx makes the decision—the soldier or the American Jew? Or do both sides of Marx participate in what he eventually decides to do?

Context: In "Defender of the Faith," why might Roth name the narrator and major character Marx? What jokes or ironies are implied by that choice? What Marxes are familiar to Roth's readers, and how does the story invoke or play with those namesakes?

Context: How does the issue of assimilation play into "Defender of the Faith"? What stance does Roth take on assimilation as opposed to hanging onto one's roots, customs, and backgrounds? Why is it hard to tell?

Exploration: Some critics have noted that a number of Jewish writers create stories that demonstrate ordinary people attempting to control their fates, even in a world that seems absurd and uncertain. Simply by making this attempt, whether they are successful or unsuccessful, they succeed. Is this a characteristic only of Jewish writers? Can you think of other works in this unit that illustrate this idea? What about other works from any of the units of *American Passages*?

Exploration: Guilt seems to play a large role in the canon of American literature. What other works focus on guilt? Where does this guilt come from? Are Americans just a guilty people? Of what are they guilty?

N. Scott Momaday (b. 1934)

Writer, teacher, artist, and storyteller, Navarre Scott Momaday has spent his life preserving the oral traditions and culture of Native American peoples. As the only child of Al Momaday (Kiowa) and Natchee Scott (part Cherokee), he grew up on Navajo and Apache reservations in Arizona and New Mexico, though he continued to visit his Kiowa family in Oklahoma. His parents, who were artists as well as teachers, taught in a small school in New Mexico's Rio Grande Valley, and he attended a variety of schools, including reservation, mission, and military, with classmates of not only Pueblo, Navajo, and Apache descent but Hispanic and Anglo as well. After earning his B.A. at the University of New Mexico in political science, he went on to receive his M.A. and Ph.D. in English from Stanford under the guidance of poet and critic Yvor Winters. In addition to visiting professorships at institutions such as Columbia University, Princeton University, and the University of Moscow, Momaday holds honorary degrees from a variety of American universities, including Yale. Well-schooled in canonical American literary traditions as well as Native American narratives, he writes as a member of many worlds, and sometimes as an exile from them all, as he tackles the effects of a post–World War II materialistic culture on his people.

Momaday uses Native American oral and European American poetic traditions, oral and written history, autobiography, and legend to create a rich panorama of Native American life. His first major work, *House Made of Dawn* (1968), is about a Native American who cannot reconcile his Pueblo heritage with city life. This Pulitzer Prize–winning novel heralded the beginning of what many scholars refer to as "the Native American Renaissance." Other works by Momaday include *The Ancient Child* (1989), a novel about a San Francisco artist struggling with his Kiowan identity; three volumes of poetry; three autobiographical works, which include *The Journey to Tai-me* (1967) and *The Way to Rainy Mountain* (1969); a collection of essays, *The Man Made of Words* (1997); and various pieces of literary criticism and works on Native American culture.

[5972] Nancy Crampton, *N. Scott Momaday Portrait* (n.d.), courtesy of Nancy Crampton.

TEACHING TIPS

■ Students may be surprised by the innovative format of Momaday's autobiography and by the way that he moves between myth and personal recollections. In an interview for *American Passages*, Momaday notes that "the voices are all around us, the three voices. You have the mythic and the historical and the personal and then they become a wheel, they revolve, they alternate. . . . Myth becomes history becomes memoir becomes myth." Ask students to prepare for a discussion on *The Way to Rainy Mountain* by reviewing the Momaday interviews in the archive.

■ Today over 11,000 Kiowa live on their reservation in Oklahoma, but Kiowa oral tradition tells of how the Kiowa originally lived and hunted in what is now Montana. The Kiowa are a Plains Indian community. Traditionally, Kiowa have lived in tipis; they have ridden horses since their introduction in the seventeenth century, and each of the six bands has its own Sun Dance ritual. Most Kiowa stories about the self customarily took the form of what critic Hertha Wong has called "communo-bio-oratory"—that is, community-life-speaking (for more on this see Unit 1). These tales include oral stories of counting coup, narrative paintings on tipis and Buffalo hides, and ledger books and pictorial calendars from the late nineteenth century. As early as the nineteenth century, Kiowa art was commissioned for exhibitions. Some of this work, along with more recent drawings, can be seen in the Smithsonian. This tradition has continued into the twentieth century and can be seen in the work of writers such as N. Scott Momaday, as well as paintings by the Kiowa Five of the "Oklahoma school": Spencer Asah, James Auchiah, Jack Hokeah, Stephen Mopope, and Monroe Tsatoke, all of whom studied at the University of Oklahoma in the late 1920s. You may find it helpful

MOMADAY WEB ARCHIVE

[4203] Anonymous, *Protest Against the Bureau of Indian Affairs (BIA)* (1970), courtesy of the Denver Public Library, Western History Collection. Along with the development of contemporary Native American writing in the late 1960s and 1970s, protest movements arose against the discrimination suffered by American Indians.

[5972] Nancy Crampton, *N. Scott Momaday Portrait* (n.d.), courtesy of Nancy Crampton. Momaday (Kiowa) spent most of his childhood on reservations in New Mexico and Arizona, where he was exposed to the rituals and traditions of tribal life, as well as the influence of postwar cultural, unemployment, and alcoholism. Momaday is part of the movement sometimes called the Native American Renaissance.

[5973] Nancy Crampton, *N. Scott Momaday 3/4 Shot* (n.d.), courtesy of Nancy Crampton. Momaday's 1968 *House Made of Dawn* won the Pulitzer Prize and is seen by some scholars as the beginning of the Native American Renaissance. His work focuses on the power of language and place that helps shape Native American identity.

[8106] Anonymous, *Girl's Dress* (c. 1890), courtesy of the Portland Art Museum, gift of Elizabeth Cole Butler. This *hoestôtse*, or Cheyenne dress, is made of leather and incorporates glass beadwork. This style was developed by the Kiowa in the mid-1800s and was copied by other Plains tribes.

[8295] N. Scott Momaday, Interview: "Becoming Visible" (2003), courtesy of *American Passages* and Annenberg/CPB. N. Scott Momaday discusses the relationships among the mythic, the historical, and the personal.

[8861] N. Scott Momaday, Interview: "Becoming Visible" (2003), courtesy of *American Passages* and Annenberg/CPB. N. Scott Momaday discusses the oral tradition.

to begin a discussion of Momaday's work by analyzing the way that a ledger book, winter count, or painted hide functions as a communo-bio-oratory.

QUESTIONS

Comprehension: Look carefully at the two-column sections (set in three different typefaces) of *The Way to Rainy Mountain*. How are we to read them? Simultaneously? One at a time? What does this arrangement suggest about the mind of the writer or the kind of thinking we need to be doing to understand him?

Comprehension: Grandparents played a crucial role in educating and acculturating children. They were important storytellers who communicated Kiowa history, legends, and religion. What role does Momaday's grandmother play in *The Way to Rainy Mountain*? What are you led to expect when Momaday invokes his grandmother early in his story? What do you find surprising in the way that he develops that part of his account? In *House Made of Dawn*, what effect does viewing Able through the perspective of Ben Benally in the third section of the book have on your understanding of Able?

Context: *The Way to Rainy Mountain* contains several accounts of Kiowa history from both a native and a non-native perspective, some of which are offered without much interpretation. Why might Momaday allow these stories to float and flow like this?

Exploration: How do Momaday's works, and Native American works in general, seem to fit this unit? How does Momaday represent local cultures and ethnic differences in his writing? Make a list of ways in which Native American cultural concerns are similar to and different from those of African Americans and Jewish Americans.

Suggested Author Pairings

RALPH ELLISON AND SAUL BELLOW

Ellison and Bellow were friends, sharing a house in rural New England when they were aspiring writers. As artists they were highly suspicious of mass movements, of slogans, of attempts to reduce identity and political questions to simple terms. Both were college-educated and respectful of a literary tradition. In echoing and responding to that tradition as they developed contrarian voices, they received high praise but also resentment from other factions in the modern and contemporary arts. Their works, which are often considered to be early glimpses of **postmodernism**, might also be connected thematically and/or stylistically.

PHILIP ROTH AND ARTHUR MILLER

Unlike Bellow and Malamud, these authors were drawn to the flashier circles of postwar American popular culture—Hollywood, the glamorous venues and residential districts of metropolitan New York, and other places where pop and literary life intersected. Though neither cultivated celebrity himself, both were connected for a time to high-profile actresses. Roth's tumultuous relationship with Claire Bloom is recounted in her autobiography; in his play *After the Fall*, Miller told, in thinly fictionalized form, the story of his marriage to and breakup from the legendary Marilyn Monroe. Over the course of their careers, Roth and Miller have moved somewhat uneasily through many sites and varieties of American life—working-class neighborhoods, suburbs, old New England towns, and the sun-drenched boulevards of Los Angeles and the new American West.

GRACE PALEY, BERNARD MALAMUD, AND PAULE MARSHALL

In the works of these three first-generation American writers, the challenge of becoming American in the years after World War II is intensified by special circumstances, one of which involves being a citizen of New York. The United States's biggest and most powerful city figures significantly in their work: their characters cope with the turbulent action of the streets, the marginalization of the elderly in a fast-paced metropolis, the nurture and segregation of ethnic neighborhoods in outlying boroughs, and the complexities of being literary in a culture obsessed with celebrity. The Vietnam War, the civil rights struggles, and the rise of the American university as an employer of writers and an arbiter of taste are all rich topics for discussion in the context of these authors.

N. SCOTT MOMADAY AND RICHARD WRIGHT

Both of these authors write about young men propelled from the world they know into a violent modernity. Momaday's best-known novel, *House Made of Dawn*, is about a Native American who cannot reconcile his Pueblo heritage with the horrors of war and the rootlessness of city life. Momaday's other works attempt a spiritual homecoming—a rediscovery of spirit and consolation in the traditional landscapes of the Kiowa (Momaday's nation) and other Native American peoples. Also a wanderer in his personal life, Richard Wright never goes home in his fiction or in his memoirs. In his novel *Native Son*, his autobiographical work *Black Boy*, and several of his short stories, a key theme is the protagonist's puzzlement as he faces a bleak and menacing future. Like Momaday, Wright depicts both the mysteriousness and the violence of modern life for people who are hurled into it suddenly, without education, family support, or psychological readiness—and both do so as members of historically oppressed minority groups.

CORE CONTEXTS

With Justice for All: From World War II to the Civil Rights Movement

From James Fenimore Cooper to Ernest Hemingway, American heroes have often been defined by their ability to defeat in battle those things and people considered "anti-American." During World War II, many non-European and non-Christian Americans displayed their patriotism by enlisting in the armed forces. Not only was their enlisting a way to gain—or publicly display—citizenship, but it was also a way of resisting government proclamations about who "the enemy" was. Even as Japanese American families were being interned as "enemies of the state," for example, Japanese American men were enlisting, fighting overseas, and being honored for their efforts. As these servicemen returned home, however, they were often recognized not so much as heroes but as racial "others." These situations have been treated by writers like Philip Roth in "Defender of the Faith," N. Scott Momaday in *House Made of Dawn*, and Ralph Ellison in *Invisible Man*.

These diverse veterans of World War II had hoped that their loyalty and service to the country might demonstrate that the stereotypical and racist attitudes held by many white Americans were unfair and undeserved. As with the war years, the decades beyond the war continued to be a time of segregation and discrimination in the United States. It took a threatened coordinated march on Washington and other major cities by African Americans in June 1941 before Franklin Roosevelt would issue Executive Order 8802, mandating full and equitable participation in defense industries, without discrimination due to race, creed, color, or national origin. This order was, however, rarely enforced over the next few years. Even after the United States entered the war, the War Department refused to integrate military units "on the grounds that it would undermine the morale of white soldiers" (*Oxford Companion to World War II* 5). African Americans who did enlist early during the war were mostly forced into servile support roles in both the army and the navy. The Army Air Corps resisted accepting African Americans until compelled to do so. Eventually, the 99th Fighter Squadron, an African American unit based in Tuskegee, Alabama, would go on to gain fame in the Mediterranean. Many other such units and individuals distinguished themselves in service to their country. By the war's end in 1945, great gains had been made in increased service and command opportunities for soldiers of color.

After the war was over, many minority veterans returned to the United States with expectations of social and cultural change, yet in instance after instance they encountered heavy resistance from whites who were determined to return race relations to a prewar state. Just

---

AMERICANS OF
FOREIGN BIRTH

IN THE

WAR PROGRAM FOR VICTORY

By

Hon. Earl G. Harrison

Including a Special Message from

President Franklin D. Roosevelt

[8600] Earl A. Harrison, *Americans of Foreign Birth in the War Program for Victory* (1942), courtesy of Special Collections, Michigan State University Libraries.

[5079] NAACP, *Sign Reading "Waiting Room for Colored Only, by Order Police Dept."* (1943), courtesy of the Library of Congress [LC-USZ62-120260 (b&w film copy neg.)]

as most of the women who worked in factories during the war were expected to give up their jobs and return to the home, African American workers were also expected to leave industrial jobs that had previously been held by whites who had gone off to war. Fights and riots related to these issues broke out in Detroit, New York, Mobile, and other cities and towns in the United States. Still, by the late 1940s, African Americans had, by working in industry, government, and military positions, made great strides economically, forming the beginnings of a black middle class. Also, in moving to northern, midwestern, and western urban areas to seek better jobs, they left many of the restrictions and the racist culture of the Jim Crow South behind. Many of these themes are seen in the works of Ralph Ellison and Gwendolyn Brooks.

The 1950s would see African Americans and other minorities strive for even more gains on cultural, political, and economic fronts in the United States. In December 1955 Rosa Parks initiated a bus boycott in Montgomery, Alabama, and one year later the Supreme Court made bus segregation illegal. In 1957, President Dwight Eisenhower sent U.S. Army troops to Little Rock, Arkansas, to enforce the desegregation of its public schools. In August 1957, Congress passed the Voting Rights Bill, attempting to ensure equal voting privileges for minorities. In early 1960, the Greensboro sit-ins began, with students protesting segregation policies at a Woolworth's lunch counter. Such protests spread to many other towns in the South. In the 1960s, mostly under the leadership of Martin Luther King Jr., Freedom Rides in the South and marches on Washington helped make the civil rights movement one of the major cultural events of the twentieth century. Still, racial discord and strife continued throughout the 1960s.

World War II also had a major impact on Japanese Americans, especially those living and working in the western United States. With the attack on Pearl Harbor on December 7, 1941, the United States entered World War II. Fears about national security, especially on the West Coast, influenced by racial ideology, led President Franklin D. Roosevelt to issue Executive Order 9066 in February 1942. All persons of Japanese ancestry, both citizens and aliens, were ordered out of the Pacific military zone to inland internment camps. Roosevelt's order affected 117,000 people, two-thirds of whom were native-born citizens of the United States. There was no distinction made between designated aliens from Japan, Japanese immigrants, and second-generation American-born citizens of Japanese descent. Many families lost their homes and possessions in the move, as they were unable to work in order to pay rents and mortgages. The struggling United States economy was greatly affected, as Japanese American farmers on the West Coast had been producing a significant amount of the country's vegetables and fruits. The effects of the Executive Order were far-reaching. Medical and legal licenses were revoked, life insurance policies cancelled, and bank accounts confiscated.

[8522] Ansel Adams, *Manzanar Relocation Center from Tower* (1943), courtesy of the Library of Congress, Ansel Adams Manzanar War Relocation Photographs [LOT 10479-2, no. 8].

independence and civic participation helped bolster women's organizing after the war, including protests for equal rights and welfare reform.

[5079] NAACP, *Sign Reading 'Waiting Room for Colored Only, by Order Police Dept.'* (1943), courtesy of the Library of Congress [LC-USZ62-120260 (b&w film copy neg.)] Martin Luther King Jr. was a brilliant orator. His skill with language was one of his most powerful weapons in the fight for civil rights. King's fight for equality was crucial to ending the "separate but equal" policy that had reigned in the southern states following Reconstruction.

[7865] Charles Keck, *Statue of Booker T. Washington* (1922), courtesy of the Library of Congress [LC-USZ62-103181]. "I am standing puzzled, unable to decide whether the veil is really being lifted, or lowered more firmly in place; whether I am witnessing a revelation or a more efficient blinding."—Ralph Ellison, *Invisible Man*. Ellison's narrator's comment reflects the debate over how African Americans should be educated. Born into slavery but freed after the Civil War, Booker T. Washington devoted his life to the advancement of African Americans. Although he was respected by both blacks and whites, Washington came under criticism for his willingness to trade social equality for economic opportunity.

[8522] Ansel Adams, *Manzanar Relocation Center from Tower* (1943), courtesy of the Library of Congress, Ansel Adams Manzanar War Relocation Photographs [LOT 10479-2, no. 8]. In 1943 one of America's best-known photographers, Ansel Adams, documented the daily life of the Japanese Americans interned at the Manzanar Relocation Center in the high desert of California.

[8523] Ansel Adams, *Loading Bus, Leaving Manzanar for Relocation, Manzanar Relocation Center, CA* (1943), courtesy of the Library of Congress, Ansel Adams Manzanar Relocation Photographs [LOT 10479-2, no. 14]. The Manzanar Relocation Center was one of nine Japanese internment camps. In what would come to be seen as among the greatest mistakes made by the U.S. government during

The inland internment camps were little more than primitive prisons, often located in remote areas. Multiple families were housed in quickly constructed and poorly made barracks with little or no privacy. Some have compared these places to European concentration camps. It took until 1945 for the order barring Japanese Americans from the West Coast to be terminated. Though many Japanese Americans were greatly angered by this treatment and some renounced their citizenship, a large number volunteered to serve in the armed forces.

It was decades before the United States government would admit to its error in this decision. In 1989, nearly fifty years after the fact, President George Bush signed the Internment Compensation Act, which awarded twenty thousand dollars to each surviving victim of the camps. A class-action lawsuit in 1993 also recognized that these citizens' constitutional rights had been violated. Many nonfiction works have been written on the subject of Japanese American internment camps, such as *Farewell to Manzanar* (1973) by Jeanne Wakatsuki Huston. Fiction dealing with this subject includes works like Yoshiko Uchida's *Journey Home* (1978) and Margaret Poynter's *A Time Too Swift* (1990).

QUESTIONS

Comprehension: Why do you think whites, especially in the South, were so reluctant to provide equal civil rights to minorities in the 1940s, 1950s, and 1960s, even to veterans who had served their country well and returned home?

Comprehension: Examine the archive image of the statue of Booker T. Washington, who founded the Tuskegee Institute for Colored Teachers in 1881 in Tuskegee, Alabama. More than 100,000 people were present when the statue was unveiled on Founder's Day, April 5, 1921. Washington, the standing figure, is larger than life. The former slave next to him has an anvil and a plow. The lifting of the veil is said to represent Washington's plan to educate recently freed slaves. How does this interpretation compare to Ralph Ellison's treatment of the veil in *Invisible Man*, chapter 2? Is the veil being lifted or lowered? Compare the veil in this statue to veil images used by W. E. B. Du Bois in *The Souls of Black Folk*.

Comprehension: Who might have benefited from Japanese Americans being placed in detention camps, which led to foreclosures on their homes and prevented them from continuing with their farming?

Context: Besides racism, why might the U.S. government have considered Japanese Americans more of a threat than German or Italian Americans? Could something similar to the internment camps happen today? Why or why not? To whom do you think it could happen?

Exploration: From the perspective of over fifty years, it is easy to look back and see that it was unjust to restrict the civil rights of certain groups. Looking back over the other units of *American Passages*, what do you see that was also obviously unfair? Fifty or sixty years from now, what might historians see as unjust about our society today?

Exploration: Why is it that so much time has to pass before societies can recognize the mistakes of their past? How is the situation of Japanese Americans during World War II similar to what happened to Jewish people in Eastern Europe? How is it different? Can it be equated to the institution of slavery in eighteenth- and nineteenth-century America? All three groups have recently used the legal and political systems to seek redress for these crimes. Why haven't descendants of African American slaves been as successful as members of the other two groups?

Suburban Dreams: Levittown, New York

Levittown, New York, is an enormous middle-income housing development built during the late 1940s and early 1950s; it epitomizes the architecturally homogeneous towns and subdivisions that popped up across the United States during the Truman and Eisenhower years. When William Levitt began erecting low-cost Cape Cod houses on potato fields east of New York City in 1946, his planned community had a population of 450; by the late 1950s, its population was 60,000. Builders liked "housing developments" such as Levittown: their lack of distinctive style made them quick and cheap to construct. Families liked them too, and not just because of their affordability: living in a house allowed for more privacy than living in an apartment building, and certainly allowed more access to the outdoors. At the same time, living in a moderately populated, planned community like Levittown, with its yards opening one onto the other, fostered feelings of instant neighborhood and shared upward mobility.

Not surprisingly, these housing developments tended to contain only white middle-class families. Black families were not welcome, and the sameness of the homes enforced, at least outwardly, the sameness of the lives lived inside them. The explosion of areas like Levittown, and suburban areas outside core cities around the country, came in large part from returning World War II veterans taking advantage of the G.I. Bill. The benefits of having served in the armed forces included money for a college education and a down payment on a new home. Federal Housing Administration mortgage policies and a better transportation infrastructure also helped accelerate the growth of suburbs. For these new homebuyers, many from lower- and middle-class backgrounds, obtaining such a home was partial fulfillment of the American Dream. Still, Levittown, social historians have said, was emblematic not only of the successes of the American Dream in the prosperous years following World War II, but also of its quieter, more insidious failures. As part of white flight from more ethnically diverse urban areas, suburban subdivisions became notorious for continuing and solidifying a trend of ethnic and class segregation across the entire nation, as well as the neglect of economically challenged and rapidly deteriorating city centers.

World War II, thousands of Japanese citizens were held in camps against their will.

[8598] War Relocation Authority, *Relocation of Japanese Americans* (1943), courtesy of Vincent Voice Library, Michigan State University. On February 19, 1942, just over two months after the Japanese bombed Pearl Harbor, President Roosevelt signed the Japanese Relocation Act and created the War Relocation Authority. The WRA removed and detained some 120,000 Japanese over the next four years. Over 60 percent of the internees were U.S. citizens; many others had resided in the country for decades.

[8600] Earl A. Harrison, *Americans of Foreign Birth in the War Program for Victory* (1942), courtesy of special collections, Michigan State University Library. Speech delivered in 1942 by Harrison to the American Committee for the Protection of Foreign Born addressing the special role of millions of non-native-born Americans in the war effort. The speech commends this group's loyalty and help to their new country. Though non-U.S. citizens could not fight in the war, they helped "provide the armed forces and the military supplies to facilitate the development of a second military front on the battlefield of Europe to ensure the complete defeat of the Nazi army."

[3024] Gottscho-Schleisner, Inc., *Levittown House of Mrs. Dorothy Aiskelly, Residence at 44 Sparrow Lane* (1958), courtesy of the Library of Congress [LC-G613-72794].

[3062] Carl Mydans, *House on Laconia Street in a Suburb of Cincinnati, Ohio* (1935), courtesy of the Library of Congress [LC-USF34-000658-D].

[2165] Ludwig Baumann, *Home Furnishings Exhibit* (1952), courtesy of the Library of Congress [LC-G612-62235].

"SUBURBAN DREAMS" WEB ARCHIVE

[2165] Ludwig Baumann, *Home Furnishings Exhibit* (1952), courtesy of the Library of Congress [LC-G612-62235]. "Cookie-cutter" communities like Levittown spread rapidly in postwar America, characterized by not only homogeneous architecture but also homogeneous furniture and lifestyle. Writers like John Cheever, John Updike, and Arthur Miller critiqued suburban life. **[2749]** John Collier, *Store Dummy Displaying Daniel Boone Hat, Fur*

Intrigued and alarmed by the paradoxical nature of these communities, a handful of American writers in the 1950s and 1960s explored the ramifications of life within suburbia. Most were critical. While authors such as John Cheever and John Updike focused on upper-middle-class suburbs and the stifled emotional and intellectual milieu of the WASPs (White Anglo-Saxon Protestants) within them, Jewish American writers looked at the suburbs from a different perspective: both in appreciation of the respite they afforded Jewish Americans striving to leave the chaotic, dirty cities and with concern about the consumerism and conformity that such communities seemed to promote. Most vexing for Jewish American writers was the move away from the expression of any distinctive religious and cultural identity that necessarily accompanied relocation into towns such as Levittown, Scarsdale, or Short Hills. Philip Roth in particular explored the uneasiness of such an assimilated Jewish American suburban family.

In *Good-bye, Columbus* (1959), protagonist Neil Klugman, a Newark, New Jersey, resident, partakes enthusiastically of the tennis courts, houses, and country club girls of suburban New Jersey, only to find that that world contains as much hypocrisy and pain as the cramped apartments of the inner city. Published a decade later, Roth's *Portnoy's Complaint* (1969) harnesses the somewhat fond and lyrical observations of his earlier work to wickedly dissect the suburban American Dream. *Portnoy's Complaint* satirizes the consumption and assimilation that had become the hallmark of the good Jew, especially the good Jew outside of the city. Touching directly on "cookie-cutter" communities such as Levittown, Alex Portnoy's mother extols her nephew, the "biggest brain surgeon in the entire Western Hemisphere," whose genius is confirmed by his possession of "six different split-level ranch type houses." Granted, her annoying praise makes us laugh, but its comical partnering of enormous professional success with duplicate dull-as-dishwater house ownership points to some of the complexities of America's suburban dream, complexities felt early in the remarkable attractions of Levittown. Issues such as the struggle over neighborhoods can be seen in other literary works, among them Lorraine Hansberry's *A Raisin in the Sun* (1959) and Jo Sinclair's *The Changelings* (1955).

QUESTIONS

Comprehension: Why were these planned communities built close to highways?

Comprehension: In what ways might a community in which all the dwellings are the same have allowed for more individualism than city dwelling?

Comprehension: What significance do you see in the fact that fences between yards were not allowed during Levittown's early years?

Context: How might the heritage shared by those who grew up in suburban housing developments differ from that shared by people who grew up in other areas of the United States? Consider, for example, the way Ralph Ellison depicts the city in *Invisible Man*.

Context: If Levittown and communities like it helped empty cities of the white middle class, what effect do you think they had on the areas in which they were built? What do you make of the fact that Levittown was built on fields that had once yielded huge potato crops? Consider the topic of "urban sprawl." How does a story like Bellow's "Looking for Mr. Green" reflect what happens in situations of "white flight" from urban centers?

Exploration: How might writers of different ethnic backgrounds react to a place like Levittown, or any suburb? Read John Cheever's "The Swimmer" and John Updike's "Separating," and compare their various visions of family life outside the city.

Exploration: How do reruns of TV programs from the 1950s and 1960s, like *Leave It to Beaver*, *My Three Sons*, or *Bewitched*, reflect on suburban life? Are there any programs from this era that are set in locations other than the suburbs? Why or why not?

Living with the Atomic Bomb: Native Americans and the Postwar Uranium Boom and Nuclear Reactions

The **Cold War** arms race between the Soviet Union and the United States created a new U.S. need for uranium to be used in the production of nuclear weapons. The Four Corners area of the Southwest, including Arizona, Utah, New Mexico, and Colorado, is rich in uranium, much of it on Navajo lands. Struggling economically after World War II, the Navajo people welcomed the jobs created by a new emphasis on uranium mining. The impact of this Cold War development for these Native Americans and their lands has, however, had devastating effects in the areas of health and environment. A significant number of the men who worked in these mines, most of them Navajos, breathed in uranium dust and were consequently exposed to small but constant amounts of radiation. Many of the mines, in their first years of operation, were very poorly ventilated. The mineworkers, unaware of the dangers, often ate and drank down in the mines. In addition, the men would often arrive at their homes after work coated in uranium dust, exposing their family members to small doses of radiation. Some of the radioactive rocks from the mines were used to rebuild houses in the villages. The mill tailings from the mines entered the local environment, contaminating ground water in the surrounding areas. According to UREO (Uranium and Radiation Education Outreach), today there are nearly 1,100 abandoned uranium mines in this region, with only around 450 having been reclaimed to some extent.

Much controversy surrounds the issues associated with uranium mining. Native Americans point out that the government did not tell the Navajos about the dangers of radiation sickness for the men work-

Trimming Detachable, Suitable for Auto Aerial Plume (Advertisement). Amsterdam, New York (1941), courtesy of the Library of Congress. [LC-USF34-081569-E]. Suburban children in 1950s America were obsessed with cowboys and romanticized stories of the Wild West; one of their favorite games was "Cowboys and Indians," and stores had a hard time keeping coonskin caps in stock.

[3024] Gottscho-Schleisner, Inc., *Levittown House of Mrs. Dorothy Aiskelly, Residence at 44 Sparrow Lane* (1958), courtesy of the Library of Congress [LC-G613-72794]. The postwar generation saw the development of so-called "Levittowns," homogeneous suburbs that were first conceptualized by William Levitt in response to the postwar housing crunch. These communities were typically middle-class and white. Jews, who were only recently being considered "white," also flocked to the suburbs during this era. Philip Roth satirizes Jewish suburban life in *Goodbye, Columbus*, and Arthur Miller dramatizes the suburban plight of Willy Loman in *Death of a Salesman*.

[3062] Carl Mydans, *House on Laconia Street in a Suburb of Cincinnati, Ohio* (1935), courtesy of the Library of Congress [LC-USF34-000658-D]. Suburban scene of houses, street, and sidewalk. This is an early example of the type of suburban neighborhood that flourished immediately following World War II.

[8844] Pancho Savery, Interview: "Becoming Visible" (2003), courtesy of *American Passages* and Annenberg/CPB. Professor Pancho Savery discusses life in 1950s America.

[6635] Skeet McAuley, *Fallout Shelter Directions* (1984), courtesy of Sign Language, Contemporary Southwest Native America, Aperture Foundation, Inc.

ing in the mines and with the tailings. While studies show that cancer rates among the Navajo living near the uranium mine tailings are much higher than the national average, some government studies from the 1980s denied that there was any widespread problem with radiation contamination. Native American writers, from Leslie Marmon Silko to Sherman Alexie, have documented the trouble caused by uranium mining, with many of these pieces collected in *American Indian Literature, Environmental Justice and Ecocriticism* (2001).

Native Americans had other issues to address in the United States. By 1953, Native American unemployment was a major fact of reservation life. The Bureau of Indian Affairs (BIA) attempted to solve this problem by persuading large numbers of Indians to relocate into urban areas, using the lure of job training and housing brochures depicting Indian families leading a middle-class life. While the initial response was enthusiastic, within five years 50 percent of those who moved had returned to their reservations.

Ironically, as with many other minority groups, Native Americans played important roles in helping to win World War II, only to be relegated to their previous status after the war was over. The story of the Navajo code-talkers is a fascinating one. This top-secret project consisted of Navajo men who joined the Marine Corps to allow their language to act as a code in military communications. Classified information was able to be more readily communicated using the Navajo code-talkers than through previous encryption methods. *Windtalkers*, a 2002 movie, uses the history of the code-talkers for its underlying story.

The story of uranium usage and atomic power in the United States also touches on the cultural paranoia that was evoked by a fear of atomic weapons. As Paul Boyer puts it in *By the Bomb's Early Light: American Thought and Culture at the Dawn of the Atomic Age* (1985), "American culture had been profoundly affected by atomic fear, by a dizzying plethora of atomic panaceas and proposals, and by endless speculation on the social and ethical implications of the new reality." The culture of the Cold War, with political adversaries such as the Soviet Union after World War II, and later communist China, convinced much of the American public that a homeland attack was not just a possibility but, indeed, a probability. The arms race became all the more serious after the Soviet Union successfully tested an

[6467] U.S. Army, *Frenchman's Flat, Nev. Atomic Cannon Test* (1953), courtesy of the Library of Congress [LC-USZ62-117031].

atomic bomb in 1949 and developed the hydrogen bomb in the 1950s. Americans and the world were all too familiar with the destructive power of nuclear weapons after they had been used against Japan at Hiroshima and Nagasaki to bring World War II to an end. American policy on the use of atomic weapons wavered over the decades. Truman vowed never to use them again as a "first strike" weapon; but the Korean War caused reconsideration of this policy. Both Truman and Eisenhower maintained that a major stockpiling of atomic weapons was necessary in the face of an expanding communist threat.

The average American's fear of a nuclear attack increased even more when the Soviet Union successfully pulled ahead of the United States in what was the beginning of the "space race" by launching the Sputnik satellite in 1957. Both countries had been improving their ability to launch and control rockets since World War II, and the success of Sputnik added to the fear that a Soviet attack could come from outer space itself.

The government and the popular press urged average Americans to construct their own backyard bomb shelters to protect against a nuclear attack. Magazines such as *Popular Mechanics* and *Life* ran articles about shelter designs and described how Americans could seek refuge from falling atomic bombs. Many public and government buildings were designated as nuclear fallout shelters, and schools and civic organizations regularly practiced defensive drills for a possible attack. In "Cultural Aspects of Atomic Anxiety," Alan Filreis suggests that "the bomb generally made mid-century Americans fear more acutely what they always already feared: that things that had been whole in their lives would now split, and that such splitting could not be controlled. Fragmentation was one fear. The loss of control was another. The bomb symbolized the two fears in one." Fragmentation, disjunction, and broken verse were modernist innovations (e.g., the poetry of Gertrude Stein or the visual break-up in cubist paintings); however, the atomic bomb "took cultural or aesthetic aspects of modern life—a 'modernism' that could be safely imagined as something threatening but very far-off or at least contained, in Paris or New York—and seemed now to bring that incoherence dramatically home, or, indeed, into the home."

In late 1962, the United States and the Soviet Union stood on the edge of an all-out nuclear conflict due to the Cuban missile crisis. The Soviet Union had constructed a number of missile sites within Cuba, allowing for a much quicker first strike against the U.S. mainland. The United States demanded that these weapons be removed, and over the course of thirteen days of threats and negotiations, Americans prepared for a nuclear war. This incident marked perhaps the height of American fears of nuclear annihilation. Just a few years later, movies such as *Dr. Strangelove* (1964) and *Fail-safe* (1964) demonstrated how these fears continued to be a part of the culture of the times. Interestingly, the documentary film *The Atomic Café* (1982) nostalgically explores the world of living with the atomic bomb during the 1950s and 1960s.

QUESTIONS

Comprehension: Many U.S. citizens make sacrifices during times of war in order to support their country. What is unique about the sit-

Navajo men, struggling economically after the war, took jobs mining uranium in the 1950s, with no warning about the dangers associated with working in these mines. Writers such as Leslie Marmon Silko and Sherman Alexie have documented the trouble caused by uranium mining.

[6467] U.S. Army, *Frenchman's Flat, Nev. Atomic Cannon Test* (1953), courtesy of the Library of Congress [LC-USZ62-117031]. Atomic detonation and resulting fireball. After the United States dropped atomic bombs on Japan during World War II, poets, novelists, and other artists began to explore the ethical issues surrounding the use of such weapons. John Hersey's *Hiroshima* depicts the horrors of August 6, 1945, in Hiroshima.

[6635] Skeet McAuley, *Fallout Shelter Directions* (1984), courtesy of "Sign Language, Contemporary Southwest Native America" Aperture Foundation, Inc. Nuclear weapons have been tested in the Southwest for over half a century. For writers like Leslie Marmon Silko, weapons-testing is not respectful to the natural world and dims humanity's hopes for renewal and regeneration.

[3075] William P. Gottlieb, *Portrait of Billie Holiday and Mister Downbeat, New York, N.Y.* (1947), courtesy of the Library of Congress, American Memory, William P. Gottlieb Collection [LC-GLB23-0428 DLC].

uation of Native Americans and their support of the country during World War II and the Cold War?

Comprehension: Why did Americans have such a fear of atomic destruction in the 1950s and 1960s?

Context: How does knowing what we do about most Native American tribes' relationship with the land shape our understanding of both the uranium mining and the relocation program?

Context: How does the move of many Native Americans to urban areas compare to migration patterns of other minority groups during this era?

Context: How honest was the American government with ordinary citizens in its approach to civil defense during the 1950s and 1960s? Could practicing "duck and cover" drills in schools, going to designated government basement bomb shelters, and building backyard shelters really have helped people during a nuclear attack? Why might the government have found this approach helpful? Could it have led to a suspicion of government, as might be seen in Arthur Miller's *The Crucible* or Ralph Ellison's *Invisible Man*, in which the narrator ends up living in an underground "shelter" of sorts?

Exploration: What problems were faced by African Americans, Native Americans, and Japanese Americans who remained in the United States during the war? How were those problems similar to and different from the problems faced by minority veterans when they returned? You might also want to compare the portrait of Native American veterans in Momaday's fiction with that of Jewish military men in Roth's short story "Defender of the Faith."

Exploration: John Hersey's book *Hiroshima* depicts the horrific and altered lives of six individuals who survived the atomic bombing of Hiroshima in August 1945. This story was first published in the *New Yorker* magazine in 1946 as an extended article. The book was a best-seller. How might its publication have led to an increased dread of an atomic attack by the American public?

EXTENDED CONTEXTS

Jazz Aesthetics

Though twenty-first-century American youth may associate jazz with "easy listening," it is important to consider jazz's revolutionary influence on the literature and aesthetics of the 1950s and 1960s. For American writers of this era, jazz referred not only to a musical style but also to a style of dance, literature, dress, and art. Jazz's rebellion could be felt in the freedom of **improvisation**, as well as the ability to take old melodies, split them apart, and make them fit a new rhythm and a new worldview.

The history of jazz is rich and complex. As a musical art form, its roots go back to African and African American musical traditions, spanning tribal drumming, slavery field chants, gospel, ragtime, and the blues. Once it entered the mainstream, jazz and the blues, often referred to together, quickly became recognized as one of the first truly original American art forms. In the 1920s, a time known as the "Jazz Age," and beyond, this musical form has enjoyed a widespread public popularity in the United States and Europe.

There are a variety of jazz styles, but most jazz is characterized by improvisation. Rhythmic jazz typically has a forward momentum called "swing" and uses "bent" or "blue" notes. Jazz often includes "call-and-response" patterns in which one instrument, voice, or part of the band answers another. Jazz musicians place a high value on finding their own sound and style, and that means, for example, that trumpeter Miles Davis sounds very different from trumpeter Louis Armstrong. Since jazz musicians play their songs in their own distinct styles and often improvise, a dozen different jazz recordings of the same song will each sound different.

The influences of jazz on the literature of the 1950s were extensive. Langston Hughes, Gwendolyn Brooks, Ralph Ellison, and James Baldwin were among the midcentury writers who incorporated jazz motifs into their works. The use of jazz may also apply more generally to postmodern notions of pastiche and rebellion. Visual artists, such as Romare Bearden, were also influenced by jazz and used it as a subject in their work.

[5479] Winold Reiss, *Drawing in Two Colors* (c. 1920), courtesy of the Library of Congress [LC-USZ64-5687].

QUESTIONS

Comprehension: How might the "improvisation" of jazz have a direct bearing on the sense of improvisation that occurs in postmodern literature?

Context: In Ellison's *Invisible Man*, what "melodies" from literature, art, music, and culture does the narrator quote? How does he remake them? You may want to begin with his use of Louis Armstrong's "Black and Blue," or compare Ellison's narrative style to other works of jazz, dance, or art.

Exploration: One writer who continuously demonstrates the influences of jazz and the blues in his poetry is Langston Hughes. Read some of Hughes's poems aloud and try to determine how this music influences his writing. Compare what Hughes does in his poetry to the prose styles of Ellison and Baldwin. Are there similarities?

Baseball: An American Pastime

When Alexander Cartwright, founder of the New York Knickerbockers team, published rules for his baseball team in 1845, a new national pastime was born. The game of baseball gained popularity throughout the rest of the nineteenth century and was featured in Mark Twain's 1889 novel *A Connecticut Yankee in King Arthur's Court*. During the second half of the nineteenth century, playing baseball became an important symbolic activity in America, as teams tied together communities and defined a new way of belonging or not belonging. As

"JAZZ AESTHETICS" WEB ARCHIVE

[3071] William P. Gottlieb, *Portrait of Ella Fitzgerald, Dizzy Gillespie, Ray Brown, Milt (Milton) Jackson, and Timmie Rosenkrantz, Downbeat, New York, N.Y.* (1947), courtesy of the Library of Congress, American Memory, William P. Gottlieb Collection [LC-GLB23-0285 DLC]. During the 1940s and 1950s, America was still a segregated nation, but jazz was one of the few areas where African Americans were accorded respect, and black and white musicians played together.

[3074] William P. Gottlieb, *Portrait of Louis Armstrong, Carnegie Hall, New York, N.Y.* (1947), courtesy of the Library of Congress, American Memory, William P. Gottlieb Collection [LC-GLB23-0024 DLC]. Audiences and musicians have called Armstrong the greatest jazz musician of all time. Raised in New Orleans, the birthplace of jazz, Armstrong was a huge influence on jazz and on later trumpet players such as Miles Davis and Dizzy Gillespie. Equal parts great musician and performer, he was sometimes criticized for his shuffle-along down-South stage personality "Satchmo." See "Note on Commercial Theatre" by

Langston Hughes for a comment on the "whiting" of black culture. Jazz was crucial to the poetry of the Black Arts movement.

[3075] William P. Gottlieb, *Portrait of Billie Holiday and Mister Downbeat, New York, N.Y.* (1947), courtesy of the Library of Congress, American Memory, William P. Gottlieb Collection [LC-GLB23-0428 DLC]. Known as "Lady Day," jazz legend Billie Holiday got her start in obscure Harlem nightclubs. The white gardenias in her hair in this photo were one of her trademarks. Gottlieb's collection includes portraits of jazz greats such as singers Sarah Vaughan and Cab Calloway, guitarist Django Reinhardt, and pianist Art Tatum. For a depiction of female blues singers, see Gwendolyn Brooks's "Queen of the Blues."

[3548] Anonymous, *Louis Armstrong Conducting Band, NBC Microphone in Foreground* (1937), courtesy of the Library of Congress [LC-USZ62-118977]. Louis Armstrong was one of the best-known jazz musicians of the 1930s. Jazz was an important theme in modernist writing and visual art. Jazz trumpeter Valaida Snow, nicknamed "Little Louis" due to her Armstrong-like playing style, is eulogized in Colleen McElroy's poem "It Ain't Blues That Blows an Ill Wind."

[5479] Winold Reiss, *Drawing in Two Colors* (c. 1920), courtesy of the Library of Congress [LC-USZC4-5687]. Offset lithograph of African American man dancing. Also titled *Interpretation of Harlem Jazz I*. German-born Winold Reiss (1886–1953) studied in Munich before moving to New York in 1913. He is best known for his portraits of African Americans and Native Americans. Poets, novelists, and painters incorporated imagery and rhythms from jazz in their work. In 1924 Aaron Douglas began studying with Reiss: the style and colors of Douglas's work reflect Reiss's influence.

early as the 1880s and 1890s, immigrants learned to play baseball in order to shed their greenhorn status and to show their enthusiasm for something truly American. This transformation is recounted in Chaim Potok's *The Chosen* (1967) and Anzia Yezierska's *Bread Givers* (1925).

The turn of the century saw the creation of the American League and the two-league system that we are familiar with today. Though professional baseball players in the early part of the twentieth century were largely drawn from colleges, by the 1920s professional players were much more likely to come from the lower and middle classes. Sons of immigrants and midwestern farm boys could rise through the expanding professional farm system and eventually shine on the diamond. These rising stars in baseball helped solidify yet another version of the popular "rags to riches" story. In the 1950s, a number of teams finally moved west, to Milwaukee, Kansas City, and Los Angeles, making the sport more locally available to a wider audience. Baseball often mirrored society at large and reflected its overall attitudes, values, and trends. Organized baseball was racially segregated for decades after its creation. Many cities created their own separate Negro baseball teams that featured outstanding players such as Cool Papa Bell, Josh Gibson, and Satchel Paige.

World War II caused people to question segregation practices and led to the opening of the game to new types of players. One important wartime innovation was the All-Girls Professional Baseball League, in existence from 1943 to 1954. Since many professional male ballplayers and other young men were off serving in the military, women were recruited to play baseball on teams mostly located throughout the Midwest. However, these careers, too, reflected trends in society at large. The codes of conduct and rules of play for these women were much different than they were for male professional players. When the men returned from the war, women baseball players were expected to return to their previous professions and lives, as were the women who took over assembly-line work during the war.

In 1947 Jackie Robinson (1919–1972) became the first African American to officially play in the major leagues. His breaking of the color line was just the beginning of a long struggle for equal status and pay. Racist comments, hate mail, segregated housing, and death threats were to be an everyday part of the game for African American major league players for years to come. When Hank Aaron broke Babe Ruth's home run record in 1974, he too received racial slurs and death threats. It wasn't until the 1980s and 1990s that African Americans entered the ranks of major league baseball management. The game of baseball tended to reflect in a highly visible public forum some of the backlash against the civil rights movement and the exclusion of people of color from other venues of society.

Jewish players had not been strictly prevented from playing baseball—Hank Greenberg played for the Detroit Tigers in the 1930s and made no effort to hide his religion—but Sandy Koufax, a pitcher for the Dodgers from 1955 to 1960, proved that Jews too could be sports heroes in American postwar culture. Other Jewish players also made a name for themselves. Buddy Myer, an infielder for the Senators, won the batting title in 1935. Al Rosen was a four-time All Star third baseman for the Indians in the 1950s, and Steve Stone, pitching for Baltimore, won the 1980 Cy Young Award. Chaim Potok's novel *The Chosen* begins its investigation into the conflict between modern orthodox and Hasidic Jews with a baseball game played by teams from the two groups.

Baseball not only reflected changes in race relations in this country, but also brought the subject of labor relations into a much broader cultural context. The "reserve clause" in baseball basically bound a player to one team throughout his career. It took away any right of "free agency," whereby a player could offer himself to the highest bidder. A Supreme Court ruling in November 1953 kept baseball's exemption from antitrust laws in place and the reserve clause in effect. In 1964, players formed a union, the Major League Baseball Players Association, and it took twenty-five more years before a form of "free agency" became available to major league players. These struggles between players and team owners reflect some of the conflict that occurred between labor unions and industry or powerful landowners that is discussed in Unit 12.

Not surprisingly, baseball functions as an important trope in the literature of this era. It stands as an icon for something truly "American." It also, along with other sports, emphasizes the skills and importance of the individual along with the necessity of group organization and collaborative cooperation. Many major American writers have used baseball as subject matter, as exemplified by Ring Lardner's *You Know Me, Al*, Bernard Malamud's *The Natural*, and Philip Roth's *The Great American Novel*.

[1992] Anonymous, *African American Baseball Players of Morris Brown College, with Boy and Another Man Standing at Door, Atlanta, Georgia* (c. 1900), courtesy of the Library of Congress [LC-USZ62-114266 DLC].

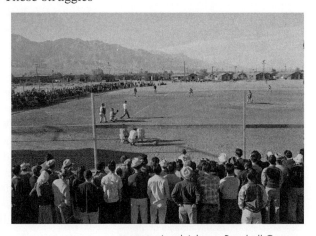

[8526] Ansel Adams, *Baseball Game* (1943), courtesy of the Library of Congress, Ansel Adams Manzanar War Relocation Photographs [LOT 10479-4, no. 22].

QUESTIONS

Comprehension: In what ways does the history of baseball in the United States play off the American Dream?

Comprehension: How does baseball reflect other aspects of American culture?

Comprehension: Baseball is an important symbol of American-ness in *Invisible Man* and *Goodbye, Columbus*. What made baseball such an important symbol of American culture?

Context: How are the individual and collaborative aspects of baseball reflective of important elements of American society at large?

Exploration: Baseball is just one example of America's preoccupation with sports and entertainment. Why do you think American culture has this keen interest? What function do sports and entertainment play in your own life? How are sports and entertainment similar to and different from literature and the arts?

"BASEBALL" WEB ARCHIVE

[1992] Anonymous, *African American Baseball Players of Morris Brown College, with Boy and Another Man Standing at Door, Atlanta, Georgia* (c. 1900), courtesy of the Library of Congress [LC-USZ62-114266 DLC]. At this traditionally African American institution in Atlanta, baseball has a long and proud history. During the second half of the nineteenth century, playing baseball became an important symbolic activity in America, as teams tied together communities and defined a new way of belonging. The sport was featured in novels such as Mark Twain's *A Connecticut Yankee in King Arthur's Court* (1889).

[5162] Dorothea Lange, *Fourth of July, near Chapel Hill, North Carolina* (1939), courtesy of the Library of Congress [LC-USF34-020010-E DLC]. Although baseball had been played widely throughout the United States, using local rules, since the early 1800s, it is said to have been "invented" when Alexander Cartwright formulated formal rules and regulations in 1845; by the 1860s it was widely thought of as America's "national pastime." People from all walks of life played baseball, from immigrants in the late nineteenth century to the depression-era men pictured here.

[6732] Kenji Kawano, *Navajo Indian Boys Playing Baseball* (2001), courtesy of Kenji Kawano. For over two centuries, baseball has been a popular American sport that has attracted players from a number of ethnic, cultural, and economic backgrounds. It wasn't until 1947, however, that major league baseball allowed non-white players.

[8500] Anonymous, *Gary Works Baseball Team* (1912), courtesy of the Calumet Regional Archives, Indiana University Northwest. Members of the baseball team sponsored by the U.S. Gary Steel Works in Indiana. Workers tried out for such teams and practiced in their free time.

[8526] Ansel Adams, *Baseball Game* (1943), courtesy of the Library of Congress, Ansel Adams Manzanar War Relocation Photographs [LOT 10479-4, no. 22]. Photograph of a baseball game in one of the Japanese internment camps. In spite of the discrimination against Japanese Americans during World War II, many claimed to wish for a chance to prove their loyalty.

ASSIGNMENTS

Personal and Creative Responses

1. *Journal and Letters:* Study some of the stories of the Tuskegee airmen of World War II. Write a letter in the voice of an African American airman at Tuskegee to someone back home. Try to imagine what it was like for a black person who had risked his life in combat, only to encounter continued racism and segregation at the airbase in Alabama. What would the atmosphere have been like? What kinds of frustrations might these airmen have encountered? What would have surprised or pleased them?

2. *Journal:* When in your life have you not fit in? How did you feel? What did you do about it? Conversely, think of instances in your life when you conformed to the expectations of society or close friends or family, without thinking about it too much. After having studied this unit, can you re-evaluate those moments of conformity? Were they mostly good or bad? Would you do the same thing again today?

3. *Journal:* Write a story from the point of view of a young person waiting inside a bomb (fallout) shelter with his or her immediate family after a possible attack warning has been issued. What would life in the bomb shelter be like? What would your concerns be?

4. *Poet's Corner:* Reread Gwendolyn Brooks's "We Real Cool." Choose a topic of your own and write a poem that imitates this style. Think about Brooks's choice of subject matter. What does her language sound like? What are the features of her verse? After you've completed your poem, write a short paragraph analyzing what you have written. What characteristics of Brooks were you trying to capture?

5. *Poet's Corner:* Write a short poem that takes on the point of view of someone who remains culturally "invisible." Perhaps the poem might show why the person actually wishes to remain invisible or perhaps it will be a lament to the ongoing invisibility.

6. *History:* After reading Momaday's *Way to Rainy Mountain*, put together a smaller project that unites your own culture, family history, and personal outlook. Use prose passages, poems, family histories and genealogies, photos, even stories from friends and anything else that helps you toward an understanding of your place within your family, your past, the places you've lived, the things you've done, and your culture.

7. *History:* Interview family members who were adults or children during the 1950s and 1960s. How do they characterize their experiences? Did men and women respond differently to the threat of nuclear attack? How did children cope with the daily fear of annihilation? Did anyone in your family build a bomb shelter?

8. *History:* Do some research on James Meredith, the first African American student to enroll at the University of Mississippi, in October 1962, and the resulting riot. Where did Meredith come from? Why did he put himself at so much personal risk to enroll at Ole Miss? How did the Kennedy administration get involved? How

does this early desegregation contrast with the recent trend of resegregating many state universities?

9. *Multimedia:* Using the *American Passages* archive, along with images available on the web (hint: use <www.google.com> and click on the "images" tab), and slide-show software, create a multimedia presentation of photos and paintings that illustrate the struggle for civil rights in the 1950s and 1960s. Write a caption for each image, explaining how the image relates to the civil rights movement.

Problem-Based Learning Projects

1. Much of this unit underscores the pressure that many people have felt to "fit in" and to "be an American"; it is ironic that a good portion of "an American's" qualities include being individualistic and self-reliant. Imagine that you are part of a major advertising agency. Your firm needs to decide whether "conformity" or "independence" sells better. Research advertisements from the popular magazines of the 1950s (*Life, Newsweek, Time*), and put together a presentation that either confirms the pressures of conformity or demonstrates a trend toward individualism.

2. You are part of a team asked to make a presentation to the U.S. Congress. The United States has never established a "national language," and today the country is recognized as being more multicultural than ever before. Still, every few years, politicians attempt to make English the "standard" legal language of the country. Prepare a presentation to be offered at a congressional subcommittee hearing that addresses this issue. Argue either for establishing English as the national language or for recommending that such a proposal be voted down.

3. The year is 1961 and you have been sent to cover the Greensboro sit-ins as a reporter. Write a magazine article in which you describe the protests. Why were the demonstrators so upset? What were their arguments? What were the arguments of the store owners and the townspeople who disagreed with the protests? Now imagine that you must present both sides of the issue to different audiences. Rewrite the article so that you can sell it to a northern liberal pro–civil rights magazine; then rewrite the article so that you can sell it to a conservative small-town magazine with mostly southern white readers. What will you need to emphasize and de-emphasize? Are you able to present all the facts in both versions of the article? Why or why not?

4. Debate has broken out among city council members because one of the oldest trees in the county, just inside the city limits, needs to be cut down for a developer to put in a parking lot. However, a contingent of African Americans want the tree preserved because it marks the location of a lynching that occurred there in the early 1940s. Research mid-century lynchings in the United States. Then write an essay that takes a stand on whether or not the tree should be

kept. Be sure to draw on your research and to consider other points of view.

GLOSSARY

assimilation   Becoming part of the dominant culture and leaving behind characteristics and qualities that would designate one as different or "other."

bildungsroman   A novel of formation or growth into maturity; a novel of education and an awakening from the innocence of youth.

Cold War   A period following World War II up to the dissolution of the Soviet Union, when communist and democratic countries vied for political control of and influence in the world. The period was marked by a nuclear arms race that guaranteed "mutual annihilation" if either side used its weapons of mass destruction.

conformity   Going along with the popular beliefs, trends, and attitudes of the dominant society of the time.

existentialist writing   Literature that embraces the view that the individual must create his or her own meaning in an unknowable, chaotic, and seemingly empty universe. French author Albert Camus proposes that in such a world, one may decide either that all efforts are futile or that the mere struggle to continue in such an absurd universe is an act of creation in itself.

improvisation   The act or art of composing and rendering music or poetry extemporaneously, in a unique or individual manner.

jazz   Music in which improvisation and soloing play an important part. There is tremendous variety in jazz, but most jazz is very rhythmic, has a forward momentum called "swing," and uses "bent" or "blue" notes. You can often hear "call-and-response" patterns in jazz, in which one instrument, voice, or part of the band answers another.

McCarthyism   Related to the period during the Cold War during which Senator Joseph McCarthy and the House Un-American Activities Committee sought out American citizens who were suspected of being members or former members of, or sympathizers with, the communist party.

metafiction   Fiction that self-consciously refers to writing and its conventions.

naturalism   Late-nineteenth- and early-twentieth-century literary approach of French origin that realistically depicts social problems and views human beings as helpless victims of larger social and economic forces.

novel of identity   Novel that addresses the question of "who am I" and "how do I fit into the society around me."

oral tradition   The passing on of oral culture, tradition, and history from one generation to the next, through stories told time and again. Oral tradition did not, and does not, cease to exist with the rise of literacy; it co-exists, especially in cultures that retain a strong sense of oral dissemination of information and culture.

postmodern literature   Literature that responds to, and is written in the context of, philosophical and socio-historical movements that challenge the progress-oriented master narratives of Enlightenment and positivist traditions. At the beginning of the twentieth century, linguists and philosophers questioned the possibility that language can truly reflect reality, or that any essential, categorical, or transcendental truth claims can be made about the world. From the unspeakable violence of the Holocaust, to the assertion of gender and other personal traits as being malleable and socially constructed, postmodernism has sought to explain the many uncertainties, ironies, contradictions, and multiple points of view that animate the world. Postmodern literature is often consciously self-reflexive, questioning the nature of the text and the authority and existence of the author, and uses techniques like pastiche, metanarrative, nonlinear constructions, absurdity, and irony. Postmodernism is at once a literary style, a critical and theoretical movement, and a description of the sociocultural world of globalized consumer capitalism.

SELECTED BIBLIOGRAPHY

Adamson, Joni. *American Indian Literature, Environmental Justice, and Ecocriticism*. Phoenix: U of Arizona P, 2001.

Boyer, Paul. *By the Bomb's Early Light: American Thought and Culture at the Dawn of the Atomic Age*. New York: Pantheon Books, 1985.

Coontz, Stephanie. *The Way We Never Were*. New York: Basic Books, 1992.

Dear, I. C. B., ed. *Oxford Companion to World War II*. Oxford: Oxford UP, 1995.

Ellison, Ralph. *Shadow and Act*. New York: Vintage, 1972.

Filreis, Alan. "Cultural Aspects of Atomic Anxiety." <dept.english.upenn.edu/~afilreis/50s/atomic-anxieties.html>. The Literature and Culture of the American 1950s [computer file and Web site]. Philadelphia: University of Pennsylvania, Dept. of English, 1995.

Spanos, William V. *The Errant Art of Moby-Dick: The Canon, the Cold War, and the Struggle for American Studies*. Durham: Duke UP, 1995.

UREO: Uranium and Radiation Education Outreach. Northern Arizona University. <www4.nau.edu/eeop/ureo/eevact.htm>.

"What Is Jazz?" Smithsonian Jazz—A Jazz Portal Intended to Preserve and Promote One of America's Greatest Art Forms—Jazz. <www.smithsonianjazz.org/class/whatsjazz/wij_start.asp>.

Whitfield, Stephen J. *The Culture of the Cold War*. Baltimore: Johns Hopkins UP, 1991.

FURTHER RESOURCES

The Atomic Café [documentary film]. Directed by Jayne Loader and Kevin Rafferty. 1982.

The Cold War: Europe and the Third World [video recording]. Produced by WGBH in association with The Metropolitan Museum of Art, New York. Santa Barbara: Intellimation, 1989.

Foertsch, Jacqueline. *Enemies Within: The Cold War and the AIDS Crisis in Literature, Film, and Culture*. Urbana: U of Illinois P, 2001.

Frascina, Francis, ed. *Pollock and After: The Critical Debate*. New York: Routledge, 2000.

Guilbaut, Serge. *How New York Stole the Idea of Modern Art: Abstract Expressionism, Freedom, and the Cold War*, trans. Arthur Goldhammer. Chicago: U of Chicago P, 1983.

Momaday: *Voice of the West* [video recording]. KCTS Television. Produced and edited by Jean Walkinshaw. Alexandria: PBS Home Video, 1996.

A More Perfect Union: Japanese Americans and the U.S. Constitution [online exhibit]; Fast Attacks and Boomers: Submarines in the Cold War [online exhibit]; Paint by Number: Accounting for Taste in the 1950s [online exhibit]; Produce for Victory: Posters on the American Home Front (1941–45) [online exhibit]. Smithsonian: National Museum of American History. <americanhistory.si.edu/>. National Mall, 14th Street and Constitution Avenue, N.W., Washington, DC. Phone: (202) 357-2700.

Moss, Joyce, and George Wilson. *Literature and Its Times*. Detroit: Gale, 1997.

Ralph Ellison: The Self-Taught Writer [video recording]. Produced, written, and directed by Rex Barnett. Atlanta: History on Video, 1995.

"The Real Thirteen Days: The Hidden History of the Cuban Missile Crisis." The National Security Archive <www.gwu.edu/~nsarchiv/nsa/cuba_mis_cri/index.html>. Digital National Security Archive <nsarchive.chadwyck.com/>. Nearly 40,000 of the most important, declassified documents—totaling more than 250,000 pages—are included in the database. UMI.

A Walk Through the 20th Century with Bill Moyers: World War II: Propaganda Battle. Created and developed by the Corporation for Entertainment and Learning, Inc., and Bill Moyers; produced in association with WNET/New York and KQED/San Francisco. Washington, DC.: PBS Video, 1983, 1988.

Authors and Works

Featured in the Video:

Allen Ginsberg, *Howl*, "A Supermarket in California" (poems)

Adrienne Rich, "Diving into the Wreck," "Power," "Transcendental Etude" (poems)

Amiri Baraka (LeRoi Jones), "Will They Cry When You're Gone, You Bet," "A Poem for Willie Best" (poems); *Dutchman* (play)

Discussed in This Unit:

John Ashbery, "And Ut Pictura Poesis Is Her Name," "Illustration," "Soonest Mended," "Self-Portrait in a Convex Mirror" (poems)

James Wright, "The Minneapolis Poem," "A Blessing," "The Journey," "With the Shell of a Hermit Crab" (poems)

Gary Snyder, "Beneath My Hand and Eye the Distant Hills. Your Body," "The Blue Sky," "Milton by Firelight" (poems)

Sylvia Plath, "Daddy," "Lady Lazarus," *Ariel* (poems); *The Bell Jar* (novel)

Audre Lorde, *Zami*, *The Cancer Journals* (prose nonfiction); "Coal," "Black Mother Woman," "Chain" (poems)

Joy Harjo, *The Woman Who Fell from the Sky*, "Call It Fear," "White Bear," "The Flood" (poems)

Lorna Dee Cervantes, *Emplumada*, "Visions of Mexico While at a Writing Symposium in Port Townsend, Washington" (poems)

Overview Questions

■ How do these authors broaden or complicate our concept of what it means to be American? What strategies do these authors use to express the predicament of marginalized peoples? How did civil rights and protest movements reshape the notion of what it means to be an American? What connections do you see between the poetry in this unit and the civil rights struggle?

■ How would you describe the mood or abiding intentions of American literature during this period? How does the experience of the Vietnam War affect the poetry of this period? What other social or political forces shaped the poetry of this time? How does feminism influence the poetry of the period? Where do you see the influence of popular culture?

■ Along with the New York school poets, the Beat poets were deeply influenced by life in the city. In the late 1940s and early 1950s, writers like Allen Ginsberg, Jack Kerouac, and Lucien Carr, all of whom had connections to Columbia University, met and discussed their new, experimental vision for poetry. New York culture, with its bustling nightlife and hosts of adventurous students, musicians, and artists, offered much for young rebels struggling to find a literary voice. By the middle 1950s, San Francisco also featured a lively and unconventional artistic community. When Ginsberg moved to San Francisco in 1954, he soon became a center of attention in a book-loving, verse-loving North Beach neighborhood where bohemian and gay lifestyles were tolerated to an extent that few other American metropolises could match. Literary historians often regard Ginsberg's first public performance of *Howl* on October 7, 1955, as the inauguration of a "San Francisco Renaissance" and a demonstration that "Beat" culture had truly arrived. For more than thirty years after that night, San Francisco and New York City were meccas for radical and experimental art in America, places where authors such as Kerouac, Gary Snyder, Ginsberg, Amiri Baraka, and Audre Lorde learned from one another and formed powerful communities of verse. How does their urban setting shape the nature and themes of their work?

■ Gary Snyder, James Wright, and Theodore Roethke are often referred to as nature poets. What relationship do you see between their work and nature poets of the American nineteenth century? Where are the key differences?

■ Many of these poets used travel as a metaphor for a spiritual journey, and works like Jack Kerouac's *On the Road* enjoyed astonishing popularity during the 1960s. What relationships do you see between this yearning for the open road and the sentiments of earlier American writers?

■ Describe some of the movements into which postwar poetry is classified. How did they develop? What interests and styles are identified with each school?

■ How does postwar poetry continue or transform the legacy of modernism? How do African American writers from this period build on ideas and politics inherited from the Harlem Renaissance?

■ How do the African American, Chicano, and Native American authors in this unit re-imagine American identity? How do they challenge the way history has been told and recorded? What other myths about America are challenged by the poets in this unit?

Learning Objectives

After students have viewed the video, read the headnotes and literary selections in *The Norton Anthology of American Literature*, and explored related archival materials on the *American Passages* Web site, they should be able to

1. discuss the political, historical, and social contexts of postwar poetry, particularly the counterculture of the 1950s and 1960s;
2. discuss several different schools of poetry represented by poets in the unit, namely the Beat movement, the New York school, confessional poetry, feminism, and the Black Arts movement;
3. recognize and describe innovations in the poetry of the period;
4. describe ways in which these poets differ from their modernist predecessors and how postwar poets continue to challenge and expand our notion of American poetry and the American idiom;

5. describe postmodernism, discuss its causes and origins, and discuss ways in which the poetry in this unit responds to the postmodern condition.

Instructor Overview

After World War II, a complex and dynamic new chapter of American cultural history began, a chapter that in many ways is neither completed nor easily describable. After the worldwide depression and violence of the 1930s and 1940s, millions of people hoped for some kind of respite, a period of peace, prosperity, and stability. Forty million people had died in places whose very names, to the generation of the 1950s and 1960s, became a litany of massacre and catastrophe: Nanking, Coventry, Pearl Harbor, Bataan, Stalingrad, Omaha Beach, Guadalcanal, Cassino, Dresden, Tokyo, Berlin, Hiroshima, Nagasaki. But the peace treaties and agreements worked out among the Allies soon gave way to a forty-year "Cold War," as the two nuclear superpowers, the United States and the Soviet Union, contended with each other for ideological control of the world.

Sorting out the various literary experiments, coteries, and insurgencies of the years between 1950 and the present would be a vast enterprise in itself, complicated by the interventions of commercialism, pop culture, fads and fashion, and the enormous expansion of the college and university system as a focus for youthful energy and as an arbiter of taste. If students are confused by the cacophony of monikers, slogans, and short-lived obsessions that can be lifted from the pages of postwar history, you might encourage them to think about long-term and conflicting characteristics of those decades. The American middle and upper classes experienced unprecedented comfort and prosperity, along with an unprecedented threat of apocalypse—that this new life of ease and gadgetry could be obliterated in a matter of minutes. Intercontinental nuclear weapons made the threat of annihilation very real from the late fifties onward. And even as the technological innovations and daily comforts of democracy seem to have eclipsed the potential enemy of the Cold War U.S.S.R., plenty of controversy remains as to whether the threat of nuclear war has subsided.

Television proliferated in the West during the 1950s and 1960s; a virtual explosion of loud, fast, and lurid media brought news and spectacle into every corner of the United States, transforming nearly every aspect of American public life—including the social impact of the writer, and the nature and duration of literary celebrity.

The works in Unit 15 reflect numerous literary groups that responded to the vast social changes taking place, including the Beats (Ginsberg, Snyder), confessional poets (Sylvia Plath, Robert Lowell, Anne Sexton), the Black Mountain poets (Charles Olson, Robert Duncan, Denise Levertov, Robert Creeley), Black Arts (Audre Lorde, Amiri Baraka), the New York school (Frank O'Hara, John Ashbery, Kenneth Koch, and James Schuyler), feminist poets (Adrienne Rich, Sylvia Plath, Audre Lorde), Chicano nationalists (Lorna Dee Cervantes), and latter-day transcendental and pastoral poets (Gary Snyder, Robert Bly, James Wright, Galway Kennell, and W. S. Merwin). To help situate students with respect to this multitude of literary movements, you might present the Beats as a wellspring of many other movements, the first widely celebrated "bohemian" experiment after World War II. Centered in Greenwich Village and San Francisco, the Beats became known for many traits and preoccupations that showed remarkable durability. New communities of artists came together with an alternative lifestyle that included drug experimentation, a fascination with Eastern religions and personal spirituality, open homosexuality, and an "anti-establishment" demeanor. Beat poetry tends to blur the line between prose and poetry, mixes registers, draws copiously on popular culture, sounds both authoritative and hip, and glorifies the experience of living on the fringes of society.

Confessional poets, like Robert Lowell, Anne Sexton, and Sylvia Plath, also sought to astonish readers by exploring deeply personal experience such as mental illness, sexuality, and hostility within the immediate family. Poets who associated with American feminist thought, including Adrienne Rich, Sylvia Plath, and Audre Lorde, are often linked to other schools of poetry as well but are distinguished by verse fiercely dedicated to expressing the predicament of modern American women. The Black Arts movement was also ignited by political struggles, specifically those linked to the civil rights and black nationalist movements of the 1950s and 1960s. The Black Mountain poets, including Charles Olson and Robert Creeley, are remembered for the short-lived experimental college in North Carolina where they taught for a while. These poets favored open forms, sudden, unexpected imagery and diction and remarkable freedom in prosody. Theirs was a verse in celebration of spontaneity. The New York school, including Frank O'Hara, John Ashbery, and Kenneth Koch, distinguished itself by its close association with the experimental painting underway in the city and its environs. From abstract expressionism, these poets learned to perceive the work of art as what critic David Perkins calls a "chronicle of the creative act that produces it." These writers were also influenced by composers dedicated to similar values, including John Cage and Igor Stravinsky.

This search for identity gave rise to the belief that the personal is political, a notion that formed in the 1960s as artists, poets, and activists used their personal lives to make political statements. In questioning American identity, these authors confront the problem of the divided self, whether it be Lorna Dee Cervantes's division between her Chicana heritage and her American life, Adrienne Rich's identification as both a lesbian and a mother, Amiri Baraka's personal variation upon doctrines of Black nationalism and American identity, or Joy Harjo's Native American heritage that highlights the tension between a native worldview and dominant American culture. The poetry of this time is also characterized by open form, conversational diction, candid subject matter, corporeal imagery and symbolism, political and social critique, and radicalism in both thought and lifestyle. Much of the poetry, with the exception of the meditative poets, also depends upon the belief that words and art should be used as political tools. The importance of poetry to so many of the political movements of this time illustrates a direct link between social environment and artistic creation.

The video, archive, and curriculum in this unit highlight intersections among art, politics, and culture. The key historical events and cultural upheavals include protest poetry, free verse, and sexual revolution. The materials also suggest ways that students might relate the authors and works to one another. Students should also be encouraged to consider the contemporary legacy of postwar poetry, including hip-hop, poetry slams, performance art, contemporary jazz, and experimental rock.

Student Overview

Not long after the devastation of World War II, Americans found themselves embroiled in the Korean War (1950–53) and the Vietnam War (1964–75). Both of these conflicts proved to be more ethically complicated than World War II, and in Vietnam guerilla warfare made the actual fighting more confusing as well. As a result, the U.S. government promoted traditional values, namely domesticity and political and cultural conservatism, to fight for stability on the domestic front in what seemed like an increasingly turbulent and threatening world. The new media, especially television, helped to enforce this domestic ideology in which family and home remained a central priority for women; indeed, the enormous subdivisions of suburban ranch houses became important symbols of American safety, pastoral happiness, and prosperity during this period. The 1950s, in many ways, marked the beginning of modern American popular culture as we now know it. By the mid-1960s, the political, social, and cultural climate had changed dramatically. With the rising popularity of rock and roll and the beginning of the sexual revolution, American youth culture seemed to diverge as never before from middle-aged, middle-class American life. Adolescence became a demographic, a separate cultural audience, a different state of mind. At the same time, undercurrents of discontent with racist, sexist, and economically inequitable American social and political practices grew into full-fledged movements, many of which skillfully exploited the media.

Led by Martin Luther King Jr., Rosa Parks, James Farmer, Shirley Chisholm, and many others, the civil rights movement became a center of national attention. Sit-ins, Freedom Rides, and other nonviolent demonstrations shared the spotlight with important court cases and national legislation to change the legal, economic, and social status of American minorities. The Vietnam-era draft took a heavy toll on black neighborhoods in major cities, and many downtown areas were devastated by riots in the years from 1965 through 1970. As anxiety and moral concern about the war spread to college campuses, thousands of schools became centers of political ferment and many forms of experimentation. A sexual revolution spread from these schools to mainstream American life, and at the same time the rights and power of women underwent a transformation unprecedented in U.S. history. By 1972, with the end of the draft and a scaling-down of the American involvement in Southeast Asia, antiwar fervor slackened and many writers and artists drifted from a common cause into a kind of discontent that seemed fragmented and desultory by comparison. Nonetheless, in art, music, student culture, and "alternative" communities, a style took hold that remains strong and recognizable to this day.

Much of the poetry of the 1960s and 1970s reflects the political and social turmoil of the time. Flamboyantly experimental work from this era is sometimes classified as "postmodern," a loose term suggesting a cultural and aesthetic break with the formal styles and values exemplified by authors writing earlier in the twentieth century. The continuing urge to "make it new" caused many artists to turn dramatically away from the long shadow of Eliot, Stevens, Auden, and even Pound himself, who had coined the phrase as a basic principle for writing in a transformed world. However, arguments persist as to whether postmodernism ever broke sufficiently with these traditions to define itself as something truly distinct from varieties of modernism. Characteristics of postmodernism include a spirit of alienation from an accelerating technological and materialist way of life, a willingness to blend voices and borrow from other world cultures and literary traditions, and a delight in reflexivity—in poems which echo or play with other poems, art which incorporates other art or found objects from the world beyond the gallery, drama which escapes the confines of the stage and the theater and mingles, one way or another, with all the media and noise reverberating in the boulevards.

Moving through *American Passages* chronologically may reveal a lot of "old" ideas in the "new" art of the Vietnam years and after, and these are to be valued. Creativity is often a process of adaptation and borrowing, and the drive for originality can take an individual artist deep into the world's cultural past. Most of the poets in this unit share a distrust of received wisdom and authority and a faith in aggressive candor. Postmodern American poetry has favored open forms, vernacular diction, personal themes, political and social struggle, and a variety of radical perspectives.

➤ **Authors covered:** Allen Ginsberg, Adrienne Rich, Amiri Baraka

➤ **Who's interviewed:** Michael Bibby, associate professor of English (Shippensburg University); Maria Damon, associate professor of English (University of Minnesota); Anne Waldman, poet and co-founder of the Jack Kerouac School of Disembodied Poetics (Naropa University, Boulder); Crystal Williams, poet and assistant professor of creative writing (Reed College)

➤ **Points covered:**

• Allen Ginsberg, Adrienne Rich, and Amiri Baraka lived for many years in alternative communities, and their poetry often reflects this alternative or contrarian lifestyle. They viewed poetry as intensely political and believed that verse could contribute to moral awakening and social change.

• The postwar period is characterized by a host of movements, including civil rights, antiwar and disarmament, Black Arts, drug legalization, and feminism. The spirit of protest that shaped the 1960s and 1970s deeply influenced these poets. Poetry often played a part in these protest movements, as Ginsberg's performance in front of the Pentagon suggests.

• In the wake of World War II and the beginning of the Cold War, America embraced capitalism and conformity. This was the era of the Red Scare, when people not only were afraid of the spread of communism but were actually blacklisting one another for sympathizing with the Soviet cause. The Beat poets rebelled against what they saw as dangerous conformity; they denounced capitalism and distrusted the government.

• Like other Beats, Ginsberg used his poetry and his lifestyle to rebel against the American status quo. In 1954, Ginsberg moved to San Francisco, where he became active in the counterculture based in Haight Ashbury. He also performed *Howl* for the first time, sparking public awareness of the Beat movement. Ginsberg shares Whitman's penchant for lengthy lines, long lists, and authoritative voice. Like Whitman, Ginsberg wrote for the general public.

• The Black Arts movement included a group of activist artists who used their work to evoke political change. Black Arts comes out of the civil rights and Black Power movements.

• Amiri Baraka is the representative figure of Black Arts in this unit. Born Everett Leroy Jones, Baraka circulated with the Beats, but eventually left the circle to devote his attention to racial issues. After Malcolm X's death, Baraka became a black nationalist, and in

1968 he became a Muslim, a conversion that resulted in the changing of his name. Much of Baraka's work, including his important play *Dutchman*, is aggressively political and full of rage.

• Adrienne Rich is an important figure in the women's movement. Her poetry and prose explore her experiences as a woman and a lesbian, issues that until this time were socially taboo. Her work has challenged assumptions about women in North American society and given many women the vocabulary to talk about their oppression. Rich helped to popularize the idea that the personal is political, meaning that the way we live our personal lives has public consequences and social ramifications that affect and shape the world around us.

PREVIEW

• **Preview the video:** The 1960s and 1970s were characterized by political and social unrest in America. Protests became a part of 1960s culture. Various demonstrations and protest movements were motivated by the civil rights struggle, the war in Vietnam, the proliferation of nuclear weapons, the deterioration of the environment, and a generalized fear that America was becoming a more conformist and materialist society. Poets like Ginsberg, Baraka, and Rich believed that poetry was intensely political, and they used literature to challenge the status quo.

• **What to think about while watching:** How did American poets respond to the political and social experience of the 1960s and 1970s? How do the poetry and lifestyle of these writers challenge mainstream American values? What legacy have these poets left for later generations? How did poetry and the public figure of the poets change during this period?

• **Tying the video to the unit content:** Unit 15 expands on the concepts explained in the video to explore further the changing social and literary traditions as they contributed to, and were affected by, the writings of the authors covered. The curriculum materials introduce students to many schools of poetry that emerged during this time, including the New York school, the Chicano movement, the feminists, Black Arts, Beats, meditative poets, and language poets. The unit also offers background on integral historical events, including the Vietnam War, the women's movement, and Black Arts, which shaped the literature and outlook of the postwar period.

	What is American literature? What are its distinctive voices and styles? How do social and political issues influence the American canon?	**What characteristics of a literary work have made it influential over time?**	**How are American myths created, challenged, and re-imagined through these works of literature?**
Compre-hension Questions	What are some of the characteristics of Beat poetry? How are the lifestyles of the Beat poets, like Allen Ginsberg, reflected in their art?	What does Adrienne Rich mean when she says that the personal is political? How does "Passage" enact this idea?	In *Dutchman* Lula calls Clay "Uncle Tom." What does she mean?
Context Questions	What is new about the poetry of this period? What kinds of values are the writers challenging?	Allen Ginsberg cited Walt Whitman as the single greatest influence on his own work. What do these poets share in terms of craft and personal style? Why would Ginsberg align himself with Whitman? How does Ginsberg represent Whitman in "A Supermarket in California"? What is this poem ultimately about?	Amiri Baraka was originally connected to the Beat movement, but he split from it to concentrate on racial issues. Compare the sections of *Howl* read in the video to "Will They Cry When You're Gone, You Bet." What similarities do you see between Baraka's poetry and Ginsberg's?
Exploration Questions	Poetry was often read at protest movements during this period. Why do you think poetry was given such high status? Is it awarded a similar place in political activism today?	How did these poets and activists change or influence what it means to be an American? What values did they help to create or promote? What would you say has been the cultural legacy of the 1960s?	While the 1950s are often associated with peace, prosperity, and homogeneity, the authors in this unit expose how the often racist, sexist, and inequitable society sustained by such rhetoric was subject to revolutionary criticism during the 1960s and 1970s. Why does the former image of the 1950s endure? How do the ideas of radical change and strict historical periodization circumscribe or expand the messages and impact of these writers?

	Texts	Contexts
1950s	Adrienne Rich, *A Change of World* (1951), "Storm Warnings" (1951), "Snapshots of a Daughter-in-Law" (1958) Allen Ginsberg, *Howl* (1956), "Sunflower Sutra" (1956), "A Supermarket in California" (1956), *Kaddish* (1959) John Ashbery, "Illustration" (1956) Gary Snyder, "Milton by Firelight" (1959), "Riprap" (1959)	Korean War (1950–53) Heyday of McCarthyism (1953–54) U.S. Supreme Court bans school segregation in *Brown v. Board of Education* (1954) Rosa Parks is arrested for refusing to give up her seat on a bus, sparks Montgomery bus boycott (1955) Supreme Court rules that bus segregation is illegal (1956) Voting Rights Bill passed by Congress (1957) President Eisenhower sends U.S. Army troops to Little Rock, Arkansas, to enforce desegregation in public schools (1957) The Soviet Union launches *Sputnik* 1, the first artificial satellite, into space (1957)
1960s	John Ashbery, "Europe" (1960) Allen Ginsberg, "To Aunt Rose" (1961) Sylvia Plath, *The Bell Jar* (1963), *Ariel* (1965) James Wright, "Autumn Begins in Martins Ferry, Ohio" (1963), "A Blessing" (1963), "To the Evening Star: Central Minnesota" (1963), "The Minneapolis Poem" (1968) Amiri Baraka, *Dutchman* (1964), "An Agony. As Now." (1964), "A Poem for Willie Best" (1964) Audre Lorde, "Coal" (1968) Gary Snyder, "Beneath My Hand and Eye the Distant Hills. Your Body" (1968), "The Blue Sky" (1969) Adrienne Rich, *Leaflets* (1969)	Greensboro sit-in protests begin (1960) Cuban Missile Crisis (1962) Civil Rights March on Washington, D.C. (1963) President John F. Kennedy assassinated (1963) Civil Rights Act (1964) Vietnam War (1964–75) Malcolm X assassinated (1965) Voting Rights Act (1965) Black Panther Party for Self Defense founded by Huey Newton and Bobby Seale (1965) Martin Luther King Jr. assassinated (1968) U.S. astronauts make first moon landing (1969)
1970s	John Ashbery, "Soonest Mended" (1970), "Self-Portrait in a Convex Mirror" (1975), "And Ut Pictura Poesis Is Her Name" (1977) Audre Lorde, "Black Mother Woman" (1971), "Chain" (1978), "Harriet" (1978) Adrienne Rich, *The Will to Change* (1971), "Diving into the Wreck" (1972), "Power" (1974), *Of Woman Born: Motherhood as Experience and Institution* (1976), "Transcendental Etude" (1977), "Twenty-One Love Poems" (1978) James Wright, *Collected Poems* (1971), "A Centenary Ode: Inscribed to Little Crow, Leader of the Sioux Rebellion in Minnesota, 1862" (1971), "With the Shell of a Hermit Crab" (1977)	Watergate scandal (1972–74) *Roe v. Wade*; Supreme Court rules abortion is legal (1973) President Richard Nixon resigns from office (1974) Moral Majority founded (1979) Iran hostage crisis (1979–81)

AUTHOR/TEXT REVIEW

Allen Ginsberg (1926–1997)

Allen Ginsberg was born in Newark, New Jersey, to Louis, a poet and high school teacher, and Naomi, who was of Russian descent. A graduate of Paterson public schools, Ginsberg developed an early friendship with the poet William Carlos Williams, who served as an important mentor during his early development. After leaving New Jersey to attend Columbia University, Ginsberg met the novelist William Burroughs, who encouraged not only his writing but also his questioning of social conformity.

After graduating from Columbia in 1948 (he was expelled twice, but did receive a degree), Ginsberg considered the following summer a turning point in his spiritual development. Feeling alone and isolated in New York City, Ginsberg reports having a vision in which he heard his own voice reciting William Blake's poetry. The hallucination became a moment of great insight for Ginsberg, and he refers to the experience as a revelation.

Perhaps the most crucial moment in Ginsberg's poetic career, however, was his decision to move to San Francisco, where a group of young writers, including Burroughs, Jack Kerouac, and Gregory Corso, were already living. Eventually, these writers

[5683] John Doss, *Allen Ginsberg at Madame Nhu Protest, 1963* (1963), courtesy of the Allen Ginsberg Trust and the Department of Special Collections, Stanford University Libraries.

were associated with the Beat movement, a term coined by Kerouac for its punning reference to "beaten down" and "beatified." Ginsberg credits Kerouac as one of his greatest influences. Through this prose writer, he came to appreciate the practice of automatic writing, in which the process of writing becomes as important as the final product; in fact, revision is discouraged. Kerouac also convinced Ginsberg to incorporate personal experience in his verse, a practice that opened the door for confessional poetry. Robert Lowell said that *Howl* forever changed how he would write poetry and made his book *Life Studies* possible. Ginsberg's poetry features colloquial language riddled with slang and obscenities, a prophetic tone, lengthy lines meant to be performed aloud, and a desire to capture the author's physical and emotional state at the time of creation.

Known for their alternative lifestyle, the Beat writers experimented freely with drugs, sex, and spirituality. Like Kerouac, Ginsberg traveled extensively, mostly during the early 1960s. His poetry is colored by this social freedom and wanderlust. Perhaps his most famous poem, *Howl* chronicles the Beat culture of the 1950s. A radical poem for its subject matter, straightforward exploration of alternative culture (particularly drug-induced experiences), and social commentary, *Howl* was in danger of being censored in 1957, but Judge Clayton Horn decided that the poem merited publication. The trial made *Howl* an instant success and brought the Beat movement new prominence.

Ginsberg, like many of the other Beat poets, was deeply interested in Eastern religions, particularly Buddhism, and studied it in India during the early 1960s. In 1965, Ginsberg returned from his travels throughout the East and began lecturing at universities around the country. He continued to hold radical beliefs and became a symbol of counterculture and intellectual freedom in the United States. He remained an avid opponent of war, consumerism, and the establishment until his death.

TEACHING TIPS

■ Beat poets were famous for their poetry performances; indeed, we might see them as precursors to currently popular "poetry slams." Have students take turns reading passages from *Howl* (the first section of the poem works well). After several students have performed the poem, ask the class to discuss the performance choices each student made. What words did they emphasize? What was the tone of the performance? Did they change the dynamics of their voice? What was it like for the students to read this poem aloud? How does the meaning change with each performance?

■ Ask students to write their own poem in the style of Ginsberg. You might get them started by asking them to make a list of the defining characteristics of their generation. Students should also consider the formal features of Ginsberg's work (long lines, blurred boundary between prose and poetry, use of many registers, including slang, erudite allusions, etc.), the often aggressive tone, the intimacy created between speaker and reader, and the political critique that drives his work. After the students have written their poems, they should write several paragraphs explaining what features or characteristics they were trying to capture. Then, have students break into small groups and share their poems. Each group should vote on the best poem. Groups should be prepared to defend their choices as they listen to all of the poems.

QUESTIONS

Comprehension: Why do you think Ginsberg chose the title *Howl*? What is the effect of the repetition of words at the beginning of lines (e.g., who, Moloch, I'm). To what does Moloch refer? Why does Ginsberg divide the poem into three parts?

Comprehension: In "To Aunt Rose," Ginsberg refers to the Abraham Lincoln Brigade, Hitler, and Emily Brontë, a seemingly eclectic set of allusions. What is the significance of each reference? How is history treated here?

Comprehension: "Sutra" is the Sanskrit word for "thread." It refers to Brahmin or Buddhist texts used for religious teaching. In Ginsberg's poem "Sunflower Sutra," what does the title mean? What does the sunflower symbolize?

Context: In "A Supermarket in California," Ginsberg repeatedly addresses the nineteenth-century poet Walt Whitman. Why does he invoke this bard? What do these poets share? If Ginsberg is determined to forge a new poetry about life on the fringes of society, why does he invoke a traditional, canonized poet?

Context: Compare Ginsberg's interpretation of the Beats' philosophy to Gary Snyder's. What techniques do the poets share, and where do they diverge?

Exploration: Review the context on "Orientalism" in Unit 10. Many of the modernist poets, particularly Ezra Pound and William Carlos Williams, were fascinated by Asian art, architecture, and poetry. The Beat poets also share an interest in Asian culture, particularly Buddhism. How do these two generations of American poets differ in their treatment of Asian culture? What techniques do they share? Why do you think this fascination with the Far East continues throughout the century? You might consider Pound's "In a Station of the Metro" and "The River-Merchant's Wife: A Letter"; William Carlos Williams's "Willow Poem"; Ginsberg's "Sunflower Sutra"; and Gary Snyder's "The Blue Sky."

Exploration: Ginsberg begins "Ego Confession" with the line, "I want to be known as the most brilliant man in America." How does that beginning affect the reader? What is the tone? What is the portrait of the poet represented here? How does Ginsberg's notion of the poet differ from that of his modernist predecessors, like T. S. Eliot (see *The Waste Land*) and William Carlos Williams (consider *Paterson*)?

Exploration: Like William Carlos Williams, Walt Whitman, Robert Frost, and a host of other writers, Ginsberg struggles to create a uniquely American poetry. What does it mean to be an American to Ginsberg? What does he value most? How does his poetic voice differ from that of other poets you've read? How is it similar?

John Ashbery (b. 1927)

John Ashbery was born in Rochester, New York, and he earned his B.A. from Harvard University. He also received an M.A. from Columbia, where he wrote his thesis on English novelist Henry Green, who is known for his detached and witty style. Ashbery studied as a Fulbright scholar in France from 1955 to 1957 and returned there in 1958. He earned a living by writing art criticism for *Art News* and the European edition of the *New York Herald Tribune*. Upon returning to America in 1965, Ashbery continued to work as editor of *Art News* for the next seven years. Since 1972, he has continued his work as art critic while also teaching at Brooklyn College.

Associated with the New York school of poetry, Ashbery is known as an experimental poet, whose impersonal, clever style is often difficult and opaque. The New York School was a group of poets including Frank O'Hara, Ashbery, Kenneth Koch, James Schuyler, and Ted Berrigan, among others, who knew each other well, made references to each other in their work, and were deeply influenced by avant-garde artists such as Jackson Pollock. Under the influence of abstract art, these writers became interested in the creative process itself. Unlike many of their contemporaries, they did not write about the social and political issues of their time. Ashbery's interest in visual art, particularly the New York school of abstract painters prolific in the 1940s and 1950s, influences his verse. Like many of these painters, Ashbery explores the relationship between nature and life, but rather than using nature as a blueprint for life, Ashbery chooses not to emphasize realism. Instead, his poems examine the creative process itself, as a poem like "And Ut Pictura Poesis Is Her Name" illustrates. Like the high modernists, Ashbery uses juxtaposition, verbal playfulness, and wit, and he rarely offers the reader commentary or analysis in his poems, instead leaving the meaning open to interpretation.

Like many other American poets, Ashbery composes his work in a conversational style reminiscent of dialogue, though the diction is rarely colloquial. His work is characterized by sudden changes in register and tone, and he often blurs the boundaries between prose and poetry. The mixture of erudite language with the discourse of popular culture also shows the influence of mass culture in modern life. Interested in different voices, he often imitates or incorporates fragments from newspapers, advertisements, business memos, scientific articles, and textbooks. In addition, Ashbery uses clichés frequently to show our inability to escape the hackneyed confines of language itself. While many poets, particularly the modernists, rely on fragmentation in their poetry, Ashbery differs because he leads the reader to expect sequence and continuity. For example, he frustrates our grammatical expectations by beginning a line with standard grammar only to use the inappropriate verb tense or referent later on. He also confuses syntax by omitting punctuation and piling up relative clauses and parentheses. Influenced by W. H. Auden, Laura Riding, and Wallace Stevens, Ashbery writes decisive yet lyrical verse, and he considers the musicality of his verse most important. Regarded as one of the most important modern poets, Ashbery has had a profound influence on a younger generation of authors known as the language poets.

[4526] Joan Miro, *The Farm* (1921–22), courtesy of the National Gallery of Art and Artist Rights Society: 1987.18.1./PA: Miro, Joan, The Farm, Gift of Mary Hemingway, Photograph © 2002 Board of Trustees, National Gallery of Art, Washington; © 2002 Successio Miro/Artist Rights Society (ARS), New York/ADAGP, Paris.

TEACHING TIPS

■ Because Ashbery's poetry is difficult, David Perkins offers two helpful approaches to reading his work. Ashbery's early work, through the 1950s, can be read in the context of modernism because it relies on the same collage technique typical of Eliot, Pound, and Williams. Also influenced by surrealism in the 1950s, Ashbery writes poems that depend upon juxtaposition, fragmentation, swift changes in register, and syntactical disruption. His later poetry seems to share more with Stevens and Auden because it is characterized by a meditative sensibility. Interested in the movement of the mind and the impossibility of representing reality, Ashbery's poems develop new techniques to broach similar problems of the nature of reality.

ASHBERY WEB ARCHIVE

[4022] Marcel Duchamp, *Nude Descending a Staircase (No. 2)* (1912), courtesy of Philadelphia Museum of Art, The Louise and Walter Arensberg Collection, and Artist Rights Society; © Artist Rights Society (ARS), New York/ADAGP, Paris/Estate of Marcel Duchamp. American audiences criticized and ridiculed this abstract painting when it was exhibited at the Armory Show in New York in 1913. It is a clear example of cubism, fragmentation, and the use of geometrical shapes, all of which are hallmarks of modernist painting.

■ Ashbery's use of the collage technique links him to earlier modernists. Have your students construct their own poems using magazine fragments.

QUESTIONS

Comprehension: Ashbery's poem "Illustration" could be read as a character sketch of the figure of the "novice." What happens to the "novice . . . sitting on a cornice"? Who is she? What does she symbolize? How does the title help us better understand the poem?

Comprehension: How does Ashbery's interest in abstract painting influence his poetry?

Comprehension: Like many of Ashbery's poems, "Soonest Mended" is inspired by a painting. What is the tone of "Soonest Mended"? Line 14 seems to mark a shift in the poem. What changes here? What is the speaker's "ambition"? What does he mean by this?

Context: Ashbery is known for writing collage-like poems, a technique also practiced by many of the high modernists, including T. S. Eliot. Like Eliot, Ashberry writes in a range of registers, experimenting with what he calls "prose voices." Compare *The Waste Land* to "Soonest Mended," looking particularly at how these poets make transitions, link material, and jump between images and registers. What technical similarities and differences do you notice?

Context: Ashbery peppers his poetry with scores of erudite allusions. In "Self-Portrait in a Convex Mirror," for example, each page contains several footnotes explaining these references to readers. Why do you think he includes so many allusions? To whom or what does he allude? Can you make generalizations about these references? What does this tell us about his intended audience?

Exploration: In *Laocoön; an Essay on the Limits of Painting and Poetry*, Gotthold Lessing argues that the sister arts of poetry and painting achieve their effects through the nature of the medium (words, paint), and to succeed, each must exploit the potential of that medium while keeping in mind its limitations. Poetry, for example, works best when representing human action, but it lacks visual vividness. In contrast, painting best adapts to the representation of idealized human beauty in repose. Owing to the nontemporal character of words and paint, neither painting nor poetry easily represents the body in action. Only by selecting the "critical" or "fruitful" moment, which simultaneously preserves physical beauty and concentrates within itself the suggestion of past and future action, can the painter or poet even indirectly represent a sequence of events in action. How does Ashbery's poetry reflect this struggle and the desire to blend media? You might consider "Self-Portrait in a Convex Mirror" in particular.

Exploration: Ashbery's poetry has been described as meditative because he rarely describes events or people; instead he is interested in representing the inner workings of the mind, especially as involved in the creative process. Like his modernist predecessors,

Auden and particularly Stevens, Ashbery struggles with the problem of representing a reality that can never be truly grasped. As critic David Perkins notes, Ashbery, like Stevens, writes about the "mind forming hypotheses about reality in general, about the ultimate truth of nature of things." While Stevens tried to represent the "supreme fiction," however, Ashbery finds it futile to seek order or structure in reality. Despite this seemingly cynical and hopeless outlook, however, Ashbery's poetry is usually positive and curious, upbeat and hopeful. Look at the surrealist paintings in the Web archive. How do these paintings compare to Ashbery's poetry? How do these visual images influence the way you read his work?

James Wright (1927–1980)

James Wright grew up in Martins Ferry, Ohio, a small midwestern town hit hard by the depression. Wright's father worked in a factory to make ends meet, and the financial hardships endured by the family influenced Wright deeply, as later evidenced by his poetry about the poor and marginalized in American society. Wright received his undergraduate degree from Kenyon College, a center for creative writing at the time led by John Crowe Ransom. Wright later served in the army during the American occupation of Japan. After returning from overseas, he earned an M.A. and Ph.D. at the University of Washington, where he was a pupil of Theodore Roethke. After studying in Vienna on a Fulbright scholarship, Wright returned to the United States, where he has taught at universities and colleges across the country.

Wright's early poetry shares a sense of seriousness of subject matter characteristic of Thomas Hardy, Edwin Arlington Robinson, and Robert Frost. Like Frost and Hardy, Wright focuses on outsiders in his poems—figures like escaped convicts, grieving widows, and convicted murderers. Many of his subjects also experience intense poverty, as "The Minneapolis Poem" suggests. Poems like "A Blessing" also illustrate Wright's affinity with nature, a feature that renders this poem reminiscent of Frost. Wright feels conflicted about America, a land filled with both promise and racism. The tensions between the beautiful natural world and a cruel, industrialized world mirror this internal struggle. Wright's anger at his social **alienation** allows him to empathize with other marginalized people, and his poems often bear an elegiac, mournful tone as he envisions the promise and opportunity that could have been.

Wright's poetry changed markedly, however, after he translated the work of Pablo Neruda, Cesar Vallejo, and Georg Trakl. He learned from them a form of surrealism in which the connections between images seem absent. Like other poets writing in the 1960s, Wright also began to reject the traditional poetic form he had embraced earlier in his career. This later poetry reflects his continued interest in portraying outsiders, however, particularly the poor and oppressed. In 1971, his *Collected Poems* won the Pulitzer Prize.

[9149] Anonymous, *Federal Wire & Steel Co.'s Plant, Cleveland, Ohio* (c. 1920), courtesy of the Library of Congress, Prints and Photographs Division, Detroit Publishing Company Collection [LC-D4-72257 DLC].

■ Like Gary Snyder, James Wright seeks an alternative to modern, industrialized society, a sentiment fueled in part by his childhood in an Ohio factory town. He looks to nature as a refuge, as poems like "To the Evening Star: Central Minnesota" and "A Blessing" suggest. His work often shows glimpses of the transcendentalism characteristic of other poets in this unit. Ask your students to read the poems mentioned above and then write a prose description of the landscape evoked in the verse. Their versions will probably be longer than Wright's poems, so ask them how they came to their conclusions. As they share their work with their classmates, notice the different interpretations that arise.

WRIGHT WEB ARCHIVE

[4528] René Magritte, *La Condition Humaine* (1933), courtesy of the National Gallery of Art and Artist Rights Society: 1987.55.1./PA: Magritte, René, *La condition humaine*, Gift of the Collectors Committee, Photograph © 2002 Board of Trustees, National Gallery of Art, Washington; © 2002 C. Herscovici, Brussels/Artist Rights Society (ARS), New York. Painting of window and easel showing landscape. This work explores the divisions between realism and representationalism. Poet James Wright learned from Pablo Neruda, Cesar Vallejo, and Georg Trakl a form of surrealism in which the connections between images seem absent.
[7397] Anonymous, *Happy Hooligan It Is to Laugh: Nothing But Fun* (1902), courtesy of the Library of Congress [POS-TH-1902. H36, no. 3]. *Happy Hooligan*, a cartoon by Frederick Burr Opper, featured a jobless character with a small tin can hat. Anthropologists have noted that traditionally powerful groups often use humor to restore and reinforce jeopardized hierarchies and power relations. Poet James Wright, writing in the mid-twentieth century, often focused on U.S. class issues.
[8618] Various, *National Vietnam Examination* (1966), courtesy of Special Collections, Michigan State University Libraries. Exam distributed by Students for a Democratic Society (SDS) and the Inter-University Committee for Debate

QUESTIONS

Comprehension: Poets often use titles as a way to suggest something gently to the reader. What is the significance of the title "A Blessing"? What or who is being blessed? What does the speaker mean by the last two lines?

Comprehension: As it is for the work of many poets in this unit, particularly the Beats and the transcendent poets, the image of the journey is central to Wright's work. Who or what is the "she" referred to in the third stanza of "The Journey"? What is the journey the speaker describes?

Comprehension: An elegy is a poem written to honor the dead. As might be expected, traditional elegies usually evoke a somber tone, employ ornate and elevated language, and offer a generally flattering portrait of the deceased. In "With the Shell of a Hermit Crab," Wright satirizes the elegy form. What is the tone of this poem? How is the reader meant to respond? Toward the end, the poem begins to sound a little more sincere. How do you account for this shift? What is the purpose of the epigraph?

Context: Both Wright and Snyder are, in many ways, poets of nature. How do their attitudes toward the natural world differ? What techniques, if any, do they share?

Exploration: James Wright's poetry often shows an awareness of working-class suffering, and his landscapes often reflect a sympathy and compassion for rural life and its hardworking inhabitants. How does his work compare to that of other poets, particularly Genevieve Taggard and Gwendolyn Brooks, who write about the working classes? While Taggard and Brooks often focus their poems on the people, Wright's poems are frequently more indirect, projecting sentiments and feelings onto a landscape instead. You might compare "Autumn Begins in Martins Ferry, Ohio" to some of Genevieve Taggard's work ("A Middle-aged, Middle-class Woman at Midnight," "Mill Town") and Brooks's "kitchenette building" and "The Bean Eaters."

Exploration: James Wright's poetry has often been described as elegiac. Elegies are usually short poems written in a formal tone upon the occasion of someone's death. However, "elegiac" can also refer to poetry of meditation, usually on love, death, or expansive philosophical topics. Some of the most famous elegies by modern American poets include Wallace Stevens's "The Owl in the Sarcophagus," Robert Lowell's "For the Union Dead," Anne Sexton's "Sylvia's Death," and Allen Ginsberg's *Kaddish*. Elegies are generally characterized by a ceremonial tone, expressions of grief and loss, praise for the deceased, an attempt to continue their memory, and consolation in natural surroundings or religious values. Many poets of the twentieth century, however, reflect modern cynicism by undermining or satirizing the traditional conventions of the elegy. Although Wright's poems are not necessarily elegies for or to specific people, they do seem to mourn the loss of a particular way of life and landscape. How do these poems fit the characteristics of a traditional elegy? Which poems seem more elegiac than others? How does Wright's work diverge from the traditional genre?

Adrienne Rich (b. 1929)

Born in Baltimore, Adrienne Rich describes her mother and grandmother as "frustrated artists," whose talents were denied expression by culture and circumstance. Perhaps their example, along with her father's encouragement, sparked her desire to become a writer at a time when women were still trying to prove themselves in a male-dominated arena. After graduating from Radcliffe in 1951, Rich was recognized for her poetry in the same year by W. H. Auden, who selected her first book, *A Change of World*, for the coveted Yale Younger Poets series. Rich's early poetry was influenced primarily by male writers, including Frost, Thomas, Donne, Auden, Stevens, and Yeats. For many young women, these men were the poets studied in high school and university classes, talked about in magazines and journals, and invited to speak at universities. Young women were exposed to relatively little poetry written by other women, and as such were taught implicitly that to write well meant to write as well as a male poet. For writers like Rich, Plath, and Sexton the struggle to find female role models and express female experience was beginning with their own work. Of course, there were examples of women poets mentoring one another, most notably the mentorship of Elizabeth Bishop by Marianne Moore, but this proved to be the exception rather than the rule. By the end of the 1950s and early 1960s, however, Rich's poetry had changed markedly as she began exploring women's issues and moving away from formal poetry toward a **free verse** that she saw as less patriarchal and more in tune with her true voice.

In the late 1960s, Rich, along with her husband, became active in radical politics, especially protests against the Vietnam War. In addition, she taught minority students in urban New York City, an experience that began her lifelong commitment to education, a subject that would return in her essays. Not surprisingly, her poetry reflected this intense interest in politics. This later verse features fragmented lan-

on Foreign Policy. The SDS was a major force in organizing protests and other forms of opposition to the Vietnam War. Many American poets protested the war, including Allen Ginsberg, Denise Levertov, Robert Bly, Robert Lowell, Adrienne Rich, James Wright, and Galway Kinnell.

[9149] Anonymous, *Federal Wire & Steel Co.'s Plant, Cleveland, Ohio* (c. 1920), courtesy of the Library of Congress, Prints and Photographs Division, Detroit Publishing Company Collection [LC-D4-72257 DLC]. James Wright was born in Martins Ferry, Ohio, across the river from Wheeling, West Virginia, where his father worked in a glass factory. Wright's poetry is saturated with images of, and commentary on, the impact of industrialization on the natural landscape.

[4312] Anonymous, *Adrienne Rich* (c. 1975), courtesy of the Library of Congress [LC-USZ62-103575].

guage, raw images, and looser form. At this time, Rich also began identifying herself and her work with the growing feminist movement; she also identified as a lesbian. This lesbian consciousness led to the development of poems such as "Transcendental Etude" and "The Floating Poem" that dealt explicitly with lesbian love and sex. In the 1970s, Rich began exploring feminism through essay writing. Her most famous collection of prose, *Of Woman Born: Motherhood as Experience and Institution*, combines personal accounts, research, and theory to reveal her thoughts on feminism. In the 1980s, Rich wrote a number of dialogue poems, the best-known of which is her "Twenty-One Love Poems." This series modernizes the Elizabethan sonnet sequences written by men to idealized women by directing the poems to an unnamed female lover. Other poems, penned to women like Willa Cather, Ethel Rosenberg, and the poet's grandmothers, explore further aspects of Rich's identity, including her experience as a Jewish woman.

Rich's work is known for its political radicalism and candid exploration of motherhood, feminism, lesbianism, and Jewish identity. Her role as poet, essayist, and critic has earned her an important place in contemporary feminism.

TEACHING TIPS

■ Adrienne Rich's use of free verse can seem deceptively simple to students. Type out one of the poems in paragraph form and ask students to break the lines where they feel they should be broken. Emphasize that there is not a right answer "here," but rather that you are curious about what their rationale will be for where lines should be broken. Have students compare their versions of the poem to the original, and have them hypothesize about why Rich broke the lines where she did.

■ In "Diving into the Wreck" Rich uses the underwater exploration of a shipwreck as a metaphor for the exploration of the self or unconscious. Like many of her poems, this work seems to be about the struggle to form an identity. Ask students to paraphrase the poem, thinking particularly about Rich's use of the first person and the symbol of the diver. What are the main points about identity in this poem? Is Rich making an argument here? Then, ask students to consider the speaker in some of Rich's other poems, like "Transcendental Etude" and "Snapshots of a Daughter-in-Law." How do the speakers in these poems differ? What is Rich saying about identity here? This activity should help students discover that women are not neatly packaged, unified selves, as often imagined by patriarchal society; Rich's poetry gives voice to an often-fractured sense of self.

QUESTIONS

Comprehension: "Snapshots of a Daughter-in-Law" is filled with allusions, but one of the most telling is the quotation in section 7 from

Mary Wollstonecraft, an early feminist who fought for equality and suffrage at the turn of the eighteenth century. What is the significance of this allusion? Why does Rich refer to this early feminist?

Comprehension: Postmodern poets often pay particular attention to the way the poem looks on the page. Look at Rich's "Power." Why does she choose to space the words as she does? What is the effect on the reader? How do her formal choices shape our reading of the content?

Comprehension: Rich appropriates lines from Emily Dickinson and John Donne in her poems "I Am in Danger—Sir—" and "A Valediction Forbidding Mourning." Why does she invoke these poets? Is she claiming to be similar to or different from these authors? How do the titles affect our expectations as readers? What significance do these literary allusions hold?

Context: The transcendental poets were interested in connections between spirituality and nature. How does Rich's "Transcendental Etude" fit into this context? How does her poem differ from Snyder's "The Blue Sky"?

Context: As an active feminist, Rich was interested in raising consciousness about all kinds of women's issues, from sexual freedom to emancipation from the domestic sphere. How might "Snapshots of a Daughter-in-Law" be viewed as a feminist, consciousness-raising poem? What symbols are characteristic of feminist poetry? How does Rich represent the female body in this work?

Context: Compare the form of "Storm Warnings" with that of "Power." How has Rich's work changed from the early poem, written in 1951, to the later 1974 poem?

Exploration: During the first and second waves of feminism, female poets mined the resources of Greek and non-Western mythologies for ways to rewrite cultural history. What mythological figures do poets like H.D. (Hilda Doolittle) use to tell their stories? Which mythological figures do Rich and her cohort (Sylvia Plath, Anne Sexton, and Audre Lorde) choose? What power does using these figures add to Rich's work?

Exploration: The women's movement brought myriad issues to the forefront and gave women the vocabulary and forum to discuss their experiences honestly. For instance, the difficult and frustrating sides of mothering and marriage became topics of conversation. Many of the female poets in this unit reflect this liberated atmosphere as they explore the experience of motherhood and childbearing with candor and objectivity. Compare some of the poems about motherhood written by Sexton ("Little Girl, My String Bean, My Lovely Woman"), Lorde ("The Woman Thing," "Black Mother Woman"), and Plath ("Morning Song"). How do they represent mothering? What is new about this poetry? What seems surprising?

Exploration: Adrienne Rich has said that poetry must "consciously situate itself amid political conditions." How does her poetry reflect this idea? How might this statement be seen as descriptive of this period of poetry more generally? How does Rich's stance on poetry and politics compare to that of other writers in this unit, particularly Baraka and the Beats?

Gary Snyder (b. 1930)

Gary Snyder was raised on a dairy farm in the Pacific Northwest. He graduated with a B.A. in anthropology from Reed College and worked as a logger in the Pacific Northwest before going to Berkeley to study Asian languages from 1953 to 1956. During this time, he also met Allen Ginsberg, Jack Kerouac, and many of the other writers identified with the Beat movement. After spending three years in California, Snyder moved to Japan for roughly eight years. Although he returned to America briefly to teach at Berkeley, he returned to Japan to study Buddhism, an experience that deeply influenced his poetry.

As his life suggests, Snyder is fascinated by travel and ancient cultures, and the metaphor of the journey appears often in his poetry. His educational background in anthropology also shapes his investigation of rituals and history. Snyder's training in Zen Buddhism seems to unite his interest in foreign cultures, ancient ritual, and the serenity of nature; Asian influences in his work align him with Pound and Williams. Unlike Romantic poets, who used nature to mirror their emotions, Snyder does not use natural images to reflect his inner feelings, but rather appreciates the serene otherness of nature. Experimental language, conversational diction, unconventional line breaks and visual spacing, and abundant dialogue also characterize Snyder's poetry. The juxtaposition of American landscapes, particularly of the Pacific Northwest, with Eastern images and allusions, makes Snyder's poetry unique and powerful.

[7377] Lee Russell, *Grant County, Oregon. Malheur National Forest. Lumberjack Hitching Cable on Log which Will Be Loaded onto Trucks* (1942), courtesy of the Library of Congress [LC-USF34-073482-D DLC].

Like Robert Bly, James Wright, and W. S. Merwin, Gary Snyder turns to nature as an antidote to the problems of modernization and industrialized civilization. His poetry celebrates the Pacific Northwest as an alternative to the fast-paced modern world that seems impossibly separated from nature, simplicity, and manual labor. Snyder looks to the American Indians and to ancient Buddhism out of a genuine desire to learn wisdom from these traditions and rituals. Nature and meditation, he believes, are windows to the self. As might be expected, Snyder's interest in nature and the Orient aligns him with imagism and Pound. His affinity with nature led him to become active in the ecological movement, and his own lifestyle, which included growing his own vegetables, cutting wood, and hunting, made him virtually independent from modern civilization. Snyder has published numerous books of poetry, as well as many translations of ancient and modern Japanese poetry. In 1975, he received the Pulitzer Prize.

TEACHING TIP

■ Gary Snyder's poetry is deeply concerned with nature and with creating a visual picture of landscapes. Ask several students to come to the chalkboard and draw what they "see" in a poem ("Riprap" works well). How do the drawings differ? What have students left out? How closely does their memory of the poem resemble the original text?

QUESTIONS

Comprehension: Poets often refer to their literary ancestors, usually to align themselves with a particular tradition or to provide context for their work. Why does Snyder refer to Milton in "Milton by Firelight"?

Comprehension: Snyder uses quotation marks in a curious manner in "Beneath My Hand and Eye the Distant Hills. Your Body." What is the effect of the unconventional grammar and syntax? What is the purpose of the spacing, line breaks, and other visual techniques on the page?

Comprehension: What is the speaker's attitude toward nature in "Ripples on the Surface"? What is the effect of the unconventional punctuation toward the end of the poem?

Context: How would you describe Snyder's treatment of nature in his work? How does he broaden our concept of the American landscape?

Context: Snyder's poetry rarely confronts political and social issues like Vietnam or civil rights. Why do you think he chooses to avoid these hot-button issues? Are there ways in which his poetry could be described as politically and socially radical?

Context: The figure of Kokopelli, the ancient Hopi god of fertility, appears frequently in Snyder's poetry. What might Snyder's purpose be in using Kokopelli, particularly in "The Blue Sky"?

Exploration: "The Blue Sky" seems to unite Snyder's interest in Buddhism, India, and Native American culture. What is the effect of blending all these influences? How do the unconventional line breaks affect the meaning of the poem?

Exploration: Snyder's reverence for physical labor aligns him with Robert Frost. Compare Snyder's "Milton by Firelight" to Frost's "Mowing" or "After Apple-Picking." What do these poets share in technique and theme? Where do they diverge? How does this respect for work and the outdoors connect to American identity?

Exploration: Snyder's interest in the Far East, particularly Zen Buddhism, along with his knowledge of the Chinese language and culture, connect him to the high modernists, particularly Ezra

Collection. Baskets play important roles in spiritual and medicinal rituals. Mabel McKay, a Pomo weaver, wove baskets under the guidance of a spirit who taught her healing songs and imbued her baskets with spiritual power. The baskets here are made from willow, sedge root, dogbane, clam shell, abalone shell, magnesite beads, and meadowlark, quail, bluebird, mallard, oriole, and flicker feathers.

Pound. Snyder's concrete, economical imagery is also reminiscent of imagism. How does Snyder's work both continue and revise these central themes of modernist poetry?

Sylvia Plath (1932–1963)

Sylvia Plath spent most of her childhood in Wellesley, Massachusetts, where she lived close to her maternal grandparents. Her father, Otto Plath, was an entomology professor at Boston University, where he was known for his pioneering work on bumblebees. In 1940, when Plath was eight years old, her father died, which forced her mother, Aurelia, to enter the workforce. Despite her efforts, however, money was tight in the Plath household. Even in light of these hardships, Plath was a precocious child who enjoyed writing, reading, and the outdoors.

To the outside world, Sylvia Plath seemed to represent the 1950s ideal. Tall, slim, and outgoing, Plath made friends easily and excelled in extracurricular activities. Always a talented student, Plath attended prestigious Smith College on a scholarship, and she quickly became known on campus as a gifted writer. Behind the social exterior, however, Plath was a perfectionist, whose drive for success proved intense. She enjoyed many accolades, placing fiction in national magazines and winning first prize in the *Mademoiselle* Fiction Contest in 1952. Despite her success, Plath suffered from depression, and after her junior year at Smith, she attempted suicide, an experience that appears metaphorically in her later poems. After graduating *summa cum laude* from Smith, she won a Fulbright to study at Cambridge University in England, where she met and married poet Ted Hughes. Plath was instrumental in helping Hughes begin his successful writing career, and their influence on one another is notable. As Plath's poems about domesticity and motherhood suggest, becoming a wife and parent brought many difficult issues to the forefront of her life. Raised with 1950s middle-class values, Plath struggled with the tensions between those domestic ideals and her own feminism, and her poetry bears the mark of the conflict between her role as artist and her role as wife/mother. Plath's struggle to represent women's issues has earned her an important place in feminism. Hughes and Plath separated in the fall of 1962, and Plath was left to raise their two children alone. During what turned out to be one of the coldest British winters on record, Plath again suffered from depression, and she committed suicide at the age of thirty.

[9154] U.S. Office of War, *Housewife Preparing Dinner in Compact Kitchen in Greenbelt, Maryland* (c. 1942), courtesy of the Library of Congress [LC-USZ62-94034].

As a student in Robert Lowell's writing workshop in the late 1950s, Plath met Anne Sexton, who was to become an important influence on her poetry. Plath admired both Lowell's and Sexton's liberating verse, in which they tackled taboo subjects like mental illness, suicide, and family relationships with candor and intensity. Known as confessional poetry, the verse pioneered by

Sexton, Lowell, John Berryman, and Theodore Roethke exposed the raw emotion and intimacy of personal experience. Although Plath's poetry is often described as confessional, her poetry proves less auto-biographical than that of her friends. While she often begins her poems with what seems like autobiographical material, her genius lies in her ability to turn that autobiography into myth and metaphor. One of the great metaphor-makers of the century, Plath uses brilliant imagery to move her poetry far beyond the personal. In addition, much of what reads like autobiographical detail in poems like "Daddy" and "Lady Lazarus" is actually a dramatized performance based only loosely on her own life.

Plath is best known for her last book of poems, *Ariel*, which was published posthumously in 1965. Most of the poems in the volume were written in the fall and winter of 1962–63 in what appears to have been an amazingly creative period. Writing during the "blue hours" of the morning, or between 4 A.M. and 7 A.M. before her children awoke, Plath penned her finest work, characterized by a distinctive poetic voice, daring subject matter, colloquial diction, and brilliant metaphor. Plath told friend and critic A. Alvarez that these poems were meant to be heard rather than read, and the cooing rhymes of "Daddy" and rep-etition in "The Applicant" capture this sentiment. Although Plath had carefully arranged the sequence of *Ariel* before her death, Ted Hughes, the executor of her estate, rearranged the material, leaving out some of the more "aggressive" poems. He has been widely criticized for what many readers and critics consider the mismanagement of her work. Plath's journals and letters were later published, and her *Collected Poems* won the Pulitzer Prize in 1981. She also wrote dozens of short stories, a semi-autobiographical novel, *The Bell Jar*, and two children's books.

TEACHING TIPS

■ Students often have difficulty separating the poet from the speaker in Plath's poems. A productive discussion of Plath's work must con-sider her relationship to confessional poetry and the place of biog-raphy within that context. While it is indisputable that Plath draws on her personal life in her poems, many of the details are purposely exaggerated or misrepresented. In other words, biography is often a starting place, but Plath's genius lies in the ability to transform the personal into something more general, or as some readers and critics have put it, into something mythical.

■ Introduce your students to the idea of a dramatic monologue by having them read Emily Dickinson's "I heard a fly buzz when I died." How does the speaker in Plath's "Daddy" perform in a similar man-ner? How might this also be read as a dramatic monologue? Try to avoid discussion of sensationalized stories about the poet's life.

■ Readers often overlook the wit and cleverness in Plath's poetry. Often quite funny and refreshingly honest, Plath is one of the great metaphor-makers in modern poetry. Begin your study of Plath with poems like "Morning Song" and "Child," which show the tender and witty side of Plath as she writes about the wonder, joy, confusion, and fear of motherhood.

QUESTIONS

Comprehension: Plath's poems about motherhood are often surprising for their objectivity. In "Morning Song," why does the speaker say "I'm no more your mother . . ."? What does she mean here? What is the significance of the image of the museum? How does this mother feel toward her new infant? Does the tone change in the poem?

Comprehension: Like many of Plath's poems, Lady Lazarus begins *"in medias res,"* or "in the middle." In other words, the reader does not immediately understand the context or situation of the poem. In "Lady Lazarus" the speaker announces, "I have done it again." What is the *it*? Who is the peanut-crunching crowd?

Comprehension: Authors carefully consider their titles, often choosing them to set the tone of the work. Why do you think Plath chose the title "Daddy"? Why didn't she use "Father," or some other epithet, instead? What tone does this create? How does it fit with the content of the poem?

Context: What is the tone of "The Applicant"? Who is the speaker? To whom is he or she speaking? What is the role of repetition in this poem? How might this poem be connected to 1950s culture?

Context: Like other feminist works, Plath's poetry frequently uses the symbol of the body. How does the body in poems like "Lady Lazarus" or "Metaphors" compare to that by other poets in this unit? You might consider Audre Lorde's "Black Mother Woman" and Lorna Dee Cervantes's "The Body as Braille."

Context: Many of Plath's poems seem to engage the theme of transcendence; often, the speaker leaves or sheds the physical body (the end of "Lady Lazarus" is a good example); and frequently, her speakers commune with nature in interesting ways. "Ariel" is ostensibly about the speaker's ride on a horse, but it seems to take on mythic qualities by the end of the poem. Is the ride a metaphor for something else? What images seem particularly strange or unique? What is the "red / Eye, the cauldron of morning"? How might this be considered a poem of transcendence?

Exploration: The cultural critic Theodor Adorno was famous for saying that there could be no poetry after Auschwitz, and indeed, many poets remained silent on the subject for many years. Plath has been widely criticized for her use of Holocaust imagery in "Lady Lazarus" and "Daddy." Why do you think she uses these images? What is the effect of the references to the Holocaust in these poems?

Exploration: Sylvia Plath has become an icon in feminism since her death in 1963. Some people argue that her sensationalized life accounts for her large following, but other critics and readers agree that her poetry appeals to a wide audience for different reasons.

Perhaps one explanation is that Plath's poetry often articulates the struggle outlined by Betty Friedan in *The Feminine Mystique*. In other words, many of Plath's speakers seem unhappy, even desperate, in a domestic space that seems to offer few outlets for creative or intellectual expression. What other reasons can you point to for Plath's popularity among both scholars and general readers? How does her work embody many of the concerns of feminism?

Audre Lorde (1934–1992)

The daughter of West Indian parents, Audre Lorde was born in Harlem. She graduated from Hunter College in 1961 and earned a Masters in Library Science from Columbia University. For the next decade, she worked as a librarian and teacher. Lorde was also poet in residence at Tougaloo College, Mississippi, and taught at a number of colleges in New York City. Although she is known primarily as a poet, her "biomythography," *Zami: A New Spelling of My Name* (1982), is an important and influential prose work that chronicles her life from her childhood in Harlem to her coming out as a lesbian. In addition, Lorde recounts her battle with cancer in her poignant book *The Cancer Journals* (1980). These works, along with many of her poems, offer Lorde's readers personal glimpses into her life and experience, a trait that aligns her with confessional writers like Adrienne Rich, with whom she enjoyed a long and artistically fruitful relationship, and also with Sylvia Plath.

As Lorde has acknowledged, she is not an easy poet to categorize. Often associated with the Black Arts movement, her poetry, like that of Amiri Baraka, is frequently fiercely political; rage and violence are not tempered in her verse. In many ways, though, her verse, like that of Nikki Giovanni and June Jordan, falls into the feminist expansion of the Black Arts movement. In the late 1960s Lorde created poems like "Coal" and "Black Mother Woman" that celebrate blackness and seek to instill a sense of pride and self-love in the African American community. She draws inspiration from African history and myth, and many readers consider her best poetry to be those works that deal most closely with myth. Lorde's poems are not just directed at her own race; indeed, much of her work, often termed **protest poetry**, is laced with social criticism meant to call all readers to action. Poems like "Chain," for example, originate from current events and their journalistic origins force readers to confront social travesties in modern society. Known for her political commitment, Lorde is widely considered one of the most powerful and radical poets of our time.

TEACHING TIP

■ Read within the context of the Black Arts movement, the political undertones of Lorde's poetry are clearly visible. The message "Black Is Beautiful," one of the hallmarks of the movement, was a

[2254] Abbie Rowe, *March on Washington for Jobs and Freedom* (1963), courtesy of the National Park Service, Historic Places of the Civil Rights Movement.

LORDE WEB ARCHIVE

[2254] Abbie Rowe, *March on Washington for Jobs and Freedom* (1963), courtesy of the National Park Service, Historic Places of the Civil Rights Movement. Throughout the 1950s and 1960s, many groups, including African Americans seeking greater equality and civil rights, used marches and nonviolent protests to make their voices heard. The sight of thousands of protesters marching in front of the White House had a powerful impact.
[3042] Anonymous, *Civil Rights March on Washington, D.C. [A Young Woman*

at the March with a Banner] (1963), courtesy of the Still Picture Branch, National Archives and Records Administration. Basic constitutional rights were denied to African Americans for well over the first 150 years of the United States's existence. "I have come to believe over and over again," poet Audre Lorde said, "that what is most important to me must be spoken, made verbal and shared, even at the risk of having it bruised or misunderstood."

[5460] Courier Lithograph Company, *Uncle Tom's Cabin—On the Levee* (1899), courtesy of the Library of Congress, Prints and Photographs Division, Theatrical Poster Collection [POS-TH-1899.U53, no. 3]. Poster for a theater production showing happy slaves dancing. Post–Civil War Uncle Tom Shows were often performed by whites in blackface. By presenting blacks as subservient, without physical, intellectual, moral, or sexual power, such shows gave the term "Uncle Tom" its current derogatory meaning.

[6237] Gemini Rising, Inc., *Clenched Fist on Red, Green, and Black Background* (1971), courtesy of the Library of Congress [LC-USZC4-4389]. The Black Arts movement of the 1960s and 1970s was closely related to the Black Power movement. Leaders of the Black Arts movement, such as Amiri Baraka, argued that ethics and aesthetics were inextricably linked and that black art ought to be politically focused and community-oriented.

[7138] Anonymous, *LeRoi Jones (Amiri Baraka) Leads the Black Arts Parade Down 125th Toward the Black Arts Theater Repertory/School on 130th Street, New York City* (1965), courtesy of *The Liberator*. Influenced by civil rights activism and black nationalism, Baraka (Jones) and other African American artists opened the Black Arts Theater in Harlem in 1965.

[7652] Anonymous, *Jim Crow Jubilee* (1847), courtesy of the Library of Congress [LC-USZ62-37348]. Jim Crow laws took their name from a character in minstrel shows that featured racist stereotypes about African Americans, depicting them as lazy and as less intelligent than whites.

radical call for the black community to nurture itself and to recognize its own self-worth. Using the archive, study the visual images that reflect the idea that "Black Is Beautiful." Alternatively, instructors could show the class representations of black Americans from the early twentieth century. Examples might include Aunt Jemima, Bojangles, minstrel shows, Uncle Ben, and the "lawn jockey." In small groups, students should consider each image, identify the stereotype the image is based on, and explain how and why a poet like Lorde chose to counter such derogatory stereotypes with her work. Is it easy for students to recognize the original stereotypes black writers were trying to challenge? If so, what does that suggest? If not, what might that suggest? Then have your students read "Coal." How does looking at the images in the archive change the way they read this poem? What new elements do they notice in the text?

QUESTIONS

Comprehension: Lorde often writes about differences between generations, particularly of women. In "Black Mother Woman," what is the speaker's relationship to her mother? What has she learned from her? What does this poem have to say about identity? What is the significance of the title?

Comprehension: Many of Lorde's poems explore the issue of being black and female. Why does Lorde title a poem "Coal"? What is the effect of isolating the pronoun "I" on the first line? What is the tone of the poem? How does Lorde portray language in this poem? What is she saying about words and their meanings? What is she saying about blackness in this poem?

Context: How is Lorde's poetry a feminist response to Black Arts poetry, such as that by Baraka? You might compare "Coal" or "Black Mother Woman" with Baraka's "An Agony. As Now." and "A Poem for Willie Best."

Context: Audre Lorde talks about using poetry to break the silence. How does her poetry push the boundaries of the genre's traditional subject matter? How might that align her with confessional poets? What differences do you see between her writing and that of confessional poets like Sexton and Plath?

Exploration: Lorde's poetry, like Baraka's, often expresses rage and violence. Discuss Lorde's intended audience. How might her poetry affect different groups of people? How does Lorde challenge conventional concepts of what it means to be an American?

Exploration: Lorde's interest in African tradition, and particularly in oral traditions, deeply influenced her work. How does oral tradition manifest itself in her poems? How does her use of the oral tradition connect her to earlier African American writers, like those of the Harlem Renaissance, or perhaps to authors of slave narratives? What techniques do these writers share?

Amiri Baraka (LeRoi Jones) (b. 1934)

Amiri Baraka was born Everett Leroy Jones in Newark, New Jersey. A creative child, he enjoyed cartooning and creative writing, particularly science fiction. Also gifted academically, Jones graduated from high school two years early and attended Howard University, where he was disappointed by what he saw as the school's attempt to train black students to be white. It was during his undergraduate years that Jones changed the spelling of his name to the more Africanized LeRoi. His later stint in the U.S. Air Force as a weatherman and gunner also proved demoralizing, as he realized the extent of white prejudice and, perhaps more disconcertingly, the prevalence of the belief that mistreatment of blacks was justified. These experiences surface in his later writing. While a graduate student at Columbia, Jones knew some of the Beat writers, with whom he shared an impulse toward living on the fringes of American society. In the late 1950s, Jones was visible on the literary scene; he and his first wife, Hettie Jones, published *Yugen*, a poetry magazine. In 1961, he helped start the American Theater for Poets. Until this point, Jones was known mostly for his poetry, through which he sought a solution to racism in American society.

However, after the assassination of Malcolm X in 1965, Jones's views changed dramatically. From that point on, Jones considered racial harmony in America impossible and urged blacks to find other alternatives. The 1960s proved a turning point in his art. Jones became increasingly interested in drama, and his most successful play, *Dutchman*, premiered on March 24, 1964, at the Cherry Lane Theatre in New York, with Jennifer West and Robert Hooks starring in the lead roles.

As racial tensions heightened in the mid-1960s, Jones became a committed activist, leaving his family to move to Harlem, where he quickly became known as a black nationalist. His commitment to the arts strengthened, and in 1965 he founded the Black Arts Repertory Theater, which produced militant drama meant for black audiences. For Jones, art was a vehicle for political change, in particular for the liberation of blacks. In 1967 Jones was arrested during the summer riots, but the charges against him were eventually dropped. In 1968 he founded the Black Community Development and Defense Organization. The members wore traditional African dress, conversed in both Swahili and English, and dedicated themselves to Islam. To mark this new political and spiritual transformation, Jones changed his name to Imamu Amiri Baraka. His controversial and radical politics have earned him an important place in the black community, and he has been influential in developing relationships between black Americans and black Africans. Identified with the Black Arts movement, Baraka's work is characterized by an angry voice that frequently calls for violence as a means to achieve liberation for blacks.

[6262] Anonymous, *LeRoi Jones (Amiri Baraka), Allen Ginsberg and John Fles* (1959), courtesy of the Department of Special Collections, Stanford University Libraries.

[4314] Leroy McLucas, *Imamu Amiri Baraka, Formerly LeRoi Jones, Head-and-Shoulders Portrait, Facing Right* (1965), courtesy of the Library of Congress [LC-USZ62-115116]. In 1965, after the assassination of Malcolm X, Amiri Baraka divorced his white wife, changed his name, and moved to Harlem, where he became a prominent figure in the Black Arts movement. Since then, Baraka has revised his black nationalist views in favor of Marxism and dropped "Imamu" (a Muslim word which means "spiritual leader") from his name.

[6262] Anonymous, *LeRoi Jones (Amiri Baraka), Allen Ginsberg and John Fles* (1959), courtesy of the Department of Special Collections, Stanford University Libraries. Jones (Baraka) and Ginsberg seated in living room with drums. Jones was originally associated with the Beat movement, but with the growth of the Black Power movement, he changed his focus to political civil rights.

[7138] Anonymous, *LeRoi Jones (Amiri Baraka) Leads the Black Arts Parade Down 125th Toward the Black Arts Theater Repertory/School on 130th Street, New York City* (1965), courtesy of *The Liberator*. Influenced by civil rights activism and black nationalism, Baraka (Jones) and other African American artists opened the Black Arts Theater in Harlem in 1965.

[7430] Anonymous, *Beat Poet Allen Ginsberg's Former Companion, Peter Orlovsky, Left, and Black Activist Poet Amiri Baraka Speak with Each Other* (1997), courtesy of the Associated Press. While a graduate student at Columbia, LeRoi Jones (Amiri Baraka) knew some of the Beat writers, with whom he shared an interest in living on the fringes of American society. However, after the assassination of Malcolm X in 1965, Baraka considered racial harmony in America impossible. Much of Baraka's work reflects this more militant perspective. His "Civil Rights Poem" was written during a homophobic period, though earlier he had been friends with a number of the gay members of the Beat Generation, and here he is featured with Ginsberg's ex-lover.

- Choose one of the longer speeches in Scene II of *Dutchman*. Practice performing the excerpt. What choices have you made about delivery? What have you chosen to emphasize? Why? What gestures, pauses, or inflections make sense to you? Why?

- Baraka's work has been controversial because it often calls for violence. Whether or not readers accept the anger and vengeance expressed in these works, it seems important to talk about audience. Have students imagine that they have been asked to do the publicity for a production of *Dutchman*. Whom do they imagine attending the play? What text would be on the flyers and in the program notes? Whom is Baraka trying to reach? Why does he feel violence and anger are successful tools? How have different groups of people responded to his work? Does his militancy affect his credibility as a thinker and artist?

QUESTIONS

Comprehension: Why does Baraka choose the subway as a setting for *Dutchman*? What is significant about his choice?

Comprehension: Were you surprised by the ending of *Dutchman*? Why do you think Baraka chose to end the play this way? What do you take away from the play? How might it be read as a politically charged drama?

Comprehension: In "A Poem for Willie Best," who is Willie Best? Why did Baraka dedicate a poem to him? Baraka uses numerous parentheses in this poem. What is the effect of this stylistic choice? Why are some of the parentheses left open?

Context: Both Amiri Baraka and Langston Hughes wrote with political agendas, though Baraka's philosophy tended to be more militant and separatist than Hughes's. Both poets also wrote about both the average black man and the black artist. Compare Hughes's "Note on Commercial Theatre," "The Weary Blues," and "Song for a Dark Girl" to Baraka's "A Poem for Willie Best," a poem about a black character actor. What techniques do these poets share? How are their works different?

Exploration: Using drama as a way to incite public action is not a new concept. Indeed, in 1907, John M. Synge's production of *Playboy of the Western World* at the Abbey Theater incited riots in Ireland because audiences felt it was offensive. Why is it that drama seems able to stir people to action? Along with Baraka and Synge, you might also consider W. B. Yeats (*Catherine Ni Houlihan*) and Arthur Miller (*The Crucible*).

Exploration: Although the Black Arts movement has waned, there are still artists and audiences who believe in black separatism. How has Baraka influenced contemporary culture? Do you see evidence of his teachings and practices today? You might consider rap music, hip-hop, and film in your answer.

Joy Harjo (b. 1951)

The daughter of a mixed Cherokee, French, and Irish mother and a Creek father, Harjo was born in Tulsa, Oklahoma. As a student and poet, Harjo has remained in touch with her Native American roots. She left Tulsa as a teenager to attend the Institute of American Indian Arts, a high school in Santa Fe, New Mexico. She earned an undergraduate degree from the University of New Mexico and an M.F.A. from the University of Iowa. Her career as an educator has led her all over the Southwest; she has held positions at Arizona State University, the University of Colorado, the University of Arizona, and the University of New Mexico.

The Harjo family has a prominent place in the history of the Creek Indians. As the great-great-granddaughter of the leader of a Creek rebellion against their **removal** from Alabama to Oklahoma, Harjo comes from a people with a painful history. Still, her poetry often emphasizes the positive aspects of Native American heritage. Harjo uses words to begin the healing process and to explain the ruptures in current society. She is interested in questions of gender and ethnic identity and her work devotes special attention to the struggles of Native American women. Her poetry is rich with myth, and she draws inspiration from nature, as well as the oral tradition and culture of her Creek heritage. She often refers to herself as a wanderer, and her poetry explores the experience of movement, relocation, and journey, both physical and spiritual.

Joy Harjo travels widely throughout the United States, playing saxophone with her band. Her poetry also resonates with the rhythms and sounds of music, particularly jazz, blues, country, and Native American dance songs. Harjo's works include *The Woman Who Fell from the Sky* (1994), *A Map to the Next World* (1991), and *How We Became Human* (2002). She co-edited *Reinventing the Enemy's Language* (1998), an anthology that celebrates the experience of Native American women. The most comprehensive anthology of its kind, it includes poetry, fiction, prayers, and memoir from Native American women, representing nearly fifty Indian nations.

TEACHING TIPS

■ Harjo's poems borrow from the Native American oral tradition and have a sense of rhythm that makes them even more powerful when read aloud. Have students read one of her poems aloud. How does the performance change the way they originally thought about the poem?

■ Harjo is a saxophonist in a jazz band that combines Native American drums and instrumentals with the jazz of the American South, the geographic homelands of the Creek Indians. Though twenty-first-century American youth may associate jazz with "easy listening," it is important to consider jazz's revolutionary influence on literature and aesthetics during the twentieth century. For American writers, jazz referred not only to a musical style, but also to a style of dance, litera-

[7432] Anonymous, *Imamu Amiri Baraka, the Former Poet-Playwright LeRoi Jones* (1974), courtesy of the Associated Press AP. This photo of Imamu Amiri Baraka was taken when he announced in Trenton on Wednesday, January 9, 1974, that the New Jersey Black Political Assembly would meet in New Brunswick, New Jersey, January 26, to select delegates to the National Black Political Convention.
[7495] Herman Hiller, *Malcolm X at Queens Court* (1964), courtesy of the Library of Congress [LC-USZ62-119478]. Portrait of Malcolm X. Malcolm X's assassination prompted Amiri Baraka to emphasize race in his art.

[7382] Duncan, *Chitto Harjo or Crazy Snake, Head-and-Shoulders Portrait, Facing Front* (1903), courtesy of the Library of Congress [LC-USZ62-111977].

[3708] Jesse Logan Nusbaum, *Entryway of House Near Guadalupe from Under Porch, Sante Fe, N.M.* (1912), courtesy of the Denver Public Library/Western History Department. Creek poet Joy Harjo attended high school in Santa Fe. One of her goals has been to make poetry and prose that is more inclusive of the experiences of people of color.

[7382] Duncan, *Chitto Harjo or Crazy Snake, Head-and-Shoulders Portrait, Facing Front* (1903), courtesy of the Library of Congress [LC-USZ62-111977]. Photograph of Creek chief Chitto Harjo, leader of dissident Creeks who opposed land allotments that violated earlier treaties. Joy Harjo is part Creek and an enrolled member of the Muscogee tribe. Harjo's work ties Native American heritage, including oral traditions, to contemporary themes.

[8313] Joy Harjo, Interview: "Native Voices and Poetry of Liberation" (2003), courtesy of *American Passages* and Annenberg/CPB. Writer Joy Harjo discusses the staying power of oral tradition.

[8314] Joy Harjo, Interview: "Native Voices and Poetry of Liberation" (2003), courtesy of *American Passages* and Annenberg/CPB. Writer Joy Harjo discusses the power of the spoken word.

ture, dress, and art. Jazz's rebellion could be felt in the freedom of improvisation, as well as the ability to take old melodies, split them apart, and make them fit a new rhythm and worldview. Harjo borrows from jazz in her poetry both in terms of the syncopated rhythms of her work and in her affinities for improvisation, call and response, and collage. Ask students to explore the importance of jazz for Harjo's verse.

QUESTIONS

Comprehension: Poets often use repetition for emphasis and to create a pattern when writing in free verse. Often the repetition is slightly different in each rendition, making the reader think about the subtle shades of meaning in language. In "Call It Fear" Harjo repeats phrases like "walk backwards," "talk backwards," "breathe backwards." What does she mean here? What is the significance of these repeated images? What is the "edge" to which she keeps referring?

Comprehension: Animals in poetry are often representative of a wilderness damaged or forgotten in the chaos of the modern world. What is the significance of the white bear in "White Bear"? What is the tone of this poem? What is the role of nature?

Comprehension: "Summer Night" is filled with beautiful, delicate imagery. What is the effect of the line breaks on the page? How does the visual pattern of the poem affect its meaning?

Context: In *The Woman Who Fell from the Sky*, Harjo relates Native American myth to contemporary life. How does her use of myth compare to that of the feminist poets in this unit, particularly Adrienne Rich ("Snapshots of a Daughter-in-Law") and Sylvia Plath ("Ariel")?

Context: Memory is an important theme in Harjo's work. Assimilation and the ever-decreasing number of people who can speak tribal languages threaten the preservation of the cultures of Native Americans, who have traditionally relied on oral tradition to transmit their heritage. Thus, it is not surprising that memory is so central to Harjo's work. How does she represent memory, both personal and collective? You might look at "The Flood" and "White Bear."

Exploration: The relationships and understanding among different generations of women are central to many women poets. This seems particularly true of writers in the women's movement. How do these poets represent the differences among generations of women? In what ways is the tone of their poems political? Consider poems by Lorde, Harjo, and Rich in your answer.

Exploration: Many of Harjo's poems bear the influence of jazz, using call and response, repetition, and visual patterns in a way reminiscent of that genre. Compare Harjo's "Summer Night" to Langston Hughes's "The Weary Blues," also influenced by jazz. What similarities or differences in technique do you notice?

Exploration: Travel is an important theme in Harjo's work. How does this theme relate to the experiences of Native Americans, both in terms of a connection to the land and with regard to Native American spiritual images that often involve flight and journey? How does recent Native American history, particularly forced removal to Oklahoma, relate to these images of travel in Harjo's poetry? How does she use this theme to bring closure to the past?

Lorna Dee Cervantes (b. 1954)

Cervantes was born in San Francisco and is of Mexican descent. Sensitive to the racial and ethnic prejudice she might encounter growing up in San Jose, her parents insisted that she speak only English both in and outside the home. She graduated from San Jose State College and for many years supported herself by writing and publishing. Cervantes founded and published a journal, *Mango*, which featured the work of Latino poets; she also wrote two volumes of poetry. Currently, she teaches at the University of Colorado at Boulder and is co-editor of *Red Dirt*, a cross-cultural poetry journal.

Both her Mexican heritage and her feminism inform Cervantes's writing. Her poetry celebrates her Mexican heritage, but it is also harshly critical of machismo and male dominance in Chicano culture and celebratory of specifically female oral traditions. She sometimes implicitly compares Euro-American dominance of Chicano people and lands with Chicano men's domination of women. Just as men and women are often at odds in her bilingual poems, English and Spanish words seem to battle on the page for space and prominence. Some poems imagine fantastical escapes from such conflict—an entirely female family, for example, or an uninhabited land. Images of birds and migration appear often in her work, particularly in her first book, *Emplumada* (1981), the title of which is a play on Spanish words connoting a bird's plumage and a writer's pen. In *From the Cables of Genocide: Poems on Love and Hunger* (1991), Cervantes uses symbols from nature to explore romantic and familial love. Her affinity for nature and landscape lend her work a unique delicacy and beauty that sometimes belie its political and social messages.

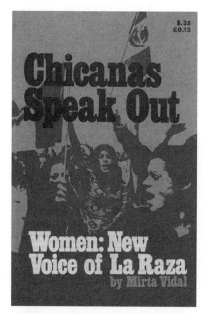

[7084] Mirta Vidal, Cover of *Chicanas Speak Out* (1971), courtesy of Duke University.

TEACHING TIP

■ Students will probably find Cervantes's poetry very accessible. Building the discussion around the idea of a dual identity will help them recognize the complicated aspects of her work. What does it mean for an American poet to write about a dual heritage? How does a poet like Cervantes explore what it means to be an American? Consider the ways in which this contemporary American poet incorporates Spanish in her work. Have your students choose one of Cervantes's poems and translate the Spanish (they can use a Spanish/English dictionary or the Internet) into English. Then have them rewrite the poem completely in English. How does this translation change the poem? What effects are lost? You might consider using "Visions of Mexico While at a Writing Symposium in Port Townsend, Washington" or "The Body as Braille" for this activity.

CERVANTES WEB ARCHIVE

[5615] Anonymous, *Disturnell Map of Mexico* (c. 1850), courtesy of Benson Latin American Collection, University of Texas at Austin. Although the treaty of Guadalupe-Hidalgo officially ended the Mexican-American War in 1848, disputes continued between the Mexican and United States governments concerning, among other issues, the border of Texas.

[6133] Anonymous, *Young Hispanic Woman* (c. 1969), courtesy of the Denver Public Library, Western History Collection. In the 1960s and 1970s, a number of Chicana women protested definitions of womanhood and American identity that excluded Chicana heritage and life.

[6710] Judith F. Baca, *La Memoria de Nuestra Tierra* (2000), courtesy of the Social and Public Art Resource Center, © Judith F. Baca, La Memoria de Nuestra Tierra, Colorado, 2000. Judith Baca is an acclaimed muralist who believes that art can be a forum for social dialogue, as well as a tool for social change. In this sense her work shares much with the writings of Gloria Anzaldúa, Cherrie Moraga, Lorna Dee Cervantes, and Helena Maria Viramontes.

[7084] Mirta Vidal, Cover of *Chicanas Speak Out* (1971), courtesy of Duke University. Chicana authors, including Cherrie Moraga and Lorna Dee Cervantes, protested exclusive definitions of womanhood and American identity that did not include Chicana heritage and life.

[7605] Anonymous, *Unidentified Woman Finishes Defiant Message* (1973), courtesy of the Denver Public Library. A young woman with long hair, wearing bellbottoms, scrawls out a message which reads, "We are not beaten . . . and we do not intend to be beaten or driven as such. . . . What has happened here is but the sound before the fury of those who are oppressed." The building pictured was damaged in an explosion that followed a shootout between Denver police and people of the Chicano community on March 16, 1973.

[8756] Eliot Young, Interview: "Exploring Borderlands" (2003), courtesy of *American Passages* and Annenberg/CPB. Eliot Young, professor of history at Lewis and Clark College, discusses Chicano and Chicana literature.

QUESTIONS

Comprehension: How do you interpret the uncle's dream in "Uncle's First Rabbit"? What is the effect of his first hunting experience? What is the tone of this poem?

Comprehension: In "For Virginia Chavez," Cervantes alludes to a string of famous poets, including Lord Byron, the Romantic poet, John Donne, the seventeenth-century poet, and popular Victorian poets Robert and Elizabeth Browning. Why would an author like Cervantes refer to canonical British writers? How is she continuing or transforming the work of those earlier authors?

Comprehension: In "Visions of Mexico While at a Writing Symposium in Port Townsend, Washington," Cervantes divides the poem into two parts, titled "Mexico" and "Washington." What is the speaker's attitude towards each place? What is the tone of the poem? Does it change? What images are associated with each place? What does that tell us about the speaker's state of mind? What is the effect of the long title?

Context: The theme of migration appears often in Cervantes's poetry, and is frequently connected to the prominence of migration within Latino history. This theme might also be seen as a reflection of Cervantes's personal migration between Mexican and American cultures. Trace Cervantes's use of migration, as both symbol and theme, in the poems in this unit. (You might look specifically at "Uncle's First Rabbit," "Visions of Mexico While at a Writing Symposium in Port Townsend, Washington," and "Emplumada.") What generalizations can you make about her treatment of this theme? How is it represented in each of the poems?

Context: The Black Arts movement is defined by a commitment to bringing the arts and community together, raising consciousness about black experience, using art to gain political and social equality for black Americans, and building a sense of pride and awareness of history in the black community. After reading Cervantes's work, think about what a Chicano aesthetic might look like. What goals might it share with the Black Arts movement?

Exploration: Like Cervantes, the Beats draw on ideas related to travel in their work. You might look specifically at Kerouac's *On the Road* and Snyder's "The Blue Sky." How does Cervantes's use of the concept of the "journey" differ from that of the Beats? What do her poems about migration have in common with works by the Beats, as well as by transcendent poets?

Exploration: Birds are a common poetic symbol for the soul, in part because of their ability to move between the sky and the earth. In other poems, birds, usually songbirds, are symbols of the poet. Some important poems that use this trope are Paul Laurence Dunbar's "I Know Why the Caged Bird Sings," Sylvia Plath's "Lady Lazarus," and John Keats's "Ode to a Nightingale." Images of birds appear throughout Cervantes's work. How do you interpret this? How do these images change in different poems? What kinds of birds appear? What specific cultural dimension do these birds have?

Exploration: Many of the poets in this unit have a keen sense of place; particular places and landscapes figure prominently in their poetry. Ginsberg, for example, writes about San Francisco and large urban areas, Harjo writes about landscapes central to Native American lore, and Wright's poems are often about rural Ohio. Similarly, Cervantes envisions the landscapes of Mexico and America in her work. Why does the land seem so important to all these poets? Are there particular historical or cultural reasons that might make them feel tied to the land? How might an interest in the land relate to ideas of transcendence and liberation?

Suggested Author Pairings

LORNA DEE CERVANTES AND AUDRE LORDE

Both these writers explode the notion that female identity is uniform and continuous. Cervantes's poetry is characterized by her dual heritage, and she frequently juxtaposes locations, languages, and imagery. Similarly, Lorde's poetry features candid speakers struggling with their experiences as outsiders because of race, gender, and sexual orientation. Comparing the way these poets use standard English alongside Spanish or black vernacular dialect also raises useful questions about what it means to connect two worlds and what it means to be an American. Both writers also recognize the political force behind poetry. Cervantes has been instrumental in creating and developing a Chicano aesthetic, just as Audre Lorde has been an important presence in Black Arts. Despite these similarities, these writers differ widely, particularly in the tone of their poems. Lorde's use of the first person creates an intimacy with the reader, whereas Cervantes's writing has a more narrative feel. How do these authors redefine what it means to be American? How does their ethnic heritage influence their ideas about America and its national values?

JAMES WRIGHT AND JOY HARJO

Both of these poets share an affinity with nature, and both write in a meditative style. While Wright looks primarily to nature as an antidote to the modern, Harjo expresses a desire to unite the past (her Native American heritage) with the present (modern times), and she uses nature as a means to connect the two. Wright and Harjo, however, do share a desire for transcendence, and might be described as meditative poets. Both poets remember and long for nature and landscapes destroyed or threatened by civilization, and both poets write with a sense of loss and reverence. In what ways can their poems be read as elegies, not for people, but for landscapes and locations? How do the different backgrounds of these poets influence their views of nature? How do they complement and diverge from one another?

AMIRI BARAKA, GARY SNYDER, AND ALLEN GINSBERG

These poets recognize the political power behind their poetry, and they use words to shock audiences, critique government institutions, and question traditional American values. Although he later became a leader of the Black Arts movement, Baraka was connected to the early Beat movement, and he knew Ginsberg and the other New York–based writers of the movement. Like the Beats, Baraka was interested in living on the fringes of society, exploding conventional ways of thinking, and using poetry for political rebellion. By the mid-1950s, however, Baraka had separated from the Beats to pursue racial themes in his poetry, and his work became increasingly militant. He also began spending more time on drama and dedicated himself to bridging the gap between the community and artists. While the Beat poets considered themselves outsiders, they did write poetry that appealed to the masses. Just as Baraka shocked audiences with his dialect, obscenities, and violence, so the Beat poets shocked their readers with similar breaches of tradition, using obscenities, slang, and references to illegal drugs. Ginsberg became the voice for the Beat movement, and Baraka, in a similar fashion, became the figure most associated with Black Arts. Both poets had lifestyles that matched their vibrant, radical, and confrontational poetry. Gary Snyder, however, joined the Beat movement later, after many of the writers had moved to San Francisco. His interest in nature and ecology set him apart from Baraka and Ginsberg. Snyder's work is also decidedly more meditative. Still, he shares their radical use of diction and subject matter, and he, too, lives on the fringes of society. Like Ginsberg, who was interested in the Far East, and Baraka, whose poetry reflects a fascination with Africa, Snyder's work also shows some marks of primitivism. Interested in the Far East, particularly China, and Native American culture, Snyder explores transcendence and spirituality in his work. How do these poets deepen our understanding of the Beat movement and its complexity? How does each poet use politics differently in his work? How have these men changed our perception of the poet as a cultural figure?

SYLVIA PLATH AND ADRIENNE RICH

These writers are considered among the most important feminist poets of our century. Both women struggle to represent female experience, and they shatter conventional notions of poetic subject matter in the process. They write openly about the female body, intimate relationships, sex, and motherhood. For both authors, questions of identity are central to their work, and readers are often struck by the conflicted sense of self represented by these poets. How do these authors challenge society's treatment of women and **sexuality**? What is experimental or innovative about their writing? Why are they so important to the feminist movement?

JOHN ASHBERY AND ALLEN GINSBERG

Both of these poets are interested in the discourse of popular culture and they both explore the boundaries between prose and verse. In addition, both Ginsberg and Ashbery avoid writing about specific events and people, choosing instead to concentrate on the workings of the mind or a representation of the creative process. But Ginsberg uses an authoritative, sweeping voice reminiscent of Whitman, whereas Ashbery's poetic voice seems detached, erudite, and witty. Ginsberg looks to jazz, Eastern religion, and drugs for poetic inspiration, whereas Ashbery draws on visual art and is particularly influenced by avant-garde painters like Jackson Pollock. Ginsberg's poetry is highly political, whereas Ashbery seems disconnected from the political turmoil of the 1960s. How do these poets represent American experience? How do they incorporate elements of popular culture? What do they envision as the goal of poetry and art?

CORE CONTEXTS

The War in Vietnam: The War at Home

America emerged from World War II as a superpower with a dramatically transformed foreign policy. The United States became, in historian Mary Sheila McMahon's words, "a more activist and outward-looking state" as it purported to defend democratic ideals. The government felt that to protect American self-interests, defend itself against the Stalinist Soviet Union and Maoist China, and promote capitalistic democracy worldwide, it had to abandon its tradition of isolationism. With the onset of the Cold War, the perceived threat of Soviet and Red Chinese aggression strengthened the government's resolve to protect its interests everywhere. This resolve led to interventions in the autonomy of other nations and increased anxiety at home about "subversive" political and social movements. After the escalation of the Vietnam War in the mid-1960s, the conflict and its heavy casualties divided the country dramatically. U.S. involvement in Vietnam killed more than 50,000 Americans and lasted longer than the fighting in both world wars combined.

The Vietnam War was a protracted struggle in jungles, swamps, and other difficult terrain, a war with no front lines and two adversaries: the North Vietnamese Army, a well-trained, well-equipped force with decades of experience in guerrilla warfare, and the Vietcong, a South Vietnamese army of dedicated irregulars, genius in the tactics of hit-and-run, and adept at blending in with a civilian population whose loyalties were always in doubt. By the middle of 1968, promises of a quick conclusion had melted away, and a series of catastrophic engagements—the Tet Offensive, the siege of Khe Sanh, the battle for Hue, which nearly destroyed the second-largest city in the Republic of Vietnam—brought many Americans to the sobering recognition that

[3043] John A. Gentry, LCpl, *Vietnam . . . Private First Class Joseph Big Medicine Jr., a Cheyenne Indian, Writes a Letter to His Family in the United States* (1969), courtesy of the National Archives and Records Administration.

[7360] Frank Moffit, SPC 5, *Vietnam . . . A Sky Trooper from the 1st Cavalry Division (Airmobile) Keeps Track of the Time He Has Left on His "Short Time" Helmet* (1968), courtesy of the National Archives and Records Administration.

the war could continue for a very long time, and that the prospects of a real victory were dim. Another source of moral conflict in the United States was the configuration of the American Armed Forces, and of American casualties, as a result of provisions of the draft. Because college students before 1970 were deferred from conscription, campuses became places of temporary and uneasy refuge, where male students were keenly aware of a countdown to graduation and a coming forfeiture of protection; meanwhile, the front-line forces in Southeast Asia were filled with young men from working-class, inner-city, and minority backgrounds, men who lacked the money and the connections to spare them from military service. As the reasons for continuing the war grew more and more confused in the minds of troops abroad and Americans at home, the resistance to the war grew exponentially in 1968 and 1969; demonstrations in Washington, D.C., New York, and other cities drew hundreds of thousands of people.

When Richard Nixon took office in January 1969, the American government implemented two strategies to cool the domestic resistance and find a way out of the conflict: (1) a "Vietnamization" of the combat forces, which meant that American troops would be gradually moved away from direct combat, and (2) a draft lottery, which ended the college deferment and determined eligibility for conscription on the basis of randomly chosen birth dates. For a while, these changes did have some of the intended effect, but the May 1970 killing of student protesters by National Guard troops at Kent State and Jackson State, two college campuses, brought about a nationwide student strike. With the support of faculty and administrators, many campuses shut down almost completely until the end of the academic year.

Many of the poets writing during this period responded directly to the Vietnam conflict or expressed a heightened distrust of authority. Repelled also by the general assumption that America could fight a major war and indulge itself materialistically at the same time, some poets looked to leftist politics for an alternate vision of what the United States could be. The Vietnam conflict and the protests against the war were also, in a sense, media events. For the first time in history, television crews could send full-color videotape quickly home from a battlefield halfway around the world, and domestic TV crews could bring violent confrontations with police and National Guardsmen directly into the living room. Not surprisingly, depictions of the human body as a site of suffering, resistance, and sacrifice turn up frequently in literature written during and about these years.

[7361] Anonymous, *Vietnam War Protesters* (1967), courtesy of the National Archives and Records Administration [NRE-21-KANSWICHCR-CR928-WICH1895].

QUESTIONS

Comprehension: What are some of the reasons Americans protested against the Vietnam War? Why did this conflict raise such opposition at home?

Comprehension: How did the Vietnam protest movements change American culture? What values are associated with the Vietnam era? How did the Vietnam War change the public's attitude towards the government?

Context: Although *Howl* was written in 1954, there are several references to capitalism and at least one reference (line 32) to communism. What is Ginsberg's attitude toward American capitalism and Soviet communism? Based on what you know of his lifestyle and the Beat movement, how do you think Ginsberg responded to the Vietnam War?

Context: Although the Vietnam War was a defining event for a generation of poets, few of the poems in this unit directly address the conflict. Why? Do you see more subtle evidence of the war's influence?

Exploration: During the height of the Vietnam protests in the late 1960s, many men and women donned Vietcong uniforms in order to make a dramatic political statement. Why do you think protesters dressed in Vietcong uniforms? What statement were they trying to make?

Exploration: Literary critic and poet Peter Sacks has argued that elegies not only memorialize the dead, but seek to take the reader and poet through a mourning process, thereby helping the reader recover from fears of mortality and move beyond loss. Some critics have argued that in the era following Hiroshima and the Holocaust, the appropriate mourner would not recover from her "melancholia," but would mourn the loss of the dead in perpetuity. Compare elegiac poems on Vietnam (e.g., Denise Levertov's "What Were They Like?") to Lowell's "For the Union Dead" and Allen Tate's "Ode to the Confederate Dead." What sources of consolation does each poet provide? What role does language play in this consolation? Do any of these poems seem to see an end to mourning?

The Beat Generation: Living (and Writing) on the Edge

> "I saw the best minds of my generation destroyed by madness, starving hysterical naked, dragging themselves through the negro streets at dawn looking for an angry fix . . ."

When Allen Ginsberg performed these first lines of *Howl* in the crowded Six Gallery in San Francisco, the 150 people in the audience began cheering. As Kenneth Rexroth remembers, Americans were feeling oppressed by what he called "an undeclared military state," a government that seemed out of control, and a culture that seemed more interested in mass consumerism than morals or aesthetics. Ginsberg's voice immediately became a voice of hope and change. Poet Michael McClure describes the immediate visceral response to *Howl*: "Everyone knew at the deepest level that a barrier had been broken, that a human voice and body had been hurled against the harsh wall of America and its supporting armies and navies and academies and

[3043] John A. Gentry, LCpl, *Vietnam . . . Private First Class Joseph Big Medicine Jr., a Cheyenne Indian, Writes a Letter to His Family in the United States* (1969), courtesy of the National Archives and Records Administration. Soldier from Company G, 2nd Battalion, 1st Marine Regiment, on a clear, search, and destroy mission near An Hoa. U.S. military destruction in Vietnam encouraged antiwar protesters and distrust of the government. Writer Grace Paley, who described herself as a "combative pacifist and cooperative anarchist," was deeply involved in the antiwar movement.

[6217] Cameron Lawrence, *It Is a Sin to Be Silent When It Is Your Duty to Protest* (1971), courtesy of the Library of Congress. Feminist and activist poet Adrienne Rich's work provokes readers to see the connections between the struggle for women's rights and other movements, including that against the war in Vietnam.

[7360] Frank Moffit, SPC 5, *Vietnam . . . A Sky Trooper from the 1st Cavalry Division (Airmobile) Keeps Track of the Time He Has Left on His "Short Time" Helmet* (1968), courtesy of the National Archives and Records Administration. Soldier, part of Operation Pershing, near Bong Son. By 1968, many Americans were ambivalent about the U.S. involvement in the Vietnam War. Most of the soldiers drafted after 1965 were troubled by their role in what they saw as a morally ambiguous conflict. A variety of American poets protested the war, including Allen Ginsberg, Denise Levertov, Robert Bly, Robert Lowell, Adrienne Rich, James Wright, and Galway Kinnell.

[7361] Anonymous, *Vietnam War Protesters* (1967), courtesy of the National Archives and Records Administration [NRE-21-KANSWICHCR-CR928-WICH1895]. Wichita, Kansas, protest against the Vietnam War. Antiwar protests were major cultural events in the 1960s and early 1970s. Many writers and artists participated, including Adrienne Rich, whose work became more explicitly political during this time.

[5681] Anonymous, *Allen Ginsberg, Gregory Corso, Jack Kerouac & Peter Lafcadio, Mexico City* (n.d.), courtesy of the Allen Ginsberg Trust.

institutions and ownership systems and power-support bases." By the time Ginsberg reached the end of *Howl*, the cheers were so loud that it was difficult to hear him read, but when he had finished, history had been made. The Beat movement had become an officially recognized force in the literary and cultural landscape.

The Beat Generation, as it came to be called, claims a number of well-known writers, including Jack Kerouac, William Burroughs, and Lawrence Ferlinghetti, the founder of City Lights Bookstore in San Francisco. The Beat authors covered in this unit include Allen Ginsberg, Gary Snyder, and Amiri Baraka (Baraka dropped his allegiance to the Beats as he began to emphasize the African American roots of his poetic voice). These writers looked to unconventional role models, or "Secret Heroes" as Ginsberg labeled them, like Charlie Parker, Dizzy Gillespie, Arthur Rimbaud, and Dylan Thomas. What all these earlier artists shared was noncanonical status, experimental artistic style, and a fast-paced, unorthodox lifestyle. The word "beat" was a slang term used by postwar jazz musicians to mean down and out, or poor and exhausted. It also suggested "dead beat" or "beat-up." The adoption of the word "beat" to describe this generation of poets is generally credited to Jack Kerouac and Allen Ginsberg, who claimed that the word meant "exhausted, at the bottom of the world, looking up or out, sleepless, wide-eyed, perceptive, rejected by society, on your own, streetwise." Kerouac later credited the term with a philosophical dimension, meaning beatitude or beatific. Proclaiming themselves the Beat Generation ironically helped these writers gain a sense of identity as outsiders. Although Ginsberg, Kerouac, and other early members of the group met in New York City, San Francisco eventually became the hub of the Beat movement. San Francisco, even more than New York City, was home to a thriving alternative culture, where radical ideas and lifestyles were welcomed.

When Ginsberg's *Howl* was eventually published in a collection, a court trial over its alleged obscenity only heightened its popularity, and the publicity it generated along with the publication of Jack Kerouac's *On the Road* (1957) brought word of the movement into the American heartland. The Beat Generation became synonymous with counterculture, rebellion, and bohemian living. These writers refused to conform to traditional middle-class values; they rejected materialism and organized religion, and searched instead for alternative ways to find spiritual understanding. The Beats looked to Eastern religion, with its emphasis on meditation and communion with nature. Some of them experimented with mind-altering drugs. Many of the Beat poets were openly homosexual, and their candor on the taboo subject of same-sex relationships helped pave the way for the gay rights movement in the 1970s.

Beat literature is characterized by a vigorous rejection of traditional social, sexual, political, and religious values. Although much writing of the time could be described as experimental, Beat writing shares a set of recognizable features, including spontaneity, a penchant for surreal imagery, juxtaposition, long lines, aggressive individualism, an interest in the writing process, the practice of automatic writing, a fascination with drug-induced states, and a general interest in life on the edges of society.

QUESTIONS

Comprehension: What are some of the features that characterize Beat poetry?

Comprehension: What kinds of values did the Beat Generation uphold?

Context: Ginsberg's poem *Howl* is often taken as a kind of manifesto for the movement. What features, formal and thematic, seem to characterize both this poem and the Beat movement as a whole?

Context: What does Baraka's poetry share with the Beat movement? How does race complicate his association with this group?

Context: How does Snyder's attitude toward nature fit in with the Beat Generation's outlook?

Exploration: William Carlos Williams was an American modernist poet known for celebrating everyday American speech and writing poems about ordinary subjects. In some ways, his compressed verse seems antithetical to the fluid, lengthy lines typical of much Beat poetry. However, Williams was an early admirer of Ginsberg's poetry. What might Williams have found attractive about this younger man's work?

Exploration: Beat writers express a strong connection to physical places and locations. America's cities and landscapes are often crucial to their work. How do these writers treat physical space? You might consider looking at Allen Ginsberg's *Howl*, Gary Snyder's "August on Sourdough, A Visit from Dick Brewer," and Amiri Baraka's *Dutchman*. With what aspects of America do these writers identify? Why is traveling so important to these poets?

Black Arts: A Separate Voice

The Black Arts movement arose alongside the Black Power movement in the 1960s. The movement flourished from 1965 to about 1975, and though it was short-lived, its legacy was long. Artists typically associated with Black Arts include Amiri Baraka, Nikki Giovanni, Ed Bullins, Harold Cruse, Adrienne Kennedy, Larry Neal, and Sonia Sanchez. Black Arts, according to writer Larry Neal, was an ethical movement, meaning that the artists, from poets and playwrights to painters and musicians, believed that art must have a political purpose and that it must be experienced by the masses. Rather than writing modernist poetry with racial themes, as poets like Gwendolyn Brooks and Robert Hayden had done in the 1940s and 1950s, the Black Arts poets worked to express a distinctly black aesthetic derived from black experience and a long African American oral tradition. Black Arts authors sought a new kind of audience; they wrote for the masses in the American ghettoes, and they wrote to bring this vast community together.

However, the Black Arts movement was controversial because it

[6254] Anonymous, *Ginsberg with Hal Chase, Jack Kerouac & William Burroughs* (c. 1944), courtesy of the Allen Ginsberg Trust.

"THE BEAT GENERATION" WEB ARCHIVE

[5681] Anonymous, *Allen Ginsberg, Gregory Corso, Jack Kerouac & Peter Lafcadio, Mexico City* (n.d.), courtesy of the Allen Ginsberg Trust. The Beat Movement arose at the height of 1950s conservatism and eventually gave birth to the more broad-based counterculture movements of the 1960s. The Beats looked to non-traditional role models like jazz artists Dizzy Gillespie and Charlie Parker, and the French symbolist poet Arthur Rimbaud.

[5683] John Doss, *Allen Ginsberg at Madame Nhu Protest, 1963* (1963), courtesy of the Allen Ginsberg Trust and the Department of Special Collections, Stanford University Libraries. Allen Ginsberg is pictured here in front of City Lights Bookstore in San Francisco, after the anti–Madame Nhu demonstration of 1963. Madame Nhu, wife of the head of the secret police in Vietnam, was the official hostess of the U.S.-controlled South Vietnamese government. When a Buddhist monk immolated himself in Saigon as a protest against the government's favoritism of Catholicism (the majority of South Vietnamese were Buddhist), Madame Nhu called the suicide a "barbecue" and offered to light the match for the next one. When she came to the University of California, Berkeley, campus in 1963, she was met with a wide variety of protests.

[6254] Anonymous, *Ginsberg with Hal Chase, Jack Kerouac & William Burroughs* (c. 1944), courtesy of the Allen Ginsberg Trust. Photograph taken near Columbia University, where many

Beat poets and writers were students. Beat writers expressed their disenchantment with American conformity.

[6505] Anonymous, *The Howl Trial, San Francisco Municipal Court, 1957* (1957), courtesy of City Lights Books. Lawrence Ferlinghetti, arrested for publishing Ginsberg's poem, comments on the *Howl* obscenity trial: "The prosecution put only two 'expert witnesses' on the stand—both very lame samples of academia—one from the Catholic University of San Francisco and one a private elocution teacher, a beautiful woman, who said, 'You feel like you are going through the gutter when you have to read that stuff. I didn't linger on it too long, I assure you.' The University of San Francisco instructor said: 'The literary value of the poem is negligible. . . . This poem is apparently dedicated to a long-dead movement, Dadaism, and some late followers of Dadaism. And, therefore, the opportunity is long past for any significant literary contribution of this poem."

[7537] Anonymous, *Allen Ginsberg Uncensored Poetry Reading in Washington Square Park* (1966), courtesy of the Associated Press AP. Allen Ginsberg was born in New Jersey in 1926 and attended Columbia University; while a student, he was greatly influenced by William Burroughs.

[8911] Michael Bibby, Interview: *American Passages: Poetry of Liberation* (2003), courtesy of *American Passages* and Annenberg/CPB. Professor Michael Bibby discusses Ginsberg's attitude toward the government and society.

[7138] Anonymous, *LeRoi Jones (Amiri Baraka) Leads the Black Arts Parade Down 125th Toward the Black Arts Theater Repertory/School on 130th Street, New York City* (1965), courtesy of *The Liberator*.

was characterized by an impulse toward separatism and militancy. In the late 1960s, a great deal of anger characterized the outlook of many African Americans. Catchphrases like "Black Pride," "Black Power," and "Black Is Beautiful" caught the attention of the black community (as well as the rest of America). Powerful symbols and images, like the Afro or the raised black fist silk-screened on shirts and posters, reinforced this new sense of racial pride. Afro-American studies departments were founded in universities across America, and English departments began to include literature by black writers on their syllabi.

The Black Arts movement had a profound impact on the poetry of the period, including poetry that emerged out of the Chicano movement, the Asian American movement, and the Native American Renaissance. Literature was judged first and foremost by its political message. Did the poetry incite action? Did the verse further the political cause for blacks? This shift in focus from aesthetics to politics was a radical moment in African American art, but in many ways, this poetry was similar to much of the other verse being written at the time by the Beats and feminists. They, like their counterparts, were protesting a whole range of societal problems. As critic David Perkins argues, the Black Arts movement "had many characteristics of an avant-garde movement. It was anti-establishment, continually self-dividing into factions, preoccupied with defining itself and its aims, prolific of manifestos and enormously confident of its own vitality and importance."

The movement lost energy in the 1970s as the political and social climate improved for blacks, thanks to the civil rights movement, and the imperative to be political and to appeal to the masses grew wearisome for many artists who wanted to grow and find new readers. The legacy of the Black Arts movement, however, remains important to current literature. The poets of the 1960s deserve much credit for changing the way the black community and the rest of society view blackness; indeed, they helped to instill a sense of pride in blacks everywhere with poems like "Coal," "Black Mother Woman," and "The Woman Thing." Their work inspired black poets to use realistic dialect and speech in their poetry, and they also urged them to express black experience more honestly than ever before. This paved the way for black poets to write in a more confessional manner, incorporating intimate personal experience into their work.

QUESTIONS

Comprehension: What are the features of the Black Arts movement? What relationship did poets and writers see between art and politics?

Comprehension: How would you describe the political and social climate within which the Black Arts movement developed?

Comprehension: What relationship do you see between the values and styles of the Black Arts movement and those of rap, hip-hop, or other musical forms in American popular culture? What is achieved when politicized art gains a mass audience? What can be lost in the process?

Context: What do you think attracted Baraka and other Black Arts writers to the Beat movement in the 1950s and 1960s? What characteristics of Beat poetry continued in the work of these African American writers?

Context: How does Audre Lorde's poetry fit into the Black Arts movement? What features does her poetry share with this new direction in poetry?

Exploration: We live in a time when entertainment and popular culture industries quickly notice, adapt, and exploit trends in alternative communities and "countercultures," to the extent that it can be difficult to tell the original or the radical from the commercial copy. In the late 1960s, rock FM radio stations sprang up across the country, and "Blaxploitation" films were produced by Hollywood to reflect and profit from the race consciousness that had grown strong in African American communities. If you are interested in the history of popular music, consider the recordings of African American groups of the late 1960s and early 1970s: Funkadelic; Sly and the Family Stone; Earth, Wind and Fire. Consider also the dramatic changes in the sound of Motown artists who were already well established by the late 1960s: The Temptations, The Supremes, Marvin Gaye, and others. If you are interested in film, sample some of the Blaxploitation films that have enjoyed a long life on video: *Shaft*, *Superfly*, *Blackula*, *Putney Swope*, *Sweet Sweetback's Baadassss Song*. Such films are often grouped together at rental outlets. As you look and listen, speculate about these works as cultural artifacts. Do they show us the sensibility of the Black Arts movement? An exploitation or caricature of that sensibility? Or some mingling of the two?

Exploration: Social historians have sometimes suggested that the ideology of the Black Arts poets was essentially counter to the values of Martin Luther King Jr., who emphasized nonviolent protest and harmony among races in America and the world. Where do you see affinity between works from the Black Arts movement and the values of King and the civil rights movement? What debt might the Black Arts movement owe to King?

Exploration: In light of what you've learned about the Black Arts movement, reread the selections from Ralph Ellison's *Invisible Man*. In the 1960s, Ellison was often vilified by younger African American writers for being too "literary" in the white sense, for emulating forms and styles of Faulkner, Joyce, Emerson, Mark Twain, and other white authors. Does Ellison nonetheless qualify as a subversive or revolutionary writer? Compare the resistance of *Invisible Man* to the resistance of the Black Arts movement. What are the strengths and limitations of each as political art?

[7140] Emory, *One of Our Main Purposes Is to Unify Brothers and Sisters in the North with Our Brothers and Sisters in the South* (c. 1970), courtesy of the Library of Congress [LC-USZC4-10248].

[6714] Romare Bearden, *The Family* (1976), courtesy of the Romaré Bearden Foundation/Licensed by VAGA, New York, NY.

"BLACK ARTS"
WEB ARCHIVE

[3011] Austin Hansen, *Eartha Kitt Teaching a Dance Class at Harlem YMCA* (c. 1955), courtesy of Joyce Hansen and the Schomburg Center for Research in Black Culture, New York Public Library. Eartha Kitt came to New York as a child and grew up in a vibrant Harlem. An acclaimed dancer, singer, international cabaret performer, and

1950s sex symbol, Kitt began her dance career with the Katherine Dunham Dance Troupe at age seventeen. Kitt was blacklisted for almost a decade after speaking out against the Vietnam War in 1968.

[6714] Romare Bearden, *The Family* (1976), courtesy of the Romare Bearden Foundation/Licensed by VAGA, New York, NY. Romare Bearden gained international recognition for the powerful visual metaphors and probing analysis of African American heritage in his collages, photomontages, watercolors, and prints. He was a member of the Harlem Artists Guild and had his first solo exhibition in 1940 at the age of twenty-nine. He had many literary friends, including James Baldwin, Ralph Ellison, and Albert Murray.

[7138] Anonymous, *LeRoi Jones (Amiri Baraka) Leads the Black Arts Parade Down 125th Toward the Black Arts Theater Repertory/School on 130th Street, New York City* (1965), courtesy of *The Liberator*. Influenced by civil rights activism and black nationalism, Baraka (Jones) and other African American artists opened the Black Arts Theater in Harlem in 1965.

[7140] Emory, *One of Our Main Purposes Is to Unify Brothers and Sisters in the North with Our Brothers and Sisters in the South* (c. 1970), courtesy of the Library of Congress [LC-USZC4-10248]. Political poster for the Black Panthers. In the 1960s and 1970s, the Black Panthers and black nationalist writers emphasized the need for solidarity among African Americans and people of African descent throughout the world.

[7234] Anonymous, "The Evil System of Colonialism and Imperialism Arose and Throve with the Enslavement of Negroes and the Trade in Negroes, and It Will Surely Come to an End with the Complete Emancipation of Black People" (c. 1970), courtesy of Library of Congress [LC-USZ62-995]. This poster shows the power of action and demonstration in effecting change for disenfranchised, marginalized, and persecuted peoples. It draws on and is titled after a quotation from Mao Tsetung.

EXTENDED CONTEXTS

The Women's Movement: Diving into the Wreck

Adrienne Rich's poem "Diving into the Wreck" encapsulates the spirit of the women's movement in the 1960s. Fighting for a voice, women, from artists to housewives, joined together and demanded to be heard. Rich's poem speaks to this sense of inclusion in the first line, where she uses the first-, second-, and third-person to address the reader, signaling that both as individuals and as a community women need to fight for their equality. In this poem, however, the battle begins with finding a voice and making sure that the "book of myths in which our names do not appear" is rewritten to include the experience of women. The intimacy between artist and reader in this poem characterizes the art produced by feminist writers like Anne Sexton, Audre Lorde, and Sylvia Plath.

Although Second Wave Feminism, or "Women's Lib," didn't gain national attention until the late 1960s, women across America were voicing protest much earlier. The prevailing domestic ideology of the 1950s not only told women that their place was in the home caring for the family, but also tried to convince them that, unless there was something wrong with them, they should find complete fulfillment in that role. For many women, these societal standards proved stifling, and as the decade progressed, some women were becoming increasingly frustrated by the standards imposed upon them and the lack of choices they could make in a culture that perceived women who were unmarried or pursuing careers as socially aberrant. In addition, with the growth of the advertising industry and a new influx of consumer products, many families wanted both spouses to earn wages in the hopes of increasing their buying power. But as women went out in search of jobs, they quickly realized that their options were limited. Although society seemed to encourage women to stay home, more women than ever before were attending college. It was not uncommon for women to receive degrees from prestigious colleges only to be told that their single option was to become housewives. By revising fairytales and myths, poets such as Sylvia Plath and Anne Sexton satirized the constrictive roles forced upon women, thereby laying the groundwork for later feminist work.

These cultural standards were so ingrained that many women either felt guilty for wanting to break the mold or found it difficult, if not impossible, to articulate their feelings of alienation and frustration. When Betty Friedan's *Feminine Mystique* hit the shelves in 1963, American society changed as Friedan's articulation of the desperation women felt resonated with women across the country. At the end of the first chapter of this radical work, Friedan outlines her argument poignantly:

> If I am right, the problem that has no name stirring in the minds of so many American women today is not a matter of loss of femininity or too much education, or the demands of domesticity. . . . It may well be

the key to our future as a nation and a culture. We can no longer ignore that voice within women that says: "I want something more than my husband and my children and my home."

Friedan's landmark book raised consciousness about women's roles and changed many Americans' view of how a household should be structured.

Despite the dominant ideology of the time, there were many women, particularly college students, who were active in what scholar Alice Echols has termed the "climate of protest." These women took part in marches, sit-ins, and speak-outs during the civil rights movement and anti-Vietnam protests. Like the earlier alliance between the abolitionist groups and suffragists, the feminist movement shared much with the other movements of the 1960s. While these female activists did not find much support for gender issues among these other groups, their participation in various movements prepared them well for their later struggle for women's liberation. They learned tactics of civil disobedience, gained practice speaking publicly, and began to see their bodies as sites of resistance. Likewise, the women's movement shared some of the philosophical underpinnings of the wider protest movement. The women's movement of this era has, however, been criticized for espousing middle-class, white values and for assuming that all female experience is similar. In fact, many groups, including the poor and African Americans, felt that the women's movement excluded them, and feminists have remained divided on issues of audience and inclusion.

Labeled Second Wave Feminism because it followed the Suffragist movement earlier in the century, the women's movement rattled American society. While this new feminism fought hard against the values forwarded by 1950s society, the liberation movement also took on more specific battles. Central to these new feminists was the fight to gain control over their own bodies. With new advances in medical technology, the birth control pill became available for the first time in 1961. For feminists, the ability to control their reproductive fate was necessary to liberation, and they fought for the right to choose abortion, to have access to birth control, and to educate women about their bodies and their sexuality. In a society that often refused to discuss sexuality or even female anatomy with any degree of candor, the feminist movement's resolve to raise consciousness about the workings of the female body itself proved radical.

Feminists also fought to change society's perceptions of women. They did not simply want to open thousands of childcare facilities, but rather they wanted to change the perception that childcare is the sole responsibility of the woman and mother. As many feminists argued, the battle for liberation had to begin at home, where women had traditionally been expected to shoulder the domestic burdens. Domestic chores and responsibilities would have to be shared by men if women were to gain equal opportunity in other spheres. Feminists also raised awareness about the objectification of women, particularly the damaging effects of unattainable standards of beauty

[7362] Phil Stanziola, *800 Women Strikers for Peace on 47th Street near the UN Building* (1962), courtesy of the Library of Congress [LC-USZ62-128465].

[6180] United Women's Contingent, *When Women Decide This War Should End, This War Will End: Join the United Women's Contingent on April 24* (1971), courtesy of the Library of Congress [LC-USZC4-6882].

[3010] Austin Hansen, *Woman and Baby Evicted from Their Harlem Apartment, 1950s* (c. 1950s), courtesy of Joyce Hansen and the Schomburg Center for Research in Black Culture, New York Public Library. This photo's echoes of the traditional iconography of the Madonna and Child comment ironically on life in inner-city New York. Gwendolyn Brooks's work addresses the struggles of raising children in poverty.

[3296] Dick DeMarsico, *Protesting A-Bomb Tests* (1962), courtesy of the Library of Congress [LC-USZ62-126854]. Demonstrators protesting U.S. testing of atomic weapons. The use of nuclear weapons in World War II prompted a variety of responses from U.S. citizens, including fear, protest, and feelings of alienation.

[6180] United Women's Contingent, *When Women Decide This War Should End, This War Will End: Join the United Women's Contingent on April 24* (1971), courtesy of the Library of Congress [LC-USZC4-6882]. Protest poster against the Vietnam War. The antiwar, civil rights, women's rights, and gay liberation movements were connected politically and artistically. In 1961, writer and activist Grace Paley founded the Greenwich Village Peace Center, which was integral to draft resistance during the Vietnam War.

[6181] Peg Averill, *When Women Become Massively Political the Revolution Will Have Moved to a New Level . . .* (1976), courtesy of the Library of Congress [CN POS 6-U.S., no. 39 (C size) <P&P>]. Poster of a woman in whose flowing hair is pictured a setting sun and silhouettes of soldiers. The woman's movement was closely allied to the peace movement. The National Organization for Women's 1966 statement of purpose began as follows: "We, men and women who hereby constitute ourselves as the National Organization for Women, believe that the time has come for a new movement toward true equality for all women in America, and toward a fully equal partnership of the sexes, as part of the world-wide revolution of human rights now taking place within and beyond our national borders."

heralded by the media and popular culture. For example, Sylvia Plath's poem "The Applicant" critiques the ways in which American culture, and particularly the world of advertising and women's magazines, objectifies women and forces them (and men) into confining roles. The women's movement struggled to expose the often painful and uncomfortable lengths women were encouraged to go to in pursuit of beauty. In protest, feminists burned bras, girdles, high-heeled shoes, and other items which they perceived as symbolic of their objectification. One of the most publicized protests occurred in September 1968 when a large group of feminists demonstrated at the Miss America Pageant in Atlantic City. Their witty slogans and fierce criticism of the event as degrading and sexist sparked debate around the country and did much to raise awareness of the movement's growing intensity.

Poetry proved important to the women's movement, in part because it helped to build solidarity and a shared set of images among women of the time. In fact, poetry readings were often integral parts of rallies and protests during this time. As literary critic Michael Bibby argues in his work on poetry in the Vietnam era, the feminist poetry written in the 1960s is characterized by a radical openness about the personal experience of women, and the poetry openly celebrates the female body and sexuality. For the first time, female poets were writing literature about menstruation, childbirth, and eroticism. The immense popularity of poets like Adrienne Rich, Sylvia Plath, and Anne Sexton illustrates the profound relationship between the personal and political. Although Plath's best-known poems were written before the women's movement really took off, her work was published posthumously from the mid-1960s on, and her defiant voice, unforgettable images, and struggle for a creative identity separate from the confines of domesticity made her work an icon of the movement. The poetry of Rich and Sexton was celebrated for the same reasons. Rich also contributed hosts of essays that have become central to feminist theory today, and her identity as a lesbian became a political statement that seemed to mark a new direction in feminism. Rich's notion of the lesbian continuum, in which sexuality is not either/or, but rather is better understood as a range, remains one of the key concepts in queer theory.

Feminist poets also responded to literary currents perceived as predominantly male. Nikki Giovanni and Audre Lorde, for example, represent female voices in the Black Arts movement, and poems like "The Woman Thing" and "Coal" offer a feminist view of the new black aesthetic. Other women of color, including Joy Harjo and Lorna Dee Cervantes, also helped to broaden the representation of women in feminist poetry. There were also several female poets associated with the Beat movement, notably Diane DiPrima. The university was also an important instrument of change. Women's studies departments emerged, syllabi were gradually broadened to include female authors, and female scholars were changing the face of literary criticism. Critics like Elaine Showalter (*A Literature of Their Own*) and Sandra M. Gilbert and Susan Gubar (*The Madwoman in the Attic*) were forcing scholars, students, and readers not only to recognize women's literature, but also to rethink the canon as a whole.

QUESTIONS

Comprehension: What was the relationship of the women's movement to other protest movements of the time?

Comprehension: What roles does the female body play in the women's movement?

Context: Scholar Wayne Booth has famously noted the rhetorical power of metaphors. By making comparisons, metaphors have influence on symbolic and emotional levels, in addition to literal ones. In "Daddy," Sylvia Plath compares the oppression of women by their fathers to the treatment of Jews by the Nazis. What is gained by this comparison? What is lost? What allusions and comparisons does Plath make in her other poems? You might look at "The Applicant," "Lady Lazarus," or "Morning Song."

Context: Audre Lorde and Adrienne Rich both identified themselves as lesbians. How does sexual orientation influence their poetry? How do you see the relationship between the personal and the political? Is there a sense in which identifying oneself as lesbian might be seen as a political statement? Why or why not?

Exploration: Sylvia Plath and Adrienne Rich are feminist poets whose work is characterized by a memorable voice, an intimate connection between reader and poetic speaker, and an honest, often raw portrayal of female experience. What is the poetic legacy of writers like Plath and Rich? Can you think of any poets writing today that seem similar to or indebted to these authors?

Exploration: Feminists saw the female body as a site of political struggle and suffering, and that vision was intensified during the Supreme Court's hearing of **Roe v. Wade** in the early 1970s. These women battled to gain reproductive rights, educate women about their bodies, raise awareness about rape and domestic violence, and encourage women to value their natural beauty. How does the body function as a symbol in feminist poetry of this period? You might look at Audre Lorde's "Black Mother Woman," Sylvia Plath's "Lady Lazarus," Adrienne Rich's "Diving into the Wreck," or Anne Sexton's "Little Girl, My String Bean, My Lovely Woman."

Poetry of Transcendence: Poets Look to the American Landscape

The postwar period was in many ways imbued with an atmosphere of spiritual searching. The younger generation in particular, which included many of the poets in this unit, was desperately seeking what they termed transcendent experience. Native American culture and religion, as well as the rise of the New Age movement, provided one answer to this spiritual searching. Poets like Gary Snyder and James Wright were particularly drawn to Native American culture, an inter-

[6182] Ivy Bottin, *Woman Power* (1965), courtesy of the Library of Congress [POS 6-U.S., no. 548 (C size) <P&P>]. Members of the women's movement sought to change the dominant perception that all women could be satisfied by lives as homemakers. Many feminists argued that the fight for liberation must begin at home, where men should share in domestic chores.

[6190] Marcia Salo, *I Am a Woman Giving Birth to Myself* (1973), courtesy of the Library of Congress [CN POS 6-U.S., no. 306 (C size) <P&P>] and the Times Change Press. For many of the women involved in the women's movement of the 1960s and 1970s, there was an intense connection between the personal and the political. Central to these new feminists was the fight to gain control over their bodies, as a woman's control of her reproductive fate was necessary for true liberation. The feminists' resolve to increase education about female anatomy and reproductive health was, at the time, radical.

[6932] Student Mobilization Committee to End the War in S.E. Asia, *Pull Him Out Now: Join with the Hundreds and Thousands of Students, GI's, Women, Unionists, Puerto Ricans, Gay People . . .* (c. 1970), courtesy of the Library of Congress. Political poster protesting U.S. military involvement in Vietnam. The antiwar movement linked and encouraged a number of other movements, including the civil rights movement, the Chicano movement, and the farm workers movement. Many American poets protested the war, including Adrienne Rich, Robert Lowell, and Allen Ginsberg.

[7362] Phil Stanziola, *800 Women Strikers for Peace on 47th St. near the UN Building* (1962), courtesy of the Library of Congress [LC-USZ62-128465]. Women protest for peace. Antiwar sentiment grew throughout the 1960s as some Americans became more critical of the Cold War mentality. Throughout the Cold War, the United States became increasingly involved in international conflicts that had high American death tolls and no apparent resolution, such as the Korean and Vietnam wars.

[4999] Anonymous, *Allen Ginsberg, Timothy Leary, and Ralph Metzer (Left to Right) Standing in Front of a Ten Foot Plaster Buddha* (1965), courtesy of the Library of Congress [LC-USZ62-119239].

est probably prompted in part by the rise of the American Indian movement, which insisted on the power of traditional ways even as it sought to make real political changes. Indian tradition, which featured sweat lodges, sun dance revivals, and other rituals, became popular during this time. Peyote, also central to Native American religion and culture, held particular interest for the Beat poets, who experimented with a wide array of hallucinogens. Peyote is a flower on a cactus that contains the drug mescaline, which is similar to LSD. As a rite of passage into manhood, Indian boys would take the drug and go on a "vision quest," during which they would wander around the wilderness for several days, experiencing drug-induced visions. Such rituals were appealing to a generation that yearned for transcendent experience and believed that the mind harbored fascinating and meaningful abilities untapped by the "normal" mode of living. Likewise, the New Age movement encouraged people to believe in alternate states of reality, to believe in crystals and visions, and to look inward for spiritual meaning.

In addition to their interest in Native American culture and New Age practices, the meditative poets were also inspired by nature and the outdoors. Alongside the fiercely political poetry written during this period, poets like James Wright, Robert Bly, and Galway Kinnell were writing verse that seemed defiantly silent on social issues. Instead of tackling the political and social shortcomings of mainstream America head-on, this group of "meditative" poets protested the state of society by turning away from civilization and looking instead to nature and the land as a source of inspiration. In an era in which

[7341] Arthur Rothstein, *Strip Mining Operations with a Thirty-Two Cubic Yard Steam Shovel. Cherokee County, Kansas* (1936), courtesy of the Library of Congress, Prints & Photographs Division, FSA/OWI Collection [LC-USF34-004274-D DLC].

mankind was not only slowly poisoning itself, but seemed also to be toying with its newfound power to destroy itself and the world, these poets saw technology as extremely dangerous. They lamented the urbanization that seemed to be creeping outward from the cities, as suburbia spread over the American landscape. During the 1950s, the government undertook the largest highway expansion program in American history, and road construction, with all its noisy machinery, unfurled across the country. The environment seemed to be under siege as reports of oil spills, strip mines, and increased pollution filled the newspapers. Rachel Carson's *Silent Spring* announced the devastating effects of DDT on the environment, and its publication triggered growing awareness about environmental and ecological problems plaguing the country and the globe. The list of endangered species grew steadily. Indeed, to many of these poets, civilization was threatening nature and the environment like never before. In the face of this modernization and a burgeoning global economy, these poets looked to nature and the wilderness as an escape and as a source of inspiration.

Drawing on the Romantics and the American Transcendentalists like Henry David Thoreau and Ralph Waldo Emerson, poets like Gary Snyder, Joy Harjo, and James Wright sought out a simpler life, where they could escape the encroachment of civilization. Their transcendental philosophy, in which humans' connection to the land becomes a source not only of peacefulness but also of artistic inspiration and spiritual renewal, is founded on quintessentially American ideals. Like Thoreau and Emerson, these poets of the 1960s saw transcendental living and writing as a way to practice American ideals like self-reliance, resourcefulness, and individualism. Snyder actually managed to live almost self-sufficiently in the mountains of Oregon and California, growing much of his own food and chopping his own wood. This connection to an earlier, yet deeply American culture explains his interest in myth, folklore, and the theme of the journey in his poetry. Although Joy Harjo's poetry seems quite different from Snyder's, her search for spirituality in nature, as well as her connections to the land and American Indian culture, aligns her with the poetry of transcendentalism. These poets were, like their predecessors, reacting against what they perceived as an intrusive and morally suspect government. In looking to nature, they were enacting an anti-establishment sentiment. Part of this interest in the land also meant an interest in non-Western cultures.

Although the confessional poets did not draw their inspiration from Native American culture or the ecological concerns characteristic of the meditative poets, they did share an interest and belief in the idea of the poet as a visionary. Robert Lowell, Anne Sexton, and Sylvia Plath all believed in a transcendent state, often induced by mental illness (mania or depression) that sparked brilliant poetry.

QUESTIONS

Comprehension: What are the features of poetry of transcendence?

Comprehension: Why were the meditative poets attracted to Native American culture and religion? What did it offer them that mainstream American culture did not?

Comprehension: How might confessional poetry be described as transcendent?

Context: Transcendental poetry features the idea of the poet as a visionary. How do Gary Snyder ("The Blue Sky"), Joy Harjo ("Eagle Poem," "The Flood"), and Sylvia Plath ("Ariel") represent this idea? What is the relationship between the poet and the creative process in these poems?

Context: How do the heritages of Harjo and Cervantes complicate their treatment of nature? Can they be classified as meditative poets?

Context: Reread Thoreau's essay on civil disobedience. How does Wright's poetry capture the flavor of civil disobedience as defined by Thoreau?

Exploration: Using the archive, look at the Hopi images and the Zen Buddhist artifacts. Why would very different traditions appeal to

larly Gary Snyder and James Wright—
were drawn to Native American belief
systems and to the use of peyote.

[7341] Arthur Rothstein, *Strip Mining
Operations with a Thirty-Two Cubic Yard
Steam Shovel. Cherokee County, Kansas*
(1936), courtesy of the Library of
Congress, Prints & Photographs Division,
FSA/OWI Collection [LC-USF34-
004274-D DLC]. Heavy machinery at
mining site. Meditative poets found
inspiration in nature and were alarmed
by increasing environmental destruction
in the United States.

[8314] Joy Harjo, Interview: "Native
Voices and Poetry of Liberation" (2003),
courtesy of *American Passages* and
Annenberg/CPB. Writer Joy Harjo discusses the power of the spoken word.

[8608] Native Alliance for Red Power,
NARP Newsletter (June/July 1969),
courtesy of the Special Collections,
Michigan State University Libraries. The
Native Alliance for Red Power (NARP)
was a Canadian organization similar to
the American Indian Movement (AIM).
Both were part of tribalism and the Pan-
Indian movement of the 1970s.
Organizations like AIM, NARP, and the
Black Panthers called for changes in the
treatment of minorities and were more
willing to use physical confrontation
than their predecessors in the civil rights
movement of the 1950s and early 1960s.

the same group of writers? What historical, political, or cultural events might have led to their fascination? How does this type of primitivism differ from that of the high modernists, like Ezra Pound and T. S. Eliot?

Exploration: The poets mentioned in this Extended Context appreci-
ated and revered Native American culture. They believed deeply in ecological preservation. They practiced traditionally American ideals like self-reliance, freedom of thought and speech, and strong individuality. Yet, many Americans considered them outsiders, or strange, misguided youth. How did these poets perceive American identity? What values did they uphold? What perceptions were they trying to change? How do their poetry and lifestyles reflect these ideas?

ASSIGNMENTS

Personal and Creative Responses

1. *Poet's Corner:* Reread Allen Ginsberg's *Howl*. Think about the values you associate with your generation. How would you describe the current youth culture? What are the defining moments in your generation? Write your own poem in which you strive to define your generation and its place in American culture and identity. If you wish, use Ginsberg's phrase, "I saw the best minds of my generation . . . ," to get you started.

2. *Journal:* Imagine that you are Sylvia Plath, but still alive today, and have recently come across some reviews of your work that are sharply critical of your use of Holocaust imagery in poems such as "Lady Lazarus" and "Daddy." How do you respond to such criticism? How do you justify your use of these images? What do you think your poems gain by invoking the Holocaust?

3. *Doing History:* Native Americans have preserved their history and heritage for hundreds of years by telling stories and using rituals to create a collective tribal memory. As the language and culture of many tribes threatens to disappear, many Native American writers feel compelled to write down these oral traditions. Using the archive, compare the oral (transcribed) and written histories of removal. How do the versions differ?

4. *Multimedia:* You have been asked to speak at a local women's col-
lege or high school. Using the archive and the poetry in this unit, develop a slide show in which you highlight important moments in the women's movement of the 1960s and 1970s. Be sure to leave your audience not only with a sense of how far women have come, but also with an idea of what might come next.

Problem-Based Learning Projects

1. You have been asked to design a retrospective of 1960s America. Using the archive and literature in this unit, choose around ten items (a poem or a single image or soundclip might count as an item) that you feel are representative of the decade. Write a few paragraphs explaining your choices. How did you decide on these items? What values seem most important in this decade? How do your chosen items reflect those? What did it mean to be an American in the 1960s?

2. You work for a standardized test company, and your team has just been asked to write a test unit on postwar America. Compose an essay exam for your students. Write three or four questions that you would like to have the students explore. What themes seem important to the period? What symbols or images have remained influential? What knowledge should a group of students be expected to have about postwar America?

3. You are a reporter for the *New York Times*, and you've been asked to write a series on the legacy of the Black Arts movement. What concepts or values from that movement are still alive? How has the perception of African Americans changed? What kinds of changes do you see? What elements of popular culture are indebted to the Black Arts movement?

GLOSSARY

alienation   The experience of feeling outside mainstream culture. Most of the poets and movements in this unit explore a sense of alienation from society that has compelled them to search elsewhere for meaning. The emphasis on Eastern religion, alternative states of reality, hedonism, and nature suggests that these poets were seeking to redefine themselves and their generation through art.

free verse   Poetry that does not have a regular rhyme scheme or meter. Some of the features of free verse include enjambment, visual patterning, and varying line lengths. Most poets in this unit write in free verse.

protest poetry   Poetry that strives to undermine established values and ideals, particularly those associated with the government and other bodies of authority. Protest poetry often aims to shock readers into political action by discussing taboo subject matter, using unconventional and often profane language, criticizing popular beliefs, and shunning formal poetic conventions.

removal   A term that refers to the American policy, spearheaded by President Andrew Jackson, which forcibly relocated major southeastern Indian tribes to Oklahoma. The Creek Indians, along with most of the other large southern tribes such as the Cherokee and Choctaw, were removed to Oklahoma during the 1830s. The Cherokee were forced to march to Oklahoma along what became known as the Trail of Tears, as over one-third of the tribe died en route.

Roe v. Wade A controversial Supreme Court case from 1973, in which the Court ruled that abortion was legal. This was a turning point in American history because it gave women more authority over their bodies. The decision met with immediate resistance from Catholic groups and Christian fundamentalists. As the decade progressed, the courts gradually qualified the decision, making more stringent rules about the time frame and circumstances under which abortions can be performed.

sex(uality) The sexual revolution was characterized not only by openness about the body and sex, but also by a willingness to engage in sexual activity outside marriage. Suddenly, the moral constraints placed on sexual activity were challenged, and sex became not just a more accepted and talked-about part of life, but also an area of experimentation and a symbol of the counterculture's rejection of mainstream values. The attitude towards sex in the 1960s revolutionized American culture and illustrates another example of the body being used as a site of radicalism and protest. This new candor about sex also ushered in the gay rights movement, which took off in the 1970s.

SELECTED BIBLIOGRAPHY

Bibby, Michael. *Hearts and Minds: Bodies, Poetry, and Resistance in the Vietnam Era*. New Brunswick: Rutgers UP, 1996.

Charters, Ann. *The Portable Beat Reader*. New York: Penguin, 1992.

Echols, Alice. *Daring to Be Bad: Radical Feminism in America, 1967–1975*. Minneapolis: U of Minnesota P, 1989.

Lee, A. Robert, ed. *The Beat Generation Writers*. Chicago: Pluto Press, 1996.

McMahon, Mary Sheila. "The American State and the Vietnam War: A Genealogy of Power." In *The Sixties: From Memory to History*. Ed. by David Farber. Chapel Hill: U of North Carolina P, 1994.

Perkins, David. *A History of Modern Poetry*, vol. II. Boston: Harvard UP, 1987.

Rosen, Ruth. *The World Split Open: How the Modern Women's Movement Changed America*. New York: Penguin, 2000.

Steigerwald, David. *The Sixties and the End of Modern America*. New York: St. Martin's Press, 1995.

FURTHER RESOURCES

The Academy of American Poets <www.poets.org>.

America's War on Poverty [videorecording]. Producer Terry Kay Rockefeller. Alexandria: PBS Video, 1995.

Brooks, Charles. *Best Editorial Cartoons of 1972: A Pictorial History of the Year*. Gretna: Pelican, 1973.

A Century of Recorded Poetry [sound recording]. Los Angeles: Rhino Records, 1996.

Greenberg, Jan, ed. *Heart to Heart: New Poems Inspired by Twentieth-Century American Art*. New York: Harry N. Abrams, 2001.

Howls, Raps & Roars: Recordings from the San Francisco Poetry Renaissance [sound recording]. Berkeley: Fantasy Records, 1993.

Our Souls Have Grown Deep Like the Rivers: Black Poets Read Their Work [sound recording]. Los Angeles: Rhino/World Beat, 2000.

Palabra: A Sampling of Contemporary Latino Writers [videorecording]. San Francisco: The Poetry Center and American Poetry Archives, SFSU, 1994.

Reflections on the Wall: The Vietnam Veterans Memorial. Harrisburg: Stackpole Books, 1987.

Sullivan, James D. *On the Walls and in the Streets: American Poetry Broadsides from the 1960s*. Urbana: U of Illinois P, 1997.

Young, Al. *Color: A Sampling of Contemporary African American Writers* [videorecording]. San Francisco: The Poetry Center and American Poetry Archives, SFSU, 1994.

Authors and Works

Featured in the Video:
Maxine Hong Kingston, *The Woman Warrior: Memoirs of a Girlhood Among Ghosts* (novel)
Sandra Cisneros, *The House on Mango Street* (novel), *Woman Hollering Creek* (short stories)
Leslie Feinberg, *Stone Butch Blues* (novel)

Discussed in This Unit:
Toni Morrison, "Recitatif" (short story)
Thomas Pynchon, "Entropy" (short story)
Toni Cade Bambara, "Medley" (short story)
Maxine Hong Kingston, from *Tripmaster Monkey: His Fake Book* (excerpt from novel)
Diane Glancy, "Jack Wilson or Wovoka and Christ My Lord," "Polar Breath" (short stories)
Alice Walker, "Everyday Use" (short story)
David Mamet, *Glengarry Glen Ross* (play)
Judith Ortiz Cofer, "The Witch's Husband" (short story)
Sandra Cisneros, "My Lucy Friend Who Smells Like Corn," "Barbie-Q," "Mericans" (short stories)

Overview Questions

■ How do minority writers distinguish their communities' values from "mainstream" values?

■ What can writers' descriptions of physical spaces, including cities, workplaces, and houses, tell us about American life in the twentieth century?

■ How do Americans use public and private memorials, such as the Vietnam Veterans Memorial or the quilts in Alice Walker's "Everyday Use," to define themselves?

■ What literary strategies are commonly used in postmodern texts?

■ How are the civil rights movement, the women's rights movement, and the queer rights movement reflected in literature?

■ How has the American family changed with the advent of the women's liberation movement? How might authors both mourn the passing of traditional ways and celebrate new developments in society?

■ How do the writers in this unit use and/or adapt strategies or stylistic devices of various oral traditions, including the Native American and Mexican American oral storytelling traditions?

■ What does it mean to be a "radical" writer?

■ How do writers incorporate specific historical events, such as wars or scientific advances, into their texts?

■ How have authors used techniques of collage in their writings, and how do these techniques echo other artistic movements?

■ How do **postmodern narratives** adapt earlier literary forms? How and why do they borrow from or reject these earlier forms?

■ How do authors use "storytelling" to transmit ideas to their readers?

■ How have women writers revised the myth of the "self-made man"?

■ How do writers use characters' belongings, homes, and careers as symbols of both heritage and values?

■ How do writers educate readers about social injustice?

■ A bildungsroman tells the story of a character's journey, often from innocence to experience (or childhood to adulthood). How do the Unit 16 writers adapt the bildungsroman to express the experiences of minority groups within American society? Is it possible to discuss ethnic subgroups as "characters" who progress through stages of development? Why or why not? What might be the benefits and pitfalls of such an approach?

Learning Objectives

After students have viewed the video, read the head-notes and literary selections in *The Norton Anthology of American Literature*, and explored related archival materials on the *American Passages* Web site, they should be able to

1. identify and analyze postmodern elements in twentieth-century prose;
2. explain how minority writers (women, ethnic and racial minorities, and sexual minorities) have used postmodern narrative techniques to define their identities;
3. discuss the relationship between individual quests for identity and the related literature;
4. analyze the connections between postmodern literature and the feminist, civil rights, and gay rights movements;
5. analyze the connections between postmodern American literature and performance art, collage, memorials, the city within the city, and gay and lesbian identities.

Instructor Overview

Like the revolutionaries who hundreds of years earlier fought for the American colonies' freedom from English rule, the Unit 16 authors have challenged the status quo to demand recognition as independent subjects with unique identities. These authors continue the work started by earlier feminist writers, such as Margaret Fuller, Charlotte Perkins Gilman, and Kate Chopin, as well as by writers who celebrated self-determination, freedom, diversity, and democracy, such as Ralph Waldo Emerson and Walt Whitman. Alongside the sweeping social revolutions of the 1970s, including the Black Power movement and the women's movement, Unit 16's authors highlight individuals' searches for identity—legal, social, cultural, sexual, and artistic. With often-innovative postmodern narrative styles, these writers have claimed places not only for themselves in the always-shifting canon of American literature, but also for the communities they represent in the popular imagination's conception of America.

In the 1970s through the early 1990s, women writers enjoyed historically unprecedented promi-nence, as government arts funding and publishing houses, many independent and run by women, recovered "lost" women authors from previous eras and gave opportunities to young women writers. "The Search for Identity: American Prose Writers, 1970–Present," the video for Unit 16, focuses on three women writers who use postmodern narrative styles to enlarge American society's definition of womanhood. In *The Woman Warrior: Memoirs of a Girlhood Among Ghosts*, Maxine Hong Kingston combines fiction and autobiography to articulate how a Chinese American adolescent negotiates her values: which of her parents' and which of the dominant culture's values will she adopt? As she grows from childhood to adulthood, she also experiences the double consciousness, to use W. E. B. Du Bois's term, of being both American and Chinese. Similarly, in *The House on Mango Street*, Sandra Cisneros writes the story of Esperanza, a nascent Chicana feminist growing up in Chicago. Cisneros's novel—actually, a collection of short vignettes that cohere to tell the story—highlights the multilayered processes of identification necessary for many Americans. This idea of identity as a process is also at the center of Leslie Feinberg's *Stone Butch Blues*. Combining fiction and autobiography, Feinberg writes of Jess Goldberg, a transgendered individual attempting to deal with her own confusion in the face of mainstream society's often hostile reaction to her sexual variance.

By discussing these and the unit's other seven authors in the context of social changes and movements from the 1970s on, Unit 16 strives to teach students how to discuss identity as fluid and multi-valent rather than static and unified. The Unit 16 archive and the curriculum materials extend the video's discussion of identity as a process, as they situate Kingston, Cisneros, and Feinberg in relation to other activist writers of their time, as well as to texts such as David Mamet's play *Glengarry Glen Ross*, whose characters tell the other side of the story—how some people in the mainstream can react to societal changes that they perceive as threatening to their ways of life.

This unit asks students to consider "identity" in racial, sexual, gendered, financial, and educational terms. It also invites students to analyze the literature in light of artistic movements (collage, performance art), cultural trends (memorials, the city within the city), and identity theory (gay and lesbian identities). The core and extended contexts can help students to better appreciate the authors' social milieus: (1) the performance art context discusses how artists expanded the definition of "art" to raise awareness of social issues; (2) the memorials context describes some of the postmodern memorials, such as the Vietnam Veterans Memorial, that were built in the late twentieth century and remain powerful; (3) the collage context explores the work of Romare Bearden and other collage artists; (4) the gay and lesbian identities context explains how the gay rights movement is related to the ideas of Judith Butler and other theorists who pioneered new ways of thinking about identity; and (5) the city within the city context introduces the idea of economic imbalances in America's urban spaces. By giving students the opportunity to read literature by authors who have been involved in these artistic and political movements, Unit 16 asks students to examine their own relationships to society by considering the roles of heritage, community, opportunity, and identity.

Student Overview

Like the revolutionaries who hundreds of years earlier fought for the American colonies' freedom from English rule, the Unit 16 authors have challenged the status quo to demand legal and cultural recognition as independent subjects with unique identities. These authors continue the work started by earlier feminist writers, such as Margaret Fuller, Charlotte Perkins Gilman, and Kate Chopin, as well as by writers who celebrated self-determination, freedom, diversity, and democracy, such as Ralph Waldo Emerson and Walt Whitman. Alongside the sweeping social revolutions of the 1970s, including the Black Power movement and the women's movement, Unit 16's authors highlight individuals' searches for **identity**—legal, social, cultural, sexual, and artistic—and for their **historical roots**. With often-innovative **postmodern** narrative styles, these writers have claimed places not only for themselves in the always-shifting canon of American literature, but also for the communities they represent in the popular imagination's conception of America.

In Unit 16's video, you will learn of the pioneering efforts of three women authors—Maxine Hong Kingston, Sandra Cisneros, and Leslie Feinberg—to revise and expand American society's definition of womanhood. By studying these and the unit's other seven authors in the context of social changes and movements from the 1970s on, you will be able to discuss identity as fluid and multivalent rather than static and unified. The Unit 16 archive and the curriculum materials extend the video's discussion of identity as a process, as they situate Kingston, Cisneros, and Feinberg in relation to other activist writers of their time, as well as to texts such as David Mamet's play *Glengarry Glen Ross*, whose characters tell the other side of the story—how some people in the mainstream can react to societal changes they perceive as threatening to their ways of life.

This unit asks you to consider "identity" in racial, sexual, gender, financial, and educational terms. It also invites you to analyze the literature in light of artistic movements (collage, performance art), cultural trends (memorials, the city within the city), and identity theory (gay and lesbian identities). The core and extended contexts can help you to better appreciate the authors' social milieus: (1) the performance art context discusses how artists expanded the definition of "art" to raise awareness of social issues; (2) the memorials context describes some of the postmodern memorials, such as the Vietnam Veterans Memorial, that were built in the mid-to-late twentieth century and remain powerful; (3) the collage context explores the work of Romare Bearden and other collage artists; (4) the gay and lesbian identities context explains how the gay rights movement is related to the ideas of Judith Butler and other theorists who pioneered new ways of thinking about identity; and (5) the city within the city context introduces the idea of economic imbalances in America's urban spaces. In this unit, then, you will have the opportunity to read literature by authors who have been involved in these artistic and political movements, and you will thereby be able to examine your own relationship to society by considering the roles of heritage, community, opportunity, and identity.

➤ **Authors covered:** Maxine Hong Kingston, Sandra Cisneros, Leslie Feinberg

➤ **Who's interviewed:** Mary Pat Brady, professor of English (Cornell University); Patricia Chu, associate professor of English (George Washington University); Sandra Cisneros, award-winning author and poet; Leslie Feinberg, transgender activist and award-winning author; Greg Sarris, professor of English (Loyola Marymount University)

➤ **Points covered:**

- Explains how women writers in the 1970s through the 1990s blurred genres (fiction and nonfiction, novels and short stories) to tell their stories.
- Connects feminist and identity movements in the 1970s and 1980s to parallel developments in literature, and explains that as women gained more political and social power, their writing also garnered more respect.
- Shows how these later writers recovered largely forgotten women writers from the past (e.g., Zora Neale Hurston) to establish a women's literary tradition.
- Addresses the challenges for ethnically diverse writers of describing their communities truthfully and questioning dominant beliefs while still identifying with these communities.
- Shows how these writers used their communities' storytelling techniques, primarily the oral tradition, in their own fiction.
- Analyzes how these writers tried to separate myths about womanhood from lived realities.
- Shows how Kingston, Cisneros, and Feinberg drew inspiration from their own lives to write fiction that would bring attention to the needs of their communities. Also expresses their desires to "give something back" to their communities, or to return one day to help those who could not leave.
- Defines postmodern narrative, transgendered identity, and feminism.

PREVIEW

- **Preview the video:** Inspired by the civil rights movement, the women's movement of the 1960s and 1970s challenged established conceptions of what it meant to be American. Partly because such works as Betty Friedan's *The Feminine Mystique* sold many more copies than publishers had anticipated, literary critics and readers began to take the work of women writers more seriously in the 1960s and 1970s. Maxine Hong Kingston's *The Woman Warrior* inspired other women writers grappling with issues of feminine, American, and ethnic identity. Like Kingston, Sandra Cisneros and Leslie Feinberg portrayed in their works characters the reading public had never before encountered. These representations challenged mainstream society's definitions of women and of American identity. Like other "postmodern" writers of the period, Kingston, Cisneros, and Feinberg experimented with form and blurred genres. A mixture of fiction and autobiography characterizes their best-known works.

- **What to think about while watching:** What is identity? What does it mean to have a dynamic rather than a rigid identity? What does it mean to say that identity is a process? How might this idea conflict with preexisting ideas about identity? What is postmodern narrative? What writing styles did these authors use and why? What does it mean to "translate" one culture's stories into the language of another culture? How did female writers challenge the meaning of being American? What does it mean to be a woman in America? How can books help women readers to realize the options available to them? How did minority women writers complicate mainstream views of their communities while also questioning these communities' dominant beliefs? What risks did these writers take in telling their stories?

- **Tying the video to the unit content:** Unit 16 includes texts by Feinberg, Cisneros, Kingston, and five additional women writers (Toni Morrison, Toni Cade Bambara, Judith Ortiz Cofer, Diane Glancy, and Alice Walker) as well as Thomas Pynchon and David Mamet. It expands the video's emphasis on shifting identities to address how diverse people—men, women, Native Americans, African Americans, children, artists, and others—use postmodern techniques to express their reactions to a changing society and to contribute to its development. Many of the texts and the accompanying questions ask students to examine their own relationships to society by considering the roles of heritage, community, opportunity, and identity. The unit asks students to consider "identity" in racial, sexual, gendered, financial, and educational terms. It also invites students to analyze the literature in light of artistic movements (collage, performance art), cultural trends (memorials, the city within the city), and identity theory (queer politics).

	What is an American? How does American literature create conceptions of the American experience and identity?	**How do place and time shape literature and our understanding of it?**	**How are American myths created, challenged, and re-imagined through these works of literature?**
Comprehension Questions	What is integration? What is assimilation? How are they different?	How many American women had entered the workforce by the mid-1970s? Why did women's writing begin to be taken more seriously in the 1970s and 1980s? How did the women's rights and women's liberation movements affect women's literature?	How does Leslie Feinberg deflate the myth that there are only two genders?
Context Questions	Why is it so important for writers to be able to build on a literary tradition? For example, in the video, Sandra Cisneros says that when she was a young writer, Maxine Hong Kingston's *The Woman Warrior* "gave her permission" to write *The House on Mango Street*. What do you think she means by this? What do the two texts have in common?	How does region affect individuals' views of the country and their own identity?	How did Kingston, Cisneros, and Feinberg use experimental styles as well as autobiography to challenge mainstream society's definition of womanhood?
Exploration Questions	How, if at all, have these authors' personal stories changed your conception of what it means to be a woman in America?	Consider the mother's cautionary tales about female sexuality in Kingston's *The Woman Warrior*. How do these writers use the stories of earlier generations in their own fiction? How do the stories change in the retelling?	These authors asked complicated, contradictory questions about themselves in order to discover their identities. What questions did they ask? What did they discover?

	Texts	Contexts
1950s		National Guard called to enforce desegregation in Little Rock, Arkansas, public schools (1957)
		USSR launches *Sputnik*, first unmanned space craft (1957)
		NASA is founded; the United States enters "space race" with the Soviets (1958)
1960s	Thomas Pynchon, *Entropy* (1960), *The Crying of Lot 49* (1966)	John F. Kennedy elected president (1960)
	Ken Kesey, *One Flew Over the Cuckoo's Nest* (1962)	18.6 percent of married women with children work outside the home (1960)
	Faith Ringgold, "Civil Rights Triangle" (1963)	FDA approves first birth control pill (1960)
	Romare Bearden, "Three Folk Musicians" (1967)	Soviet cosmonaut Yuri Gagarin is first man in space (1961)
		Alan B. Shepard Jr. is first American in space (1961)
		Project Apollo to put a man on the moon is launched (1961)
		John Glenn is first American astronaut to orbit the earth (1962)
		First telecommunications satellite launched into orbit (1962)
		Beatlemania begins (1963)
		Reverend Martin Luther King Jr. leads civil rights march on Washington, D.C.; over 250,000 people participate (1963)
		President Kennedy assassinated (1963)
		Digital Equipment Corporation introduces PDP-8, the first successful mini mainframe computer (1963)
		Civil Rights Act passed (1964)
		Vietnam "conflict" escalates (1965)
		Malcolm X assassinated (1965)
		Martin Luther King Jr. leads civil rights march from Selma to Montgomery, Alabama (1965)
		Watts riots in Los Angeles (1965)
		Edward H. White Jr. is first American to conduct a space walk on the Gemini 4 mission (1965)
		Black nationalist organization the Black Panthers founded by Bobby Seale and Huey P. Newton (1966)
		National Organization for Women (NOW) founded (1966)
		First floppy disk developed by IBM (1967)
		Democratic National Convention in Chicago; nationally televised riots (1968)
		Riots in 125 cities around the world (1968)
		Martin Luther King Jr. and Robert F. Kennedy assassinated (1968)

	Texts	Contexts
		John Lennon and Yoko Ono hold "bed-in" to protest the Vietnam war (1969)
		Apollo 11 mission realizes President Kennedy's vision for the U.S. space program; astronauts Neil A. Armstrong and Buzz Aldrin land on moon and complete moonwalk (1969)
		Woodstock Festival held in New York state; 500,000 people attend (1969)
		Nixon initiates "Vietnamization" policy for the war (1969)
1970s	Alice Walker, "Everyday Use" (1973) Laurie Anderson, "Object, Objection, Objectivity" (1973) Maxine Hong Kingston, *The Woman Warrior: Memoirs of a Girlhood among Ghosts* (1976) Romare Bearden, "Family," "The Return of Ulysses" (1976) Toni Cade Bambara, "Medley" (1977)	Four student antiwar protesters killed by National Guard troops at Kent State University, Ohio, setting off protests at campuses around the United States (1970) American Indian Movement (AIM) founded (1970) Voting age lowered from 21 to 18 (1970) 30.3 percent of married women with children work outside the home (1970) Compact disc (CD) developed (1970) Environmental Protection Agency (EPA) created (1970) Disney World opens in Orlando, Florida (1971) Watergate scandal (1972) Equal Rights Amendment approved by Congress (1972) Military draft ends (1973) United States withdraws from Vietnam (1973) *Roe v. Wade* Supreme Court decision legalizes abortion (1973) President Nixon resigns in the wake of the Watergate scandal to avoid impeachment (1974) Sex Discrimination Act passed (1975) U.S. Bicentennial (1976) First Apple personal computer (1976)
1980s	David Mamet, *Glengarry Glen Ross* (1982) Alice Walker, *The Color Purple* (1982) Toni Morrison, "Recitatif" (1983), *Beloved* (1987) Sandra Cisneros, *The House on Mango Street* (1984) Maxine Hong Kingston, *Tripmaster Monkey: His Fake Book* (1989)	45.1 percent of married women with children work outside the home (1980) Former Beatle John Lennon murdered (1980) First space shuttle flight (1981) Sandra Day O'Connor becomes first woman appointed to the U.S. Supreme Court (1981) AIDS officially recognized in the United States (1982) Equal Rights Amendment fails to be ratified as the 28th amendment to the U.S. Constitution (1982)

Texts	Contexts
	Vietnam Veterans Memorial, designed by artist Maya Lin, dedicated in Washington, D.C. (1982)
	IBM personal computer marketed (1982)
	Sally Ride becomes first American woman astronaut in space (1986)
	U.S. Space Shuttle *Challenger* explodes (1986)
	Nuclear disaster at Chernobyl, USSR (1986)
	Berlin Wall falls; Soviet Union collapses; Cold War ends (1989)
	People's Republic Army massacre of pro-democracy demonstrators in Tianamen Square, Beijing, China (1989)
1990s Sandra Cisneros, *Woman Hollering Creek*, including "My Lucy Friend Who Smells Like Corn," "Barbie-Q," "Mericans" (1991)	East and West Germany reunified (1990)
Diane Glancy, *Firesticks*, including "Jack Wilson or Wovoka and Christ My Lord" and "Polar Breath" (1993)	Nelson Mandela freed from prison after twenty-seven years in captivity (1990)
Judith Ortiz Cofer, *The Latin Deli*, including "The Witch's Husband" (1993)	Apartheid officially ends in South Africa (1991)
Leslie Feinberg, *Stone Butch Blues* (1994)	Soviet Union dissolved (1992)
Laurie Anderson, "Stories from the Nerve Bible" (1994)	Los Angeles riots following Rodney King beating verdict (1992)
	World Wide Web established (1992)
	Bill Clinton elected president (1992)
	Guillermo Gomez-Peña and Coco Fusco begin performing "Two Undiscovered Amerindians" (1992)
	Nelson Mandela elected president in South Africa's first multi-racial democratic election (1994)
	61 percent of married women with children work outside the home (1994)
	In "Come With Me," Puff Daddy samples Led Zeppelin's "Kashmir" (1998)
	Installation of Judith Baca's *La Memoria de Nuestra Tierra* in Denver International Airport (1999)

AUTHOR/TEXT REVIEW

MORRISON WEB ARCHIVE

[2254] Abbie Rowe, *March on Washington for Jobs and Freedom* (1963), courtesy of the National Park Service, Historic Places of the Civil Rights Movement. Throughout the 1950s and 1960s, many groups, including African Americans seeking greater equality and civil rights, used marches and nonviolent protests to make their voices heard. The sight of thousands of protesters marching in front of the White House was powerful and made causes like that of these marchers hard to ignore. This nonviolent approach contrasts with the radicalism of Black Arts movement writers and the Black Panthers.

[3042] Anonymous, *Civil Rights March on Washington, D.C. [A Young Woman at the March with a Banner]* (1963), courtesy of the Still Pictures Branch, National Archives and Records Administration. The civil rights marches in Washington, D.C., and throughout the South during the late 1950s and 1960s made the cause of equality for African Americans visible to the nation. Beyond the right to vote and equal education, African Americans demanded access to good jobs, homes, and other basic opportunities and constitutional rights. "I have come to believe over and over again," poet Audre Lorde said, "that what is most important to me must be spoken, made verbal and shared,

Toni Morrison (b. 1931)

Unlike many African American authors, Toni Morrison has set most of her fiction not in the rural South or the urban North but in Lorain, Ohio, where she was born as Chloe Anthony Wofford in 1931. She attended Howard and Cornell Universities before beginning careers in teaching and editing. While teaching, Morrison counted among her students civil rights activist Stokeley Carmichael and prominent literary and cultural critic Houston A. Baker Jr.; while editing for Random House, she worked with Muhammad Ali and Toni Cade Bambara. Her novels include *The Bluest Eye*, *Song of Solomon*, *Tar Baby*, *Jazz*, and *Sula*. One of the most prominent African American woman authors in the nation's history, Morrison was the first African American woman to win the Nobel Prize, which she did in 1993.

Morrison is best known as the author of the 1987 Pulitzer prize–winning novel *Beloved*, which tells the story of Sethe, an ex-slave haunted by memories and by the ghost of her daughter, Beloved, whom she killed as an infant because she did not want her to live as a slave. Morrison's portrayals of the brutality of the slave system recall the atrocities depicted in Harriet Jacobs's and Frederick Douglass's slave narratives. The novel sparked discussion about how the nation should attempt to heal from the wounds caused by slavery: was it best to literally live with the past, like Sethe, or to try to move into the future, like other characters in the novel?

In "Recitatif," too, Morrison explores the role of memory in shaping women's consciousness. Morrison tells the stories of two childhood friends, one white and one black, as they move into adulthood during the civil rights era. The twist is that she does not identify which woman belongs to which race. While some readers have felt that this "trick" is unnecessarily manipulative, by denying this information to the reader, Morrison highlights the human urge to categorize people. Without diminishing the very real consequences of racial difference, Morrison points out the absurdities of racial stereotyping by providing racial "markers" that serve to confuse rather than clarify her characters' races.

TEACHING TIPS

■ When you assign "Recitatif" to your class, provide background historical information about racial desegregation in schools (you can consult an online encyclopedia and/or see Unit 15) or ask students to briefly research the topic themselves. You might start by asking them to find out what "segregation" was. If your students are familiar with the topic before class discussion, you will be able to address the picketing scenes in a more sophisticated way. For example, you can ask your students to discuss the "sides" of the battle: Why did some people want desegregation? Why did some not want it?

■ Students will want to attempt to identify Twyla's and Roberta's races, so this is a good opportunity to discuss how and why people stereotype each other as well as the pitfalls of doing so. You could start your discussion by assigning certain pages to groups of students and asking them to identify where Morrison uses phrases or ideas that could be considered "racial markers."

QUESTIONS

Comprehension: What does "recitatif" mean? Why does Morrison use it for the title of her story?

Comprehension: Identify Roberta's and Twyla's races based on textual clues. How do you know? Are you *sure*? Why or why not? How does any uncertainty affect your reading of the story?

Comprehension: Why do Roberta and Twyla have to live in the orphanage as children? How are they different from the other children there?

Context: Why did some people oppose and some support racial desegregation in schools? What issues were involved?

Context: In the story, the town of Newburgh has changed dramatically because of an influx of IBM employees. For example, the Food Emporium stocks very different types of food for the new residents. Consider these changes in relation to "urban renewal" and "urban relocation."

Context: Think about this story while you analyze images of protesters in the archive. Interpret the language of picketing signs, as well as the picketers' facial expressions and body language. What are they "saying"?

Exploration: Why are Twyla's and Roberta's diverging memories of Maggie so important? Consider Maggie's race, her muteness, and her abuse by the schoolgirls. What does Morrison suggest about why people remember things in certain ways?

Exploration: Roberta and Twyla picket over the issue of racial desegregation in schools, each holding signs that are as much about their personal relationship as they are about the larger issues. In Twyla's words, "People changed signs from time to time, but Roberta never did and neither did I. Actually my sign didn't make sense without Roberta's." What do their signs mean and why do they make sense only together? Also, think about the prevalence of marches and protests at this time. Why did people march for rights? Was it effective?

Exploration: Newburgh has changed since its former sleepy days, but James's family has fond memories of an earlier time in the community, and Twyla "can see them all together on the Hudson in a raggedy skiff." Compare the "old" and "new" Newburgh to the "old" and "new" Hudson River Valley community in Washington Irving's "Rip Van Winkle." Consider the narrators' roles in shaping these histories.

even at the risk of having it bruised or misunderstood."

[3266] National Park Service, *John F. Kennedy's Address to the Nation on Civil Rights* (1963), courtesy of the National Archives and Records Administration. On June 11, 1963, President Kennedy addressed the United States following the use of National Guard troops to enforce the ruling of a federal court allowing two African American students to attend the University of Alabama. "I hope that every American, regardless of where he lives, will stop and examine his conscience about this and other related incidents," Kennedy said. "This nation was founded by men of many nations and backgrounds. It was founded on the principle that all men are created equal, and that the rights of every man are diminished when the rights of one man are threatened."

[3603] Harriet Jacobs, Frontispiece from *Incidents in the Life of a Slave Girl, Written by Herself* (1861), courtesy of *Incidents in the Life of a Slave Girl*. *Incidents in the Life of a Slave Girl* was the first female-authored slave narrative published in the United States. Focusing on the specific plight of enslaved African American women, Jacobs's autobiography uses the discourse of sentimentality to appeal to a white female readership. In the late twentieth century, Toni Morrison's *Beloved*, in many ways influenced by slave narratives, describes the brutality of slavery and looks to ways the nation might attempt to heal from the wounds of its past.

[6187] Anonymous, *Congress to Unite Women, May 1, 2, 3, '70: Intermediate School, 333 W. 17 St., N.Y.C.* (1970), courtesy of the Library of Congress. From the same year that Toni Morrison and Alice Walker published their first novels, this poster calls women to one of the many conferences organized to formulate plans of action against oppression. In her article "Playing in the Dark," Morrison writes: "My work requires me to think about how free I can be as an African-American woman writer in my genderized, sexualized, and wholly radicalized world. [F]or me, imagining is not merely looking or looking at; nor is it taking oneself intact into the other. It is, for the purpose of the work, *becoming*."

Thomas Pynchon (b. 1937)

Thomas Pynchon has become famous as the man who does not want to be famous. Little is known about this author's personal life: we know only that Pynchon was born in 1937 on Long Island, New York, and that he graduated from Cornell University in the 1950s, after which he served in the navy. Though he is notoriously reclusive, he reportedly lives somewhere in northern California. Devoted fans track Pynchon sightings much like the Elvis Presley fans who record rumored appearances by "the King." Unlike Elvis, though, Pynchon most certainly is still alive, and because of his insistence on remaining private, he has figured in debates about the importance of biographical information in literary analysis. For critics who believe that an author's life events is essential to understanding his/her writing, Pynchon's silence leaves a frustrating information gap. However, some are less bothered, including critics who believe that an author's biography is immaterial when compared to a text's "cultural" history—that is, the general history of politics, entertainment, social issues, cultural trends, and the like during the years of the text's composition.

Pynchon is known for writing densely detailed, nonlinear narratives that mirror the complexity of the postmodern condition. His plots are complicated, as are his themes, so his texts can be challenging for even the most careful readers. His works are also known for their humor; in Pynchon's short story "Entropy," soldiers crash Meatball's party to find communists but end up joining the fun. Pynchon's novel *The Crying of Lot 49* offers a good entrance into his longer fiction, because it combines a complex structure with an engaging wit as it explores the nature of being American: the heroine tries to determine a connection between a mysterious legacy left to her and a similarly mysterious, secret alternative to the U.S. postal service.

TEACHING TIPS

■ If you have students who are majoring in the sciences or interested in science fiction, try to get them involved in these discussions. These students rarely have the opportunity to discuss their areas of expertise in literature classes, and they can help their fellow students to better understand Pynchon's allusions. Also, you may have students who can provide updated information about the theories and scientists mentioned in the text.

■ Students who rely heavily on biographical information when they read and interpret literature may wish to know more about Pynchon before interpreting his writing. This would be a good time to briefly teach students about the New Critics' approach to reading literature, including their ideas about the intentional fallacy. You might emphasize the importance of close reading—students should learn how to think about and discuss not only the general ideas in a text but also its language. Choose a phrase or sentence, and ask them to discuss the connotations of each word. As for the intentional fallacy, ensure that students do not assume that a text means a certain thing because that interpretation agrees with the author's biography: it is impossible to ever truly know the author's intention.

Comprehension: What is "entropy"? Why is it an apt title for Pynchon's story?

Comprehension: What is a "lease-breaking" party? Why is this detail important? What does this days-long party tell us about Meatball Mulligan and his friends?

Comprehension: The perspective shifts frequently and abruptly between "upstairs" and "downstairs" scenes. Mark the locations of the shifts to determine why Pynchon intersplices the narratives in this way. How does this technique affect your understanding of both stories? What do upstairs and downstairs characters represent?

Context: Why do the soldiers say they're looking for communists? Consider this in relation to [6240] ("Look behind the mask! Communism is death" poster) and [6241] (anti-communist poster).

Context: The story takes place in February 1957, in Washington, D.C., a center for those involved in the civil rights movement as well as for intellectuals, the military, and protesters. Pynchon shows interactions among a wide variety of such characters, from freewheeling musicians to U.S. Navy enlisted personnel. Discuss the importance of Washington, D.C., and other urban areas as gathering places for people with disparate ideas.

Context: Saul talks about how "Miriam has been reading science fiction again. That and *Scientific American*. It seems she is, as we say, bugged at this idea of computers acting like people." Consider how twentieth-century technological innovations such as space travel have brought the stuff of science fiction to life. How do these innovations and ideas affect our notions of reality and the meaning of life? Consider the 1969 Apollo 11 moonlanding [6899] as an example of reality pushing the boundaries of the imagination.

Context: The musicians downstairs are described as wearing "horn rimmed sunglasses and rapt expressions." They "smoke funny-looking cigarettes which contained not, as you might expect, tobacco, but an adulterated form of *cannabis sativa*." What is *cannabis sativa*? Discuss how Pynchon uses this reference to the drug culture to characterize these men. Why do you think the narrator uses the Latin ("scientific") name? What does it say about his relationship to drug culture?

Exploration: Pynchon is famously secretive about his own life, so we have to analyze the story without any information about his biography or cultural or literary influences. Why do you think an author might wish to remain unknown? How does the lack of information about him affect your reading of the story?

Exploration: Pynchon's characters discuss scientists and scientific

[6241] Anonymous, *Anti-Communist Poster Showing Russian Soldier and Joseph Stalin Standing over Graves in Foreground; Cannons and People Marching to Siberia in Background* (1953), courtesy of the Library of Congress [LC-USZ62-117876]. Thomas Pynchon's work is rife with references to contemporary and historical events, popular culture, and politics. "Entropy" opens with a description of a supposedly cosmopolitan and urbane group in Washington, D.C.—a passage that admits its own irony in what is perhaps a reference to the politics of the anti-communist McCarthy era.

[6899] Neil A. Armstrong, *Moon Landing, Apollo 11* (1969), courtesy of the National Aeronautics and Space Administration. Photograph of astronaut Edwin E. Aldrin Jr. and the Lunar Module (LM) taken by Neil A. Armstrong with a 70mm Hasselblad lunar surface camera. Writer Thomas Pynchon's works are full of scientific language and allusions and explore the shifting demarcations between science and science fiction.

[7105] *New York Times* Paris Bureau Collection, *London Has Its Biggest Raid of the War* (1941), courtesy of the National Archives and Records Administration. Thomas Pynchon's *Gravity's Rainbow* has four main plots and many subplots. World War II London, however, is a prominent setting in this work. Pynchon's fascination with science and technology, as well as popular culture, animates this novel which includes an investigation into the V2 rocket program developed by Germany for bombing England during the war.

ideas to make sense of the world. Research one of these scientists or ideas (Gibbs, Boltzmann, entropy, thermodynamics, etc.) to better understand the story.

Exploration: Analyze the conversations that appear throughout the story in relation to Saul and Meatball's discussion of communication theory, including the ideas of "noise" and "leakage." When speaking to each other, how can people differentiate meaning from the surrounding noise and leakage?

Exploration: Aubade (her name means "a morning song") hears in the hothouse "a motif of sap-rising": "That music rose in a tangled tracery: arabesques of order competing fugally with the improvised discords of the party downstairs, which peaked sometimes in cusps and ogees of noise." What is a fugue? How does Pynchon use fugue-like structure in this story? Locate his "melodies" and "counter-melodies" and compare them to those in a fugue by a musician such as Bach.

Toni Cade Bambara (1939–1995)

In addition to writing many stories and novels, Toni Cade Bambara was a civil rights activist, teacher, and editor. She lived in Harlem for the first ten years of her life, and her fiction reflects her intimate knowledge of city spaces. She also traveled extensively in adulthood, making trips to Cuba and Vietnam and a move to Atlanta. Bambara was committed to using her skills as a writer not only to entertain, but also to educate and contribute to social and political movements. When not writing, she was fervently devoted to activism in other forms. Early in her life she worked "in the trenches" to help minority city dwellers, and late in her life she made activist films, including a television documentary that spotlighted police brutality. In the 1970s and 1980s, she was also involved in the women's and black liberation movements, and before her death she encouraged many young southern writers to continue to use literature as a tool for social revolution.

In her fiction, Bambara told stories about African Americans in the rural South and the urban North and of immigrants from the Caribbean. She depicted vibrant, though certainly not trouble-free, black communities whose residents were coming to terms with the changes in American society. In an 1982 taped interview with Kay Bonetti of the American Audio Prose Library, Bambara said, "When I look back at my work with any little distance the two characteristics that jump out at me is one, the tremendous capacity for laughter, but also a tremendous capacity for rage." Both are apparent in most of her works. In "Medley," for example, we see the laughter shared by women sipping drinks together as well as the frustrations felt by Sweet Pea, the main character, when the men around her act as if her opinion is meaningless. A young feminist who is dedicated to her dream of building a home for herself and her daughter, Sweet Pea, like many nascent feminists at the time, feels uncomfortable "neglecting" or leaving behind the man in her life. Bambara knew that in order to thrive—not just survive—women would need to learn how to adapt to society's

[7154] Danny Lyon, *Atlanta, Georgia—High School Student Taylor Washington Is Arrested at Lebs Delicatessen—His Eighth Arrest* (1963), courtesy of the Library of Congress [LC-USZC4-4843].

ever-changing rhythms without sacrificing their own identities in the process. In both her fiction and her personal life, Bambara refused to give up the fight, and she continued to work after a cancer diagnosis until her death. She was the epitome of the "liberated woman"—an educated, socially dedicated, creative individual who in every way used the personal to political effect. Bambara's works include the short story collections *Gorilla, My Love* (1972) and *The Birds Are Still Alive* (1977), as well as the novel *The Salt Eaters* (1978).

TEACHING TIPS

■ While some students are uncomfortable talking about sexual scenes and issues in class, it is important to address this story's "shower scenes." You may want to isolate one of these scenes and read through it with the class, focusing on how Bambara parallels the music that Sweet Pea and Larry create together with their physical intimacy. It may be useful to note that although Sweet Pea seems sexually satisfied, she nonetheless decides that she needs to leave her relationship.

■ Discuss Sweet Pea's decision to leave her relationship with regard to some of the feminist images provided in this unit and on the *American Passages* Web site. For example, you could analyze her statements about personal independence in light of the following images: [6182] (*Woman Power* poster); [6190] (*I Am a Woman Giving Birth to Myself*); and [6191] (*Women are Happening*). Ask your students to think about Sweet Pea's struggle for self-determination as part of a larger women's movement represented in the posters.

■ While the narrative only briefly mentions the Vietnam War, Sweet Pea's comment about getting "that bloodsucker off our backs" could open the door to a discussion about how and why she identifies with the conflict. Students may be familiar with Muhammad Ali's stand against the war, and you can use this knowledge as an entrée into a discussion about how and why disenfranchised people frequently sympathize with each other in opposing "the man." You may also refer interested students to Michael Bibby's *Hearts and Minds: Bodies, Poetry, and Resistance in the Vietnam Era*, in which he discusses identification between black nationalists and the Vietcong.

QUESTIONS

Comprehension: What does Sweet Pea do for a living? Why do the gamblers pay her so much for her service?

Comprehension: As Sweet Pea tells Pot Limit and Sylvia about her return to Larry's apartment, she admits that she "embroider[s] a little on the homecoming tale" to play to her audience. What does this comment indicate about her reliability as narrator?

Comprehension: How do we know when Sweet Pea is *remembering* as opposed to *storytelling*? What is the difference between the two and why is it important?

Context: Locate Sweet Pea's statements of self-empowerment and

Bambara was a social activist whose novel *The Salt Eaters* demonstrates the importance of storytelling in shaping healthy communities.

[6217] Cameron Lawrence, *It Is a Sin to Be Silent When It Is Your Duty to Protest* (1971), courtesy of the Library of Congress. Feminist and activist poet Adrienne Rich's work provokes readers to see the connections between the struggle for women's rights and other movements, including that against the war in Vietnam.

[7154] Danny Lyon, *Atlanta, Georgia—High School Student Taylor Washington Is Arrested at Lebs Delicatessen—His Eighth Arrest* (1963), courtesy of the Library of Congress [LC-USZC4-4843]. Photograph of a police officer restraining a young protester. Many writers in the 1960s and 1970s were profoundly affected by the civil rights movement, including activist Toni Cade Bambara. Bambara's writing focuses on the need for societies to adapt without sacrificing their identities.

resistance to societal double standards for men and women, and consider these statements in relation to Marcia Salo Rizzi's 1973 poster *I Am a Woman Giving Birth to Myself* [6190]. Also consider Sweet Pea in relation to Melinda Beck's drawing, *Racism/Sexism* [6178]. Do you think that Sweet Pea is "a woman giving birth to herself"? What does this mean?

Context: Muhammad Ali famously refused to fight in the Vietnam War, saying, "Man, ain't got no quarrel with them Vietcong." Research Ali's stance and its aftermath. Also, relate his position to Sweet Pea's comment that "my nephew'd been drafted and it all seems so wrong to me, our men over there in Nam fighting folks who fighting for the same things we are, to get that bloodsucker off our backs." Who or what is the bloodsucker, and who is the "our" to whom she refers? Consider Sweet Pea's opinions and relate them to [6180] (*When Women Decide This War Should End, This War Will End* poster) and [6217] (*It Is a Sin to Be Silent When It Is Your Duty to Protest* poster). Should Sweet Pea be more active in opposing the war, or does she have enough to worry about in her personal life?

Context: Compare Sweet Pea's self-empowerment in "Medley" to Dee/Wangero's self-empowerment in Alice Walker's "Everyday Use." How are they the same? How different? How do you know?

Exploration: Compare Bambara's use of music, including jazz, in this story to Langston Hughes's (see Unit 10) and Amiri Baraka's (see Unit 15) use of jazz in their poetry.

Exploration: Why does Bambara include Larry and Hector's "best story" about Bam's funeral? Does it matter that Hector is "not what you'd call a good storyteller"? Consider Sweet Pea's comment, "There was something in that story about the civil rights workers wanting to make a case cause a white cop had cut Bam down. But looked like Hector didn't have a hold to that part of the story, so I just don't know." Why does Sweet Pea comment on what Hector *doesn't* say?

Exploration: Sweet Pea says that her friendships with Pot Limit and Sylvia help her recover from difficult days, but that she worries that no one will "intervene" for Larry in the same way. Consider the role of the African American community in this story. Use the text to identify the values of this community, including its strengths and limitations. You might also compare Bambara's depiction of community to Zora Neale Hurston's in *Their Eyes Were Watching God*.

Maxine Hong Kingston (b. 1940)

Maxine Hong Kingston, née Maxine Ting Hong, was born in Stockton, California, to Chinese immigrant parents who left successful careers in China to raise their children in the United States. Her fiction thematically deals almost exclusively with her heritage as a Chinese American woman, including the struggles of trying to balance her parents' cultural values with American customs and expectations. It also more broadly addresses the challenge for all Americans of living in a country in which so many different cultures coexist. Kingston combines fact and fiction in her writing, culling from her mother's stories about China while adding elements of history, legend, autobiography, and "outsider" observation.

While most famous for her first novel, the 1976 National Book Critics Circle award–winning *The Woman Warrior: Memoirs of a Girlhood Among Ghosts*, which addresses the complex issues facing Chinese American women, Kingston also wrote a companion novel, *China Men*, that does the same for Chinese American men. Kingston is adept at weaving China's **oral tradition** of storytelling into her fiction, but her fiction says as much about mainstream America as it does about Chinese Americans. She is also a keen observer of the ways people interact with and judge each other and, like Toni Morrison, provides provocative critiques of how people from all ethnic groups are guilty of stereotyping rather than sincerely trying to know each other.

In *Tripmaster Monkey*, Kingston returns to the locale of her college days, Berkeley, California, to tell the story of a struggling Chinese American playwright. We see in the sometimes-disagreeable character Wittman Ah Sing that Kingston is not afraid to tackle complicated issues that may cause some discomfort for readers both within and outside of Chinese American communities. Kingston's stories are not only for or about Chinese Americans: she strives to create literature that illuminates what it means to be an American, period, and as such resonates with readers from any ethnic group.

[7437] Eric Risberg, *Author Maxine Hong Kingston* (2001), courtesy of the Associated Press.

TEACHING TIPS

■ Many students seem to automatically sympathize with a story's protagonist. While Wittman Ah Sing is a sympathetic character in many ways, you may want to discuss his own areas of blindness or prejudice. Consider, especially, his discussion of "F.O.B." Chinese Americans and his reasons for contacting Nanci Lee. Ask your students to think about why Kingston chooses to depict Wittman as she does. Consider that Wittman has one perspective, but the narrative on the whole may have another. Use this story to teach students how to distinguish the main character's biases from the text's.

■ Ah Sing is a fifth-generation Chinese American man. Look at the early-twentieth-century photographs of San Francisco Chinatown in the archive; these could be very similar to the San Francisco homes and neighborhoods of Ah Sing's ancestors. Compare these images to Ah Sing's descriptions of San Francisco and Chinatown in the 1980s.

QUESTIONS

Comprehension: What does "F.O.B." mean? Who uses this term and why?

Comprehension: Of all the women that he knew at college, why does Ah Sing choose to call Nanci Lee?

Comprehension: Ah Sing and Nanci Lee discuss the problems they face in trying to become successful; for example, Nanci Lee, an

KINGSTON WEB ARCHIVE

[6166] Anonymous, *Police and Detectives Guarding Chinatown, July 6, 1909* (1909), courtesy of the Library of Congress [LC-USZ62-69697]. Writing at the turn of the twentieth century, Sui Sin Far (Edith Maud Eaton) made efforts to combat stereotypes of Chinese immigrants as "heathen," "unclean," and "untrustworthy." She provided insight into the unique culture of America's Chinatowns.

[6170] Anonymous, *Chinese New Year* (1909), courtesy of the Library of Congress [LC-USZ62-120168]. Chinese immigrants brought their traditions and customs to America, where they established strong communities to provide support in an unfamiliar world. Maxine Hong Kingston offers personal and deeply reflective portraits of how Chinese immigrants' experiences, from the mid-nineteenth century through the present, have affected their sense of American identity.

[6171] Arnold Genthe, *Children Were the Pride, Joy, Beauty, and Chief Delight of the Quarter, Chinatown, San Francisco* (c. 1896–1906), courtesy of the Library of Congress, Prints and Photographs Division [LC-USZC4-5265]. Four children in traditional Chinese clothing on a sidewalk in San Francisco's Chinatown. Writing about the time this photograph was taken, Sui Sin Far (Edith Maud Eaton) sought to make the lives of Chinese immigrants understandable to white audiences.

[6501] Marc Cohen, Cover: *The Woman Warrior* by Maxine Hong Kingston (1989), courtesy of Vintage International. Maxine Hong Kingston published her first novel, *The Woman Warrior*, in 1976. Kingston was born in California to Chinese parents and grew up speaking Say Yup, a Cantonese dialect. Her prose is infused with Chinese rhythms and Chinese American speech.

[7437] Eric Risberg, *Author Maxine Hong Kingston* (2001), courtesy of the Associated Press. "We approach the truth with metaphors."—Kingston, from "An Imagined Life." Kingston draws much of the inspiration for her writing from the stories her mother told her as a child, which kept Chinese tradition alive for her.

[8183] Anonymous, *The Voyage, No. 8* (c. 1920), reprinted in *Island: Poetry and History of Chinese Immigrants on Angel Island, 1910–1940*, courtesy of the University of Washington Press. "How has anyone to know that my dwelling place would be a prison?" asks this poem, one of many written on the walls of the Angel Island detention center by Chinese immigrants who were held there for extended periods by U.S. authorities. Maxine Hong Kingston's *China Men* focuses on the stories of early Chinese American immigrants.

actress, is frustrated by the roles that she receives. What is the problem? Why is she frustrated?

Comprehension: Ah Sing tells us his family history and, at the same time, allows us insight into white stereotypes about and expectations of Chinese Americans. Read the story closely to come up with a description of Chinese Americans as Ah Sing thinks whites see them. Consider phrasing such as "credits to our race."

Context: Compare Ah Sing's representation of the Chinatown community to Toni Cade Bambara's representation of an African American community in "Medley." What do they tell us about the significance of minorities living in a "city within a city"? Consider those who may be excluded from these communities (e.g., Nanci Lee) and why.

Context: Why do you think Kingston uses such detail about Nanci Lee and Ah Sing's conversation, as well as Ah Sing's thoughts during the conversation? Think about their conversation in light of the "communication theory" discussed by Saul and Meatball in Thomas Pynchon's "Entropy."

Context: Consider Ah Sing's reading on the bus as an example of performance art. What is he trying to accomplish by reading aloud? Why do you think he chooses this medium to communicate? Do you think this is a successful performance?

Exploration: In naming her main character Wittman Ah Sing, Kingston seems to invite us to identify him with the nineteenth-century American poet Walt Whitman, who is famous for celebrating America's democracy and diversity. In fact, as Wittman reads Rilke on the bus, his fellow passengers are described as "Walt Whitman's 'classless society' of 'everyone who could read or be read to.'" What does this mean? Read Whitman's "I Hear America Singing." What does it mean to "sing"? Write a poem or song that represents Wittman Ah Sing's "song" or your own.

Exploration: Ah Sing again recalls Walt Whitman (who included many long lists in his poems) when he lists the writers and texts that he would like to read on various trains that traverse the American West. What is the significance of this list? Read all or part of one of the texts that he lists and compare its representation of the American West or California to Kingston's in *Tripmaster Monkey*.

Exploration: In *The Souls of Black Folk*, W. E. B. Du Bois explains the difficulty of "double consciousness" for African Americans: "One ever feels his two-ness,—an American, a Negro; two souls, two thoughts, two unreconciled strivings; two warring ideals in one dark body, whose dogged strength alone keeps it from being torn asunder." Can we adapt this idea to better understand Wittman Ah Sing as both an American and a Chinese American? You might also consider how Leslie Feinberg references Du Boisian double-consciousness to discuss both race and gender issues in *Stone Butch Blues*.

Diane Glancy (b. 1941)

Born in Kansas City, Diane Glancy is a poet, short story writer, playwright, and professor. She received her B.A. from the University of Missouri in 1964, her M.A. from Central State University in 1983, and an M.F.A. from the University of Iowa's Writer's Workshop in 1988. Currently, she teaches creative writing at Macalester College in St. Paul, Minnesota. Her father's Cherokee heritage is evident throughout her fiction; Glancy concentrates much of her writing on her dual identity as a mixed-heritage Native American. Her stories, including "Jack Wilson or Wovoka and Christ My Lord," address the difficulties of being "half" rather than "whole": half white, half Native American, her narrator defiantly wrestles with her position as both insider and outsider within her community.

Glancy's characters are honest—some readers have commented that they feel as if the characters are personal friends making confessions. For example, in "Jack Wilson or Wovoka and Christ My Lord," the narrator, using the informal (some say conversational) language that is typical of Glancy's characters, tells us, "I believe in being generous up to a point and then I think to say things like they are." Glancy often uses such colloquial language, sometimes with unusual punctuation, to tell stories about her identity, her family, and her spirituality. Her writing style often echoes the Native American oral tradition and, like oral storytelling, her fiction provides details that appeal to all five senses: she writes evocatively of the sights, sounds, smells, tastes, and feelings that her characters experience, thus drawing her audience more intimately into the work. Glancy's publications include *Trigger Dance* (1990) and *Firesticks* (1993), from which the stories in *The Norton Anthology of American Literature* are taken.

[4203] Anonymous, *Protest Against the Bureau of Indian Affairs (BIA)* (1970), courtesy of the Denver Public Library, Western History Collection.

TEACHING TIPS

■ Students may have a difficult time understanding some of Glancy's writing because of its nontraditional punctuation. You may want to teach them to read the more confusing sentences as if they were poetry. Also, ask them to read sentences aloud so that they can more easily find the rhythm and, accordingly, the meaning in the prose.

■ Discuss the importance of oral tradition in Native American cultures. You could pair these stories with earlier Native American texts. You could also ask student volunteers to read aloud from the stories and, while doing so, to remember that they're not just reading aloud: they're *storytelling*. For more information about the Native American oral tradition, see Unit 1.

■ Students may more usefully discuss elements of oral storytelling and other Native American beliefs/traditions in Glancy's stories if they have some background first. Wovoka, also known as Jack Wilson (c. 1856–1932), was a Native American prophet, considered by some to be a messiah, of the Paiute tribe. After receiving a command from God during a fever- and delirium-induced vision, he taught his tribe members a "ghost dance" that was to help them live prosperously and peacefully, recover their lost lands, and regain contact with their

GLANCY WEB ARCHIVE

[4203] Anonymous, *Protest Against the Bureau of Indian Affairs (BIA)* (1970), courtesy of the Denver Public Library, Western History Collection. "To look upon that landscape [Rainy Mountain] in the early morning, with the sun at your back, is to lose the sense of proportion," writes N. Scott Momaday in *The Way to Rainy Mountain*. "Your imagination comes to life, and this, you think, is where Creation was begun." Along with the expansion and development of contemporary Native American writing in the late 1960s and 1970s, protest movements arose against the discrimination suffered by American Indians.
[4219] Western Photograph Company, *Gathering Up the Dead at the Battle Field of Wounded Knee, South Dakota* (1891), courtesy of the Smithsonian Institution. U.S. soldiers, gathering bodies from the battlefield at Wounded Knee, standing in front of a wagon full

of dead Sioux. A blizzard delayed the burial of the dead. Eventually, the Sioux were buried in a mass grave, with little effort made to identify the bodies.

[5595] Gales and Seaton's *Register, Register of Debates, House of Representatives, 23rd Congress, 2nd Session, Pages 1007 through 1010, Cherokee Memorial* (1835), courtesy of the Library of Congress. This is a record of the reception of the Memorial of the Cherokee Council by Congress. Despite the eloquence of the petitions and their invocation of the republican ideals of natural rights and independence, the Cherokee people were brutally forced off their ancestral lands in 1838.

[8008] Greg Sarris, Interview: "Native Voices" (2003), courtesy of *American Passages* and Annenberg/CPB. Greg Sarris, author, professor of English, and Pomo Indian, discusses the trickster figure Coyote.

[8101] Blackfeet, *Dress* (c. 1890), courtesy of the Portland Art Museum, gift of Elizabeth Cole Butler. The Blackfeet of Montana are a Plains Indian confederacy of three politically independent tribes: the Peigan (Poor Robes), Bloods (Kainai or Many Chiefs), and North Blackfeet (Siksika or Blackfoot). Blackfoot author James Welch helped start the Native American Renaissance with works like *Winter in the Blood*, *Fools Crow*, and *Riding the Earthboy 40*. This woman's dress, made of leather, glass beads, and wool cloth, is similar to what women would have worn during the Ghost Dance movement of the 1890s.

[8688] Arch C. Gerlach, editor, *Map of Early Indian Tribes, Culture Areas, and Linguistic Stocks*, from *The National Atlas of the United States*, U.S. Dept. of the Interior, Geological Survey (1970), courtesy of the General Libraries, University of Texas at Austin. The Cherokee originally lived in the southeastern part of what is now the United States, but after the unsuccessful petitions of the Cherokee Memorials, they were removed to Indian Territory (present-day Oklahoma). Contemporary writer Diane Glancy is of Cherokee descent; her 1996 novel, *Pushing the Bear*, is about the Trail of Tears, the Cherokees' long, forced march to Indian Territory, during which thousands died.

ancestors. You might start a discussion of Glancy by asking your students to read one or two of the Ghost Dance songs or a selection from Black Elk.

QUESTIONS

Comprehension: In "Jack Wilson or Wovoka and Christ My Lord," Glancy's punctuation is untraditional and her language is colloquial. How do these formal techniques influence your understanding of the stories?

Comprehension: Why do you think the narrator of "Jack Wilson" so frequently reminds us of her mixed-race heritage?

Comprehension: What happens to the old woman at the end of "Polar Breath"?

Context: The narrator of "Jack Wilson" tells about an Indian man who "can't fly really so heavy with his heritage." What does this mean? Compare this passage to Alice Walker's "Everyday Use," in which Dee/Wangero tells Maggie, "You just don't understand . . . your heritage." What is heritage and what does it mean to these characters? Is it a blessing or a burden?

Context: The female narrator of "Jack Wilson" states of her relationship with men: "if he's willing to stay you usually let him empty as the house is even with him in it." And consider that although the old woman in "Polar Breath" seems to enjoy her solitude, she eventually moves toward reunion with her late husband. Compare these descriptions to Bambara's description of Sweet Pea and Larry's relationship in "Medley." Why do the women seem to want to be alone, yet return to these men?

Context: Analyze [4203], in which Native American students protest the Bureau of Indian Affairs in 1970 (the BIA is an often-criticized governmental agency charged with handling matters related to Native Americans). What do you make of the signs in this image, especially "Indians Are Red/B.I.A. What Are You" and "Stop Persecuting Indians"? Why might these people have been protesting?

Exploration: The narrator of "Jack Wilson" tells us that the "changing surviving ole Coyote finally teaches in the end that there's no ultimate reality no foundation and whatever he/she believes is true." What are the implications of a belief in shifting realities, or of an ideology characterized by relativism? What would it mean for there to be no "absolutes"?

Exploration: Compare Emily Dickinson's poetry with Glancy's prose, for example, when Glancy says, "Me and all the runny-nosed reservation children suffering alcoholism poverty want close-mindedness growing up to engender the same in their own." How do these authors' unique punctuation and word use either restrict or enlarge the possible meanings of their works? Why might they reject traditional punctuation and grammar?

Exploration: The mixed-race narrator of "Jack Wilson" says, "it was years before I started saying what I thought" and "I saw right away I was invisible to him." In *One Flew Over the Cuckoo's Nest*, Ken

Kesey's narrator Chief Bromden is also half white and half Native American. Chief pretends to be deaf and mute, making him, in a sense, invisible. Read *One Flew Over the Cuckoo's Nest* and compare Chief's experiences with those of Glancy's narrator. What does it mean to be "invisible"? Is silence an effective mode of resistance in an oppressive society? What does it mean when the bird in "Jack Wilson" says, "presence. Substance. Something visible"?

Exploration: The old woman in "Polar Breath" is described as "an exile in herself." What does this mean? How, if at all, is this possible? What is the significance of her dead husband and the spirits? Is she really alone?

Alice Walker (b. 1944)

Born in rural Eatonton, Georgia, but educated in the North, Alice Walker has been able to analyze the rural South, the focus of most of her writing, as both an insider and an outsider. In her works, which include novels, short stories, poetry collections, and essays, she has drawn inspiration from her own life experiences, including an abortion and a visit to Africa while she was attending Sarah Lawrence College. Walker also participated actively in the civil rights movement, during which she met civil rights lawyer Mel Leventhal. After she and Leventhal married, they fought discrimination against their interracial relationship. As a professor at Wellesley College, Walker taught one of the first women's studies courses in the nation, and she has been integral in bringing greater attention and appreciation to the work of early-twentieth-century anthropologist and writer Zora Neale Hurston, who, like Walker, skillfully wove folk materials into her narratives.

Walker won the 1983 Pulitzer Prize for her best-known novel, 1982's *The Color Purple*, which in 1985 was transformed into a successful movie starring Whoopi Goldberg and Oprah Winfrey. In *The Color Purple*, Celie, an African American woman, learns to assert her rights in relationship to her husband and comes to terms with her desire for another woman, Shug. While Walker has sought to describe black women's struggles to find agency and self-determination, she was criticized for too harshly portraying black men in the novel, a charge that shocked and dismayed her.

Walker's works include *In Love and Trouble* (1973), *Meridian* (1976), *In Search of Our Mothers' Gardens* (1983), and *Possessing the Secret of Joy* (1992).

TEACHING TIPS

■ Start by asking your students what kinds of heirlooms their families have, if any, and why they're meaningful. Pay attention to their reasons: some students may provide sentimental reasons (like Maggie's), some may provide "cultural" reasons (like Dee/Wangero's), and some may provide financial reasons ("it may be worth something someday").

[6187] Anonymous, *Congress to Unite Women, May 1, 2, 3, '70: Intermediate School, 333 W. 17 St., N.Y.C.* (1970), courtesy of the Library of Congress.

WALKER WEB ARCHIVE

[3090] Harriet Powers, *Pictorial Quilt* (c. 1895–98), courtesy of the Museum of Fine Arts, Boston. Copyright 2002 MFA, Boston. Harriet Powers (American, 1837–1911). United States (Athens, Georgia), 1895–98, pieced, appliqued, and printed cotton embroidered with cotton and metallic yarns, 175 x 266.7 cm (68 7/8 x 105 in.), Museum of Fine Arts Boston, bequest of Maxim Karolik, 64.619. Many slave and freed women used quilts to record their histories. Some quilts communicated messages: for example, quilts using the color black indicated a safe house on the Underground Railroad. Like slave narrative authors, African American quilters often used biblical themes and references in their work.

[4819] Alan Lomax, *Zora Neale Hurston, Rochelle French, and Gabriel Brown, Eatonville, Florida* (1935), courtesy of the Library of Congress [LC-USZ61-1777 DLC]. Used with the permission of the Estate of Zora Neale Hurston. Hurston is pictured here interviewing residents of her hometown, the all-black community of Eatonville. While studying at Barnard, Hurston worked with renowned anthropologist Franz Boas and, in 1927, under Boas's direction, traveled to Louisiana and southern Florida to study and collect African American folktales. *The Eatonville Anthology*, an anthropologically based narrative, sketches vivid images of Hurston's hometown and reveals her skill as an anthropologist.

[6187] Anonymous, *Congress to Unite Women, May 1, 2, 3, '70: Intermediate School, 333 W. 17 St., N.Y.C.* (1970), courtesy of the Library of Congress. From the same year that Toni Morrison and Alice Walker published their first novels, this poster calls women to one of the many conferences organized to formulate plans of action against the web of racial, heterosexual, and patriarchal oppression. In her article "Playing in the Dark," Morrison writes: "My work requires me to think about how free I can be as an African-American woman writer in my genderized, sexualized, and wholly radicalized world. [F]or me, imagining is not merely looking or looking at; nor is it taking oneself intact into the other. It is, for the purpose of the work, *becoming*."

[6949] Harriet Powers, Bible Quilt (c. 1886), courtesy of the Smithsonian Institution, National Museum of American History. Harriet Powers, a black woman from Athens, Georgia, made quilts like this one before and after her emancipation. Her biblical scenes reflect how both slaves and freed people turned to Christianity to interpret their hard circumstances and find hope.

■ Students might be interested in thinking about the quilt as an heirloom in relation to the phenomenon of "antiquing." You could start this discussion by talking about the PBS television series *Antiques Roadshow*. On the show, people bring family heirlooms, relics from their attics, mysterious found objects, and the like to antique appraisers. Usually, an object's owners tell the story of how the object came into their possession, and then the appraisers explain the object's cultural history (as far as they can tell) and provide estimates of its financial worth. Each episode of the show thus demonstrates many different types of valuation: personal (family stories, family heirlooms, sentimental value), cultural (historical value, the antique's place in larger narratives about the country, wars, places, etc.), and financial. What makes some antiques more "valuable" than others? Whose definition of "value" is most important? And why are television viewers so interested in watching other peoples' junk be appraised?

QUESTIONS

Comprehension: The story begins with a dedication that reads: "For Your Grandmamma." How does this dedication shape your understanding of the text? Who does the "your" refer to here: the reader? Someone in the story? And why "Grandmamma"? What is being suggested here?

Comprehension: Why does the story begin with such a detailed description of the yard?

Comprehension: Why have Dee and her boyfriend changed their names to "Wangero" and "Hakim-a-barber"? Why did Dee reject her birth name? What is the significance of the new names? Also, consider Dee/Wangero's new clothes.

Context: Closely read Walker's descriptions of the family's house and compare it to [7030], a photograph taken in 1958. These two houses were categorized as "good enough for Negro occupancy" (later, a housing project was built in their place). What does "good enough" mean? "Read" the photo, as well. What is behind the girl in the foreground? Note her clothes, her stance. Consider the condition of both the house and the yard.

Context: Consider the quilts as "collages" of the family's history. What different elements are brought together in the quilt? You might also consider how the quilts serve as memorials to earlier generations. Are the quilts more a memorial to a person, Grandma, as Maggie seems to believe, or a culture, as Dee/Wangero seems to believe?

Context: Dee/Wangero seems to feel contempt for her family because they have not, in her opinion, "progressed" into modernity. Compare her anxieties to those expressed in phrases about "F.O.B." Chinese Americans in Maxine Hong Kingston's *Tripmaster Monkey*. Discuss these characters' fears of seeming unassimilated, unsophisticated, and uncultured.

Exploration: Early in the story the narrator offers a frank description of herself as a "big-boned woman with rough, man-working hands."

She goes on to catalog her various features. Why does she do this? What is she trying to suggest and what does she ultimately accomplish by revealing these things about herself? Do you think that her self-description is meant to convince the reader that she is a certain type of person and, therefore, to be trusted? *Are* certain types of people inherently more trustworthy than others?

Exploration: When Dee/Wangero arrives at her mother's homestead, she begins collecting the things she wants to bring back with her. What do the things she wants tell us about her? What does she want to do with them, and why are her intentions here significant?

Exploration: How might we read the argument between Dee/Wangero and her mother over the quilts as a commentary on the function of art and/or heritage? What is each character suggesting about the meaning and purpose of the quilts? What does each believe they should be "used" for? Does the text encourage us to side with one or the other? If so, how does it manipulate our sympathies?

Exploration: Two characters in a story can be called "doubles" when they represent two perspectives about one issue. Some readers have suggested that Maggie and Dee/Wangero are doubles who embody different positions in mid- to late-twentieth-century debates about African American culture and progress. Consider Maggie's statement that "I can 'member Grandma Dee without the quilts" and Dee/Wangero's statement, "You just don't understand . . . your heritage. It's really a new day for us."

David Mamet (b. 1947)

David Mamet was born on the Jewish south side of Chicago. His plays have been performed throughout the country, in his hometown as well as in New York City, where Mamet studied the Stanislavsky method of acting. He has said that this method made him aware of how "the language we use, its rhythm, actually determines the way we behave, more than the other way around." It is important, then, for Mamet's audiences and readers to pay close attention to his use of language.

David Mamet's language in his plays and films is so distinctive that it is now known as "Mametspeak." His characters talk through, around, and over each other, sometimes clarifying and sometimes obliterating meaning, and his works have been described as perfect for "people who love words." In *Glengarry Glen Ross*, for which he received the 1984 Pulitzer Prize, Mamet tells the story of a desperate man attempting to keep his job in a profession that, for better or worse, has passed him by. The play uses the business of sales as a metaphor for the American condition, as characters jostle for position in an office where there are only so many "leads" to go around. For these men, who have been defined by their work, the end of a career could necessitate a new search for identity in a world that may seem as if it no longer has room for them.

In 1988's play *Speed the Plow*, in which Madonna was the original lead actress, Mamet used his experience as a screenwriter to stage a

[7030] Anonymous, *These Two Houses Were Among the Structures in Washington, D.C. . . .* (1958), courtesy of the Library of Congress [LC-USZ62-124134]. These two Washington, D.C., houses were classed as "good enough" for occupancy by African Americans until they were demolished so that a housing project could be built in their place. In the foreground a young girl stands near an old wooden well.

[8958] Alice Walker, Interview: "Rhythms in Poetry" (2003), courtesy of *American Passages* and Annenberg/CPB. Author Alice Walker discusses Langston Hughes's writing.

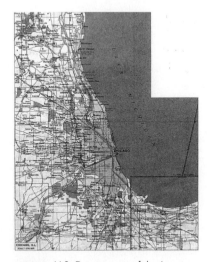

[9072] U.S. Department of the Interior, *Map of Chicago, 1970*, from the *National Atlas of the United States of America*, U.S. Geological Survey (1970), courtesy of the General Libraries, University of Texas at Austin.

scathing critique of the truth behind Hollywood's glamorous façade. The film world has nonetheless treated him well. Since beginning his screenwriting career in 1981, Mamet has succeeded equally in films and in theater. Unlike many other writers who have attempted to "go Hollywood," Mamet has maintained his reputation as a legitimate writer. His film credits include *The Untouchables* (1987), *Glengarry Glen Ross* (1992), *The Edge* (1997), and *Wag the Dog* (1997). Mamet's plays include *The Duck Variations* (1972), *Sexual Perversity in Chicago* (1974), *American Buffalo* (1977), and *Oleanna* (1992).

TEACHING TIPS

■ One of the best ways to get your students interested in drama is to have them act out scenes for the class. You can choose the scenes or allow the students to pick their own. Remind them to pay close attention to both their vocal performances and their body language. To reinforce the play's themes, ask them to follow up their dramatic performances with analyses (including close readings) of the scenes that they acted out.

■ Mamet has written many screenplays and many of his plays have been made into films. Choose a scene or two from one of these plays, and ask your students to analyze the characters' language. You might ask them to come up with a list of characteristics of Mamet's work that they can compare to *Glengarry Glen Ross* after they read the play. Also, after the students read *Glengarry Glen Ross*, you could show a scene from the movie and ask them to compare the reading experience to the viewing experience. What does the film bring to or take from the play?

■ Many students have a hard time engaging with literature if they don't "like" any of the characters, and Mamet is famous for creating generally unsympathetic characters. Encourage students to find ideas in the text to which they can relate. Or, ask them if Mamet's representations seem "realistic." Do the students know people like this? Or, do the students know people who *talk* like this?

QUESTIONS

Comprehension: What is Glengarry? What is Glen Ross? Why are they important in the play?

Comprehension: What do these characters do for a living? What is "the board"? What are "leads"?

Comprehension: How do the salesmen attempt to deal with James Lingk's desire to renege on his contract? Why does Roma become so angry with Williamson?

Context: Analyze the play's first words from Levene to Williamson (or choose another scene) in terms of Thomas Pynchon's ideas in "Entropy" about "noise" and "leakage." How much of Levene's speech is just noise and how much is communication? Is there a difference between the two? Does any language or utterance communicate something? If so, what?

Context: In stories by Maxine Hong Kingston, Sandra Cisneros, and other writers in this unit, characters are on the receiving end of ethnic and racial slurs. In this play, David Mamet's characters are often on the giving end—they actually make the derogatory comments. Why? What is Mamet suggesting about why people participate in and perpetuate stereotyping? For example, if we interpret Moss's comments about Indians in light of his job insecurity, are they more understandable and/or less offensive? Why or why not?

Context: When James Lingk attempts to cancel his deal, the salesmen are dismissive of his arguments, especially when he mentions his wife's role in the family's decision making. Consider their reactions in relation to Toni Cade Bambara's "Medley," in which Sweet Pea says that men ignore her while they "conduct business" in her presence. Consider Roma's comments to Lingk: "You have a life of your own. You have a contract with your wife. You have certain things you do jointly. . . . and there are *other* things. Those things are yours." What "things" does Roma suggest are Lingk's?

Exploration: Figuratively speaking, what does it mean to "get on the board"? Why is it so important to get and stay on the board, and how does Mamet suggest this be accomplished? What are "leads" and how can we get them? Is it possible for people without "leads" to succeed? What is he saying about American values and corporate, financial, and monetary systems? If "sales" are a metaphor for American capitalist society, what is Mamet suggesting about American values, opportunities, and achievements?

Exploration: When Levene crows about his sale to Bruce and Harriet Nyborg, he explains their agreement: "It was like they wilted all at once. . . . they both kind of *imperceptibly slumped*." Thus, his victory is their defeat. At what cost has Levene seized his own "opportunity"? Are the Nyborgs sympathetic characters? How, if at all, does your opinion of them change after you learn of their history with salespeople?

Exploration: In the nineteenth century, Henry David Thoreau wrote that "the mass of men lead lives of quiet desperation" because they spend too much time worrying about money, material goods, and worldly achievement. Here, David Mamet tells of twentieth-century desperate men who resort to desperate measures because they are part of the system of "corporate slavery." Why do you think achievement and financial success are so important to these characters? Also consider the ideas about manhood and masculinity that recur throughout the play, e.g., "It's not a world of men." What does it mean to be a man according to these characters and/or according to this text?

Exploration: Compare the salesmen in *Glengarry Glen Ross* to Willy Loman in Arthur Miller's play *Death of a Salesman*. Consider how the salesmen in these plays are depicted as archetypal victims and, simultaneously, perpetrators of American capitalism and consumer culture.

Leslie Feinberg (b. 1949)

Like her character Jess Goldberg, Leslie Feinberg was born in Buffalo, New York, where she grew up before the 1969 Stonewall Rebellion, which many observers consider the watershed moment in the twentieth-century movement to secure the rights of nonheterosexual people. Feinberg struggled to find her identity in a culture that seemingly had no place for her as a transgendered individual. Now, as a journalist and author as well as an activist for the rights of gay, lesbian, bisexual, and transgendered individuals, she has stated that her written work is often an attempt to answer her own questions about why some people feel that they need to punish those who are different.

Following in the tradition of writers like Toni Cade Bambara, Feinberg's novel *Stone Butch Blues* endorses the belief that writing can be revolutionary. Simply by sharing this story with others, Feinberg extends her activist reach by educating her readers. In *Stone Butch Blues*, she combines autobiography and fiction in a narrative structured as a letter to an ex-girlfriend. Her character Jess Goldberg struggles to come to terms with her identity and sexuality in a society that provides no models and no safe refuge for her. Thus, even as its startling depictions of brutality and cruelty may be uncomfortable for some readers, the novel answers a need in the queer community for testimonials that establish a common history and reveal stories that had for so long remained untold.

[7947] Deirdre Griswold Strapp, *Leslie Feinberg Speaking at Madison Square Garden Theater as a Founder of Rainbow Flags for Mumia* (2000), courtesy of Deirdre Strapp.

TEACHING TIPS

■ You will probably need to spend some time clarifying the terms "queer," "transgender," "transsexual," "gender variant," "butch/femme," and other phrases that students have questions about. For more information, see the "Gay and Lesbian Identities in Contemporary American Writing" extended context in this unit and consult an introduction to queer studies, such as Annamarie Jagose's *Queer Theory: An Introduction* (New York UP, 1997).

■ To exhibit the hatred toward gender-variant individuals that Feinberg describes, you could show an excerpt of the 1999 movie *Boys Don't Cry*, for which Hilary Swank won an Academy Award for Best Actress. You could ask the students to compare the rape scenes in the movie and in *Stone Butch Blues*. Or, students who may not be ready for such graphic descriptions could compare the scenes in which Swank's character cross-dresses to similar scenes in the novel.

■ Many students even at college age are uncomfortable talking about sexuality in general, so you may have to teach them how to do so usefully and constructively. Also, because of the persistence of homophobia, be prepared for the possibility that some students may make stereotypical and perhaps offensive comments. With this issue more than perhaps any other, it is important to remain sensitive to the probability that students are personally dealing with these matters, and some in the group are probably coming to terms with their own sexual identities and orientations.

Comprehension: What does it mean to be transgendered? What does it mean to be **gender variant**?

Comprehension: How does Jess realize that she is not like the other children?

Comprehension: What are butch and femme identities? What are **identity politics**?

Context: Relate Jess's difficulties dealing with the mainstream community to the difficulties experienced by Chinese Americans Nanci Lee and Wittman Ah Sing in Maxine Hong Kingston's *Tripmaster Monkey*. How are their experiences similar? What makes them different?

Context: Compare Feinberg's forthright, public image to Thomas Pynchon's near-invisibility. Feinberg seems to *need* to tell her own story as well as Jess's. Why might she consider her own story so important? You might want to think about your answer in relation to the statement, "The personal is political" (see Unit 15).

Exploration: Why do you think Jess Goldberg tells her story in letter form? Why is her audience, her former girlfriend, so important? How does this audience shape the content, tone, and style of the narrative? Do you think that the letter, or epistolary, form allows a narrator to relate details more intimately, or do you think that a specific audience (i.e., the recipient of the letter) can actually limit the narrator's revelations? If you have read *Portnoy's Complaint* by Philip Roth, you could compare Feinberg's narrative letter to Roth's narrator's address to his therapist.

Exploration: The video for this unit expressed the idea that identity is not a stable, fixed thing but rather a process. What does this mean? Consider this idea in relation to Jess's story. What are the steps of her identity process? Has she resolved her identity at the novel's end? Is it ever possible to resolve identity or does the process continue until death?

Exploration: Cultural theorist Marjorie Garber explains that a "category crisis" occurs when the borders between things often positioned as binary opposites—such as black and white, old and young, new and used—are revealed to be permeable. In *Stone Butch Blues*, Feinberg shows that the line between man and woman can be (and is) crossed. What other categories are in crisis in Feinberg's novel? Consider gender, sexuality, race, education level, class, and any other category by which people are identified and/or judged.

Judith Ortiz Cofer (b. 1952)

Judith Ortiz Cofer was born in Hormingueros, Puerto Rico, and was educated in the United States, primarily New Jersey. Her fiction incorporates elements of memoir as well as of the oral storytelling tradition that she learned, and that comforted her, while she was growing up in Puerto Rican communities. As a writer of fiction, poetry, and essays, Cofer has merged her Latin and Anglo experiences to express the dual

[7419] Anonymous, Cover: *The Liberty Press* (1996), courtesy of The Liberty Press. Cover of a 1996 issue of *The Liberty Press*, a gay/lesbian newspaper. Headline reads, "Leslie Feinberg tops the bill." Feinberg's novel *Stone Butch Blues* works from the premise that writing can be a tool for social change.

[7422] Anonymous, *Leslie Feinberg*, photo (n.d.), courtesy of The Liberty Press. The protagonist of Leslie Feinberg's *Stone Butch Blues* struggles to find her identity in a culture that does not seem to have a place for her as a transgendered individual.

[7766] Chris Hampton, Newspaper article: "Leslie Feinberg a Powerful Presence at Lesbigays OK Awareness Week." *The Liberty Press*, May 1996 issue [Vol. 2 No. 9] (1996), courtesy of The Liberty Press, Wichita, Kansas. Feature article from a 1996 issue of *The Liberty Press*, a gay/lesbian newspaper, which also includes "a full report on anti-gay marriage activity in our capital." Leslie Feinberg, a journalist and activist, has sought to understand why so many in the United States feel hatred for those who do not fit neatly into gender categories.

[7947] Deirdre Griswold Strapp, *Leslie Feinberg Speaking at Madison Square Garden Theater as a Founder of Rainbow Flags for Mumia* (2000), courtesy of Deirdre Strapp. Leslie Feinberg has gained recognition as a writer and activist. This is a photograph of her speaking at a rally for Mumia Abu-Jamal, a former Black Panther and radio journalist convicted in the shooting death of a police officer and who is now on death row.

[8985] Leslie Feinberg, Interview: "Search for Identity" (2003), courtesy of *American Passages* and Annenberg/CPB. Author Leslie Feinberg discusses identity as a process.

identity engendered by living in two cultural spheres. In her work, she adapts for new readers the Spanish and classical myths that provided the foundation for the stories she heard as a child. For example, in "The Witch's Husband," Cofer uses a double-narration technique that allows us to share the perspectives of both the storyteller Abuela and her granddaughter. Cofer is adept at crafting fiction that honors the traditions and stories of the older generations while remaining sensitive to the post–women's liberation views of the younger generation.

Cofer also builds bridges between generations as a professor of English and creative writing at the University of Georgia: she teaches students about the importance of their ancestors' stories even as she guides them in creating their own. In addition, she regularly gives lectures on biculturalism in America and on the importance of encouraging diverse voices to contribute to American literature. Cofer's works include *Terms of Survival* (1987), *Reaching for the Mainland* (1987), *The Line of the Sun* (1989), *Silent Dancing* (1990), *The Latin Deli: Prose and Poetry* (1993), and *Woman in Front of the Sun: On Becoming a Writer* (2000).

TEACHING TIPS

■ You may want to start a discussion of "The Witch's Husband" by relating it to the oral tradition of Cofer's culture. Discuss how Abuela's story may be even more effective if spoken, and encourage students to read passages aloud.

■ Students will be curious about what Abuela ("Grandmother") might have done during her year in New York. While you may effectively entertain a few suppositions, this would be a good place to emphasize Abuela's role not just as a character but also as a *storyteller*. She decides to leave out these details for a reason. Why? Are they not important to the story?

QUESTIONS

Comprehension: Why does the narrator's family think she will be able to talk "sense" into her grandmother?

Comprehension: Why did Abuela go to New York for a year and what did she do there?

Comprehension: Why do you think the story is called "The Witch's Husband" and not, for example, "The Witch"? Is the story more about Abuela or her husband? Or is it actually about the narrator? Also, what does it mean to be a "witch"?

Context: Think about how Cofer uses storytelling as a memorial to earlier generations, as a means of remembering and honoring ancestors. How does Abuela's ability to tell a good story, including her knowledge of her audience's values, affect her granddaughter's impressions of old age?

Context: Compare this narrator's appreciation of her grandmother's "folk wisdom" to Dee/Wangero's simultaneous disdain and reverence for her mother's way of life in Alice Walker's "Everyday Use." You might also think about the way the homes, and setting more generally, function in a story, particularly Cofer's use of the hammock, Walker's use of the butter churn, and both authors' use of yards.

Context: Compare Abuela to the "big-boned," down-home woman in Alice Walker's "Everyday Use." They are both earthy, sensual women, but in very different ways. They each fulfill some traditional gender roles and expectations but break others, and they each (as far as we know) expand their opportunities relatively privately, e.g., by wearing masculine clothes, attending secret witches' meetings, or taking an extended break from the family. Consider their decisions to act privately in relation to archive item [6181] ("When women become massively political, the revolution will have moved to a new level" poster). Could these women do more "good" for the women's movement if they were more public about their **feminism**? Why or why not?

Exploration: Compare Abuela's storytelling approach of keeping memories to the more methodical approach—the "art of memory"—used by the father in Li-Young Lee's poems, especially "This Room and Everything in It."

Exploration: Abuela's story ends, "And in time, the husband either began forgetting that he had seen her turn into a witch or believed that he had just dreamed it." How does this ending affect the story's meaning? Is his forgetting positive or negative? If he no longer recognizes her "powers" as real, does this mean he has lost his hard-earned wisdom?

Exploration: The narrator tells us that in Puerto Rico, a "good woman" is willing to martyr herself to the interests and needs of those around her—and no woman has been better in this way than Abuela, whose "life has been entirely devoted to others." Do you agree that this kind of self-sacrifice makes a woman "good"? Think about this definition in relation to the following passage from British novelist and essayist Virginia Woolf, who wrote that when she began her career, she had difficulty because she was haunted by a phantom that she called "the Angel of the House." The angel whispered, "My dear, you are a young woman. . . . Be sympathetic; be tender; flatter; deceive; use all the arts and wiles of our sex. Never let anybody guess that you have a mind of your own. Above all, be pure." Is this good advice? Consider why this way of thinking could be difficult for both Woolf and Abuela, who seem very different.

Exploration: Consider "The Witch's Husband" in relation to other stories about witches in American society, including Arthur Miller's *The Crucible* (about the Salem witch trials). Do you think that stories like "The Witch's Husband" allow us to interpret witchcraft and "possession" as a form of resistance for women? In what sorts of societies might such forms of resistance be necessary? You might consult I. M. Lewis's *Ecstatic Religion*, which discusses how witchcraft, shamanism, and possession can enable women to resist.

York Public Library, Astor, Lenox and Tilden Foundations. Van de Velde was a seventeenth-century Dutch artist. Beginning with the introduction of tobacco to Europe in the 1500s, smoke began to appear in artwork to allegorize the five senses, most often taste, as well as the notion of fleeting time. This etching shows a shift both in perceptions of tobacco and in representations of evil. The scene was intended to expose the darker and more unnatural side of tobacco by placing tobacco pipes in the hands of goblins and feminine minions of the devil.

[2245] Alexandre-Marie Colin, *The Three Witches from Macbeth* (1827), courtesy of Sandor Korein. Shakespeare's influence on the popular American imagination has been profound. Paintings like this one resonate with the nineteenth-century interest in the occult and fear of what was seen by some as the supernatural power of women.

[6181] Peg Averill, *When Women Become Massively Political the Revolution Will Have Moved to a New Level* . . . (1976), courtesy of the Library of Congress [CN POS 6-U.S., no. 39 (C size) <P&P>]. Poster of a woman in whose flowing hair is pictured a setting sun and silhouettes of soldiers. The women's movement was closely allied to the peace movement. The National Organization for Women's 1966 statement of purpose began as follows: "We, men and women who hereby constitute ourselves as the National Organization for Women, believe that the time has come for a new movement toward true equality for all women in America, and toward a fully equal partnership of the sexes, as part of the world-wide revolution of human rights now taking place within and beyond our national borders."

[8990] Greg Sarris, Interview: "Search for Identity" (2003), courtesy of *American Passages* and Annenberg/CPB. Greg Sarris, author, professor, and Pomo Indian, discusses the task of integrating diverse cultures and viewpoints.

Sandra Cisneros (b. 1954)

Sandra Cisneros was born in Chicago but spent most of her childhood and youth moving back and forth between Chicago and Mexico. By addressing themes of identity, poverty, and gender in lyrical and sensual language, she has become one of the nation's most well-known and respected **Chicana** authors. Nonetheless, her vibrant style has not always been welcome, as she faced a battle with her San Antonio neighbors when she painted her historic King William District home purple. A *Houston Chronicle* article quoted the city commissioner as saying, "If you, because of your heritage, are allowed to paint your house purple, then we have no rules." Cisneros eventually agreed to paint her Victorian-era home in an approved, "authentic" color combination: pink with red trim.

[6394] José Guadalupe Posada, *Altar de la Virgen de Guadalupe* (1900), courtesy of the Library of Congress, Prints and Photographs Division [PGA-anegas, no. 127 (AA size)].

Like many of the writers in this unit, Cisneros uses fiction to point out how some Americans actively exclude or passively forget to include people unlike themselves when they define what it means to be American. Cisneros has stated that while she refuses to make concessions to Anglo readers, such as translating all Spanish language words in her texts into English, she nonetheless wants to open doors so that readers of any background can appreciate her stories and their implications for one's understanding of "Americanness."

By creating a voice and style uniquely her own, Cisneros tells stories that reflect her interests as well as those of her community. Cisneros's novel *The House on Mango Street* modifies stories that she heard throughout her life, especially those she witnessed firsthand while working as a counselor for inner-city high school children in Chicago. The novel's innovative style—it is a collection of short, poetically phrased vignettes—allows her to depict urban life in a unified way while representing the varied influences that shape the feminist consciousness of her main character, Esperanza.

Much of Cisneros's writing asks how women have been complicit in permitting the perpetuation of their own oppression. She writes frequently about sex and relationships between men and women, focusing on the dangers incumbent in many women's hyper-romanticized notions of sex, love, and marriage. If our girls play games in which they practice fighting over men, Cisneros seems to ask in "Barbie-Q," then why are we surprised when they grow up and make men the centers of their lives? It is impossible to separate the Chicana and feminist elements in Cisneros's work, and many readers believe that one of her greatest contributions has been to bring more attention to the needs of women of color, who have sometimes been overlooked by women's movements. Cisneros's works include two books of poetry, *My Wicked Wicked Ways* (1987) and *Loose Woman* (1994), and a collection of short stories, *Woman Hollering Creek* (1991).

■ Some students may have very fond memories of playing with Barbie dolls as children. This may make them both especially resistant and especially attracted to "Barbie-Q." Use your students' memories of childhood play to help steer conversation toward two ideas that Cisneros seems to be questioning: (1) Barbie dolls themselves as models for women, and (2) the sorts of modeling young children see that encourages them to play in certain ways, e.g., having their dolls fight over men.

■ Along the same lines, you might bring a Barbie doll to class (or ask students to bring one of their childhood Barbie dolls) to compare Barbie's physical dimensions with an actual woman's (some analysts have claimed that no real woman could exist with Barbie's dimensions). Also, you might note that in 1998, the Mattel toy company introduced new Barbie dolls, some of which had wider waists and hips, flatter chests, thinner lips, and flatter feet than the traditional Barbies. Why might the company have introduced these new dolls?

■ Ask your students why Cisneros might use stories about children to tackle very adult themes: same-sex desire, sexism, and racism. You might also want to discuss the challenges of writing from a child's perspective. Do your students think Cisneros does a good job of capturing children's "voices" through her child narrators? Why or why not?

QUESTIONS

Comprehension: Why does the narrator of "My Lucy Friend Who Smells Like Corn" want her skin to "get so dark it's blue where it bends like Lucy's"? Why does she like Lucy so much?

Comprehension: The narrator asks a series of questions in the final paragraph of "Barbie-Q." For whom does the narrator speak? Who is the audience of these questions? Is Cisneros directly challenging the reader?

Comprehension: In "Mericans," why does the narrator call her relative the "awful" grandmother?

Context: Compare the writing style and punctuation in "My Lucy Friend Who Smells Like Corn" to Diane Glancy's in "Jack Wilson." Why might these writers independently choose these similar styles? Or, why might they choose *not* to write with textbook grammar and punctuation?

Context: In "Barbie-Q," why do the children make their Barbies act in certain ways (e.g., fighting over a nonexistent man, the missing Ken doll) and wear certain clothes? If the girls are modeling behavior that they've witnessed, who are the models?

Context: In "Mericans," the grandmother and narrator visit a Catholic church, where the narrator describes icons that have survived attacks: "La Virgen de Guadalupe on the main altar because she's a big miracle, the crooked crucifix on a side altar because that's a little miracle." What does this statement mean? Compare these descriptions of the church and its altar (see archive item [6394]— "Altar de la Virgen de Guadalupe") to the picture. What are the most

[6394] José Guadalupe Posada, *Altar de la Virgen de Guadalupe* (1900), courtesy of the Library of Congress, Prints and Photographs Division [PGA-anegas, no. 127 (AA size)]. This print, on fuschia ground-wood paper, shows an image of la Virgen de Guadalupe on an altar surrounded by potted plants and candles. In Sandra Cisneros's "Mericans," the narrator visits a Catholic church with her grandmother and describes the "big miracle" of La Virgen de Guadalupe.

[6502] Lorraine Louie, Cover: *The House on Mango Street* (1984), courtesy of Random House/Vintage Contemporaries Books. Sandra Cisneros spent her childhood moving with her parents and six brothers between Chicago and Mexico City. In her most widely read novel, *The House on Mango Street,* Cisneros draws on this background to explore the experience of growing up in Chicago's Mexican American community.

[6525] Wayne Alaniz Healy and David Rivas Botello, "La Familia" Mural (1977), courtesy of SPARC (Social and Public Art Resource Center). This mural shows a Chicano family standing in the center of a starburst, surrounded by images of life in Mexico and in the United States. Many Chicanos and Chicanas have struggled to understand their hybrid identity within the dominant white culture. Sandra Cisneros writes primarily about the experiences of Chicanas growing up in the United States.

[6528] Mario Torero, *We are NOT a minority!!* (1978), courtesy of SPARC (Social and Public Art Resource Center). Mural depicting a billboard. A young Chicano man points at the viewer in the typical "Uncle Sam" recruitment pose, with lettering that reads, "We are NOT a minority!!" Writers, including Gloria Anzaldúa and Sandra Cisneros, strive to give a voice to the Chicano/a experience.

[6638] Dana Tynan, *Sandra Cisneros After an Interview* (1991), courtesy of the Associated Press (AP), AP/Wide World Photos. Sandra Cisneros spent her childhood moving with her parents and six brothers between Chicago and Mexico City. In her most widely read novel, *The House on Mango Street,* Cisneros draws on this background to explore the experience of growing up in Chicago's Mexican American community.

significant similarities and differences? Why have an altar in a home in addition to one in a church?

Exploration: In "My Lucy Friend Who Smells Like Corn," it seems like the narrator fantasizes about a woman-only utopia when she envies Lucy's all-girl family: "There ain't no boys here." What is appealing about Lucy's family community? Why does the narrator want to be one of the sisters? What does it mean to be sisters?

Exploration: "Barbie-Q" presents, in doll form, many different "types" of women by listing different Barbie dolls and outfits: "mean-eyed," "bubblehead," "Career Gal," "Sweet Dreams," "Bendable Legs." You can find other "types" by visiting the doll aisle in a toy store. Is Cisneros criticizing the makers of dolls such as Barbie or the culture that buys into these images of women? What is she saying about the importance of clothes in constructing identity?

Exploration: Are the girls in this story weak or crybabies? Do they go along with the boys' games so as not to be left out? Consider the comment, "I'd rather play flying feather dancers, but if I tell my brother this, he might not play with me at all." Why are the girls always the sidekicks in these games? Does Cisneros seem to blame the boys for imposing their games on the girls, or the girls for going along with the boys? Is she also critiquing gender conditioning in American society—are boys and girls "trained" to act a certain way?

Exploration: At the story's end, the children have become a spectacle—a tourist attraction for out-of-place visitors who want to take pictures as souvenirs. The tourist is surprised when she learns that the young Chicano children can speak English. Why does she think they are not Americans and cannot speak English? What is Cisneros saying about what it means to be an American? What does an American look like, sound like, *do*? Consider these questions in relation to archive items [6525] (*La Familia* mural) and [6528] (*We Are Not a Minority* mural).

Suggested Author Pairings

SANDRA CISNEROS AND TONI CADE BAMBARA

Ask students to compare the children's ideas about womanhood in Cisneros's short stories, especially "Barbie-Q," to Sweet Pea's adult perspective in Bambara's "Medley." While the stories do not have a one-to-one correspondence, they can help you shape a discussion about the development of two authors' feminist thinking in America. The children seem to believe that women are defined by their clothing and that any man—even a nonexistent "idea" of a man, like the absent Ken doll—are worth fighting over. But Sweet Pea resists such ideas and scoffs at the men who attempt to fight over her. Sweet Pea probably would not identify herself as a feminist, but her instinct is to take care of herself and her child before the man in her life (though you might want to discuss her lingering worries about Larry's ability to survive alone). These characters could help you define feminism for many students who are still wary of the label "feminist." Ask students to identify and discuss Sweet Pea's statements of independence and self-determination.

THOMAS PYNCHON, MAXINE HONG KINGSTON, AND DAVID MAMET

While the texts by these writers are quite dissimilar in many ways, you could teach students how to make connections by focusing on the importance of conversation in each of them. Begin by reading Pynchon's "Entropy," and discuss Saul's ideas about "communication theory" (including "noise" and "leakage"). Then, ask your students to use Saul's theory to analyze the conversation between Nanci Lee and Wittman Ah Sing in *Tripmaster Monkey* and virtually any snatch of dialogue in *Glengarry Glen Ross*. Your students may want to discuss why they agree or disagree with the theory. This would also be a good opportunity to address genre questions: they can compare how dialogue functions in prose as opposed to drama, and compare actual "snatches" of conversation from the texts. How do different characters speak? Are they recognizable by their speech patterns: the words they choose, the examples they use, the length of their sentences?

JUDITH ORTIZ COFER, DIANE GLANCY, AND ALICE WALKER

With "The Witch's Husband," "Polar Breath," and "Everyday Use," you can discuss how similar characters function in different texts. Ask your students to compare Cofer's Abuela, Glancy's old woman, and Walker's mother. How are they similar and different? You could discuss their feminist sensibilities, including their relative awareness, or lack thereof, about feminism. Ask the question: does a woman have to call herself a feminist to be one? What does it mean to be a feminist? These stories also offer a good opportunity to discuss how the characters address aging and marriage. Why do the older women seem more confident about themselves? Think about how Abuela and Walker's mother deal with their young female relatives. In addition, for genre discussions, it would be useful to address the importance of storytelling in each culture. How do these authors (particularly Cofer and Glancy) mimic the oral tradition in their written stories? How do their uses of oral tradition differ?

SANDRA CISNEROS AND MAXINE HONG KINGSTON

Use "Mericans" and *Tripmaster Monkey* to discuss how these texts addresses urban life for minorities. Compare Cisneros's and Kingston's depictions of whites as seen by the Chicano children and Wittman Ah Sing. What tensions are apparent within the "city within a city" in each text? You might discuss the child's rejection of the "awful grandmother" and Wittman's derogatory comments about "F.O.B." Chinese immigrants. Also, closely consider the authors' descriptions of physical places. Ask students if they can picture these communities based only on the writers' word-paintings. Ask students to use phrases from the texts to describe the smells, sights, sounds, tastes, and textures of these communities.

CORE CONTEXTS

Escaping Their Cages: Performance Artists in the Twentieth Century

Imagine that you arrive for a concert, only to see all of the musicians do, well, nothing—no singing, no playing, no dancing. Would you feel you had been cheated out of a show, or would you feel invigorated by the concert's daring "newness"? Many performance artists would hope for the latter. Unrestricted by the bounds of traditional materials and freed from the need for museum space to display their work, performance artists often turn to their own bodies and environments to create art that many observers find both innovative and unsettling. In many cases, artists seek to discomfit viewers, forcing them to confront not only visual images but also ideas, ideologies, and people that might otherwise remain unacknowledged or, in a very real sense, invisible in the mainstream.

Beginning with the earliest performance artists, such as experimental musician John Cage (1912–1992), one of performance art's important goals has been to disrupt societal apathy by demanding audience participation in the performance. Cage used sounds made by machines, nature, people, found objects such as bottles, and virtually anything else he could locate, to produce experimental music that many listeners called "noise." He wanted his listeners to participate in the composition by finding the music within the noises. At times he went even further, once conducting a piece in which none of the members of his orchestra ever lifted their instruments—it was the audience's responsibility to fill in the silence with their own music. We can see the musicians in Thomas Pynchon's "Entropy" working out this theory for themselves. Duke, for instance, decides to write a song with "no piano, man. No guitar. Or accordion. . . . Nothing to listen to. . . ." Meatball, horrified, realizes that "the next logical step" is, in Duke's words, "to think everything." When Meatball protests, Duke replies that "there are a few bugs to work out," but that Meatball and, presumably, all other naysayers, will "catch on." Like Duke, performance artists are not, for the most part, unaware of potential resistance from their audiences but, like all revolutionaries, they hope that their new ideas eventually will prevail.

Alongside works that exist primarily to rattle the complacency of viewers, other performance art pieces exist independent of any audi-

[6123] John Whitworth, *Protest for Legislature to Improve Conditions* (1969), courtesy of the Denver Public Library, Western History Collection.

ence at all or with ephemeral audiences who may not even realize that they have participated in or witnessed a performance. Wittman Ah Sing, in Maxine Hong Kingston's *Tripmaster Monkey*, reads aloud from Rainer Maria Rilke's *Notebooks of Malte Laurids Brigge* on a public bus in San Francisco. Kingston's narrative provides the excerpts that Wittman reads aloud so that readers, too, can "witness" his performance. Wittman does not ask for applause or recognition: he complacently observes that "some of those present on the Muni were looking at [him], some had closed their eyes, some looked out the window, everyone perhaps listening." It is enough, then, that "none of the passengers was telling Wittman to cool it." He is pleased simply because they allowed him to continue reading. Sometimes, then, tolerance can be defined simply as allowing others to exist. Ah Sing's "performance" recalls real-life performances by other writers and poets, such as AIDS sufferer and activist Essex Hemphill in the poetry that he performs in Marlon Riggs's poignant and controversial film *Tongues Untied* (1989).

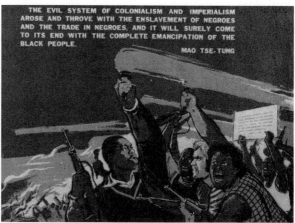

[7234] Anonymous, *The Evil System of Colonialism and Imperialism . . .* (c. 1970), courtesy of the Library of Congress [LC-USZ62-995].

Some audience-free performance art, however, argues that such passive acceptance from the audience (i.e., society), while sometimes freeing, also can indicate blindness or apathy. In 1969, New York City performance artist Vito Acconci (b. 1940) enacted a "private" performance that consisted of his following random, unaware pedestrians through the streets of New York until they entered buildings, at which point he chose new "leaders" to follow. If no one knew about his journey, what could this performance possibly accomplish? Acconci saw himself as a "marginal presence . . . tying in to ongoing situations," and, as such, he demonstrated through his art that people and, by extension, society may be involved in revolutionary acts even without their own knowledge, much less their permission. While Acconci's performance itself was harmless, it also reminds us that people, preoccupied by the day-to-day comings and goings of life, could also be blithely complicit in allowing reprehensible acts or ideas to continue unabated.

Perhaps most significantly, then, performance art in the United States has been used by artists from disenfranchised or minority groups, including women, ethnic and racial minorities, and sexual minorities, to combat such apathy as well as prejudice and injustice. Frustrated by their absence or misrepresentation in American history textbooks and mainstream popular culture, these artists have created works to counter the history books and to make their presence and perspectives known. In a "living diorama" titled "Two Undiscovered Amerindians" (1992–94), which they performed during national celebrations of Columbus's arrival in the New World, Chicano performance artist Guillermo Gomez-Peña (b. 1955) and Cuban American performance artist Coco Fusco (b. 1960) dressed in grass skirts, painted their faces, wore tribal headdresses, and locked themselves inside a cage. They mocked the idea that the continent had not been discovered until Columbus arrived, exposed the specific nineteenth-century practice of "caging" indigenous peoples for display, and protested "cages" such as discrimination and stereotypes that still exist. Karen Finley (b. 1956) and Laurie Anderson (b. 1947) also have provided commentaries on myriad social issues, and as two of the most influential feminist performance artists, they frequently offer scathing critiques of society's continued marginalization of women. Their different methods highlight the flexibility of performance art: it bends to fit the talents of its various performers. Finley has created installation pieces and delivered monologues about pornography, sexual excess, and sexual repression and deprivation. Anderson, on the other hand, has combined autobiography with architecture, photography, and music. Her "Object, Objection, Objectivity" (1973) collects her photographs of men who insulted her with unwanted sexual comments.

In addition to addressing societal inequalities, performance artists also confront specific issues and causes. Before becoming famous as Beatle John Lennon's wife, Yoko Ono (b. 1933) was already well known in performance art circles in the early 1960s for her feminist, avant-garde perspective and for the art shows that she held in her downtown New York City loft, starting in 1961. Her influence on Lennon increased the visibility of performance art in popular culture, as seen in his "Revolution 9" (from the Beatles' 1968 *White Album*), which was inspired by John Cage's music and composed entirely of preexisting sounds. Lennon's mainstream fame allowed their 1969 weeklong honeymoon bed-in for world peace to become one of the world's most widely seen performance art events. Over thirty years later, recordings of this anti–Vietnam War protest can be purchased on video, and Lennon's song "The Ballad of John and Yoko" (1969) immortalizes their position: "The news people said / 'Hey, what you doin' in bed?' / I said, 'We're only tryin' to get us some peace.'" By subverting the public's expectations and enduring widespread ridicule, Ono and Lennon successfully used performance art to bring visibility and support to a cause in which they believed.

Some observers argue that they and subsequent performance artists have been *too* successful and that American culture has changed so much that performance art has lost its shock value and "strangeness." But artists continue to perform, believing that because of its flexibility and fluidity, performance art by definition can never be irrelevant; it is, by its very nature, not only innovative but also politically, socially, and culturally revolutionary.

QUESTIONS

Comprehension: What is performance art? Why does it continue to be appealing as an alternative to more traditional forms of art?

Comprehension: How have Karen Finley and Laurie Anderson used performance art to bring visibility to feminism? Relate their performances to the feminist posters [6182] (*Woman Power* poster) and [6183] (*Feminism Lives!* poster).

Context: Compare John Cage's theory of noise and music to the theory

---

"ESCAPING THEIR CAGES" WEB ARCHIVE

[3043] John A. Gentry, LCpl, *Vietnam . . . Private First Class Joseph Big Medicine Jr., a Cheyenne Indian, Writes a Letter to His Family in the United States* (1969), courtesy of the National Archives and Records Administration. Soldier from Company G, 2nd Battalion, 1st Marine Regiment, on a clear, search, and destroy mission near An Hoa. U.S. military involvement in Vietnam encouraged antiwar protest and distrust of the government.

[6123] John Whitworth, *Protest for Legislature to Improve Conditions* (1969), courtesy of the Denver Public Library, Western History Collection. Men and women, both Hispanic and white, set the stage for a protest with tents, furniture, and other household items near the Colorado Capitol Building in Denver. A placard reads, "Denver Witnesses for Human Dignity."

[6182] Ivy Bottin, *Woman Power* (1965), courtesy of the Library of Congress [POS 6-U.S., no. 548 (C size) <P&P>]. The women's movement sought to change the dominant perception that all women could be satisfied by homemaking. Many feminists argued that liberation must begin at home, where men should share domestic chores.

of noise and communication set forth by Thomas Pynchon in "Entropy" (1960). How can we differentiate music, or meaning, from surrounding "noise" and "leakage"? Also consider Duke, Meatball, and Pac's conversation about "think[ing] everything."

Context: In Kingston's *Tripmaster Monkey* (1989), Wittman Ah Sing performs live readings of Rilke while riding public transportation. What do these readings accomplish? The audience is basically passive: does this indicate that they somehow accept the readings or just that they're apathetic? If the audience would react violently, would the performance be more successful or effective?

Exploration: Because so much of life is made up of various kinds of performance, how can we determine which performances are "art"? Does a categorization depend on the author's intention? The audience's reaction? Other factors?

Exploration: What do you think Vito Acconci was trying to accomplish with his virtually invisible performance? To find out, follow in his footsteps for an afternoon or even just ten minutes. What was your experience like? Did you perceive your environment and those around you differently?

Exploration: The growth of technology, including photo-imaging software, increasingly sophisticated recording equipment, and the Internet, has created new sites of experimentation for technologically savvy artists who "perform" by using computers to manipulate images, visual space, and text. Do you think performance art and computers are a good match? Why might a performance artist turn to the Internet, for example, to display his/her work? And is it really "performance" if it's on the computer?

Exploration: As performance art has become more accepted and seemingly a part of the mainstream, some might argue that it has concurrently become less shocking and, thus, less effective at delivering social messages. What happens when a fringe movement enters the mainstream? What do you think it loses and gains in the process?

Exploration: Performance art tends to stir up a lot of controversy, as its artists and subjects often push the limits of "acceptable" mainstream behavior. Specific works of performance art or exhibitions often are held up as ridiculous by people who want to discontinue government funding for the arts. Why do you think performance art may be controversial? Do you think that the government should limit its funding of artists to "traditional" art forms? If so, how would you define traditional? If not, why not? How should the government decide which artists it funds?

Memorials: The Art of Memory

Houses can be robbed, physical bodies assaulted, and rights taken away, but memory, we like to think, is inviolable. We are formed and defined by what and how we remember, and when our memories are called into question, so too are our identities as individuals. For exam-

[6183] Anonymous, *Feminism Lives!* (c. 1973), courtesy of the Library of Congress, Prints and Photographs Division. Poster declaring "Feminism Lives!" in pink, above a black-and-white photograph of women fighting for suffrage. In the 1960s, a second wave of feminist activism washed over the United States, spearheaded by such figures as Betty Friedan, whose 1963 book *The Feminine Mystique* created solidarity among the many women who were dissatisfied with the role society had mapped out for them.

[6525] Wayne Alaniz Healy and David Rivas Botello, "La Familia" Mural (1977), courtesy of SPARC (Social and Public Art Resource Center). This mural shows a Chicano family standing in the center of a starburst, surrounded by images of life in Mexico and in the United States. Many Chicanos and Chicanas have struggled to understand their hybrid identity within the dominant white culture. Sandra Cisneros writes primarily about the experiences of Chicanas growing up in the United States.

[7234] Anonymous, *The Evil System of Colonialism and Imperialism . . .* (c. 1970), courtesy of Library of Congress [LC-USZ62-995]. This poster shows the power of action and demonstration for dispossessed, marginalized, and persecuted peoples. Its quotation from Mao reads, "The evil system of colonialism and imperialism arose and throve with the enslavement of Negroes and the trade in Negroes, and it will surely come to its end with the complete emancipation of the Black people." Questions of action, audience, apathy, politics, and affect permeate performance art.

[8619] Various, *Don't Mourn, Organize: SDS Guide to Community Organizing* (1968), courtesy of Special Collections, Michigan State University Libraries. Students for a Democratic Society's *Guide to Community Organizing.* Some of the articles in this guide address organization and resistance to the war beyond draft dodging, the original focus of SDS actions. One discusses responses of poor whites to black rebellion and violence during the ghetto uprisings in the summer of 1967.

[9161] Historic American Buildings Survey, *View of the Memorial from the Southwest End—Vietnam Veterans Memorial* ([1982] 1996), courtesy of the Library of Congress [HABS, DC, WASH, 643-10].

ple, consider how in Toni Morrison's "Recitatif," Twyla is never more distressed than when she realizes that for years she may have been misremembering important events in her life. To guard against such potentially disturbing lapses in memory, the speaker in Chinese American poet Li-Young Lee's "This Room and Everything in It" (1990) attempts to perfect his father's "art of memory." The speaker uses this method both to pay tribute to his father and to mentally file his memories so that he can prepare for "certain hard days ahead, / when I'll need what I know so clearly this moment." His very personal, emotionally invested process reflects how many people think memory works: it is individual and private, and it allows us to keep our senses of self intact even in difficult times.

But what about collective memory? Some American sites, such as Monticello, Thomas Jefferson's home in Virginia, and Graceland, Elvis Presley's home in Tennessee, serve purposes that are as diverse as the people who visit them. As centers of learning, recreation, and nostalgia, these sites are more than just houses previously occupied by the famous: they are memorial grounds for national and cultural icons. When a nation or group of people formally recognizes an event, person, or idea, the memorialized subject—be it a person, a house, or a monument—becomes part of the nation's "official memory." America is crowded with these memorials, including the Lincoln Memorial, tombs of unknown soldiers, Mount Rushmore, John F. Kennedy's gravesite, and still-preserved Revolutionary War and Civil War battlegrounds. In general, these memorials were built not only to celebrate the dead but also to celebrate the supposedly righteous causes for which they died and to honor the nation.

But in more recent years, memorials have been built that honor the dead without necessarily honoring the cause of death. One of the most often-visited, haunting, and cherished national monuments is the Vietnam Veterans Memorial in Washington, D.C. Maya Lin, the architect and sculptor who designed the memorial, knew that she needed to recognize the deep mourning and unhealed wounds of surviving loved ones, Vietnam veterans, and a nation divided by an unpopular war. Unlike World War II memorials, for example, which celebrated America's victory and righteous involvement in the battle as well as its fallen soldiers, Lin had to honor the sacrifices of the dead without celebrating the war itself. Her design solved this dilemma by emphasizing the names of the more than 56,000 Americans who died during the war. Since its dedication in 1982, the memorial's somber black granite surface has been perpetually marked by splashes of color—the flowers, photographs, letters, and tokens left behind by the war's survivors, other veterans, loved ones of the dead, and tourists including schoolchildren, families, and international visitors. This monument serves as a public and private mourning wall, a site of convergence for the shared regret and deeply private grief of a nation and its citizens.

Sometimes, artists and communities create memorials as historical correctives, to celebrate, as mural artist Judith Baca put it in a *New York Times* interview, "people who were excluded from history." These memorials hope to remind the public that while the country has moved toward greater diversity and equality for all of its people, there is still work to be done. To pay tribute to the efforts of Chicano rights activists César Chavez and Corky Gonzalez, Baca incorporated their images into "La Memoria de Nuestra Tierra," a mural located in Denver's International Airport [6710]. The nation has not officially memorialized Chavez and Gonzalez, who practiced civil disobedience to fight for Chicano and farmworker rights in the 1960s, but since its installation in 1999, Baca's painting has increased public awareness of the still-ongoing fight for Chicano rights in America.

The AIDS quilt, first unveiled in 1987, is another memorial that educates while it recalls the past. The quilt is, in many ways, the quintessential postmodern memorial: its location is not fixed, its content and dimensions are constantly shifting, and its myriad panels break down stereotypes about AIDS by displaying its victims—through photographs, letters, and personal items—as individuals with families, dreams, and distinct identities. The AIDS quilt is also inherently democratic; it is continually added to and changed "by the people" when each victim's loved ones contribute their 12-foot-square panels, many of which use collage techniques to tell stories about the victims' lives. Though the quilt has a permanent home in Atlanta, Georgia, sections of panels can be displayed simultaneously at different locations throughout the country. In fact, at nearly 50 square miles and 50 tons, it is the world's largest work of community folk art, and it would be nearly impossible for any one venue to display the entire piece. Its form, then, serves its function: like AIDS itself, the quilt is almost too large to fathom, and it grows along with the number of people lost to the disease. As a highly personal, portable, and emotionally affective memorial, the quilt is, in its founder Cleve Jones's words, "a silent, stunning display that helps heal, educate, and inspire."

It is important to remember that memorials need not be monuments or tangible objects: literature, music, and dance, for instance, can also be used to memorialize cultural stories, traditions, and values. In *Woman Hollering Creek* and "Mericans," Sandra Cisneros memorializes the Chicano practice of praying to the Virgin of Guadalupe for healing. Alice Walker memorializes the traditional African American rural home in "Everyday Use" by carefully describing its features: the yard, the butter churn, and the quilts. In a sense, every reader of the story "visits" this memorial. In the absence of official memorials, writers such as Cisneros and Walker, along with lobbyists, activists, and other citizens, remind us daily of past heroes and horrors and call our attention to important social issues. People who wear red ribbons for AIDS victims or pink ribbons for breast cancer victims; Chicano families that build altars to Catholic saints in their homes; bereaved survivors who preserve rooms as shrines to lost loved ones: these people all practice memorializing in their everyday lives.

QUESTIONS

Comprehension: Why did Maya Lin's Vietnam Veterans Memorial have to be different from memorials to previous wars?

[7974] Janjapp Dekker, *Sandra Cisneros with Virgen de Guadalupe Boots* (n.d.), courtesy of *El Andar Magazine*.

"MEMORIALS" WEB ARCHIVE

[2161] Eero Saarinen, *Saarinen's Conceptual Drawing of the Gateway Arch* (1948), courtesy of the National Park Service, Jefferson National Expansion Memorial. The Gateway Arch was built to commemorate the westward expansion of the United States and to inspire like-minded ambition. Just below the arch sits the courthouse where the Dredd Scott decision declared that slaves were not human, a stark reminder of the costs of America's growth.

[6710] Judith F. Baca, *La Memoria de Nuestra Tierra* (2000), courtesy of the Social and Public Art Resource Center, © Judith F. Baca, La Memoria de Nuestra Tierra: Colorado, 2000. Judith Baca is an acclaimed muralist who believes that art can be a forum for social dialogue, as well as a tool for social change. In this sense, she shares much with Gloria Anzaldúa, Cherríe Moraga, and Helena Maria Viramontes and builds on the work of Mexican muralist Diego Rivera.

[7163] Esther Bubley, *Inside the Lincoln Memorial* (1943), courtesy of the Library of Congress, Prints and Photographs

Division [LC-USW3-040346-D]. After Lincoln's assassination, his image became iconic in the North and among African Americans, appearing in ceremonies; popular songs and prints; statuary, including his templelike memorial; and poetry such as Whitman's "Oh Captain! My Captain!" and "When Lilacs Last in the Dooryard Bloom'd."

[7974] Janjapp Dekker, *Sandra Cisneros with Virgen de Guadalupe Boots* (n.d.), courtesy of *El Andar* magazine. Sandra Cisneros spent her childhood moving with her parents and six brothers between Chicago and Mexico City. Here we see her wearing boots bearing images of La Virgen de Guadalupe, a vision of the Virgin Mary that appeared to an Indian convert in the sixteenth century. Cisneros writes about La Virgen in "Guadalupe the Sex Goddess" and "Little Miracles, Kept Promises." Cisneros currently resides in San Antonio, Texas.

[9161] Historic American Buildings Survey, *View of the Memorial from the Southwest End—Vietnam Veterans Memorial* ([1982] 1996), courtesy of the Library of Congress [HABS, DC,WASH,643-10]. The design specifications for the Vietnam Veterans Memorial said that the work must "make no political statement regarding the war and its conduct" and that it must include the name of each of the 57,661 Americans who died in the conflict. Maya Lin's winning design was controversial, but the then-twenty-one-year-old Yale architectural student persevered in seeing it through to completion. Viewed within the tradition of land art, the memorial makes a sharp cut into the sloping land, with a gravestone-like surface of polished granite that literally reflects viewers back into the open wound through which they walk.

[9164] Historic American Buildings Survey, *Panels 37F and 38E—Vietnam Veterans Memorial* ([1982] 1996), courtesy of the Library of Congress [HABS, DC,WASH,643-70]. Thousands of veterans, the families and friends of those who died in the Vietnam War, and visitors to Washington, D.C., come to the memorial each year to pay tribute. Over 57,000 Americans died in the war, and they are all named on the panels of the monument.

Comprehension: How is the AIDS quilt a postmodern memorial?

Comprehension: How can memorials be both public and private?

Context: Read the "Collage" context in this unit and analyze the AIDS quilt as a collaborative collage. Consider its form as well as its function. Relate the quilt's message to the messages of Romare Bearden's collages and to urban graffiti collages.

Context: Some writers compose elegies, or mournful poems, to remember the dead. The stories themselves, as well as their subjects, can also be "memorials" to previous generations. Analyze the writing styles and themes in Judith Ortiz Cofer's "The Witch's Husband," Diane Glancy's "Jack Wilson" and "Polar Breath," and Alice Walker's "Everyday Use." How do the writers' styles serve as memorials to the traditions of the authors' cultures (including oral tradition)?

Context: Consider the quilts in Alice Walker's "Everyday Use" as memorials to the family's ancestors. Do you think it is more appropriate to pay tribute to the grandmother's way of life by using the quilt, as Maggie would do, or by preserving and displaying it, as Dee/Wangero would do? Consider Dee/Wangero's comments about heritage.

Exploration: The AIDS quilt is a testimony to both the personal diversity of individual victims, as well as to the unfathomable reach and effect of the virus on modern humanity. The quilt is often displayed in parts at different locations around the world. The AIDS Memorial Quilt organization, which manages these appearances, has also made a vast Web site (www.aidsquilt.org) that includes a database of the individual panels. How is this site a part of the memorial? What are some of the positive and negative features of the site? How does the Internet affect the way we think about the possibilities of time and space as it relates to memory, testimony, and memorial?

Exploration: Research another national memorial, such as John F. Kennedy's gravesite, the National Holocaust Museum, the Trail of Tears National Historic Trail, or the St. Louis Arch. What does the memorial encourage us to remember? What is its most important message? Also consider researching the debates about constructing a memorial to the African Americans who were legally enslaved for decades in the United States. What political issues are at stake? What would such a memorial signify? Could the absence of such a memorial demonstrate a lack of national healing—could this void itself be an abstract memorial to the struggles perpetuated by the legacy of slavery?

Exploration: In Toni Morrison's Nobel and Pulitzer Prize–winning novel *Beloved* (1987), the character Sethe imagines that some places and events are so powerful that they never really go away. She says, "Some things go. Pass on. Some things just stay. . . . If a house burns down, it's gone, but the place—the picture of it—stays, and not just in my memory, but out there, in the world. . . . If you go there—you who never was there—if you go there and stand in the place where it was, it will happen again; it will be there for you, waiting for you."

What do you think Sethe means? Do you agree that some events "memorialize" themselves by lingering in the air, like smoke after a fire? Have you ever experienced anything like what Sethe is describing here?

Exploration: Some cultural scholars have argued that memorials serve to replace the dead with an object and thereby help the living move past their melancholia. Do you think memorials are more "about" remembering the dead or comforting the living? If they are about the living, do you think that memorials do, indeed, help us to "move past" melancholia, or do they simply prolong it by providing concrete (sometimes *literally* concrete) reminders?

Exploration: While more memorials are built across the nation every year, some people believe that Americans have a tendency to over-memorialize. For example, it took a surprising amount of effort to build a World War II memorial on the Washington Mall in Washington, D.C., and late-night comedians regularly joke about the proliferation of commemorative "days." Do you think that Americans tend to memorialize too much, too soon? If so, why? What sort of response (if any) would you find more appropriate, and why?

Collage: Putting the Pieces Together

When young children cut pictures out of magazines and glue them haphazardly to poster board, they probably do not realize that their projects grow out of an artistic movement invested in an aesthetic of social change. Like performance art, assembly and collage have allowed artists to explore the ways in which individuals and communities negotiate radical societal changes. To create assembly pieces, which are usually three-dimensional, artists combine preexisting elements (e.g., furniture, garbage, food) to form new pieces. In the final "assemblies," the individual elements are usually recognizable, yet have been recontextualized to communicate new meaning. Collage uses similar techniques but in two dimensions. The artist's primary role is to "see" differently: he or she must recognize how unexpected combinations might work to reveal new perspectives on important issues. Collage, then, is a distinctly postmodern art form in that it allows its artists to transcend conventions and represent reality as shifting rather than stable.

One collage master, African American artist Romare Bearden (1914–1988), was a cubist early in his career but had no formal artistic training. He brilliantly nuanced the collage form to represent the lives of African Americans in the twentieth century, confronting stereotypes during the civil rights movement by representing the complexities of the African American experience. While referencing the works of artists such as Picasso, he mixed genres (primarily painting and photography) and staked out a completely new African American artistic tradition by combining the imagery of two traditional African American imaginary homes: the rural South and the urban North (partic-

[6714] Romare Bearden, *The Family* (1976), courtesy of the Romare Bearden Foundation/Licensed by VAGA, New York, NY.

ularly Harlem). His works profoundly affected their viewers, many of whom found that his collages represented African American life even more accurately than representational photographs.

In the years Bearden was painting, depictions of African Americans in the mainstream media frequently focused on the hardships of their daily lives, including poor education, violence at home and on the streets, and meager living conditions. Even those with the best intentions often saw African Americans as lacking basic necessities and skills. While Bearden did not ignore such difficulties in his art, he often chose to celebrate the unique, vibrant contributions of African Americans to broader currents of U.S. culture and society. His technique perhaps can best be understood in relation to another image of African American life in the mid-twentieth century. The photograph "Two Negro Houses" (1958) [7030] shows two Washington, D.C., houses in which African American families lived during the 1950s. The houses look old, broken down, and even premodern (the girl stands in front of an old-fashioned water well), emphasizing what these families lacked: proper housing, water, sanitation, and modern amenities. Bearden's paintings, however, consist of multiple overlapping images and focus on what black Americans *had*. For example, in "The Family" (1976) [6714] and "Playtime—Inner City" (1976) [6717], Bearden uses vibrant colors, and his images evoke the joys of music, family attachments, and play within African American communities. Significantly, his characters confront the viewer by staring directly out from the canvas: these are faces that show pride and vitality, not hopelessness.

Like Bearden, writers use collage techniques to enhance readers' perceptions of American life. In "Recitatif," Toni Morrison's narration jumps back and forth in time as her main characters' lives intersect over many years. Just as Bearden leaves it to the viewer to decipher many details in his crowded paintings, Morrison never identifies the races of her main characters except to clarify that one is white and one is black. This information gap forces readers into the uncomfortable position of confronting their own stereotypes as they attempt to determine the race of each character. By overlapping different characters' versions of shared history, Morrison shows what can happen when two people's diverging memories of the same event bump up against each other. When Roberta and Twyla discover that they have startlingly different memories of an important event in their childhood, Twyla asks, "I wouldn't forget a thing like that. Would I?" Her uncertainty points to the story's theme—the insecurity and instability of memory—that is also conveyed formally via narrative collage.

Similarly, Thomas Pynchon's style in "Entropy" also may cause discomfort for some readers, as the author zigzags between two narratives that occur simultaneously in the upstairs and downstairs apartments of the same house. It may seem that he has randomly cut and pasted two stories together, but close reading reveals that his placement of the textual elements is just as deliberate as Bearden's placement of images in his works. The effect is the same in literature as in visual art: the audience is forced to consider two seemingly unrelated images simultaneously. Thus, comments made by downstairs characters can help the reader to better understand upstairs characters, and vice versa.

Mainstream culture also offers numerous examples of collage in action. One of the most familiar forms of pop-culture collage is usually illegal: for years, urban graffiti artists have used spray paint to decorate buildings, benches, buses and trains, and other public areas. Often, artists paint new images adjacent to or even on top of previous images, sometimes obliterating previous pictures, thus creating "collaborative" collages that change as the communities change. Sometimes called "train-bombing" by its New York City subway practitioners, this art form allows artists, working quickly to avoid detection by authorities, to use relatively inexpensive materials on the seemingly limitless canvas of urban objects.

While graffiti artists have been active for decades, in recent years perhaps the most visible—or, rather, audible—form of popular collage has been the "sampling" practiced by hip-hop musicians. By inserting samples, or short "quotes," from other musicians' songs into their own compositions, musicians pay tribute to earlier musical styles while updating them for a new generation of listeners. Sampling produces effects in music similar to those of collage in visual art and literature: it unites ostensibly different (both racially and sonically) musical forms. For example, Puff Daddy (now P. Diddy) fused 1990s rap with 1970s hard rock when he sampled Led Zeppelin's "Kashmir" in his 1998 song "Come With Me," which he performed on TV's *Saturday Night Live* with Zeppelin's Jimmy Page on guitar. Like artists such as Romare Bearden and writers who use collage-type layering in their narratives, hip-hop artists use "collage" in their music to build bridges between themselves and past masters, to show off their skills, and to express the diversity and energy of their communities.

QUESTIONS

Comprehension: What is collage? How is this art form different from assembly?

Comprehension: What does it mean to discuss reality as "shifting" rather than "stable"?

Comprehension: How have authors adapted collage techniques to their literature?

Context: In his paintings, Romare Bearden attempted to portray African American communities from the "inside." Compare his representations to those in Toni Cade Bambara's "Medley," in which she also provides an insider's view of a predominantly black community. Consider her descriptions of her home, the nightclub, and the gambler's home.

Context: In Diane Glancy's "Polar Breath," the old woman's death scene could be read as a collage: she sees "her husband in his icehouse fishing in winter" while "inside her head, birds flew from the wall" and "up the road, the church steeple hung like a telephone

"COLLAGE" WEB ARCHIVE

[6513] Pablo Picasso, *A 1912 List, Written by Pablo Picasso, of European Artists to be Included in the Armory Show of 1913* (1912), courtesy of Walt Kuhn Family Papers and Armory Show Records 1882–1966, Archives of American Art, Smithsonian Institution. Handwritten list of artists to be included in the Armory Show. Modernist writers and visual artists, including Dos Passos, Picasso, and Braque, used combinations of disparate pieces to create a whole image and message.

[6714] Romare Bearden, *The Family* (1976), courtesy of the Romare Bearden Foundation/Licensed by VAGA, New York, NY. Romare Bearden gained international recognition for the powerful visual metaphors and probing analysis of African American heritage in his many collages, photomontages, watercolors, and prints. He was a member of the Harlem Artists Guild and had his first solo exhibition in 1940 at the age of twenty-nine. He had many equally distinguished friends, such as James Baldwin, Ralph Ellison, and Albert Murray.

[6715] Romare Bearden, *The Return of Ulysses* (1976), courtesy of the Romare Bearden Foundation/Licensed by VAGA, New York, NY. Romare Bearden's painting and collages distinguished him within the twentieth-century African American aesthetic tradition. Derek Walcott's poem *Omeros* is a Caribbean retelling of the Odysseus (Ulysses) myth. Bearden often drew on his past in Mecklenburg County, North Carolina, for his powerful images.

[7030] Anonymous, *These Two Houses Were Among the Structures in Washington, D.C. . . .* (1958), courtesy of the Library of Congress [LC-USZ62-124134]. These two Washington, D.C., houses were classed as "good enough" for occupancy by African Americans until they were demolished so that a housing project could be built in their place. In the foreground a young girl stands near an old wooden well.

pole pulled crooked by its wires after an ice storm." How does collage help Glancy to portray her character's death? Do you think the technique is effective?

Exploration: Some critics claim that musicians who use sampling are actually plagiarizing other artists' work. How do we distinguish between artistic sampling and criminal plagiarizing? Is a work of art that incorporates sampling any less original than works of art that draw their inspiration from less obvious sources?

Exploration: Why do you think graffiti is more appealing to some urban artists than other art forms, such as traditional painting or sculpture?

Exploration: Many Americans frequently use collage techniques, from schoolchildren completing class art projects to adults creating scrapbooks that contain collages of photographs, letters, souvenirs, and other personally meaningful items. Scrapbooking in particular has become a national phenomenon of sorts, with entire companies and stores devoted to providing tips and selling materials. Why do you think people have so readily adopted collage techniques to memorialize their personal histories? Are collages such as family scrapbooks "art"?

EXTENDED CONTEXTS

Gay and Lesbian Identities in Contemporary American Writing

In the cultures of the West, the literary arts have been energized by a gay presence for as long as there have been arts at all. Over the course of American cultural history, however, that presence, and its importance, have not always been recognized and understood. In the American Renaissance, Walt Whitman stands out as a powerful representative of a gay identity and poetic voice, but in the reconstruction of American literary history he is presented, for most of his long career, as an isolated figure, working courageously and almost alone. From the earlier years of the twentieth century, Willa Cather is remembered in much the same way—as an artist whose life and work were complicated and intensified by a condition of isolation, an imperative to keep her own sexuality in the background of her art and her public life. Before the end of the 1960s, in Britain and America, there were brief periods in which gay and lesbian literary communities found or created a context in which to express themselves together and in the open, and to affirm every dimension of who they were as Americans and artists. London in the early 1890s was such a place; the "Bohemian" neighborhoods of lower Manhattan before World War I were another. More often than not, however, a gay or lesbian author who wanted to be "out" as an individual and an artist had to seek safety away from the public gaze, away from local police and repressive laws. Many of the expatriate artists of the 1920s and after (including

[8171] Anonymous, *Gays Kissing* (n.d.), courtesy of the Gay, Lesbian, Bisexual, Transgender Historical Society.

Gertrude Stein, James Baldwin, and Elizabeth Bishop) spent much of their time in Paris, in South America, and in other far-off places where they could live and work with a measure of freedom unavailable in much of the United States, where old Puritan values hung on strongly.

It is not surprising, therefore, that the so-called "Stonewall Riots" of July 1969, a confrontation with the New York City police in and around a gay bar in Greenwich Village, have been remembered by some social historians as "the Boston Tea Party of the gay and lesbian rights movement." What they came to signify was the full arrival of civil-rights militancy for gay communities in major American cities. The "sexual revolution" of the later 1960s had been strongly heterosexual; now it took on a new cast, especially in cities where the arts flourished—San Francisco, Seattle, Chicago, Boston, and New York. In these and other venues, there was a renaissance of literary life in which gay and lesbian sexuality and identity were foregrounded. In poetry, in drama, in film, and in dance, there was unprecedented experimentation with these new possibilities and values in mind.

By the early 1980s, however, the celebratory mood had shifted towards the tragic. Slowly, awareness spread that the HIV virus was a lethal danger, and that AIDS was already a death sentence to thousands of gay Americans. There were no effective treatments for HIV exposure and infection for the first decade of the epidemic, and as the disease devastated gay populations that had flourished so recently before, mainstream America began to recognize the price that was being paid not only in human lives, but also in its collective imaginative and cultural life.

At the same time, along with social and legislative activism, changes have begun and continue with regard to the reading and criticism of literature by gay and lesbian authors and about gay experience. This new field of study is often referred to as "queer theory." One primary objective is to find a language appropriate to discussing this art, as well as to locate aesthetic values and assumptions which are not unduly inflected by centuries of cultural habit, a long tradition of commentary which either ignored the importance of sexual preference in artistic expression, or which repressed that importance. For instance, Hollywood studios and independent filmmakers have participated in the national dialogue about gay identity with varying levels of intensity, sometimes as adversaries, sometimes not. The 1980s and 1990s brought a return of the transvestite as a subject in such mainstream films as *The Crying Game* (1992), as well as in popular films from much smaller production companies, including *Paris Is Burning* (1990), *Priscilla, Queen of the Desert* (1994), and *Boys Don't Cry* (1999). Marjorie Garber describes this popularity as signaling a "category crisis" not only with respect to sexual identity, but also elsewhere in society: in her view, transvestites represent a permeable border between the male and the female and the possibility that other binary oppositions—upper and lower classes, black and white races, Jews and Christians, masters and slaves, gays and straights—may also be much less sure than we have been led to believe.

Also writing about transvestite and contemporary gay life, Judith

[6229] Anonymous, *Together: A Gay Game for Everybody* (1973), courtesy of the Library of Congress.

[6229] Anonymous, *Together: A Gay Game for Everybody* (1973), courtesy of the Library of Congress. Poster depicting two interlocking "woman" symbols, which form a board game. Beginning in the 1960s, a number of "homophile" organizations began to form, inspired by militant black civil rights groups. Such activists as Franklinn Kameny and Barbara Gittings protested discriminatory employment practices, and by 1970 several thousand people had joined the more than fifty homophile organizations that had been established.

[8171] Anonymous, *Gays Kissing* (n.d.), courtesy of the Gay, Lesbian, Bisexual, Transgender Historical Society. A gay couple kisses in the background of this photograph; in the foreground are two lesbian women. In the second half of the twentieth century, homosexuals began to demand equal protection under U.S. law.

[8172] Anonymous, *Gay Parade* (n.d.), courtesy of the Gay, Lesbian, Bisexual, Transgender Historical Society. The gay rights movement really came to life when, in 1969, New York City police raided a gay bar in Greenwich Village called the Stonewall Inn. The patrons of the Stonewall fought back, and three nights of rioting ensued, bringing unprecedented support for the homosexual liberation movement. By 1973 there were more than 800 homosexual groups in the United States; today there are more than 5,000 organizations fighting for gay rights.

[8179] Anonymous, *Lesbians Kissing* (n.d.), courtesy of the Gay, Lesbian, Bisexual, Transgender Historical Society. Photograph of a lesbian couple kissing. Although progress has been made in securing rights for homosexuals, a reactionary movement has consistently tried to slow that progress down. For example, in 1977 a gay rights ordinance was repealed in Florida due to the efforts of singer Anita Bryant. Political and religious figures including Jesse Helms and Jerry Falwell have fought to revoke rights for homosexuals and prevent them from securing protection under the law.

Butler has described gender, in contemporary culture, as a role that is performed rather than a transcendent identity. In her view, gender is or has become such a performance, such that people can choose to cause "gender trouble" by dressing, acting, and behaving in ways that resist traditional expectations—for example, by "voguing." If sexuality is not who we *are* but what we *do*, and if sexual activities or desires do not equal sexual identities, there is no need for rigid categories such as "heterosexual" or "homosexual."

Filmmaker Marlon Riggs's *Tongues Untied* (1989) reveals another snapshot of the diversity of gay life in America, and the special predicament of gay African Americans. The film features the work of poet Essex Hemphill and confronts the challenges of interracial love, self-hatred, and persecution within African American social contexts. With the popularity of TV shows such as *Will and Grace* and *Queer as Folk*, which both focus primarily on gay characters, and *Buffy the Vampire Slayer* and *Felicity*, which both include gay characters among their ensemble casts, gay culture has found entrance into the mainstream.

QUESTIONS

Comprehension: What happened at the Stonewall Inn in 1969?

Comprehension: Describe the various meanings and contexts in which the word "queer" can be used. How is its current meaning different from "gay" or "lesbian"?

Context: Consider the relationship between the young narrator and Lucy in Sandra Cisneros's story "My Lucy Friend Who Smells Like Corn." What is the nature of their relationship?

Context: In *Stone Butch Blues*, Leslie Feinberg's character Jess writes about her perspective on Stonewall, 1970s activism, and the difficulties experienced by transgendered people within the gay rights movement. In what ways do you see her "performing" gender? At what point do you think she is most "true" to herself? Is it possible to identify a specific point or do you think this exercise goes against the very idea of identity as a process?

Context: Another Unit 16 core context, "Memorials," describes the AIDS quilt. How do you think that the AIDS quilt may contribute to struggles for gay and lesbian rights? You might also consider AIDS elegies, or poetic memorials to the dead, such as those by Mark Doty.

Exploration: Explore the gay rights posters and other images in the archive. What do the images tell you about the struggles of the gay and lesbian movement? Choose one or two posters and analyze their text and imagery to identify their messages. Whom do the posters target?

Exploration: Using online resources, compare the organization, style, and intention of gay arts communities over a longer historical period: London in the 1890s, New York's "Bohemian Period" (c.1900–17), Bloomsbury in the 1920s and 1930s, San Francisco in the 1980s and after. What similarities and differences do you observe? What could latter-day communities learn from their historical forebears?

Locking the Gates: The City within the City

The "city within the city" has long been understood to mean urban enclaves with names like Little Italy, Chinatown, the Barrio, or Boystown. The literature included in this unit contains richly descriptive accounts of such communities, including Maxine Hong Kingston's Chinatown, Sandra Cisneros's Chicano neighborhoods, and Leslie Feinberg's queer district. These authors' characters, like their real-life counterparts, have found acceptance, cultural touchstones, and inspiration in these communities.

In recent years, however, while many of these ethnic, racial, or identity-based communities have continued to thrive, another definition of the "city within the city" has begun to take hold, inspired by another striking urban division: the economic imbalance between the "haves" and the "have-nots." Disparities in income have delineated new cities within the city with boundaries defined not by identity markers so much as by widely varying living conditions and opportunities. Like Disney World, a self-enclosed, sanitized, comfortable space that provides everything its visitors need—food, shelter, entertainment, and, perhaps most importantly, security—new urban designs promoted by the wealthy and sometimes billed as "urban renewal" seemingly offer many benefits: meeting places, museums, restaurants, arts, and diversions. But these ostensible improvements mask the growing economic disparity between the rich and the poor and often physically displace the poor from their homes.

In many cities, including Los Angeles and New York, physical barriers literally separate the classes, creating fortresses that insulate the "safe" areas from "dangerous" ones. As urban theorist Mike Davis sees it, the "pleasure domes" of new malls, apartment complexes, office buildings, and art centers depend upon the "social imprisonment of the third-world service [workers] who live in increasingly repressive ghettoes and barrios." While ambition and creativity are still evident in these economically depressed neighborhoods, as seen in the more than 3000 murals (primarily painted by Hispanic Americans) that decorate Los Angeles's walls, these previously vibrant urban communities have been devastated by widespread drug use, crime, and poverty. In 1903, W. E. B. Du Bois predicted that "the problem of the Twentieth Century [would be] the problem of the color line." Now, at the beginning of a new millennium, urban theorists warn that the problem of the twenty-first century will be the problem of these abject cities within the city.

QUESTIONS

Comprehension: What are some potential negative effects of creating urban "pleasure domes"?

[6166] Anonymous, *Police and Detectives Guarding Chinatown, July 6, 1909* (1909), courtesy of the Library of Congress [LC-USZ62-69697]. Writing at the turn of the twentieth century, Sui Sin Far (Edith Maud Eaton) made efforts to combat stereotypes of Chinese immigrants as "heathen," "unclean," and "untrustworthy." She provided insight into the unique culture of America's Chinatowns.

[6171] Arnold Genthe, *Children Were the Pride, Joy, Beauty, and Chief Delight of the Quarter, Chinatown, San Francisco* (c. 1896–1906), courtesy of the Library of Congress, Prints and Photographs Division [LC-USZC4-5265]. Four children in traditional Chinese clothing on a sidewalk in San Francisco's Chinatown. Writing about the time this photograph was taken, Sui Sin Far (Edith Maud Eaton) sought to make the lives of Chinese immigrants understandable to white audiences.

[6527] Judith F. Baca, *Pickers from Guadalupe Mural* (1990), courtesy of SPARC (Social and Public Art Resource Center). © Judith F. Baca, Farmworkers of Guadalupe, 1989. Since 1976, muralist Judith Baca has worked as the founder and artistic director of the Social and Public Art Resource Center in Los Angeles. She has headed a number of large-scale projects dealing with interracial relations, such as the construction of *The Great Wall*, of which this image is a part.

[7746] Danny Lyon, *Young Men of the Second Ward, El Paso's Classic Barrio Near the Mexican Border* (1972), courtesy of the National Archives and Records Administration. This photograph was taken by Danny Lyon for the Environmental Protection Agency's *Documerica* project. Lyon, hailed as one of the most creative documentary photographers of the late twentieth century, photographed the Rio Grande Valley and the Chicano barrio of South El Paso, Texas. Tejanos, or Chicanos from Tejas (Texas), have developed a rich tradition of arts and literature that develops out of their lives in this border again.

Context: Explore the photos of early-twentieth-century Chinatown [6164, 6166, 6167]. Compare the clothing worn by people pictured in these images to Wittman Ah Sing's descriptions of Chinese Americans in Kingston's *Tripmaster Monkey*: "Immigrants. Fresh Off the Boats out in public. Didn't know how to walk together. . . . So uncool. You wouldn't mislike them on sight if their pants weren't so highwater, gym socks white and noticeable. F.O.B. fashions—highwaters or puddlecuffs. Can't get it right. Uncool. Uncool." Why is fashion so important to Wittman? What did the traditional Chinese clothes worn at the turn of the twentieth century signify, and what does Wittman think the "F.O.B." clothes say about their wearers?

Exploration: Compare Wittman Ah Sing's descriptions of "F.O.B." Chinese Americans to Anzia Yezierska and Abraham Cahan's discussions of clothing and "greenhorns" in Unit 9.

Exploration: Research the construction, condemnation, and reconstruction of Chicago's Cabrini Green housing project. What does this project's history tell us about changes in theories of urban planning and development? Why do you think the architectural style of Cabrini Green and similar housing developments has fallen out of favor with city planners and residents? Use online resources including <www.voicesofcabrini.com> as well as sites created by former and current residents.

ASSIGNMENTS

Personal and Creative Responses

1. *Journal:* In Toni Cade Bambara's "Medley," when Sweet Pea criticizes Hector's storytelling, she also provides her criteria for effective storytelling, including the need for names and details. What elements do you think are necessary for a good story? Create a definition or list; then use it to analyze any story that is meaningful to you (a family story, movie, novel, etc.). Does the story meet all your criteria? If not, how does the discrepancy affect your definition?

2. *Journal:* In David Mamet's *Glengarry Glen Ross*, Roma asks a series of questions in Act 1, Scene 3, including "what is our life?" and "what is it that we're afraid of?" Consider his statement, "All it is is THINGS THAT HAPPEN TO YOU." In your journal, answer his questions and offer an interpretation and opinion of his statement.

3. *Journal:* Do you think Abuela, "the witch" of "The Witch's Husband" by Judith Ortiz Cofer, spent long enough in New York (one year)? What do you think she did there? Was this enough of a taste of freedom to allow her to remain happy in Puerto Rico? Do you think it would just whet her appetite for even more freedom? How feminist is she, if at all, according to your own definition of feminism?

4. *Creative Writing:* In "Polar Breath," Diane Glancy depicts the old woman's death using images of birds, the icehouse, frigid water, and spirits. Do these images seem appropriate for the old woman? Choose a person or character from another story in this unit, and write a story or create a visual representation of his/her death using character-appropriate imagery.

5. *Creative Writing:* Write a new version of Alice Walker's "Everyday Use" from Dee/Wangero's point of view. What was it like to grow up in the house and see it burned? Why did you change your name and clothes? Describe your visit home. Why are the quilts so important to you? Why are you so frustrated with your family?

6. *Acting and Performance:* As a young actor, David Mamet was influenced by the Stanislavsky method of acting, also called "method acting," with which actors attempt to make their work as *real* as possible. Research the Stanislavsky method further. With a group of students, choose a scene from *Glengarry Glen Ross* and use method acting to rehearse and perform it for the class.

7. *Acting and Performance:* Alone or with a small group of students, produce performance art of any kind to relay a message to your class. Before you begin, answer the following questions: What message are you trying to convey? Why? How can you best communicate your ideas? How can performance art afford you a new perspective or suggest new ways of thinking to your audience?

8. *Multimedia:* Imagine that you are part of a performance art group that needs new members. To convince talented artists to use performance art methods, create a presentation that reports on the activities of one performance artist mentioned in this unit. Using the *American Passages* multimedia resources, Internet research, and your knowledge of performance artists, create a slide show of the artist's work, a video capturing audience reactions, and/or print materials to explain the artist's themes, ideas, and methods. Explain why performance art is the most successful means of reaching some audiences.

9. *Modified "Show and Tell":* Think about the importance of the quilts in Alice Walker's "Everyday Use." Choose an object that is personally meaningful to you, and prepare a multimedia presentation explaining its significance. Is the object functional? Is it "worth more" than the dollars you could get if you sold it? Design visuals and a narrative that speak to the object's aesthetic, sentimental, cultural, and financial value.

Problem-Based Learning Projects

1. It is 1975 and you belong to a local feminist group that has convinced many women to join your cause and actively promote women's rights. However, you have had less success recruiting men. Your job is to design a public relations campaign directed at young men. You need to convince them that feminism is not just a

women's issue. Design a campaign—including a slogan, logo, pamphlet, and posters—that persuades young men to join their mothers, sisters, girlfriends, and friends in fighting for women's equality.

2. You are a member of your school's drama club, and you want to produce David Mamet's play *Glengarry Glen Ross*. However, some members of the campus community (including parents and wealthy alumni, among them the drama club's most consistent financial contributor) oppose the play because it contains strong language and offensive slurs. Create a skit aimed at these opponents, explaining why you think the play is appropriate and asking for their support. To be persuasive, you may need to analyze Mamet's language and content for your audience.

3. You are an artist who wants to paint a mural representing your neighborhood on the side of a local building. The building's owner has approved your plan and your design, except that she does not like your idea to incorporate existing graffiti into the mural. She thinks that the graffiti is vandalism and that it should be covered. Write a letter in which you convince her that the graffiti is actually art and that it is essential to your design.

4. Imagine that you are a prominent urban planner and designer. Your city has decided to erect a memorial to the victims of the September 11, 2001, terror attacks, and you have been hired to determine where to place the memorial and what it should look like, including its form, size, and any text that might be included. Prepare a report of your findings that you can present at the next city meeting. Include visual representations of your ideas to support your report.

GLOSSARY

Chicano/a   A once derogatory term that has been reclaimed by Mexican Americans. Implies a more radical definition of Mexican Americans' subjectivity than the term "Hispanic."

feminism   Feminism is an extremely broad and diverse term that focuses on the examination of sex and gender. It captures an expansive history of, and debate about, personal identity, political action, philosophical inquiry, and literature and literary studies. Feminism itself can be characterized as a movement, a mindset, or a way of being; feminists have examined topics ranging from the unequal treatment of women in almost every aspect of daily life, to the restrictions of patriarchal culture and its oppression of women, to the intersecting forces of race, gender, sex, and class as they impact the possibilities of knowledge, representation, lived experience, cultural and historical interpretation, and the constitution of reality itself. Contemporary feminism can be traced through an extended history of women's activism, particularly the "sexual revolution" of the 1960s and 1970s. Critics have assailed what they argue is a single-minded, righteous, or anti-male intention within feminism, as the movement itself continues to expand and develop with both clarity and contradiction.

gender variant   An individual who does not fit into the categories "male" or "female." The person's genital sexuality may not match his/her gender identity. Can include transsexual and transgendered individuals.

historical roots   The values, myths, and culture that often form the foundation of an individual's identity.

identity   An individual's consciousness of his/her own being. Can include personality traits as well as an allegiance to social categories such as race, ethnicity, gender, sexual orientation, and religion.

identity politics   Movements that focus on securing rights for people from various identity groups, such as women, ethnic and racial minorities, and sexual minorities.

oral tradition   Passing cultural wisdom and values from one person or one generation to another through oral storytelling. Unlike written communication, the oral tradition necessarily involves person-to-person contact and is thus by definition community based and performative. The oral tradition was an early stage in virtually every language system and is still prominent in Native American and Chicano cultures, among others.

postmodernism   A philosophical and socio-historical movement that challenges the progress-oriented master narrative of Enlightenment and positivist traditions. At the beginning of the twentieth century, linguists and philosophers questioned the possibility that language can truly reflect reality, or that there can be any essential, categorical, or transcendental truth claims made about the world. From the unspeakable violence of the Holocaust, to the assertion of gender and other personal traits as being malleable and socially constructed, postmodernism has sought to explain the many uncertainties, ironies, contradictions, and multiple points of view that animate the world. Postmodern art and literature is often self-consciously reflexive, questioning the nature of the text and the authority and existence of the author; it uses techniques like pastiche, metanarrative, nonlinear constructions, absurdity, and irony. Postmodernism is at once a literary style, a critical and theoretical movement, and a description of the socio-cultural world of globalized consumer capitalism.

postmodern narrative   A story that may not have a linear structure and that incorporates postmodern ideas about form and reality.

SELECTED BIBLIOGRAPHY

Blumenfeld, Warren J., and Diane Raymond. *Looking at Gay and Lesbian Life*. Boston: Beacon, 1988.

Chadwick, Whitney. *Women, Art, and Society*. 3rd ed. New York: Thames and Hudson, 2002.

Davis, Mike. *City of Quartz: Excavating the Future in Los Angeles*. New York: Verso, 1990.

Feinberg, Leslie. *Stone Butch Blues*. Ithaca: Firebrand Books, 1993.

Goldberg, Roselee. *Performance Art: From Futurism to the Present*. 3rd ed. New York: Thames and Hudson, 2001.

Lucie-Smith, Edward. *Movements in Art since 1945*. 5th ed. New York: Thames and Hudson, 2001.

Phillips, Lisa. *The American Century: Art and Culture, 1950–2000*. New York: Whitney Museum of Art in association with W. W. Norton and Company, 1999.

Pohl, Frances K. *Framing America: A Social History of American Art*. New York: Thames and Hudson, 2002.

FURTHER RESOURCES

Abelove, Henry, Michele Aina Barale, and David Halperin, eds. *The Lesbian and Gay Studies Reader*. New York: Routledge, 1993.

Before Stonewall and *After Stonewall*. Films produced by John Scagliotti.

hooks, bell. *Feminism Is for Everybody: Passionate Politics*. Cambridge: South End, 2000.

Butler, Judith. *Bodies That Matter*. New York: Routledge, 1993.

———. *Excitable Speech*. New York: Routledge, 1997.

———. *Gender Trouble*. New York: Routledge, 1990.

Garber, Marjorie. *Vested Interests: Cross-Dressing and Cultural Anxiety*. New York: Routledge, 1992.

Halperin, David M. *Saint Foucault: Towards a Gay Hagiography*. Oxford: Oxford UP, 1995.

Hemphill, Essex, ed. *Brother to Brother: New Writings by Black Gay Men*. Boston: Alyson Publications, 1991.

LeGates, Richard T., and Frederic Stout, eds. *The City Reader*. 2nd ed. New York: Routledge, 2000.

Leitch, Vincent B., et al., eds. *The Norton Anthology of Theory and Criticism*. New York: W. W. Norton and Company, 2001.

Riggs, Marlon. *Tongues Untied*. Film/documentary. PBS: 1989.

Trujillo, Carla, ed. *Chicana Lesbians: The Girls Our Mothers Warned Us About*. Berkeley: Third Woman Press, 1991.

Wittig, Monique. *The Straight Mind and Other Essays*. Boston: Beacon Press, 1992.

Zukin, Sharon. *The Culture of Cities*. Cambridge: Blackwell, 1995.

```
┌─────────────────────────────────────────┐
│              APPENDIX                     │
├─────────────────────────────────────────┤
│          WRITING ABOUT                    │
│                                           │
│          LITERATURE                       │
└─────────────────────────────────────────┘
```

Getting Started

At some point, almost everyone has suffered from writer's block. One professional used this trick to beat it: he would force himself to sit in front of the computer for an hour a day and not allow himself to get up for snack or bathroom breaks, read or send e-mail, or otherwise engage in what sociologists call "frittering" and the rest of us just call wasting time. The next day he would do the same, but he had to write for an hour: it could all be garbage ("I don't know what I want to say, I don't know what I want to say"), but he had to write something. After doing this for a few days, he usually had something he could work with. Another way to end writer's block is to brainstorm before you begin writing. Contrary to what you may have been told, outlines for books, chapters, or essays don't usually spring fully formed from the heads of writers, like the goddess Athena from the head of Zeus. Most people find it helpful to reflect on the topic informally first. One form of reflection is free writing—that is, writing down all your thoughts on the subject without your internal editor nagging you about spelling, grammar, and so on. To figure out how to organize the jumble that results from free writing, you may find it helpful to cluster your ideas.

Thesis Sentences

Your thesis sentence tells your reader where your piece is headed. Professor Gail Sherman (English, Reed College) makes an analogy between your argument and a train ride: like passengers, your readers will enjoy the ride much more if they know where the trip is headed and don't need to guess whether each stop is the final destination or merely a resting point in a longer journey. Without a thesis sentence, both you and your reader would be lost and confused. A thesis sentence limits the scope of what you have to cover in your essay.

Here are some tips:

1. A thesis sentence is a **debatable assertion** that you seek to prove in the body of your essay. A thesis sentence is not a statement of fact. "Emily Dickinson is one of the most important early American women poets" is a fact, not a thesis, as is "Emily Dickinson's poetry is full of ambiguity." Dickinson *is* one of the most important early female American poets, and her work *is* ambiguous. An essay that argued otherwise would be pointless.

There is no need to argue the obvious. A better thesis sentence might be something like "Emily Dickinson's 'I heard a Fly buzz—when I died—' employs the gothic art of 'telling it slant.'"

2. A thesis sentence is very **specific**. Notice how narrow the above claim is: the essay is not trying to prove that *all* of Dickinson's poems "tell it slant"—a job much too large for four or five pages—just that one of her poems does.

3. A thesis sentence helps you **organize your thoughts** and foreshadows for your reader what you will cover in the body of your essay. To prove this assertion you could explain what the gothic is, explicate what you mean by "telling it slant" (see Dickinson's poem 1129), and then support your claim that Dickinson avoids discussing her subject directly in poem 465. Read Dickinson's poems 465 and 1129, and complete the following outline in a way that supports the given thesis sentence:

Sample Student Brainstorming for Essay on Poem 465

Thesis:	**"Emily Dickinson's 'I heard a Fly buzz—when I died—' (poem 465) employs the gothic art of 'telling it slant.'"**
Introduction:	Background on the gothic and the **Thesis Sentence**. Gothic literature is not merely about the occult and mysterious: it is about crossing the line between this world and the next, the known and the unknown, the speakable and the unspeakable. Through the appearance of a fly at a deathbed, Dickinson's poem 465 indirectly approaches the unknown that follows death.
Body ¶ 1:	Explication of Dickinson's poem "Tell all the Truth . . ." (poem 1129) suggests that the question of what happens after death is too dangerous to ask directly and is a subject better raised circuitously.
Body ¶ 2:	Stanza 1—The poem opens with an implicit but unspoken question: what is the significance of the fly the speaker hears as she dies? Does it mean the dying speaker is saved, doomed to hell, or neither? Dickinson does not answer this question directly but hints at its significance through the "stillness of the room."
Body ¶ 3:	Stanza 2—_____
Body ¶ 4:	Stanza 3—_____
Body ¶ 5:	Stanza 4—_____
Conclusion:	_____

Notice that this student has more than three body paragraphs in her essay. The organization of her essay is organic: that is, it follows the logic of the poem and her argument, rather than some preconceived cookie-cutter idea of what an essay should be.

1. Which of the following statements are facts and which are thesis sentences?
   - Mary Rowlandson's *Narrative* uses typology.
   - Mary Rowlandson's *Narrative* has withstood the test of time as a key Puritan document.
   - Mary Rowlandson's *Narrative* predicts the end of the world.
   - Mary Rowlandson's *Narrative* uses typology to confirm the Puritan mission.
2. What makes each of these statements potentially weak as a thesis sentence?
3. Rewrite these statements so that they can better serve as strong thesis sentences.
4. Write your own thesis sentence and outline to answer the question "How does Mary Rowlandson use typology in her captivity narrative?"

Introductions

There is no easy way to write an interesting essay: in all cases it will take creativity and thought. The following ideas are suggestions for ways to avoid a beginning that might lead the reader to fear that your essay will be simplistic or boring.

First, it is important to think about the kind of first impression you are making on your reader. After reading the introduction, your reader may ask herself the following types of questions: Does this essay interest me? Is the writing clear or will I have a hard time following this paper? Is the writer just "going through the motions" or does the style show energy and vitality? Does the writer seem well informed? Do I like this writer as a person or am I put off by her manner? Here are some ways to gain your reader's interest and sympathy:

- Begin with an interesting story or anecdote. Explain how the story relates to the question you will explore in your essay.
- Describe a scene that arouses curiosity.
- Use a provocative quotation: explain it and use the explanation to develop the thesis of the essay.
- Begin with a simple, definite statement.
- Ask a rhetorical question that you answer with your thesis. Note that thesis sentences that are questions are rarely effective as it is hard to guide readers through an argument if they don't know what stand you are taking.

For more help on writing introductions, consult Richard Marius's *A Writer's Companion* and John Trimble's *Writing with Style*.

Making Arguments

Once you have brainstormed about the theme of your essay, you may want to consider how you will support your argument. In his *Rhetoric* Aristotle distinguishes between three means of persuasion that can be produced by the rhetorician's art: (1) the character of the speaker (*ethos*); (2) the disposition created in the hearer or reader (*pathos*); (3) the argument (*logos*).

Ethos

The *ethos* or moral character of your argument is the way you present yourself to your readers. This is the primary means by which you gain your readers' trust. Do you come across as scholarly and insightful or as clichéd and scattered? Part of your ethos is your presentation of the work: Is it stapled? Clearly printed? Written in a reasonably sized font? As Christopher Carey points out in "Rhetorical Means of Persuasion," there are six traditional ways that authors create persuasive characters for themselves. The following are worth looking for anytime you read an essay or speech: appeals to age and experience, reverence for civic virtue, patriotism and public-spiritedness, displays of piety, following the rules of decorum (for example, avoiding delicate subjects), and modest restraint. Narrators in fiction and nonfiction also use these tricks of the trade: for example, you might consider how Frederick Douglass in *Narrative of the Life* or Ishmael in *Moby-Dick* gains sympathy for his cause.

As a writer, your ethos is also determined by the diction you choose. Diction is a powerful tool in writing analytical essays. For example, read the following sentences and write a brief character sketch of the narrator:

> *Speaker 1:* Ever since the dawn of time, the American Southwest has been a melting pot: in addition to the huge numbers of tribes that live there, Spanish and British settlers and strip miners, and even nuclear scientists have settled there. But out of this place came a new literature that was made from both the oral tradition and explored contemporary issues.
>
> *Speaker 2:* For millennia, the American Southwest has been the crossroads of cultures: it is the home of ancient civilizations, Zuni, Hopi, Navajo, Pueblo, and then Conquistadors, cowboys, strip miners, nuclear scientists. From this landscape, a new Native American literature emerged, based on very ancient oral traditions but exploring contemporary issues of integration, assimilation, and identity.

Which of these speakers carries more authority and why? What strategies does she use to construct her authority? It is important to remember that being authoritative is not the same as being wordy: clear, direct prose can convey authority, whereas prose that clouds its meaning can raise the reader's suspicion that the writer is hiding something. Rewrite the following sentences so they are more authoritative and direct:

> *Sentence 1:* Literature before 1700 was weird. All the people who lived in the colonies had oral traditions, and diaries, and letters, and such, but they didn't have the good stuff: fiction.
>
> *Sentence 2:* Learning, Tolerance, and Progress: these doctrines are key to anyone's understanding of what America is or what it means to be an American. But if you were the kind of person who lived in the South during the era of Reconstruction, you could be considered a subversive. In spite of all of these hindrances, ways to speak the truth were invented by these writers.

Pathos

Pathos is the second key to a strong rhetorical argument. Pathos is the emotional response you invoke in your reader, or as Aristotle puts it in his *Rhetoric*, it is the process of "creating a certain disposition in the audience." There are standard ways in which speakers and writers use emotional appeals to secure the goodwill of the hearer. For example, as Christopher Carey notes, the speaker can lay claim to qualities that the audience will respect, stress the disadvantages of the speaker's situation as a claim to pity, arouse hostility against an opponent, generate prejudice against the opponent through tangential or irrelevant information, incite fear, or plead for pity. Which of these ploys are used in the opening of Mary Rowlandson's *Narrative*?

> On the tenth of February 1675, came the Indians with great numbers upon Lancaster; their first coming was about sunrising; hearing the noise of some guns, we looked out; several houses were burning, and the smoke ascending to heaven. There were five persons taken in one house; the father, and the mother and a sucking child, they knocked on the head, the other two they took and carried away alive. There were two others, who being out of their garrison upon some occasion were set upon; one was knocked on the head, the other escaped; another there was who running along was shot and wounded, and fell down; he begged of them his life, promising them money (as they told me) but they would not hearken to him but knocked him in the head, and stripped him naked, and split open his bowels.

QUESTIONS

1. Does the speaker (Rowlandson) lay claim to qualities that the audience will respect?
2. Does she stress disadvantages of the speaker's situation as a claim to pity?
3. Does she arouse hostility against an opponent?
4. Does she generate prejudice against the opponent through tangential or irrelevant information?
5. Does she incite fear?
6. Does she plead for pity?

Before Rowlandson has even met her captors, we have a great deal of concern that she might not survive her captivity. Think how differently one of the attacking party would have described the incident and what sympathies he might have instilled!

Although you may think of academic prose as unemotional and stolid, pathos can be a powerful tool for persuading your audience. Consider the following openings to two student essays on the topic "What is poetry?":

> *Essay 1:* Poetry is distinguished from other forms of writing by an author's use of poetic conventions. A poetic convention is an established or customary usage of language as found in what has already been accepted as poetry. Verse, rhyme, rhythm, and meter are common prominent poetic conventions. Onomatopoeia and alliteration also help distinguish poetry from other forms of writing, but they do not adequately define what poetry is.

Essay 2: "Somebody who should have been born is gone." Anne Sexton's "The Abortion" wrenches our hearts, but it is also art. There are two poles in poetry, the dichotomy between impulse and craft, what I think of as "hot" and "cold." "Hot" is the pure emotional force, the energy driving the poem, while "cold" refers to the element of sculpting language as an art form: the process of refinement, the filter of artistic decision which transforms the feeling into a harmonious piece of work.

Nonprofessional writers often forget that part of their goal is to make the reader *want* to continue reading. Which of the above essays would you want to read if given the choice? Don't be afraid to try to gain your reader's interest.

Logos

The logic you use to persuade your audience is perhaps the most central part of persuasion: in fact, Aristotle calls **logos** the "proper task of rhetoric." How do you know if your logic is persuasive? This question is perhaps best answered by asking whether your logic ever fails. That is, does it contain any logical fallacies?

In his 1958 book *The Uses of Argument*, Stephen Toulmin outlines a six-part model for the structure of an argument. Toulmin proposes that three elements are essential to all arguments: (1) the **claim**; (2) the **data** (or support); and (3) the **warrant**. In addition, arguments may contain one or more of the following: (4) the **backing**; (5) the **rebuttal**; and (6) the **qualifier**. Let's deal with the three essential parts first. Imagine the logical structure of your essay as a Greek Temple, or to use an American example, the Supreme Court building.

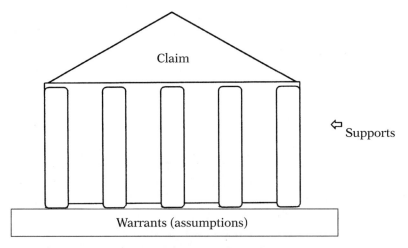

Your argument (temple) has three main levels: the foundation, the columns, and the triangular pediment at the top. At the top of the argument (temple) is the claim you aim to prove: your thesis sentence or your hypothesis. For example, in the Dickinson essay discussed above, the claim would be **"Emily Dickinson's 'I heard a Fly buzz—when I died—' employs the gothic art of 'telling it slant.'"** The pillars **support** this claim through the use of evidence, expert opinions, facts, data, personal narratives, quotations, analysis, and the like. At the foundation of your argument (temple) lie the warrants or assumptions upon which the argument is based. This is the trickiest part of your argument as it is often unstated.

To better understand the use of warrants (and rebuttals, qualifiers, and backings) let's look at an example from the middle of Michael Wigglesworth's poem "The Day of Doom." In this section we find the "goats" (the unsaved) standing before Christ arguing for their salvation:

> A wond'rous crowd then 'gan aloud,
>   thus for themselves to say,
> "We did intend, Lord to amend,
>   and to reform our way:
> Our true intent was to repent,
>   and make our peace with Thee;
> But sudden death stopping our breath,
>   left us no liberty.
>
> "Short was our time, for in his prime
>   our youthful flower was cropped:
> We died in youth, before full growth,
>   so was our purpose stopped.
> Let our good will to turn from ill,
>   and sin to have forsaken,
> Accepted be, O Lord, by Thee,
>   And in good part be taken."   (Stanzas 107–108)

The parts of the argument above are as follows:

Claim: "Let our good will to turn from ill, / and sin to have forsaken, / Accepted be, O Lord, by Thee . . ." That is, save us by allowing our desire to repent to be enough.

Data/Support: "Our true intent was to repent . . . / But sudden death stopping our breath"; "We died in youth, before full growth, / so was our purpose stopped."

Warrants: If we had had more time, we would have repented. There wasn't enough time. Others repented because they were given enough time to live by God. If everyone is to be judged on the same basis, it is only fair to take into account that everyone didn't have the same amount of time to repent.

A **rebuttal** points out the weaknesses in an argument: it states what is invalid or wrong. Most of the time rebuttals take the form of an attack against the warrants of an argument. Your job as a writer is to anticipate these refutations and to make a counterclaim in the form of a qualifier and backing. Let's use Christ's rebuttal of the goats from "The Day of Doom" as an example:

> To whom the Judge: "Where you allege
>   the shortness of the space
> That from your birth you lived on earth,
>   to compass saving grace:

It was free grace that any space
    was given you at all
To turn from evil, defy the devil,
    and upon God to call.

"One day, one week, wherein to seek
    God's face with all your hearts,
A favor was that far did pass
    the best of your deserts.
You had a season, what was your reason
    such precious hours to waste?
What could you find, what could you mind
    That was of greater haste?"   (Stanzas 109–110)

Here Christ refutes the goats by arguing that they did have sufficient time. Notice, however, that his rebuttal takes the same form, with a claim, support, and warrants. What are Christ's claims? What are Christ's supports? What are Christ's warrants? What are the goats' warrants that Christ refutes?

In order to refute (or head off) a rebuttal, an argument may back its warrants by making them explicit and supporting them with evidence of their own, or an argument may qualify its language so that it claims that something is probable rather than certain. Brainstorm how, for example, the goats might back their warrants above or qualify their support or claim. A final strategy is to attack the warrants of the rebuttal itself. What is the backing of the goats' warrants? How are the goats' claims or supports qualified? How are Christ's warrants refuted?

After you have completed this exercise, you might want to check "The Day of Doom" to see if the real goats succeeded as well as you have. An important step in composing your argument will be to outline the structure of your argument, brainstorm on your underlying warrants, refute any rebuttals, and qualify your assertions. For further help on making and strengthening arguments see Nancy Wood's *Writing Argumentative Essays*, particularly the chapter "Argument and Literature."

Paragraphs

Checking your paragraph structure is a great way to see if the *logos* of your argument is coming across effectively. In some ways, paragraphs are like miniature essays: at the very least they should contain a hypothesis ("topic sentence"), evidence, analysis of the evidence, and a conclusion. One of the problems that writers face is a lack of cohesion between paragraphs. In addition to providing road maps for the paragraphs, topic sentences should make sense if placed next to each other. It is often helpful to map out your argument by writing your thesis and topic sentences on a separate piece of paper. This can allow you to see any gaps in your logic. If the map of your argument is working, readers should feel that they have been taken through the logical steps in a proof and that the conclusion is justified.

A second paragraph-related problem that writers face is a lack of sufficient analysis. As a rule of thumb, the proportion of evidence (quotations and the like) to analysis should be 1 to 4. That is, for every line you quote, you should have at least four lines of analysis. You may find it helpful to create a map of your individual paragraphs as well.

Comparisons

The goal of a comparison essay is not to argue that two items are "similar but different": after all, everything is "similar but different" on some level! The goal of a comparison is to get at the deeper issues of the text—that is, to further analysis. Most beginning writers organize comparison essays in an "A B A+B" structure. For example, an essay comparing Dickinson's "I'm Nobody! Who are you?" (poem 260) and the opening of Whitman's "Song of Myself" would contain one paragraph on Dickinson (A), one on Whitman (B), and one on Whitman and Dickinson together (A+B). While this structure is acceptable when one is pressed for time (for example, when taking an essay exam), it hinders strong analysis of the materials by keeping separate the items that need to be compared (namely the authors' works). Instead, you might want to consider arranging your paragraphs so that you are comparing parallels in the works, themes, or the like. Look at this outline for a paper on Dickinson and Whitman. Notice how the more thematic structure helps strengthen the analysis.

    I.   Introduction
   II. The self in "I'm Nobody" and stanza 1 of "Song of Myself"
       a. The lyric I
       b. Romanticism and the narcissistic self
       c. Selfhood and godhood
  III. The crowd in "I'm Nobody" and stanza 1 of "Song of Myself"
       a. Embracing and rejecting multitudes
       b. A community of two?
  IV. The natural world in "I'm Nobody" and stanza 1 of "Song of Myself"
       a. The bog versus the bank
       b. The me and the not me
   V. Conclusion

By structuring the essay around themes, rather than around authors, the student has made a more convincing analysis.

Conclusions

After you have summarized your argument, what can you do with your conclusion? Traditionally, authors have used conclusions as a place to expound on the significance of their argument or its relationship to the "big picture." You may find it helpful to raise a new idea that, while related to your topic, takes it in a slightly new direction and shows how it fits into the larger context.

Alternatively, your conclusion may raise further questions that are related to the specific topic, but are more general in scope. Your conclusion may also serve as the fulfillment of your argument structure. For example, if your essay has been an objective analysis or argument, discuss a situation from your own experience that is analogous to or exemplary of the issue about which you have written. If your essay has been a discussion of a problem, your conclusion may propose a solution. Another interesting possibility is to use a quotation that reflects the conclusion the essay has made. You should be cautious if you choose to repeat the opening quotation. You will want to make sure you show how the reader's perception of it should have changed as a result of reading your essay.

Revising and Peer Editing

Most pieces of professional writing have been through an extensive revision process, and their authors have usually received feedback from a variety of readers. Exchanging papers with your classmates or friends is a useful way to learn how to become a better reader of your own work. While time consuming, peer editing can be valuable. The following self-evaluation may help you begin the revision process:

SELF-EVALUATION

1. If you had another day to work on this essay (or Web site, or slide show), what would you do to improve it?
2. Why did you decide to write on this topic? If there was only one choice of topic, what have you done to make it your own?
3. What do you like about this piece of writing so far? Is it comparable in quality to the other work you have done?
4. Which parts still seem weak or underdeveloped to you and why?
5. Is there anything that you wanted to include that isn't currently represented?
6. Does the opening fit with the rest of the piece or did you change direction after writing the introduction?
7. How would you summarize the piece's main point?
8. What sentence-level errors do you often make in your writing? Have you proofread for these?

Taking Exams

Exams are not meant to be a form of punishment, though they can feel that way. Rather, they are designed to test your retention of the reading materials and core concepts and to assess your ability to apply the information you have learned in new ways. Doing well on an exam takes both preparation before the exam as well as organization during it so that you can display what you have learned in the most convincing way possible.

Ideally, preparation for exams will not include rereading or—even worse—reading for the first time, the course materials. Your lecture and reading notes should help you review quickly the important characters, themes, issues, and historical and cultural landmarks. When you finish reading a book, spend ten or fifteen minutes listing five or six memorable moments, key themes and characters, and recurrent symbols or motifs. One place to make such notes is inside the back cover of your books. These notes are helpful not only for class discussion but also for studying for exams.

Two common kinds of exam questions are analyses (or identifications) of a passage and essay questions that require you to compare themes or characters from a series of texts. It is always worth asking the form of the exam ahead of time. If you know the exam will ask you to identify passages, review the "memorable moments" that you've jotted down at the back of each book as well as the passages mentioned in lecture or during class discussion. You may find it helpful to compare your "memorable moments" with those of your classmates or to quiz one another with them. If you know the exam will consist of comparative essay questions, you may find it helpful to make a grid like the following one:

Relevant Texts	Literary Movement	Significant Contexts	Theme/Issue: _____ Guiding Question: _____
Title Author			(examples, passage, position taken)
Title Author			
Title Author			
Title Author			

You can make a similar chart that compares texts across historical periods or for each book.

Once you have the exam in front of you, your job is to give the right answer in a way that is intelligible and clear. Here's a four-step process for taking essay exams:

1. Brainstorm for five minutes on scratch paper. Most essay questions will ask you to take a stand on an issue or to assess whether a claim is valid. Brainstorming will let you get all of your thoughts out on paper without worrying about how they sound or whether they are spelled correctly.

2. Read your brainstorm. Which side did you have the most (and best) evidence to support?
3. Write an outline and thesis. Yes, you need a thesis sentence even on in-class exams. Your thesis should clearly state which side of the issue you are choosing. Your outline should organize your brainstorming in a coherent manner. This is the point at which you will want to consider whether you will be making concessions to the other side of the argument. Quickly check to make sure your thesis directly answers the question. Revise your thesis if necessary.
4. Write! Make sure that your handwriting is legible. If you have time, proofread.

For more advice on how to prepare for and take essay exams, see Edgar Roberts's *Writing about Literature*.

Grammar and Punctuation Tips

Since most word processors give grammar advice, one would think you wouldn't need to know the rules; yet no grammar program would score 100 percent on a grammar quiz. So here are some of the most common errors and how to fix them:

1. **Infinitives:** Don't split infinitives: It is actually "to go boldly," not "to boldly go."
2. **Idioms of Comparison:** You need both halves of the following phrases: "not only . . . but also," "just as . . . so too." For example, "He is not only my brother, but also my friend." "Just as Harriet Beecher Stowe makes appeals to the sentimental tradition, so too Harriet Jacobs uses tropes and plot devices from sentimental novels."
3. **Quotations:** Commas and periods go inside quotation marks. For example, "Sacvan Bercovitch argues, 'The jeremiad is an important American tradition.'"
4. **Pronouns:** A pronoun must refer clearly to a single nearby antecedent: "Mark Twain grew up in Hannibal, Missouri. **He** harkened back to this town in the setting of a number of his novels." Here is an example of an unclear pronoun: "Huckleberry Finn and Tom Sawyer are two of the most unforgettable characters in all of American literature. He represents the classic story of a 'foundling,' or orphaned child." To correct the above sentences you would need to clarify to whom "He" refers.
5. **Which/That: That** is for clauses that are necessary for the meaning of the sentence. **Which** is for nonrestrictive clauses—clauses that add information that is interesting but is not necessary to maintain the essential meaning of the sentence. For example:
   ■ Many of Joel Chandler Harris's biographers suggest that his early insecurities led to lifelong shyness, **which** he compensated for by writing humorous stories and playing practical jokes.
   ■ On the other hand, the Trickster tales **that** Uncle Remus narrates are characterized by poetic irony and a subtle critique of oppression and prejudice.

6. **It's/Its: It's** is a contraction of **it** and **is**. **Its** is the possessive form of **it**.
   - During the civil rights movement, nonviolent demonstrations, sit-ins, and legal trials shocked American society to **its** core.
   - **It's** also important to realize that Jonathan Edwards actually managed to live in accordance with his strict beliefs: his devotion to family, rigorous dedication to study, and lifelong focus on God testify to the conviction that underlay his rhetoric.

Writing Web Pages

It is no longer enough to know how to write a paper; your assignments may also include writing either a Web page or a series of Web pages. The comments here pertain only to the style and usability of Web pages: software may be necessary for the actual composition process. As with essays, it is important to plan and organize your materials before you begin composing your pages.

If you are creating just one page, ask yourself what information you want the page to contain, as well as what other pages you would like to link to. Creating a Web page is like publishing a book: although you may have an intended audience in mind, you never know exactly who will read your work. Make sure that you include information about the purpose or goal of the page, who you are (your school, year in school, major), contact information in case people have questions (e-mail and/or phone number), and the date the page was created or updated. You may also want to let people know on what authority your information is based; perhaps include a short bibliography or a list of relevant coursework or "real world" experience. Like a piece of writing, your Web page will be judged based on *ethos* (your character) and *pathos* (the emotions you invoke in your reader), as well as its *logos* (logic). Make your page crowded, busy, and hard to read only if you intend to invoke the anger or frustration of your reader. To create your own style guide, you may want to look at two or three Web pages that you admire and answer the following questions:

1. What is the purpose of these pages? How do you know? How does this compare to your goals?
2. Who created the page and when?
3. How many colors does each page use?
4. What font, type size, and color do the pages use for the text? What type size, font, and color do they use for emphasis?
5. Is the background white, colored, or patterned?
6. Is the page easy to navigate? What features help you navigate it?
7. Does the page tell you where to go if you have questions?

After answering these questions, you should have a better understanding of what the goal of your own page is and how style can help you achieve it.

If your page will contain more information than could be printed out on one page, you may want to consider creating multiple pages. When building a multi-page Web site, you should create a diagram that shows how people can move through the Web site. This is called a "wire frame." Here is an example:

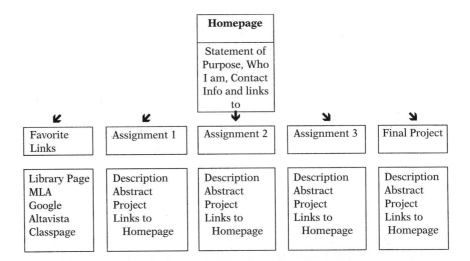

In *Web Teaching Guide: A Practical Approach to Creating Course Web Sites*, Sarah Horton suggests putting the information you want your page to contain on separate flashcards and dividing them into groups until the organization feels logical. Use these cards to test your organization on friends or classmates; ask the "testees" if the card groupings are logical.

Creating a Slide Show

The *American Passages* Web site includes software that will take you through the creation of a slide show using images and sound files from the *American Passages* archive. You can save this slide show and edit it later, or you can send it to your classmates and professor. Creating a successful slide show takes clarity of purpose and organization. As with any presentation, you want to make your organizing principles apparent to the viewers. Like an essay, a slide show should have an introduction with a thesis, supporting evidence (most likely images, sound files, and text passages), and a conclusion that reiterates the main points of the presentation. It is important not to present too much information on one slide, so you will want to make sure that you divide your evidence into digestible chunks. As when you design a Web site, you will probably find it helpful to write an outline of how you want your presentation to appear and to use flashcards as dummy slides. Here's an outline of a sample student presentation comparing sentimentality in Harriet Jacobs's *Incidents in the Life* and artifacts from everyday life in the nineteenth century.

■ Title: "Am I Not a Woman? Slavery and the Cult of True Womanhood," by Claude Stiles. Image #5476, *Am I not a Woman and a Sister?*
■ Introduction: Thesis: To convince readers that Jacobs is worthy of sympathy, Harriet Jacobs's *Incidents in the Life* uses the same tropes of the Cult of True Womanhood that we find in the popular culture of nineteenth-century America.

- Outline: Definition
  Topic 1. Motherhood
  Topic 2. Homemaking
  Topic 3. Piety
  Topic 4. Purity
- Definition of Cult of True Womanhood: "This influential ideal of femininity stressed the importance of motherhood, homemaking, piety, and purity. While men were expected to work and act in the public realm of business and politics, women were to remain in the private, domestic sphere of the home."
  - Topic 1: Motherhood
    Details about this topic from text
    Supporting information and examples from popular culture
  - Topic 2: Homemaking
    Details about this topic from text
    Supporting information and examples from popular culture
  - Topic 3: Piety
    Details about this topic from text
    Supporting information and examples from popular culture
  - Topic 4: Purity
    Details about this topic from text
    Supporting information and examples from popular culture
  - What This Means
    Slavery was justified using the logic that slaves were not humans. By appealing to the Cult of True Womanhood, Jacobs convinces readers that she is not only human but also a woman and hence deserving of their sympathy.
  - Conclusion

This student might find it helpful to break down Topics 1–4 into more individual slides, particularly if the passages selected are lengthy. For example, Topic 1 might actually appear as follows:

- **Topic 1: Motherhood—Outline of Steps**
- Details about this topic from text: Even though the physical costs are high, Jacobs decides to spend seven years in an attic in order to be able to watch over her children.
  Image: Floor plan of the attic
- Supporting information and examples from popular culture: In the ideal of motherhood found in the artifacts from nineteenth-century America, women were often not only educators of children but also guardians of family ideals, as seen in this image of republican motherhood.
  Image: Mother reading to her children
- Supporting information and examples from popular culture: Jacobs's time in the attic debunks representations from nineteenth-century racist literature that argued that African Americans had no "family values."
  Image: Frontispiece from nineteenth-century southern novel
- Summary: Jacobs's sacrifice on behalf of her children reinforces her humanity and appeals to the sympathy of her readers.

The more thought you put into planning your slide show before you begin to build it, the more likely it is that the slide show will persuade your readers that your interpretation is logical and thoughtful.

A Brief Overview of MLA Style

You may have been told that it is important to cite your sources in order to avoid plagiarizing them. It is also important to cite your sources because it gives your writing greater authority. Let's face it: if a famous critic or historian makes a claim that supports your case, your case will carry more weight than if you have come up with the idea on your own. After all, the critic or historian has had years more education and time spent researching the topic than you have, and she already has a large audience who respects her opinion. Citing her work will only enhance your presentation of yourself as someone who has researched the topic and has thought carefully about sources. So, how does one properly cite material?

You need to cite your sources if you quote or paraphrase a concept from a source, as long as that idea isn't common knowledge. Thus, you don't have to provide a citation for the fact that World War II ended in 1945, but you do have to tell us how you know that Jonathan Edwards married "Sarah Pierrepont, a woman renowned for her devotion to spiritual matters, and started what would become a family of eleven children" (*American Passages Study Guide* 197).

Rules for citation vary from field to field, but most literary critics use the style in the *MLA Handbook for Writers of Research Papers*. MLA style dictates that citations will appear parenthetically at the end of the sentence in which the quotation appears, or at the end of the paraphrased material. This citation consists of the author's last name and the page number upon which the material appears. If there is no author, you may use the title of the work instead. The full bibliographic information then appears at the end of the work under the heading "works cited." These entries are listed alphabetically and are in the following format:

- Last name of author, First name. *Title*. Where published: Publisher, year published.

For example:

Novak, Barbara. *Nature and Culture: American Landscape Painting, 1825–1875*. Oxford: Oxford UP, 1980.

Journal articles are in the following format:

- Last name of author, First name. "Title of article." *Title of journal* volume (year): page numbers of article.

For example:

Blondell, Carey. "High Style in Wharton's *House of Mirth*." *Critical Inquiry* 6 (Fall 1988): 323–41.

SELECTED BIBLIOGRAPHY

Carey, Christopher. "Rhetorical Means of Persuasion." In *Persuasion: Greek Rhetoric in Action*. Ed. Ian Worthington. London: Routledge, 1994.

Gibaldi, Joseph. *MLA Handbook for Writers of Research Papers*. 6th ed. New York: Modern Language Association of America, 2003.

Horton, Sarah. *Web Teaching Guide: A Practical Approach to Creating Course Web Sites*. New Haven: Yale UP, 2000.

Marius, Richard. *A Writer's Companion*. 4th ed. Boston: McGraw-Hill College, 1999.

Roberts, Edgar V. *Writing about Literature*. 8th ed. Englewood Cliffs, NJ: Prentice Hall, 1995.

Toulmin, Stephen E. *The Uses of Argument*. Updated ed. New York: Cambridge UP, 2003.

Trimble, John R. *Writing with Style: Conversations on the Art of Writing*. 2nd ed. Upper Saddle River, NJ: Prentice Hall, 2000.

Wood, Nancy. *Writing Argumentative Essays*. 2nd ed. Upper Saddle River, NJ: Prentice Hall, 2001.